STRATEGIC MARKETING MANAGEMENT CASES

FOURTH EDITION

David W. Cravens
Charles W. Lamb, Jr.
M. J. Neeley School of Business
Texas Christian University

IRWIN

Homewood, IL 60430
Boston, MA 02116

This symbol indicates that the paper in this book is made from recycled paper. Its fiber content exceeds the recommended minimum of 50% waste paper fibers as specified by the EPA.

Senior sponsoring editor: Stephen M. Patterson
Editorial coordinator: Lynn M. Nordbrock
Marketing manager: Scott J. Timian
Project editor: Karen Smith
Production manager: Diane Palmer
Designer: Larry J. Cope
Art coordinator: Mark Malloy
Compositor: Bi-Comp, Incorporated
Typeface: 10/12 Century Schoolbook
Printer: R. R. Donnelly & Sons Company

Library of Congress Cataloging-in-Publication Data

Cravens, David W.
    Strategic marketing management cases / David W. Cravens, Charles W. Lamb, Jr.—4th ed.
       p.   cm.—(The Irwin series in marketing)
    Rev. ed. of: Strategic marketing management cases and applications. 3rd ed. 1990.
    Includes index.
    ISBN 0-256-10531-6
    1. Marketing—Case studies. I. Lamb, Charles W. II. Cravens, David W. Strategic marketing management cases and applications.
III. Title. IV. Series.
HF5415.C6944 1993
658.8′02—dc20   92–6750

Printed in the United States of America
1 2 3 4 5 6 7 8 9 0 DOC 9 8 7 6 5 4 3 2

To M. J. Neeley

THE IRWIN SERIES IN MARKETING

Consulting Editor Gilbert A. Churchill, Jr.
University of Wisconsin, Madison

Preface

Gaining a competitive advantage in marketing is a continuing challenge. An important part of this challenge is analyzing and strategically responding to rapidly changing environmental opportunities and threats. This requires marketing professionals to develop effective strategic analysis, planning, implementation, and control skills.

Marketing is the responsibility of everyone in an organization, not just those in marketing and sales positions. A market-driven company gains business advantage through customer satisfaction. Marketing strategy is the process of selecting market targets and integrating an organization's customer influencing capabilities to meet the needs and wants of the targeted buyers.

External pressures are adding new demands to marketing strategy:

- The needs and wants of buyers are becoming fragmented and increasingly complex. New technologies are rapidly expanding customers' choice alternatives.
- Major changes are taking place in consumer markets due to demographic shifts, geographical movement of people, and new lifestyles.
- Deregulation of financial services, transportation, and telecommunications has created new marketing requirements in these industries.
- High-performance marketing strategies have become essential because of escalating costs and declining productivity in many businesses.
- Intensive global competition for market position exists in many industries such as automobiles, consumer electronics, appliances, aerospace, steel, apparel, and construction equipment.
- Strategic restructuring (industry consolidation, downsizing) is occurring in many companies to cope with pressures for change from customers and competitors.
- Interorganizational marketing relationships are transforming traditional concepts for competing in domestic and foreign markets.

Cases place students in business situations requiring the use of marketing analysis and the development of action recommendations. These cases, representing a wide array of business and nonprofit organization situations, enable the student to expand his or her understanding of marketing strategy concepts, decision processes, and their application. We have purposely avoided focusing heavily on decisions facing large corporations. Many of the cases in this book concern decisions facing small and medium-sized organizations. Many also illustrate problems and decisions facing multinational firms.

USING STRATEGIC MARKETING MANAGEMENT CASES

This book can serve as a teaching-learning resource in several ways. It can be used as the primary text for advanced or capstone marketing management and strategy courses. In addition to helping meet the needs of instructors developing new courses in strategic marketing, it offers instructors a way to expand the strategic emphasis of marketing management courses beyond the coverage in traditional marketing management texts and casebooks. Of course, *Strategic Marketing Management Cases* also contains many cases that examine traditional marketing management areas. The book can also be used with a marketing management book to create a text and case combination for use in undergraduate advanced marketing management and strategy courses, and in MBA marketing management and strategy courses. Four chapters, which cover a step-by-step approach to marketing analysis and planning, financial analysis, and case analysis, provide useful foundation materials. These chapters are particularly helpful in the absence of a companion text.

Computer Software. A software disk has been shrink wrapped with the text. It contains Lotus 1-2-3® templates for 12 of the cases, including 2–1, Food Lion, Inc.; 2–3, Rockingham Memorial Hospital; 2–5, Makhteshim Chemical Works; 2–11, The Simons Lumber Company; 3–6, Algonquin Power and Light Company (A); 4–1, The North Face; 4–5, Vancouver Public Aquarium; 4–8, Airwick Industries; 5–4, Zayre Corporation; 5–7, Paper Mate; 6–1, Leykam Mürztaler; and 6–10, Robert N. Maxwell Memorial Community Hospital. These cases provide a wide range of opportunities for computer analysis. The basic template material can also be expanded depending on the instructor's preferences and the students' capabilities.

The fourth edition of *Strategic Marketing Management Cases* represents a major revision based on feedback from users and nonusers of the second and third editions. Major features new to the fourth edition include:

- Two thirds of the 64 cases in *Strategic Marketing Management Cases* are new to this edition.
- Over three fourths of the cases describe situations taking place in 1985 or more recently; about one-fourth describe situations that marketing decision makers faced in the 1990s.
- A major emphasis is placed on international/global case decisions. These cases offer instructors materials for examining various global marketing issues.
- To meet the needs of instructors who wish to use the case analysis process described in Chapter 4, we have continued the case format followed in previous editions. Instructors have a wide range of short- and medium-length new and old favorite cases to choose from. As in previous editions, we have selected cases that illustrate strategic marketing problems and decisions faced by large, medium sized, and small organizations, goods and services sellers, manufacturers and channel intermediaries, industrial and consumer products companies, profit and nonprofit organizations, and domestic, foreign, and multinational companies. To ensure strong student interest, each case was evaluated on interest and difficulty by a student team.
- To meet the needs of instructors who wish to use cases in a question-and-answer format or to use them for exam purposes, about one third of the teaching notes in the Instructor's Manual are formatted in terms of discussion questions and answers. These discussion questions are not listed at the end of the cases. Past users of the text and respondents to a marketing management casebook survey indicate that they prefer not listing the questions with the case so that students will focus their attention on the entire situation and decisions facing management rather than on answering specific questions. The new format enables instructors to adopt either a question focus or broad case discussion approach.
- The Instructor's Manual provides detailed analyses and supporting materials for each case. Suggestions are included for course design. Transparency masters are also included to aid in class discussion of selected cases. Information updating several case situations is provided in the manual.

ACKNOWLEDGMENTS

In addition to the important contribution made to the book by the authors of the cases, we want to acknowledge several others whose assistance and support were invaluable. We appreciate the permission of the editors of *The Wall Street Journal* and the *Fort Worth Star Telegram* to reprint their articles. Steve Patterson, sponsoring editor, assisted in all phases of the revision. Gilbert A. Churchill, Jr., University of Wisconsin–Madison, as consulting editor, also provided many helpful suggestions. We were also fortunate to have the benefit of detailed reviews by the following instructors in developing this edition and previous editions:

Seymour T. R. Abt	McGill University
Scott Alden	Purdue University
Benny Barak	Hofstra University
E. Wayne Chandler	Eastern Illinois University
Jack R. Dauner	Fayetteville State University
Lawrence P. Feldman	University of Illinois–Chicago
Betsy Gelb	University of Houston
Ken Grant	Monash University
Max Lupul	California State University–Northridge
Thomas J. Page, Jr.	Michigan State University
Charles R. Patton	University of Texas at Brownsville
A. M. Pelham	University of Northern Iowa
William N. Rodgers	University of San Francisco
Patrick L. Schul	Memphis State University
Carol A. Scott	University of California–Los Angeles
R. Viswanathan	University of Northern Colorado

Several of our graduate assistants have made essential contributions to this edition of the book—especially Suzy Ewing, Michael Hobbs, and Paul Lauritano. Special thanks are due Fran Eller and Mary Tidwell for typing the manuscript and for their assistance in other aspects of the project. We are greatly appreciative of the support and encouragement provided by our dean, H. Kirk Downey and department chair, Bill Moncrief, without whose help the development of this book would not have been possible. Finally, we want to express our appreciation to Eunice West and her late husband, James L. West, and to M. J. Neeley and his late wife, Alice, for the endowments that help support our positions and enable us to work on projects like this book.

We are indebted to all of these people and to the many authors and publishers who gave us permission to use their materials. We also appreciate the support and suggestions we have received from adopters of previous editions of this book. While the final result is our responsibility, the assistance provided was essential in completing the project.

> **David W. Cravens**
> **Charles W. Lamb, Jr.**

CASE CONTRIBUTORS

We appreciate the opportunity to include the cases of the following academic colleagues.

Larry Alexander, Virginia Polytechnic Institute and State University

Robert Anderson, The College of Charleston

John Bargetto, University of Notre Dame

Franz Bea, University of Tubingen

Daniel Bello, Georgia State University

Thomas Bertsch, James Madison University

Bobby Bizzell, University of Houston, Downtown

Lew Brown, University of North Carolina at Greensboro

Victor Buell, University of Massachusetts

Janet Caswell, University of Virginia

Sherry Chaples, George Mason University

Gilbert Churchill, Jr., University of Wisconsin, Madison

Valorie Cook, Stanford Graduate School of Business

Robert Crowner, Eastern Michigan University

Robert Davis, Stanford University

Don DeCoster, University of Washington

Barbara Dixon, Dartmouth University

Jim Dooley, Seattle University

Peter Doyle, Bradford University

Maureen Fanshawe, University of Michigan

Neil Ford, University of Wisconsin, Madison

Christopher Gale, IMEDE

Walter Good, University of Manitoba

John Grant, Southern Illinois University–Carbondale

Holly Gunner, Management Analysts Center, Inc.

Robert Haas, San Diego State University

Michael Hayes, University of Colorado at Denver

Sharon Henson, University of Alabama

Per V. Jenster, University of Virginia

Jim Kerlin, University of Alabama

Daniel Kopp, Southwest Missouri State University

Thomas Kosnik, IMEDE

Alfred Kotzle, University of Tubingen

Peter LaPlaca, University of Connecticut at Storrs
Earl Levith, Edlon Products, Inc.
John Little, University of North Carolina at Greensboro
Stewart Malone, University of Virginia
Barry Mason, University of Alabama
Morris Mayer, University of Alabama
Philip McDonald, Northeastern University
Patricia McDougall, Georgia Institute of Technology
Gary Mezzatesta, Stanford University
Joseph Mills, American Safety Razor Co.
Michael Mokwa, Arizona State University
Patrick Murphy, University of Notre Dame
James Nelson, University of Colorado
Valerie Pandak, James Madison University
Penny Paquette, Harvard University
John Pearce II, George Mason University
Grant Poeter, University of British Columbia
James Brian Quinn, Dartmouth College
Bernard Reimann, Cleveland State University
Kendall Roth, University of South Carolina
Adrian Ryans, The University of Western Ontario
Donald Scotton, Cleveland State University
Richard Sharpe, University of Tennessee at Knoxville
Shannon Shipp, Texas Christian University
Lois Shufeldt, Southwest Missouri State University
Neil Snyder, University of Virginia
Stephen Tax, University of Manitoba
Arthur Thompson, University of Alabama
Orville Walker, University of Minnesota
Allan Waren, Cleveland State University
Charles Weinberg, University of British Columbia
Richard White, University of North Texas
William Woolridge, University of Colorado
Thomas Wotruba, San Diego State University
John Wright, Georgia State University
William Wynd, Eastern Washington University

Contents

CASES

PART 2   Coordinating Business and Marketing Strategies

PART 3   Marketing Situation Analysis

PART 4   Market Targeting

PART 5   Marketing Strategy and Program Development

PART 6   Planning, Organizing, Implementing, and Controlling Marketing Strategy

STRATEGIC MARKETING MANAGEMENT CASES

PART 1

Strategic Marketing Management

Chapter 1

Analyzing Competitive Strategies and Market Structure

While favorable market and competitive conditions clearly enhance market performance, these factors do not explain why some firms' marketing strategies are successful and others are not. Top performing companies can be found in many different industries. Examples include American Airlines in air transportation, Honda in automobiles, The Gap in men's and women's apparel, AST Research in personal computers, and Rubbermaid in housewares. Industry experts expressed negative opinions about Honda's plan to enter the European-dominated luxury import segment of the automobile market. Two years after the Acura Legend entered the U.S. market in the 1980s, it gained first place in sales and customer satisfaction ahead of BMW, Mercedes-Benz, Volvo, and Audi.

Companies gain competitive advantage in a wide range of product and market situations. Market success does not result from a single characteristic such as company size, industry structure, or market attractiveness. Successful strategy choices are guided by the evaluation of market structure and growth rates, the differences in the needs of buyers, the structure and intensity of competition, the organization's skills and resources, and other important situational factors.

This chapter and the following one examine the process of developing effective marketing strategies. First, a step-by-step approach to marketing strategy selection is presented. Next, the nature and scope of market entry barriers are discussed, and their impact on strategic choices is considered. A look at different types of competitive situations follows. Next, product-market definition and analysis are considered, followed by discussion of market segmentation in different competitive situations.

Chapter 2 begins with an analysis of the sources of competition, industry structure, product life cycle implications, strategic group analysis, and key competitors. An examination of how competitive advantage varies for different competitive situations follows. Finally, matching the organization's competitive advantage with appropriate market targeting and positioning strategies shows how marketing strategy is guided by the specific market and competitive situations confronting an organization.

STRATEGY AND COMPETITIVE ADVANTAGE[1]

The choice of marketing strategies for different competitive situations is affected by the specific business environment of an organization. Nevertheless, a step-by-step strategy choice process can be used by management to identify the critical strategy issues and the key strategic decisions that must be made. This process is examined, followed by a discussion of strategy choice criteria.

Strategy Selection Process

An organization's marketing strategy identifies the buyers to be targeted and the positioning strategy (product, distribution, price, and promotion strategies) to be used for each customer target selected by management. The major steps in the strategy selection process are shown in Exhibit 1–1.

Market Definition and Analysis.   Buyers' needs and the products that meet these needs determine the structure of the "product-market."[2] Product-market boundaries are established by identifying the buyers' needs of interest to management and the product(s) that satisfies these needs. For example, the product-market for meeting the needs for away-from-home eating includes fast-food retailers, full-menu restaurants, and other food services. Needs can be further specified by the food consumption occasion such as business meetings, family occasions, and entertainment.

Market Segmentation.   Buyers in many markets have different needs. Understanding these differences is essential in guiding marketing strategy targeting and positioning decisions. Segmentation analysis identifies customer groups within a product-market. Each segment should include buyers with similar preferences for the product offer-

EXHIBIT 1–1   Selecting Marketing Strategy

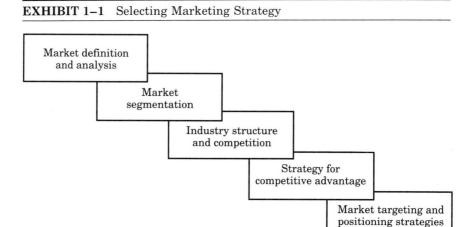

ings in the product-market. For example, Procter & Gamble has six different marketing campaigns targeted to different customer groups for Crest toothpaste.[3] P&G applies market segment analysis methods to identify customer segments and the buying preferences of customers in each segment.

Industry Structure and Competition.   The product-market structure and segments within the product-market define the arena of active competition. There is also the potential threat of new competition. Industry structure analysis indicates the nature and scope of the organizations serving the product-market. Competitor analysis considers the specific firms competing in the segments of interest to the organization.

Strategy for Competitive Advantage.   Competitive advantage results from offering superior value to customers through: (1) lower prices than competitors for equivalent benefits; and/or (2) unique benefits that more than offset a higher price.[4] Competitive advantage often occurs within specific segments rather than spanning an entire product-market. For example, Dell Computer quickly obtained a position in the personal computer market by targeting selected organizational buyers. Founded in 1984, Dell's sales in 1991 were approaching $700 million. Dell's targeting strategy is to sell PCs by mail at competitive prices. The company offers a 30-day money-back guarantee, a one-year warranty, and guaranteed 24-hour on-site service.[5] These service features provide Dell an important competitive advantage with small-

and medium-size business buyers. Other mail order PC marketers do not offer comparable services.

Market Targeting and Positioning Strategies.   Product-market analysis, segmentation, industry and competitor analysis, and deciding how to compete (e.g., low prices or unique benefits) establish key guidelines for deciding which buyers to target and selecting a positioning strategy (product, distribution, price, and promotion) for appealing to each group of targeted buyers. Buyers position the brands serving the target market based on their preferences for various product attributes (e.g., price). Management may decide to target a single segment, a few segments, or many of the segments in the product-market. For example Hartmarx targets many segments in the men's apparel market with its various brands. Included are Austin Reed, Hart Schaffner & Marx, Hickey-Freeman, Racquet, and several other brands.

Strategy Choice Criteria

Many factors influence the choice of a particular marketing strategy. Evaluating each alternative against a complete set of choice criteria assures that the important influences on strategy are considered by management. These criteria help to focus attention on the various strategic influences regardless of the marketing strategy situation. A series of strategy questions identifies the criteria that are important in strategy selection.[6]

Sustainable Competitive Advantage.   This is a key consideration in selecting a strategy. Does the proposed strategy offer an opportunity to gain a sustainable advantage over competitors? For example, experience indicates that the market pioneer (first firm to enter a market) often has a competitive edge over later entrants. An important issue in assessing potential advantage is evaluating the attractiveness of the market opportunity targeted by the strategy. An excellent example of selecting a strategy that offered sustainable competitive advantage is the entry by Domino's Pizza into the home delivery market. The founder targeted and positioned Domino's to meet the needs of buyers seeking rapid and reliable home delivery of pizza. No major competitor was satisfying this need when Domino's entered the market. The home delivery industry was highly fragmented.

Realistic Assumptions.   Marketing strategies are designed to obtain favorable responses from the buyers targeted by an organization. The assumptions underlying a proposed strategy must be sound. These premises may include anticipating the responses of competition, estimating market growth, and evaluating the capabilities of the organization. Realism is important in assessing the probable revenue and cost implications of a proposed strategy including the probable responses of competition. Critical review of assumptions is particularly important when entering new markets and when competing in rapidly changing markets. These turbulent environments can drastically alter the effectiveness of strategies.

Skills, Resources, and Management Commitment.   The ability of the organization to develop and implement a strategy and the commitment of operating managers toward achieving a successful strategy are important success determinants. For example, when the management of a small organization decides to enter a mature product-market, it is essential to evaluate the skills and resources required to successfully launch this new venture. Even a large firm with substantial resources may lack the necessary skills to compete when entering a product-market that is new to the firm. The willingness of the management team to favorably support the strategy is also very important.

Cie, Generale des Ets, Michelin, the giant tire maker, experienced difficulties in attempting to expand its market position in the United States in the early 1980s. Michelin's management underestimated the competitive barriers and marketing skills that were necessary to dominate the market.[7] The European tire maker irritated tire dealers and was unable to meet its sales forecasts using higher prices than U.S. tire brands. The Michelin brand name did not have the influence on buyers and dealers anticipated by management. The company had to revise its marketing strategy to build consumer and dealer support.

Cohesiveness of the Strategy.   Market targeting and positioning strategies must be carefully coordinated. The positioning strategy must be designed to favorably influence targeted buyers. The cohesiveness of the marketing components (product, distribution, price, and promotion) is an important success factor in marketing strategy selection. Advertising and personal selling efforts are often difficult to coordinate toward a common positioning theme. Marketing program cohesiveness is more difficult when external participants are involved such as a manufacturer selling its products through independent sales agents who are compensated by a commission on sales. The Gillette case (5–5) provides an interesting description of the design and implementation of a cohesive marketing strategy for the Sensor razor, introduced in 1990.

Risks and Contingencies.   Two considerations are important in assessing risk: (1) the importance of each aspect of risk to the strategy choice, and (2) the extent of control that management has over the risk factor.[8] The more important the risk factor and the less control exercised by the organization over the factor, the more vulnerable the strategy is to the risk. The potential trade barriers that may be exercised by the European Community nations beginning in 1993 are illustrative of a risk factor that may affect U.S. and Japanese companies competing in unified Europe.

Flexibility/Adaptability.   The widespread turbulence in the business environment expected in the 1990s highlights the critical importance of selecting strategies that are adaptable to changes in the environment. Making good decisions in a constantly changing business environment is essential for competing in the 1990s. Flexible and adaptable strategies are necessary to adjust to constantly changing customer requirements and competitive conditions. The global supply networks used by retailers like Bombay Company and Pier 1 are examples of flexible strategies. Bombay contracts most of its furniture production to producers in several different countries. The company monitors product quality and distribution.

Value Added.   Finally, the financial attractiveness of the strategy must be assessed. Will the proposed strategy add value to the organization? The Gillette Sensor razor venture is an example of a strategy designed to "maximize shareholder value."[9] The company spent more than $200 million to develop and start manufacturing the razor. Advertising in 1990 totaled $110 million. If successful, the new product would achieve management's value-added objective. If the product did not deliver the sizable returns expected by management, it would be criticized for wasting a larger amount of money. By early 1991 the Sensor was performing above management's expectations.

These seven choice criteria are useful in screening the marketing strategies under consideration by management. They provide a checklist for review by the management team responsible for strategy selection and implementation.

MARKET ENTRY BARRIERS

Entry barriers prevent or make difficult the entry of new competitors into an existing product-market. Market entry analysis is important in deciding *whether* to compete in a market of interest to an organization and in deciding *how* to compete. Understanding of the barriers that are present in a particular competitive situation is essential for both existing firms and potential entrants.

The firm(s) already serving the market often have a competitive advantage over a company planning to enter the market.[10] Advantage is created by the market entry barriers that the new entrant will encounter when attempting to gain a position in the market. Entry barrier analysis consists of: (1) identifying the specific barriers confronting an organization and establishing the relative importance of each barrier, (2) estimating the effect of the barriers on entry at different stages of product-market maturity, and (3) examining how the entry barriers vary in different product-markets (e.g., consumer and industrial products).

Entry Barriers

Six barriers represent the major sources of influence on market entry decisions.[11] These are shown in Exhibit 1–2 with accompanying definitions. The definitions shown in Exhibit 1–2 indicate several specific factors that contribute to each entry concept. For example, cost advantage may be achieved through volume production, design efficiency, and experience. A brief discussion of each entry barrier follows.

Cost Advantage. Cost advantage is gained in various ways by the firms operating in a product-market. The means of achieving favorable costs include production volume efficiencies, design advantages, experience, access to raw materials, and government subsidies. A barrier exists when a new market entrant has substantially higher costs than the incumbent firms. Cost reduction strategies are used by existing firms to discourage new market entrants.

Product Differentiation. The brand images established with buyers for the products of established firms often create important entry barriers. These advantages may result from customer awareness and satisfaction, product features, and other methods of brand differentiation. Rubbermaid, in houseware products, is a familiar name to almost everyone. This powerful consumer franchise is a strong deterrent to new competition. Differentiation of brands may prevent new competition in market segments as well as the entire product-market. For example, Nucor Corp. has a strong segment position for steel building joists in the Sunbelt. This provides Nucor a competitive advantage against the giant steel producers.

Capital Requirements. The Gillette Sensor razor venture is an excellent illustration of the high costs of entering some markets. Competing in certain markets requires large financial resources. The stakes required for market entry may be so high that new firms will not be willing or able to enter the market. Many large, mature product-markets such as consumer electronics, tires, automobiles, and appliances

---

EXHIBIT 1–2 Market Entry Barriers

Concept	Definition
Cost advantages of incumbents (CAI)	The advantages include the decline in unit cost of a product as the absolute volume of production per period increases as well as the reduction in unit cost resulting from product know-how, design characteristics, favorable access to raw materials, favorable locations, government locations, government subsidies, and learning or experience curve.
Product differentiation of incumbents (PDI)	Established firms have brand identification and customer loyalties stemming from past advertising, customer service, product differences, or simply being first into the market.
Capital requirements (CR)	The need to invest large financial resources to enter a market and compete in that market.
Customer switching costs (CSC)	One-time costs to the buyer due to switching from one supplier to another (i.e., employee retraining costs, cost of new ancillary equipment, need for new technical help, product redesign, etc.).
Access to distribution channels (ADC)	The extent to which logical distribution channels for a product are already served by the established firms in the market.
Government policy (GP)	The extent to which government limits or forecloses entry into industries with such controls as licensing requirements and limits access to raw materials (i.e., regulated industries and Environmental Protection Agency laws).

Source: Fahri Karakaya and Michael J. Stahl, "Barriers to Entry and Market Entry Decisions in Consumer and Industrial Goods Markets," *Journal of Marketing,* April 1989, p. 85.

require huge capital resources for entry. Moreover, the risks of competing may be too high for those firms that have the resources necessary to compete. In contrast, entry into apparel markets such as women's clothing can be accomplished without large capital investments in production equipment.

Customer Switching Costs. This barrier is particularly important for business-to-business products and services. While a consumer may be willing to change brands for frequently purchased products, persuading a manufacturer to purchase from a new and unproven supplier is often difficult. Established relationships between buyers and sellers are often hard to penetrate by new suppliers. Weaknesses in the current buyer-seller relationship must be found in order to get customers to switch to a new supplier. The use of single-source suppliers and just-in-time inventory systems further strengthen buyer and seller relationships.

Access to Distribution Channels.   Many small firms have the skills and resources necessary to produce various products. A major constraint on market entry for these firms is gaining access to distribution channels. Marketing middlemen often reject new products from unknown suppliers because they do not have established brand identities in the marketplace. Many consumer products and services are distributed through distribution networks that are owned or managed by a single company. These vertical marketing systems also are used for various industrial products.

Government Policy.   Governments may impose various constraints on market entry. The most extreme competitive barrier is the granting of a monopoly. While deregulation of industries in the United States and other countries has removed entry barriers in several instances, government controls and policies continue to impose important entry constraints in a wide range of product-markets. For example, the unification of Western Europe in 1992 presents a variety of market entrance issues for firms in countries that are not members of the 12-nation European Community.

The importance of the entry barriers varies. One research study using a sample of Fortune 500 executives in a simulated environment found that each of the six entry barriers in Exhibit 1–2 was considered relevant by the respondents.[12] Cost advantages were perceived as the most important entry barrier with capital requirements second and product differentiation third. No distinct relative importance pattern was found for the remaining three factors.

The Timing and Type of Market Entry

The market pioneer (first to enter) often gains a sustainable competitive advantage over subsequent firms entering the market.[13] Early entry must include good strategy choices to achieve advantage. Simply being first is not enough. And entering the market first does not assure the pioneer of a favorable market and profit position. Initial entry offers an opportunity for rewards but is also risky. The successful pioneer must select and implement effective strategies for sustaining competitive advantage.

Research findings indicate that there are differences in the importance of the six entry barriers between consumer and business markets.[14] Each barrier, except capital requirements, varies in importance for early entry into industrial and consumer markets. Product differentiation and access to distribution channels appear to be more influential for early entry into consumer markets. Variation in the importance of the entry barriers does not change significantly at the late entry stage. Customer switching costs are the only barrier that the study participant found more important in late entry than in early entry.

COMPETITIVE SITUATIONS

A variety of factors in the business environment creates different competitive situations. Influences affecting the competitive situation include product-market characteristics, the stage of industry maturity, the structure of the industry, the geographic scope of competition, and the competitive position of an organization. These influences change as the market moves through different stages of evolution. First, several market situations are examined to highlight the differences in competitive situations. Next, the forces of change that are affecting the business environment are considered. This is followed by a discussion of restructuring actions by organizations seeking to improve their competitive advantage in the turbulent and rapidly changing business environment.

Types of Market Situations

The stage of maturity of a market provides a useful basis for considering different competitive situations. These stages include *emerging, growth, mature,* and *global* market situations.

Emerging Markets.   A new market opportunity may be of interest to the founder of a new enterprise or to an existing company. A new product-market is at the introductory stage of its life cycle. Buyers needs are not well-defined, and there is no base of experience about market behavior:

> Emerging industries are newly formed or re-formed industries that have been created by technological innovations, shifts in relative cost relationships, emergence of new consumer needs, or other economic and sociological changes that elevate a new product or service to the level of a potentially viable business opportunity.[15]

A new product-market is created for one of two reasons. The most common reason is a product innovation that results in an alternative technology for meeting an existing need in the market place. The second reason for a new product-market is an innovation that satisfies a previously unmet need. Examples of new product-market developments that offer alternative solutions to existing buyers' needs include surgical stapling (alternative to needle and suture), word processing equipment and software (alternative to the electric typewriter), and the use of plastics instead of metals in various product applications. Innovations that satisfy previously unmet needs include human heart transplants and portable lap-top and briefcase computers.

"The most pervasive feature of emerging markets is uncertainty about customer acceptance and the eventual size of the market, which process and product technology will be dominant, whether cost declines will be realized, and the identity, structure, and actions of competitors."[16] Buyers' needs are not highly differentiated in the early stages of product-market development because buyers do not have experience with the product. Forecasting the future scope and direction of growth of product-market development may be difficult. For example, in the early stages of the personal computer (PC) market, use of the PC for entertainment in the household was considered to be a strong growth area. Instead, the primary area of growth in the 1980s was business use of the PC. Anticipated growth in household use of PCs did not occur.

Growth Markets.   A new market either moves into the growth stage or dies. The transition from the new market to the growth stage often occurs within a short time span. A rapid growth rate is assumed in this discussion, recognizing that various rates of growth may occur. The growth stage of market development creates several important marketing strategy and competitive advantage issues.

The typical assumption is that the rapidly growing market provides an attractive opportunity for existing firms and potential market entrants. The growth stage product-market is better defined and there is less uncertainty than is present in the emerging stage. Nevertheless, growth creates rapid changes and uncertainties. In the growth stage, buyers gain experience with the product, and sales response patterns are developed. Since the market is not stable, further changes are likely. The size and scope of the market are better defined than in the earlier stage. Management can obtain market information to guide decisions.

Identification of the factors that influence market trends in the growth market is important in evaluating the current and future attractiveness of the market. Business and marketing planning efforts should be closely coordinated to target the most promising growth and competitive advantage opportunities. Market segment identification and analysis become increasingly important as the product-market moves through its life cycle. Differences in buyers' requirements should start to develop in the growth stage if they were not present in the emerging stage.

Mature Markets.   The firms remaining in the industry at the maturity stage of the product-market typically represent a subset of the competitors that previously entered the market. A shakeout often occurs during market maturity. All of the firms who enter the emerging and growth stages of the market do not survive. The needs and characteristics of buyers may also change. Consider, for example, the differences in the size and composition of the personal computer market during its life-cycle stages. The market that emerged in the middle 1970s served the information processing needs of hobbyists. By the late 1970s, a substantial market for PCs in home entertainment had developed. The 1980s marked a major shift toward the business use of PCs. By 1990 business needs dominated the market. Market entry by new competitors in the mature stage is less likely than in previous life-cycle stages. The firms that remain in the industry are successful in gaining and keeping a competitive advantage.

The attractiveness of the product-market may be significantly altered at the maturity stage. Because of this, three important strategic evaluations are essential: (1) monitoring the external environment for new opportunities that match the organization's skills and resources; (2) identifying potential competitor threats to existing technologies (e.g., surgical stapling as a substitute for needle and suture); and (3) identifying opportunities within specific segments of the product-market for new and improved products.

Global Markets.   Gaining knowledge about global markets is important even if management decides to compete only in a domestic market, since domestic markets often include international competitors. Many companies are expanding beyond national boundaries to pursue market opportunities throughout the world. The increasingly smaller world linked by instant communications capabilities, global supply networks, and international financial markets requires the managements of all firms to evaluate global threats and opportunities. Global markets may correspond to any of the product-market maturity stages discussed above.

Competing in global markets creates two important strategic issues. First, slow domestic growth and intense competition in domestic markets encourage companies that have the skills and resources to expand into international markets. Global opportunities are available to firms of various sizes, not just industry giants. Second, competing effectively in domestic markets requires knowledge of competitive forces in the global marketplace.

The unification of Europe in 1992 is illustrative of the changes occurring in markets throughout the world. The elimination of trade barriers in the 12 participating European countries requires major alterations of business and marketing strategies. These changes affect the organizations within the 12-nation group and business firms from other nations that plan to compete in the unified market. Evaluating the need to obtain a European Community partner is an example of the many strategic issues facing U.S. managers. Various issues must be resolved concerning trade protection, advertising strategy, product design variations, pricing, and distribution systems. Nations within the trade group are moving rapidly to gain market leadership. Seimens, the German electronic giant merged with Nixdorf Computer in 1989, an action intended to strengthen both firms for competing against American and Japanese computer makers.

Analyzing the Forces of Change[17]

A major study conducted by the Conference Board Inc. of 64 Canadian, European, Japanese, and U.S. corporations shows the widespread global trend toward strategic refocusing.[18] A related survey of 271 companies headquartered in 34 countries indicates that 61 percent of managers expect their business will broaden in scope, 26 percent forecast a shift in focus, and 13 percent anticipate a narrowing of business scope.[19] Constant change is expected across a wide range of organizations and business environments during the 1990s. Refocusing occurs because of industry consolidation, new patterns of competition, shifts in customer needs/wants, and competitive pressures for improved performance. Not surprisingly, market-related changes are the most common restructuring influences.

Customer Satisfaction.   Shifts in customer needs and wants require restructuring of the marketing organization to improve the effectiveness of sales and marketing efforts. Getting closer to the customer is a high priority for top management in the global struggle for market leadership. Important changes in markets include: (1) greater differentiation of customer needs within markets, creating a greater number of markets and more complex market segments; (2) demand for product/service quality improvement at competitive prices; and (3) expansion in the supporting services provided by the suppliers. IBM's redeployment of employees into the field in the late 1980s was designed to gain closer and stronger relationships with customers. The large number of nonsales personnel involved in this redeployment required an extensive training program in selling and sales support activities.

Industry Structural Changes.   The nature and scope of competition may change because of the consolidation of firms in an industry, insider buyouts, strategic alliances, and other adjustments to the organizations in an industry. The emergence of new forms of competition may also create structural changes in existing industries. Restructuring affects the marketing strategies of the units involved, resulting in changes in product scope, revision of distribution channels, merging two or more sales forces, redeployment of selling effort, and reduction in the size of the sales force.

Distribution Trends.   Methods of distribution in various industries may affect marketing strategies. Examples include the formation of vertical marketing systems (channels owned or controlled by one firm), adoption of single-source supply relationships, just-in-time inventory systems, and the establishment of strategic alliances between independent organizations. These integrated channel strategies create cohesive and closely coordinated distribution networks from producer to end user. The marketing strategy of the firm seeking to manage its distribution channels must be designed to cover all levels of influence in the distribution network.

Environmental Influences.   Various changes in the international and domestic environment create opportunities and threats that require restructuring actions. These influences include public policy changes (e.g., deregulation), social forces, technology advances, and economic performance. Cooperative trade agreements are illustrative responses to environmental influences. New technology may lead to industry and corporate restructuring.

Changes in Business and Marketing Strategies

Market turbulence may result in: (1) adjusting the size of the business; (2) changing product and/or market scope; or (3) creating new working relationships with other organizations. Several possible strategic responses are examined.

Rapid Growth/Retrenchment.   Reducing or rapidly expanding the number of employees of a company or business unit while retaining the existing product mix and market scope is one form of strategic response to an altered business environment. This change affects the size rather than the scope of the organization. Size adjustments may require a new organizational structure and the redeployment of people. For example, Vallen Corporation, the leading firm in the fragmented safety equipment distribution industry is rapidly expanding its nationwide network by opening branches and acquiring small safety equipment distributors. Acquisitions are reducing the number of firms in the industry.

Changing the Product Mix.   Altering a company's mix of products may affect its business operations and marketing strategy. Product expansion may be achieved through internal development or by acquisition. Maytag's additions to its kitchen appliance lines is illustrative. Industry trends in the 1980s toward a small number of full-line manufacturers caused Maytag to expand from its core line of laundry equipment into ranges, refrigerators, and related appliance lines. One consequence confronting Maytag's management is deciding how to market multiple brands of the same appliance. For example, Maytag acquired several refrigerator brands. Marketing strategy issues for Maytag include using a single salesforce or one for each brand, determining wholesale and retail scope of distribution, selecting brand positioning strategies, and developing advertising strategies.

Altering Market Scope.   This situation involves changing market focus using the same product mix. Illustrative actions include expanding into new international markets, altering domestic geographic scope, and targeting new customer groups. Tandy Corp.'s targeting of its personal computer line at the business market in the mid-1980s is illustrative. Tandy's prior targets consisted of consumer and small-business buyers served through retail stores. It was necessary to train and deploy a marketing and sales organization to serve organizational buyers. Larger commercial buyers require direct contact by field salespeople.

Repositioning.   Turbulent market pressures may cause management to reposition the company, business, or product with the targeted customers. The purpose of repositioning is to change how customers and prospects perceive an organization and its brands. Product, distribution, price, and promotion strategies may be affected. These positioning components may also be changed to maintain the same perception of buyers but to do so in a more efficient way. For example, telemarketing may be used to supplement face-to-face selling.

Distribution Channel Integrative Strategies.   An organization in a distribution channel may decide to vertically integrate the channel members (raw materials suppliers, producers, and marketing middlemen) through ownership, creating a vertical marketing system. Cooperative arrangements other than ownership may be established between independent organizations. Regardless of the mechanism used for integration, a major result of these strategies is that the distribution channel forms a competitive unit. The organization that manages the channel must restructure to effectively coordinate and manage the distribution system. For example, The Limited, Inc., coordinates a worldwide distribution network of women's apparel suppliers, warehouses, and retail stores capable of moving a new fashion design from idea to retail stores in 60 days!

Diversification.   Despite the poor performance record of many diversification strategies, some corporations continue to expand into new product and market areas.[20] Diversification actions may include expansion into product and market areas related to the core business or into unrelated products and markets. Diversification requires performing all business functions in a new organization. The firm's existing organizational structure normally cannot serve the needs of a diversification unit. For example, the current salesforce is not experienced in the new product and market areas. Because of this, a typical strategy is to acquire a business already serving in the product/market area targeted for diversification.

Strategic Alliance.   A cooperative alliance between two or more independent companies is intended to create a competitive advantage for each organization. For example, the salesforces of Squibb and McNeil Pharmaceuticals have collaborated to sell Capoton, a high blood-pressure medication, in direct competition with industry leader Merck, Sharp and Dohme. A strategic alliance may vary according to the time span of the agreement, the closeness of operating ties, the number of businesses linked together, the organizational level, the product/market involvement, and the type of marketing ties between the participants.[21]

Each of the strategic responses to market turbulence has a unique impact on the organization involved. The scope of actions may affect the corporate strategy, business unit strategy, and/or marketing strategy. The diversification and strategic alliance situations are corporate in scope whereas other refocusing situations typically affect only business unit and marketing strategies.

The different types of market situations, forces affecting the business environment, and accelerated restructuring of business and marketing strategies illustrate the various competitive situations that may affect an organization. Next, we consider the impact of product-market structure on strategy selection (Exhibit 1–1).

PRODUCT-MARKET DEFINITION AND ANALYSIS

Marketing strategy decisions require a clear definition and understanding of the product-market structure that contains the buyers to be targeted by the organization. Mapping the *entire* market is necessary to guide strategy decisions and anticipate market changes. "Equipped with this map, a company can be in a position to examine all of the players serving the arena and anticipate what changes may occur between and among the segments of the map."[22] Incorrect market definition may result in faulty marketing decisions such as poorly targeted new products, failure to find competitive weaknesses, and ineffective use of marketing resources. Market knowledge provides essential information for marketing strategy design and implementation.

Deciding how to define a market is very important since alternative definitions are possible. There is a tendency to define a market too narrowly, thus excluding potential competitors. Market boundaries change because of differences in buyers' needs and products. The definition of the market should be based on buyers' needs that are satisfied by available products. Thus, a product-market consists of people with needs and product benefits that satisfy those needs. First, the determination of product-market boundaries is considered. Next, the product-market characteristics of different competitive situations are discussed.

Determining Product-Market Boundaries[23]

The differences in buyers' needs and the many alternative brands and types of products that may satisfy the needs of buyers may create a complex product-market structure. Starting with a broad generic need and determining the types of products (or services) that can satisfy the need assure that the market is properly defined. This broad perspective helps to identify potential competitive threats, and opportunities. For example, Western Union's management failed to recognize the impact of facsimile transmission of information as a competitive threat to Western Union's services. The rapid development of fax communications virtually eliminated Western Union's competitive advantage in the late 1980s.

Generic Product-Market. The starting point in product-market definition is to specify the need/want that a group of products satisfy. The generic "product-market" includes all products (or services) that can satisfy a broad need such as consumer needs for short-term cash investment. Specific types of services that may meet this need include checking accounts, money market funds, bank CDs and Treasury Bills. The objective is to define the generic product-market and then break out the various specific needs and products that satisfy the needs. This establishes the product-market structure within which an organization's brand(s) compete.

Product Type Product-Market. This level of market structure is a product category or classification that offers a unique set of benefits and cost, which is intended to satisfy a buyer's need or want in a specific way. Thus, two different product concepts or technologies that satisfy a particular need represent two different product type product-markets. A checking account becomes one product type and money market funds another product type product-market. Within the product type, there may be variants such as money market funds offered by brokers, banks, and mutual funds. Market segments may exist within each variant category.

A product-market structure for consumers' needs for short-term loans is shown in Exhibit 1–3. The various services satisfy different types of buyers, loan requirements, and use situations. The objective is to define the array of needs and products that satisfy these needs so that the entire structure of the product-market is shown. More complete diagrams of the type shown in Exhibit 1–3 can be used for this purpose.

EXHIBIT 1–3 Product-Market Structure Illustration

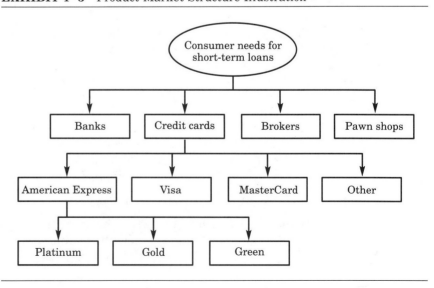

Stages of Product-Market Development

The nature and scope of product-markets vary in different competitive situations. For example, market definition may be more difficult in emerging markets than in mature markets. Mature markets often display stable characteristics and are typically well-defined. Buyers' needs and wants, product scope and differentiation, distribution characteristics, rate of change of the product-market, and forecasting complexity are affected by different competitive situations. Several illustrative characteristics of product-markets are shown in Exhibit 1–4 to highlight the variations that occur at different stages of market maturity.

EXHIBIT 1–4   Product-Market Characteristics for Different Competitive Situations

---

Emerging Markets

Market definition:
Product-market boundaries are not clearly established when the product is new to the world. Market scope may be relatively narrow if the product is intended to satisfy a previously unmet need. Emerging markets for substitutes (e.g., alternative technologies) of existing products may be defined in reference to the existing product-market.

Buyers' needs/wants:
Needs are relatively similar since buyers have had limited experience with the new product/service. Some differentiation may occur depending on brand alternatives and product differentiation.

Product scope and differentiation:
Range of models and applications are often limited. Alternative design concepts may be used by competing firms (e.g., Betamax and VHS video cassette player/recorder systems).

Distribution characteristics:
Channel systems will have to be developed for products that satisfy previously unmet needs. Substitute products may benefit from existing distribution channels.

Rate of change of product-market:
Product-market scope and structure are likely to change during the emerging stage, particularly if the rate of buyer acceptance is high. Change will not be as rapid as in the growth stage of the market. The size of the market and growth rate will be influenced by the market potential for the product.

Forecasting complexity:
Determining the future scope and direction of growth of the product-market may be difficult during the emerging stage. There is often a tendency to overestimate the speed and magnitude of market growth.

EXHIBIT 1–4   *(continued)*

Projections are often very optimistic concerning the rate of acceptance of the new product.

Growth Markets

Market definition:
Product-market structure is more clearly defined than in the emerging stage, but continues to change because of buyer and competition influences. Competitor structure is influenced by entry and exit of competitors.

Buyer needs/wants:
As buyers gain experience with the product, their needs/wants display differences. These variations create opportunities for segmentation.

Product scope and differentiation:
Models and applications expand during the growth stage. Brand offerings multiply as a result of entry of new competitors. Lack of standardization of brands continues to prevail.

Distribution characteristics:
Channel structure begins to develop during this stage. Experimentation in alternative channels may occur. Direct distribution to end-users may be used for appropriate products.

Rate of change of product-market:
Rapid growth during this stage may create demand and supply gaps. Rapid acceptance of the product by buyers may cause short-term shortages. Overreaction by competitors may occur, leading to capacity expansion.

Forecasting complexity:
Uncertainty continues to exist about the future size of the product-market. Broad determinants of market size may be identifiable. Large forecasting errors are likely.

Mature Markets

Market definition:
Market structure should be clearly established at this stage. Buyers' characteristics should be available and variations in purchasing patterns established.

Buyers' needs/wants:
Substantial variation in buyers' requirements and preferences is characteristic in mature product-markets. Segmentation opportunities are generally favorable and selective targeting may be essential for competing by small market share firms.

Product scope and differentiation:
Product variations do not expand at this stage. Differentiation is often used to target the needs of specific segments. Brands have established positions with buyers. Consolidation among industry members may occur.

EXHIBIT 1–4   (*concluded*)

Distribution characteristics:
  Distribution networks should be well developed at this stage. These may involve direct sales forces and/or use of middlemen. Entry by new competitors may be difficult due to entry barriers.

Rate of change of product-market:
  The product-market should display slow and relatively stable growth patterns. Market saturation may occur. Market decline may eventually occur.

Forecasting complexity:
  Forecasting should be accurate at this stage with the determinants of market size clearly established. Market segment forcasting is necessary since size and growth potential normally vary across segments.

MARKET SEGMENTATION

The next step in the marketing strategy selection process is segmenting the product-market (Exhibit 1–1). Market segmentation is a requirement for competing in many product-markets. "Segmenting the marketplace is one of the most important strategic moves that can be made by high-tech companies, industrial firms, and firms that sell services to other businesses."[24] Buyers often display different preferences for products and services. Finding out what these customer satisfaction requirements are and grouping people (organizations) with similar preferences is important in guiding marketing strategy decisions. Creative segmentation is often a key to gaining competitive advantage. Market segmentation provides an opportunity for a small organization to target buyers where the firm's advantages are most favorable. Large companies use segmentation as a basis for market domination by targeting multiple segments.

Segmentation is the process of dividing a product-market into subgroups of buyers, each group displaying some degree of similarity of buyers' preferences toward specific product attributes. Management may decide to target one or more segments. Segmentation helps a company to match its capabilities to buyers' requirements and improves customer satisfaction by focusing efforts on specific needs. Customer satisfaction creates competitive advantage.

The automobile market illustrates the importance of segmenting and selectively targeting buyers. In 1965, the sales of General Motors' best selling model, the Chevrolet Impala, were 1.5 million units compared with 300,000 units for the 1987 sales leader, the Chevrolet Celebrity. Thus, the best selling GM brand in 1987 was one fifth of 1965 sales. The mass markets of the 1960s and 1970s are gone. Finely tuned market segmentation strategies are essential in today's complex marketplace. Competing in the 1990s will demand penetrating analysis of buyers' needs and the identification of strategically important segments. Segmentation analysis is critical to deciding where to compete, when to compete, and how to compete.

Segmentation is examined at various stages of market development to demonstrate how segmentation is affected by different competitive situations.[25]

Segmenting Emerging Markets

The similarity of buyers' needs in a new product-market often limits the depth of segmentation. It may be possible to identify a few broad segments. For example, heavy, medium, and low product usage creates segments in a new-product-market where usage varies across buyers. In some instances segmentation may not be feasible. An alternative is to define and describe an average or typical user, delaying segmentation analysis until the market develops further.

A segment of an existing product-market may develop to create a new product-market variant. The segment category becomes large enough to become a new product-market. The market for lap-top computers is illustrative. This market is developing so rapidly that it has become a distinct product-market within the personal computer market. Segments in the market reflect differences in use requirements, product features, and price/quality variations.

Segmenting the new product-market into broad user groups may be feasible using judgmental rather than analytical methods. One approach for the market pioneer is to identify the most promising user group(s) and to focus marketing efforts on one or a few segments that display the primary opportunity for early sales. For example, the market for microwave cookware was initially determined by microwave oven ownership coupled with factors influencing heavy usage (e.g., two working spouses, large family, etc.). Age was also useful in targeting early adopters. Older people were unsure about the safety of microwave cooking.

Continuous monitoring of the emerging market is essential to spot important directions of future development and the formation of groups of buyers with similar requirements. Adaptability of competing firms to the changing needs of buyers is critical to maintaining a competitive edge. Failure to respond to changes in the marketplace during the emerging stage may weaken a firm's market position and lead to failure in the growth stage of the market. Early awareness of trends in segment formation provides an important competitive advantage.

Segmenting Growth Markets

If not already beginning to develop in the emerging market, segments should start to form in the growth stage. "Customers with homogeneous needs begin to be identified, which allows marketing effort to be targeted more precisely, and experience with the product, process, and materials technologies leads to greater efficiency and increased standardization."[26] The market environment is moving from highly uncertain to moderately uncertain. Of course, further change is likely, but the direction of change is toward better knowledge about the forces that influence the size and composition of the product-market. The boundaries of a product-market become more distinct in the growth stage. Patterns of use can be identified, and the characteristics of buyers can be related to their use patterns. Segmentation by type of industry and/or type of application may be feasible in industrial markets. Characteristics such as age, income, and family size may identify broad segments for consumer products such as food and drugs. Analysis of existing buyers may indicate market potential guidelines.

Market composition often changes during the growth stage. The entry of new competitors, coupled with buyers' experience, creates various differences in both customers and product offerings. Anticipating the directions of change is very important in keeping a competitive advantage. The potential for segment growth and stability must be evaluated by management.

Segmenting Mature Markets

Segmentation is essential at the maturity stage of the product-market life cycle. The product-market should be clearly defined, indicating the differences in buyers' needs and preferences. The market should have generally stable characteristics. Change during maturity should be much slower and more predictable than during the growth stage. The factors influencing market growth should be apparent. The market is not likely to expand or decline rapidly unless an unusual external influence occurs. A severe oil supply shortage due to a Middle East conflict is illustrative of an unusual influence.

Identification and evaluation of market segments are essential to choosing market targets that offer unique competitive advantages. Experience should be available concerning buyers' responses to the marketing efforts of the firms competing in the product-market. This information helps to establish market segments. Knowledge of the effects of environmental influences on the segments in the market should enable accurate forecasts. Marketing research information is useful to identify who the existing (and potential) buyers are, growth trends, gaps in customer satisfaction, and competitor strengths and weaknesses. Standardized information services are available for various mature markets such as food and drugs, pharmaceuticals, automobiles, and computers. These services provide marketing research data on a subscription basis to participating companies.

Mature markets contain buyers with experience. Buyers have information about competing brands and often display preferences for particular brands. The key marketing issue is developing and sustaining brand preference since buyers are aware of the product type and its features. Buyers recognize their needs in mature markets. The challenge is matching the firm's product offerings to the needs they can satisfy. Mature markets are often quite large. This enables a firm to find attractive sales opportunities within one or a few segments. Consider, for example, the markets created for microwave cookware and food products by the nearly 80 percent of U.S. households that use microwave ovens.

Segmenting Global Markets

The product-markets in any developed country typically are composed of market segments. The prior discussion of segmenting markets at different maturity stages generally applies to international markets. There may also be advantages to segmenting across domestic boundaries if buyers' needs and wants remain similar. For example, segmentation is an important strategic issue for the organizations planning to compete in the European market after unification in 1992.

There may be similarities in consumer behavior across national boundaries in some or all of the European Community countries.[27] Nevertheless, there are many cultural, historical, institutional, physical, and economic differences among the 12 countries. Unification will not eliminate these differences. The identification of similarities will enable Pan-European segmentation for some products and services. Moreover, similarities will probably increase over time between buyers in particular segments across the country boundaries of the EC countries.

SUMMARY

This chapter considers how to analyze competitive situations and determine market structure. It provides a foundation for selecting marketing strategies in different competitive situations. The chapter begins with a step-by-step approach to marketing strategy selection (Exhibit 1–1), which provides a guide to marketing strategy analysis and selection. Several important criteria in strategy selection are discussed. For example, one important factor in strategy selection when entering new markets is recognizing the entry barriers that may be present.

The discussion moves next to examination of different types of market situations (emerging, growth, mature, and global markets). An analysis of the factors that cause changes in market and competitive situations follows. These changes are examined to identify how they affect business and marketing strategies.

The chapter concludes with a discussion of product-market definition and analysis at different stages of evolution and market segmentation. Market segmentation is a requirement for competing in many product-markets. Segmentation at different stages of market evolution is discussed.

Chapter 2 continues the examination of the marketing strategy development shown in Exhibit 1–1. It considers industry structure and competition, competitive advantage, and selection of market targeting and positioning strategies.

NOTES

1. This process and the discussion of strategy choice criteria are drawn from David W. Cravens, *Strategic Marketing,* 3rd. ed. (Homewood, Ill.: Richard D. Irwin, Inc., 1991), chapter 8.
2. The term *product* refers to both physical goods and services.
3. Zachary Schiller, "Stalking the New Consumer," *Business Week,* August 28, 1989, pp. 54–58 and 62.
4. Michael E. Porter, *Competitive Advantage* (New York: The Free Press, 1985), p. 3.
5. Andy Zipser, "Can Dell, CompuAdd Broaden Niches?" *The Wall Street Journal,* January 5, 1990, pp. B1 and 6.
6. These criteria are suggested by George S. Day, "Tough Questions for Developing Strategies," *Journal of Business Strategy,* Winter 1986, pp. 60–68.
7. Thomas Kamm, "Michelin is Revamping Its Strategy in Bid to Inflate Its Position in the Tire Industry," *The Wall Street Journal,* December 12, 1984, p. 30.
8. Day, "Tough Questions for Developing Strategies," pp. 66–67.
9. Lawrence Ingrassia, "Face-Off: A Recovering Gillette Hopes for Vindication in a High-Tech Razor," *The Wall Street Journal,* September 29, 1989, pp. A1 and 4.
10. Michael Porter, "Industry Structure and Competitive Strategy: Keys to Profitability," *Financial Analysis Journal,* July–August 1980, pp. 30–41.
11. Michael Porter, *Competitive Strategy* (New York: The Free Press), 1980.
12. Fahri Karakaya and Michael J. Stahl, "Barriers to Entry and Market

Entry Decisions in Consumer and Industrial Goods Markets," *Journal of Marketing,* April 1989, pp. 80–91.

13. See, for example, Ibid., and William T. Robinson, "Sources of Market Pioneer Advantages: The Case of Industrial Goods Industries," *Journal of Marketing Research,* February 1988, pp. 87–94.

14. Karakaya and Stahl, "Barriers to Entry," pp. 80–91.

15. Porter, *Competitive Strategy,* p. 215.

16. Mary Lambkin and George S. Day, "Evolutionary Processes in Competitive Markets: Beyond the Product Life Cycle," *Journal of Marketing,* July 1989, p. 4.

17. The discussion in this section is drawn from David W. Cravens, Raymond W. LaForge, and Thomas N. Ingram, "Sales Strategy: Charting a New Course in Turbulent Markets," *Business,* December–January 1991, pp. 3–9.

18. James K. Brown, *Refocusing the Company's Business,* Report No. 873 (New York: The Conference Board, Inc., 1985), p. 1.

19. Harold Stieglitz, *Chief Executives View Their Jobs: Today and Tomorrow,* Report No. 871 (New York: The Conference Board, Inc., 1985).

20. Porter, Michael E., "From Competitive Advantage to Corporate Strategy," *Harvard Business Review,* May–June 1987, pp. 43–59.

21. See Lee Adler, "Symbiotic Marketing," *Harvard Business Review,* November–December 1966, pp. 59–71; and P. "Rajan" Varadarajan and Daiel Rajaratnam," Symbiotic Marketing Revisited," *Journal of Marketing,* January 1986, pp. 7–17.

22. William E. Rothschild, "Surprise and Competitive Advantage," *The Journal of Business Strategy,* Winter 1984, p. 10.

23. The following discussion is based on Cravens, *Strategic Marketing,* chapter 4.

24. James D. Hlavacek and B. C. Ames, "Segmenting Industrial and High-Tech Markets," *The Journal of Business Strategy,* Fall 1986, p. 39.

25. The following discussion is drawn from Cravens, *Strategic Marketing,* chapter 8.

26. Lambkin and Day, "Evolutionary Processes in Competitive Markets," p. 14.

27. John A. Quelch, Robert D. Buzzell, and Eric R. Salama, *The Marketing Challenge of 1992* (Reading, Mass.: Addison-Wesley Publishing Company, 1990), pp. 69–71.

Marketing Strategies for Different Competitive Situations

The discussion of different competitive situations, market structure, and segmentation in Chapter 1 identifies important guidelines for marketing strategy development. Chapter 2 considers industry structure and competition at different stages of market evolution, selecting a strategy for competitive advantage, and choosing targeting and positioning strategies. These topics complete the remaining steps in the analysis and strategy development process introduced by Exhibit 1–1 in Chapter 1.

INDUSTRY STRUCTURE AND COMPETITION

Defining and analyzing the competitive arena is necessary to determine what the competition is doing and what existing and potential competitors are likely to do in the future. Competitor identification, analysis, and evaluation serve several purposes.[1] Study of the competition helps management to avoid surprises and to identify threats and opportunities. Knowledge of competitor strengths and weaknesses helps to gain competitive advantage by decreasing reaction time. Finally, competitor analysis enables management to understand its own company better. Industry structure and competition are examined in different competitive environments.[2]

Competing in Emerging Markets

There is no industry structure when the market pioneer enters the market, unless the new product-market emerges from an existing segment of a product-market. The rate of new industry development depends on the attractiveness of the market and entry barriers. "The emerging phase of the industry is usually accompanied by the presence of the greatest proportion of newly formed companies (to be contrasted with newly formed units of established firms) that the industry will ever experience."[3]

New enterprises are more likely to enter a new product-market than are large, well established companies. The exception is the development of a major innovation in a large company coupled with strong entry barriers to prevent other companies from entering the market. The pioneers that develop new product-markets "are typically small new organizations set up specifically to exploit first-mover advantages in the new resource space."[4] These entrepreneurs often have limited access to resources and must focus on product-market opportunities that require low levels of investment and simple organizational designs. The early stages of the personal computer software market included such entrepreneurs.

The development of the industry is influenced by various factors including the rate of acceptance of the product by buyers, entry barriers, the performance of firms serving the market, and the future expectations of market opportunity. The possession of proprietary technology by the pioneer may make entry by others impossible until they can gain access to the technology. Xerox, with its copying process, and Polaroid, with its instant film, held monopoly positions for several years. In contrast, the use of standard components and open architecture enabled many new firms to enter the personal computer market in the 1980s.

Industry formation may be affected by various situational factors. Porter cites several problems that may constrain industry development:[5]

Inability of firms to obtain raw materials and components and/or rapid escalation of supply prices.

Absence of established distribution network, support services, and other infrastructure inadequacies.

Lack of product standardization and erratic product quality.

Customers' confusion due to lack of experience and perceptions of possible obsolescence of the product.

High costs due to supply constraints and learning costs.

Financial and regulatory constraints.

An emerging industry may develop along various lines depending on how the above factors affect the industry structure. The initial period of development may include many changes in industry structure, creating both high risks and high rewards for the firms that enter. Major change during the initial years is a common feature of emerging industries. Some potential entrants may decide to observe industry development before considering entry. For example, established companies typically delay entry until the market moves into the growth phase.

Competing in High-Growth Markets

The prevailing assumption is that high-growth markets are very attractive, and that early entry offers important competitive advantages. There are also potential problems for industry participants in high-growth product-markets:

> First, a visible growth market can attract too many competitors—the market and its distribution channel cannot support them. The intensity of competition is accentuated when growth fails to match expectations or eventually slows. Second, the early entrant is unable to cope when key success factors or technologies change, in part because it lacks the financial skills or organizational skills.[6]

Success is highly influenced by making the right decisions to exploit the opportunities and to avoid the risks inherent in a rapidly expanding product-market. Making generalizations about industry structure in growth markets is difficult. Normally, the number of competitors will increase rapidly, and business failures are likely because of the crowding of opportunities and the lack of skills and resources needed to gain competitive advantage.

There is some evidence that large, established firms are more likely to enter markets at the growth stage rather than at the emerging stage. The large firms may not be able to move as quickly as small specialist firms in exploiting the opportunities in the emerging product-market.[7] Since the large organizations have skills and resource advantages for achieving market leadership, these powerful firms can overcome some of the timing advantages of the market pioneers. They also have the advantage of evaluating the attractiveness of the product-market during its initial development. The uncertainties about the size and scope of the emerging market may encourage a wait-and-see position by large potential competitors.

Competing in Mature Markets

Companies in mature industries: (1) create intense competition for market share; (2) place heavy emphasis on cost, service, and profits; (3) make adjustments in business and marketing strategies, (4) may slow new product flows, (5) may experience international competition; and (6) may experience increases in the power of channel organizations linking manufacturers with end-users.[8] Deciding how to compete successfully in a mature product-market is a demanding challenge. Maturity is a common situation in a wide range of markets.

The typical mature industry structure consists of a few companies that dominate the industry and a variety of companies pursuing market selectivity and/or product differentiation strategies. Entry into a mature product-market is often limited by major barriers coupled with unattractive opportunities for sales and profits. Entry occurs primarily by firms that pursue market or product selectivity strategies. Acquisition may be used for market entry rather than to internally develop products and marketing capabilities. Mature industries are increasingly attractive targets for global consolidation. Examples include automobile tires, computers, foods, household appliances, pharmaceuticals, and consumer electronics.

Another industry form that may occur in mature markets is the fragmented industry. This industry structure consists of many firms, none of which holds a strong industrywide position. The fragmented industry is made up of a large number of small- and medium-sized companies.[9] Fragmented industries exist in services, retailing, distribution, wood and metal fabrication, and agricultural products. These industries may offer important opportunities for a firm to create a strong market position by expanding its scope through acquisition and geographic expansion. ChemLawn, in lawn care, adopted this strategy in the 1970s. Vallen Corp., in safety equipment distribution, is currently expanding its market position.

Dimensions of Global Competition

Chief executives in a wide range of industries recognize that competing internationally is a requirement for sustaining competitive advantage. Several factors contribute to the importance of expanding into international markets. A *Wall Street Journal* survey of 433 CEOs from the United States, Europe, Japan, and the Pacific Rim cites the following reasons for global expansion:[10] increasing revenue, increasing profitability, achieving technological leadership, diversifying into new businesses, lowering business costs, and improving product quality. American executives are less concerned with global expansion than executives in Europe, Japan, and the Pacific Rim. For example, only 27 percent of U.S. executives consider global expansion a way to increase profitability compared with 53 percent of European and Japanese CEOs and 40 percent of Pacific Rim CEOs. Other surveys indicate very similar responses. The complacency that contributed to the loss of market positions in the 1980s continues to prevail in many U.S. firms.

The success of Japanese companies in penetrating American and European markets requires consideration of their marketing methods. Japanese businesses have developed very effective customer-driven management processes. Key strengths of Japanese organizations are their team-oriented multifunctional business processes. Interestingly, the marketing approaches of Japanese companies are traditional, based on concepts and methods developed in the United States and Europe.[11] These companies have achieved high levels of customer satisfaction through study and analysis of buyers' needs coupled with impressive implementation of the strategies selected. These competitors recognize that customer satisfaction is a continuing, long-term responsibility of everyone in the organization.

SELECTING A STRATEGY FOR COMPETITIVE ADVANTAGE[12]

Market definition and analysis, market segmentation, and analysis of industry structure and competition provide important information for deciding how to gain competitive advantage for a particular competitive situation (Exhibit 1–1). The intensity of competition in the markets throughout the world highlights the importance of achieving and sustaining competitive advantage. Jack Welch, chairman of the General Electric Company states, "If you don't have a competitive advantage, don't compete."[13] His restructuring actions in the 1980s moved GE out of consumer electronics and other businesses that did not represent attractive opportunities for GE. It is increasingly clear that a strong relationship exists between business performance and competitive advantage. Day and Wensley emphasize the importance of defining competitive advantage to include both the state of advantage and how it is gained:

> This integrated view is based on positional and performance superiority being a consequence of relative superiority in the skills and resources a business deploys. These skills and resources reflect the pattern of past investments to enhance competitive positions. The sustainability of this positional advantage requires that the business set up barriers that make imitation difficult. Because these barriers to imitation are constantly eroding, the firm must continue investing to sustain or improve the advantage.[14]

Competitive advantage is an ongoing process rather than a one-time consequence. Deciding how to gain and keep competitive advantages requires (1) understanding the sources of competitive advantage, (2) evaluating existing competitive advantage, and (3) determining what is required to sustain advantage.

Sources of Advantage

Competitive advantage indicates the differences among competitors or uniqueness in the case of a firm holding a monopoly position. The sources of advantages are superior skills and superior resources.[15]

Superior Skills.   Superior skills help an organization to develop and implement strategies that will differentiate the firm from its competition. Skills include technical, managerial, and operational capabilities. Consider, for example, the very successful Pentech International, Inc., a small producer of crayons and specialty pens. The company targets children and their mothers.[16] The innovative chairman and management team develop products that offer a unique advantage but may not generate enough sales to be of interest to large companies. Pentech's 1990 sales were $30 million compared with $18 million in 1989. The company's products include erasable marking pens and Gripstix pencils that have special grooves to fit a child's fingers.

Superior Resources.   This source of advantage may include strong distribution networks, brand image (e.g., Rubbermaid), production capability, marketing power (experienced salesforce), technology, and natural resources. De Beers' control of 85 percent of the world supply of uncut diamonds is illustrative. The firm's monopoly position enables it to control the flow and prices of diamonds throughout the world.

Both skills and resources contribute to gaining advantage. Strength in one source can overcome the limitations regarding the other sources. The economic performance of Singapore in Southeast Asia is particularly impressive, considering the country's lack of natural resources. The skills of Singapore's leaders, the work ethic of the population, and the country's strategic location have overcome major resource constraints. For example, Singapore Airlines is one of the most profitable air carriers in the world.

Competitive advantage results from cost leadership and/or differentiation that creates superior value for customers (Exhibit 2–1). Cost advantage enables a firm to offer superior value by pricing an equivalent product at a lower price than its competitors. Office warehouse chains have been very successful in competing with traditional high-margin office supply retailers using this strategy.

EXHIBIT 2–1   Sources of Competitive Advantage

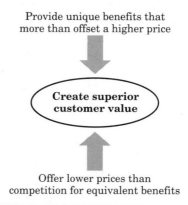

Provide unique benefits that
more than offset a higher price

**Create superior
customer value**

Offer lower prices than
competition for equivalent benefits

Source: Based on Michael E. Porter, *Competitive Advantage* (New York: The Free Press, 1985), p. 3.

Differentiation that corresponds to buyers' preferences provides unique benefits that more than offset a higher price. Differentiation may be achieved through innovative products, brand image, special features, and other types of differentiation. Mercedes automobiles and Rolex watches are examples of products that are marketed using successful differentiation strategies. The Limited, in women's apparel, uses a combination of innovative styling and attractive prices to create superior customer value.

An important factor in gaining advantage is deciding *where* and *how* to compete. Buyers in market segments often vary in their preferences for different product attributes. For example, the decision of Snap-on-Tools' management to serve professional mechanics' hand tool needs, resulted in targeting a market segment that is willing to pay premium prices for high quality products supported by responsive customer services delivered to the customer's auto repair facilities. During the 1970s and 1980s the company avoided head-on competition with mass merchandisers and Asian suppliers of low priced tools.

Value Chain Analysis.   "The value chain disaggregates a firm into its strategically relevant activities in order to understand the behavior of costs and the existing and potential sources of differentiation."[17] The activities that an organization performs to design, produce, market, deliver, and support its products or services represent its value chain. The producer of a product is part of a system of value chains consisting of its suppliers and distribution network (e.g., distributors, dealers, retailers). Competitive advantage occurs when the organization performs the value chain activities (e.g., marketing and sales, technology development, production) at lower costs or better than the competing firms.

The purpose of value chain analysis is to evaluate each key activity to determine competitive advantage. Advantage gaps target high priority activities for management. For example, reducing the time from placing an order to delivery is desired by most buyers. High performance wholesalers of medical supplies have developed fast and cost-effective electronic ordering systems for their retail customers.

Sustaining Competitive Advantage

"For a producer to enjoy a competitive advantage in a product/market segment, the difference or differences between him and his competitors must be felt in the market place: that is they must be reflected in some *product/delivery attribute* that is a *key buying criterion* for the market."[18] A capability gap is the difference between a firm's capability and the strongest competitor for a key buying criterion. An organization has a competitive advantage when its capability exceeds the strongest competitor for a key buying criterion. Management must identify an aspect of differentiation that the customer will perceive as a superior value and an advantage that cannot be easily duplicated by the competition. This represents a sustainable competitive advantage. Capability gaps fall into four categories:[19]

Business system gaps are due to the ability of a company to perform individual functions better than competitors and the difficulty competitors have in eliminating the gap. American Airlines SABRE reservations system is widely acknowledged as the best in the industry.

Position gaps occur because of prior decisions, actions, and circumstances. Rubbermaid's strong brand image in housewares is illustrative. The name is familiar to almost all buyers. This image was created during a long time span.

Regulatory/legal gaps are created through special treatment of an organization by government. Examples include patents, quotas, operating licenses, import quotas, and consumer safety laws.

Organizational or managerial quality gaps display an organization's ability to consistently innovate and adapt more quickly and effectively than the competition. The Limited, in women's apparel retailing, can identify new clothing trends, produce the clothing, and move it to retail stores much faster than its competitors.

Competitors are constantly trying to reduce (or eliminate) the capability gap. Striving for continuous improvement in the value offered to buyers and/or the costs of providing the product or service are requirements for sustaining advantage. New products that meet buyers' needs better than existing products create advantage. Japanese companies have been particularly impressive in using this strategy in the camera and consumer electronics markets.

There are often important differences in competitive advantage at various stages of market evolution. The following discussion considers advantage strategies in emerging, growth, mature, and global markets.

Strategy for Competitive Advantage in Emerging Markets

Competitive advantage for a firm entering a new product-market is often achieved by offering buyers unique benefits rather than lower prices for equivalent benefits.[20] Cost may be the basis of superior value when the new product is a lower-cost technology compared with an existing product. For example, the availability of fax communications offers a lower-cost method of sending a small amount of printed information to distant locations compared to overnight express services.

The choice of when to enter a new product-market may result in a competitive advantage. Research concerning the order of market entry indicates that the pioneer has a distinct advantage over firms entering the market after the pioneer.[26] These studies estimate that the second firm entering the market will obtain 60 to 70 percent of the share of the pioneer. The pioneer can develop entry barriers, making it more difficult and costly for others to enter. The advantage of entering after the pioneer is the opportunity to evaluate the pioneer's performance and thus reduce the risk of entry failure. Entry timing may also depend on the firm's resources and skills.

Advantage may be gained in various ways in an emerging industry.[22] Management's lack of experience in the market offers no clear guide to strategy selection. The uncertainty about how buyers will react to product offers results in different product designs, positioning concepts, distribution strategies, and supporting activities. The absence of product standards is typical in emerging markets. Differences in personal computer operating systems occurred in early stages of this product-market, which caused different computer brands to be incompatible. Similar variations often occur in new consumer electronics products.

The uncertainties that exist in an emerging industry acknowledged, experience suggests, "that more successful or longer-living firms engage in less change than firms which fail."[23] Successful pioneering firms select and follow a consistent strategy on a continuing basis. If these findings in the minicomputer industry apply across a broad range of new ventures, then the choice of an appropriate entry strategy is very important. Of course, some adjustments in customer targeting and positioning strategies are often necessary over the product life cycle.

Business strategies in new markets can be classified according to market targeting scope and market penetration actions.[24] The former may range from a broad coverage of the product-market to a narrow segment focus. The latter refers to the degree of aggressiveness in the use of resources to achieve market penetration. Factors influencing the choice of strategy include the organization's capabilities and resources, the competitive opportunity, and management's risk-reward assessment. Market focus may offer less risk and greater flexibility in adapting to changing conditions. Greater market scope offers more power for influencing the future direction of the market and creating entry barriers.

Strategies for Competitive Advantage in Growth Markets

A comparative analysis of strategies at different product-market life cycle stages is shown in Exhibit 2–2. The "developing" market category in Exhibit 2–2 corresponds to the growth stage discussed in this chapter. Analysis of the historical performance of successful strategies suggests that the early followers with established businesses in related markets are often the best performers in developing (growth) markets. Johnson & Johnson's later entry into the surgical stapler market pioneered by U.S. Surgical Corporation (see Case 4–2) is illustrative. Established firms have experience in a related market that can be quickly applied in the growth product-market.

EXHIBIT 2–2   Competition and Selection in Developing Markets: Strategies for Success*

Niche Configuration	Embryonic	Developing	Maturing
Population density	Low	Increasing	High
Size and rate of environmental change	High	Reducing	Low
Predominant organization form	r-specialists	K-generalists	K-generalists
Other forms	r-generalists	Polymorphists	K-specialists
Best performers	r-specialists	K-generalists	K-generalists

* r-specialists are small-scale pioneers, and r-generalists are large-scale pioneers. K-generalists are early followers with established businesses in related markets. Polymorphists are early followers with widely diversified portfolios. K-specialists are small-scale late entrants occupying narrow market segments.

Source: Mary Lambkin and George S. Day, "Evolutionary Processes in Competitive Markets: Beyond the Product Life Cycle," *Journal of Marketing*, July 1989, p. 12.

A study of the firms entering and exiting the minicomputer industry highlights two performance characteristics in the rapid growth stage of the product-market: (1) survival rates are much higher for aggressive firms competing on a broad market scope compared with conservative firms competing on the same basis, and (2) survival rates are high (about three-quarters) for both aggressive and conservative specialists.[25] In this industry survival requires aggressive action by firms that seek large market positions in the total market, while the other competitors are likely to be more successful using market selectivity strategies. Similar strategies may be appropriate in other growth markets.

Strategies for Competitive Advantage in Mature Markets

Management of companies in mature product-markets typically follow objectives seeking to *stabilize, turnaround,* or *harvest* the business. The stabilize objective may be pursued by cost reduction, selective targeting, and/or product differentiation. Restructuring the corporation is undertaken to try to improve (turn around) financial performance. Harvesting is the decision not to compete. These objectives may be achieved by gaining advantage via market position or specialization.

Market Position Advantage.   In markets where volume production and experience lower costs, a few large firms often dominate the market. This represents the oligopolistic industry discussed in economics. For example, the global tire-making industry is dominated by Michelin (France), Goodyear, and Bridgestone (Japan). Consolidation of tire producers through mergers, acquisitions, and restructuring occurred during the 1980s. Michelin is the market leader. The three giants will battle for market domination during the 1990s. Advantage of the market leaders includes scale economies, brand position, experience, and resources.

Companies that are at a disadvantage in mature markets are the small-scale subunits of large diversified companies and smaller specialists that entered the market at the growth stage and cannot compete in a highly competitive market.[26] These companies may be forced to exit the market during the stage of product-market maturity. Segment domination of the specialist is often a critical success factor.

Specialization.   A firm that does not possess a market position advantage in a mature market must usually adopt a specialization strategy. Regardless of available skills and resources, it is very difficult (and costly) to gain a large market share position in a mature market. Instead, market focus is often a more successful strategy. Of importance is the likelihood of segments where opportunities exist for specialization. The market leader(s) may dominate the market and not satisfy the needs of all buyers:

> Typically, a generalist strategy appeals to some common denominator across all areas of the markets in order to maximize economies of scale. The cost advantage of such a strategy, however, may be offset by an inability to cater to segments of the market that have heterogeneous requirements.[27]

Examples of successful specialization strategies in mature markets include Cooper Tire in automobile tires and Convex Computer in mini-supercomputers. Cooper targets the replacement-tire segment while Convex targets scientists and engineers with applications requiring extensive numerical calculations.

Gaining Advantages in Global Markets

Companies competing in international markets may target a single country, several countries, or compete on a global basis. Top management must decide whether to compete internationally, and, if so, how to compete. Competing with a domestic focus also requires an understanding of relevant global influences on the domestic strategy.

Multinational and global strategies reflect different strategic perspectives. The multinational company adapts its home-country strategy to foreign markets. The global corporation considers the entire world as the competitive arena. It may be located anywhere and it uses its resources and capabilities in a worldwide network of manufacturing and marketing operations.[28] The multinational corporation develops its domestic strategy for each of the countries targeted rather than developing a coordinated strategy for competing in global markets. The distinction between the two concepts centers more on strategic perspective than on differences in specific targeting and positioning actions. End-user customer targets differ across national boundaries as well as within each country.

Deciding how to compete in international markets is an important strategy issue. Buzzell and Quelch identify three strategic options that may be considered by a multinational threatened by global competition.[29] One option is to convert to a global strategy. Examples of companies shifting toward global strategies include IBM, Michelin, Sony, and Black and Decker. A second option is establishing a strategic alliance with other companies. This combination of partners is intended to achieve global scope. Examples of international alliances include Volvo and Renault in automobiles and Texas Instruments and Hatachi in semiconductors. A third option is to target a market segment that a company can dominate and for which a company can build entry barriers against global competitors. The segment strategy may be domestic or international in scope. Producers of expensive Swiss watches appear to be following this strategy.

TARGETING AND POSITIONING STRATEGIES[30]

Deciding targeting and positioning strategies is the final step in selecting a marketing strategy for the organization's particular competitive situation (Exhibit 1–1). Management must select an effective market target and positioning strategy for gaining a strong market position in the competitive situation confronting the firm. Identifying targets that offer opportunities for advantage to an organization is an important strategic challenge. These targets are often market segments within the total market. Targeting may range from domination of a single segment to strong multisegment positions in one or more product-markets. Examples of effective targeting and positioning strategies exist in all kinds of businesses.

Targeting Strategy

The choice of market target(s) determines the people (organizations) in a product-market that a business will target with its positioning strategy. The alternatives range from targeting a single segment to targeting several segments. Study of the product-market, buyers' requirements, segment preferences, the structure of competition, and opportunities for competitive advantage assist management in making the market target decision. Each segment of interest must be studied to identify the key product attributes desired by buyers. Finding gaps between buyers' preferences and existing competitive offerings creates opportunities for advantage. Positioning strategy seeks to provide a product and supporting service offering that meets the needs of buyers in the targeted segment.

Positioning Strategy

The positioning process is described in Exhibit 2–3. The choice of the market target guides the positioning strategy. The *positioning concept* selected by management is the product (brand) meaning derived from the needs of the buyers in the market target.[31] For example, the positioning concept used for Kodak's Ektar film is the benefit of a very high quality photograph that retains sharpness for enlargements as large

---

EXHIBIT 2–3 The Positioning Process

Positioning concept
The product (brand) meaning derived
from the needs of the buyers
compromising the market target.

Position effectiveness
The extent to which
management's positioning
objectives are achieved in the
market target.

MARKET
TARGET

Positioning strategy
The combination of marketing
actions used to portray the
positioning concept to
targeted buyers.

Position of the brand
The positioning of the brand by
the buyers in the market target.

Source: David W. Cravens, *Strategic Marketing,* 3rd. ed. (Homewood, Ill.: Richard D. Irwin, Inc., 1991), p. 266.

as posters. Selecting a good positioning concept may require research to determine buyers' perceptions about attributes of competing brands and identify gaps between their needs and product offerings. The *positioning strategy* is the combination of marketing actions used to influence the perceptions of brands by the targeted buyers. The components of a positioning strategy include the physical product, supporting services, distribution channels, price, and promotion. Buyers may position a brand using physical product attributes as well as other attributes (e.g., prestige). The *position* of the brand is determined by the buyer's perceptions of the firm's positioning strategy (and perceptions of competitors' strategies). Positioning may focus on an entire company, a mix of products, a specific line of products, or a particular brand. Positioning is often centered at the brand level. *Position effectiveness* considers the extent to which management's positioning objectives are achieved for the market target of interest.

The discussion that follows considers targeting and positioning strategies at different stages of market evolution. The objective is to identify important targeting and positioning issues at each market stage rather than indicating actual strategies that should be used. These strategies should be selected for the actual competitive environment of a particular company.

Marketing Strategy in Emerging Markets

Marketing strategies are initially developed, implemented, and evaluated. The uncertainties and risks are high. Changes are made to adapt to company experience and the altered requirements of buyers as they gain experience in using the product. The adjustments may affect both targeting and positioning strategies. Targeting changes may include expanding targets to include new customers and achieving better targeting by identifying segments within the product-market. Positioning changes may require increasing the amount of resources for the marketing program as well as shifting how the resources are allocated to marketing-mix components.

Targeting.   Targeting strategy may be relatively broad in an emerging market. All surgeons operating in major hospitals were targeted by U.S. Surgical when the company initially entered the surgical stapler market. If the initial targeting is too narrow, an organization may fail to develop its capabilities in areas where growth is promising. Primary initial users are identified and targeted. Market monitoring enables refining targeting as the product-market gains experience and structure.

Apple Computer illustrates the importance of adjusting targeting strategies as the market develops. Apple first targeted the hobbyist and household users of PCs for home entertainment. Later in the development of the market Apple targeted both individuals and small businesses. Apple was threatened in the mid-1980s by the explosive growth in business use of PCs. MS/DOS operating systems were popular with business users. Management responded quickly to business market needs with its desktop publishing capabilities and simple-to-use equipment. These actions enabled the firm to maintain its competitive position. Targeting often changes as the market develops. Anticipating and reacting to buyers' needs and requirements demands close contact with the marketplace and the monitoring of competitors' actions.

Positioning.   Competing in a new product-market requires developing a positioning concept and designing a marketing mix. The effectiveness of the mix components is often uncertain. Major changes in product, distribution, price, and promotion composition are likely during the early years of market development. Nevertheless, these early positioning decisions should consider the future directions of marketing strategy during the life cycle of the product-market. Park and Zaltman comment on the long-term management of individual products and services using the strategic brand concept:

. . . it addresses the need to determine, prior to market entry, how positioning strategies at each stage should proceed. This advanced planning enables the firm to develop the appropriate resources at each stage so that a positioning strategy at the next stage can be better implemented.[32]

Positioning and mix composition decisions are affected by whether the firm is first to enter a market or instead is a later entrant. The information available to the pioneer is limited to the needs (often uncertain) of the customer targets and management's knowledge about product alternatives that satisfy the same needs targeted by the new entry. Later entrants have the advantage of watching the pioneer. They can evaluate the targeting and positioning actions and the results of earlier entrants.

The quality of products often varies in an emerging market because of lack of production experience and differences in standards used by producers. High technology products may change rapidly in the early stages of market entry as a result of improvements in design. Distribution channels must be established unless entry is by an existing firm that can use its distribution network. Pricing decisions are influenced by management's assessment of the amount that buyers may be willing to pay and the costs of producing and marketing the product. Management may attempt to quickly recover development costs with high prices or instead try to build market position via relatively low prices. In some situations it may be necessary to price at or below cost to initially gain market position. Both prices and costs typically decline as the product-market moves through its life cycle. Promotion expenditures are normally high for market entry. The nature and scope of the market targets selected will affect the amount of promotion required to perform necessary communications with buyers and other people who influence the purchase of the product.

A pricing strategy of "buying in" to gain control of a market has been successful in some domestic and international markets.[33] The objective is to bind the buyer to the supplier through initially low prices and other inducements to tie customers to their suppliers for long periods. The strategy has been used primarily in the industrial products area and in international markets. For example, the strategy was used by Europe's Airbus Industrie to gain access to U.S. airline business for the A–300 aircraft. The company provided training and other services to facilitate the transition to the new aircraft.

Marketing Strategy in Growth Markets

Growth markets present some interesting marketing strategy issues regarding the choice of market targets and positioning strategies. Strategic development is affected by whether a company is already competing in the product-market or instead deciding to enter the market.

Targeting.   The major influences on targeting decisions in growth markets include: (1) the capabilities and resources of the organization; (2) the competitive environment; (3) the extent to which the product-market can be segmented; (4) the future potential of the market; and (5) the market entry barriers confronting potential competitors. Exhibit 2–2 suggests three possible targeting strategies: extensive market coverage by firms with established businesses in related markets (k-generalists); extensive coverage by firms with diversified product portfolios (polymorphists); and selective targeting by small organizations serving one or a few market segments.

A focused targeting strategy may be appropriate when buyers' needs are differentiated or when product differentiation occurs. A new market entrant may identify segments that are not served by large competitors. These buyers provide an opportunity for the small firm to gain competitive advantage. The market leader(s) may not find small segments attractive enough to allocate the skills and resources necessary to gain a position in the segment. If all of the buyers in the market display similar needs, a small organization may gain advantage through product specialization. This strategy would concentrate on a specific product or component.

A company that seeks to appeal to most of the buyers in the market must determine how much variation there is in buyers' needs and wants. The choice of specific targets depends on the segments that exist in the market. During the growth stage of the business market for personal computers, the three major segments were small-, medium-, and large-size companies. Microsegmentation (many segments) in a growth market is typically not necessary. A small number of segments can be identified by one or a few general characteristics (e.g., size of business). When no segments are apparent, broad market scope targeting is guided by a general profile of buyers. This average-buyer profile becomes the target.

Positioning Strategy.   Several characteristics of positioning strategies for narrow market scope targeting and broad market scope targeting are shown in Exhibit 2–4. These strategies are illustrative since many factors may influence the choice of a particular strategy. For example, major differences exist in the use of positioning components in consumer and industrial markets. Personal selling is often used when business firms are targeted because the number of buyers is small (compared to consumer markets) and the size of purchase is large. Advertising consumes a much larger portion of the marketing budget than personal selling in many consumer products firms. The

---

EXHIBIT 2–4   Illustrative Positioning Strategies in Growth Markets

	Narrow Market Scope	*Broad Market Scope*
Product	Product designed for segment target or focused on a specific product or component in non-segmented market.	Broad product line designed to meet multiple needs of wide range of buyers.
Channel	Typically a single channel using intermediary or direct contact with end users.	Multiple channels likely to be used unless a single channel network provides extensive market coverage.
Price	Price determined by value provided by product. Margins should be relatively high.	Pricing strategies likely to vary between market targets. Intensity of competition may impose price pressures.
Promotion	Advertising targeted for cost effectiveness. Personal selling may target middlemen or end-users.	Advertising may be broad in scope or focused depending on targets. Personal selling varies according to targets and role in marketing program.

Source: David W. Cravens, *Strategic Marketing,* 3rd. ed. (Homewood, Ill.: Richard D. Irwin, Inc., 1991), p. 307.

role of sales promotion (e.g., coupons, contents, premiums, etc.) varies considerably by type of product and market. Sales promotion represents a major part of total promotion expenditures. The amount spent for sales promotion in the United States exceeds advertising expenditures.

Competing in Mature Markets

Both targeting and positioning strategies may be adjusted when moving from the growth to maturity stages of the product-market. Targeting changes may reflect new priorities of targeted segments. Positioning within a targeted market may be fine tuned to improve customer satisfaction and operating performance. When the product-market reaches maturity, management is likely to place heavy emphasis on efficiency. Since the market is growing slowly and competition is heavy, the challenge is to manage for performance.

Targeting.   Segmentation analysis is essential for all firms competing in the product-market. Selecting the segment(s) to target is crucial for small firms seeking to gain marketing advantage against the industry giants. Market maturity may create new opportunities and threats in the firm's market target(s). Even the firms pursuing extensive targeting strategies may eliminate certain segments as targets. Those targets retained in the segment portfolio are assigned priorities to guide resource allocations for positioning actions such as product research and development, channel management, pricing strategy, advertising expenditures, and selling-effort allocations. Elimination of targets and shifts in targeting priorities by large competitors may create new opportunities for firms following selective targeting strategies.

Positioning.   At this stage there should be well established operating guidelines concerning the role and relationships among all components of the marketing mix. During maturity, management places more emphasis on control than on planning. Changes in the positioning components are usually small unless operating results are unsatisfactory. In a mature market, there is an extensive base of experience about the relationship between marketing effort and market response. Regular audits of marketing effectiveness are essential to fine tune performance and identify problem areas.

The WD–40 Company is an interesting example of how a small company can gain competitive advantage in a mature industry. The company produces and markets the WD–40 lubricant. The company has a leading position in this specialized lubricant segment. Sales were approaching $100 million in 1992. Profits are strong and the company has no long-term debt.

Restructuring Strategies in Mature Markets

Many companies restructured during the 1980s. Changes in customer requirements, intensity of competition, poor performance, unfavorable market trends, and other pressures may cause management to alter business strategy. These changes normally require major targeting and positioning adjustments. Since environmental turbulence and business restructuring are considered in Chapter 1, the present discussion centers on the impact of restructuring on marketing strategy. Several organizational restructuring changes and their impact on market targeting and positioning are shown in Exhibit 2–5. The

EXHIBIT 2–5 Illustrative Impacts of Business Restructuring on Targeting and Positioning Strategies

Changes in Business Strategy	Market Targeting Impact	Positioning Impact
Rapid Growth/Retrenchment	Market scope may not change, although targets may be increased or reduced.	Substantial changes in resource allocation (e.g., advertising expenditures, organizational design, and sales force size).
Changing the Product Mix	No change is necessary unless increase in product scope creates opportunities in new segments.	Changes in product strategy, methods of distribution, and promotional strategies may be necessary.
Altering Market Scope	Targeting is likely to change to include new targets.	Positioning strategy must be developed for each new target.
Repositioning	Should not have a major effect on targeting strategy.	Product, distribution, price and promotion strategies may be affected.
Distribution Channel Integration	Should have no effect on targeting strategy.	Primary impact on channel, pricing, and promotion strategies.
Diversification	Targeting strategies must be selected in new business areas.	Positioning strategies must be developed (or acquired) for the new business areas.
Strategic Alliance	Targeting strategy may be affected based on the nature and scope of the alliance.	Operating relationships and assignment of responsibilities must be established.

Source: David W. Cravens, *Strategic Marketing,* 3rd. ed. (Homewood, Ill.: Richard D. Irwin, Inc., 1991), p. 311.

changes must be analyzed and operating strategies developed to implement the desired restructuring actions.

Eastman Kodak Company made major restructuring changes during the 1980s to improve the firm's performance in the global photography markets. For example, in 1989 the salesforce for Kodak's battery line was merged into the U.S. sales group that sells film and cameras and has strong relationships with retailers.[34] This action was designed to improve Kodak's market position and profitability in the battery product-market. Kodak held an 8 percent share in 1989 compared to 42 percent for Duracell, 34 percent for Eveready, and 9 percent for Rayovac. The salesforce restructuring required product training, territory realignment, redeployment of selling effort, and other operating changes. Kodak faces a major challenge to effectively compete in this market. Kodak's problems in gaining market position with its battery line illustrates the difficulty of entering a market at the mature stage.

Defensive Strategy

Deciding how to defend against the entry of new competitors is an important strategic issue. The discussion in Chapter 1 on barriers to market entry examines various obstacles confronting a potential entrant. The present discussion considers the defensive strategies available to a firm when a new competitor enters the market. Management must decide whether a change in marketing strategy should be made to defend against a new market entrant.

Market incumbents' reactions to entry may be aggressive, passive, or accommodating.[35] The *aggressive* strategy is intended to make entry more difficult. The *passive* strategy involves no change in the existing positioning strategy. The *accommodating* strategy is designed to make entry easier for the new entrant. Consider, for example, Tylenol's aggressive response to Datril's entry into the nonaspirin market in 1975. Tylenol's high profit margin was a major reason for Datril's entry. Tylenol used an aggressive counterentry strategy. Bristol-Myers lost $10 million in its attack on Tylenol, whose aggressive price strategy matched Datril's market entry price.[36] Tylenol's price defense was successful against Datril. Interestingly, Tylenol did not lose market position. In early 1983, Bristol-Myers tried again with Datril 500, spending $3 million on advertising during the first six weeks. The ads stated that Extra-Strength Tylenol was priced 25 to 45 percent higher than Extra-Strength Datril, based on a national survey. Management indicated that achieving a 2 to 3 percent market share for Datril would indicate strong performance. Datril obtained about a 1 percent market share a year after introduction.

Hauser offers several general guidelines concerning defensive strategy that are supported by research findings. The two assumptions underlying the following defensive responses are that the attacker knows what the defender's reaction will be, and the strategies of all other firms in the market remain constant. These are Hauser's suggested directions of change for the defender:

- Distribution and awareness advertising should be decreased.
- Price strategies are independent of distribution and awareness advertising strategies but not vice versa.
- Profits always decrease as the result of a new competitive brand.[37]

An important consideration is whether the new competitor selects the same market target(s) as the defending firm. If head-on competition for a market target is assumed and if consumer tastes are uniform, Hauser's research findings suggest that at the margin (a particular market position) defensive profits change as follows:

- Increase for price decreases.
- Increase for product improvements along the defending brand's relative strengths.
- Increase for increases in repositioning advertising along the defending brand's relative strengths.[38]

These findings offer only general guidelines. More specific directions of change research in a particular competitive arena is necessary to develop strategy guidelines.[39] Interestingly, although defensive actions through marketing-mix changes appear to be useful in defending against competitive entry, analysis of experience indicates that companies often pursue passive strategies. For example, Robinson, in an analysis of Profit Impact of Market Strategy (PIMS) data, found that the typical reported defender's strategy during the first year of market entry by a new competitor was no reaction.[40] Caterpillar's initial passive reaction to Komatsu's entry into the U.S. earthmoving market is illustrative.

Global Market Entry Strategies

International markets can be entered in various ways based on management's desired market scope, company resources and capabilities, entry barriers, and other considerations. Several entry strategies are described to indicate the major features of each.

Exporting.   A producer's products can be shipped to the targeted country with marketing and distribution functions performed by an independent distributor or importer or by the producer's marketing subsidiary. Independent agents provide a popular entry strategy for small firms that do not have international experience. The company-owned marketing organization requires more investment but offers greater control over operations.

Licensing.   In pursuing a licensing strategy "a company assigns the right to a *patent* (which protects a product, technology, or a process) or a *trademark* (which protects a product name) to another company for a fee or royalty.[41] This strategy is used by Löewenbräu AG to market its beer worldwide. The Miller Brewing Company is licensed in the United States to produce the Löewenbräu brand. Licensing agreements include fee arrangements and other marketing requirements such as the levels of advertising support to be provided by both parties. Licensing has low resource requirements and provides market access through the licensee's established distribution network.

Joint Ventures.   This strategy is used by a company that decides to share management with one or more collaborating foreign firms.[42] The joint venture, like licensing, greatly limits the political and economic risks of the company entering the market. Certain countries require joint venture establishment as a condition of market entry. The strategy is sometimes used by firms in different countries that have complementary competitive advantages.

Strategic Alliance.   The alliance establishes a cooperative arrangement between two independent corporations that may involve ownership. This strategy is similar to the joint venture but normally does not involve the creation of an organization with a local partner. Drucker describes the strategic alliance:

> Alliances of all kinds are becoming increasingly common, especially in international business: joint ventures; minority holdings (particularly cross-holdings, in which each partner owns the same percentage of the other); research and marketing compacts; cross-licensing and exchange-of-knowledge agreements; syndicates, and so on. The trend is likely to accelerate. Marketing, technology and people needs all push it.[43]

The success of the alliance depends on the effectiveness of the coordination between the participating organizations. Explicit operating guidelines and responsibilities are essential. The use of strategic alliances by American, European, and Japanese companies escalated during the late 1980s.

Complete Ownership by the Entering Company.   This strategy consists of creating a wholly owned manufacturing and marketing subsidiary by the entering company. A major investment is required and is subject to the environmental threats of the country. The subsidiary may involve either establishing a new entity or acquiring an existing company. Several examples of foreign ownership exist in the United States, Europe, and other countries.

SUMMARY

Marketing strategy should be guided by analyzing how several important factors affect market target and positioning strategies in different competitive environments. Exhibit 2–1 describes the major steps in the process. Strategy selection begins with product-market definition and analysis followed by market segment identification and analysis of industry structure and competition. Next, competitive advantage is evaluated for each market target under consideration. Finally, market targeting and positioning strategies are selected, taking into account the situational variables that affect the strategies that are implemented.

There are important variations in targeting and positioning strategies at various stages of market evolution. Competitive strategies must recognize the various factors that enhance and inhibit marketing strategy in different competitive environments. In addition to the degree of market maturity, the characteristics and capabilities of the organization developing (or revising) the marketing strategy are important influences on strategy selection. Exhibit 2–2 examines competition and strategy selection in different markets by alternative forms of organizations.

The core marketing strategy decisions are selecting the buyers to be targeted and deciding how to form a positioning strategy for each target. Product, distribution, price, and promotion strategies work together to position the organization's product in the mind of the targeted buyers. Since many markets contain buyers whose needs and wants are not the same, market segmentation analysis is essential in guiding targeting decisions. Depending on the stage of market evolution and the organization's capabilities and resources, management may decide to target one, a few, or most of the segments in the market. Many targeting strategies tend toward the two ends of the continuum (e.g., few versus many).

Positioning strategy considers the needs and preferences of the buyers in each market target. Management must combine the marketing-mix components into a coordinated positioning strategy. A strategy must be developed for each market target. Multiple targets require multiple positioning strategies. The strategies may be totally unique or may share some common marketing-mix characteristics.

Marketing strategy is affected by various situational factors. This is illustrated by considering strategies for entering and competing in new, growth, and mature product-markets. Restructuring actions of organizations in mature markets are also examined to illustrate the impact of these changes on market target and positioning strategies. Strategies for defending an existing market position against new entrants are discussed. Surprisingly, the reactions of existing competitors to new entrants is often passive. Finally, the expanding importance of competing in international markets is considered and the dimensions of global competition are discussed. Strategies for competing in global markets are examined.

NOTES

1. Howard Sutton, *Competitive Intelligence,* Research Report No. 913 (New York: The Conference Board, Inc., 1988).
2. The following discussion is drawn from David W. Cravens, *Strategic Marketing,* 3rd ed. (Homewood, Ill.: Richard D. Irwin, Inc., 1991), chapter 8.
3. Michael Porter, *Competitive Strategy* (New York: The Free Press, 1980), p. 218.
4. Mary Lambkin and George S. Day, "Evolutionary Processes in Competi-

tive Markets: Beyond the Product Life Cycle," *Journal of Marketing,* July 1989, p. 13.

5. Porter, *Competitive Strategy,* pp. 221–25.

6. David A. Aaker and George S. Day, "The Perils of High-Growth Markets," *Strategic Management Journal,* Vol. 7, 1986, p. 419.

7. Lambkin and Day, "Evolutionary Processes in Competitive Markets," p. 11.

8. Porter, *Competitive Strategy,* pp. 238–40.

9. Ibid., chapter 9.

10. George Anders, "Going Global: Vision vs. Reality," *The Wall Street Journal,* September 22, 1989, pp. R20–21.

11. Philip Kotler, Liam Fahey, and Somkid Jatusripitak, *The New Competition: What Theory Z Did Not Tell You About Marketing* (Englewood Cliffs, N.J.: Prentice Hall, Inc., 1988).

12. The material in this section is drawn from Cravens, *Strategic Marketing,* chapter 2; and David W. Cravens, "Designing Marketing Strategies in Different Competitive Environments," in H. E. Glass, ed., *Handbook of Business Strategy,* 3rd ed. (New York: Warren, Gorham and Lamont, 1992).

13. As quoted in Stratford P. Sherman, "The Mind of Jack Welch," *Fortune,* March 27, 1989, p. 50.

14. George S. Day and Robin Wensely, "Assessing Competitive Advantage: A Framework for Diagnosing Competitive Superiority," *Journal of Marketing,* April 1988, p. 2.

15. The following discussion is drawn from Ibid., pp. 2–4.

16. "Hot Growth Companies," *Business Week,* May 22, 1989, p. 90.

17. Michael E. Porter, *Competitive Advantage* (New York: The Free Press, 1985), p. 33.

18. Kevin P. Coyne, "Sustainable Competitive Advantage—What It Is, What It Isn't," *Business Horizons,* January/February 1986, p. 55.

19. The following discussion is based on Ibid., pp. 57–58.

20. Competitive advantage for different market situations is adopted from Cravens, *Strategic Marketing,* chapter 8.

21. See for example, William T. Robinson and Claes Fornell, "Sources of Market Pioneer Advantages in Consumer Goods Industries," *Journal of Marketing Research,* August 1985, pp. 305–15; and Glen L. Urban, Theresa Carter, Steven Gaskin, and Zofia Mucha, "Market Share Rewards to Pioneering Brands: An Empirical Analysis and Strategic Implications," *Management Science,* June 1986, pp. 645–59.

22. Porter, *Competitive Strategy,* p. 217.

23. Elaine Romanelli, "New Venture Strategies in the Minicomputer Industry," *California Management Review,* Fall 1987, p. 161.

24. Ibid.

25. Ibid., pp. 170–72.

26. Lambkin and Day, "Evolutionary Processes in Competitive Markets," p. 15.

27. Ibid., p. 14.

28. Jeremy Main, "How to Go Global—and Why," *Fortune,* August 28, 1989, p. 70.

29. Robert D. Buzzell and John A. Quelch, *Multinational Marketing Management* (Reading, Mass.: Addison-Wesley Publishing Company, 1988), pp. 7–8.

30. The following discussion of marketing strategy for different competitive situations is based on Cravens, *Strategic Marketing,* chapter 8. See also Cravens, "Designing Marketing Strategies in Different Competitive Environments."

31. C. Whan Park, Bernard J. Jawerski, and Deborah J. Macinnis, "Strategic Brand Concept-Image Management," *Journal of Marketing,* October 1986, pp. 135–45.

32. C. W. Park and Gerald Zaltman, *Marketing Management* (Hinsdale, Ill.: The Dryden Press, 1987), p. 249.

33. Robert E. Weigand, " 'Buying in' to Market Control," *Harvard Business Review,* November-December 1980, pp. 141–49.

34. Clare Ansberry, "Kodak is Standing by Its Battery Line As Merged Sales Force Finds Success," *The Wall Street Journal,* February 16, 1989, p. B6.

35. William T. Robinson, "Marketing Mix Reactions to Entry," *Marketing Science,* Fall 1988, pp. 368–85.

36. "Datril Again Tries Price Vs. Tylenol," *Advertising Age,* March 21, 1983, pp. 2 and 52.

37. John R. Hauser, *Theory and Application of Defensive Strategy,* Marketing Science Institute, Report No. 85–107, August 1985, p. 16.

38. Ibid., p. 16.

39. John R. Hauser and S. P. Gaskin, "Application of 'DEFENDER' Consumer Model," *Marketing Science,* Fall 1984.

40. Robinson, "Marketing Mix Reactions to Entry," pp. 368–85.

41. Jean-Pierre Jeannet and Hubert D. Hennessey, *International Marketing Management* (Boston: Houghton-Mifflin Company, 1988), p. 279.

42. Philip R. Cateora, *International Marketing,* 7th ed. (Homewood, Ill.: Richard D. Irwin, Inc., 1990).

43. Peter F. Drucker, "From Dangerous Liaisons to Alliances for Progress," *The Wall Street Journal,* September 8, 1989, p. A8.

Chapter 3

Financial Analysis for Marketing Decisions

Accounting is a scorecard of business, portraying the activities of a company by using a set of objective numbers that indicate how the firm is performing.[1] The finance function interprets the accounting scorecard when evaluating organizational performance and planning for the future. An understanding of the use of basic financial analysis methods is required of marketing executives. Consider, for example, how the pricing strategy of Burroughs Wellcome Company's life-prolonging AIDS drug, AZT, affects the financial performance of the company.

The profits of Burroughs Wellcome doubled during the three-year period ending in 1988.[2] AZT was priced at $8,000 for a one-year supply. At this price, analysts estimated AZT sales could increase to $1 billion by 1992, half of which would be net profit. Not surprisingly, Burroughs Wellcome received widespread criticism from patients and their advocates about the pricing of AZT. Unknown to many critics, the company is 75 percent owned by a charitable organization. About one fourth of Burroughs Wellcome's earnings is distributed in dividends; the rest is spent on research and development of experimental drugs for a wide range of diseases. The criticism continued, and the company announced a 20 percent price reduction in September of 1989. Critics argued that further cuts should be made because of the drug's huge market potential and the opportunity to lower costs and recover development costs. Financial analysis of alternative price strategies is clearly a high priority management issue at Burroughs Wellcome.

Several kinds of financial analyses are needed for marketing planning and control activities. Sales and cost information is used in financial analyses for marketing management. Such analyses represent an important part of your case preparation activities. In some instances it will be necessary for you to review and interpret the financial information provided in the cases. In other instances you may actually prepare analyses to support your recommendations.

This chapter considers financial analysis activities and methods that are used to (1) gauge how well marketing strategy is working, (2) evaluate marketing decision alternatives, and (3) develop plans for the future. Special considerations that may affect marketing financial analyses are also discussed. The methods covered in this chapter represent a group of tools and techniques for use in marketing financial analysis. Throughout the discussion we are assuming that you have a basic understanding of accounting and finance fundamentals.

ANALYSIS ACTIVITIES

While many kinds of financial analyses underlie marketing operations, most of them fall into four categories. The *financial situation analysis* is intended to determine how well marketing activities are doing. It involves the study of trends, comparative analyses, and assessments of present financial strengths and limitations for the entire business or a unit, brand, or some other component of the business. *Financial evaluation of alternatives* involves the use of financial information to evaluate whether to introduce a new product, expand the sales force, eliminate a mature product, or move into a new market.

EXHIBIT 3–1   Financial Analyses

Situation analysis:
  Sales and cost analyses
  Profit-contribution and net profit analyses
  Liquidity analysis

Evaluation of alternatives:
  Sales and cost forecasts
  Break-even analyses
  Profit-contribution and net profit projections
  Return on investment

Financial planning:
  Sales and cost forecasts
  Budgets
  Pro forma income statement

Financial control:
  Sales and cost analyses
  Actual results to budgets
  Profit performance

Financial planning involves projections concerning activities that marketing management has decided to undertake. For example, if it has been decided to introduce a new product on a national basis, management must prepare sales and cost forecasts, budgets, and other financial planning and control tools. Finally, in *financial control*, actual results are compared to planned results. The objective is to keep the gap between actual and planned results as narrow as possible. Several illustrative financial analyses are shown in Exhibit 3–1.

Unit of Financial Analysis

Various units that can be used in the financial analysis of marketing are shown in Exhibit 3–2. Two factors often influence the choice of a unit of analysis: (1) the purpose of the analysis and (2) the costs and availability of the information needed to perform the analysis. We shall briefly examine each influence to see how it affects the choice of each unit used for analysis activities.

In a marketing situation assessment, more than one unit of analysis is often needed. Marketing management may be interested in examining the financial performance of several of the units shown in Exhibit 3–2. In contrast, the unit used in the financial evaluation of alternatives should correspond to the alternative under consideration. For example, if an expansion of the sales force is being analyzed, the salesperson is a logical basis of analysis. If a product is a candidate for elimination by a firm, an analysis should be performed to assess the revenue and cost impact of dropping the product. The analysis should include the drop candidate plus other products that would be affected. Finally, in financial planning and financial control, the unit or units of analysis often correspond to products and/or organizational units (branches, departments, business units, etc.) since budgeting and forecasting analyses are typically prepared for these units.

EXHIBIT 3–2   Alternative Units for Financial Analysis

Market	*Product/Service*	*Organization*
Total market	Industry	Company
Market niche(s)	Product mix	Segment/division/unit
Geographic area(s)	Product line	Marketing department
Customer groups	Specific product	Sales unit
Individual customers	Brand	Region
	Model	District/branch
		Office/store
		Salesperson

The most readily available sales and cost information for financial analysis is that which corresponds to the formal financial reporting practices in the given firm. Units that are used for internal reporting often include product categories, business units, and subparts of the sales organization (regions, districts, etc.). When the desired unit of analysis does not correspond to one that is included in the firm's information system, both the cost and the difficulty of obtaining information increase significantly. For example, if the cost accounting system has not tabulated costs by individual products, obtaining such information may require a substantial effort. Fortunately, the information needed for marketing analysis can often be estimated at accuracy levels suitable for that purpose.

Sales and Cost Information

The data base for marketing financial analysis is obtained by accumulating historical sales and cost data for the various units shown in Exhibit 3–2. The data base can be used in forecasting future sales and costs. In addition to the sales and cost data, marketing management often wishes to examine sales and cost trends. Among the widely used bases for the analysis of such trends are dollar and unit sales, percent-

---

EXHIBIT 3–3   Dillard Department Stores on the Move

**A. The top five growth chains
(1982-1986)**
(in square-feet percent gains)

Dillard
15.5%

May
13.3%

Federated
11.3%

Nordstrom
11.3%

D.H. Holmes
7.9%

**B. The top five growth chains
in sales growth
(1982-1986)**
(in sales dollars percent gains)

Nordstrom
26.1%

Dillard
25.6%

Dayton-Hudson
14.9%

Jacobson
11.9%

May
11.2%

Source: Michael Totty, "Growth-Minded Dillard Draws Notice," *The Wall Street Journal*, March 16, 1988, p. 6.

age growth rates, and market share. Note, for example, the competitor sales analysis for Dillard Department Stores Inc., shown in Exhibit 3–3. Sales trends can be examined for each of the retailer's key competitors. The chart illustrates the trends in total sales and sales per square foot.

Cost information is not very useful for marketing financial analysis unless it is combined with revenue (sales) data to perform various kinds of profit analyses. While in some instances we can analyze historical costs such as the average cost required to close a sale, the analysis is incomplete unless we compare costs to what they have accomplished.

EVALUATING FINANCIAL PERFORMANCE

Several factors are involved in evaluating financial performance. The discussion begins by examining some accounting fundamentals. This is followed by a review of the basic financial reports. Next, several important financial ratios are defined. Finally, a financial analysis model is presented, and some additional marketing performance measures are noted.

Some Fundamentals

Costs.   As we move through the discussion of financial analysis, be sure to recognize the type of costs being used in the analysis. Using accounting terminology, costs can be designated as fixed or variable. From basic accounting you will recall that a cost is *fixed* if it remains constant over the observation period, even though the volume of activity varies. In contrast, a *variable* cost is an expense that varies with sales over the observation period. Costs are designated as semivariable in instances when they contain both fixed and variable components.

Break-Even Analysis[3].   This is a technique for examining the relationship between sales and costs. An illustration is given in Exhibit 3–4. Using sales and cost information, you can easily see from a break-even analysis how many units of a product must be sold to break even. In this example 65,000 units at sales of $120,000 are equal to total costs of $120,000. Any additional units sold will produce a profit. The break-even point can be calculated in this manner:

$$\text{Break-even units} = \frac{\text{Fixed costs}}{\text{Price per unit} - \text{Variable cost per unit}}$$

EXHIBIT 3–4   Break-Even Analysis

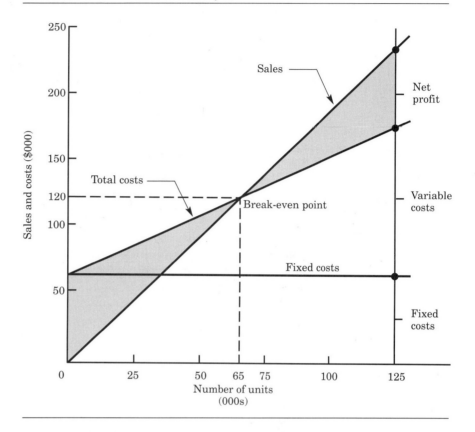

Price in the illustration shown in Exhibit 3–4 is $1.846 per unit, and variable cost is $0.769 per unit. With fixed costs of $70,000, this results in the break-even calculation:

$$\text{Break-even units} = \frac{\$70,000}{\$1.846 - \$0.769} = 65,000 \text{ units}$$

This analysis is not a forecast. Rather it indicates how many units of a product at a given price and cost must be sold to break even. Some important assumptions that underlie the above break-even analysis should be recognized:

1. We have assumed that fixed costs are constant and that variable costs vary at a constant rate.
2. We have assumed that all costs are either fixed or variable.
3. The analysis considered only one selling price. A higher price would yield a lower break-even point, and a lower price would yield a higher break-even point.

When the above assumptions do not apply, the analyst must modify the basic break-even model shown in Exhibit 3–4. The model can be expanded to include nonlinear sales and costs as well as alternative price levels.

Contribution Analysis.   When the performance of products, market segments, and other marketing units is analyzed, an examination of the profit contribution generated by a unit is often useful to management. Contribution margin is equal to sales (revenue) less variable costs. Thus contribution margin represents the amount of money available to cover fixed costs, and the excess available is net income. For example, suppose a product is generating a positive contribution margin. If the product is dropped, the remaining products would have to cover fixed costs that are not directly traceable to it. Contribution margin analysis is shown in Exhibit 3–5. In this example, if Product X were eliminated, $50,000 of product net income would be lost. If the product is retained, the $50,000 can be used to contribute to other fixed costs and/or net income.

Gross and Net Profit Margins.   Gross and net profit margins are used to gauge company and business unit financial performance and to budget for future operations. Gross and net profit are shown on the profit and loss or income statement. Margins on sales can be calculated by dividing gross or net profit amounts by sales in dollars. The income statement is used to report financial performance to stockholders and to compute taxes. An illustrative statement is shown in Exhibit 3–6.

Basic Financial Reports

These reports are typically prepared for a company and its major subdivisions:

1. *Balance sheet:* A statement of financial position at a particular time (e.g., December 31, 1992), indicating total assets by category, short- and long-term liabilities, and stockholders' equity.

EXHIBIT 3–5   Contribution Margin Analysis for Product X ($000)

Sales	$300
Less:	
Variable manufacturing costs	100
Other variable costs traceable to Product X	50
Equals: Contribution margin	150
Less: Fixed costs directly traceable to Product X	100
Equals: Product net income	$ 50

EXHIBIT 3–6   Profit and Loss (Income) Statement ($000)

Sales revenue	$752
Less: Cost of goods sold	492
Equals: Gross profit margin	260
Less: Selling and administrative expenses	140
Equals: Net profit before taxes	120
Less: Taxes	50
Equals: Net profit	$ 70

EXHIBIT 3–7   Composition of the Balance Sheet ($000)

Cash	$ 100	Current liabilities	$ 75
Accounts receivable	200	Short-term debt	125
Inventory	150	Long-term debt	1,000
Total current assets	450	Total liabilities	1,200
Property and equipment	1,500	Net worth	1,050
Other assets	300	Total liabilities	
Total assets	$2,250	and net worth	$2,250

2. *Income statement:* This report covers a period of time (e.g., year ending December 31, 1992). It indicates sales minus all relevant costs, and the difference is net income (see Exhibit 3–6).
3. *Cash flow statement:* Sometimes referred to as the sources and uses of funds, this report starts with a beginning cash balance for a period (e.g., a quarter) plus all cash receipts minus all cash expenditures. It ends with a net cash balance for the period.

Since these reports and future forecasts (pro forma projections) are prepared for a company and its major parts or segments, the reports are normally not part of the marketing plan. Nevertheless, it is important that marketing executives understand the composition and relationships among major financial reports for the enterprise.

Several of the ratios discussed in the next section use information from the balance sheet; you will need to review its composition. An example is shown in Exhibit 3–7.

Key Financial Ratios

Financial information is more useful to management if it is prepared so that comparisons can be made. James Van Horne comments upon this need:

To evaluate a firm's financial condition and performance, the financial analyst needs certain yardsticks. The yardstick frequently used is a ratio or index, relating two pieces of financial data to each other. Analysis and interpretation of various ratios should give an experienced and skilled analyst a better understanding of the financial condition and performance of the firm than he would obtain from analysis of the financial data alone.[4]

As we examine the financial analysis model in the next section, note how the ratio or index provides a useful frame of reference. Typically, the ratio is used to compare historical and/or future trends within the firm or to compare a firm or business unit with an industry or specific firms.

Several financial ratios that are often used to measure business performance are shown in Exhibit 3–8. Note that these ratios are primarily useful as a means of comparing:

1. Ratio values for several time periods for a particular business.
2. A firm to its key competitors.
3. A firm to an industry or business standard.

There are several sources of ratio data.[5] These include data services such as Dun & Bradstreet, industry and trade associations, government agencies, and investment advisory services.

Financial Analysis Model

The model shown in Exhibit 3–9 is useful for examining financial performance and identifying possible problem areas. The model combines several important financial ratios into one equation. Let's examine the model, moving from the far right to the left. Assuming that our performance target is return on net worth, the product of return on assets and financial leverage determines performance. Increasing either ratio will increase return on net worth. This can be accomplished by increasing leverage (e.g., greater debt) or by increasing profits. Next, note that return on assets is determined by the product of profit margin and asset turnover. Thus, greater expense control or faster asset turnover (e.g., inventory turnover) can improve return on assets. The values of these ratios will vary considerably from one industry to another. In grocery wholesaling, for example, profit margins are typically very low, whereas asset turnover is very high. Through efficient management and high turnover a wholesaler can stack up impressive returns on net worth.

Note how the equation incorporates the major parts of the balance sheet and the income statement. An illustration using the model ratios plus other financial ratios is provided in Exhibit 3–10. The variations by type of wholesaler highlight the importance of comparative analysis

EXHIBIT 3–8 Summary of Key Financial Ratios

Ratio	How Calculated	What It Shows
Profitability ratios:		
1. Gross profit margin	$\dfrac{\text{Sales} - \text{Cost of goods sold}}{\text{Sales}}$	An indication of the total margin available to cover operating expenses and yield a profit.
2. Operating profit margin	$\dfrac{\text{Profits before taxes and before interest}}{\text{Sales}}$	An indication of the firm's profitability from current operations without regard to the interest charges accruing from the capital structure.
3. Net profit margin (or return on sales)	$\dfrac{\text{Profits after taxes}}{\text{Sales}}$	Shows after-tax profits per dollar of sales. Subpar profit margins indicate that the firm's sales prices are relatively low or that its costs are relatively high or both.
4. Return on total assets	$\dfrac{\text{Profits after taxes}}{\text{Total assets}}$ or $\dfrac{\text{Profits after taxes} + \text{Interest}}{\text{Total assets}}$	A measure of the return on total investment in the enterprise. It is sometimes desirable to add interest to after-tax profits to form the numerator of the ratio, since total assets are financed by creditors as well as by stockholders; hence it is accurate to measure the productivity of assets by the returns provided to both classes of investors.
5. Return on stockholders' equity (or return on net worth)	$\dfrac{\text{Profits after taxes}}{\text{Total stockholders' equity}}$	A measure of the rate of return on stockholders' investment in the enterprise.

Ratio	Formula	Description
6. Return on common equity	$\dfrac{\text{Profits after taxes} - \text{Preferred stock dividends}}{\text{Total stockholders' equity} - \text{Par value of preferred stock}}$	A measure of the rate of return on the investment that the owners of common stock have made in the enterprise.
7. Earnings per share	$\dfrac{\text{Profits after taxes} - \text{Preferred stock dividends}}{\text{Number of shares of common stock outstanding}}$	Shows the earnings available to the owners of common stock.

Liquidity ratios:

Ratio	Formula	Description
1. Current ratio	$\dfrac{\text{Current assets}}{\text{Current liabilities}}$	Indicates the extent to which the claims of short-term creditors are covered by assets that are expected to be converted to cash in a period roughly corresponding to the maturity of the liabilities.
2. Quick ratio (or acid-test ratio)	$\dfrac{\text{Current assets} - \text{Inventory}}{\text{Current liabilities}}$	A measure of the firm's ability to pay off short-term obligations without relying upon the sale of its inventories.
3. Cash ratio	$\dfrac{\text{Cash \& marketable securities}}{\text{Current liabilities}}$	An indicator of how long the company can go without further inflow of funds.
4. Inventory to net working capital	$\dfrac{\text{Inventory}}{\text{Current assets} - \text{Current liabilities}}$	A measure of the extent to which the firm's working capital is tied up in inventory.

Leverage ratios:

Ratio	Formula	Description
1. Debt-to-assets ratio	$\dfrac{\text{Total debt}}{\text{Total assets}}$	Measures the extent to which borrowed funds have been used to finance the firm's operations.
2. Debt-to-equity ratio	$\dfrac{\text{Total debt}}{\text{Total stockholders' equity}}$	Provides another measure of the funds provided the creditors versus the funds provided by owners.
3. Long-term debt to equity ratio	$\dfrac{\text{Long-term debt}}{\text{Total stockholders' equity}}$	A widely used measure of the balance between debt and equity in the firm's overall capital structure.

EXHIBIT 3–8 *(concluded)*

Ratio	How Calculated	What It Shows
4. Times-interest-earned (or coverage ratios)	$$\frac{\text{Profits before interest and taxes}}{\text{Total interest charges}}$$	Measures the extent to which earnings can decline without the firm's becoming unable to meet its annual interest costs.
5. Fixed charge coverage	$$\frac{\text{Profits before taxes and interest} + \text{Lease obligations}}{\text{Total interest charges} + \text{Lease obligations}}$$	A more inclusive indication of the firm's ability to meet all of its fixed-charge obligations.
Activity ratios:		
1. Inventory turnover	$$\frac{\text{Cost of goods sold}}{\text{Inventory}}$$	When compared to industry averages, it provides an indication of whether a company has excessive inventory or perhaps inadequate inventory.
2. Fixed-assets turnover*	$$\frac{\text{Sales}}{\text{Fixed assets}}$$	A measure of the sales productivity and utilization of plant and equipment.
3. Total-assets turnover	$$\frac{\text{Sales}}{\text{Total assets}}$$	A measure of the utilization of all the firm's assets; a ratio below the industry average indicates the company is not generating a sufficient volume of business given the size of its asset investment.
4. Accounts receivable turnover	$$\frac{\text{Annual credit sales}}{\text{Accounts receivable}}$$	A measure of the average length of time it takes the firm to collect the sales made on credit.
5. Average collection period	$$\frac{\text{Accounts receivable}}{\text{Total sales} \div 365}$$ or $$\frac{\text{Accounts receivable}}{\text{Average daily sales}}$$	Indicates the average length of time the firm must wait after making a sale before it receives payment.

* The manager should also keep in mind the fixed charges associated with noncapitalized lease obligations.

Source: Adapted from Arthur A. Thompson, Jr., and A. J. Strickland III, *Strategy and Policy* (Homewood, Ill.: Business Publications, 1981), pp. 216–18.

EXHIBIT 3–9 Financial Analysis Model

$$\frac{\text{Net profits (after taxes)}}{\text{Net sales}} \times \frac{\text{Net sales}}{\text{Total assets}} \rightarrow \frac{\text{Net profits (after taxes)}}{\text{Total assets}} \times \frac{\text{Total assets}}{\text{Net worth}} = \frac{\text{Net profits (after taxes)}}{\text{Net worth}}$$

| Profit margin | Asset turnover | Return on assets | Financial leverage | Return on net worth |

of ratios. For example, comparisons between grocery wholesalers are more appropriate than comparing a grocery wholesaler to an industrial distributor.

Productivity Measures

Various units of analysis can be used to measure the productivity of marketing activities. Examples include sales per square foot of retail floor space, occupancy rates of hotels and office buildings, and sales per salesperson. As an illustration, Kmart had 1987 sales per square foot of $183 compared to Wal-Mart's $213 and Target's $193.[6] Interestingly, 75 percent of the adults in the United States shop at Kmart at least once every three months. The key to increasing Kmart's sales is to sell these buyers more merchandise. Space productivity measures can be obtained for individual departments in retail stores that offer more than one line, such as department stores.

Another widely used productivity measure is inventory turnover (net sales divided by inventory). Exhibit 3–10 indicates inventory turnover for six types of wholesalers. Inventory turnover equals sales divided by inventory, which indicates whether or nor a firm has excessive or inadequate inventory levels. Note, for example, the high turnover rates for grocery wholesalers (16.1×). Exhibit 3–11 shows a performance profile for several types of wholesalers.

Distribution Channel Margins

Often, it is necessary to determine the amount of markup or margin a particular product incurs as it moves through the distribution channel from the producer to the end user of the product. Markup is the amount the seller adds to the cost of the product to determine the selling price. This amount can be stated as percentage either of selling price or of

EXHIBIT 3–10 Financial Ratios for Six Types of Wholesalers, 1988

Financial Ratios	Drug Wholesalers	Grocery Wholesalers	Hardware Wholesalers	Electrical Distributors	Plumbing, Heating, and Air Conditioning Distributors	Industrial Distributors
Strategic profit model ratios:						
Net profits (before taxes)/sales	3.4%	1.1%	2.4%	3.1%	2.5%	2.4%
Sales/total assets	2.8×	5.7×	2.5×	2.6×	2.7×	2.4×
Net profits (before taxes)/total assets	9.5%	6.3%	6.0%	8.1%	6.8%	5.8%
Total assets/net worth	2.9×	3.3×	2.7×	2.8×	2.7×	2.7×
Net profits (before taxes)/net worth	27.6%	20.8%	16.2%	22.7%	18.4%	15.7%
Liquidity ratios:						
Current assets/current liabilities	1.5×	1.4×	1.7×	1.6×	1.6×	1.6×
Current assets (minus inventory)/current liabilities	.7×	.7×	.8×	.9×	.9×	.9×
Cash/current liabilities	10.0%	10.2%	11.3%	10.5%	10.2%	11.9%
Net profits (before interest and taxes)/interest (median)	3.0×	2.6×	3.1×	3.5×	3.1×	2.7×
Working capital ratios:						
Sales/accounts receivable	9.5×	19.4×	7.8×	6.8×	7.3×	7.0×
Sales/inventory	6.8×	16.1×	5.8×	7.2×	6.8×	6.3×
Accounts payable/inventory	63.5%	72.8%	52.9%	72.8%	62.3%	62.7%
Sales/net working capital	10.8×	27.5×	7.7×	8.8×	8.4×	7.8×
Balance sheet items (percent of assets):						
Cash	5.3%	5.2%	5.6%	5.5%	5.3%	5.9%
Accounts receivable	29.8%	29.2%	32.4%	38.6%	37.1%	34.8%
Inventory	41.9%	35.3%	43.5%	36.8%	39.8%	38.6%
Fixed assets	11.9%	20.8%	11.6%	11.3%	10.1%	13.0%
Notes payable	19.4%	17.4%	19.0%	16.9%	17.8%	17.6%
Accounts payable	26.6%	25.7%	23.0%	26.8%	24.8%	24.2%
Long term liabilities	12.8%	18.4%	12.6%	12.6%	10.6%	13.8%
Net worth	34.0%	30.7%	37.7%	35.1%	37.5%	36.8%

Source: Robert Morris Associates and Distribution Research Program, University of Oklahoma.

EXHIBIT 3–11   Performance Profile of Selected Wholesalers (strategic profit model ratios, 1988)

Type of Wholesaler	Net Profits/ Net Sales	Net Sales/ Total Assets	Net Profits/ Total Assets	Total Assets/ Net Worth	Net Profits/ Net Worth
Appliance distributors	1.9%	2.4×	4.6%	3.0×	13.8%
Automotive jobbers	2.2	2.2	4.8	2.7	13.0
Electronics distributors	1.7	2.4	4.1	2.9	11.9
Furniture wholesalers	2.6	3.4	8.8	3.1	27.3
Lumber and building materials wholesalers	2.3	3.4	7.8	2.8	21.8
Medical and dental equipment distributors	3.0	2.7	8.1	3.1	25.1
Sporting goods wholesalers	2.5	2.1	5.3	2.9	15.4
Tire distributors	1.8	2.6	4.7	3.8	17.9
Tobacco wholesalers	1.1	6.2	6.8	2.8	19.0

Source: Robert Morris Associates and Distribution Research Program, University of Oklahoma.

---

cost. The most common practice is expressing margin on a percentage of the selling price:

Margin as a percentage of *selling price:*

Cost + Margin = Selling price
Margin = %/100 × Selling price

Margin as a percentage of *cost:*

Cost + Margin = Selling price
Margin = %/100 × Cost

If the selling price of a product is $10 and cost is $8, the margin is $2. Margin as a percentage of selling price is $2/$10 × 100 = 20%. However, if one is computing margin as a percent of cost, then margin = $2/$8 × 100 = 25%.

To determine the total markup from the manufacturer to the ultimate consumer, one must take off margins one at a time. It is incorrect to total percentages and subtract the total amount from the retail selling price to determine manufacturer's selling price. Costs and selling prices must be determined by starting at one point in the channel (e.g., retailer) and working through each channel level to the level of interest (e.g., manufacturer). An example of a markup chain and channel pricing is shown in Exhibit 3–12. Markup is expressed as a percentage of the selling price.

EXHIBIT 3–12   Example of a Markup Chain and Channel Pricing

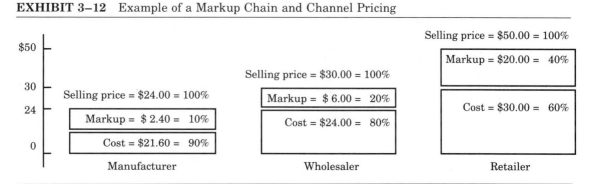

Source: E. J. McCarthy and W. D. Perreault, *Basic Marketing,* 8th ed. (Homewood, Ill.: Richard D. Irwin, Inc., 1984), Figure 20-1.

FINANCIAL PLANNING

Financial planning involves two major activities: (1) forecasting revenues and (2) budgeting (estimating future expenses). The actual financial analyses and forecasts that are included in the strategic marketing plan vary considerably from firm to firm. Those that are often placed in the financial analysis section of the plan include:

- Sales and market-share analyses and forecasts by product, market segment, areas, and other categories.
- Budget projections for marketing operations.
- Break-even and profit contribution projections by marketing planning unit (e.g., market target, product line, market area).
- Return on investment projections by marketing planning unit.
- Capital requirements.

The choice of the financial information to be used for marketing planning and control will depend upon its relationship with the corporate or business unit strategic plan. Another important consideration is the selection of performance measures to be used in gauging marketing performance. Our objective is to indicate the range of possibilities and to suggest some of the more frequently used financial analyses.

IMPORTANT FINANCIAL ANALYSIS ISSUES

Selecting Performance Criteria

Companies vary considerably as to how they gauge marketing performance. Consider these five examples of profitability measures used by different firms:[7]

1. A diversified manufacturing company currently expects an operating margin on sales of at least 5 percent for all products.
2. Management in a chemicals company now looks for return on investment (ROI) of at least 15 percent from each product line, and considers an ROI figure of less than 11 percent as calling for close review and possible divestment.
3. A consumer packaged-goods company has the general objective that any product's marginal profit before advertising and promotional expenditures should be a minimum of 20 percent higher than fixed and variable costs.
4. A manufacturer of capital equipment demands at least 25 percent ROI from each product or operating unit.
5. Another capital goods producer, employing the ratio of direct costs to sales price as a means of measuring relative profit performance, classes a ratio of 60 percent as satisfactory and one over 70 percent as unsatisfactory.

How exactly should management measure the financial performance of marketing operations? What criteria should be used: return on investment, sales, profit contribution, or what? Many firms use volume attainment and profitability as criteria although, surprisingly, those using ROI seem to be in the minority.[8] This may result from several difficulties in attempting to apply the technique to gauge marketing performance:

> Because there are innumerable variations of profit levels, a proper question initially is, "*What return* is being used for the measure?" Examples of profit levels are profit before royalties (including or excluding interest payments), profit before taxes, cash flow, division profit contribution, factory contribution, or sales region or district contribution.
>
> Any of the above are useful, depending upon the investment base being used.
>
> Again, one could ask, "Return on *what investment*?" It may be total parent company investment, total investment of subsidiary, total assets, manipulative assets (excluding intangibles), funds employed (tangible working capital), or selected bases (receivables, inventories, cash, etc.).
>
> The remaining question is, "*Whose investment*?" The investment of the stockholder differs in concept with the operating investment of the firm. Use of each may give startlingly different results, especially in the case where tangible funds employed in a firm are contrasted with the stockholder's investment if large amount of goodwill has been capitalized.[9]

Once these questions are answered, ROI measures provide an important gauge of marketing performance.

Marketing's decision-making information needs often do not correspond to traditional managerial accounting reporting procedures, so some give-and-take negotiations may be necessary between top management, marketing, and accounting. Issues as to how to allocate revenues and costs, the extent of disaggregation of both revenues and costs, and many other questions must be resolved to obtain relevant information for financial analysis. Revenue and cost information has two dimensions, the past and the future. Accumulating and analyzing past information are necessary to measure the effectiveness of past strategies. Developing future estimates is needed to evaluate proposed strategies.

Finally the time period of analysis must be selected. Most strategic marketing decisions extend from a few to several years into the future, so financial analysis must take into account the time value of money and the flows of revenue and costs over the relevant time horizon. The high rate of inflation expected during the next decade adds another complicating factor to financial projections.

Marketing's Influence on Financial Performance

Marketing strategy, once it is implemented, affects the financial performance of the corporation by generating sales and by incurring costs. An examination of a basic financial analysis system widely known as the Du Pont investment model will place marketing's impact upon financial performance into perspective. This model is shown in Exhibit 3–13. The heavy-lined boxes indicate that marketing has some effect upon the area. Note that ROI in Exhibit 3–13 corresponds to net profits (after taxes) divided by investment, measured by total assets. By following the arrows, you can trace marketing's influence on revenues and costs all the way to return on investment. Exhibit 3–13 can be expanded to include more details. For example, the investment box can be broken down into fixed assets (cash, marketable securities, accounts receivable, and inventories). Likewise, selling, general, and administrative expenses can be divided into specific expense components.

Eliminating Information Gaps

You will rarely find all the information that you would like to have for use in financial analysis in a case. This parallels the state of affairs in business practice. Marketing management must often eliminate information gaps by estimating the values of information needed in an analysis. You should proceed in a similar manner when necessary (and appropriate) in performing various kinds of financial analyses for the cases in this book.

An example will be useful in illustrating how information gaps can be eliminated. Suppose you have a company with three products: A, B, and C. You want to perform break-even analysis for Product B, but the

EXHIBIT 3–13 ROI Model

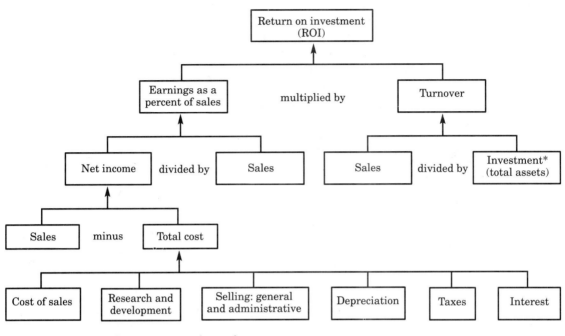

* Other measures of investment can be used.

fixed-cost information provided is for the entire company. Since you have sales for each product, one way to proceed is to assume that fixed costs can be allocated to each product based on the percentage of total sales accounted for by that product. For example, if Product B represents 20 percent of sales, then it would be assigned 20 percent of fixed costs. Using this fixed-cost estimate and per unit selling price and variable cost, break-even for Product B can be estimated. While the fixed-cost estimate may not be exact, it is probably adequate to give a close approximation of break-even.

You should note that other bases for allocating fixed costs may be appropriate in a given situation. The important consideration is that the assumptions underlying your estimating procedure be logical and, if possible, supported by facts provided in the case.

In estimating needed information, you should proceed with caution. A key requirement is that you have some basis for what you do. You should not make unrealistic guesses about the values of the information you need. In general, a good rule to follow is to be conservative with your estimates. It is sometimes helpful to estimate a range of values of the unknown factor. For example, if you are projecting the sales of a new product for the next three years, you might make three estimates: an optimistic estimate, a pessimistic estimate, and a most-likely estimate of sales for each of the three years.

Finally, it may be helpful to determine how sensitive your analysis is to the information you are estimating. Referring again to Product B, if the break-even level is not affected very much by different assumptions about how to allocate fixed costs, then any reasonable assumption about allocation should be acceptable. Alternatively, if the outcome of the financial analysis is affected significantly by small changes in the value you are estimating, then you should carefully assess the probable accuracy of your estimates.

Impact of Inflation

The double-digit inflation rates of the late 1970s and early 1980s signal the importance of proper treatment of the impact of inflation on marketing financial analysis. Conventional financial reporting using historical cost accounting suffers from two inadequacies during inflationary periods: (1) the dollar does not represent a constant or stable measuring unit over time; and (2) prior to sale, no recognition is given to changes in the prices of the assets held by a firm.[10] Some alternative methods of inflation accounting are shown in Exhibit 3–14.

Perhaps the most significant implication is the apparent emphasis by top management on the total level of asset commitment to specific products and markets. This, of course, will have its greatest impact on

EXHIBIT 3–14   Alternative Inflation Accounting Methods

	*Nominal Dollars**	*Constant Dollars*
Historical cost	1. Method used in conventional financial reporting	2. Dollars restated to dollars of constant general purchasing power
Current cost	3. Dollar amounts reported in terms of current replacement cost of specific assets	4. Same as 3 except that all amounts in 3 are restated to a constant-dollar basis

* Actual dollars received at sale of product and expended when inventory and equipment were acquired.

Source: Adapted from Frederick E. Webster, Jr., James A. Largay III, and Clyde P. Stickney, "The Impact of Inflation Accounting in Marketing Decisions," *Journal of Marketing*, Fall 1980, pp. 9–17.

products and markets requiring heavy capital investments in fixed assets and working capital.[11]

Time Value of Money

The time value of money represents another influence on the evaluation of the financial performance of marketing operations. Since several sources provide extensive coverage of this topic, we shall only note its importance in marketing financial analysis, particularly when dealing with uneven cash flows over long time periods.[12]

SPREADSHEET ANALYSIS—USING PERSONAL COMPUTERS

The increased availability of computers provides a powerful tool of analysis. With the most basic of personal computers, the business student has the capability to simplify lengthy and repetitive analyses and evaluation of multiple alternatives. Customized programs and graphing features are widely used by businesses, along with electronic spreadsheet software.

Spreadsheet Capabilities

The electronic spreadsheet—marketed under names such as Lotus 1-2-3®, Borland Quattro, and others—provides the basic tools of analysis in an easy-to-use software program. Text, formulas, and numbers can be fed into the computer to develop ratio analyses, sales forecasts, reconciliations, accounting statements, and cost data. The major advantage of the spreadsheet is the ability to conduct analysis while changing various assumptions and to arrive at an answer or conclusion without manually repeating the calculations.

Some software packages, including Lotus 1-2-3, have computer graphics capabilities. Graphs, pie charts, bar charts, and other visual comparisons can be prepared. For example, the analysis shown in Exhibit 3–15 was prepared in only a few minutes on an IBM XT computer, using Lotus 1-2-3. The analyst needs only to type in the ranges for each product group, the range for time periods, and appropriate titles. A graphic comparison of the sales projections is shown in Exhibit 3–16.

EXHIBIT 3–15

ESTIMATED ANNUAL SALES BY PRODUCT GROUP

PRODUCT GROUP	ANNUAL GROWTH RATE	ANNUAL SALES 1992	PROJECTED ANNUAL SALES 1993	1994	1995	1996
A	5.0%	$ 870,000	$ 913,500	$ 959,175	$ 1,007,134	$ 1,057,490
B	-2.0%	$ 767,000	$ 751,660	$ 736,627	$ 721,894	$ 707,456
C	12.0%	$ 583,000	$ 652,960	$ 731,315	$ 819,073	$ 917,362

How Spreadsheet Analysis Is Set Up

To illustrate its features, a more detailed description of the mechanics of spreadsheet analysis is necessary. The spreadsheet is a matrix of cells that can be filled with text, formulas, or numbers. Data can be manipulated by referencing a cell. This includes the row and column

EXHIBIT 3–16

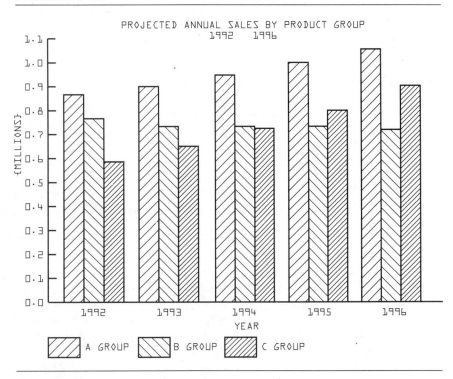

location denoted by numbers and letters respectively. It is this feature that allows formulas to be calculated based upon whatever number is entered in a cell, not just relying on a number that may need to be replaced should an assumption or key figure be changed.

For example, assume that a firm produces Products A and B and that the firm wishes to calculate the total revenue from these products. For each product, one cell would contain the price of a product and another the amount sold. The cell that would display the total revenue would contain the formula: number of units of A sold times the price, added to the number of units of B sold times the price. If the formula was entered using the numerical values of the prices and units sold, then if any of these values should change, the formula would have to be reentered in the cell to display the correct total revenue accounting for the changes. However, if the formula was entered using the cell location for the values of the number of units of A and B sold and the prices of A and B, the total revenue figure would be changed automatically. Any change in the price or amount sold of A or B would be entered in the appropriate cell. The computer would recalculate the total revenue based upon this change and display the answer in the cell for total revenue. Setting up the formulas based upon cell locations rather than values is especially useful where there are complex, lengthy formulas and when conditions are likely to change or there is a desire to see the proposed effect of certain changes in variables.

Using the Spreadsheet in Case Analysis

The electronic spreadsheet is very useful in case analysis. Ratios, break-even points, or forecasts can be determined from balance sheet and income statement data entered on the spreadsheet from the case information. The analyst can change key assumptions or figures in the balance sheet or income statement and immediately see the effect of these changes on any calculations. A standard financial analysis format can be established, and data from any case can be entered on the spreadsheet. The possibilities are endless, limited only by your imagination and the data provided in the case.

SUMMARY

This chapter develops a foundation for marketing financial analysis. A variety of financial analysis methods were examined. Emphasis has been on application rather than method, since we have assumed that you already have an understanding of basic managerial accounting and finance. To supplement the coverage in the chapter, several sources are cited in the footnotes.

It is clear that marketing executives' financial analysis responsibilities are expanding rapidly, demanding a capability in using new concepts and techniques as well as interpreting financial analyses provided by others:

> To respond to these pressures positively, marketing managers will need a better understanding of accounting and financial management than that of their predecessors. The characteristic marketing manager's emphasis in analysis and action on sales volume, gross margin, and market share must be replaced by a more general management focus on bottom-line profitability and return on investment. Top management will think increasingly in terms of total resource allocation across products and markets, assessing the total product portfolio in terms of complex trade-offs between business growth opportunities in markets requiring additional investment for future profitability versus cash generation now in markets with limited or negative investment.[13]

As you move through the analysis of the various cases, you may find it helpful to refer to this chapter when you analyze financial information provided in a case or prepare your own financial analyses. Building upon the materials discussed in this chapter, Chapter 4 considers various aspects of case analysis.

NOTES

1. Robert C. Higgins, *Analysis for Financial Management* (Homewood, Ill.: Business One Irwin, 1983), p. 3.
2. Marilyn Chase, "Pricing Battle: Burroughs Wellcome Reaps Profits, Outrage from Its AIDS Drug," *The Wall Street Journal,* September 15, 1989, pp. A1, A4.
3. This illustration is drawn from David W. Cravens, Gerald E. Hills, and Robert B. Woodruff, *Marketing Decision Making: Concepts and Strategy*, rev. ed. (Homewood, Ill.: Richard D. Irwin, Inc., 1980), pp. 335–36.
4. James C. Van Horne, *Fundamentals of Financial Management*, 4th ed. (Englewood Cliffs, N.J.: Prentice Hall, 1980), pp. 103–4.
5. A useful guide to ratio analysis is provided in Richard Sanzo, *Ratio Analysis for Small Business* (Washington, D.C.: Small Business Administration, 1977).
6. Francine Schwadel, "Kmart Is Trying to Put Style on the Aisle," *The Wall Street Journal*, August 9, 1988, p. 6.
7. David S. Hopkins, *Business Strategies for Problem Products* (New York: Conference Board, 1977), p. 11.
8. Sam R. Goodman, *Financial Analysis for Marketing Decisions* (Homewood, Ill.: Business One Irwin, 1972), p. 88.
9. Ibid., pp. 102–3.
10. Frederick E. Webster, Jr., James A. Largay III, and Clyde P. Stickney,

"The Impact of Inflation Accounting on Marketing Decisions," *Journal of Marketing*, Fall 1980, p. 10.

11. Ibid., p. 14.

12. An excellent discussion of evaluating investment opportunities is provided in Higgins, *Analysis for Financial Management*, chaps. 8 and 9.

13. Webster et al., "The Impact of Inflation Accounting," pp. 16–17.

Financial Analysis Exercises

Exercise 3–1   Snapamatic Camera Company (A)

This exercise presents a situation requiring several basic financial calculations. It is a useful means of identifyng where to review financial analysis methods.

Snapamatic Camera Company has introduced a new line of low-priced cameras called "Click Quick," and the information for that product line is given below.

a. Retail selling price	$25 per unit
b. Retailer's cost	$20 per unit
c. Wholesaler's cost	$15 per unit
d. Manufacturer's variable selling expense as % of age of selling price	10%
e. Fixed selling and advertising expense	$800,000
f. Annual sales for Snapamatic	150,000 units
g. Estimated market size for low-priced cameras	800,000 units
h. Variable manufacturing cost	$2.50 per unit
i. Fixed manufacturing cost	$100,000

Discussion Questions

1. What is the variable cost per unit of Click Quick for Snapamatic Camera Company?
2. What is Snapamatic's contribution margin per unit?
3. Calculate the break-even volume in units and in dollars.
4. Estimate the market share that Click Quick has to command in order to (a) break even and/or (b) attain a before-tax target profit of $600,000.

Exercise 3–2 *Snapamatic Camera Company (B)*

The management of Snapamatic Camera Co. is considering introduction of a new product called "Click-O-Matic," which is to be marketed in addition to Click Quick. This is intended for a higher-priced (meant for the more avid and sophisticated photographer) segment of the market. The following information has been compiled for managerial decision making:

a. Retailer's margin	20%
b. Jobber's margin	15%
c. Wholesaler's margin	$5 per unit
d. Variable selling expense as % age of sales	10%
e. Retailer's selling price	$60
f. Incremental fixed selling expense	$300,000
g. Promotion and advertising for Click-O-Matic	$500,000
h. New equipment required	$500,000 (to be depreciated over 10 years)
i. Direct factory labor	$4 per unit
j. Raw materials	$5 per unit
k. Factory and administrative overhead	$3 per unit (at a 50,000 unit volume level)

Discussion Questions

1. What is the contribution margin per unit for the Click-O-Matic line?
2. Calculate the break-even sales in dollars and in units.
3. How much sales volume in dollars should Snapamatic Camera Company attain on Click-O-Matic to get 15 percent return on the equipment?
4. Customers initially may be very sensitive to the higher price of $60, so it is considered worthwhile performing an analysis using a unit price of $55 per unit and raise the retail margin to 25 percent. What is the break-even volume in units?

Exercise 3–3   Supersonic Stereo, Inc.

"At this rate, I'll be looking for a new job," thought Bob Basler, sales manager of Supersonic's Atlanta district. "Our sales are stagnant, and what's worse, our profits are down." Sales and profit results for the last five years did not measure up to objectives established for the Atlanta district (see Exhibit 1). Basler knew that very shortly he would be hearing from Pete Lockhart, Supersonic's national sales manager, and that the same question would be asked: "When are you going to turn the Atlanta district around?"

Bob was faced with another problem that added to his worries. One of his sales representatives, Charlie Lyons, was very upset and was threatening to quit unless he received a substantial salary increase. Lyons felt that since he led the district in sales volume, he should be amply rewarded. "I have to find out what's happening in the Atlanta district before I go and make recommendations for salary increases," Basler thought. "Besides, if I make such a recommendation, Pete will think that I have taken leave of my senses. He will not approve any salary increases for anybody as long as the Atlanta district's performance is so weak."

Supersonic Stereo is one of the country's leading manufacturers of stereo equipment. Since its formation in 1962, Supersonic has experienced rapid growth, based largely on its reputation for high-quality stereo products. Prices were competitive, although some dealers engaged in discounting. Supersonic distributed its stereo equipment on a selective basis. Only those dealers who could provide strong marketing support and reliable servicing were selected by Supersonic. Dealers were supported by Supersonic's national advertising campaign. Advertising averaged 5 percent of sales, somewhat more than what other stereo manufacturers spent for this item.

Supersonic's sales force was compensated with salary plus commission of 6 percent based on gross margin. Gross margin was used to discourage sales representatives from cutting prices. Accounts were assigned to sales representatives based on size. New sales representatives were usually assigned a number of small accounts at first. As they progressed they were assigned larger accounts. The more experienced sales representatives were assigned the larger, more desirable accounts. In some cases, a sales representative would have only three or four accounts, each averaging $250,000 a year.

The average base salary for the sales force reached $26,500 in 1989,

Source: Gilbert A. Churchill, Jr., Neil M. Ford, and Orville C. Walker, Jr., *Salesforce Management* (Homewood, Ill.: Richard D. Irwin, Inc., 1990), pp. 781–85.

EXHIBIT 1 Total Sales and Profits for the Atlanta District, 1985–1989

	1985	*1986*	*1987*	*1988*	*1989*
Total sales	$2,641,081	$2,445,120	$2,610,029	$2,514,113	$2,638,340
Net profit	13,873	14,050	15,381	16,511	14,383

and commissions averaged $9,500. Total average sales-force compensation was $36,000 in 1989. Travel expenses were paid by Supersonic. The total package was considered by one executive to be too plush. This executive, Stella Jordan, felt that not enough was expected from the sales force. "I know of one sales representative who calls on three accounts and in 1983 earned $38,563," she stated at a recent meeting. "If we want to improve our profits, then we need to either reduce our base salaries or cut back our commission rate."

Jordan's suggestion was not favorably received by Basler, who felt that such a move would have a disastrous effect on sales force motivation. Stella countered by pointing out that motivation must be lacking since the Atlanta district's performance is so poor. "If salaries or commissions cannot be reduced, at least let's not raise them," she suggested. "Maybe we should consider raising quotas and not pay commissions until sales representatives exceed their quotas. Or," she continued, "maybe a management by objectives approach should be developed."

Basler knew that Jordan's comments demanded a response. He also knew she was talking about Charlie Lyons when she mentioned a sales representative with three accounts earning $38,563. Basler suggested that he should be allowed time to do a complete cost analysis by sales

EXHIBIT 2 Profit and Loss Statement, Atlanta District, 1989

Sales		$2,638,340
Cost of goods sold		2,014,485
Gross margin		$ 623,855
Expenses:		
Salaries	$177,000	
Commissions	37,431	
Advertising	131,915	
Packaging	43,642	
Warehousing and transportation	76,374	
Travel expenses	59,340	
Order processing	770	
Rent	83,000	
Total expenses		609,472
Net profit (before taxes)		$ 14,383

EXHIBIT 3   Allocation of Natural Accounts to Functional Accounts, Atlanta District

| | | Functional Accounts | | | | | |
Natural Accounts		Selling Direct Costs	Selling Indirect Costs	Adver- tising	Order Proces- sing	Ware- house and Trans- porta- tion	Pack- aging
Salaries	$177,000	$106,500	$47,500		$12,000		$11,000
Commissions	37,431	37,431					
Advertising	131,915			$131,915			
Packaging	43,642						43,642
Warehousing and transportation	76,374					$ 76,374	
Travel expenses	59,340	57,340	2,000				
Order processing	770				770		
Rent	83,000		18,500		4,500	40,000	20,000
Total expenses	$609,472	$201,271	$60,000	$131,915	$17,270	$116,374	$74,642

representative before adopting any corrective action. Jordan agreed and offered her assistance. Salaries for the others were as follows: Sand $24,500, Gallo $27,500, and Parks $26,000.

Basler's first activity was to identify available information for his district. He was able to secure a profit and loss statement for the Atlanta district (see Exhibit 2). Jordan suggested that since Basler was interested in sales-force profitability, his next step should be to allocate the natural accounts in Exhibit 2 to their appropriate functional accounts. Exhibit 3 shows the results of this step.

EXHIBIT 4   Product Line Sales and Costs

Product	Selling Price per Unit	Cost per Unit	Gross Margin per Unit	Number Sold in Period	Sales in Period	Adver- tising Expendi- tures	Pack- aging
Receivers	$250	$212	$38	3,151	$ 787,750	$ 40,000	$ 6,302
Turntables	85	64	21	12,079	1,026,715	50,000	24,158
Speakers	125	87	38	6,591	823,875	40,000	13,182
				21,821	$2,638,340	$130,000	$43,642

EXHIBIT 5   Sales Calls, Orders, and Units Sold, by Salesperson

Salesperson	Number of Sales Calls	Number of Orders	Number of Units Sold			Total
			Receivers	Turntables	Speakers	
Paul Sand	85	60	668	2,652	1,534	4,854
Diane Gallo	105	85	823	3,270	1,582	5,675
Kathy Parks	110	60	816	3,131	1,578	5,525
Charlie Lyons	170	75	844	3,026	1,897	5,767
	470	280	3,151	12,079	6,591	21,821

"If we are going to do an analysis by sales representative, we need much more information," Stella indicated. To help in this regard, she compiled product sales data (see Exhibit 4).

Basler provided data for each sales representative, showing number of sales calls, number of orders, and unit sales by product line (see Exhibit 5). The next step would be to compile the data to develop a profitability analysis by sales representative.

The problem with Charlie Lyons is still there, mused Basler. He wants more money, and Stella Jordan thinks he is overpaid and underworked. Since Charlie Lyons is something of a focal point, we ought to do a profitability analysis for each of his customers. Basler's next step was to compile data by customer. Exhibit 6 presents customer data for each of Lyons's three accounts.

Preparing guidelines for allocating costs to sales representatives and customers was Basler's next task. Based on his review of several distribution cost and analysis textbooks and further conversations with Stella Jordan, Basler developed the following guidelines:

EXHIBIT 6   Customer Activity Analysis for Charlie Lyons

Customers of Charlie Lyons	Number of Sales Calls	Average Time Spent on Each Call (minutes)	Number of Orders	Number of Units Purchased			Total
				Receivers	Turntables	Speakers	
American TV	65	55	40	422	1,513	854	2,789
Appliance Mart	55	45	15	337	1,058	569	1,964
Audio Emporium	50	45	20	85	455	474	1,104
	170	50	75	844	3,026	1,897	5,767

Functional Cost Item	Basis of Allocation
Direct selling	Number of calls × Average time spent with each customer
Commissions	6 percent of gross margin
Travel	Total travel costs divided by number of calls; this figure is then multiplied by individual salesperson calls or customer calls
Advertising	5 percent of sales dollars
Packaging	Number of units × $2
Warehousing and transportation	Number of units × $3.50
Order processing	Number of orders × $2.75

Basler's next step is the development of the necessary accounting statement, which will permit a detailed analysis of each sales representative's profitability. From there he will proceed to a customer profitability analysis for Charlie Lyons's customers.

Exercise 3–4   *Winkleman Manufacturing Company*

In a recent staff meeting, John Winkleman, president of Winkleman Manufacturing Company, addressed his managers with this problem:

> Intense competitive pressure is beginning to erode our market share in handhelds. I have documented 11 large orders that have been lost to Backman and Wiston within the past three months. On an annual basis this amounts to nearly 10,000 units and $1.5 million in lost opportunities. Within the last 18 months, at least 16 serious competitors have entered the market. Two-thirds of these DMMs have continuity indicators. The trend is the same for European and Japanese markets as well. Our sales of handheld DMMs in fiscal year 81 is forecast to grow only 1.7 percent. According to Dataquest projections, the handheld DMM market will grow 20.9 percent for the next five years. I think that figure is conservative. Our competitors are gaining attention and sales with added features, particularly at the

Source: Prepared by Jim Dooley, under the supervision of Dr. William L. Weis. Albers School of Business, Seattle University. Copyright © 1981 by Jim Dooley and William L. Weis.

present time with continuity indicators. Since a new Winkleman general-purpose, low-cost handheld is two years from introduction, it is important that something be done to retain the profitable position of market leader in our traditional direct and distributor channels. Next meeting I want some ideas.

The Winkleman Manufacturing Company is a major electronics manufacturer in the Northwest, producing many varied products. The three products that most concern Mr. Winkleman are the Series A handheld digital multimeters (DMMs). As an innovator in the field of handheld DMMs, Mr. Winkleman saw his business flourish over the last two years. But now, with his three most successful products in late stages of maturity and a recession in full swing, times are not looking as rosy.

The three multimeters of concern are model numbers 1010, 1020, and 1030. These three models form a complementary family line. The 1010 is a low-cost unit containing all standard measurement functions and having a basic measurement accuracy of .5 percent. The 1020 offers identical measurement functions but has an improved basic measurement accuracy: .1 percent. The top of the line is the 1030. In addition to a basic accuracy of .1 percent, the 1030 offers several additional features, one being an audible continuity indicator. (See Exhibit 1 for sales and projected sales of these three models.)

At the next staff meeting, one of the newer management team members, Dave Haug, presented his ideas for tackling the lost-market problem:

What we need is a face-lift of our existing product line to hold us over the next two years. Changes in color, a new decal, some minor case modifications, and most important an audible continuity indicator in the 1010 and 1020 should give us two more years of product life to tide us over. We can call this Series B to retain continuity in switching from the old to the new. As my analysis indicates, Winkleman's decline in 1010/1020 sales could be reversed and show a modest increase in market share over the next two years with the inclusion of the Series B features [see Exhibit 2]. Discussions with large-order customers indicate that Winkleman could have won 40–60

EXHIBIT 1   Selected Sales and Projections (number of units)

Model	FY 80 (actual)	FY 81 (forecast)	Percentage
1020	67,534	61,800	−8.4%
1010	37,455	35,500	−5.5
1030	25,602	35,500	+39.0
Total	130,591	132,800	+1.7%

EXHIBIT 2   Series A and B—Projected Comparison (number of units)

Model	Unit Price	Series A FY 81	Series B FY 81	Change (percentage)	Total Sales* (change *)
1020	$179	61,800	66,000	4,200 (+6.8%)	$11.81 (+.75)
1010	139	35,500	40,000	4,500 (+12.6%)	$ 5.56 (+.63)
1030	219	35,500	36,000	500 (+1.4%)	$ 7.88 (+.11)
Total		132,800	142,000	9,200	$25.25

* Dollars in millions.

percent of the lost large orders that were mentioned at our last meeting if our entire handheld family featured audible continuity. As you well know, the popularity of continuity indication has been confirmed in several other studies conducted over the past two years.

An estimate of sales of Series B has been generated from inputs from field sales, distribution managers, and discussions with customers. Conservative estimates indicate that sales of Series B will increase 6.9 percent above current Series A levels, with a marginal revenue increase of $1.5 million at U.S. list and assuming the same list prices as the current Series A models. During this current period of tight economic conditions, the market is becoming increasingly price sensitive. I am aware that our normal policy dictates multiplying the factory cost by three for pricing purposes and that the added factory cost of an audible continuity indicator is $5.00; but for income purposes we should not tack this on to the current prices. My analysis indicates that an increase of $5.00 would reduce incremental sales by 20 percent, and an increase of $10.00 would reduce incremental sales by 80 percent.

Also remember that we must pay for some nonrecurring engineering costs (NRE) [see Exhibit 3]. These must come out of our contribution margin—which at Winkleman is calculated by taking the total dollar sales less the 28 percent discount to distributors less factory cost for those units. I believe that increasing these prices will reduce our margins significantly, hindering our ability to cover the NRE, let alone make a profit. Therefore I propose we go ahead with Series B and hold the line on prices.

Dennis Cambelot, a longtime Winkleman employee, spoke up with a comment on Dave's proposal:

Dave, I think this Series B idea shows a lot of potential, but pricewise you are way out of line. We have always added the standard markup to our products. We make quality products, and people are willing to pay for quality. The only thing your fancy MBA degree taught you was to be impractical. If you had gotten your experience in the trenches like me, your pricing theories would not be so conservative, and this company could make more money.

EXHIBIT 3   Engineering Costs and Schedule

Objectives for Series B, Models 1010, 1020, and 1030:
  All case parts molded in medium gray
  New decal for all units
  Pulse-stretched beeper for 1010 and 1020
  Rubber foot on battery door
  Positionable bail
  Manuals updated as necessary
For these objectives, NRE costs will be:

Manual (updated schematics for 1010, 1020, along with instructions for operation of beeper; model number and front panel changes for all units)	$ 3,500
Battery door mold (add three units)	12,000
Battery door foot die	3,000
Decal	1,900
Bail improvement	8,600
Photo lab	250
PCB fab (prototypes)	500
Engineering labor (25 man-weeks)	81,000
Hard model run	6,000
Total	$116,750

At the close of the meeting, Mr. Winkleman asked that each manager consider the Series B proposal. He directed that this consideration include: (1) whether or not to adopt the B series; (2) if yes, at what price level; (3) alternative suggestions.

Discussion Question

How would you respond at the next meeting?

Exercise 3–5   Time Unlimited, Inc.

The Microcomputer Division of Time Unlimited, Inc., manufactures and sells two models of computers. The smallest one, the RAM–64, and 64K internal memory, two double-density 5½-inch floppy disk drives

---

Source: Professor Mary Ziebell, Seattle University, and Professor Don T. DeCoster, University of Washington.

with 197K bytes each, a detachable full typewriter keyboard, and a 12-inch video display of 80 columns × 24 rows with scrolling capability. In addition, it includes as standard software a profit plan, a household budget program, a word-processing system, and two computer games of the customer's choice. It can be used either as a home computer or in a small business where the data-processing needs are not extensive. The other model, the RAM–128, is larger than the RAM–64 and has greater capacity, including two 8-inch double-sided, double-density disk drives holding over 700K bytes. In addition to the software package offered with the RAM–64, a complete accounting program and a sophisticated statistical analysis package are included as part of the standard software. However, it still is classified as a microcomputer. The RAM–128 is purchased by businesses that want a small computer with the additional data-processing capabilities that the smaller model does not offer. Time Unlimited, Inc.'s prices are higher than their competitor's because the RAM computers offer processing and programming features not available from competitors, as well as a superior warranty and service program. Time Unlimited usually announces any price changes after the competition has posted theirs for the year.

Late in 1981 the Computer Division managers held a meeting where the following discussion took place. In attendance were:

Jon Patric—marketing manager

Andrea Suzanne—chief accountant

Ross Edwards—vice president of the Computer Division

Jim Mathews—production manager

Jon Patric: In a few months we are going to raise the price of the RAM–64 from $1,800 to $2,000 per unit, while our competition will be raising their prices from $1,700 to $1,850 per unit. In addition, the price of the RAM–128 will go from $13,500 to $15,000 per unit. By contrast, our competition is planning on raising their prices from $12,500 to $14,000. We project that our microcomputer sales division should sell at least 40,000 units of the RAM–64 at $1,800 per unit; at $2,000 per unit we should sell at least 20,000 units. Our market studies also indicate that at $13,500 per unit we should sell at least 4,000 units of RAM–128, while at $15,000 per unit we project sales of at least 2,000 units. I'm very concerned about this decrease in our volume of sales and question the advisability of raising our prices at this time.

Andrea Suzanne: The reason we are increasing the prices of the RAM–64 and RAM–128, Jon, is due to the fact that labor and material prices have gone up about 12 percent over the last year. Our increase in price just reflects the cost of inflation. I have finished compiling some current data (Exhibit 1) through June of 1981, if anyone is interested. One idea to decrease cost would be to cut the 10 percent sales commission to 7 or 8 percent. That's

EXHIBIT 1 Estimated Cost Comparisons of RAM–64 and RAM–128 at Different Production Volumes through June 1981

A. RAM–64

Expenses	Volume (units)				
	10,000	20,000	30,000	40,000	50,000
Raw materials	$ 144	$ 144	$ 144	$ 144	$ 144
Purchased parts	160	160	160	160	155
Direct labor	510	500	490	485	490
Departmental overhead					
Direct*	35	34	32	33	33
Equipment depreciation	144	72	48	36	29
Indirect†	235	120	80	60	48
General overhead‡	127	125	120	122	123
Production costs	1,355	1,155	1,074	1,040	1,022
Marketing and administration§	677	578	537	520	511
Total costs	$2,032	$1,733	$1,611	$1,560	$1,533

B. RAM–128

Expenses	Volume (units)				
	1,000	2,000	3,000	4,000	5,000
Raw materials	$ 1,450	$ 1,450	$ 1,450	$ 1,450	$ 1,450
Purchased parts	1,740	1,740	1,740	1,730	1,720
Direct labor	4,600	4,500	4,350	4,400	4,500
Departmental overhead					
Direct*	400	380	373	365	370
Equipment depreciation	870	435	290	218	174
Indirect†	1,305	652	435	326	261
General overhead‡	1,110	1,100	1,087	1,095	1,100
Production costs	11,475	10,257	9,725	9,584	9,575
Marketing and administration§	5,738	5,129	4,858	4,793	4,788
Total costs	$17,213	$15,385	$14,583	$14,377	$14,363

* Power, supplies, repairs.
† Supervision, interest, rent, property taxes.
‡ Allocated on the basis of 25 percent of direct labor.
§ Allocated on the basis of 50 percent of production costs.

all our competitors are paying their sales staff. Also our service warranty costs have increased from 4 percent to approximately 7 percent of sales. We really need to know the cause of this increase.

Ross Edwards: Jon, if we kept both models at the current price, would the competitors keep their prices at the current level, or would they still raise their prices? We really need to know this. Also it seems from the attached income statement (Exhibit 2) that the RAM–128 line is not as profitable as the RAM–64 line. Perhaps we should be concentrating our marketing efforts on the RAM–64. It also seems to me we should seriously consider Andrea's suggestion on reducing sales commissions.

Jon Patric: Our competition would probably raise their prices even if we kept ours the same, though perhaps not as much as originally planned, Ross. We are currently in a strong market position (Exhibit 3), and I would not like to see this market share lost. In response to Andrea's suggestion, I am certain that a decrease in the level of commissions would seriously affect our market share because of salespeople's decreased motivation.

Jim Mathews: From a product-line evaluation standpoint, we are not making much money on the RAM–128. Maybe we should drop it and produce only the RAM–64 or develop another model. I realize we cannot transfer all of the equipment that is used in manufacturing the RAM–128 to the manufacture of the RAM–64, but we can transfer the labor that is used to produce the RAM–128 to produce the RAM–64. However, your question on increasing warranty costs, Andrea, is harder to answer. Up through 1980 we have always considered 4 percent of the sales price of both the micros a reasonable estimate of our costs of servicing the computers under the one-year warranty, and this proved accurate in the past. But with the increase in parts and labor costs as well as some small problems in this year's production process, it's not surprising that warranty costs have increased. In fact I'm rather surprised the increase wasn't more. It is

---

EXHIBIT 2

TIME UNLIMITED, INC.
Income Statement
For Year Ending December 31, 1980
($000)

	*RAM–64**	*RAM–128**	*Total*
Gross sales	$54,600	$40,500	$94,500
Expenses			
Raw materials	$ 3,880	$ 3,915	$ 7,795
Purchased parts	4,320	4,698	9,018
Direct labor	12,960	11,745	24,705
Direct overhead	864	980	1,844
Equipment depreciation	1,440	870	2,310
Indirect overhead	2,160	1,174	3,334
General overhead	3,240	2,935	6,175
Marketing and administration	14,364	13,114	27,478
Total expenses	$43,228	$39,431	$82,659
Income	$10,772	$ 1,069	$11,841

* Sold in 1980: 30,000 units of RAM–64; 3,000 units of RAM–128.

EXHIBIT 3   Time Unlimited, Inc., Market Position

	Sales Volume		Price (per unit)	
Selling Year	Industry Totals	Time Unlimited	Competition's Average Price	Time Unlimited
RAM–64 model				
1978	40,000	5,000	$ 5,000	$ 6,000
1979	75,000	10,000	2,500	2,700
1980	150,000	30,000	1,700	1,800
1981	200,000	—	1,850	—
RAM–128 model				
1978	7,500	500	$20,000	$23,000
1979	15,000	1,500	15,000	16,500
1980	25,000	3,000	12,500	13,500
1981	35,000	—	14,000	—

important, given our current marketing strategy, that we maintain the highest possible reputation in this area. At least that's what Jon is always telling me.

Andrea Suzanne: To get back to the idea of dropping the RAM–128 line, we really may want to give that further consideration. Our records show that the nontransferable RAM–128 equipment has a book value of $4,350,000. We should be able to sell this equipment for around $2 million. This would give us a good cash inflow, enough perhaps to develop a new product line.

Jim Mathews: Great idea, Andrea. Our current plant capacity is 50,000 units of the RAM–64 and 5,000 units of the RAM–128. With the cash from the sale of the RAM–128 equipment, we could expand our plant capacity to 70,000 units of the RAM–64. It would cost about $3 million for an additional building and equipment, give or take a little.

Ross Edwards: Well, I can see from our discussion that there are several options open to us. I do have an additional concern. After reviewing the data brought in by Andrea, I'm not exactly sure how much it is costing us to produce and sell either of our models. We really need this piece of information. And while you are thinking about that, please keep one important point in mind. Our divisional goal is an income of 12 percent of sales, so we should consider that when seeking solutions to the questions that were brought up in today's meeting. It is reasonably urgent that we come up with a suitable analysis as soon as possible. We are almost through the year now and must make some decisions for the coming year. I'll see you back here in one week.

Chapter 4

Guide to Case Analysis

A case presents a situation involving a managerial problem or issue that requires a decision. Typically, cases describe a variety of conditions and circumstances facing an organization at a particular time. This description often includes information regarding the organization's goals and objectives, its financial condition, the attitudes and beliefs of managers and employees, market conditions, competitors' activities, and various environmental forces that may affect the organization's present or proposed marketing strategy. Your responsibility is to carefully sift through the information provided in order to identify the opportunity, problem, or decision facing the organization; to carefully identify and evaluate alternative courses of action; and to propose a solution or decision based on your analysis.

This chapter provides an overview of the case method. It begins with a discussion of the role that cases play in the teaching/learning process. This is followed by a series of guidelines for case analysis. After carefully reading this material, you should be prepared to tackle your first case analysis. Even if you have had previous experience with cases, this chapter will provide a useful review.

WHY CASES?

The case method differs substantially from other teaching/learning approaches such as lecture and discussion. Lecture- and discussion-oriented classes provide students with information about concepts, practices, and theories. In contrast, cases provide an opportunity to *use* concepts, practices, and theories. The primary objective of the case method is to give you a hands-on opportunity to apply what you have learned in your course work.

Consider this analogy: Suppose that you want to learn to play a musical instrument. Your instruction might begin with several classes and reading assignments about your particular instrument. This could include information about the history of the instrument and descriptions of the various parts of the instrument and their functions. Sooner or later, however, you would actually have to play the instrument. Eventually you might become an accomplished musician.

Now suppose you want to become a marketing professional, instead of a musician. You started with classes or courses that introduced you to the foundations of marketing management. Your prior studies may have also included courses in areas of specialization such as marketing research, buyer behavior, and promotion, as well as other business disciplines such as management, finance, accounting, economics, and statistics. You need practice and experience to become a professional. This is precisely the purpose of the case method of instruction. The cases in this book will give you opportunities to apply your knowledge of marketing and other business subjects to actual marketing situations.

Case studies help to bridge the gap between classroom learning and the practice of marketing management. They provide us with an opportunity to develop, sharpen, and test our analytical skills at:

- Assessing situations.
- Sorting out and organizing key information.
- Asking the right questions.
- Defining opportunities and problems.
- Identifying and evaluating alternative courses of action.
- Interpreting data.
- Evaluating the results of past strategies.
- Developing and defending new strategies.
- Interacting with other managers.
- Making decisions under conditions of uncertainty.
- Critically evaluating the work of others.
- Responding to criticism.

In addition, cases provide exposure to a broad range of situations facing different types and sizes of organizations in a variety of industries. The decisions that you encounter in this book will range from fairly simple to quite complex. If you were the managers making these decisions, you would be risking anywhere from a few thousand to several million dollars of your firm's resources. And you could be risking your job and your career. Obviously the risk, or the cost of making mistakes, is much lower in the classroom environment.

A principal difference between our earlier example of learning to play a musical instrument and the practice of marketing lies in what might be called consequences. A musician's expertise is based on his or her ability to perform precisely the same series of actions time after time. The outcome of perfect execution of a predetermined series of actions is the sought consequence: a beautiful melody. Marketing, on the other hand, is often described as a skillful combination of art and science. No two situations ever require exactly the same actions. Although the same skills and knowledge may be required in different situations, marketing executives must analyze and diagnose each situation separately and conceive and initiate unique strategies to produce sought consequences. Judgment, as opposed to rote memory and repetition, is one key to marketing success. When judgment and a basic understanding of the variables and interrelationships in marketing situations are coupled, they form the core of an analysis and problem-solving approach that can be used in any marketing decision-making situation.

THE CASE METHOD OF INSTRUCTION

The case method of instruction differs from the lecture/discussion method that you have grown accustomed to since you began your formal education 14 or more years ago. It is only natural that you are a bit anxious and apprehensive about it. The methods of study and class preparation are different, your roles and responsibilities are different, and the "right" answers are much less certain. The case method is neither better nor worse than alternative methods; it is just different.

The case method is participative. You will be expected to take a more active role in learning than you have taken in the past. The case method is based on a philosophy of learning by doing as opposed to learning by listening and absorbing information. Case analysis is an applied skill. As such it is something you learn through application, as opposed to something someone teaches you. The more you practice, the more proficient you will become. The benefit you receive from case analysis is directly proportional to the effort you put into it.

Your Responsibilities

Your responsibilities as a case analyst include active participation, interaction, critical evaluation, and effective communication.

Active Participation.   We have already noted that the case method is participative. It requires a great deal of individual participation in class discussion. Effective participation requires thorough preparation. This entails more than casually reading each case before class. The guidelines in the next section of this chapter will assist you in preparing case analyses. Also, keep in mind that there is a difference between contributing to a class discussion and just talking.

Interaction.   Interaction among students plays an important role in the case method of instruction. Effective learning results from individual preparation and thinking combined with group discussion. Whether you are assigned to work independently or in groups or teams, most instructors encourage students to discuss cases with other students. This, of course, is common practice among managers facing important business decisions. Case discussions, in and out of class, are beneficial because they provide immediate feedback regarding individual perspectives and possible solutions. Other important benefits of case discussions are the synergism and new insights produced by group brainstorming and discussion.

Critical Evaluation.   One of the most difficult responsibilities of student case analysts is learning to critique their peers and to accept criticism from them. Typically, students are reluctant to question or challenge their classmates or to suggest alternatives to the perspectives proposed by others in the class. Students find this difficult because they are generally inexperienced at performing these functions and are also unaccustomed to being challenged by their peers in the classroom. However, the case method of instruction is most effective when all parties engage in an open exchange of ideas. Good cases do not have one clear-cut superior solution. Don't be shy about expressing and defending your views. Moreover, the reasoning process you use and the questions you raise are often more important than the specific solution that you recommend.

Effective Communication.   Each of the three responsibilities discussed above requires effective communication. It is important that you organize your thoughts before speaking. You will develop and refine your communication skills by making class presentations, participating in case discussions, and writing case analyses. Furthermore, the focus of the case method is the development and sharpening of quantitative and qualitative analytical skills. Your analytical skills will improve as you organize information, diagnose problems, identify and evaluate alternatives, and develop solutions and action plans.

Case analysis plays an important role in your overall education. What you learn in a course that uses the case method may be your best preparation for securing your first job and launching your career. If you ask a sample of recruiters to assess the students who are completing undergraduate and graduate programs in business administration today, you will probably hear that these students are extremely well-trained in concepts and quantitative skills but that they lack verbal and written communication skills and decision-making skills. The case method offers students an excellent opportunity to enhance and refine those skills.

A GUIDE TO CASE ANALYSIS

There is no one best way to analyze a case. Most people develop their own method after gaining some experience. As with studying, everybody does it a little bit differently. The following suggestions are intended to give you some ideas of how others approach cases. Try these suggestions and make your own adjustments.

Begin by reading each case quickly. The purpose of the first reading should be to familiarize yourself with the organization, the problem, or the decision to be made, the types and amount of data provided, and in general to get a feel for the case. Your second reading of the case should be more careful and thorough. Many students find it helpful to underline, highlight, and make notes about symptoms, potential problems and issues, key facts, and other important information.

Now you should be in a position to investigate the tabular and numerical data included in the case. Ask yourself what each figure, table, or chart means, how it was derived, whether or not it is relevant, and whether further computations would be helpful. If calculations, comparisons, or consolidations of numerical data appear useful, take the necessary action at this time.

A large part of what you will learn from case analysis is how to define, structure, and analyze opportunities and problems. The following information is intended to provide you with a general framework for problem solving. In essence, it is the scientific method with some embellishment. If your instructor does not assign a preferred analytical framework, use the approach shown in Exhibit 4–1. A discussion of each step follows, and a detailed outline of analytic issues and questions is provided in the appendix to this chapter.

Step 1: Situation Audit

The situation audit phase of the problem-solving process is basically a synopsis and evaluation of an organization's current situation, opportunities, and problems. This phase of case analysis is typically handled in a worksheet form rather than as a formal part of the written case. The primary purpose of the audit is to help you prepare for problem definition and subsequent steps in the problem-solving process. The situation audit interprets and shows the relevance of important case information. Thus it is important that your situation audit be diagnostic rather than descriptive.

It is descriptive to recognize that, "Company A's current and quick ratios are 1.03 and 0.64, respectively." A diagnostic look at these figures indicates that Company A may not be able to meet maturing obligations. The poor quick ratio shows that without inventory, the

EXHIBIT 4–1   An Approach to Case Analysis

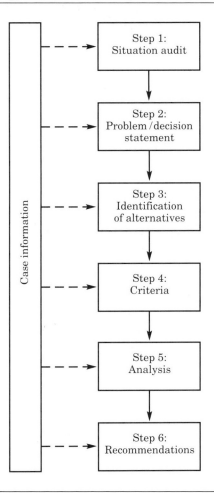

company's least liquid asset, short-term obligations could not be met. In other words, Company A is insolvent. If you have information about a number of different problems or challenges facing Company A, knowing that the company is insolvent helps you to focus your attention on those that affect the firm's short-term survival needs.

The breadth and depth of an appropriate situation audit are determined by the nature and scope of the case situation, and your instructor's specific instructions. Each case will require a situation audit that is a little different from any of the others because of the information available and the decision to be made.

There are at least two philosophies regarding the appropriate depth and scope of a situation audit. One philosophy holds that the situation audit should include a thorough and comprehensive assessment of the organization's mission and objectives; each business unit of interest; present and potential customers and competitors; the organization's market-target objectives and strategies; its marketing program positioning strategy; its product, distribution, pricing and promotion strategies; current planning, implementation and management activities; its financial condition, and an overall summary of the organization's situation. If your instructor favors a thorough and comprehensive situation audit, you will find the outline for case analysis in the appendix to this chapter quite helpful in organizing your work.

Some instructors, however, feel that the situation audit need not be a thorough and comprehensive study, but rather a short, concise analysis of the organization's major strengths, weaknesses, opportunities, and threats—reserving the comprehensive effort for the analysis step. Some call this a SWOT analysis, and recommend including only information that is crucial in preparing to analyze the case. The emphasis here is on *analysis*, *diagnosis*, *synthesis*, and *interpretation* of the situation. In a written assignment you should be able to present this in less than two pages.

A Note on Gathering More Data and on Making Assumptions. Students often feel that they need more information in order to make an intelligent decision. Decision makers rarely, if ever, have all the information they would like to have prior to making important decisions. The cost and time involved in collecting more data are often prohibitive. Decision makers, like you, therefore have to make some assumptions. There is nothing wrong with making assumptions as long as they are explicitly stated and reasonable. Be prepared to defend your assumptions as logical. Don't use lack of information as a crutch.

For example, an assumption that Company A, mentioned previously, cannot borrow large sums of money is both reasonable and defendable. To assume that it could borrow large sums of money would require a clear explanation of why some lender or investor would be willing to lend money to, or invest money in, a firm with a quick ratio of 0.64.

Step 2: Problem/Decision Statement

Identification of the main problem, opportunity, or issue in a case is crucial. To paraphrase from *Alice In Wonderland*, if you don't know where you are going, any solution will take you there. If you don't properly identify the central problem or decision in a case, the remainder of your analysis is not likely to produce recommendations necessary to solve the organization's main problem.

You may become frustrated with your early attempts at problem/decision identification. Don't feel alone. Most students and many experienced managers have difficulty with this task. Your skill will improve with practice.

A major pitfall in defining problems/decisions occurs in confusing symptoms with problems. Such things as declining sales, low morale, high turnover, or increasing costs are symptoms that are often incorrectly identified as problems. You can frequently avoid incorrectly defining a symptom as a problem by thinking in terms of causes and effects. Problems are causes, and symptoms are effects. The examples cited above are the effects or manifestations of something wrong in the organization. Why are sales declining? Why is morale low? Why is turnover high? Why are costs increasing? The key question is why. What is the cause? Sales may be declining because morale is low and turnover is high. Why is morale low, and why is turnover high? These effects may be caused by an inadequate compensation plan, which in turn may be caused by inadequate profit margins. Profit margins may be low because products have been incorrectly priced or because the distribution system is outdated. As you can see, symptoms may appear in one part of the overall marketing program, and the true problem may lie elsewhere in the program. Keep asking why, until you are satisfied that you have identified the problem (cause) and not just another symptom (effect).

Think about this analogy. You are not feeling well, so you make an appointment to see your physician. The physician will ask you to describe what is bothering you. Suppose you say you have a headache, a sore throat, chills, and a fever. The physician will probably take your temperature, look in your throat, and perhaps examine you in other ways. The goal, of course, is to diagnose your problem so that a remedy can be prescribed.

How does this relate to case analysis? Your headache, sore throat, chills, and fever are symptoms of something wrong. They are signals to you to seek help. This information also assists your physician in making his or her diagnosis. These symptoms are similar to the declining sales, poor morale, high turnover, and increasing costs that we discussed earlier. They are the effects of some underlying cause. Your role in case study, like the role of your physician, is to analyze the combination of symptoms that can be identified, and then to determine the underlying problem.

Let's carry the analogy a bit further. Suppose the physician's diagnosis is that you have a common cold. Since there is no cure for a cold, all he or she can do is prescribe medication to treat the symptoms. The cold will cure itself in a matter of days.

Now suppose the diagnosis of the cause is incorrect. Instead of just a common cold, you contracted malaria during a recent vacation in Southeast Asia. If the physician treats the symptoms or effects, they will be temporarily reduced or eliminated, but they will soon reappear. Each time they reappear they will be more severe, until the ailment is properly diagnosed or you die. This is precisely what will happen in an organization if a symptom is incorrectly identified as a problem. Treating the symptom will temporarily reduce its dysfunctional impact on the organization, but sooner or later it will reappear. When it reappears it will probably be more severe than it was previously. This is why carefully identifying the root problem, decision, or issue in your case analysis is so important.

When you identify more than one major problem or decision in a case, ask yourself whether or not the problems or decisions are related enough to be consolidated into one problem/decision statement. You may not yet have reached the central problem. If, however, you have identified two or more problems that are not directly associated with one another, we recommend that you rank them in the order of their importance and address them in that order. You may find that although the problems do not appear to be closely linked, the solutions are related. One solution may solve multiple problems.

A final suggestion regarding defining problems or decisions is to state them concisely and, if possible, in the form of a question. Try to write a one-sentence question that is specific enough to communicate the main concern. For example:

- Should Brand A be deleted from the product line?
- Should General Mills implement a cents-off campaign, or should it use coupons to stimulate trial of its new cereal Gold Rush?
- Which two of the five candidates should be hired?
- How should Magic Chef define its marketing planning units?
- What is the best marketing program positioning strategy for Agree creme rinse?

In addition to your problem/decision statement, you may find it useful to provide a brief narrative describing the main parameters of the problem/decision. This is helpful when you have a compound problem/decision that can be subdivided into components or subproblems.

Step 3: Identification of Alternatives

Alternatives are the strategic options or actions that appear to be viable solutions to the problem or decision situation that you have determined. Often, more than two seemingly appropriate actions will be available. Sometimes these will be explicitly identified in the case, and sometimes they will not.

Prepare your list of alternatives in two stages. First, prepare an initial list of alternatives that includes all the actions that you feel might be appropriate. Group brainstorming is a useful technique for generating alternatives. Be creative, keep an open mind, and build upon the ideas of others. What may initially sound absurd could become an outstanding possibility.

After you have generated your initial list of alternatives, begin refining your list and combining similar actions. Use the information that you organized in your situation audit regarding goals, objectives, and constraints, to help you identify which alternatives to keep and which to eliminate. Ask yourself whether or not an alternative is feasible given the existing financial, productive, managerial, marketing, and other constraints and whether or not it could produce the results sought. That is, does the alternative directly address the problem or decision you identified in Step 2? If your problem/decision statement and your alternatives are inconsistent, you have erred in one step or the other. To help avoid this mistake, be explicit in showing the connections between the situation audit, the problem/decision statement, and the final set of alternatives.

Doing nothing and collecting more data are two alternatives often suggested by students with limited case experience. These are rarely the best actions to take. If you have identified a problem or a decision that must be made, ignoring the situation probably will not help. Likewise, recommending a survey, hiring a consultant, or employing some other option associated with gathering more data is rarely a viable solution to the central problem or issue. In some cases, a solution may include further study, but this will normally be part of the implementation plan rather than part of the solution. Most cases, at least those included in this book, are based on real business situations. You have the same information that was available to the decision maker when the decision was made. The major difference is that your data are already compiled and organized. If complete information were available, decisions would be easy. This is not the case in business situations, so it may help you to become familiar with making decisions under conditions of uncertainty. Executives, like case analysts, must rely on assumptions and on less-than-perfect information.

Step 4: Criteria

Next you should develop a list of the main criteria that you will use to evaluate your strategic options. By expressly stating the criteria you intend to use in evaluating alternatives, you make clear the measures you plan to use in assessing and comparing the viability of your alternative courses of action.

Perhaps the best place to start in identifying criteria is to ask yourself what factors, in general, should be considered in making a strategic decision regarding this particular problem. For example, assume that your task is to identify the most attractive product-market niche. Your alternatives are niches X, Y, and Z. Your question then would be: What criteria should be employed in assessing the choices of product-market niches? An appropriate set of criteria might include (for each niche) potential sales volume, variable costs, contribution margins, market share, total niche sales, business strength, and niche attractiveness. This will provide an evaluation relative to the market and to competition.

The single most important factor in many decisions is profitability. Since profits are a principal goal in all commercial organizations, nearly every marketing decision is influenced by monetary considerations that ultimately affect profits (or expected profits). Sometimes several profit-oriented criteria are involved. These may include future costs and revenues, break-even points, opportunity costs, contribution margins, taxes, turnover, sales, and market share, for example.

Many criteria are only indirectly linked to profits. Such things as the impact of a decision on employees, the local economy, the environment, suppliers, or even customer attitudes may not directly affect profits. Because profits are almost always the overriding criterion, all factors bearing on them, directly or indirectly, must be considered.

Step 5: Analysis

Analysis is the process of evaluating each alternative action against the issues that were identified in Step 4. Often, analysis includes assessment of advantages and limitations associated with each issue. A tendency exists when first starting a case analysis to identify important issues carefully and then to analyze each issue superficially. The consequence is a weak analysis. Your analysis will be much more penetrating and comprehensive if you use the same criteria in assessing each alternative.

One way of assuring that you assess each alternative in terms of each critical issue is to organize your analysis in outline form as follows:

Step 5:   Analysis
   Alternative A: (Specify the alternative)
      1. Identify the criterion and thoroughly discuss Alternative A in terms of criterion number 1.

  2. For the remaining criteria, follow the same procedure.
Alternative B: (Specify the alternative)
  1. Criterion 1. Thoroughly discuss Alternative B in terms of critical issue number 1.
  2. Criterion 2–n. Follow the same procedure.

Following is a brief, unedited example from a student paper. The problem/decision was whether Wyler Foods, a powdered soft-drink subsidiary of Borden, should introduce a new line of unsweetened powdered drink mixes to compete with the market leader, Kool-Aid. One alternative was to introduce the product and attempt to compete head-to-head with Kool-Aid. Criteria identified by the student were:

1. Projected profit impact.
2. Long-term growth implications.
3. Competitor reactions.
4. Resource requirements.
5. Competitive advantages and/or disadvantages.

Analysis of the alternative in terms of each criterion follows. (*Note that exhibits identified in the analysis are not included.*)

Step 5: Analysis
  Alternative A. Head-to-head competition with Kool-Aid
  1.1 *Projected profit impact.* The profit potential for head-to-head competition with Kool-Aid does not seem promising. Assuming that the product will perform nationally as it did during test marketing, it should achieve a 4 percent share of the $143.51 million unsweetened powdered drink mix (UPDM) market (see Exhibit 1).

    This represents sales of $5.74 million. Long-term share could be as low as 2.5 percent of the overall market. A retail price of 12 cents per packet, and cost of goods sold of 9.4 cents per packet will produce a contribution margin of approximately $1.24 million (see Exhibit 2). This level of contribution margin will not be sufficient to cover advertising and sales promotion expenditures, which will exceed $4 million, and could rise to $8–10 million.

    Quantity allowances to stimulate grocer acceptance will have to be in the $800,000 area. Adopting this alternative would lead to substantial first-year losses, minimally in the $4–5 million range, and possibly much higher (see Exhibit 3).

  1.2 *Long-term growth implications.* Long-term corporate growth factors are dependent upon how deeply the new product can penetrate the Kool-Aid-dominated UPDM market. If the product performs no better than the test market results indicate, this strategy would be a long-term money loser. The product will have to capture roughly 15.4 percent of the UPDM market to break even (see Exhibit 4).

  1.3 *Competitor reactions.* Kool-Aid can be expected to spend $10–12 million more on advertising and sales promotion than is proposed for the new product in its first year. Kool-Aid can also be expected to emphasize its traditional position as the favored UPDM. The leading brand is able to exercise considerable influence in established distribution channels to keep the new product line off the grocers' shelves, necessitating huge quantity allowances to achieve penetration. Through 50 years of acclimation, the consumer is now at the point of utilizing the Kool-Aid product as the taste benchmark; this imperils the new product line even before the contest starts. Perhaps of greatest importance, Kool-Aid may opt for price competition. Because of sales volume considerations, Kool-Aid can cut prices and maintain profitability. Wyler simply could not afford to match Kool-Aid's potential price cuts. To do so would further darken its bleak profit outlook (see Exhibit 5).

1.4 *Resource requirements.* Wyler seems to be short on financial resources necessary to implement this alternative (see Exhibit 5). Substantial cash infusions would be needed for some time before any cash outflows would be generated. Wyler's personnel seem to be capable of executing the strategy.

1.5 *Competition advantages and/or disadvantages.* Implementation of this alternative involves doing battle with Kool-Aid on Kool-Aid's home ground. Rather than exploiting a key Wyler strength, this alternative seems to favor Kool-Aid's strengths and Wyler's weaknesses. Wyler will be playing by Kool-Aid's rules, which isn't likely to produce a successful outcome.

Although this is a fairly simple example without any financial comparisons, it illustrates a useful approach for evaluating alternative actions. Note that each alternative should be evaluated in terms of each criterion. After the alternatives are analyzed against each criterion, you should complete your analysis with a summary assessment of each alternative. This summary will provide the basis for preparing your recommendations.

One approach that students sometimes find useful in preparing their summary analyses is illustrated in Exhibit 4–2. Its preparation involves the following five steps:

EXHIBIT 4–2 ABC Company Summary Assessment

Criteria	Relative Weights	Alternatives (ratings)		
		(1)	*(2)*	*(3)*
Corporate mission & objectives	(.2)	(5)	(2)	(3)
Market opportunity	(.3)	(2)	(3)	(5)
Competitive strengths/weaknesses	(.2)	(2)	(3)	(2)
Financial considerations	(.3)	(1)	(1)	(4)
Index: Relative weight × Rating		2.3	2.2	3.7

Step 1: List criteria on one axis and alternative actions on the other axis.

Step 2: Assign a weight to each criterion reflecting its relative importance on the final decision. For convenience, assign weights that add up to one.

Step 3: Review your analysis and rate each alternative on each criterion using a scale of one to five with one representing very poor and five representing very good.

Step 4: Multiply the weight assigned to each criterion by the rating given to each alternative on each issue.

Step 5: Add the results from Step 4 for each alternative.

It is important to understand that this type of analytical aid is *not* a substitute for thorough, rigorous analysis, clear thinking, and enlightened decision making. Its value is in encouraging you to assess the relative importance of alternatives and criteria, and helping you to organize your analysis.

Step 6: Recommendations

If your analysis has been thorough, the actions you recommend should flow directly from it. The first part of your recommendations section addresses what specific actions should be taken and why. State the main reasons you believe your chosen course of action is best, but avoid rehashing the analysis section. It is important that your recommendations be specific and operational. The following example of a recommendation deals with whether a manufacturer of oil field equipment should introduce a new product line.

> The key decision that management must make is whether viscosity-measurement instrumentation represents a business venture that fits into the overall mission of the firm. The preceding analysis clearly indicates that this would be a profitable endeavor. If AOS concentrates on the high-accuracy and top end of the intermediate-accuracy range of the market, sales of $500,000 appear feasible within two to four years, with an estimated contribution to overhead and profits in the $145,000 range. This is assuming that manufacturing costs can be reduced by 20 to 25 percent, that effective marketing approaches are developed, that further product development is not extensive, and that price reductions per unit do not exceed 10 percent.

The second part of your recommendations section addresses implementation. State clearly who should do what, when, and where. An implementation plan shows that your recommendations are both possible and practical. For example:

> AOS should initially offer two instruments. One should provide an accuracy of 0.25 percent or better; the second should be in the accuracy range of 0.1 to

0.5 percent. Top priority should be assigned to inland and offshore drilling companies. Next in priority should be R&D laboratories in industry, government, and universities, where accuracy needs exist in the range offered by AOS. Based on experience with these markets, other promising targets should be identified and evaluated.

AOS needs to move into the market rapidly, using the most cost-effective means of reaching end-user markets. By developing an original-equipment-manufacturer (OEM) arrangement with General Supply to reach drilling companies and a tie-in arrangement with Newtec to reach R&D markets, immediate access to end-user markets can be achieved. If successful, these actions will buy some time for AOS to develop marketing capabilities, and they should begin generating contributions from sales to cover the expenses of developing a marketing program. An essential element in the AOS marketing strategy is locating and hiring a person to manage the marketing effort. This person must have direct sales capabilities in addition to being able to perform market analysis and marketing program development, implementation, and management tasks.

The last part of your recommendations section should be a tentative budget. This is important because it illustrates that the solution is worth the cost and is within the financial capabilities of the organization. Too often, students develop grandiose plans that organizations couldn't possibly afford even if they were worth the money. Budgeting and forecasting are discussed in Chapter 2.

Your instructor realizes that the numbers used in your tentative budget may not be as accurate as they would be if you had complete access to the records of the company. Make your best estimates and try to get as close to the actual figures as possible. The exercise is good experience, and it shows that you have considered the cost implications.

Students often ask how long the recommendations section should be and how much detail they should go into. This question is difficult to answer because each case is different and should be treated that way. In general it is advisable to go into as much detail as possible. You may be criticized for not being specific enough in your recommendations, but you are not likely to be criticized for being too specific.

APPENDIX   *An Outline for Case Analysis*

The outline shown here is an expanded version of the approach to case analysis discussed in this chapter. Although reasonably comprehensive, the guide can be shortened, expanded, and/or adapted to meet your needs in various situations. For example, if you are analyzing a business unit that does not utilize channels of distribution, section VIII B of the outline will require adjustment. Likewise, if the salesforce represents the major part of the marketing program, then section VIII E should probably be expanded to include other aspects of salesforce strategy.

This guide is not intended to be a comprehensive checklist that can be applied in every case. Instead, it is illustrative of the broad range of issues and questions you will encounter in analyzing the strategic decisions presented in this book and elsewhere. The key is to *adapt the outline to the case*, not the case to the outline.

Step 1. Situation Audit

I. Corporate mission and objectives.
   A. Does the mission statement offer a clear guide to the product-markets of interest to the firm?
   B. Have objectives been established for the corporation?
   C. Is information available for the review of corporate progress toward objectives, and are the reviews conducted on a regular (quarterly, monthly, etc.) basis?
   D. Has corporate strategy been successful in meeting objectives?
   E. Are opportunities or problems pending that may require altering marketing strategy?
   F. What are the responsibilities of the chief marketing executive in corporate strategic planning?

II. Business unit analysis.
   A. What is the composition of the business (business segments, strategic planning units, and specific product-markets)?
   B. Have business strength and product-market attractiveness analyses been conducted for each planning unit? What are the results of the analyses?
   C. What is the corporate strategy for each planning unit (e.g., growth, manage for cash)?
   D. Does each unit have a strategic plan?
   E. For each unit, what objectives and responsibilities have been assigned to marketing?

III. Buyer analysis.
   A. Are there niches within the product-market? For each specific product-market and niche of interest to the firm, answer items B through I.
   B. What are estimated annual purchases (units and dollars)?
   C. What is the projected annual growth rate (five years)?
   D. How many people/organizations are in the product-market?
   E. What are the demographic and socioeconomic characteristics of customers?
   F. What is the extent of geographic concentration?
   G. How do people decide what to buy?
      1. Reason(s) for buying (What is the need/want?).
      2. What information is needed (e.g., how to use the product)?
      3. What are other important sources of information?
      4. What criteria are used to evaluate the product?
      5. What are purchasing practices (quantity, frequency, location, time, etc.)?

H. What environmental factors should be monitored because of their influence on product purchases (e.g., interest rates)?

I. What key competitors serve each end-user group?

IV. Key competitor analysis. For each specific product-market and each niche of interest to the firm, determine:

A. Estimated overall business strength.

B. Market share (percent, rank).

C. Market share trend (five years).

D. Financial strengths.

E. Profitability.

F. Management.

G. Technology position.

H. Other key nonmarketing strengths/limitations (e.g., production cost advantages).

I. Marketing strategy (description, assessment of key strengths and limitations).

1. Market-target strategy.

2. Program positioning strategy.

3. Product strategy.

4. Distribution strategy.

5. Price strategy.

6. Promotion strategy.

V. Market-target strategy.

A. Has each market target been clearly defined and its importance to the firm established?

B. Have demand and competition in each market target been analyzed, and key trends, opportunities, and threats identified?

C. Has the proper market-target strategy (mass, niche) been adopted?

D. Should repositioning or exit from any product-market be considered?

VI. Market-target objectives.

A. Have objectives been established for each market target, and are these consistent with planning-unit objectives and the available resources? Are the objectives realistic?

B. Are sales, cost, and other performance information available for monitoring the progress of planned performance against actual results?

C. Are regular appraisals made of marketing performance?

D. Where do gaps exist between planned and actual results? What are the probable causes of the performance gaps?

VII. Marketing program positioning strategy.

A. Does the firm have an integrated positioning strategy made up of product, channel, price, advertising, and salesforce strategies? Is the role selected for each mix element consistent with the overall program objectives, and does it properly complement other mix elements?

B. Are adequate resources available to carry out the marketing program? Are resources committed to market targets according to the importance of each?

C. Are allocations to the various marketing mix components too low, too high, or about right in terms of what each is expected to accomplish?

D. Is the effectiveness of the marketing program appraised on a regular basis?

VIII. Marketing program activities.

A. Product strategy.

1. Is the product mix geared to the needs that the firm wants to meet in each product-market?

2. What branding strategy is being used?

3. Are products properly positioned against competing brands?

4. Does the firm have a sound approach to product planning and management, and is marketing involved in product decisions?

5. Are additions to, modifications of, or deletions from the product mix needed to make the firm more competitive in the marketplace?

6. Is the performance of each product evaluated on a regular basis?

B. Channels of distribution strategy.

1. Has the firm selected the type (conventional or vertically coordinated) and intensity of distribution appropriate for each of its product-markets?

2. How well does each channel access its market target? Is an effective channel configuration used?

3. Are channel organizations carrying out their assigned functions properly?

4. How is the channel of distribution managed? What improvements are needed?

5. Are desired customer service levels reached, and are the costs of doing this acceptable?

C. Price strategy.

1. How responsive is each market target to price variation?

2. What roles and objectives does price have in the marketing mix?

3. Does price play an active or passive role in program positioning strategy?

4. How do the firm's price strategy and tactics compare to those of competition?

5. Is a logical approach used to establish prices?

6. Are there indications that changes may be needed in price strategy or tactics?

D. Advertising and sales promotion strategies.

1. Are roles and objectives established for advertising and sales promotion in the marketing mix?

2. Is the creative strategy consistent with the positioning strategy that is used?

3. Is the budget adequate to carry out the objectives assigned to advertising and sales promotion?

4. Do the media and programming strategies represent the most cost-effective means of communicating with market targets?

    5. Do advertising copy and content effectively communicate the intended messages?

    6. How well does the advertising program meet its objectives?

  E. Salesforce strategy.

    1. Are the roles and objectives of personal selling in the marketing program positioning strategy clearly specified and understood by the sales organization?

    2. Do the qualifications of salespeople correspond to their assigned roles?

    3. Is the salesforce the proper size to carry out its function, and is it efficiently deployed?

    4. Are salesforce results in line with management's expectations?

    5. Is each salesperson assigned performance targets, and are incentives offered to reward performance?

    6. Are compensation levels and ranges comparable to those of competitors?

IX. Marketing planning.

  A. Strategic planning and marketing.

    1. Is marketing's role and responsibility in corporate strategic planning clearly specified?

    2. Are responsibility and authority for marketing strategy assigned to one executive?

    3. How well is the firm's marketing strategy working?

    4. Are changes likely to occur in the corporate/marketing environment that may affect the firm's marketing strategy?

    5. Do major contingencies exist that should be included in the strategic marketing plan?

  B. Marketing planning and organization structure.

    1. Are annual and longer-range strategic marketing plans developed and used?

    2. Are the responsibilities of the various units in the marketing organization clearly specified?

    3. What are the strengths and limitations of the key members of the marketing organization? What is being done to develop employee skills? What gaps in experience and capability exist on the marketing staff?

    4. Is the organizational structure for marketing appropriate for implementing marketing plans?

X. Financial analysis.

  A. Sales and cost analyses and forecasts.

  B. Profit contribution and net profit analyses and projections.

  C. Liquidity analyses.

  D. Break-even analyses.

  E. Return on investment.

  F. Budget analyses.

  G. Pro forma statements.

XI. Implementation and management.

  A. Have the causes of all performance gaps been identified?

  B. Is implementation of planned actions taking place as intended? Is implementation being hampered by marketing or other functional areas of the firm (e.g., operations, finance)?

C. Has the strategic audit revealed areas requiring additional study before action is taken?

XII. Summary of the situation.

Has the situation audit revealed opportunities which would enable the organization to gain a competitive advantage based upon its distinctive competencies?

A. What are the major opportunities available to the organization?

B. What are the major threats facing the organization?

C. What are the requirements for achieving success in selected product-markets?

D. What are the organization's and the principal competitors' distinctive competencies regarding these requirements? Do these areas of strength complement a given opportunity, or do strategic gaps exist that serve as barriers to pursuing the opportunity?

E. What strategic gaps, problems, and/or constraints relative to competitors appear?

F. What time and resources are required to pursue an opportunity or close a strategic gap?

G. Does the organization's mission (or objectives) need to be redefined?

XIII. Opinions and assumptions.

A. Are opinions or assumptions provided by others? Are they reasonable, given the source?

B. Is it necessary to make assumptions about the organization's objectives, competition, the environment, or something else?

Step 2. Problem/Decision Statement

A. What are the symptoms that suggest a problem exists?

B. What is the major problem or decision that must be addressed?

C. Are there secondary problems or decisions?

Step 3. Identification of Alternatives

A. What actions might provide viable solutions to the problem or decision?

B. Can actions be combined?

C. Can actions be eliminated without further consideration?

Step 4. Criteria

What criteria should be used to evaluate the strategic options? Any of the items listed in the situation audit may be relevant issues in analyzing the alternatives.

Step 5. Analysis

A. Examine each alternative in terms of each criterion.

B. What are the relative advantages and disadvantages of each choice in terms of each of the criteria?

Step 6. Recommendations

    A. What specific actions, including the development of marketing or other plans, should be taken and why?

    B. Who should do what, when, and where?

    C. What are the expected costs and returns associated with your recommendations?

    D. What contingencies may alter the attractiveness of your recommendations?

PART 2

Coordinating Business and Marketing Strategies

The importance of developing market-driven business strategies became clear during the turbulent 1980s. Restructuring of corporations was widespread throughout the business sector. Slow growth in many industries, intensive global competition, and scarce financial resources spelled out the challenge facing corporate managements. Strategic planning with a market-centered focus has become essential to survival in complex economic environments.

Strategic planning for the enterprise demands perceptive insights about customers' needs and wants, as well as ways of achieving customer satisfaction through the firm's marketing offer (product distribution, price, and promotion strategies). Thus, a close working relationship between marketing strategists and executives responsible for the strategic planning of the enterprise is essential.

Unfortunately, the glamour and mystery often associated with strategic planning may mask what should be viewed as a demanding yet logical process: deciding the mission and objectives of the enterprise and then devising strategies for reaching those objectives.

WHAT IS STRATEGIC PLANNING?

An overview of business planning is shown in Exhibit 1. The process is a continuing one, beginning with an assessment of the situation faced by a corporation. This leads to an examination of corporate mission and objectives, which may over time be changed to respond to the findings of the situation assessment. Strategies are required to accomplish mission and objectives. These strategies are developed for the product and market areas that determine the composition of the busi-

---

EXHIBIT 1   Business Planning Overview

```
┌──────────────────┐
│  Analyze the     │
│  situation       │──┐
└──────────────────┘  │
     ┌────────────────────────────┐
     │ Develop mission statement  │
     │ and objectives             │──┐
     └────────────────────────────┘  │
          ┌────────────────────────────┐
          │ Determine composition      │
          │ of the business            │──┐
          └────────────────────────────┘  │
               ┌────────────────────────────┐
               │ Make strategic analysis    │
               │ of business units          │──┐
               └────────────────────────────┘  │
                    ┌────────────────────────────┐
                    │ Select business  unit      │
                    │ objectives and strategy    │──┐
                    └────────────────────────────┘  │
                         ┌────────────────────────────┐
                         │ Prepare business           │
                         │ unit strategic plan        │
                         └────────────────────────────┘
```

---

ness. An important part of planning in a firm that is made up of more than one product-market area is regular evaluation of the different business areas. These business units often have different objectives and strategies, representing a portfolio of businesses. The strategic plan for each unit spells out what its assigned role is in the corporation and how that role will be fulfilled. Underlying the plan are strategies for marketing, finance, operations, and other supporting areas. Strategies are implemented and managed. Regular assessment of the strategic situation completes the cycle.

SITUATION ASSESSMENT

A corporate situation assessment provides a foundation for developing the strategic plan. The analysis should clearly describe the present situation faced by the organization, and should include the following information:

1. Analysis of external forces that do (or will) influence the corporation. These include economic, technological, social, governmental, and natural factors.

2. Analysis of demand, customers, industry, and distribution structure.
3. Evaluation of key competitors.
4. Objective assessment of corporate capabilities and limitations, highlighting key differential advantages over competition.
5. Identification of strategic opportunities and threats.

A useful format for combining this information is a situation assessment *summary* that considers the strategic implication of each item in the summary. It should be specific, pointing to areas that may affect the corporate mission and objectives, business composition, strategic analysis of business units, and business unit strategies.

CORPORATE MISSION AND OBJECTIVES

The path(s) that management chooses to follow in the development of the firm establishes key guidelines for strategic planning. The choice of mission and objectives should spell out where the company is going and why:

> Management must initially establish the nature and scope of a firm's operations and adjust these decisions as necessary over time. Strategic choices about where the firm is going in the future, taking into account company capabilities and resources and opportunities and problems, establish the mission of the enterprise.[1]

The Mission Statement

A useful means for communicating business purpose and objectives is the mission statement. The following are examples of its contents.[2]

1. The reason for the company's existence and the responsibilities of the company to stockholders, employees, society, and various other stakeholders.
2. The customers' needs and wants to be served with the firm's product or service offering (areas of product and market involvement).
3. The extent of specialization within each product-market area (e.g., deciding to offer just Tootsie Rolls rather than a variety of candies).
4. The amount and types of diversification of product-markets desired by management.

---

[1] David W. Cravens, *Strategic Marketing* (Homewood, Ill.: Richard D. Irwin, 1991), p. 37.

[2] Ibid.

5. Management's performance expectations for the company.
6. Other general guidelines for overall business strategy, such as the role of research and development in the corporation.

An overriding influence upon the mission decision is: What does management want the business to be? Acknowledging the constraining nature of capabilities, resources, opportunities, and problems, management is left with much flexibility in making the decision as well as changing it in the future. Uncontrollable factors may create the need for alteration of mission. Peter Drucker has noted that:

> Defining the purpose and mission of the business is difficult, painful, and risky. But it alone enables business to set objectives, to develop strategies, to concentrate its resources, and go to work. It alone enables a business to be managed for performance.[3]

In addition to a mission statement, long-range objectives should be indicated so that the performance of the enterprise can be gauged. Objectives for the corporation are often set in the following areas: marketing, innovation, resources, productivity, social, and financial.[4] Examples include sales growth and market-share expectations, human resources training and development, new-product targets, return on invested capital, earning growth rates, debt limits, energy reduction objectives, and pollution standards. Objectives should be realistic and specific so that management can measure progress toward achieving them.

Corporate Development Alternatives

Most companies start business operations in some core business area. Success often leads to expanding into related areas and sometimes into entirely new product-market areas. The major corporate development options are shown in Exhibit 2. There are, of course, many specific strategies and combinations of these options.

Core Business.   Many firms start out serving one product-market. The product or service may be a single product or a line of products. The initial venture is the core business, as food products were in the case of General Mills, and women's apparel was in the case of The Limited. This strategy, when it involves a single product-market, offers the advantages of specialization but contains the risks of being dependent upon one set of customer needs. As a corporation grows and

---

[3] Peter F. Drucker, *Management* (New York: Harper & Row, 1974), p. 94.
[4] Ibid., p. 100.

EXHIBIT 2   Corporate Development Options

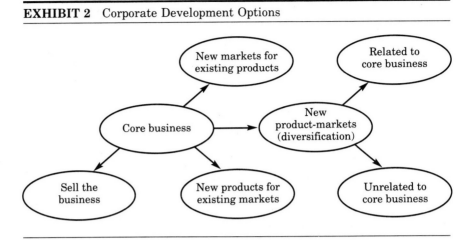

---

prospers, management often decides to move into other product and market areas as shown in Exhibit 2.

New Markets for Existing Products.   One way to expand away from the core business is to serve other needs and wants, using the same product or a similar product. The Maytag Company is a leading manufacturer of home *and* commercial laundry equipment. A. T. Cross markets its line of writing instruments to consumers—and to organizations for incentives, employee recognition, and other uses. For many companies, this is a natural line of development. The strategy reduces the risks of depending upon a single market, yet it allows the use of existing technical and production capabilities. The major demands arising from this strategy are adequate resources for expansion and the capabilities for developing a new marketing strategy. Since it may be difficult to acquire a marketing capability or to turn it over to a marketing intermediary, the requirements for internal marketing strategy development should be recognized when adopting this alternative. The primary caution to be exercised is to be sure the new market opportunity is carefully evaluated as to its feasibility and attractiveness.

New Products for Existing Market.   Another strategy for shifting away from dependence upon one product-market is to expand the product mix offered to the firm's market target. This can be achieved either by acquiring companies or products or by internal new-product development. A disadvantage of this strategy is the continued dependence upon a particular market area.

Diversification.   The distinction between diversification and product or market expansion is that the former involves movement into a new product-market area by either internal development or acquisition. Often the riskiest and costliest of the options shown in Exhibit 2, it may be attractive if existing product-market areas face slow growth, if resources for diversification are available, and if good choices are made. Diversification, once it has been successfully implemented, offers the advantage of spreading business risks over two or more segments of business. Diversification may follow one of two avenues: (1) movement into different, yet related, product-market areas or (2) building the corporation into a conglomerate consisting of unrelated product-market areas.

BUSINESS COMPOSITION

Understanding the composition of a business is essential in both corporate and marketing planning. When firms serve multiple markets with multiple products, grouping similar business areas together facilitates planning. Several guidelines to use in forming business planning units are shown in Exhibit 3. Management, of course, has some flexibility in deciding how to divide the business into planning units. A note of caution is in order: Forming too many planning units can be more

---

EXHIBIT 3   Guidelines for Forming Business Units

Inventory the products offered by the corporation to identify specific products, product lines, and mixes of product lines. Determine the end-user needs that each product is intended to satisfy.

Identify which products satisfy similar needs (e.g., foods for main meals). Also determine which products satisfy the needs of more than one user group.

Form units composed of one or more products or product lines that satisfy similar needs (e.g., food preparation appliances). The products that form a planning unit should have major strategic features in common, such as distribution channels, market target, technology, and/or advertising and salesforce strategies.

Determine if there are management, market, operating, or other advantages to combining two or more planning units into a division, group, or business segment.

Review the proposed scheme to determine if it offers both operational and strategic advantages. Do the potential benefits of the scheme exceed the costs?

---

harmful than useful. A large number of units will require a correspondingly large number of strategies and management structures that are expensive and probably not cost effective.

BUSINESS UNIT STRATEGY

Management must decide whether (1) to maintain or strengthen its market position, (2) to attempt to shift into a more desirable position, or (3) to exit from a business unit. Of course, as a product-market matures, strategic position may be altered due to a decline in the attractiveness of the product-market. Management must select a strategic plan for each strategic business unit (SBU), taking into account strategic position, available resources, forecasts of future competitive and market conditions, and the relative attractiveness of available opportunities.

Selecting a Strategy

After completing the analysis of an SBU, the following questions should be answered:

- What is the strategic situation of the business unit in terms of product and market maturity?
- How has the business unit performed during the past three to five years?
- How attractive will the product-market opportunities be in the next three to five years?
- How strong is our business unit position compared to that of our competition?
- What should be the future strategy of the business unit over the next three to five years?

The use of a three- to five-year time span will vary among firms, depending upon the planning horizon used. The decision will depend on the rate of change in markets, competition, and other external factors.

The strategy options for an SBU range from an aggressive growth strategy to maintaining market position to exiting from the business area. In a multiunit corporation, the strategies for SBUs will normally be determined as a part of the corporation's total portfolio strategy.

The Business Unit Plan

Top management should establish guidelines for long-term strategic planning. In a business that has two or more strategic business units, decisions must be made at two levels. Top management must first decide what business areas to pursue, and then establish priorities for allocating resources to SBUs. Decision makers within SBUs must determine the appropriate strategies for delivering the results that management expects.

Most businesses that have multiple SBUs have specific guidelines for business units to use in developing strategic and tactical plans. The strategic plan outline shown in Exhibit 4 covers the major issues commonly addressed in business unit plans.

EXHIBIT 4   Plan Outline—A High-Technology Products Manufacturer

I. Management summary
II. Business definition
   A. Mission
   B. Purpose
   C. Role
III. Progress report
   A. Comparison of key financial and market indicators
   B. Progress made on major strategies
IV. Market and customer analysis
   A. Potential versus served market
   B. Market segmentation
V. Competitive analysis
   A. Description of three major competitors
   B. Analysis of competitors' strategies
VI. Objectives, strategies, and programs
   A. Key objectives
   B. Major strategies to accomplish the objectives
   C. Action programs to implement strategies
   D. Major assumptions and contingency programs
   E. Market share matrix
VII. Financial projections
   A. Financial projections statement
   B. Personnel projections

Source: Rochelle O'Connor, *Facing Strategic Issues: New Planning Guides and Practices*, Report No. 87 (New York: The Conference Board, Inc. 1985), p. 32.

CONCLUDING NOTE

We have examined the major steps in developing business plans shown in Exhibit 1. Business planning begins with the corporate situation assessment. Consideration of the corporate mission and objectives, determination of business composition, analysis of business units, selection of objectives and strategies for business units, fitting these strategies into plans, and then implementing and managing the strategic plans follows.

The planning process shown in Exhibit 1 generally corresponds to the approaches used in business firms and other goal-directed organizations. It demonstrates marketing's rapidly increasing role in business planning, and it provides essential guidelines to marketing management.

Cases for Part 2

The 13 cases in Part 2 focus on corporate and marketing strategy issues.

CASES

The first case, Food Lion, Inc., is an interesting analysis of a successful regional supermarket chain. Management has developed a unique positioning concept. Deciding how to compete in the future is a vital concern of management. The case highlights several strategic analysis and planning issues.

Case 2–2, RJR Nabisco, examines a large international conglomerate after restructuring by a new market-driven CEO. The case considers important challenges confronting top management in a corporation comprising several business areas.

Case 2–3, Rockingham Memorial Hospital, describes how management in a regional hospital is considering whether or not to develop and implement a sports medicine program. Local population statistics and anticipated expense and revenue data are provided.

Case 2–4, Amtech Corp., considers the business and marketing strategy challenges confronting a small company that is pioneering a new market for electronic identification systems. Management faces important decisions concerning which markets to pursue, such as toll road applications.

Case 2–5, Makhteshim Chemical, presents an interesting international market entry situation in the business-to-business sector. The small Israeli company is a specialty chemical producer seeking to penetrate the American market with a flame-retardant chemical. Management is concerned with developing an effective strategy for this market.

Case 2–6, Kmart Stores, examines a large discount retailer confronted with important business and marketing strategy decisions.

Analysis requires evaluating strategies for competing in the 1990s in an increasingly challenging and demanding retail environment.

Case 2–7, Campbell Soup Company, describes Campbell's business unit portfolio. It also considers the CEO's strategic priorities. The case examines several important business portfolio management issues, and discusses various food-processing industry trends.

The Limited Inc. (Case 2–8) is one of America's power retailers in the women's apparel market. The case examines several strategy issues that management must consider in deciding how and where to compete in the 1990s. The company competes in several retail market segments.

Case 2–9, MacTec Control AB, is a rapidly growing Swedish firm that markets computer hardware and software for the monitoring and control of pressurized water flows. Municipal water departments and industrial firms represent the primary target markets for MacTec's Aqualex System. The case discusses whether or not MacTec should enter the U.S. market.

Sony Corporation (Case 2–10) is a large Japanese corporation that produces consumer and industrial electronics and other products and services. Management's new strategy for competing in the "post-Morita era" is described. The case provides insights into the challenges of competing in global consumer and business markets.

Case 2–11, Simons Lumber Company, presents a small, family-owned business that has been successful for over 100 years. The president, Stephen Simons, is trying to decide on a future direction and a strategy for the company. Simons is reasonably confident that the company can continue to earn satisfactory profits over the next five years with minimal supervision on his part. On the other hand, expansion will dictate many major changes in personnel and the way the company currently operates.

Case 2–12, Pier 1 Imports, Inc., provides a look at the development of a successful specialty retailer of home furnishings. The company repositioned during the 1980s, targeting medium-to-high income women. The case considers several of management's strategy challenges and offers insights into the corporate culture.

Case 2–13, Kinder-Care, is about a chain of preschool education centers in the United States and Canada that experienced phenomenal growth over its relatively short history. The national director of marketing considers how to continue growing, evaluating the possible impact of changing demographics on Kinder-Care's marketing strategy.

Case 2–1   Food Lion, Inc.*

In 1957 three former Winn-Dixie employees opened their first supermarket in Salisbury, North Carolina, under the name Food Town. Cofounders Ralph Ketner, Brown Ketner, and Wilson Smith all had considerable retail experience in the grocery industry; however, Food Town struggled in its early years. Various marketing gimmicks were implemented (the company gave away trading stamps and even free automobiles), but the stores failed to win the loyalty of customers. In fact, Ralph Ketner had to close 9 of the 16 stores during the first 10 years of operation. He blamed much of this failure on the underpricing techniques of Winn-Dixie. By 1966, only seven Food Town stores remained.

In response to the problem, Ketner decided to slash prices on all items sold in the stores. He realized that a drastic increase in volume would be necessary to make this approach work and keep the company afloat. The company theme of LFPINC or "Lowest Food Prices in North Carolina" became popular as both customers and sales increased greatly. Sales rose 54 percent to $8.9 million, and profits rose 165 percent to $95,000 in the first year under the new pricing strategy.[1]

In 1970 the company went public. Etablissements Delhaize Freres et Cie, a Belgium grocery chain, purchased 47.6 percent of the stock in 1974. Today, Delhaize controls 50.6 percent of the voting stock and has 5 of the 10 seats on the board of directors.[2] The company changed its name to Food Lion in 1983 to avoid confusion with another similarly named chain. Also, the company began implementing its expansion program.

Today, Food Lion operates in eight states, from Delaware to Florida, and is considered to be one of the fastest growing retail grocers in the country. (See Exhibit 1.) Food Lion President and CEO Tom E. Smith explains, "Our goal is to bring extra low grocery prices to as many people in the Southeast as possible."[3]

Food Lion has 27,000 employees, and continues to operate conventional size stores (21,000–29,000 square feet) and to offer discount prices. The company remains committed to expansion throughout the

---

* Prepared by Janet L. Caswell under the direction of Professor Neil H. Snyder, both of the University of Vigrinia. © 1988 by Neil H. Snyder.

[1] Richard Anderson, "That Roar You Hear Is Food Lion," *Business Week,* August 24, 1987, p. 66.

[2] Ibid.

[3] *1987 Food Lion, Inc. Annual Report,* p. 1.

EXHIBIT 1 Store Distribution

Location	Stores	Percent of Total
North Carolina	233	49.1%
Virginia	112	23.5
South Carolina	74	15.6
Tennessee	29	6.1
Georgia	19	4.0
Florida	6	1.3
Delaware	1	0.2
Maryland	1	0.2
Total	475	100.0%

Source: *Standard & Poor's Stock Report,* p. 3905.

Southeast and has avoided moving into the sales of general merchandise in its stores. A food consultant's comments highlight the company's success in the aforementioned areas. He states that Food Lion is "probably the best example of commitment to a format and operating style in the industry today. And although it is a conventional store operator, it also stands as an excellent practitioner of niche marketing. The stores aren't fancy, but beat everyone on price, and the company doesn't make many mistakes."[4]

Ralph Ketner

Since cofounding Food Lion, Ralph Ketner has continued to be a force behind its success. In 1968 it was his idea to adopt the strategy of discount pricing and his LFPINC theme which promoted the company. He acted as chief executive officer until 1986, when he passed the reins to President Tom Smith. Despite giving up his CEO title, Ketner still exerts considerable influence over the operation of Food Lion. He remains chairman of the board of directors, and plans to retain this position until 1991. In addition, Delhaize signed an agreement in 1974 to vote with Ketner for 10 years. This agreement was later extended and was in effect until 1989.[5]

---

[4] Richard DeSanta, "Formats: Growing Apart, Coming Together," *Progressive Grocer,* January 1987, p. 37.

[5] "Ketner Gives Up Food Lion Reins," *Supermarket News,* January 6, 1986, p. 18.

Tom E. Smith

President and CEO Tom E. Smith is very much responsible for Food Lion's growth and success. This is largely attributed to his involvement with the company since his youth. At age 17, Smith began as a bag boy at Food Lion's first store. He attended night school at Catawba College and graduated in 1964 with a degree in business administration. He spent the next six years working for Del Monte, when he was hired as Food Lion's sole buyer. Smith developed the successful strategy of stocking fewer brands and sizes than his competitors. He also took advantage of wholesaler specials by purchasing large volumes at discount prices. He was named vice president for distribution in 1974, and later became executive vice president in 1977. His continued success in these areas led to his promotion to president in 1981, at the age of 39. In 1986 he was named CEO.

Smith views himself as a planner who carefully molds the company's growth while keeping a close eye on the operations. This style has enabled him to react to and resolve any problems quickly and effectively. He has been a primary reason for Food Lion's constant commitment to its overall strategy of discount pricing and cost reduction. Smith has also become well-known through his participation in over 50 percent of the Food Lion commercials. This media exposure has brought him recognition not only in the Southeast, but as far away as San Francisco and even Scotland from visiting customers.[6] These commercials portray Smith as a hard-working and very trustworthy manager.

FOOD LION'S ATTITUDE TOWARD
SOCIAL RESPONSIBILITY

Food Lion is recognized as a corporate neighbor, and it takes pride in performing charitable acts. In 1986 the company received the Martin Luther King, Jr., Award in recognition of its humanitarian efforts. Food Lion received the award for its role in donating trucks to aid southeastern farmers during a prolonged drought; the trucks enabled the farmers to transport hay from Indiana. Also, the company was cited for providing equal opportunity employment and establishing express lanes for handicapped customers.[7]

---

[6] Anderson, "That Roar You Hear Is Food Lion," p. 65.
[7] *1986 Food Lion, Inc. Annual Report,* p. 4.

THE SUPERMARKET INDUSTRY

Several trends in the supermarket industry were of concern to many retail grocers. During 1987 there was a decline in the percentage of disposable income spent for food at home. After discounting inflation, real sales did not increase from 1986. As Exhibit 2 shows, food-at-home spending accounted for more retail sales than any other category in 1983. However, slow growth has caused a reduction in this percentage, leaving food stores in second place behind auto dealers. The percentage of retail sales for eating and drinking establishments during this same period has trended upward.

The grocery industry is also experiencing competition from other types of stores. Discount department and drug stores are starting to sell more packaged foods. Many fast-food restaurants continue to sell a larger variety of prepared foods for takeout. Sales from specialty shops, which concentrate on one particular type of food, have increased as well. Wholesale clubs have also been of concern to retail grocers. These clubs have been effective at luring many customers away from conventional supermarkets. Those supermarkets stressing discount prices have been hurt most by the emergence of the wholesale clubs.

In response to the trends, most grocery chains are stressing the idea of one-stop shopping. New store formats and product offerings are abundant. These ideas are an attempt to obtain a product mix that stresses higher margin items and services, as well as creating an atmosphere causing consumers to view the supermarket as more than a place to buy groceries. Items such as flowers, greeting cards, videocassettes, and pharmacy items are appearing more frequently in many supermarkets. There has also been a greater emphasis on stocking perishables.

EXHIBIT 2   Percentage of U.S. Retail Sales by Type of Establishment

Type of Establishment	1983	1984	1985	1986	1987*
Food stores	22.0%	21.1%	20.6%	20.4%	20.3%
Eating and drinking	9.9	9.6	9.7	10.0	10.1
Drug and proprietary	3.5	3.4	3.4	3.4	3.6
General merchandise	11.1	11.0	10.9	10.7	11.0
Furniture and appliance	4.6	4.8	5.0	5.4	5.5
Auto dealers	19.8	21.6	22.6	22.9	22.2
Hardware and lumber	4.4	4.7	4.8	5.2	4.7
Clothing	5.3	5.3	5.4	5.5	5.8
Gas stations	8.5	7.8	7.3	6.1	5.7
All others	10.9	10.7	10.4	10.4	11.2

* First six months.

Source: Bureau of the Census (Revised) 1987.

EXHIBIT 3   Chain Executives' Opinions on Prospects for New Formats

	Percent		
	Excellent	*Good*	*Fair/Poor*
Superstores	56%	36%	8%
Combination	38	53	9
Convenience stores	26	39	35
Super warehouse	22	39	39
Hypermarkets	10	33	57
Specialty	8	37	55
Wholesale clubs	6	30	62
Conventional	4	35	59
Warehouse stores	1	17	79

Source: *Progressive Grocer,* April 1988.

However, the biggest trend in the industry is the shift to bigger stores. Several experts believe that increased size is necessary to provide the variety that many consumers desire. One chain president expressed this sentiment: "Customer satisfaction starts with the store design: one-stop shopping, complete service departments, and integrating a drugstore and pharmacy into the store."[8] Much of the one-stop shopping trend is a result of increases in the numbers of working women, dual-income families, single parents, and singles living alone. Time and convenience are two characteristics that consumers fitting into these groups often desire.

The one-stop shopping concept has resulted in several new store formats. Combination stores offer consumers a variety of nonfood items. These stores can be as large as 35,000 square feet, and 25 percent of the space is devoted to nonfood and pharmacy items. Superstores are similar to the combination stores in that they offer a wide selection of general merchandise items. These stores are all greater than 40,000 square feet, and are thought to be the strongest format for the near future. Exhibit 3 shows chain executives' views on the prospects for the various formats that exist today.

The newest and largest of the formats is the hypermarket. Currently, 55 of these stores exist in the United States. The typical hypermarket ranges in size from 125,000 to 330,000 square feet and requires $25 to $50 million in sales per year just to break even.[9] Normally, 40 percent of the floor space in hypermarkets is devoted to grocery items and the remaining 60 percent is used for general merchandise. Free-

---

[8] "Retail Operations: The New Basics," *Progressive Grocer,* September 1987, p. 56.

[9] David Rogers, "Hypermarkets Need Something Special to Succeed," *Supermarket Business,* May 1988, p. 26.

EXHIBIT 4 Store Attributes Desired by Consumers

Rank	Characteristic
1	Cleanliness
2	All prices labeled
3	Low prices
4	Good produce department
5	Accurate, pleasant clerks
6	Freshness date marked on products
7	Good meat department
8	Shelves kept well stocked
9	Short wait for checkout
10	Convenient store location

Source: *Progressive Grocer,* April 1988.

way access, population density, and visibility are all key variables contributing to a hypermarket's success. A majority of the stores are run by companies which are not U.S. food retailers. For example, Wall-Mart has opened several stores under the Hypermarket USA name. Also, Bruno's, a retail grocery chain, is teaming up with Kmart to build a store in Atlanta.[10]

Because of the trend to expand store size, the number of stores declined for the first time in years. However, the larger store sizes resulted in an increase in actual square footage. Many small units have been closed due to the openings of larger stores. In many market areas, there continue to be too many stores and too few customers to support them. This is going to be an even bigger concern given the advent of the combination stores and hypermarkets, since they tend to attract customers from a wider area than the conventional stores.

Although the majority of retailers believe that the bigger stores are necessary to be successful in the future, there is a large group that believes the industry is going overboard in its attempt to provide one-stop shopping. Chain executive Carole Bitter believes that the emphasis on size is unfounded. "There has been an ego problem in the industry that has led to overbuilding and has driven up store sizes and has increased the number of formats."[11] Proponents of conventionals claim that the larger stores are too impersonal to be attractive to everyone. They also believe that many consumers desire the conventional type of store, and that this format will continue to be successful. Although many consumers claim that they want more service departments, studies have shown that the shoppers are not willing to pay enough for

---

[10] Ibid.

[11] "Retail Operations: The New Basics," p. 62.

such departments to make them profitable. Exhibit 4 reveals what the average shopper desires. One-stop shopping capabilities rates only 26th on the list.

COMPETITION

In recent years, competition in the Southeast has become quite intense. Previously, this area was characterized by predominantly conventional stores. Combination and superstores were scarce. However, many retailers realized that the Southeast was a prime location for the newer formats. In 1984 Cub Foods opened three large, modern stores in the Atlanta area in an attempt to challenge Kroger's dominance in the Southeast. This move marked the beginning of several competitive shakeups in the South.

Kroger

Kroger operates 1,317 supermarkets and 889 convenience stores in the South and Midwest. In 1987 sales were nearly $18 billion. More than 95 percent of the floor space is either new or has been remodeled during the past 10 years.[12] This is a result of the chain's move to larger combination and superstore formats. Kroger has not been as successful as it would like. The company realizes a net profit margin of approximately 1 percent. This is partly due to its new outlets cannibalizing its existing stores and has caused same-store sales comparisons to be relatively flat.[13]

In response to the disappointing profit margins, Kroger is planning to decrease its capital spending plans by about $300 million. It is hoped that this will reduce interest costs as well as keep start-up expenses down. Also, the firm is cutting corporate overhead 20 percent. As for future store designs, Kroger is considering the curtailment of the new super-warehouse stores. These stores combine low grocery prices with high-priced service departments and have not appealed to a large segment of the market. Furthermore, the company is planning to reduce store remodeling in mature market areas.[14]

---

[12] *Standard & Poor's Standard Stock Reports*, p. 1318.
[13] *Value Line Investment Survey*, 1987, p. 1511.
[14] Ibid.

Winn-Dixie

Winn-Dixie is the fourth largest food retailer in the country with sales of nearly $9 billion. The chain operates 1,271 stores in the Sunbelt area, with the heaviest concentration of stores located in Florida, North Carolina, and Georgia. During the past few years, Winn-Dixie has been hurt by the influx of competition in the Southeast. As a result, profit margins have dipped to just over 1 percent. Net income also declined in 1987. Management points to a lack of investment in new stores and a rather slow response to competitors' underpricing methods as the main reasons for the decline in profits.[15]

Management has adopted several new strategies to combat the competition. Foremost is the move to larger store formats. In the past, the chain operated mostly conventional stores and depended on operating efficiencies to realize sizable profits. However, management believes that it is now necessary to alter the stores in response to changing consumer needs. At the end of 1987, the average supermarket was 27,700 square feet. There are approximately 250 new stores in the 35,000–45,000-square-feet range, and they are expected to account for nearly half of all sales in the next five years.[16] The units in the 35,000-square-feet category are combination stores operated under the Winn-Dixie name. The 45,000-square-feet stores employ the superstore format and use the name Marketplace. Emphasis is being placed on service departments as well as price-sensitivity.

Other changes involve management. Last year, the company eliminated a layer of management that resulted in 60 layoffs. The firm is also adopting a decentralized strategy which divides the company into 12 operating units. Each division is allowed to develop its own procedures and image. It is hoped that this will help the stores cater to the consumers in each market area more effectively.

Lucky Stores

Lucky operates nearly 500 supermarkets throughout the country. The majority of these are located in California; however, the chain does operate 90 stores in Florida. In 1986 Lucky began a major restructuring. This resulted in the sale of all the nonfood businesses. Also, the company has concentrated on increasing the store size to enable the sale of more service and nonfood items. The average size of the stores at the end of 1986 was 31,000 square feet.[17]

At the end of the year, there was much speculation that American Stores Company would begin to pursue an unsolicited tender offer for

[15] *Standard & Poor's,* p. 2491.

[16] "Winn-Dixie Strategy," *Supermarket News,* March 3, 1987, p. 12.

[17] *Standard & Poor's,* p. 1387.

EXHIBIT 5   Selected Statistics for Major Southeastern Supermarket Chains, 1987

	Kroger	Lucky	Winn-Dixie	Bruno's	Food Lion
Stores	2,206	481	1,271	111	475
Employees	170,000	44,000	80,000	10,655	27,033
Sales ($ million)	$17,660	$6,925	$8,804	$1,143	$2,954
Sales/employee	103,881	157,386	110,049	107,265	109,267
Net profit ($ million)	$246.6	$151	$105.4	$31	$85.8
Net profit margin	1.4%	2.2%	1.2%	2.7%	2.9%
Gross margin	22.4	25	22	20.8	19.2
Current ratio	1.1	.83	1.65	1.63	1.41
Return on equity	24.5	46.3	15.2	15.4	25.3
Return on assets	5.5	11.8	7.9	10.3	10.6
Long-term debt/equity	.69	.38	.03	.04	.26
Earnings per share	$3.14	$3.92	$2.72	$.79	$.27
Average price/earnings ratio	15.1	10.2	13.9	23.1	35.3

Source: Standard and Poor's.

all outstanding shares of Lucky common stock. American is a leading retailer in the country and operates mostly combination food and drug stores.

Bruno's

Bruno's operates approximately 100 supermarkets and combination food and drug stores in the Southeast. This chain pursues a strategy of high-volume sales at low prices. Another strategy involves the use of four different formats under various names. Consumer Warehouse Foods stores are relatively small warehouse stores which emphasize lower prices and reduced operating costs. Food World stores are large supermarkets which offer a variety of supermarket items at low prices. Bruno's Food and Pharmacy stores promote the idea of one-stop shopping through the combination store format. Finally, FoodMax stores are superwarehouses which offer generic and bulk foods in addition to the national labels.[18]

The company is also well-known for its innovative forward buying program. Bruno's is able to purchase goods at low prices because of its 900,000-square-feet distribution center which houses excess inventory. This strategy has been very successful as the company boasts high operating and net profit margins.[19] Exhibit 5 presents comparative statistics for Food Lion and its four major competitors.

[18] Ibid., p. 3358M.
[19] John Liscio, "Beefing Up Profits," *Barron's*, May 25, 1987, p. 18.

EXHIBIT 6   Food Lion's Growth and Expansion (in thousands)

Year	Stores	Sales	Net Income
1987	475	$2,953,807	$85,802
1986	388	2,406,582	61,823
1985	317	1,865,632	47,585
1984	251	1,469,564	37,305
1983	226	1,172,459	27,718
1982	182	947,074	21,855
1981	141	666,848	19,317
1980	106	543,883	15,287
1979	85	415,974	13,171
1978	69	299,267	9,481

Source: Food Lion annual reports.

EXPANSION AT FOOD LION

Food Lion has continued to grow and expand in the Southeast. During 1987 the chain opened 95 new stores while closing only 8, bringing the total to 475. With the exception of four supermarkets, Food Lion operates its stores under various leasing arrangements. The number of stores has grown at a 10-year compound rate of 24.1 percent.[20] With this expansion has come a 29.7 percent compound growth rate in sales and a 30.9 percent compound growth rate in earnings—see Exhibit 6.[21]

The existence and further development of distribution centers serve as the core for continued expansion. At the end of 1987, four such centers had been completed. These are located in Salisbury and Dunn, North Carolina; Orangeburg County, South Carolina; and Prince George County, Virginia. Two additional centers are planned for Tennessee and Jacksonville, Florida. These distribution centers enable Food Lion to pursue expansion using its "ink blot" formula. Using this strategy, new stores are added to an existing market area in order to saturate the market. "If anyone wants to go to a competitor, they'll have to drive by one of our stores," explains CFO Brian Woolf.[22] Despite the emergence of new stores, cannibalization has not been a problem. In fact, same-store sales increase approximately 8 percent annually. When Food Lion enters a new area, the strategy of underpricing the competitors is employed. Such a strategy has caused average food prices to decline 10–20 percent in some parts of the country.[23] Every new store is constructed no further than 200 miles from a distribution

[20] *1987 Food Lion, Inc. Annual Report,* p. 9.

[21] Ibid.

[22] Liscio, "Beefing Up Profits," p. 19.

[23] "Food Lion's Roar Changes Marketplace," *Tampa Tribune,* April 5, 1988, p. 1.

center. With continued expansion, new distribution centers whose radiuses overlap an existing distribution territory are erected to keep warehouse and transportation costs down.

Moreover, Food Lion continues to employ a cookie-cutter approach to its new stores. Rather than purchase existing stores, the firm much prefers to build new ones from scratch. All the stores fall into the conventional store category. The majority are 25,000 square feet and cost only $650,000 to complete. These stores emphasize the fruit and vegetable departments. Approximately 40 percent of the new stores are 29,000 square feet and contain a bakery/delicatessen. These are placed after careful consideration is given to the demographics and psychographics of the area. Normally, new stores turn a profit within the first six months of operation. In comparison, most competitors construct slightly larger stores which cost over $1 million to complete.[24]

The standard size of the stores has allowed the company to keep costs down while sticking to basics. Aside from the bakery departments, Food Lion has stayed away from service departments such as seafood counters and flower shops. Such departments are often costly due to the increase in required labor. Also, Food Lion has remained a retail grocery chain, shunning the idea of moving into the general merchandise area.

With the steady increase in stores over the past 10 years comes an increase in the need for quality employees. In an interview last March, Smith expressed concern over the high dropout rate of high school students.[25] Food Lion relies heavily on recent graduates, and the current trend may signal a decline in the quality of the average worker. Food Lion has responded to the labor problem by setting up an extensive training program for its 27,000 employees. These programs range from in-store training at the operational level to comprehensive training programs for potential managers. In addition, the firm continues to offer programs at headquarters to upgrade the work of the upper staff. Management is also attempting to increase the use of computers within the company. More specifically, Smith is hoping to utilize computer systems to handle much of the financial reporting aspects in the individual stores in an attempt to lessen the need for more employees.

ADVERTISING

Rather than employ costly advertising gimmicks, such as double coupon offers, Food Lion's advertising strategy combines cost-saving techniques with an awareness of consumer sentiment. Smith is the company's main spokesman, appearing in over half of the television

---

[24] Anderson, "That Roar You Hear Is Food Lion," p. 65.
[25] "Food Lion, Inc.," *The Wall Street Transcript,* March 28, 1988, p. 88890.

commercials. Not only has this method kept advertising expenses down, but it has also made the public aware of both Smith and his discount pricing policy. By producing most of the ads in-house and using only a few paid actors, the cost of an average TV spot is only $6,000. Also, the company policy of keeping newspaper ads relatively small results in annual savings of $8 million. Food Lion's advertising costs are a mere 0.5 percent of sales, one fourth of the industry average.[26]

The content of the ads is another reason for Food Lion's success. Many of the TV spots feature some of the cost-cutting techniques used by the firm. One often-mentioned theme at the end of ads is "When we save, you save." Another commonly used theme states, "Food Lion is coming to town, and food prices will be coming down." Before moving into the Jacksonville, Florida, area, Food Lion launched a nine-month advertising campaign. Many of these ads focused on innovative management methods which permit lower prices to be offered in the stores. For example, one ad demonstrates how a central computer is used to help control freezer temperatures. Other ads attempt to characterize Food Lion as a responsible community member. One such spot describes the importance that management places on preventive maintenance for its forklifts and tractor trailers.

Smith has also used the media to react to potential problems. For instance, Winn-Dixie launched an advertising attack against Food Lion reminding customers how competitors have come and gone. The company countered with an ad featuring Tom Smith in his office reassuring consumers. "Winn-Dixie would have you believe that Food Lion's low prices are going to crumble and blow away. Let me assure you that as long as you keep shopping at Food Lion, our lower prices are going to stay right where they belong—in Jacksonville."[27] Smith also reacted quickly to a possible conflict in eastern Tennessee in 1984. Several rumors circulated which linked the Food Lion logo to Satanic worship. In response, Smith hired Grand Ole Opry star Minnie Pearl to appear in the Tennessee advertisements until the stories disappeared.[28]

INNOVATIONS

The grocery industry is characterized by razor-thin margins. While most retail grocery chains have failed to introduce new innovations in the industry, Food Lion has employed several techniques which enable

---

[26] Anderson, "That Roar You Hear Is Food Lion," p. 65.

[27] "Food Lion, Winn-Dixie in Animated Squabble," *Supermarket News,* September 14, 1987, p. 9.

[28] Anderson, "That Roar You Hear Is Food Lion," p. 66.

the firm to offer greater discounts on nearly all its products. These innovations help Food Lion to realize a profit margin of nearly 2.9 percent, twice the industry average. The company's credo is doing "1,000 things 1 percent better."[29] Such a philosophy has resulted in keeping expenses at 14 percent of sales as compared to the industry average of 20 percent.

Examples of the company's cost-cutting ideas are abundant. Rather than purchase expensive plastic bins to store cosmetics, Food Lion recycles old banana crates. These banana boxes are also used for storing groceries in warehouses. These innovations save the company approximately $200,000 a year.[30] Furthermore, the firm utilizes waste heat from the refrigerator units to warm part of the stores. Also, motion sensors automatically turn off lights in unoccupied rooms. Costs are further reduced by Food Lion's practice of repairing old grocery carts rather than purchasing newer, more expensive models. Perhaps the greatest savings can be attributed to the carefully planned distribution system. This system allows management to take advantage of wholesalers' specials. The centralized buyout-and-distribution technique allows products for all stores to be purchased at one volume price.

Moreover, labor costs remain lower than those of many competitors. Smith is vehemently opposed to the use of unionized labor. Despite protests from the United Food and Commercial Workers International Union claiming that Food Lion's wages are well below union standards, management has continued to please its workers and avoid unionization. In fact, Smith believes its employee-benefit package is unequaled in the industry. A profit-sharing plan linking an employee's efforts in making Food Lion profitable with wealth accumulation for the future is already in use. Plans to improve long-term disability insurance benefits are underway.[31] In contrast, several other chains have experienced problems solving labor union problems. For example, a month-long strike by Kroger's Denver-area employees resulted in concessions on wages, benefits, and work rules. Safeway employees were also given quick concessions after threatening to close down several stores.[32]

Other innovations are designed to increase sales. Food Lion often sells popular items such as pet food and cereal at cost in an attempt to draw more customers into the stores. The company makes $1 million a year selling fertilizer made from discarded ground-up bones and fat. Lower prices are also feasible due to the policy of offering fewer brands

---

[29] Ibid., p. 65.

[30] "Ad Series Heralds First Florida Food Lion," *Supermarket News,* March 2, 1987, p. 12.

[31] *1986 Food Lion, Inc. Annual Report.*

[32] *Value Line Investment Survey,* August 28, 1987, p. 1501.

and sizes than competitors. The company has increased its private label stock, which now includes at least one unit in every category. These two methods allow the company to price its national brand products below many competitors' private brands. As mentioned earlier, the smaller store size and sale of mostly food items have contributed to the high profit margin realized by the company.

FINANCE

Food Lion has been able to expand without becoming overextended or burdened with heavy debt repayments. The firm's capital structure consists of 26 percent long-term debt and 74 percent equity. The majority of growth has been financed through internally generated funds. The company does not want to grow at the expense of profits. Exhibit 7 presents selected financial ratios for the company.

The growth in Food Lion's stock price also reflects the sound financial position of the company. This growth illustrates the continued confidence of investors in the future productivity of the firm. In response to the rapid rise of Food Lion's stock price, management has declared two stock splits since late 1983, when the two separate classes of stock were formed from the previous single class. These splits are designed to keep the price of the stock low enough to be attractive and affordable to all investors. The price/earnings ratio indicates how much investors are willing to pay for a dollar of the company's earnings. In 1987 Food Lion's P/E ratio was the 83rd highest of all the companies listed in the Value Line Investment Survey.

EXHIBIT 7   Selected Financial Ratios for Food Lion, 1978–1987

Year	Operating Margin	Net Profit Margin	Return on Assets	Return on Equity	Long-term Debt as a Percent of Capital
1987	6.8%	2.9%	14.2%	32.4%	26.0%
1986	6.9	2.6	14.1	29.8	24.0
1985	6.3	2.6	14.4	29.1	20.5
1984	6.3	2.5	13.6	30.2	22.8
1983	5.9	2.4	13.0	28.3	25.9
1982	5.6	2.3	15.7	28.1	18.0
1981	6.7	2.9	18.1	32.3	12.4
1980	5.9	2.8	17.7	33.4	15.5
1979	6.7	3.2	20.0	39.0	19.0
1978	6.9	3.2	19.5	38.3	22.8

Source: *1987 Food Lion Inc. Annual Report.*

FUTURE

Next week, Tom Smith is meeting with the board of directors to discuss and present his ideas for the next few years. Given the recent troublesome trends in the grocery industry as well as the increasing competition in the Southeast, he is reviewing the future strategy of Food Lion. Foremost in his mind is the extent to which Food Lion should continue to expand operations of its conventional stores in this area. He is also pondering movement into other market areas. Smith wants to be sure that the company will be able to finance future growth without greatly changing its current capital structure. Although the current success of Food Lion is quite impressive, Smith realizes that other grocery chains have experienced problems by not responding to the changing environment. He wants to be certain that this does not happen to Food Lion.

Case 2–2   *RJR Nabisco**

Among the casual shoppers in Aisle 3 of the Tom Thumb supermarket one recent Thursday morning, Louis V. Gerstner Jr. stands out. He is wearing a suit. He is acompanied by a young executive with a clipboard. And he is thinking of spending, say, $200 million.

Mr. Gerstner, chief executive officer of RJR Nabisco Holdings Inc., is scouting for small, food-company acquisition candidates. Bread, cakes, cereals, spices and a dozen other categories all draw a look.

When Mr. Gerstner is intrigued by what he sees on the shelf, he lingers a moment to engage his strategy chief, Stephen Wilson, in rapid-fire dialogue about profit margins and market share. When Mr. Gerstner is unimpressed, he walks on, forcing Mr. Wilson to abandon all talk of that acquisition idea, flip ahead in his notes and start afresh.

This is the new RJR: A no-nonsense, impatient company where top-level strategy meetings are sometimes held on the linoleum aisles of supermarkets. Bureaucracy, flamboyant spending and intra-company rivalries are out. Teamwork, urgency and a Japanese-style fixation on quality are in.

RJR Nabisco might not be quite as much fun or as innovative as a few years ago, when it had far more debt and the freewheeling F. Ross

* Source: George Anders, "Back to Biscuits," *The Wall Street Journal,* March 21, 1991, pp. A1, 4. Reprinted by permission of *THE WALL STREET JOURNAL,* © 1991 Dow Jones & Company, Inc. All Rights Reserved Worldwide.

Johnson ran the show. He was willing to spend billions on new plant technology and a smokeless cigarette that flamed out. And in legendary style, Mr. Johnson put sports celebrities on the payroll for big bucks and little work and built up a fleet of 11 corporate jets known as the RJR Air Force.

But competitors, analysts and customers all say that today's RJR is a lot more efficient. Propelling all these changes is the 49-year-old Mr. Gerstner, a one-time McKinsey & Co. management consultant and the former president of American Express Co. Selected in early 1989 to run RJR Nabisco by its major shareholder, the buy-out firm of Kohlberg Kravis Roberts & Co., Mr. Gerstner instantly got broad authority. "We're financial people," says KKR partner Henry Kravis. "Lou makes the long-run operating decisions."

Much more than most new guys, Mr. Gerstner finds himself at a company whose ups and downs have become a subject of national fascination. The 1988 takeover battle for RJR produced countless headlines and a best-selling book. The company's new stock, recently listed on the New York Stock Exchange, regularly is among the most actively traded. Mr. Gerstner's $2.9 million salary, and his bountiful package of RJR stock and options (worth $58 million at current prices) raise the question: Is he worth it?

For the moment, the financial markets' answer is yes. RJR's stock already has surged about 50% to $11 a share. Operating profit rose 31% last year, to $3.43 billion. While the company posted a net loss of $480 million for 1990 because of big interest bills, its giant LBO debt is being paid down ahead of schedule. Just this week, the company formulated plans to retire yet another $1.5 billion of its junk bonds. Analysts expect RJR Nabisco to be back in the black either this year or next.

Mr. Gerstner's style—a mixture of charm and cajoling, broad strategic thoughts and sudden intrusions into the nitty-gritty of business— holds lessons for almost any new manager.

But after two years at RJR, he can't claim to be a hero yet. The company's biggest money-maker, the Winston cigarette, has been losing market share for years. And RJR's debt burden doesn't allow it to make the kind of big acquisitions in the food business being made by its major rival, Philip Morris Inc. What's more, the company's free-spending bureaucratic culture has been so ingrained that Mr. Gerstner won't be rid of it anytime soon. Reshaping RJR, he told managers in a closed-door briefing last fall, "is like crossing the Sahara. It just goes on and on and on."

When Mr. Gerstner took over RJR in March 1989, its executive suite was desolate. A host of top managers had quit in the wake of the failed bid for the company by Mr. Johnson, who lost out to KKR. Since then, Mr. Gerstner has filled these slots with his kind of people, bringing in a general counsel from American Express and a chief administrative officer from H. J. Heinz, and hiring as his head of tobacco operations a former RJR hand who had left during the mid-1980s for a post at Citicorp. Gone are the pranks and profanity that caused the company's old Atlanta executive offices to be known as the Fraternity. People now start work at 8 a.m., show an occasional sparkle of dry wit, and otherwise favor such a serious, collegial tone that executives now suggest that headquarters be known as the Seminary.

In two stages in 1989 and 1990, Mr. Gerstner moved RJR's headquarters out of Atlanta to four floors of unremarkable rented space in a midtown Manhattan bank building. Small signs of penny-pinching can be found. Paneling is mahogany where visitors might notice, stained hardwood where they won't. Busy hallways are lined with cheap industrial green carpeting. Walls are covered with rayon.

Gone are the elaborate printed reports operating divisions once sent to headquarters, such as one immense briefing ensemble that Mr. Gerstner derisively calls "the rainbow." It came in red, green and blue binders, telling the CEO everything that had happened the previous month. "If I'm doing my job, I'm talking to division managers all the time," Mr. Gerstner says. "I know what's in that book weeks before all the numbers are typed in."

Such headquarters triumphs are small stuff, though, in the overall sweep of RJR. Even after some buyout-related divestitures, the company's sales exceed $13 billion a year, and its vast work force sprawls throughout the U.S., Latin America, Canada and Western Europe. Drawing on his McKinsey training, Mr. Gerstner spent much of his first year learning RJR Nabisco's business from the bottom up. He logged 250,000 miles visiting bakeries from Chicago to Beijing, attending salesmen's conferences and eating dinner with low-level managers.

Starting early last year, Mr. Gerstner pulled back and tried to develop a broad strategy for the company. The R.J. Reynolds tobacco business was hugely profitable but losing market share. The food company was a financial success, but showed more in-fighting and complacency than Mr. Gerstner wanted.

In speech after speech, Mr. Gerstner aired his strategic thoughts to groups of employees: Cut bureaucracy. Act with a sense of urgency. Emphasize quality and teamwork. He printed up pale gray cards with eight such points and mailed them to all 64,000 employees. Partly because of the boss's personality and partly because of RJR's debt load, the Gerstner agenda, at least for now, includes no big risks, no big innovations: It centers on running the current operations to maximum efficiency.

The full program isn't clicking yet. In Winston-Salem, N.C., for example, domestic tobacco chief James Johnston says he is "disappointed" at progress so far in changing his unit's corporate culture. Mr.

Johnston, the 44-year-old Gerstner hire from Citicorp who once ran Reynolds's Japanese operations, says he is eager to stir up creative problem-solving among all his employees. But he says many employees still seem most comfortable awaiting directives from their boss, answering with a snappy "Yes, sir," and then going off to do a task whether they believe in it or not.

The clearest collision between the strategies espoused by Messrs. Gerstner and Johnston and the time-honored practices at Reynolds is to be found with Winston. America's No. 1 brand until 1974, Winston finished last year with an 8.8% market share, a 1.9-point drop since the company's leveraged buy-out and a huge distance behind Marlboro's industry-leading 26%.

The new managers have cut the Reynolds work force by 2,300 employees, in RJR's only major job reduction, a move executives say was related to shrinking cigarette demand and not the LBO debt. Reynolds, which had been known as one of North Carolina's most reliable employers, offered a minimum of eight months' pay, an unusually large severance package, to laid-off tobacco workers. Reynolds' biggest round of tobacco layoffs, in August 1989, was seen as a jolt in Winston-Salem at the time. But current and former workers say anxieties about RJR's new direction subsided after a few months.

While making job cutbacks, Reynolds executives have plowed nearly half of the $115 million in annual labor-cost savings back into trying to make Winston a better cigarette.

In the past year, RJR has spent $30 million on better tobacco blends for Winston, bought brighter wrapping paper for cigarettes and smoothed out the edges of cigarette cartons. It has packed more tobacco into each Winston so that the "puff count"—a measure of how long a cigarette takes to be fully smoked—has risen 10%.

Whether consumers care is an open question. Some marketing experts regard the quality campaign as just a holding action, designed to slow the desertion from Winston but not really win new smokers. Mr. Johnston talks only about stabilizing the brand rather than making a major run at Marlboro. In the past 10 years, marketers have tried and failed with a lot of ideas for Winston, from slogans like "Big Red" and "Real taste" to $1 million giveaways with cigarette packages.

Salomon Brothers Inc. analyst Diana Temple estimates that even in Winston's current condition, its contribution to RJR's operating earnings—or profit before interest, taxes and amortization—is $700 million a year. That's nearly as much as the entire Nabisco food company contributes. Says Mr. Gerstner: "Winston is very important for us to fix."

RJR is in much better shape on the food side, which requires, and wants, less redirection from Mr. Gerstner. The food division has raised operating profit about 50% since the buy-out and held market share with brands that include Oreo and Chips Ahoy! cookies, Premium and Ritz crackers, Fleischmann's margarine and Grey Poupon mustard.

Mr. Gerstner has stepped carefully with Nabisco. He began a recent Dallas speech to Nabisco sales managers by saying: "I'll go anywhere to be with salesmen." He praised the cookie operations as "a tower of strength" and added: "When I joined the company, I heard within 20 minutes that you guys were really good. It's true."

Yet once he wins people's trust, Mr. Gerstner begins goading, prodding. When Dallas sales manager Wayne Yowell proudly mentioned that Nabisco's local market share had risen 1.7 percentage points in the past year, to 49.7%, Mr. Gerstner quickly asked if that figure will top 50% this year. "That's our goal," Mr. Yowell said, slightly taken aback. "But it gets harder once you get near 50%."

"No it doesn't," Mr. Gerstner calmly replied. "It gets easier. Think how little the next guy has."

Again and again these days, Mr. Gerstner talks of his belief that Nabisco can pull further ahead of the competition if it steps up its use of "information technology," a strategy that draws heavily on his American Express experience. Computers and data bases, he argues, can tell Nabisco a lot about what kinds of consumers buy its products, how to win their attention and how to focus marketing. Recently, RJR hired McKinsey consultants for a six-month study of ways this might reshape Nabisco's business.

Nabisco executives are intrigued, but a little skeptical. Among them, ideas like electronic subsitutes for "cents-off" coupons, which appeal to Mr. Gerstner, evoke shudders. They worry that such easy-to-use coupons may just cut into profits without winning extra customers.

In marketing, too, Nabisco's executives have strong ideas about what works. A clear example came last summer when top management reviewed a potential new Fig Newton commercial. In the ad, an English boy named Randolph is upbraided by his mom for eating cookies in bed. "It's not a cookie, Mother," Randolph replies, "It's a Fig Newton."

Mr. Gerstner, who doesn't think that children should sass their parents, found the ad distasteful. He tried to talk Nabisco executives out of airing it, to no avail. The child may be a brat, says John Greeniaus, Nabisco's chief executive, "but he's sold a lot of Fig Newtons for us."

Whatever the minor jockeying between Nabisco and headquarters, Mr. Gerstner appears to be making major headway in getting the company's two big operating units, tobacco and food, to work together for the first time since they were joined in a 1985 merger. A few years ago, the tobacco operations were "the enemy," recalls Nabisco's Mr. Greeniaus. Tobacco and food executives competed for marketing and capital-spending dollars and maligned each others' projects.

Now, Nabisco shares its expertise in 800 phone numbers with Reynolds executives who want to set up a toll-free line for Winston customers. Reynolds, in turn, has let Nabisco tap into sophisticated coupon-analysis models to figure out how many cents off are needed to win customers for new cereal brands.

The way the buy-out of RJR was structured, Messrs. Greeniaus and Johnston each control 1.5 million shares of RJR. Each man's stake is now worth $16.5 million today, and a lot more if the stock continues its rise. Little wonder that Mr. Greeniaus says: "It's not a question of climbing the old corporate ladder. It's a question of having our equity be worth something."

Two years after taking on huge debt and going private in the leveraged buy-out, RJR now is doing its best to position itself to investors as a "normal" company. The public currently owns about 18% of RJR's fully diluted stock, and will own a further 7% if RJR completes a 75-million-share equity offering it announced yesterday. RJR management owns about 5%, KKR's investment partnerships own 59%, and various convertible securities and warrants account for the rest of the stock. Debt has been cut to $17 billion from more than $25 billion (see Exhibit 1).

Because of the remaining debt, however, acquisitions are a problem. When Messrs. Gerstner and Wilson scouted targets in the Texas grocery store, their spending limit was less than $1 billion and their likely timetable was two or three years in the future.

"I don't think we're close to having a framework yet [for acquisitions] that has me comfortable," Mr. Gerstner concedes. "But we've got time to do it."

RJR also spends more cautiously in upgrading its factories. Mr. Gerstner, his lieutenants—and especially his KKR shareholders—insist that's for the best. In its pre-buyout days, RJR Nabisco was so awash in cash that it planned to spend $2.4 billion on two entirely new bakeries, each known as Cookieville. Among the planned features was a computerized system to pluck minor ingredients like onion flavor out of storage bins, convey them 100 feet across a warehouse area and dump them into giant mixing vats for crackers. But that $10 million feature would have replaced only one worker and one forklift truck.

Cookieville got canceled right after the buy-out. In its place, Nabisco is spending about $1.4 billion over the next seven years for much more modest upgrades of its bakeries. Newer, wider ovens will be installed. But there won't be any optical sensors or mechanical arms to pluck out the occasional defective Oreo; two workers in hairnets will still do that.

A former Nabisco executive says the Cookieville project might have lowered Nabisco's operating costs considerably over time. Mr. Gerstner and KKR's Mr. Kravis aren't convinced. "This is a great example" of smarter capital spending in a buyout, Mr. Kravis says. "When man-

EXHIBIT 1   RJR Nabisco Gains Ground under Gerstner

It has pared down debt . . .
Quarterly long term debt, in billions

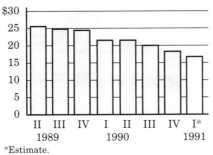

*Estimate.

And boosted profit margins . . .
Quarterly earnings before interest, taxes
and amortization as a percent of sales

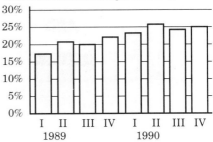

Causing its stock to soar . . .
Price of RJR warrants through Feb. 1;
RJR when-issued stock thereafter

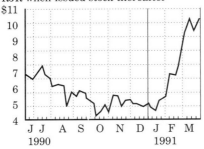

Though challenges persist.

• Winston and Salem cigarettes are seen
  as declining brands.

• Cash for acquisitions is still scarce.

• Domestic tobacco market shrinks
  2% to 4% a year.

• Corporate culture isn't changing as
  fast as new executives would like.

agement has its own money at risk, people don't just spend it for the sake of spending."

Like most chief executives of financially successful leveraged buyouts, Mr. Gerstner now sits on a paper fortune from stock that he bought at cheap prices in the early days of the buy-out. Yet he stubbornly refuses to count himself a winner yet. "The way I look at it, I'm $6.5 million in the hole," he says, referring to the cash he spent for RJR stock in 1989. "That money is spent. Gone. I haven't received one dollar back." Under agreements with the company, he can't sell any of his RJR stock until 1994. "In no way do I feel financially secure," Mr. Gerstner says.

Case 2–3   Rockingham Memorial Hospital*

Rockingham Memorial Hospital has made patient care its primary objective. Through practical application of this philosophy, the Physical Therapy Department has provided education, treatment, and rehabilitation of patients. To fulfill this goal more effectively, the department is considering expansion into a sports medicine program. This particular service would provide education, treatment, and rehabilitation for injuries resulting from sports and fitness-related activities.

Research measures have been started to check into the feasibility of starting a full department for sports medicine. The supervisor of the Physical Therapy Department, the hospital President, and the Vice President of Operations and Planning contacted various individuals to determine interest in such a program and facility. The hospital's organizational structure is illustrated in Exhibit 1.

In-depth discussions with the local county school superintendents, coaches, and athletic directors revealed a sincere interest in this type of program. The hospital administrators also attended conferences concerning the development of sports medicine clinics. In addition, they visited a few successful sports medicine clinics to discuss issues involved in the formation of such a facility.

A portion of Rockingham Memorial Hospital's service area was selected to survey. The total service area includes seven counties plus three cities. However, the City of Harrisonburg plus Rockingham County were selected because they seemed to be the best serviced areas. Within the survey area are five high schools, five junior high schools, three colleges, and two recreation departments.

Information regarding the possibility of a sports medicine clinic was presented initially to the superintendents of schools, then to the coaching staffs. During this informational process, data was obtained from the schools concerning their knowledge and need for sports medicine. Since the early reactions were favorable and more information was requested, meetings were conducted with various principals and athletic directors. As a result of the positive feedback, interviews were also conducted with coaching staffs and trainers. The schools were able to identify seven areas considered important enough to include in the educational services of such a facility:

---

* This case was prepared by Valerie Pandak, Research Associate, and Thomas Bertsch, Professor of Marketing at James Madison University.

EXHIBIT 1   Organizational Structure

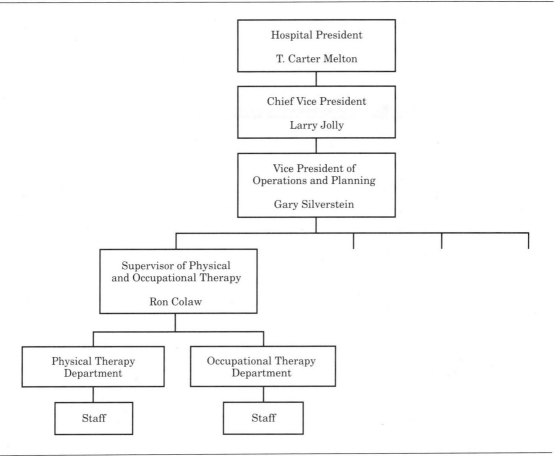

1. Preseason screenings and evaluations to include flexibility and strength, and functional tests to augment the routine physicals by physicians.
2. Assistance with conditioning programs.
3. Equipment evaluations, plus assistance in purchasing new equipment.
4. Student trainer programs.
5. Assistance with specific rehabilitations, plus guidelines to follow for sports injuries.
6. Seminars on immediate care of injuries, first aid, and safety considerations.
7. Specific testing plus assistance with criteria for returning to play.

The results of the research revealed frustrations encountered by coaches regarding prevention, care, and treatment of their athletes. Each school has some form of conditioning or rehabilitating equipment, but many of the facilities were neither well equipped nor properly monitored. All in all, the coaches involved in the survey were extremely enthusiastic, as well as supportive of a sports medicine facility opening in the area.

Other information provided by the survey is shown in Exhibit 2. The 10 percent market share excludes minor injuries, which would not require a physician's care and ultimately would not require the care given in a sports medicine rehabilitation program. The data seemed to

EXHIBIT 2   Local Population Statistics

*Schools**	*Number of Athletes*	*Estimated 30% Injury Rate*	*10% Market Share of Injuries*
Harrisonburg High School and Thomas Harrison Junior High	408	122.4	12.2
Broadway High School and J. C. Myers Junior High	300	90.0	9.0
Spotswood High School and Montevideo/Elkton Junior High	342	102.6	10.2
Turner Ashby High School and John Wayland Junior High	320	96.0	9.6
Eastern Mennonite High School	240	72.0	7.2
Bridgewater College	200	60.0	6.0
Eastern Mennonite College	185	55.5	5.5
Totals	1,995	598.5	59.7

Service Area	*Total Population*	*30% of Recreation Athletes*	*15% of Estimated Injuries*	*10% Market Share of Injuries*
Rockingham County	54,000	16,200	2,430.0	243.0
Harrisonburg	25,700	7,710	1,156.5	115.65
Surrounding area	44,300	13,290	1,993.5	199.35
Totals	124,000	37,200	5,580.0	558.0

Organized Recreational Populations

Rockingham County	5,844
Harrisonburg	1,612
Totals	7,456

* The populations of students and athletes from the area's university are not included due to the already existing athletic training program there.

indicate a significant population size for the types of services being considered.

The Sports Medicine Center would provide educational services in addition to actual treatment. The educational programs include: ongoing educational opportunities for health professionals involved with sports medicine, seminars for scholastic coaches plus trainer visits to sports events; community education regarding aspects of injury prevention relating to sports; and the ongoing education of injured athletes during their progression through rehabilitation. The center's staff members serve as consultants regarding conditioning programs and equipment purchases by schools.

The actual treatment of the patient at the sports medicine center can be broken down into five areas: evaluations; acute treatment of injury; subacute/chronic treatment; rehabilitation postsurgery; and testing capabilities. Within each of these areas, the services to the patient will depend on the type and extent of injury.

To provide the forementioned services, a variety of equipment would be required. A list of the equipment and prices is provided in Exhibit 3. However, the list does not include the costs of renovating the facility area needed to provide an adequate setting for the program. These projected renovation costs are listed in Exhibit 4.

The initiation of the sports medicine program would necessitate hiring the following staff:

1. Physical therapist experienced in the treatment of athletic injuries.
2. Athletic trainer with experience as well as current knowledge of sports-related injuries.
3. Attendant to assist both the therapist and the trainer.

The evaluation and development of specific therapeutic programs by the physical therapist coupled with the taping, screening, and prevention program skills of the athletic trainer would provide a well-rounded program of care and rehabilitation. The salary expenditures are listed in Exhibit 5.

For the Sports Medicine Center to be successful, it would have to be highly visible in the early stages of development. In order to educate potential users, the staff members would visit schools in the area on a frequent basis to further promote awareness of the program. During these visits, the staff would establish the groundwork for a good relationship with the coaches and athletes of these schools. Programs for the general public would include speeches to area Boosters' Clubs, community organizations, and recreational groups. A list of recreational organizations is provided in Exhibit 6. Participants of the recreational organizations would be sent a promotional brochure along with an invitation to visit the sports medicine facility shortly after its completion. Physicians of all specialties and medically related staff would

---

EXHIBIT 3   Projected Equipment Expenses

Equipment Item	*Price*
Computer—software	$ 250
Computer—IBM PC	4,000
Ortho Tron II	8,495
Filtron	1,095
UBE	1,995
Eagle equipment	
Chest press	2,345
Shoulder press	2,195
Lateral pulldown	1,945
Leg extension	2,395
Leg curl	2,295
Multi-hip	2,295
Leg press	4,295
Ice machine	3,000
Whirlpool—large 46 × 24 × 25	1,800
Whirlpool—small 25 × 13 × 15	1,575
Whirlpool table 47 × 43	295
Ultrasound/electrical stimulation (2 machines)	6,290
Hot packs	945
Hot pack rack	215
Treatment tables 3 @ $376 each	1,128
Small treatment table	286
Wall pulleys	615
Cryotemp	1,000
Multi-ankle-exerciser	500
Hand weights	
Dumbell—weights & rack	400
Velcro—wrist and ankle with rack	335
Rowing machine	2,000
Universal exercise equipment	8,000
Treadmill	11,000
Television, VCR and VCR camera	2,000
Shoe insert fabrication machine	*
Miscellaneous items	3,016
Total	$78,000

* No estimate available.

---

also be sent a brochure and invited to an open house. Other individuals that would be invited to visit the facilities on different occasions would include: Hospital Auxiliary members, church leagues, high school boosters, county and city school boards, athletic coaches, and school principals.

EXHIBIT 4 Renovation Expenses

Expense Item	Projected Amount
Baseboard	$ 153
Floor covering 24 × 82	3,500
Floor covering 24 × 18	589
Ceiling and labor	2,700
Wall and door	2,000
Light fixture and labor	750
Ceiling fixture	2,000
Desk work area	400
Wall covering	700
Cubical curtain	400
Curtain rods	400
Heating connectors, other fixed equipment, and miscellaneous costs	46,408
Total	$60,000

The local news media would be invited during the initial week of service to encourage publicity coverage. Advertisements would be placed in the local newspapers in addition to school publications. Later, radio ads would be used to promote special events involving the Sports Medicine Center. T-shirts would be given to patients on their initial visit to the Center.

EXHIBIT 5 Salary Expenses

Next year	One full-time licensed physical therapist for ½ year: $10,800 One full-time athletic trainer for ½ year: $8,850
Following year	Licensed physical therapist: $21,800 Athletic trainer: $17,700
Yearly	Licensed physical therapist: $21,800 Athletic trainer: $17,700 Physical therapist/athletic trainer: $20,000 Part-time secretary/aide: $7,300

Notes: Salary expenses include 8 percent pay increases each year on January 1.

Employee benefits are projected at 26 percent of total salary cost. This forecast assumes that when employees are on vacation, it will be necessary to provide additional coverage.

Training and travel expenses are projected to increase 5 percent annually.

Utilities, housekeeping, and maintenance are budgeted at the hospital's cost of $17.84 per square foot. The sports medicine program area will require approximately 2,400 square feet. These costs will increase at 5 percent per year.

Medical supplies are projected at $1,000 for the first full year.

Depreciation is projected with a 10-year life on equipment.

EXHIBIT 6   Recreational Organizations

Valley Wellness Center—over 2,100 members
2 golf courses
3 dance studios
Track/running club
Bicycle club
Bowling alley
Tennis leagues
2 fitness centers
2 baseball leagues
Swim team
Competitive ski team
Summer sports camps at 2 colleges
Roller skating club
Bowhunters club

The program's success would rely heavily on its visibility with physicians. Each patient would have to have a physician's referral, before he or she could receive treatment at the clinic.

The projected market share figures for the first seven years of operation are listed in Exhibit 7. In Exhibit 8, a projected income statement for these initial seven years of the Sports Medicine Center of Rockingham is illustrated. The figures in Exhibits 7 and 8 have been projected by Rockingham Memorial Hospital's finance department. However, the figures would require a revision each year as more experience was gained with the program.

EXHIBIT 7 Market Share Analysis

Market Features	Program Year						
	1	2	3	4	5	6	7
Recreational athletes							
Population of area served	124,000	124,000	124,000	124,000	124,000	124,000	124,000
Percentage of recreational athletes	30%	30%	30%	30%	30%	30%	30%
Estimated recreational athletes	37,200	37,200	37,200	37,200	37,200	37,200	37,200
Injury rate	15%	15%	15%	15%	15%	15%	15%
Annual estimated injured recreational athletes	5,580	5,580	5,580	5,580	5,580	5,580	5,580
Estimated market share (percent)	10%	15%	25%	30%	30%	30%	30%
Recreational athletes participating in sports medicine program	558	837	1,395	1,674	1,674	1,674	1,674
Visits/Athlete	7	7	7	7	7	7	7
Total recreational athlete visits	3,906	5,859	9,765	11,718	11,718	11,718	11,718
Scholastic athletes							
Estimated scholastic athletes	1,995	1,995	1,995	1,995	1,995	1,995	1,995
Injury rate	30%	30%	30%	30%	30%	30%	30%
Annual estimated injured scholastic athletes (total recreational athlete visits)	599	599	599	599	599	599	599
Estimated market share (percent)	10%	15%	25%	30%	30%	30%	30%
Scholastic athletes participating in sports medicine program	60	90	150	180	180	180	180
Visits/Athlete	7	7	7	7	7	7	7
Total scholastic athlete visits	420	630	1,050	1,260	1,260	1,260	1,260
Total scholastic and recreational athlete visits	4,326	6,489	10,815	12,978	12,978	12,978	12,978

EXHIBIT 8 Projected Income Statement

				Program Year				
Financial Issues	*1**	*2*	*3*	*4*	*5*	*6*	*7*	*Total of Years 1–7*
Revenue								
Price per visit	$ 30.00	$ 31.50	$ 33.08	$ 34.73	$ 36.47	$ 38.29	$ 40.20	$ 244.27
Number of visits	2,163	6,489	10,815	12,978	12,978	12,978	12,978	71,379
Total revenue (price × visits)	$64,890	$204,404	$357,760	$450,726	$473,308	$496,928	$521,716	$2,569,732
Bad debts	$ 3,245	$ 10,220	$ 17,888	$ 22,536	$ 23,665	$ 24,846	$ 26,086	$ 128,486
Net revenue	$61,645	$194,184	$339,872	$428,190	$449,643	$472,002	$495,630	$2,441,166
Expenses								
Salaries	$19,750	$ 39,500	$ 69,960	$ 75,557	$ 81,602	$ 88,130	$ 95,180	$ 469,679
Employee benefits	5,135	10,270	18,190	19,645	21,217	22,914	24,747	122,118
Training and travel	1,600	1,600	1,764	1,852	1,945	2,042	2,144	12,947
Marketing	7,000	1,000	1,000	1,000	1,000	1,000	1,000	13,000
Utilities, housekeeping, and maintenance	21,408	44,058	47,205	49,565	52,043	54,645	57,377	326,301
Medical supplies	500	1,000	1,050	1,103	1,158	1,216	1,277	7,304
Miscellaneous expenses	1,000	1,000	1,000	1,000	1,000	1,000	1,000	7,000
Depreciation—equipment and renovation	5,650	12,300	13,600	13,600	13,600	13,600	13,600	85,950
Total expenses	$62,043	$110,808	$153,769	$163,322	$173,565	$184,547	$196,325	$1,044,379
Net income	($398)	$ 83,376	$186,103	$264,868	$276,078	$287,535	$299,305	$1,396,867
Discounted annual cash flows								
Cash inflows present value @ 10%	($377)	$ 71,538	$144,506	$186,212	$175,667	$165,640	$156,106	$ 899,292
Less start-up cash outflow								
Equipment								(78,000)
Renovation								(60,000)
Total cash outflow								(138,000)
Net present value								761,292
Break-even charge	14.35	15.07	15.82	16.61	17.44	18.31	19.23	
Break-even volume	1,035	3,104	5,173	6,208	6,208	6,208	6,208	

* The first-year data is for only six months.

Case 2–4   Amtech Corporation*

On the way to making his first $10 million, 37-year-old David P. Cook has broken a lot of rules.

He dropped out of college his freshman year and never went back. He garnered his first venture capital, $100,000, before even drafting a business loan.

And rather than zeroing in on an industry, like most entrepreneurs, Cook jumped from writing software to renting videos to making electronic identification tags—all in the span of five years.

"We've got a saying around here," said David Druckenbrodt, one of Cook's colleagues. "When everybody says we're doing the wrong things, we know we're getting close."

At a time when market testing, target groups and endless financial analyses control more and more business decisions, Cook's approach is often refreshingly old-fashioned: He follows his instincts.

He taught himself how to program a computer and develop economic models. And in 1978, when a friend urged him to start a software company that would cater to the oil industry, he figured he could do a better job than the current players, so why not?

Cook Data Services later went public and became the No. 1 firm in its field, selling $120,000 computer models to the oil patch.

When his ex-wife wanted to open a video store, Cook looked around and concluded that the fragmented, mom-and-pop industry was ripe for plucking. After a detailed evaluation, he decided to create a national chain of video rental superstores—a concept that retailers and analysts scoffed at.

But today Blockbuster Entertainment Corp., the company Cook started, is the industry leader, with a market value well over $1 billion.

"You'd like to think your life has some plan to it," Cook said. "But the last thing I ever thought was that I'd be in the video rental business.

"The world is so diverse—why limit yourself?"

When his dad told him that scientists in Los Alamos, N.M., had created an interesting technology that tracked livestock in the fields, Cook investigated. His firm ended up buying the patent rights and control of the company, and raised $21.7 million to develop commercial applications.

---

* Source: Mitchell Schnurman, "Innovator's Firm Is Ready to Forge New Industry with Electronic Tags," *Fort Worth Star-Telegram,* August 6, 1989, pp. 4–1, 7, 8.

Now, the Dallas firm, Amtech Corp., is making electronic identification tags for cargo containers, railroad cars and automobiles that use tollways around the world.

Amtech appears on the verge of creating a new industry—and perhaps becoming the third public company to be started by this mild-mannered fresh-faced young man.

"People don't realize how versatile and flexible they can be," Cook said from his spacious office in Highland Park, just north of downtown Dallas. "They'll spend their whole career chasing the one thing they studied in school, just because they don't believe they can do anything else.

"It's the fear factor that freezes them."

Cook hardly seems like the fearless sort. His thin body, fair complexion and black-rimmed glasses make him look more like a bashful librarian than a blazing entrepreneur.

He doesn't play the stock market, even though he puts his net worth "at well over $10 million." He prefers to keep his money in certificates of deposit.

Cook doesn't want to be called an entrepreneur because the label is so common today.

"Suddenly everybody is an entrepreneur," he said.

And unlike many motivators, Cook speaks softly, rarely raising his voice, and he absolutely never pounds a table.

The one time he can remember snapping at an employee—a programmer who made a costly error in 1981—Cook said he was so upset that he caught a plane to San Diego and spent five days on the beach—"decompressing."

"I told myself there was no room in my company for a manager who manages like that, even if it was me," he said.

Cook clearly made the adjustments that were needed. At Cook Data Services, annual revenues doubled in each of its first five years, reaching $6.1 million in 1982, with earnings of $901,000.

In early 1983, the company completed a public offering that swelled its corporate treasury to $8.4 million, money earmarked for expanding the business internally and through acquisitions.

But then the bottom fell out of the energy industry, and Cook refused to pump money into it. He spun off the software unit to management, gaining almost $10 million to invest in a new business.

In 1984, he put up $500,000 for the patent rights to Amtech, which had been started by a group of scientists who had worked on electronic identification for 12 years. The U.S. Department of Agriculture provided the initial financial backing for the scientists, hoping to develop a system to locate roaming livestock and monitor their body temperatures.

Cook and Kenneth Anderson—a veteran of the corporate world who joined Cook's firm in 1983—believed there were many commercial applications in electronic identification tags. Over the next few years, Cook's firm invested another $1.7 million into the program's early development and, as board members, Cook and Anderson monitored its progress.

But after examining roughly 300 investments, Cook and Anderson decided to put their money into video rental stores. The business had no dominant players, they concluded, and the concept of a superstore for videos could be replicated easily in markets throughout the country.

The plan called for initially spending up to $700,000 on each store, vs. the $50,000 that smaller players raised for their rental businesses. The money would stock each store with up to 10,000 titles, allow Cook to design the interiors for much larger volumes, put bar codes on each tape to speed check-outs, and pay for staffing to keep the shops open until midnight, seven days a week.

Cook figured that what Home Depot did to hardware and supermarkets did to grocery shopping, he would do to video rental.

But critics had a field day slamming Cook's Blockbuster idea, and the sharp criticism of a *Barron's* columnist helped kill its 1986 public offering. Cook was forced to raise money privately, which ultimately cost him control of the company.

But time has proven him correct.

Blockbuster, controlled by a trio of investors who bought out Cook and Anderson in early 1987, now has 790 outlets nationwide. It earned more than $8 million in the first six months of 1988, and revenues doubled to $74 million.

The Blockbuster venture also was a major score for Cook and his backers, who walked away with returns of up to 1,000 percent, he said.

"David has done a lot of things that have surprised me," said Robert Glaze, a private investor who, in 1978, put up the first $100,000 for Cook's software company. "But all his coups attest to one fact—he's a winner."

Cook's track record is attracting the kind of support he needs now, in building the foundation of a technology firm whose revenues are expected to jump tenfold this year.

Among the investors who have answered his call: H. Ross Perot, who bought a 14.9 percent stake in Amtech (a share slightly smaller than Cook's); Japanese giant Mitsubishi Corp. and American President Companies, a major transportation firm, which each pumped in $6 million for 13-percent stakes.

Cook also is talking with a few railroads that are considering joining the venture.

And with Amtech needing to raise $15 million in the next several months, he now is weighing a public offering—and says it would fly.

"If you do a couple of successful companies," Cook said, "people believe in you as much as the concept."

But the concept for Amtech is also a big part of the attraction.

Amtech's technology provides a function that is similar to bar codes on groceries and magnetic strips on credit cards. All three technologies identify objects, but Amtech uses radio signals to send and receive information.

Amtech's advantage is that it can electronically read tags at a good distance, at great speeds and regardless of whether dirt, snow or other debris cover the device.

The company's primary market is tagging shipping containers transported by ship, rail and truck. A few months ago, Amtech's system was selected as the industry standard for identification tags in this so-called intermodal container industry. One reason: Its system was the only candidate that could read a tag at a distance of 40 feet, the minimum set by the industry.

Being named the industry standard is expected to vault the company's revenues from $1.4 million in 1988 to more than $10 million this year—and eventually more than $100 million annually, Cook said.

Amtech also is trying to become the standard for tags on railroad cars, which typically are traded among rail companies and can be difficult to track. Currently, rail companies videotape their lines as they pass a location, then spotters study the tapes to compile inventories.

With electronic tags on the rail cars, a receiving antenna could be installed along the track to count each car automatically as it passes.

A third market is in trucking. Amtech is conducting a study in New Mexico, tagging trucks that travel Interstate 40. Eventually, trucks and weigh stations could have equipment that would allow trucks to pass through the stations at standard cruising speeds.

The fourth-largest market is tollways, which happen to be the most visible among typical consumers. Amtech's system uses a small, credit card-size device, called a tolltag, which is placed on the inside of a car windshield.

As the car approaches a tollgate, an Amtech antenna automatically reads the tag and flashes the go sign. Customers, who are billed monthly on their credit cards, don't have to scramble for change or roll down their windows at the gate—a convenience and a timesaver.

In Dallas, the North Dallas Tollway last week expanded its Amtech tag readers to each of its 12 lanes at the Wycliff Avenue exit. Drivers are charged the usual toll, plus a 5-cent fee for each time the card is used.

They also must pay a $2 monthly charge for the card. For a small fee, they can receive a printout of all the tolls they paid that month—a useful record for drivers who deduct car expenses on their tax returns.

Almost 5,000 Dallas drivers have purchased tolltags since the system started two months ago. Amtech operates similar programs in New Orleans and New York City, and recently was selected to provide the network for a tollway in Oslo, Norway.

The foreign project touched off an international incident when Norway's government tried to force Oslo officials to give the $4.5 million contract to a Norwegian firm, even though Amtech's system had performed better on tests and was less costly.

Cook said the dispute has not yet been resolved, but Amtech is proceeding as if it still has the contract. The company, which employs about 125 people—55 in its research and development unit in Santa Fe, N.M.—will have to gear up for the project.

While Amtech is hoping to sell up to 20,000 tolltags in Dallas to cover its costs, the Norway contract calls for an initial order of 200,000 tags.

The deal is one example of the growth that may lie ahead for Amtech. And Cook seems prepared for it.

With Blockbuster, Cook raised eyebrows by spending $6 million on a computer system for Blockbuster's tape distribution. But when the company rolled out a national expansion, the system seemed a bargain.

At Amtech, the company is investing millions in research and development and computer software, and Cook has assembled a deep management team. It includes Chairman Michael Corboy, former top executive of Tocom Inc., a maker of cable television converters that was sold to General Instrument Corp.; and President Russell Mortenson, a lawyer who was managing partner of 2M Cos., an investment firm headed by former EDS executive Morten Meyerson.

Cook likes to compare Amtech today to Blockbuster's stage of development three years ago. Like Blockbuster in 1986, Amtech is likely to lose about $6 million this year, but Cook said the company will turn the corner in early 1990.

After that, its markets could explode. And Amtech has to position itself, through its capital base and management, to respond if the surge in demand comes.

"The future belongs to the people who conceive it," said Cook, "not those who wait for it."

Case 2–5   *Makhteshim Chemical Works**

"To say that we are unhappy with our progress to date would be an understatement," admitted Mr. Ilan Leviteh, vice president of Makhteshim Chemical Works, a small Israeli specialty chemicals company. In 1987, Makhteshim faced a key decision: "Our penetration of the U.S. market has not gone well, and we have to decide what to do about it. We have to be here," he emphasized. "The U.S. market is just too important."

For the last three years, M&T Chemicals (M&T), a U.S. company, had marketed the F–2000 Series of brominated polymeric flame retardants for Makhteshim. If Makhteshim wanted to exercise its cancellation option in its contract with M&T for the sale of its flame retardant product line in the United States, it had to do so soon. Another major U.S. flame retardant company has asked Makhteshim to produce a generic product for them. Determined to be in what they regarded as a vital market, Makhteshim's management was reassessing its entry strategy.

MAKHTESHIM CHEMICAL WORKS

Makhteshim Chemical Works was established in Israel in 1952. Makhteshim was the majority shareholder of Agan Chemical Manufacturers in 1987. When combined, the two companies operated as Makhteshim-Agan. Makhteshim-Agan was the chief chemical producer within Koor Chemicals, Ltd., the chemical division of Koor Industries, Ltd.

Koor Industries, Ltd. was Israel's largest industrial manufacturing firm. Koor Industries, Ltd. had worldwide sales of over $2.1 billion in 1986, and ranked 262nd on the Fortune 500 list of non-U.S. companies. It had over 100 manufacturing facilities, and over 180 marketing,

* This case was prepared by Patricia P. McDougall of Georgia Institute of Technology, Earl H. Levith of Edlon Products, Inc., and Kendall J. Roth of the University of South Carolina as the basis for class discussion rather than to illustrate either effective or ineffective handling of a management situation. Mr. Levith served as the 1985–86 Director of the Fire Retardant Association. The authors wish to thank Dr. William R. Sandberg for his helpful comments.

Distributed by the North American Case Research Association. All rights reserved to the author and the North American Case Research Association. Permission to use the case should be obtained from the author and the North American Case Research Association.

EXHIBIT 1   Organizational Structure

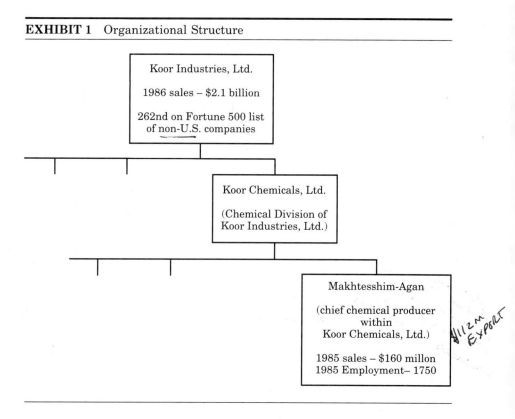

financial, and commercial companies within the group. An organizational structure diagram is presented in Exhibit 1.

Makhteshim Chemical Works and Agan Chemical Manufacturers, Ltd. were both parts of the chemical branch of Koors Industries. Together they operated three manufacturing facilities in Israel and had 1,750 employees.

Outside of Israel, Makhteshim and Agan operated somewhat as a joint company—Makhteshim-Agan—sharing offices, staffs, and communication facilities. The agricultural chemicals sales and marketing forces of the two companies were joined in the United States; however, they were not joined for the non-agricultural chemicals in the United States.

Makhteshim-Agan had three regional sales offices which were located in Europe, the United States, and Brazil. The company had attained distribution of its products in 65 countries through more than 40 distribution centers on five continents. Sales in Israel accounted for only 10 percent of Makhteshim-Agan's production. Sales in 1985 were $160 million, with export sales accounting for 70 percent of the sales

---

EXHIBIT 2   1985 Makhteshim-Agan Export Percentages

	Sales Dollars	*Production*
Export	112,000,000 (70%)	90%
Local markets	48,000,000 (30)	10
Total sales	160,000,000	

Source: Company documents.

dollars (Exhibit 2). The distribution of sales among the company's main product groups is shown in Exhibit 3.

In Israel, Makhteshim Chemical Works and Agan were run as basically two different companies, each with separate headquarters and staffs. They competed with each other and other Koors subsidiaries for the resources from the parent company. Agan dealt primarily in agricultural chemicals and household pesticides. Makhteshim, on the other hand, produced agricultural chemicals, fine chemicals,[1] flame retardants, polymer intermediates, and other industrial chemicals. A diagram of their operating structure within Israel is presented as Exhibit 4.

Because of their different product focuses, the marketing approaches and operating philosophies of these two organizations were different. The agricultural chemical business tended to be more tightly focused, with fewer suppliers competing in a relatively homogeneous marketplace for chemicals. The number of customers tended to be smaller and more stable, and ongoing relationships could be built up on the business side of customer companies. Agan sold primarily chemical compounds of known technology and enjoyed widespread recognition for providing quality products. There was little interaction between Agan's R&D staffs and the customers' technical people. In most parts of the world, Agan's technical people generally limited their contacts to demonstrating the application of herbicides and pesticides, along with general agronomic techniques. Thus, Agan had developed a marketing approach that did not require great technical sales expertise, but relied on price. This strategy had been successful for Agan.

Makhteshim, on the other hand, sold a diverse product line in many markets. One common element in these markets was their strong technological orientation. Makhteshim's management believed the com-

---

[1] Fine chemicals are specialty chemicals made in very small volumes. They are usually used in complex reactions, have high profit margins, and are extremely expensive. For example, a fine chemical may be made in a 50 gallon batch and sell for $20 per pound, while a commodity chemical would be made in a continuous process and may sell for $20 per ton.

EXHIBIT 3   Makhteshim-Agan 1987 Main Product Groups

Product	Percentage of Revenues
Agrochemicals and household pesticides	88.0%
Fine chemicals and intermediates	5.0
Polyester and flame retardants	3.0
Photographic chemicals	2.0
Industrial chemicals	2.0
Total	100.0%

Source: Company documents.

pany enjoyed a strong technological position based primarily on its work in bromine and phosgene chemistry. They considered Makhteshim's technical staff to be of excellent quality and its laboratory facilities to be "world class." They had backed these resources with an $80 million capital investment program begun in 1986 and were confident that Makhteshim did fine technical work when it was aware of a problem or issue confronting a customer industry. Makhteshim had been successful in its European and Far East markets using a low cost strategy. Makhteshim had used Israeli nationals in these markets.

EXHIBIT 4   Operating Structure within Israel

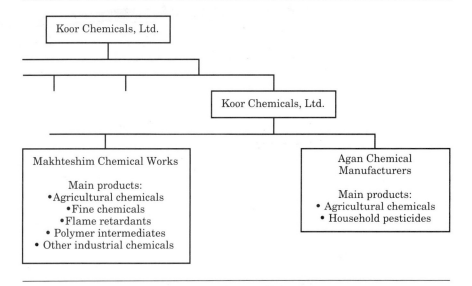

GATEKEEPER

PRODUCER

U.S. IS A LONG WAY FROM LABS.

A second common element in Makhteshim's markets was the incorporation of chemicals, such as flame retardants, into the customer's end product. In this environment the customer's technical staff (who specify the components of the end product) played a key role in the purchasing decision. In the flame retardant industry, suppliers typically hired technically trained salespeople, as competitive pressures required that salespeople be familiar with the product technology and various issues facing the customer's industry. Knowledge of a customer's technology and the nature of its end product were also important since rival sellers of flame retardants often used alternate technologies to perform the same function. Additional information on the U.S. flame retardant industry is provided in the Appendix.

In the opinion of its management, Makhteshim operated at a disadvantage in its ability to incorporate chemicals into the customer's end product. The company's technical staff was not part of its marketing program. Instead, they remained in their laboratories with limited interaction with customers or industry peers, tending toward isolation from industry issues and trends. Their contacts with Makhteshim's sales force were limited, generally consisting of responding to the latter's requests for specific technical information. Management believed that this state of affairs made it difficult for the technical staff to develop an overall picture of industry trends or an understanding of how they might make better commercial use of their technical skills.

Some elements of Makhteshim's management believed the company has failed to recognize opportunities and to obtain the resources required to implement its own strategy because many of its overseas activities were combined with Agan. Instead, Makhteshim had been forced to adopt a low-cost strategy that limited the resources committed to its technical sales function and to the regulatory and political conflicts that surrounded some of its products. Sometimes this had meant bringing new products to market with limited technical support.

In entering the U.S. market, Makhteshim had attempted to overcome this shortcoming by arranging for M&T to market its F–2000 flame retardant product line. Flame retardant products comprised less than 5 percent of Makhteshim's sales. The flame retardant products were very profitable.

While M&T was not considered by industry sources to be one of the strongest players in the flame retardant marketplace, it was considered to have a good technical staff that called regularly on customers and would easily be able to handle the F–2000 line. M&T was a specialty chemicals company. Industry sources described their technical department as "competent" and "credible," but lacking technological leadership. M&T's good cost position was viewed as its primary competitive advantage, with its products marketed primarily on the basis of price. One industry expert referred to M&T's product line as "copy-cat products," and noted that the deal with Makhteshim afforded M&T the opportunity to buy into a high-tech line. M&T manufactured its own product line, which included Thermoguard. In some respects Thermoguard was competitive with Makhteshim's F–2000 flame retardant product line. M&T simply added the F–2000 product line to its own narrow flame retardant product line and tried to sell it as an additional product. No major emphasis was given to the F–2000 line.

Makhteshim had expected to gain a significant (>15 percent) market share of the U.S. flame retardant market within its first two years, but the product had thus far not been incorporated into a major customer's end product. M&T's position was that Makhteshim expected too much too soon. M&T pointed to a recent major customer order as a breakthrough in the marketing program. Although the initial order was small, M&T attested that the fact the customer had developed a new product line based on Makhteshim's product offered the potential of continuing sales for a long time.

While Makhteshim was committed to the U.S. flame retardant market, the Israelis were increasingly concerned about the style and cost of doing business in the U.S. marketplace. They were unfamiliar with a large sales force. They were not accustomed to large bills for dinners, tended to stay in less expensive hotels, and controlled entertainment expenses tightly.

As the deadline for exercising its cancellation option in M&T's contract approached, Makhteshim's management was reassessing its basic strategy in the U.S. flame retardant market. In particular, some now doubted the efficacy of distributor marketing when it was not backed with knowledge of the market and strong support from their own manufacturing operations. All recognized that any request for more resources would undergo intense scrutiny by Koor management, and would be questioned vigorously by other groups within Koor, who were all competing for the same limited resources. A clear consensus was at present not available.

Appendix: *U.S. Flame Retardant Industry Note*

In 1987, the flame retardants industry in the United States was an $850 million dollar business growing at annual rates in excess of 15 percent per year (see Exhibits A–1 and A–2). Gross profit margins were about 40 percent. In comparison to the U.S. market, the profitability of other world markets was about 75 percent of the U.S. levels. Major competitors in the industry included Occidental Chemical, Ethyl-Saytex, and Great Lakes Chemical.

The purpose of flame retardants was to slow down the development and spread of a fire, allowing sufficient time for people to react to the fire situation.

EXHIBIT A–1   U.S. Sales of Flame Retardant Substances, 1986

	Pounds (millions)	Sales (millions, U.S. $)
Organic		
Chlorinated	100	$ 70
Brominated	150	260
Inorganic		
Aluminum trihydrate	400	80
Antimony oxide	40	60
Other	350	380
Total	1040	$850

Source: Interviews with industry experts.

Flame retardants were used in a multitude of end-use applications, from electrical wire insulation, connectors, and circuit boards to carpet backing, children's clothing, plywood paneling, and plastic plumbing. With the continuing increase in the use of new materials, and new applications for existing materials, industry experts predicted that the U.S. flame retardant chemical industry would grow to over $2 billion by the year 2000.

U.S. FLAME RETARDANT INDUSTRY CHARACTERISTICS

The flame retardant industry was a high-profit, value-added industry, and had three major characteristics. It was (1) created by regulation, (2) driven by technology, and (3) sustained by supplier commitment.

The flame retardants industry was *regulation created*. Few consumers of flame retardants would use them if they were not required to do so. Flame

EXHIBIT A–2   Flame Retardant End Use 1987 U.S. Market Growth Rates

	Percent
Carpet backing	(5)
Wire/cable	>15
Unsaturated polyester	8–10
Thermoplastics	6–10
Flexible PVC	>10
New applications/polymers	>20

Source: Interviews with industry experts.

retardants added cost to the end product, changed and degraded properties of the base polymer, and were generally inconvenient to work with. However, with the increasing rash of highly publicized fires taking their toll in both lives and property, and the increasing use of polymers in critical applications, flame and fire retardants were increasingly demanded by building codes, insurance regulators, the military, large consumers, and government bodies at all levels.

Standards had been set by Underwriters Laboratories, the U.S. military, the states of California and New York, Factory Mutual, the EEC, and a multitude of countries around the world. For example, laws had been passed in California regulating mattresses sold in the state. In 1987, New York passed laws requiring testing and registration of plastic products containing flame retardants used in New York. The upholstered furniture industry had accepted standards governing their products. The VIC (Verband Chemische Industrie, Germany's principal industry trade group) had announced that its members would stop further development of plastics containing poly brominated diphenyl oxides[2] until a toxicity issue was resolved.

While Israel had been successful negotiating a free trade agreement with the United States, a notable exception to this success was in the area of bromine chemicals and flame retardant chemicals. Industry sources had described Israeli testimony and efforts as "surprisingly" poor.

Most industry analysts foresaw increasing regulation as a certainty, with more and more governmental entities concerning themselves with the issues of smoke emissions and toxic gasses from plastics in fires. It had been estimated that the cost of compliance with current and proposed regulations in the United States alone, would be in the amount of hundreds of millions of dollars. As a consequence of this governmental involvement, political issues had overwhelmed technology, creating a severe threat to some products and technologies, and a golden opportunity for others.

The flame retardants industry was *technology driven*. The customers for flame retardants had a single objective—to meet a specific flame retardant performance requirement at the lowest possible cost, giving them a competitive advantage in a specific application. They were relatively indifferent to the product or technology which gave them this level of flame retardant performance. However, the flame retardant user had a variety of performance requirements which they were attempting to satisfy simultaneously. Thus, a product that gave them flame retardancy alone, but degraded other performance characteristics they were trying to achieve, was unacceptable. For example, aluminum trihydrate (ATH) was an inexpensive flame retardant for wire insulation. However, to reach a high level of flame retardancy, so much ATH had to be used in the wire, that the wire became stiff and difficult to bend. Unless this could be overcome with other additives, ATH would not be the product of choice in wire insulation, no matter how well it performed as a flame retardant.

---

[2] Makhteshim's F–2000 series had received full clearance on toxicology and would not be affected by this action.

The flame retardant manufacturer had to be aware of and be able to address the properties of the total polymer system. They had to know the effects of their products on the polymer, the interaction of their products with other additives and modifiers, and the total system cost and performance characteristics. This usually resulted in a close working relationship between the flame retardant manufacturer and the customer. The technical people of the customer, those actually developing new products for the marketplace, had to feel comfortable that the flame retardant supplier understood his problems and could help solve them. The flame retardant supplier was expected to be able to give technical assistance to the customer on the application of his products. The marketing and business people of the flame retardant supplier were expected to know the end-users of the products, and the characteristics of the industry being served by their customers. They, too, had to be sufficiently knowledgeable in the industry technology to understand and deal with the technical issues. An example of the distribution chain can be found in Exhibit A–3.

The third major characteristic of successful flame retardant businesses was the importance of the customer's perception of a long-term *commitment* from the supplier. A customer's new products could require years of research to develop. They were highly proprietary, and rarely patentable. It could take at least a year and easily over $200,000 to get the necessary UL or MILSPEC certifications before the product could be sold for a specific application. Often, a flame retardant supplier would run many of the tests for his customer before the customer would submit them for official testing. Once the official testing

---

EXHIBIT A–3   Flame Retardant Producers' Distribution Chain

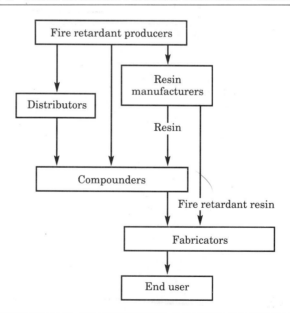

was completed (usually a UL test was required), it could take an additional year or more before the customer certified the product and incorporated it into its product line. A customer would not likely undertake the development of a new product with a supplier that the customer felt lacked either the commitment or staying power to assure the new product's continued availability.

FLAME RETARDANT INDUSTRY SITUATION

Marketing

The flame retardant industry was a specialty chemicals business which sold a performance characteristic rather than a chemical product. Sales of products for flame retardant purposes to the polymers industry in the United States in 1986 were on the order of $850 million, with an industry growth rate in excess of 15 percent. Pricing levels ranged from a low of $.15 per pound in aluminum trihydrate to specialty fluoropolymers costing $15 to $20 per pound. Halogen flame retardants (chlorine or bromine based) were typical in the wire/cable markets, and were priced in the $2.25–$2.75 per pound range. Synergist (e.g., antimony oxide) cost around $1.90 (see Exhibit A–4). Operating profit in the flame retardant specialty additives business was high, typically running 20–40 percent on sales.

A key point to understand, however, was that there was no universal flame retardant for all polymer systems. Each flame retardant system had performance advantages and disadvantages in any particular polymer system. For example, halogenated systems (bromine or chlorine in combination with antimony oxide as a synergist) had been the primary flame retardant systems in polypropylene, polyethylene, and nylon in the United States due to their ability to withstand the high processing temperatures required. Phosphorus systems had served a similar market in Europe along with bromine and chlorine. Aluminum trihydrate had been used primarily in carpet backing and some wire/cable applications due to its low cost relative to halogens and its acceptable performance characteristics. Opportunity in the flame retardant industry depended on the performance of the given technology in a particular application.

EXHIBIT A–4   Flame Retardant Product Pricing, 1986

Type	$/Lb.
Flourine compounds	15.00—20.00
Chlorine/bromine compounds	.50— 3.05
Phosphorus compounds	1.10— 1.80
Antimony	1.50— 1.90
Aluminum trihydrate	.10— .30

Source: Interviews with industry experts.

Key Marketing Trends

There were currently three trends which were radically changing the character of the industry and redefining the opportunities available to the participants. These were:

- Increasing politicization.
- Industry consolidation.
- Technological change.

There was *increasing politicization* of the regulatory standards in which the flame retardants industry must function. Toxic gas and smoke emissions in a fire environment were becoming critical to the nontechnical community due to the rather spectacularly publicized deaths in recent hotel fires. The fire at the MGM Grand Hotel in Las Vegas, Nevada, in 1981, and the DuPont Hotel fire in Puerto Rico in 1986 were particularly vivid examples of publicized horror. The public was demanding a "safe" fire environment, and was demanding that technology provide a solution. Some flame retardant systems would probably be regulated out of existence, not on the scientific merits of their products, but on the political issues at hand. Primarily at risk were some brominated products which were also under attack in Germany as dioxin creators. All halogen-based systems were at risk due to their high smoke levels and their evolution of acid gasses.

The second major trend was that of recent industry consolidation. Major players were consolidating their strengths.

Finally, the issue of market obsolescence due to technological change would have a profound effect on certain market segments. Ten years ago, Occidental Chemical had sold several million pounds of their product, Dechlorane® Plus to the polypropylene market. In 1987, less than one tenth of that amount was sold in that segment. This was due to new polymers being used in the previous applications and to engineering redesigns to remove the need of flame retardancy altogether. A similar situation was occurring in carpet backing, as major carpet manufacturers were conducting research and development to make the carpet fiber itself flame retardant.

Technology

Technology, brought to play in the marketplace, was considered by most industry experts to be the single most important factor of success in the flame retardant business. New regulations for smoke and toxic gas emissions required technological improvements in existing products. The acid gasses (HCl, HBr) that developed during a fire not only posed a threat to lives, but could do considerable damage to expensive electronic equipment. When a New York city telephone switching station burned, over $50 million of equipment was destroyed, not by flames, but by the acid gasses released in the fire. Also, because halogens acted primarily in the vapor phase, large amounts of smoke were generated, hampering escape from the fire. For these two primary reasons, regulators and consumers were driving the flame retardant industry away from halogen systems. Aluminum trihydrate was the main beneficiary of this effect, as its primary mechanism was that of a heat sink in the early stage, and later decomposing into innocuous water vapor.

New polymers were constantly being brought to market, replacing other construction materials (wood, metal), as well as other polymers. With these new polymers came increasing challenges for flame retardancy. Some of these challenges were higher processing temperatures, polymer and copolymer compatibility, and smaller particle size for thinner sections.

The flame retardant companies were addressing these technology issues with significant research programs in surface modifications and coating, fine particle grinding technology, encapsulation techniques, concentrates, and chemical/matrix modifications. Industry associations such as the Fire Retardant Chemical Association (FRCA) and the Society of Plastics Industry (SPI), as well as groups of individual producers, were addressing the questions of regulation and toxicity.

Manufacturing

Manufacturing plants for fire retardant chemicals tended to be small (annual capacities of 10–50 million pounds) and flexible. Several products were made using the same equipment. Their $5–$20 million capital cost was considered low by chemical industry standards. The plants often required specialized equipment, and production was usually campaigned, resulting in significant inventory levels. In campaigned production, plants made up to about a six months' supply of a specific chemical before changing the equipment over to make a different chemical. This allowed the plant to take advantage of long production runs and reduced the set-up cost and the cost of the extensive cleaning of the equipment that was necessary to avoid cross-contamination. A plant's location was usually not a factor in competition because transportation costs, even from overseas, were small relative to value added. For example, Occidental's Dechlorane® Plus sold for approximately $2.60 per pound. Transportation, duty, and handling costs to most parts of the world rarely exceeded $.05 per pound. Product quality and consistency, however, were critical. Raw materials tended to be a small part of the overall cost of the products (15–25 percent). While a strong raw materials base might be a competitive advantage, it was not a requirement for success.

Other Key Points

Several other key points must be made in order to understand the industry situation. First, the flame retardants business was a *worldwide business*, both in terms of markets and producers. Companies based in West Germany, Israel, and Japan had established strong marketing presences in the United States, just as U.S. companies have done overseas. Applications technology was the name of the game, and technology transfers were rapid and efficient.

Second, while the industry was large in dollar terms, it was a *very small industry* in people and organizational terms. Everyone in the industry knew everyone else, what they were doing, and with whom they were doing it. There were very few secrets for very long. This required that market participants have strong leadership, with clearly defined plans and objectives, as execution of plans had to be clean and sure. False starts or hesitation in execution could cause the loss of an opportunity or of a competitive position.

Finally, the *rapid change* of the rules by which the industry had lived for the last 30 years, had thrown the industry into confusion. Managers who were used to dealing with technical performance issues were somewhat at a loss in dealing with political regulatory bodies. Newer managers seemed to face these issues more effectively. However, industry management was currently in a generational transition and remained for the most part ill equipped to deal in this new arena. Thus, companies that could deal with the public policy makers had an opportunity to influence regulation in the direction most beneficial to their products and technologies.

Case 2–6   *Kmart Stores**

INTRODUCTION

The S.S. Kresge Company opened hundreds of Kmart stores throughout the United States after its first store opened for business in the early 1960s. The company maintained a practice of keeping the stores very uniform in layout and appearances throughout most of this period. Each store was a simple box-like building usually located as freestanding away from shopping malls. Kmart stores sold low to medium quality merchandise that was priced lower than its competitors. This approach proved to be very successful, especially among price conscious shoppers who left full service department stores to shop at Kmart and other discounters. The Kmart logo itself became a symbol of low prices in the minds of many shoppers.

In the dynamic 1980s, important changes were taking place in the retail industry. Younger shoppers had become more discriminating than their parents and many had a greater amount of disposable income to spend. These younger shoppers wanted higher quality mer-

---

* This case was written by John L. Little, Assistant Professor of Strategic Management at the University of North Carolina at Greensboro, and Larry D. Alexander, Associate Professor of Strategic Management at Virginia Polytechnic Institute and State University. Copyright © 1988 by John L. Little and Larry D. Alexander.

chandise and they were willing to pay for it. While Kmart stuck with its traditional approach, other retailers had moved in to satisfy this new consumer group. In the process, these competitors created a retail environment that had never been more competitive. Furthermore, the successful market penetration of warehouse clubs and specialty stores into the retailing industry meant even more intense competition for discount stores such as Kmart.

How Kmart should respond to these and other issues remained unclear. One thing did seem certain. Unless Kmart made changes to remain aligned with a changing retail environment, its future financial performance would probably decline.

HISTORY

The S.S. Kresge Company was founded in 1899 with the opening of a single store in downtown Detroit, Michigan. Its founder, Sebastian Kresge, who followed a slogan of "Nothing over ten cents," rapidly opened more stores in new locations. He standardized the mix of merchandise, continued to emphasize low prices, and centralized the purchasing function. This latter move greatly increased the bargaining power that Kresge had over suppliers while at the same time reducing administrative overhead. This made the opening of new stores easier by spreading startup costs over a wider base. Kresge soon developed operating procedures that permitted centralized control over a growing number of uniform stores. The lower prices charged by Kresge caused individual store volume to increase and profits to rise, which provided the necessary funds to open still more stores. When the company was incorporated in 1912, Kresge's "five and ten" style stores numbered 85 and had a combined annual sales of more than $10 million.

Variety stores, which carried a variety of inexpensive kitchen, stationery, toy, soft-good items, and hard goods, grew in popularity throughout the 1920s and 1930s as a more convenient means of shopping than the earlier established specialty stores. A number of variety store chains had been established by 1940, with their limited selection of a wider array of product lines. The greater buying power available to these chain stores allowed them to underprice the specialty stores that concentrated in just one product line. The combination of lower prices and a wider selection of different product categories was a powerful attraction to customers. Furthermore, since more and more shoppers had their own cars, they were willing to travel further from home to save money.

During the 1950s, the introduction of shopping centers and supermarkets began to draw customers away from variety stores. To counter this, some variety retailers began looking for new ways to attract customers. In 1954, for example, Marty Chase converted an old mill in Cumberland, Rhode Island, into a discount store named Ann and Hope. The store sold ribbon, greeting cards, and women's clothing. As other discount stores opened throughout the 1950s, then Kresge President, Harry Cunningham, began to consider a similar approach. Finally, in 1962, Kresge responded by opening its first Kmart discount store in Garden City, Michigan.

Kmart discount stores were nothing more than a large scale version of the earlier Kresge retail stores. They still emphasized low prices, a wide selection, and low overhead costs which combined to create profits. The first Kmart stores were stocked primarily with Kresge merchandise. A number of licensees, who operated departments within the store, added their merchandise to the selection. Later, licensee merchandise was replaced entirely with Kmart's own merchandise. The initial stores were a great success, and by 1966, they numbered 162 with a combined sales of over $1 billion.

The Kmart success formula remained relatively unchanged for many years. Many new stores were added each year, sometimes by the hundreds. Almost all of them were uniform, freestanding stores located away from large shopping centers. By erecting simple, freestanding buildings in suburban areas, Kmart opened its stores more quickly than competitors, who had to wait for shopping centers to be completed. This also helped to keep overhead costs down since its freestanding stores were not located in expensive shopping malls, where rent was high. Over time, Kmart stores became located in almost all major U.S. metropolitan areas. During the 1960s and 1970s, annual sales grew by an average of 20 percent per year, primarily due to the fact that consumers found Kmart's blend of low price and wide selection very attractive. The company's smaller Kresge stores, unlike its Kmart stores, were not as profitable and many were closed during this period.

By 1976, the Kresge Company had become the second largest general merchandise retailer in the United States, behind only Sears. During the next year, the corporate name was changed from the Kresge Company to the Kmart Corporation because Kmart stores accounted for 94.5 percent of all corporate sales.

By the late 70s, several problems were impacting on Kmart. Good locations for new Kmart stores were becoming more difficult to find. Other discount chains were drawing some Kmart shoppers away. Industry surveys indicated that the needs of the customers were changing. While other discounters started upgrading their stores and started emphasizing brand name merchandise, Kmart continued to sell primarily low-priced Kmart private label and generic goods in their same austere-looking stores. Furthermore, during these same years, Kmart sales growth started to flatten.

In 1980, Bernard Fauber was named Kmart's new chief executive officer. He replaced an unusual arrangement in which three men shared the office of the president. Fauber quickly moved to refurbish its dated Kmart stores, and to upgrade the quality of goods which it carried. New display racks, better point of purchase displays, and improved traffic flow through the stores helped to make Kmart stores more attractive to customers.

FUNCTIONAL AREA STRATEGIES WITHIN THE KMART STORES

Marketing

Early on, Kmart stores emphasized low prices as an important marketing weapon. Its low prices often meant that the product being offered was of a lower quality. For hard goods such as kitchen appliances, this usually meant that just the basic product was carried, without the extra features that competing retailers' higher priced models offered.

Kmart focused on satisfying the needs of low- and middle-income families with limited budgets. Customers in this market segment were unwilling to pay higher prices for similar products with extra features. Still, it was estimated in the 1980s that 80 percent of all Americans shopped at Kmart at least once during a calendar year.

The sales promotion of Kmart's products was accomplished in several ways. First, sales promotion was emphasized by more attractive in-store, point of purchase displays. Second, Kmart's well known "blue light specials" were used to promote specific products for short periods of time during the day. Third, its products were promoted in numerous newspaper ads.

Kmart relied heavily on newspaper advertising to promote its goods. Newspaper inserts were designed at corporate headquarters and sent to newspapers throughout the country for publication. Advertising copy was sent to store managers in advance so they could prepare for the sales. The company placed approximately 120 million inserts in 1,700 different newspapers each week throughout the United States by the mid-1980s. While the company continued to emphasize newspapers, increased attention was being given to television advertising. This advertising only became relatively economical once Kmart had opened thousands of stores across the nation.

With its high level of market penetration, Kmart initiated a new effort to get customers to buy more goods per trip. Management felt this would be possible because disposable family income of many Kmart customers was rising. This rise in family income was partially the result of a significant increase in the number of two-income families. Kmart estimated that 19 percent of its customers were from households with annual incomes of at least $40,000; however, this customer group typically bought only low-priced items such as tennis balls, batteries, and shampoo at Kmart.

Kmart added more national brand merchandise and higher quality private labels, and then displayed them in a more attractive manner. Brand name products such as Casio, Minolta, Nike, MacGregor, Wilson, and General Electric were increasingly found throughout the store. Kmart hoped that this action would help attract higher income customers to other product areas and increase their per sale purchases. At the same time, the company hoped to retain its less affluent customers by continuing to offer an assortment of lower priced, lower quality merchandise.

Kmart did extremely well in certain departments, but performed weakly in others. It was the leader in housewares and the second largest appliance retailer behind only Sears. Many customers were attracted to its brand name appliances and housewares by Kmart's low prices. These same customers, however, were turned off by Kmart's cheap clothing, which had a low image among many consumers. Its apparel departments, in fact, had been a major shortcoming for Kmart throughout the years. Kmart tried to address this problem by upgrading many lines of clothing. Furthermore, the responsibility for ordering apparel was taken away from store managers and given to professional staff buyers at corporate headquarters, who were more knowledgeable about fashion.

Kmart had also moved into specialty discount stores through several acquisitions. The first Designer Depot, which was a discount price specialty apparel store, was started in Detroit during 1982. These stores sold quality brand-name merchandise at discounts of 20 percent to 70 percent. Some stores also sold shoes, while others sold bedroom and bathroom soft goods.

The company also acquired several other impressive specialty chains. Waldenbook Company, Inc., another Kmart acquisition in 1985, operated 943 stores in all 50 states. Builders Square, Inc., a warehouse type home improvement center chain, was acquired in 1984. By 1985, the company had 25 stores located in eight states. Fredrick Stevens, executive vice president of specialty retailing operations, argued that 400 locations across the country could support the volume requirements of these huge discount builders' supply warehouses. Builders Square was hoping to capture a 25 percent share of that market.[1]

---

[1] "Kmart: A Look inside the Nation's Largest Discounter," *Mass Market Retailers*, December 16, 1985, p. 42.

Pay Less Drug Stores Northwest, another Kmart acquisition in 1985, was the 10th largest drug chain in the nation. Pay Less was a discount chain, supported by a very cost efficient operation, and strong management. With sales approaching $1 billion and 176 stores, the chain hoped to penetrate rapidly in its present markets in California, Oregon, Washington, Idaho, and Nevada.

Two final Kmart acquisitions were in the restaurant industry. Furr's Cafeterias, acquired earlier in 1980, and Bishop Buffets, acquired in 1983, had a total of 162 units by 1985. Due to slow growth in the cafeteria industry, however, future growth for new cafeterias in this acquisition was expected to be limited to 10 percent per year.

Kmart Corporation had limited involvement in overseas markets. It did have, however, a 20 percent interest in G.L. Coles and Coy Limited, a food and general merchandise retailer in Australia. It also had a 44 percent interest in Astra, S.A., which operated a food and general merchandise chain in Mexico.

Store Operations

During the 1980s, Kmart was approaching market saturation, with its stores located almost everywhere throughout 48 states. Its 2,332 stores by the end of 1985 were located in 250 of this country's 255 Standard Metropolitan Statistical Areas (SMSA). From a record 271 new stores opening in 1976, only 18 new Kmart stores were opened in 1985.

Because of market saturation, Kmart switched its emphasis from opening new stores to renovating existing ones. This effort, which started in the early 1980s, was intended to increase productivity as well as to upgrade the store image. Wider and taller display cases carried more merchandise and made better use of cubic space. This allowed for a wider assortment of merchandise to be displayed within the same square footage. It also reduced the need for additional back-room storage. A new store layout was developed around a wide center aisle which let consumers walk through every department without leaving the aisle. As one Kmart store manager put it, "We want to encourage people to go into areas where they would not normally go . . . to pass by merchandise they were not planning to buy!"[2]

All Kmart stores were designed around the same basic floor plan, as shown in Exhibit 1. As shoppers entered the store, they were no longer confronted with the smell of popcorn and the sight of gumball machines. Instead, they might be greeted by the jewelry department with a wide selection of watches and jewelry of various price ranges. The

---

[2] Ibid., p. 20

EXHIBIT 1   Typical Kmart Store Floor Layout

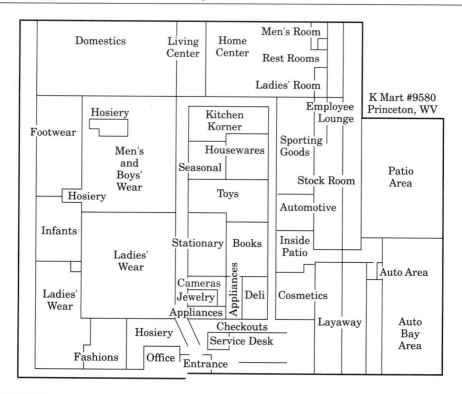

Source: Kmart pamphlet, 1985.

main aisle down the center of the store separated soft goods from hard goods. Located on the soft goods side of the store were women's apparel, then men's apparel, with infants' wear, and children's clothes nearby. Popular crafts and yarn were also located on this side, where homemakers were most likely to look for them. In the hard goods half of the store, housewares, sporting goods, automotive supplies, and hardware were located at the rear of the store, drawing men and women past the high impulse, high margin merchandise in the greeting cards, jewelry, and toy departments. The health and beauty items and the pharmacies, for the minority of stores that had them, were typically located in the right front section of the store.

Electronic communications systems connected all stores to 10 enormous regional distribution centers. These centers were located in California, Nevada, Texas, Kansas, Minnesota, Michigan, Indiana, Ohio, Pennsylvania, and Georgia, as shown in Exhibit 2. These highly automated distribution centers contained a combined 15 million square feet of warehouse space. Together, they operated a fleet of 250 tractors and 1,000 trailers, which provided weekly delivery to every Kmart store requesting it.

Approximately 25 percent of Kmart's merchandise was handled by these distribution centers. In contrast, 75 percent of all store purchases were shipped directly from suppliers to the stores in order to minimize shipping cost. The delivery of products from suppliers was usually fast in order to keep such a large account as Kmart satisfied. This reduced inventory level requirements at stores to minimum levels. A significant reduction in reorder time had been achieved by installing optical scanners on cash registers at Kmart stores. Scanning, coupled with a company-wide computer network, permitted automated replenishment of merchandise, and made it possible to differentiate the seasonal needs of each region.

As part of its efforts to upgrade its image, Kmart was completing a major remodeling program of store interiors to present a more modern store appearance to shoppers. This new effort, called "The Kmart of the

EXHIBIT 2   Store Distribution Network

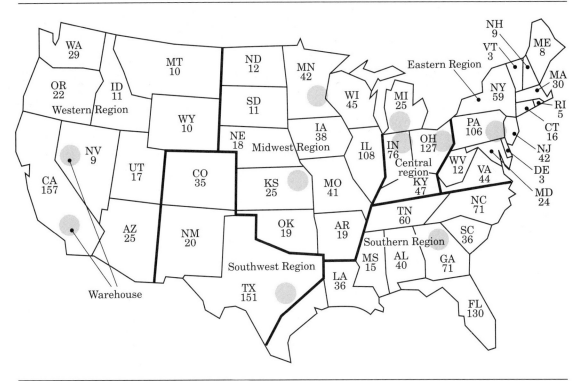

Source: *Mass Market Retailers*, December 16, 1985, p. 42.

Eighties," incorporated a new color scheme on interior walls and floors, broader aisles, and more attractive displays. Low-volume lines were dropped or consolidated to achieve a store within a store format. The Kitchen Corner, Home Care Center, and Domestic Center were arranged along the back wall and emphasized fashion and style at discount prices. The early success of the plan was encouraging. Sales per square foot had risen from $139 in 1980 to $168 four years later. While this was superior to the $128 per square foot typical among discounter department stores, it was far behind such discounters as Target and Wal-Mart.

Product categories no longer in demand were eliminated. For example, Kmart's 360 automotive service departments in rural stores were closed in 1982. Unprofitable stores were closed altogether, freeing up more than $1 million each in capital for use elsewhere in the corporation.

The more than 2,000 Kmart stores were organized into six regions, each of which had from 266 to 422 stores. Each region was comprised of about 20 districts, while each district had from 10 to 20 stores.

Kmart stores came in five basic sizes. The smallest was the 40,000-square-foot-size store, which was placed in smaller markets. At the other end, the jumbo 120,000-square-foot store was placed in large metropolitan markets. These freestanding stores were located in suburban areas with large parking lots, and were usually leased rather than owned. Buildings usually were erected by local contractors, but a Kmart subsidiary built several stores each year to allow the company to remain knowledgeable about building costs and procedures.

Kmart's decision to avoid shopping center locations was part of its low overhead philosophy. Leasing costs at shopping centers were very high compared to Kmart locations. Shopping centers generally did not want discounters as tenants anyway, due to the negative image associated with them. Also, specialty stores did not want to locate next to a discount store because of the significant price difference between their products and a discounter's. Sometimes, Kmart would buy existing buildings in shopping centers or develop properties in good locations and sublease retail space to specialty stores.

FINANCE

Total sales for the Kmart Corporation, as shown in its consolidated statement of income in Exhibit 3, were $22.4 billion for fiscal year 1985, which ended on January 29, 1986. This represented a 6.3 percent increase over the sales for the previous year. Net income after taxes for that same year was $221.0 million. The consolidated balance sheet for fiscal 1985 and 1984 is shown in Exhibit 4. Finally, a comparison of

EXHIBIT 3

Kmart Corporation
Consolidated Statements of Income
(millions, except per-share data)

	Fiscal Year Ended		
	January 29, 1986	*January 30, 1985*	*January 25, 1984*
Sales	$22,420	$21,096	$18,598
Licensee fees and rental income	225	207	191
Equity in income of affiliated retail companies	76	65	57
Interest income	24	40	38
	22,745	21,408	18,884
Cost of merchandise sold (including buying and occupancy costs)	16,181	15,260	13,447
Selling, general and administrative expenses	4,845	4,428	3,880
Advertising	567	554	425
Interest expense:			
Debt	205	147	84
Capital lease obligations	191	193	189
	21,989	20,582	18,025
Income from continuing retail operations before income taxes	756	826	859
Income taxes	285	327	366
Income from continuing retail operations	471	499	493
Discontinued operations	(250)	—	(1)
Net income for the year	$ 221	$ 499	$ 492
Earnings per common and common equivalent share:			
Continuing retail operations	$3.63	$3.84	$3.81
Discontinued operations	(1.90)	—	(.01)
Net income	$1.73	$3.84	$3.80

Source: Kmart Corporation, *1985 Annual Report*, p. 30.

EXHIBIT 4

Kmart Corporation
Consolidated Balance Sheets
(millions)

	January 29, 1986	January 30, 1985
Assets		
Current Assets:		
Cash (includes temporary investments of $352 and $294, respectively)	$ 627	$ 492
Merchandise inventories	4,537	4,588
Accounts receivable and other current assets	363	231
Total current assets	5,527	5,311
Investments in affiliated retail companies	293	188
Property and equipment—net	3,644	3,339
Other assets and deferred charges	527	220
Investments in discontinued operations	—	204
Total assets	$9,991	$9,262
Liabilities and Shareholders' Equity		
Current Liabilities:		
Long-term debt due within one year	$ 15	$ 2
Capital lease obligations due within one year	76	74
Notes payable	127	235
Accounts payable—trade	1,908	1,917
Accrued payrolls and other liabilities	548	362
Taxes other than income taxes	218	200
Income taxes	198	99
Total current liabilities	3,090	2,889
Capital lease obligations	1,713	1,780
Long-term debt	1,456	1,107
Other long-term liabilities	345	163
Deferred income taxes	114	89
Shareholders' equity	3,273	3,234
Total liabilities and shareholders equity	$9,991	$9,262

Source: Kmart Corporation, *1985 Annual Report*, p. 31.

sales and various financial data for Kmart over a 10-year period are presented in Exhibit 5.

Retail sales at Kmart were extremely seasonal with a high proportion of sales and profits coming during the Christmas shopping season. For example, some 33 percent of Kmart's 1984 sales and 41 percent of its profits came during the fourth quarter alone.

EXHIBIT 5 Kmart Corporation—10-Year Financial Summary

	1984	1983	1982	1981	1980	1979	1978	1977	1976	1975
Summary of operations (millions)										
Sales	$21,096	$18,598	$16,772	$16,527	$14,204	$12,731	$11,696	$9,941	$8,382	$6,798
Cost of merchandise sold	$15,260	$13,447	$12,299	$12,360	$10,417	$9,283	$8,566	$7,299	$6,147	$4,991
Selling, general and administrative expenses	$4,982	$4,305	$4,049	$3,810	$3,326	$2,839	$2,503	$2,085	$1,750	$1,409
Interest expense—net	$300	$235	$219	$230	$200	$149	$132	$116	$103	$89
Income before income taxes	$820	$854	$419	$323	$436	$625	$634	$564	$484	$395
Net income	$499	$492	$262	$220	$261	$358	$344	$298	$262	$196
Per-share data (dollars)										
Earnings per common and common equivalent share	$3.84	$3.80	$2.06	$1.75	$2.07	$2.84	$2.74	$2.39	$2.11	$1.61
Cash dividends declared	$1.24	$1.08	$1.00	$.96	$.92	$.84	$.72	$.56	$.32	$.24
Book value	$25.87	$23.35	$20.89	$19.81	$18.99	$17.79	$15.68	$13.56	$-1.62	$9.69
Financial data (millions)										
Working capital	$2,422	$2,268	$1,827	$1,473	$1,552	$1,403	$1,308	$1,231	$1,074	$904
Total assets	$9,262	$8,183	$7,344	$6,657	$6,089	$5,635	$4,836	$4,489	$3,983	$3,336
Long-term obligations—Debt	$1,107	$711	$596	$415	$419	$209	$209	$211	$211	$210
—Capital leases	$1,780	$1,822	$1,824	$1,752	$1,618	$1,422	$1,294	$1,266	$1,155	$989
Shareholders' equity	$3,234	$2,940	$2,601	$2,456	$2,343	$2,185	$1,916	$1,649	$1,409	$1,169
Capital expenditures-owned property	$622	$368	$306	$361	$302	$292	$217	$162	$123	$112
Depreciation and amortization-owned property	$203	$168	$157	$141	$119	$93	$77	$65	$56	$52
Average shares outstanding	126	125	124	124	123	123	122	122	121	121

Source: Kmart Corporation, *1984 Annual Report*, pp. 16, 17.

Kmart did not offer a charge card and did not encourage credit sales. By comparison, approximately 58 percent of arch rival Sears' sales were on credit. MasterCard and VISA credit cards were accepted at Kmart and limited in-house credit was provided on appliance sales. Many Kmart stores required customers to follow a rigid two-step procedure for writing checks. The customer first had to get approval from the service desk, and then wait at a checkout line to pay for the purchased items.

Kmart's policy for granting exchanges or refunds, on merchandise which did not satisfy the customer, was quite liberal. Most items could be returned for cash by customers without a hassle. This policy was inherited from the old Kresge variety stores. Similarly, Kmart customers could get a rain check on any advertised item not found in stock at the time of the sale.

INNOVATION

The Kmart approach to innovation was to adopt new ideas only after they had been developed and proven successful by someone else. This approach avoided risk and had served Kmart well throughout the years. Once a good idea was identified, however, Kmart showed its genius in applying and perfecting it. For example, when the discount store idea emerged, Kresge was the first to refine the concept with its Kmart stores. Kmart pursued rapid expansion while other retailers looked on with amazement. The idea of standardizing the store floor plan and layout was another example of how Kmart borrowed a good idea from elsewhere and perfected it.

HUMAN RESOURCES/PERSONNEL

Kmart Corporation employed more than 290,000 people in 1985, but tried to encourage a small business feeling within its individual stores. Loyalty among store managers was unusually high; consequently, their turnover rate was low. Many Kmart managers had never worked for any other employer, and 25-year-service pins were common. Furthermore, promotion to managerial positions was almost entirely done from within. For those selected, management training consisted of a 16-week program on all phases of a Kmart store's operation. After the program, the trainees became assistant managers with responsibility for several departments. Typically, trainees were rotated through various departments and stores for 6 to 10 years before they were ready to manage their own stores.

The opportunity for promotion was strong in the 1970s when new stores were being opened at the rate of several per week. That changed in the 1980s when Kmart greatly curtailed its new store openings. This threatened to increase employee turnover as assistant managers became impatient to move up. At the same time, Kmart was reducing the number of assistant managers from three to two per store in order to cut administrative costs.

Kmart relied heavily on part-time employees to operate its stores. The company goal was to have 60 percent part-time and 40 percent full-time employees within each store. This gave the store manager greater flexibility in matching the work force with the amount of traffic during different periods of the day. Also, the labor costs for part-time employees were considerably lower because they started at minimum wage and were not paid benefits. The great majority of these employees were women who preferred to work part-time because of their family obligations. The company, however, did have an employee savings plan even for part-timers in which Kmart contributed 50 cents in Kmart stock for every one dollar that the employee contributed.

MANAGEMENT

Harry Cunningham developed the basic Kmart strategy and led the company during its rapid growth from 1962 to 1972. When he stepped down in 1972, he appointed Kmart's Robert Dewar, Ervin Wardlow, and Walter Tennga to collectively run the company. Dewar, with 32 years of legal and financial background but no store experience, was named chairman. Wardlow, with strong merchandising experience, was named president. Finally, Tennga, a real estate and financial executive, was named vice chairman. These three executives ran the company for eight years. Although sales tripled during this period, the three could not agree on which direction Kmart should take.

In 1980, Bernard Fauber was named the new chief executive officer at the suggestion of Dewar, who felt that Kmart needed a store man at the top, rather than a staff man. Since then, Kmart has made dramatic changes in its approach to business. As Fauber conceded:

> For 20 years we had been just about the most successful retailer in America, so it was not easy getting our people to admit that some changes were advisable and others were necessary.[3]

In explaining the reasons behind Kmart's decision to diversify into other areas, Fauber added:

---

[3] Ibid., p. 54.

We realized that we must do something else for growth since it was no longer possible to open 100 to 120 Kmart stores each year.[4]

Fauber, like all but one previous CEO, was not a college graduate. He first came to work for the company in 1941 as an 18-year-old stockroom boy in a Kresge store. Nine years later, he joined the management training program. Later he gained experience as a store manager and district manager, and in 1968 became vice president of the Western Region. Like nearly all Kmart executives, Fauber had never worked for any other company.

Kmart's philosophy was to train their store managers as generalists, then allow them wide discretion in running their stores. They had an incentive plan based on store profits to avoid the mistake Sears made in the 1970s when it tied its department managers' incentive plan to sales volume. The Sears incentive system, which has since been changed, caused its managers to focus on low-margin merchandise which boosted sales and their bonuses, but which hurt profits.

Store managers at Kmart were encouraged to involve themselves and the store in community activities, such as the United Way. One socially responsible effort Kmart undertook was its "Lost Child Program" in 1985. The prime exposure available nationwide at its stores made Kmart a good vehicle for the program and enhanced the corporate image.

THE RETAIL INDUSTRY

Market Segments

The retail industry was divided into several general segments which somewhat overlapped one another. There were full-line department stores, discount department stores, discount drug stores, specialty stores, supermarkets, and convenience shops. Exhibit 6 shows the top 15 general merchandise chains for 1985, which include many of these store types. The trend towards one-stop shopping had blurred the distinctions among these various kinds of stores in recent years. For example, shoppers could find food items in drugstores and discount stores, and clothing and hardware in supermarkets. Within the discount department store category, the emerging warehouse stores were the fastest growing segment along with discount specialty stores.

---

[4] Ibid.

EXHIBIT 6   Top 15 General Merchandise Chains for 1985

Rank and Company	Net Sales ($000)	Net Income ($000)	Earnings per Share	Location of Headquarters
1. Sears Roebuck	$40,715,300	$1,303,300	$3.53	Chicago
2. Kmart	22,420,002	221,242	1.73	Troy, Mich.
3. J. C. Penney	13,747,000	397,000	5.31	New York
4. Federated Department Stores	9,978,027	286,626	5.88	Cincinnati
5. Dayton Hudson	8,793,372	283,620	2.92	Minneapolis
6. Wal-Mart Stores	8,580,910	327,473	1.16	Bentonville, Ark.
7. F. W. Woolworth	5,958,000	177,000	5.50	New York
8. BATUS	5,881,408	163,532	—	Louisville
9. Montgomery Ward	5,388,000	(298,000)	—	Chicago
10. May Department Stores	5,079,900	235,400	5.38	St. Louis
11. Melville	4,805,380	210,812	3.90	Harrison, N.Y.
12. Associated Dry Goods	4,385,019	119,696	3.00	New York City
13. R. H. Macy	4,368,386	189,315	3.69	New York City
14. Wickes Companies	4,362,454	76,130	0.47	Santa Monica, Calif.
15. Allied Stores	4,135,027	159,275	3.70	New York City

Source: "The 50 Largest Retailing Companies," *Fortune*, June 9, 1986, pp. 136–37.

External Threats

By the mid-1980s, the retail environment was extremely competitive. Retailers were also being squeezed by two powerful factors. One factor was slower growth in customer demand for general merchandise in recent years. Industry forecasts suggested a continuing trend in this direction with a declining proportion of disposable income being spent on general merchandise in coming years. The other factor was the excess number of stores that existed in the industry. These two realities along with several others were making retail merchants somewhat worried about the future.

The decline in the teenage population had decreased per capita spending on apparel. Apparel chains, which had expanded so rapidly in the 1960s and 1970s to capitalize on the lucrative teenage market, were now facing an older customer base with less interest in fashion. As Americans grew older, their spending patterns were shifting toward health and leisure services and away from general merchandise.

Another source of trouble for retailers was the extremely high level of consumer credit in the mid 1980s. Some industry observers feared this would lead to a decline in consumer spending and increased woes for retailers. Part of this was due to the catch-up spending that people did for consumer durables after the 1981–1983 recession.

Competition

A recent challenge within the retail industry was wholesale clubs and specialty stores. They were at opposite ends of the retailing spectrum. Still, both of these store types were very profitable, and they were making it harder for stores in the middle.

The wholesale club concept was first introduced in 1976 by Sal and Robert E. Price with their first Price Club in San Diego. For a $25 membership fee, small businessmen could buy such diverse goods as food, office supplies, and appliances at wholesale prices. This membership approach meant that the Price Club got an interest-free loan in advance and locked in the customer with switching costs if they decided to move to another such club. By stocking 4,000 high-moving items, as compared to 60,000 items found in typical discount stores, Price Club stores turned over their inventory 15 times a year, compared to just 5 times for a full-line discount store. The Price Club had grown to 25 stores, and the concept was being copied by other retailers.

Specialty stores enjoyed strong growth in the early 1980s. A number of large retailers had established chains of small stores specializing in single product lines like shoes, women's apparel, and books. Woolworth had found success in stationery supplies with Harold's Square, Lucky Stores with its Minnesota Fabrics, and Allied Stores with its Catherine's Stout Shoppes. The attraction of such stores was the greater depth of choice in a specific line for which many consumers were willing to pay extra.

Between the wholesale clubs and the specialty stores were full-line department stores. This was where the primary battle within the retailing industry was taking place. The saturation of the market with these one-stop shopping stores had caused many changes. For example, both Sears and J. C. Penney had curtailed most new store openings. Instead, they both were moving to upgrade their existing stores with higher quality, higher priced merchandise. Both sought to establish a fashion image to differentiate themselves from the discount chains.

Sears

Kmart's greatest competition came from Sears Roebuck & Co., the world's largest retailer with its 435 full-line departments stores, 397 medium-sized department stores, and 1,971 catalog sales offices. Sears stores generated sales of $21.5 billion in 1985, which rose to a staggering $40.7 billion when all other Sears strategic business units were included. For its full-line department stores, Sears' breadth in departments was unsurpassed by any competitor.

During the 1970s, Sears first moved to higher priced, more stylish merchandise. This confused many customers who preferred to go to discounters for lower prices and specialty shops for greater product line depth. Under CEO Edward Telling, who took office in 1978, the company made drastic changes. Twenty percent of its work force was cut, 200 stores were closed, and the remaining stores renovated. Many Sears clothing labels were replaced by fashion labels associated with such names as Arnold Palmer, Joe Namath, and Cheryl Tiegs.

With its move into financial services, Sears envisioned the day when a customer could walk into a Sears store and buy a house through its Coldwell Banker realty division, insure it through its Allstate Insurance division, and furnish it before he or she left. Sears' charge card was already held by 58 percent of Americans. Visa cards, on the other hand, were held by only 53 percent of all households. The opportunity existed for Sears to convert its ordinary credit accounts into savings and checking accounts. Furthermore, the deregulated banking environment of the 1980s made it possible to offer multiple financial services in retail stores, an option Sears seemed to be pursuing.

J. C. Penney

While Sears had its strength in hard goods, J. C. Penney Company, Inc., had a well-established reputation for quality in soft goods. The company got its initials J. and C. from G. Johnson and T. Callahan, who founded the firm back in 1902. During the 1960s, and 1970s, Penney's tried to move into hard goods to counter Sears' well established strength there. Penney's did this in several key instances by teaming up with well-known suppliers. For example, it formed an alliance with General Electric to sell its washers, dryers, refrigerators, stoves, etc., in its retail stores.

During 1985, when Penney's had total sales of approximately $13.7 billion, it made a retrenchment of sorts. It discontinued its auto accessories department, eliminated children's toys, and even discontinued selling many hard goods such as G.E. appliances. Instead, it renewed its commitment to emphasize soft goods in its 574 metropolitan market stores, 133 metropolitan market soft-line stores, and 696 geographic market stores in nonmetropolitan markets. With this move, the firm refocused its efforts on selling quality clothing to men, women, boys, girls, and infants. In addition to clothing, Penney's continued to emphasize its towels, sheets, etc., for which it was noted.

Discount Chains

In 1985, there were more than 8,700 general merchandise discount stores in the United States. Exhibit 7 gives a comparison of profitability and growth performance of the top discount, variety, and department store chains. The average discount store had 55,792 square feet of selling space, which had been rising in recent years. The average customer transaction was $12.35. The annual sales per square foot, as shown in Exhibit 8, varied from the $603 in the photography department of $132 in men's and boy's wear.

There were a number of regional chains within the discount segment of the retail industry. They included Mervyn's in the West, Target in the Midwest, Caldor in New England, and Richway in the Southeast. For the most part, they had done very well by differentiating themselves from Kmart. Some firms had accomplished this by appealing to the high end of the discount market. Other discounters sold department store quality merchandise at discount prices in attractive stores. As a result, they succeeded in attracting many affluent shoppers who would not normally shop at Kmart.

One of the most successful retailers in recent years was Wal-Mart, a discount chain headquartered in Bentonville, Arkansas. Much of its success was due to the location of its stores. Its 834 discount stores and 19 Sam's Warehouse Clubs were concentrated in small towns in the South and Midwest. By clustering up to 150 stores within several hours drive of a central warehouse and stocking only name brand merchandise, Wal-Mart consistently led the industry in return on investment.

SUPPLIERS

Retailers dealt with thousands of suppliers to stock the wide range of merchandise they carried. This was due in part to the fact that most retailers did not manufacture the merchandise they carried. The bargaining power of large retail chains in relation to their suppliers was great. Sears, J. C. Penney, Kmart, and others, were such large and welcome customers that suppliers often became overly dependent on them.

Each year, many new products were introduced by the major chains, replacing old products which were discontinued. Each supplier knew that their products were expected to generate targeted levels of sales. Those that didn't achieve these goals were dropped with little regard for the supplier. On occasion, suppliers were encouraged to increase production capacity only to find their product dropped a short time later on. Often, orders were cancelled at the last minute, leaving sup-

EXHIBIT 7 General Merchandise Retailers, 1985—Yardsticks of Management Performance

Company	% in —Segment— Sales/Profits	Profitability—Return on Equity			Debt as % of Equity	Net Profit Margin	Growth—Sales			Earnings per Share		
		Rank	5-Year Average	Latest 12 Months			Rank	5-Year Average	Latest 12 Months	Rank	5-Year Average	Latest 12 Months
Department stores:												
R. H. Macy	●/●	1	21.4%	16.3%	14.0%	4.3%	4	14.2%	7.5%	2	2.1%	−15.6%
Lucky Stores	25/13	2	19.2	17.5	61.3	1.1	12	9.5	6.5	12	−0.3	12.8
Dillard Dept. Stores	●/●	3	18.6	19.8	70.4	3.9	1	25.2	49.3	1	40.5	32.0
Mercantile Stores	●/●	4	16.3	15.0	28.0	5.0	7	10.9	6.8	4	17.5	4.2
May Dept. Stores	68/72	5	16.0	17.3	41.2	4.4	10	9.8	10.2	5	14.6	9.3
Federated Dept. Stores	67/89	6	14.6	13.1	27.9	3.3	8	10.8	8.0	10	3.5	11.0
Allied Stores	●/●	7	12.8	15.3	70.9	3.9	5	13.8	5.7	9	3.9	25.5
J. C. Penney	79/NA	8	12.7	10.1	54.7	2.9	13	3.0	2.3	8	13.3	−18.6
Strawbridge	●/●	9	12.5	16.0	125.8	3.7	6	11.5	12.5	3	20.1	16.6
Associated Dry Goods	61/73	10	11.8	12.2	33.8	2.8	2	19.6	9.5	6	13.6	−0.7
Carson Pirie Scott	50/45	11	10.8	13.4	104.2	2.0	3	19.6	23.2	11	4.2	132.5
Sears Roebuck	67/57	12	10.6	10.7	87.4	2.9	9	10.4	4.6	7	13.5	−19.9
Carter Hawley Hale	73/52	13	9.4	7.3	84.6	1.6	11	9.6	−2.0	13	−0.3	−50.0
Equitable of Iowa	41/2	14	7.0	4.3	9.2	2.6	14	2.7	4.9	14	−15.0	−10.2
Alexander's	●/●	15	1.4	7.4	87.0	1.0	15	1.9	0.5		NM	24.7
Medians			12.7	13.4	61.3	2.9		10.8	6.8		13.3	9.3
Discount and variety:												
Wal-Mart Stores	●/●	1	34.9	30.7	49.6	3.9	1	39.9	32.2	1	43.0	24.1
SCOA Industries	84/●	2	24.8	22.6	88.5	2.9	8	10.4	5.1	8	9.3	9.8
Ames Dept. Stores	●/●	3	23.1	19.7	60.6	3.1	2	20.1	30.8	5	23.5	19.4
Stop & Shop Cos	48/73	4	19.2	12.8	52.8	1.3	7	11.2	12.8	2	33.6	−26.9
Dayton-Hudson	71/73	5	16.8	16.1	43.2	3.3	4	19.0	12.2	9	9.1	10.3
Zayre	70/65	6	15.7	19.0	46.5	2.6	5	16.0	19.9	3	28.7	22.1
Rose's Stores	●/●	7	15.6	14.2	16.6	2.1	6	14.0	9.2	4	28.1	−13.9
Kmart	●/●	8	13.2	12.4	89.3	1.8	9	10.0	13.4	7	10.5	−23.2
Household International	26/8	9	12.0	13.6	236.0	2.6	10	9.1	5.3	10	4.7	−4.6
Associated Dry Goods	38/26	10	11.8	12.2	33.8	2.8	3	19.6	9.5	6	13.6	−0.7
Heck's	86/DD	11	9.3	def	89.3	def	11	2.0	6.5		NM	P-D
F. W. Woolworth	68/39	12	3.5	14.5	35.4	2.6	13	−5.6	3.2		NM	20.6
Cook United	●/DD	13	def	def	NE	def	12	−2.8	−47.7		NM	D-D
Medians			15.6	14.2	49.6	2.6		11.2	9.5		10.5	−0.7

Source: Industry Survey-Retailing, *Forbes*, January 13, 1986, p. 202.

EXHIBIT 8   Discount Store Sales by Category

Category	Volume ($ billions)	Sales per Store ($ millions)	Annual Sales per Sq. Ft.	Annual Turns	Initial Markup (%)	Gross Margin (%)
Women's apparel	$14.3	$1,763	$176	4.6	48.0%	37.2%
Men's and boys' wear	8.2	1,011	132	3.4	44.6	36.0
Housewares	6.3	777	135	3.2	41.1	30.2
Consumer electronics	5.9	728	316	3.2	31.4	19.4
Health and beauty aids	5.6	691	219	4.5	26.9	20.5
Automobile	5.2	641	279	2.8	34.9	28.7
Hardware	4.8	592	184	2.4	41.9	32.1
Toys	4.1	506	202	3.1	36.5	28.4
Sporting goods	3.8	469	187	2.0	36.9	26.9
Photo camera	3.3	407	603	3.2	24.5	16.6
Domestics	3.2	395	126	2.5	43.4	35.3
Personal care	2.9	358	421	3.3	30.4	20.0
Stationery	2.1	259	140	3.5	46.7	40.1
Paint	1.8	222	175	2.4	43.9	35.2
Electric housewares	1.7	210	238	3.4	33.2	21.4
Jewelry	1.4	166	290	1.8	49.9	37.7
Glassware	0.7	80	129	4.0	40.7	34.9

Source: *Standard & Poor's Industrial Survey*, July 4, 1985, p. 120.

pliers in a difficult position. At times, chain retailers would take merchandise on a consignment basis, paying for it only if sold, thus shifting the risk to the supplier. Payment to the suppliers was, at times, delayed by retailers in order to enhance cash flow and obtain free short-term financing.

Sears and Kmart were good examples of firms making sizeable use of private label merchandise. Often their private label products were made by a brand name manufacturer to similar or the exact same specifications as the brand label. The manufacture of private label products could then be contracted out to other manufacturers, giving a great deal of leverage to the retailer and reducing the bargaining power of suppliers.

In spite of such treatment by chain retailers, many suppliers were willing to take the risk and abuse. In return, they hoped to get enormous volume and nationwide distribution which high volume retailers could provide. In response to this one-sided relationship, a number of general merchandise manufacturers had broadened their product lines. By producing a wide variety of items, a supplier could reduce dependence on a single product and increase its bargaining power with the retailer.

BUYERS—THE NEW CONSUMERS

Several important demographic shifts were affecting retailers during the mid 1980s. Population shifts from the cities to the suburbs were reducing the sales volume of urban stores while helping suburban stores. Population shifts from older industrialized areas of the Northeast to the Sun Belt states had similar effects. The baby-boom teenagers of the 1960s were approaching middle age. Better educated than their parents, their perception of value, attitude towards quality merchandise, and response to promotional techniques were changing the way retailers did business.

Price still remained a key consideration, but quality and brand image had increased in importance. Many consumers were willing to trade dollars for time, as was proven by the demand for fast-food, microwave ovens, and other time-saving products and services.

While the number of households was growing rapidly, the population growth was slowing. This caused changes in the type of merchandise demanded, the way to market it effectively, and the price/quality trade-off. Health-related products, prescriptions, and leisure products were in greater demand reflecting the needs of older customers. At the same time, the market for baby food, toys, and children's clothing had declined.

Women were working in greater numbers than ever before. This contributed to the rise in discretionary income, and increased the demand for products needed by working women, such as clothes and cosmetics. A Kmart survey showed that the percentage of Kmart customers with household incomes from $25,000 to $40,000 had increased from 23.3 percent in 1980 to 28.1 percent in 1984.[5] Some 18.9 percent of Kmart's customers in 1984 came from households with incomes greater than $40,000 as compared to 8.3 percent in 1980. A profile of who shops at a Kmart, broken down by income, occupation, education, sex, and age is shown in Exhibit 9.

With more women working, men were doing retail shopping more than ever before. Men tended to be less value conscious and more likely to trust the advertising of national brands. The trend was clearly towards a more mature, affluent customer with a preference for value, quality, and fashion in merchandise.

KMART AND THE FUTURE

Sales at the average Kmart store were good, but there was tremendous room for improvement. Overall, Kmart's per store sales were about one third that of Sears stores. Kmart's appliances and housewares depart-

EXHIBIT 9   Demographics of Kmart Shoppers

	Percent of Kmart Shoppers
Occupation:	
Professional	12.5%
Technical	5.5
Manager	13.4
Clerical	4.5
Salesworker	6.4
Craftsman	11.7
Operative/kindred worker	9.8
Service worker	4.7
Laborer	3.1
Retired	20.7
Income:	
Over $20,000	38.7
Under $20,000	60.6
Education:	
High school or less	52.2
Some college or more	46.5
Sex:	
Male	46.6
Female	53.4
Age:	
Under 25	12.8
25–34	24.1
35–44	19.6
45–54	12.7
55–64	14.5
65+	15.3

Source: *Chain Store Age*, December 1984, p. 54.

ments were strong areas; however, its clothing and other soft goods, which took up almost half of the typical Kmart store, had low appeal to many customers. Clearly, Kmart needed to address its clothing dilemma, perhaps by reducing store space allocated for it or by improving the clothing being offered. Overall, Kmart needed to decide which product lines and departments should be emphasized. Exhibit 10 provides a breakdown of total retail trade by major product areas.

---

[5] Kmart Corporation, *1984 Annual Report*, p. 3.

EXHIBIT 10   Total Retail Trade (in millions of dollars)

	1984	% Charge 1983–84	10-Year Growth Rate
Retail trade total	$1,297,015	+10.5%	+ 9.0%
Durable goods	464,287	+17.1	+ 9.6
Nondurable goods stores total	832,728	+ 7.1	+ 8.8
General merchandise group	153,642	+10.2	+ 7.9
General merchandise stores	144,575	+10.6	+ 8.4
Department stores	129,284	+10.9	+ 8.6
Variety stores	9,067	+ 5.1	+ 1.8
Apparel group	66,891	+10.8	+ 8.8
Men's and boy's wear stores	8,432	+ 5.9	+ 3.1
Women's apparel accessory stores	27,899	+13.9	+ 9.3
Family & other apparel stores	17,567	+13.8	+11.1
Shoe stores	10,339	+ 5.6	+ 9.9
Furniture & appliance group	63,581	+16.3	+ 8.9
GAF total	325,938	+11.7	—
Automotive group	277,008	+19.0	+ 9.5
Gasoline service stations	100,997	+ 2.2	+10.2
Lumber, building material hardware	59,304	+15.2	+ 9.7
Eating and drinking places	124,109	+ 8.2	+10.8
Food group	269,959	+ 5.9	+ 8.3
Drug and proprietary stores	44,165	+10.3	+ 9.2
Liquor stores	19,494	+ 2.5	+ 6.3

Source: *Standard & Poor's Industrial Survey*, July 4, 1985, p. 111.

Since the appointment of Bernard M. Fauber as chief executive officer in 1980, Kmart had made a number of substantial changes. By the end of 1985, the store renovation program had been going for some time, and the move toward higher quality national brand merchandise was well underway. Still, as 1986 began, there were a number of important issues still facing Kmart. Would the repositioning program succeed in attracting more affluent customers to buy its higher priced name-brand merchandise? What additional steps could be taken to upgrade Kmart's stores? Would the new image result in a substantial loss of lower income customers which had historically been the backbone of its business? Might Kmart customers be confused by the move as happened to Sears in the 1970s? How could Kmart improve the performance of its clothing and soft goods? If it did, could fashion-seeking customers really be convinced that Kmart was a trendy place to shop? These and other questions came to mind as CEO Fauber looked ahead to the remainder of the 1980s and into the 1990s.

Case 2–7   *Campbell Soup Company**

In mid-1985, five years after he had been appointed president and chief executive officer of Campbell Soup Company, Gordon McGovern decided it was time to review the key strategic theme he had initiated— new product development. Shortly after he became Campbell's CEO, McGovern reorganized the company into autonomous business units to foster entrepreneurial attitudes; his ultimate objective was to transform Campbell from a conservative manufacturing company into a consumer-driven, new-product-oriented company. As a result of McGovern's push, Campbell had introduced 334 new products in the past five years—more than any other company in the food processing industry.

During the 1970s Campbell's earnings had increased at an annual rate just under 9 percent—a dull performance compared to the 12 percent average growth for the food industry as a whole. With prior management's eyes fixed mainly on production aspects, gradual shifts in consumer buying habits caused Campbell's unit volume growth to flatten. McGovern's five-year campaign for renewed growth via new product introduction had produced good results so far. By year-end 1984 sales were up 31 percent—to $3.7 billion—and earnings had risen by 47 percent—to $191 million. But now it appeared that Campbell's brand managers may have become so involved in new product development that they had neglected the old stand-by products, as well as not meeting cost control and profit margin targets. Campbell's growth in operating earnings for fiscal year 1985 fell far short of McGovern's 15 percent target rate. Failure to control costs and meet earnings targets threatened to leave Campbell without the internal cash flows to fund its new-product strategy. Exhibit 1 offers a summary of Campbell Soup's recent financial performance.

THE FOOD PROCESSING INDUSTRY

In the early 19th century small incomes and low urban population greatly limited the demand for packaged food. In 1859 one industry— grain mills—accounted for over three fifths of the total U.S. food processing. Several industries were in their infancy: evaporated milk,

---

* Prepared by graduate researcher, Sharon Henson, under the supervision of Professor Arthur A. Thompson, The University of Alabama. Copyright © 1986 by Sharon Henson and Arthur A. Thompson.

EXHIBIT 1 Financial Summary, Campbell Soup Company, 1979–1985 (in $ thousands)

	1979	1980	1981	1982	1983	1984	1985
Total sales (includes interdivisional)	n.a.	$2,566,100	$2,865,000	$2,995,800	$3,359,300	$3,744,600	$4,060,800
Net sales (excludes interdivisional)	$2,248,692	2,560,569	2,797,663	2,955,649	3,292,433	3,657,440	3,988,705
Cost of products sold	1,719,134	1,976,754	2,172,806	2,214,214	2,444,213	2,700,751	2,950,204
Marketing and sales expenses	181,229	213,703	256,726	305,700	367,053	428,062	478,341
Administrative and research expenses	94,716	102,445	93,462	136,933	135,855	169,614	194,319
Operating earnings	253,613	276,869	280,355	309,283	349,116	378,316	389,488
Interest—net	1,169	10,135	30,302	21,939	39,307	26,611	32,117
Earnings before taxes	252,444	257,532	244,367	276,863	306,005	332,402	333,724
Taxes on earnings	119,700	122,950	114,650	127,250	141,000	142,200	135,800
Net earnings, after taxes	119,817	134,582	129,717	149,613	165,005	191,202	197,824
Percent of sales	5.3%	5.3%	4.6%	5.1%	5.0%	5.2%	5.0%
Percent of stockholders' equity	13.8%	14.6%	13.2%	14.6%	15.0%	15.9%	15.0%
Per share of common stock	1.80	2.04	2.00	2.32	2.56	2.96	3.06
Dividends declared per share	.86	.93	1.02	1.05	1.09	1.14	1.22
Average shares outstanding	66,720	65,946	64,824	64,495	64.467	64,514	64,572
Salaries, wages, pensions, etc.	$ 543,984	$ 609,979	$ 680,946	$ 700,940	$ 755,073	$ 889,450	$ 950,143
Current assets	680,955	861,845	845,343	921,501	932,099	1,063,330	1,152,761
Working capital	362,187	405,628	368,246	434,627	478,899	541,515	579,490
Plant assets—gross	1,134,571	1,248,735	1,368,663	1,472,693	1,607,634	1,744,866	1,856,122
Accumulated depreciation	520,603	560,730	613,643	657,315	718,478	774,004	828,662
Plant assets purchased and acquired	159,603	155,796	155,275	175,928	178,773	201,864	222,321
Total assets	1,325,823	1,627,565	1,722,876	1,865,519	1,991,526	2,210,115	2,437,525
Long-term debt	36,298	137,879	150,587	236,160	267,465	283,034	297,146
Stockholders' equity	900,017	958,443	1,000,510	1,055,762	1,149,404	1,259,908	1,382,487
Depreciation	60,360	67,958	75,118	83,813	93,189	101,417	119,044

Source: Annual reports of Campbell Soup Company.

canning, candy, natural extracts, and coffee roasting. From 1860 to 1900 the industry entered a period of development and growth that made food processing the leading manufacturing industry in the United States. The driving forces behind this growth were increased urbanization, cheaper rail transport, and the advent of refrigeration and tin can manufacturing.

At the beginning of the 20th century the food processing industry was highly fragmented; the thousands of local and regional firms were too small to capture scale economies in mass production and distribution as was occurring in other industries. During the 1920s industry consolidation via acquisition and merger began; the process was evolutionary not revolutionary and continued on into the 1960s and 1970s. Companies such as Del Monte and Kraft, whose names have since become household words, were established, as were the first two multiline food companies—General Foods and Standard Brands (later part of Nabisco Brands). With consolidation came greater production cost efficiency and national market coverages. Following World War II the bigger food companies made moves toward more product differentiation and increased emphasis on advertising. Some became multinational in scope, establishing subsidiaries in many other countries. Starting in the 1960s and continuing into the 1980s the industry went through more consolidation; this time the emphasis was on brand diversification and product line expansion. Acquisition-minded companies shopped for smaller companies with products having strong brand recognition and brand loyalty.

Then in the 1980s giants began acquiring other giants. In 1984 Nestlé acquired Carnation for $3 billion. In 1985 R. J. Reynolds purchased Nabisco Brands for $4.9 billion (and then changed its corporate name to RJR Nabisco), and Philip Morris acquired General Foods Corporation for $5.7 billion—the biggest nonoil deal in U.S. industry. In 1985 the U.S. food processing industry had sales over $100 billion and combined net profits of over $4 billion. Exhibit 2 (pp. 202–3) shows data for leading companies in the industry in 1985.

COMPANY BACKGROUND

Campbell Soup Company was one of the world's leading manufacturers and marketers of branded consumer good products. In 1985 the company had approximately 44,000 employees and 80 manufacturing plants in 12 nations, with over 1,000 products on the market. Its major products were Prego spaghetti sauces, Le Menu frozen dinners, Pepperidge Farm baked goods, Mrs. Paul's frozen foods, Franco-American canned spaghettis, Vlasic pickles, and its flagship red-and-white-label canned soups.

Founded in 1869 by Joseph Campbell, a fruit merchant, and Abram Anderson, an ice box maker, the company was originally known for its jams and jellies. In 1891 it was incorporated as the Joseph Campbell Co. in Camden, New Jersey. In 1899 John T. Dorrance, a brilliant 24-year-old with a Ph.D. from MIT, developed a process for canning soup in condensed form. He was also a master salesman who came up with the idea of attaching snappy placards to the sides of New York City streetcars as a way of promoting the company's products.

From 1900 to 1954 the company was owned entirely by the Dorrance family. It was incorporated as the Campbell Soup Company in 1922. When Dorrance died in 1930 after running the company for 16 years, he left an estate of over $115 million, the third-largest up to that time. He also left a company devoted to engineering, committed to supplying value (in recessions it would rather shave margins than lower quality or raise prices), and obsessed with secrecy. John T. Dorrance, Jr, ran the company for the next 24 years (1930–54) and few, if any, important decisions were made at Campbell without his approval. In 1954 the company went public, with the Dorrance family retaining majority control. In 1985 the Dorrance family still held about 60 percent of Campbell's stock and picked the top executives of the company. In 1984 John Dorrance III became a member of the board. The more than eight decades of family dominance contributed to what some insiders described as a conservative and paternalistic company culture at Campbell.

Over the years Campbell had diversified into a number of food and food-related businesses—Swanson frozen dinners, Pepperidge Farm bakery products, Franco-American spaghetti products, Recipe pet food, fast-food restaurant chains, Godiva chocolates, and even retail garden centers. Still, about half of the company's revenues came from the sale of its original stock-in-trade: canned soup. Throughout most of its history, the company picked its top executives from among those with a production background in the soup division—most had engineering training and good track records in furthering better manufacturing efficiency. One such person, Harold A. Shaub, a 30-year veteran of the company, was named president in 1972. An industrial engineer, Shaub placed a premium on controlling production cost while maintaining acceptable product quality. There were occasions when Shaub, during unannounced inspection tours, had shut down a complete plant that didn't measure up to the strict standards he demanded.

During his tenure Shaub began to set the stage for change at Campbell, acknowledging that "The company needed changes for the changing times."[1] He restructured the company into divisions built around

---

[1] *The Wall Street Journal,* September 17, 1984, p. 1.

EXHIBIT 2 The Top 15 Companies in the Food Processing Industry, 1985 ($ millions)

Company*	Year	Sales	Profits	Assets	Return on Common Equity	Example Brands
1. RJR Nabisco	1985	$ 16,595	$2,163	$16,930	20.3%	Nabisco, Del Monte
	1984	12,974	1,619	9,272	22.1	
2. Dart & Kraft	1985	9,942	466	5,502	17.0	Velveeta, Parkay,
	1984	9,759	456	5,285	16.5	Miracle Whip
3. Beatrice	1985	12,595	479	10,379	21.8	Swiss Miss, Wesson,
	1984	9,327	433	4,464	20.4	Tropicana
4. Kellogg	1985	2,930.1	281.1	1,726.1	48.0	Mrs. Smith's, Eggo,
	1984	2,602.4	250.5	1,667.1	27.0	Rice Krispies
5. H. J. Heinz	1985	4,047.9	266	2,473.8	22.6	Star-Kist Tuna,
	1984	3,953.8	237.5	2,343	21.0	Heinz Ketchup
6. Ralston Purina	1985	5,863.9	256.4	2,637.3	26.7	Hostess Twinkies,
	1984	4,980.1	242.7	2,004.2	23.1	Meow Mix
7. Campbell Soup	1985	3,988.7	197.8	2,437.5	15.0	Prego, Le Menu,
	1984	3,657.4	191.2	2,210.1	15.9	Vlasic pickles

Company	Year					Brands
8. General Mills	1985	4,285.2	(72.9)	2,662.6	(6.5)	Cheerios, Betty Crocker
	1984	5,600.8	233.4	2,858.1	19.0	
9. Sara Lee	1985	8,117	206	3,216	20.5	Popsicle, Bryan, Rudy's Farm
	1984	7,000	188	2,822	19.4	
10. CPC International	1985	4,209.9	142.0	3,016.6	10.5	Mazola, Skippy, Heilmann's
	1984	4,373.3	193.4	2,683.4	14.7	
11. Borden	1985	4,716.2	193.8	2,932.2	14.3	Wyler's, Bama, Cracker Jack
	1984	4,568	182.1	2,767.1	13.7	
12. Pillsbury	1985	4,670.6	191.8	2,778.5	17.3	Green Giant, Häagen-Dazs
	1984	4,172.3	169.8	2,608.3	17.0	
13. Archer Daniels	1985	4,738.8	163.9	2,967.1	10.8	LaRosa, Fleischmann's
	1984	4,907	117.7	2,592.7	NA	
14. Quaker Oats	1985	3,520.1	156.6	2,662.6	20.3	Gatorade, VanCamp's
	1984	3,334.1	138.7	1,806.8	19.8	
15. Hershey Foods	1985	1,996.2	112.2	1,197.4	16.6	Delmonico, Hershey's Chocolate
	1984	1,848.5	108.7	1,122.6	17.3	
Industry composite	1985	$101,669	$4,004	$58,294	16.5%	

* Ranking is by market value of common stock according to *Business Week*, April 18, 1986. Financial data is from annual reports.
NA = Not available.

major product lines. Then in 1978, realizing that Campbell's marketing skills were too weak, he hired aggressive outsiders to revitalize the company's marketing efforts. That same year Campbell purchased Vlasic Foods, Inc., the largest producer of pickles in the United States.

Also in 1978 Campbell launched Prego spaghetti sauce products, the first major new food items introduced by Campbell in 10 years. The former Campbell policy required that a new product had to show a profit within a year and the pay-out on Prego was expected to be three years. But because the policy held back new product development, Shaub changed it and set a goal of introducing two additional products each year.

In 1980 Campbell broke a 111-year-old debt-free tradition, issuing $100 million in 10-year notes. Until then the company had relied primarily on internally generated funds to meet long-term capital requirements.

Because of company tradition, everyone expected Shaub's successor to come from production. Thus it came as a surprise to Gordon McGovern, president of Connecticut-based Pepperidge Farm and a marketing man, when Shaub called him into his office and said, "I'd like you to come down here and take my place."[2] When McGovern became Campbell's president and CEO on December 1, 1980, Shaub remained on the board of directors.

McGovern was at Pepperidge Farm when the company was bought by Campbell in 1961. He was in business school when Margaret Rudkin, founder of Pepperidge Farm, spoke to his class. She told how she had built her bread company from scratch in an industry dominated by giants. McGovern was impressed. He wrote to Rudkin for a job, received it in 1956, and began his climb through the ranks. When Campbell acquired Pepperidge Farm in 1961 it had sales of $40 million. When McGovern became its president in 1968 sales had reached $60 million. When he left to become president of Campbell in 1980, Pepperidge Farms' sales had climbed to $300 million. McGovern brought some of what he considered Pepperidge's success strategy with him to Campbell: experimentation, new product development, marketing savvy, and creativity.

MANAGEMENT UNDER McGOVERN

Every Saturday morning McGovern did his family's grocery shopping, stopping to straighten Campbell's displays and inspect those of competitors, studying packaging and reading labels, and trying to learn all he could about how and what people were eating. He encouraged his

---

[2] *Forbes,* December 7, 1981, p. 44.

managers to do the same. Several board meetings were held in the backrooms of supermarkets so that afterward directors could roam the store aisles interviewing customers about Campbell products.

McGovern's style of management was innovative to a company known as much for its stodginess as for its red and white soup can. For decades Campbell Soup operated under strict rules of decorum. Eating, smoking, or drinking coffee was not permitted in the office. Managers had to share their offices with their secretaries, and an unwritten rule required executives to keep their suitcoats on in the office. When McGovern joined Campbell he drove to work in a yellow Volkswagen that stuck out in his parking space so much that the garagemen quietly arranged to have it painted. Finding the atmosphere at headquarters stifling, he promised a change.

He began wandering through the corridors every day, mingling easily among the employees. McGovern's voluble personality and memory for names made him popular with many employees. But not everyone was impressed by McGovern's style. Some production people were suspicious of his marketing background. Others believed that his grocery trips and hobnobbing with employees were ploys calculated to win him support and a reputation. But McGovern pressed forward with several internal changes: (1) a day care center for the children of employees (complete with Campbell Kids posters on the wall), (2) a health program including workouts in a gymnasium, and (3) an unusual new benefit program which covered adoption expenses up to $1,000 and gave time off to employees who adopted children—in the same way that women were given maternity leave. He appointed the first two women vice presidents in the company's history; one of these, a former director of the Good Housekeeping Institute, was hired to identify consumers' food preferences and needs.

McGovern decentralized Campbell management to facilitate entrepreneurial risktaking and new product development, devising a new compensation program to reward these traits. He restructured the company into some 50 autonomous units and divided the U.S. division into eight strategic profit centers: soups, beverages, pet foods, frozen foods, fresh produce, main meals, grocery, and food service. Units were encouraged to develop new products even if another unit would actually produce the products. Thus, the Prego spaghetti sauce unit—not the frozen food group—initiated frozen Mexican dinners. And although it wasn't his job, the director of market research created "Today's Taste," a line of refrigerated entrees and side dishes. "It's like things are in constant motion," the director said. "We are overloaded, but it's fun."[3]

---

[3] *The Wall Street Journal*, September 17, 1984, p. 10.

The new structure encouraged managers, who had to compete for corporate funding, to be more aggressive in developing promising products. According to McGovern:

> These integral units allow the company to really get its arms around chunks of the business. The managers are answerable to the bottom line—to their investments, their hiring, their products—and it's a great motivation for performance.[4]

As part of this motivation, Campbell began annually allotting around $30 million to $40 million to support new ventures, each requiring a minimum of $10 million. This strategy was intended to encourage star performers while enabling management to weed out laggards. McGovern felt that this was much easier to determine when everyone knew where the responsibilities lay—but that it was no disgrace to fail if the effort was a good one. An employee noted that McGovern was endorsing "the right to fail," adding that "it makes the atmosphere so much more positive."[5]

Every Friday McGovern held meetings to discuss new products. The fact-finding sessions were attended by financial, marketing, engineering, and sales personnel. Typical McGovern questions included: "Would you eat something like that?" "Why not?" "Have you tried the competition's product?" "Is there a consumer niche?" The marketing research director noted that in Shaub's meetings the question was "Can we make such a product cost-effectively?"[6]

Under Shaub the chain of command was inviolable, but McGovern was not hesitant about circumventing the chain when he felt it was warranted. He criticized one manager's product to another manager, expecting word to get back to the one with the problem. Although this often motivated some to prove McGovern wrong, others were unnerved by such tactics. When he became aware of this, McGovern eased up a bit.

In the past under prior CEOs, cost-cutters got promoted; now in McGovern's more creative atmosphere, the rules weren't so well defined. As one insider put it, "There's a great deal of uncertainty. No one really knows what it takes to get ahead. But that makes us all work harder."[7]

When hiring managers McGovern, himself a college baseball player, tended to favor people with a competitive sports background. "There's teamwork and determination, but also the idea that you know how to lose and get back up again. 'Try, try, try' is what I say. I can't stress how important that is."[8]

---

[4] *Advertising Age,* January 3, 1983, p. 38.
[5] Ibid.
[6] *The Wall Street Journal,* September 17, 1984, p. 10,
[7] Ibid.
[8] *Advertising Age,* January 3, 1983, p. 38.

STRATEGY

The strategic focus was on the consumer—considered to be the key to Campbell's growth and success in the 1980s. The consumer's "hot buttons" were identified as nutrition, convenience, low sodium, price, quality, and uniqueness—and managers were urged to "press those buttons." General managers were advised to take into account the consumer's perceptions, needs, and demands regarding nutrition, safety, flavor, and convenience. Key strategies were: (1) improving operating efficiency, (2) developing new products for the modern consumer, (3) updating advertising for new and established products, and (4) high quality.

When he took over, McGovern developed a five-year plan that included four financial performance objectives: a 15 percent annual increase in earnings, a 5 percent increase in volume, a 5 percent increase in sales (plus inflation), and an 18 percent return on equity by 1986. His long-range strategy included making acquisitions every two years that would bring in $200 million in annual sales. Campbell's acquisition strategy was to look for small, fast-growing food companies strong in product areas where Campbell was not and companies on the fast track that were in rapidly growing parts of their industries. Under McGovern Campbell made a number of acquisitions:

1982
- Mrs. Paul's Kitchens, Inc., a processor and marketer of frozen prepared seafood and vegetable products, with annual sales of approximately $125 million (acquired at a cost of $55 million).
- Snow King Frozen Foods. Inc., engaged in the production and marketing of a line of uncooked frozen specialty meat products, with annual sales of $32 million.
- Juice Bowl Products, Inc., a Florida producer of fruit juices.
- Win Schuler Foods, Inc., a Michigan-based producer and distributor of specialty cheese spreads, flavored melba rounds, food service salad dressings, party dips and sauces, with annual sales of $6.5 million.
- Costa Apple Products, Inc., a producer of apple juice retailed primarily in the Eastern United States, with annual sales of $6 million.

1983
- Acquired several small domestic operations at a cost of $26 million, including:
- Annabelle's restaurant chain of 12 units in the southeastern United States.
- Triangle Manufacturing Corp., a manufacturer of physical fitness and sports medicine products.

1984
- Mendelson-Zeller Co., Inc., a California distributor of fresh produce.

EXHIBIT 3 Examples of Major Acquisitions in the Food Processing Industry, 1982–1985

Buyer	Acquired Company	Year	Price (millions of dollars)	Products/Brands Acquired
Beatrice	Esmark	1984	$2,800	Swift, Hunt-Wesson brands
CPC	C. F. Mueller	1983	122	Makes CPC biggest U.S. pasta maker
ConAgra	Peavey	1982	NA	Jams & syrups
	ACLI Seafood	1983	NA	
	Armour Food	1983	166	Processed meats
	Imperial Foods' Country Poultry	1984	18	
Dart & Kraft	Celestial Seasonings	1984	25	Herbal teas
Esmark	Norton Simon	1983	1,100	Hunt-Wesson
General Foods	Entenmann's	1982	315	Baked goods
	Otto Roth	1983	NA	Specialty cheeses
	Monterey	1983	NA	
	Peacock Foods	1983	NA	
	Ronzoni	1984	NA	Pasta
	Oroweat	1984	60	Bread
McCormick	Patterson Jenks	1984	53	Major British spice and food distributor
Nestle	Carnation	1984	3,000	Evaporated milk, Friskies pet food
Philip Morris	General Foods	1985	5,750	Jell-O, Maxwell House
Pillsbury	Häagen-Dazs	1983	75	Ice cream
	Sedutto	1984	5	
Quaker Oats	Stokely-Van Camp	1983	238	Baked beans, canned goods
Ralston Purina	Continental Baking	1984	475	Hostess Twinkies, Wonder Bread
R. J. Reynolds	Nabisco Foods	1984	4,900	Oreo cookies, Ritz crackers,
	Canada Dry	1984	175	ginger ale, soda, tonic

NA = Not available.
Data compiled from various sources.

1985

- Continental Foods Company S.A. and affiliated companies which produced sauces, confectioneries, and other food products in Belgium and France; the cost of the acquisition was $17 million.

Campbell was by no means alone in adding companies to its portfolio; many major mergers in the food industry were taking place (see Exhibit 3). Several factors were at work:

- Many food companies had been stung by ill-fated diversification forays outside food. In the 1960s when industry growth had slowed, it was fashionable to diversify into nonfoods. Many of the acquired companies turned out to be duds, draining earnings and soaking up too much top management attention. Now food companies were refocusing their efforts on food—the business they knew best.
- Even though the food industry was regarded as a slow-growth/low-margin business, the fact remained that stable demand, moderate capital costs, and high cash flows had boosted returns on equity to almost 20 percent for some companies. Food processors discovered that they were earning better returns on their food products than they were earning in the nonfood businesses they had earlier diversified into.

While companies such as Beatrice, the nation's largest food company, and Nestlé, the world's largest, paid substantial sums to buy out large established companies with extensive brand stables, others—such as Campbell—followed the route of concentrating on internal product development and smaller, selective acquisitions to complement their existing product lines. In fact Campbell was considered the leader among the food processors who were striving to limit acquisitions in favor of heavy, in-house product development. Campbell's emphasis on new product development was not without risk. It took $10 to $15 million in advertising and couponing to launch a brand. Because of the hit-or-miss nature of new products, only about one out of eight products reaching the test market stage were successful. Moreover, industry analysts predicted that the continuing introduction of new products would lead to increased competition for shelf space and for the consumer's food dollar.

MARKETING

The outsiders Shaub had hired to revitalize Campbell's marketing included a vice president for marketing who was an eight-year veteran of a New York advertising firm and a soup general manager who was a former Wharton business school professor. In addition to those hired by

Shaub, the rest of McGovern's marketing-oriented executive team included: a frozen foods manager (a former marketing manager with General Foods), the head of the Pepperidge Farm division, and the head of the Vlasic Foods division (both marketing men from Borden). This team boosted Campbell's marketing budget to $428 million by 1984 (up 57 percent from 1982). Advertising spending grew from $67 million in 1980 to $179 million in 1985. Prior to McGovern, Campbell used to cut ad spending at the end of a quarter to boost earnings. Besides hurting the brands, it gave the company an unfavorable reputation among the media. In 1985 the marketing expenditures (including advertising and promotion) of some of the leading food companies were: Campbell—approximately $488 million, Quaker—$619 million, Heinz—$303 million, Pillsbury—$365 million, and Sara Lee—$594 million.

In 1982 McGovern was named *Advertising Age's* Adman of the Year for his efforts in transforming Campbell into "one of the most aggressive market-driven companies in the food industry today."[9] *Advertising Age* noted that McGovern had almost doubled the advertising budget and had replaced the company's longtime ad agency for its soups, leading to a new ad campaign that helped reverse eight years of flat or lower sales. The new campaign emphasized nutrition and fitness, as opposed to the former "mmm,mmm,good" emphasis of taste. Print ads included long copy that referred to major government research studies citing soup's nutritional values. The new slogan was: "Soup is good food." New products and advertising were aimed at shoppers who were dieting, health conscious, and usually in a hurry. In keeping with the new fitness image, the 80-year-old Campbell Kids, although still cerubic, acquired a leaner look. Campbell's marketing strategy under McGovern was based on several important market research findings and projections:

- Women now comprised 43 percent of the workforce and a level of 50 percent was projected by 1990.
- Two-income marriages represented 60 percent of all U.S. families. These would take in three out of every five dollars earned.
- Upper-income households would grow 3.5 times faster than total household formations.
- More than half of all households consisted of only one or two members.
- There were 18 million singles, and 23 percent of all households contained only one person.
- The average age of the population was advancing with the number of senior citizens totaling 25 million-plus and increasing.

---

[9] Ibid.

- The percentage of meals eaten at home was declining.
- Nearly half of the adult meal-planners in the United States were watching their weight.
- Poultry consumption had increased 26 percent since 1973.
- Ethnic food preparation at home was increasing, with 40 percent, 21 percent, and 14 percent of households preparing Italian, Mexican, and Oriental foods, respectively, at home from scratch.
- There was growing consumer concern with food avoidance: sugar, salt, calories, chemicals, cholesterol, and additives.
- The "I am what I eat" philosophy had tied food into lifestyles along with Nautilus machines, hot tubs, jogging, racquet ball, backpacking, cross-country skiing, and aerobic dancing.

In response to growing ethnic food demand, Campbell began marketing ethnic selections in regions where interests were highest for particular food types. For instance, it marketed spicy Ranchero Beans only in the south and southwest and planned to market newly acquired Puerto Rican foods in New York City.

The product development priorities were aimed at the themes of convenience, taste, flavor, and texture. The guidelines were:

- Prepare and market products that represent superior value to consumers and constantly strive to improve those values.
- Develop products that help build markets.
- Develop products that return a fair profit to Campbell and to customers.

In support of these guidelines, Campbell adopted several tactics:

- Use ongoing consumer research to determine eating habits by checking home menus, recipe preparation, and foods that are served together. Study meal and snack eating occasions to determine which household members participate so that volume potential can be determined for possible new products and product improvement ideas.
- Develop new products and produce them in small quantities that simulate actual plant production capabilities.
- Test new or improved products in a large enough number of households which are so distributed throughout the United States that results can be projected nationally. Once the product meets pretest standards, recommend it for market testing.
- Once packaging and labels have been considered, design and pretest introductory promotion and advertising.
- Introduce a new product into selected test markets to determine actual store sales which can be projected nationally.
- If test marketing proves successful, roll out the new product on a regional or national plan using test market data as a rationale for expansion.

EXHIBIT 4   Campbell's Leading New Products (total of $600 million in sales for fiscal 1985)

	1985 Ranking	*Year Introduced*
Le Menu Frozen Dinner		1982
Prego Spaghetti Sauce		1982
Chunky New England Clam Chowder		1984
Great Starts Breakfasts		1984
Prego Plus		1985

Source: *The Wall Street Journal,* August 14, 1985.

A key part of the strategy was the "Campbell in the Kitchen" project, consisting of some 75 homemakers across the country. Three to five times a year Campbell asked this "focus group" to try different products and give opinions. McGovern regularly dispatched company executives to the kitchens of these homemakers to observe eating patterns and see how meals were prepared. He sent Campbell's home economists into some of the households to work with the cooks on a one-to-one basis.

All this was in sharp contrast to the preMcGovern era. Campbell averaged about 18 new product entries a year through the late 1970s. Many of these were really line extensions rather than new products. Substantial numbers flopped, partly because they had often been subjected to only the most rudimentary and inexpensive tests. Sometimes the testing had consisted only of a panel of the company's advertising and business executives sipping from teaspoons.

In 1983 Campbell was the biggest new products generator in the combined food and health and beauty aids categories with a total of 42 new products. Second was Esmark, 36; followed by Lever/Lipton, 33; Nabisco Brands, 25; Beatrice and General Foods, 24 each; American Home Products, 23; Quaker Oats, 21; Borden, 19, and General Mills and Noxell, 17 each. Exhibit 4 shows Campbell's leading new products from 1982 to 1985.

PRODUCTION

McGovern summarized Campbell's philosophy on quality: "I want zero defects. If we can't produce quality, we'll get out of the business."[10] In 1984 Campbell held its first Worldwide Corporate Conference dedi-

---

[10] *Savy,* June 1984, p. 39.

cated to quality. Hundreds of Campbell managers from all levels and most company locations spent three days at this conference. Campbell believed that the ultimate test of quality was consumer satisfaction and its goal was to maintain a quality-conscious organization at every employee level in every single operation.

Before McGovern took over, Campbell used to emphasize new products compatible with existing production facilities. For example, a square omelet was designed for Swanson's frozen breakfasts because it was what the machine would make. After McGovern's appointment, although low-cost production was still a strategic factor, consumer trends—and not existing machinery—were the deciding factors for new product development. Other important factors considered in the production process included:

- The growing move toward consumption of refrigerated and fresh produce in contrast to canned or frozen products.
- The emerging perception that private label and/or generic label merchandise would drive out weak national and secondary brands unless there was a clear product superiority and excellent price/value on the part of the brands supported by consumer advertising.
- The polarization of food preparation time with long preparation on weekends and special occasions, but fast preparation in between via microwaves, quick foods, and instant breakfasts.
- The cost of the package—especially metal packaging—which was outrunning the cost of the product it contained.
- Energy and distribution costs—these were big targets for efficiency with regional production, aseptic packaging, and packages designed for automatic warehouse handling and lightweight containers becoming standard.

The bulk of $154 million in capital expenditures in 1983 went into improvement of production equipment, expenditures for additional production capacity, the completion of the $100 million canned foods plant in North Carolina, and the start of a mushroom-producing facility at Dublin, Georgia. In 1984 construction began on a $9 million Le Menu production line in Sumter, South Carolina. Capital expenditures in 1985 totaled $213 million. Most of this went into improvements of production equipment, packaging technology, and expenditures for additional production capacity.

Campbell was considered a model of manufacturing efficiency. Production was fully integrated from the tomato patch to the canmaking factory. Campbell was the nation's third largest can manufacturer behind American Can Company and Continental Group. Yet Campbell, which made the red and white soup can with the gold medallion an American institution, had recently concluded that food packaging was headed in the direction of snazzier and more convenient containers. McGovern compared sticking with the can to the refusal of U.S. automobile makers to change their ways in the face of the Japanese challenge:

> There's a tremendous feeling of urgency because an overseas company could come in here with innovative packaging and technology and just take us to the cleaners on basic lines we've taken for granted for years.[11]

Other soup companies—including Libby, McNeill & Libby, a Nestlé Enterprises, Inc., unit that made Crosse & Blackwell gourmet soup— had already started experimenting with can alternatives. Campbell's testing was considered the most advanced, but a mistake could mean revamping production facilities at a cost of $100 million or more.

Researchers at the Campbell Soup Company's DNA Plant Technology Corporation were working toward the development of the "perfect tomato." They were seeking ways to grow tasty, high solids tomatoes under high-temperature conditions that would cause normal plants to droop and wither. They also hoped to crossbreed high quality domestic tomatoes with tough, hardy, wild tomatoes that could withstand cold weather. A breakthrough in this area could result in two harvests a year. Conceding that they were latecomers (Heinz began similar research several years after Campbell), Campbell researchers estimated that they were four to five years ahead of Heinz.

Campbell believed its key strengths were: (1) a worldwide system for obtaining ingredients, (2) a broad range of food products that could be used as a launching pad for further innovation, and (3) an emphasis on low-cost production.

CAMPBELL'S OPERATING DIVISIONS

Campbell Soup Company was divided into six operating units—Campbell U.S., Pepperidge Farm, Vlasic Foods, Mrs. Paul's Kitchens, Other United States, and International. Sales and profit performance by division are shown in Exhibit 5.

CAMPBELL U.S.

In 1985 the Campbell U.S. Division was Campbell's largest operating unit, accounting for almost 62 percent of the company's total consolidated sales. Operating earnings increased 5 percent over 1984. Unit volume rose 7 percent in 1983, 9 percent in 1984, and 4 percent in

---

[11] *Business Week,* November 21, 1983, p. 102.

EXHIBIT 5   Sales and Earnings of Campbell Soup, by Division, 1980–1985 ($ millions)

	1980	*1981*	*1982*	*1983*	*1984*	*1985*
Campbell U.S.:						
Sales	$1,608	$1,678	$1,773	$1,987	$2,282	$2,500
Operating earnings	205	190	211	250	278	292
Pepperidge Farm:						
Sales	283	329	392	433	435	426
Operating earnings	29	35	41	43	35	39
Vlasic Foods:						
Sales	130	137	149	168	193	199
Operating earnings	8	10	12	13	14	16
Mrs. Paul's Kitchens:						
Sales				108	126	138
Operating earnings				10	14	11
Other United States:						
Sales	35	27	56	64	84	81
Operating earnings	1	(1)	(1)	(1)	(2)	(3)
International:						
Sales	512	694	643	599	624	716
Operating earnings	33	46	46	33	34	35

Source: Campbell's annual reports.

1985. The Campbell U.S. division was divided into eight profit centers: Soup, Frozen Foods, Grocery Business, Beverage Business, Food Service Business, Poultry Business, Fresh Produce Business, and Pet Foods Business. Exhibit 6 shows the brands Campbell had in this divison and the major competitors each brand faced.

The soup business group alone accounted for more than 25 percent of the company's consolidated sales (as compared to around 50 percent in the 1970s). Campbell's flagship brands of soups accounted for 80 percent of the $1 billion-plus annual canned soup market; in 1985 Campbell offered grocery shoppers over 50 varieties of canned soups. Heinz was second with 10 percent of the market. Heinz had earlier withdrawn from producing Heinz-label soup and shifted its production over to making soups for sale under the private labels of grocery chains; Heinz was the leading private-label producer of canned soup, holding almost an 80 percent share of the private-label segment. See Exhibit 6 for information on competitors and their brands.

Although the soup business was relatively mature (McGovern preferred to call it underworked), Campbell's most ambitious consumer research took place in this unit. McGovern planned to speed up soup sales by turning out a steady flow of new varieties in convenient pack-

EXHIBIT 6 The Campbell U.S. Division: Products, Rival Brands, Competitors

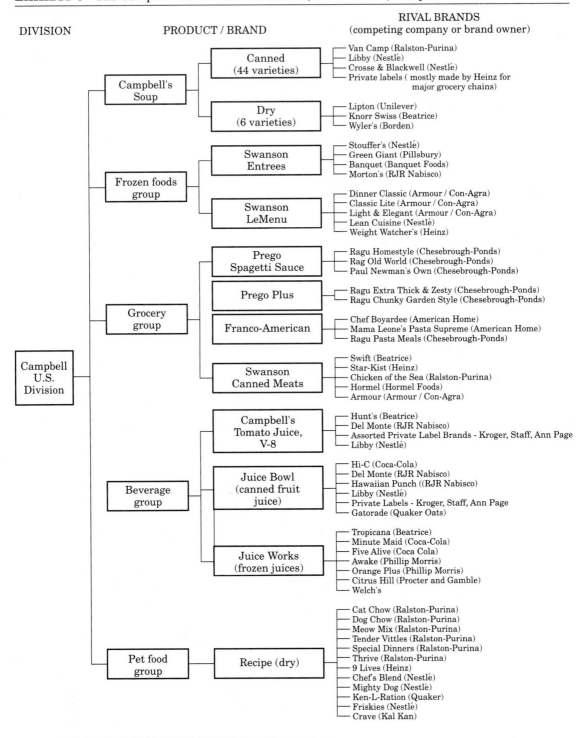

DIVISION	PRODUCT / BRAND	RIVAL BRANDS (competing company or brand owner)
	Campbell's Soup → Canned (44 varieties)	Van Camp (Ralston-Purina) / Libby (Nestlé) / Crosse & Blackwell (Nestlé) / Private labels (mostly made by Heinz for major grocery chains)
	Dry (6 varieties)	Lipton (Unilever) / Knorr Swiss (Beatrice) / Wyler's (Borden)
	Frozen foods group → Swanson Entrees	Stouffer's (Nestlé) / Green Giant (Pillsbury) / Banquet (Banquet Foods) / Morton's (RJR Nabisco)
	Swanson LeMenu	Dinner Classic (Armour / Con-Agra) / Classic Lite (Armour / Con-Agra) / Light & Elegant (Armour / Con-Agra) / Lean Cuisine (Nestlé) / Weight Watcher's (Heinz)
Campbell U.S. Division	**Grocery group** → Prego Spagetti Sauce	Ragu Homestyle (Chesebrough-Ponds) / Rag Old World (Chesebrough-Ponds) / Paul Newman's Own (Chesebrough-Ponds)
	Prego Plus	Ragu Extra Thick & Zesty (Chesebrough-Ponds) / Ragu Chunky Garden Style (Chesebrough-Ponds)
	Franco-American	Chef Boyardee (American Home) / Mama Leone's Pasta Supreme (American Home) / Ragu Pasta Meals (Chesebrough-Ponds)
	Swanson Canned Meats	Swift (Beatrice) / Star-Kist (Heinz) / Chicken of the Sea (Ralston-Purina) / Hormel (Hormel Foods) / Armour (Armour / Con-Agra)
	Beverage group → Campbell's Tomato Juice, V-8	Hunt's (Beatrice) / Del Monte (RJR Nabisco) / Assorted Private Label Brands - Kroger, Staff, Ann Page / Libby (Nestlé)
	Juice Bowl (canned fruit juice)	Hi-C (Coca-Cola) / Del Monte (RJR Nabisco) / Hawaiian Punch ((RJR Nabisco) / Libby (Nestlé) / Private Labels - Kroger, Staff, Ann Page / Gatorade (Quaker Oats)
	Juice Works (frozen juices)	Tropicana (Beatrice) / Minute Maid (Coca-Cola) / Five Alive (Coca Cola) / Awake (Phillip Morris) / Orange Plus (Phillip Morris) / Citrus Hill (Procter and Gamble) / Welch's
	Pet food group → Recipe (dry)	Cat Chow (Ralston-Purina) / Dog Chow (Ralston-Purina) / Meow Mix (Ralston-Purina) / Tender Vittles (Ralston-Purina) / Special Dinners (Ralston-Purina) / Thrive (Ralston-Purina) / 9 Lives (Heinz) / Chef's Blend (Nestlé) / Mighty Dog (Nestlé) / Ken-L-Ration (Quaker) / Friskies (Nestlé) / Crave (Kal Kan)

ages: "Ethnic, dried, refrigerated, frozen, microwave—you name it, we're going to try it."[12]

In 1985 Campbell began an assault on the $290 million dry-soup mix market dominated by Thomas J. Lipton Inc., a unit of the Anglo-Dutch Unilever Group. This move was made because dry-soup sales in the United States were growing faster than sales of canned soup. Lipton's aggressive response to test marketing of an early Campbell dry-soup product resulted in Campbell's rushing a six-flavor line into national distribution ahead of schedule.

In 1982 McGovern caused a stir when he announced publicly that Campbell's Swanson TV-dinner line was "junk food": "It was great in 1950, but in today's world it didn't go into the microwave; it didn't represent variety or a good eating experience to my palate."[13] He maintained that consumers had discovered high-quality options to the TV-dinner concept. The market niche for more exotic, better quality entrees was being exploited by Nestlé's Stouffer subsidiary and Pillsbury's Green Giant division (Exhibit 6).

Campbell's Frozen Foods group answered the challenge by producing its own frozen gourmet line, Le Menu. Campbell committed about $50 million in manufacturing, marketing, and trade promotion costs on the basis of encouraging marketing tests. In the five years prior to Le Menu, Swanson's sales volume had slipped 16 percent, its biggest volume decline (23 percent) was in the area that had been its stronghold: sales of dinners and entrees. Overall industry sales in dinners and entrees grew to $2 billion during 1982. The single dish entree market had increased 58 percent since 1978 with sales being dominated by Stouffer's Lean Cuisine selections.

Le Menu—served on round heatable plates and consisting of such delicacies as chicken cordon bleu, al dente vegetables, and sophisticated wine sauces—produced 20 percent growth in the frozen meal unit with sales of $150 million during its first year of national distribution (1984). This was double Campbell's earlier projection of sales.

Under Project Fix Swanson dinners were overhauled, putting in less salt and more meat stock in gravies and adding new desserts and sauces. The revamped line had new packaging and a redesigned logo. The Frozen Foods Business Unit reported an overall volume increase of 3 percent in 1983, 27 percent in 1984, and 2 percent in 1985. In 1985 the unit had a 52 percent increase in operating earnings as sales rose 10 percent.

Meanwhile, Pillsbury had targeted the $4 billion-a-year frozen main meal market and the rapidly expanding market in light meals and

---

[12] *Business Week,* December 24, 1984, p. 67.
[13] Ibid.

snacks as vital to its future. In 1984 Pillsbury purchased Van de Kamp's, a market leader in frozen seafood and ethnic entrees for $102 million. During 1985 Van de Kamp's became the number one seller of frozen Mexican meals. Pillsbury also sold more than one third of the 550 million frozen pizzas consumed in the United States in 1985 and made substantial investments in quality improvements and marketing support to maintain the number one position in frozen pizza.

The Grocery Business Unit's star was Prego Spaghetti Sauce that in 1984 had obtained 25 percent of the still growing spaghetti sauce market and was the number two sauce, behind Chesebrough-Pond's Ragu. (Exhibit 6 lists competing brands.) Chesebrough had recently introduced Ragu Chunky Gardenstyle sauce to try to convert cooks who still made their own sauce (about 45 percent of all spaghetti sauce users still cooked their own from scratch). The new Ragu product came in three varieties: mushrooms and onions, green peppers and mushrooms, and extra tomatoes with garlic and onions. Campbell had no plans for a similar entry because copying Ragu wouldn't be innovative. However, a Prego Plus Spaghetti Sauce line completed its first year of national distribution in 1985. To show "old-fashioned concern," all three sizes of Prego sauce came in jars with tamper-evident caps; Campbell would buy back from grocery shelves all jars that had been opened.

The Beverage Group's 1985 operating earnings were affected by a slower-than-anticipated introduction of Juice Works—a line of 100 percent natural, no-sugar-added, pure, blended fruit juices for children. This was attributed to intense competitive pressure and major technological problems. Campbell's Tomato Juice and V-8 Cocktail Vegetable Juice also reported disappointing earnings. Juice Bowl, however, showed improved earnings in 1985. Campbell's competition in this area came from Hunt's, Del Monte, and private label brands (Exhibit 6).

The Poultry Business Unit sales were up 13 percent in 1985. Operating earnings for the year were positive, compared to a loss in 1984. These results stemmed from the national rollout of frozen "finger foods"—Plump & Juicy Dipsters, Drumlets, and Cutlets—and sales of Premium Chunk White Chicken. Some of the competitors were Banquet's Chicken Drum-Snackers and Tyson's Chick'n Dippers.

PEPPERIDGE FARM

Pepperidge Farm, Campbell's second-largest division with 12 percent of the company's consolidated sales, reported a decline in operating income and a sales gain of less than 1 percent between 1983 and 1984. In 1980 it was one of the fastest growing units; sales had risen 14 percent annually, compounded.

1984's disappointing results were largely blamed on losses incurred in the apple juice (Costa Apple Products, Inc., purchased in 1982) and "Star Wars" cookies businesses. When Pepperidge Farm introduced Star Wars cookies, McGovern called them a "travesty" because they were faddish and did not fit the brand's high-quality, upscale adult image. Plus, at $1.39 a bag, he maintained that it was a "lousy value." But he didn't veto them because, "I could be wrong."[14] As the popularity of the movie series waned, so did sales.

The frozen biscuit and bakery business unit volume was also down. New products such as Vegetables in Pastry and Deli's reportedly did not receive enough marketing support.

To remedy the division's growth decline, a number of steps were taken:

- Apple juice operations were transferred to the Campbell U.S. Division Beverage Unit.
- During the year Pepperidge divested itself of operations that no longer fit into its strategic plan, including Lexington Gardens, Inc., a garden center chain.
- Deli's went back into research and development to improve quality.
- By the start of the 1985 fiscal year a new management team was in place and a comprehensive review of each product was being conducted in an effort to return emphasis to traditional product lines and quality standards which accounted for its success and growth in the past.

At the end of 1985 Pepperidge Farm showed an 11 percent increase in operating earnings over the previous year in spite of a 2 percent drop in sales. This was considered a result of the transfer of Pepperidge Farm beverage operations to the Campbell U.S. Beverage Group and the sale of the Lexington Gardens nursery chain. During 1985 sales in the Confectionery Business Unit increased 22 percent and seven Godiva boutiques were added. Goldfish Crackers and Puff Pastry contributed to a volume increase in the Food Service Business Unit, while some varieties of Deli's and the Snack Bar products were discontinued.

One of Pepperidge Farm's major competitors in frozen bakery products was Sara Lee, which had 40 percent of the frozen sweet goods market and an ever-increasing 33 percent share of the specialty breads category. Pepperidge Farm's fresh breads and specialty items competed against a host of local, regional, and national brands. Exhibit 7 presents more details.

---

[14] *Business Week,* November 21, 1983, p. 102.

EXHIBIT 7   The Pepperidge Farm Division: Products, Rival Brands, Competitors

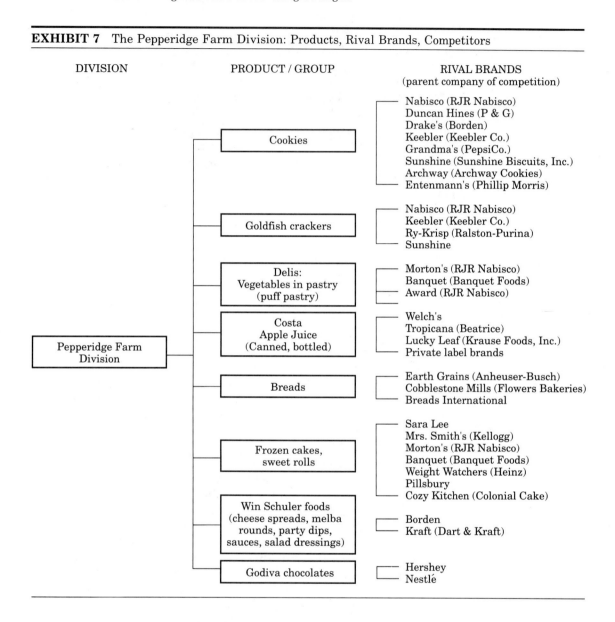

| DIVISION | PRODUCT / GROUP | RIVAL BRANDS (parent company of competition) |

VLASIC FOODS

Campbell's third largest domestic division enjoyed an 11 percent increase in operating earnings in 1985. Vlasic maintained its number one position with a 31 percent share of the pickles market. Seventeen percent of Vlasic's sales were in the food service category.

EXHIBIT 8 Vlasic Division: Products, Rival Brands, and Competitors

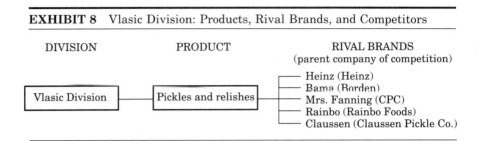

DIVISION	PRODUCT	RIVAL BRANDS (parent company of competition)
Vlasic Division	Pickles and relishes	Heinz (Heinz) Bama (Borden) Mrs. Fanning (CPC) Rainbo (Rainbo Foods) Claussen (Claussen Pickle Co.)

In 1985 Vlasic implemented new labels which used color bands and a flavor rating scale to help consumers find their favorite tastes quickly on the supermarket shelf. Taking advantage of their marketing research, which indicated consumer desires for new and interesting flavors, Vlasic introduced "Zesty Dills" and "Bread & Butter Whole Pickle" lines in 1985. Heinz was Campbell's leading national competitor in this area (Exhibit 8), but there were a number of important regional and private label brands which competed with Heinz and Vlasic for shelf space.

Win Schuler, the Vlasic subsidiary purchased in 1982, reported flat sales in 1984 due to a general economic decline in the Michigan and upper midwest markets where its products were sold. In 1985 it was moved to Campbell's Refrigerated Foods Business Unit where there were plans to begin producing a wider range of food products under the Win Schuler brand name.

MRS. PAUL'S KITCHENS

Sales of this division for 1984 were up 16 percent over the previous year, operating earnings increased 36 percent, and unit volume increased 9 percent. Mrs. Paul's sales represented just over 3 percent of Campbell's total business; all results exceeded goals set for the year. However, strong competitive pressure on its traditional lines was blamed for the unit's drop in operating earnings for 1985. Competing brands included Hormel and Gorton's (Exhibit 9).

When Campbell acquired Mrs. Paul's in 1982, it was rumored that Heinz and Pillsbury, among others, were considering the same acquisition. Shortly after the acquisition, Campbell responded to consumer preferences for convenience seafood products that were nutritious, low in calories, microwavable, and coated more lightly, by introducing Light & Natural Fish Fillets in 1983. Quality improvements were made to existing products, and a promising new product, Light Seafood Entrees, was introduced in 1984. Market share increased about 25 percent over 1983, and Light Seafood Entrees went national in 1985.

EXHIBIT 9   The Mrs. Paul's Kitchen Division: Products, Rival Brands, National Competitors

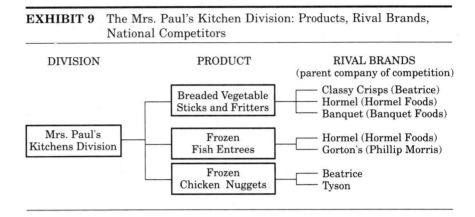

DIVISION	PRODUCT	RIVAL BRANDS (parent company of competition)
Mrs. Paul's Kitchens Division	Breaded Vegetable Sticks and Fritters	Classy Crisps (Beatrice) Hormel (Hormel Foods) Banquet (Banquet Foods)
	Frozen Fish Entrees	Hormel (Hormel Foods) Gorton's (Phillip Morris)
	Frozen Chicken Nuggets	Beatrice Tyson

This line, which featured seven varieties of low-calorie, microwavable, seafood dishes, accounted for 11 percent of 1985's volume. However, sales of the company's established product lines of breaded frozen seafood items dipped below the 1984 level.

CAMPBELL'S OTHER U.S. BUSINESSES

Beyond the base of Campbell's main operating groups there were several additional small businesses: Triangle Manufacturing Corp., a health and fitness products manufacturer; Campbell Hospitality, the restaurant division; and Snow King Frozen Foods, Inc., a manufacturer of frozen meat specialty products.

In 1984 the Hospitality Division, encompassing 59 Pietro's restaurants, 15 Annabelle's, and 6 H. T. McDoogal's, reported an operating loss slightly less than 1983. During the year the division added one H. T. McDoogal's, two Annabelle's, and nine Pietro's units.

In 1985 Annabelle's experienced a 14 percent increase in sales and a 43 percent rise in operating earnings. During the year Campbell announced its intention to sell four H. T. McDoogal's restaurants. Snow King reported a sales decline of 19 percent and an operating loss of almost $1 million.

Competing food companies in the restaurant business included General Mills and Pillsbury. General Mills' Red Lobster unit was the nation's largest full-service dinner-house chain. Red Lobster had 1985 sales of $827 million—an all-time high—and its operating profits also set a record. Pillsbury's Restaurants Group was comprised of Burger King and Steak & Ale Restaurants; both achieved record sales and earnings in 1985. Pillsbury opened 477 new restaurants in 1985—the most ever in a single year—bringing the total to 4,601.

Triangle, Campbell's physical fitness subsidiary, in its second full year of operation in 1985, reported that sales had more than tripled, but that increased marketing costs aimed at securing brand recognition resulted in an operating loss. Sales growth was a result of doubling the size of Triangle's distribution system. It's best known product line, "The Band" wrist and ankle weights, maintained the number two position in its category with a 14 percent market share. Triangle planned to build on its strengths by entering the exercise equipment category and by marketing its products internationally.

CAMPBELL'S INTERNATIONAL DIVISION

Campbell's International Division provided 18 percent of the company's consolidated sales in 1984. Campbell had subsidiaries in 11 foreign countries and was planning to expand further. Total restructuring of the International Division was in progress with goals of increasing sales and earnings and building a solid base for growth.

In 1985 steps were taken toward the division's goal of contributing 25 percent of Campbell's corporate sales and earnings. A number of operations were consolidated, and new businesses were added. Other international objectives were to improve Campbell's presence in all international markets and to make Campbell into a premier international company.

RECENT EVENTS

During 1985 the market price of Campbell's stock reached a new high of $80.50 a share. In July the stock was split two for one. At year-end 1985 the market price was $51.50 and the stock price was up $4 during one December week. Analysts were puzzled by this sudden rise in market price, and there were rumors of a takeover.

Analysts observed that the company had been hurt by fierce competition in 1985, an increasing softness in many of its markets, and mistakes on new product introduction. In its *1985 Annual Report* Campbell acknowledged increased competition in the marketplace:

> The supermarket has become an arena of intense competitive activity as food companies introduce a steady stream of new consumer-oriented products and support them with massive marketing dollars in an attempt to carve out a first or second place position in the respective categories. That competitive activity is keeping the pressure on Campbell's operating results.

Case 2–8   Limited Inc.*

Leslie Wexner has an obsession with size. Just look at his houses.

He has a palatial abode in Columbus, Ohio, which he considers home. For weekend getaways, he has one of the biggest ski retreats in Aspen. And he has two Manhattan townhouses, one a seven-story edifice that had been a private school. All pale, however, beside the 60,000-square-foot mansion he is building in a Columbus suburb. "The biggest home ever in central Ohio," trumpeted Columbus Monthly magazine recently.

In Mr. Wexner's retailing dynasty, too, size appears to be everything. In the past 27 years, Mr. Wexner's company, Limited Inc., has expanded to 3,290 stores nationwide, making it one of the country's fastest-growing, most ambitious specialty-store companies. Last year, Limited generated $4.6 billion in sales, nearly four times those of the Saks Fifth Avenue chain.

But many think that the best days for U.S. retailing are over. They blame too many malls, a weakening economy and increasingly cautious consumers.

Mr. Wexner knows all this. Yet he's still expanding as fast as he can. And so far, Limited's earnings are impressive; for the August 4 quarter, the company reported yesterday a 24 percent gain in net income to $79 million, or 22 cents a share, on a 17 percent rise in sales to $1.16 billion.

"It is our clear intention to become a $10 billion company with 10 percent after-tax profits by the mid-1990s," Mr. Wexner, Limited's chairman, told banner-waving shareholders at its annual meeting. "That is our dream, that is our common vision, and that is what we are working toward."

Yet even as the grandest houses can weather, so too is Mr. Wexner's empire showing signs of wear and tear. In June and July, dollar sales at its flagship division's stores that had been open at least one year declined 5 percent from a year earlier, analysts estimate. Partly as a result, Limited's stock has lost more than 20% of its market value since a June stock split. It closed yesterday at $19.50 a share, unchanged on the day. Although other retail stocks have also slumped, this is the first time Wall Street has expressed such doubts about Mr. Wexner since women rejected short skirts three years ago.

---

* Source: Jeffrey A. Trachtenberg, "Merchant in a Rush," *The Wall Street Journal,* August 15, 1990, pp. A1, 4. Reprinted by permission of *THE WALL STREET JOURNAL,* © 1990 Dow Jones & Company, Inc. All Rights Reserved Worldwide.

"Investors have been convinced that the Limited is invincible," says Janet Mangano, an analyst at Jesup, Josephthal & Co. in New York. "But the company's core businesses need to be updated if they are going to maintain their levels of profitability. The economy is slowing. It's tough times ahead for people selling discretionary items, including the Limited."

Mr. Wexner considers the doubters short-sighted. Bigger is better, both for consumers and for the company, he says. "Customers go where the inventories are."

Since Mr. Wexner founded Limited in 1963, he has prospered by appealing to retailing's refugees. His stores draw teenagers (Limited and Express), fans of sexy lingerie (Victoria's Secret) and big women ignored by the likes of Calvin Klein (Lane Bryant). Limited also lures working women who want to shop on Fifth Avenue (Lerner New York) and preppy men who don't want to pay Ralph Lauren prices (Abercrombie & Fitch). The exception is Henri Bendel, whose affluent customers are already served by many retailers.

Mr. Wexner's obsession with growth, however, could be the company's Achilles' heel. Over the past five years, he has acquired Lerner, Bendel and Abercrombie & Fitch, all troubled businesses. Like an old-fashioned 1960s conglomerateur, Mr. Wexner believes that top performers such as Victoria's Secret and Express can carry the laggards. He also thinks that his keen fashion touch and low-cost offshore factories will transform the acquisitions into mall superstars.

But the turnarounds are taking longer than some observers expected.

Although the new Lerner stores are jazzy and upbeat, the big chain continues to perform below potential, company executives say. Abercrombie & Fitch is still deciding whether it's a men's store or a fancy gift shop. And Bendel, which once appealed to a small universe of tiny-waisted women, is searching for roots in meat-and-potatoes markets such as Chicago and Columbus. Earlier this year, its much-touted former president departed under pressure.

Adding to Mr. Wexner's difficulties, a critical new clothing line at the company's flagship Limited division has proved a slow seller. And even Lane Bryant, which has long dominated the large-size business, is stirring concern.

The man behind Limited Inc. seems driven partly by a powerful mixture of anger and pride. Nearly 30 years ago, his late father, Harry Wexner, abruptly fired him from the family's small clothing store in Columbus. "He told me I was clumsy as an ox and didn't have any aptitude for the business," says Mr. Wexner, now 53 years old. "It was a very stereotypical father-and-son conflict."

The company Mr. Wexner says he launched to prove his father wrong reflected his modest resources. "It was early-Midwest family room with beams and stucco," recalls Carol Farmer, a retail consultant who grew up in Columbus. "But you had to shop there. Les had taste, and he worked like a demon." Mr. Wexner named his store the Limited because the offerings were limited to cheap but trendy women's sportswear—blouses with Peter Pan collars, madras shorts, Shetland sweaters.

Limited blossomed along with the nation's growing freeway system, which provided access to regional malls. One store became two, two became four. As he expanded, Mr. Wexner sought out older, more experienced businessmen for advice. How far could you expand out of town? he asked. Could you go little by little, or could you leapfrog over geographical areas?

"Success fanned his emotions," says Gordon Schiffman, an original board member. "He always wanted to be the best women's clothier in the country. He was intense, a bundle of enthusiasm. Finally, though, he asked me to step down. 'Gordie,' he said, 'I appreciate everything you've done, but I need somebody with a bigger attitude.' "

As long as the U.S economy was in overdrive. Mr. Wexner could translate his ambitions into double-digit gains in annual sales and earnings. But now shoppers are cutting back. Real-estate prices are down. Unemployment has risen to 5.5 percent. Talk of a recession is growing. Bankruptcy filings have stalled classy competitors such as Rich's and Bloomingdale's.

Mr. Wexner has weathered such storms before, but this one is hitting just when he is pushing an unprecedented expansion. This year, he is adding 2.75 million square feet of new selling space to his 14.4-million square-foot base. He intends to add over three million more square feet in 1991. The building is necessary if Mr. Wexner is to achieve $10 billion in sales and earnings of $1 billion by 1995—the pledge that had fueled much of the stock gains.

Mr. Wexner is building bigger stores and more of them because he believes that customers short of time will flock to stores set up to meet all their needs. "People's attitudes and social habits change," he says. "Customers going to a shopping center today would rather go to a store of preference, where they can find what they want, rather than 10 specialty stores."

But his bigger-is-better theory, which worked so well for so long at the Limited's flagship division, isn't infallible.

In early summer, as temperatures began to climb above 80 degrees in the Northeast, Limited managers began to ship truckloads of heavy fall blazers, coats and pants bearing the new, hard-to-pronounce Paul et Duffier label. This was well in advance of competitors. The chain's Forenza label, which once conveyed the latest in street fashion from Milan and Paris, was being phased out, and its buyers wanted to move as fast as possible with as much as possible.

It proved a mistake.

June sales at stores open at least one year unexpectedly dropped an estimated 5 percent at the Limited group. Because this division produces nearly one third of corporate earnings, shareholders panicked. In one day, the stock plunged nearly 10 percent. Since the June stock split, Mr. Wexner himself has suffered a paper loss of more than $500 million on his 103.5 million shares (nearly 30 percent of the common shares outstanding).

A recent walk through the Limited store on New York's stylish Madison Avenue found the racks crowded with Paul et Duffier wool blazers marked down from $149 to $89. Upstairs, a group of Paul et Duffier fall coats was $225 instead of $350, But even at these discounts, little was selling. One saleswoman, dressed in a linen blouse and cotton skirt, looked across a department devoid of customers and said, "It's too hot to try those clothes on."

Limited insists that the promotions are part of a plan to introduce the new line and that it will fine-tune the mistakes. But shrewd competitors, such as the Gap, offered customers brighter colors in lighter-weight fabrics. And in the image-driven fashion business, first impressions are often lasting impressions. (See Exhibit 1.)

"Forcing sale prices on shoppers today is stealing business from the future," says Kurt Barnard, publisher of Barnard's Retail Marketing Report. "It's grim news for them, no question about it. The Limited apparently bought a great deal of this merchandise, and it isn't selling."

Behind Limited's stumble is a bold attempt to lure older, more affluent consumers instead of teen-agers and women in their early 20s.

Sipping coffee in one of his East Side Manhattan townhouses, Mr. Wexner says he has the world's best job. But he may be one of retailing's most aloof monarchs. This committed bachelor has said he never has had time to settle down. Here, where the living-room walls are covered with a special egg-shell crackle wallpaper, Picassos compete with De Koonings for space. It is a serene tableau but devoid of photographs of friends or family.

Mr. Wexner is an enigma in the often-glamorous world of retailing, where jaunty personalities such as Marvin Traub of Bloomingdale's have become society figures. After rejecting his second White House dinner invitation because it interfered with business plans, Mr. Wexner was told he wouldn't be asked again. That didn't upset him. "I didn't think my presence was necessary at a sit-down dinner for 300," Mr. Wexner says blandly.

Even in Columbus, he rarely joins the formal-dinner set. "I don't think there are many people here who know him well," says one prominent hostess, requesting anonymity because her husband is a business associate of Mr. Wexner's. "The man is a workaholic. Everything else is basically a distraction."

EXHIBIT 1   The Limited Inc. Confronts Competitive Times

The Limited's many divisions . . .
Estimated fiscal 1989 sales, by division, in millions

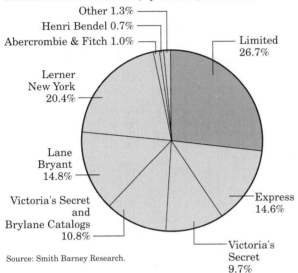

Other 1.3%
Henri Bendel 0.7%
Abercrombie & Fitch 1.0%
Limited 26.7%
Lerner New York 20.4%
Lane Bryant 14.8%
Victoria's Secret and Brylane Catalogs 10.8%
Express 14.6%
Victoria's Secret 9.7%

Source: Smith Barney Research.

Still earn money . . .
EstimAted fiscal 1989 operating profit, by division, in millions

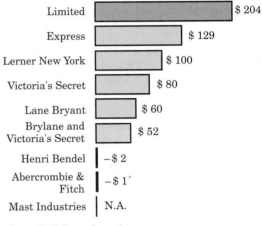

Limited	$ 204
Express	$ 129
Lerner New York	$ 100
Victoria's Secret	$ 80
Lane Bryant	$ 60
Brylane and Victoria's Secret	$ 52
Henri Bendel	−$ 2
Abercrombie & Fitch	−$ 1
Mast Industries	N.A.

Source: Smith Barney Research.

But face slower growth . . .
Comparison of The Gap and the Limited division, monthly change in store sales, in percent

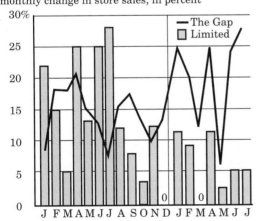

— The Gap
▢ Limited

J F M A M J J A S O N D J F M A M J J

Sources: Smith Barney Research; The Gap.

And recent investor wariness.
The Limited, weekly closing stock price

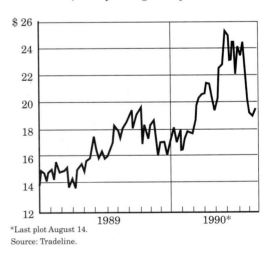

*Last plot August 14.
Source: Tradeline.

But if Mr. Wexner lacks social ambition, he evidently hungers for the status accorded people who succeed at managing big department-store chains.

Twice he has failed in efforts to acquire the Carter Hawley Hale chain. Last year, he approached executives at R.H. Macy & Co. about taking an equity stake in that huge retailer. Most recently, he secretly backed a management-led buy-out attempt at Marshall Field. Had that bid succeeded, he would have emerged as a substantial minority shareholder.

Meanwhile, Mr. Wexner continues to tinker with Henri Bendel and Abercrombie & Fitch. Recently he even suggested that both could well become $1 billion companies—very big by retailing standards. This is why some have begun to wonder whether his fixation on upper-crust customers may be affecting his judgment.

"He seems to believe that if he is going to be a legend, he needs to attract the affluent, fashionable, mature woman," suggests George Rosenbaum, president of Leo J. Shapiro, a Chicago-based market-research firm. Referring to the Henri Bendel chain, Mr. Rosenbaum adds:

"We're talking about serving the princesses of America. These aren't the neglected women Mr. Wexner has nurtured in the past. He relishes a test, but this is a much riskier thing than he has ever done before. There's reason to be dubious."

Admittedly, Mr. Wexner has frequently surprised skeptics. Many analysts deem his retailing skills second only to those of Wal-Mart founder Sam Walton. Eventually, both Henri Bendel and Abercrombie & Fitch may indeed emerge as hits. "He has enough income to support what amounts to research and development," says New York investment banker Gilbert Harrison. "He won't give up."

But the uncertain futures of those chains underscore Mr. Wexner's problem. At some point, sales and profits at even Express and Victoria's Secret, among the company's strongest divisions, will begin to mature. And Mr. Wexner can't be sure what will replace them.

This is why he is experimenting with a raft of niche businesses. Besides Henri Bendel and Abercrombie & Fitch, these include bath shops, men's clothing shops, children's businesses and yet more lingerie under the Cacique label. William Smith and Margaret McKenna, analysts at Smith Barney, Harris Upham & Co., also think that Mr. Wexner may soon launch a cosmetics and related-products line.

"The thing about Les is that he really believes that trees grow to the sky," one close adviser says. "They don't. He owns some remarkable businesses today, but there are no guarantees that he will be able to build new ones."

But Mr. Wexner is characteristically upbeat. In early August, he opened a new Henri Bendel store at the Atrium in Chestnut Hill, a Boston suburb chockablock with luxury-goods retailers. To ensure that his entry is noticed, Mr. Wexner has graced it with a grand staircase, tons of marble and a gilded dome over the cosmetics department. And with 40,000 square feet spread over three levels, it's the biggest store in the mall.

Case 2–9   MacTec Control AB*

Georg Carlsson is president of MacTec Control AB, a Swedish firm located in Kristianstad. Georg began MacTec in 1980 with his wife, Jessie. MacTec grew rapidly and now boasts of 30 employees and annual revenues of about $2.8 million. Since 1985, MacTec has been partly owned by the Perstorp Corporation whose headquarters are located nearby. Perstorp is a large manufacturer of chemicals and chemical products, with operations in 18 countries and annual revenues of about $600 million. Perstorp has provided MacTec with capital and managerial advice, as well as chemical analysis technology.

MACTEC's AQUALEX SYSTEM

MacTec's product line centers around its Aqualex system: computer hardware and software designed to monitor and control pressurized water flow. The water flow consists mostly of potable water or sewage effluent as these liquids are stored, moved, or treated by municipal water departments.

The system employs MacTec's MPDII microcomputer (see Exhibit 1) installed at individual pumping stations where liquids are stored and moved. Often these stations are located quite far apart, linking geographically dispersed water users (households, businesses, etc.) to water and sewer systems. The microcomputer performs a number of important functions. It controls the starts, stops, and alarms of up to four pumps, monitors levels and available capacities of storage reservoirs, checks pump capacities and power consumptions, and records pump flows. It even measures the amount of rainfall entering reservoirs and adjusts pump operations or activates an alarm as needed. Each microcomputer can also easily be connected to a main computer to allow remote control of pumping stations and produce a variety of charts and graphs useful in evaluating pump performance and scheduling needed maintenance.

The Aqualex system provides a monitoring function that human operators cannot match in terms of sophistication, immediacy, and cost. The system permits each individual substation to: control its own

---

* This case was written by Professor James E. Nelson, University of Colorado. © 1989 by the Business Research Division, College of Business and Administration and the Graduate School of Business Administration, University of Colorado, Boulder, Colorado, 80309-0419.

EXHIBIT 1

The Aqualex System is based on the MPDII which controls and monitors the pumping stations

An MPDII microcomputer is installed at a pumping station and works as an independent, intelligent computer. When required, it can go online with the central computer and report its readings there.

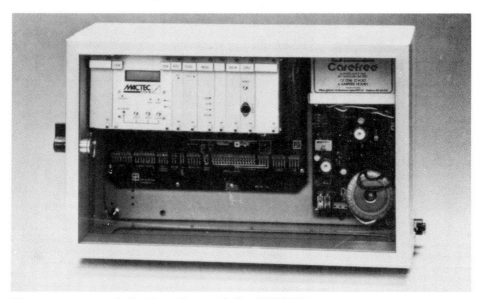

Here are some of the functions of the MPDII:

— It governs the starts, stops, and alarms of up to four pumps, controlled by an integrated piezo-resistive pressure-level sensor.

— It checks the sump level.

— It checks pump capacity and changes in pump capacity.

— It activates an alarm when readings reach preset deviation limits.

— It registers precipitation and activates an alarm in case of heavy rain.

— It constantly monitors pump power consumption and activates an alarm in case of unacceptable deviation.

— It registers current pump flow by means of advanced calculations of inflow and outfeed from the sump.

— It can register accumulated time for overflow.

— It switches to forward or reverse action, even by remote command.

— It stores locally the last nine alarm instances with time indications. These may be read directly on an LCD display.

— It can be remotely programmed from the central computer.

An MPDII does a great job, day after day, year after year.

pumping operations; collect, analyze, and store data; forecast trends; transmit data and alarms to a central computer; and receive remote commands. Alarms can also be transmitted directly to a pocket-size receiver carried by one or more operators on call. A supervisor can continually monitor pumping operations in a large system entirely via a computer terminal at a central location and send commands to individual pumps, thereby saving costly service calls and time. The system also reduces the possibility of overflows that could produce disastrous flooding in nearby communities.

MacTec personnel work with water and sewage engineers to design and install the Aqualex system. Personnel also train engineers and operators to work with the system and are available 24 hours a day for consultation. If needed, a MacTec engineer can personally assist engineers and operators if major problems arise. MacTec also offers its clients the option of purchasing a complete service contract whereby MacTec personnel provide periodic testing and maintenance of installed systems.

An Aqualex system has several versions. In its most basic form, the system is little more than a small "black box" that monitors two or three lift station activities and, when necessary, transmits an alarm to one or more remote receivers. An intermediate system monitors additional activities, sends data to a central computer via telephone lines and receives remote commands. An advanced system provides the same monitoring capabilities but has forecasting features, maintenance management, auxiliary power back-up, and data transmission and reception via radio. Prices for the three different types in early 1989 are $1,200, $2,400, and $4,200.

AQUALEX CUSTOMERS

Aqualex customers can be divided into two groups—governmental units and industrial companies. The typical application in the first group is a sewage treatment plant having 4 to 12 pumping stations, each station containing one or more pumps. Pumps operate intermittently and, unless an Aqualex or similar system is in place, are monitored by one or more operators who visit each station once or twice each day for about half an hour. Operators take reservoir measurements, record running times of pumps, and sometimes perform limited maintenance and repairs. The sewage plant and stations are typically located in flat or rolling terrain, where gravity cannot be used in lieu of pumping. If any monitoring equipment is present at all, it typically consists of a crude, on-site alarm that activates when fluid levels rise or fall beyond a preset level. Sometimes the alarm activates a telephone dialing function that alerts an operator away from the station.

Numerous industrial companies also store, move, and process large quantities of water or sewage. These applications usually differ very little from those in governmental plants except for their smaller size. On the other hand, there are considerably more industrial companies with pumping stations and so, Georg thinks, the two markets often offer close to identical market potentials in many countries.

The two markets desire essentially the same products, although industrial applications often use smaller, simpler equipment. Both markets want their monitoring equipment to be accurate and reliable, the two dominant concerns. Equipment should also be easy to use, economical to operate, and require little regular service or maintenance. Purchase price often is not a major consideration. As long as the price is in an appropriate range, customers seem more interested in actual product performance than in initial cost outlays.

Georg thinks worldwide demand for Aqualex systems and competing products will continue to be strong for at least the next 10 years. While some of this demand represents construction of new pumping stations, many applications are replacements of crude monitoring and alarm systems at existing sites. These existing systems depend greatly on regular visits by operators, visits that often continue even after new equipment is installed. Most such trips are probably not necessary. However, many managers find it difficult to dismiss or reassign monitoring personnel that are no longer needed; many are also quite cautious and conservative, desiring some human monitoring of the new equipment "just in case." Once replacement of existing systems is complete, market growth is limited to new construction and, of course, replacements with more sophisticated systems.

Most customers (and noncustomers) consider the Aqualex system the best on the market. Those knowledgeable in the industry feel that competing products seldom match Aqualex's reliability and accuracy. Experts also believe that many competing products lack the sophistication and flexibility present in Aqualex's design. Beyond these product features, customers also appreciate MacTec's knowledge about water and sanitation engineering. Competing firms often lack this expertise, offering products somewhat as a sideline and considering the market too small for an intensive marketing effort.

The market is clearly not too small for MacTec. While Georg has no hard data on market potential for Western Europe, he thinks annual demand could be as much as $9 million. About 40 percent of this figure represents potential, the rest is demand for replacing existing systems. Industry sales in the latter category could be increased by more aggressive marketing efforts on the part of MacTec and its competitors. Eastern European economies represent additional potential. However, the water and sewer industries in these countries seem less interested in high-technology equipment to monitor pumping operations than do

their Western counterparts. Additionally, business is often more difficult to conduct in these countries. In contrast, the U.S. market looks
very attractive.

MACTEC STRATEGY

MacTec currently markets its Aqualex system primarily to sewage
treatment plants in Scandinavia and other countries in northern and
central Europe. The company's strategy could be described as providing technologically superior equipment to monitor pumping operations
at these plants. The strategy stresses frequent contacts with customers
and potential customers to design, supply, and service Aqualex systems. Superior knowledge of water and sanitation engineering with
up-to-date electronics and computer technology is also important. The
result is a line of highly specialized sensors, computers, and methods
for process controls in water treatment plants.

The essence of MacTec's strategy is demonstrating a special competence that no firm in the world can easily match. MacTec also prides
itself on being a young, creative company, without an entrenched bureaucracy. Company employees generally work with enthusiasm and
dedication; they talk with each other regularly and openly. Most importantly, customers—as well as technology—seem to drive all areas
of the company.

MacTec's strategy in its European markets seems fairly well-de-
cided. That is, Georg thinks that a continuation of present strategies
and tactics should continue to produce good results. However, one
change is the planned creation of a branch office conducting sales and
manufacturing activities somewhere in the European Community
(EC), most likely the Netherlands. The plan is to have such an office in
operation well before 1992, when the 12 countries in the EC (Belgium,
Denmark, France, Greece, Ireland, Italy, Luxembourg, the Netherlands, Portugal, Spain, United Kingdom, and West Germany) would
mutually eliminate national barriers to the flow of capital, goods, and
services. Having a MacTec office located in the EC would greatly simplify sales to these member countries. Moreover, MacTec's presence
should also avoid problems with any protective barriers the EC itself
might raise to limit or discourage market access by outsiders.

Notwithstanding activities related to this branch office, Georg is
considering a major strategic decision to enter the U.S. market. His
two recent visits to the United States have led him to conclude that the
market represents potential beyond that for western Europe and that
the United States seems perfect for expansion. Industry experts in the
United States agree with Georg that the Aqualex system outperforms
anything used in the U.S. market. Experts think many water and

sewage engineers would welcome MacTec's products and knowledge. Moreover, Georg thinks U.S. transportation systems and payment arrangements would present few problems. The system would be imported under U.S. Tariff Regulation 71249 and pay a duty of 4.9 percent.

Entry would most likely occur in the form of a sales and service office located in Philadelphia. The Pennsylvania and New York state markets seem representative of the United States and appear to offer a good test of the Aqualex system. The two states together probably represent about 18 percent of total U.S. market potential for the system. The office would require an investment of $200,000 for inventory and other balance sheet items. Annual fixed costs would total close to $250,000 for salaries and other operating expenses; Georg plans to employ only a general manager, two sales technicians, and a secretary for at least the first year or two. Each Aqualex system sold in the United States would be priced to provide a contribution of about 30 percent. Georg wants a 35 percent annual return before taxes on any MacTec investment, beginning no later than the second year. The issue is whether Georg can realistically expect to achieve this goal in the United States.

MARKETING RESEARCH

Georg had commissioned the Browning Group in Philadelphia to conduct some limited marketing research with selected personnel in the water and sewage industries in the city and surrounding areas. The research had two purposes: To obtain a sense of market needs and market reactions to MacTec's products, and to calculate a rough estimate of market potential in Pennsylvania and New York. Results were intended to help Georg interpret his earlier conversations with industry experts and perhaps facilitate a decision on market entry.

The research design employed two phases of data collection. The first consisted of five one-hour, tape-recorded interviews with water and sewage engineers employed by local city and municipal governments. Questions included:

1. What procedures do you use to monitor your pumping stations?
2. Is your current monitoring system effective? Costly?
3. What are the costs of a monitoring malfunction?
4. What features would you like to see in a monitoring system?
5. Who decides on the selection of a monitoring system?
6. What is your reaction to the Aqualex system?

Interviewers listened closely to the engineers' responses and probed for additional detail and clarification.

Tapes of the personal interviews were transcribed and then analyzed by the project manager at Browning. The report noted that these results described typical industry practices and viewpoints. A partial summary from the report appears below:

> The picture that emerges is one of fairly sophisticated personnel making decisions about monitoring equipment that is relatively simple in design. Still, some engineers would appear distrustful of this equipment because they persist in sending operators to pumping stations on a daily basis. The distrust may be justified because potential costs of a malfunction were identified as expensive repairs and cleanups, fines of $10,000 per day of violation, lawsuits, harassment by the Health department, and public embarrassment. The five engineers identified themselves as key individuals in the decision to purchase new equipment. Without exception, they considered MacTec features innovative, highly desirable, and worth the price.

The summary also noted that the primary purpose of the interview results was for construction of a questionnaire to be administered by telephone.

The questionnaire was used in the second phase of data collection, as part of a telephone survey that contacted 65 utility managers, water and sewage engineers, and pumping station operators in Philadelphia and surrounding areas. All respondents were employed by governmental units. Each interview took about 10 minutes to complete, covering topics identified in questions 1, 2, and 4 above. The Browning Group's research report stated that most respondents were quite cooperative, although 15 people refused to participate at all.

The telephone interviews produced results that could be considered more representative of the market because of the larger sample size. The report organized these results under the topics of monitoring procedures, system effectiveness and costs, and features desired in a monitoring system:

> All monitoring systems under the responsibility of the 50 respondents were considered to require manual checking. The frequency of operator visits to pumping stations ranged from monthly to twice daily, depending on flow rates, pumping station history, proximity of nearby communities, monitoring equipment in operation, and other factors. Even the most sophisticated automatic systems were checked because respondents "just don't trust the machine." Each operator was responsible for some 10 to 20 stations.
>
> Despite the perceived need for double-checking, all respondents considered their current monitoring system to be quite effective. Not one reported a serious pumping malfunction in the past three years that had escaped detection. However, this reliability came at considerable cost—the annual wages and other expenses associated with each monitoring operator averaged about $40,000.

Respondents were about evenly divided between those wishing a simple alarm system and those desiring a sophisticated, versatile microprocessor. Managers and engineers in the former category often said that the only feature they really needed was an emergency signal such as a siren, horn, or light. Sometimes they would add a telephone dialer that would be automatically activated at the same time as the signal. Most agreed that a price of around $2,000 would be reasonable for such a system. The latter category of individuals contained engineers desiring many of the Aqualex System's features, once they knew such equipment was available. A price of $4,000 per system seemed acceptable. Some of these respondents were quite knowledgeable about computers and computer programming while others were not. Only four respondents voiced any strong concerns about the cost to purchase and install more sophisticated monitoring equipment. Everyone demanded that the equipment be reliable and accurate.

Georg found the report quite helpful. Much of the information, of course, simply confirmed his own view of the U.S. market. However, it was good to have this knowledge from an independent, objective organization. In addition, to learn that the market consisted of two, apparently equal-size segments—of simple and sophisticated applications—was quite worthwhile. In particular, knowledge of system prices considered acceptable by each segment would make the entry decision easier. Meeting these prices would not be a major problem.

An important section of the report contained an estimate of market potential for Pennsylvania and New York. The estimate was based on an analysis of discharge permits on file in governmental offices in the two states. These permits are required before any city, municipality, water or sewage district, or industrial company can release sewage or other contaminated water to another system or to a lake or river. Each permit showed the number of pumping stations in operation. Based on a 10 percent sample of permits, the report estimated that governmental units in Pennsylvania and New York contain approximately 3,000 and 5,000 pumping stations for waste water, respectively. Industrial companies in the two states were estimated to add 3,000 and 9,000 more pumping stations, respectively. The total number of pumping stations in the two states (20,000) seemed to be growing at about 2 percent per year.

Finally, a brief section of the report dealt with the study's limitations. Georg agreed that sample was quite small, that it contained no utility managers or engineers from New York, and that it probably concentrated too heavily on individuals in larger urban areas. In addition, the research told him nothing about competitors and their marketing strategies and tactics. Nor did he learn anything about any state regulations for monitoring equipment, if indeed any existed.

However, these shortcomings came as no surprise, representing a consequence of the research design proposed to Georg by the Browning Group six weeks ago, before the study began.

THE DECISION

Georg's decision seems difficult. The most risky option is to enter the U.S. market as soon as possible; the most conservative is to stay in Europe. The option also exists of conducting additional marketing research.

Case 2–10   *Sony Corporation**

It's a Sony, say the ads, and fans of the company's fancy electronics understand. But if the ads were for the corporation itself, the line might be different: It's a *new* Sony.

The old Sony was strictly a maker of consumer items, however remarkable in their novelty; the new Sony serves industry as well, with products like powerful work-station computers.

The old and very proud Sony wouldn't dream of selling something that didn't carry its brand; the new one is doing a thriving business selling components to other manufacturers.

The old Sony would hand the world a technology—Betamax videocassette recorders—and wait for rival electronics makers to follow its lead; the new Sony, much chastened by that costly flop, persuaded more than 100 other concerns to join in the research before launching another VCR format, 8 millimeter.

And in perhaps the biggest switch of all, the new Sony is out to sell not simply hardware but also the entertainment software that runs on it; with its CBS Records acquisition last year, Sony is already the world's largest music producer, and it now is shopping intently for a movie studio.

All these changes reflect a Sony that is beginning to move beyond the era of its famous chairman, Akio Morita. Sony's image has been inextricably linked to the white-haired, extroverted Mr. Morita, who

---

* Source: "New Format: A Changing Sony Aims to Sell the 'Software,' Too," *The Wall Street Journal*, Dec. 30, 1988, pp. A1, A4.

with a co-founder built a company based on the twin ideas of innovative technology and selling to the West. Mr. Morita is 67 years old, and he now spends much of his time traveling to espouse his views on trade friction and competitiveness. The post-Morita era is coming.

Already vanishing is the notion that Sony can simply invent nifty products for needs people don't know they have—then show them why they want the things. This won't do in an age of ever-toughening competition, both at home and from other Asian nations. The new, humbler Sony pays more attention to what both the public and the other companies in its industry want built.

This is the approach of the man who increasingly runs the company today, Sony president Norio Ohga. The 58-year-old Mr. Ohga wasn't trained as an engineer; he was an opera singer, and he came to Sony's attention decades ago as a music student full of opinions on how to make a good tape recorder. He still looks at things from the customers' viewpoint, Sony people say. "He defines the application first, then says, 'Let the technologists get us there,'" explains Tsutomu Sugiyama, Sony's corporate communications manager.

An example is the way Sony is trying to support its newest VCR technology. The company's latest small wonder is the Video Walkman, a product designed to enable people to indulge their addictions to video wherever they happen to be. A portable videocassette player and tiny television set, the Video Walkman is not much bigger than a long paperback book.

Its technology, however, is 8mm—more compact than the prevailing VHS of most VCRs, but not a format with many movies or videos available. And that presents a problem. "Unlike TV or radio, the equipment that's on the rise now is the kind that is worthless on its own without software," notes Akihiko Tsuda, senior manager of corporate planning at Toshiba Corp. This is one of the bitter lessons from the VHS-Betamax "video wars," in which Sony's Betamax lost out when software makers produced more movies for VHS, the format Sony's rivals had united behind.

"We learned from Betamax about the importance of software," says Michael Schulhof, vice chairman of Sony Corp. of America. Now, if Sony had its own film library, it could control the format in which the movies were put on tape; that could give a strong edge to 8mm over the technology it competes against, a compact version of VHS called VHS-C. "To have a balanced company, the one piece we are missing is a major movie studio," Mr. Schulhof says.

So last fall, Sony went after MGM/UA Communications Inc., which has a library of close to 1,000 United Artists films and a national distribution system. The choice surprised some analysts because MGM/UA is Hollywood's weakest studio, but Sony executives familiar with the talks say their company believed MGM could be rebuilt in two years with a $300 million infusion. Although the talks broke down in November, the courtship may not be over.

An alternative target could be Columbia Pictures, which would also provide a good film library and national distribution system, although its management has been in disarray. Columbia, 49 percent owned by Coca-Cola Co., denies any interest in selling but says it would have to listen to a decent offer. Meanwhile, MCA Inc. is expected to be up for sale before long as its chairman, Lew Wasserman, nears retirement.

Buying a film company should make Sony stronger in the future, industry analysts say, just as the $2 billion acquisition of CBS Records did (the records unit contributed 16 percent of Sony's sales in the six months ended in September). But it won't be easy. The entertainment-software business is not only risky but costly; a top-tier studio like MCA might cost $6 billion, analysts say.

And Sony doesn't have a clear field because other Japanese electronics companies are moving in the same direction, notably archrival Victor Co. of Japan. "We can't say there isn't a possibility that we'd consider buying a foreign movie company," acknowledges a JVC managing director, Masanobu Ikeda.

Even if Sony overpaid for a movie company, the purchase might work out, analysts in Japan say. For one thing, there may be big domestic payoffs from a video-software library after 1990, when Japan begins 24-hour satellite TV broadcasting and has to fill air time for 12 or 13 channels instead of the current seven.

Meanwhile, Sony's base—its hardware innovation—faces increased competition. When it introduces something new, other electronics concerns catch up quickly. South Korean and Taiwanese firms are taking over bread-and-butter products like VCRs, for instance. In addition, Sony makes about 70 percent of its sales abroad, and though it is raising its overseas production, trade friction remains a threat.

These are arguments for diversification, and that is what Sony is pursuing. Entertainment software is one example. Computers are another. Sony has been producing the office-use computers known as work stations for about two years. It claimed about 20 percent of the Japanese workstation market in the year ended last March 31. This year, Sony expects to almost double its sales to 6,000 units.

Then there is the selling of components, a major reversal of strategy also pursued during Mr. Ohga's presidency. Sony's previous insistence on selling only under its own brand was a venerable tradition. In 1955, Mr. Morita brashly turned down a windfall order for 100,000 tape recorders and microphones from Bulova Watch Co. because Bulova wanted to market them under its name. Mr. Morita insisted Sony had to build its own name recognition.

But as part of a corporate restructuring carried out by Mr. Ohga, Sony now includes a division created specifically to market components. Sony's semiconductors, once made only for its own products, now go to competitors both at home and abroad. In just four years, parts have come to claim an 11 percent share of Sony's sales, excluding CBS Records.

"We started not from zero, but very small," says Junichi Kodera, managing director of the components marketing group. New he predicts that Sony will soon be delivering more parts outside the company than to its own consumer-products groups.

This amounts to "a more offensive approach" to Sony's technology, explains Shawn Layden, a communications officer. "We changed 180 degrees from the defensive strategy of patenting and protecting our technology to developing new market segments."

Selling hardware is also one goal of Sony's push into entertainment software, of course. CBS Records' global distribution network is a springboard "to ultimately expand into a world-wide software distribution company through which we can market audio and video hardware," says Mr. Schulhof.

The continuing stress Sony puts on inventive hardware is evident in the way it prepared the ground for 8mm camcorder technology, its entry in the latest round of video wars. (Its rival, the VHS-C format, has the advantage that its tapes can be played on standard VHS players with a simple adapter; 8mm tapes can't be played on either VHS or Beta, but the technology can record for up to four hours.)

In the mid-1970s, when Sony introduced its pioneering Betamax video technology, it proudly presented the format to its competitors as a *fait accompli* and urged them to accept it as the standard. But that isn't the way things are done in group-oriented Japan, and to rivals it only confirmed the impression they already had that Sony was arrogant. Competitors such as Hitachi, Toshiba and Matsushita Electric Industrial (Panasonic's maker) instead banded together behind VHS. "The VHS-Beta battle was decided on some other grounds than technical advantage," concedes an executive at one Sony rival.

This time, Sony did things right: From the start of its foray into 8mm, it rounded up more than 100 companies to undertake research on the technology. It agreed to sell 8mm camcorders to be marketed under other brands. "Sony said, 'I'll take a smaller margin and less technological pride in exchange for less risk,'" says Toshiaki Kaminogo, a Japanese business writer. "They learned a lesson."

And Sony is trying to fit in better in other ways, too. Within its work force it has long discouraged hierarchy and encouraged employees to think up ideas—approaches that, while pleasing many employees, made them seem "foreign" to other Japanese companies. Now Sony preaches good manners; an in-house newsletter runs a cartoon in which a Sony mascot admonishes salesmen to hold elevator doors and not smoke in the halls.

As for the 8mm camcorder, the jury is still out on whether it will win out over VHS-C. But Sony's new cooperativeness appears to be paying off. After a slow start in 1985, Sony's production of 8mm camcorders will jump an estimated 30 percent in the current fiscal year to 1.8 million units. The 8mm format now claims 50 percent of Europe's camcorder market, 30 percent of Japan's and 20 percent of North America's, says Kurt Hahn, an analyst at Hoare Govette Japan. And software is coming: 500 or so 8mm video titles are available to Japan, about half that number in the U.S. and about 800 in Europe.

Says Sony's Mr. Sugiyama: "To be unique is not the only solution anymore. You have to be a trend setter, but you also have to go with the rest to establish good business."

The shifts in strategy have yielded some good numbers. After a 42 percent drop in earnings in the year ended March 31, 1987—largely because of the stronger yen's damage to exports—Sony saw its net rise nearly 47 percent in fiscal 1988. CBS Records is contributing in the current year, earlier than expected. (See Exhibit 1 for data comparisons.)

The push into entertainment software is a project of Mr. Ohga, the president, and its success is one reason for thinking he may someday succeed Mr. Morita as chairman. But Sony is a puzzle in this regard, because it has little experience with succession.

Started in 1946 as Tokyo Tsushin Kogyo Co., the company was led for decades by the founders, Mr. Morita and Masaru Ibuka, and an early colleague, Kazuo Iwama. So intent were they on selling to the West that they changed the name in 1958 to one Americans could remember better; "Sony" was based on the Latin word *sonus* (sound) and the American slang "sonny boy." Mr. Ibuka now is retired. Mr. Ohga became president with the unexpected death of Mr. Iwama six years ago.

Even if Mr. Ohga became chairman, Mr. Morita's imprint wouldn't be erased. So speculation focuses on who would become president in that case. Many analysts bet on Mr. Morita's 61-year-old brother, Masaaki, a Sony deputy president who started research into Betamax technology and became chairman of Sony Corp. of America in 1987. His age works against him, though, they say, and his elder brother is reportedly leery of promoting a family member.

Others think a new name will emerge. Possible contenders are the senior corporate-planning officer, Ken Iwaki, 52, who takes a logical, straightforward economist's approach, and Nobuo Kanoi, 57, a strong-willed engineer and audio expert, now senior managing director for product coordination. Yet for at least the next five years, analysts see little reason to expect Mr. Ohga to move either up or out.

For all the changes going on within Sony, it may be a while before retail customers sense a difference. They, inevitably, still think of

EXHIBIT 1 Sony Masters Its Lesson in Humility

Sales came back . . .
In billions of dollars*

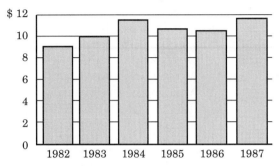

*Translated from yen at 125 yen per dollar.

Earnings recovered . . .
In millions of dollars*

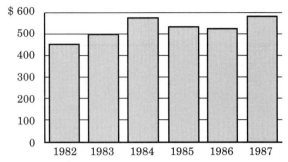

*Translated from yen at 125 yen per dollar.

It spent on R & D . . .
Research and development spending as
a percentage of sales.

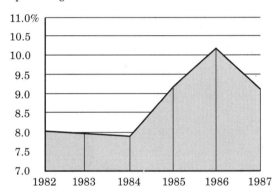

Its stock surged . . .
Sony vs. index of Japanese electronics companies
(indexed to Jan. 2, 1987 = 100)

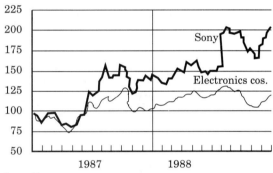

Source: Datastream.

Domestic sales gained . . .
Percentage of sales by region.

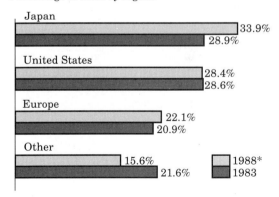

Japan 33.9% / 28.9%
United States 28.4% / 28.6%
Europe 22.1% / 20.9%
Other 15.6% / 21.6%

1988*
1983

*First six months.

And it diversified.
Percentage of sales by product.

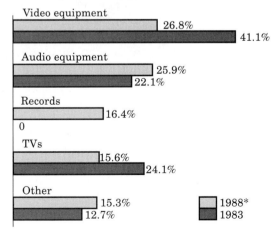

Video equipment 26.8% / 41.1%
Audio equipment 25.9% / 22.1%
Records 16.4% / 0
TVs 15.6% / 24.1%
Other 15.3% / 12.7%

1988*
1983

*First six months.

Sony as simply a vendor of equipment with a reputation for quality. Typical is Ikuo Sakurai, a 35-year-old store clerk stopping one evening at Sony's fancy showroom in Tokyo's Ginza district.

"I don't want to have the same thing as everyone else. That's why I like Sony," Mr. Sakurai says. He owns a Sony tape recorder, TV set, stereo, Beta VCR and 8mm camera. But of Sony the music or movie kingpin, he knows nothing. Peering into the screen of a Sony word processor, he says, "I'm thinking of getting one of these next."

Case 2–11   The Simons Lumber Company*

"I guess we are in a predicament that many of our competitors would envy," said Stephen Simons. "Our company's reputation is among the best in the industry, we make a respectable profit in both good and bad economic times, and we know our business, but it is very difficult to enlarge our niche without running into competition from a national wholesaler or manufacturer."

Simons had spent the past 16 years of his life in this company, although in the past four years he spent only 20 percent of his time at the business, having started an unrelated venture in 1982. Now, as this new venture was taking more of his time, Simons was trying to decide the best course of action for the lumber business. Whereas his father had focused on managing the "top line" of the income statement, Stephen Simons had focused primarily on the "bottom line." Stephen Simons now wondered whether his emphasis had been carried too far and if it was time for a change in focus. Should he try to plot a course of planned expansion or should he be content to continue dominating the niche the company now occupies? Given the difficulty of obtaining market information on a narrow product line in a limited geographic area, Simons is not even sure that his firm is dominating its selected niche. He thought his company still had the largest market share in its products, but he suspected that position may be eroding.

---

* Copyright © 1987, Stewart C. Malone, McIntire School of Commerce, University of Virginia.

THE WHOLESALE LUMBER INDUSTRY

Wholesale lumber companies provide the linking pin between the lumber producer and retailer or end-user of the lumber. These wholesale companies are generally small, family-owned businesses, although the past 20 years have seen the rise of larger national or regional wholesalers. Even the larger wholesalers tend to be privately owned, and currently only one lumber wholesaler's stock is traded publicly.

There are at least two dimensions on which lumber wholesalers may differ (Exhibit 1). The first dimension is the breadth of product line handled. Full-line wholesalers carry the entire spectrum of lumber and building products. Studs, plywood, and dimension lumber for building are major product lines for these firms. These products are often regarded as commodities, and the profit margin per unit may be extremely small; but the market for these products is large, and they tend to sell in large blocks. Given the financial resources and exposure in this type of business, full-line wholesalers tend to be larger than average in size.

As opposed to the full-line wholesaler, the specialty wholesaler has an extremely narrow product line, often only one or two products. Specialty wholesalers are generally found where there is a high degree

---

EXHIBIT 1

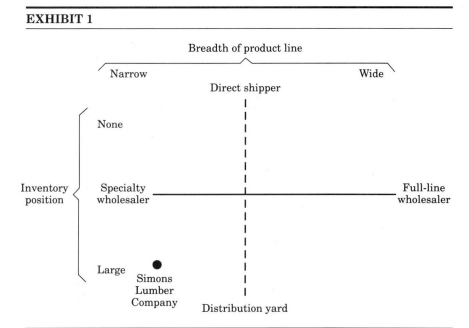

of product or market knowledge required. Sales volumes are usually smaller for a specialty wholesaler, but markups are generally higher.

A second dimension that distinguishes wholesalers is their inventories. Direct shippers are wholesalers that seldom take physical possession of the products they sell. Their function is to obtain an order from a customer, place it with a mill for production, and the mill then ships it directly to the wholesaler's customer. A distribution yard wholesaler, however, maintains a physical inventory of the product line, in the geographic market where business is conducted. Because of the financial risk and requirements of maintaining a physical inventory, profit margins are generally considerably higher for a distribution yard wholesaler.

Some wholesalers (primarily distribution yards) add additional value to their products by remanufacturing or altering the size, shape, finish, and so on of certain products. It is much easier to enter the wholesale business as a direct shipper than as a distribution yard, because the requirements for entry are limited to mill and customer contacts, as well as credit line for working capital. Many wholesale lumber businesses are started by a sales representative leaving an established firm to start his own direct-shipper company. Often, if the new venture is successful, the new wholesaler will then add distribution yard facilities to his company.

In actual practice, the distinctions between direct shippers and distribution yards should be considered a continuum since many companies may have both direct and distribution yard sales. The 1982 Census of the Wholesale Trade showed 1,317 lumber wholesalers without a yard (direct shippers) and 1,950 wholesalers with a yard (distribution yards).

The North American Wholesale Lumber Association reported that a survey of its members for 1983 showed that average sales per distribution yard were approximately $6.5 million, a 26 percent increase over the previous year. The average sales of the membership companies (both direct and distribution yards) were approximately $21 million in 1983.

The industry still depends heavily on person-to-person contact for developing relationships between customers and suppliers. Wholesalers maintain lists of active, inactive, and potential customers, which are then used by their sales representatives to solicit orders. While face-to-face contact was once the most prevalent method of soliciting business, telephone contact is now far more prevalent, given the cost of travel. One wholesale trade association survey estimated the average lumber wholesaler's telephone expense during 1983 was $84,000. Obviously, the telephone expense is dependent on the intensity of the firm's marketing area and its geographic trading area.

EXHIBIT 2   New Housing Units Started 1977–1984 (in thousands)

1978	*1979*	*1980*	*1981*	*1982*	*1983*	*1984*
2,036	1,760	1,313	1,100	1,072	1,712	1,753

Inasmuch as lumber is an undifferentiated product, suppliers in this industry compete heavily on price and service (product expertise, advantageous delivery schedules, etc.). Those products which are regarded as commodities, such as 2×4s and plywood, are exceedingly price sensitive, and most customers have little loyalty to a particular manufacturer or wholesaler. Specialty items are somewhat more differentiated, and a customer may be dependent on a wholesaler for highly technical information. Brand or supplier loyalty is somewhat greater in this class of product.

The major market for lumber in the United States is the housing industry, and the wholesale lumber industry shares many characteristics with it. First, housing demand is highly interest-rate sensitive. Generally, when mortgage rates increase, the demand for new housing falls. Thus, given the swings in interest rates, both the housing and lumber markets are highly cyclical. (See Exhibit 2.)

While demand for lumber may be cyclical, there have been certain changes in the industry in the past 10 years that have affected competition. With energy costs increasing through the 1970s and freight carriers deregulated in the 1980s, the cost of transportation became a significant portion of the lumber cost. Many wholesalers, especially those dealing in price-sensitive commodity items, found it necessary to add a traffic manager to their staffs in order to remain competitive. Increased transportation costs also led wholesalers to focus on species of lumber that were geographically closer to the consuming market. In the last 20 years, the amount of lumber from the Pacific Northwest shipped to markets east of the Rockies declined dramatically, while southern pine and eastern Canadian woods increased their market share in the eastern half of the United States.

COMPANY HISTORY

In 1894 Robert Simons joined with partner Bernard Taylor to open a lumberyard in downtown Baltimore. With a small inventory and two delivery wagons, the two men soon prospered. After 15 years of successful operation, Simons bought out Taylor to establish Robert Simons & Sons. The company followed a typical growth path for a lumberyard; that is, serving a wider and larger range of customers. Individual consumers, building contractors, and, later, industrial accounts were sought. As the company entered the 1920s, its customer base was centered around the building contractor and industrial trade. This period of prosperity led to profitable years at the company, but Simons' son, who was now president, followed the same conservative financial methods as his father. Thus, the Great Depression was a serious, but not catastrophic, event for the company.

By World War II, the company entered its fastest growth period, supplying material for the war effort. Its largest single customer was the federal government, with large contractors and shipbuilders making up the balance. As the war ended, the nation's attention turned to home building. The pent-up demand during the Depression and the war years produced a huge surge in building, and, by this time, the company had evolved into a large, full-line retailer, carrying the inventory of plywood, studs, roofing materials, etc., as well as a wholesale supplier of timbers to other retail lumber companies within a 50-mile radius.

As the 1950s ended, the third Simons to manage the company was facing increasing competitive pressure from much larger retail lumber companies. Sales volume was at a record high for the company, but profits were down due to margins eroding under competitive price cutting. Since Simons was well known and respected by the lumber retailers (he had just completed a three-year term as president of their national trade association), he decided to eliminate the high-volume, high-exposure retail business and concentrate on wholesaling or supplying the needs of his former competitors. A year after the switch was made, annual sales had dropped 70 percent, with profits down 10 percent.

The business continued basically unchanged through the 1960s until 1969, when the fourth Simons joined the company as a salesman. The difference between the two generations was apparent by the approach each took to the company. The elder Simons focused on sales and customer relations, even though many of the sales were not very profitable. The younger Simons concentrated on smaller, high-profit segments of the market. Profit, not total sales, was the emphasis of the young Simons. At that time, the company's customer base was approximately 40 percent retail yards and 60 percent large contractors and industrials. Throughout the early 1970s, the company focused on developing the higher-margin retail lumber customer and deemphasizing the contractor business, where sales were always subject to competitive bidding. The geographic trading area was expanded to a 200-mile radius of Baltimore. Products were added that were more architectural and less industrial in nature.

ORGANIZATION/MANAGEMENT

The company is currently managed by the fourth generation of the Simons family, Stephen Simons. Simons had spent his entire adult life in the business, with the exception of the period he was away working toward a graduate degree. The small size of the company prevented even a functional organization, since each employee had to be able to do several jobs, which might have been unrelated. The office was located in suburban Baltimore, and at this location were the president, the two inside salespeople, and a secretary. Simons handled all of the purchasing and financial duties as well as those sales calls which required engineering or technical information. Karen Welsh and Jane Watson, the two salespeople, handled the more routine orders and inquiries as well as shipping details. Mrs. Welsh and Mrs. Watson had both started with the company as secretaries approximately six years ago. As they became increasingly familiar with the company's customers and products, they began to assume increasing sales responsibilities. The secretary/bookkeeper took care of general office work and the operation of the company's minicomputer.

The yard and sawmill were located on an eight-acre site in an industrial section of Baltimore. Over the years, the market value of this property had increased dramatically, and Simons wondered whether it was still economically feasible to operate a lumber company from this site. The property consisted of the building where the millwork machines were housed and another small storage building where some of the finished lumber was stored. Most of the lumber was stored outside, and the lack of inside storage had limited the types of products which the company could consider carrying in its inventory.

The yard foreman and six workers were employed at this location. Joe David, the yard foreman, had been employed by the company for 10 years, having taken over from a predecessor who had been there for 40 years. David was given a great deal of discretion in the operation of the yard. Unless there was a special requirement, David scheduled all production as well as maintained the elderly and specialized sawmill machines. He was generally responsible for the hiring, management, and discipline of six subordinate employees.

The company enjoyed a high degree of loyalty from most of its employees. The office salespeople and the yard foreman received annual bonuses based on the company's profit, and, in good years, these bonuses were in the range of 25 percent of base salary. Unlike a large number of its competitors, the company did not lay off its yard employees during the slow winter months, and Simons believed this steady employment policy helped maintain the workers' loyalty. The company also contributed a certain amount to a qualified profit-sharing trust for the employees' retirement.

CORPORATE PHILOSOPHY

In its long history, the company had gone through several expansions/contractions, yet its objective had always been to focus on high-profit and fairly small types of markets, where its flexibility and ability to provide specialized service allowed it to compete successfully. Simons' philosophy had been to avoid marketing wars with major wholesalers and manufacturers and to compete in those market segments which appeared too small or unattractive to its bigger competitors. When Simons Lumber shifted from a retailer to a wholesaler in the late 1950s, the company adopted a policy of not competing with its customers. This policy, which had earned it a high degree of customer loyalty, had also had its costs. On a number of occasions, Simons had lost orders to other wholesalers who bid the job direct to the contractor (thus eliminating the retailer). During the 1960s, Stephen Simons had considered buying a treating plant, which chemically preserved the lumber. Simons correctly believed that this field was a high-growth area but did not follow through with the acquisition because it would have meant competing with one of the company's largest customers at the time. As it turned out, this customer was later lost, and Simons regretted not having entered the treating business.

In terms of financial philosophy, Simons had always followed a conservative path. For the past several years, the company had carried no long-term debt, and generally has retained almost all of its current earnings each year.

Through its philosophy of operating in sheltered niches, as well as its highly conservative financial posture, Simons Lumber had always generated a profit and seldom, if ever, incurred a loss.

PRODUCT LINE

The company marketed three main types of products: timbers, laminated beams, and roof decking. As of 1984, timbers, laminated beams, and decking accounted for 50 percent, 35 percent, and 15 percent of total sales, respectively. These products were used on expensive single-family construction as well as commercial buildings. The timbers were generally used for structural purposes, such as exposed beam ceilings. Simons bought this material from lumber mills in the Pacific Northwest and often remilled the lumber to the customers' specifications. Although the timbers carried a high profit margin, they also had high handling and manufacturing costs associated with them. Demand for this product had been fairly stable over the past 10 years and had shown very little growth.

The laminated beams were used in applications very similar to that of the solid-sawn timbers, but the laminated beams (or glulams) offered significantly greater strength than a solid-sawn timber and had greater dimensional stability and aging characteristics. These advantages had a price, however, in that a laminated beam was about 50 percent more expensive than a comparable piece of solid-sawn timber. Generally speaking, glulams were used in more contemporary types of architecture, whereas solid-sawn timbers were seen in more rustic or traditional structures. The market for laminated beams had grown steadily over the past five years, even with the entry of new competitors.

Roof decking was a product that was generally applied over exposed beams to form the ceiling of the structure. After the decking was nailed down, insulation and roofing shingles were applied to complete the roof of the structure. Decking was produced in a variety of sizes and grades, but Simons carried only the premium grades since the appearance of the ceiling was so critical in these applications.

MARKETING PROMOTION

The marketing effort of Simons Lumber Company was concentrated in the Middle Atlantic area of the United States. Because lumber had a fairly high weight-to-value ratio, freight costs made it difficult for the company to be competitive much more than 250 miles from its distribution yard. The company's primary customers were retail lumber dealers. While chain retailers bought from the company, approximately 80 percent of the company's sales were to independently owned retail lumber dealers. When a builder needed a timber-type product, he generally contacted the lumber retailer who was supplying the other construction lumber on the job. This retailer then asked for quotations from suppliers like Simons.

Up until the 1960s, the geographic scope of the business was limited enough that personal sales calls were the main thrust of the company's marketing effort. As the geographic area expanded, customers were seen personally on a less frequent basis and increasing emphasis was placed on telephone sales. The bulk of the telephone contacts consisted mainly of order taking; that is, quoting price and availability to customers. Technical or large jobs were handled either by Stephen Simons or the senior salesperson. Simons was worried that too much of the telephone contact was coming in from the customers, rather than being initiated by his sales personnel. While he had sent the two salespeople to several telemarketing seminars sponsored by the telephone company, outgoing calls generally increased for a time and then subsided.

Advertising the company and its products had been frustrated by the lack of an effective medium for this effort. Until very recently, there was no publication for the wholesale trade that focused on the company's geographic area. The use of a national publication was judged too costly to be effective. For these reasons, the company had relied on exhibiting at the one annual trade show that was located in the Middle Atlantic market as well as using direct mail. The direct-mail efforts, undertaken on a somewhat sporadic basis, had generally been successful in temporarily increasing the sales of existing products, but Simons realized that these efforts must be more consistent and regular if they were to have a major and long-lasting effect. At the current time, Simons had initiated a program of a direct mailing to retail lumber dealers on a once-a-month level of frequency. Additionally, the two salespeople had been assigned a number of accounts, which they were to contact and solicit on a regular basis.

A LOOK AT COMPETITORS

While competition was keen in the wholesale lumber industry, the niches in which the Simons Company operated were somewhat protected. The company did, however, face different competitors in each of its product lines.

Over the past 15 years, the number of competitors in the timber portion of the business had declined. Major competitors in New York and Washington failed in the last housing recession. While some benefit accrued to the company from the failings of its competitors, direct shippers and new products prevented this occurrence from being a major windfall. The increasing popularity of treated yellow pine timbers had resulted in the loss of market share in certain very small timber sizes. Likewise, a large national wholesaler had started to carry a small inventory of popular-size timbers that cost significantly less than Simons'. While the quality of the competitor's timber was so much lower that they could not be used for exposed applications, the competitor's cost advantage had resulted in the loss of a certain amount of business where the appearance of the lumber was not important. Finally, packaged home kits which featured exposed beams had also increased competition for Simons since some homebuyers opted for a packaged home, which did not contain Simons beams, rather than a custom-built home, which Simons might have been able to supply.

In the laminated sector of the market, the company had competed with several of the largest wholesalers in the country who operated in the Baltimore area over the past 15 years, only to see these wholesalers exit the market in disarray. While laminated beams carried a high profit margin, this product normally sold in fairly small quantities (compared to the commodity products these wholesalers were used to) and required a substantial amount of technical expertise and advice. The most successful competitor, Rogers Supply, was another small (but larger than Simons) wholesaler located approximately 60 miles away. Like Simons, this wholesaler supplied a quality product and technical information; but, unlike Simons, Rogers distributed the product to anyone, retailer or builder. While Rogers' distribution technique angered retailers who may have been eliminated from a sale, these retailers often continued to buy from Rogers if the price was advantageous.

Competition in the decking market depended on the size and grade of decking being considered. Of the three products that Simons handled, decking had less value added than any of the other products and was considered by some to be almost a commodity product. For this reason, profit margins were about half of what Simons received on its other two product classes.

Two-inch-thick decking constituted the majority of decking sales in the Simons' market area, and this product was carried by a number of small and large competitors. Especially in the lower grades, competition was fierce, and price alone often determined which supplier got the order. Simons concentrated on the premium appearance grade of decking, which highly complimented the timbers and beams that it sold. The competition was somewhat less rigorous than in the lower grades, and profit margins were better, although total sales volume was smaller.

A smaller portion of the total decking market was 3-inch-thick decking, which was used on very large residential jobs as well as commercial construction. Simons was one of the few wholesalers in the area to stock this product, and when small quantities were needed or the material was needed rapidly, Simons had little competition. On larger jobs (a truckload or more) when the material was not needed immediately, Simons faced competition from direct-shipment wholesalers and from the lumber manufacturers themselves. Whereas a sale from inventory carried a markup of 15 to 20 percent, a direct sale often carried a markup of 5 percent or less, depending on the order size. Simons often quoted the larger jobs on a direct-shipment basis, but the main focus had been on the smaller orders where little competitive pressure exists.

FINANCIAL INFORMATION

The stock of the company was owned by Stephen Simons (33 percent) and his father (67 percent). While the elder Simons had not been active in the company since his retirement 13 years ago, he controlled the

EXHIBIT 3

SIMONS LUMBER COMPANY
Balance Sheet
For the Years 1981–1985

	1981	1982	1983	1984	1985
Assets					
Current assets:					
Cash	$ 148,213	$ 250,524	$ 599,944	$ 695,267	$ 418,391
Marketable securities	423,102	401,362	135,645	180,006	1,048,743
Accounts receivable/trade	154,242	220,227	146,880	161,234	189,082
Accounts receivable/other	14,366	23,741	94,688	95,638	100,825
Inventory	529,948	582,436	427,128	515,288	505,727
Life insurance	120,777	141,824	166,546	296,334	313,962
Total current assets	1,390,648	1,620,112	1,570,831	1,943,767	2,567,731
Fixed assets (net):					
Land	158,460	158,460	85,500	85,500	85,500
Buildings	0	0	0	0	0
Machinery and equipment	54,857	61,617	47,150	37,797	36,072
Transportation	70,999	64,192	12,067	7,148	0
Office fixtures	17,301	13,384	16,944	4,830	6,264
Total fixed assets	301,617	297,652	161,662	135,274	127,836
Total assets	$1,692,265	$1,917,765	$1,732,492	$2,079,041	$2,704,566

**Liabilities and
Stockholders' Equity**

Current liabilities:

Accounts payable—trade	$ 300,711	$ 359,026	$ 15,861	$ 28,624	$ 284,939
Accrued salaries	52,060	33,964	0	121,410	220,362
Federal and state taxes payable	11,353	(276)	42,839	27,090	26,344
Accrued profit-sharing pay	34,200	34,200	11,400	57,000	45,600
Total current liabilities:	398,324	426,915	70,101	234,124	577,245
Stockholders' equity:					
Preferred stock (2,394 shares 7% cumulative—$100)	239,400	239,400	239,400	239,400	239,400
Common stock (978 shares outstanding)	185,820	185,820	185,820	185,820	185,820
Retained earnings	868,722	1,065,630	1,237,172	1,419,697	1,702,102
Total stockholders' equity	1,293,942	1,490,850	1,662,392	1,844,917	2,127,322
Total liabilities and stockholders' equity	$1,692,265	$1,917,765	$1,732,492	$2,079,041	$2,704,566

EXHIBIT 4

SIMONS LUMBER COMPANY
Income Statement
For the Years 1981–1985

	1981	1982	1983	1984	1985
Sales	$2,441,559	$2,478,704	$2,115,194	$2,808,037	$3,124,242
Cost of goods sold	1,576,373	1,614,939	1,241,359	1,734,360	1,998,253
Gross profit	865,186	863,765	873,835	1,073,677	1,125,989
Yard expenses:					
Payroll and payroll taxes	175,750	176,700	176,493	185,820	193,840
Maintenance	38,243	25,095	18,445	20,340	51,619
Delivery expenses	8,370	11,558	12,470	2,544	4,590
Gas and oil	14,343	19,492	16,205	16,958	16,931
Electricity	6,998	6,205	6,283	8,402	9,893
Depreciation	30,997	50,287	31,445	26,408	22,813
Total yard	274,700	289,338	261,341	260,471	299,687
Administrative expenses:					
Payroll and payroll taxes	198,489	218,198	218,717	267,803	267,030
Group insurance	19,521	22,215	26,963	22,048	16,942
Office rent	10,501	12,369	13,994	15,650	16,255
Office supplies	16,781	11,290	15,324	13,631	21,307
Advertising	3,350	3,002	1,395	1,132	1,845

	(1)	(2)	(3)	(4)	(5)
Insurance	24,229	33,953	38,293	40,157	38,663
Professional expenses	10,606	5,206	8,797	3,059	3,040
Local taxes	10,784	8,989	8,512	8,170	7,877
Travel and entertainment	1,628	2,504	10,456	16,199	23,839
Dues and subscriptions	5,666	5,273	6,625	5,974	7,230
Contributions	846	8,398	190	243	276
Pension expense	90,223	87,231	83,706	78,181	70,161
Profit-sharing expense	45,600	57,000	11,400	34,200	34,200
Interest expense	0	5,105	5,341	5,210	5,200
Telephone	22,637	21,709	20,281	17,961	15,130
Bad debts	1,353	561	950	10,406	1,102
Miscellaneous expense	0	0	0	0	4,342
Total administrative	536,950	556,193	470,942	486,833	459,701
Operating profit	289,353	257,013	141,552	87,594	130,785
Other income:					
Interest income	99,058	80,186	67,097	83,249	65,092
Rental income	0	1,520	18,240	23,370	25,080
Purchase discounts	0	0	26,828	31,160	29,826
Miscellaneous	3,612	5,360	(2,831)	5,159	2,784
Total other income	102,670	87,066	109,334	142,937	122,782
Net profits before taxes	392,023	344,079	250,886	230,531	253,566
Federal and state taxes	47,500	44,916	51,602	42,231	39,900
Net profits after taxes	$ 344,523	$ 299,163	$ 199,283	$ 188,300	$ 213,666

majority of the stock and still came to the office every day. Any major changes in the company's operations had to meet with his approval.

Stephen Simons had found it difficult to assess the company's performance relative to its competitors. Since most of its competitors were closely held, there were few financial comparisons available, and much of the data published in secondary sources were based on companies that are very different in size, geographical scope, and product specialization. During the late 1970s, the industry trade association collected information from member companies and published averages that Simons found very useful. These reports showed that, compared to industry averages, Simons Lumber had lower total sales per employee, a lower growth rate, and among the highest gross margin per employee and the highest return on sales. Simons found this data very useful, but the reports were discontinued in 1982 because so few wholesalers were willing to release sensitive financial information.

The company had always followed a conservative financial policy. Suppliers had always valued their relationship with the company, since it had discounted every invoice since its founding. At the present time, the conservative financial posture had become dysfunctional. The company, like other closely held firms, had seldom paid a dividend. Until 1975, earnings were small enough that this did not pose a problem. However, the past 10 years had seen a large increase in the level of earnings without a corresponding increase in cash usage. Now, the IRS was suggesting that the amount of cash retained was unreasonable and wanted the company to pay a sizable dividend.

Balance sheets and income statements for the past five years are presented in Exhibits 3 and 4 (pp. 254–57). Several facts should be noted about the financial statements:

1. Starting in 1984, purchase discounts were netted against the company's purchases, rather than presented separately.
2. The pension expense represents payments to employees who retired prior to the inception of the current pension plan.
3. Federal and state taxes are not a constant percentage of profits due to various credits and adjustments.
4. Inventory values are calculated on a LIFO basis.
5. The life insurance figure is the cash surrender value of policies on the officers.

FUTURE OUTLOOK

The future of the Simons Lumber Company is highly dependent on the choices made in the next year. Given the fairly stable nature of the company's products and personnel, Simons is reasonably confident that

---

EXHIBIT 5   Organization Chart

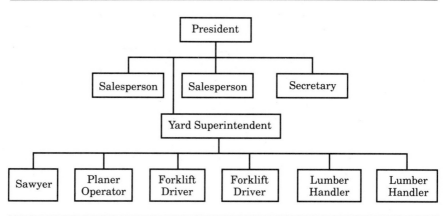

---

the company can continue to earn a satisfactory profit over the next five years with minimal supervision on his part. On the other hand, expansion would dictate many major changes in personnel and the way the company currently operates. (An organization chart is shown in Exhibit 5.)

Case 2–12   *Pier 1 Imports, Inc.**

In many places, Pier 1 Imports Inc. still conjures up the image of psychedelic pillows, scented candles, beaded curtains, and other cheap furnishings for counterculture digs.

But yesterday's Sgt. Pepper generation has grown up and, after a time, so has Pier 1. Now its stores are piled to the rafters with pricey wicker settees, French stemware, and decorative Italian tables that appeal to the stores' new customers—college-educated women between the ages of 25 and 44 who earn more than $35,000 a year. With nearly 400 stores in 37 states, the Fort Worth, Texas-based chain is the only specialty home-furnishing outfit that can claim national status.

To remake its image, Pier 1 has turned itself inside out, remodeling its stores, sprucing up its advertising and bringing in tough, corporate

---

* Source: Michael Totty, "For Pier 1, the Days of the Counterculture Are Gone," *The Wall Street Journal,* April 27, 1988, p. 6.

management. "They had to wrench themselves into the '80s and they spent the whole '70s doing it," says Chris LaBastille, a growth-company analyst for Shearson Lehman Hutton Inc.

The company is now so Establishment, in fact, that last week the industry was thick with rumors that such All-American retailing giants as Sears, Roebuck & Co., J. C. Penney Co., and Kmart Corp. might seek to acquire Pier 1, which racked up about $327 million in sales last year.

Pier 1's stock soared to $11.25 a share from $8.75 in composite trading on the New York Stock Exchange last week after the company announced an unsolicited inquiry from an unnamed retailer seeking to buy it. Pier 1 immediately hired Drexel Burnham Lambert to help it weigh offers. Yesterday, Pier 1 closed at $10.75, up 12.5 cents, giving the company an indicated value of $326.8 million based on 30.4 million shares outstanding.

Pier 1 has approval from its major owner, Intermark Inc., to sell the company, but only if the price is "substantially" above its current market price, says Charles Scott, Intermark's president and chief executive. An offer of $13 "wouldn't even pique our interest," he says.

Sears and the other retailers won't discuss any plans they might have to acquire Pier 1. But last year Sears created a specialty stores division and recently acquired several specialty retailers. A Sears spokesman says the company "is committed to expanding" into specialty retailing, and Sears has compelling reasons to do so. Like most other big retailers, it is finding it tough to increase earnings internally; profit for its merchandise group peaked in 1984 and has slipped since. Pier 1, in contrast, is expected to grow at a heady 25 percent a year clip for at least five years.

"The big retailers don't have that kind of growth out in front of them," says Bo Cheadle, a specialty retailing analyst for Montgomery Securities in San Francisco. "They're all reaching out and looking for some segment of retailing that they can grow in."

In recent months, Sears bought a small chain of women's clothing stores, a Texas-based eye-care company, and is wrapping up its purchase of the Western Auto automotive parts chain. Penney also has ventured into specialty stores, buying a 20 percent stake in the Alcott & Andrews women's apparel outlets.

There's plenty of reasons why Pier 1 is suddenly attracting attention. Since new management took over three years ago, sales have climbed 23 percent and profits 40 percent. Pier 1's gross profit margins, a measure of just how high a retailer can mark up its goods, reached an enviable 57.3 percent in fiscal 1988. And the company is expanding by leaps and bounds, having opened 179 new stores under its new management. Pier 1 plans another 87 new stores this year and expects to have 500 stores across the United States and Canada by 1990. And as

EXHIBIT 1   Growth at Pier 1

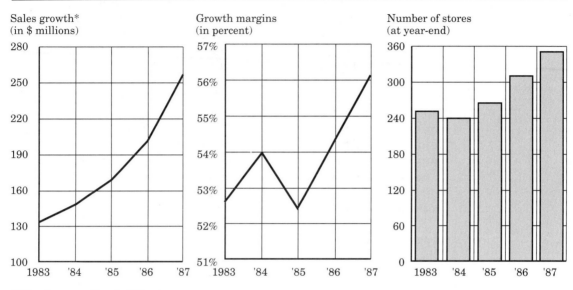

Sales growth*
(in $ millions)

Growth margins
(in percent)

Number of stores
(at year-end)

* Fiscal year ending in February.

an importer, it has buying and manufacturing capabilities in about 60 countries that competitors would be hard pressed to duplicate (see Exhibit 1).

Pier 1 also dominates a niche it created—exotic imported furniture and housewares that, experts predict, will continue to enjoy rapid growth as baby boomers reach their peak home-furnishing years.

Yesterday's "flower children" are still flocking to Pier 1 because its stores offer the unique and the exotic. The difference is that Pier 1's patrons today own their own homes and have the money to fix them up. "Pier 1 appeals to the innate snobbishness of the group for uniqueness," says Carl Steidtman, chief economist at Management Horizon, a retail consulting unit of Price Waterhouse.

Charles Tandy, founder of Tandy Corp., opened the first Pier 1 in 1962 as an outlet for a little-known San Francisco importer of Far Eastern pottery and housewares. Soon, the stores blossomed as the flower children of the 60s flocked to Pier 1 in search of "far-out" furnishings that reflected their distaste for tradition. By the end of the decade, Pier 1 was the recognized outfitter of college dorms and hippie pads—the Ralph Lauren of the bead-and-incense set.

But as its former customers left college, cut their hair, and climbed the corporate ladder, the company began to founder. From 1971 to 1980, the number of sales dropped by half. In desperation, stores tried to win back shoppers with art supplies, wine and spirits—even tropical fish. All of these retailing experiments failed miserably.

Pier 1's unconventional style extended even to its annual reports. Its 1984 report resembled a National Geographic magazine which informed shareholders of the company's "gypsy team" that scoured such exotic places as Java and Bali in search of ethnic clothing and accessories.

Pier 1 badly needed a new sense of direction—and quickly. Clark A. Johnson, a former president of Wickes Furniture—a company battered by the severe recession in the 1970s—was brought in to turn Pier 1 around. Mr. Johnson instilled a market-driven, by-the-numbers approach to the business, and pushed Pier 1 to upgrade its merchandise and quadruple its size by the end of the century. "We wanted to hurry up and increase our stores so that the company was positioned to take advantage of that growth," says Mr. Johnson.

That was an ambitious undertaking for a company that, like love beads and day-glow posters, had become passé. Pier 1's shoppers, if they remembered Pier 1 at all, recalled dingy stores reeking of incense and crowded with college-dorm furnishings. "It was like visiting a poorly lit bazaar in some Third World country," says Stan Richards of Richards Group, Pier 1's outside advertising agency.

To shed its Third World image, floors were painted red and store layouts were redone to a less-cluttered look. Fluorescent fixtures gave way to focused spots that highlighted merchandise. And candles and incense were relegated to corners of the stores.

In changing its image, however, Pier 1 didn't completely reject its past. The large Japanese paper lanterns still hang prominently from the ceilings, and rattan emperor chairs, albeit with higher price tags, are still popular. Such items "really defined the company in a way that we hoped people would recognize," explains Thomas Christopher, Pier 1's senior vice president for operations.

Pier 1's "new image" advertising highlights merchandise with brightly colored photos of umbrellas, pillows and kitchenware. Black-and-white newspaper advertisements that simply stated "Sale $29.99," were replaced by eye-catching color ads in Sunday supplements that promised "the best swiveling rocker since Elvis."

All the company's efforts aren't lost on former customers who are finding their way back. Joe Crews, a Dallas attorney who used to buy his window shades and bedspreads at the store while in college, now shops for end tables and lampshades while his wife buys cotton clothing.

On a recent visit, they were looking at bedspreads for a new king-size bed. "When I first came back (a few years ago), I had the impression it was cheaper and poorer quality stuff," Mr. Crews recalls as he browses through some bedspreads priced at about $70 at one of Pier 1's Dallas emporiums. In the old days, the bedding selection would have been largely limited to India print spreads that sold for about $5.

Mr. Crews, like a lot of Pier 1 shoppers who used to shop there during his college days, seemed impressed. "I've seen it go from a lot of little baskets and candles to better-quality furniture," he says. "The styles are substantially different."

Case 2–13   Kinder-Care Learning Centers, Inc.*

INTRODUCTION

"Good morning, Rob." Rob Hartley looked up from his desk. Perry Mendel, the president and founder of Kinder-Care Learning Centers walked in the office carrying two cups of coffee. "I thought you could use some coffee after last night," Mr. Mendel said. "Congratulations!"

"Thanks," Rob said as he reached for the cup. Mr. Mendel always took time to praise an employee for a job well done. Rob had gotten home late the night before from an out-of-town awards ceremony. At 33, Rob was Kinder-Care's national director of marketing. He had been honored to accept *Sales and Marketing Management's* "1982 Outstanding Achievement Award for Service Marketing" for the new Kindustry program he had developed.

Rob had joined Kinder-Care in April 1981. He remembered sitting in Mr. Mendel's office and hearing the Kinder-Care story. Mr. Mendel had recalled, "Right from the start I expected it to be big, like Holiday Inns. I would not have gone into it unless I thought I would have an opportunity to accomplish the *vastness* of what I dreamed about." Now Mr. Mendel's dream had turned into 723 child-care centers in 36 states and in one Canadian province, as shown in Exhibit 1.

Mr. Mendel sat down with a warm smile on his face. "Rob," he began slowly, "I've asked a few of the board members to set up a meeting with you next week. I really value your judgment. I would like you to put forward your ideas for our marketing program over the next five

---

* J. Barry Mason and Morris L. Mayer, *Modern Retailing: Theory and Practice,* 3d ed. (Plano, Tex.: Business Publications, 1984), pp. 922–33. This case was prepared by Jim Kerlin.

EXHIBIT 1   Number of Centers in Each State

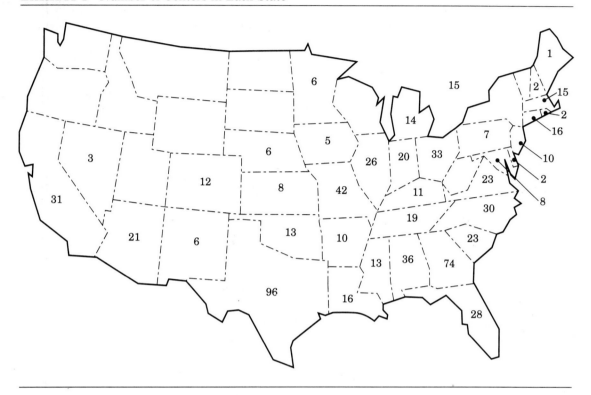

years." Rob felt buoyant, and then he felt distressed. He sensed what was about to be said.

"We have quite a challenge ahead of us," Mr. Mendel continued. "The demographics may start to turn against us by then. I want us to be in a position to meet that challenge head-on."

After a brief pause, Rob managed to say, "You can count on me, Mr. Mendel." "I have a lot of confidence in you, Rob," Mr. Mendel countered as he stood to leave, "and once again, congratulations!" Rob felt relieved as Mr. Mendel left the office. He leaned back in his swivel chair and took a sip of coffee.

"Donna," Rob called to his secretary, "bring me my marketing development file please." He spun around and peered out the window. It was beautiful outside, and he began to muse about Kinder-Care: how it came so far so fast, what it was now, and where it was going. Donna brought in the file and laid it on his desk. "Thanks, Donna," he said as he opened it.

GROWTH AND FINANCIAL HIGHLIGHTS

The first thing Rob noticed was the importance that demographics had played in the founding of Kinder-Care. After World War II, Perry Mendel had joined his three brothers-in-law in the family auto parts business. Several years later one of the three went into real estate development, building shopping malls and 250 homes a year. Later Perry Mendel switched to the more profitable real estate business with Aaron as it began to prosper from the population migration to the Sun Belt. In studying population demographics as part of his new job, Mendel began to realize that women's liberation, a soaring divorce rate, and economic necessity were sending mothers back into the work force in record numbers.

Excited by an article he had read on the potential of child care, Mendel and eight business associates raised the first $200,000 to start Kinder-Care. The first center opened in July 1969. By the end of the first year, seven centers were operating. Early in 1970, after franchising proved to be an unprofitable means of financing development, Mendel sold 40 percent of the equity for $2.8 million to go public. It was not enough. By October Mendel sold out reluctantly to Warner National Corporation for $1.5 million in stock.

With his financing worries out of the way, Mendel began to concentrate his efforts on the real estate aspect of Kinder-Care. Soon he began using a sale/leaseback method to get local investors to finance expansion. Kinder-Care guaranteed the investor a nice income on a 20-year lease. The investor earned about 15 percent pretax on his investment, and Kinder-Care grew. By 1973 there were 48 centers in 10 states. In 1974 the present corporate office was built. By year-end, Kinder-Care had 4,250 children enrolled in 62 centers.

By 1976 Mendel wanted Warner National to relinquish its 72 percent interest in Kinder-Care. He borrowed $2.25 million from banks and raised $2.25 million from 19 individuals. Armed with $4.5 million cash, he cinched the deal by throwing in all of his Warner stock. In 1977 Taft Broadcasting bought a 20 percent interest for $3.6 million. Kinder-Care later managed to obtain a $5 million mortgage loan commitment to develop 20–25 centers over the next two years. In August 1977 Kinder-Care acquired 15 day-care centers from AID, Inc. for $2.7 million. Its year-end earnings were nearly $750,000 on $12.8 million in sales. Sales and earnings history of the firm is shown in Exhibit 2.

By 1978 Kinder-Care's stock had grown so much that the board voted a 2-for-1 stock split. It also formed a subsidiary, Kinder Life Insurance Company, to provide life insurance to children enrolled in the centers and to employees. Recent stock and dividend data are shown in Exhibit 3.

EXHIBIT 2   Sales and Earnings History

Year	Revenues	Net Income	Earnings per Share
1973	$ 2,268,551	$ 216,800	$0.15
1974	4,663,346	346,516	0.24
1975	6,088,993	369,247	0.26
1976	9,108,769	509,787	0.35
1977	12,820,884	745,180	0.18*
1978	19,744,208	1,320,761	0.29*
1979	28,591,345	2,173,226	0.46
1980	56,577,767	3,499,495	0.55†
1981	87,037,734	4,290,743	0.56
‡	23,326,538	(2,737,979)	—
1982	116,467,200	6,654,637	0.66

Note: The actual loss was $1,797,856 for the period, with an accounting debit of $940,133 due to a cumulative-effect accounting change. Comparable year-earlier results are $14,196,954 in sales and $311,111 net income, or $0.05 earnings per share after stock-split adjustment.

* Adjusted for 2-for-1 stock split.

† Adjusted for 5-for-4 stock split.

‡ Results of a 13-week "short year" caused by the changing of the fiscal year-end from the last Friday in May to the last Friday in August. The new year-end is in harmony with the beginning of the fall enrollment period and employee incentive programs.

Source: *The Wall Street Journal,* Earnings Digests.

Kinder-Care's expansion continued in 1979 with the acquisition of Mini-Skools Limited of Canada for $16 million in cash and stock. It gained 88 centers in the United States and Canada. The next year, it entered the New England states when it bought Living and Learning Centers for $3.6 million in cash and notes. It acquired 87 centers for $10 million in cash and notes from American Creative Schools and Creative Day Schools of North Augusta, Georgia. It added 33 centers in the Southwest with the purchase of American Pre-Schools for an undisclosed amount. All of this growth was partially financed by a 450,000-share offering in March at $9.13 per share and a 750,000-share offering at $16.25 per share in October. The May year-end net was nearly $3.5 million.

Taft Broadcasting offered 1,422,217 shares of Kinder-Care at $12.50 in late 1981. The board decided to change the year-end to the last Friday in August at that time. By then Kinder-Care had over 700 centers. In May 1982 a $32 million convertible debt offering which paid 11 percent interest was issued to allow even more expansion.

EXHIBIT 3

Recent Stock and Dividend Data

Year	Price Range	Dividends
1977	$12.75–$11.00*	$0.02
1978	18.25– 9.00†	0.03
1979	15.25– 7.75	0.07
1980	20.00– 8.37‡	0.09
1981	17.50– 10.25	0.10

Note: 8,081,878 shares outstanding at 1981 end.
* After 100 percent stock dividend, previously a range of $18.25–$13.25.
† After 100 percent stock dividend, previously a range of $29.25–$11.75.
‡ After 25 percent stock dividend, previously a range of $17.75–$8.37.

Source: *Moody's OTC Industrial Manual 1982*, p. 1515.

Consolidated Income Account
($000)

	Year ended		
	5/29/81‡	*5/30/80†*	*6/1/79*
Operating revenues	$ 87,038	$ 56,578	$ 28,591
Direct operating expenses	74,625	46,808	23,883
General and administrative expenses	1,749	1,184	718
Operating profit	10,664	8,586	3,990
Other income	1,220	665	586
Total	1,883	9,251	4,575
Interest	6,468	4,654	1,473
Income taxes	1,415	1,295	1,040
Equity earnings	291	117	111
Net income	4,291	3,449	2,173
Previous retained earnings	8,323	5,281	3,390
Dividends	711	407	283
Retained earnings	11,902	8,323	5,281
Earnings, common share*	$0.56	$0.55	$0.37
Year-ending common shares	8,081,878	5,632,458	4,713,520

* As reported on 7,702,948 (1980, 6,274,099; 1979, 5,889,765) average common shares adjusted for 25 percent stock dividend 12/80.
† Reflects change in accounting for interest capitalization and includes Mini-Skools Limited acquired as of August 31, 1979, on purchase basis.
‡ Includes Living and Learning Centers, Inc. (acquired August 31, 1980), 41 day-care centers (acquired August 1, 1980), and 11 day-care centers (acquired May 1981) from dates of acquisition.

EXHIBIT 3   (*concluded*)

Subsidiaries (wholly owned): Kinder Care–Eagle Properties, Inc.; Kinder-Care Merchandise, Inc.; Kinder Life Insurance Co.; Kinder Canada Ltd.

Officers

Perry Mendel, president	F. E. Montgomery, vice president
R. J. Grassgreen, executive vice president, secretary, and treasurer	Emanuel Kulbersh, vice president
	H. L. Cohen, vice president

Directors

Perry Mendel	L. E. Wallock	W. L. Gauntt
R. J. Grassgreen	Fred Berman	E. L. Lowder
A. M. Aronov	Mark Sabel	C. S. Mechem, Jr.

Auditors: Peat, Marwick, Mitchell & Co.

Consolidated Balance Sheet
($000)

	5/29/81	5/30/80
Assets		
Cash	$ 4,966	$ 3,840
Certificate of deposit	8,092	3,450
Receivables	1,520	523
Prepays	1,709	671
Total current assets	$ 16,288	$ 8,483
Property, etc., net	85,924	70,928
Excess cost acquired	1,458	2,138
Equity in subsidiary†	2,572	2,281
Other assets	9,101	3,544
Total	$115,345	$87,375
Liabilities		
Notes, etc., payable	4,018	2,032
Accounts, etc., payable	3,543	3,180
Total current liabilities	$ 7,561	$ 5,212
Long-term debt	58,172	49,157
7½s, convertible debentures	9,985	10,000
Deferred rent	1,017	376
Deferred income taxes	3,944	3,217
Common stock ($0.50)	4,041	3,057
Additional paid-in capital	18,721	7,972
Retained earnings	11,902	8,323
Reacquired stock*	—	dr 540
Total	$115,345	$87,375
Net current assets	8,727	3,271

Note: Above statements include accounts of company's Canadian subsidiaries which have been translated to U.S. dollars.

* 481,389 shares at cost.

† Equity in Kinder Life Insurance Company, a wholly owned subsidiary formed in May 1978.

Source: *Moody's OTC Industrial Manual 1982,* p. 1515.

Further, in August 1982 a three-year, $25 million revolving credit facility was established with Bank of America for long-term or sale/leaseback financing. It included a five-year term loan.

As Rob Hartley looked at the previous two years' financial statements he felt confident of Kinder-Care's position. The common stock had traded over-the-counter at a red-hot 25 times earnings. Return on equity was 12.4 percent last year and 18.3 percent in 1980. The debt-equity ratio had fallen from a 3.64 high in 1980 to a moderate 2.33 : 1 in 1981. Kinder-Care anticipated earnings to be $8.6 to $8.9 million in 1983 or earnings per share of $0.84 to $0.88 after a 25 percent stock dividend in November. The number of centers was expected to continue its nearly 30 percent growth rate to over 950 centers by year-end.

MARKETING STRATEGY

Next, Hartley reviewed Kinder-Care's marketing strategy. He realized that one key to Kinder-Care's success was its location decisions. Two board members were experienced real estate developers. Many Kinder-Care centers were located on land adjacent to shopping malls which they developed. Naturally Kinder-Care benefited from the marketing research and land development expertise offered by the firms. Locations were on a side street not far from the McDonald's-type locations, but near a neighborhood and less expensive. Kinder-Care's construction teams built centers according to the latest prototype layout as shown in Exhibit 4. They also dealt with equipment manufacturers to purchase swing sets, seesaws, and other playground equipment. Some centers in warmer climates even had small swimming pools in a separate fenced-in area.

The second aspect of the strategy was the prepackaged educational plans. Consultants in nutrition, physical fitness, early childhood education, and health helped develop Kinder-Care's exclusive GOAL program (Growth Opportunities for Achievement and Learning). The program had various "discovery areas" within each center: library, home living, construction, math, music, creative arts, manipulations, science, sound table, and woodworking. All teachers were given a monthly guide with materials for each day's activities. The material covered was consistent throughout the nation. It was shipped approximately one month in advance, with two months of material to a shipment. Parents were given a three-month "Kinder Calendar" of the upcoming activities, a sample of which is shown in Exhibit 5. Among the professional packages offered in the program were the respected Lippincott "Beginning to Read, Write, and Listen" for five-year-olds and Rowland's "Happily Ever After" series of children's tales for four-year-olds.

EXHIBIT 4   Latest Prototype Design

After-school klubmates 6-12-year-olds	Baby room	Toddlers
	Rest room / Rest room	
5-year-olds	Kitchen	2-year-olds
	Rest room / Rest room	
	Storage closet	
4-year-olds	Teacher's lounge / Office	3-year-olds
	Entrance	

The final aspect of the strategy was the center itself, a prototype of which is shown in Exhibit 4. Many promotional image-building services were offered, including early education, life insurance, and mail-order catalog merchandise. Staff was paid the minimum wage. Center directors received a modest salary. Consequently turnover was high. Teacher-pupil ratios were kept at a low 1 to 10. Each state had regulations to control pupil ratios, building codes, discipline, and the like. The centers were designed to hold a capacity of either 80, 100, or 120 children. Kinder-Care's enrollment now was over 50,000. Rob was pleased his fall enrollment campaign had increased occupancy. Over

EXHIBIT 5

February '83
Scents, Cents, and Senses

WEEKS:	Monday	Tuesday	Wednesday	Thursday	Friday
Jan. 31-Feb. 4 They Number 5 **"E"**	1 Nose · 2 Ears · 2 Eyes · 2 Hands · 1 mouth = 5 ? ? ? ? ? ? ? ? ? ? Sniff, Sniff, the ROSE — Wouldn't it be terrible if we didn't have a nose?	A pair of ears . . . better to hear you with, my dear	Groundhog Gala Seeing is Believing Brush up on dental care! Children's Dental Health Month	Hands There are things that hands do that feet never can Did you know? Winter is half over on February 6th?	Mouth I wish I had two Little mouths just like my 2 little feet — One to talk with and one just to eat!
February 7-11 Let's Play Store **"M"** Review	What Shall it Be? A donut shop The supermarket A toy store or better yet, a place to eat	It Pays to Advertise Coupon Power Coin Display	Label Fun Penny Power (Making change)	Resource Person (Sharing of Coin Collection) Cents, Cents, and more Cents (Make play money for Trade Day)	TRADE DAY
February 14-18 Love Makes the World Go Round **"L"**	Cupids, Candies, Flowers and Cards	Making flowers for someone we LOVE February is American Heart Month VALENTINE'S DAY	Everything is Coming Up Rosy! Discover pink Make someone happy — send a Happy Gram	Bottle Music Make lovable Characters	Candy Making And would you believe it's even healthy?
February 21-25 Imagination and Me **"I"**	What Would Happen if . . . CREATIVE EXPRESSIONS	Inside, outside, upside down (Spatial concepts) Looby Lou will teach me right and left.	Wacky Wednesday Artful Me Tin Can Band	Mystical Magnets Backwards Day	Chef's See & Do Using my Thinking Cap

KinderCare

---

500 centers had achieved their base or better from last spring. Rates were competitive for comparable services offered elsewhere. The rates are shown in Exhibit 6.

Rob knew that Kinder-Care was three times larger than its nearest competitor, La Petite Academies of Kansas City, Missouri. He did not

---

EXHIBIT 6   Rates

Infants and toddlers	$46 per week
Age 2	$40 per week
Age 3 and older	$36 per week
"Klubmates" (ages 6–12)	$12 per week after school
Optional transportation	$6–8 per week

Note: Klubmates are part of the Kindustry program.

---

consider churches or other tax-exempt places which simply baby-sat to be real competition. He was proud that Kinder-Care had become known as "the child-care centers for children of schoolteachers." He believed this gave credence to the educational programs. In order to improve Kinder-Care's competitive position, the Kindustry program was developed.

Kindustry was designed to help corporations solve two growing problems: (1) valuable employees were quitting to raise a family, and (2) working couples were complaining they did not know what to do with youngsters before and after school. Kinder-Care's solution was to have a staff member pick up a child in the morning and take him to school and after school to deliver him to the nearest center where he could be taught such things as first aid until his parent took him home. Kinder-Care introduced a red schoolhouse logo for the program, dubbed the youngsters (ages 6 to 12) "Klubmates" and created special areas within the centers for them alone.

Next, Kinder-Care organized a sales force and designed a pilot program. First, a sales force was set up with three zone marketing managers (one each in California, Texas, and North Carolina), 16 regional managers, and 65 district managers (each assigned to about 12 centers). No one had sales experience except the zone managers. Training skills were taught. The Equitable Life Assurance company began testing the program in Atlanta, Albuquerque, and Columbus, Ohio. The employer paid 20 percent of the cost for 1,200 eligible employees. Kinder-Care billed the company, which in turn deducted the remainder of the cost from paychecks. The new tax law helped encourage this program even further. It expanded the tax credit to 20–30 percent of the costs of child care. For a family with income over $28,000, for example, as much as $480 for one child or $960 for two or more children could be deducted.

After its initial success, Kinder-Care expanded the program to include a dozen hospitals, several insurance companies, and a dozen industrial firms. A major development was the opening of a center at

Walt Disney World. It provided care for the children of the 13,000 employees and the children of the theme park guests. The Klubmates now made up about 20 percent of total enrollment.

Another service offering was life insurance. Kinder Life Insurance offered two policies which were underwritten by Republic National Life. Kinder-Care developed promotional literature to explain the policies. Kinder-Care pays the first year's premium. One policy is $5,000 whole life paid up at 80. Semiannual premiums are $10.50 to age 21 and $32.50 thereafter. The other policy is a 17-year convertible term policy for $16,000. Rates vary depending upon the parent's age. For example, a mother of age 23–26 would pay $18.01 semiannually.

Yet another service was the mail-order catalog. Kinder-Care marketing had expanded this to include items such as T-shirts, watches, tote bags, sportswear, and huggable "Kinderoo" kangeroo dolls. Kinderoo had been Kinder-Care's answer to Ronald McDonald: a giant, dressed-up kangaroo to open each new center and to serve as a goodwill

---

EXHIBIT 7 Demographic Data on Location, Age, and Unit Size

	1970	1980
U.S. resident population (in millions)		
Total persons	203.2	226.5
Urban	149.3	167.0
Rural	53.9	59.5
In SMSAs	153.7	169.4
Percentages	(75.6%)	(74.8%)
Central cities	67.9	67.9
Suburbs	85.8	101.5
In nonmetro areas	49.6	57.1
Age of population (in millions):		
Under 5	17.2	16.3
5–9	n.a.	16.6
10–14	n.a.	18.4
15–19	n.a.	21.1
20–24	n.a.	21.3
25–29	24.9	19.4
30–34	n.a.	17.7
Median age	28.0	30.0
Unit size		
Persons per household	3.14	2.75
Persons per family	3.58	3.28

n.a. = Not available.

EXHIBIT 8 Demographic Data on Projections, Participation Rates, and Miscellaneous

---

U.S. Population Projection (in millions)*

	Fertility Rate Assumed		
	2.7	2.1	1.7
1980	224	222	221
1985	239	233	229
1990	255	244	236
1995	269	253	242
2000	283	260	246

	1970	1980
Miscellaneous data		
One-person households	17.0%	22.5%
Female householder	26.8%	36.6%
Birth rate per 1,000	18.4	16.2
Marriages per 1,000	10.6	10.9
Divorces per 1,000	3.5	5.3
Labor force participation rates		
Married men, spouse present	86.9%	81.0%
Married women, spouse present	40.8	50.2
With children under 6	30.3	45.0

* Based on base year 1976, population 215 million.

EXHIBIT 9 Various Child-Care Data

	1970	1980
Enrollment (in millions)*		
Nursery school	4.3	2.4
Elementary school	32.7	28.3

	1983	1985
Projected enrollment (in millions)*		
Elementary and kindergarten	31.2	31.4
Public	27.6	27.8
Private	3.6	3.6

Number of Establishments	Receipts ($000)	Annual payroll ($000)	Employees
14,172	$759,554	$338,781	87,510

* 1977 Census of Service Industries, SIC 835 Child Care

ambassador. A song was even developed by Perry Mendel called "Let's All Be Little Kinderoos" to rival Mickey Mouse's theme song. Other promotional literature given with the catalog included magazine subscription forms for parents, bumper stickers, and a brochure explaining Kinder-Care programs like Kinder-Camp, a summer camp program for children through age five. In addition Kinder-Care had started fund-raising projects to help "Jerry's Kids" at MDA. The 1980 contribution was over $126,000, and in 1981 over $104,000 was raised. Overall Rob felt Kinder-Care had a very good marketing mix.

CHANGING DEMOGRAPHICS

Now Rob Hartley turned his attention to the problem at hand. He wanted to be ready for his meeting, so he began to browse through various demographic and kindergarten enrollment data he had accumulated as shown in Exhibits 7, 8, and 9. He was looking for trends and implications. He tried to think of ways his present marketing mix could be improved or which aspects he should emphasize. New ideas also began to come to mind: Kinderoo camps with retreats for his Klubmates to pick up summer enrollment, Kinder-Care computer centers for adults after work hours, and shopping services for single-parent households. He knew he must be careful in any diversification strategy. He felt that if he moved too far from his prime target market—14 million working women of childbearing age in middle- to upper-income households—that Kinder-Care might not reach its occupancy goals.

PART 3

Marketing Situation Analysis

The objective of marketing situation analysis is to provide information to assist management in developing and managing marketing strategy. It includes defining and describing the product-market of interest such as personal computers for business users. Industry and competitor analysis are also important aspects of the situation analysis.

The failure of the Western Union Corporation's management to identify significant technological and regulatory changes illustrates the negative consequences of not conducting market situation analyses on a regular basis. Advantages in telecommunications technology eliminated Western Union's competitive advantage.[1] The company's telex business was devastated by the exploding use of facsimile communications throughout the World.

DEFINING AND ANALYZING PRODUCT-MARKETS

Market opportunity analysis serves two purposes. It enables management to understand markets before deciding whether and how to serve them. Equally important, it enables the firm to track product-market trends to determine when shifts in targeted customers, or adjustments in marketing efforts, are needed. For example, this kind of market tracking could have been used by Western Union's management.

Four kinds of information are normally included in a market opportunity analysis:

---

[1] Janet Cuyon, "S.O.S. Western Union, Saved by a Junk Bond Deal, Needs Recovery Again," *The Wall Street Journal*, October 3, 1989, pp. A1, A4.

1. As much information as possible about the people/organizations that use the product. (These profiles of customers are useful in designing marketing strategy and tactics.)
2. The present size of each product-market and how fast it is growing.
3. The firms that supply products and services at each level, including both similar types of firms (e.g., manufacturers) and those functioning at different levels in channels of distribution (e.g., distributors, retailers).
4. An assessment of major competitors (essential to guiding marketing strategy decisions).

The analysis should help management decide what market-target strategy to adopt and the marketing program positioning strategy to use. (The terms market-target and target-market can be used interchangeably.)

Customer Profiles

Answers to these four questions will supply essential information about customers:

1. Who are the existing/potential customers?
2. What are their characteristics?
3. How do they decide what to buy?
4. What factors, other than customer characteristics and company marketing efforts, influence buying?

Identifying and describing the people or organizations that constitute the market for a product (questions 1 and 2) are the first steps in product-market analysis. Typically, demographic and socioeconomic characteristics are used to identify potential users in product-markets. Characteristics such as family size, age, income, geographical location, sex, and occupation are often useful in identifying customers in consumer markets. A variety of factors can be used to identify end users in industrial markets, including type of industry, size, location, and product application.

Many published sources of information are available to identify and describe customers; for example, United States census data, trade association publications, and studies by advertising media (TV, radio, magazines). The important task is to find those characteristics that will identify potential customers. In some situations, research studies may be necessary.

In examining how customers decide what to buy, it is useful to observe how people move through the sequence of steps leading to a decision to purchase a particular brand. Buyers normally begin by recognizing a need. Next, they seek information. Third, they identify and evaluate alternative products. Finally, they choose a brand. This process varies, based upon a number of factors, including the importance of the purchase, whether it is an individual or group decision, and whether it is a first-time purchase or a repeat purchase. Essential in studying buyer behavior is learning what criteria people use in making decisions. Determining why people buy offers important insights for marketing strategy.

The final step in building customer profiles is to identify external factors that may alter buyers' needs and wants. Environmental influences include the government, social change, economic shifts, technological changes, and other macroenvironmental forces. Typically, these factors cannot be controlled by the buyer or the firms that market the product.

Size and Growth Estimates

Two market-size estimates are often used in product-market analysis. One is a measure of the potential that exists in a market. Since in most instances an opportunity is never fully realized by the firms serving the product-market, a second measure is needed. This is a forecast of what is likely to occur for the time period under consideration. The potential represents an upper limit; the forecast normally is something less than total potential. In addition to size estimates, expected growth rates over the planning period are very useful in planning.

Industry and Distribution Analyses

The ways in which products and services reach end users should be identified and analyzed. Normally an analysis is conducted from the point of view of a particular firm. For example, a department store chain such as Dayton-Hudson or Dillards would include other retailers in its industry analyses. Two kinds of information are needed:

1. Study of the industry of which the company is a part.
2. Analysis of the distribution channels that link together the various organizations serving end users' needs and wants.

Starting first with the industry analysis, the following information is needed:

- Industry characteristics and trends, such as sales, number of firms, and growth rates.
- Operating practices of the firms in the industry, including product mix, services provided, barriers to entry, and related information.

A knowledge of distribution channels is essential to understanding and serving product-markets:

- When do producers go directly to their end users?
- When do producers work through distribution channels?

Key Competitors

Normally a company does not compete with all firms in an industry, so it is necessary to find out which are key competitors. Also, if specific customer needs can be satisfied by product categories from other industries, potential competitors should be included in the analysis. Information that is obtained from a key-competitor analysis often includes:

- Estimated overall business strength of each key competitor.
- Present market share and past trends.
- Financial strengths and performance.
- Management capabilities (and limitations).
- Technical and operating advantages (e.g., patents, low production costs, new products).
- Description and assessment of marketing strategy.

Keeping up with what the competition is doing is one of management's most important responsibilities. The above information should be obtained and studied on a regular basis.

Market Segmentation Analysis

Identifying and analyzing the segments that constitute a product-market are also important situation analysis activities. Segments are subgroups of buyers within a total market. Each segment has similar preferences concerning the product category of interest. Segmentation is further discussed in the introduction to Part 4.

CONCLUDING NOTE

Understanding product-markets is essential to making good marketing decisions. The activity of defining and analyzing product-markets is probably more critical to making sound planning decisions than any other activity in the enterprise. The uses of these analyses are many and varied. Defining and analyzing product-markets includes examining customer profiles, making size and growth estimates for the product-market and industry, conducting distribution analyses, analysis of key competitors, and developing marketing strategy guidelines.

Cases for Part 3

The 12 cases in Part 3 examine market and competitor analysis. The cases also highlight several marketing strategy issues.

CASES

The Daimler–Benz case (3–1) considers the company's truck business. It provides an opportunity to conduct a marketing situation analysis for a global industry. The case also identifies several international strategy issues confronting Daimler–Benz in the truck market.

Case 3–2, Survival Aids, Ltd., describes the operations of a small British company that specializes in equipment and training for survival against the elements. The case examines an interesting strategic planning situation. Management is concerned about what should be the future strategy of the firm.

The Marriott Corp. case (3–3) considers the company's move into the medium-price segment of the lodging market with its Courtyard chain of hotels. The research and market analysis information guiding management's decisions are presented and the market targeting and positioning strategies are outlined.

Case 3–4, Metropol Base-Fort Security Group, considers the competitive challenges in the security services market in Canada. The case highlights important strategy concerns confronting the firm. Management is trying to determine how to effectively compete against large multinationals such as Pinkertons.

Frito-Lay, Inc. (Case 3–5) examines the use of marketing research and information systems by the leading snack food producer. It emphasizes management's commitment to user-driven product development. The case offers an interesting view of the role of marketing research in a successful consumer products firm.

Algonquin Power and Light Company (Case 3–6), a metropolitan gas and electric utility, is considering whether to begin manufacturing compost for sale from tree and shrubbery trimmings. Management must decide whether to pursue this business opportunity, and if so, whether to target the retail market, the wholesale market, or both.

Case 3–7, La-Z-Boy Chair Company, looks at company operations and strategic challenges. The La-Z-Boy brand name is widely recognized in the United States. The case describes the furniture industry and presents an interesting strategy analysis situation. Extensive industry and company financial data are included in the case.

Toyota Lexus (Case 3–8) is an analysis of the luxury European style automobile market segment and a discussion of Toyota's entry with its new Lexus line of cars. The case examines several market analysis, competitive advantage, and marketing strategy issues including the positioning of a Japanese brand against Mercedes and BMW.

Case 3–9, The Michigan League, concerns a University of Michigan food service operation that has been experiencing a decrease in business. Pat Lawson, manager of the Michigan League for the past six years, is interested in discovering why fewer customers are eating in the League's cafeteria and coffee shop and is making plans to reverse that trend.

American Safety Razor (Case 3–10) describes the divestment of the business by Phillip Morris and the actions taken by the insider management team that purchased the small razor producer. Management must develop strategies to achieve financial stability and profitable performance in an industry dominated by Gillette.

Case 3–11, The Cleveland Clinic, describes a highly successful medical services organization attempting to geographically diversify into Florida from its Ohio core market. The case provides an opportunity to examine competitive issues in the professional services area.

Japan, Inc. (Case 3–12) examines Japan's global business strategies that have been used to become a world-class competitor in global markets. The case describes the Japanese social environment and considers several future competitive challenges for nations competing with Japan in the race for economic preeminence.

Case 3–1   *Daimler–Benz AG**

Dr. Gerhard Liener, Daimler–Benz's managing director for acquisitions and foreign operations, was analyzing the international strategy of the firm's truck group, headquartered in Stuttgart, West Germany. It was on January 29, 1986, and he wondered how long his company would be able to maintain its strength in the face of increased global competition posed by European and American truck companies, international joint ventures, and the lurking threat of Japanese export of large commercial vehicles.

HISTORY OF DAIMLER–BENZ

Daimler–Benz was the product of a merger between two German automobile manufacturers, Benz et Cie and Daimler Motoren Gesellschaft, in 1926. Karl Benz and Gottlieb Daimler, both pioneers in the automotive industry, set up their respective companies in 1883 and 1890. Both firms manufactured expensive cars as well as commercial vehicles and large engines for locomotives, ships, and zeppelins.

Shortly after the merger, Daimler–Benz began to grow rapidly. Production increased from 10,829 vehicles in 1927 to over 42,000 by 1938. Innovations in diesel power, success in racing, and a revival of the German economy all contributed to this growth. Unfortunately, this expansion was abruptly halted when most of the company's production facilities were destroyed in World War II. Daimler–Benz was quick to rebuild, however, and by 1950 production had exceeded the prewar high.

In the years that followed, Daimler–Benz saw even more phenomenal growth. Output increased from 104,000 units in 1956 to over 300,000 units by 1969. A commitment to quality was the trademark of this company, which produced a highly specialized line of commercial vehicles. Expansion and acquisitions internationally kept the supply of vehicles growing with the demand for them. By 1985, Daimler–Benz produced 541,039 cars (up 13.1 percent over 1984) and 220,213 commercial vehicles (up 4.4 percent from 1984), of which 65,407 (down 3.8 percent) were trucks over 6 tons. The total concern achieved 1985

---

* This case was written by Dr. Per V. Jenster, McIntire School of Commerce, University of Virginia, Charlottesville, 22923; Dr. Alfred Kotzle, Institute for Planning and Organization, University of Tubingen, Tubingen, G-7400, West Germany; and Dr. Franz X. Bea, Institute for Planning and Organization, University of Tubingen, Tubingen, G-7400, West Germany.

revenues of DM51,900 million (up 19 percent), of which DM37,079 million came from cars and commercial vehicles. Daimler–Benz exported 53.6 percent of its production.

DAIMLER–BENZ AND THE TRUCK INDUSTRY

Over the years, the commercial vehicle market had evolved into a complex and competitive arena. With an emphasis on quality and reliability, Daimler–Benz was the largest producer of diesel trucks in the world as well as Europe's largest commercial vehicle producer. Daimler–Benz had a long tradition of truck assembly overseas, which had been forced by "local content" rules (i.e., rules specifying that a certain part of the value-added process must reside locally). For this and other reasons, Daimler–Benz over the years established truck and bus plants in Brazil and Argentina, as well as in Turkey, Spain, Yugoslavia, Indonesia, Saudi Arabia, Nigeria, and Hampton, Virginia. Additionally, there were 23 assembly plants worldwide in which Daimler–Benz had no ownership.

Daimler–Benz had increasingly realized the strategic importance of a global presence, and this had led it to pursue acquisition candidates in America, the world's largest market for commercial vehicles. This process resulted in the 1977 acquisition of Euclid (a heavy-equipment manufacturing subsidiary of White), which was divested in 1983; Freightliner, Inc., Oregon, 1981; and a 49 percent stake in Fabrica de Autotransportes Mexicana (FAMSA), Mexico, in 1985. Dr. Liener explained this effort to *Financial Times:* "We must think of our sons," suggesting that the long-term health and development of the truck group was at stake.

FAMSA employed 865 office and factory workers and had a production capacity of 15,000 commercial vehicles, although the expected 1986 sales would not exceed 4,000 vehicles due to the poor Mexican economy. When asked why Daimler–Benz chose Mexico for this operation, Mr. Hans-Jurgen Hinrichs, sales director of FAMSA, clarified that "The white spot on the map annoyed us." He suggested that "Daimler–Benz's policy of trying to be everywhere in the world, even when the prospects in the short term don't appear to be too great," would continue to pay dividends of the type the group collected when its patience and persistence in the Middle East was rewarded in the startling truck sales boom after the mid-1970s oil price rise. It was also acknowledged that there were still some gaps in Daimler–Benz's world coverage, but that it had been talking seriously to the Chinese about truck sales and assembly there.

COMPETITION

The nature of the competitive environment had changed over the last 10 years. Daimler–Benz was now facing a three-pronged assault from Western Europe, Japan, and the United States in the international truck industry. Exhibit 1 presents the 1984 production of heavy-duty trucks by the major manufacturers.

EXHIBIT 1 Heavy Trucks: International Production by Major Manufacturers, 1984

Manufacturer	Where Produced	Units	Manufacturer	Where Produced	Units
Daimler–Benz	Germany	38,000	General Motors	USA	18,000
(66,000 units in 1983)	USA/Canada	20,000	(13,000 units in 1983)	Korea	1,000
	Brazil	6,000		Great Britain	500
	Argentina	1,000		Brazil	500
		65,000			20,000
IHC (Navistar)	USA/Canada	35,000	Nissan	Japan	19,000
(23,000 units in 1983)	Australia	1,000	(17,000 units in 1983)		
		36,000	Fiat IVECO	Italy	14,000
			(19,000 units in 1983)	Germany	3,000
Volvo	Sweden	26,000		France	750
(30,000 units in 1983)	USA	10,000		Argentina	1,000
		36,000		Brazil	250
Paccar	USA/Canada	30,500			19,000
(19,000 units in 1983)	Mexico	1,000	Isuzu	Japan	17,000
	Great Britain	500	(15,000 units in 1983)		
		32,000	Renault RVI	France	15,000
Mack	USA/Canada	29,000	(20,000 units in 1983)	Spain	1,500
(14,000 units in 1983)				Great Britain	500
Mitsubishi	Japan	22,000			17,000
(17,000 units in 1983)			MAN	Germany	11,000
Saab–Scania	Sweden	22,000	(12,000 units in 1983)	Austria	1,000
(17,000 units in 1983)					12,000
Hino	Japan	21,000			
(15,000 units in 1983)					
Ford	USA	19,500			
(12,000 units in 1983)	Great Britain	1,000			
	Brazil	500			
		21,000			

The idea of international competition was actually much more complex than the Europe–United States–Japan triad might suggest, due to the fact that ownership interests often crossed national boundaries. For instance, many of America's largest truck producers were under European control. Renault had a large stake in Mack Trucks, which itself had many subsidiaries in foreign markets. The Swedish Volvo's recent purchase of White Motor Corporation and Daimler–Benz's 1981 purchase of Freightliner, Inc., gave these large European firms a very strong foothold in the U.S. market. Similarly, Iveco, a Fiat subsidiary, was increasing its presence in the United States as well.

In 1985, the first signs of Japanese interest in the European truck market had become apparent. Hino, Mitsubishi, Isuzu, Mazda, and Toyota all displayed commercial vehicles at the Brussels motor show at the beginning of the year. And while all except Hino had been making increasing inroads into Europe's light commercial vehicles, Hino's exhibits were in weight ranges up to 15 tons.

In the United States, Japanese truck producers were moving swiftly into market niches that the domestic manufacturers had abandoned, thinking they would be too expensive to supply with American vehicles. Significantly, the Japanese are being aided and abetted in this process by the U.S. producers. For example, Nissan Diesel signed an agreement to supply a new generation of medium-weight trucks to International Harvester, now Navistar, and distribute them through Navistar's 850 dealers. At the same time, Nissan planned to sell through its own distribution company based in Texas.

General Motors, which held nearly 40 percent of the shares in Isuzu, decided to start selling Isuzu class 3 lightweight trucks through its own network of 250 dealers in 20 states. Ironically, GM seemed to be filling out gaps in its own range because it believed that Hino and Toyota would aggressively attack the diesel sectors (classes 3–8) in the States. For its U.S. venture, Hino had linked up with Mitsui, the major Japanese trading house, which had long been associated with Toyota but had also been selling trucks through its own distribution network. Between the two distribution networks, they saved more than 20 dealerships on sales in excess of 1,000 trucks per year, with an expected increase of 4,000 by 1990.

By the same token, General Motors and Ford each had many subsidiaries in Europe, especially in the United Kingdom, producing commercial vehicles that had large shares of their markets as well. Paccar, which manufactured Kenworth and Peterbilt trucks, had affiliates in Europe, Africa, and the Middle East. Navistar and Mack also sold a large number of their vehicles to foreign customers.

It was apparent from the large number of subsidiaries, acquisitions, joint ventures, and assembly plants located throughout the world that the European and U.S. truck manufacturers found it effective for several reasons to maintain a strong global presence with production and assembly taking place in multiple locations. The Japanese produced and exported trucks at an increasing rate without relying on foreign manufacturing subsidiaries or joint ventures.

Export of commercial vehicles from Japan increased by nearly 40 percent from 1979 to 1980. More importantly, while North America was the largest market for these vehicles, sales to EEC countries increased by 34 percent that year, and sales to other European countries jumped a staggering 92 percent. "Led by the traditional Japanese powers, Toyota, Nissan, and others, this nation is making the true run at the world truck market."[1]

FREIGHTLINER, INC.

On July 31, 1981, Daimler–Benz completed its acquisition of Freightliner Corporation, previously a subsidiary of Consolidated Freightways, Inc. (CFI). The $300 million transaction gave Daimler–Benz full ownership of Freightliner's four truck assembly plants (located in Portland, Oregon; Mt. Holly, North Carolina; Indianapolis, Indiana; and Burnaby, British Columbia, Canada) along with Freightliner's parts manufacturing plants in Portland, Oregon; Gastonia, North Carolina; and Fremont, California. Freightliner's two Vancouver financial subsidiaries, Freightliner of Canada, Ltd., and Freightliner Financial Services, Ltd., were also included in the deal.

Freightliner, headquartered in Portland, Oregon, manufactured and sold mainly heavy-duty trucks of the class 8 variety, signifying a gross weight of at least 33,000 pounds. The Freightliner acquisition gave Daimler–Benz an immediate 10 percent share of the class 8 truck market to add to its existing lines of class 6 and class 7 trucks, sold through Mercedes–Benz of North America. Freightliner has also been previously involved in sales of medium-duty trucks as a result of its truck-marketing ties with Volvo. As a result of the Daimler–Benz acquisition, however, this collaboration was terminated.

Freightliner was formed by Consolidated Freightway, Inc., in 1939 in order to design and build trucks more suitable to the long-haul traffic in the West, where the majority of CFI's driving was done. During the 1950s, Freightliner began to sell to other truckers as well, with sales to CFI gradually making up a smaller percentage of total revenue.

---

[1] *Financial Times,* November 29, 1985.

Freightliner's trucks were marketed by White Motor for over 20 years but were never distributed in the eastern United States. In 1977, Freightliner set up its own organization of 207 dealers after White Motor began to lose market share. In order to achieve increased sales, it was decided that improved eastern service was needed; and, to help accomplish this, a new plant was opened in Mt. Holly, North Carolina, in 1979. This was followed by the closing of the Chino, California, assembly plant in September 1980. The closing was blamed partly on the sharp decrease in demand for heavy-duty trucks experienced after the peak reached in 1979. This decrease in demand caused a sales drop of 36 percent early in 1980, which led to the dismissal of Freightliner's president, William Critzer.

Critzer's successor was Ronald Burbank, who had just been named chief operating officer of CFI. He continued on as president and chief executive officer after the acquisition by Daimler–Benz; and, aided by a rise in heavy-duty truck demand, an improved product range, and strong sales efforts, he was able to greatly expand sales, thus reaching full capacity in 1984. However, its inability to fully meet demand caused the U.S. market share to decline somewhat in 1984, whereas its Canadian share continued to increase.

The demand for heavy-duty trucks of 134,000 vehicles declined slightly in 1985 from 138,000 in 1984 (compared to 80,000 in 1983), whereas 145,000 medium-heavy vehicles were sold in both years. Despite the growing competition, Freightliner was able to sell 20,809 (against 20,526 in 1984) heavy-duty vehicles in North America, producing sales of $1.6 billion. This meant an improvement in Freightliner's U.S. market share from 12.8 percent to 13.5 percent, whereas the Canadian market share dropped to 12.3 percent from 13.2 percent. Exhibit 2 provides an overview of the market share for the various U.S. competitors. Freightliner furthermore saw a 10 percent reduction in employees to 5,439 from 6,059 in 1984.

EXHIBIT 2   U.S. Market Shares for Class 8 Trucks

Manufacturer	1980	Manufacturer	1985
IHC	20.4%	IHC (Navistar)	21.3%
Mack	19.5	Mack	19.1
Paccar	15.4	Paccar	16.3
GMC	14.4	**Freightliner**	**13.5**
Ford	12.0	Ford	11.6
Freightliner	**9.0**	GMC	9.0
White	9.0	White	8.2
Others	1.3	Others	0.7

THE FUTURE OF DAIMLER–BENZ

Daimler–Benz had weathered the 1980–83 world recession that sent sales of most truck manufacturers plummeting, and sales at Daimler–Benz had even been relatively stable. Its expansion policy had been one of wise acquisitions and cautious movement into new markets. Its reputation for quality, value, and innovation had up until now been unequaled. The question for Dr. Liener was how to sustain the strategic position in a global industry where competition was increasing.

Case 3–2   Survival Aids, Ltd. *

Nicholas Steven was born March 20, 1949, in Purlev, Surrey, England. In 1960, he moved with his family to Cumbria, where he attended Austin Friars School in Carlisle. There he studied physics and chemistry. He took an active part in the local Army Cadet Force, and, in 1967, he entered Sandhurst, the Royal Military Academy, where he participated in judo, shooting, and other sports.

After receiving a commission into the Royal Signals in 1969, Nick was awarded the Agar Memorial Prize for academic achievement and the Signals Sword for all-round performance while at Sandhurst. In early 1970, he was posted to Germany for a tour as a line troop commander before entering the Royal Military College of Science in October. Nick was awarded a degree in applied science in 1973 and went on to command a VHF radio troop in the United Kingdom (U.K.), a specialist information team with 22 SAS in the Oman, and an independent signal troop in the Caribbean. He also instructed at the School of Signals and served as adjutant of the 16th Signal Regiment in West Germany.

In 1979, Nick Steven decided to leave the military and begin another career. He considered a number of different occupational options and finally decided to start his own business. Throughout his military career Nick had been involved in survival training but had found that good quality survival equipment was practically unobtainable. His plan, therefore, was to build a company specializing in equipment and training for survival against the elements.

---

* This case was prepared by Robert L. Anderson, the College of Charleston, and Bobby G. Bizzell, University of Houston-Downtown, as a basis for class discussion. Copyright by Robert L. Anderson and Bobby G. Bizzell; distributed by North American Case Research Association. All rights reserved to the authors and the North American Case Research Association.

By 1987, Survival Aids, Ltd., was a successful and thriving business. Survival Aids had grown from a business with a single product to one with nearly 1,400 different items, which generated £2.5 million in revenue (turnover) in 1987. Nick had been more successful than even he had anticipated, but he now had to decide what to do with his company. Nick could sell Survival Aids to another larger company, he could acquire one or more of his smaller competitors, he could place more emphasis on retail outlets, he could expand his product line, he could expand into other countries, or he could do nothing and let his company continue its steady growth.

HISTORY

Nick's military career had been very successful—he was told that he would probably have become a major general had he stayed in the service; however, the service had not prepared him to start and operate his own business. In an effort to learn what he could about business, Nick entered his business plan in an Enterprise competition, which won him a free business course at Durham University Business School. Once Nick felt that he was ready to start his business, he and his partner, Michael Hunting (whom Nick bought out after the business was formed), took the £5,000 available to them and formed Survival Aids, Ltd., with its one product.

Initial Product

Survival Aids was a company built around one product. The initial product was a compact, lightweight Survival Ration Pack suitable for use by those who indulge in outdoor pursuits. The sealed emergency pack contained specially selected high energy foods and drinks as well as solid fuel, matches, instructions, and other necessities. The kit contained 14 different items sealed in an airtight aluminum container, which could be used to hold hot food and drinks. The Survival Ration Pack was introduced in August 1979 at a press reception in London, which featured a wild foods buffet. The pack was originally sold through camping and outdoor leisure shops to both civilians and military personnel.

Location

When Nick began his search for a suitable building to serve as both the office and production area for his new company, he established several criteria to guide him. First, he wanted a location in a rural area that would provide jobs for people who might otherwise have difficulty finding work. Second, he believed that his company should be located in an area that offered many outdoor activities. Third, he needed a facility that was inexpensive. As a first step he selected a building owned by a relative near Carlisle in Cumbria but hoped later to find a building large enough for his current and future needs.

Being located near the Lake District, Survival Aids was able to sell its product to outdoor retailers while Nick continued his search for a more ideal location. Using the same initial criteria, Nick found a suitable building in Morland, near Penrith, which would be adequate for several years, since it contained two buildings, one which could be used for offices and a larger building that could be used for production and warehousing.

Product Line and Sales

Although Survival Ration Packs were selling well, Nick realized that his company could not grow with only one product. Therefore, he decided to expand his product line, and he began selling some 10 products by mail order. In 1980, Survival Aids published its first typewritten mail order catalog, which featured some 68 items and contained one black-and-white photograph. In that same year, the company exhibited for the first time at the national Camping and Outdoor Leisure trade show at Harrogate. Catalogs, each better than the previous one, were published every six months and distributed to a rapidly growing list of customers.

In January 1983, a quarterly mini-catalog and magazine *Survival News* were launched and distributed free to customers. The catalog was now published annually, with supplemental catalogs published as needed. The 36-page 1985 catalog was produced in full color for the first time, and the 48-page 1986 catalog was distributed to well over 100,000 customers. Nick did not want all of Survival Aids' sales to be from mail order customers, so he began wholesaling to dealers while looking out for new markets.

Nick realized that soldiers were becoming an increasingly important customer group; therefore, in 1983, the company exhibited at the Rhine Army Summer Show. Survival Aids was the first company to develop alternative professional equipment that soldiers could purchase by mail. In 1984, the Survival Aids Liaison Team conducted a series of survival lectures and equipment briefings around the U.K., culminating with Nick's presentation to 1,200 survival enthusiasts in Watford Town Hall. Catalog sales and other selling efforts were successful, and Survival Aids enjoyed a turnover in excess of £1 million for the first time in 1985.

COMPANY OPERATIONS

The sales figures for 1985 had not been unanticipated or surprising. Turnover continued to increase, and sales for 1987 reached the £2.5 million mark. Survival Aids, Ltd. was now an established, successful company that was a dominant force in its industry. The company enjoyed a national reputation, and its products were of the highest quality available. Survival Aids would continue to expand its product line and would broaden its selling techniques.

Products and Services

Survival Aids now sells approximately 1400 different products to outdoor enthusiasts. Most products are made by other companies for Survival Aids; however, many products are made to the company's specifications and, in some cases, the company has exclusive rights to other manufacturers' products.

Products.   The following products, by major category, are sold by Survival Aids:

Protection
  Shell clothing
  Footwear
  Outer thermal clothing
  Inner thermal clothing
  Immediate care
  Bivis, bags, blankets
  Sleeping systems

Location
  Navigation, signaling
  Time
  Distance
  Light

Water
  Water purification
  Water carriers

Food
  Rations
  Cooking equipment

Tools
  Knives
  Kits and accessories
  Pouches and firestarters

Survival Skills
  Books and courses

Military
  Combat clothing
  Waterproofs
  Boots
  Bergens
  Webbing
  Kits and accessories

Product Selection.   Products that do not sell well are usually dropped from the catalog, and new ones are added. The following criteria or policy statements were used to select new products included in the 1986 catalog:

1. "No new products are to be offered for sale until they have been thoroughly tested, costed, sourced, sampled, packaged, and stocked."
2. "We want more own/exclusive products in our own packaging but will accept certain high quality products from companies such as Tekna and Pains Wessex."
3. "New products should have reasonable wholesale margins."
4. "Quality has become a key feature of the company's inventory. Suppliers must be reliable, and alternative sources must be developed."
5. "No new products may have any assembly requirement. They must be supplied ready for sale."
6. "New products and existing products must have better instructions, labelling, packaging, and documentation in 1986."

Services. In 1982, Nick decided to begin a survival training school that would teach outdoor enthusiasts basic survival skills and would provide some exposure for the company. Initially, Survival Aids would offer 20 courses a year to teach the following skills: expedition training, survival, combat survival, executive development, and civil defense. Nick estimated that the survival school would eventually generate revenue of about £100,000 per year. There were other benefits to be derived from the school. First, Survival Aids employees could be exposed to outdoor activities. Second, the school could provide facilities for R & D. Third, students would be potential customers for the company's products. Finally, the school would be good advertising.

The training programs that were presented to people from age 14 up were somewhat successful. The programs did meet some of the established goals; however, the survival school was not sufficiently profitable to continue. The program was eventually sold to Outward Bound, another organization in the same training business. Other services, such as seminars and equipment demonstration programs, are still provided when needed.

Organization and Personnel

From a business with no personnel and no structure, Survival Aids has grown to a company employing 35 people that has a fairly well-developed organizational structure (see Exhibit 1). Since unemployment in the area is relatively high, it is not difficult to hire capable employees. It is somewhat more difficult to hire managers with technical skills, because of the company's rural location; however, Nick assembled a very professional staff capable of managing the company through future growth stages.

EXHIBIT 1   Organization Chart of Survival Aids, Ltd., 1988

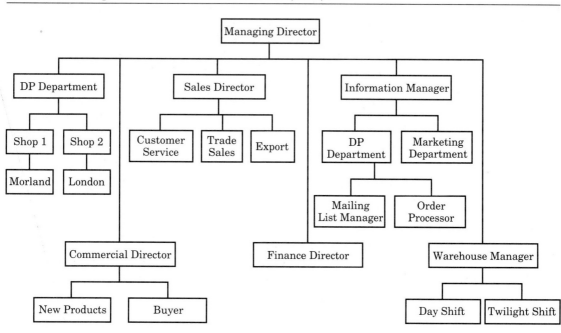

The company provides very comfortable working conditions, the management style is participative, and the employees are well paid. In addition to above average wages, all employees participate in a profit-sharing plan. Nick decided to set aside in perpetuity 15 percent of pretax profits for worker incentive. Employees would receive a percentage of that lump sum, based on their personal performance (graded very good, satisfactory, or unsatisfactory) and their base salary. Nick has even considered letting his managers buy stock in the company (at present, he owns 100 percent of the company's stock), because he believes that all employees should share in the success of the company.

Marketing and Distribution

Selling survival packs through camping and outdoor leisure shops was satisfactory in the early stages of Survival Aids' development; however, when the product line expanded, Nick realized that he should have more direct control over the selling and distribution of his merchandise. To gain this control, Nick decided that mail order selling was most appropriate for Survival Aids.

Selling. The majority of sales of Survival Aids' products comes from mail order customers. The heaviest selling season is from September to March, when the company averages about 150 orders per week. Since the quality of merchandise is high and the products are well described in the catalog, very few items are returned. Nick expects mail order to continue to be an important source of sales, because he believes that its advantages outweigh the disadvantages. The following are some of the adantages of mail order selling for Survival Aids:

Full price paid.

Cash in advance.

Few bad debts.

Wide range of customers. No dependence on major accounts.

Lack of stock does not usually lose sale.

Cash sales and credit purchase reduce working capital requirements.

Best and sometimes only way to approach military customers.

Small items are suited for mail order.

Location is not a disadvantage.

Catalog is an easy and inexpensive way to introduce new products.

Direct contact with end user.

While mail order selling seemed to have several advantages over other selling techniques, it also had some drawbacks. The following are some of the disadvantages of relying on mail order selling:

Small orders may be uneconomic to process, especially if paid for by credit card.

Returns could be expensive.

Customers cannot really "examine" products before they are purchased.

It is necessary to maintain a large and growing mailing list.

Nick realized that Survival Aids would need to utilize more than one selling technique if it was to reach the most potential customers. In February 1986, the first Survival Shop, a retail outlet for Survival Aids products, was opened in the company's Morland facility. This shop was quite profitable, especially during the six summer weeks when many tourists visited the Lake District. To further test the profitability of retail outlets, Nick opened a shop in a major London train station in 1987. Early indications are that the shop will be profitable, leading Nick and his managers to contemplate opening additional shops in London and other parts of the country.

Nick had also tried some other selling techniques with varying degrees of success. The company tried contract sales (selling to the military, government agencies, and the like), but very little continuity was obtained from this method of selling. Nick identified the following problems associated with contract selling: Survival Aids does not manufacture products; contract business is not repetitive; it is time consuming; and one-of-a-kind orders do not fit into Survival Aids' system. While contract selling would be continued, it would receive very little budget support. Survival Aids had also been represented at several trade shows, usually with exposure and advertising value outweighing profitability. The company now sells through mail order, contract sales, and retail shops, and it continues to wholesale its products to independent camping shops and the NAAFI (the equivalent to U.S. military post exchanges).

Competition.   Several companies sell items similar to those offered by Survival Aids, but no single company has a product line as complete as Survival Aids'. Companies that compete do so on the basis of price, rather than quality or service. Nick is aware of a few companies that could expand their product lines to compete with Survival Aids; however, he is confident that good service and high-quality products will keep Survival Aids ahead of the competition.

Advertising.   The target market for Survival Aids is primarily military personnel and people (primarily males) interested in any outdoor activity. To attract this market, Survival Aids relies mainly on its catalogs; however, it does use other advertising media. The company advertises in weekly, monthly, and quarterly magazines, such as *Great Outdoors, Soldier,* and *Y.H.A. News.* Advertisements are also placed in other local publications. Advertising is important, but effective public relations also sells products. Survival Aids has been the subject of many news and television reports, and company employees have written numerous articles that have appeared in national magazines. Survival seminars have considerable PR value, and Nick and his managers are often asked to speak to local organizations and business schools.

Catalogs.   The lifeblood of any mail order company is its catalog. The catalog offered by Survival Aids in 1987 does not even resemble the first one published in 1980. From a simple typewritten document listing 68 items, the catalog has progressed to a full-color, 48-page annual publication describing more than 1,400 items (most manufactured in the U.K.) purchased from 200 suppliers. In 1987, Survival Aids ordered 200,000 catalogs at a cost of 0.45 each. The mailing list, with approximately 130,000 names, is actively maintained. Customers who have not purchased anything for six months are sent a "last catalog" notice. Customers who have received such notice are dropped from the mailing list if they do not make a purchase within a reasonable amount of time. People who request their first catalog are sent the latest edition, which includes incentives to recommend Survival Aids to their friends.

Besides being informative, the catalog is also instructive. For example, the 1987 catalog provides information about such topics as "how to keep warm in a British winter" and "what to wear in hot wet climates." The catalog has also been used to try to expand the target market. The cover of the 1987 catalog featured a woman for the first time in the company's history. The description of the cover noted that the "Front cover picture shows 22-year-old Heather Morris from Chirbury, Shropshire, taking part in Operation Raleigh. Heather was on the Black River Expedition in Honduras, in April 1985." The catalog has not been circulated enough to know whether the picture of a woman hiking through the jungle will encourage more females to buy from Survival Aids.

Automation

Processing customer orders, maintaining an extensive mailing list, keeping records, and several other operations eventually became too cumbersome to do manually; therefore, in 1986, a computer was purchased. The company installed a sophisticated mini-computer, which provided on-line order processing, stock control, dispatch control, marketing information, office automation, and accounting packages. So many routine functions were computerized that the company soon needed a larger, more powerful machine. Since customer service is so important to Survival Aids' continued growth, manual backup procedures are in place should the computer be unavailable.

The introduction of the computer created no problems for Survival Aids. The company was particularly fortunate to have on its staff a person who was interested in computers and whose expertise has grown to keep pace with Survival Aids' data processing needs. Other employees had to be trained to use the computer. Even though the employees were not computer literate, they soon learned enough about the hardware and software to function efficiently. Now most staff have terminals on their desks and four employees have completed programming courses.

EXHIBIT 2   Survival Aids Ltd., Five-Year Summary

	1983	1984 (12 months)	1985	1986 (18 months)	1987 (12 months)
Profit and loss:					
Turnover	£410,648	£787,063	£1,237,847	£2,600,939	£2,584,936
Operating profit	16,726	37,339	42,669	61,570	102,100
Interest	(1,827)	(2,406)	(11,543)	(20,875)	(22,700)
Profit before tax	£ 14,899	£ 34,933	£ 31,126	£ 40,695	£ 79,400
Assets employed:					
Fixed assets	£ 22,039	£ 45,818	£ 50,233	£ 96,104	£ 141,891
Net current assets (liabilities)	2,847	(6,485)	12,524	15,336	37,584
Creditors due after more than one year	(18,576)	—	(1,883)	(19,386)	(45,130)
Deferred taxation	(1,309)	(9,338)	(9,020)	(11,000)	(11,000)
Shareholders' funds	£ 5,001	£ 29,995	£ 51,854	£ 81,054	£ 123,345

EXHIBIT 3   Survival Aids Ltd., Profit and Loss Account for the Year Ended 30 September 1987

	Year Ended 30 September, 1987	Eighteen Months to 30 September, 1986
Turnover	£2,584,936	£2,600,939
Cost of sales	(1,647,910)	(1,684,201)
Gross profit	937,026	916,738
Distribution costs	(86,665)	(131,809)
Administrative expenses	(748,261)	(723,359)
Operating profit	102,100	61,570
Interest payable	(22,700)	(20,875)
Profit on ordinary activities before taxation	79,400	40,695
Tax on profit on ordinary activities	(22,690)	(11,495)
Profit on ordinary activities after taxation	56,710	29,200
Extraordinary item	(14,419)	—
Profit for the financial period	42,291	29,200
Retained profit, beginning of period	55,053	25,853
Retained profit, end of period	£ 97,344	£ 55,053

EXHIBIT 4   Survival Aids Ltd: Balance Sheet—30 September 1987

	1987	*1986*
Fixed assets:		
Tangible assets	£141,891	£96,104
Current assets:		
Stocks	489,500	353,571
Debtors	153,097	113,540
Cash at bank and in hand	503	460
Total	643,100	467,571
Creditors: Amounts falling due within one year	(605,516)	(452,235)
Net current assets	37,584	15,336
Total assets less current liabilities	179,475	111,440
Creditors: Amounts falling due after more than one year	(45,130)	(19,386)
Provisions for liabilities and charges	(11,000)	(11,000)
Net assets	£123,345	£81,054
Capital and reserves:		
Called-up share capital	£ 26,001	£26,001
Profit and loss account	97,344	55,053
Total capital employed	£123,345	£81,054

Financial Information

For the last six years Survival Aids has been a profitable company (see Exhibit 2) with turnover nearly doubling each year and profit increasing from £5,000 to nearly £80,000 in 1987. The company's net profit for 1986 (18 months) was £29,200 (see Exhibit 3), and it had tangible assets worth £141,891 (see Exhibit 4). Finally, the source and application of funds is included in Exhibit 5.

THE FUTURE

Survival Aids, Ltd., has been successful and profitable since its founding. The company's sales have nearly doubled each of the past five years, with 1987 sales reaching £2.5 million and 1988 sales expected to be approximately £3.5 million. The products sold by Survival Aids are of the highest quality, management and staff are very capable, and no competitors pose a serious threat to the company. Although the company has been successful in the past, Nick is not sure that it will continue to grow without some changes. There are several options

EXHIBIT 5   Survival Aids Ltd., Statement of Source and Application of Funds for the Year Ended 30 September 1987

	Year Ended 30 September, 1987	Eighteen Months to 30 September, 1986
Source of funds		
Profit on ordinary activities after taxation	£ 56,710	£ 29,200
Add (deduct) items not involving the movement of funds during the period:		
Depreciation	45,018	25,990
(Profit) loss on disposal of tangible fixed assets	(5,518)	1,392
Deferred taxation charge	—	1,980
Total funds from operations	96,210	58,562
Funds from other sources:		
Proceeds from disposal of tangible fixed assets	28,000	1,028
Increase in long-term portion of hire-purchase creditor	25,744	17,503
Increase in creditors falling due within one year	139,242	144,345
Total	289,196	221,438
Application of funds		
Extraordinary item after taxation	14,419	—
Purchase of tangible fixed assets at cost	113,287	74,281
Increase in stocks	135,929	183,447
Increase in debtors	39,557	5,507
	303,192	263,235
Net application of funds	£(13,996)	£(41,797)
Increase (decrease) in net liquid funds		
Cash at bank and in hand	£ 43	£ (28)
Bank overdraft	(14,039)	(41,769)
	£(13,996)	£(41,797)

being considered to make Survival Aids even more dominant in its market. The following are some of those options.

Retailing. The company has been a retailer for just over a year; however, indications are that retailing could be successful and allow Survival Aids to continue to grow. Expanding retail operations would require several changes in the company's strategies and policies.

Franchising. If retailing proves to be successful, Nick might consider franchising his business. He realizes that this is a fast-growth option, and that he might lose some control of his business.

Manufacturing. Survival Aids has always sold products manufactured by other companies; however, it might be possible and profitable for the company to begin manufacturing some of the products it sells.

Expand the product line. It might be advantageous to offer outdoorsmen a larger variety of products. For example, Survival Aids could increase its product line to include guns, boating accessories, mountain climbing equipment, and so on. Several customers had requested these types of items in the past, and Nick felt that there would be substantial demand for them in the future.

Acquire other companies. Acquiring complementary companies would provide instant growth and could expand the product line at the same time. For example, there is a relatively small but profitable company that manufactures tents, rucksacks, and climbing hardware. Such a company might be an attractive acquisition candidate.

Sellout. Rather than buying another company, Nick could sell Survival Aids. He had been approached on several occasions by people who expressed an interest in buying his company. Nick could sell Survival Aids to another company and either remain as a key executive or leave and pursue other interests.

Export. Survival Aids catalogs are now distributed in several foreign countries, and orders are received from abroad, but international sales have never amounted to more than 10 percent of total turnover. Nick is particularly interested in exporting to the United States. At one point, the company was represented at a trade show in Chicago, and an advertisement was placed in *Soldier of Fortune* magazine. Sales in the United States were too meager to justify any further selling effort; however, Nick feels that he and Survival Aids may now be ready to make a concerted effort to become established in the United States.

Go public. Since Nick is the sole owner of Survival Aids, he could realize a significant profit and foster company growth by selling Survival Aids stock to the public.

Do nothing. Nick could make no significant changes and simply let things remain as they are. Survival Aids would continue its steady growth, and there would be no pressure on the employees to "grow" and accept change.

Case 3–3   Marriott Corp.*

In early 1982, Marriott Corp. started building the prototype of a new mid-priced hotel chain, something more modest than its usual hotels. Sample rooms with movable walls were assembled and furnished in the company's Gaithersburg, Maryland, hotel. Hammers and calculators labored in unison as Marriott executives slid walls back and forth, settling on three possible room shapes.

Then, over several weeks, hundreds of prospective customers were herded through the test rooms and quizzed. They howled at the idea of a room a foot shy on width, but they made nary a peep when length was trimmed 18 inches.

That little discovery should save Marriott more than $80,000 on each hotel property, or at least $24 million over the life of the project. It also says a lot about the changing nature of the hotel industry. In the late 1970s, market research wasn't in such vogue. Marriott, like most hoteliers, had grown easily with one sort of hotel that it duplicated again and again.

But a building boom has left several cities and some market segments saturated. And many hotel companies have spent the last few years researching and retooling in order to develop new growth strategies that are just now becoming clear. The new hotels themselves— and the development of the new systems needed to operate them— portend vast changes for this $33 billion industry.

Holiday Corp., for example, is entering three new market segments. Hyatt Corp., Ramada Inns Inc., Imperial Group PLC's Howard Johnson Co., and Manor Care Inc.'s Quality Inns International have all targeted new groups of customers. "What all of us are trying to do," says Darryl Hartley-Leonard, the executive vice president of Hyatt, "is steal some market share."

No lodging company is more ambitious than Marriott. (Exhibit 1 shows financial information for 1984.) The Bethesda, Maryland, company, which also owns contract food-service businesses and owns and franchises Big Boy and Roy Rogers restaurants, plans to build 300 "Courtyard by Marriott" hotels by the early 1990s in a bid to take market share away from mid-priced mainstays, Holiday Inns and Ramada Inns.

---

* Source: Steve Swartz, "Basic Bedrooms: How Marriott Changes Hotel Design to Tap Mid-Priced Market," *The Wall Street Journal,* September 18, 1985. Reprinted by permission of *THE WALL STREET JOURNAL,* © 1985 Dow Jones & Company, Inc. All Rights Reserved Worldwide.

EXHIBIT 1   Marriott Corp.—1984

Sales	$3.5 billion
Net income	$139.8 million
Employees	140,000
1984 lodging revenue	$1.6 billion
Resort hotels	21
Convention hotels	12
Other hotels	114
Rooms	65,279

In addition, Marriott is expanding its downtown convention network, launching a line of suites-only hotels and testing the time-share condominium market. Still on the drawing board: a retirement-community business that would incorporate the features of a nursing home, and a scaled-down model of its regular, full-service hotel aimed at smaller markets.

The stakes are high. The outcome of this segmentation movement could dramatically affect the makeup of this industry for the next decade and beyond. Some chains, such as Howard Johnson and Ramada, have already gone through hard times. Independent operators, who provide about half the hotel rooms in the country, also are feeling the heat as industry giants fight it out. "Some old-line chains will gradually lose market share, and some newer, more aggressive chains are going to gain market share," says J. W. Marriott Jr., the company's president and chief executive officer. "The question for us is: How successful will we be with these new products?"

The biggest question for Marriott is Courtyard, a two-story 150-room suburban hotel aimed at the $45- to $65-a-night market. (A traditional Marriott hotel room rents for $65 to $100 a night.) Analysts say many properties in the midpriced sector are old and could be vulnerable to a new competitor, and success here would vastly broaden Marriott's customer base.

But such an ambitious invasion of new turf has its risks. Marriott is committing more than $2 billion over the next several years to build Courtyard. What's more, Marriott is entering a market with different pricing and marketing strategies, different service labels, and a different clientele.

The company hasn't taken the move lightly. It spent about three years researching Courtyard before a test model was built. "I must have slept in a couple hundred midpriced facilities," says Donald A. Washburn, the vice president for market development.

Marriott's research indicates that room quality and outdoor surroundings matter most to a would-be guest. So Marriott is trying to keep Courtyard's rooms as close as possible in quality to its full-service rooms, while throwing in a landscaped courtyard with serpentine walkways and, of course, a swimming pool.

Most of the cost cutting has come out of public space and service. A Courtyard hotel has a tiny lobby and lounge, just one restaurant, a couple of small meeting-rooms, and no doorman, bellman or room service. Marriott now has six test-Courtyards in Georgia and boasts of an average occupancy rate of 90 percent. "You get a room that's worth more than you're paying for it," says John J. Rohs, a vice president for research at Wertheim & Co. Adds an executive at a competing chain, "If Bill Marriott builds 300 of those, he could hurt a lot of people."

Marriott spent many years in the highly competitive, low-profit-margin family restaurant business before building its first hotel in 1957. And its aggressive interest in market segmentation stems in part from an intense desire to set itself apart from the rest of the hotel industry. While most hotel chains grow primarily through franchising, Marriott likes to keep to itself by designing, building, financing, and managing (but not owning) its hotels. The hotels usually are sold to limited partnerships or institutions and managed by Marriott. It rarely uses outside consultants, and its doesn't like to hire general managers from competing hotels.

Unions are grudgingly tolerated at most companies, but Marriott fights them on every front. Its only unionized hotel, at San Francisco's Fisherman's Wharf, is neither owned nor managed by Marriott. (It is one of the few hotels Marriott has franchised.) Many chains publicly release occupancy rates; Marriott generally won't, though Courtyard has been an exception. "It's a competitive world we live in," says Mr. Marriott.

Such attitudes have led to allegations of arrogance and union busting, but few disparage Marriott's achievement. The hotel division, which accounted for about half of Marriott's $327.7 million pretax operating profit last year, has increased both revenue and profit at an annual rate of 20 percent for the past 20 years.

Since 1980, the hotel chain has more than doubled in size to 147 properties. More important, it has become the largest single operator of hotel rooms in the United States, and its lucrative management contracts have made Marriott one of the industry's most profitable companies. "Right now," says a rival executive, "they're the darlings of the industry."

The source of drive for the company has always been a workaholic member of the Marriott family. The first was J. Willard Sr., a devout member of the Church of Jesus Christ of Latter-day Saints, who founded the company as a root-beer stand in 1927 and who died [in 1985] at age 84. Also a Mormon, Mr. Marriott's eldest son—known as Bill—became chief executive in 1972. He remembers spending the vacations of his youth with his father in California visiting several family restaurants a day in search of ideas to take back to the East Coast.

Now Bill Marriott . . . emulates his father's practice, visiting about 100 Marriott hotels a year and about that number of competitors' hostelries. While the younger Mr. Marriott is expanding the chain at a much faster pace, the hotels are still run in the same old way: rigidly centralized and with great attention to the bottom line.

Mr. Marriott recalls a visit to a small luxury chain earlier this year. Despite its 10 percent occupancy, the hotel insisted on putting fresh flowers in every room. "The only person who saw [most of] them was the maid who took out the dead ones and put in the fresh ones," he says. "This happens more than you think in this industry."

But it couldn't happen at a Marriott. Marriott hotels are "run by the book, and the book is controlled by central people," says Gary L. Wilson, who recently left his post as Marriott's chief financial officer for a similar job at Walt Disney Productions. "The book" is in fact a dozen or so encyclopedia-like tomes detailing, among other operations, how to remove hair from bathroom sinks. The "central people" are numerous. Hyatt, traditionally Marriott's most direct competitor, estimates that for every two hotel executives it employs, Marriott has seven. No ingredient in hotel food may be changed without the explicit approval of headquarters. "We test our recipes," says Mr. Marriott. "We know what they cost. We won't let anyone mess with the food specs."

While concentrating on operations, however, Marriott, like most of its competitors, historically did little else. Consumer research and extensive marketing were rare. Room decor was chosen according to the personal taste of Marriott's decorators, and with a nod from Bill Marriott. The company got quite a jolt in the early 1980s, when its first forays into consumer research showed those decor decisions weren't going over with guests. Marriott's trademark reds and loud patterns were thereupon scrapped in favor of subtle shades of rust and beige.

"You might say the hotel industry grew in spite of itself," says Mark V. Lomanno, the associate director of research at Laventhol & Horwath, the consulting and accounting firm.

That changed with the onset of the 1980s, however, when many lodging companies began forecasting tough times. Tax incentives, in the form of investment tax credits and accelerated depreciation, lured scores of investors into hotel construction, often in areas where it wasn't needed. Marriott was running out of places to put its standard hotel, a 300- to 400-room, full-service facility located near an airport or a large suburban population center. In search of new markets, "we had to make the shift from a purely operations-driven company to a marketing-oriented company," says Frederic V. Malek, the executive vice president for hotels who had been a White House aide in the Nixon administration.

For Marriott, the move has meant bolstering the marketing staff, altering promotion paths and compensation scales to keep its best people selling, and starting a frequent-guest bonus program that costs $16 million a year to operate, according to a study done by a competing chain. It has also meant automating its hotel operations to allow more efficient tracking of guests, and attempts at jazzing up Marriott's rather staid image.

The company's internally designed hotels, for example, had a reputation for efficiency and consistency, but not for style or chic. So Marriott has been acquiring and building more resort properties, and it has turned to outside architects. John C. Portman, Jr., known for his cavernous atriums, glass elevators and other extravagances, designed the new Marriott Marquis hotels in Atlanta and New York.

Fashion, however, has its price. The Times Square property, which opened this month, cost $400 million and thus is one of the most expensive hotels ever.

But the key change, and the most difficult, has been the development of new operating cultures needed to succeed in new markets. When the first Courtyard was built, for example, Marriott moved the Courtyard management team from the hotel division and put it in a division that includes the company's fast-food chains, hoping to foster more creativity. "We make some decisions without all our flanks covered," says A. Bradford Bryan, Jr., the Marriott vice president in charge of Courtyard. He concedes that such a statement would be heresy in the hotel division.

In fact, none of the hotel division's traditions seems sacred at Courtyard. All-cotton towels, a hallmark of Marriott's hotel chain, have given way at Courtyard to cheaper fabric. Even a biography of the company founder, free for the taking in other Marriott hotel rooms (right beside the Bible), is sold at Courtyard vending machines, for 75 cents.

The hard part for Courtyard executives, however, is just beginning. Marriott plans to open 30 Courtyards in 1986 and about one a week thereafter, for the next several years.

Of course, competitors aren't taking this frontal assault lightly. Holiday Corp. is refurbishing some of its older properties, building about 50 Holiday Inns a year and throwing out an equal number of marginal properties. Says Richard Gonzalez, Holiday's director of new-business planning: "Marriott may find that there's some very, very strong competition in the midscale market."

Some of Marriott's stiffest challenges may be internal. There are some thorny marketing issues. To consumers, "the Marriott name may just mean expensive," says Daniel R. Lee, a senior analyst at Drexel

Burnham Lambert Inc. Francis W. Cash, a Marriott executive vice president, acknowledges that the company must condition potential guests to expect fewer frills and less service with Courtyard. "If you think [Courtyard] is the little Marriott," he says, "you're going to be disappointed."

The company is attempting to run the smaller, less complicated hotels with managers who have much less experience than its traditional general managers. And it plans to deviate from tradition by hiring managers from competing chains.

As the time to begin "mass production" approaches, Courtyard executives continue to tinker with the "product." For example, a fully equipped office for guest rental has failed and will be replaced, probably by an exercise room. And a large game room, designed to create a "home away from home" atmosphere, has been shrunk to the size of an extra-large closet. Marriott found that Courtyard guests didn't go for Ping Pong and pool, so a few video games should do nicely.

Case 3–4   *Metropol Base–Fort Security Group**

Pat Haney, president of Metropol Base-Fort Security Group (Metropol), was sitting in his office contemplating the future direction of his company. Metropol, a leading Canadian security firm whose services included the provision of uniformed security guards, mobile security patrols, polygraph testing, insurance and criminal investigations and a broad range of specialized services, was faced with a number of challenges which threatened its future profitability. "Increasing competition, especially from large multinationals such as Pinkertons, is further reducing already low industry margins," offered Pat. He was also concerned about Metropol's reliance on the commodity-like security guard business for 90 percent of its revenue. "We have to find some way to meaningfully differentiate our services from those of our competitors," Pat observed. "That is essential if we are to achieve the kind of growth we desire."

* Written by Stephen S. Tax, M.B.A., under the supervision of Professor W. S. Good, as a basis for classroom discussion rather than to illustrate either effective or ineffective handling of an administrative situation. Copyright by the Case Development Program, Faculty of Management, University of Manitoba. Support for the development of this case was provided by the Canadian Studies Program, Secretary of State, Government of Canada.

COMPANY BACKGROUND

Metropol was founded in Winnipeg, Manitoba, in 1952 by George Whitbread, a former R.C.M.P. officer. He perceived the need and profit potential in providing security services to the business sector, particularly at large industrial sites such as hydro installations and mines in northwestern Ontario. At the time most businesses security needs were not being met.

By 1970 the company had grown to such an extent that Mr. Whitbread could not run and control the operation on his own, so he hired a couple of assistants. That turned out to be a big mistake, as the assistants proved to be relatively ineffective.

In 1975, Mr. Whitbread had become so frustrated trying to manage the business on his own that he hired former Manitoba Premier Duff Roblin to act as a consultant to the firm. Mr. Roblin ended up purchasing the company.

Pat Haney joined the firm in 1976. He was hired to run the Winnipeg operation, which at the time was 80 percent of the firm's business. It was also expected that Pat would develop an overall marketing program for the company. "My experience was in the computer field," declared Pat. "When I first heard about Metropol Security I thought it was a stocks and bonds company."

In the late 1970s and early 80s Metropol expanded into Saskatchewan and Alberta and was aggressively seeking acquisitions. Finally, in 1984 it merged with Base-Fort Security, the leading security firm in Alberta and a major competitor in B.C. and a number of other areas in Canada. Pat believed this move offered economies of scale as well as other benefits and was an important step toward making Metropol a national company.

Sales topped $30 million in 1985 making Metropol the third largest security company in Canada. Offices were maintained in B.C., Alberta, Saskatchewan, Manitoba, Quebec, the N.W.T., and Newfoundland with 70 percent of their business coming from western Canada.

THE SECURITY INDUSTRY

Security products and services were purchased by individuals and businesses as a means of reducing the risk of loss or damage to their assets. The amount of security purchased depended upon individual risk preferences, their perception of the degree of risk involved, and the value of the assets to be protected. Security, therefore, was very much an intangible product subject to individual evaluation.

The industry offered such services as unarmed uniformed security guards, mobile patrols, investigations, consulting and education as well as "hardware" products such as alarms, fences, locks, safes, and electronic surveillance devices (ESDs) and monitoring equipment. Most companies purchased a package combining various services and hardware systems. "It would not make much sense to have 50 television monitors and only one person watching them," Pat pointed out, "nor would it be wise to have 50 security guards roaming around a building which had no locks on the doors."

There were a number of factors which contributed to the competitive nature of the security industry. All a firm needed to enter the business was to open an office. Start-up costs were minimal and no accreditation was required by the company or its employees. Clients considered the cost of switching from one firm to another quite low, so the business

---

EXHIBIT 1   Forecast Market Growth for Security Guard and Private Investigation Services, Electronic Security Devices (ESDs) and Hardware Products in the United States, 1985–1995*

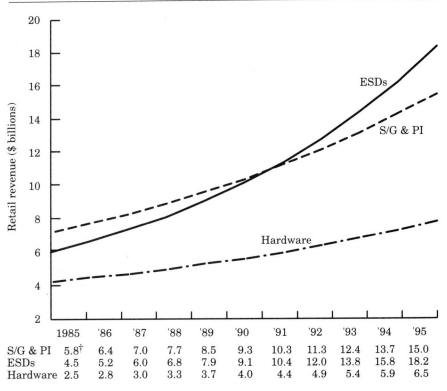

	1985	'86	'87	'88	'89	'90	'91	'92	'93	'94	'95
S/G & PI	5.8†	6.4	7.0	7.7	8.5	9.3	10.3	11.3	12.4	13.7	15.0
ESDs	4.5	5.2	6.0	6.8	7.9	9.1	10.4	12.0	13.8	15.8	18.2
Hardware	2.5	2.8	3.0	3.3	3.7	4.0	4.4	4.9	5.4	5.9	6.5

* The Canadian growth rate for each type of service/product was expected to be similar to the U.S. pattern.
† All figures are in $ billions.

Source: Metropol research.

often went to the lowest-cost provider. Most customers really did not understand the difference in services provided by the various competitors in the security business which made differentiation very difficult. Pat found in studying the financial statements of the large multinational security firms that most security companies earned pretax profit margins of about 4 percent on gross sales.

The 1985 security guard and private investigation markets in Canada were worth about $400 million retail. ESDs and other types of hardware added close to another $400 million to this figure at retail prices.

Growth was expected to continue in the security field for a variety of reasons including: a general increase in the level of risk around the world, the rising cost of insurance, economic growth, technological innovation which created new security problems, and an increasing sophistication among security system purchasers. The ESD and security guard segments were expected to outpace basic hardware sales growth (Exhibit 1).

On the negative side was the industry's poor reputation for the quality and reliability of its services. This perception threatened to limit growth and provide an opportunity for new competitors to enter the market.

COMPETITION

Metropol's competition came in both a direct and indirect form from a variety of competitors. "We compete with other firms who primarily offer security guard services as well as a number of company's that provide substitute products and services," observed Pat.

There were literally hundreds of security guard businesses in Canada ranging in size from one or two ex-policemen operating out of a basement to large multinational firms like Pinkertons, Burns, and Wackenhut. Metropol was the third largest firm in the country with a 7.0 percent market share (Exhibit 2). It was the leading firm in western Canada with a 25 percent share of that market.

Hardware products served as the foundation of a good security system. While items such as fencing, lighting, alarms, safes and locks, were to some extent complementary to the security guard business, they also competed with it—firms could substitute some proportion of either their security guard or hardware expenditures for the other.

Insurance had long been a favorite substitute for security and other loss prevention services. Business spent more on insurance than all forms of security products combined. However, falling interest rates, a series of major disasters around the world, and a trend to more generous damage awards by the courts were making insurance a more ex-

---

EXHIBIT 2   The Largest Security Guard Companies Operating in Canada, Ranked by Market Share

Company Name	Canadian Revenue ($ millions)	Employees	Market Share (%)
1. Pinkertons	50	4600	12.5
2. Burns	30	4500	7.5
3. Metropol Base-Fort	30	2000	7.0
4. Wackenhut	12	2000	3.0
5. Canadian Protection	12	1700	3.0
6. Barnes	12	1500	3.0
7. Phillips	10	1200	2.5
Canada	400	40,000*	100%

* In-house guards could raise this figure by as much as 100 percent. However a better estimate would be 50–60 percent, as in-house accounts use more full-time staff. This means that there are more than 60,000 people working as guards or private investigators at any time. Further, with turnover at close to 100 percent annually, there are over 100,000 people working in this field over the course of a year.

Source: Metropol research.

---

pensive alternative. Faced with higher premiums, lower limits and higher deductibles, businesses were likely to consider spending more on loss prevention products and services.

The various levels of government also provided some basic protection services to companies (fire, police, etc.). However, their services were geared more to personal than business protection. These government services tend to set the base level of risk in a community. Tight budgets were not permitting these services to keep pace with the growth in crime and the increase in the value of corporate assets. This provided the private security business with an opportunity to fill the void.

Businesses were spending almost as much for ESDs and related services as for security guard services. There were a number of different ESD products ranging from small electronic gadgets to the very popular central station monitoring systems. ESDs were the fastest growing segment of the security industry. The principal attribute of these products was that they provided accurate and reliable information to whoever was responsible for responding to a problem situation. Thus, to a large extent, these products were really productivity tools that enhanced the performance of security guards, the fire department and/or the police force. They did tend to reduce the amount of security guard service needed. Some security-conscious firms with large-scale security needs hired their own internal (in-house) specialists. In most cases they would also hire guards from companies like Metropol to do the actual patrolling.

The primary basis of competition in the security business was price. However, this was as much the fault of small, poorly managed firms and large multinationals trying to purchase market share as it was a fundamental characteristic of the industry. "I've seen companies bid under cost," observed Pat, "and they did not necessarily know they were doing it. It is a very unprofessional business in that sense. If you offer superior service and give a customer what he wants, in most cases you don't have to offer the lowest price. Just recently the Air Canada Data Centre job went to the highest bidder. Lowering your price is very easy, but not the way to succeed in this business." However, since price was a key factor in getting jobs, cost control became crucial if profits were to be made. Pretax margins of 4–8 percent quickly disappeared if unanticipated costs occurred.

MARKET SEGMENTS

The market for security products and services could be segmented in a variety of ways such as by type of service, type of business, geographic location, sensitivity to security needs, government versus private companies, and occasional versus continuous needs. Metropol segmented their customers and the rest of the market using a combination of the above bases as outlined below and in Exhibit 3.

Large security conscious organizations (private and public). The common feature among these companies was that they had the potential for heavy losses if security was breached. They typically had high value assets, such as computers or other high-tech equipment, or valuable proprietary information as in the case of research and development firms. These buyers were usually quite knowledgeable about security and rated quality over price. This group included firms in both local urban and remote, rural locations.

Organizations for whom security was a low priority. This group was dominated by local companies, commercial property management companies, and branches of firms which were headquartered elsewhere. They were less knowledgeable about security and tended to have limited security programs. They were price sensitive and principally utilized low-cost security guards.

Government organizations. Government organizations (nonhospital) typically awarded contracts based on a tendered price for a predetermined period of time, usually 1–2 years. The price for these

EXHIBIT 3   Security Guard Service Market Segmentation by Gross Margins and Guard Wages

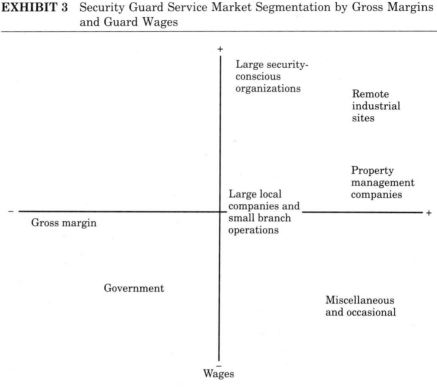

contracts was commonly in the vicinity of the minimum wage plus 5 percent.

Occasional services. These included anything from sporting or entertainment events to social or emergency services. Contracts in seasonal, as with a C.F.L. or N.H.L. sports team or one time affairs. Wages paid to the security personnel were usually quite low but profit margins to the firm were above average.

BUYER BEHAVIOR

The buyer of security services was commonly in the stronger position. This resulted from a multitude of firms offering what buyers perceived to be largely undifferentiated products and services and sellers trying to "win" business by providing the lowest price. Further the cost of switching suppliers was low because of the customer's perceived similarity of their services. It was also quite simple for firms to bring the security function in-house if they believed they could achieve substantial cost savings or other improvements in their security programs. In addition, some buyers tended to give security considerations a low priority in their budgeting.

Firms purchasing security products and services had three levels of decisions to make: (1) a general policy on the role and risk-cost framework security would play in their firm, (2) a decision regarding the types of products and services to be purchased, and (3) the selection of suppliers.

Each decision level involved new groups or individuals within the organization. Policy decisions were generally made at the senior executive level, while the product/service and supplier decisions tended to be made at the local level.

Most purchases were straight tender purchases based on a sealed bidding process. Firms with whom security was a low priority and most government agencies tended to choose the lowest bidder. Companies who took a greater interest in the quality of their security program considered attributes other than price when deciding upon their security supplier.

As part of a study on the security industry, Metropol surveyed buyers' ratings of the importance of several factors in choosing a security firm. They also had buyers rate Metropol's performance on those performance factors. Among the most significant decision-making criteria identified were consistency and reliability, availability of service

---

EXHIBIT 4   Customer Decision-Making Criteria—Survey Results*

How important are the following attributes to you
when making a decision on security services?

	Not Important			Very Important		Average Score
	1	2	3	4	5	
Consistency and reliability	—	—	—	3	14	4.824
Quality of service representatives	—	—	—	5	12	4.706
Price competitiveness	—	—	3	8	6	4.176
Company reputation	1	1	—	7	8	4.176
Emergency services	—	2	4	7	4	3.765
Full range of products and services	—	4	2	6	5	3.706
Consulting services	—	6	6	3	2	3.059
National coverage	4	4	6	2	—	2.375

* The survey was a convenience sample of Metropol customers.

Source: Metropol research.

EXHIBIT 5   Customer Decision-Making Criteria—Survey Results

How would you rate Metropol Security on the following attributes?

	Poor	Fair	Sat.	Good	Excellent	Average Score
	1	2	3	4	5	
Consistency and reliability	1	1	5	7	3	3.588
Quality of service reps.	—	2	—	11	4	4.000
Price competitiveness	—	1	4	10	2	3.765
Company reputation	—	—	2	10	5	4.176
Emergency services	1	1	6	7	3	3.556
Full range of products and services	1	2	7	6	1	3.235
Consulting services	—	4	5	5	2	2.944
National coverage	1	—	7	3	—	3.091

representatives, and price. Metropol scored highest on the quality of their representatives and the customers' view of the firm's reputation (Exhibits 4 and 5).

METROPOL

Metropol organized its operations on a regional (provincial) basis. The Manitoba headquarters developed a centralized policy and operating guidelines procedure which was instituted in all offices. While sales representatives dealt with the day-to-day needs of customers, top management was involved in making sales presentations to large accounts.

Services

Despite Metropol's variety of services, supplying unarmed, uniformed security guards accounted for most of their revenue. Their sales revenue breakdown by service type was:

Security guards	90%
Mobile security checks	8
Other (investigation, polygraph testing, retail services, consulting, and education)	2
	100%

Providing security guard services involved more than just sending guards to industrial or office sites. Metropol had to train, pay, uniform and insure the guards. They also had to supervise and dispatch their people as well as provide reports to their clients.

"We have attempted to provide greater value to our customers than our competitors have," stated Pat. "For example, we have a 24-hour dispatch service, while all the other firms use an answering service. There is a $100,000 (annual) difference in cost, but we can respond much faster to any situation. Some customers will say they just consider price in their purchase decision but end up linking and buying the extra service."

Metropol also gave their guards special training on the procedures to follow in the case of such emergencies as bomb threats, hostage takings, and fire evacuations. Again, this was an attempt to differentiate their services from those of other security guard companies.

The mobile security business was contracted out to local firms. This market was not considered to be a growth area, and Metropol did not invest a great deal of resources in it.

Investigative and polygraph services were contracted out to a couple of ex-R.C.M.P. officers. Metropol had maintained these investigators on its staff at one time but found that demand for these services was not great enough to justify having the high-salaried people as full-time employees.

Education programs were another means Metropol used to create added value and increase switching costs for their customers. Pat explained, "We give seminars on such topics as 'The Protection of Proprietary Information' for our clients and even invite some companies we don't current serve. We want our clients to realize that if they switch security firms they will be losing something of value."

Metropol did not sell hardware products such as fences, alarms and locks. However, it could arrange the purchase of such equipment for their clients. It was presently considering working in conjunction with a systems engineer so the company would be able to provide a total security package to their customers.

Costs

Metropol divided its costs into two groups, direct and administrative. A "typical" job had the following cost characteristics:

Direct costs	83–86%
Selling and administrative costs	8–9
Pretax profit margin	4–7

Given the above figures, cost control was a key success factor for Metropol and the security industry in general. Metropol's margins were, in fact, higher than the industry average of approximately 4 percent. "We use a job costing process," volunteered Pat. "Every pay period (two weeks) we look at what we made on each job. We consider and analyze every expense item very closely to see if there was any deviation from what was budgeted."

Direct costs included wages, uniforms, bonding, transportation and supervision. Metropol did a good job of keeping its costs as low or lower than its competitors' despite offering a higher level of service. Some of this was a result of economies of scale in purchasing such items as uniforms, achieved because of their comparatively large size. The company also did a superior job in collecting their outstanding receivables within a two-week period.

Pricing

Prices were determined by identifying the direct costs associated with a job, allowing for a contribution to selling and administrative overhead, and providing for a profit margin. Consideration was also given to any particular reason there may be for pricing a bid either particularly high or low. "We once bid at very close to our direct cost for a job in a town where we had no competition in order to discourage other firms from entering that market," noted Pat. He also suggested that it was important to anticipate competitors' likely pricing strategy when bidding on a job as well as recognizing that some projects had greater potential for cost overruns.

Promotion

Metropol individually identified the companies in each of their trading areas that were potential clients and concentrated their promotional efforts on that group. In Manitoba this "club" amounted to about 500 firms.

Once these firms were identified, strategies were developed to either sell to those potential accounts which presently had no security service or to become the logical alternative for those businesses who were using competitive services. "We want to put pressure on these incumbent firms to perform," explained Pat.

Metropol used, among other things, their educational seminars to stress to their clients that they offered superior services. At times firms using competing security companies were invited as a means of encouraging them to switch to Metropol.

Employees

Metropol employed almost 2000 people, 1900 of whom were security guards and 100 who were selling, administrative or management personnel.

Security guards came principally from three backgrounds; (1) young people [18–25] who could not find other work, (2) older people [50–65] looking for a second career, or (3) ex-military or police personnel who liked the quasi-military nature of the job.

Annual employee turnover in the security guard industry was very high, estimated to be in the vicinity of 100 percent. Metropol's turnover rate was in the same range. Reasons for the high level included a combination of low wages, generally boring work, and a lack of motivation or support from senior management.

"We have some employees who have been with the company for 15 years," Pat pointed out. "However, the wages we pay are based on our billing rate, which often only allows for minimum wages to be paid to our employees." Intense competition and clients who wanted to pay a bare minimum for security guard services forced companies to pay their guards the legal minimum wage. This caused high turnover rates which, evidently, did not bother some clients. Other customers, concerned with employee turnover, specified a higher minimum wage rate which the security company had to pay its guards. Pat liked this attitude because it allowed him to pay his people a higher wage and still be competitive.

Metropol's supervisors and customer service representatives (salespeople) did a good job servicing their accounts and handling any crisis that arose. They helped maintain Metropol's reputation as a competent and reliable security company despite the generally poor reputation of the industry.

The Future

Pat turned his attention to the future. He believed that the way business was conducted in the security guard industry would not significantly change in the near future. He did expect the business to become somewhat more professional with guards being trained in formal, standardized programs. The pressure on profit margins was expected to continue and perhaps even intensify as the larger, multinational firms fought for market share and smaller independents struggled for survival. Pat was thinking about how he could use Metropol's present position and reputation in the security guard sector to expand into more profitable segments of the industry or improve the company's general standing within the guard sector. Some of the opportunities he was considering included:

- Geographic expansion.
- Focused strategy.
- Expanding the range of security products and services offered by the company.
- Diversification into other service areas outside the security field.
- Serving the consumer home security market.

Geographic Expansion. "To be a national company in Canada you need a presence in southern Ontario," observed Pat. Even though many companys' security needs were handled at the local level, there was considerable potential for a national accounts program. To be involved in providing a national service, a company had to be active in the Toronto area, where most national companys' security decisions were made. In addition the Ontario market offered substantial local business. Pat explained, "We handle Northern Telecom's security guard needs throughout western Canada, but not in Ontario. Northern Telecom has three times the business volume there as it does in all of the western provinces combined."

There were three ways Metropol could enter the Ontario market: (1) by purchasing a local security firm, (2) through merging with another company, or (3) bidding on contracts in Ontario and opening up an office once a contract was obtained.

Pat believed that the "merger method" was the most appealing since it offered the potential for increased profits with virtually no additional cash investment. He had discussed the possibility with two firms that had head offices in Ontario and were also minor competitors in the Winnipeg, Edmonton, Calgary, and Vancouver markets. The western offices of the merged firm could be closed down and the business operated under the Metropol name. "The gross margin on their western contracts would go right to the bottom line," suggested Pat. "Because all the current Metropol offices could meet their administrative needs and absorb any incremental expenses."

A restricting factor in this strategy was Metropol's limited product/ service line. To provide a complete security package for any company on a national basis, it was necessary to offer the hardware and ESD packages in addition to the security guards.

Focused Strategy. This alternative was really a continuation of Metropol's current strategy. Following this approach Metropol's principal objective would be to become the fastest growing security guard firm in western Canada, with the highest profit margin and return on equity, the lowest employee turnover, and the most satisfied customers in the business of providing contract, unarmed security personnel. This strategy required an increased emphasis on developing a formal marketing program and increasing the value added of Metropol's security guard and support services. Tighter control of costs and employee motivation would be critical success factors, as would be the need to carefully segment the market and identify the most profitable clients.

The strategy would be designed to match the distinct competencies and resources of Metropol with the needs of the marketplace. Pat believed that while the strategy "sounded good," it would be very difficult to implement. "Even if you offer the highest quality service, you might not get the job," he offered. "Too many contracts, particularly those involving the government sector and crown corporations, are based solely on price, and simply supplying a higher service level in the provision of security guards is not likely to change that."

Expansion of Security Products and Services. From the customer's point of view there was an advantage to having one firm coordinate and provide the complete security coverage required by his business; the security system was more effective and efficient. If the customer had to contract with different firms for guards, fences, locks, lights, alarms, and ESDs, there was likely to be a lot of overlap and, in some cases, gaps in the overall system. Also, it was likely to be more expensive. Pat considered an investment in the production of hardware equipment much too costly given his firm's limited resources, but he was investigating the possibility of arranging a deal with a large multinational distributor of security hardware and ESD products.

Pat explained, "We would like to have an exclusive relationship whereby they (large multinationals) would provide us, at wholesale, with all the hardware and ESD equipment we needed on a private label basis (Metropol brand) and they would train our people. We could offer them our monitoring services and access to new markets." Metropol would package the system, which would include hardware, software, and people in whatever mix its clients needed. The products would be sold to the client or leased on a five-year arrangement.

The expanded product line strategy would deliver significant benefits to Metropol. Hardware and ESD equipment offered better margins than security guard services and, in some cases were subject to becoming obsolete. This provided opportunities to sell up-graded systems. For example, television monitoring devices had already gone through several generations of change despite their relatively recent entry into the security product mix. Service contracts to maintain the equipment would provide another source of additional revenue. Finally, the need of these systems for close monitoring and servicing increased the dependence of the customer on Metropol. This higher dependence meant that switching costs for the customer were much higher than with security guard services. This would be especially true if the equipment was leased for a five-year period.

Diversification into Other Service Areas. This alternative would capitalize on Metropol's skills in hiring people for contract type jobs and administering a payroll. Their current product line could be expanded to include one or all of the following additional services which could be provided on a contractual basis: secretarial services, nursing care, janitorial services, or landscaping services. The commercial sector would continue to be their primary target market.

Several years ago Metropol got into the dry cleaning business with poor results. "Businesses like janitorial and landscaping services are beyond our particular expertise," revealed Pat. "However, we are looking at providing people and handling the payroll for temporary clerical or nursing services. In those cases, we would be taking our established skills to another market."

Pat sited Drake International's experience as evidence that the strategy could work. That company went from providing temporary help to the provision of security guards.

The Consumer Market. Another alternative for Metropol would be to expand into the consumer market for security products and services. The major products of interest to residential customers were locks, supplementary lighting, fences, mobile home checks, house sitting, and alarm systems. This segment was growing slower than the business sector, but still offered substantial opportunity.

Pat was currently exploring Metropol's opportunities as a franchisor of home alarm systems to the numerous small Canadian alarm system dealers. "We would become the Century 21 of the alarm business," Pat suggested.

The alarm business in Canada was made up of a large number of small independent dealers and a few large multinationals. The "small guys" would buy their alarms from wholesalers in small lots which precluded much discounting. They also had to contract out their alarm monitoring to their competition, the large multinationals, because they could not afford the central station monitoring equipment. In most cases advertising and financing of installations for customers was too expensive to be carried out on a significant basis.

Pat thought a Metropol alarm franchise offered a number of important strategic advantages to independent alarm dealers: (1) by arranging with a large alarm manufacturer to produce a private label Metropol brand alarm line they could pass on volume discounts to their dealers, (2) franchisees would have the Metropol name behind them, (3) co-op advertising would provide greater exposure, (4) an arrangement for consumer financing could be established, and (5) Metropol would set up a central monitoring system.

Consideration was also being given to making locksmiths subdealers of Metropol alarm systems. "Normally a customer must call a locksmith and an alarm specialist to secure his home," suggested Pat. "It would be more effective, especially from a selling perspective, if the locksmith could do both."

Conclusion

Pat realized that the alternatives he was considering were not merely incremental changes in Metropol's strategy. In fact each option represented a distinct direction for the firm's future development. "We have to define our business's mission more specifically," Pat thought to himself. "Then we can choose and implement the strategy that best suits that mission."

Case 3–5   Frito-Lay*

In a marketing think tank [in Dallas] where a bare light bulb symbolizes the next bright idea, Howard Davis sizes up a visiting potato-chip "user."

"You're somewhat in the Ruffles camp," says Mr. Davis, chairman of Tracy-Locke, the market-research and advertising agency for the munch moguls at Frito-Lay Inc. He then takes a closer look at his guest's boat shoes, khaki pants and red tie. "You *must* have confidence to dress that way, so flat chips aren't for you."

But he also considers the user's plain blue shirt, noting the absence of stripes, the predictable navy socks and matching plastic pen. "You aren't taking a trip on the wild side, though; not exciting enough for jalapeno-flavored. Maybe on a Friday night you'll try cheddar to really step out. Bean dip too if you loosen up."

Knowing what consumers crave and tailoring products to fit those needs will be more important to marketers in the 1990s than ever before. One reason: It is the most efficient way to sell. Consumers are more demanding about the products they buy. They are more jaded about advertising come-ons. And it is harder to significantly influence consumers at reasonable cost amid a blaze of advertising in general.

The result, in some sense, is a reversal of the ad strategy that prompted Vance Packard's 1950s classic, "The Hidden Persuaders."

* Source: Robert Johnson, "In the Chips," *The Wall Street Journal,* March 22, 1991, pp. B1–B2. Reprinted by permission of *THE WALL STREET JOURNAL,* © 1991 Dow Jones & Company, Inc. All Rights Reserved Worldwide.

Rather than trying to manipulate consumers to buy their products, companies increasingly are letting the consumers manipulate them. This doesn't mean entirely abandoning the use of persuasion in advertising. But it does mean relying less on these tactics alone to move the goods.

To do this, marketers like Frito-Lay are exploring every facet of consumer behavior—from obvious things such as taste preferences, to more subtle psychological desires. In the process, they hope to come up with products that they won't have to beg consumers to buy.

At Frito-Lay, this approach has become something of an obsession. Snack-food research and development costs at the company have about doubled in past decade—to between $20 million and $30 million a year. At the same time, the company says it is spending proportionately less on advertising than it did in the past.

"I'm not much interested" in big ad campaigns anymore, says Robert Beeby, Frito-Lay's president.

The company must be doing something right: Its potato-chip market share has risen to 33.5% from about 25% a decade ago, and is more than double its nearest competitor, Borden Inc., according to *Snack Food Magazine*. Pretax profit margins approach a whopping 20 cents on every retail-sales dollar.

Moreover, this is in a $4 billion market that itself is booming. Potato-chip consumption in 1991 will top just over six pounds per person in the U.S.—the equivalent of about 100 of the one-ounce bags sold in vending machines, according to the Snack Food Association, an industry trade group. Consumption has been growing about 5 percent a year for the last decade.

"Young people are learning to graze on potato chips, the ways cows eat grass," says George Rosenbaum, a marketing consultant based in Chicago. His recent consumer survey of potato-chip eaters shows that people under 30 years old "expect the potato chip to be there as on-demand feeding," he says. "Like soft drinks, they are expected to be within reach and instantly available."

All of this from a product that Herman Lay toted around in one-ounce bags in a 1929 Model A. Back then, Mr. Lay learned about customer preferences primarily through informal conversations with a few grocery and gas-station managers.

Frito-Lay is now a subsidiary of PepsiCo Inc., and has a sales force of 10,000, each equipped with a hand-held computer that can advise headquarters in Plano, Texas, immediately about a supply shortage or a competitor's new flavor. It sells about 85 varieties of potato chips. And the informal conversations have evolved into nearly 500,000 consumer interviews a year.

"We have to reflect the vast increase in choices available all around us," says Mr. Davis. "The nation has gone from three networks, *Life* and *Look,* chocolate and vanilla, to hundreds of cable channels, regional magazines everywhere and Rain Forest Crunch."

Inside Frito-Lay's "Potato Chip Pentagon," a boxy, closely guarded building near Dallas, nearly 500 chemists, engineers and psychologists toil. Leaving no consumer preference to guesswork, they use a $40,000 simulated human mouth made of aluminum to measure the jaw power it takes to crunch single chips. By comparing consumer preferences in taste tests with results from the aluminum mouth, researchers calculate that most people prefer a chip that breaks under about four pounds of pressure per square inch. The company tests a few chips from nearly every batch at its 22 factories to make sure that standard is met.

Quality-control engineers measure the thickness of chips to $^{36}/_{1000}$th of an inch for flat chips and $^{91}/_{1000}$ths for Ruffles. Consumers have complained about chips that were cut $^{8}/_{1000}$ths of an inch too thick or thin, researchers say.

Other engineers test the chemical reactions of single chips on a computer screen that shows "flavor patterns" in eight colors. The printouts give results of roughly 50 chemical compounds in a single chip, showing, for instance, just how much more vinegar an experimental new barbecue flavor could stand before it becomes unpalatable to most people. Among other things, scientists experiment with compounds that will reduce the notorious bad breath associated with corn and tortilla snacks and certain flavors of potato chips. ("Frito Breath" and "Dorito Breath" are privately acknowledged problems within Frito-Lay.)

"We have to have a fanaticism about this to deliver just the right feeling to the mouth, enough satisfaction per ounce," says Dennis Heard, senior vice president of technology at Frito-Lay, and holder of a doctorate in chemistry. "We have to be perfect; after all, no one really *needs* a potato chip."

But many people *want* them by the bagful—thanks to Mr. Heard. His seasoning department develops 24 new flavor variations a year; they go through more than 6,000 consumer taste tests in their quest to develop about six new types of a chip that actually reach the national market each year.

Knowing more about consumers than the consumers themselves know is an important goal at Frito-Lay. "A lot of people who say they feed their families only alfalfa sprouts also eat potato chips," says Mr. Davis of Tracy-Locke. "They don't lie, exactly, they just have a certain self-image of what they ought to be doing."

To get in the right mood for creating ads, Tracy-Locke executives prepare a dozen or so videotapes depicting the types of people who they think eat various Frito-Lay snacks. The videos—shown only to Tracy-Locke copywriters—are scenes from current ads for hundreds of products. They are assembled based on interviews with 1,000 or more Frito-

Lay consumers. (In some of the interviews, for instance, consumers are shown photographs of people in various situations, and are asked whether these people are likely to eat potato chips. Among the responses: A person with an umbrella is unlikely to eat chips, as is a construction worker; someone playing softball is slightly more likely to eat chips; and a person watching television is very likely.)

The videos reflect distinct personality differences among eaters of various snacks. Some examples:

Lay's Potato Chips: Consumers of these flat chips are seen as "affectionate, irresistible, casual and a fun member of the family." Scenes show bubbling streams, puppies, flowers, a couple exchanging wedding vows, a farmer driving mules and a little girl stroking a cat. The music theme is the soft-rock "Little Pink Houses" by John Cougar Mellencamp.

Ruffles Potato Chips: Customers are depicted as "expressive, aware, confident enough to make a personal statement." Scenes show people getting into a BMW and other new cars, a man opening champagne, wind surfers and a woman working out in a fashionable outfit. The music is the fast-paced soundtrack from "Caddyshack."

Dorito Tortilla Chips: The scenes are of various actors talking about dating and love, Matt Dillon looking for a seat by the pool in "The Flamingo Kid," Prince doffing his shirt, and someone writing on a blackboard: "I want."

Such personality differences, moreover, are only a small part of a complex snack-food equation. The basic snack-chip market remains "anyone with a mouth," says Mr. Davis. But the impulses behind that hunger for snack food are increasingly diverse. "There's really no national snack-food market anymore," he says.

That's why some of Frito-Lay's 85 kinds of potato chips are sold regionally. For example, vinegar-flavored chips are sold mainly in the Northeast. Mesquite flavor, a sort of barbecue, is mainly for the Southwest and California. Sour-cream flavor is most popular in the Midwest. And Northerners like their chips fried a bit longer than the typical $2\frac{1}{2}$ minutes—making them a little browner than the ones most popular in the Sun Belt.

Little wonder that some consumers can barely keep up with all their options. When Frito-Lay set up a display of its new Cheetos "Paws"—a corn snack in the shape of a cheetah's foot—near the petfood aisle, confusion set in. "Are Paws for my cat, or for me?" one shopper demanded. Distributors resolved to steer Paws well clear of the pet food.

Marketers also have to be more wary these days of health and environmental concerns. One ounce of potato chips, about 18 morsels, contains 150 calories, or roughly 7% of the daily total recommended for most adults. The real health villain of chips is their fat—one ounce contains about 10 grams, or 14% of the recommended daily allowance.

"The chip debases the potato—a vegetable that's essentially fat-free and contains no sodium," says Michael Jacobson, executive director at the Center for Science In the Public Interest, based in Washington, D.C. "As a vegetable, the best thing you can say about the potato chip is it's better than ketchup."

To satisfy concerns that salt is also a health villain, Frito-Lay has reduced the salt content of its chips by about one-third in the last 10 years. But it doesn't publicize those efforts, partly because some consumers already complain of too little salt. The revelation that salt content is dwindling could bring even more griping, the company fears.

But Frito-Lay *is* promoting its new reduced-oil Lite Ruffles chips. Reducing oil is a more common health concern than trimming salt, consumer surveys have found. But there's a limit. Taste tests found that the company could reduce the amount of vegetable oil by one-third, at most. "Less than that, they taste lousy, and consumers won't sacrifice taste for health in snacks," says Dwight Riskey, a psychologist and Frito-Lay's vice president of market research.

Frito-Lay has also made great efforts to avoid using the word "fried." It was once a virtue in potato-chip ad copy—practically synonymous with "crisp" and "crunchy." But don't speak of "frying" around Frito-Lay executives anymore; the word has been stricken from marketing-research papers, brainstorming sessions and consumer interviews. Explains Mr. Heard with a slight grimace, "We say 'cooked,' not 'fried.'"

(They may not *say* it, but they still *do* it. So Frito-Lay portrays its products as a slightly naughty temptation. "Betcha Can't Eat Just One," the Young & Rubicam ad line from 1966, persists on Lay's packages today. The occasional customers who phone the company's hotline operators to report that they *did* stop after eating one chip find only more temptation as their reward: coupons for more snacks.)

What else has Frito-Lay learned about its consumers? For one thing, 65 percent of all chips are eaten in private. "When one is alone on a Friday night, potato chips confer some of the merriment and excitement of snacks eaten previously at a party or other fun event," says John Cacioppo, a psychologist who studies social behavior at Ohio State University.

Most people also expect their potato chips to reach a certain level of excellence in appearance, size, shape and taste. They expect more from potato chips than certain other foods, say Mr. Riskey. That's because consumers figure that if they are going to eat unhealthy food, they better get a *lot* of pleasure from it.

The result is a persnickety customer. People hate broken potato chips. (Of the 80,000 or so complaints Frito-Lay gets a year, the most concern broken or oversalted chips.) People also don't like chips that are too big or too small: They can't be bigger than the diameter of a softball, or smaller than the diameter of a golf ball.

About 64 percent of potato-chip eaters go for only the flat chips, Frito-Lay research shows. The thicker, ridge-style chips are eaten exclusively by 12 percent of the market, and 24 percent concede to eating both. Plain-flavored chips retain a 70 percent market share, but that is falling so fast it may be 50 percent within a decade.

Under ideal psychological conditions—relaxing at a movie with a soft drink nearby—a typical adult eats about 72 potato chips, or four ounces, at a sitting. Frito-Lay researchers arrived at that figure by renting theaters and offering thousands of consumers free tickets and unmarked bags of chips. The company collected the bags as consumers left and counted the uneaten chips. The test results show that consumers eat about one-third more chips at a sitting than they admit to in interviews.

The marketing lesson for Frito-Lay's future: Push bigger bags, even if they don't seem to catch on at first. "Potato chips today are where soft drinks were 30 years ago," says Mr. Beeby, the company's president. "No one walks around with a 6½-ounce Pepsi anymore. That's a child's size—an embarrassment. We want that to be true of small bags of potato chips too. We want to load the consumer up with bigger bags," he says.

Frito-Lay also goes to great lengths to make sure its packaging conforms to its consumer insights. For instance, it tested hundreds of shades of blue in focus groups to achieve the right bold, cheerful color on its new Ruffles packages. The bag, trimmed in a gold shade that also received extensive testing, "is a powerful statement about the chip and the person who uses it," says Mr. Riskey.

To embolden that power statement, many of its chip packages have replaced the clear plastic windows in favor of photos depicting larger-than-life chips. The perfectly photographed large chips jump out at a shopper as they walk by the bag. "It gets the chip closer to the customer," reasons Mr. Riskey.

Ironically, all this concern results from a dish that began as a joke. In 1853, Cornelius Vanderbilt, the railroad magnate, was vacationing at Saratoga Springs, a resort in upstate New York. At dinner, Mr. Vanderbilt complained that the fried potatoes were too thick, and he returned them to the kitchen. The chef, George Crum, took offense and replied by slicing the potatoes paper-thin and frying them to a crisp in hot oil. But to his surprise, the Vanderbilt crowd loved them.

Chip sales have boomed ever since. Kevin Knowles, a Frito-Lay route man in Dallas, says he sells $18,000 of snacks a week through five supermarkets, compared with $13,000 five years ago. The 30-year-old Mr. Knowles, who says he grew up sprinkling his personal chips with extra salt and pepper, claims such store-aisle innovations as a one-ton display that reached all the way to a ceiling, and another display decorated as a football field, complete with artificial turf.

But for all his expertise, he is unprepared for the query by a 10-year-old girl about why the store isn't stocked with packs of Ruffles Lights that can fit in a lunch box. "We'll get them in for you this week," he promises, noting the request on his hand-held computer.

Mr. Knowles also observes that with warm weather coming, he will have to stock a larger percentage of potato chips and less corn snacks. Potato chips weigh less than corn chips, and thus sell better in summer, he says. "I got a little sick eating Fritos one 95-degree day. They just sort of got to me," he confesses. Brightening, he adds, "Potato chips won't do that."

Case 3–6   Algonquin Power and Light Company (A)*

BACKGROUND

Allan Beacham is the marketing director for the Algonquin Power and Light Company, a large public utility providing gas and electric service to a major metropolitan area whose market is more than 1.5 million people.

Beacham is studying a report sent to him by Donald Orville, the company's forester. Orville is employed by Algonquin Power and Light to manage reforesting and reseeding of company construction projects. Possessing a degree in forestry from Syracuse University, Orville is acknowledged as a real authority in the forestry community.

Like many other public utilities across the country, Algonquin Power and Light Company conducts a maintenance program on its existing power lines. Trees, shrubs, and scrub are cut away from the lines to prevent chances of damage and subsequent power shortages. This maintenance program is directed by Donald Orville, and he estimates that the company's maintenance crews collect 100 tons of waste wood residue (cuttings) each week as a result of the line-clearing program.

Orville has developed a compost from these tree and shrub cuttings in his company laboratory. In his mind, this compost provides an organic soil amendment that is in much demand in the county. In his

* Reprinted by permission from Robert W. Haas and Thomas R. Wotruba, *Marketing Management: Concepts, Practice and Cases* (Homewood, Ill.: Richard D. Irwin/Business Publications, Inc., 1983), pp. 324–32.

report, Orville states, "Waste wood-chip residue can be converted into a humus material superior in quality to the organic peats, leaf molds, and composted redwood products being marketed in the county. An accelerated composting process will convert this waste material into a marketable soil amendment in a matter of 6 to 10 weeks." The Orville report continues, "Composted trimming wastes have properties superior to the various redwood products. Leafy vegetative matter is included in the chip residue resulting in a more complete composting of the material. This product has a low carbon to nitrogen ratio, which is desirable in composts." Orville firmly believes the compost can be marketed profitably and this is the reason he has submitted his report to Allan Beacham.

PAST COMPANY TREE CUTTINGS DISPOSAL PRACTICES

Up to this time, the company has simply taken its line maintenance cuttings to county-operated dumps or disposal sites. An average of 50 loads of wood chips is produced each week by the cutting crews, and the county assesses a dump charge against each truckload of waste hauled to the dump. This amounts to an annual disposal charge of $3,000.

In addition, each time a trip is made to the dump, an average of one hour of productive crew time is lost. Based on 50 such trips a week, crew time involved costs the company an additional $55,000 annually.

Orville contends that these costs could be eliminated if the waste wood material was processed into the soil amendment compost. Line-clearing equipment would then be based at the processing site or sites. The company would realize a profit on its sales of such compost.

Reading through Orville's report, Beacham is impressed with the logic of Orville's argument. To date, Algonquin Power and Light Company has paid money to dispose of product components that may be in great demand. In addition, Beacham believes such a program may have ecological advantages to the utility—the company would be converting a previously wasted resource into a valuable soil amendment.

COSTS OF OPERATING A COMPOST OPERATION

In his report, Orville foresees the need for two pieces of equipment to convert the waste wood residue into marketable humus composting material. Equipment required will be: (1) a 75-cubic-yard-per-hour shredder. Waste materials will pass through the shredder and would

---

EXHIBIT 1   Annual Cost of Operation of the Compost Program

Capital Base	Annual Capital Cost Factor*	Equipment Operation Expense	Annual Revenue Requirements
Land			
($60,000) (0.1969)†	$11,814.00		$11,814.00
Loader			
($25,000) (0.3251)†	8,127.50	(1,500 hrs.) ($1.197) = $1,795.50	9,923.00
Shredder			
($15,000) (0.2626)†	3,939.00	(1,000 hrs.) ($1.197) = $1,197.00	5,136.00
Land and equipment revenue requirements			$26,873.00

Labor (special equipment operator)		
Annual labor factor	Overhead (33% of base labor)	
$10,836.96	$3,576.20	$14,413.16
Insurance estimate (from company insurance department)		500.00
Miscellaneous expense factors:		
Supervision, sales, etc.		5,000.00
Total annual return requirements, including return on equity		$46,786.16

* Levelized annual capital cost factors include a return on equity of 15 percent.
† Rates used by the company to compute annualized capital costs.

---

then compost in long windrows on a packed earth surface. After composting, the material will be reshredded and screened. Such a shredder costs $15,000; (2) a size 1½-cubic-yard loader will be needed to load the wood chips into the shredder and the compost into waiting trucks. The cost of this loader is $25,000.

Labor studies conducted by Orville indicate that a single man working with the mobile processing equipment can operate the compost program. In his report, Orville outlined what he believes the annual cost of operation to Algonquin Power and Light Company would be. His estimate of $46,786.16 is derived in the manner shown in Exhibit 1.

In his report, Orville estimates that the 100 tons of waste wood residue collected each week will convert into 10,000 to 15,000 cubic yards per year of marketable compost. He also believes that a "virtually unlimited market exists for all locally produced humus material at a bulk price of $8.50 per cubic yard." Using a 10,000 cubic yard forecast, he computes the return to the company from such a program to be $96,000 based on the following:

$ 85,000	10,000 cubic yards of finished compost @ $8.50/yard
−47,000	Operation expenses of a subsidiary operation
$ 38,000	Direct profit from sale of compost
+58,000	Savings in residue hauling and dumping fees
$ 96,000	Return to the company

While Beacham is impressed with Orville's report, he is suspicious of some of the figures. He is particularly concerned with Orville's demand computations. For example, he questions Orville's contention that the compost could be sold at a bulk price of $8.50 per cubic yard. He also wonders if 10,000 cubic yards could in fact be sold in a year. Before he makes any decision regarding the compost program, Beacham wants his concerns to be addressed. He respects Orville's cost and technical expertise, but he questions his market knowledge and expertise. In short, Beacham requires more information before he makes a decision.

MARKETING ORGANIZATION

Algonquin Power and Light Company's marketing organization is headed by Allan Beacham who holds the position of director of marketing. Reporting to Beacham are three marketing program managers, Bob Morton, Ed Walton, and Carlos Berlozzi. These marketing program managers function very much like product managers—each is responsible for developing and implementing assigned specific marketing programs. For example, Berlozzi has responsibility for the utility's energy-conservation program while Walton manages the industrial-applications program. In addition to these three marketing program managers, the department includes Marjorie Haskins, the marketing research manager, who supervises a staff of three research analysts, and Edward Robinzes, the advertising manager. Both Haskins and Robinzes provide staff assistance to Beacham and the three marketing program managers. Beacham decides to give the compost project to Bob Morton and calls him to his office.

THE MEETING BETWEEN ALLAN BEACHAM AND BOB MORTON

Allan Beacham briefed Bob Morton on Orville's findings and recommendations and handed him a copy of the forester's report. "Bob," Beacham said, "I would like you to check this out. Orville may have something here, but we need more definitive market information. Look into it, and get back to me with a feasibility report and a strategy recommendation either to enter or not to enter this compost business. Back up your recommendation with some research data so that we will have some facts to fall back on. I will alert Marjorie Haskins so that she knows you need her help. Get with her as soon as you can and then get back to me. In the meantime, I will put Orville on hold." With that, Bob Morton returned to his office to study Orville's report. From the tone of Beacham's conversation, he knew this was a high priority project and that he would have to act soon. After thoroughly studying Orville's report, he scheduled a meeting with Marjorie Haskins, the marketing research manager.

RESEARCH REQUIREMENTS

In his meeting with Haskins, Morton outlined what he thought were his research requirements. Specifically, he wanted to know:

1. The approximate size of the total county compost market, both for commercial and residential users.
2. Competitive prices in both the commercial and residential markets.
3. Present producers of compost sold in the county and their locations.
4. Resellers and/or middlemen involved in marketing compost in the county.
5. The willingness of prospective customers to switch to Algonquin's compost from their present product.

Morton outlined these requirements to Haskins and impressed upon her the need for prompt information. She knew of the project's priority because Allan Beacham had briefed her, too. She promised Morton she would schedule a meeting with her staff immediately and would have information back to him within a month. Morton was pleased with Haskins' cooperation, and he left the meeting with a positive feeling that Haskins would provide him with the type of information he needed.

RESEARCH FINDINGS

About three weeks after their meeting, Haskins called Morton to inform him that the research had been completed by her department. Through the use of a "build-up" research methodology, Haskins had discovered seven basic markets for compost in the county. These are shown in Exhibit 2, which also indicates estimates of annual compost demand for each market. She considered the estimate of 78,641 cubic yards to be conservative yet realistic.

EXHIBIT 2   Estimates of County Demand for Compost by
Type of Customer

Customer Type	Estimate of Cubic Yards Used per Year
Topsoil companies	36,800
Retail nurseries:	
Specialty nurseries	11,400
Chains and discounters	4,816
Growers: Farms, orchards, etc.	19,200
Landscape contractors and gardeners	6,425
Manufacturers and distributors	Unable to ascertain
Government	Unable to ascertain
Total demand	78,641

Note: A limited number of manufacturers did use compost, but it was
often purchased indirectly through landscapers, topsoil companies, etc.
Local distributors also handled compost, but since they resold to other
demand components (retailers, etc.), much of their demand was also
duplicated in the demand of other components. Interviews with government buyers at city, county, and state levels indicated that government
did at times purchase quantities of compost from outside suppliers.
However, they also composted their own trimmings. Thus reliable estimates of compost purchased from outside suppliers could not be obtained. In view of these considerations, the estimate of 78,641 cubic
yards is viewed as a conservative estimate.

Breaking down the markets into retail and wholesale/user segments, she provided Morton with information showing brands and
products presently being purchased, their sources and suppliers, and
prices paid. These data may be seen in Exhibits 3 and 4.

From field interviews with prospective customers, Haskins developed a list of product specifications that the compost must meet if
customers were to seriously consider Algonquin compost as a substitute for existing competitive products already on the market. These
specifications may be seen in Exhibit 5.

The field research also revealed some concerns or fears expressed by
potential users. Some of the most commonly expressed fears were:

1. Could Algonquin Power and Light provide compost in the required quantities over time? Many prospective customers were reluctant to switch because they were afraid they might later find that the
utility could not provide quantities required. This was a particular
concern of large growers and topsoil companies mainly because the
utility company's policy of underground power lines in new areas
would in the long run reduce the source of compost materials.

2. How good would Algonquin's quality control be? The utility was
seen as a novice in the soil amendment business. Many potential buy-

EXHIBIT 3 Potential Competition in the Wholesale and/or User Market based on Selected Field Interviews

Business Operation Interviewed	Products Presently Being Purchased	Quantities Purchased Annually	Sources and Locations of Suppliers	Present Price Being Paid
Maynard Sand and Material Company (topsoil company)	Douglas fir wood chips 3/8" or less in size	24,000 cu. yd.	Local county distributor	$2.50 per cu. yd.
Dave Parker Supplies (topsoil company)	Redwood shavings 3/8" or less in size	3,600 cu. yd.	Local sawdust company (in county)	$4.50 per cu. yd.
	Used sawdust	500–1,500 cu. yd.	Stall sweepings from local horse ranches	$1.00 per cu. yd.
	Nitrolized fir compost 1" or less in size	250–750 cu. yd.	Both bought from out-of-county distributor 200 miles away	$5.50 per cu. yd. + $3.00 per cu. yd. freight
	Redwood compost 1" or less in size	250–750 cu. yd.		$6.00 per cu. yd. + $3.00 per cu. yd. freight
Green Thumb Nursery (wholesale nursery grower of small ornamentals)	Redwood compost 1/8" or less in size	100 cu. yd.	Local sawdust company (in county)	$4.50 per cu. yd.
Marlowe's Nursery (wholesale nursery grower of trees and large shrubs)	Redwood compost 1/4" or less in size	1,000 cu. yd.	Local sawdust company (in county)	$3.50 per cu. yd. bought on a 40 cu. yd. basis
Garden Valley Nursery (wholesale nursery grower of 1- and 5-gallon plants)	Nitrolized redwood and fir compost 1/4" or less in size	2,000–3,000 cu. yd.	Local sawdust company (in county)	$4.00 per cu. yd.
County government	Redwood R.S.A. nitrogen-treated compost bulk	Unable to determine	Local county distributor for small orders / Out-of-county sawdust company for large orders	$5.75 per cu. yd. delivered on a 35 cu. yd. basis / $4.90 per cu. yd. delivered on a 60–65 cu. yd. basis

EXHIBIT 4 Potential Competition in the Retail Nursery Business based on Selected Store Samplings

Type of Store	Brand Name of Competitive Product(s) Presently Stocked	Producer and/or Supplier of Present Products	Form in Which Product Is Sold to Consumers	Retail Price Charged
Discount Store A	Hawaiian Magic (redwood compost)	Out-of-county fertilizer Producer A	70 lb. bags	$1.19 per bag
	Garden Pride redwood soil conditioner	Out-of-county fertilizer Producer B	2 cu. ft. bags	$1.99 per bag
Specialty Nursery A	Garden Humus Bark Compost	Out-of-county fertilizer Producer C	3 cu. ft. bags	$2.49 per bag
Specialty Nursery B	Redwood Garden Mulch	Local fertilizer Producer A (in county)	4 cu. ft. bags	$4.00 per bag
Discount Store B	University Formula Redwood Compost	Out-of-county fertilizer Producer D	60 lb. bags	$2.17 per bag
Department Store A	Redwood Compost	Private brand—no producer listed on bags	60 lb. bags	$2.49 per bag
Chain Drug A	Hawaiian Magic (redwood compost)	Out-of-county fertilizer Producer A	70 lb. bags	$2.29 per bag
	Organic compost	Out-of-county fertilizer Distributor A	65 lb. bags	$2.49 per bag
Specialty Nursery C	Redwood Garden Mulch	Local fertilizer Producer A (in county)	4 cu. ft. bags	$2.97 per bag
Discount Store C	Viva Redwood Compost	Local fertilizer Producer A (in county)	4 cu. ft. bags	$2.99 per bag
Discount Store D	Viva Redwood Compost	Local fertilizer Producer A (in county)	4 cu. ft. bags	$2.99 per bag
Specialty Nursery D	Bandini 101 Redwood Compost	Bandini (national producer and sold through local distributor)	4 cu. ft. bags	$3.79 per bag
Discount Store E	Red Star Redwood Compost	Out-of-county fertilizer Producer E	4 cu. ft. bags	$2.26 per bag

---

EXHIBIT 5   Required Product Specifications for Compost Soil Amendment

Based on field interviews with such potential customers as topsoil companies, retail nurserymen, growers in the nursery industry, landscaping personnel in city, county, and state governments, and others, the compost produced would have to meet the following specifications if it is to be seriously considered as a substitute for existing competitive products already on the market:

- Its ability to sustain and stimulate plant life must be demonstrated.
- It should contain 1 to 2 percent nitrogen content.
- It should be a dark earthy color.
- It should be fine in content. Nursery customers would like compost to be capable of passing through a 1/4″ screen and preferably through a 1/8″ screen. Topsoil companies require a compost that will pass through a range of 1/2″ to 3/8″ screen, preferably the latter.
- It must be free of weed, seed, dust, and other objectionable materials.
- It must be friable—properties that allow it to be easily crumbled.
- It must be stable over time. Changes in content because processing batches were different would have adverse effects in all markets.
- Its source of supply must be reliable over time.
- It must hold moisture well.
- It must not contain any cuttings that might be harmful to plant life, such as oleander, eucalyptus, and hardwoods.
- It may contain other ingredients, such as peat moss and leaf mold, but it must *not* contain steer manure.
- It must be bagged and labeled for the retail-nursery business but can be sold in bulk for growers and topsoil companies.
- It must be certified by an independent laboratory.

---

ers expressed a fear concerning the company's production and quality-control capabilities.

3. How would the Algonquin compost compare to redwood compost? Most of the prospective customers interviewed did not think the compost would be as good as redwood compost, despite Orville's contentions that it was. The major concern was that the Algonquin compost would break down quicker than redwood compost. This was a particularly big point with growers of trees and large ornamental shrubs who use exclusively redwood compost. They argued that redwood compost allowed them to grow their plants in a pot to the desired sale size with a single planting because the break-down period of the redwood was the same as the growing time. If they switched to the Algonquin compost, they would have to replant during the growing period because the new compost's break-down period was considerably shorter. This, of course, meant increased cost to these growers. Growers of small plants expressed no such concerns.

Despite the concerns, most prospective customers who were interviewed were interested. All were concerned about future sources of redwood compost as the supply of redwood is limited, and all were looking for comparable competitive products that could be purchased at lower prices.

In summary, Haskins felt the compost market for Algonquin looked promising and she told that to Morton. After receiving Haskins' research findings, Morton called Donald Orville on the phone. He wanted to hear the forester's reaction to the required product specifications that the research uncovered. Specifically, he wanted to know if Orville's compost could meet those specifications. Orville's reaction was most positive. While the compost's present form did not meet those exact specifications, there was little problem in changing it to meet them. The present compost is light brown but could easily be given a dark earthy color. It could easily be nitrolized to meet the 1 to 2 percent nitrogen content requirement, and it could also be screened to any size desired. Other than that, the present compost could support plant life, and Orville had evidence of that in his laboratory. The certification requirement was no problem, and Orville had already met with a local chemical lab on such certification. Orville believed the compost could meet the required specifications with very little modification.

Armed with the research findings provided him by Haskins' department and Orville's positive reaction, Bob Morton starts to prepare the feasibility report that Beacham requested, and he considers strategy recommendations he would make for Orville's compost. Based on the research findings, Morton believes that any strategy recommendations must consider both the retail and the wholesale-user markets. Advise Bob Morton on what strategy approach is most appropriate.

Case 3–7 La-Z-Boy Chair Company*

One of the most widely recognized trademarks in the United States, La-Z-Boy seems to connote a relaxed, lazy atmosphere. Is the La-Z-Boy Chair Company (LZB) like the visions its trademark suggests? Hardly! Consider the percent increase in net sales and percent increase in net profit in the last six years. Exhibits 1 and 2 show the Income Statements and Balance Sheets for the years 1983 through 1988, respec-

* This case was prepared by Robert P. Crowner, associate professor of management of Eastern Michigan University, as a basis for class discussion. Copyright © 1988 by Robert P. Crowner. Distributed by the North American Case Research Association. All rights reserved to the author and the North American Case Research Association.

EXHIBIT 1

LA-Z-BOY CHAIR COMPANY
Income Statement
For Years Ending April 30
(in thousands of dollars)

	1983	1984	1985	1986	1987	1988
Net sales	$196,973	$254,865	$282,741	$341,656	$419,991	$486,793
Costs and expenses:						
Cost of sales	136,952	167,387	191,312	235,524	289,779	352,069
Selling, general, and administrative	38,595	45,962	54,713	65,610	85,469	91,354
Interest expense	1,031	963	1,146	1,570	1,877	4,008
Total	176,578	214,312	247,171	302,704	377,125	447,431
Operating income	20,395	40,553	35,570	38,952	42,866	39,362
Other income	2,062	3,037	3,117	2,807	2,081	2,662
Income before taxes	22,457	43,590	38,687	41,759	44,947	42,024
Income taxes:						
Federal:						
Current	237	14,790	9,201	14,797	19,558	17,931
Deferred	8,717	4,010	6,508	2,809	(1,175)	(4,832)
State	732	1,505	1,619	1,143	1,900	2,444
Total taxes	9,686	20,305	17,328	18,749	20,283	15,543
Net income	$ 12,771	$ 23,285	$ 21,359	$ 23,010	$ 24,664	$ 26,481
Net income per common share	0.69	1.16	1.17	1.26	1.34	1.45

EXHIBIT 2

LA-Z-BOY CHAIR COMPANY
Balance Sheets
For Years Ending April 30
(in thousands of dollars)

	1983	1984	1985	1986	1987	1988
Current assets:						
Cash	$ 1,115	$ 3,220	$ 2,062	$ 2,419	$ 1,393	$ 2,207
Short-term investments	14,973	25,957	18,250	13,305	21,172	14,740
Receivables	70,762	79,557	92,167	106,638	116,952	135,560
Less allowances	2,140	2,300	2,445	2,814	3,118	4,976
Net receivables	68,622	77,257	89,722	103,824	113,834	130,584

EXHIBIT 2 (*concluded*)

	1983	1984	1985	1986	1987	1988
Inventories						
Raw materials	11,463	11,992	12,209	15,305	19,541	24,522
Work in process	6,740	8,965	11,630	14,771	17,143	23,323
Finished goods	4,563	5,147	4,097	5,157	8,791	18,977
Total	22,766	26,104	27,936	35,233	45,475	66,822
Other current assets	452	585	2,985	3,229	5,037	5,085
Total current assets	107,928	133,123	140,955	158,010	186,911	219,438
Other assets	500	2,572	7,726	18,095	9,488	6,737
Fixed assets:						
Land	$ 1,954	$ 2,197	$ 2,344	$ 2,842	$ 3,586	$ 5,266
Buildings	28,853	31,316	37,314	44,088	52,782	64,637
Machinery	29,024	33,410	40,248	51,041	66,821	69,437
	59,831	66,923	79,906	97,971	123,189	139,340
Less depreciation	27,535	31,095	35,157	41,082	49,701	55,180
Net fixed assets	32,296	35,828	44,749	56,889	73,488	84,160
Goodwill						26,257
Total assets	$140,724	$171,523	$193,430	$232,994	$269,887	$336,592
Current liabilities:						
Notes payable			$ 1,077	$ 3,682	$ 6,099	$ 10,744
Current portion of long-term debt	$ 936	$ 1,098	1,087	1,717	979	7,039
Accounts payable	10,414	10,966	15,470	11,033	20,134	16,815
Payroll	6,173	7,987	8,265	13,144	15,941	16,046
Other liabilities	4,345	4,182	6,383	7,478	10,014	13,098
Income taxes	993	4,655	1,185	2,392	7,168	1,764
Deferred income taxes	6,649	9,321	12,016	12,196	11,241	6,868
Total cur. liab.	29,510	38,209	45,483	51,642	71,576	72,374
Long-term debt	11,763	13,222	11,165	24,463	23,270	76,215
Deferred income taxes	2,136	3,474	7,288	9,917	9,687	9,238
Equity:						
Common stock, $1 par value	18,641	18,641	18,641	18,641	18,641	18,641
Capital in excess of par value	5,168	5,540	5,514	5,783	6,054	6,493
Retained earnings	73,984	92,862	108,354	124,951	142,485	161,629
Currency adjustments	(131)	(271)	(654)	(659)	(449)	320
	97,662	116,772	131,855	148,716	166,731	187,083
Less treasury shares	347	154	2,361	1,744	1,387	8,318
Total equity	97,315	116,618	129,494	146,972	165,344	178,765
Total liabilities and equity	$140,724	$171,523	$193,430	$232,994	$269,877	$336,592

EXHIBIT 3   Acquisitions and Their Annual Sales

Burris Industries, Inc.—acquired July 1985	$10.6 million*
Rose Johnson, Inc.—acquired January 1986	$20.0 million
Hammary Furniture, Inc.—acquired September 1986	$22.0 million
Kincaid Furniture, Inc.—acquired January 1988	$85.0 million

   * Sales in the year prior to acquisition.

---

tively. This dramatic growth, which made LZB number three in the furniture industry and the largest producer of upholstered furniture, was achieved by acquiring four other companies as well as by internal growth. The four acquisitions are shown in Exhibit 3, with their annual sales in the year prior to acquisition.

While the furniture industry sales grew by 52 percent in the last 10 years from sales of $9.7 billion in 1978 to $14.8 billion in 1987, LZB sales grew at a much faster rate of 216 percent. During the 10-year period, the top 10 manufacturers moved from 20 percent to 33 percent of the total market growing by 139 percent. During this same 10-year period, LZB moved from eighth to third place in the industry. Can this performance be continued? What can LZB do for encores?

COMPANY BACKGROUND

LZB was founded by Edward M. Knabusch and his cousin Edwin J. Shoemaker in 1927 as a partnership known as Kna-Shoe Manufacturing Company in Monroe, Michigan. In 1928, the first reclining chair was developed as a wooden-slat porch chair. Although the Lion Store in Toledo, Ohio, refused to handle it, the buyer suggested that if it were an upholstered chair it would have a much wider market year round. The two partners followed the suggestion and produced and patented the first "La-Z-Boy Chair" in 1929. In that same year the company was incorporated as the Floral City Furniture Company, the name selected because Monroe was then known as the "Floral City" since it was the home of the world's two largest nurseries.

During the depression years of the 1930s, the chair was leased to established companies on a royalty basis, with Floral City retaining the rights for Monroe County. In 1938, a new mechanism was developed which was so revolutionary that new patents had to be secured. Floral City took back the patent in 1939 and continued to manufacture chairs through 1941. La-Z-Boy Chair Company was formed in 1941 to separate the production function from the merchandising activity. Beginning in 1942 and continuing through World War II, LZB produced seats for military vehicles and naval vessels.

In 1947, chair production began again and sales grew to $52.7 million by 1970. The first out-of-state plant was built in Newton, Mississippi, in 1961. Edward Knabusch, who died in 1988, continued as president of LZB until 1972, when he was succeeded by his son Charles. Edwin Shoemaker continues to be active in LZB as vice chairman of the board and executive vice president of engineering.

SALES AND MARKETING

Sales and marketing are under the direction of Patrick H. Norton, senior vice president. Norton, who is 66 years old, joined LZB in September 1981, following a successful career with Ethan Allen, Inc. Exhibit 4 shows the organization chart for the upper management of LZB. In addition to the activities of advertising and sales communication, residential sales, contract sales, and sales for Burris Industries, the following activities also report to Norton: corporate interior design for Showcase Shoppes, national merchandising manager, sales and service administration, manufacturing services manager, sales and marketing research, product design, and store development for Showcase Shoppes. Norton's strategy is responsible for the dramatic expansion of LZB into the broader lines of furniture since he arrived. He believed that for LZB to continue to expand and be competitive it must offer a full line of furniture.

Sales

Sales are divided into two broad categories. The Residential Division, which is by far the largest segment of the business, sells a complete line of reclining chairs and other upholstered chairs, sofas and sleep sofas and modular seating groups. The Burris Division sells upscale upholstered furniture to the residential market, which is complemented by an extensive line of wooden occasional tables sold by the Hammary Division. Within these divisions traditional, transitional, and contemporary styles are sold.

The Contract Division sells desks, chairs, and credenzas to the general business market. The Rose Johnson Division complements the contract division by providing office panel walls, chairs, and work centers.

Residential sales are carried out by 100 independent manufacturer's representatives who are under annual contract to sell the LZB line exclusively within their geographic area. These reps are paid by commission equivalent to 3 percent of direct shipments plus 2 percent from an incentive pool for performance against an order goal. The incentive

EXHIBIT 4 Organization Chart, La-Z-Boy Chair Company

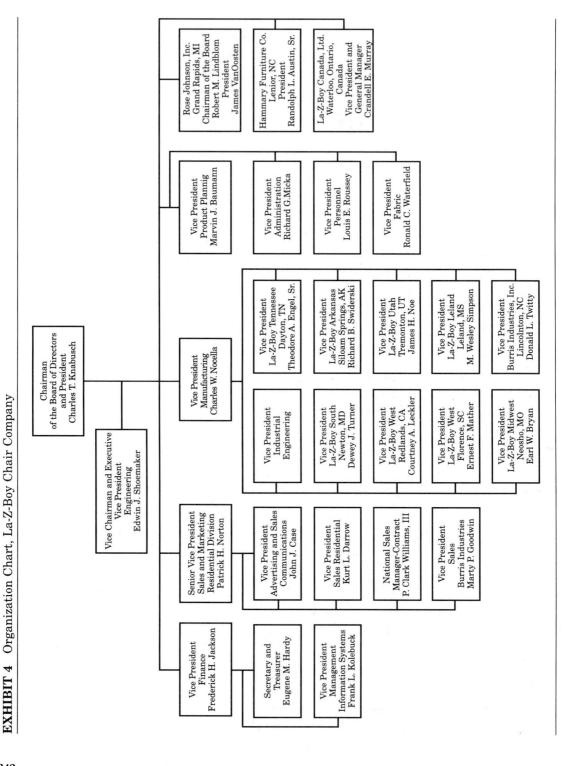

begins when the rep reaches 70 percent of the goal and reaches the full 2 percent when 100 percent of the goal is attained. Sales in excess of the goal receive a commission of 7 percent. The established goal is based upon history and the corporate target regarding market share and growth. The rep can protest the goal. LZB's new sales strategy is to reduce the size of the exclusive territories, often limiting them to a county in populous areas. Therefore, over time, the number of reps has been increased. This is accomplished by only changing territories as existing reps retire or are dismissed.

The reps are managed by four regional managers—South Central, Eastern, Midwest, and Western. The regional managers spend two to three days per week on the road working with sales reps. The regional manager breaks the region's sales goal down into goals for individual sales reps. LZB has the right to interview and approve any "associates" whom the sales reps may hire to work with them.

The yearly sales goal is developed by using a demographic profile. Factors considered are age groups, racial groups, since minorities historically have purchased few chairs, home owner status, since the major market is home owners or those living in single family dwellings, and furniture dollars spent within an area. The average customer is in the middle class, with chair customers being 35 and older as contrasted with sleeper customers being younger, newly married, and renters.

To determine each region's goal, a regional factor is applied. Marketing Statistics, a firm located in New York, is used to obtain a buying power index for each county as a percent of the total U.S. market. A separate index is used for recliners and for sleepers. The American Furniture Manufacturers Association collects and provides information about the industry. Industrial Marketing Research in Chicago provides quarterly and annual customer surveys which are useful. Sales for LZB are about equally divided between the first and second halves of its fiscal year.

Distribution for LZB is divided into three major categories. General furniture dealers account for about 50 percent of sales. The Gallery Program, which currently includes about 75 stores, 25 percent of the general furniture market, and is increasing, is featured with the general dealers. Under this program, the dealer must dedicate 3,500 square feet to LZB products, and LZB designs the area. The dealer is licensed on an open-end basis by location. Department stores, which do 20 percent of the total furniture business, have been a weak category for LZB. Department stores always want special pricing and LZB does not engage in discounting.

National accounts make up 10 percent of sales. The largest single account is Montgomery Ward, which is handled by the home office, but a 3 percent commission is paid the local sales rep for servicing the account. Most accounts are regional, such as Art Van in Detroit and Macy's.

LZB Showcase Shoppes, which number about 265, account for about 35 percent of sales. A Showcase Shoppe is licensed on an open-end basis by location. Location is everything—that is, the site should be located in an area where the city is growing, with a reasonable concentration of quality homes, apartments, or condominiums which are less than 15 years old within a seven-mile radius; the activity in the surrounding area should be conducive to retail activity; the street should be a heavily traveled major artery that is well known to everyone; the site should be readily visible and located near the street with maximum window frontage and should be easily accessible and convenient to shoppers; and the building should be free-standing. Small strip centers can be effective, but large strip centers or regional malls are ineffective. The minimum showroom size is 6,000 square feet, with the normal Shoppe expected to be 7,000 to 10,000, with an additional 1,500 to 2,400 square feet on site area required for warehouse, office space, and so on. An initial investment of $132,000 is typical, of which $75,000 is required for working capital and the balance for capital improvements. LZB provides the Shoppe with an operating manual, which includes advice on advertising, personnel policies, freight, service, interior design, and signage.

Contract sales are handled through a different group of manufacturers's reps who do not handle LZB products exclusively. These reps typically have other employees working for them. Sales of subsidiaries are handled in a manner similar to the residential sales with their own reps.

Advertising

John J. Case, vice president of advertising and sales communications, joined LZB in 1977 as assistant national accounts manager and progressed through several positions to his present one in 1985. He is responsible for all of LZB's national corporate advertising and public relations for the residential, office products, and Burris divisions, as well as the sales training program for dealers and sales representatives. He graduated from Michigan State University with a B.A. degree in telecommunications.

Prior to 1982, LZB spent money on corporate advertising and on retail advertising materials but had no control over its image in the local marketplace. Its corporate image and its local image were not compatible. Retail outlets bought seasonally and promoted seasonally. As a result, manufacturing was adversely affected by the two peak sales periods in May and November.

Beginning in 1982, LZB began to regain control over its local image by combining "retail" and "corporate" budget strength, harnessing dealer advertising dollars, and maintaining the corporate message. To accomplish this, it was necessary to force advertising in March and September. This was done by creating four sales events a year, instead of the previous two for Father's Day and Christmas. A national LZB Recliner Sale in March and a Fall Sale in September were developed, which eventually smoothed out the manufacturing cycle.

Each sale was supported with national retail advertising that contained the dealer name and location in Sunday supplement magazines. These local supplements were supported by a heavy national television campaign. Alex Karras was used as an effective salesman in the ads. Not only did he have the obvious sports image for men but, even more important, he appealed to women who usually make the final decision when purchasing furniture. He seemed to have a friendly "teddy bear" image for women. In 1987, four 15-second TV spots, one for each sales event, were made by Alex, as well as the effective TV commercial called "Facts."

In addition to the national TV advertising and Sunday supplements, LZB provided dealers, who signed up for the sales event, with a Point-of-Sale Kit, including newspaper slicks, counter cards, hang tags, window banner, wall poster, and ceiling danglers. Colorful Hi-Fi preprints were available for each sale. A total of 16, 30-second radio spots which could be customized and the TV commercial "Facts" and the 15-second national TV spots could be ordered and tagged with the dealer's own message. LZB offered co-op advertising help for its participating dealers and offered four all-expense paid one-week trips for two to Hawaii to those who tied in with their local advertising and shared the results with LZB. In 1987, all of these plans were summarized in a 34-page, 11-inch by 14-inch colored Advertising Planning Calendar, which was sent to each of the 3,200 dealers. Co-op usage ran from 65 percent to 90 percent in recent years. Advertising expense for LZB runs about 3 percent of net sales.

In addition to these four major sales events, LZB promotes its full line of residential products in national home and family magazines. Ross Roy, Inc., located in Detroit, is the advertising agency used by LZB for its magazine and TV advertising.

COMPETITION

There has been a consolidation going on within the furniture industry over the last few years, with the top 10 companies now controlling 33 percent of the market. Through a series of mergers many small and medium-sized companies have been absorbed into larger companies. Exhibit 5 shows statistics for the top 10 U.S. furniture manufacturers, as of 1987, according to *Furniture/Today* April 4, 1988. Exhibit 6 (page 349) shows comparative ratios for LZB and the upholstered household furniture industry (SIC 2512) for the years 1984 through 1987.

EXHIBIT 5   Top 10 U.S. Furniture Manufacturers

Rank	Company	1987 Revenues in $ Millions	1987 Market Share (%)	1986 Revenues in $ Millions	1986 Market Share (%)
1	Interco	$ 1,100	7.4%	$ 635	4.6%
	St. Louis-based, publicly held conglomerate, powered by last April's acquisition of Lane (Action, Hickory Business Furniture, Hickory Chair, Hickory Tavern, HTB, Lane, Pearson, Royal Development and Venture), became industry's first manufacturer to exceed $1 billion in furniture. Entered furniture arena in 1978–80 with purchase of Ethan Allen and Broyhill. Added Highland House in 1986.				
2	Masco	600	4.0	335	2.4
	Since mid-1966 furniture entry, this publicly held, Detroit-based home products powerhouse has assembled, mainly through aggressive acquisition, an array of companies now including Baldwin Brass, Drexel Heritage, Frederick Edward, Henredon, Hickorycraft, La Barge Mirrors, Lexington (Dixie, Henry Link, Link-Taylor and Young-Hinkle). Maitland-Smith, Marbro Lamp, Marge Carson, The Roberts Co. and Smith & Gaines.				
3	La-Z-Boy	538	3.6	418	3.0
	Publicly held motion chair specialist, based in Monroe, Mich., further broadened product reach with acquisition early this year of solid wood furniture maker Kincaid. Burris, Hammary and Rose Johnson also acquired since mid-'80s. Revenues for 1987 include $85 million from Kincaid.				
4	Mohasco	507	3.4	460	3.3
	Publicly held furniture/carpet company, relocated last year from Amsterdam, N.Y., to Fairfax, Va. Furniture operations are Chromcraft, Cort Furniture Rental, Mohasco Upholstered Furniture (Avon, Barcalounger, Stratford, Stratolounger and Trendline), Monarch, Peters-Revington and Super Sagless. Cort, a retail rental chain, accounts for about one-fifth of furniture revenues.				

Rank	Company	1987		1986	
		Revenues in $ Millions	*Market Share (%)*	*Revenues in $ Millions*	*Market Share (%)*
5	Bassett	475	3.2	423	3.1
	Broadly diversified, publicly held furniture company based in Bassett, Va. Divisions are Basset Bedding, Bassett Contract, Bassett Furniture, Commonwealth Contract, Impact, Montclair, MCI, National/Mt. Airy and Weiman.				
6	Universal	399	2.7	191	1.4
	Publicly held wood furniture specialist, with Far East supply based and U.S. headquarters in High Point, expanded into upholstery last year by acquiring Benchcraft and its casual dining unit, Cal-Style. Acquisition accounted for $162 million of 1987 sales.				
7	Ladd	387	2.6	379	2.7
	Publicly held, broadly diversified furniture company based in High Point. Owns Lea, American Drew, Daystrom, American of Martinsville, Barclay, Clayton Marcus, Lea Lumber & Plywood and Ladd Transportation.				
8	Armstrong	361	2.4	314	2.3
	Publicly held furniture/floorings/ceiling company based in Lancaster, Pa. Furniture operations, based in Thomasville, N.C., are Armstrong, Thomasville, Gilliam and Westchester. Westchester, with about $12 million in annual sales, was acquired late last year.				
9	Chicago Pacific	245	1.7	111	0.8
	Publicly held, Chicago-based furniture/appliance company entered furniture in 1986 with purchase of Pennsylvania House, Kittinger and McGuire. Last year, added over $100 million to volume with acquisition of contract specialist Gunlocke and summer-and-casual major Brown Jordan. Established Charter Group for hotel-motel market in January 1988.				

EXHIBIT 5 *(concluded)*

Rank	Company	1987		1986	
		Revenues in $ Millions	Market Share (%)	Revenues in $ Millions	Market Share (%)
10	Sauder Woodworking	255	1.5	203	1.5
	Privately owned ccmpany based in Archbold, Ohio, specializes in ready-to-assemble furniture.				
	Top 10 total	$ 4,837	32.6%	$ 3,469	25.1%
	U.S. Industry total	$14,830	100%	$13,820	100%

* Ranked by total 1987 furniture revenues of companies or subsidiaries whose principal revenue source is household furniture manufacturing. Totals include all component, bedding, retail or contract sales.

Notes:

Company revenue figures were compiled by Furniture/Today market research from financial statements of publicly held companies and other information supplied by authoritative industry sources. Totals reflect results of 1987 calendar year—except for Bassett (Nov. 30 fiscal year-end), La-Z-Boy (Jan. 23 trailing 12 months) and Interco (Feb. 29 fiscal year-end).

Totals for companies making acquisitions within past fiscal year are pro forma, including full 12-month revenues of companies acquired.

For market-share calculations, F/T used the recently revised estimates of U.S. Department of Commerce for shipments by producers of wood, upholstered and metal household furniture, excluding bedding and contract furniture. The computations preceded any rounding of figures.

The good results in 1987 are the result of several factors: a strong 1986 housing market, continued consumer confidence, the diversion of spending from a saturated automobile market, and an increase in furniture exports. The outlook for growth in the upholstered furniture business in 1988 and 1989 is about 3.2 percent annually, or about 1 percent in constant dollars, according to the American Furniture Manufacturers Association. The aging of the "baby boomers," which will be the fastest growing segment of the population between 1987 and 1992, should have a positive impact on consumer demand during those years. Further consolidation at the manufacturing level for furniture suppliers is expected in the future. These large firms are expected to use national multimedia advertising to create home-furnishing-company images in addition to individual brand-name identification.

Furniture exports increased 15 percent in 1987 after declining at a compound rate of 9 percent per year from 1981 to 1986. In contrast, furniture imports slowed for the third consecutive year. Taiwan, which is the largest foreign furniture supplier, experienced a competitive disadvantage when its currency appreciated against the dollar, causing a 24 percent decline in the value of the dollar. Even so, Taiwan was expected to increase its shipments to the United States to over the one billion mark in 1987. Strong furniture demand is being experienced in Canada, and the decline in the value of the dollar versus European and Japanese currencies has helped U.S. exports.

EXHIBIT 6   Comparative Ratios: La-Z-Boy Chair Company versus Upholstered Household Furniture (SIC #2512) from Dun's Key Ratios

			1984	*1985*	*1986*	*1987*
$\dfrac{NP}{NW}$	%	Company	16.5	15.7	14.9	17.4
		Industry	14.3	13.3	16.1	14.3
$\dfrac{NP}{NS}$	%	Company	7.6	6.7	5.9	5.4
		Industry	2.8	2.4	3.1	3.0
$\dfrac{NP}{TA}$	%	Company	11.0	9.9	9.1	7.9
		Industry	7.7	6.3	7.9	7.1
$\dfrac{CA}{CD}$		Company	3.1	3.1	2.6	3.0
		Industry	2.1	2.2	2.3	2.1
Quick Ratio		Company	2.5	2.4	2.0	2.1
		Industry	1.0	1.0	1.1	.9
$\dfrac{FA}{NW}$	%	Company	34.6	38.7	44.4	55.2
		Industry	41.4	35.2	36.1	42.4
$\dfrac{CD}{INV}$	%	Company	162.8	146.6	157.4	108.3
		Industry	104.4	110.9	99.8	98.5
$\dfrac{TD}{NW}$	%	Company	49.4	58.5	63.2	97.4
		Industry	75.8	84.1	74.6	86.5
$\dfrac{CD}{NW}$	%	Company	35.1	35.1	43.3	47.4
		Industry	59.7	59.1	52.5	58.4
$\dfrac{NS}{NW}$		Company	2.2	2.3	2.5	3.2
		Industry	5.3	5.5	5.2	4.8
$\dfrac{NS}{NWC}$		Company	3.0	3.2	3.6	3.3
		Industry	8.5	8.1	8.2	8.8
$\dfrac{NC}{INV}$		Company	10.1	9.7	9.2	7.3
		Industry	9.6	10.1	10.3	10.5
$\dfrac{TA}{NS}$	%	Company	68.4	68.2	64.3	69.1
		Industry	33.1	34.5	31.6	30.5
C.P.	Days	Company	115.8	110.9	98.9	97.9
		Industry	27.7	30.3	29.0	27.2
$\dfrac{AP}{NS}$	%	Company	5.5	3.2	4.8	3.5
		Industry	4.6	46.3	4.0	4.3

Note: La-Z-Boy's fiscal year is changed to the previous calendar year above.

At the retail level, the major trend is clearly toward gallery programs, which were pioneered by Ethan Allen. Galleries are independent manufacturer-directed outlets or stand-alone displays in furniture or department stores. *Furniture/Today* estimated that there were 2,400 installed galleries by the end of 1986 and expected the number would increase to 5,700 by 1991. Shipments by manufacturers to galleries are expected to increase from 21 percent in 1986 to 43 percent in 1991. The increasing competition for retail floor space will require manufacturers to provide more support to the retailers.

According to a survey made in 1985 by *Better Homes & Gardens*, most customers (89.4 percent) shop at more than one store when buying furniture. The survey also showed that 58.2 percent of the customers took a month or more to make a purchase commitment. To get ideas before they bought, 75 percent said they shopped various stores. Decorating information was considered important to purchasers, although 90 percent said they did not hire an interior designer the last time they decorated their homes. About half admitted they needed advice. About 80 percent of married purchasers indicated that it was important for the spouse to be pleased and, therefore, they usually shopped together. Other data regarding furniture purchases are shown in Exhibits 7 and 8.

In a marketing research report in 1985 done by the Marketing Research Bureau, consumers raised ethical issues regarding in-store designers. They believed there was a potential conflict of interest in that the designer might be motivated by the desire to sell more furniture, rather than solving the customer's problems. The same survey indicated that the usual shopping procedure was for customers to visit their local home furnishing dealer, obtain numbers of the desired furniture, and then buy the furniture from discount outlets at a substantially lower price.

Unlike LZB, the competing brands of Action Chair, which is a division of Lane Chair, LZB's largest competitor, specialize in selling through department stores. Department stores like to have exclusives, which is one of the reasons LZB does not use them as dealers. Most of LZB's competitors are not fully integrated in manufacturing and typically buy their mechanisms from Leggett & Platt, Super Sagless, or Hoover.

MANUFACTURING

Charles W. Nocella, vice president of manufacturing, is responsible for the extensive manufacturing organization shown in Exhibit 4, which includes all plants except the Waterloo, Canada; RoseJohnson; Kincaid; and Hammary. In addition to the activities shown, Nocella is responsible for purchasing, safety, and traffic. The plants operate quite autonomously under the direction of a vice president in each plant. The

EXHIBIT 7   Influences on Buying, La-Z-Boy Chair Company

Influences on Buying: Although consumers cite price as the "most difficult" factor about buying furniture, construction, comfort and durability are considered to be stronger influences in the furniture buying decision.

	Very Important	Somewhat Important
Construction	85.3%	14.7%
Comfort	93.8	6.0
Durability	87.3	12.3
Fabric	68.0	31.0
Finish on wooden parts	64.4	32.2
Styling/design	65.2	32.9
Soil and stain resistant fabrics	67.3	30.3
Material used	65.7	31.3
Guarantee/warranty	59.1	36.1
Retailer's reputation	39.5	46.9
Size	52.6	40.9
Manufacturer's reputation	45.9	42.8
Price	59.4	35.6
Brand name	26.0	56.5
Delivery time	21.9	44.4
Decorator/designer	7.5	29.6

Shopping Activities: Before making a furniture purchase, 75% of consumers visited home furnishings stores for ideas. It tops activities leading to a final selection.

Shopped stores to get ideas	75.0%
Watched local newspaper ads for furniture	59.6
Looked in a Sears', Penney's, or Ward's catalog to check prices	39.4
Looked in a manufacturer's catalog I have (such as one for Ethan Allen, Pennsylvania House, etc.)	37.0
Got suggestions from friends, relatives, etc.	27.6
Clipped manufacturers' ads and tried to locate a specific piece of furniture	16.3
Telephoned different local stores about prices and brands	15.9
Talked to a decorator from a local store	13.9
Sent for manufacturers' brochures featured in magazine ad	12.0
Talked to a decorator other than one in store	7.7
Called "800" toll-free number to see what local store carried a certain brand	2.6
Other	2.4
No answer	2.6

Quality Measures: Construction features are considered by consumers to be the best measure of quality of a piece of furniture.

Construction features (coil construction, joint construction, etc.)	87.3%
Brand name	68.5
Finish on wood surface	61.1
Price	28.4
Salesperson's recommendation	23.1
Friends' and relatives' recommendations	22.4
Just by looks	18.3
Other	2.6
No answer	0.2

* Source: *Better Homes & Gardens.*

EXHIBIT 8 Information Sources for Furniture Purchases, La-Z-Boy Chair Company

Information Sources: Consumers rate magazines (65.9) as the most important source of information in planning home furnishings purchases. Magazines are closely followed by regular newspaper advertisement (65.7 percent).

	Very Important	Somewhat Important	Neither Important Nor Unimportant	Somewhat Unimportant	Very Unimportant	No Answer
Advertisements or circulars that are delivered to your home	9.4%	45.0%	29.7	6.0%	7.0%	2.9%
Advertisement supplements or circulars which are included in your Sunday newspaper	12.7	52.7	22.6	4.3	4.8	2.9
Regular newspaper advertisements in your Sunday newspaper	11.3	54.4	24.0	4.3	2.6	3.4

Regular newspaper advertisements in your daily newspaper					
Regular newspaper advertisements in your daily newspaper	9.4	49.3	29.8	3.8	2.9	4.8
Magazine ads	14.9	51.0	26.2	3.1	4.8	2.9
Catalogs	14.2	49.8	23.6	4.3	3.1	5.0
Radio advertisements	2.2	23.3	43.3	14.9	9.1	7.2
TV advertisements	5.5	34.7	38.9	9.4	6.0	5.5
Friends' and neighbors' opinions	16.8	36.3	26.9	6.5	7.2	6.3

Buying Factors: Price is the "most difficult" factor about buying furniture for the home, according to a *BH&G* consumer panel.

Cost of furniture	52.9%
Determining quality	30.3
Choosing a style	21.9
Choosing a fabric	15.9
Choosing a color	11.8
Other	1.9
No answer	1.0

* Source: *Better Homes & Gardens.*

14 plants employ about 6,650 people, with a combined floor space of 4,536,000 square feet. Much of this floor space was constructed quite recently—527,800 in 1987, 74,000 in 1985, and 120,000 in 1984, plus the additions made through acquired companies. A listing of the plants is shown in Exhibit 9, with pertinent information as of April 25, 1987.

EXHIBIT 9   Manufacturing Plants, La-Z-Boy Chair Company

Location	Floor Space (square feet)	Operations Conducted	Built	Employees
Monroe, MI	215,200	Home office, research, and development	1941	415
Newton, MS*	464,200	Recliners, rockers, and hospital seating	1961	678
Redlands, CA	179,900	Assembly of recliners and rockers	1967	289
Florence, SC*	407,900	Recliners and hospital seating	1969	801
Florence, SCI	48,400	Fabric processing center and parts warehouse	1975	19
Neosho, MO*	473,400	Residential and contract furniture	1969	992
Dayton, TN	564,200	Recliners, sofas, sleepers, and modular seating	1973	1,076
Siloam Spgs., AK	189,600	Recliners and sleepers	1943	246
Tremonton, UT*	402,400	Recliners and contract	1979	617
Leland, MS*	153,500	Desks and contract	1985†	130
Waterloo, OT	209,800	Recliners, rockers, sofas, and contract	1979†	412
Lincolnton, NC	379,000	Upholstered furniture	1986†	299
Grand Rapids, MI	428,000	Manufactures office furniture and panels	1986†	223
Lenoir, NC	420,800	Upholstered products, case goods, and hospitality furniture	1986†	453
Praire, MS	453,800	Distribution center and small parts warehouse	1986†	6
Hudson, NC	730,000	Solid wood bedroom and dining room furniture	1987*	1,427

* These plants and the Fabric Processing Center at Florence are leased on a long-term basis. All other plants are owned by LZB.
† Year acquired as a result of purchasing a company.

LZB manufacturing is characterized by backward integration. Lumber for the furniture framing is purchased from sawmills and kiln dried at the plants. LZB makes its own chair mechanisms and purchases its sleeper mechanisms from Leggett & Platt. Metal for the recliner mechanisms is purchased in coils, and the parts made at the plants. Fabric is purchased direct from the mills in large quantities to fulfill the needs of all plants. It is received, stored, and shipped from the Fabric Processing Center in Florence, South Carolina, to all plants for use in upholstering. The center has automated storage and is controlled by computer, so little manpower is required to operate this centralized facility.

LZB's manufacturing philosophy could be characterized as rather conservative. LZB usually waits until a new technique is thoroughly perfected before beginning to use it. For instance, computerized cutting of fabric at the plants was only instituted within the last two years, even though the concept had been around for over 10 years. The punch presses and methods used in the pressrooms in the plants have not been updated in the last 20 years.

The manufacturing process is twofold, involving both wood and metal. The wooden parts are manufactured from kiln-dried hardwood lumber. The raw boards are brought into the wood room, where they go through the rip saw operation. Here, the lumber is cut into predetermined lengths, with the knot-holes and major blemishes being removed. Only the good portions of the lumber are used. An 80 percent yield is strived for, but 65 to 70 percent is normally attained.

Following cutting, the wood pieces go through a series of planing, squaring, and sizing operations. Then the pieces are measured and glued together, parallel to the long side to provide wood slabs, which are again trimmed and cut into the final subassembly sections. From here, the pieces go through a series of operations, which include drilling dowel holes, contouring specific shapes on band saws, and sanding. Wood assembly is the final operation, wherein the various pieces are doweled, glued, and pressed together into frames. These wooden frames are then ready for subassembly with metal parts.

The metal parts are produced in the punch press room, where coils and strips of unhardened steel are run through dies to produce engineered components. The metal parts are not heat-treated, because hardness is not required, but some must be painted if they will be visible on the final product. The metal parts are then riveted together as required and go to the "metal-up" department, where they are assembled. The metal parts are then combined with the wooden parts to form a subassembly ready to be upholstered in the "frame-up" department. The marriage of metal and wood working together as one unit is what has provided LZB with its quality reputation.

All of the plants except—Monroe, Michigan; Florence, South Carolina; and Waterloo, Ontario—are not unionized, which is unusual in the upholstered furniture industry. Factory workers have been paid on a "piece work" concept from the beginning. Typically, one employee upholsters the seat and back of a chair and a second employee does the body, since there are too many styles for one employee to do the whole chair. A base rate is paid based on local wage surveys, but each employee has the opportunity to make quite a bit more depending on the number of pieces produced.

Each plant employs two to four time-study engineers to keep the piece rates up to date. Normal time was changed to 150 percent to facilitate the 150 percent normal performance. The company's policy is to never retime a job just because people are making money on the standard rate. Rather, jobs are retimed when there has been a change in methods or design. A complaint procedure is in place, so anyone can grieve a rate they believe is unfair. One rule of thumb is that the rate is good if the standard for the day can be made in five hours. Employees are reluctant to change jobs, because it temporarily cuts into their incentive performance.

LZB is very committed to quality, which is made somewhat trickier to accomplish by the incentive program. Constant vigilance is required by supervision. Piece rates are only paid for producing the item once— employees must rework their defective production on their own time. Each part is distinctively marked by the employee, so it can be traced back to him if a quality problem develops. There is about one inspector for every 125 chairs produced per day. A typical plant produces 1,200 to 1,300 chairs per day and some produce 300 to 400 sleeper sofas per day. A rule of thumb for planning purposes is one and three quarter chairs can be produced per man day. One employee can upholster about 10 chairs per day and another employee can frame 15 per day.

Products are basically produced to order, with only about 2.5 percent made for inventory. There is a 14-week window used for computer scheduling in Monroe by the manufacturing services manager. Two weeks before the product is to be in its shipping box, the fabric is shipped to the plant and subsequently cut. For actual plant scheduling, order tickets are used, which are accumulated for individual items in the same style. Fabrics are grouped by a lay (40 sheets of fabric) for cutting of a given pattern. Sometimes different fabrics can be combined, but stripes and plaids have to be cut separately. The optimum layout of pieces on a sheet of fabric is determined by the pattern layout department via computer transmission from Monroe. The material is actually cut by CNC (computer numerical control) equipment in the plant. Foremen meet informally each morning at each plant to develop a mutually beneficial daily schedule. The foremen of cutting and sewing work together to balance the load in sewing. Most dealers do not want to receive an early shipment, so the shipping schedule is the controlling element.

As stated before, each plant operates quite autonomously and often with a unique management style. LZB does not have a strong corporate policy regarding management, but in general it is loosely knit, and with a friendly small-town atmosphere. Edward Knabusch's philosophy was "to treat people like people." The style could be said to be somewhere between participative and authoritarian, although some of the most successful plants are more authoritarian.

PRODUCT PLANNING AND DEVELOPMENT

Marvin J. Baumann, vice president for product planning and development, is responsible for product development, product engineering, and the mechanical engineering and test laboratories, all of which employ 75 people. Development has been aided by product development's use of CAD/CAM. LZB is somewhat unique in its industry, in that it extensively tests its products. Recently an independent testing lab (ETL) was added to test such products as the Lectra-Lounger and the Lectra-Lift Chair.

All product designs are developed internally. A natural process for design is utilized; an idea is developed, the parts are framed, an approval process is followed leading to final approval, and then the design is implemented at the plants with appropriate training. New versions of the reclining mechanism are being developed, since the patent has expired. New ideas for furniture design are often found through sales and marketing techniques like consumer demand surveys, furniture markets, and travel into Europe. In fact, the most popular current style of chair is the Eurostyle, the plush overstuffed look. Competitors have the impression that LZB overengineers its products, but LZB believes that good engineering can only result in good quality. An annual review of LZB's products with the vendors is made. Cost, styling, and convenient transportation are considered in developing a new style. The removable-back reclining chair is an example of convenient transportation, because the back can be separated from the rest of the frame, allowing more chairs to be loaded on a truck.

Once a style is approved, technicians use computerized pattern layout systems to generate the cutting patterns for upholstery fabrics. The objective is to minimize waste by maximizing the number of pattern pieces attainable from a given sheet of fabric. The resulting patterns become part of an electronic library store in the company's central computer. On demand, digitized cutting instructions are down-loaded to fabric cutting machines at LZB's plants. Currently, some 700 patterns are available on-line. A subsequent step will be to up-load data from the cutting machines to analyze actual efficiencies.

FABRIC DEPARTMENT

LZB is unique in the industry, in that it has a separate fabric department. This department has provided special attention to purchasing attractive, durable fabrics for upholstering. LZB uses about 11 million yards of fabric per year to produce 7,140 units per day. At any one time LZB has a fabric purchasing commitment of 6.4 million yards on hand or on order.

LZB has five committees to make fabric decisions. These committees are the following: chairs and sofas, office furniture for contract sales, Rose Johnson, Burris, and LZB Canada, which is separated because color trends and style are about 18 months behind the United States. While the look of the fabric is important, of even greater importance is the production practicality of the fabric. A fabric is tested for nominal wear and the minimum standards for a fabric must be surpassed after color or pattern have been determined. Fabric lines are reviewed twice a year for all product divisions except the Contract Division, which is reviewed annually.

FINANCE

Frederick H. Jackson, vice president of finance, who is 60 years old, has been a director of LZB since 1971 and was the treasurer prior to election to vice president in 1983. Reporting to Jackson are the secretary and treasurer, the vice president of management information systems, and the director of corporate taxes.

LZB has a very conservative financial philosophy. The balance sheet is stated conservatively (i.e., assets are written down rapidly). Contingency liabilities, such as warranties, are shown on the balance sheet. All cash discounts on accounts payable are taken but not paid earlier than necessary. The current ratio has historically been in the 3 to 4 range, with 2 as a minimum. The current debt-to-equity ratio target has been not to exceed 40 percent.

Cash management has become more important in recent years. Gene Hardy, the treasurer, believes cash management is an art and forecasts cash receipts by month for a year's period. He is shooting for a weekly forecast. Short-term investments are made in certificates of deposits and commercial paper, with the overriding concept being to not risk the principal. He deals with the banks with whom LZB has a working relationship—National Bank of Detroit, Manufacturers Bank, Monroe Bank and Trust, Mellon Bank of Pittsburgh, and First Union Bank of North Carolina. Working capital is forecasted on a corporate basis.

Normal terms of sale are 2 percent, 30 days, net 45 days, but only 15 percent of LZB's sales are made on this basis. The four sales events each year are billed with a 2 percent discount at 90 to 120 days as determined by the sales department. Nine people follow up on delinquent accounts after they are 15 days past due. At 30 days past due a letter is sent requesting payment within 10 days. Continuing problem accounts are put on a credit hold and eventually submitted to Dun & Bradstreet for collection and are written off the books at that time. In May of 1988 approximately 9.5 percent of the accounts were overdue, and the figure has been as high as 11 percent at Christmas. Accounts are noted by one of four different risk codes to facilitate credit management.

Capital expenditures are evaluated by using the payback method, with two to three years being considered an acceptable payback. The internal rate of return (IRR) is calculated, but LZB does not have a hurdle (minimum) rate that projects must meet. A Request for Authorization form is made out for each project, including a narrative with plants being able to approve up to $5,000, corporate officers approving up to $100,000, and the board of directors approving all expenditures over $100,000. Capital expenditures are projected for a three-year period by plant.

Budgets are made up for each plant by the treasurer, with input from the plants for the last eight years. The individual departments in the plants typically have only limited involvement in the budgeting process.

Inventory is stated on a LIFO basis. Semiannual physical inventories are taken. Cycle counts are taken of fabric at the Fabric Center. Inventory turns are measured for lumber and fabric, which are maintained on a perpetual inventory basis. LZB is moving in the direction of setting guidelines for inventory levels at the plants. Kincaid, which was acquired in January 1988, builds inventory to stock while most LZB divisions build to order.

The general, selling, and administrative expenses are running at 20 percent of sales, which is considered alarming by the treasurer. However, commissions are 5 percent or a quarter of the total. He would like to see the figure in the 15 percent to 16 percent range.

LZB paid $53 million to acquire the stock of Kincaid Furniture Company, Inc. The book value of Kincaid's assets at the time of purchase was $27 million. As a part of the net assets acquired, Kincaid had $12 million in debt.

MANAGEMENT

The chairman of the board and president is Charles Knabusch, who is the son of the founders of LZB and is 48 years old. He has been a director of the company since 1970. He literally grew up with LZB and has been a part of the growth and maturing of the company. He has been described as a "shirt sleeves manager."

The board of directors is composed of six inside members and four outside members, as noted in Exhibit 10.

Approximately 30 percent of the common stock is controlled by the Monroe Bank & Trust, of which about half belongs to the founders. The Knabusch family owns about 13.4 percent of the common stock and Edwin Shoemaker owns about 6.6 percent. Other officers and directors own 0.7 percent.

LZB believes in treating each employee as an important person. The fact that LZB has labor unions at only 2 of its 11 plants attests that this policy works and is appreciated by the employees. LZB believes that the values of the manager make the company. Time is taken out of the busy schedules to make other people feel good. Programs to keep communication flowing between employees and management are stressed, such as "Lunch with the Boss." Vacant positions within the company are posted and employees may apply for the position. Most of management has been with the LZB for an extended time, having been promoted from within.

Supervisory, technical, and clerical employees are paid by rating jobs, using a point factor method. Jobs are matched against common factors, such as education, related experience, mental skill, human relations responsibility, complexity and impact of work decisions, and necessity for accuracy. Employees are evaluated regularly on achievement of their department's mission statement and how the goals were achieved. To foster continued individual growth, required training is used to equip people to rotate into new positions.

EXHIBIT 10   LZB Board of Directors

Director	*Position*
Charles T. Knabusch	Chairman and president
Edwin J. Shoemaker	Executive vice president of engineering
Gene M. Hardy	Treasurer and secretary
Frederick H. Jackson	Vice president of finance
Patric H. Norton	Senior vice president, sales and marketing
Lorne G. Stevens	Vice president of manufacturing, retired
Warren W. Gruber	Retail businessman
David K. Hehl	Public accountant
Rocque E. Lipford	Attorney
John F. Weaver	Executive vice president of Monroe Bank & Trust

LZB is committed to the concept of incentive pay. Factory workers are paid on a piece rate concept. Office workers are included in profit sharing and receive merit pay based on performance. Executives and middle managers receive bonuses for quality work. All employees have a comprehensive benefit plan, including paid vacations, health and dental insurance, prescription medicine program, term life insurance, and a defined benefit retirement plan.

THE FUTURE

Forbes magazine in its February 22, 1988, issue ran an article entitled "Takeover Bait?" in which it listed LZB as 1 of 22 likely prospects for a takeover. It fits the picture of high cash reserves, low debt, a low price/earnings ratio, and a strong cash flow from operating income. Is LZB worried? Gene Hardy says such defense measures as staggered three-year terms for directors and 67 percent stockholder vote required for approval of any merger are already in place. Perhaps most important is the distribution of stock among family and friends, although a leveraged buyout could occur under the right circumstances. The price range for LZB stock for recent years is shown in Exhibit 11.

As might be expected, Charles Knabusch does not wish LZB to be acquired. He said, "We are happy doing our thing, our way." His goals for the company are to continue growing while remaining profitable. But how is this to be accomplished in an industry that is becoming increasingly concentrated and with a stable but aging population?

EXHIBIT 11   Price Range of LZB Stock

Fiscal Year	Price Range
1983	$2\frac{5}{8}$– $7\frac{7}{8}$
1984	$7\frac{7}{8}$–$12\frac{1}{8}$
1985	$6\frac{3}{4}$–$10\frac{5}{8}$
1986	$10\frac{7}{8}$–$16\frac{7}{8}$
1987	$15\frac{5}{8}$–$20\frac{1}{8}$
1988	$13\frac{1}{8}$–$22\frac{5}{8}$

Case 3–8 Toyota Lexus*

Despite the festive air surrounding the preview here of Toyota Motor Corp.'s new Lexus luxury cars, the wine glasses placed atop an LS 400 sedan weren't for anyone's enjoyment.

Instead the glasses were props to prove that the $35,000 Lexus car purrs on the highway. Lexus officials filled the glasses with water, elevated the rear wheels so the car wouldn't zoom away and gunned the 32-valve, V-8 engine to 157 miles per hour. The water in the glasses didn't even ripple.

"I'm pretty numb to new cars," said John C. Salagaj, a vice president of Diversified Services Inc. of Ft. Lauderdale, Fla., a big Budget Rent-a-Car Corp. licensee. "But these grabbed my attention."

That, of course, was the whole idea behind last week's unveiling, where the trappings went beyond the hyperbole that's typical at such events. On Monday, Lexus officials played host for a lunch at the Pebble Beach resort and brought in former first lady Nancy Reagan to speak. They also brought in competitors' cars—Honda Motor Co.'s Acura Legend, the Mercedes-Benz 420 SEL and the BMW 735i—to give attending fleet managers, auto writers and dealers a chance to compare firsthand.

Standing out in the luxury car market, which has been flat or shrinking in recent years, will be especially tough in the 1990 model year. The new entries include a more responsive version of Ford Motor Co.'s boatlike Lincoln Town Car, Volkswagen AG's four-wheel-drive Audi V-8 Quattro and Mercedes-Benz's sleekly restyled SL convertible. Not to mention the soon-to-debut Infiniti entries from Toyota's archrival, Nissan Motor Co.

In this flooded market, Lexus has an important strength: a big price edge on its German competitors. But with the luxury market soft and consumer confidence about making car purchases waning, that may not be enough to establish a strong presence. The line also faces the challenge of forging an identity—one distinct not only from Lexus's rivals but also from Toyota itself.

The Lexus and Infiniti cars are priced about the same, but the two companies are taking radically different marketing approaches. Infiniti is trying to define "Japanese luxury," with Zen-like advertising featuring rocks and pussy-willow buds, and rice-paper screens in its

---

showrooms. Toyota's approach is far less esoteric: Lexus is supposed to be a reasonably priced and better-performing version of Mercedes and BMW models that cost as much as $80,000.

"These cars are coming at a time when buyers are already ridiculing the price-value of German cars," says John Morzenti, a Porsche-Audi dealer near Philadelphia. "We're going to see a bloodbath over the next couple of years. The Japanese have never been beaten in any market they've attempted to attack."

The German makers argue that Lexus lacks character. The wine-glass demonstration, they say, only shows that Lexus makes driving an antiseptic experience compared with German luxury cars, which are engineered to give drivers a feel for the road. What's worse, "they have no tradition," sniffs Gunter Kramer, head of BMW's U.S. sales and marketing arm. "At this end of the market, a tradition of prestige is what brings in buyers."

J. Davis Illingworth, head man at Lexus, retorts: "If I were Mercedes or BMW, I'd say the same thing about our lack of tradition. But we have the 50-year heritage of Toyota's production of quality cars, and [Lexus is] the best car the company has ever produced."

Toyota worked on the two Lexus models—the LS 400 and the smaller ES 250, priced at $21,050—for six years. It put them through 2.5 million miles of test driving. The cars are equipped with such antiaging features as stainless-steel exhaust pipes, to prevent corro-

---

EXHIBIT 1   The Crowded Luxury Car Market

Share of the standard luxury car segment by brand name in 1988

- Cadillac
- BMW 1.4%
- Jaguar 1.6%
- Audi 3.1%
- Other 3.2%
- Chrysler
- Volvo
- Acura
- Mercedes-Benz
- Buick / Oldsmobile
- Lincoln

26.9%
5.2%
5.9%
7.2%
7.3%
19.5%
18.8%

Base prices of Lexus LS 400 sedan and competitive luxury sedans:

Lexus LS 400	$35,000
Mercedes 420 SEL	61,210
BMW 735i	54,000
Jaguar XJ6	43,500
Infiniti Q45	38,000
Cadillac Fleetwood 60 Special	34,325
Acura Legend Sedan LS	29,960
Lincoln Continental	29,910

Source: J. D. Power & Associates, Agoura Hills, Calif.

sion. All of the leather in each car comes from the hide of the same individual cow, Toyota says, to prevent uneven fading. The full general warranty lasts for four years or 50,000 miles, except for the engine and transmission warranty, good for 72,000 miles.

The ES 250 model looks much like the Acura Legend and, like the Legend, has front-wheel drive. But the LS 400 has rear-wheel drive, like the European cars against which it will compete, to better handle the output of the 250-horsepower engine. Still, the LS 400 gets 23 miles a gallon, avoiding the federal "gas-guzzler" tax paid on some European luxury cars.

The engines on both Lexus models are mounted on liquid-filled braces, to reduce vibration and noise. In strategic places, the cars feature "sandwich steel"—a layer of plastic placed between two layers of metal. Lexus officials extol the importance of this by rapping the stuff with a screwdriver, producing a thud instead of a metallic ping. "I don't think you've driven a quieter car in your life," says Richard Chitty, manager of parts and service.

Optional equipment includes traction control, which, Toyota says, grips the road to prevent the car from spinning out when accelerating on wet pavement, and a cellular telephone that automatically mutes the sound of the stereo radio when phone calls are made.

But Lexus's biggest attribute may be timing. It is hitting the market at a time when European auto makers are reeling from prices that began shooting up when the dollar dropped three years ago. BMW has held its own, but Mercedes sales plunged 18 percent through July from a year earlier, after falling 7.4 percent in 1988. And Porsche AG's sales are running 44 percent below last year, when they declined 33 percent from 1987.

"Brand loyalty in the luxury car market is very shaky," says Lexus's Mr. Illingworth. "People have paid tremendous amounts of money on European cars, and they're questioning why."

But it's too early to judge whether Lexus will duplicate the market success of Honda's Acura division. Creating a new image from scratch won't be easy. Toyota cars, while technically sound, lack the panache of Honda models. And by borrowing exterior and dashboard-styling cues from Mercedes-Benz, say some experts, Lexus risks getting a "copycat" label instead of a distinct identity.

Also, while Lexus's prices compare favorably with those of European cars, they don't look particularly attractive alongside the prices of Ford's Lincoln line and General Motors Corp.'s Cadillac division. Both domestic luxury nameplates have scored some big successes recently: Lincoln with the Continental, and Cadillac with the restyled and lengthened Fleetwood and DeVille. Lexus's target buyer for the LS 400 is 43 years old and has a household income of $100,000 a year. But many people fitting that description are swamped with mortgage payments and staring at big college tuition bills—and thus may conclude they can live without a $35,000 car no matter how good it is.

Another challenge will be keeping the dealers profitable. Acura cars have sold well, but some dealers have been so overwhelmed by expenses that they've put their franchises on the market. Lexus hopes to have 90 dealers by year end, sell 16,000 cars for the balance of this year, and 70,000 to 75,000 next year. That's as many as BMW sold in the United States last year.

Lexus is drawing plenty of lookers. Superior Lexus in Kansas City, Mo., reported giving so many test drives that it couldn't close until 11 P.M. on its opening day last week. Longo Lexus in El Monte, Calif., stayed open until 11:30 P.M. one day recently.

Vaughn Szarka, a real-estate broker from Cleveland, flew to Monterey last week to test drive an LS 400 on the nearby Laguna Seca Raceway before buying one. Mr. Szarka has owned 60 different cars in his life and frequently trades for newer models. For the past five years, he has owned BMWs, but he now thinks BMW prices are "ridiculous."

For years BMW catered more to its cars than to its customers, but now it's going to find people won't take that anymore," Mr. Szarka says "Americans are thinking twice about what they're really getting for their money."

Case 3–9   *The Michigan League**

Pat Lawson has been manager of the Michigan League for six years. She is in charge of the operation and maintenance of the League building. She acts as purchasing agent and is in charge of the accounting and financial management of the League's activities. As business manager, Pat Lawson is responsible to a board of governors and to the vice president for finance. She is expected to report regularly to both.

Recently the staff has noticed a continuing decrease in the number of customers in the cafeteria and coffee shop. However, at the same time the other League functions (conferences, banquets, special events) are operating near capacity. Pat is interested in finding the underlying causes of the decrease in the customer count. She would like to develop courses of action to reverse this trend.

---

* Prepared by Maureen Fanshawe, in James D. Scott, Martin R. Warshaw, and James R. Taylor, *Introduction to Marketing Management*, 5th ed. Copyright © 1985, by Richard D. Irwin. Reprinted by permission of the publisher.

BACKGROUND

The Michigan League is one of three University Activity Centers in Ann Arbor. The other two centers are the North Campus Commons and the Michigan Union. The Michigan League was built in 1929 with funds raised by University of Michigan women. At the time of the League's construction, women were not permitted to use the Michigan Union. In response to the women's need, the University alumnae built the Michigan League "for the purpose of promoting the social and recreational welfare of the women students in the university." Through the years the emphasis has shifted, and presently for both men and women the primary student building (receiving the major university funding) is the Michigan Union. Currently the Michigan League serves not only the campus community but also the general public.

The League is centrally located one block from the main street of the campus area. It is situated on a highly trafficked street and is very visible. A large sign near the sidewalk advertises the cafeteria and other services. In addition to the cafeteria and coffee shop, the League building has a gift shop, study rooms, conference rooms, a ballroom, several large banquet rooms, student organization offices, and, on the fourth floor, hotel service consisting of 21 rooms. Over the past four years there has been a significant increase in the use of the building by students for study and meeting space.

CAFETERIA

The cafeteria is open Monday–Saturday, 11:30 A.M.–1:15 P.M. and 5:00 P.M.–7:15 P.M. Dinner is served on Sunday from 11:30 A.M. to 2:15 P.M. A full menu is provided for both lunch and dinner. Meal prices range from approximately $3.00 for lunch to $4.25 for dinner. The cafeteria does not serve alcohol. The League has a limited conference liquor license for scheduled events. A daily special is offered in addition to the other items. The luncheon and dinner entrees are on a three-week cycle and offer a different variety daily. Although there is no table service, the cafeteria maintains a full staff. The cafeteria has a pleasant atmosphere and emphasis is placed on cleanliness.

NATURE OF THE MARKET

The Michigan League is available to the general public as well as the campus community. Throughout the school year the cafeteria serves approximately 388 lunches and 350 dinners daily. The coffee shop serves 800–1,200 people daily. During the summer months the daily totals are considerably lower. Peak seasons are directly associated with the academic year. From May through August there is a steady decline in business (Exhibits 1 and 2). Special functions scheduled at the League are also affected by the "seasonality" factor. During the months of May–August the League facilities for weddings operate at capacity.

Hill Auditorium and Powers Center are university cultural performance centers, each within one block of the League. Plays, concerts,

---

EXHIBIT 1

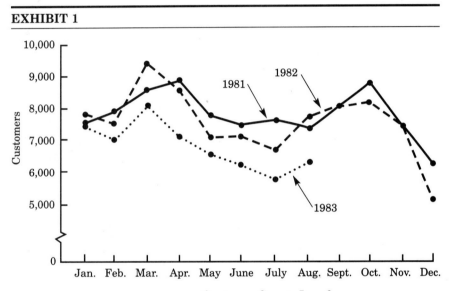

	Customer Count: Lunch		
	1981	*1982*	*1983*
January	7,641	7,648	7,487
February	7,883	7,586	6,989
March	8,725	9,403	8,067
April	8,816	8,780	7,125
May	7,675	7,267	6,610
June	7,440	7,221	6,290
July	7,659	6,795	5,722
August	7,435	7,724	6,236
September	8,144	8,049	*
October	8,900	8,418	*
November	7,667	7,682	*
December	6,422	5,227	*

* Customer count not yet taken for September–December 1983.

EXHIBIT 2

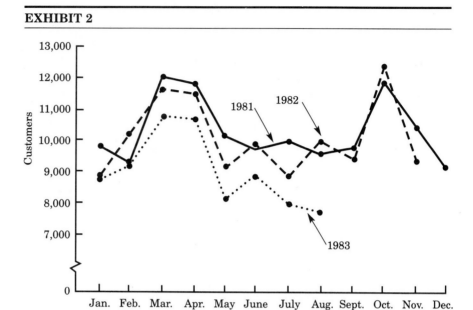

| | Customer Count: Dinner | | |
	1981	*1982*	*1983*
January	9,757	8,666	8,635
February	9,265	9,849	9,074
March	11,946	11,636	10,779
April	11,664	11,552	10,718
May	9,894	9,170	8,098
June	9,688	9,838	8,941
July	9,943	8,766	7,925
August	9,628	9,844	7,812
September	9,673	9,572	*
October	12,152	12,164	*
November	10,778	9,168	*
December	9,253	7,555	*

* Customer count not yet taken for September–December 1983.

---

and ballet are frequently run. On performance nights the League adjusts its regular schedule and menu. There is an increase in the cafeteria customer count on these evenings. This increase is not as high as Pat believes it could be. She has attributed this fact to the large number of area restaurants serving alcohol which are available to the Hill Auditorium and Powers Center patrons.

The results of a 1978 survey performed by the League cafeteria revealed that present customers use the cafeteria on a regular basis

EXHIBIT 3   Survey Results for Michigan League, 1978

	Tuesday Noon (170 surveys)	Tuesday Night (128)	Thursday Night (130)	Sunday (140)
How Often				
First time	2	2	2	4
Infrequent	40	19	25	33
Often	125	107	88	102
Enjoy				
Food	128	117	101	132
Location	154	105	85	98
Cafeteria	126	98	86	122
No tipping	117	100	87	116
Atmosphere	91	91	88	117
Music				
Prefer music	41	54	43	37
Prefer no music	41	27	5	46

Cumulative Results (568 surveys)

How Often		*Enjoy*		*Music*	
First time	10	Food	478	Prefer music	175
Infrequent	117	Location	432	Prefer no music	119
Often	422	Cafeteria	432		
		No tipping	426		
		Atmosphere	387		

EXHIBIT 4   Frequent Comments

Positive		*Negative*	
Enjoy the food	74	Dull variety	23
Variety	25	Too much gravy	13
Reasonable price	32	Student special	19
International night	17	Prices too high	28
Service	51	Cold food	25
Atmosphere	18	Service	
		Long, slow lines	38
		Discourteous staff	21
		Small portions	38
		Parking	20

and for the following reasons: they enjoy the food, location, no tipping feature, cafeteria-style service, and atmosphere. Also provided by this survey were positive and negative comments about the cafeteria (Exhibits 3 and 4).

A third and final part of the survey requested customer suggestions. Many of the suggestions were for bigger salads, a salad bar, to expand the variety of vegetarian dishes and specials, and to include a vegetable or salad with the student special. Presently the League has comment and suggestion cards available in the cafeteria, coffee shop, and hotel rooms. After each special function, a short rating and suggestion card is sent to the person who made the arrangements.

SPECIAL FEATURES AT THE CAFETERIA

The League cafeteria offers daily specials. These specials are available to the students at a reduced price. A luncheon special costs $2.50, and a dinner student special costs $2.75. The cafeteria sells approximately 125 luncheon and 60 dinner specials daily. The student specials are less than the cost of dormitory dinners. Students find it the "best food for the price in town." Over the years, the board has felt "that providing good food to students at the lowest possible cost in an attractive university setting was an important responsibility of the League." The League has a student tax discount but does not have senior citizen discounts.

From October through July, every Thursday evening at the cafeteria is "International and American Heritage Night." Each Thursday night the menu consists of foods from the featured country or state. International night has been successful. On this night the cafeteria serves an average of 475 customers.

The Michigan League cafeteria "Command Performance dinner" offered the customer a unique dining experience. The customers were encouraged through advertisements to make requests for their favorite foods, to be served at the Command Performance dinner. From these nominations the most requested items were selected to make up the menu for the evening. This special feature has been offered twice and was successful.

Sunday dinner at the cafeteria is served from 11:30 A.M. to 2:15 P.M. White linen cloths and fresh flowers are placed on the tables. The Sunday customer profile at the cafeteria is primarily senior citizens.

COMPETITION

The Michigan League is centrally located on the Michigan campus one block from the campus shopping street and three blocks from downtown Ann Arbor. There are approximately 143 restaurants in the downtown area. Eighty of these restaurants provide full service. The League cafeteria's 1982 share of the Ann Arbor restaurant market was 1.9 percent. In a recent report the board of governors recommended that, "The university administration officially recommend that all university departments use the university centers (League, Union, and North Campus Commons) food services, both within these buildings and for catering wherever needed on the university campus."

In direct competition with the League cafeteria is the Michigan Union. The recent revitalization of the Union is expected to affect the League. Food revenue may decline as Union revenue increases. The Union University Club offers a menu similar to the League's, with prices approximately one dollar higher per meal at lunch and two dollars higher at dinner. The Union has table service and serves alcohol. Every Sunday night at the Union from 5:30 P.M.–8:00 P.M. is an "all-you-can-eat" Italian Festival for $3.99. The Italian Festival night is successful. A recent addition to the Union's lower level, the Michigan Union Grill (MUG), has a variety of food counters and primarily caters to student clientele. The prices are relatively low, to meet the students' budgets, and a student tax discount is offered. Dormitory food service does not operate on Sundays. The other area restaurants have a wide variety of menus but are priced slightly higher than the League. The recent restructuring of dorm food service to include breakfast and flexible hours affected the League's student count adversely.

The recent construction of the Ingalls Street pedestrian mall has drastically decreased parking availability for League patrons. Ingalls Street (which runs adjacent to the League) previously had 45 open-meter parking spaces. More than half of the spaces were destroyed. This loss of parking has been a problem for League patrons. There are two public parking structures, each within one block of the League. It costs two dollars to park in the garage. Across the street from the League is a staff parking lot. Parking is permitted in this lot only after 5:00 P.M. Street parking on North University after 5:00 P.M. has recently been permitted, adding about 12 spaces.

PROMOTION

The League's 1982 advertising budget was $5,500. Of this budget, 91 percent was allocated to the cafeteria. The objective of the cafeteria advertising is to increase awareness in the community. The emphasis of weekly advertisements is usually placed on special-feature nights at the cafeteria. The Command Performance dinner was advertised twice in the *Ann Arbor News*. The League purchased a 2″ × 5″ ad (space is sold by column inch, $7.50 per inch) and ran the ad the week preceding the event. When the League is not advertising for a feature night, a 1½″ × 2″ ad is purchased for $22.50 and run once a week.

For several years the League ran a weekly advertisement for the cafeteria, using a limerick theme. Readers would compose an advertising limerick for the cafeteria and mail their suggestions to Julie, Pat Lawson's administrative assistant. She would then select the best limerick entry weekly, to be used in the advertisement. The winning entry received two free dinners at the cafeteria. The League employed this promotional strategy for five years prior to its discontinuance in July 1983. The League staff felt that although they had received a tremendous response, the theme had become overused and repetitive and, as a result, had lost effectiveness.

Presently the League has no measurement of ad effectiveness. In addition, their promotional strategy uses a mass appeal, with minimal attention given to individual market segments. The staff wonders whether the advertising dollars could be more effectively spent by placing emphasis on slow nights rather than on already successful feature nights. To increase the customer count on slow nights, Pat is considering the extension of the feature-night concept to these nights. She also senses a need for an advertising strategy to define her key potential customers and then to target the advertising efforts to this market.

The League also advertises in the *Observer,* a monthly newspaper publication. The cafeteria is listed in the Restaurant Guide section. The price is 6 months for $25 for a four-line listing. The ad is clearly visible but is listed with many other Ann Arbor restaurants. A one-fourth page display advertisement in the *Observer* costs $246 (for a one-month edition). However, the *Observer* offers a frequency rate discount. The League has never purchased display ad space in the *Observer.* Presently they purchase only the service ad in the restaurant guide.

The *Michigan Daily* is a student-run newspaper on the Ann Arbor campus of The University of Michigan. The *Daily* has approximately 5,000 subscribers. Advertising space costs $4.75/inch. Presently the League does not advertise in the *Michigan Daily*.

The remaining balance of the advertising budget is used to purchase flyers for the League cafeteria and coffee shop. These flyers are distributed to all new students and staff. Included on this flyer is a coupon for a free beverage, which is heavily used by students. The International and American Heritage Nights schedule is printed on a $2'' \times 3''$ card and is available throughout the university.

FINANCIAL RESOURCES

The University Activities Centers—North Campus Commons, Michigan Union, and the Michigan League—are owned by the university. The League uses earned revenue to meet its operating expenses. Financial support from the university is made available through allocations. All improvements have been financed from reserves and university loans. Loans are repaid on schedule, and there is only a small balance outstanding. Presently the student fee allocation to the League is $3.50 per student.

The number of customers served at the cafeteria and coffee shop is declining. A statement of the League's revenues and expenses for the year 1982–83 is shown in Exhibit 5. Revenue for the Michigan League for fiscal year 1982–83 was 6 percent greater than for fiscal year 1981–82. This includes: guest room rentals (up 2 percent), meeting room rentals (up 25 percent), banquets and parties (up 16 percent), catering (up 79 percent), and beverages (up 12 percent). However, despite these growth areas cafeteria revenue is down $25,437 (3 percent) and coffee shop revenue is down $6,145 (2 percent). Food costs are in line, but labor costs are 50 percent of total earned income. In a report to the board of governors, Pat Lawson states, "A major staff training program is currently under way to increase productivity, but with an already lean, hard-working staff, it is unrealistic to expect much of a reduction in labor costs because of the AFSCME (union) wage rates."

The staff is presently considering several cafeteria improvement projects. The League is unwilling to borrow additional funds until the current loan is repaid. Alternative sources considered are: "A search for major donors (fund-raising committee and fund drive)" and addi-

---

EXHIBIT 5

MICHIGAN LEAGUE
Statement of Revenue and Expense
June 1983 and Fiscal 1982–83

	June 1983	June 1982	7/1/82– 6/30/83	7/1/81– 6/30/82
Revenue				
House:				
Guest room rentals	$ 14,368	$ 14,335	$ 194,569	$ 189,848
Meeting room rentals	8,273	9,809	120,757	96,540
Front desk merchandise	7,976	8,877	113,718	113,372
Sundry	193	2,920	7,316	10,707
Food:				
Cafeteria	59,191	67,692	725,102	750,539
Coffee shop	18,355	22,178	272,373	278,518
Banquets and parties	38,867	47,081	414,803	357,603
Catering	23,315	4,897	105,701	59,095
Beverage	6,401	15,487	83,757	74,582
NCC administrative services	450	450	5,400	5,400
Total operating revenue	$177,389	$193,726	$2,043,496	$1,936,204

EXHIBIT 5   *(concluded)*

	June *1983*	*June* *1982*	*7/1/82–* *6/30/83*	*7/1/81–* *6/30/82*
Expense				
House:				
Salaries and wages	$ 22,004	$ 21,360	$ 184,593	$ 174,272
Front desk merchandise	9,435	6,272	85,585	79,147
Supplies and general	991	1,214	9,893	10,300
Equipment repairs	1,306	92	4,010	4,327
Laundry	602	634	11,476	10,268
Food:				
Coffee shop salaries and				
wages	11,194	11,438	116,170	100,338
Food, salaries, and wages	70,128	68,385	652,021	617,413
Food cost	37,276	41,201	533,873	540,594
Transportation	-0-	-0-	2,531	2,452
Supplies and general	4,260	2,187	37,275	35,429
Equipment repairs	383	704	9,940	9,353
Laundry	2,182	2,644	35,476	29,638
Beverage	(293)	5,163	25,692	27,192
General:				
Administrative salaries	11,781	18,599	137,432	131,137
Maintenance wages	2,198	2,182	20,587	23,316
Office	930	613	7,936	6,002
Telephone	(82)	(150)	7,722	8,386
Building maintenance	4,475	4,877	37,901	41,978
Board of Governors	56	415	712	1,443
Publicity	419	281	4,245	5,970
Sales tax	3,485	4,270	51,312	45,618
Insurance	74	148	9,094	10,626
Unemployment insurance	-0-	-0-	2,107	503
Bad debts	-0-	-0-	17	60
Miscellaneous	2,408	850	17,479	15,243
Total operating expense	185,842	193,379	2,005,079	1,931,005
Net operating income (loss)	$ (8,453)	$ 347	$ 38,417	$ 5,199
Other Income and Expense				
U-M allocation	$ 17,781	$ 48,877	$ 319,761	$ 295,919
Interest on investments	33,898	26,430	33,898	26,430
Development fund	6,376	100	62,707	200
Utilities	(12,486)	(15,255)	(214,863)	(204,080)
Student awards	(629)	-0-	(629)	(549)
Debt retirement	-0-	(4,837)	(58,272)	(58,040)
Equipment reserves	(950)	(397)	(11,393)	(4,761)
Building reserves	(1,570)	(466)	(18,854)	(5,589)
Total other income and expense	42,420	54,452	112,355	49,530
Net income (loss)	$ 33,967	$ 54,799	$ 150,772	$ 54,729
Total salaries and wages	$117,305	$121,964	$1,110,803	$1,046,476

tional financial assistance from the university. The League's fund raising for 1982 collected $69,000. The League is developing a cookbook for sale. The book will be ready for sale in June 1984 and is expected to earn $50,000–$100,000. Pat Lawson believes that although revenue generated by the cafeteria is the most important source of operating funds, it is not a source of funds for projects that might be undertaken in the future.

FURTHER CONSIDERATIONS

In her report to the board of governors, Pat Lawson stated a need for financial assistance to meet necessary kitchen modernization costs (new appliances). The projected need totals $500,000. However, Pat is considering a complete remodeling of the cafeteria within the next three years. Total costs for complete remodeling are approximately $750,000. The project would include the necessary kitchen equipment, line restructuring, and a complete redecoration of the cafeteria. The plans for the cafeteria line restructuring are to change it from a straight line to an "open"-style square line (scramble system). This would improve efficiency and provide additional customer convenience by eliminating unnecessary waiting. Customers would be able to proceed directly to the section of items they desired. The development of an "open" line would decrease seating capacity. The cafeteria presently seats 250 persons.

As Pat considers the remodeling plans, she is also hoping to include plans to build a small extension to the cafeteria, which would help to recover the seating lost to the line restructuring. The extension as a "greenhouse"-style design is being considered. She believes that the extension should be built at the same time as the other remodeling is undertaken so that shutdown time is minimized. The greenhouse room is to extend from the front of the League building, which faces the main street.

Pat believes that the new room would provide several benefits: (1) make the League cafeteria more visible, (2) provide a direct entrance from the street to the cafeteria, (3) increase seating, and (4) improve cafeteria attractiveness. If remodeling plans include construction of the greenhouse room, estimated total costs could be approximately $1 million. Pat is interested in determining the feasibility of the League financing the remodeling project. She believes that the League's opportunities are limited to income provided by loans, fund raising, cookbook sales, and increased business at the cafeteria.

Case 3–10   American Safety Razor Company*

American Safety Razor Company's fight for survival was one of Virginia's biggest business news stories in 1977. Philip Morris, the parent company of American Safety Razor (ASR), had been seeking a buyer for the troubled subsidiary. However, sale was not easy because profits of ASR had declined each of the previous three years (see Exhibit 1). Philip Morris also insisted that prospective buyers guarantee to retain all 870 ASR employees. The Bic Pen Company had agreed to buy ASR; however, the Federal Trade Commission blocked the sale and claimed that such an agreement would be in restraint of competition.

Since no other purchase offers were considered acceptable, Philip Morris decided to close ASR. Manpower was reduced drastically as part of Philip Morris's liquidation plan. In operations alone, one third of the work force was laid off. The national sales force was cut from 80 people to 30. Then, in September 1977, ASR's president John R. Baker and eight other company executives finalized an agreement to purchase ASR from Philip Morris. The executives paid $600,000 of their own money and $15 million which they had borrowed from two banks and a federal aid program.

COMPANY STRATEGY

Baker's initial marketing strategy after acquisition of ASR was to offer lower prices than Gillette and Schick and to expand ASR's share of the existing female market with the unique woman's razor, Flicker. From 1960 to 1976 ASR had focused on increased advertising expenditures, expansion of the sales force, greater consistency in product quality, competitive pricing, and development of new products. However, the new owners could not afford expensive, high-risk marketing strategies because of the financial strain of purchase and the need to pay off company debts that amounted to over $1 million a year in interest alone.

Baker expected ASR to "bounce back" and grow. He believed that ASR had an advantage over competition because the new owners were

---

* This case was prepared by Joseph R. Mills, customer service manager of American Safety Razor Company, and Thomas M. Bertsch, associate professor of marketing at James Madison University. Confidential information has been disguised.

EXHIBIT 1

AMERICAN SAFETY RAZOR COMPANY
Five-Year Comparative Income Statement
($000)

	1973	1974	1975	1976	1977*
Net sales	$22,909	$26,089	$28,008	$27,917	$30,286
Royalties and other revenues	24	27	94	75	51
Total operating revenues	22,933	26,116	28,102	27,992	30,337
Less:					
Variable cost	8,768	9,692	9,924	9,965	11,225
Shipping expense	630	618	579	653	794
Fixed manufacturing	4,001	4,602	4,767	4,086	4,278
Available contribution margin	9,534	11,204	12,832	13,288	14,040
Operating expenses:					
Advertising	1,616	1,601	1,744	1,882	1,324
Sales force and promotion	4,503	5,571	7,451	8,070	8,462
Marketing research/marketing					
administration	379	449	453	417	346
General and administrative	1,290	1,320	1,720	1,397	1,479
Research and development	506	547	599	702	627
Total operating expenses	8,294	9,488	11,967	12,468	12,238
Operating profit	1,240	1,716	865	820	1,802
Interest expense	0	0	0	0	0
Other expenses	245	432	24	118	723
Profit before taxes	$ 995	$ 1,284	$ 841	$ 702	$ 1,079

* Amounts projected prior to management purchase in September.

the company's managers and the existing work force was determined to succeed. However, management continued to search for ways to speed the improvement of company profits and market share.

COMPANY SALES COMPOSITION

As indicated in Exhibit 1, ASR's sales were approximately $28 million for the year prior to management purchase of the firm. Seventy percent of company sales were in the "wet shave" consumer market. Its own brands provided more than three fourths of the dollars obtained by ASR from that market segment.

Industrial products provided the largest portion of ASR sales revenue. Twenty-seven percent of company business was in the industrial market segment. Sales growth since 1967 was attributed largely to the efforts of ASR to serve industrial consumers regardless of how unique the product might be.

The surgical blade market segment accounted for less than 5 percent of ASR's sales. Although the demand was not large, surgical blade sales were consistent in volume.

The remainder of company sales revenue came from foreign markets. By 1977 ASR's international sales had almost reached $2 million. Shaving blade products accounted for approximately 60 percent of the sales dollars from exports, and industrial products accounted for the rest.

BLADE MARKETS

Domestic Consumer Market

In 1977 the U.S. wet-shave market was estimated by the health and beauty aid industry to be $400 million per year at the retail level. That year, Gillette was holding 55 percent of the shaving blade market. Schick claimed 22 percent, and ASR held 11 percent. The remainder of the wet-shave market was divided between Bic and Wilkinson.

Little market growth was expected for at least the next 10 years because of the slow rate of population growth. Opportunities were increasing in the women's market segment because teenage girls were shaving at an earlier age and more frequently than they did during the early 1970s. However, males were shaving less frequently. Beards were more widely accepted in the late 1970s than they were in the early 1970s, and the popularity of the bearded look had increased. Very few electric-razor users switch to blades, so that market segment did not represent a significant area of possible growth for ASR. Firms in the blade industry expected most new domestic consumer business to come from either increasing market share of their company or opening up new markets.

Industrial Blade Market

The industrial blade market in the United States was estimated by industry leaders to be in the $40 million to $50 million range. ASR held about 20 percent of that market, which made it one of the largest manufacturers of industrial blades in the United States. Ardell Industries, Crescent Manufacturing, and Winsor Manufacturing had 10 percent, 5 percent, and 2 percent, respectively, of the industrial blade market. Exacto and Durham, which offered a limited product line, each had gross sales in the $5 million to $6 million range. Of the four major producers of shaving blades, only ASR competed in the industrial market.

Surgical Market

The surgical blade market was estimated at only $6 million. Bard-Parker was the sales leader with a 59 percent share of the market; ASR was a distant second with 29 percent, followed by Beaver with 8 percent. Proper, a foreign company that exports large quantities of blades to the United States, was next with 2 percent of the market. The surgical blade market was very small compared to the wet-shave consumer market.

International Market

The sales potential of foreign wet-shaving markets was estimated by one industry leader to be 10 times the actual dollar sales to the U.S. market. In 1977 Gillette accounted for between 80 and 90 percent of the foreign sales of U.S. blades. Schick, Wilkinson, and ASR also competed in the overseas market, but Gillette had taken the lead in teaching people to shave.

ASR has had mixed results from its efforts to penetrate foreign markets. The company had approximately half of the shaving blade market in Puerto Rico. However, high labor costs forced closing of its production facility in Scotland, and its efforts in Brazil to provide technical assistance for blade manufacturing did not meet expectations. Even though setbacks were encountered in several foreign markets, the new owners of ASR still believed that some international markets could be highly profitable for ASR.

PRODUCT STRATEGY

ASR offers over 500 different versions of packaged shaving, industrial, and surgical blade products. See Exhibit 2 for a list of product line changes made by ASR.

Products by Gillette have become the industry standards for comparison. Therefore ASR's shaving blade products are judged against Gillette's products and are designed to meet those standards. However, ASR's shaving systems, such as Flicker and Double II, are designed to be distinctive in appearance.

Typically, major competitors in the blade industry denied that they

EXHIBIT 2   Major Product Line Changes of ASR, as of 1977

Year Introduced	Product	Status
1875	Star safety razor	Replaced with Gem razor
1889	Gem safety razor	Continued, with modification
1915	Ever-Ready shaving brush	Continued
1919	Gem, Star, and Ever-Ready shaving blades	Continued
1933	Lightfoot soap	Discontinued in 1973
1934	Electric shaver	Discontinued in 1934
1935	Pile wire-carpet	Discontinued in 1977
1935	Surgical blades and handles	Continued
1947	Double-edge shaving blade	Continued
1948	Injector shaving blade	Continued
1963	Stainless steel coated blade	Continued
1969	Face Guard shaving blade	Continued
1970	Personna tungsten steel blades	Continued
1971	Flicker	Continued
1973	Personna Double II shaving system	Continued
1974	Personna Injector II blade	Continued
1975	Double Edge II	Discontinued in 1976
1975	Lady	Continued
1977	Single II shaving system	Continued

developed products in response to the introduction of a new product by a competitor. Company representatives usually stressed that they were responding to consumer needs, not actions of competitors. The industry practice, though, was for major producers to follow quickly a competitor's innovative product with a competing product. When Wilkinson introduced its stainless steel blade in the early 1960s, all major competitors followed with similar products. In 1969 Gillette introduced its Platinum Plus blade, and competitors followed with versions of the platinum-chromium blade. Eighteen months after ASR introduced Flicker to the women's wet-shaving market, Gillette introduced Daisy. The time between introduction of a new type of product and introduction of a similar product by a major competitor is now only 10 to 12 months.

New product introductions are one way for a firm to increase market share. However, a new, better shaving blade product may not gain much market share. This fact became painfully clear to ASR soon after the introduction of twin-blade systems in 1971. Gillette's introduction in this product category was the Trac II. Schick called its introduction Super II. ASR decided that it had one of three choices: make no introduction, make the same design as Gillette and offer it under a different name, or make a slightly different product. ASR's management decided it had to make an introduction because of the large market potential involved. The ASR version came out eight months later and was called Double II.

Since ASR was late in entering this new consumer market segment, management chose to try a modified twin-blade system. The new version was a double-edge bonded blade system, which offered twice as many shaves as the Trac II and Super II. The shaving system uniquely featured a gap between the bonded blades that permitted the cut hair to be washed away. With discounts offered, the consumer could buy the ASR system at the same price as Trac II. ASR's new product was a good one, according to consumer tests, but Double II did not pick up the 16 percent market share expected (see Exhibit 3).

The major marketing emphasis in the industry since the middle 1960s has been directed toward the marketing of "shaving systems" versus razors and blades. One of the newest systems to be introduced is the disposable razor. Some market analysts estimated that the disposable razor category could build into a 20 percent segment of the estimated $400 million blade market. By 1978 Wilkinson and Schick had followed Bic and Gillette into the low-priced disposable razor market with their own versions of a disposable razor.

ASR offered industrial blades for the carpet industry, utility knife blades, and specialty blades for the food, textile, and electronic industries. There was also an industrial line of injector, single-edge, and double-edge blades. The company had been able to convince its industrial customers that disposable blades mean a quality product and a reduction of machine downtime. The strategy of ASR was to find new industrial users for disposable blades, but the market was specialized, so customized orders were common.

ASR offers a full line of surgical blades and handles. Since competitors have not made any recent introduction of new products for this market, ASR has devoted its efforts to technological and quality improvements. Consistent processing effort is expended to improve the sharpness and durability of its surgical blades.

EXHIBIT 3   Market Performance of Twin-Blade Systems

Product	Date of Introduction	1971–1973 Advertising ($ millions)	January 1974 Share of Total Razor Blade Market	1973 Sales ($ millions)
Trac II (Gillette)	1971	$117	23.2%	$10.9
Super II (Schick)	1972	4	6.3	2.5
Double II (ASR)	1973	3	1.3	0.6

Although standard-brand shaving blade products and industrial blades were sold in the international market, many products were especially prepared for each market. For instance, in South America many double-edge blades are sold one at a time; therefore ASR individually wrapped and packaged each blade for that market. Package labels for Europe were printed in four languages: English, French, Portuguese, and German. In the Far East, a single-edge blade with an extra-thick back for easier handling was sold instead of the standard single-edge blade. Customized orders were accepted in the hope of building repeat business.

DISTRIBUTION STRATEGY

Most razors and razor blades in the United States were sold in retail groceries and drugstores. New retail accounts were solicited directly on the basis of their expected volume. ASR had decided to concentrate on large accounts. Therefore it used distributors to serve small accounts, but it sold direct to large accounts. Much of the industry was dominated by large accounts such as chain drugstores and supermarkets.

The company was hesitant to reject requests for dealer labels. Management felt that ASR could not compete unless its product offerings were in a dominant position on the shelf. This was particularly true of wholesalers and retailers, who were willing to push their own brand considerably more than a manufacturer's brand.

In general, demand for manufacturers' brands of blades was not growing significantly. However, ASR saw an opportunity to increase its market share in the dealer-brand segment of the market. A product was considered eligible for dealer labels if it had at least 8 to 10 percent of the branded market. All dealer label accounts were handled by a small corporate department which performed the necessary marketing functions. ASR held 75 percent of this growing market segment.

ASR sold its surgical blades through a national hospital supply company, which acted as exclusive distributor for the blades. The distributor was permitted by contract to ship to any location in the world. The 1976 contract between the two firms also included renewal clauses.

ASR's industrial products were sold to both users and distributors. Brokers were used to sell less than 20 percent of the products. ASR's industrial sales force concentrated its efforts on the large-volume customers and distributors. Many of the direct customers were manufacturers in the electronics, textile, and food industries.

The International Marketing Division utilized distributors in most countries because ASR did not employ an international sales force. ASR preferred to sell to many distributors within a country in order to obtain wide distribution and to avoid dependence on a single distributor; however, many foreign distributors had exclusive selling rights in their country. The most active accounts were in Latin America, Canada, and Japan.

PRICING STRATEGY

ASR's prices for unique products, such as Flicker and single-edge blades, were competitive with the prices of other shaving products in the market. If a retailer did any local promotion of ASR's brands of products, then cooperative advertising was arranged. ASR's double-edge, injector, and Double II products were priced less to retailers than similar items offered by competitors.

ASR was the price leader for industrial blades. Since dealer promotions and national advertising were not used for industrial blades, this market segment was a consistent contributor to profitability.

The company's surgical products were priced low in relation to competition. The national distributor established the resale prices, and the wholesale prices were renegotiated annually.

ASR's products were sold in foreign wholesale markets for approximately one third less than they were sold for in the United States. Price quotes on export orders did not include shipping costs, although domestic prices included shipping charges.

PROMOTION STRATEGY

The amount spent by ASR on national advertising varied according to the newness of the product. Established products, such as single-edge blades, were not advertised. However, a product such as Flicker did receive attention. Flicker was both a relatively new product and one which was dominant in the market. Therefore ASR allocated $1 million for promotion of its Flicker ladies' shaving system in 1977.

Razors and razor blades were typically marketed with large expenditures for promotion. Gillette, for example, spent $6 million on promoting its new Good News! shaver in 1977. Gillette also planned to support its new Atra (automatic tracking razor) with a $7.7 million advertising campaign in 1977. Major competitors of ASR had spent large sums of money on consumer-directed advertising and promotion to maintain strong national brand preference.

The Bic Pen Company, which had been blocked from buying ASR, decided in 1976 to compete in the American branded blade market. It planned a large and expensive introductory marketing program for 1977, budgeting $9 million for sales and promotion of its single-blade,

EXHIBIT 4 Marketing-Sales Organization

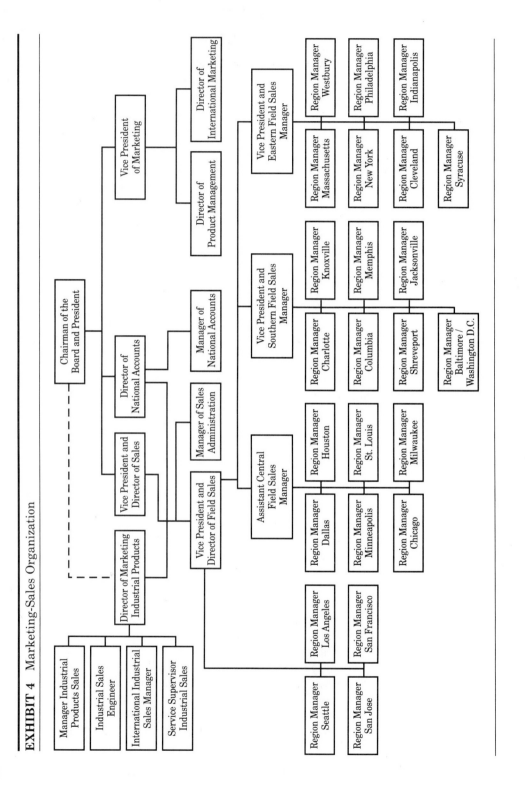

lightweight razor, which is completely disposable. Part of the promotional strategy was to give away a disposable razor and blade to 40 percent of the U.S. households.

Promotional methods used by major producers of blades included give-aways, rebates, cents-off programs, couponing, cooperative advertising with retailers, special displays, and volume discounts. The industry relied heavily on the use of TV advertising. However, several other advertising media were used, including full-page magazine ads and Sunday newspaper supplement ads.

MARKETING ORGANIZATION

Prior to the planned liquidation of ASR by Philip Morris, the marketing group consisted of brand managers, assistant brand managers, a marketing administrator, a single marketing researcher, and an assistant researcher. By 1978 the group had been reduced to the vice president of marketing, the director of product management, and the director of international marketing (see Exhibit 4). ASR's top management felt that the smaller marketing team could handle the reduced advertising budget and the target market segments.

Both the sales group and the marketing group were based in Staunton, Virginia. The vice president of sales reported to the company president. The directors of field sales, industrial products, and national accounts reported to the vice president of sales. Three field sales managers reported to the director of field sales. Twenty-four regional managers reported to the field sales managers. ASR had four selling divisions: Branded Products, Private Label Products, Industrial and Surgical Products, and International Marketing.

The sales force represented the only link between the company and large retail accounts, such as chain drugstores and supermarkets. Chain stores were very important since they represented the key strategic approach of the ASR shaving blade business. Each regional sales manager was expected to spend much of his time in developing sales to the big chains.

Until late 1974 ASR's field salespeople received a compensation package composed of straight salary plus fringe benefits. Then, in 1975, an incentive system was introduced which included a monthly commission, a semiannual incentive for participation in company promotional programs, and annual compensation opportunities related to regional profitability. The new compensation package was introduced to help both the sales managers and the salespersons. By 1978 the sales managers felt that ASR was attracting better quality, experienced salespersons and that the sales personnel liked the new incentive rewards.

Case 3–11   The Cleveland Clinic*

For years, Ohio's Cleveland Clinic has ranked with the top world-class providers of medical care. It pioneered coronary bypass surgery and developed the first kidney dialysis machine. King Hussein of Jordan uses the clinic, so too the royal family of Saudi Arabia.

But to Diran M. Seropian, chief of the medical staff of the largest hospital in Broward County, Fla., the clinic is the Carl Icahn of medicine—"a hostile corporation with a hostile corporation mentality." Its unforgivable mistake, in Dr. Seropian's view: It opened an outpatient facility here 18 months ago as part of a plan to expand into this market. Local politicians and businesses cheered the idea. But many local physicians were outraged, and an extraordinary campaign to keep the clinic out was begun.

The battle between the Cleveland Clinic and the South Florida physicians is part of a larger war sweeping the health care industry and can ultimately be boiled down to one issue: competition. Big-name health-care institutions are after new markets for their state-of-the-art medicine, and are posing a new threat to local physicians. The expansions are also disrupting traditional relationships between physicians and their patients, physicians and their hospitals and physicians and their fellow physicians.

In the Cleveland Clinic's case, Carl C. Gill, the chief executive of the Clinic's Florida enterprise, and a surgeon who has done 4,000 open-heart operations, was denied local hospital privileges. The credentials committee of Broward General Medical Center said he lacked enough experience in the emergency room, among other things. In fact, for 15 months, the clinic was blocked from conducting heart surgery in Florida. When one hospital finally opened its doors, some local physicians, apparently in protest, began snubbing the facility and referring their patients elsewhere. And when some patients told their local physicians that they wanted to consult physicians at the clinic, they were handed their medical charts and told not to come back.

In a recent full-page advertisement in the Miami Herald, Dr. Seropian, who has led the charge, pulled out the stops. He likened the clinic to Dingoes—wild Australian dogs—"that roam the bush eating every kind of prey."

In May, the clinic filed suit in federal district court in Fort Lauder-

---

* Source: Ron Winslow, "Medical Clash: Big Hospitals Move into New Territories, Draw Local Staffs' Ire," *The Wall Street Journal,* August 18, 1989, pp. A1, 4. Reprinted by permission of *THE WALL STREET JOURNAL,* © 1989 Dow Jones & Company, Inc. All Rights Reserved Worldwide.

dale, charging, among other things, that some physicians had conspired to "hamper" its entry into Broward County. In a countersuit, Amjad Munim, a pulmonologist and one of two individual defendants named in the complaint, maintained the clinic had tried to recruit him to spy on his fellow physicians so it could build a legal case against them. Meanwhile, the Federal Trade Commission is investigating whether the battle has involved violations of antitrust laws.

The Cleveland Clinic, which had revenue of $672 million in 1988, isn't alone in its desire to expand. The Mayo Clinic, based in Rochester, Minn., has recently set up satellite operations in Jacksonville, Fla., and Scottsdale, Ariz. The M. D. Anderson Cancer Center in Houston is negotiating to open a branch in Orlando, Fla. Several other, smaller institutions and academic centers have also established regional branches, intended to feed patients to their main facilities.

In part, these institutions are victims of their own success. Many once-exotic procedures that they invented are now routinely available across the country, reducing the need for patients to travel to the medical meccas. For instance, the Cleveland Clinic might once have had a hold on coronary bypass surgery, but no more: Last year more than 250,000 patients had the operation at hospitals throughout the United States.

"These clinics used to be the court of last resort for complex medical cases," says Jeff Goldsmith, national health-care adviser to Ernst & Whinney, the accounting firm. "Now, the flooding of the country with medical specialties and high-technology equipment has forced them to adopt a different strategy."

Their expertise and reputation spell formidable competition for the local medical community. On one level, says Jay Wolfson, a health-policy expert at the University of South Florida in Tampa, "it's like bringing in a McDonald's. If you're a mom-and-pop sandwich shop on the corner, you could get wiped out."

In Fort Lauderdale, physicians insist they aren't threatened by the Cleveland Clinic. Instead, they say they resent what they see as special favors the institution was given to invade their turf. They also maintain the clinic will lure fully insured patients from local hospitals, leaving behind the burden for indigent care. And they bristle at the suggestion that the clinic dispenses a better brand of medicine. "They've implied the doctors here are dummies, that they're bringing enlightened medicine to the hinterlands," Dr. Seropian says.

Since its founding in 1921, the not-for-profit Cleveland Clinic has built its business taking on complex, high-risk cases, and leaving more routine primary care to family physicians. In addition to treating patients, its salaried physicians do research and train new physicians, tasks the clinic says set it apart from everyday medical practice. "Basic fee-for-service practice doesn't advance medicine," says Dr. Gill.

Clinic physicians claim they aren't interested in stealing patients. But they make no apology for provoking a battle with their fee-for-service brethren that is both cultural and economic. Says Dr. Gill: "Let's let the marketplace sort out what the best way to deliver health care is."

The conflict began early in 1986 over modest ambitions: a proposed joint venture between the clinic and the North Broward Hospital District, a tax-supported agency that operates Broward General and three other county hospitals. Under the plan, the clinic would build an out-patient facility adjacent to Broward General Medical Center. The medical center would provide surgical and other major services.

But word of the idea leaked prematurely and a hastily-arranged meeting to explain it to the district's physicians erupted into a verbal pummeling of William Kiser, chairman of the Cleveland Clinic Foundation board of governors. Soon after, hospital officials halted the negotiations.

"The [physicians] really had a problem with a bunch of carpetbaggers from the North," Dr. Kiser said.

The clinic, however, moved ahead with its expansion plans. Like any business, it keeps close tabs on its core market, and the outlook wasn't all that bright. Seven states provide 90 percent of the clinic's business and population growth in that region is expected to be flat through the year 2000. But not so southeastern Florida, where the population is still growing and, in many areas, is highly affluent (Exhibit 1).

On the surface, the region—Dade, Broward, and Palm Beach Counties—is a dream market. Yachts lining the canals of the Intracoastal Waterway and a ubiquitous building boom reflect wealth and growth so palpable that clinic officials have come to call it "immaculate consumption." Moreover, about 20 percent of the 3.7 million residents in Dade, Broward and Palm Beach Counties are over 65 years old. By the year 2000, about 50 percent of the population will be over 45—a potential motherlode of patients.

"We felt there was room for us," Dr. Kiser said. "We decided to go on our own rather than wait to be invited."

Others have been drawn by the same flame. Throughout the 1970s, for-profit hospital chains rushed here to cash in on the growing elderly population, whose medical tab was paid in full by Medicare. But in 1983, when the U.S. instituted new medicare payment guidelines called DRGs, or diagnosis related groups, to control surging medical costs, hospital occupancy rates began to plummet. Now, the region is glutted with health care: There are 240 physicians for every 100,000 residents in southeastern Florida—the national average is 189—and a surplus of 3,500 hospital beds.

Glut or not, the clinic drew up big plans: a $200 million complex,

EXHIBIT 1   Projected Population Growth 1990–2000 in the Cleveland
Clinic's Markets

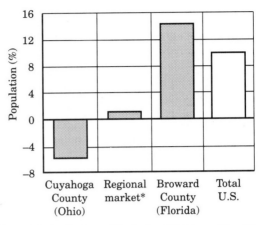

* Includes portions of Ohio, Indiana, Kentucky, Michigan, New York, Pennsylvania
and West Virginia

Sources: Cleveland Clinic Foundation; Broward Economic Development Board, based on U.S.
Bureau of the Census data.

anchored by a state-of-the-art, 400-bed hospital. Health planners
blanched, but the business community was enthralled.

"We looked at this as a world-class health facility that we would use
to build business around," said James Garver, president of the
Broward Economic Development Board.

In May 1987, with help from a politically connected law firm and
after some of its physicians had made about $2,000 in campaign contri-
butions to local legislators, the clinic won passage of crucial legislation: a law granting it tax-exempt status and waiving the state medical exam for 25 senior physicians who would move from Cleveland to
launch the new facility.

Local physicians were enraged. "Twenty-five thousand physicians
have taken that exam to practice in this state," fumes Dr. Seropian.
The Cleveland physicians shouldn't have been exempted, he says.

The clinic says it received the same consideration previously afforded the Mayo Clinic and academic institutions hiring out-of-state
faculty. (Ultimately, 13 of its physicians accepted exemptions before
the waiver expired.)

With the bill's passage, the clinic pressed forward to build its outpatient facility, which opened in February 1988. But more battles
loomed. For one, to build its proposed hospital, which it hoped to open
in the early 1990s, the clinic had to get a "certificate of need" from the

state, proving that the community actually needed the services. The local hospital association and health planners allied with local physicians to oppose it.

The clinic's physicians meanwhile had no place to operate, and started hunting for a hospital that would open its doors. The clinic found two allies, one of which was North Beach Hospital, a 153-bed facility that was filling only 28 of its beds. There was just one problem: North Beach lacked a certificate of need for cardiac service.

Enter Richard Stull, the chief executive of the Nort Broward Hospital District. Mr. Stull had played a key role in the early joint-venture discussions between the clinic and the District, and he held steadfast to his hope of an affiliation with the clinic.

"In this county there are 20 acute-care hospitals that are known for nothing," Mr. Stull says. "All I was looking for was adding something so that we'd stand out." He was also worried about offsetting competition from a new source: Some of his own physicians were setting up clinics that siphoned off outpatient business from the hospital.

When a cardiac team left Broward General at the beginning of 1988, Mr. Stull thought the clinic's heart specialists could fill the void. But once again, the hospital's medical staff was opposed.

In the resulting battle:

- The hospital's credentials committee denied practice privileges to the clinic's five-person cardiac team, including Dr. Gill, because the clinic is "an acknowledged potential competitor" of the hospital, the committee said.
- The district's board, in the face of political pressure, overruled the committee and last January signed a five-year contract with the clinic to provide cardiac services at Broward General. In protest, some physicians apparently diverted their patients to other hospitals, helping to depress February revenues at Broward General $3.5 million below projections.
- When the clinic asked for privileges for its other specialists to consult on cardiac cases, the local credentials committee refused to act. Mr. Stull had to fly in a panel of physicians from outside the area to approve their qualifications.

On May 15, more than 14 months after the clinic's outpatient facility opened, Dr. Gill performed the first open heart operation at Broward General for the Cleveland Clinic Florida.

But that victory was tempered by a serious setback. In January, state health officials denied the clinic a certificate of need for its hospital. They said there were already too many surplus hospital beds in the area, and rejected the clinic's claim that it offered unique services.

For now, the clinic's hospital plans are on hold. But, in the meantime, it says its Florida practice is thriving. More than 12,000 patients have sought treatment since it opened; some wait as long as three months for an appointment with one of its 48 physicians.

Specialty-care and exotic procedures remain its stock-in-trade. In one recent operation, three clinic surgeons replaced a Fort Lauderdale resident's cancerous throat with a piece of his small intestine. In another, a physician used two ribs to make a new forehead for a man whose own had been removed to relieve pressure in his brain. Then there is Beth Acker. Told by a local neurosurgeon that she had an inoperable spinal cord tumor and four months to live, the 29-year-old mother went to the clinic where she had successful surgery. "They handled it like an everyday thing," she said.

Gradually, local physicians are sending patients its way, the clinic says, but the vast majority come in on their own. That is prompting the clinic to expand its services and add a general medical practice to its group of specialists.

Case 3–12   Japan, Inc.*

They are the world's new plutocrats, buying up Rembrandts and real estate with their rock-hard yen—the new highfliers in an age of high technology, the new elite in an era in which money is a major measure of power.

They are an insecure people from an insular nation no bigger than California, hiding their national vulnerabilities behind a veil of yen, escaping their crowded cities to roam a world in which they increasingly are resented and even reviled—ambassadors of a nation notably devoid of the idealism or ideology that has motivated great powers in the past.

They are the richest of people and the poorest of people; the most envied of leaders and the most eager of followers; the strongest of global competitors and the most fragile of global powers. In the increasingly intense struggle for world leadership, Japan is winning many of the battles. But can it win the war?

The Japanese miracle is well-known. A country that only a generation ago was disparaged as a producer of tinny transistor radios has

---

* Source: Karen Elliott House, "The '90s & Beyond: Though Rich, Japan Lacks Ideology, Arms for Global Political Leadership," *The Wall Street Journal,* January 30, 1989, pp. 1, A8. Reprinted by permission of *THE WALL STREET JOURNAL,* © 1989 Dow Jones & Company, Inc. All Rights Reserved Worldwide.

turned itself into one of the wealthiest and most technologically advanced on Earth, a transformation accomplished through sheer hard work and a social organization so cohesive and centrally managed that an Italian journalist here laughingly calls Japan "the only communist nation that works."

Unburdened by defense spending or, until recently, a consumer culture, Japanese saved and invested in industry. With methodical precision and market perceptivity, Japan began industry by industry to take leadership, moving rapidly from heavy industries on to high technology. Now, finally, the yen has replaced the dollar as the symbol of financial strength, enabling Japan to go on an unprecedented global buying binge (see Exhibit 1).

This lock-step national march from war-torn poverty to economic prominence has set off an urgent debate in the West: Is this seemingly invincible economic engine destined in the next generation to simply roll over the world, establishing Japan's unchallenged dominance? Or do Japan's limits—the scarcity of its natural resources, the narrowness of its political vision and the animosity it stirs—foreclose true global leadership? Japan's future is a question that weighs not only on experts but on ordinary individuals: What American or European consumer hasn't felt, along with admiration for a Japanese car or VCR, a twinge of fear for his own country's future?

"At the rate things are going, we are all going to wind up working for the Japanese," says Lester Thurow, an economist at Massachusetts Institute of Technology.

EXHIBIT 1   Good Neighbor Policy?

Japanese and American 1987 merchandise trade balance with Asian countries, in billions of dollars; minus sign indicates trade deficit.

	Japan's 1987 Trade Balance with Country	*U.S. 1987 Trade Balance with Country*
Hong Kong	$7.37	$−6.51
South Korea	5.17	−9.89
Taiwan	4.86	−16.01
Singapore	3.98	−2.34
Thailand	1.17	−0.84
China	0.86	−3.41
India	0.43	−1.26
Philippines	0.05	−0.88
Malaysia	−2.63	−1.16
Indonesia	−5.48	−2.95

Source: *Directions of Trade Yearbook.*

EXHIBIT 2   Japan's Emergence as a Financial Power

The Yen's dramatic rise . . .
Number of dollars 1,000 yen buys

Fueled big U.S. investments . . .

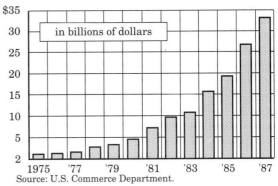

Source: U.S. Commerce Department.

While Japanese savings rate . . .
1987 personal savings as a percentage of
disposable personal income

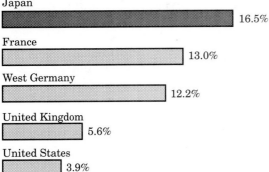

Japan 16.5%

France 13.0%

West Germany 12.2%

United Kingdom 5.6%

United States 3.9%

Source: CIA.

Easily finances its deficit.
1987 central government deficit as a
percentage of GNP

United States 3.5%

Japan 2.7%

France 2.4%

West Germany 1.4%

United Kingdom 1.1%

Source: OECD.

"Japan will be the No. 1 financial power in the next generation,"
declares Alfred Herrhausen, chairman of Deutsche Bank, in his office
atop its shimmering new Frankfurt headquarters, from which he
tracks the rise of Japanese banking (see Exhibit 2). (Nine of the world's
10 largest banks, ranked by 1987 assets, are Japanese.)

Yet despite all this yen-inspired awe, Japan obviously hasn't replaced the United States as the preeminent global power—and it probably never will. This is the conclusion that emerges from talks with
more than a hundred government officials, scholars and other experts
in the United States, Russia, Europe and Asia. There are dissenting
voices, certainly, but the predominant view is that while Japan will

wield greater influence, especially economic, a broader global leadership will elude it. Japan's deficiencies are simply too great.

For starters, Japan is a one-dimensional power. Its economic might isn't bolstered by either military, political or ideological clout, elements that have always been essential for a nation to shape international events. Nor is there much prospect of Japanese rearmament in the next generation, so opposed is the entire world even four decades after World War II. While the international community does insist Japan play a larger political role, Japanese so far lack the confidence or will to do so. Japan keeps its head down. It is content to have a Mitsui policy, not a Mideast policy; a foreign-exchange policy, but not a true foreign policy.

In the few instances where Japan has tried to expand its political role, as it did recently in offering proposals for handling Third World debt, the international reaction has ranged from skepticism to hostility. That is largely because Japan is seen as standing for no ideal other than a quest for self-enrichment, hardly a globally appealing philosophy.

"The Japanese will find out money isn't everything just as we found out armaments aren't everything," says Soviet deputy foreign minister Anatoli Adamishin.

Even in the field where the Japanese are strongest, economics, it is far from clear they are winning. For Japan's wealth is dependent on access to others' markets, a dependency that makes it vulnerable. By contrast, America's enormous domestic market provides greater self-sufficiency, as well as leverage over Japan and others who rely on it.

"Japan is like a thin-bottomed pan on a hot fire—very vulnerable to external forces," says Chung Hoon Mok, president of Hyundai Construction Co., over dinner in Seoul.

Many in the United States, of course, worry these days about Japan's feats on the frontiers of high technology, once virtually the exclusive preserve of America. Having some years ago all but abandoned consumer electronics to big Japanese companies like Sony, Toshiba and Hitachi, U.S. industry now is being challenged in futuristic technologies like fiber optics, genetic engineering and superconductivity. These are fields that require heavy investment in research and development, and they lend themselves to the kind of cooperation among industrial giants that is a hallmark of Japanese success.

Regardless, many businessmen who envy Japan's technological prowess and marketing might remain confident the high-tech battle is far from lost. One reason is America's preeminence in the realm of pure science where technologies are born. "We still have a commanding lead in pushing the frontiers of science," says Bobby Inman, chairman of Westmark, an electronics holding company in Texas. "Where we've fallen short frequently is in the speed with which we turn technology into product. But we're waking up."

Much of Japan's success has been based on rapid commercialization of technology developed in America. But these days American companies are working harder to protect their patents, to cooperate in the development of new technologies and to turn their discoveries into products more quickly. Government and industry have begun to work together on research too, though at a level far below that of Japan. The Bush administration has signaled that helping U.S. industry compete in technology is a top priority.

"Six years ago I was pretty pessimistic," says Mr. Inman, former deputy director of the Central Intelligence Agency. "Today I am cautiously optimistic because of the level of attention I see the problem beginning to get."

It's even more fashionable in America these days to lament Japan's frequent and flashy purchases of pieces of America and of American corporations. In fact, this buying spree is as much a manifestation of Japanese weaknesses as of strength. It's true the low dollar makes U.S. assets cheap, but the Japanese also rush to America for what they can't find at home.

"The U.S. is a land of opportunity and Japan is a land of lack of opportunity," says Jiro Tokuyama, senior adviser to the Mitsui Research Center. "We close our market because opportunities are scarce and we don't want to share them with others. Already our college graduates don't have the same opportunities as those 20 years ago." But, he adds, "being closed is a weakness. This is our dilemma."

Indeed, Japanese investment at levels America is likely to tolerate is a blessing, not a curse. Ironically, given America's low savings rate (less than one-fourth that of Japan), it is Japanese money that is financing the investment that is rebuilding America's competitiveness, including new thrusts in high-tech fields. Also, for all the concern about buying of U.S. assets, Japanese investment in America still ranks below that of Britain and Holland. (More broadly, total American ownership of assets abroad is about $1 trillion, while total foreign ownership of American assets stands at about $1.5 trillion.)

Most important, there is the obvious fact that the assets so avidly purchased by Japanese these days remain in America. "We sold the top of these two buildings to the Japanese," says Citicorp Chairman John Reed in his glass-walled New York office. "But these two buildings are in Manhattan, and the fact that they own them doesn't mean very much."

Just as some fret that there is too much Japanese investment in the United States, others worry that it might suddenly end. "Even a rumor that investment might stop sends the market into a tizzy," says Fred

Bergsten, director of the Institute for International Economics in Washington. "We are hostage to foreigners."

While possible, an investment halt is hardly likely. Japan is at least as reliant on the American consumer market for its exports as America is dependent on Japanese investment. An abrupt end to Japanese lending to America could precipitate a U.S. recession that most economists believe would rapidly send shock waves through Japan's economy.

"An American recession affects the whole world," says Toyoo Gyohten, Japan's vice minister of finance. "Nobody wants an American recession."

Moreover, many individual Japanese investors and companies have spent so heavily in America they can ill afford to stop supporting its currency and economy. "The more the Japanese invest, the more committed they are to the American economy," says John Welch Jr., chairman of General Electric Co. "If you buy a home in my neighborhood, you care how I keep my neighborhood. If the Japanese own our assets, they don't want values to drop or currencies to drop."

Mitoji Yabunaka, an America-watcher in Tokyo's foreign ministry, acknowledges the U.S. leverage: "It's a very tough decision for Japanese investors. They've already invested so heavily that if they stop and get a free fall of the dollar, they lose a lot."

The Japan-will-win school relies on yet another facile assumption. In the next century, this theory goes, Japan will lead an Asian bloc— two billion hard-working, self-sacrificing people, a full two-thirds of the world's population, all harnessed to Japan's economic ambitions. In reality, this 1990s version of the 1930s Greater Co-Prosperity Sphere imposed by Japan's armies grows less likely every day. For as Japan gets stronger, so does Asian suspicion, resentment, and fear (see Exhibit 3).

"Japanese may feel patriotic sentiments when they see the rising sun on Japan's flag," says Wu Ningkun, a professor at Beijing's Institute of International Relations. "But to Chinese it is just blood and murder." (He then launches into a recitation of Japan's wartime brutalities, which he says killed 30 million Chinese.)

In no sense is Asia a monolith. Culturally and historically, its divisions are far deeper than those in Europe. And the distances among those diverse neighbors are great. Europeans, using the code term "1992," talk ceaselessly these days of economic unity. Asians do not. At New York conferences of the Council on Foreign Relations, in university seminars and even in some corporate board rooms, experts discuss with great seriousness the emergence of a new Asian trading bloc. But here in Asia, a visitor finds that concept draws only blank stares. When it is explained, the reaction is a combination of horror and bemusement.

EXHIBIT 3   On Japan's Future

"At the rate things are going, we are all going to wind up working for the Japanese."

—Lester Thurow
Economist at MIT

"If you think what exists today is permanent and forever true, you inevitably get your head handed to you."

—John Reed
Chairman of Citicorp

"Japan's view is always a flying-geese format with Japan as the head goose."

—Ding Xinghao
Shanghai's Institute of International Studies

"Japan is too big to be under the U.S. umbrella and too vulnerable to be on its own. We need each other."

—Zbigniew Brzezinski
Former U.S. National Security Adviser

"We can sell cars and VCRs, but who loves Japan? We are winning the battle but losing the war."

—Jiro Tokuyama
Mitsui Research Center

"Why should Americans be so pessimistic, so defeatist, as to believe you can't keep pace with Japan?"

—Helmut Schmidt
Former West German chancellor

"It's simply not possible for Asian nations to be a viable bloc. . . . You have one giant, Japan, and many peanuts."

—Park Ungsuh
South Korean economist

"Closing the gap with America was easy. Now the race begins."

—Wataru Hiraizumi
Member of Japanese parliament

"Japan's view is always a flying-geese format with Japan as the head goose," says Ding Xinghao, director of American studies at Shanghai's Institute of International Studies. "Our memories are long, so we aren't about to fly in Japan's formation."

Korean economist Park Ungsuh offers a practical, if less colorful, analysis. "It's simply not possible for Asian nations to be a viable bloc," he says, "because there is too much disparity between economies. You have one giant, Japan, and many peanuts."

Statistics underscore the point that, unlike Europe, Asia isn't a region of nearby neighbors and near-equals. The two largest economies in Asia are Japan, with annual per capita income of more than $13,000, and China, with only $270. Other economies, while booming, are dwarfed by these two; the increase in China's economic output in 1984 exceeded the entire gross national product of South Korea.

The same point is made by many others who look beneath the statistics on Japan's trade surpluses with most of the rest of Asia. A 1989 world economic survey by Coopers & Lybrand, the big American accounting firm, stresses that "no unified 'Pacific Rim' exists." It argues that the region is "simply a collection of high-growth, competitive countries that have yet to achieve any sense of economic coherence."

Beyond practical obstacles to an Asian bloc are even greater political ones. Generally, proximity to Japan raises, rather than reduces, anti-Japanese sentiment. If Europe reacts to Japan with cool envy and America with occasional angry outbursts, in Asia, from businessmen to bar girls, it's open season on Japan.

At the Cotton Club, a Bangkok bar that caters to Japanese businessmen, Thai hostesses dressed in pseudo-kimonos tell Western visitors how much they despise the Japanese men who pay them for drinks and dances.

In the glistening Seoul headquarters of Luck Gold Star, a Korean electronics and chemical products company, corporate president Lee Hun Jo frets over predictions emanating from America that Japan will play a greater role in Asia: "If that's so, I'm afraid we won't have a very stable next decade."

Zhao Fusan, a vice president of the Chinese Academy of Social Sciences in Beijing, is more blunt. A picture of the Virgin Mary adorns his cluttered office but doesn't temper his harsh views of Japan. "The Japanese are an aggressive people," he says. "They exploited us in the '40s with force and now with finance. They sell us inferior goods and deny us technology to try to keep China backward. But Asians have memories that can't be rubbed out with money."

A group of young Chinese economists at Shanghai's Asia Institute gleefully predict those memories will more and more manifest themselves in anti-Japanese government policies. "As democracy spreads in Asia, the people's hatred of Japan will carry more and more weight," predicts Chen Lebo, an economist at the institute.

Almost certainly, the greatest problem confronting Japan in the next several decades is the Japanese. Felix Rohatyn, a New York investment banker who believes Japan's economic power already exceeds America's, says, "Japan may have trouble adjusting to victory. The Japanese are going to have to give a lot back to the world. There's no history of their doing so."

Former West German Chancellor Helmut Schmidt echoes the point. "If I were Japanese, my top priority would be establishing friendly relations with my neighbors by learning to say, 'I'm sorry.' They never have."

Japanese acknowledge this constraint on their nation. "We can sell cars and VCRs but who loves Japan? Who loves Japanese?" says Mr. Tokuyama. "We are winning the battle but losing the war."

In view of all this, there seems little justification for the American elite's attraction to the idea of Japanese invulnerability and inevitable dominance. That analysis largely rests on taking a snapshot of Japan's sudden, sharp accumulation of wealth in the last eight years and projecting it forward into the future, forgetting that in 1980 Japan had a trade deficit of $10 billion, not today's $80 billion surplus.

"I'd guess that the next decade may not be as favorable for Japan as this one has been," says Citicorp's Mr. Reed. The costs of commodities Japan imports such as oil and coal have been low in much of the 1980s, he notes, while the prices of Japanese exports like cars and computers have been relatively high. Besides, he adds, three-quarters of the $90 billion swing in Japan's fortunes between 1980 and 1988 was due to currency realignments and only 25 percent to increased export volume. "If you think that what exists today is permanent and forever true, you inevitably get your head handed to you," says Mr. Reed.

The Japanese know better than anyone that the race for economic preeminence is only now beginning. For the past 40 years, Japan has mainly followed in America's footsteps, doing, in the words of management guru Peter Drucker, "better what the West was already doing well."

"Closing the gap with America was easy," says Wataru Hiraizumi, a member of the Japanese parliament. "Now the race begins."

That race almost certainly isn't as lopsided as some handicappers think. America's economy remains nearly twice the size of Japan's. Japan's annual economic growth, which averaged 11% in the '60s and just under 5% in the '70s, has slowed to a modest 3.8% in the '80s, almost exactly the same as America's.

Japan no longer boasts the low labor costs of a developing country and the high labor productivity of a developed one. Labor costs in America now are lower than in Japan, and productivity higher. Just as in America a decade ago, labor costs are prompting Japanese industries to move offshore, taking jobs with them, to Korea, Singapore, Taiwan—even the United States. And Japan's hoard of dollar assets has lost 60% of its value in just three years through the U.S. currency's decline.

Beyond all that, Japan's vaunted corporate loyalty is fraying as its job opportunities decline and Japanese business leaders seek to reward initiative, not longevity. After all, to excell, Japan now has to innovate, not imitate. Yet nothing in its educational system or, until very recently, its corporate culture encourages independent thinking or creativity. So, significantly, Japan is once again imitating America, this time by trying to motivate individual excellence, not reward group unity.

But it is America, not Japan, for which Asians cheer. That's not merely because they like America more, though many do, but because they need America more. America, not Japan, is Asia's major market. And it is America only that offers a counterweight to both Soviet and Japanese ambitions in Asia.

"America is far more trusted than Japan," says South Korean Foreign Minister Choi Kwang Soo. "Japan harbors ambitions to be a major power, and that worries not just us but the Soviets and China."

And, short of their unlikely full-scale rearmament, Japan, too, needs America. "The next decades will be marked by competition between the U.S. and Japan rather than confrontation between the U.S. and the Soviets," says Mr. Ding, the America expert at Shanghai's Institute of International Studies. "But the world hasn't yet reached a point where military power isn't required to maintain global equilibrium, and that's America's task."

PART 4

Market Targeting

The selection of market targets is one of management's most demanding challenges. Should a company attempt to serve all customers that are willing and able to buy, or selectively go after one or more subgroups of customers? An understanding of a product-market is essential in selecting the market-target strategy. The market targeting process includes:

- Deciding how to form segments in the product-market.
- Describing the people/organizations in each segment.
- Evaluating market-target alternatives.
- Selecting a market-target strategy.

The possibilities for selecting the firm's target group of customers range from attempting to appeal to most of the buyers in the market to targeting one or a few segments within the market.

A market segmentation strategy assumes that people or organizations within a product-market will vary as to their responsiveness to any marketing program. The objective is to identify two or more subgroups within the product-market. Each subgroup represents people or organizations that respond similarly to a marketing offer. A segmentation strategy can be implemented by going after a single segment or by designing a separate marketing program to appeal to each segment of interest.

FINDING AND DESCRIBING SEGMENTS

Using a segmentation strategy, a company may gain worthwhile advantages—including higher profitability and strength over competition—through better use of the firm's capabilities and resources. By selecting niches of the product-market, each containing people or organizations that exhibit some degree of similarity, management can gain

greater customer responsiveness from effort expended than by directing the same marketing effort to the whole product-market.

Management must somehow identify possible segments and then,
for each segment of interest, determine which marketing program positioning strategy will obtain the most favorable profit contribution,
net of marketing costs. Since there are many ways to divide a product-
market and several marketing program combinations that might be
used for each niche, finding the very best (optimal) market target and
marketing program strategy is probably impossible.

Criteria for Segmentation

An important question is whether segmentation is worth doing. Since
there are many ways to form segments, how does the planner make the
choice? Five criteria are useful. First is the responsiveness to a company's efforts. If little or no variation exists between four selected consumer groups, then the way they respond (e.g., amount, frequency of
purchase) to any given marketing program should be the same. If four
(or any) segments actually exist in this selection, their responses will
be different—and a different marketing program strategy will work
best for each group.

After meeting the first condition—measuring responsiveness to a
company's efforts—the other requirements come into play. Second, it
must be feasible to identify two or more different customer groups, and
third, a firm must be able to aim an appropriate marketing program
strategy at each target segment. Fourth, in terms of revenue generated
and costs incurred, segmentation must be worth doing. Fifth, the segments must exhibit adequate stability over time so that the firm's
efforts via segmentation will have enough time to reach desired levels
of performance.

If we fail to meet the five requirements, a segmentation strategy
may be questionable. The ultimate criterion is performance. If a niche
scheme leads to improved performance (profitability) in a product-market, it is worthwhile. The advantage of meeting the requirements for
segmentation is that we are more certain the strategy will lead to
improved performance.

Forming Segments

Much of the information obtained from product-market analysis can be
used in describing market niches. The starting point in describing
niches is the definition and analysis of the product-market (customer

profiles) that were discussed previously. The objective is to identify key characteristics that will be useful in distinguishing one niche from another.

Describing the Segments

It is important to identify key characteristics of the people or organizations that occupy each niche. Factors such as those used in dividing product-markets into segments are also helpful in describing the people in the niches. You will recall from the discussion of market analysis in Part 3 that the following information was needed:

- Market profiles of customers.
- Size and growth estimates.
- Distribution channels.
- Analysis of key competitors.
- Product- or brand-positioning strategy.

This same information is needed for each segment of interest to better evaluate its potential value.

Evaluating Market-Target Alternatives

Market-target alternatives range from a mass strategy to a strategy directed toward one, more than one, or all segments. When serving several niches, the marketing program positioning strategy used for a segment may be totally different from that used for other segments, or each program may overlap to some extent programs for other segments. Thus, a firm may use a unique combination of the product offering, distribution approach, price, advertising, and personal selling to serve each segment, or some of the marketing mix components may be used for more than one segment. For example, the same airline services are used to appeal to business and pleasure travelers, although different advertising and sales efforts are aimed at each user group.

Once segments are formed, each one should be evaluated to accomplish three purposes:

1. Since there is often more than one marketing program that can be used for a given segment, a selection of the best program alternative is necessary for each candidate.
2. After evaluation is complete, those segments which still look attrac-

tive as market-target candidates should be ranked as to their attractiveness.

3. Finally, the evaluations will help management decide which buyers to target.

SELECTING A MARKET-TARGET STRATEGY

Assuming that segments can be identified, management has the option of selecting one or more niches as market-targets. Several factors often affect this decision including characteristics of the product-market and company characteristics.

Product-Market Characteristics

The market that a firm decides to serve has a strong influence upon the choice of a market-target strategy. When buyers' needs and wants are similar there is no real basis for establishing niches. Market complexity is another consideration, overlapping to some extent the other factors. The more complex the market situation as to competing firms, variety of product offering, variation in user needs and wants, and other factors, the more likely that a useful niche scheme can be found.

Company Characteristics

A firm's market share is an important factor in deciding what market-target strategy to use. Low market-share firms can often strengthen their position over competition by finding a segment where they have (or can achieve) an advantage over that competition.

The success of some small market-share firms such as Southwest Airlines lends strong support to this position. Also important in choosing a market target strategy are the resources and capabilities of a firm. With limited resources a niche strategy may be essential, as is also the case when the firm's capabilities are in short supply.

Other Considerations

Selection of an appropriate strategy must also take into account the number of competing firms and the capabilities of each. Intense competition often favors a niche strategy, particularly for low-share firms. Finally, production and marketing-scale economies may influence management in choosing a strategy. For example, large volume may be required to gain cost advantages, and scale of production may also affect marketing and distribution programs.

CONCLUDING NOTE

The market-target decision sets into motion the marketing strategy. Choosing the right market-target is a most important decision affecting the enterprise. This decision is central to properly positioning a firm in the marketplace. Sometimes a single target cannot be selected for an entire strategic business unit when the SBU contains different product-markets. Moreover, locating the firm's best competitive advantage may first require detailed segment analysis. Market-target decisions connect corporate and marketing planning. These decisions establish key guidelines for planning, and the market-target decision provides the focus for the remaining marketing-planning decisions.

When it appears feasible to identify segments in a product-market, management should form niches, evaluate them, and then consider feasible targeting strategies. We have developed several guidelines to assist in segment identification and evaluation. Likewise, important considerations in choosing targeting strategies were discussed.

Cases for Part 4

The 10 cases in Part 4 focus primarily upon market-target decisions and strategies.

CASES

The North Face (Case 4–1) is a high-quality outdoor equipment and clothing manufacturer. It is a market leader in three of its four product categories. The focus of the case is how The North Face can continue to grow; whether it should introduce a new ski wear line and, if so, what strategy should be used.

Case 4–2, U.S. Surgical Corp., describes a rapidly growing company in the surgical supply business. It recently introduced a new line of surgical sutures, a product market dominated by Johnson & Johnson's Ethicon division. This new product line pits U.S. Surgical directly against Ethicon in three major segments of the surgery business. The case describes the competitive environment in which this battle for market share is taking place.

The TenderCare Disposable Diaper case (4–3) concentrates on the planned introduction of a superior diaper. Lawrence Bennett, vice president of marketing at Rocky Mountain Medical Corporation, must quickly decide upon market-target and marketing program positioning strategies for the new product.

L. A. Gear (Case 4–4) founder, chairman and president Robert Greenberg has publicly stated his objective of making L. A. Gear America's number one family brand of athletic footwear. To do this he must attract large numbers of customers with very divergent tastes and preferences. The case provides an overview of some of the challenges facing L. A. Gear and Mr. Greenberg's plans for addressing them.

The Vancouver Public Aquarium (Case 4–5) has just completed its most successful year in history, setting attendance records and opening major new exhibits. But success brings problems. This case describes some of the problems, challenges, and tradeoffs facing this successful nonprofit organization.

Case 4–6 describes Citicorp's effort to launch a new product called POS (point-of-sale) Information Services that would aid marketers in refining their market targeting strategies, monitoring the success of their promotional programs, and provide a host of useful competitive information. In its first six years, the new product lost about $180 million. Management still believes in the innovative product and expects a turnaround. The case describes many of the problems POS Information Services has had in the past and why officials think the program is now on the right track.

Case 4–7, American Greetings, describes the greeting card company's efforts to achieve rapid growth during the early and mid 1980s. In 1986, however, the environment was changing. The focus of the case is on formulating new long-term objectives and strategies.

Case 4–8, Airwick Industries, focuses on the marketing strategy for a product called Carpet Fresh, a rug and room deodorizer. Mike Sheets, president of Airwick, and Wes Buckner, executive vice president of the Consumer Products Division, are interested in developing a plan to increase sales and maintain the brand's competitive position.

The J. C. Penney case (4–9) illustrates problems that Penney's management has had in upgrading the retailing chain's image. Both customers and suppliers have shied away from Penney's because of its past image. Although Penney's has experienced some successes, sales per square foot lag substantially behind industry leaders. What should J. C. Penney management do now?

The final case in Part 4, Minnesota Mining & Manufacturing Co. (4–10), describes 3M's recent growth in foreign sales and the strategies that it uses to enter new markets. The case illustrates 3M's global marketing strategy and results of its commitment to increase efficiency and improve quality.

Case 4–1   The North Face*

The North Face was a privately owned company which designed, man-ufactured, and sold high-quality outdoor equipment and clothing. It began as a specialty mountain shop in San Francisco in 1966, and started manufacturing in Berkeley in 1968. Since that time, the company had emphasized quality backpacking and mountaineering equipment featuring state-of-the-art design and functional detail. The North Face soon dominated this market and became the market leader in three of the four product categories it manufactured—tents, sleeping bags, backpacks and clothing. Sales in 1980 were in excess of $20 million (see Exhibits 1 and 2 for historical financial statements). All items were produced domestically at the company's manufacturing facility in Berkeley. In the early 1980s The North Face operated five well-located retail stores and two factory outlets in the San Francisco Bay area and Seattle. In addition, it employed 14 independent sales representatives who covered 10 sales territories in the United States.

EXHIBIT 1   Profit and Loss Comparisons (in 000s)

	1977	1978	1979	1980
Sales				
Manufacturing	$11,437	$13,273	$15,153	$17,827
Retail	2,254	2,570	2,879	3,368
Total	$13,691	$15,843	$18,032	$21,195
Cost of sales	9,337	11,188	12,443	13,964
Gross margin	4,354	4,655	5,589	7,231
Selling and operating expense	2,186	2,320	2,646	3,306
Contributing to overhead	2,168	2,335	2,943	3,925
Corporate G&A expense	686	685	777	924
Interest expense	242	268	438	658
Incentive compensation and ESOP	235	204	253	330
Total	$ 1,163	$ 1,157	$ 1,468	$ 1,912
Total pretax profits	$ 1,005	$ 1,178	$ 1,475	$ 2,013
Total aftertax profits	$ 498	$ 609	$ 776	$ 1,019

---

* This case was written by Gary Mezzatesta and Valorie Cook, Stanford Graduate School of Business, under the supervision of Professor Robert T. Davis. Reprinted with permission of Stanford University Graduate School of Business, Copyright 1983 by the Board of Trustees of the Leland Stanford Junior University.

EXHIBIT 2   Comparative Balance Sheets (year ended September 30—in 000s)

	1977	1978	1979	1980
Assets				
Current				
Cash	$ 110	$ 149	$ 201	$ 370
Accounts receivable	2,765	3,765	3,910	4,573
Inventories	4,496	4,494	4,452	5,947
Other	319	329	229	196
Long term	803	1,012	1,256	1,437
Other assets	65	68	100	104
Total assets	$8,558	$9,817	$10,148	$12,627
Liabilities				
Current				
Notes payable to bank	$2,624	$3,180	$ 2,563	$ 2,613
Accounts payable	2,019	2,186	2,109	2,231
Accrued liabilities	693	589	627	783
Income taxes payable	318	339	360	568
Current portion LT debt	141	159	222	316
Other				
Long-term debt	351	302	360	1,103
Deferred income taxes	33	73	143	230
Stockholders' equity				
Common stock—A	1,687	1,687	1,687	1,687
Common stock—B	0	2	2	2
Retained earnings	692	1,300	2,075	3,094
Total liabilities	$8,558	$9,817	$10,148	$12,627

Its dealer structure consisted of about 700 specialty shops throughout the United States, as well as representation in 20 foreign countries.

The company's desire for continued growth in the face of a maturing backpacking market prompted Hap Klopp, president of The North Face and the driving force behind its success to date, to investigate expansion into new products related to the current backpacking business. One avenue of growth which appeared to have significant potential was that of Alpine (downhill) ski clothing. This opportunity was pursued, with the result that The North Face Skiwear Line was being readied for formal introduction in fall 1981.

The uppermost question in management minds at this point was, what was the most effective way to distribute the new skiwear line?

EARLY HISTORY

Hap Klopp, 39-year-old president of The North Face and a graduate of the Stanford MBA program, purchased the original company in 1968, following a brief period as manager of another backpacking retail outlet in the San Francisco Bay area. At that time the operation consisted of three retail stores and a small mail-order business. The firm sold a line of private-label backpacking and brand-name downhill ski equipment. Klopp closed two stores, brought in equity, and opened a small manufacturing facility for the production of down-filled sleeping bags in the back of the main store in Berkeley, California. Sales in 1969 were just under $500,000.

Prior to 1971, most of the retail sales were in Alpine (downhill) ski equipment, where competition had depressed the margins. To gain relief, management decided to concentrate on the backpacking and ski touring (cross country) markets, where margins were higher and such adverse influences as seasonality, fashion cycles, and weather conditions were less damaging.

THE NORTH FACE PRODUCTS

The North Face manufactured four key lines for the backpacking market: Sleeping bags, packs, outdoor clothing, and tents. All products stressed quality, design, and durability and were priced for the high end of the market. All products carried a full lifetime warranty.

Sleeping Bags

North Face sleeping bags ranged from "expeditionary" models (designed to provide protection to −40° F) to bags offering various combinations of lightness and warmth (aimed at satisfying the needs of the vacationing, leisure-oriented backpacker). The North Face bags were considered superior to competitive products in construction and durability and offered the optimal trade-off between warmth and weight. As the company grew, TNF expanded the variety of sleeping bags offered to meet virtually every environmental condition that a backpacker could expect in the United States. The quality of down used, the nylon fabric thread count, the unique coil zippers, and the stitching were key points of differentiation. Goose down bags retailed from $162 to $400, with the price escalating as the warmth of the bag increased. Initially, the bags were only down-filled, but in recent years, a complete line of synthetic-filled models was introduced. Synthetic fills were preferred by some for damp weather environments and where weight and compressibility were of lesser importance. Synthetic bags ranged in retail price from $75 to $205—also the top end of the competitive market.

From the start, the company had manufactured only two sizes of sleeping bags instead of the usual three found in the industry. This policy not only simplified production but also reduced retailers' stocking needs and retail stock-outs. When TNF began, sleeping bags had been the fastest growing segment of the backpacking industry, but this growth had begun to slow during the early 1970s.

Parkas and Other Outdoor Clothing

Parkas and functional outerwear were the growth leaders for The North Face in 1981. Their line included a range of parkas designed to appeal to the serious backpacker. Design stressed maximum comfort over a wide temperature range and contained convenient adjustments for ventilation control. Other features such as pocket design, snap-closed flaps over zippers, and large over-stuffed collars further enhanced the line. As the industry grew and fashion became more of an element, a much wider range of color surface fabrics were incorporated into the line. Materials such as Gore-Tex (a breathable yet waterproof material) had been introduced, which offered a functional advantage over existing products on the market. Two types of parkas were offered: those which afforded primary protection from cold, damp conditions (generally of synthetic material); and those which were intended to withstand cold, dry conditions (primarily of down). As in fabrics, a number of new, strongly promoted synthetics, such as Thinsulate, Polarguard, and Hollofill, had been incorporated into the line to meet expanding consumer base and desires. Parkas varied in price from approximately $50 for a synthetic-filled, multipurpose vest to $265 for a deluxe expeditionary model. The company was in the process of trying to sell a system of clothing called "Layering," which utilized multiple layers of clothing combined in a variety of ways to meet climatic conditions.

Tents

In 1981, The North Face had revolutionized the world market for lightweight backpacking tents with its geodesic designs. With assistance from well-known design engineer, R. Buckminster Fuller, the company's employees had created and patented geodesic tents. These tents provided the greatest volume of internal space with the least material and the highest strength to weight ratio of any tent design. They also had more headroom, better use of floor space, and better weather shedding. Because geodesics are free-standing, they also required less anchoring to the earth. Competitors throughout the world were beginning to copy the products; but to date, the company had not legally pursued its patent protection. Other special tent features included reinforced seams and polymer-coated waterproof fabric that management believed provided three times the tear strength and superior performance at subfreezing temperatures. The company had helped develop unique tent poles that were available nowhere else in the world. The North Face still carried two A-frame tents for the purpose of price and continuity of line at $200 and $240 price points while the geodesic line had eight tents ranging from $220 to $600. As with the other North Face products, these were at the high end of the price spectrum; but management was convinced that consumers were getting very good value for their money.

The market for tents had accelerated recently with the introduction of the geodesics, which met new customers' needs better than did A-frame tents. Management felt that two to four years of rapid growth in geodesic tent sales would continue while A-frames were becoming obsolete, and then the market would return to its former modest levels of growth.

Backpacks

The North Face divided the pack market into three segments:

Soft Packs/Day Packs.

Internal Frame Packs.

External Frame Packs.

The North Face introduced the first domestically made internal frame pack, which created a market niche and produced extremely good sales for the company. Retail price ranges from $45 to $115 were at the high end of the scale, but management was sure that the quality details (including extra strength nylon, bartack stitching, extra loops and straps, high-strength aluminum, etc.) made these good values for the money.

In the soft-pack area, there were fewer features to distinguish the company's products from its competitors'. Price competition—with competitors' prices from $16 to $37—was much more noticeable.

In the external frame market, historically dominated by Kelty, the company had introduced a remarkably different, patented product called the Back Magic. It was an articulated pack with independent shoulder and hip suspension, which placed the weight of the pack closer to the backpacker's center of gravity than other packs had done. Although offering an expensive product ($150 to $160) and encountering some bothersome contractor delays, the company was significantly increasing its market share in this category.

Additionally, to expand this category of the company's sales and to open up a whole new market for its dealers, The North Face introduced a complete line of soft luggage in 1981. The company was attempting to capitalize upon the peripatetic nature of its customers and its belief that customers wanted the much higher quality traditionally found in luggage shops. Features such as binding in all seams, leather handles on nylon webbing, shoulder straps with leather handles, and numerous zippered internal pockets were incorporated. Prices ranged from $40 to $65.

MARKETING PHILOSOPHY

The North Face promoted more than just a product, it fostered a way of life. Throughout the ranks of management one found a cadre of outdoor enthusiasts.

It is important to note how Hap Klopp viewed his company's business:

> (The North Face) may be selling bags, tents, packs, boots, or parkas, but I suggest that people are buying better health, social contact, sunshine, adventure, self-confidence, youth, exercise, romance, a change of pace, or a chance to blow off steam and escape from the urban degeneration of pollution, economic collapse, and congestion.

One central theme served as the foundation for The North Face's corporate strategy. It was best summarized by Hap Klopp: "Make the best product possible, price it at the level needed to earn a fair return, and guarantee it forever." Hap contended that profits were not made from the first sale to a customer. After all, it took considerable effort and money to attract that purchase in the first place. Rather, the customer had to be treated well once he had been attracted. Repeat sales were the key to this business's profitability. Hence, there was the need to provide a product that would always satisfy.

A key conceptual tool that North Face used to analyze the backpacking market and similar specialty markets is what Klopp called "the pyramid of influence" (Exhibit 3). Within this hierarchy, management believed that word-of-mouth communication flowed down a chain of expertise from the mountaineer, to the backpacker, to the secondary user, and finally to the general camping public. Those at the high end of the chain, the "technocrats," tended to influence the buying decisions of the average outdoorsman, who relied upon recommendations and brand image rather than his own research. The North Face characterized the market pyramid as follows:

Segment	Use	Price	Preferred Product Characteristics
Mountaineer	Frequent, Hard	No object	Durable Functional Perfect workmanship
Backpacker	Frequent, Careful	Value conscious	Lightweight Repairable Comfortable Brand more important
Secondary user	Inconsistent, Careful	Value conscious	Durable Multipurpose Comfortable Brand name
General camper	Inconsistent, Careless	Price sensitive	Simple Sturdy Multipurpose Brand name

The Company believed that a number of its competitors had made serious marketing blunders in changing their distribution and products to meet the needs of the larger, lower strata, thereby ignoring the pattern of influence of the pyramid and the foundation of the business. This led to the erosion of their name and franchise in all of the strata. In contrast, The North Face's long-term strategy was to maintain an orientation toward the top of the pyramid and quietly broaden the line

EXHIBIT 3   Market Pyramid of Influence

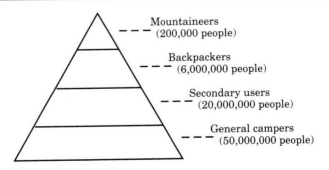

Mountaineers (200,000 people)

Backpackers (6,000,000 people)

Secondary users (20,000,000 people)

General campers (50,000,000 people)

so that its existing dealers would be able to meet the needs of both the peak of the pyramid and the emerging customers.

The North Face adamantly declared that the pattern of influence in specialty markets only worked one way—downward. By designing and selling high-quality, functional items focused at the top of the pyramid, a firm could systematically build a strong market image hinging on credibility. Klopp discounted the integrity and wisdom of the switch from a "top down" to a "bottom up" strategy. Many companies short-sightedly looked at the financials associated with each segment and changed their distribution network and products to meet the larger, lower strata. This process, he claimed, eventually led to failure, since ignoring the foundations of the business eventually caused a "franchise erosion" at all levels of the pyramid. In short, lowering the quality of product and service to maintain sales growth was a no-win game which would inevitably lead to erosion of market and image and to the advancement of someone who was at the top of the cone. If a company wanted to maintain its commitment to a market and customer group for the longer term, it had to stick to the "top down" approach.

Because of its strict adherence to this philosophy, The North Face approached the marketplace with the following strategy: enter specialty markets; nurture them carefully; focus R&D at the top of the pyramid; use specialty shops to skim the market; target promo efforts for trendsetters. Once a dominant position in a market was established growth was sought via two paths:

1. Finding new geographical or new use markets.
2. Introducing new quality products.

The company led the backpacking industry with the following market shares (estimated from available data) in 1980:

	Market Share	*Industry Ranking*
Outerwear/Clothing	47%	1
Sleeping bags	48%	1
Tents	28%	1
Packs	20%	3

The North Face accounted for 21.9 percent of the sales of backpacking products to specialty stores in 1980, while its closest competitor achieved a 13.5 percent market share. In summary, the company's distinctive competence, which distinguished it from its competition, was the manufacture of high-quality, functional products of classic design, which sold at a premium price and carried a lifetime warranty. The key success factors were thought to be the company's reputation as a specialty supplier of quality products, its strong relationship with its

EXHIBIT 4 U.S. Industry Specialty Store Sales of Backpacking Products (wholesale prices—in 000's)*

Year	Total Sales
1971	$15,400
1972	21,600
1973	27,400
1974	40,700
1975	44,800
1976	57,050
1977	65,850
1978	70,400
1979	77,500
1980	81,700
1981†	84,300
1982†	86,900
1983†	90,100
1984†	92,400
1985†	95,100

* Domestic sales only.
† Estimated.

distribution network, and its high-caliber management team. The North Face was generally recognized as having the best management team in the industry, due to its depth of industry knowledge and length of time in the business.

While the backpacking industry had enjoyed substantial growth over the past decade, from total U.S. industry specialty store sales of $15,400,000 in 1971 to $81,700,000 in 1980, the backpacking market appeared to be maturing, with total sales forecasted to grow to $95,100,000 by 1985. (See Exhibit 4 for historical and projected market size.) Klopp believed that the industry was out of the high-growth stage of the product life cycle, heading toward the maturity stages; the increasing difficulty the company reported in achieving product differentiation seemed to validate this observation.

CHANNELS OF DISTRIBUTION

The North Face's reliance on the "pyramid of influence" also dictated its handling of distribution channels. Since they were in specialized markets, The North Face preferred to build its brand name carefully by using specialty stores as a foundation. Once this foundation was established, The North Face attempted to nurture it carefully by providing the dealers with new products and techniques (via training classes) to attract new customers. The company only used the more general sporting goods stores (e.g., Herman's, EMS) when it needed geographic coverage in a particular area, and even then tried to limit distribution to certain outlets of the chain. The firm avoided mass merchandising stores as much as possible. TNF felt that specialty shops developed brand awareness and consumer franchise for their products, while general shops exploited their brand name. Thus, it relied heavily upon the prosperity of these specialty outlets. Careful control of the channels lay at the cornerstone of The North Face's marketing strategy.

Wholesaling

Backpacking industry sales were distributed among retail stores in the following proportions:

	Dollar Value	*Number of Outlets*
Backpacking specialty stores	50%	40%
Sports specialty stores	25	30
General sporting goods stores	10	5
Ski shops, department stores, etc.	15	25

Sales were fairly evenly distributed among the Pacific, North Central, and Northeast regions of the United States, with lesser proportions falling in the Mountain and Southern states.

The North Face sold primarily to approximately 700 retail stores, 75 percent of which specialize in backpacking and mountaineering equipment and the rest in general sporting goods. Wholesale distribution by The North Face was handled by 14 independent sales representatives who carried hiking, mountaineering and cross-country skiing lines. These representatives covered 10 sales territories in the United States and were paid on commission. The North Face products were their major source of income. Management felt that this network was especially valuable as a conduit for information about market conditions, product knowledge, retail management programs, and competition. It was estimated that 55–60 percent of all consumer purchases resulted from word-of-mouth endorsement from a satisfied friend or from a sales presentation in the store. Thus, the primary marketing thrust of The North Face was to (1) sell dealers on the company's products and markets; and (2) provide information and point-of-sale aids to help floor salespeople.

The representatives were crucial to this effort and all were carefully chosen by the sales and marketing vice president and cofounder, Jack Gilbert. As a group, the reps had an average of seven to eight years' experience in the industry, were avid backpackers and lovers of the outdoors, and had been with The North Face since its inception. The reps were highly successful and had been well-treated by the company through the years. Over that time, the nature of their responsibilities had evolved from pioneering or prospecting for new accounts to training existing accounts in industry and management techniques, having established The North Face as the authority in the backpacking field.

The company long pursued a policy of building stable, ongoing relationships with carefully selected dealers. It followed a limited distribution policy, seeking to maintain a balance of dealers and market demand in any geographic area. The company individually reviewed and approved all potential dealer locations, including new locations of existing accounts, and was committed to maintaining and strengthening its dealers. In seeking new product areas in which to expand, it was considered important for The North Face to evaluate the potential of its current dealers to sell the products under consideration.

Retailing

The North Face's retailing objective was to use its own retail stores to attain its desired market share and profit objectives only where wholesaling was unable to achieve satisfactory market penetration and where the policy had no adverse impact on wholesale distribution. To meet this objective, the strategy was to expand existing outlets and introduce new outlets in an orderly fashion, locating only where conflict with the wholesale division was minimized. This strategy was reinforced in the following policy statement:

> The Retail Division will continue to examine expansion possibilities on a local basis. The Retail Division will not expand into any domestic geographic area which will have a significant adverse effect on the wholesale sales of The North Face. The focus of expansion efforts will only be around those areas where The North Face presently has established stores.

The North Face currently owned and operated five well-located retail stores and two factory outlets in the San Francisco Bay area and Seattle. In 1980, the mail order operation was closed down due both to its lack of profitability and its perceived conflict with the wholesaling operations. In recent years, the Retail Division had enjoyed considerable increases in sales and profits, significantly above the industry average:

	1977	1978	1979	1980
Company stores (in 000s):				
Sales	$2,189	$2,574	$2,884	$3,368
Gross margins	N/A	974	1,156	1,446
Profits/contribution	N/A	104	220	364
Inventory turns	1.6X	1.7X	2.1X	2.1X
Transfers to stores	$ 918	$ 908	$ 770	$1,120
(Sales from company wholesale to company retail)				

It should be noted that the "transfer" figures represent sales from company wholesale to company retail. Management felt that not all of these sales would have gone to independents if the company stores did not exist. This is important to consider in looking at The North Face's total profitability. The significance of these figures was underscored by the comparison that the average North Face store bought $200,000 from wholesaling while the average wholesale account bought slightly over $30,000 annually. Additionally, the Retail Division test-marketed some promotional programs and products and, through its factory outlets, took nearly $500,000 of seconds—which otherwise would have created image problems if sold through wholesale channels—as well as products that were made out of overstocked materials supplies. While the exact impact on corporate profit of these activities was hard, if not impossible, to calculate, it was thought to be considerable.

CONFLICT BETWEEN RETAILING AND WHOLESALING

A continual conflict existed between retail and wholesale because of the feeling that retail might expand into an area which was beyond its domain. In part to alleviate this problem, the Retail Division closed down its mail-order operation. The retail expansion into Seattle caused the loss of some wholesale business and was used as a lever by some competitive reps; but since The North Face did not terminate any existing dealers, the issue died. Although there were a number of good wholesale accounts left, The North Face did not sell to them because of the geographical protection it had granted its dealers. The company felt it received increased loyalty and purchases because of this protection and would lose them if its accounts were increased randomly.

Differing opinions on the subject of further retail expansion existed even at the highest levels of the company. At one point, at least, Klopp felt that retail expansion was the most effective means of generating market share and promoting brand-name allegiance, while Jack Gilbert, the sales and marketing vice president, had serious reservations in three areas:

1. *The Impact on the Dealers.* Gilbert felt that retailers in this industry were "very paranoid" that manufacturers would expand their retail operations. Indeed, competitive reps in the industry were known to advise dealers not to "give too much of your business to The North Face because they are out there gathering information about your market area in order to expand their retail operation." He believed that a North Face retail expansion would damage the company's excellent relationship with its dealers.
2. *The Profit Implications.* While the going margin at retail was 40 percent compared to a target margin at wholesale of 30 percent, entry into expanded retail operations was not a profitable strategy in the short run. The initial investment for a store was $40,000 in fixtures and capital improvements, plus $100,000 of inventory at retail prices. It took three years for an individual store to make the contribution management wanted—12 percent contribution to overhead and 8 percent to pretax profits.
3. *Growth.* Finally, Gilbert was concerned about whether The North Face could meet its growth objectives by going both the wholesale and retail routes, particularly given the company's limited financial resources.

Additional concerns regarding inventory control and the development of capable store managers via a training program were voiced by John McLaughlin, financial vice president for The North Face.

OUTLOOK TOWARD GROWTH

Maintaining a healthy rate of growth was also a major goal of management. The style of the company was aggressive and entrepreneurial. Hap and his management team did not want to risk frustrating the young, energetic staff they had gathered. As mentioned earlier, the backpacking industry seemed to be entering the maturity phase of the product life cycle. Over the past few years, the total market was growing only at a 5 percent compound annual growth rate. The North Face had grown at a faster rate than the overall market, consistently gaining market share, but it was evident that this situation would not last forever, especially given the company's reliance on the "pyramid of influence" theory.

In evaluating potential new markets, management looked for opportunities that could fulfill the following objectives:

- An overlap with current customer base.
- A product compatible with current machinery capabilities.
- A line that would complement seasonal production peaks.
- A market in which "top down" strategy would work.
- A line which matched with the interests and expertise of the existing management team.
- A line that would maintain and strengthen The North Face's current dealer network.
- A line that would not threaten or cannibalize the base business.

TNF's decision-making style added further complexity to the situation. The firm espoused a collaborative style of strategy formation and implementation. Employee input and consensus were essential. Hap fostered this environment by utilizing a paternalistic management style. In fact, each individual felt as if he or she had influence on the direction of TNF. In the context of the approaching decision, this meant that marketing needed to receive a general approval before entering a new business.

THE SKIWEAR LINE

The company's desire for continued growth in the face of this maturation of the backpacking market spurred management to investigate expansion into new products. In looking at manufacturing and marketing growth opportunities, the company analyzed its own sales, those of its dealers, and the markets highlighted, to see what opportunities were not being completely exploited. Interestingly, the company found that, although it never manufactured or marketed its products specifically for skiing, it held nearly 2 percent of the skiwear market; in some categories, such as down vests, it had nearly 5 percent. It was also discovered that over two thirds of all dealers handling The North Face products also sold skiwear. Most appealing was the fact that the market appeared to be highly fragmented.

As shown in the table below, and as pointed out in an industry-wide

Market size (1980—in 000s):	
Adult down parkas/vests	$ 30,000
Adult nondown parkas/vests	54,000
Adult bibs and pants	21,000
Shell pants	1,600
X-Country ski clothing	2,600
	$109,200

study published in May 1980: "Most skiwear categories have one or two market leaders, but in all areas no one brand dominates the market. In fact, in all categories studied, it required between 9 and 12 brands to make up 70 percent of the market share in dollars." Exhibits 5 and 6 contain details on the skiwear market.

These factors, coupled with an increasing number of requests for uniforms "which work" (i.e., functional, durable, and warm) from ski instructors, ski patrollers and other professional users thought to influence the market, led The North Face to introduce its skiwear line. The company's strategy in skiwear was predicated on the same strategy as its backpacking business—functionally designed, classically styled clothing. The skiwear was targeted to the "professional skier" (not the racer), since management felt that a Trendsetter and Uniform Program targeted to ski patrollers and lift operators would serve to trigger sales in the same manner that using mountaineers impacted the backpacking pyramid of influence.

EXHIBIT 5   Skiwear* Market Sales 1979–80 (in millions)

	Dollars	*Market Share*
1. White Stag	$ 27.0	12.5%
2. Roffee	19.0	8.8%
3. Skyr	13.5	6.3%
4. Head Ski & Sportswear	13.0	6.0%
5. Aspen	12.5	5.8%
6. Gerry	12.0	5.5%
7. Swing West (Raven)	10.0	4.6%
8. Alpine Designs	9.0	4.2%
9. Obermeyer	8.0	3.7%
10. Sportscaster	7.5	3.5%
11. Beconta	7.0	3.3%
12. Bogner America	7.0	3.3%
13. C.B. Sports	6.0	2.8%
14. Serac	5.0	2.3%
15. Profile	5.0	2.3%
16. Demetre	5.0	2.3%
17. Woolrich	4.5	2.0%
18. The North Face	4.0	1.9%
19. Other	41.0	18.9%
	$216.0	100.0%

* Excluding underwear.

EXHIBIT 6 Estimated Market Share by Segments of Skiwear Market

Down Parkas		Nondown Parkas		Bibs	
Men's	Women's	Men's	Women's	Men's	Women's
1. Gerry 21.7%	1. Gerry 15.0%	1. Roffee 14.6%	1. Roffee 12.4%	1. Skyr 13.7%	1. Roffee 15.0%
1. Roffee 8.6%	2. Slalom 9.8%	2. White Stag 8.7%	2. White Stag 12.3%	2. Roffee 12.4%	2. Skyr 14.6%
3. Alpine Designs 7.4%	3. Roffee 8.7%	3. Skyr 8.0%	3. Skyr 10.6%	3. White Stag 11.0%	3. White Stag 9.1%
4. Powderhorn 5.4%	4. Head 7.8%	4. Head 7.7%	4. Head 10.2%	4. Head 7.2%	4. Head 6.6%
5. Head 5.3%	5. Mountain Goat* 6.1%	5. C.B. Sports 7.2%	5. Slalom 6.2%	5. Beconta 5.2%	5. Slalom 6.5%
6. White Stag 4.7%	6. White Stag 4.7%	6. Serac 5.9%	6. Swing West 5.0%	6. Swing West 4.9%	6. Swing West 4.6%
7. Mountain Goat* 3.6%	7. Tempco 4.2%	7. Cevas 4.6%	7. Bogner 4.4%	7. Gerry 4.1%	7. No. 1 Sun† 4.6%
8. C.B. Sports 3.3%	8. Sportscaster 3.9%	8. Slalom 4.2%	8. Cevas 3.2%	8. Slalom 3.9%	8. Beconta 4.4%
9. Obermeyer 3.1%	9. No. 1 Sun† 3.4%	9. Swing West 4.2%	9. No. 1 Sun† 3.0%	9. No. 1 Sun† 3.8%	9. Gerry 3.8%
10. Sportscaster 2.8%	10. C.B. Sports 3.1%	10. No. 1 Sun† 3.8%	10. C.B. Sports 2.6%	10. Alpine Designs 3.7%	10. Bogner 3.1%
11. All other 33.6%	11. All other 33.8%	11. All other 31.1%	11. All other 30.1%	11. All other 30.1%	11. All other 27.7%

* Second brand name of White Stag.
† Second brand name of Head.

ISSUES WITH SKIWEAR

The decision to introduce skiwear was also not without some problems. Although a majority of the dealers carried skiwear, some did not. The latter might oppose "The North Face" trade name going into another local store, even if it was part of a product line they did not carry. Further, the current dealers were not always the most influential top end shops required to build a market, and their ski departments might not take The North Face's ski-oriented products as seriously as they did the company's backpacking offerings. Similarly, some of the best ski shops which influenced the entire market were not presently The North Face outlets. Out of a total market size of over 3,000 Alpine ski dealers, only about 475 were currently carrying The North Face products. Moreover, the sales reps already had a very extensive line and it was a concern of management that they might have difficulty pushing the ski items during the critical start-up phase. Further, this expansion into a new area in effect required the established sales reps to "start over" again with prospecting for new accounts, a task which might tax their capabilities and desires.

Different complications arose in each of TNF's markets. The following example from a metropolitan center in California highlights some critical issues.

At the time of the skiwear decision, TNF distributed its backpacking products primarily through one large, specialty backpacking/skiing shop in the city. Suburban neighborhood stores were utilized for additional coverage. The city store ranked amongst the top 20 percent of TNF dealers. In the past, TNF had rewarded this supplier by withholding merchandise from direct competitors.

TNF serviced this account with regular visits of the local sales representative, frequent visits by sales managers, an annual dealer seminar, and periodic information-gathering visits by top management. The store's annual sales topped $1 million, with 65–70 percent of this deriving from backpacking products. Sales of TNF items accounted for the majority of backpacking revenue. TNF management felt that this shop, as the largest specialty shop in the area, "made" the area backpacking market. TNF developed consumer awareness via close association with this outlet and by regular co-op advertisements. In short, if a serious local backpacker needed equipment, he would most likely shop at this store.

In backpacking, this shop had little formidable competition. Some second-tier specialty shops existed, but they offered less ease of access and a narrower product range. A wide variety of general sporting goods shops also competed in the territory. These stores each had backpacking sections but did not emphasize service. TNF did not associate with these stores.

EXHIBIT 7   Partial Organization Chart

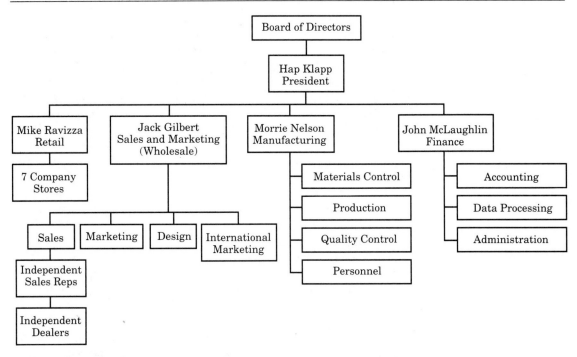

Backgrounds:
Mike Ravizza, Retail—Joined The North Face in 1969; Stanford undergraduate.
Jack Gilbert, Sales & Marketing—Co-founder of The North Face in 1968; Stanford undergraduate.
Morrie Nelson, Manufacturing—Joined The North Face in 1975; University of Washington undergraduate, Santa Clara MBA.
John McLaughlin, Finance—Joined The North Face in 1970; Dartmouth undergraduate, Stanford MBA.

Unfortunately, the skiing market was much more fragmented in this territory. Although TNF's key backpacking account also sold skiing products, it did not have a dominant position. The store was one of the handful of large dealers that handled skiwear. It did not "make the market." Instead, it often reacted to the environment in setting pricing, merchandising, and product selection policies. In addition, five comparably sized ski specialty shops (no backpacking gear at all) competed in this territory. Each shop carried roughly the same product line frequently featuring loss leadership on hardware (Rossignol, Nodica, Lange, etc.). Soft goods were the primary profit maker. The offerings emphasized aesthetics and functionality.

TNF management obviously faced a serious problem in introducing the skiwear line in this market. On the one hand, TNF owed special consideration to its key backpacking account. But management also realized that this account alone would not develop sufficient brand awareness as a pioneer for the skiwear line. The key account's owner was concerned about losing backpacking sales if TNF decided to offer its products to other area shops. In this territory, as in others, TNF needed to act quickly and carefully.

Case 4–2   U.S. Surgical Corp.*

Leon Hirsch, the chairman of U.S. Surgical Corp., sold 100,000 of his company's shares last August at $45 apiece. He sold too soon. The stock now fetches $122.50.

But Mr. Hirsch isn't looking back. Riding his company's growing reputation for innovative technology and its soaring sales, he is declaring war on Johnson & Johnson, the king of surgical supplies.

At a big meeting of nurses in Atlanta last week, U.S. Surgical unveiled its first line of sutures. J&J's Ethicon division makes more than 80 percent of the sutures sold in the United States and claims two thirds of the $1.3 billion business worldwide, but Mr. Hirsch isn't daunted. "Our sutures come out of the package straight and smooth," he says. "Theirs come out kinked and rough."

Nearly a decade of research went into developing the new sutures, and Mr. Hirsch is betting that a lot of surgeons will switch to his line. But Ethicon, acknowledging the kink problem, countered by rolling out its own kink-free sutures at the nurses' meeting.

The showdown involves a lot more than stitching. For the first time, U.S. Surgical can go head-to-head against Ethicon in three major segments of the surgery business. It dominates the other two: staplers, used for closing incisions and other tasks, and so-called endoscopic instruments, used in a fast-growing technique in which doctors do gallbladder and other surgery through small holes instead of wide gashes in the abdomen.

The U.S. market for the three segments could triple to $3 billion by 1995, and some analysts think that by then U.S. Surgical will overtake Ethicon as the top supplier to the nation's surgeons. But as the new,

* Source: Ron Winslow, "Major Operation," *The Wall Street Journal*, April 16, 1991, pp. A1, 4. Reprinted by permission of *THE WALL STREET JOURNAL*, © 1991 Dow Jones & Company, Inc. All Rights Reserved Worldwide.

minimally invasive procedures grow from 70,000 last year to an expected two million or more a year by the mid-1990s, the real prize will be leadership in the technological changes transforming surgery.

Reflecting U.S. Surgical's dominant status in endoscopy equipment—by far the fastest-growing segment of the surgery market—the company is expected to report today that its first-quarter earnings soared more than 60 percent from a year earlier. For all of last year, earnings climbed 50 percent to $46 million and revenue 49 percent to $514.1 million. Some analysts expect U.S. Surgical to be a $1 billion company by next year (see Exhibit 1).

EXHIBIT 1   U.S. Surgical: Trying to Sew Up a Market

To keep profit rising . . .
Annual net income, in millions

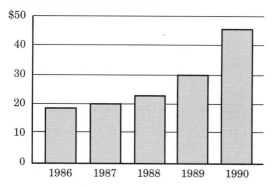

In a competitive market . . .
Domestic surgical supply market share, in percent

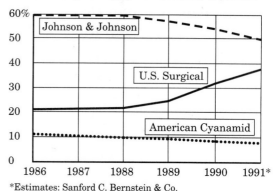

*Estimates: Sanford C. Bernstein & Co.

It goes after sutures . . .
Estimated 1991 domestic suture market, in percent

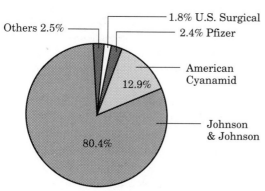

Tries to make investors happy.
Monthly closing price of U.S. Surgical's stock

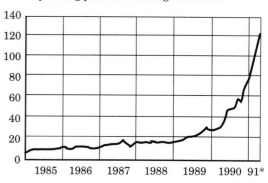

*Estimates: Sanford C. Bernstein & Co.

Caught flat-footed at first by the pace of change, Ethicon currently runs a distant second in instruments for endoscopic surgery (often called laparoscopy). But it recently pledged a major offensive to close the gap; among other moves, it plans to quadruple its engineering staff from 1989 levels to 230 this year, and a slew of new products are starting to hit the market.

"Our effort will be as focused, intense and ambitious as any we have ever embarked upon," vows Ralph S. Larsen, J&J's chairman and chief executive. "We are prepared to do whatever it takes to assure success."

Doctors and buyers for hospitals hail the rivalry as a spur to innovation and quality and a potential check on price. Both companies are "very hungry," says Jonathan Sackier, director of surgical endoscopy at Cedars Sinai Medical Center in Los Angeles. "They're pushing out extremely good new products at an amazing rate."

Although other companies are also scrambling for this business, the main event will be between J&J and Mr. Hirsch, whom Kurt Kruger, a Hambrecht & Quist securities analyst, calls "the pit bull of the wound-closure business." As each company takes aim at the other's strength, the combat has intensified to surgery's version of the cola wars.

The University of California at Davis has to run an "Ethicon Day" and a "U.S. Surgical Day" in its courses that train doctors in new surgical techniques because Mr. Hirsch, like an incumbent ahead in the polls, won't share such a platform with Ethicon. "We're happy to go head-to-head," says David Murray, Ethicon's vice president for marketing.

When administrators at Johns Hopkins Hospitals signed a contract with Ethicon for staplers a couple of years ago, U.S. Surgical salespeople complained to doctors, who, in turn, complained to Mr. Hirsch. He then traveled to Baltimore to dress down the institution's purchasing officials. "The surgeons kept asking for our product and they were given Ethicon's," he says.

To defend its suture line, Ethicon contested every request U.S. Surgical made to the Food and Drug Administration to exempt its sutures from lengthy clinical trials. Ethicon lost all seven decisions and several appeals, but the legal maneuvers delayed U.S. Surgical's marketing plans by two years.

Mr. Hirsch, a former peddler of coin-operated dry-cleaning equipment, is no stranger to conflict. But until U.S. Surgical's stock surged, he made more headlines in tussles with animal rights groups opposed to the company's use of dogs in research and sales training and with the Securities and Exchange Commission than with competitors.

In 1984, the SEC charged the company with overstating earnings by falsifying purchase orders, shipping unordered products to hospitals while booking them as sales, and other securities-law violations. The company didn't admit to any wrongdoing, but it restated three years of earnings and consented to a court order barring future violations. By settling, the company avoided $10 million in legal fees, Mr. Hirsch says, but the incident cost him $317,000 in bonuses and years of respect on Wall Street. He says the matter was provoked by a disgruntled former employee and "was just plain hogwash."

Such controversies, however, didn't distract the company from relentlessly pursuing its most important constituency: surgeons. Its 650-person sales force—including 375 in the United States—has taught thousands of doctors how to use staplers, which it invented more than 20 years ago and has developed into a business running $400 million a year and growing 20 percent annually. Its salespeople spend much of the workweek in surgery, providing what Mr. Hirsch calls "technical assistance" to doctors using the company's products.

Sometimes, says Bruce Wolfe, chief of gastrointestinal surgery at UC Davis, the salespeople "are a little too forward in telling doctors how to do their surgery." But Dr. Wolfe adds: "They've been highly trained in how to use their equipment, and surgeons in these parts respect them."

That respect has paid huge dividends to U.S. Surgical as doctors begin to switch to minimally invasive surgery for gallbladder patients. Most of the 15,000 doctors who learned the operation last year did so at courses supported by U.S. Surgical and staffed by sales representatives demonstrating its products.

Among those products are trocars, sharp-pointed tubes that serve as ports of entry into the abdominal cavity for surgical instruments and a tiny camera that displays a patient's innards on a monitor. The doctor watches the monitor while manipulating the instruments. The typical gallbladder procedure requires four keyhole-sized slits, not the traditional six- to eight-inch incision.

Last year, 70,000 patients underwent the procedure, and most of the 600,000 people who have gallbladder surgery each year are considered candidates for it.

In addition, some doctors use the technique for appendectomies, hysterectomies and treatments for hernias, ulcers and other ills. It's possible that, in a few years, trocars could be used in two million cases annually. Trocars, as well as many trocar-compatible instruments on the market or under development, are used just once and discarded. Both U.S. Surgical and Ethicon sell disposable gallbladder kits that include most of the required accessories, and they plan similar packages for other procedures.

And, seeking to develop new instruments, they are working closely with physicians they consider leaders in various fields. For example, Ethicon engineers are working with Thierry Vancaillie, who with colleagues at the Texas Endoscopy Institute in San Antonio has started using endoscopy for colon surgery.

Ethicon is stepping up its support of physician training courses, and it expects to benefit from the clout of its parent, J&J. For instance, an anti-adhesion compound already on the market for other uses and a wound-healing agent under development in another division may be included in the kits for various endoscopic procedures. J&J even makes a surgical drape especially designed for the operation.

In a market so new, the company insists, an early lead means little. "In the long run," says David Clapper, Ethicon's vice president for product management, "the endoscopy explosion is the best thing that's happened to Ethicon."

U.S. Surgical, however, currently claims about 90 percent of the endoscopic business. Its clip applier, used to seal off ducts and vessels, is preferred by doctors because it holds several clips; Ethicon's must be removed from the abdomen and reloaded after each use.

While the endoscopic business is expected to grow 40 percent a year, sutures plod along, with sales rising only about 5 percent annually. Sutures involve a broad range of special technologies ranging from microneedles used in eye surgery to the wire thread used to close chests after bypass operations. Bought in bulk, they are more price-sensitive than other U.S. Surgical products. Kaiser Permanente, the big Oakland, Calif., health-maintenance organization, puts price tags on sutures in surgical supply rooms to encourage doctors to avoid a $12 stitch if a $2 one will do.

But thanks to sutures, Ethicon's domestic sales last year exceeded $1.5 million per salesperson, compared with less than $1 million at U.S. Surgical. Moreover, Ethicon often ties discounts on sutures to purchases of its staplers and trocars, an attractive deal for hospitals seeking to cut costs and control inventories.

With its own sutures, U.S. Surgical can blunt that advantage. Its sutures are packaged in a maze-like circular channel, and as a nurse pulls one out, it hangs straight. By contrast, Ethicon's absorbable Vicryl sutures used to come in a figure-eight package that caused the thread, when pulled out, to kink up like an accordion.

Mr. Hirsch claims other advantages: a smoother, stronger thread that passes easily through tissue and a needle that is sharper and readily accessible when the package is opened. A comparison of the products staged by sales reps at U.S. Surgical headquarters last month appeared to convince a small group of doctors.

But the doctors didn't see Ethicon's improved line. Needles made with a new, proprietary alloy are sharper, and some have grooves on the inside of the shaft to provide a firmer grip. The absorbable suture retains 40 percent of its strength in the body after three weeks, against 20 percent previously. And its new "relay" package gives nurses easy access to the needles and replaces the figure-eight with an "oval wind" that practically eliminates kinks.

In the early 1980s, when Ethicon had about 30 percent of the U.S. suture market against the then-dominant Davis & Geck division of American Cyanamid Co., Ethicon launched a new, coated version of Vicryl. Its salespeople prowled hospital corridors, wads of string dangling from their pockets, to buttonhole doctors, and they propelled Ethicon to its current dominance in sutures. Says Mr. Clapper: "You go to the ultimate customer—the surgeon—and sell, sell, sell."

Mr. Hirsch couldn't have said it better.

Case 4–3   *TenderCare Disposable Diapers**

Tom Cagan watched as his secretary poured six ounces of water onto each of two disposable diapers lying on his desk. The diaper on the left was a new, improved Pampers, introduced in the summer of 1985 by Procter & Gamble. The new, improved design was supposed to be drier than the preceding Pampers. It was the most recent development in a sequence of designs that traced back to the original Pampers, introduced to the market in 1965. The diaper on his right was a Tender-Care™ diaper, manufactured by a potential supplier for testing and approval by Cagan's company, Rocky Mountain Medical Corporation (RMM). The outward appearance of both diapers was identical.

Yet the TenderCare diaper was different. Just under its liner (the surface next to the baby's skin) was a wicking fabric that drew moisture from the surface around a soft, waterproof shield to an absorbent reservoir of filler. Pampers and all other disposable diapers on the market kept moisture nearer to the liner and, consequently, the baby's skin. A patent attorney had examined the TenderCare design, concluding that the wicking fabric and shield arrangement should be granted a patent. However, it would be many months before results of the patent application process could be known.

As soon as the empty beakers were placed back on the desk, Cagan and his secretary touched the liners of both diapers. They agreed that there was no noticeable difference, and Cagan noted the time. They repeated their "touch test" after one minute and again noted no difference. However, after two minutes, both thought the TenderCare diaper to be drier. At three minutes, they were certain. By five minutes, the

---

* This case was written by Professor James E. Nelson, University of Colorado. Some data are disguised. © 1986 by the Business Research Division, College of Business and Administration and the Graduate School of Business Administration, University of Colorado, Boulder, Colorado 80309-0419.

TenderCare diaper surface seemed almost dry to the touch, even when a finger was pressed deep into the diaper. In contrast, the Pampers diaper showed little improvement in dryness from three to five minutes and tended to produce a puddle when pressed.

These results were not unexpected. Over the past three months, Cagan and other RMM executives had compared TenderCare's performance with 10 brands of disposable diapers available in the Denver market. TenderCare diapers had always felt drier within a two- to four-minute interval after wetting. However, these results were considered tentative because all tests had used TenderCare diapers made by RMM personnel by hand. Today's test was the first made with diapers produced by a supplier under mass manufacturing conditions.

ROCKY MOUNTAIN MEDICAL CORPORATION

RMM was incorporated in Denver, Colorado, in late 1982 by Robert Morrison, M.D. Sales had grown from about $400,000 in 1983 to $2.4 million in 1984 and were expected to reach $3.4 million in 1985. The firm would show a small profit for 1985, as it had each previous year.

Management personnel as of September 1985 included six executives. Cagan served as president and director, positions held since joining RMM in April 1984. Prior to that time he had worked for several high-technology companies in the areas of product design and development, production management, sales management, and general management. His undergraduate studies were in engineering and psychology; he took an MBA in 1981. Dr. Morrison currently served as chairman of the board and vice president for research and development. He had completed his M.D. in 1976 and was board certified to practice pediatrics in the state of Colorado since 1978. John Bosch served as vice president of manufacturing, a position held since joining RMM in late 1983. Lawrence Bennett was vice president of marketing, having primary responsibilities for marketing TenderCare and RMM's two lines of phototherapy products since joining the firm in 1984. Bennett's background included an MBA received in 1981 and three years' experience in groceries product management at General Mills. Two other executives had also joined RMM in 1984. One served as vice president of personnel; the other as controller.

Phototherapy Products

RMM's two lines of phototherapy products were used to treat infant jaundice, a condition experienced by some 5 to 10 percent of all newborn babies. One line was marketed to hospitals under the trademark

Alpha-Lite. Bennett felt that the Alpha-Lite phototherapy unit was superior to competing products because it gave the baby 360-degree exposure to the therapeutic light. Competing products gave less complete exposure, with the result that the Alpha-Lite unit treated more severe cases and produced quicker recoveries. Apart from the Alpha-Lite unit itself, the hospital line of phototherapy products included a light meter, a photo-mask that protected the baby's eyes while undergoing treatment, and a "baby bikini" that diapered the baby and yet facilitated exposure to the light.

The home phototherapy line of products was marketed under the trademark Baby-Lite.™ The phototherapy unit was portable, weighing about 40 pounds, and was foldable for easy transport. The unit when assembled was 33 inches long, 20 inches wide, and 24 inches high. The line also included photo-masks, a thermometer, and a short booklet telling parents about home phototherapy. Parents could rent the unit and purchase related products from a local pharmacy or a durable-medical-equipment dealer for about $75 per day. This was considerably less than the cost of hospital treatment. Another company, Acquitron, Inc., had entered the home phototherapy market in early 1985 and was expected to offer stiff competition. A third competitor was rumored to be entering the market in 1986.

Bennett's responsibilities for all phototherapy products included developing marketing plans and making final decisions about product design, promotion, pricing, and distribution. He directly supervised two product managers, one responsible for Alpha-Lite and the other for Baby-Lite. He occasionally made sales calls with the product managers, visiting hospitals, health maintenance organizations, and insurers.

TenderCare Marketing

Right now most of Bennett's time was spent on TenderCare. Bennett recognized that TenderCare would be marketed much differently than the phototherapy products. TenderCare would be sold to wholesalers, who in turn would sell to supermarkets, drugstores, and mass merchandisers. TenderCare would compete either directly or indirectly with two giant consumer-goods manufacturers, Procter & Gamble and Kimberly-Clark. TenderCare represented considerable risk to RMM.

Because of the uncertainty surrounding the marketing of Tender-Care, Bennett and Cagan had recently sought the advice of several marketing consultants. They reached formal agreement with one, a Los Angeles consultant named Alan Anderson. Anderson had extensive experience in advertising at J. Walter Thompson. He had also had responsibility for marketing and sales at Mattel and Teledyne, specifically for the marketing of such products as IntelliVision,™ the Shower Massage,™ and the Water Pik.™ Anderson currently worked as an independent marketing consultant to several firms. His contract with RMM specified that he would devote 25 percent of his time to Tender-Care the first year and about 12 percent the following two years. During this time, RMM would hire, train, and place its own marketing personnel. One of these people would be a product manager for Tender-Care.

Bennett and Cagan also could employ the services of a local marketing consultant who served on RMM's advisory board. (The board consisted of 12 business and medical experts who were available to answer questions and provide direction.) This consultant had spent over 25 years in marketing consumer products at several large corporations. His specialty was developing and launching new products, particularly health and beauty aids. He had worked closely with RMM in selecting the name TenderCare, and had done a great deal of work summarizing market characteristics and analyzing competitors.

MARKET CHARACTERISTICS

The market for babies' disposable diapers could be identified as children, primarily below age 3, who use the diapers, and their mothers, primarily between ages of 18 and 49, who decide on the brand and usually make the purchase. Bennett estimated there were about 11 million such children in 1985, living in about 9 million households. The average number of disposable diapers consumed in these households was thought to range from zero to 15 per day and to average about seven.

The consumption of disposable diapers is tied closely to birth rates and populations. However, two prominent trends also influence consumption. One is the disposable diaper's steadily increasing share of total diaper usage by babies. Bennett estimated that disposable diapers would increase their share of total diaper usage from 75 percent currently to 90 percent by 1990. The other trend is toward the purchase of higher-quality disposable diapers. Bennett thought the average retail price of disposable diapers would rise about twice as fast as the price of materials used in their construction. Total dollar sales of disposable diapers at retail in 1985 were expected to be about $3.0 billion, or about 15 billion units. Growth rates were thought to be about 14 percent per year for dollar sales and about 8 percent for units.

Foreign markets for disposable diapers would add to these figures. Canada, for example, currently consumed about $0.25 billion at retail, with an expected growth rate of 20 percent per year until 1990. The U.K. market was about twice this size and growing at the same rate.

The U.S. market for disposable diapers was clearly quite large and growing. However, Bennett felt that domestic growth rates could not be maintained much longer because fewer and fewer consumers were available to switch from cloth to disposable diapers. In fact, by 1995, growth rates for disposable diapers would begin to approach growth rates for births, and unit sales of disposable diapers would become directly proportional to numbers of infants using diapers. A consequence of this pronounced slowing of growth would be increased competition.

COMPETITION

Competition between manufacturers of disposable diapers was already intense. Two well-managed giants—Procter & Gamble and Kimberly-Clark—accounted for about 80 percent of the market in 1984 and 1985. Bennett had estimated market shares at:

	1984	1985
Pampers	32%	28%
Huggies	24	28
Luvs	20	20
Other brands	24	24
	100%	100%

Procter & Gamble was clearly the dominant competitor with its Pampers and Luvs brands. However, Procter & Gamble's market share had been declining, from 70 percent in 1981 to about 50 percent today. The company had introduced its thicker Blue Ribbon™ Pampers recently in an effort to halt the share decline. It had invested over $500 million in new equipment to produce the product. Procter & Gamble spent approximately $40 million to advertise its two brands in 1984. Kimberly-Clark spent about $19 million to advertise Huggies in 1984.

The 24 percent market share held by other brands was up by some 3 percentage points from 1983. Weyerhaeuser and Johnson & Johnson manufactured most of these diapers, supplying private-label brands for Wards, Penneys, Target, Kmart, and other retailers. Generic disposable diapers and private brands were also included here, as well as a number of very small, specialized brands that were distributed only to local markets. Some of these brands positioned themselves as low-cost alternatives to national brands; others occupied premium ("designer") niches with premium prices. As examples, Universal Converter entered the northern Wisconsin market in 1984 with two brands priced at 78 and 87 percent of Pampers' case price. Riegel Textile Corporation's Cabbage Patch℠ diapers illustrated the premium end, with higher prices and attractive print designs. Riegel spent $1 million to introduce Cabbage Patch diapers to the market in late 1984.

Additional evidence of intense competition in the disposable diaper industry was the major change of strategy by Johnson & Johnson in 1981. The company took its own brand off the U.S. market, opting instead to produce private-label diapers for major retailers. The company had held about 8 percent of the national market at the time and decided that this simply was not enough to compete effectively. Johnson & Johnson's disposable diaper was the first to be positioned in the industry as a premium product. Sales at one point totaled about 12 percent of the market but began to fall when Luvs and Huggies (with similar premium features) were introduced. Johnson & Johnson's advertising expenditures for disposable diapers in 1980 were about $8 million. The company still competed with its own brand in the international market.

MARKETING STRATEGIES FOR TENDERCARE

Over the past month, Bennett and his consultants had spent considerable time formulating potential marketing strategies for TenderCare. One strategy that already had been discarded was simply licensing the design to another firm. Under a license arrangement, RMM would receive a negotiated royalty based on the licensee's sales of RMM's diaper. However, this strategy was unattractive on several grounds. RMM would have no control over resources devoted to the marketing of TenderCare: the licensee would decide on levels of sales and advertising support, prices, and distribution. The licensee would control advertising content, packaging, and even the choice of brand name. Licensing also meant that RMM would develop little marketing expertise, no image or even awareness among consumers, and no experience in dealing with packaged-goods channels of distribution. The net result would be that RMM would be hitching its future with respect to TenderCare (and any related products) to that of the licensee. Three other strategies seemed more appropriate.

The "Diaper Rash" Strategy

The first strategy involved positioning the product as an aid in the treatment of diaper rash. Diaper rash is a common ailment, thought to affect most infants at some point in their diapered lives. The affliction usually lasted two to three weeks before being cured. Some infants are more disposed to diaper rash than others. The ailment is caused by "a reaction to prolonged contact with urine and feces, retained soaps and topical preparations, and friction and maceration" (Nelson's *Text of Pediatrics,* 1979, p. 1884). Recommended treatment includes careful washing of the affected areas with warm water and without irritating soaps. Treatment also includes the application of protective ointments and powders (sold either by prescription or over the counter).

The diaper rash strategy would target physicians and nurses in either family- or general-practice and physicians and nurses specializing either in pediatrics or dermatology. Bennett's estimates of the numbers of general or family practitioners in 1985 was approximately 65,000. He thought that about 45,000 pediatricians and dermatologists were practicing in 1985. The numbers of nurses attending all these physicians was estimated at about 290,000. All 400,000 individuals would be the eventual focus of TenderCare marketing efforts. However, the diaper rash strategy would begin (like the other two strategies) where approximately 11 percent of the target market was located—California. Bennett and his consultants agreed that RMM lacked resources sufficient to begin in any larger market. California would provide a good test for TenderCare because the state often set consumption trends for the rest of the U.S. market. California also showed fairly typical levels of competitive activity.

Promotion activities would emphasize either direct mail and free samples or in-office demonstrations to the target market. Mailing lists of most physicians and some nurses in the target market could be purchased at a cost of about $60 per 1,000 names. The cost to print and mail a brochure, cover letter, and return postcard was about $250 per 1,000. To include a single TenderCare disposable diaper would add another $400 per thousand. In-office demonstrations would use registered nurses (employed on a part-time basis) to show TenderCare's superior dryness. The nurses could be quickly trained and compensated on a per-demonstration basis. The typical demonstration would be given to groups of two or three physicians and nurses and would cost RMM about $6. The California market could be used to investigate the relative performance of direct mail versus demonstrations.

RMM would also advertise in trade journals such as the *Journal of Family Practice, Journal of Pediatrics, Pediatrics,* and *Pediatrics Digest.* However, a problem with such advertisements was waste coverage because none of the trade journals published regional editions. A half-page advertisement (one insertion) would cost about $1,000 for each journal. This cost would be reduced to about $700 if RMM placed several advertisements in the same journal during a one-year period. RMM would also promote TenderCare at local and state medical conventions in California. Costs per convention were thought to be about $3,000. The entire promotion budget as well as amounts allocated to direct mail, free samples, advertisements, and medical conventions had yet to be decided.

Prices were planned to produce a retail price per package of 12 TenderCare diapers at around $3.80. This was some 8 to 10 percent higher than the price for a package of 18 Huggies or Luvs. Bennett thought that consumers would pay the premium price because of TenderCare's position: the pennies-per-day differential simply would not matter if a physician prescribed or recommended TenderCare as part of a treatment for diaper rash. "Besides," he noted, "in-store shelf placement of TenderCare under this strategy would be among diaper rash products, not with standard diapers. This will make price comparisons by consumers even more unlikely." The $3.80 package price for 12 TenderCare diapers would produce a contribution margin for RMM of about 9 cents per diaper. It would give retailers a per-diaper margin some 30 percent higher than that for Huggies or Luvs.

The Special-Occasions Strategy

The second strategy centered around a "special-occasions" position that emphasized TenderCare's use in situations where changing the baby would be difficult. One such situation was whenever diapered infants traveled for any length of time. Another occurred daily at some 10,000 day-care centers that accepted infants wearing diapers. Yet another came every evening in each of the 9 million market households when babies were diapered at bedtime.

The special-occasions strategy would target mothers in these 9 million households. Initially, of course, the target would be only the estimated one million mothers living in California. Promotion would aim particularly at first-time mothers, using such magazines as *American Baby* and *Baby Talk*. Per-issue insertion costs for one full-color, half-page advertisement in such magazines would average about $20,000. However, most baby magazines published regional editions where single insertion costs averaged about half that amount. Black-and-white advertisements could also be considered; their costs would be about 75 percent of the full-color rates. Inserting several ads per year in the same magazine would allow quantity discounts and reduce the average insertion cost by about one third.

Lately, Bennett had begun to wonder if direct-mail promotion could instead be used to reach mothers of recently born babies. Mailing lists of some 1 to 3 million names could be obtained at a cost of around $50 per 1,000. Other costs to produce and mail promotional materials would be the same as those for physicians and nurses. "I suppose the real issue is, just how much more effective is direct mail over advertising? We'd spend at least $250,000 in baby magazines to cover California while the cost of direct mail would probably be between $300,000 and $700,000, depending on whether or not we gave away a diaper." Regardless of Bennett's decision on consumer promotion, he knew RMM would also direct some promotion activities toward physicians and nurses as part of the special-occasions strategy. Budget details were yet to be worked out.

Distribution under the special-occasions strategy would have TenderCare stocked on store shelves along with competing diapers. Still at issue was whether the package should contain 12 or 18 diapers (like Huggies and Luvs) and how much of a premium price TenderCare could command. Bennett considered the packaging and pricing decisions interrelated. A package of 12 TenderCare diapers with per-unit retail prices some 40 percent higher than Huggies or Luvs might work just fine. Such a packaging/pricing strategy would produce a contribution margin to RMM of about 6 cents per diaper. However, the same pricing strategy for a package of 18 diapers probably would not work. "Still," he thought, "good things often come in small packages, and most mothers probably associate higher quality with higher price. One thing is for sure—whichever way we go, we'll need a superior package." Physical dimensions for a TenderCare package of either 12 or 18 diapers could be made similar to the size of the Huggies or Luvs package of 18.

The Head-On Strategy

The third strategy under consideration met major competitors in a direct, frontal attack. The strategy would position TenderCare as a noticeably drier diaper that any mother would prefer to use anytime her baby needed changing. Promotion activities would stress mass advertising to mothers, using television and magazines. However, at least two magazines would include a dollar-off coupon to stimulate trial of a package of TenderCare diapers during the product's first three months on the market. Some in-store demonstrations to mothers using "touch tests" might also be employed. Although no budget for California had yet been set, Bennett thought the allocation would be roughly 60 : 30 : 10 for television, magazines, and other promotion activities, respectively.

Pricing under this strategy would be competitive with Luvs and Huggies, with the per-diaper price for TenderCare expected to be some 9 percent higher at retail. This differential was needed to cover additional manufacturing costs associated with TenderCare's design. TenderCare's package could contain only 16 diapers and show a lower price than either Huggies or Luvs with their 18-count packages. Alternatively, the package could contain 18 diapers and carry the 9 percent higher price. Bennett wondered if he really wasn't putting too fine a point on the pricing/packaging relationship. "After all," he had said to Anderson, "we've no assurance that retailers or wholesalers would pass along any price advantage TenderCare might have due to a smaller package. Either one or both might instead price TenderCare near the package price for our competitors and simply pocket the increased margin!" The only thing that was reasonably certain was TenderCare's package price to the wholesaler. That price was planned to produce about a 3-cent contribution margin to RMM per diaper, regardless of package count.

Summary of the Three Strategies

When viewed together, the three strategies seemed so complex and so diverse as to defy analysis. Partly the problem was one of developing criteria against which the strategies could be compared. Risk was obviously one such criterion; so were company fit and competitive reaction. However, Bennett felt that some additional thought on his part would produce more criteria against which the strategies could be compared. He hoped this effort would produce no more strategies; three were plenty.

The other part of the problem was simply uncertainty. Strengths, weaknesses, and implications of each strategy had yet to be given much thought. Moreover, each strategy seemed likely to have associated with it some surprises. An example illustrating the problem was the recent realization that the Food and Drug Administration (FDA) must approve any direct claims RMM might make about TenderCare's efficacy in treating diaper rash. The chance of receiving this federal agency's approval was thought to be reasonably high; yet it was unclear just what sort of testing and what results were needed. The worst-case scenario would have the FDA requiring lengthy consumer tests that eventually would produce inconclusive results. The best case could have the FDA giving permission based on TenderCare's superior dryness and on results of a small-scale field test recently completed by Dr. Morrison. It would be probably a month before the FDA's position could be known.

"The delay was unfortunate—and unnecessary," Bennett thought, "especially if we eventually settle on either of the other two strategies." In fact, FDA approval was not even needed for the diaper rash strategy if RMM simply claimed (1) that TenderCare diapers were drier than competing diapers and (2) that dryness helps treat diaper rash. Still, a single-statement, direct-claim position was thought to be more effective with mothers and more difficult to copy by any other manufacturer. And yet Bennett did want to move quickly on Tender-Care. Every month of delay meant deferred revenue and other postponed benefits that would derive from a successful introduction. Delay also meant the chance that an existing (or other) competitor might develop its own drier diaper and effectively block RMM from reaping the fruits of its development efforts. Speed was of the essence.

FINANCIAL IMPLICATIONS

Bennett recognized that each marketing strategy held immediate as well as long-term financial implications. He was particularly concerned with finance requirements for start-up costs associated with the California entry. Cagan and the other RMM executives had agreed that a stock issue represented the best option to meet these requirements. Accordingly, RMM had begun preparation for a sale of common stock through a brokerage firm that would underwrite and market the issue. Management at the firm felt that RMM could generate between $1 and $3 million, depending on the offering price per share and the number of shares issued.

Proceeds from the sale of stock had to be sufficient to fund the California entry and leave a comfortable margin remaining for contingencies. Proceeds would be used for marketing and other operating expenses as well as for investments in cash, inventory, and accounts receivable assets. It was hoped that TenderCare would generate a profit by the end of the first year in the California market and show a strong contribution to the bottom line thereafter. California profits would contribute to expenses associated with entering additional markets and to the success of any additional stock offerings.

Operating profits and proceeds from the sale of equity would fund additional research and development activities that would extend RMM's diaper technology to other markets. Dr. Morrison and Bennett saw almost immediate application of the technology to the adult incontinent diaper market, currently estimated at about $300 million per year at retail. Underpads for beds constituted at least another $50 million annual market. However, both of these uses were greatly dwarfed by another application, the sanitary napkin market. Finally, the technology could almost certainly be applied to numerous industrial products and processes, many of which promised great potential. All these opportunities made the TenderCare situation that much more crucial to the firm; making a major mistake here would affect the firm for years.

Case 4–4   L.A. Gear*

Here in the Galleria, the infamous mecca for pubescent mall prowlers, L.A. Gear Inc.'s trademarked pastel sneakers and screaming fluorescent togs have been marked down at some stores. "They have the stuff that's, like, yesterday's news," says 17-year-old Jennifer Vanderbort, a salesgirl at the mall.

At Nautilus/Aerobics Plus in Studio City, where many young women in Spandex body suits used to wear L.A. Gear's silver and gold lame workout shoes, L.A. Gear "had its time. But Nike is the hottest thing out now," says Diana Garrett, the health club's 22-year-old receptionist. In nearby Flintridge, high-schooler Kate Krappman, 14, says of L.A. Gear: "They're going downhill really fast."

If some Valley Girls are getting bearish on L.A. Gear, so are some traders and investors on Wall Street.

The price of L.A. Gear's stock, the Big Board's largest gainer in the first nine months of 1989, nearly tripled to $46.75 a share. Then in the past few weeks it sank by almost a third as investors were unnerved by a string of surprises: a criminal investigation into alleged underpayment of customs duties, the lowering of earnings estimates by a securities analyst, and the resignation last Friday of the company's chief financial officer. Yesterday the stock closed down 87.5 cents at $33.75 a share, which is nearly 30 percent below its 1989 high.

Short-sellers, spreading rumors of ruin, have played their part. The management's effort to discredit them hasn't been helped by insider selling.

None of this might have made so much difference but for L.A. Gear's dependence on the whims of fashion.

It took founder, Chairman and President Robert Greenberg only six years to parlay a $5,000 license to market "E.T.: The Extra Terrestrial" shoelaces—he sold $3 million worth—into a shoe and clothing business with $600 million in sales. But L.A. Gear could tumble down in a fraction of that time if its hot sneakers with their sunshiny good looks suddenly got frosted in the malls.

Many investors remember what happened to the stock of Reebok International Ltd. when its earnings dropped last year. After peaking

---

* Source: David J. Jefferson, "Fashion Victim? L.A. Gear, a Firm Built on Fads, Fades a Bit with Both Investors and Sneaker Buyers," *The Wall Street Journal*, December 8, 1989, pp. 1, A4. Reprinted by permission of *THE WALL STREET JOURNAL*, © 1989 Dow Jones & Company, Inc. All Rights Reserved Worldwide.

at $18.375 a share, Reebok stock plunged to $10.50. It since has recovered, closing unchanged yesterday at $18.75.

Not to worry, says Mr. Greenberg, 49, who along with the rest of L.A. Gear's executives favors open-collar Italian linen shirts and slacks. "People criticize us for being a trend company. But General Motors depends on trends and fads, Pepsi does, Coke does. Diet drinks and small cars—aren't those trends and fads?" Actually, Mr. Greenberg adds, L.A. Gear really doesn't *set* any trends. "That's too risky," he says. "We follow the trends, and we don't bet the farm on them."

Any erosion in the consumer market has yet to appear in L.A. Gear's financials. Its sales for the fiscal year ended Nov. 30 are estimated to have reached some $600 million, up from $223.7 million in 1988. The order backlog nearly tripled, too, to an estimated $240 million. If the year's net income amounted to $3.10 or so a share—Merrill Lynch's latest estimate, lowered from $3.25—it still would have more than doubled fiscal 1988's adjusted $1.29 a share (see Exhibit 1).

Mr. Greenberg is so flush with success that he now boasts he'll make L.A. Gear "America's No. 1 family brand," sprinting past Reebok and Nike in athletic footwear. He has printed up "L.A. Gear: 1 in '91" T-shirts and caps for his executives.

But first, he must guide his young, quirky company through a tricky transition, attracting more men and adult women buyers and enhancing L.A. Gear's name overseas. At the same time he must create newer and funkier styles to keep the teen-agers *totally* satisfied.

And the competition is tough: Nike still keeps its grip on the market for performance sneakers, while Reebok is battling in L.A. Gear's backyard with an expanding Los Angeles design office to stay atop West Coast trends.

To lessen its dependence on teen-age girls by selling more men's shoes, L.A. Gear has signed on basketball stars Kareem Abdul-Jabbar, Akeem Olajuwon and Karl Malone as L.A. Gear pitchmen. To attract women outside the 13- to 25-year-old group, the company has signed actress Priscilla Presley. To keep the teens happy and broaden its international appeal, the company has entered into a two-year, $20 million-plus contract with Michael Jackson for a Jackson line of shoes and clothes.

International sales have jumped to $52 million from $20 million in fiscal 1988. L.A. Gear soon will sell in 100 countries, including the Soviet Union. Sales of L.A. Gear apparel and fashion watches accounted for an estimated 7.5 percent of all fiscal 1989 sales, up from less than 1.5 percent in 1988. Many of the clothes are generic "blanks," made in the Far East, with an L.A. Gear logo slapped on to bring a hefty markup domestically.

The battle for the men's market is uphill. The company has had trouble breaking away from its teeny-bopper roots, and men's athletic

EXHIBIT 1   L.A. Gear: Has the Runner Stumbled?

Sales keep growing . . .
Revenue in millions of dollars

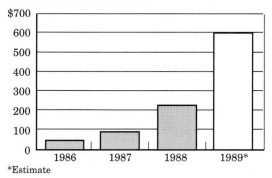

*Estimate

It's a success in the market . . .
Estimated share of 1989 U.S. market
for athletic shoes

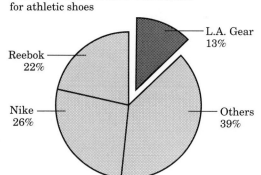

Reebok 22%
L.A. Gear 13%
Nike 26%
Others 39%

And earnings keep climbing . . .
Net income in millions of dollars

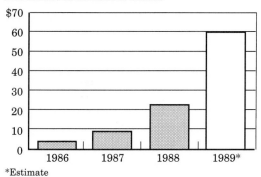

*Estimate

But its stock dropped recently.
Monthly close

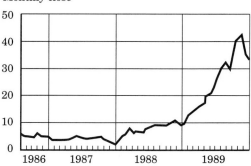

shoes constitute only 23 percent of its sales; they make up about 70 percent of the sales of other athletic footwear companies.

"I maybe still have some reservations that they can just go in and penetrate that men's market," says James Hines, vice president and corporate director of marketing footwear for Oshman's sporting goods chain. Oshman's has done limited test-marketing of L.A. Gear in its California stores. "There're a lot of people who've been in there a long time, and it's pretty hard to go in from a dead start and compete," Mr. Hines says.

The push to be all things to all consumers threatens to blur L.A. Gear's identity. "First they sign Kareem and position themselves as a performance product, and now they sign Michael Jackson, who is the consummate rock star and probably the person who would most appeal to the teen-agers of the world. What does that say about the image of the company? Are they themselves getting confused?" asks John Gillis, communications vice president of a fledgling sneaker maker, Ryka Inc., and a former spokesman for Reebok. Reebok learned the hard way about blurring its identity with a disastrously oblique "U Be U" marketing campaign.

Mr. Greenberg sees no such problems for L.A. Gear. "This company is not a sporting-goods company like Nike and Reebok," he says. "It's a fashion company. It's about looking pretty for women and looking good for men."

Mr. Greenberg has ridden fads and fashions since he enrolled in a Boston beauty school as a teen-ager. In the 1960s he imported wigs from the Orient to capitalize on the popularity of *faux manes*. He got into skin-tight jeans, and then into roller skates after a visit to the Venice Beach boardwalk, a palm-lined strip in Los Angeles that resembles a roller derby for the barely clad. When he couldn't move more skates he sold the shoelaces alone, and bagged his $3 million from the E.T. craze in just three months.

His shoelace coup gave birth to the existing company. It began in early 1983 as a manufacturer and grew into a retail clothing outlet with lots of neon and loud music on trendy Melrose Avenue in Los Angeles. There Mr. Greenberg and crew peddled sportswear embossed with a name and logo they felt conveyed the active, breezy Southern California life style. The L.A. Gear logo features a sunburst seal encircling a scene of Los Angeles' obelisk-like City Hall surrounded by palm trees.

Mr. Greenberg decided to get into sneakers in 1984, when Reebok, in Canton, Mass., was taking off, and L.A. Gear's Melrose store was losing money. His key decision was to sell not only to sporting goods stores, the usual outlet for brand-name athletic shoes, but also to department stores and women's shoe chains.

When Reebok found itself unable to fill orders for its popular black and white athletic shoes in 1987, L.A. Gear met the demand with its flashy sneakers. Its advertisements featured young California blondes in skimpy attire, inspiring the nickname "L.A. Rear."

That was coined by John Horan, publisher of the Sporting Goods Intelligence trade publication. The industry truism that athletic shoes are made more for marketing than for running and jumping was one that "L.A. Gear recognized right up front," Mr. Horan says. "So L.A. Gear goes over to the Far East, buys a basic shoe, puts funny trim on it, or a leather doohickey, and then spends the rest on advertising. And forgetting my personal opinion about the ads, there's a very close association between L.A. Gear's marketing and its sales success."

It costs roughly $15 to produce a typical pair of L.A. Gear sneakers that sells at wholesale for $30 and at retail for $60.

The company will spend $50 million on advertising this fiscal year, up from $30 million in fiscal 1989; Reebok and Nike each have spent about $60 million on advertising in the past year. L.A. Gear executive vice president Sandy Saemann, who grew up and still lives in nearby Manhattan Beach, directs and produces the company's commercials inhouse, rather than employ Madison Avenue, and creates much of the advertising himself.

A large man with a silver necklace and emerald pinky ring, Mr. Saemann takes pride in having no formal artistic training. He says he won awards for his product displays when he was a grocery clerk. "It's just a natural thing I have," he says.

Michael Jackson was sold on dealing with L.A. Gear by its tight control over the creative process, Mr. Saemann says, slapping a new L.A. Gear/Jackson sneaker, the "Unstoppable," on his desk. The black and white hightop, available in stores next spring, resembles a space boot from Mr. Jackson's 3-D Disney movie "Captain E-O," but with "L.A. Gear" embossed prominently in five places. "He loves the way we market him," Mr. Saemann asserts.

L.A. Gear nurtures its marketing muse in an environment not given to understatement. The just-departed financial officer's white Mercedes-Benz coupe has a license plate that reads "GEAROTC"—a play on "erotic" and on "Gear—Over the Counter," where its stock was once traded. At a meeting in Marina del Rey last month, L.A. Gear's 150 sales representatives cheered like students at a pep rally as blondes in fluorescent L.A. Gear beachwear bounced through a haze of dry-ice vapor down a lighted runway to the beat of an old tune by the Jackson 5, Michael's family.

The company cultivates its ability to pounce on trends. In a design studio that resembles an art school, just behind Mr. Greenberg's office at L.A. Gear's Marina del Rey headquarters, a dozen artists in their 20s turn fads into footwear. A woman works on a prototype with fringe, buckles and cute little cartoon coyotes—sneakers a la Tex-Mex. Another dons a brown bolero hat and new pair of black sneakers with chains and studs, which she'll wear to a nearby disco to gauge the reaction from the Madonna wanna-be's.

A mirrored conference room is stacked with designs: sneakers with black chiffon laces, sneakers with clown faces, sneakers that look like Army boots, even sneakers that look like sneakers. Mr. Greenberg, who visits shopping malls and sometimes poses as a shoe salesman to monitor teens' tastes, creates many of the ideas. "The lines now are just the yummiest lines we've ever had," he says.

Some have asserted that the atmosphere at L.A. Gear is too free and easy. In a complaint in a wrongful termination suit in October 1987, filed in California state court and since settled, former national sales manager Dino Lamparello alleged that he "began to observe the practice of using of illicit drugs, particularly cocaine and marijuana, by defendant employer's top executives . . . both in social settings and, on occasion, in the office." An attorney for L.A. Gear calls the assertions "scurrilous allegations, which all of the defendants have denied."

On Wall Street, L.A. Gear's rapid rise owed as much to its tightly controlled image-making as it did to its earnings performance. From early on, the company made a point of letting investors know how well it was doing, and quarter after quarter volunteered its earnings projections to the Dow Jones News Service.

In making itself so visible the company also has exposed itself to criticism. Rumors that in many cases may have been generated by short sellers have dogged it, despite being aggressively challenged by the company. Last summer rumor had it that a shipload of L.A. Gear sneakers had sunk into the Pacific. It hadn't, but Elliot Horowitz, then chief financial officer, quickly informed Wall Street that he insures all shipments at full retail price.

Last month another rumor had it that L.A. Gear was offering retailers special incentives to take deliveries before the end of the fiscal year. The company denied it, although it is offering such incentives this month, as it did last December.

Another rumor has more basis in fact.

The buzz from Wall Street bears last week was that Mr. Horowitz had sold 70,000 shares of his L.A. Gear stock just prior to the company's announcement of a Massachusetts federal grand jury investigation into the possible underpayment of customs duties on shipments from Taiwan a few years back. In an interview last week, Mr. Horowitz said he did sell some stock on Nov. 10, five days before the announcement, but that the 70,000 figure is "way off."

He declined to provide other specifics, but he noted that he still held options on 250,000 shares. He is one of several executives who have taken some profits on their holdings in recent months.

People close to the federal customs-duty investigation say that, at worst, L.A. Gear could be hit with a $1 million penalty.

On Monday, L.A. Gear announced that Mr. Horowitz had resigned after the board proposed a new employment contract. It would have cut his pay. His former contract awarded him bonuses tied to the company's earnings, giving him compensation of about $4.5 million this past year.

Messrs. Greenberg and Saemann had similar contracts, but have now negotiated new one-year agreements that cap their pay. The caps are $5 million for Mr. Greenberg and $4.5 million, plus the value of stock options, for Mr. Saemann. The unrealized profit on Mr. Greenberg's 3.6 million shares had shrunk in recent weeks to a low of $115 million from a peak of nearly $170 million.

Mr. Greenberg acknowledges that he has lots of tinkering to do at L.A. Gear, but he says he and the company are in business for the long haul. "It's kind of like nuclear fission," he says. "If you get it right it works forever. But it's a very delicate balance."

Case 4–5   *Vancouver Public Aquarium**

Richard Knight, public relations director for the Vancouver Public Aquarium, reread the memo he had just received from Elizabeth Dewey, the aquarium's educational programs coordinator. Ms. Dewey had proposed that, starting the following fall, the Vancouver Aquarium restrict weekday admissions to only school tours during the hours from 10:00 A.M. to 3:00 P.M., and exclude the general public during those hours.

During the 1986–87 school year, the Vancouver Public Aquarium (VPA) offered five formal educational programs for students from kindergarten to grade 12. Further, the aquarium's trained guides (docents) gave children guided tours which included various performances offered to the general public. Though these tours were successful, there was evidence that both individual visitors and the schools felt that the aquarium could be better utilizing their facilities. For instance, some members of the general paying public found it irritating to browse through the galleries with "all the screaming kids around." Also, the teachers felt that the feeding performances, one of the highlights of the aquarium, could be geared more to the predominantly younger weekday market. Because the school market was important to the aquarium and weekday attendance by the general paying public was low, Mr. Knight felt that he must examine the proposal fully before giving Ms. Dewey a response.

BACKGROUND

31 YEARS

The VPA opened its doors on June 3, 1956, in Vancouver's Stanley Park, a popular recreational area adjacent to downtown Vancouver (Exhibit 1). Accessible by bus or car, the park was centrally located

---

* This case was prepared by Grant N. Poeter and Charles B. Weinberg of the University of British Columbia. Used with permission.

EXHIBIT 1 Aquarium Location Map

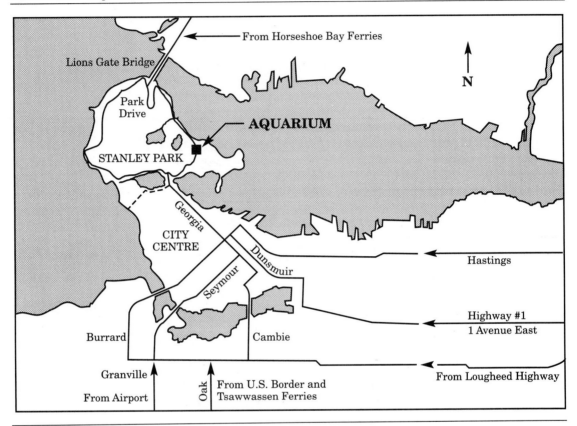

within the Greater Vancouver Regional District (GVRD), an association of Vancouver and its surrounding communities (Burnaby, North Vancouver, Richmond, West Vancouver, and others). Most of the GVRD's population of 1.3 million people lived within ten miles of Stanley Park.

The aquarium's facilities had undergone numerous renovations in the 30 years following its opening. In 1967, the B.C. Telephone Pool was constructed to hold dolphins, but the aquarium acquired a killer whale (orca) instead. It quickly became evident that the pool was unsuitable for such a large mammal, and so in 1972, the killer whale pool was opened. In conjunction with these outdoor "gallery" changes, the aquarium continued to improve its indoor exhibits. Perhaps the most significant indoor change was the addition of the Amazon Gallery, which recreated the environment of an Amazon River valley. Opened in 1983 by Queen Elizabeth II, the Amazon Gallery, with its 2,200 specimens, was the only indoor exhibit of its kind in the world. Designed and constructed to house only killer whales, this exhibit set what many experts viewed as the world standard in both exhibit philosophy and animal husbandry.

DANGER OF ONE A ONE TSTK SPOT

With Expo '86, Vancouver's 100th birthday, and the aquarium's 30th birthday, 1986 was a record year for attendance with 876,825 visitors (Exhibit 2). Increasing attendance beyond that level was a challenge that faced Mr. Knight.

EXHIBIT 2   Annual Attendance, 1982–1986

Attendance	*1982*	*1983*	*1984*	*1985*	*1986*
Paid					
Adults	216,161	257,400	237,312	248,742	329,334
Youths & senior citizens	76,123	84,276	70,713	79,285	—
Groups	43,465	45,665	46,605	34,983	55,280
Education programs	10,580	6,226	8,983	14,638	—
Family rate	166,696	181,107	166,736	120,409	196,481
Children & seniors	—	—	—	—	86,186
Youths	—	—	—	—	22,784 *@ 2.25*
	513,025	574,674	530,349	498,057	690,065
Other attendance					
Members	54,783	91,891	73,604	66,963	73,148
Other	70,399	89,003	99,614	87,162	113,612
Total	638,207	755,568	703,567	652,182	876,825
Single admission					
Adults	$ 4.25 ea	$ 4.50 ea	$ 4.50 ea	$ 5.00 ea	$ 5.25 ea
Senior citizens	$ 2.00 ea	$ 2.25 ea	$ 2.25 ea	$ 2.50 ea	$ 2.75 ea
Youths (5–18 yrs.)	$ 2.00 ea	$ 2.25 ea	$ 2.25 ea	—	—
Youths (12–18 years)	—	—	—	$ 3.75 ea	—
Youths	—	—	—	—	$ 4.00 ea
Children	—	—	—	$ 2.50 ea	$ 2.75 ea
Group admission					
Family	$10.00	$11.00	$11.00	$13.00	$13.25
Adults, 10–34 persons	$ 3.00	$ 3.25	$ 3.25	—	—
35 or more	$ 2.50	$ 2.75	$ 2.75	—	—
Adults, 10 or more	—	—	—	$ 3.75	$ 4.00
Youths, 10 or more	$ 1.25	$ 1.50	$ 1.50	$ 2.00	$ 2.25

CURRENT OFFERINGS

In 1987, the aquarium housed some 7,100 specimens (669 species) of marine and aquatic life. Its sea otter breeding program was most successful and had helped to preserve this once endangered species; since 1983, five pups had been born at the aquarium. The aquarium saw itself as being on the leading edge of both marine research and display of mammals and Northern Pacific marine species.

The main product offered to visitors by the aquarium was the opportunity to see its collection of aquatic life. Related species were housed in "galleries," usually by geographic region. In addition, the aquarium offered whale shows, films, tours, and special showings (such as "Fishes of China"), all included in the admission price. There were no restaurants or food services on the aquarium's grounds, although a number of food stands were located nearby in Stanley Park.

The aquarium also offered several secondary products. It had rented its facilities for social functions; companies could have staff parties, meetings, and dinner/dances in the various galleries; for children, birthday parties, complete with cake, were available. The aquarium also offered special lectures and school programs on aquatic life. Members could take advantage of whale watching tours, beach walks, and special previews. These programs had been very successful.

The aquarium also ran a retail operation, the Clam Shell Gift Shop, which sold aquarium-related books, animal prints, nature calendars, and numerous aquarium souvenirs.

MISSION

The VPA stated its mission as follows:

> The Vancouver Aquarium is dedicated to the preservation and enhancement of aquatic life through education, recreation, and research. It is a private, non-profit society, and is completely self-supporting.

> This mission statement was the driving force behind the aquarium. Every program had to fit into one of the three categories in the statement; all staff were required to follow its guidelines. As expressed by VPA staff and literature, the aquarium's main business was to educate the public about aquatic life. The aquarium accomplished this through such activities as demonstrations and interpretive programs. In particular, the VPA offered numerous programs—such as lectures, tours, and beach walks—to educate school children, teens, and adults.

MARKETS

During the past two years, the aquarium's average weekday attendance in winter had been 550 patrons per day (Exhibit 3). Weekends were busier, with Saturdays averaging 1,300 patrons and Sundays averaging 2,100. Mr. Knight felt that Saturday's attendance could be higher, possibly reaching Sunday's levels.

During the summer, there was still a difference between weekdays and weekends but general attendance levels were higher. In fact, the weekday levels were more than double those of the winter months.

The aquarium had at least six significant markets: schools, members, general admissions, donors, volunteers, and scientists. Mr. Knight felt that the first five markets would be affected by any decision relating to school tour admissions.

Members

By the end of 1986, the Vancouver Public Aquarium Association had 39,360 members, based on the sale of 15,077 memberships (up from 11,850 in 1985) to individuals, couples, and families. Members accounted for 73,148 of the aquarium's total attendance of 876,825.

Diverse programs were offered to this group, which ranged from special educational programs to free admission to the aquarium; educational programs included whale watching in Johnstone Strait, previews of special displays, Galiano Island beach walks, and behind-the-scenes tours. Members received a 10 percent discount on giftshop purchases and an informative newsletter, called the *Sea Pen*, about once a month.

Mr. Knight realized that the membership was vital to the aquarium's finances and philosophy. He wondered how the members would react to not being allowed to use "their" aquarium on demand.

General Admissions

According to the 1986 Annual Report, the general admissions category accounted for 61 percent of revenues (Exhibit 4). A recent study of summer visitors found that 97 percent of those surveyed felt they had received good value for their entertainment dollar. The aquarium offered various programs to educate and entertain this public. For example, there were feeding shows, interpretive talks, films, and volunteers to answer exhibit enquiries. In addition, the aquarium was open for extended hours during the summer.

EXHIBIT 3   Average Daily Attendance for 1985 and 1986

Month	Monday	Tuesday	Wednesday	Thursday	Friday	Saturday	Sunday	Holidays	Total
1985									
January	436	493	400	391	434	1,399	2,157	1,036	26,147
February	725	545	395	376	949	1,301	2,622	0	26,644
March	832	712	707	818	1,042	2,139	2,866	1,293	44,267
April	928	812	746	858	888	1,944	2,508	2,420	54,335
May	1,458	1,041	1,085	1,214	1,283	2,144	3,081	3,105	50,452
June	1,883	2,157	1,646	1,882	2,155	2,365	3,189	0	66,664
July	4,361	3,314	3,822	3,694	3,357	3,858	4,181	4,052	119,047
August	3,731	3,801	4,221	3,477	3,268	4,161	4,992	5,436	123,214
September	957	1,121	1,081	968	1,489	2,287	3,265	3,883	49,136
October	957	678	578	419	957	1,764	1,694	1,687	28,271
November	405	274	498	378	347	925	1,961	2,831	21,916
December	340	341	359	249	254	532	1,475	1,482	29,263
Winter average*	616	507	491	439	664	1,343	2,129	1,388	29,418
Total average	1,418	1,274	1,296	1,227	1,369	2,068	2,833	2,269	53,280
1986									
January	447	401	350	311	535	1,426	2,289	1,452	28,341
February	475	401	585	494	750	1,027	1,675	0	21,622
March	687	523	553	709	758	1,798	2,596	2,633	41,076
April	672	641	684	635	586	1,261	1,741	2,162	34,483
May	1,614	1,997	2,613	2,080	1,928	3,244	3,366	4,746	79,204
June	3,396	3,825	3,711	3,662	3,496	4,409	4,763	0	117,200
July	6,342	5,615	5,819	5,173	5,715	6,472	6,950	4,609	182,367
August	6,238	5,810	6,142	5,290	4,944	5,450	6,622	7,550	180,315
September	2,152	1,966	2,361	2,711	2,231	3,417	4,304	5,209	82,848
October	688	978	1,041	869	1,202	2,005	2,813	2,740	43,540
November	406	442	535	327	555	1,029	1,277	1,840	22,021
December	434	443	341	382	307	523	1,216	1,832	29,402
Winter average*	523	531	568	515	685	1,301	1,978	1,750	31,000
Total average	1,963	1,920	2,061	1,887	1,917	2,672	3,301	2,898	71,868

* January, February, March, October, November, December.

454

EXHIBIT 4 Annual Financial Reports, 1982–1986 (in 000s)

Revenue	1982 $	1982 %	1983 $	1983 %	1984 $	1984 %	1985 $	1985 %	1986* $	1986* %
Admissions	$1,612	70%	$1,989	70%	$1,855	71%	$1,937	69%	$2,786	61%
Gross margin/store	268	12	303	11	308	12	313	11	894	20
Membership fees	198	9	300	10	278	11	288	10	409	9
Deferred income transfer	101	4	100	4	—	—	—	—	—	—
Donations; grants	84	4	84	3	83	3	148	5	226	5
General operating revenue	44	2	69	2	74	3	134	5	232	5
Total	$2,308	100%	$2,844	100%	$2,599	100%	$2,820	100%	$4,548	100%
Expenditure										
Specimen care; display	$ 670	29%	$ 868	31%	$ 790	30%	$ 563	20%	$ 941	25%
Engineering; operations	597	26	714	26	668	25	751	27	—	—
Administration	359	15	414	15	392	15	673	24	—	—
Attendance; membership	353	15	398	14	414	15	385	14	—	—
Education; research	344	15	404	14	425	16	407	15	—	—
Life support/building operations	—	—	—	—	—	—	—	—	875	23
Administration; services	—	—	—	—	—	—	—	—	652	17
Store; admissions	—	—	—	—	—	—	—	—	513	14
Education; visitor services	—	—	—	—	—	—	—	—	339	9
Promotion	—	—	—	—	—	—	—	—	229	6
Member services	—	—	—	—	—	—	—	—	130	3
Scientific studies	—	—	—	—	—	—	—	—	109	3
Total	$2,323	100%	$2,798	100%	$2,698	100%	$2,779	100%	$3,789	100%

* In 1986, the VPA implemented a new accounting system with redefined accounts.

The VPA's primary market was the Greater Vancouver Regional District. This area accounted for 28 percent of summer admissions and for 65 percent of off-season visitors (see Appendix). A second market was the province of British Columbia, outside Greater Vancouver.

Other areas served included the Pacific Northwest of the United States to the south and the province of Alberta to the east. Though no programs were designed for these markets, visitors from these areas did patronize the aquarium during the summer months.

During the summer months, visitor parking, although free, could be a problem. Unfortunately, the VPA could do little to alleviate this problem because adjacent land in Stanley Park could not be appropriated for extra parking.

Donors

The donor market was seen as very important for the aquarium. Without donor support, many of the aquarium's capital projects could not have been completed. For instance, some 17,000 individuals, 130 corporations, 4 foundations, and the federal government contributed more than $4.3 million to build the Max Bell Marine Mammal Centre. The aquarium recognized donors in various ways, including plaques, exhibit names (like the H. R. MacMillan Tropical Gallery), and publication of donors' names in VPA publications.

Volunteers

72 HRS on average

The 180 VPA volunteers, made up of Aquarium Association members and their families, volunteered 13,000 hours to the aquarium in 1986. They supervised educational tours, served as docents for school tours, and worked in the Clam Shell gift shop. Management believed that the main attractions for volunteers were their sense of pride in the aquarium and genuine concern for its success.

Schools

Over 7,500 students took part in the following VPA educational programs in the most recent year:

Water Wonders (kindergarten, grades 1 and 2).

Secrets of Survival (grades 3 and 4).

Mysterious Marine Mammals (grades 5, 6, 7).

Spineless Wonders (a laboratory program) (grades 5, 6, 7).

B.C.'s Marine Invertebrates (a laboratory program) (grades 11 and 12).

Royaume Aquatique (French-speaking groups).

Travelling Teacher (outreach program—an aquarium teacher visiting schools).

In addition to these formal programs, tours of the aquarium, films, and interpretive workshops were offered to school groups. To accommodate French immersion classes, the aquarium offered French-language tours. There was also a "travelling teacher," employed by the aquarium, who toured the province teaching students in out-of-town schools about aquatic life and the work being done by the aquarium.

To make teachers aware of the aquarium's programs, each school in the Vancouver area received a descriptive brochure at the beginning of the school year. During the third week of September, the VPA offered an "Open House for Educators" that gave teachers the opportunity to participate in workshops, preview the programs offered, and pick up various resource materials. Afterwards, teachers could book their classes into the programs and tours.

These programs were very popular. Usually most available spaces for the formal programs were filled by the second week in October. During the school year, the aquarium averaged five school tours per day. At present, the aquarium could handle no more than six tours in a day. Though school groups were given special group rates and a volunteer was provided to guide the tours, no other special accommodations were offered by the aquarium.

Ms. Dewey's memo offered one possible response to the popularity of these programs. Her memo read, in part, as follows:

> During the recent professional development programs, held by my department, many teachers expressed some disappointment in their inability to book their students into the aquarium's programs . . . With such a demand for these programs, an increase in service to the children of Vancouver will be beneficial to both parties. First, if the aquarium were to offer more programs, the aquarium would increase exposure and also help revenues. Second, the children would be more aware of the work done by the aquarium and may become active aquarium members in the future.
>
> To accomplish this increase in school programs, we would need to set aside certain hours for the use by students. Since most school tours are conducted in the mornings and early afternoons, we propose that these tours be run between the hours of 10 A.M. and 3 P.M. During these hours only children and their supervisors would be able to view the galleries . . . This would at least double our current capacity for handling school tours. If such a program were adopted, the feedings and interpretive segments could be targeted to a younger population. Though it would be more work at the beginning, I feel that such a program could be very successful.

Ms. Dewey's proposal would require the VPA to alter its presentations (such as the killer whale feedings) to better suit a school-age audience and to restrict the VPA's galleries to school children until 3 P.M. on weekdays. Closing the galleries to the general public on school days would have two effects on the VPA's operation. First, the "conflict" between the general public and school tours would be eliminated; the public would not be fighting the crowds of school children. However, the frustrations of aquarium members and the general admission market might shift from annoyance with the school children to anger at not being allowed admission at all. Secondly, the Clam Shell Gift Shop's hours of operation could be reduced; the shop would not need to be open during the hours of school tours. Currently, the aquarium used two full-time salaried employees and one part-time staff member, in addition to volunteers, to handle admissions and run the gift shop during weekdays. If the proposal were adopted, the aquarium's staffing needs could be reduced by at least one paid position during the school tour periods.

Mr. Knight sat down to do a preliminary study to see if the proposal was economically feasible. During the winter months, an average of 550 people per day visited the aquarium on weekdays. Of these 550, roughly 70 percent were "general admissions" (385 persons). A "typical" weekday group consisted of two adults ($5.50 each) and one child ($3). Mr. Knight felt that for the school proposal to be implemented, revenues from the school programs would have to be increased to cover at least part of the $1,700 loss of general admissions revenues. Of course, some proportion of the weekday visitors would come another time. There was also the possibility of opening the aquarium to general admission after 3 P.M., but currently few winter visitors came at that time.

School admissions were priced at $2.50 per student and the average school group's size was 34 students. Mr. Knight wondered if the aquarium, particularly the volunteer guides, could handle a significant increase in school tours. If not, could the aquarium attract new volunteer docents? He was relatively confident that the aquarium would not have to hire more paid staff.

PRICING AND PROMOTIONS

VPA's prices were to be increased by an average of 10 percent on April 1, 1987 (Exhibit 5). Adult admission would then cost $5.50, a price that included both the killer whale and beluga whale shows, tours, seal feedings, films, and entrance to all galleries.

Pricing policy was ultimately determined by the Vancouver Public Aquarium Association membership through its Board of Governors.

EXHIBIT 5   Price List (as of April 1, 1987)

General Admission	Price	Membership Fee	Price
Adult	$ 5.50	Adult	$20.00
Youth or Senior	$ 4.25	Special*	$15.00
Child	$ 3.00	Couple†	$30.00
Family	$14.00	Family	$35.00
Groups (10+)			
Adult	$ 4.25		
Child	$ 2.50		
School	$ 2.50		

* This group included students, out-of-province residents, and seniors.

† A senior couple could purchase a membership for $15.00.

Source: Vancouver Public Aquarium's Annual Report.

Though the board had the final say, most pricing changes were initiated by VPA staff. The pricing policy was cost-oriented. The aquarium budgeted its expenditures for the coming year and then set ticket prices, membership fees, etc., to balance these expenses. Discounting practices were usually reserved for the aquarium's membership and groups of 10 people or more.

The aquarium had two short-term promotional pricing programs. Both were offered in December and were marketed as the aquarium's gift to the city. During the first week in December, general admission was free. In 1986, 6,906 people took advantage of this opportunity. There were occasional other free days. For example, on March 9, 1987, the aquarium had a free day to thank Vancouver for its generous support of the Tropical Fish Gallery restocking. An astounding 12,000 people visited the aquarium.

The second promotion was the Christmas train program, which the aquarium participated in for the first time in 1986. In conjunction with Vancouver's Stanley Park Zoo, the aquarium had special nightly openings during one week of the Christmas holiday period. Patrons purchased a train ticket, entitling them to ride on a specially decorated miniature train. The train ride ran through a portion of Stanley Park as a tourist and family attraction. For most of the year, the train was run only during daylight hours. After the ride, the VPA offered admission to the aquarium and special performances of killer whale shows at a reduced price. The program helped increase awareness of the aquarium, but rain during four of the five nights kept attendance down to only 860 people.

COMMUNICATION

The aquarium's communication objective was to increase awareness of VPA programs. The membership was kept informed through special direct mail communication and regular quarterly editions of *Sea Pen* magazine. The local, nonmember segments were exposed to PSA advertisements on both radio and television. In addition, newspaper advertising was used to promote special events/exhibits. Aquarium brochures were available at Tourist Information Centres, Grayline Tour Booths, and at the Vancouver Travel Infocentre. During the summer months, billboard advertising was used.

Advertising budgets were set in December for the following year, with few changes in the mix from year to year (Exhibit 6).

Relations with the media were very good—so good that sometimes things got a little hectic. Along with regular coverage of aquarium events by local news media, major promotions generated wider coverage. The opening of the new Killer Whale Habitat, the appearance of the killer whales in the Vancouver Bach Choir/Vancouver Symphony Orchestra's "In Celebration of Whales" concert, the birth of two sea otters, and the major "Fishes in China" display all received national coverage in 1986. When an act of vandalism wiped out almost the entire tropical marine collection in late 1986, media around the world picked up the story. In addition to news coverage, TV programs like "Midday," "Sesame Street," and "The Nature of Things" featured segments on the Vancouver Public Aquarium. "Danger Bay," the CBC/Disney series, was filmed at the aquarium for a third season in 1986, continuing the adventures of Grant Roberts and his family.

The aquarium had recently started to track its visitors and ask how they found out about the aquarium. For instance, in a summer 1986 survey, 24 percent of people surveyed stated that they had seen an aquarium brochure. However, 54 percent stated that they hadn't seen any advertising. With a 1987 budget of $120,000, Mr. Knight wondered how he could be more effective in increasing awareness.

OPERATING HOURS

The aquarium had three distinct sets of operating hours. During the summer, the aquarium was open from 9:00 A.M. to 9:00 P.M., seven days per week. VPA managers felt that the extended summer hours increased attendance and also took advantage of the longer daylight hours. However, a 1982 study found that only 28 percent of visitors were aware of the extended summer hours. During the spring and fall,

EXHIBIT 6 Fiscal Budget 1986: Public Relations/Advertising

	Jan.	Feb.	March	April	May	June	July	August	Sept.	Oct.	Nov.	Dec.	Total
Radio			600		700	700	500	500	300	300	500	500	4,600
Television				1,500									1,500
Newspapers			500		500	200	500		500	300		500	3,000
"Thank-you"*					5,000								5,000
Magazines	18,860	1,670	170	580	7,580	1,980	1,910	860	580	720	670	1,220	36,800
Brochures		3,000	20,000										23,000
Brochure distribution	325	325	325	325	729	729	729	729	379	379	325	325	5,624
Photography		1,000	1,000	1,000	1,000	1,000							5,000
Passes		250			250			250			250		1,000
Billboards						6,300	6,300	6,300					18,900
Store displays		200			400		400		400		400		1,800
Schedules				5,000									5,000
Contingency	1,000	1,000	1,000	1,000	1,000	1,000	1,000	1,000	1,000	1,000	1,000		11,000
Total month	20,185	7,445	23,595	9,405	17,159	11,909	11,339	9,639	3,159	2,699	3,145	2,545	122,224

* "Thank-you" was budgeted as a full-page advertisement to thank contributors for their support in building the Max Bell Marine Mammal Centre.

461

the aquarium was open from 10:00 A.M. to 6:00 P.M. Management felt that the public would not patronize the aquarium during winter evenings, so for winter months, the hours were further reduced to 10:00 A.M. to 5:00 P.M. To increase revenues, the aquarium offered evening and restricted daytime rentals of the facilities from September to May. The typical fee ranged from $100 for a luncheon meeting using a small room in the aquarium to $1,700 for use of the entire facility during an evening. (Food was provided by outside caterers.) In 1986, the VPA received more than $200,000 in rental revenue.

Though the aquarium had used these opening hours in the past, Mr. Knight had heard of other nonprofit groups who had altered their hours to "fit" the working public. In essence, these institutions would not be open in the mornings or early afternoons but would keep their facilities open during the evening to accommodate the working public.

Weekend hours could be kept as is or extended into the evening. This might allow the aquarium to keep its present weekend customers, and if the public knew that the aquarium was open until the same hour every night, awareness of the later hours would increase. If management were to set the same operating hours for the whole year, much of the confusion caused by the changing hours might be alleviated.

THE DECISION

At February's board meeting, various alternatives for more effective use of aquarium facilities had been raised. Board approval would be required prior to implementation of any recommendation to change opening hours significantly. Also, all programs had to be compatible with the aquarium's mission statement. Though the VPA had been successful in the past, Mr. Knight felt that a new approach to marketing could improve usage of the aquarium.

He recognized that Ms. Dewey's proposal had merit and that the survey results might help the aquarium better target its winter markets.

As Mr. Knight drove home, he wondered, "Can I solve these problems?" Specifically, he needed to answer these questions:

1. How could the $120,000 promotional budget be better spent?
2. How could the aquarium boost its attendance on weekdays and on Saturday?
3. Should Elizabeth Dewey's school program proposal be implemented? If so, what communications would have to be done to minimize the risks associated with it and maximize the benefits? If not, how should the issues Ms. Dewey raised be addressed?

APPENDIX   Selected Results from January 1987 Questionnaire*

WINTER

Question	Response	Weekday	Weekend
1. Are you a resident of the Greater Vancouver Regional District?	Yes	71	60
	No	51	20
2. Are you currently a member of the Vancouver Public Aquarium?	Yes	26	34
	No	96	46
3. Is this your first visit to the aquarium?	Yes	47	23
	No	75	57
4. Was your last visit to the aquarium within the last two years?	Yes	23	46
	No	52	11
5. On average, how much time did you spend on this visit?	Less than ½ hour	0	0
	½–1 hour	44	30
	1–3 hours	72	50
	Over 3 hours	6	0
6. Are you alone or are you visiting with others?	Alone	9	4
	With others	113	76
7. How did you first learn about the aquarium?	Friend/relative	29	15
	TV	9	0
	Radio	2	0
	Tourist magazine	2	0
	Brochure	8	4
	Newspaper	0	1
	Magazine article	2	0
	Billboard	0	0
	"Discovered"	14	10
	"Just knew"	40	40
	Other	16	10
8. Do you feel that you have received your entertainment dollar value at the aquarium?	Yes	122	78
	No	0	2
9. Sex:	Male	85	47
	Female	37	33
10. What is your age group?	18–25	22	4
	26–30	34	18
	31–35	14	18
	36–40	22	14
	41–50	10	10
	51–60	12	8
	Over 61	8	8

[handwritten annotations: "SMALL WEEKDAY MEMBER" next to Q1/Q2; "REPEATERS" next to Q3; "?" next to Q4; "WOW!!" next to Q8]

* Total number of respondents: Weekdays: 122, Weekends: 80

Source: Based on a survey conducted during 2 weeks in January 1987. Interviewers were stationed near the exit and asked visitors, as they were leaving, to answer a brief questionnaire.

Case 4–6 Citicorp*

It seemed like a marvelous idea at the time: Grocery shoppers would use an ID card that, combined with the electronic scanners at the checkout line, would tell marketers exactly who bought what.

Maxwell House would have the name and address of coffee-drinkers who bought Folgers. *People* magazine could send a discount offer to everyone who bought *People* at the grocery store. Gerber would know who was loading up on baby food.

Not only that, but the effort was the work of the deep-pocketed executives of Citicorp, the big banking company with plenty of talent, experience, and patience.

But six years later, the effort looks as if it could turn out to be one of Citicorp's biggest follies. The POS (for point-of-sale) Information Services unit has spent about $200 million, generated just $20 million at best in revenue and made a mess of relationships with many grocery chains and consumer goods producers. Citicorp is hitting the brakes. In November, it abruptly canceled its most ambitious program, fired 174 staffers and shunted aside a gung-ho chief executive it had brought in 2½ years earlier to run the program.

Citicorp says it still believes in the program and looks for a turn-around. But it has quietly set a deadline for real progress. And many industry observers believe the time for Citicorp's plan has come and gone.

"I'm probably more guilty than anyone," says the former POS chief executive, Gerald Saltzgaber—and many observers agree with him. But, he adds, "you cannot talk about this without overpromising. It's such a dynamite concept."

At first glance, this seems an odd business for Citicorp, which last year had $14.6 billion in revenue, mostly from banking. Information gathering, though, was part of a futuristic goal laid out by former Chairman Walter Wriston in 1984 and put into action by his successor, John Reed, after a mountain of consultants' reports.

The "skunk works" POS operation, begun in 1985 to mine data from grocery stores, was one such venture. Initially, it was going to help supermarkets electronically keep track of and get reimbursement for all the paper coupons turned in by shoppers. Then it hit on the idea of collecting the names of shoppers and selling those lists to consumer

---

* Source: Fred R. Bleakley, "Citicorp's Folly?," *The Wall Street Journal,* April 3, 1991, pp. A1, 4. Reprinted by permission of *THE WALL STREET JOURNAL,* © 1991 Dow Jones & Company, Inc. All Rights Reserved Worldwide.

goods companies. "This was absolutely breakthrough stuff," says Barry Shereck, one of the group's first executives. Manufacturers would pay dearly to know the heavy users of rival brands, he and others at Citicorp figured.

To get those prized names, Citicorp would offer merchandise, cash rebates, check cashing or bank-account debiting so shoppers would present a scannable store card. Citicorp's ambitious goal was a data base of 40 million active grocery shoppers. "It was a marketer's nirvana," says Wes Bray, managing partner of Market Growth Resources in Wilton, Conn., a consumer goods marketing consultant.

When coupons are mass distributed, already-loyal customers take advantage and much of the rebated money is wasted. But a manufacturer could offer two or three times the normal coupon rebate with much greater success if it could target just buyers of a rival brand.

That could take target marketing to new heights. Targeting was already moving to replace mass marketing because, with so many products competing over so many channels of communication, tailored promotion messages needed to be aimed at particular audiences.

Citicorp's first shot at name gathering, a program called Coupon Bank, promised a whole new way for coupons to work. Instead of clipping coupons in the newspaper, shoppers could receive cash after the scanner electronically tabulated any purchases eligible for coupons. Besides giving manufacturers a more efficient way to spend the billions that go into paper coupons, electronic couponing could save hundreds of millions of dollars in mistakes by store clerks who redeem coupons that are out of date or don't accompany a purchase.

Electronic couponing and other shopper ID programs were still in the developmental stages when, in 1988, Richard Braddock, then head of consumer banking and now Citicorp's president, asked Mr. Saltzgaber, then a consultant in Chicago, to write up a business plan for the fledgling unit. The two had been friends at General Foods Corp., where Mr. Saltzgaber, now 54, had been a marketing executive.

Impressed with the proposal, Mr. Braddock hired Mr. Saltzgaber in 1988 to take over the 40 staffers headquartered in Stamford, Conn. Mr. Saltzgaber thought big—and spent big. According to people familiar with POS, the unit's budget was $10 million in 1987 and $17 million in 1988, but then the unit's budget jumped to $40 million in 1989 and $125 million in 1990. Mr. Saltzgaber had originally asked for $200 million in 1990. (Citicorp officials decline comment.)

The money went into larger and larger quarters, dozens of salespeople, more than 100 computer programmers, liberal expense accounts, bonuses and tens of millions of dollars worth of computers and workstations. High salaries—$100,000 to $150,000—were paid to middle managers. Mr. Saltzgaber drew a $250,000 salary and $150,000 bonus in 1989, according to one former executive. (He'll say only that his salary was less than $250,000, declining to comment on the bonus figure.)

Citicorp was spending big because it believed the POS unit could be a huge moneymaker. Not everyone agreed. "I had trouble seeing where there would ever be more than $150 million a year in revenues," Mr. Shereck says. "Yet presentations were being made saying it was a billion dollar a year business. I never saw a detailed plan on how it would get there."

When Mr. Saltzgaber joined POS, it was already working with customer identification programs at supermarkets in Los Angeles, Dallas, Chicago, Denver and Richmond. He quickly championed a new program called Reward America. By awarding cash rebates monthly to customers buying a certain number of specific products, it had the advantage of combining the concept of electronic coupons with a frequent-shopper program, presumably strong incentives for shoppers to identify themselves. In addition, the cost of running Reward America was borne by the participating manufacturers, thus encouraging the likelihood, Citicorp thought, that more stores would get behind the program.

Reward America had been proposed before. Mr. Shereck, now a consultant to troubled companies, says he had rejected it because there wasn't enough in it for everyone, especially the retailers.

Mr. Shereck, who was the senior operating executive of the POS unit in 1987 and much of 1988, recalls disagreements he had with Mr. Saltzgaber over the pace of growth. "Jerry thought the business could be grown faster by spending more money. He said he had approval from Rick Braddock to spend $150 million over three years," says Mr. Shereck. (Mr. Saltzgaber denies saying that or having such authority, and says he had strict performance and budget reviews with Mr. Braddock every six months.)

"I said that was wrong. I didn't think spending vast amounts of money was the answer," Mr. Shereck recalls. "Better to keep a low profile and work out problems quietly." He added that the sign-up of stores and shoppers, as well as management of the data, for the unit's other programs were not going as well as had been expected even then.

Reward America and other POS unit programs had some basic flaws. Grocers didn't sign up in the numbers expected, and some that did join were lukewarm in promoting it to customers. Many didn't want to see manufacturers gain access to shopper names because that would surrender more control over promotions, a longstanding tussle. In addition, if the data were going to be sold, the grocers wanted the revenue. Citicorp insisted on owning exclusive marketing rights, so some big chains, like Super Valu Stores, opted out.

Worse, Citicorp made grocers pay for the use of data generated from their own stores. Mr. Saltzgaber says Citicorp paid stores to share customer purchase information, but doesn't dispute that Citicorp also charged them for its use.

Bart Foreman, president of Group 111 Marketing in Wayzata, Minn., says grocers also didn't like Reward America because, by rewarding shoppers for buying specific brands, it "generates incremental sales for some brands, but the retailer nets out with very little. Yoplait yogurt might do well, but it's at the expense of Dannon, for instance."

Then, too, there was what one grocer calls a "We're Citicorp" attitude that smacked of arrogance. Part of that perception stemmed from the contrast between free-spending big-city bankers and the penny-pinching regional grocers. Some retailers were shocked by the large, well-furnished offices of the POS executives when they visited Stamford. "Remember, these were guys who were working out of 10-by-10 space that still had furniture from the '30s," says one marketing consultant.

Without strong store support, shopper participation in Reward America also was disappointing. Most of those who signed up lost interest. Each month they were told what they had bought and how many more of each item they would need to buy to receive a cash rebate of, say, a few dollars. "It was too complex. They wanted instant gratification," says James McConnell, an executive with Donnelley Marketing.

Rather than spotting those problems early, Citicorp POS, after the pilot program of 27 stores that began in October 1989, quickly launched successive Reward America phases that included first 90 stores and then a total of more than 200.

Although the Reward America activity was less than had been projected, it sent the POS unit's technology into overload. It couldn't write enough software or handle all the data that flowed in from scanners recording tens of thousands of shopping carts full of groceries daily. "It became their Achilles' heel," says Mr. McConnell. "If they ever get up to the levels they are shooting for, they will dim the lights in the city where they are processing."

Mr. Saltzgaber wishes he had stayed with the initial 27-store pilot before proceeding so quickly. "We would be in better shape if I had not pushed Reward America so fast," he says. "The data was pouring in. I misjudged how difficult it would be to come up the learning curve."

That miscalculation doomed Reward America. "Their marketing and sales teams were out selling before they had the technology in place," says Mr. Bray, the consultant. "Citicorp offered tantalizing capabilities and did not deliver."

Shoppers were refusing to provide much demographic data about themselves, for one thing. There weren't enough of them, for another. And, because so many were dropping out along the way, there was little continuity of purchase patterns by household name. Even worse, the POS unit had not lined up "control" stores without the program, so manufacturers could see what difference Reward America was making.

Clients soon were complaining. The data were late and the promised national data base nowhere in sight. A POS client survey showed that companies like Scott Paper Co., Campbell Soup Co. and Reynolds Metals Co. weren't getting what they had expected. Colgate-Palmolive Corp. vowed it would "never again do business" with the Citicorp unit, according to the study. "What Colgate said they experienced was total disorganization and bad service," the study reported.

Mr. Saltzgaber maintains that manufacturers were happy with Citicorp's programs and on average posted 8 percent gains in sales at the stores that participated. Still, he knew there were problems. He took his staff to task in January 1989 at a conference in Ryebrook, N.Y. There, quoting a line from what he said was his "favorite 'Nam movie," "Full Metal Jacket," he said, "You've got to walk the walk, not talk the talk."

The hiring juggernaut continued nonetheless. During the first three months of last year, the POS staff, which had already jumped from 40 to 294 people under Mr. Saltzgaber, leapt to 444, a 50 percent increase. POS has become "exponentially overstaffed for its market potential," says Joseph Fenton, an executive with Computerized Marketing Technologies, Hicksville, N.Y. Suddenly, Mr. Saltzgaber admitted he had overexpanded. In a March 26, 1990, memo to his staff, he said, "Earlier this year, the management of POS received the clear message from you (and ourselves) that we were trying to do too much . . . We should have taken one more action—slowed down the hiring."

But retrenchment was not in the air even then. In mid-May, the unit signed an 11-year lease on 136,000 square feet of space covering five of the seven floors in a new luxury Stamford office building. It took an option, good until Dec. 1, for the other two floors.

Despite all the new spending, largely for Reward America, the POS unit fell well short of its goals. Mr. Foreman of Group 111 Marketing says he had seen Citicorp projections that envisioned the entire POS group ending 1990 counting purchases by 4.8 million households from 800 stores. Instead, the count, including Reward America, was slightly more than half that.

The writing was already on the wall when the headquarters staff assembled last July for the "State of the Business Review." The group was told that the company had posted only $2 million in revenue for the first six months, which made it highly unlikely it would reach its $29 million goal for the year. "When I heard they had projected $29 million, I knew they were dreaming. It was like someone went crazy on a Lotus spreadsheet and hit the exponential key," says one staffer.

At the same meeting, the results of an employee survey showed that only 54 percent of them were happy with their jobs, and half felt "the pace of change is becoming too difficult to manage." Mr. Saltzgaber's optimism caused him to have blind spots, say some line managers who reported to him. One says, "He didn't want to hear bad news." As a result, says another, "Everyone was trying to please Jerry; they weren't solving problems or surfacing the reactions from clients." (Mr. Saltzgaber says he can understand the criticism because he does tend to look on the bright side.)

That mood persisted despite Mr. Saltzgaber's casual dress code, which gave the Stamford office the air of a California software firm. Although Mr. Saltzgaber usually wore jeans, a collarless shirt and ankle-high boots, there was still a lot of tension about him, former staffers say. One described that combination as "sort of like PLO chic."

What was missing at POS, say several former executives, was the creative, problem-solving give-and-take that should exist in an entrepreneurial operation.

Last November, Citicorp pulled the plug on Reward America. Mr. Saltzgaber was replaced in day-to-day control of POS by Bert Einloth, also from General Foods. Mr. Saltzgaber remains chairman, concentrating on "long-range planning." The budget was cut to $65 million this year.

Citicorp officials maintain POS now is on the right track. James Bailey, who oversees the unit and also heads Citicorp's enormously profitable credit-card business, says the POS unit still has the edge over competitors because of the lessons it has learned, the systems it has in place and ongoing programs at supermarkets in six cities that will be expanded.

The unit already has made progress getting purchase data into the hands of clients sooner, says Mr. Einloth. "We now can turn around data in a few weeks," he says. "A year ago it took a few months, and our goal is a few days." Current clients say they like what they see so far.

But even Mr. Saltzgaber concedes that to be effective, POS must build a data base of at least 10 million households, nearly five times what it now has. And the amount of money the current crop of clients is spending is a fraction of what will be needed to support the business and pay back the investment Citicorp has made.

"We are learning a lot from testing with Citicorp, but the results do not indicate we will do something big next year," says Jim Spector, director of consumer promotions for Philip Morris Cos. "It depends on how effective other vehicles are." Besides other forms of electronic target marketing, he says, "a lot is going on in telemarketing and selective magazine bundling."

The clock is ticking on POS. Indicating that a make-or-break date has been set, Mr. Bailey says that "at the end of 1992 if all goes as we expect, and we believe it will, this thing will continue."

The irony is that many competitors are finding that target marketing really *is* a marvelous idea—and are building businesses by learning from Citicorp's mistakes. Supermarkets now are setting up their own, similar programs. So are big consumer-goods companies. Helping them is a bevy of large and small marketing companies. Catalina Marketing Corp. of Anaheim, Calif., for one, is already entrenched in 3,500 supermarkets with an electronic checkout coupon program.

One thing all have in common: They work with the supermarkets and don't charge them for information, making cooperation much more likely. Other direct marketers, says one former POS executive, "saved millions of dollars in being able to see where Citicorp went wrong."

Case 4–7   *American Greetings**

"We're in touch" and the corporate rose logo identify the world's largest publicly owned manufacturer of greeting cards and related social-expression merchandise, American Greetings (AG). In 1981, President Morry Weiss announced the formulation of a corporate growth objective to achieve $1 billion in annual sales by 1985, which would represent a 60 percent increase over 1982 sales of $623.6 million. The battle for market share dominance between the two industry leaders, Hallmark and American Greetings, had escalated and intensified. Previously, the two leading firms peacefully coexisted by having mutually exclusive niches. Hallmark offered higher-priced, quality cards in department stores and card shops, and American Greetings offered inexpensive cards in mass-merchandise outlets. However, in 1977 American Greetings formulated a growth strategy to attack the industry leader and its niche.

* This case was prepared by Daniel C. Kopp and Lois Shufeldt. It is intended as a basis for classroom discussion rather than to illustrate effective or ineffective handling of an administrative situation. The authors would like to acknowledge the cooperation and assistance of American Greetings. Used by permission from Daniel C. Kopp.

THE GREETING CARD INDUSTRY

In 1985, Americans exchanged more than 7 billion cards—around 30 per person, marking the highest per capita card consumption ever. With the average retail price per card of a dollar, that made "social expression" a $7 billion business. According to the Greeting Card Association, card senders gave 2.2 billion Christmas cards, 1.5 billion birthday cards, 850 million valentines, 180 million Easter cards, 140 million Mother's Day cards, 85 million Father's Day cards, 80 million graduation cards, 40 million Thanksgiving cards, 26 million Halloween cards, 16 million St. Patrick's Day cards, and about 10 million Grandparent's Day cards. Everyday, nonoccasion cards now account for more than half of all industry sales, and they're on the rise. People living in the northeast and the north-central parts of the country buy more cards than average, and Southerners 30 percent fewer. People who buy the majority of them tend to be between 35 and 54 years of age, come from large families, live in their own homes in the suburbs, and have an average household income of $30,000. Changes in society—demographic and social—are fueling the growth of alternative cards. These changes have included increases in the numbers of blended families, single-parent households, working women, divorces and remarriages, and population segments which traditionally have included the heaviest greeting card users—35 to 65 years old.

Women purchase over 90 percent of all greeting cards. Women enjoy browsing and shopping for cards, and tend to purchase a card only if it is appropriate, when the card's verse and design combine to convey the sentiment she wishes to express. However, because an increasing number of women are working, these women are shopping less frequently and buying less impulse merchandise.

The growth rate for the industry has been 5 to 6 percent annually over the past several years. Sales of unorthodox cards aimed at 18–35 year old baby boomers have grown 25 percent a year. However, sales of greeting cards for the past few quarters have been lackluster. The industry is mature; sales are stagnant at about 7 billion units. According to *Chain Store Age,* the channels of distribution have been moving away from specialty stores to mass merchants.[1] Now, department stores are cutting back square footage and dropping cards altogether. Mass market appeal now has growth—one-stop shopping. Hallmark has been pushing its Ambassador line through mass merchants such as Wal-Mart and Target, in addition to diversifying into other areas.

---

[1] "Who Holds the Cards in the Greeting War?" *Chain Store Age,* April 1985, pp. 85–87.

AG is concentrating on the social expressions business: it has launched a massive national television advertising campaign to firmly position itself in all aspects of the greeting card industry. On the other hand, Hallmark, whose recent acquisitions are unrelated to the social expressions industry, is shifting its emphasis. Irvine O. Hockaday, Hallmark's CEO, said recently that he prefers outside businesses to contribute 40 percent of total Hallmark revenues, instead of the 10 percent it now contributes. Cards accounted for 64 percent of AG's 1985 sales. According to some industry experts, Hallmark is now playing follow the leader in card innovations and character licensing.

Overall slowdown in retail traffic has resulted in reduced sales. Generally, there is a soft retailing environment. The retailing industry is overstored and promotion oriented, which may result in retailers asking greeting card suppliers for lower prices to assist them in keeping their margins from shrinking. Retailers are losing their loyalty to manufacturers that supply a full line of products—cards, gift wrap, etc., and are looking instead for the lowest cost supplier of each, according to Kidder, Peabody & Company.[2] The competition in the industry has become and will continue to be intensified, especially in the areas of price, sales promotion, distribution, and selling.

More new cards have been introduced in 1986 than in any other previous year, according to the Greeting Card Association. More "feelings" type of cards, such as the "In Touch" line by AG, have been introduced. Since men buy only 10 percent of all cards sold, they are the prime target for many of the new types of cards.

Hallmark and AG are experimenting with different styles, fabricating novel reasons for people to buy their wares and using new technology that enables cards to play tunes or talk. According to *Time,* Hallmark offers 1,200 varieties of cards for Mother's Day, while AG boasts of 1,300.[3] The product ranges from a traditional card with a picture of flowers and syrupy poetry for $1 or less, to a $7 electronic version that plays the tune, "You Are the Sunshine of My Life."

Hallmark has introduced several lines of personal-relationship-oriented cards, commemorating such milestones as the wedding anniversary of a parent and a stepparent. In 1984, Hallmark introduced its Honesty Collection, which has been discontinued, with messages that reflected the nature of modern day relationships. In May 1985, AG's primary competitor brought out its Personal Touch line of cards, with intimate, conversational prose displayed on the front with no message

---

[2] E. Gray Glass III, Research Reports on American Greetings and Greeting Card Industry, Kidder Peabody and Company, May 16, 1986; May 20, 1986; December 11, 1986; and January 20, 1987.

[3] "Greetings, One and All," *Time,* May 13, 1985, p. 54.

inside. The Greeting Card Association found that 83 percent of all card senders do something—add a snapshot or a newspaper clipping or jot a note—to personalize a card, and Hallmark has been quick to supply a vehicle to take advantage of this opportunity.

Forbes has reported that there are more than 400 firms in the greeting card industry, but the two major ones, Hallmark and American Greetings, control approximately 75 percent of the market.[4] Gibson Greetings is the third major firm in the industry. Approximate market shares for the three industry leaders have been:

Company	1977	1984	1985
Hallmark	50%	45%	40–45%
American Greetings	24	33	30–35
Gibson	5	na	8–10

Analysts expect AG to keep increasing its market share. Over the last five years, unit growth rate at AG has been 4 to 5 percent a year, against industrywide growth rate of 1 to 2 percent. Industry expert E. Gray Glass III of Kidder, Peabody & Company, has indicated that AG has been showing good growth at 15 percent or better annually.[5] Furthermore, *Chain Store Age* has projected that AG will continue to take some of Hallmark's market share, but that it will take a long time for AG to pass it.[6]

The *New York Times* has reported that Hallmark has been successful in freestanding card shops, which account for about 40 percent of all greeting cards sold.[7] Fastest growth for AG has been big drugstores and supermarket chains. Growth has been slower at variety stores, traditional department stores, and gift shops, which account for about 30 percent of AG sales.

According to *Investor's Daily,* AG and Hallmark have been increasing their market shares at the expense of smaller card companies, which have been forced out of the market due to the high costs of selling, distributing, and marketing, as well as the lack of extensive computerized inventory monitoring systems that only large companies can afford.[8] Industry analysts, however, have predicted that small

[4] "New Markets-New Products," *Forbes,* July 30, 1984, p. 102.

[5] E. Gray Glass III, Research Reports on American Greetings and the Greeting Card Industry, Kidder Peabody and Company, May 16, 1986; May 20, 1986; December 11, 1986; and January 20, 1987.

[6] "Who Holds the Cards in the Greeting War?" *Chain Store Age,* April 1985, pp. 85–87.

[7] "Marketplace: Greeting Cards and Earnings," *New York Times,* June 18, 1984, p. 43.

[8] *Investor's Daily,* May 18, 1984, p. 19.

firms with a focus niche and geographic area, will continue to enter the industry and can be profitable.

Richard H. Connor, AG Executive Vice President, stated that AG has been gaining ground on Hallmark, although he wouldn't say by how much: "If you compare the businesses that are similar with both companies, we are closing the gap. Between the both of us, we have 75 percent of the market, and some of our growth must be at their expense."

Both Hallmark and AG are being challenged by Gibson, which is the fastest growing company in the industry. Gibson scored a coup with Walt Disney Productions when they secured the rights to use Mickey Mouse and his friends, who previously had been featured by Hallmark. Gibson also has licensed Garfield the Cat and Sesame Street characters, but Hallmark's line of Peanuts cards remains one of the industry's most successful.

HISTORY OF AMERICAN GREETINGS

The story of American Greetings is one of the "American Dream" of an immigrant from Poland who came to the land of promise and opportunity to seek his fortune. Jacob Sapirstein was born in 1884 in Wasosz, Poland and because of the Russian-Japanese war of 1904, was sent by his widowed mother, along with his seven brothers and one sister to live in America.

Jacob, also known as J.S., began his one-man business buying postcards made in Germany from wholesalers and selling them to candy, novelty, and drug stores in Cleveland in 1906. From a horse-drawn card wagon, the small venture steadily flourished.

J.S. and his wife, Jennie, also a Polish immigrant, had three sons and a daughter; all three sons became active in their father's business. At the age of nine, Irving, the oldest, kept the family business afloat while J.S. was recovering from the flu during the epidemic of 1918. The business had out-grown the family living room and was moved to a garage at this time.

J.S. had a basic philosophy of service to the retailer and a quality product for the consumer. He developed the first wire rack as well as rotating floor stands to make more attractive, convenient displays. In the 1930s, the Sapirstein Card Company began to print its own cards to ensure the quality of its product. The name of the company was changed to American Greeting Publishers to reflect the national stature and functioning of the company. Their first published line of cards under the American Greetings name, the Forget Me Not Line, went on sale in 1939 for a nickel. One card, which remains the company's all-time best seller, was designed by Irving.

The company saw great expansion throughout the 1940s, as loved ones found the need to communicate with World War II soldiers. The most significant effect of this was the widespread use of greeting cards by the soldiers. In the past, cards had been primarily a product utilized by women, thus the expansion to the male market was a significant breakthrough for the card industry.

The 1950s marked the first public offering of stock and the name change to American Greetings Corporation. Ground was broken for a new world headquarters, which led the way for expansion to world markets. The company made connections with several foreign markets and acquired a Canadian plant.

In 1960, J.S. stepped down at the age of 76. His son Irving succeeded him as president. Under Irving's leadership and with the assistance of his brothers, Morris and Harry Stone (all three brothers had changed their names from Sapirstein, meaning sapphire, to Stone in 1940 for business reasons), the company has continued to expand into gift wrapping, party goods, calendars, stationery, candles, ceramics, and perhaps, most importantly, the creation of licensed characters.

Expansion into these related items has somewhat diminished AG's recession-proof profits. Greeting card sales typically increase during recessions as people refrain from gift buying and instead remember others with a less expensive card. The supplemental items now constitute one third of the company's sales, not enough to seriously jeopardize AG during down economies, but greatly augment the company's sales during good economic times.

AG's world expansion became a major pursuit throughout the 1960s and 1970s. Morry Weiss, a grandson-in-law of J.S., became the new president of AG in 1978 with Irving continuing to act as the CEO and Chairman of the Board of Directors. Morris Stone continues to serve as Vice Chairman of the Board, and Harry Stone remains as an active Board member.

OBJECTIVES

In 1981 at the first national sales meeting ever held by AG, President Morry Weiss announced the formulation of a major corporate objective: to achieve $1 billion in annual sales by 1985. During fiscal 1985, AG strengthened its position as a leader in the industry: that year marked the seventy-ninth consecutive year of increased revenue—total revenue increased to $945.7 million, while net income increased to $74.4 million. This record of success represented a 300 percent increase in total revenue during the past 10 years, 613 percent increase in net income during the past 10 years, and a 315 percent increase in dividends per share in the past 10 years, with two increases in fiscal 1985.

EXHIBIT 1 International and Subsidiary Operations

United States

A. G. Industries, Inc.
Cleveland, Ohio
Charles H. Nervig, President

AmToy, Inc.
New York, New York
Larry Freiberg, President

Drawing Board Greeting Cards, Inc.
Dallas, Texas
Selwin Belofsky, President

Plus Mark, Inc.
Greeneville, Tennessee
Ronald E. Clouse, President

The Summit Corporation
Berlin, Connecticut
Robert P. Chase, President

Those Characters From Cleveland, Inc.
Cleveland, Ohio
John S. Chojnacki, Thomas A. Wilson,
   Co-Presidents

Tower Products Company, Inc.
Chicago, Illinois
Melvin Mertz, President

Canada

Carlton Cards Ltd.
Toronto, Ontario
William L. Powell, President and
   Chairman of Canadian Operations

Plus Mark Canada
Toronto, Ontario
Richard L. Krelstein, President

Rust Craft Canada, Inc.
Scarborough, Ontario
Gary Toporoski, Vice President,
   Managing Director

Continental Europe

Richard C. Schulte
Director of Operations

Grako Oy
Helsinki, Finland
Risto Pitkanen, Managing Director

A/S Muva Grafiske Produkter
Oslow, Norway
Aage Dahl, Managing Director

Muva Greetings B.V.
Heerlen, The Netherlands
Huub Robroeks, General Manager

Susy Card
Hamburg, West Germany
Charles Wightman, Managing Director

Mexico

Felicitaciones Nacionales S.A. de C.V.
Mexico City, Mexico
Felix G. Antonio, President

Monaco

Rust Craft International S.A.
Michel Bourda, Managing Director

United Kingdom

Rust Craft Greeting Cards (U.K.) Ltd.
Dewsbury, England
David M. Beards, Managing Director and
   Chairman of U.K. Operations

Andrew Valentine Holdings Ltd.
Dundee, Scotland
Alistair R. L. Mackay, Managing Director

Celebration Arts Group Ltd.
Corby, England
W. George Pomphrett, Managing Director

Denison Colour Ltd.
Guiseley, England
Brian Holliday, Managing Director

According to Morry Weiss, President and Chief Operating Officer:

AG today is positioning itself for transition from a greeting company to a total communications company. For years, AG was thought of only as a greeting card maker. That narrow description no longer applies to the world's largest, publicly owned manufacturer of greeting cards and related social-expression merchandise. Today we are diversified into other major product lines, including gift wrap, candles, stationery, ceramics, party goods, and calendars. In addition, we lead the industry in licensing characters, such as Holly Hobbie, Ziggy, Strawberry Shortcake, Care Bears, and Care Bear Cousins, which are featured on thousands of retail products and on television and in motion pictures.

Irving Stone, Chairman of the Board and Chief Executive Officer added:

AG is aggressively pursuing growth in our core business, concentrating specifically on increasing market share and unit volume, and continued margin. We'll grow through our retailers by providing the programs that will generate sales and make the greeting card department the most profitable area in their store. We'll grow through our consumers by understanding their needs and providing them with products they want and enjoy buying. We'll grow by constantly improving our operations and productivity through creativity, innovation, and technology.

We expect growth and are planning for it throughout the corporation. In the past four years we have invested heavily in increased capacity, plant expansion, new equipment, and new technology. Almost two years ago, we completed an equity offering that substantially strengthened our financial position; an additional offering is not expected in the near future. Today we see no problem financing our growth while at the same time increasing our dividends.

A flurry of acquisitions occurred in the 1980s. A full list of subsidiaries, as well as AG's international operations is displayed in Exhibit 1.

MARKETING STRATEGIES

Product

AG produces a wide product line including greeting cards, gift wrap, party goods, toys, and gift items. Greeting cards accounted for 66 percent of the company's 1986 fiscal sales. The breakdown of sales by major product categories is as follows:

Everyday greeting cards	37%
Holiday greeting cards	29%
Gift wrap and party goods	18%
Consumer products (toys, etc.)	7%
Stationery	9%

It is the belief of AG that one of the keys to increased sales is to have a product line that offers a wide variety and selection of cards, such that a consumer can always find the right card for that special person. Each year AG offers more new products than ever before. The creative department produces over 20,000 different designs to ensure the wide selection.

AG's creative staff is one of the largest assemblages of artistic talent in the world. The department has over 400 designers, artists, and writers who are guided by the latest research data available from computer analysis, consumer testing, and information from AG's sales and merchandising departments. Careful monitoring of societal changes, fashion and color trends, and consumer preferences provides further guidance to product development. AG also gives uncompromising adherence to quality—in papers, inks, and printing procedures.

AG pioneered licensing and now dominates the industry of character licensing. Their strategy has been to maximize the potential of their creative and marketing expertise. Holly Hobbie was the first licensed character in 1968; Ziggy in 1971; and Strawberry Shortcake in 1980. When introduced, Strawberry Shortcake was the most popular new character in licensing history. Sales for Strawberry Shortcake will soon exceed $1 billion in retail sales, a revenue larger than that of any other character. In 1983, AG introduced Care Bears and Herself the Elf. The product was launched with General Mills and 23 licensees supported by an $8 million advertising and promotional campaign, including a half-hour animated television special. The Care Bears license identifies ten adorable cuddlies, each with a message on its tummy.

Another licensing creation, Popples, added a new dimension to a field crowded with look-alikes. Popples literally "pop out" from a plush ball to a lovable, furry, playmate. A plush toy that folds into its own pouch, Popples enables children to make its arms, legs, and fluffy tail appear and disappear at will. Two new toys from AmToy are reaching another new and undercultivated market: My Pet Monster and Madballs. They were the hits of the 1986 Toy Fair show. These creatures are designed to delight the millions of young boys who prefer the bizarre to the cuddly.

Forty companies initially signed up to manufacture other products such as clothing, knapsacks, and books featuring the new characters. AG and Mattel spent about $10 million promoting the characters, including a half-hour Popples television special. The licensed product industry is $50 billion strong.

According to *Forbes,* all AG licensed characters have not been successful.[9] One flop, Herself the Elf, was perceived by retailers as being

---

[9] "Making of a Popple," *Forbes,* December 16, 1985, pp. 174–175.

too much like Strawberry Shortcake; it also missed the Christmas season because of production problems. Another failure was Get Along Gang, which tried to appeal to both little girls and boys.

Distribution

AG distributes its products through 90,000 retail outlets located throughout the free world, which has increased from 80,000 in 1983. Additionally, there has been growth in the channels of distribution where AG is dominant. Consumers have been seeking greater convenience and one-stop shopping, channels in which AG is strong—chain drugstores, chain supermarkets, and mass merchandise retailers. Thirty-nine percent of AG sales went to drugstores, with the remaining sales (in order of rank) going to mass merchandisers, supermarkets, stationery and gift shops, variety stores, military post exchanges, combo stores (food, general merchandise, and gift items), and department stores. During the last five years, sales to drug, variety, and department stores as a percent of total revenue have declined, while sales to supermarkets, mass merchandisers, combo stores, and military post exchange units have increased, and stationery and gift shops have remained constant.

Promotion

In 1982, AG became recognized nationwide, first through television commercials and then through a new-corporate identity program. The new logo is now featured prominently at retail outlets; the updated corporate rose logo is now a standard and highly recognizable feature greeting AG customers on all product packaging, store signage, point-of-purchase displays, and even the truck fleet. The year-round advertising campaign included the promotion of the major card-sending holidays and nonseasonal occasions during daytime and prime-time programming.

Supporting marketing is a promotion generator out of which flows seasonal and special displays, special signs, sales catalogues, national television advertising, media and trade journal exposure, television programming, and special events featuring AG's exclusive characters. Results can be seen in increased support for AG's sales personnel, greater consumer awareness, improved relations with retail dealers, greater visibility within the financial community, and improved relations with employees and communities where plant facilities are operating.

The aim of AG's national consumer advertising and public relations programs is to remind people to send cards, in that one of AG's chief competitors is consumer forgetfulness. AG is the only company in the industry to sponsor national consumer retail promotions. These consumer-directed programs serve to establish brand identity and generate retail store traffic.

In 1983 AG employed 1,600 full-time salespeople, in addition to 7,000 part-timers, all of whom have been directed through 15 regional and 66 district sales offices in the United States, the United Kingdom, Canada, Mexico, and France. AG employs a large force of retail store merchandisers who visit each department at regular intervals to ensure that every pocket in every display is kept filled with appropriate merchandise.

The AG sales force is meeting the unique and challenging needs of their customers: no other company in the industry has sales and marketing personnel assigned to specific channels of distribution to give retailers the advantage of working with specialists who understand their markets, their customers, and their specific marketing needs.

The success of AG's aggressive marketing programs is explained by William E. Schmitt, Group Vice President, Marketing:

> First we have the creativity to develop the best products in the industry. Every year we prove this with new characters, new card lines, and other products and programs that attract consumers and increase sales for our customers and ourselves. Second, we have a close relationship with our customers. The retailer support programs we offer—including terms, display fixtures, advertising and merchandising programs, promotional support, and inventory controls—are unsurpassed in the industry.

Programs are tailored for individual retailers to help plan their greeting card locations, department sizes, and displays. AG shows the retailers how to merchandise innovative ideas and enhance visibility by means of proven promotional programs.

Computer technology is helping AG's salespeople to project retailers' needs better, which has resulted in improved sell-through of the product at retail. MIS, the data processing unit for the AG Division, is playing a vital role in increasing sales for AG's products at the retail level. In 1984, AG began implementing a computer-to-computer reordering system that allows retail accounts to control inventories and turnaround time by electronic transfer of data to AG's headquarters data center.

Good retail presentation is a key to card sales; AG has created a unique identification for the greeting cards department. It is called the Total Retail Environment, and it uses a completely planned and coordinated approach to integrate display cabinets, signage, lighting, product packaging, and even products to create a stunning new AG look.

The purposes of this new system are to establish greater consumer awareness of the AG card department, to provide a distinctive look and appeal, and to provide an attractive and enjoyable place to shop.

AG also possesses the most favorable terms-of-sale program in the industry. To improve the retailer's return-on-inventory investment, AG has successful merchandising plans, retail store merchandisers, and computerized inventory controls. AG also sports a direct product profitability (DPP) concept to evaluate productivity and space allocation for products in stores. DPP takes gross margin and return-on-inventory investment analysis a step further by reflecting revenue after allowances and discounts and subtracting all costs attributable to the product, including labor and freight. AG's salespeople can then demonstrate to retailers that their greeting card department returns a high rate of profit for the space allocated.

Richard H. Connor, AG Executive Vice President, recently announced:

> To increase market share, AG revamped its sales force and created one sales department that specializes in independent retail accounts and another sales department that specializes in selling to retail chains. A third department will stock and service all types of accounts. This will give greater selling strength where it's needed and lowers our selling costs.

AG has created a new retail communications network (RCTN) that conducts research that will better enable AG to identify for accounts the appropriate products to meet the needs of their customers. Data are compiled by monitoring product sales and space productivity from a chain of nationwide test stores that encompasses all demographic and geographic variables and represents all channels of distribution. The RCTN then interprets data as it would apply to an account's specifications, including type of store, size, location, and consumer profile. This total merchandising approach to achieving maximum sales and space potential is unique in the industry.

PRODUCTION STRATEGIES

AG has 49 plants and facilities in the United States, Canada, Continental Europe, Mexico, Monaco, and the United Kingdom.

AG has been concerned with reducing production costs in order to remain the industry's lowest cost producer through efficient manufacturing operations while maintaining quality and service to their customers. According to Robert C. Swilik, Group Vice President, Manufacturing, "Improved control of our manufacturing process through planning and scheduling enable us to improve productivity, reduce manufacturing costs, and reduce inventory. Increased productivity is the result of our growing sense of shared responsibility. The relationship between management and the work force is excellent."

Quality improvements have been consistently made. Some of the major improvements have been:

1. Upgraded die cutting and embossing capabilities with the purchase of nine high-speed Bobst presses costing $1 million each.
2. Added capacity to the hot stamping and thermography operations.
3. Streamlined order filling in both everyday and seasonal operations.
4. Completed a 200,000 square-foot warehouse addition to the Osceola, Arkansas, plant and began operations in an addition to the Ripley, Tennessee, plant, which increased its capacity by 20 percent.
5. Installed a Scitex system that will dramatically improve product quality and increase productivity; new electronic prepress system enables creative department to interact with manufacturing at the creatively crucial prepress stage.
6. Installed additional high-speed and more powerful presses to further improve quality of die cutting and embossing at the Bardstown, Kentucky, plant; a 300,000 square foot addition is also planned.
7. Installed new computer graphics system called Via Video for design and layout functions for a variety of in-house publications and brochures (this gives the artist freedom to create while quickly and inexpensively exploring options and alternatives, thus increasing productivity).

MANAGEMENT

In 1983, AG underwent a major management restructuring to permit top officers of the company more time to concentrate on strategic planning. The company was reorganized from a centralized structure to a divisional profit center basis. Each division has its own budget committee, while an executive management committee composed of five senior executives approves the strategic plans for all the divisions. Strategic plans are established in one-, three-, ten-, and twenty-year time frames. Corporate AG maintains strict budgetary and accounting controls.

The basic domestic greeting card business was placed under the AG Division. Foreign and U.S. subsidiaries and the licensing division have become a second unit, with corporate management a third. Restructuring has allowed corporate management to step back from day-to-day operations and focus on the growth of American Greetings beyond the $1 billion annual revenue.

According to Irving Stone:

The prime function of corporate management is to plan and manage the growth of the entire corporation, developing capable management and allocating corporate resources to those units offering the greatest potential return on investment. Greeting cards has been our basic business for 78 years and remains today our largest business unit; there are smaller business units, which complement the greeting card business and are deserving of our attention.

American Greetings is composed of the following divisions.

American Greetings Division. This division encompasses the core business of greeting cards and related products, including manufacturing, sales, merchandising, research, and administrative services. It produces and distributes greeting cards and related products domestically. The same products are distributed throughout the world by international subsidiaries and licensees.

Foreign and Domestic Subsidiaries. Two wholly owned companies in Canada, four in the United Kingdom, six in Continental Europe, and one in Mexico. Licensees use AG designs and verses in almost every free country in the world. Subdivisions include:

Canadian Operations—Two companies, Carlton Cards and Rust Craft.

United Kingdom Operations—British are largest per capita senders of greeting cards in the world. Three AG companies in the UK— Rust Craft, Celebration Arts, and Andrew Valentine.

Continental European Operations—Five companies wholly owned.

Those Characters From Cleveland—Licensing division of AG. Characters and new television series, The Get Along Gang.

Plus Mark—Began producing Christmas promotional products such as gift wrap, ribbon, bows, and boxed Christmas cards in an industry selling primarily to mass merchandisers.

AmToy—Sells novelties, dolls, and plush toys.

AG Industries—Produces display cabinet fixtures in wood, metal, or plastic for all AG retail accounts and growing list of external clients.

FINANCE STRATEGIES

Exhibits 2 through 4 contain relevant financial information for American Greetings. The financial condition of AG has been exemplary over the years. However, AG's financial performance in 1986 was disap-

EXHIBIT 2

AMERICAN GREETINGS
Consolidated Statements of Financial Position
February 28, 1985, and 1986
($000)

Assets	1982	1983	1984	1985	1986
Current assets					
Cash and equivalents	$ 3,367	$ 19,950	$ 62,551	$ 66,363	$ 26,853
Trade accounts receivable, less allowances for sales returns of $57,382 ($42,198 in 1985) and for doubtful accounts of $3,378 ($2,900 in 1985)	131,996	148,018	146,896	173,637	240,471
Inventories:					
Raw material	53,515	47,636	48,738	59,197	59,343
Work in process	52,214	54,756	43,929	53,728	60,179
Finished products	97,221	122,167	139,275	152,543	181,237
	202,950	224,559	231,942	265,468	300,759
Less LIFO reserve	55,051	59,345	63,455	71,828	76,552
	147,899	165,214	168,487	193,640	224,207
Display material and factory supplies	11,724	12,245	11,532	20,809	26,826
Total inventories	159,623	177,459	180,019	214,449	251,033
Deferred income taxes	18,014	24,847	26,517	33,016	36,669
Prepaid expenses and other	2,057	3,524	4,187	4,795	6,228
Total current assets	315,057	373,798	420,170	492,260	561,254
Other assets	22,063	32,866	34,820	31,634	47,085
Property, plant and equipment					
Land	3,380	5,427	6,621	6,822	7,523
Buildings	110,479	118,598	133,868	143,671	165,241
Equipment and fixtures	115,927	133,731	158,507	182,101	222,718
	229,786	257,756	298,996	332,594	395,482
Less accumulated depreciation and amortization	75,052	83,745	95,092	108,591	130,519
Property, plant and equipment—net	154,734	174,011	203,904	224,003	264,963
Total assets	$491,854	$580,675	$658,894	$747,897	$873,302

Liabilities and Shareholders' Equity

Current liabilities					
Notes payable to banks	$ 4,564	$ 29,836	$ 4,647	$ 4,574	$ 15,921
Accounts payable	39,016	40,568	52,302	56,840	66,685
Payrolls and payroll taxes	17,224	16,914	23,160	26,761	28,675
Retirement plans	5,696	7,405	10,362	12,612	11,697
State and local taxes	3,278	2,448	2,811	2,796	2,763
Dividends payable	1,918	2,641	3,304	4,622	5,317
Income taxes	12,177	8,841	23,672	27,465	18,988
Sales returns	9,241	16,423	17,795	21,822	23,889
Current maturities of long-term debt	6,531	6,998	6,432	4,359	4,786
Total current liabilities	99,645	132,074	144,485	161,851	178,721
Long-term debt	148,895	111,066	119,941	112,876	147,592
Deferred income taxes	15,530	21,167	28,972	47,422	64,025
Shareholders' equity					
Common shares—par value $1:					
Class A	12,293	27,996	28,397	28,835	29,203
Class B	1,413	3,080	3,070	3,046	2,982
Capital in excess of par value	37,690	76,851	80,428	87,545	93,055
Cumulative translation adjustment	(3,829)	(7,179)	(9,158)	(13,688)	(16,801)
Retained earnings	180,217	215,620	262,759	320,010	374,525
Total shareholders' equity	227,784	316,368	365,496	425,748	482,964
Total liabilities and shareholders' equity	$491,854	$580,675	$658,894	$747,897	$873,302

Source: American Greetings.

EXHIBIT 3

AMERICAN GREETINGS
Consolidated Statements of Income
Years Ended February 28 or 29, 1981–1986
($000 except per share amounts)

	1981	1982	1983	1984	1985	1986
Net sales	$489,213	$605,970	$722,431	$817,329	$919,371	$1,012,451
Other income	9,052	17,634	20,252	22,585	26,287	23,200
Total revenue	498,272	623,604	742,683	839,914	945,658	1,035,651
Costs and expenses:						
Material, labor and other production costs	222,993	276,071	310,022	339,988	377,755	416,322
Selling, distribution and marketing	140,733	179,021	217,022	246,456	274,095	308,745
Administrative and general	61,033	76,494	96,012	112,363	123,750	131,928
Depreciation and amortization	10,863	12,752	13,890	15,507	18,799	23,471
Interest	13,548	21,647	24,086	16,135	15,556	19,125
	449,170	565,985	661,032	730,449	809,955	899,591
Income before income taxes	49,102	57,619	81,651	109,465	135,703	136,060
Income taxes	22,587	24,776	37,069	49,807	61,338	61,635
Net income	$ 26,515	$ 32,843	$ 44,582	$ 59,658	$ 74,365	$ 74,425
Net income per share	$ .97	$1.20	$1.54	$1.91	$2.35	$2.32

Source: American Greetings.

pointing, with revenue growth estimated to be at 7 percent and earnings to be similar to those of 1985. AG's revenue and earnings growth rate for the previous five years increased at compound annual rates of 17 percent and 29 percent, respectively. AG's stock declined sharply after the disappointing financial report.

According to the research department of the Ohio Company, the reasons for the change in sales and revenues were attributed to:

1. Weak retail environment—decline in retail traffic.
2. Heavy investment in display fixtures—intense competition has forced larger investments than anticipated.
3. Reduced licensing revenues—short life cycle of products and greater competitive pressures reduced licensing revenues.
4. Increased accounts receivables and inventory due to slower collections and weak ordering by retailers.
5. Increased interest expense due to increased accounts receivable and inventory levels.

Irving Stone remarked about the company's finances:

> In fiscal 1986, the retailing picture was a rapidly changing mosaic, featuring a generally poor environment marked by a substantial drop-off in store traffic. As a result, sales of many of our products, which are dependent upon store traffic and impulse buying, fell below our expectations. Nevertheless, total revenue increased for the 80th consecutive year, primarily due to increased greeting card sales. This is a proud record that few business enterprises can match. While this increase established a new corporate revenue milestone, it did not meet our performance goals, and earnings were flat for the first time in 10 years.

FUTURE OF AG

Although AG has had significant growth in the past, events in its external environment are clouding the long-term picture.

Again, from Irving Stone:

> We foresee opportunities to expand our business and profitability. Recent management restructuring provides key officers with the time necessary to concentrate on long-term strategic planning in order to identify specific opportunities, seize upon them, and transform them into bottom-line results. Much growth potential lies ahead in our basic greeting card business, both domestically and internationally. We will strengthen our growing number of subsidiaries, improve efficiency, and increase productivity. Sales increases and expanded distribution in all channels of trade are key objectives. Licensing will continue to flourish, extending our horizons further and further.

Morry Weiss further added: "Our future growth plans include aggressively pursuing growth in our core business, concentrating specifi-

EXHIBIT 4   Selected Financial Data for Years Ended February 28 or 29, 1976–1986 ($000 except per share amounts)

Summary of Operations	1976	1977	1978	1979
Total revenue				
As reported	$ 255,770	$ 277,985	$ 315,644	$ 373,487
Adjusted for general inflation*	511,223	525,318	560,333	615,852
Material, labor and other production costs	114,190	118,252	131,769	161,654
Depreciation and amortization	6,329	6,982	7,544	8,453
Interest expense	4,970	5,423	3,935	5,911
Net income				
As reported	14,601	16,787	19,926	22,911
Adjusted for specific inflation*				
Net income per share				
As reported	.53	.62	.73	.84
Adjusted for specific inflation*				
Cash dividends per share				
As reported	.13	.15	.19	.22
Adjusted for general inflation*	.26	.28	.34	.36
Fiscal year end market price per share				
As reported	5.07	4.69	5.25	5.75
Adjusted for general inflation*	9.83	8.68	9.08	9.12
Purchasing power gain from holding net monetary liabilities*				
Increase (decrease) in value of assets adjusted for specific inflation compared to general inflation*				
Translation adjustment*				
Average number of shares outstanding	27,292,484	27,292,484	27,292,036	27,293,376
Average consumer price index	161.2	170.5	181.5	195.4
Financial Position				
Accounts receivable	$ 53,258	$ 48,920	$ 54,634	$ 67,651
Inventories	52,581	53,741	71,581	98,075
Working capital	99,643	90,308	98,188	119,421
Total assets	233,572	247,503	256,297	305,746
Capital additions	15,150	7,630	20,586	25,205
Long-term debt	66,048	41,855	45,929	54,845
Shareholders' equity				
As reported	122,608	135,370	150,242	167,168
Adjusted for specific inflation*				
Shareholders' equity per share	4.49	4.96	5.51	6.12
Net return on average shareholders' equity	12.5%	13.0%	14.0%	14.5%
Pretax return on total revenue	10.2%	11.7%	13.3%	12.0%

* In average fiscal 1986 dollars.

Source: American Greetings.

	1980	1981	1982	1983	1984	1985	1986
	$ 427,469	$ 498,272	$ 623,604	$ 742,683	$ 839,914	$ 945,658	$ 1,035,651
	633,535	650,499	737,611	827,715	906,904	979,399	1,035,651
	190,135	222,993	276,071	310,022	339,988	377,755	416,322
	10,070	10,863	12,752	13,890	15,507	18,799	23,471
	9,716	13,548	21,647	24,086	16,135	15,556	19,125
	25,638	26,515	32,843	44,582	59,658	74,365	74,425
	23,024	17,495	21,349	34,817	52,298	63,860	63,630
	.94	.97	1.20	1.54	1.91	2.35	2.32
	.84	.64	.78	1.20	1.67	2.02	1.98
	.25	.26	.27	.31	.40	.54	.62
	.37	.34	.32	.35	.43	.56	.62
	5.69	5.50	9.63	18.69	23.69	33.06	35.62
	7.99	6.87	11.03	20.60	25.16	33.75	35.05
	9,750	9,391	9,366	4,739	1,784	1,438	1,843
	9,625	(15,935)	(4,981)	2,693	(10,605)	(16,067)	(5,642)
			(3,867)	(4,701)	(2,289)	(5,881)	(3,653)
	27,302,686	27,314,594	27,352,342	28,967,092	31,240,455	31,629,418	32,059,851
	217.4	246.8	272.4	289.1	298.4	311.1	322.2
	$ 76,629	$ 114,051	$ 131,996	$ 148,018	$ 146,896	$ 173,637	$ 240,471
	122,279	133,836	159,623	177,459	180,019	214,449	251,033
	135,443	167,772	215,412	241,724	275,685	330,409	382,533
	344,395	433,204	491,854	580,675	685,894	747,897	873,302
	34,516	22,768	26,720	33,967	46,418	43,575	61,799
	75,994	113,486	148,895	111,066	119,941	112,876	147,592
	186,043	205,550	227,784	316,368	365,496	425,748	482,964
	421,248	422,991	432,781	518,955	559,395	602,350	642,767
	6.81	7.52	8.31	10.18	11.62	13.35	15.01
	14.6%	13.7%	15.4%	17.1%	17.8%	19.2%	18.5%
	11.2%	9.9%	9.2%	11.0%	13.0%	14.4%	13.1%

cally on increasing market share and unit volume, and continued margin improvement."

However, according to William Blair and Company, AG's earnings growth will moderate significantly from the high-earning growth rate over the past five years.[10] This is due in part to cyclical factors in the economy, but also because of slowdowns in expansion of market share, licensing revenues, and more intense competition. Furthermore, there are two conflicting trends for AG's operating margins: gains should be made from increased productivity, but the increasing competitive nature of the industry with increased promotion might well erode such productivity increases.

Furthermore, according to industry expert, E. Gray Glass, III of Kidder, Peabody, & Company, there are some positives in the industry such as demographics and promising Christmas sales.[11] However, major concerns exist which include:

- Aggressive price competition that was only modest in the past (mark up for greeting cards is 100 percent between factory and retail outlet).
- High account turnover as retailers look for most profitable lines, and card companies fight intensely for large chain retail accounts (AG recently acquired the Sears' account while Hallmark secured Penney's).
- Increased cost pressure due to increasing advertising and distribution (racks, point-of-purchase, etc.) costs (Hallmark will spend in excess of $40 million in television and magazine ads for Hallmark merchandise and benefits of sending cards. AG will spend $33 million).
- Market share gains at the expense of other firms which come at high cost to the winner.
- Growth rate of past five years will not be matched over the next five years.
- New, viable, and growing competitors will emerge.
- Investment decisions will have to be made more carefully.
- Speculation exists that Hallmark may be formulating some counterattack strategies.

---

[10] Research Report on American Greetings, William Blair & Company, March 27, 1986.

[11] E. Gray Glass III, Research Reports on American Greetings and Greeting Card Industry, Kidder Peabody and Company, May 16, 1986; May 20, 1986; December 11, 1986; and January 20, 1987.

Merrill Lynch recently reduced AG's earnings estimates for fiscal 1987 and 1988 because of the above conditions, difficulties in production and shipment of the Christmas line to retailers, and higher-than-expected new business expenses.[12] Needless to say, the executive committee of AG is concerned about the future growth potential and is in the process of formulating long-term objectives and strategies.

Case 4–8 *Airwick Industries: Carpet Fresh**

In late fall of 1982, Mike Sheets, president of Airwick Industries, and Wes Buckner, executive vice president of the Consumer Products Division, were considering what to do next to strengthen the profitability, competitive position, and sales of Carpet Fresh.

PRODUCT BACKGROUND

Carpet Fresh, a rug and room deodorizer, was one of the most successful products in Airwick's history, far exceeding even optimistic sales expectations when it was first introduced in 1978. Used to freshen the smell of a rug and room when sprinkled on a carpet and vacuumed up during household cleaning, it had created an entirely new household product category. From a market size of zero before its launch in June 1978, the rug and room deodorizer category had grown to approximately $74 million in 1982 (Exhibit 1).

Retail sales in 1978 of $20.2 million belonged entirely to Carpet Fresh, which then enjoyed 100 percent market share. The market grew rapidly in 1979 but increased very slowly afterwards. After 1979, unit sales grew between 6 and 7 percent per year. Airwick's market share in 1982 was expected to be 48 percent (Exhibit 2) because several competitors entered the market after Airwick had pioneered the category. Airwick's share consisted primarily of Carpet Fresh sales, although one eighth of the sales was accounted for by Glamorene Rug Fresh, a lower-priced, unadvertised brand that Airwick introduced in May 1979 to counter competitive entries.

---

[12] Research Report on American Greetings and Greeting Card Industry, Merrill Lynch, September 1986 and December 1986.

* This case was developed by Holly Gunner of Management Analysis Center, Inc., in collaboration with Professor Philip McDonald, College of Business Administration, Northeastern University, Boston, Massachusetts. Copyright © 1983 by Northeastern University. Reprinted by permission.

EXHIBIT 1   Total Rug and Room Deodorizer Market

	Dollars (millions)*	Units (millions of ounces)†	
		Ounces	Change (%)
1977	$ 0.0	—	—
1978	20.2	—	—
1979	70.2	546	—
1980	68.5	584	+7.0
1981	66.1	628	+6.9
1982‡	74.0	666§	+6.1§
1983‡	80.0	—	—

* Food stores sales, at retail prices.
† Food store sales.
‡ Estimated.
§ Based on data as of 6/26.

Source: Airwick Industries (9/82).

At about $32 million in revenues (at the manufacturer's selling price), Carpet Fresh accounted for almost 30 percent of Airwick's consumer product sales in 1982. The brand also enjoyed the lowest cost of goods of any Airwick product and was a substantial contributor to company profits. Determining how to increase sales and maintain the brand's competitive position was thus a critical decision for Mike Sheets and Wes Buckner.

EXHIBIT 2   Airwick's Rug and Room Deodorizer Market Share*

Year	Carpet Fresh	Glamorene Rug Fresh	Total
1978	100.0	—	100.0
1979	65.4	8.4	73.8
1980	46.9	8.3	55.2
1981	42.9	5.8	48.7
1982	42.2	5.6	47.8

* Percentage of retail grocery store dollar sales.

Source: Airwick Industries (3/83).

COMPANY BACKGROUND

In its early years Airkem, Inc. (Airwick Industries' original name) had focused its internal R&D and marketing efforts on sanitary maintenance items for industrial and institutional markets. Airwick Liquid, an odor-controlling consumer household product, had been marketed for Airkem by outside companies until 1963. When Ciba-Geigy acquired the company in the second half of 1974, Airwick had three major business lines: institutional, consumer, and aquatic (swimming-pool treatment chemicals).

Shortly after the acquisition, each line of business accounted for roughly one third of Airwick's $47 million in sales. The Consumer Brands Division's sales in 1973 were highly dependent on air freshener products (Airwick Solid, Airwick Liquid, and Airwick Spray), which accounted for 97 percent of that division's net sales. All the division's profits came from Airwick Solid and Liquid. In late 1974 the patent on Airwick Solid ran out, and competitors S.C. Johnson and Drackett soon introduced solid air-freshener products that, according to one Airwick executive, "nearly put us out of business in 1975." The company ended 1975 with a loss and was saved only by the financial strength of Ciba-Geigy, its new parent.

Against this backdrop Mike Sheets was recruited in May 1975 to head the Consumer Product Division. Ciba-Geigy had acquired Airwick with the express purpose of diversifying into the consumer products (particularly household products) market. Mike had been vice president of marketing at the R.J. Reynolds Food Division and previously had held management positions with Gardner Advertising and McCann-Erickson, specializing in consumer packaged goods accounts. Mike perceived his marching orders as a mandate to "build the business," and he recognized the urgency of developing new product ideas that would successfully expand the division's narrow product line and diversify its exposure to competitive threats. He sensed that Ciba-Geigy was disappointed in what it had bought, but that it still had a very supportive attitude and was willing to provide the financial backing necessary to turn the business around. Nonetheless, Mike knew that the division had to get some home runs by 1980, or it would be divested.

Before there could be any home runs, Mike found he had to deal with the prior problem of simply fielding a team. Because of its historical emphasis on commercial and institutional products, the existing Airwick R&D group lacked the experience to develop materials highly suitable to the consumer market, and there was a dearth of viable consumer product concepts. Most of the ideas were aimed simply at adapting existing commercial products to sizes and forms thought suitable for household use. The one exception was Stick-Ups, another air freshener product that was successfully launched in late 1976 and helped the company finally achieve black ink for 1977.

Mike worked with Wes Buckner, vice president of marketing in the division (who came to Airwick from Ciba-Geigy's Madison Labs in late 1974) to create an R&D/marketing team that could get the job done. First, they engaged two well-known advertising agencies. Then they brought in Jim Smith to build a new R&D department, initially composed of one chemist with consumer product experience. Jim had once worked for Lehn & Fink, a competitor. Finally, Mike and Wes recruited one product manager, Dick Bankart, from outside the company. Together they set out to develop a product that would turn the division around. Standard practice in the industry was to have marketing people develop the product concept and then turn it over to R&D for physical development. But Mike believed strongly that the best products grew out of a collaborative effort between the two functions. "There's no reason why a chemist can't have marketing insights just because he's a chemist," he said.

SELECTION OF CARPET FRESH

Before considering various product ideas, strategic selection criteria were set. To pass the screen, a product would have to do the following:

Incur delivered costs (variable manufacturing, freight, warehousing, and royalties) no greater than 40 percent of sales, to provide enough gross margin for advertising and promotion expenses.

Achieve minimum annual sales of $10 million and a maximum of $100 million, to be big enough to sustain advertising and interest the trade, but not so big as to bring Airwick into direct competition with industry giants such as Procter & Gamble.

Be protectable by a patent.

Fill a specialized niche in the household or health product class.

Be differentiable in a meaningful way to the consumer, not a "me too" entry.

Entail a new application of known chemistry.

The group considered and eliminated several product ideas, including liquid floor cleaners, other air freshener ideas, and a pot-and-pan soaker. They generated a lot of ideas and checked them out using consumer group interview techniques; but they recognized that the small size of their group meant they had to place their bets on just one or two product candidates.

In May 1976, shortly after Jim Smith was hired, he had a friend from the Center for New Product Development (a small entrepreneurial firm) bring in a powdered substance that had been around for several years—and which had been rejected at one point or another by almost every company in the household products industry. The fragranced powder could be sprinkled on a rug and vacuumed up, thus freshening both the rug and the air in the room, as air was exhausted from the vacuum. Wes, Mike, and Jim were attracted by the idea because it constituted a new product category that was void of competitors, yet it fit well with Airwick's existing business. Nonetheless, they realized that consumers had no recognition of odors in rugs, the primary reason that other companies had rejected the product in the past. "We had a great answer to no problem," commented Mike. But there were no other good ideas, either, and time was ticking away. The team felt that this product might present a real opportunity, and so decided to pursue the idea.

POSITIONING CARPET FRESH

Product Concept

Concept testing to determine how best to position the product began in July 1976 and continued until a solution was reached in March of the next year. Through a market research technique of one-on-one interviews with 450 consumers responding to two different videotaped commercials, the team tried different ways to position the product. By using Airwick secretaries to act in the videotaped commercials, the team was able to modify the commercial messages rapidly as new information and problems came to light. Ad agency, marketing, and R&D people watched the interviews together behind a one-way mirror and collaborated in solving each problem that surfaced. In this way the group was able to fine-tune the product by using consumers' reactions to its physical characteristics (scent and texture), package design, name, and attributes.

Two primary concepts were developed and tested. One—the "single-minded" concept—characterized the product simply as a rug and room deodorizer. The other—the "three-way" concept—described it as deodorizing the rug and room, decreasing static electricity, and keeping carpets clean longer. One problem encountered was finding a way to get homemakers to recognize that rugs picked up odors and held them. This was essential in order to build a perceived need for a rug and room deodorizer. Homemakers thought primarily in terms of cooking, smoking, and other odors in the air. Another problem was to move consumers away from the idea that the product was a rug cleaner, as rug cleaners abounded and Carpet Fresh didn't really clean rugs.

After nearly nine months of commercial and concept testing, a correlation was found in March 1977 between pet ownership and positive reaction to the product by homemakers in the research sample. This suggested a solution to both problems: use the single-minded concept, show odor sources on the rug, and then show odors in the air. As June was the date targeted for beginning a market test, this solution came none too soon.

Packaging and Shelf Position

While concept testing was going on, some needed modifications were made in the product's physical characteristics, and a packaging consultant was brought in to help design a package that would support the concept. The team thought it important to use a novel shape and a color that would convey the idea that this was neither a rug cleaner nor an air freshener, but a totally new and serious product. (Exhibit 3 depicts one package the team considered and also shows the one actually chosen.) In addition, the package chosen was of sufficient height to

---

EXHIBIT 3   Carpet Fresh Packaging

Considered

Chosen

---

place the brand next to Lehn & Fink's $75 million Lysol Spray, a "serious" product with a high shelf price that was comparable to the price of Carpet Fresh. Lysol Spray was a fast-moving product normally placed on store shelves very near, but not in the middle of, air fresheners. The team did not want Carpet Fresh to be shelved directly alongside air fresheners, since this would undermine the concept of a totally new "rug and room deodorizer" product category, and price comparisons would also have been very unfavorable. Nor did they want Carpet Fresh to be shelved with rug cleaners, for the same reason. Furthermore, associating Carpet Fresh with rug cleaners was to be avoided because rug cleaners were purchased only once or twice a year.

Name and Price

The team believed the product also needed a highly descriptive name to help consumers understand what this novel product did. After considering the possibility that a very descriptive name would run the risk of being too generic, eventually weakening the value of the trademark, the name "Carpet Fresh" was selected. It was decided to introduce 9-ounce (aimed at initial purchases) and 14-ounce sizes and to price them for the market test at a retail price of $1.29 and $1.79, respectively. While the field market test was in progress, a laboratory test conducted by Yankelovich, Skelly & White gauged consumer attitudes and reaction to three sets of price points (Exhibit 4). The highest price evaluated—$1.99 for the 14-ounce size—was set not to exceed the price of Lysol Spray. In April 1977, prior to field testing, sales and profit levels were projected for a national introduction in March 1978 of the 9-ounce and 14-ounce sizes priced at $1.29 and $1.79, respectively, as shown in Exhibit 5. Retail prices tested included a 28 percent trade margin, standard for similar household product categories.

Capital Request and National Launch Target Date

In the April 1, 1977, marketing plan that Mike and Wes prepared to request capital funds from the Ciba-Geigy Executive Committee, a recommendation was made to commit $440,000 for manufacturing equipment that Airwick would provide to outside production contractors. Excerpts from the plan follow.

> Ideally, because of the market factors still to be checked out, we should not commit capital resources on Carpet Fresh until we have at least the controlled laboratory test market readings.

EXHIBIT 4   Memo about Consumer Attitudes

Date: June 20, 1977
To: W. Buckner
From: F. La Ronca
Subject: Yankelovich Lab—Carpet Fresh Trial

The trial phase of the Yankelovich lab is complete, and the results are very encouraging, as the table shows:

	Respondent Base	Trial	Rate (%)
Cell 1: High price ($1.39/1.99)	250 (coupon)	113	45
Cell 2: Regular price ($1.29/1.79)	175 (coupon)	90	51
	175 (no coupon)	70	40
Cell 3: Low price ($.99/1.39)	253 (coupon)	136	54
Total	853	409	48

Yankelovich is hesitant to give a normative range because there are significant variations by category and nothing directly comparable to Carpet Fresh. However, a 48 percent unfactored laboratory trial* is considered very healthy.

The coupon had a positive effect at all three price levels. However, the 40 percent trial rate with no coupon at the regular price is still very strong.

Carpet Fresh is seen to be price sensitive but not to a significant degree among the three ranges tested. Focus groups revealed that consumers did not consider the price too high and accepted the pricing, as there is no direct base of comparison. The repeat phase will be key to determining whether the brand could be more profitabily marketed at the higher price level.

Steve Rose is scheduled to discuss results of data in more detail the week of 6/20.

* "Unfactored laboratory trial" is the total rate of consumer trial for all price levels, with and without coupons.

However, the critical path to product availability for a national launch, once the investment decision is made, is currently estimated at 52 to 57 weeks.

If we were to make an investment decision by April 18, 1977, on the basis of information now available, we would be able to launch the product nationally sometime between April 15, 1978, and May 20, 1978.

EXHIBIT 5 Carpet Fresh Projections (4/1/77)

Year	Cases (thousands)*			Annual Profit ($MM)	Gross Sales ($MM)
	Total	*9 oz.*	*14 oz.*		
1978 (9 mos.)	676	434	242	$(1,501)	$ 8.6
1979	871	560	311	478	11.1
1980	950	610	340	2,189	12.1

* 1 case = 1 dozen packages.

Source: Airwick Industries (4/77).

If, on the other hand, we were to wait until September 5, 1977, after availability of Yankelovich information, our national introduction date would be sometime between September 1, 1978, and October 6, 1978. Since we would be introducing the product just before the Halloween/Thanksgiving/Christmas period, we might be well advised, under this alternative, to delay introduction until early 1979.

A delay in the national introduction of Carpet Fresh until late 1978 or early 1979 would not seem to be consistent with the urgent need for the Airwick Products Division to bring successful new products to the national market with all practical speed.

Also, we know that a major competitor is working on a possibly related product. For maximum Carpet Fresh success, it is vital that we are the first rug and room deodorizer on the market.

In view of these considerations, we propose that we accept the significant business risk and make the decision to commit, on or before April 18, 1977, the necessary resources to proceed on the critical path to a national product launch.

This investment decision is estimated to amount to $440,000.

On about September 1, 1977, we will have controlled laboratory test-market readings on the product. If at that time there would be reason to interrupt or terminate development of the capital equipment, it is estimated that approximately 33 percent, or $138,000, of the original commitment could be recovered.

During the early months of the field market test, an industry market intelligence service included a description of the Carpet Fresh product, price points, and market test in one of its reports.

THE MARKET TEST

A 36-week field market test was conducted for Airwick by AdTel in two test markets, Bakersfield, California, and Quad Cities (Davenport, Moline, Rock Island, East Moline), beginning at the end of May 1977. AdTel was a market research firm that set up actual market tests in cities where it had established relationships with grocery stores. It could arrange for shelf space in those stores and track product sales. AdTel also had an ongoing arrangement with 2,000 families in each test market city to keep diaries of monthly purchases of all products. From the diaries, AdTel could determine trial and repeat purchase cycles.

A primary objective of the Carpet Fresh market test was to gauge consumer acceptance of the product. Another key objective was to see if the positioning and advertising strategies would work to produce strong enough sales to project a target sales level of $8.6 million (based on the $1.29 and $1.79 price points) for the first nine months of the national launch in 1978. A target market share was also set at 12.3 percent of the air freshener category ($106 million in 1977), as there was no rug and room deodorizer category to use as a yardstick.

Shelf space in 81 grocery stores was obtained directly by AdTel without going through food brokers, as Airwick would do if it decided to introduce the product later. This method was chosen in part because going through food brokers would add three or four months to the waiting period before test data would begin to come in. Heavy TV advertising support was scheduled, with 19 spot commercials per week to be shown at four-week intervals. Because of the need to educate consumers about an unfamiliar product, 60-second spots were required rather than the more standard 30-second spots. In addition, 30¢-off coupons were to be sent by direct mail to stimulate trial. The coupons were sent to households that, according to market research studies, were heavy users of household products.

The Yankelovich laboratory market test was initiated at the same time. It could provide information on buyer demographics and price-point effects. Most importantly, the laboratory test could yield data by September 1977.

Market test results went far beyond even the most optimistic expectations. In September 1977, Wes reported on results through August of both the AdTel market test and the Yankelovich laboratory test. During the first 14 weeks of the AdTel test, two flights of TV advertising had been aired and 30¢-off coupons had been mailed. Average weekly sales were running at 142 percent of Airwick's original goal for the market test. The original target for Carpet Fresh's share of the air freshener market after national introduction had been 12.3 percent, but results indicated that it had actually garnered a 43.5 percent share of the test market. In addition, the size of the air freshener market in the test area had expanded by 90 percent. In one test period, Carpet Fresh had even topped sales of fast-moving Lysol Spray by 16 percent!

The Yankelovich test results provided some positive signs as well. Consumers expressed high intent to repurchase the product after initial trial, in comparison to other household products. Price sensitivity

---

EXHIBIT 6 Yankelovich Laboratory Test—Consumer Trial of Carpet Fresh

Price Points (dollars)	Consumers Who Purchase (%)
$1.39/1.99	45
$1.29/1.79	51
$ .99/1.29	54

---

for initial purchase after viewing the commercial was not very strong, as illustrated by the test results in Exhibit 6.

The laboratory test also showed that the 14-ounce package obtained a larger-than-expected percentage of initial purchases. This fit with data from the AdTel test, in which the 14-ounce size accounted for 52 percent of total sales. Initial expectations were that the 9-ounce size would account for 54 percent of sales.

On the basis of these early results, Wes increased the unit sales

---

EXHIBIT 7 Combined Bakersfield and Quad Cities Test Markets: Carpet Fresh Monthly Unit Sales (40 panel stores)

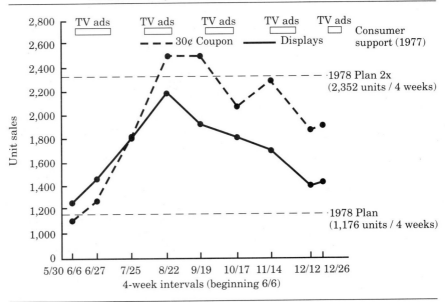

Source: Airwick Industries.

EXHIBIT 8   Memo about Out-of-Stocks

Date: October 18, 1977
To: W. Buckner
From: J. Goren
Subject: Carpet Fresh Out-of-Stocks in Test Markets

This summarizes the information provided by Ken Robb concerning out-of-stocks in the Carpet Fresh test markets.

Conclusions

The Brand believes the moderately depressed Carpet Fresh volume levels, especially on the 14-oz. size exhibited in the test markets for the weeks ending 9/26 and 10/3, can be attributed to retail out-of-stocks.

Indicated Action

1. The Brand will work closely with R&D, Marketing Services, and Manufacturing in an attempt to avoid test market out-of-stocks.
2. The out-of-stock conditions in the test markets for the weeks ending 9/26 and 10/3 will be taken into consideration in The Brand's evaluation of the Carpet Fresh test market.

Findings

1. Quad Cities
   a. Audit stores: During the week ending 9/26 (9/19 to 9/26), 5 of the 20 audit stores were temporarily out of stock, primarily on the 14-oz. size.
   b. Distribution stores: No deliveries were made to distribution stores during the week ending 9/26. This contributed to 12 of the 24 stores in this panel being out of stock on at least one size of Carpet Fresh for most of the week.
2. Bakersfield: No out-of-stocks have been reported in the Bakersfield test market during the week ending 9/26.
3. Market Audits believes that a residual out-of-stock effect would be expected in at least the Quad Cities test market for the week ending 10/3.

---

volume projections for 1978, the year of national introduction, to 1,408,000 cases, more than twice the original plan (646,000 cases). Given the additional revenue this volume would yield, he also increased the planned advertising expenditure to $6.6 million from $3.7 million.

AdTel results through the end of 1977 are shown in Exhibit 7 in relation to the original 1978 sales plan projections. The exhibit also shows the timing of TV ads, coupon mailings, and special in-store displays. Exhibits 8 and 9 provide additional information on the AdTel and Yankelovich tests.

Given the strong, positive test results, a decision was made to prepare for a national launch, and a late March 1978 date for initial shipments was announced to the trade. Airwick did not have a strong position with brokers. The company had historically distributed its products in only a few regional markets, and the volume of Airwick products had never been a very important factor to brokers. For these

---

EXHIBIT 9   Memo about Test Market Data

Date: October 21, 1977
To: M. Sheets
From: W. Buckner
Subject: Carpet Fresh Test Market Data

We have just received some top-line information from the Carpet Fresh test markets that is extremely encouraging. The table (below) outlines the top-line data from the consumer attitude and awareness study that was conducted among current Carpet Fresh users in the two test markets. This is the first consumer information that we have from people who have actually purchased the product in the stores in the market. The study was conducted in mid-September, and by that point, we had a total of seven weeks of advertising.

There was a trial level of 9 percent and an awareness level of 55 percent. Both scores are good but not outstanding. The unaided awareness score of 97 percent among users is extremely high. The 55 percent is the awareness of the brand among all the people that were contacted in order to find 200 users and 200 "aware but nonusers."

The purchase intent scale showing 82 percent for the top two boxes is extremely high. The research company indicated that in the 15 years that it has been conducting this type of market research, the 52 percent top box is the highest score it has ever received. The 82 percent purchase intent is deemed exceptional.

The likes and dislikes about the product are also shown in the table and are concerned primarily with the fragrance, the pleasant odor, and the effectiveness of Carpet Fresh. The dislikes are extremely low.

All of these data are very consistent with the previous work on Carpet Fresh that has been done during the past year, including the "one-on-ones," the consumer product use test, and the Yankelovich laboratory test.

It is the opinion of the research company that with the extremely high purchase intent we have achieved, additional advertising money would probably double the trial level and increase the awareness from 55 percent to 85–90 percent. In other words, we have a product that delivers satisfaction; therefore, one of the primary goals is to obtain a higher

EXHIBIT 9   *(concluded)*

level of trial and awareness in a shorter period of time in order to "pre-empt" this market from any competitors.

These data very definitely confirm our decision to increase the advertising expenditure from the original plan.

Carpet Fresh Awareness/Usage/Attitude Study*

Trial	9%	
Awareness	55%	
Unaided awareness among users	97%	

Purchase intent:		*Among Users*
Definitely will buy		52% ⎱ 82%
Probably will buy		30 ⎰
Might or might not		9
Probably not		4
Definitely not		5

		Aware
Likes:	*Triers*	*Nontriers*
Pleasant odor/clean fresh smell	64%	31%
Eliminates odor	45	48
Easy to use, convenient	21	10
Brightens/freshens carpet look	8	8

Dislikes:	
Smells too strong	8
Too expensive/used up too fast	8
Odor not last	5
Hard to shake out	4
No dislikes	66

* Top-line data from study conducted mid-September 1977, seven weeks of advertising, starting June 1977.

reasons the team expected difficulty in gaining broker acceptance for Carpet Fresh. Broker commissions for Carpet Fresh would be 5 percent of net sales (manufacturer's selling price), standard in the industry for household products of this type.

MANUFACTURING

Larry Graf, senior vice president of Operations, and Rich Roscelli in Manufacturing were given the job of scaling up to produce large quantities of Carpet Fresh. Airwick's policy was to use outside companies to produce and package new products and to gradually develop in-house manufacturing capacity once the product was established. Producing commercial quantities of Carpet Fresh involved locating outside fillers and blenders, ordering tooling for plastic bottles and caps, ordering labeling equipment, and arranging for transportation of chemicals to powder producers, raw plastic material to molders, packaging to fillers, and finished cases of the product to distribution points. The logistics were complex, as manufacturing locations were dispersed in New Jersey and Ohio. Outside contractors had to be located near freight and warehouse facilities.

Roscelli described the situation faced by the Operations group at the time. Carpet Fresh was "totally beyond anything we had ever dealt with before." It involved the biggest scope of materials handling ever for Airwick. "It was staggering to see how many million pounds of powder we needed. Most of our products before were liquid, mostly water. . . . Scaling up for the test market involved only small quantities, and the problems we would run into for the national launch never really surfaced." The national launch was, in fact, delayed by two months. It was not possible to get all the equipment delivered to Airwick's outside contract manufacturers and have it running properly in time to build up the minimum inventory level required—enough to fill the pipeline and have 25 percent of projected first-year sales on hand in each warehouse. "We would have liked to delay it even longer to build a more comfortable inventory level, but a date had been announced to the trade, and we had to go ahead."

For the first six weeks after national introduction in June 1978, sales levels were not very encouraging. Then 30¢-off coupons were mailed to consumers, and demand took off. Roscelli later recalled that "it was a struggle for the first six to nine months because we had only about 10 people in our group to cope with the need for speeding up production and increasing capacity, even before the national launch." These people worked full-time on Carpet Fresh for several months, but they also had responsibility for other products. They worked 12 to 14 hours a day, and several were in Ohio during the worst winter in its history. "The roof literally blew off one manufacturing facility, and we were snowed in for four days," Roscelli recalled.

Sales projections were constantly being increased (see Exhibit 10), beginning after the AdTel test started, and they continued to be increased well after the market launch. Before the test Marketing had projected 676,000 cases for 1978, with one third in the 14-ounce size and two thirds in the 9-ounce size. Year-end sales for 1978 were actually 1,867,000 cases, and the mix of sizes was roughly two thirds 14-ounce and one third 9-ounce. Molding machines for each package size differed. Actual case sales for 1979 were 2,341,000, with a backlog of 400,000 cases; 2,000,000 cases were originally projected for 1979. The response of brokers to Carpet Fresh had been unexpectedly positive,

EXHIBIT 10 Carpet Fresh Sales Projection Revisions

Projection	Cases (thousands)			($000)
	9 oz.	14 oz.	Total	
Original (4/1/77)				
1978*	434	242	676	8,589
1979	560	311	871	11,064
1980	610	340	950	12,071
Revised (9/13/77)				
1978*	n.a.	n.a.	1,408	18,755
1979	n.a.	n.a.	2,000	27,504
1980	n.a.	n.a.	2,100	28,879
Revised (9/19/77)				
1978*	n.a.	n.a.	1,872	n.a.
1979	n.a.	n.a.	2,000	n.a.
1980	n.a.	n.a.	2,100	n.a.
Revised (8/18/78)				
1978	814	853	1,667	n.a.
1979	n.a.	n.a.	2,000	n.a.
1980	n.a.	n.a.	2,100	n.a.
Revised (10/78)				
1979	n.a.	n.a.	4,675	78,915
1980	n.a.	n.a.	4,647	79,000
Revised (11/78)				
1979	n.a.	n.a.	3,375	57,000
1980	n.a.	n.a.	n.a.	n.a.

* Nine months only.
n.a. = Not available.

Source: Airwick Industries internal memoranda.

particularly because Carpet Fresh gave them substantial new product sales volume without cutting into the sales of products they already carried. Airwick's position with existing brokers improved markedly, and a new group of more aggressive brokers developed an interest in handling Carpet Fresh.

Once sales took off in the summer of 1978, Manufacturing managers had to work very hard to provide Marketing people with information on product availability and location so that the sales department could allocate whatever was available to the most critical markets. Larry Graf explained, "We learned a useful lesson from the Carpet Fresh experience because we had only a manual system for keeping track of product at the time. Today we have an automated MIS system to provide faster updates." Airwick also increased its capacity to produce

Carpet Fresh (eventually brought in-house) to a level of 7.5 million cases per year for a total capital investment of $2.1 million. Actual sales in 1982 were just under 2 million cases, requiring a 3-million-case capacity to meet peak demand.

COMPETITIVE ENTRIES

Before launching Carpet Fresh nationally, the team tried to anticipate which competitors would enter the market and how. An early and strong response was expected from S.C. Johnson, the makers of Glade air freshener. They were the biggest in the business, and very aggressive; Drackett, with its Renuzit air-freshener brand, was viewed as the second potential threat. There was also a possibility that Boyle-Midway (makers of the Wizard air-freshener brand) might enter with a rug and room deodorizer product.

There seemed to be two likely ways to position competing entries: with a lower price and with fragrances. The team considered how it would respond to each of these. A decision was made to stay with just the regular Carpet Fresh scent, to avoid becoming "just another air freshener" and to avoid diluting the "serious" Carpet Fresh image by adding different fragrances. To prepare to meet price competition, in November 1978 Mike came up with the idea of launching another, less expensive "fighting" brand, which would not be associated with Carpet Fresh. Because Airwick had recently bought the Glamorene brand name, it was decided to introduce a rug and room deodorizer product called Glamorene Rug Fresh in a plain, cylindrical, 15.5-ounce package priced at $1.59. The brand would be supported by trade deals but no advertising. The Glamorene line in 1978 included a few household products (a rug cleaner, aerosol upholstery cleaner, and drain opener) that together accounted for less than $1 million in sales, plus Spray 'N' Vac, with $10 million in sales. The Glamorene name was well known, but its image was not that of an innovator.

Airwick had planned to introduce a 22-ounce size of Carpet Fresh on May 1, 1979, requiring additional tooling and production capacity. Because production executives were already working feverishly just to fill current demand for existing sizes (each day of stockouts cost $30,000 in lost contribution), a decision was made to postpone the 22-ounce introduction until October 1979 and to concentrate instead on tooling up for a May 1 introduction of Rug Fresh. Word had reached Airwick that Lehn & Fink, makers of Lysol Spray, were preparing to launch a rug and room deodorizer product, and the race was on to beat it to market. The Production personnel redoubled their efforts and managed to get Rug Fresh into production by March 1979. Lehn & Fink's brand, Love My Carpet, reached the market at the very end of

April, and Rug Fresh was out on the shelves within a few days after. Love My Carpet was priced slightly less than Carpet Fresh in comparable sizes. Later that year, Wizard came out with a brand in floral and herbal fragrances priced at $1.29. The Wizard product had little advertising support. In 1980 Love My Carpet, holding to the same sizes, introduced two additional fragrances and added a third in 1982. By late 1982 the fragranced segment had grown to 17 percent of the total rug and room deodorizer market, and Love My Carpet had reduced Wizard to 3 percent of total market share. At one point Renuzit market tested a product but opted not to introduce it nationally. S.C. Johnson, originally thought to be the most likely competitor for Carpet Fresh, never entered the rug and room deodorizer market. Mike and Wes eventually learned through the trade press that S.C. Johnson was making major investments in health and beauty aids rather than in household products.

In August 1981 Arm & Hammer came out nationally with a baking-soda "Carpet Deodorizer" in a square, orange shaker box, with this message: "Absorbs odors with no cover-up perfume." The 21-ounce size was priced at 99¢, compared to Carpet Fresh's price of $2.19 for the 14-ounce size. Private label brands also entered the market in that year. In 1982 Arm & Hammer began regional market testing of a "light scent" version of its product, and it added a 30-ounce size. Carpet Fresh prices in 1982 were $1.49 (9-ounce), $2.09 (14-ounce), and $2.99 (22-ounce).

Exhibit 11 shows competitors' price points, product and size characteristics, sales, dollar-and-ounce market share, advertising expenditure levels, and percent penetration of grocery stores. Exhibit 12 provides information on Carpet Fresh income and expenditures. Total product category advertising by all companies in 1979 was $20 million but was reduced to $10 million by 1981. In the first six months of 1982, category advertising expenditures were at an annual level of $12 million. Airwick planned to spend $6 million on advertising for the year and another $1.5 million on promotion. In analyzing the competitive situation, Airwick executives indicated that Love My Carpet, because of its name, was able to generate a higher level of consumer awareness than Carpet Fresh at one third the advertising expenditure. Market share trends are shown in Exhibit 13.

Between 1979 and 1982 Airwick adjusted its marketing approach in response to various competitor moves (see Exhibit 14 for unit sales and selling price). In April 1979 it was decided to emphasize the "antisoil" properties of Carpet Fresh in order to differentiate it from Love My Carpet. The words "patented anti-soil formula" were added to the label, although the patented ingredient had always been part of the product. Television commercials were developed to support this approach, but the product was not really a cleaner, and the shift from

EXHIBIT 11 Competitive Situation in 1981

Competitor	Sales* Year	Sales* ($millions)	Share (percent) Ounces	Share (percent) (Dollars)	Advertising Year	Advertising ($millions)	Percentage of Grocery Store Distribution
Love My Carpet							
12 oz., $1.35	1979	$13.9	20.2	$20.4	1979	$4.8	12-wk. SARDI (4/3/81)
20 oz., $2.08	1980	19.9	30.9	29.8	1980	4.8	
	1981	16.3	25.3	26.2	1981	3.5	Brand total 89%
Regular, Floral, Citrus	1982	13.8	21.4	22.3	1982	3.2	Regular 12, 61%
(pricing strategy is to	1983	12.0	18.6	19.3	1983	3.0	Regular 20, 45
slightly undersell Car-							Citrus 12, 25
pet Fresh on a unit							Citrus 20, 14
basis)							Floral 12, 32
							Floral 20, 14
Arm & Hammer							n.a.
21 oz., $.99	1979	0	0	0	1979	0	Estimated 65% based
30 oz., $1.35 (est.)	1980	0	0	0	1980	0	on test market;
(pricing strategy is to	1981	4.1	14.5	6.5	1981	2.4	dual size may be
undercut all competi-	1982	5.1	18.0	8.1	1982	.5	higher.
tors by holding 21 oz.	1983	3.4	12.0	5.4	1983	.5	
under $1.00 while							
maintaining a pre-							
mium to regular							
baking soda)							
Wizard							
Super (20 oz.), $1.99	1979	3.4	4.9	4.8	1979	1.3	Brand total 41%
Floral (12 oz.), $1.29	1980	6.7	9.6	9.3	1980	2.7	SF 11½, 7%
	1981	3.6	5.0	4.8	1981	.5	SF 17½, 8
	1982	2.9	4.0	3.9	1982	.3	Herbal 11½, 9
	1983	2.0	3.0	2.9	1983	.1	Herbal 17½, 11
Super, Floral, Herbal							Super 17½, 21
(pricing strategy is to							
claim 25% more than							
the leading brand)							

* SAMI sales expanded by ±35 percent to account for nonfood and discounted by 25 percent margin.
n.a. = Not available.

Source: Airwick Industries (1981). Figures for 1982 and 1983 are projections.

EXHIBIT 12   Carpet Fresh Profit-and-Loss Statements (thousands of dollars)

	1978		1979	1982†
	Plan*	Actual	Actual	Actual
Gross sales	$ 8,589	$27,224	$50,619	$32,271
Less: discounts, rebates, and allowances	1,365	3,830	6,173	4,791
Net sales	$ 7,224	$23,394	$44,476	$27,791
Variable manufacturing costs	2,444	6,663	12,480	6,400
Gross margin	$ 4,780	$16,731	$31,966	$21,391
Variable expenses:				
Freight and warehousing	631	1,534	4,097	1,920
Royalties and commissions	696	1,818	3,048	2,880
Variable contribution	$ 3,453	$13,379	$24,821	$16,591
Marketing expenses:				
Advertising	$ 3,700	$ 5,884	$13,692	$ 6,000
Consumer promotion	570	1,441	1,083	320
Trade promotion	45	230	47	1,600
Selling and merchandising aids	50	44	47	32
Other marketing	125	54	166	320
Contribution before overhead expenses	$(1,037)	$ 5,726	$ 9,786	$ 8,319

Note: Exhibits 12 and 13 can be used to calculate what the gross margin and variable contribution would be at different levels of unit sales. The variable contribution is the amount available for marketers to use in stimulating product purchase. It is also possible to speculate about the effect on unit sales of various price levels and to see their impact on variable contribution—hence the amount available to stimulate purchase.
* Original plan, April 1, 1977.
† 1982 figures are estimated.

EXHIBIT 13   Room and Rug Deodorizers' Dollar Share of Market*
           (percentage)

	1979	1980	1981	Year to Date† 1982
Carpet Fresh	65.4	46.9	42.9	41.1
Love My Carpet	20.4	29.8	29.0	30.3
Arm & Hammer	—	—	7.8	10.0
Glamorene Rug Fresh	8.4	8.3	5.8	5.3
Private label	—	4.0	6.5	7.4
All other	5.8	11.0	8.0	5.9

* Retail grocery store sales.
† Period ending 1/8/82–6/26/82.

Source: Airwick Industries (8/82).

EXHIBIT 14   Carpet Fresh Unit Sales and Manufacturer's Selling Prices

	Unit Sales (cases)*		
Size	*1978*	*1979*	*1982*
9 oz.	907,467	1,066,439	379,564
14 oz.	944,506	2,035,929	1,057,942
22 oz.	—	129,265	286,109
	Manufacturer's Selling Price†		
	1978	*1979*	*1982*
9 oz.	$12.00	$12.00	$12.86
14 oz.	17.16	17.16	18.88
22 oz.	—	22.32	25.92

* One case = 12 packages.
† Per case, before discounts, rebates, and allowances.

Source: Airwick Industries.

"deodorizer" to a "cleaner" message proved confusing to consumers. However, later that year Airwick brought suit for patent infringement against Lehn & Fink, to prevent its claims that Love My Carpet also had anti-soil properties. In 1981 Airwick concentrated its marketing funds on fending off competition.

THE NEXT STRATEGIC DECISION

After Arm & Hammer's 1981 introduction, Wes and Mike began to wonder if this low-price brand might serve to expand the market by stimulating trial of the category among consumers who would subsequently trade up to Carpet Fresh. Because by 1982 only a fraction of all potential consumers used a rug and room deodorizer, one issue was whether Airwick should avoid marketing tactics that might interfere with Arm & Hammer's potential to expand the market as a whole. Alternatively, Airwick might try a tactic of its own to stimulate primary demand by positioning either Carpet Fresh or a line extension to bring in new buyers. Market research on homemakers' use of rug and room deodorizer products provided the following data:

- 45 to 50 percent had never used the product.
- 35 percent had used the product in the last year.
- Of the 35 percent who used it in the last year:
  1. One third used one can per year.
  2. One third used two or three cans per year.

3. One third used more than three cans per year (accounting for approximately 50 percent of unit sales).

Another option was for Airwick to extend its line into fragrances or to lower Carpet Fresh prices to fend off further share erosion by Love My Carpet and Arm & Hammer. Alternatively, Airwick could assume that market growth was virtually over for the category and gradually reduce advertising expenditures to make funds available for other products.

Case 4–9   J. C. Penney*

Huddled around a rack of silk ties at the NorthPark Mall here [Dallas], Deanna Woolley and Janet Weidenbach express the divided loyalties of the J. C. Penney shopper.

Ms. Weidenbach buys her hosiery at Penney. Last Christmas, Ms. Woolley bought a sweater for her mother here, and she often buys shirts and ties for her father at the store. Both women admire the tonier merchandise and the snazzy chrome-and-glass fixtures that have come with Penney's attempt to upgrade its image. "I didn't used to like to come to J. C. Penney at all," Ms. Woolley confesses as she selects a $16 yellow tie for her father. "It was old-looking, kind of like going to Sears."

Score one for the new Penney's. But ask the 21-year-olds where they buy their own clothes and almost in unison they answer, "The Limited"—the trendy specialty retailer. For Penney, a formerly frumpy mass merchant and the nation's fourth-largest retailer—with $16.4 billion in 1989 sales—the combination of praise and snub is all too common.

While other big retailers tangled with corporate raiders during the 1980s—often with disastrous results—Penney was undergoing face lifts and tummy tucks in an effort to remake itself into a department-store beauty queen. In some ways the effort has worked, and earnings have rebounded sharply.

But Penney still lags behind many of its rivals in sales per square foot of floor space. It has yet to persuade many makers of chic women's wear to supply it with the clothing and accessories it needs to help shake its reputation as a low-price purveyor of linens, children's clothing and hard goods. "Over the past decade, no major retailer in America has changed as much as J. C. Penney," company Chairman William R. Howell told investors in March. But, he added later, "you don't change 90 years of consumer perceptions in less than a decade."

Penney's experience is a sobering lesson for other old-line retailers, such as Sears, Roebuck & Co. and Montgomery Ward & Co. They also need to change the way shoppers and suppliers view them to survive in a crowded industry. In its mass-merchandising heyday, Penney joined Sears and Ward in selling cookie-cutter basics to middle-income Americans whose choices were determined by price and reliability. But discounters stole away many of the price-conscious, while regional malls gave the quality-conscious more—and more fashionable—alternatives.

Penney recognized the shift in the mid-1970s, when Mr. Howell, then director of domestic development, headed a task force charged with putting Penney's stores back in touch with middle America. Armed with "a blank sheet of paper and four offices," the task force interviewed dozens of consultants and hundreds of employees and customers, and scouted more than 70 competitors. The conclusion: The company was trying to do too many things in the wrong places.

While it had grown up as the all-purpose store in small towns, Penney had spent the 1950s and 1960s snapping up choice locations in the new regional shopping malls. But the shoppers flocking to those malls went to buy clothes and accessories, not car batteries, refrigerators or lawn mowers. They also wanted brand names, which Penney had booted out years before in favor of higher-margin private labels. Penney, it was decided, needed to become a fashionable national department store for middle-income and upper-middle-income customers.

The transition has hardly been painless. Penney closed down its appliance, lawn and garden, paint, hardware and automotive lines in 1983 and its home electronics and sporting goods lines in 1988, surrendering more than 1.5 billion in annual sales. The company says it also cut $60 million from its annual budget and reinvigorated its management ranks by moving its headquarters to Dallas from New York two years ago. The move cost some 1,250 New Yorkers their jobs.

The company has slowly changed. Tile floors in stores have given way to parquet and carpet. Penney has installed a state-of-the art video satellite network to display new merchandise to its buyers and also to potential customers. The system permits Penney to test-market new styles and has made store buying and inventory control more efficient. In expanded men's and women's fashion departments, $7.99 polyester ties and $29.99 women's shifts have given way to $22 silk neckwear and $80 career dresses.

The result: From a garden-variety mass merchant, Penney has blossomed into something glossier.

Over the past five years, while the number of Penney stores shrank by 10 percent, annual revenue has grown 16 percent and net income has more than doubled to $802 million. Though its stock price languishes at 10 times earnings, compared with 20 times earnings for hot retailers such as Wal-Mart Stores, The Limited and The Gap, Wall Street is generally upbeat about Penney's future. "I would sign a blood oath that says Penney is improving its business and will have up earnings for three years," says Oppenheimer analyst Bruce Missett. "I wouldn't do that for Kmart, even in pencil."

For all its efforts, however, Penney's yearly sales per square foot, a measure of retailing productivity, are a disappointing $128 at metropolitan stores, and even less if other stores are included. By contrast, Dayton's and Hudson's department stores and Mervyn's both sell about $202 of merchandise a square foot; May department stores do $159.

To get a more respectable $150 to $175 a square foot, securities analysts say, Penney buyers must continue to improve the merchandise mix and exploit fashion trends. Some analysts also suggest that Penney needs to close more stores, though it has shut 270 smaller ones, mostly outside malls, in the past five years.

Penney hasn't discovered the marketing elixir that would win over women who now buy towels, men's shirts and children's clothes at Penney and then scurry off to The Limited or a rival department store to shop for themselves. Part of the problem remains the lack of coveted brand names. The biggest brand in Penney's most fashionable women's area is its own house label, Jacqueline Ferrar; the biggest name at the cosmetics counter is little-known French maker Fernand Aubry. "It's difficult to categorize yourself as a department store when you don't have Clinique makeup," says Margo McGlade of Paine-Webber.

Though Penney has more than 1,300 stores and an unusual reputation for paying bills on time, its executives still must travel the country begging big-name suppliers to treat them like May and Dayton Hudson, not Sears and Montgomery Ward. That has been a tough sell, mainly because many apparel and cosmetics makers fear that the chain will discount their goods or otherwise cheapen their images.

Mr. Howell recalls his first approach to Levi Strauss & Co. in 1979 about selling its jeans through Penney. Saying "I'm here to plead with you," he promised that Penney stores were going to "change dramatically in the 1980s." Mr. Howell says the room went "very quiet, and that was about the end of the meeting."

Levi, aware that it might be missing a huge group of customers, finally agreed to sell to Penney—three years later. Penney now claims to be Levi's largest customer, selling about $100 million a year of the Dockers brand alone. But the move cost Levi some business. R. H. Macy & Co. stores dropped Levi's jeans, reasoning that the brand had lost its exclusiveness by appearing at a mass marketer, and still doesn't sell the line today.

Other manufacturers have been even harder to persuade. Top women's brands such as Elizabeth Arden, Estee Lauder, Liz Claiborne and Evan-Picone still shun Penney. Officials of those companies won't say why. Bernard Chaus, chairman of an upper-moderate women's apparel maker bearing his name, applauds Penney's improving image, but says that the prices of his clothing still are too high for Penney stores. "Perhaps someday we'll do business with them," he says.

Penney officials say that cosmetics and women's apparel makers seem concerned that other customers might suddenly consider them declasse. The attitude frustrates and puzzles those at Penney who have worked to upgrade its merchandise. While a few men's suits still sell for $149.99, most cost $175 to $350. Bridal departments at many stores have been converted to career boutiques selling women's suits at prices between $250 and $340. A hot-selling $12 leather purse was dropped because its look clashed with more expensive pocketbooks.

The company's efforts, combined with competitor's travails, have yielded some gains. After years of lobbying with manufacturers, the company this year is adding Haggar and Van Heusen brands to its men's department, Oshkosh B'Gosh to children's and Maidenform and Warner's to lingerie lines. Some manufacturers concede their decision to sell to Penney was accelerated by the bankruptcy filing of Campeau Corp. chains and by other financial problems in the retailing business.

Even some of those who have committed to a Penney connection remain skittish about the relationship, however. A designer whose line will move into Penney stores this summer calls the company "a force in the 1990s." Then he asks not to be cited by name for fear of being too closely identified with Penney. "That wouldn't be good for our name or our business," he says, evoking the memory of the late designer Halston. Designers say he lost some cachet after marketing clothing exclusively through Penney in the mid-1980s. Penney says the relationship improved its image, and blames financial and ownership problems for Halston's fate.

For years, Maidenform Inc. has made Penney's private-label lingeries. Beginning in July, it will sell its own brand at Penney, too. But this took Penney six years of wooing. "The argument that won the day until recently was that we had a brand to protect," says Robert A. Brawer, Maidenform president. "We asked ourselves, are we prepared to suffer the consequences, to lose a couple of million dollars in department store business?"

There were several heated Maidenform management meetings. Then, Mr. Brawer says, a visit from top Penney executives, and the remodeling of Penney stores to better highlight name-brand merchandise, finally convinced Maidenform that Penney would display its products well. Other department stores haven't reacted strongly to the decision, he says, and "I don't think we're going to get hurt."

As the courting of manufacturers continues, so do the physical makeovers of stores. Large-size and petite women's departments have grown. Penney is replacing novelty goods of the airport-gift-shop type with $35 picture frames, desk sets and $280-and-up glass collectibles.

Last year, it tried to improve its cosmetics lines by dumping so-called drugstore lines like Max Factor, L'Oreal and English Leather that had accounted for $21 million a year in sales. Still, the cosmetics department remains a sore spot, producing only about 2½ percent of a Penney store's sales, compared with the 10 percent or so that cosmetics produce for competitors.

So Penney has added to its cosmetics training staff and increased its sales promotion with direct mail and scented fliers in its charge-card bills. At new and remodeled stores, Penney is moving the cosmetics counter to the main mall entrance. At the NorthPark store in Dallas, the move has lifted the sales 36 percent this year.

Penney women's departments of the past seemed "a sea of racks that didn't have a clear definition," says Marshall Beere, divisional vice president for women's sportswear. Two years ago, displays were rearranged to separate goods that appeal to the more fashion-conscious from those aimed at shoppers more concerned with quality or price. Buyers' jobs were redefined; instead of buying all women's tops or junior bottoms, for instance, a buyer now picks products only for customers in a specific target group. Womens sales are up, and the junior department recorded sales gains last year in the high-teens category.

Yet women shoppers, who buy more window coverings and towels at Penney than from any other retailer in the United States, remain reluctant to buy their dressy clothes there. Laquilla Cheek, a Dallas homemaker shopping for graduation gifts, says she hasn't looked at Penney's women's clothes in 10 years. "My mother wore plaid Penney shirtwaist dresses for years," she says, and she still envisions Penney's clothes as designed for "dowdy old women." She does buy children's and men's clothes at Penney.

Susan Seiter, a corporate investor-relations specialist, says she buys lingerie and linens at Penney. She recently stocked up on pantyhose at a Hurst, Texas, store, but then spent $400 on Jones of New York and other brands on sale at another department store. "The few times I've looked [at Penney], there might be an attractive blouse," she says, "but it will be polyester and look hot, like it would smell like New Jersey if you wore it in the summer."

Penney believes that such women and the manufacturers who cater to them eventually will see the light. "We'd like to have Clinique at J. C. Penney" along with other brands, says Penney Chairman Howell.

He believes the years of changes will eventually produce a break-through. "I'm confident that there will be a day when all of those options will be at our disposal," he says. "Just as the Berlin Wall came down very quickly, I'm very optimistic."

Case 4–10   *Minnesota Mining & Manufacturing Co.*

The 725 workers at Minnesota Mining & Manufacturing Co.'s two factories here are helping to propel a U.S. export boom.

Judy Zenk works on plastic connectors for telephone-company wires in India and China. Kathy Schroepfer zaps rubber splices with electricity to make sure they will withstand the electric load in an English utility's underground cables. And Brian Kuester inspects Stormscope thunderstorm detectors before sending them to private pilots in Germany.

Spurred by a historically cheap dollar and a newfound ability to make and sell products that foreign customers want, U.S. manufacturers increased their exports last year to $316 billion from $287 billion in 1989 and $168 billion in 1985. Despite now-slowing growth abroad, 94 percent of manufacturers surveyed by the National Association of Manufacturers expect further increases.

3M, which makes tape, sandpaper, medical products and many other things, has been a leader in this export surge. In the past five years its shipments abroad have doubled to $1.2 billion, making it a major American exporter. And last year its international sales, which include products made abroad, expanded to 49 percent of its total volume of $13.02 billion.

The growth in the St. Paul, Minn., company's foreign business promises to be even more important this year. Though the company recently predicted lower first-quarter earnings, partly because of flat domestic sales and economic turmoil in Brazil, it expects a 5 percent to 6 percent real increase in international sales for the quarter.

The U.S. economy is getting a big payoff from the efforts of firms like 3M. The export boom is fueling growth in much of the so-called Rust Belt, keeping the recession from being worse than it is, and helping trim the trade deficit to the lowest level since 1983. Increased exports

---

accounted for almost all of real (inflation-adjusted) economic growth last year.

Nevertheless, the United States is still far from achieving its export potential. According to the Commerce Department, fewer than one fifth of America's exporters sell to more than five foreign markets.

3M's export machine runs on simple notions. It lets others pursue what Allen F. Jacobson, its chief executive, calls "MBA-ish ideas about market size or critical mass." Its strategy rests on two typically home-spun credos: "FIDO," for First In (to a new market) Defeats Others, and "Make a little, sell a little."

The company enters a market with a modest investment and pushes one basic product, such as reflective sheeting for traffic signs in the Soviet Union or scouring pads in Hungary. It then adds new products one at a time while making use of every possible resource, from local managers in foreign markets to logistics managers and lobbyists back home.

"We don't have a lot of brain surgeons," says Greg L. Lewis, a middle manager recently returned from a stint marketing 3M's popular Post-it notes in Europe. "We have nice, well-rounded individuals who care about the business."

The company didn't always care about exports. Like many others, it long treated foreign sales as an afterthought. As recently as the 1950s, 3M had a special place for rolls of tape rejected for the domestic market; it shipped them abroad. The attitude toward foreign customers was "here it is, and it's good for you," says Mr. Jacobson, a Nebraska native known as "Jake."

3M first ventured abroad in the 1920s, selling $189 worth of its waterproof "Wetordry" sandpaper to a European auto maker. For three decades, it exported through a holding company jointly owned with eight other U.S. sandpaper makers.

Its first big thrust into international business came after a court ordered the breakup of Durex Corp. in 1950. 3M took over a number of Durex operations, including a sandpaper plant in England, a small tape plant in France and an empty building in Germany. With them came its first real effort to expand beyond sandpaper and adhesive tape.

Durex proved useful as a model for setting up operations abroad. 3M typically started by shipping semifinished goods, such as huge rolls of tape. Local workers cut and packaged the material. The initial investment was usually small; it took two people and $110,000 to open the Colombian subsidiary in 1961. "We never rush in," Executive Vice President Harry A. Hammerly told a Commerce Department export seminar last month. "We ease in."

By making products abroad and hiring local workers and managers, 3M helped reduce anti-American sentiment. It also learned what would sell in a market. As business grew and more production was shifted abroad, 3M's steady flow of new products from its research labs created new export possibilities. From its adhesive and coating technologies came items as diverse as magnetic recording tape, carpet stain preventers and surgical drapes, which cover the patient to prevent infection.

3M soon found it couldn't leave all the marketing decisions to its multiplying foreign subsidiaries. "It was a free-for-all" of local managers picking and choosing what to sell, Mr. Jacobson says. In the 1980s, headquarters cracked down; executives in charge of various product groups decided which of some 40,000 exported products would get the most attention.

The result: "global strategic plans," even for such low-tech products as Post-it notes. The sticky yellow note pads are one of the most successful new products in 3M's history—and worth pushing hard around the world. When 3M first exported Post-it notes in 1981, it planned to "sample the daylights out of the product," as a company report later put it. It told local managers to find the best way to do it. They hired office cleaning crews to pass out samples in England and Germany and turned to office-products distributors in Italy. In Malaysia, young women went from office to office to deliver the pads.

By 1984, volume in Europe was sufficient to begin manufacturing *"les papillons jaunes"*—the yellow butterflies—in France. Post-it proliferation ensures new exports. When 3M introduced Post-it page markers at a U.S. office-products show in 1988, some foreign dealers wouldn't wait for exports to begin. They bought from U.S. distributors—a Post-it black market that the company frowned on but couldn't stop until it began exporting the markers in 1989.

Sharpening the global marketing strategy was only part of the battle. If efficiency didn't improve in its factories, competitors would underprice and outsell 3M in a wide range of products. Between 1985 and 1990, 3M slashed the labor needed to make its goods by 35 percent and the time required by 21 percent.

At New Ulm, the efficiency drive sparked one of the biggest investments since 3M arrived in 1962. The company spent $30 million for a state-of-the-art operation that combined molding and assembly of items such as electrical connectors.

At one of 3M's two plants in this community of 14,000 people, jolts of electricity administered by Ms. Schroepfer turn up no bugs in the splices headed for Britain's Eastern Electricity PLC. 3M has reduced to negligible numbers the defects on the molded rubber gadgets, which join, seal and insulate underground electric cables. 3M says its special rubber compound helps the splices stretch easily and retain elasticity. "When I bag these splices, I know they're getting an excellent product," Ms. Schroepfer says proudly.

EXHBIT 1   3M Finds Business All around the World

Export operations . . .

3M's export operations:
1990 sales by geographic area

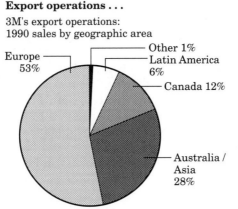

Have blossomed . . .

Annual export revenue as a percent of total revenue

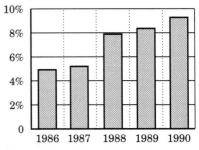

For its businesses . . . .

$13.02 billion 1990 revenue by business segment

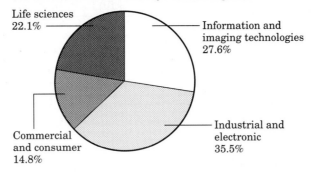

Some 29 percent of the plant's splices are sent abroad (see Exhibit 1). They are trucked to 3M's sprawling international distribution center in St. Paul, where they join some 5,400 orders the center receives each week. Workers unload everything from overhead projectors to plastic insulation for windows, then sort by destination. They pack the splices along with other British orders and then load them on a 40-foot container for the railroad trip to port in Norfolk, Va.

In 1985, it took 11 days to get most export orders through the distribution center. By the end of last year, that was down to 5½ days, even though volume had swelled 89 percent to 166 ocean containers a week. Over the same six years, shipping mistakes plunged 71 percent.

As late as the mid-1970s, each 3M subsidiary in Europe hired its own truck lines, and they crisscrossed all over the map. "Service was terrible," says Richard L. Herreid, executive director of logistics services. So, 3M set up a distribution center in Breda, the Netherlands, that acts much like an airline hub. U.S. exports from ports such as Norfolk are trucked to 3M's 19 European subsidiaries.

Last year, logistics officials persuaded 3M to spend up to $1 million extra a year for daily truck service to each subsidiary. They proved that even if some trucks go with partial loads, the savings from lower inventories and faster deliveries offset the cost of additional trucks.

A survey of 18,000 customers in Europe showed they want even faster delivery. Nevertheless, the increasingly sophisticated transportation system should prove valuable when European economies unify. "We're ready" for 1992, M. J. Monteiro, 3M's top international executive, told State Department officials earlier this month.

In Eastern Europe, 3M has sold its goods since 1969 from its 3M East subsidiary in Switzerland. When customers lacked hard currency, 3M arranged to swap goods for as much as 30 percent of its East European trade. Back at headquarters, employees visiting the company store in the basement often saw items such as rocking chairs from Romania alongside Scotch tape and Scotchgard fabric protector.

Now, 3M is easing deeper into those newly freed economies. In 1986, it hired Michael Wolski, a former trade official in East Germany, for its office there. Last year, he helped recruit 10 new sales representatives. Mr. Jacobson, 3M's chief executive, was so impressed with its ambitious new employee that he invited him to St. Paul in November to address its top officials. As if to emphasize the changes in the economic landscape, Mr. Wolski handed each a piece of the Berlin Wall and a strand of barbed wire—encased in clear plastic made by 3M.

Elsewhere in Eastern Europe, Hungarians may soon scrub pots and pans with Scotch-Brite scouring pads cut and packaged in their own country. 3M plans to import the raw material, along with other goods such as telecommunications connectors and reflective signs. The initial investment is vintage 3M: $3 million.

In Washington, 3M officials call on Hungary's ambassador to the United States. Mr. Monteiro, a 40-year 3M veteran with a brusque manner and Buddha-like expression, has brushed up on his small talk. He knows from his briefing book that the ambassador, Peter Zwack, is a former businessman and has seven children. The visit is billed as a courtesy call, but the 3M man quickly gets beyond small talk and pushes his latest project.

3M has exported to Hungary for years, he tells the ambassador. It likes to start small: "Make a little. Sell a little."

The ambassador scribbles notes.

The company prefers to hire nationals; just 160 of its 39,500 foreign employees are from the United States. It's big on research and development—6.5 percent of sales.

The ambassador likes that.

The company is full of people, Mr. Monteiro says, who, like himself, started with nothing. They advanced themselves and 3M through persistence and hard work. In Hungary, the company plans to hire 20 people by the end of 1992.

The ambassador promises to call Budapest and inquire about the paperwork.

"He's going to help us," Mr. Monteiro tells his lobbyist as they leave the embassy. In early March, as the splices were going to one of 3M's oldest foreign operations, 3M got the green light in its newest— Hungary.

PART 5

Marketing Strategy and Program Development

Marketing strategy consists of:

- Choosing a strategy for each market target to be served by the business unit.
- Setting objectives for each target market.
- Designing a marketing program positioning strategy for each target market.
- Implementing and managing the marketing strategy.

We examined target-market strategy in Part 4. Part 5 is concerned with setting objectives and with marketing program design. In Part 6 we shall consider developing marketing plans and implementing and controlling marketing strategy.

A marketing program positioning strategy consists of more than a product, or even a line of products. Distribution, price, and promotion strategies must be combined with product strategy to form an integrated marketing mix.

SETTING OBJECTIVES

An objective indicates something that marketing management wants to accomplish, such as increasing market share in target market A from 21 percent last year to 28 percent during the next three years. Objectives should address various areas such as sales, expenses, profit contribution, and human resources. Each objective should indicate a desired level of performance, how it will be measured, and who will be responsible for meeting it. We shall examine some characteristics of good objectives and then discuss how to set objectives.

Characteristics of Good Objectives

Well-stated objectives possess several important characteristics. When evaluating objectives, ask the following questions:

- Is each objective relevant to overall results? For example, if market-share gain is an objective, will increasing advertising awareness contribute to the market-share objective?
- Is each objective consistent with the other marketing objectives and with nonmarketing objectives as well? One inconsistent objective may work against another objective.
- Does each objective provide a clear guide to accomplishment? Well-stated objectives should enable management to determine the extent to which the objective has been achieved for it to be of value. Has the objective been quantified and a time frame specified?
- Is the objective realistic? Is there a reasonable chance of meeting the objective? Objectives should represent achievable results.
- Is responsibility for each objective assigned to someone? Are joint responsibilities indicated?

Setting good objectives is one of management's prime responsibilities. The task is demanding, and it requires close coordination among the people in the marketing organization to assure that all objectives correspond to the marketing mission.

Setting Objectives

There are essentially two kinds of objectives:

1. Those that specify end results (e.g., profit contribution).
2. Those that, if accomplished, will (or should) help to achieve end results (e.g., add 10 new retail outlets by January 1, 1995).

Objectives should cover market position, productivity, resources, profitability, and other important end results.

Among the troublesome problems encountered in setting objectives are the interrelationships among objectives and the shared responsibility for achieving objectives. Each objective does not fit neatly into an isolated box. Thus, considerable skill is required in determining a balanced set of objectives for different organizational levels and across different functional areas (e.g., advertising and personal selling).

Marketing objectives are normally set at the following levels:

1. The entire marketing organization within a particular company or business unit in a diversified firm.
2. Each market target served by the company or business unit.

3. The major marketing functional areas such as product planning, distribution, pricing, and promotion.
4. Subunits within particular functional areas (e.g., individual sales-people).

The extent to which the above levels are relevant in a particular firm will depend on the size and complexity of the organization.

MARKETING PROGRAM POSITIONING STRATEGY

A marketing program positioning strategy is how marketing objectives are accomplished in a firm's target markets. Product, distribution, price, and promotion strategies represent an integrated bundle of actions aimed at customers/prospects in the target market. An overview of the decisions that make up a positioning strategy is shown in Exhibit 1. We shall briefly examine each program area, beginning with product/service strategy.

Product/Service Strategy

A product/service strategy consists of:

- Deciding how to position a business unit's product/service offering (specific products and/or services, lines, or mixes) to service its target market(s).
- Setting strategic objectives for the product and/or service offerings.
- Selecting a branding strategy.
- Developing and implementing strategies for managing new and existing products and/or services.

Product Positioning and Objectives.   Product positioning consists of deciding how to compete with a product or line of products against key competitors in the market targets selected by management. Key decisions about quality, price, and features establish guidelines for product development and improvement. Closely associated with positioning decisions are the strategic objectives for the product strategy. Examples of objectives are: market penetration, profit contribution, and establishing a reputation for quality.

Branding Strategy.   The major alternatives in the branding decision by a manufacturer are:

- Make no attempt to establish brand identity, and instead rely on intermediaries to establish brand reputation.

EXHIBIT 1   Positioning-Strategy Overview

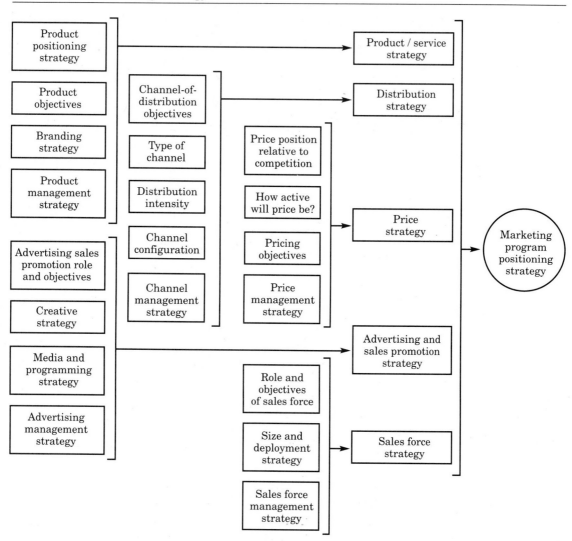

- Produce products which have the private brands of retailers on them.
- Use the corporate name (e.g., Deere & Co.) as an umbrella identity for all of the firm's products.
- Establish brand names for lines of products, as with Sears' Craftsman tools.
- Build a strong brand identification for individual products, as in the case of Procter & Gamble.
- Use a combination of the above strategies.

Marketing intermediaries often use the company and/or brand identity of manufacturers. Alternatively, if they have the resources, retailers and other intermediaries may choose to establish private brand identities.

Product Planning and Management.   Firms are continually faced with the management of their product portfolios. Decisions include new-product development, product improvement, product repositioning, and product elimination. Increasingly, firms are formalizing their product planning and management activities to more closely link product strategies with corporate, business unit, and marketing strategies.

Distribution Strategy

A manufacturer's distribution strategy consists of first deciding whether to go directly to end users, using a company sales force, or to work through marketing intermediaries, such as wholesalers, distributors, dealers, and retailers. The latter strategy requires additional decisions such as the type of channel of distribution to be used, the intensity of distribution, and the types and number of intermediaries to include at each level in the channel.

The channel decision rests heavily on the role of the manufacturer in the channel. If the firm has a strong market position and adequate resources, management may decide to manage the channel. Ethan Allen, in furniture, has built a strong network of independent retailers. These dealers have been instrumental in the success of the company. Small firms with limited resources may be restricted to finding distribution channels to which they can gain access.

Price Strategy

The nature and scope of price strategy will be established by two decisions: the decision on price position relative to competition, and the decision on how active price will be in the marketing program. The first is closely linked to several other aspects of the positioning strategy—including product quality, distribution strategy, and advertising and personal selling programs. The second decision establishes, for example, how price will be used in advertising and personal selling efforts. Once these two decisions are made, guidelines can be established for price objectives and for the management of pricing activities.

Promotion Strategy

Advertising, personal selling, publicity, and sales promotion are communication efforts to inform and persuade buyers and others involved in the purchase decision. Each communication medium has certain assets and limitations. Management's task is to shape a promotion mix using the available elements. A key issue is selecting the role and objectives of advertising and personal selling in the marketing program. Once this is resolved the remaining decisions in advertising and sales force strategies are those shown in Exhibit 1.

CONCLUDING NOTE

Developing a marketing program positioning strategy requires the blending of product, distribution, price, advertising, and personal selling strategies. Shaping this bundle of strategies is a major challenge to marketing decision makers. Here we have sorted out the issues involved in marketing programming and shown how programming is linked to the other two key aspects of marketing strategy: market-target selection and setting objectives.

As cases are studied, you should keep in mind several characteristics of the marketing mix variables. They are both supplementary and complementary in nature. Some must work together, such as using advertising to develop product awareness. Other elements can to some extent serve as substitutes for each other. For example, pricing can be used in a promotional role through the use of promotional pricing (e.g., cents-off coupons). However, recall that each mix component may set some constraining guidelines for those decisions that remain.

Cases for Part 5

The 14 cases in Part 5 focus primarily on the marketing strategy and program development needs of a wide range of different organizations.

CASES

Case 5–1, Rockwood Manor, describes the supply of, and demand for, retirement home facilities in Spokane, Washington. Don Chapman, administrator for Rockwood Manor, must make a set of recommendations to his board of directors regarding whether or not to build additional units, and if so, how these units should be marketed and to whom.

The Holly Farms case (5–2) describes a new product failure that could and should have been avoided. The case analyst's challenge is to evaluate the positioning strategy Holly Farms management used to introduce the new product, identify and evaluate alternative strategies, and advise management what to do now.

The Atlanta Cyclorama case (5–3) describes a well-known and recently renovated visitor attraction in Atlanta, Georgia, that seeks to boost attendance sharply over the next few years. Dennis Walters, director of the Cyclorama, must develop both short- and long-term strategies for attracting visitors.

The Zayre Corporation case (5–4) describes the interesting strategy situation of a company competing in several retail sectors. The challenge facing management is to develop a strategy for success in the intensely competitive retail environment.

Case 5–5, Gillette Company, describes the development of the Sensor razor and the risks and investment required to bring this product to the market. The case analyst's challenge is to evaluate Gillette's positioning strategy for Sensor, identify components of the strategy that should be used in the future, and recommend any changes that would enhance the success of this new product.

In Case 5–6, Elmer C. Meider, president of Highlights for Children, Inc., faces a declining sales and profit situation primarily in the direct sales area. Environmental changes have had a detrimental impact on the effectiveness of the direct sales force. Meider has asked various managers for their suggestions on ways to improve Highlights' financial performance and is considering several options that have been proposed.

Case 5–7, Paper Mate, focuses on whether or not to introduce a revolutionary new pen containing truly erasable ink. Derek Coward, vice president of marketing, must weigh several risks and trade-offs before making a final recommendation to the division's president.

Recently Comshare, Inc. (Case 5–8), has changed its major emphasis from providing time-sharing services to decision support systems software for use in corporate planning and other business decision-making activities. Comshare's current concern is developing a strategic marketing plan for its new software product called System W.

The Gap (Case 5–9) brand of men's, women's and children's clothing is now the third largest selling label in America. The Gap's recent increase in sales and market share is attributed by some to a "return to the basics." The case describes Gap's strategy for increasing market share and its situation at the end of 1990.

Thompson Respiration Products, Inc. (TRP)(Case 5–10), is a small manufacturer of portable respirators. Victor Higgins, executive vice president, has posed several short-term strategic issues to consider over the weekend. He also recognizes that broader questions regarding TRP's market target, marketing objectives, and positioning must be addressed in its strategic marketing plan.

Case 5–11, Northern Telecom, reviews the rapid, successful growth of the company. The case outlines those factors that have contributed to rapid growth, changes facing the telecommunications industry, and the changing nature of competition. Numerous exhibits provide information to be used to analyze Northern Telecom's position and to suggest steps that management might consider in changing marketing strategy.

Case 5–12, J. W. Thornton, Ltd., concerns a British manufacturer and retailer of high-quality chocolate and sugar confectionery. Fluctuations in the fortunes of the company have made the board of directors aware that the company needs a longer-term strategy to give firmer direction to the business.

Lee Co. (Case 5–13), has experienced boom and bust periods over the last 30 years. While the company has the second largest market share in the U.S. jeans industry, management is not happy with present performance levels. The case reviews recent trends in the industry and some of Lee's strategic moves. The real question is, "what should Lee Co. do now?"

Color Tile (Case 5–14) presents an interesting analysis of the floor covering market and the company's plans for expansion into new markets. Market definition and analysis are keys to developing an appropriate marketing strategy.

Case 5–1   *Rockwood Manor**

Dan Chapman, administrator for Rockwood Manor retirement facility, sat in his Spokane, Washington, office contemplating a recommendation to his board of directors on how Rockwood could meet the apparent demand for housing to accommodate the active elderly in Spokane County. He knew the board would ask several important questions: What is the size of the market for retirement facilities? What kind of housing facilities do active elderly want? And how should those facilities be priced?

Dan had observed the increase in elderly both nationally and locally. Many of the newly retired were healthy, active people who looked forward to a physically active lifestyle. Although they did not wish to move into a dormitory-style facility, they did want to get out from under the burdens of maintaining a home. They wanted to be free to move about as they pleased, yet have a private secure place they could call home.

In his tenure at Rockwood, Mr. Chapman had also observed that seniors were concerned about financial matters. Some wanted to build an estate for their children while others felt they should spend their hard-earned money on themselves. The current pricing schedule for rooms and health care at the manor accommodated both these two viewpoints. He was not sure how pricing would be handled in a different housing/service configuration.

NATIONAL TRENDS

The nation's population of the elderly is on the rise. According to *U.S. News and World Report,* "One of every five Americans is 55 years or older, and that figure will climb to one in every three and one-half over

* This case was prepared by William R. Wynd, Professor of Marketing, Eastern Washington University. Used by permission.

the next 40 years."[1] This increase is attributed to several factors. One is a decline in the death rate of 2 percent annually since 1970, due largely to improved public health care measures. A declining birth rate over the last decade has also contributed to a higher proportion of elderly in the population. Projections indicate that by the year 1990, 30 million people will be over age 65, accounting for 28 percent of the U.S. population.

Older Americans are increasingly well off financially when they reach retirement. Women currently account for an estimated 49 percent of the work force, and, with the increased number of women working, the income from a second pension is by far one of the most important factors in the maintenance of an upward trend in income among the elderly.

Business Week recently reported a study speculating that spending by the elderly since the mid-70s may have been extensive enough to depress the national personal saving rate.[2] Those elderly currently 65 and older make up about 16 percent of all adults, but they received more than half of all interest income and close to one third of all capital gains reported to the IRS in 1982. Furthermore, while the average family held $18,695 in liquid assets in 1983, families headed by persons 65–74 averaged $30,666.

With an average age of 74, the nation's elderly can expect at least 10 more years of life. Common sense would indicate a tendency to spend their discretionary income. Most are in reasonably good health (though they hate to climb stairs), their spouse is still living, and they have the time to enjoy a wide variety of leisure activities.

Indeed, the elderly are apparently spending more of their money on housing and transportation. The Department of Labor publishes three budgets for a retired couple made up of hypothetical lines of goods and services that were specified in the mid 1960s to portray three relative levels of living: lower, intermediate, and higher. The categories include food, housing, transportation, clothing, personal care, medical care, and other family consumption. In 1981 the percentage spent on housing, transportation, and clothing increased as income increased.

Although a growing elderly population constitutes a potential market for a wide variety of goods and services, the segment represented by active, affluent seniors is being increasingly cultivated by a wide variety of providers. A. T. Sutherland, advertising manager for *Mod-*

---

[1] Mary Gallean et al., "Life Begins at 55," *U.S. News and World Report,* September 1, 1980, pp. 51–60.

[2] "Are the Elderly the Key to the Savings Puzzle? " *Business Week,* December 31, 1984, p. 17.

ern Maturity, indicates that the maturity market (50+) accounts for 25 percent of all consumer expenditures—purchasing 3 percent of all domestic cars, 30 percent of all food consumed at home, 25 percent of all cosmetics and bath products, 25 percent of all alcoholic beverages, 41 percent of all toaster ovens and food processors, 37 percent of all slenderizing treatments and health spa memberships, and 31 percent of all automobile tires.[3]

Contrary to the belief that many senior citizens are inclined to migrate to the sunbelt regions, evidence shows that many seniors prefer to live in the home they have lived in for years. Change becomes less appealing as time passes. Hence, many elderly wish to remain in familiar surroundings for as long as they can. According to the U.S. Department of Housing and Urban Development, 70 percent of the population 65 and over live in their own homes, 5–7 percent live in retirement homes, 18–20 percent live in apartments or government-subsidized housing, and 5 percent live in institutions.[4]

Those elderly who opt to sell their homes have a wide variety of new concepts available to them, including condominium retirement settings, mobile home courts, and group homes as well as the traditional retirement center facilities. If they move to a new geographic location they are often drawn toward the less populous urban centers where the cost of living is usually more reasonable.

THE SETTING

Spokane, Washington, is one of the nation's most beautiful cities and has many attractions as a retirement community. Located in northeastern Washington state, Spokane was the site of the 1974 World's Fair. Conservative and rural in nature, the region is among the nation's most fertile wheat-producing areas. Most of the urban population is employed in wholesale and retail trade, financial services, and health care servicing a number of sparsely populated counties in northeastern Washington and northern Idaho. Most Spokanites reaching retirement age stay in Spokane. Taxes, costs of maintaining a household, availability of doctors and sophisticated medical facilities, and low crime rate are among the attractions.

---

[3] Misdirected Advertising Prevents Marketers from Taking Bite from 'Golden Apple' of Maturity Market," *Maturity News,* October 26, 1984, p. 19.

[4] U.S. Department of Housing and Urban Development, Office of Policy Development and Research, *Characteristics of the Elderly,* Washington, D.C.: Government Printing Office, February 1979, pp. 1–73.

EXHIBIT 1   1980 Census and Population Projections for Spokane County for 1985 and 1990

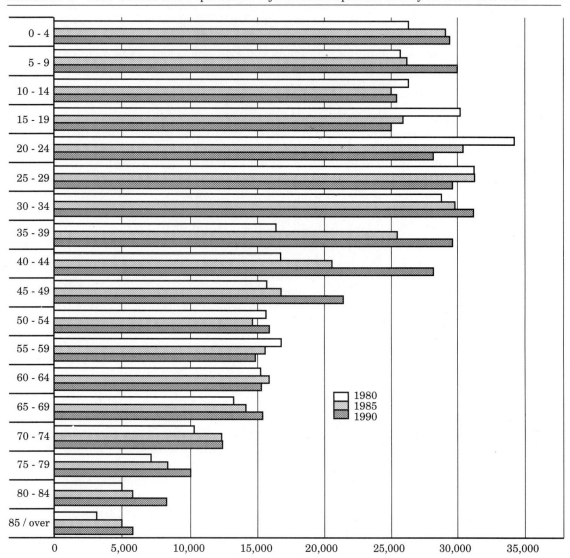

Source: Population, Enrollment, and Economic Studies Division, Office of Financial Management, November 1982.

According to the 1970 census, 44,440 of the 287,487 total county population were aged 60 or over. The 1980 census counted 54,436 of the 341,058 total county population as aged 60 or over. The number of persons 60 or over increased by 9,996 in the 10 years between the

EXHIBIT 2   1990 Population Projection for Spokane County

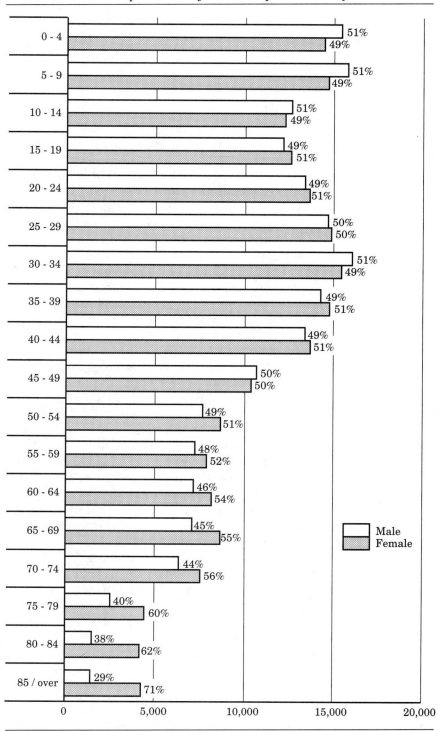

Source: Population, Enrollment, and Economic Studies Division, Office of Financial Management, November 1982.

censuses. Exhibit 1 is a bar chart showing the 1980 population in Spokane County with projections for 1985 and 1990. The population by age group and sex is shown in Exhibit 2.

ROCKWOOD MANOR

Rockwood Manor is a residential health facility that offers a full spectrum of services to meet the housing, nutrition, health, social, and spiritual needs of older persons. It is operated by a nonprofit corporation related to the United Methodist Church but receives no financial assistance from the church or any other organization. Residents purchase the privilege of living in a unit of their choice. Prices are based upon the charge for a standard living unit of 300 square feet. Living units may be purchased for cash or under terms of a time payment contract. A minimum down payment is required for a living unit under terms of the contract. The balance, plus interest on the declining balance, is amortized for a term of 84 months. In addition, residents pay a monthly services fee.

Residents of Rockwood Manor must be independently ambulatory and able to care for themselves at the time of admission. There is a per diem charge for infirmary care beginning with the 11th day of confinement during any one month. The amount of this per diem charge is equal to the audited cost of day's care in the infirmary. If a resident becomes a permanent patient in the infirmary, and his living unit is paid for in full, he may then surrender his living unit to the corporation, in which case he will then receive the infirmary care for the current monthly services fee of a standard living unit.

Rooms are also available for those residents who are not bed patients but who need assistance in the activities of daily living such as bathing and dressing. These rooms are attended by a special corps of aides under the supervision of the Director of Nursing Services. A per diem charge is made for this intermediate health care.

A resident may cancel his contract by giving 60 days notice in writing, except during illness. If the living unit has been paid for in full, the "unearned balance"[5] is refunded upon the resale of the unit. If the unit has been purchased under terms of a time payment contract, no refund is made. A time payment contract terminates with death.

---

[5] Unearned balance is calculated by dividing the amount paid by the tenant by the number of months the tenant is expected to live as shown by actuarial tables in use by major life insurance companies. The quotient is multiplied by the number of months the tenant occupied his/her unit. This amount is kept by Rockwood, the remainder (unearned balance) is returned to the tenant.

Rockwood Manor enjoys a reputation of being one of the finest retirement homes in the region. Its physical plant is clean, neat, and well maintained. Its personnel are pleasant, helpful, and professional. The location is an exclusive residential area, and relatively high fees project an "elite" image.

Rockwood owns enough land to develop a variety of housing configurations catering to the active elderly. Another high rise, condominiums, duplex units or cottages were all possibilities. Construction costs per square foot were greatest for cottages, least for a high rise apartment.

THE MARKET

An increasing elderly population represents a diverse market for a wide variety of retirement centers. Traditional retirement centers have almost always been operated by not-for-profit organizations, usually church affiliated. These centers normally sign a contract with the resident for lifetime care and promise that no one will be asked to leave due to financial problems.

According to a survey by the national accounting and consulting firm of Laventhol and Horvath, the future of the nation's life care/continuing care retirement industry is rapidly changing as entrepreneurs enter the expanding market.[6] These newer facilities, though still in the minority, offer a variety of possibilities. Some still offer the life care contract, but with totally or partially refundable entry fees. Others concentrate on renting units. They have no entry or endowment fees, and health care is usually provided strictly on a pay-as-needed basis.

Increasing costs and a growing market have brought together investors and not-for-profit organizers. An increasingly common partnership occurs when an investor group finances the development in return for the tax advantages. When these are exhausted, the not-for-profit organization purchases the development for fair market value.

Since 1975, marketing for the typical life-care center development usually precedes construction by a full year. Most developments presell half their units and achieve 66 percent occupancy within 6 months after completion and 95 percent within 18 months.

The results of a recent survey of the capacity of establishments listed in the Yellow Pages of the Spokane County Telephone Book under the heading "Retirement and Life Care Communities and Homes" is summarized in Exhibit 3.

---

[6] Aaron M. Rose, "Entrepreneurs Reshaping Lifecare," *Modern Healthcare,* July 1984, pp. 148–53.

EXHIBIT 3   Capacity of Retirement and Life Care Facilities in Spokane County, 1985

	Apartments	Beds	Total	Percent of Total
Subsidized	832	551	1,383	44
Private	1,031	711	1,742	56
	1,863	1,262	3,125	100

Nearly half the retirement apartments and beds available in Spokane County are subsidized (beyond Medicare or Medicaid) by Federal or State Government. Occupancy of both apartments and beds is nearly 100 percent.

Competition in the current Spokane market to serve relatively high income retirees comes from two other not-for-profit organizations and one recently constructed for-profit condominium apartment complex with minimum health care. The retirement complex most similar to Rockwood Manor just announced a duplex/multifamily addition designed for the active elderly. Their existing and planned units are either apartments, condominiums, or duplex units. Although the existing facilities were full and often enjoyed a waiting list, what additional capacity would do to occupancy rates was a matter of conjecture. An estimated 250 new units would be added by the latest development.

PRICING CONSIDERATIONS

Life care communities have an obligation to provide housing and health care for the life of their residents. This obligation can be separated into two financial cost components: housing and services. Costs in the housing component consist of debt service, maintenance, and periodic renovation (see Exhibit 4). Costs for monthly services cover such items as food service, laundry, recreation, and utilities. But the largest single portion of the cost of services is health care.

Dan Chapman knew that setting a fee to fund the real estate portion of the obligation would be fairly straightforward. The fee would reflect the value of discounted cash flows for debt service, maintenance, and renovation. Establishing a monthly fee for service, however, posed a problem because the aging of the community affects the cost of health care. A young community would be relatively more healthy than a "maturing" group. As the average age of the community increases so does the largest single component of monthly service. Dan wanted to

EXHIBIT 4   Construction and Garage Costs Single Family Detached*

	House	Garage	Total Cash Costs	Total Value with Land
1,250 sq. ft.	$68,750	$10,368	$107,249	$112,249
1,000 sq. ft.	55,000	7,776	86,155	91,155
750 sq. ft.	41,250	5,184	65,060	70,060

* Construction costs for condominium units would average 12 percent less, including garages.

treat the residents fairly and at the same time keep the monthly service fee consistent with the "market" he was trying to reach. With this in mind he saw three possible pricing methodologies aimed at the new group of active elderly.[7]

Pay as You Go

Under this methodology fees would be set annually on the basis of next year's anticipated expenses and the revenue short fall or surplus of the current period. Fees would be low to start because the group would be young and healthy. As they matured health care costs and fees would increase. Although new entrants would moderate the aging of the community, the vagaries of inflation would insure inequity.

Open Group

This methodology dictates that discounted cash flows be anticipated for a relatively long period, say 20 years. Young entrants replace those deceased, thus moderating health care costs. Overall fees set by this methodology are likely to be higher than pay as you go when the communities are young but lower as they mature. Insuring equity is difficult but not impossible.

---

[7] Howard E. Winklevoss and Alwyn V. Powell, *Continuing Care Retirement Communities: An Empirical, Financial, and Legal Analysis* (Homewood, Ill.: Richard D. Irwin, 1984).

Closed Group

In the closed group method, cash flows are anticipated for the actuarial life of residents in a cohort group (typically a group of new residents). This method differs from the open-group method because it centers on a specific cohort and requires that fees be self-supporting without the benefit of new entrants. Fees are the highest when set by this pricing methodology but by definition they are most equitable to all residents.

Dan wasn't sure which pricing methodology to recommend in setting monthly service fees. He knew that any fee below what residents in the Manor were paying would likely anger them. On the other hand any fee above that would have to be justified to potential new residents.

Case 5–2   Holly Farms, Inc.*

Holly Farms Corp. thought it had created the Cadillac of poultry with its roasted chicken.

The fully cooked bird seemed just the ticket for today's busy consumers: a modern, more convenient alternative to raw chicken. It scored big in a year of test marketing.

The company began phasing in national distribution of the product last fall. But it fared so dismally that the planned expansion into more markets was halted so Holly Farms could reconsider its marketing strategy.

One analyst, Bonnie Rivers of Salomon Brothers Inc., cites the blunder as a major reason she recently slashed her estimate for Holly Farms' profit for the year ending May 31 by 22 percent, to $2.25 a share from $2.90. Higher feed and persistently low chicken prices also contributed to the lower profit projection, she says. In fiscal 1987, the Memphis, Tenn.-based poultry and food concern earned $71.7 million, or $4.31 a share, on revenue of $1.42 billion.

Company executives acknowledge that the roasted chicken product will hurt fiscal 1988 earnings, but they won't make any projections.

---

* Source: Arthur Buckler, "Holly Farms's Marketing Error: The Chicken that Laid an Egg," *The Wall Street Journal*, February 9, 1988, p. 34. Reprinted by permission of *THE WALL STREET JOURNAL,* © 1988 Dow Jones & Company, Inc. All Rights Reserved Worldwide.

"We're just losing a lot of business," says John Creel, Holly Farms' senior director of sales and marketing. Grocers are buying far less of the product than Holly Farms had hoped, he says, because they believe it doesn't last long enough on the shelf. Until this problem is solved, Holly Farms decided not to expand distribution of its roasted chicken, now available in about 50 percent of the nationwide market.

Holly Farms' experience is a classic example of how a food company can stumble in launching a product. While the extensive test marketing identified strong consumer support for the product—22 percent of Atlanta women surveyed said they had tried it, and of those, 90 percent said they would buy it again—the company failed to detect the concerns and resistance of its front-line customer, the grocer.

Several grocers concur that the problem isn't with the roasted chicken itself. Ray Heatherington, meat merchandising manager for Safeway Stores Inc.'s Northern California division, calls the product—which comes in Cajun, barbecue and original flavors—"outstanding." But his stores dropped it after several weeks, because of the short shelf life.

Holly Farms says the chicken's quality lasts for a good 18 days. So to be safe, it marks the last sale date 14 days after the chicken is roasted. But it can take as long as nine days to get the chicken to stores from the North Carolina plant, which Holly Farms spent $20 million to build just for the roasted chicken product. That doesn't give grocers much lead time. To avoid being stuck with an outdated backlog, many are waiting until they run out before reordering.

In the case of raw chicken, shelf life isn't a factor because the product's high volume means it is sold in the first few days after delivery and grocers know from experience how much to stock.

A general suspicion of new products also has probably hurt the effort. "It's a hard sell to get into the supermarket, particularly if you've got a new product that the consumers and retailers haven't seen before," says Joe Scheringer, an editor at *Grocery Marketing* magazine. The meat department is probably the most resistant to change, he adds.

Some competitors believe Holly Farms didn't do enough preliminary groundwork with retailers. Holly Farms acknowledges it probably didn't go far enough to tailor its marketing program to each supermarket chain or spend sufficient time educating meat managers.

But it plans to mend fences soon. Hoping to lengthen the shelf life by five to 10 days, Holly Farms is developing a system to pack the chickens using nitrogen instead of air. To shorten delivery time, the company is considering giving the product its own distribution system, instead of delivering it along with raw poultry.

Holly Farms also plans to shift a hefty portion of its marketing budget out of television and radio and into the grocery store in the form of promotions, coupons, consumer demonstrations, and contests for meat managers. Nearly two thirds of Holly Farms' roughly $14 million in fiscal first-half marketing expenditures for the product went to media advertising; that proportion is being lowered to about one half, the company said.

Holly Farms still believes the roasted chicken product will be a blockbuster. So does Salomon Brothers' Ms. Rivers, who says: "I definitely agree with what they're doing and why they're doing it."

At least one competitor is reserving judgment: Tyson Foods Inc. of Springdale, Ark., which is test marketing a similar chicken product in Indianapolis, says it has no immediate plans to broaden distribution, in part because of Holly Farms' experience.

Case 5–3   *Atlanta Cyclorama**

Dennis Walters, director of the Atlanta Cyclorama, was sitting in his Grant Park office speculating over his greatest challenge, namely devising the 1987 promotional plan for the Cyclorama and long-range strategies for the attraction for future years. Attendance would have to be increased from an estimated 342,000 in 1986 to 500,000 in 1989, and sales would have to exceed $1 million per year by 1990.

THE ATLANTA CYCLORAMA

Before the invention of motion pictures, opportunities for the general public to view past events were definitely limited. One vehicle for accomplishing this desire was the cyclorama, defined as "a 360 degree circular painting which when viewed from its interior gives the illu-

---

* This case was prepared by John S. Wright and Daniel C. Bello, professors of marketing at Georgia State University. Reprinted by permission. Copyright © 1987 by John S. Wright and Daniel C. Bello. Revised in 1989.

sion that the viewer is in the scene." Hundreds of these cycloramas were painted and shown in American cities in the latter half of the 19th century. By 1987, however, only 14 survived throughout the world. In the United States, in addition to the Atlanta Cyclorama, panoramas were on exhibit at the Gettysburg Battlefield in Pennsylvania and in the Metropolitan Museum of Art in New York.

The Atlanta Cyclorama was created in 1885 and depicted the 1864 Battle of Atlanta, familiar to all who have seen the movie *Gone with the Wind*. The masterpiece was a 50-foot-high, 400-foot circumference painting in the round with a three-dimensional diorama complete with figures added by the W.P.A. in the 1930s. The Cyclorama was first displayed in a frame building in Grant Park in 1912. In 1921, the painting was moved to its present building. After years of use and limited maintenance, the attraction had fallen into an advanced state of disrepair so serious that by 1979 the Cyclorama had to be closed. Extensive restoration ensued at a cost of $11 million. For two and a half years, workers repaired the tears and flaws in the painting and revamped the three-dimensional diorama that served as the painting's foreground. The restoration effort also included the installation of a revolving viewing platform as well as the refurbishing of the building that housed the painting. The exhibit reopened to the public on June 3, 1982. In addition to the famous painting, visitors could also admire other exhibits related to the Civil War: for instance, the famous locomotive "Texas," winner of the "great locomotive chase" (the same train that a group of Confederates drove to Ringgold to chase Union raiders who had stolen the locomotive "General"). Thus, the Atlanta Cyclorama was part historical museum, part artwork and part Confederate memorial. The Cyclorama shared its Grant Park location with the Atlanta Zoo, thus providing a combination sight-seeing opportunity. Cyclorama attendance was 195,000 in 1982 and 300,000 in 1983. Attendance figures for 1984–86, broken down by ticket class, are shown in Exhibit 1.

Grant Park was located three miles south of the downtown hotel district. In past years, the zoo had exerted a negative influence on attendance at the Cyclorama because local media stories highlighted the fact that the zoo had fallen into a state of disrepair and that animals had been poorly treated. Fortunately, civic pride had lead to a revitalization program for the zoo in 1985, and a major renovation similar to that experienced by the Cyclorama had been completed by late 1986. Zoo attendance had increased steadily with the renovation efforts, growing from 280,000 in 1984 to almost 570,000 in 1986 (Exhibit 2).

The Cyclorama was owned and operated by the Atlanta City Govern-

EXHIBIT 1 Breakdown of Cyclorama Attendance and Revenue by Ticket Sales

Ticket Class	1984		1985		1986	
	Attendance	Revenue	Attendance	Revenue	Attendance	Revenue
Adult ($3.00)	117,000	$351,000	129,005	$387,015	146,789	$440,367
Adult group & senior citizens ($2.50)	82,463	206,158	77,030	192,575	82,325	205,813
Children ($1.50)	20,446	30,669	22,465	33,698	25,840	38,760
Child group ($1.00)	7,096	7,096	6,637	6,637	6,122	6,122
Free	41,217	—	37,578	—	42,120	—
Tour groups	30,000	57,483	29,315	67,891	38,900	90,098
Total	298,222	$652,406	302,030	$687,816	342,096	$781,160

$2.2 $2.28 $2.28

EXHIBIT 2   Attendance Figures for the Atlanta Zoo

Year	Attendance
1986	567,269
1985	344,087
1984	279,805
1983	448,397
1982	402,118
1981	347,828
1980	363,433
1979	388,832
1978	452,051

ment. In addition to a director and an associate director, there was a staff of 17 persons. The director was a professional, chosen by civil service procedures. The city council authorized the budget and exercised control over the other activities.

THE PRODUCT AND ITS MARKET

Every year, a very diversified crowd visited the Cyclorama. The admission price in 1987 was $3.00 for adults ($2.50 if in groups of 10 or more), $2.50 for senior citizens, $1.50 for children ($1 if in groups of 10 or more). Children under six and school groups were admitted free. There was no charge for parking.

Attendance could be segmented into four categories: tour groups (consisting mainly of senior citizens and school groups), conventioneers, visitors and tourits, and finally local residents. These market segments all exhibited particular characteristics.

Tour Groups.   Tour groups tended to visit the Cyclorama on weekdays. For both school children and senior citizens, the visit usually occurred once a year.

Conventioneers.   Atlanta was the third largest convention city in the United States in terms of numbers of conventions hosted. In 1985, 1.5 million conventioneers came to Atlanta (Exhibit 3). Mostly, they stayed in the downtown area and remained in Atlanta about three days. The main problem they encountered was lack of activity and entertainment close to downtown. At the heart of the convention area in Atlanta was the Georgia World Congress Center, opened in September 1976. At that time, it offered 350,000 square feet of exhibition space. But with the convention market booming, it soon proved to be

EXHIBIT 3 Atlanta Conventioneers' Attendance and Expenditures per Year

Year	Conventions Hosted	Attendance	Average Daily Expenditure per Conventioneer
1985	1400	1,500,000	$141
1984	1200	1,110,000*	141
1983	1100	1,300,000	135
1982	1000	1,150,000	126
1981	1150	1,128,000	110
1980	1090	1,002,900	99
1979	970	876,800	81
1978	800	850,000	77
1977	760	760,000	73
1976	725	635,000	70

* Note: The drop in attendance in 1984 was ascribed to organizations sending fewer representatives due to economic conditions.

insufficient. In April 1985, the Georgia World Congress Center officially celebrated its expanded opening: 650,000 square feet of exhibition space, and over one million square feet of floor space. The center was one of the world's top meeting/exhibit facilities, with its ballroom, auditorium, corporate conference center, and 70 meeting rooms.

Tourists and Sightseers. This market was more than twice the size of the conventioneer market. Summer was the favorite season to visit Atlanta; 43 percent of all tourists visited during June, July, and August. Exhibit 4 presents Cyclorama percentage attendance by month. Many Atlanta visitors came to meet with family (45%); others (39%) came to sightsee, with 14 percent specifically mentioning tourist sites and 3.5 percent mentioning cultural sites. Their stay was shorter; one to two days, but many of them enjoyed two or three attractions during their visit.

EXHIBIT 4 Cyclorama Average Monthly Attendance

Month	Percent of Total	Month	Percent of Total
January	5	July	14
February	5	August	16
March	7	September	10
April	7	October	8
May	6	November	6
June	13	December	3

EXHIBIT 5   Number of Visitors to the Atlanta Welcome Center

Year	Number of Visitors	Year	Number of Visitors
1985	11,600	1980	4,763
1984	10,995	1979	3,498
1983	7,638	1978	5,229
1982*	2,035	1977	6,219
1981	5,119	1976	6,605

* Note: In 1982 budget cuts closed some stations and reduced hours at others.

Another tourist group consisted of people who drove through Atlanta as they traveled to and from the state of Florida. Atlanta was located on two interstate highways, I-75 and I-85, which provided corridors for traffic to and from the Northeast and Midwest sections of the United States. Large numbers of tourists living in these regions spent their vacations in Florida, and the state of Georgia had tried for many years to convince these persons to "Stay and See" Georgia. For example, a number of welcome centers were set up at the state borders where information about tourist attractions in the state was distributed. Exhibit 5 shows the trends in the number of visitors to the Atlanta Welcome Center. Sporadically, the state had done media advertising in such areas of origin as Ohio and Michigan. In 1985, the state of Georgia tripled its tourist advertising budget to $2.1 million, using "Adventures in the great unknown—Georgia" as a campaign theme.

Local Residents and Their Out-of-Town Guests.   Atlanta and its metropolitan area encompassing 18 counties contained an estimated population of 2,326,000 at the end of 1984, up from 2,138,231 people in 1980, 1,684,200 in 1970, and 1,247,649 in 1960. The city was growing rapidly, but the expansion was taking place mostly at the northern perimeter of the city, far from downtown. However, the population in Atlanta was very mobile: most Atlantans were from other states, and many had only been in Atlanta for a short period of time.

CONSUMPTION PATTERNS AND ATTITUDES

Visitors to the Cyclorama sought to fulfill four different types of needs: education, enjoyment of art, history, and entertainment. But each segment exhibited specific trends which affected the attractiveness of the Cyclorama.

Conventioneers.   One major pattern observed was that Atlanta conventioneers very seldom brought their spouses with them, and only 18 percent brought their children. When planning tours, convention planners sought attractions with overall appeal, uniqueness, ability to accommodate large groups, and accessible parking. The Cyclorama fitted all these needs remarkably well, plus it had that "Old South" charm that was so appealing to conventioneers. Furthermore, the Cyclorama could be rented to a private group. It accommodated up to 180 people at a time on its rotating platform.

Tourists and Sightseers.   Tourists almost always had access to a car and they were looking for a day-long entertainment schedule. Attributions that were salient in their choice of attractions were: accessible from freeway, parking, fun for the whole family, near other attractions, and uniqueness. Once again, the Cyclorama fared well on all criteria.

The Cyclorama was a stop on the tour lists of six different Atlanta operators: Atlanta Tours, Arnell Tours, Brewster Motor Coach, Gray Line of Atlanta (a picture of the diorama was featured in their promotional brochure), Metro Tours and Southeastern Stages. Furthermore, many school groups and senior citizens groups visited the Cyclorama.

Residents and Guests.   This segment was looking for a full day experience offering a good time/value ratio. The closeness to the zoo and the low admission price were in the Cyclorama's favor. However, the guests' host would likely influence their choice, and the Cyclorama was visited at most once a year by local residents.

The Cyclorama was unique, but it also had many competitors among local tourist and cultural attractions. In the past, the Cyclorama had cooperated with other historical/cultural attractions by the use of cross-promotion techniques such as distributing each other's brochures. Additional Atlanta attractions included: (1) Stone Mountain Park, with over 5.6 million visitors, (2) Six Flags Over Georgia, an amusement park that admitted over 2.5 million visitors, (3) Fernbank Science Center which attracted 700,000 visitors, and (4) The Martin Luther King, Jr. Center with its 500,000 visitors. In 1986, the Carter Presidential Library opened to the public and proved to be a popular attraction. Other competing activities in which visitors could participate were shopping, theatre, and nightlife.

PAST EXPERIENCE WITH COMMUNICATIONS ELEMENTS

Advertising

In 1986, most of the Cyclorama's promotional budget was allocated to advertising. Ads were run for three months in *Southern Living* and for seven months in the weekly "Saturday Leisure Guide" of the *Atlanta Journal-Constitution*. In addition, advertising in connection with spe-

EXHIBIT 6 Sample Newspaper Ad

cial events was scheduled. In 1986, $40,000 was budgeted for routine advertising, plus $6,000 for special advertising. Advertising for the Cyclorama tended to be simple, staid, and dignified. Print ads were of the reminder type, treating it as a presold product. Exhibit 6 is an example of the print ad that ran in the local newspaper. Budgetary restrictions had prevented the use of personal selling to promote the Cyclorama.

Sales Promotion

Sales promotion tools used in 1986 were information brochures and cents-off coupons. The brochures were mostly distributed at welcome centers and at Atlanta Convention and Visitors Bureau booths.

The brochures were factual and focused on the historical appeal. They, too, had a dignified serious tone generally associated with cultural and historical attractions. Couponing had been directed primarily at conventioneers and $2,000 of the 1986 budget was spent on media for this purpose. Effectiveness studies had yet to be undertaken.

Publicity/Public Relations

The Cyclorama had been the subject of many articles in local magazines and newspapers. It had also been featured in public service announcements on radio and television. The Cyclorama was also doing cross-publicity with other national attractions such as the Gettysburg Cyclorama, the Boston Fine Arts Building, the Milwaukee Historical Society, and the Atlanta Historical Society.

MEDIA COST AND AUDIENCE INFORMATION

The Atlanta area was served by a variety of print and broadcast media. Exhibit 7 shows some cost and audience data for the major print vehicles in the Atlanta area. The major newspaper was the *Atlanta Journal-Constitution* which published a morning and evening edition. A single 3-inch ad cost $277 and ran in both the morning and evening papers. In terms of magazines *Southern Living* was very popular, containing articles on travel, cooking, and history. An advertiser could place a full or fractional page ad in a statewide edition or a full page ad in a metro Atlanta edition. The three magazines, *Atlanta Magazine, Business Atlanta,* and *Georgia Trends,* were slick periodicals that reached an upscale suburban family or business audience. The two magazines *Where* and *Key* were "What to do in Atlanta" periodicals and were distributed free to hotel guests.

Exhibit 8 shows cost and audience data for the TV networks and for Atlanta's five biggest radio stations. The radio stations had different creative formats in addition to different costs and audiences.

A serious constraint facing the director of the Cyclorama as he set about designing the 1987 promotional plan for the Cyclorama was in the area of budget. The Atlanta City Council had authorized an expenditure of $50,000 for a publicity fund. The amount was available for media advertising and sales promotion efforts. Personal selling and

EXHIBIT 7   Atlanta Area Print Media Cost and Audience Data—Black and White Print Ads

	Cost		Number of Readers (000s)		
	1 Time	52 Times	All Adults	Women	Men
Newspaper: 3-inch ad:					
Atlanta Journal-Constitution	$ 277	$14,404	963	475	488
Magazines: ⅓-Page ad:					
Southern Living					
Georgia edition	2,090	12,540	190	133	57
Atlanta edition (full page ad only)	3,930	21,240	100	70	30
Atlanta Magazine	1,025	5,670	33		
Business Atlanta	755	4,110	24	21	
Georgia Trends	850	4,530	24		
Where/Atlanta	850	4,260	60		
Key/Atlanta	115	690	10		

EXHIBIT 8   Atlanta Area Broadcast Media Cost and Audience Data, 7:00 A.M. to
9:00 A.M. Weekdays

	Cost	*Rating**	*Number of Viewers/Listeners (000s)*		
			All Adults	*Women*	*Men*
Television 30-second spot (morning news programs):					
WSB (ABC, Good Morning America)	$350	4.0	108	64	44
WAGA (CBS, Morning News)	125	1.3	36	22	14
WXIA (NBC, Today Show)	375	3.4	92	56	36
Radio 60-second spot (morning drive time):					
WZGC (Top 40)	250	1.3	36	19	17
WQXI (Adult Rock)	350	1.9	51	27	24
WSB (Contemporary)	200	1.4	38	20	18
WFOX (Rock Oldies)	150	.9	24	13	11
WKHX (Country)	250	1.9	51	26	25

* Rating is a measure of audience size expressed as a percentage of 2,699,800 adults, the survey area's population base for 1987.

publicity activities were carried out by the director and associate director as part of their overall duties. A separate printing budget of
$25,000 paid for brochures and similar forms of direct advertising.
   The director realized that the budget allocated to the Cyclorama was
not sufficient given the task of generating an appreciable increase in
attendance, and was fully aware of the importance of making the right
decisions as he designed the Cyclorama's promotional plan.

Case 5–4   *Zayre Corporation**

Soon after Mr. Maurice Segall became CEO of Zayre Corporation, . . .
he instituted a number of changes which repositioned Zayre Corporation in its various marketplaces. Critical corrections were made
quickly, but "without a bloodbath."

* Case copyright © 1985 by James Brian Quinn. Research associate, Penny C.
Paquette; research assistant, Barbara Dixon. The generous cooperation of the Zayre
Corporation is gratefully acknowledged.

EXHIBIT 1 Zayre Corporation Financials: Selected Financial Data (dollars in thousands except per share amounts)

For Fiscal Year Ended Last Saturday in January	1985	1984	1983	1982	1981 (53 weeks)
Summary of operations:					
Net sales	$ 3,123,008	$ 2,613,667	$ 2,139,616	$ 1,797,139	$ 1,594,235
Cost of sales, including buying and occupancy costs	2,372,467	1,986,559	1,616,889	1,361,753	1,209,179
Selling, general and administrative expenses	574,599	486,053	425,991	365,611	327,683
Interest costs:					
Debt	17,970	19,709	25,812	25,162	20,950
Capital leases	7,270	7,609	7,095	6,987	7,434
Total expenses	$ 2,972,306	$ 2,499,930	$ 2,075,787	$ 1,759,513	$ 1,565,246
Income before income taxes	$ 150,702	$ 113,737	$ 63,829	$ 37,626	$ 28,989
Provision for income taxes	70,386	52,311	28,653	15,479	11,415
Net income	$ 80,316	$ 61,426	$ 35,176	$ 22,147	$ 17,574
Number of common shares for earnings per share computations:					
Primary	20,108,771	19,254,852	16,286,334	14,335,790	13,795,560
Fully diluted	20,186,983	19,257,456	17,197,673	15,406,211	15,374,975
Net income per common share:					
Primary	$3.99	$3.19	$2.16	$1.53	$1.26
Fully diluted	$3.98	$3.19	$2.05	$1.46	$1.18

Stores in operation—end of year:					
Zayre Discount Department Stores	290	275	264	258	248
Hit or Miss	401	356	267	245	240
T.J. Maxx	156	118	86	64	43
Other financial data:					
Net income as a percent of sales	2.57%	2.35%	1.64%	1.23%	1.10%
Current assets	$ 697,750	$ 563,591	$ 449,246	$ 398,829	$ 347,646
Current liabilities	381,006	298,825	193,735	191,991	148,844
Working capital	316,744	264,766	255,511	206,838	198,802
Total assets	1,108,889	908,005	747,649	643,444	560,737
Long-term obligations, including capitalized leases	217,824	193,434	248,446	245,128	232,426
Shareholders' equity	468,071	395,457	294,762	199,232	174,110
Long-term debt-to-equity ratio, excluding capitalized leases	.31:1	.31:1	.58:1	.87:1	.90:1
Post-tax return on average equity	18.60%	17.80%	14.24%	11.86%	10.62%
Capital expenditures, excluding capitalized leases	$ 98,518	$ 76,279	$ 63,658	$ 54,914	$ 48,279
Number of common shares outstanding at year-end	19,779,981	17,953,297	8,393,173	5,411,615	5,209,166
Equity per common share	$23.66	$20.02	$15.96	$13.70	$12.39
Dividends per common share	$ .39	$ .27	$ .18	$ .15	$ .12

Note: All per-share data and number of common shares for earnings-per-share computations reflect the 10% stock dividend paid May 31, 1984; the two-for-one stock split paid June 29, 1983; and the 20% stock dividend paid June 10, 1982.

Source: Zayre Corporation, Annual Report, 1984.

553

EXHIBIT 1 *(continued)*   Selected Information: Major Business Segments
(in $000)

For Fiscal Year Ended	January 26, 1985	January 28, 1984	January 29, 1983
Net sales:			
Discount department stores	$2,195,740	$1,902,146	$1,615,999
Specialty stores	927,268	711,521	523,617
	$3,123,008	$2,613,667	$2,139,616
Operating income:			
Discount department stores*	$ 122,246	$ 90,847	$ 55,059
Specialty stores	64,156	54,768	46,945
	$ 186,402	$ 145,615	$ 102,004
General corporate expense†	17,730	12,169	12,363
Interest expense	17,970	19,709	25,812
Income before income taxes	$ 150,702	$ 113,737	$ 63,829
Identifiable assets:			
Discount department stores	$ 744,630	$ 609,748	$ 555,268
Specialty stores	293,987	257,705	143,843
Corporate (cash and market-able securities)	70,272	40,552	48,538
	$1,108,889	$ 908,005	$ 747,649
Depreciation and amortization:			
Discount department stores	$ 28,754	$ 25,702	$ 24,371
Specialty stores	11,375	8,054	4,007
	$ 40,129	$ 33,756	$ 28,378
Capital expenditures:			
Discount department stores	$ 63,932	$ 43,848	$ 36,331
Specialty stores	34,586	32,431	27,327
	$ 98,518	$ 76,279	$ 63,658

* The discount department stores use the last-in first-out (LIFO) method of valuing hardgoods inventories. (See Note B to the consolidated financial statements for further information.)

† Expense in fiscal 1983 includes a $1.7 million reserve for certain notes receivable. In fiscal 1984 the company recovered $1 million of the amount reserved. The net results of the company's test of a new prototype, a wholesale warehouse outlet, are included in general corporate expense.

Source: Zayre Corporation, *Annual Report,* 1984.

EXHIBIT 1 *(continued)*   Segment Information for Fiscal Year Ending January ($millions, except number of stores)

	1985	1984	1983	1982	1981	1980
Zayre Corporation						
Sales volume	3123	2614	2140	1797	1594	1550
Number of stores	847	749	620	567	531	528
Zayre Disct Dept Stores*						
Sales volume	2196	1902	1616	1433	1348	1345
Identified assets	745	610	555	506	463	443
Capital expenditures	64	44	36	41	41	37
Number of stores	290	275	264	258	248	254
Zayre Specialty Stores*						
Sales volume	927	712	524	364	246	205
Identified assets	294	258	144	115	61	41
Capital expenditures	35	32	27	14	8	4
Number of stores	557	474	353	309	283	274
T.J. Maxx	156	118	86	64	43	30
Hit or Miss	401	356	267	245	240	244

* Security analysts estimated that Zayre Stores units averaged about 72,000 ft^2 of space and had sales of about $8 million. They estimated T.J. Maxx averaged some 24,000 ft^2 and $5 million per unit, while Hit or Miss averaged only 3,500 ft^2 and $750,000 per unit.

Source: Zayre Corporation, *Annual Report,* 1984, 1983, 1981.

The entire retail environment shifted rapidly in 1978. As the Iranian revolution brought on a tripling of oil prices, rapid inflation and the highest interest rates in history hit the United States. Many discounters did not survive this difficult period. In 1978 there were over 65 discount chains with volumes over $100 million. Five years later, one third of them did not exist. But Zayre's sales soared to $3.1 billion in 1985 with profits of $80.3 million (see Exhibit 1). Bradlee's, Caldor, and Kmart moved toward higher-income customers. Zayre Stores stayed with its traditional customers and became one of the few successful chains selling to "center city" populations. Many such areas had strong ethnic preferences. As one Zayre executive said, "We had to solve the problem of maintaining the advantages of chain retailing, yet cater to the needs of individual locations, a really difficult task."

BARRACUDAS OR FOSSILS

By 1983, Chicago was Zayre Stores' biggest market, and sales in the lower-middle income "southside" had grown from $25 million to $100 million in only five years. The original remodeling and upgrading

EXHIBIT 1 *(concluded)*   Store Locations—January 1985

State	Zayre Stores	T.J. Maxx	Hit or Miss	State	Zayre Stores	T.J. Maxx	Hit or Miss
Alabama	7	6	2	Mississippi	1	0	0
Arizona	0	0	3	Missouri	0	0	1
Colorado	0	3	7	Nebraska	0	1	0
Connecticut	5	8	12	New Hampshire	7	1	1
Washington, D.C.	0	0	2	New Jersey	0	5	32
Florida	63	11	19	New York	7	3	35
Georgia	14	4	12	North Carolina	10	6	7
Illinois	35	16	36	Ohio	17	16	25
Indiana	12	2	7	Oklahoma	0	1	3
Iowa	1	1	4	Pennsylvania	13	8	24
Kansas	0	1	0	Rhode Island	8	1	6
Kentucky	4	3	4	South Carolina	0	2	5
Louisiana	0	2	5	Tennessee	9	5	10
Maine	11	1	4	Texas	0	7	28
Maryland	8	0	12	Vermont	4	0	1
Massachusetts	35	14	38	Virginia	11	7	16
Michigan	2	15	25	West Virginia	0	0	2
Minnesota	0	2	7	Wisconsin	6	4	6
				Total	290	156	401

Source: Zayre Corporation, *Annual Report,* 1984.

budget for Zayre Stores had grown to $100 million. Change was constant during this period. As Malcolm Sherman, Zayre Stores president said, "If ever there was an industry that responds to Darwin's theory of survival of the fittest, it's retailing. A new retailer starts as a young barracuda, and can end up as a fossil 10 years later."

In this respect, off-price merchandising was to the early 1980s what discount stores had been to the 1960s and early 1970s. Off-price chains sprang up all over, specializing in women's apparel, family apparel, shoes, housewares, linens and domestics, and so on. These stores had a special appeal to the "white collar market" to whom brand names and styles were more important. T.J. Maxx boomed in its markets and by 1985 had become the second largest (to Marshall's $1.2 billion) retailer of off-price, brand name apparel in the United States according to *Standard & Poor's Corporate Descriptions,* December 1984. By 1985 the increased number of Maxx stores had called for a 300,000 ft^2 distribution center in Worcester, Mass., to supplement its original 450,000 ft² complex.

Although performance of off-price chains was highly variable, the best such chains achieved some $200 sales per square foot, with an 8–10 times inventory turnover, and net profits before taxes of 5 percent of sales. *Chain Store Age* estimated total off-price sales of some $17 billion by 1990. Unlike other retail trends started by entrepreneurs, the off-price chains all had big money behind them. U.S. Shoe, Melville, Dayton Hudson, and Zayre were among the big players. In addition to competing with more prestigious retailers such as Marshall Field and Lord & Taylor, off-price stores competed directly with the private brands sold by Sears, J.C. Penney, or Montgomery Ward— often made by the same manufacturers to the buyers' specifications. At first, buyers obtained off-price merchandise strictly from manufacturers' overruns, closeouts, returns, previous season's merchandise, irregulars (etc.). But increasingly, buyers could obtain excellent prices on large orders placed directly with manufacturers.

Hit or Miss had changed too. It now targeted mid-to-better-income females who wanted recognized merchandise at a lower price. It offered current season, first-quality women's sportswear (casual pants, shirts, blouses, etc.) and ready-to-wear dresses, coats, and suits in both brand names and private labels at about 50 percent off regular prices. (Reed Hunter was one of H or M's private labels.) The store focused on the somewhat conservative, youthful, professional, career-minded woman, who was very fashion conscious but had to watch costs. Although Hit or Miss had been "repositioned" extensively from 1978–85 and expanded to 356 units in 31 states, the chain seemed to lack a distinctive personality or loyal clientele and was still not a roaring success in 1985.

THE NEW ZAYRE

By 1985, Zayre Corporation had changed markedly. Even with Zayre's powerful recent growth and strong balance sheet (see Exhibit 1), Mr. Segall was still pointing for new horizons. His goal was a 20 percent per year compounded growth rate. Despite his easy-to-meet style and great personal charm, he was described by *Forbes* as "all business, clearly a workaholic, but he had to be to bring about such major changes [from 1978–84]. . . . Clear thinking, tough decisions, well executed"[1] were said to be his hallmark. Mr. Segall described his style somewhat differently:

---

[1] "Making Money at the Low End of the Market," *Forbes,* December 17, 1984, p. 42.

I want growth in a disciplined fashion. . . . Everyone in this company knows what our goals are. We stand up once a year and I talk to 1,500 people—from mail clerks to executive VPs—and they know what our goals are. We don't keep secrets here. We continue to refine our mission statements, our target customers, and so on. We introduced three-year plans, which were tied to clear three-year income, sales, ROI, and operating objectives. . . . I don't want anything left to chance. I want us to be in control. All of us must execute the basics—not only with the highest of standards, but better than our competitors.

We have business plans for each segment of the business which pull all these together in a consistent way. We have also developed extensive incentive plans tied directly to these. I believe in incentive plans. Everyone has incentive plans, but ours can be very generous [see Exhibit 2]. Although I'm well paid, our key people can also make a lot of money, and we have made some millionaires. . . . I think that's great as long as the stockholder makes out better as a result.

Zayre's policy was to pay competitive base salaries, while putting significant emphasis on variable forms of compensation. The exact mix of salary, incentives, and other compensation varied, based upon the manager's organization level and job responsibilities. Three objectives underlay the Zayre compensation program: (1) to pay competitive basic and total compensation scales; (2) to reward exceptional individual performance, and (3) to ensure that the compensation program was cost effective by closely tying it to well-communicated business plans. Exhibit 2 summarizes Zayre's basic incentive plans.

In addition, Zayre used four types of long-term incentives to retain and reward its key executives: stock options, career shares, restricted stock, and long-term cash bonuses. Key executives could buy career shares for book value with a company-provided loan. Sale and conversion restrictions lapsed on these at 20 percent per year. A tax-free conversion to common shares could occur on this schedule at a predetermined exchange ratio. Zayre's Long Range Management Incentive Plan (LRMP) was a three-year cash incentive plan tied to company results for those who could influence intermediate-term performance. At the beginning of each three-year period, a three-year target was established for net income (75%) and net income/sales (25%) at divisional levels and net income (75%) and ROI (25%) at corporate levels. Incentives peaked sharply in a fashion similar to those set forth in Exhibit 2.

Hits and Questions

While T.J. Maxx and Zayre Stores were growing and profitable in 1984–85, Hit or Miss still had problems. Mr. Segall said, "We're not executing properly there. We are currently struggling with the division's real mission. I'm still persuaded there is a market for our kind of store for the career-oriented young woman between 20 and 40. But we need a much better distinctive concept and better execution for our present target market. In 3,500 ft^2 you have very little room to make a statement, and we're making too many statements."

"In the case of T.J. Maxx, we're very pleased with the execution to date, but we're facing a different competitive environment. The T.J. Maxx concept was really designed 8–9 years ago. By definition, that design has to be obsolete now. The problem is how to position this excellent chain for the 1990s and execute that positioning effectively."

Other Ventures

By 1985, Zayre's management had begun to ask itself some very basic questions about the future. "Where do we go from here as a total corporation? What kind of company should we be in the 1990s? Should Zayre start some new ventures or acquire some? We started exploring a wide range of opportunities. When all was said and done we decided to take a crack at BJ's Wholesale Club, which was our version of the Price Club on the West Coast. But this is only the beginning."

Self service, cash-and-carry "wholesale clubs" (or warehouses) like BJ's offered a "limited membership" (of small businesses) access to name-brand goods at genuine wholesale prices. For an annual fee, a business could buy at posted wholesale prices. Noncommercial buyers could buy under a group membership which involved no annual fee, but required purchase prices 5 percent above posted prices. The key to wholesale club operations was abnormally low merchandise margins, extremely efficient operations, in a bare-bones, pseudo-warehouse environment. Mr. Segall noted, "In this kind of operation, there is no room for error. But the concept offers low prices and sound values; and that is what retailing is all about." Sumner Feldberg commented, "It isn't as if we are discovering America here; it happens to be a form of retailing developed over the course of the past few years with which some people have had great success. I'm very impressed with these operations by the remarkable volume they can generate." Sales per square foot of Price Club units were estimated at well over $500.

The Price Club in California had opened its first "wholesale club" warehouse store in 1976 and by 1983 grossed some $630 million and was widely imitated. (See Exhibit 3.) Experts thought this concept would grow to at least $20 billion by 1990.[2] Minimum volumes for

---

[2] "Membership Retailing Trend Taking Off," *Chain Store Age Executive,* November 1984, p. 17.

EXHIBIT 2 Example Incentive Plans, 1985

Recipient	As Percent of Salary Target/Maximum	Performance Criteria	Below Goal Performance/ Award	Over Goal Performance/ Award	Administration
Store manager	20%/100%	Controllable Income	99%/95%	101%/104%	Adjusted for every 1% change in performance
Assistant store manager	10%/40%		98%/80% 95%/30% 90%/0	110%/140% 120%/180% Above = 6% for each 1% improvement	
Zone manager	30%/45%	New income and NI/sales for zone and individual goals	Same as store managers	+6% for every 1% over goal until 110% perf. Then +8% per 1% change to 115% perf.	Award adjusted upward or downward by 6% of the target award per 1% var. in NI/sales vs. NI beyond a 5% range, but <2x target award. 50% in financial goal, 50% on individual.
Zone merchandising manager	25%/50%				
Zone personnel manager	20%/40%				

Senior merchandising manager					
Buyer	21%/42% 15%/100%	Sales 25% + Gross profit 75% + Inventory levels	−16% per −1% sales variance, −11.1% per −1% gross profit variance	+16% per +1% sales variance, +11.1% per +1% gross profit variance	Sales award max 106% of goal. Gross profit award max 109% of goal. Adj. by −2.5% per +1% var. in year-end inventory goal if <5%. Max. penalty = 25%.
Zayre Stores division management:					
President Managers	32.5%/65% 15%/30%	85% 75% NI 25% NI/S 15% indiv. perf. goals	−5% per −1% NI below goal	+6⅔% per +1% NI above goal	Adjusted for NI/sales on same basis if <90% or >105% of goal. Adjusted by performance appraisal vs. individual goals.
Zayre corporate management	100%/115–120%	85% 75% NI 25% ROI 15% indiv. perf. goals	−5% per −1% NI below goal, −8⅓% per −1% of ROI goal	+5% per +1% NI above goal, +8⅓% per 1% ROI above goal	Awards apply outside ±3% limits on ROI. Adjusted by performance vs. individual goals.

Source: Company records.

EXHIBIT 3 Wholesale Membership Clubs: Comparative Data 1984

Company	Current Locations	Proposed Locations	Membership Policy	
			Wholesale	Retail
BJ's Wholesale Club (Zayre)	Hialeah, Fla. Medford, Mass. Johnston, R.I.	Hartford, Conn.	$30 annual fee—up to 2 additional memberships $10 each	5% markup
Club Wholesale (Elixir)	Boise, Idaho Las Vegas, Nev.	2 locations	$25 annual fee	5% markup
Costco	Anchorage, Alaska Clearwater, Fla. Fort Lauderdale Tampa Bay West Palm Beach Portland, Ore. Seattle (3) Spokane Tacoma Salt Lake City	Honolulu (10–12 units)	$25 annual fee	5% markup
Metro Cash & Carry of Illinois	Chicago (3)	No expansion plans	No fee	5% markup
Money's Worth	Greensboro, N.C.	1 in North Carolina	$25 annual fee	5% markup
Pace	Denver (2) Colorado Springs Tampa/St. Petersburg	Denver Tampa/St. Petersburg (2) Jacksonville Atlanta (3) Augusta Des Moines Omaha Greensboro, N.C. Raleigh Chattanooga Knoxville	$25 annual fee	5% markup

Company	Cities	Fee	Additional
Price Club	Phoenix Mesa, Ariz. Tucson Los Angeles (5) Orange County, Calif. Sacramento (2) San Diego (4) San Francisco (2) Norfolk, Va. Richmond Albuquerque	$25 annual fee	$15 fee +5% markup
Price Savers Wholesale Club	Anchorage, Alaska Salt Lake City Seattle Tacoma Honolulu	$25 annual fee	5% markup
Sam's Wholesale Club (Wal-Mart)	Birmingham, Ala. Jacksonville, Fla. Kansas City, Mo. St. Louis Oklahoma City Charleston, S.C. Dallas (2) Houston (3) Atlanta Wichita Louisville Tulsa Knoxville Memphis Nashville	$25 annual fee	5% markup
Warehouse Club (joint partnership W.R. Grace)	Chicago Akron Columbus Dayton Pittsburgh Detroit	$25 annual fee	5% markup
Wholesale Club	Indianapolis Cleveland Milwaukee Detroit (4) Cleveland	$30 annual fee	5% markup
Wholesale Plus	Fort Lauderdale —	$25 annual fee	5% markup
Value Club	Austin El Paso San Antonio (3) —	$25 annual fee	$5 fee +5% markup

Source: Reprinted by permission from *Chain Store Age Executive*, November 1984. Copyright © 1984 by Lebhar-Friedman, 425 Park Avenue, New York, NY 10022.

early stores were $25 million to $30 million, but some units were selling annual volumes of over $100 million. At first, estimates were that each store needed 400,000 to 600,000 people in its market area to be profitable, but this could drop as the concept caught on and operations were "debugged." A typical store operated on 10 to 11 percent merchandise margins and sold a major portion of its volume to smaller businesses, restaurants, groceries, drugstores, offices, etc. BJ's units opened with $3 to $4 million in inventory each and sought break-evens within one year. Most chains sought 60/40 business/group sales. BJ's Mervin Weich, an MIS data processing expert, noted that inventory turnover goals would be some 16X per year—based on the Price Club experience. Parking for some 400 cars was *de rigueur*, with start-up costs of $5 million to $8 million per store being common. Most wholesale chain clubs targeted staffing levels per store at 70 to 200 people.

"Deep discounting" at 40 to 60 percent off suggested retail prices was also spreading rapidly in drug items, foods, auto parts, books, stationery, and so on. There were some 200 such units in 1985, but 1,000 were expected by 1990. They operated in 20,000 to 30,000 ft² formats with very restricted lines and inventories purchased mainly on "deals" from suppliers. Direct-mail selling was also growing at 10 to 15 percent per year. And Zayre was actively expanding its direct-mail operation, Chadwick's, begun in 1983. Sumner Feldberg said, "The first catalog effort was terrific and the customer response was excellent. But Chadwick's is primarily viewed as a means for the company to gain experience in mail order, something we have not been in before, as opposed to our long experience as chain-store operators."[3]

1985 COMPETITION

What did Zayre's main competitors look like in 1985?

Sears Roebuck.   With $38.8 billion in sales, Sears was still the largest retailer by far with a continuing mission "to provide customers with more quality goods and services than any other organization of its kind." Sears sales consisted of $29.5 billion in merchandise, $9 billion Allstate Insurance, $2.5 billion Dean Witter financial services, and $1 billion from real estate and world trade activities. Sears had developed its "Store of the Future" concept with expanded product lines, more exciting displays and an emphasis on modernized and improved service levels at the point of sale. It had shifted its merchandise mix more

---

[3] "Sumner Feldberg: Maxx-imizing Potential," *Chain Store Age Executive,* January 1984, p. 19.

to upscale apparel and home furnishings, with relative deemphasis on hard-good lines. It was experimenting with smaller (8,000 to 30,000 ft^2) stores to sell its own franchised products. Sears had also added some specialty stores (100 Business Centers and 4 Paint and Hardware Centers). Its total number of stores was down to 792 from 831 in 1982 with 391 full-line, 355 medium-line, and 52 hard-line stores.

Kmart. Zayre's closest competitor was Kmart with sales of $21.1 billion from 2,400 general merchandise discount stores and 1,120 specialty outlets. Kmart discount stores operated in 48 states with an average 57,000 ft^2 format. Its stated strategy was "to provide a broader offering of brand names, larger assortment of high-value goods, and a more contemporary presentation of merchandise" because customers wanted better-quality merchandise at lower prices. Its customer mix had moved slightly upscale since 1977. Kmart had diversified *within* retailing into: *Designer Depot,* an off-price family apparel chain following the Marshall's and T.J. Maxx format; *Waldenbooks,* at 900 stores and 5 discount units the largest book retailer in 50 states (acquired for $300 million and expected to sell $1 billion in 1990); *Builders Square,* large (80,000 ft^2) warehouse home centers for contractors and do-it-yourselfers (15 outlets acquired for $88 million); *Pay-Less Drug Stores,* one of the largest retail drug chains (104 units plus discount outlets acquired for $500 million); *Financial Services,* available in 275 Kmarts with 1,000 projected by 1990; *Cafeterias,* 158 units in 2 chains expected to be $1 billion in sales by 1990; and *Kmart Trading* for export of U.S.-made goods.

J.C. Penney. In metropolitan areas Penney's now had 564 department stores averaging 157,000 ft^2 representing 60 percent of its sales, and 205 soft-line stores having 7 percent of sales. It also had 801 small-town stores averaging 25,000 ft^2 (13 percent of sales), catalog sales (14 percent), and drug stores (14 percent). It was continuing to expand in fashions using its own designer labels and remodeling its stores accordingly. It was closing down its food, hardware, and car accessory departments.[4] Penney's financial services subsidiary, while still small and primarily involved in insurance sales (now through over 200 in-store centers), also operated the J.C. Penney National Bank and five Financial Centers in California. It had $22 million in net income.

Wal-Mart. Wal-Mart had grown to $4.7 billion in sales with 642 stores in 20 states. Its average store now had 50,000 ft^2 and plans

---

[4] "New Fangled Stores for Fussy Buyers: American Retailing," *Economist,* April 30, 1983.

EXHIBIT 4   Comparative Chain Performance

		Kmart Corp.	*Wal-Mart Corp.*	*Zayre Corp.*
Sales ($ millions)				
FY ending	1/85	21,096	6,401	3,123
	1/81	14,204	1,643	1,594
	1/77	8,382	479	1,161
Net income ($ millions)				
FY ending	1/85	499	271	80
	1/81	261	56	18
	1/77	262*	16*	10*
Total assets ($ millions)				
FY ending	1/85	9,262	2,205	1,109
	1/81	6,089*	592	561
	1/77	3,983*	168*	435*
Merchandise inventory ($ millions)				
FY ending	1/85	4,588	1,104	603
	1/81	2,846	280	296
	1/77	1,738	89	211
Number of stores				
FY ending	1/85	3,365[c]	756[a]	847
	1/81	2,327[c]	330	531
	1/77	1,646	153	451[b]
Square feet of space (millions)				
FY ending	1/85	131.5[f]	41.9[d]	26.6[g]
	1/81	114.5[c]	15.5	19.7
	1/77	80.3	6.5	19.5

* Restated from original reported figures in later years' annual reports.
[a] 1984 figure includes 3 wholesale clubs; 1985 figure includes 11 clubs.
[b] Figures include On Stage/Nugent/Bell and Beaconway stores but exclude supermarkets and gas stations.
[c] Figures include shoe stores, Designer Depots, Waldenbooks, and Builders Square stores but exclude cafeterias.
[d] Figures include wholesale club space.
[e] Figures include only general merchandise space.
[f] Figures include both general merchandise and specialty store space.
[g] Rough estimates based on information provided in Annual Reports concerning Zayre Stores, Hit or Miss, and T.J. Maxx.

Source: Various years' Annual Reports for Wal-Mart Corp., Kmart Corp., and Zayre Corp.

called for 100 new stores in 1985. *Forbes* still showed Wal-Mart as first in its key financial return statistics (see Exhibit 4). Wal-Mart's basic strategy was unchanged, but it had moved into 11 wholesale clubs in 1985, opened its first drug discount store, and was testing a 25,000 ft² format for even smaller towns.

The Second Cluster

Among the second cluster of discounters, variety and diversity were most notable. Gemco-Memco stores in California grossed an amazing $23 million per store, including foods. And Target Stores owned by Dayton Hudson averaged $12 million per store. Elsewhere there were numerous local "piperack retailers" who could be successful for short periods of time by selling what the industry considered "schlock" merchandise. These units were very successful in specific locations, but Zayre was distinctly differentiated from these, and was by far the most successful chain with minority customers in the central cities of the United States. See Exhibits 4, 5, and 6 for some comparative data on various chains.

WHERE IS THE FUTURE?

Retailing would undoubtedly undergo many more changes in the late 1980s. See Exhibit 7 for data on some selected trends. Key executives at Zayre added some broad perspectives on how these might fit into their company's future.

Mr. Segall said, "We're all going to have to be sensitive to the extraordinary acceleration in the birth, growth, maturity, and decline cycle of American retailers. The pace is just incredible. The old-line retailer is gone, and today's successful patterns will be tomorrow's disasters. For us any aspect of retailing is fair game. The only thing we preclude is nonretail—no steelmaking, no broadcasting. Retailing will always be one of the largest business segments in our economy."

But excess capacity and market saturation was a real problem as each major company continued to expand. By 1985 retailing was characterized by "intertype marts with a pharmacy in the rear. Grocery stores carried both pharmacy and general merchandise items. Sears had moved out into financial services, as had Kmart and some J.C. Penney units. And so on. Meanwhile specialized flea markets, off-price catalogs, house-to-house selling, party plans, and telemarketing were expanding at wild rates. And specialized discount retailers—such as Toys "R" Us and Bata (shoes)—were establishing a clear presence in their markets.

In March 1985, Mr. Segall noted, "One of the most exciting developments in U.S. retailing in 50 years is the potential purchase by Americans of $100s of billions worth of electronics in the years to come. Increased household formations, a bulge in the educated 25–45-year-old group, more use of the home as an entertainment base, the growth of cable communication, new technologies, home computers, etc., mean this is the largest single-growth category in U.S. retailing." Marketing

EXHIBIT 5 Selected Productivity Measures by Retailer Classification, 1983–1984

*1983 Estimated Sales per Labor Hour**

	Total (105) %	Discount (17) %	Drug (18) %	Super-market (26) %	Depart-ment (18) %	Home Center (16) %	Specialty (10) %
Less than $25	8	—	6	4	6	6	40
$25–$50	24	29	28	12	33	25	20
$51–$75	15	18	22	4	6	31	20
$76–$100	19	12	17	42	11	6	10
$101 +	5	6	—	12	—	6	—
Refused comment	13	12	6	15	17	19	10
Don't know/no answer	16	24	22	12	28	6	—
(MEAN)	$(60.3)	(61.1)	(55.5)	(80.2)	(48.6)	(57.5)	(40.9)

*1983 Estimated Sales per Net Square Foot**

	Total (78) %	Discount (14) %	Drug (14) %	Super-market (10) %	Depart-ment (27) %	Home Center (6) %	Specialty (7) %
Less than $50	8	—	14	40	—	—	—
$51–$100	13	36	7	—	7	33	—
$101–$150	28	29	29	—	41	17	29
$151–$200	15	14	21	—	18	17	14
$201–$250	5	—	7	10	4	17	—
$251–$300	3	—	—	10	4	—	—
$301–$350	—	—	—	—	—	—	—

	Total (83) %	Discount (13) %	Drug (19) %	Super-market (16) %	Depart-ment (13) %	Home Center (11) %	Specialty (11) %
$351–$400	—	—	—	—	—	—	—
$401 +	5	7	—	10	—	—	29
Refused comment	14	14	7	20	11	17	29
Don't know/no answer	9	—	14	10	15	—	—
(MEAN)	(151.5)	(139.6)	(127.7)	(158.6)	(145.0)	(135.0)	(265.0)

1983 Estimated Sales per Gross Square Foot*

	Total (83) %	Discount (13) %	Drug (19) %	Super-market (16) %	Depart-ment (13) %	Home Center (11) %	Specialty (11) %
Less than $50	10	—	5	38	—	—	9
$50–$100	13	23	5	—	15	46	—
$101–$150	24	46	37	—	23	9	27
$151–$200	11	—	21	6	8	18	9
$201–$250	4	—	10	—	8	—	—
$251–$300	2	—	5	6	—	—	—
$301–$350	4	8	5	—	—	—	9
$351–$400	2	—	—	—	—	—	18
$401 +	5	—	—	12	—	9	9
Refused comment	17	15	5	19	31	18	18
Don't know/no answer	8	8	5	19	15	—	18
(MEAN)	(160.8)	(130.0)	(161.2)	(159.0)	(132.1)	(144.4)	(235.0)

* For chains using this system.

Source: *Chain Store Age Executive*, September 1984. Reprinted by permission of *Chain Store Age Executive*. Copyright 1984 by Lebhar-Friedman, 425 Park Avenue, New York, NY 10022.

EXHIBIT 6 Sales and Earnings for Quarter Ended in September or October

	Sales ($ millions)		Percent Change
	1984	1983	
Chain—General merchandise:			
Sears[1]	$6,463	$6,190	4.4%
Kmart	4,993	4,331	15.3
J.C. Penney	3,211	2,914	10.2
Federated	2,266	2,071	9.4
Dayton Hudson	1,868	1,659	13.0
Woolworth	1,404	1,353	3.8
Wal-Mart	1,584	1,167	36.0
May	1,133	1,003	13.0
Macy	1,011	929	8.8
ADG	951	905	5.0
Allied	932	883	5.5
CHH[2]	906	758	20.0
Zayre	777	659	17.8
Supermarkets and convenience stores:			
Safeway	4,584	4,300	6.6
Kroger	4,623	4,505	2.6
Southland	3,085	2,430	26.9
Lucky	2,191	2,027	8.1
Winn-Dixie	1,732	1,648	5.1
A&P[3]	1,377	1,192	15.5
Drug chains:			
Walgreen	684	595	15.0
Jack Eckerd	637	543	17.3
Revco	511	453	12.6
Longs	328	291	12.7
Specialty stores:			
Melville	1,066	985	8.2
Tandy	596	583	2.1
U.S. Shoe	416	375	10.9
Limited	349	271	29.0
Toys "R" Us	322	221	45.7
Edison[4]	269	249	7.8
Zale	217	198	9.6

[1] Sears Merchandise Group sales only. Operating profits from this group amounted to $163.8 million, or a 3.1% increase over the $158.9 million of a year earlier.
[2] Actual earnings increased 59%. Earnings per share declined because of actions taken by CHH to fight off a takeover attempt by Limited Inc.
[3] Before extraordinary credits in both years.
[4] Without a nonrecurring after-tax gain from the sale of Handyman Store properties in Texas and Oklahoma, earnings per share would have been 73¢ in the 1984 quarter, a 28.8% decrease.

Source: *Chain Store Age Executive*, January 1985. Reprinted by permission of *Chain Store Age Executive.* Copyright 1985 by Lebhar-Friedman, 425 Park Avenue, New York, NY 10022.

EXHIBIT 7 Trends in Retailing

Sales by Store Classification (yearly sales in $ millions)

Type of Store	1972	1976	1977	1979	1980	1981	1982	1983
Food store	100718	144912	157941	195710	219399	242763	268352	278427
Supermarket	93298	134534	147758	183860	206121	227756	252094	261732
Eating/drinking establishment	36885	56852	63276	76751	87310	96417	107484	118935
General merchandise store	65065	94748	93948	112400	123157	135518	139654	147354
Department store	51056	75247	76965	93620	106698	111561	115969	120686
Appliance/accessory store	24741	36796	35564	43103	44999	48849	50593	54648
Furniture/home furnishing/appliance store	22534	34790	33177	40823	44162	47124	46105	52188
Furnishing/home furnishing store	14059	21239	20320	25049	26627	28754	27725	30895
Automotive dealer	90029	123417	149952	175508	169808	182841	172669	203052
Gasoline service station	33655	47513	56468	72122	93801	103447	107540	107978
Building materials/hardware store	23844	33081	38859	50506	49381	53818	52711	59410
Drugstore	15599	21529	23198	28668	31986	34075	37232	39124
Total retail sales	459031	661749	723134	887519	965746	1056107	1100750	1186387
Effective buying income		1176240		1618643	1814167			2329210

Sales by Product Classification (yearly sales in $ millions)

Product	1972	1976	1977	1979	1980	1981	1982	1983
Men's/boys' clothing	14999	22161	23057	26854	29656	32417	33497	35743
Women's/girls' clothing	25923	38110	37055	46278	47612	52052	53758	57502
Footwear	7677	11348	10941	13762	14120	15336	15916	17026
Audio equipment/musical instruments/supplies			9575		12733	13696	13718	15172
Television	8174	12291	4386	15014	5834	6296	6327	6952
Major household appliances	7341	11022	9565	13661	12773	13816	14019	15210
Health and beauty aids			11593		15813	17171	18407	19367
Drugs	15660	22021	12703	29175	17475	18710	20257	21362
Total retail sales	459031	661749	723134	887519	965746	1056107	1100750	1186387

Source: Compiled from Sales and Marketing Management, *Survey of Buying Power Data Service*, various years.

Science Institute estimated that home appliance, radio, TV, and electronic store sales would grow from $12 billion in 1980 to $52 billion in 1990.

All of these opportunities were being eyed by well-heeled, well-managed, aggressive, large corporations looking for new entries. Mr. Segall said, "Never before have so many professionals surveyed so many new kinds of developments, ready to pounce on the attractive ones with huge war chests for financing." But each new retailing approach was also reaching maturity faster than ever before, creating ever greater pressure for precise timing, positioning, and care in choosing what directions to pursue.

Macro-Trends

J. Sheth in the *Journal of Retailing* cited other macro trends in the field:

1. The United States was becoming a very affluent, diverse, adult-oriented society with highly individualistic life-styles in which time—rather than money—had become the scarce resource.
2. Competition in retailing was becoming more global in both sourcing and distribution. And a changing focus toward deregulation was allowing very large oligopolistic companies to exploit this trend.
3. The single middle-class U.S. society was becoming more a dual class, 25 percent affluent and 60 to 70 percent average-income society whose basic functional needs were easily met; demand was shifting to psychological satisfactions in products over sheer functionality—to wants over needs.
4. With the emergence of nontraditional households with dual or multiple incomes, more goods were being demanded at individualistic, rather than shared levels—with foods, leisure items, clothing, and services all being heavily affected.
5. For demographic and technological reasons, it would be increasingly common not to separate the time and place of work, home, and shopping activities.
6. As technology dropped the relative price of many appliances, the distinction between shopping goods and convenience goods would blur, and customers would increasingly depend on manufacturers as their guarantors of quality.[5]

---

[5] J. Sheth, "Emerging Trends for the Retailing Industry," *Journal of Retailing,* Fall 1983, p. 6.

Another source referred to these trends as "life-style retailing" tailored to the life-styles of specific target markets, rather than "supplier-driven" retailing. Demographically, the 35- to 45-year-old population and the over-80 population were growing most in percentage terms, while the under-20 group was falling in the late 1980s. This bulge represented the best-educated, most affluent, and culturally diverse population in U.S. history. During the past 10 years the black U.S. population had grown 17 percent and the Hispanic population had grown 61 percent.[6] But Mr. Stanley Feldberg pointed out that there were strongly divergent regional and local trends. For example, the Northeast industrial investment and production base had radically declined and its relative working population had decreased. But the emergence of new companies and service industries—and transfer payments by governments—had given Zayre strong Northeastern sales even in areas where major shutdowns had occurred. He observed, "Our total marketplace is so complex and rapidly changing that we must be constantly ready to adapt to new modes of retailing and specific customer needs as they develop. I doubt that we—or anyone else—can analyze now exactly what the customer will want and what new retailing structures will provide in the early 1990s."

The Retail Revolution

The Retail Revolution cited other powerful trends. Mass advertising and computerized technologies seemed to provide such overwhelming advantages to large retailers that its authors thought that—with few exceptions—the small independent retailer could soon be doomed. Both forces tend to create enormous barriers to entry and to affect margins so substantially that large scale becomes a prerequisite to competitiveness. Large-scale and high technologies were already affecting employment skill levels, management sophistication, and organizational and cost structures in profound ways—and were likely to be more important in the future. Government policies originally designed to protect small retailers through resale-price-maintenance agreements (allowing producers to fix retail prices on their goods) and Robinson-Patman regulations (producers must be able to justify price differences to customers on the basis of differential costs) had perversely created the very price umbrellas that made bigness possible and indeed essential. All these forces had significantly impacted both the supplier and distribution structure of the retail industry. *The Re-*

---

[6] Blackwell and Talarzyk, "Life-Style Retailing: Competitive Strategies for the 1980s," *Journal of Retailing,* Winter 1983.

tail Revolution ends with a query as to whether these forces will lead in the next 15 years to a point where "a handful of mammoth corporations will be left to constitute the distributive network in the nation. . . . Behind the glitter and glamour of modern department stores is a saga of dramatic change and adaptation that we are only beginning to comprehend."[7]

ZAYRE IN THE FUTURE

As Mr. Segall looked to the future he said, "Zayre is almost 30 years old, a maturing young company in its prime. I have tried hard to generate a spirit in the company about itself and the future. This business is all people, and I have a lot of confidence in the people in this company. For the outside world, I only state a few objectives. One is that we are intent on achieving a 20 percent profit growth per year for many years to come. We intend to keep saying that and to posture ourselves accordingly. Our second goal is the image and reality of a well-administered organization and a thoughtful merchant. We must not ever rest on our laurels, but continue to progress with our customers and markets—and to administer competently. The next 5 to 10 years at Zayre will be exciting, interesting, and challenging. That I can promise you."

Appendix A   Some Organizational Terms in Retailing

Merchandising embraces the entire group of decisions and tasks involved in determining what merchandise is offered, acquiring it, and having it available in the right assortments at the right places to maximize the store's marketing objectives. In many retail operations, merchandising includes the functions of buying, receiving, marketing, and handling all merchandise as well as controlling inventory levels and mixes in the stores. In some large or complex chains, some of these activities may be split off as specialized functions or be decentralized regionally.

Buying is a major line activity in retailing. Buying decisions include what merchandise should be purchased, in what quantities, at what prices, under what terms, and when it should be purchased and received. In some stores the buyer also determines prices, markups, markdowns and closeouts, and plans and coordinates a department's special sales. Buying can be organized according to the class of merchandise purchased, store type, or location served. In most department stores buyers are in charge of all merchandising for their

---

[7] Bluestone, et al., *The Retail Revolution*. Boston: Auburn House Publishing Co., 1981.

particular departments as well as directing the sales forces in these departments. In some decentralized operations, buying and local sales force management may be separated.

Operations includes all those activities necessary to maintain the quality and appearance of the physical facilities of the enterprise. In some highly decentralized retail concerns, these activities—as well as supervision and control of local salepeople and inventory-handling functions—are the responsibility of Operations. Service and support activities locally may report either to Operations or directly to other centralized line or administrative functions.

Sales is the face-to-face presentation of the product to the customer and the first recording of that transaction on the store's books through the cash register, sales slip, or electronic charge system. In some cases, salespeople report to the buying or merchandise heads; in others they are separated from these functions and report either through Operations or a centralized sales unit.

Promotion generally includes advertising, publicity, displaying of merchandise, and any tactics (other than merchandise selection and pricing) which will induce profitable sales volume. Special attraction techniques such as store signs, catalogs, premiums, trading stamps, and nonrecurring interest breaks are considered promotions. Store layout, design, traffic flow planning, rack displays, wall and floor coloring, lighting presentations, etc. are important aspects of in-store promotion which clearly impact the effectiveness of all other line activities.

Case 5–5   Gillette Company*

In the lobby of Gillette Co.'s razor and blade factory, a glass case displays artifacts from shaving over the ages: An Egyptian bronze razor from 1500 B.C., a Turkish crescent razor from 1190, a straight razor from the Franco Prussian War in 1870.

Then there is the first safety razor invented by company founder King C. Gillette in 1903, the Gillette Blue Blade (1932), the Trac II twin-blade razor (1971).

Soon, Sensor, a new razor, will be added to the case. With twin blades mounted on tiny springs so they can move independently—the better to reach every nook and cranny on your face—Sensor is being touted as providing the smoothest and closest shave man has ever known. Gillette believes the new razor will be snapped up by millions.

* Source: Lawrence Ingrassia, "Face-Off: A Recovering Gillette Hopes for Vindication in a High-Tech Razor," *The Wall Street Journal,* September 29, 1989, pp. A1, A4. Reprinted by permission of *THE WALL STREET JOURNAL,* © 1989 Dow Jones & Company, Inc. All Rights Reserved Worldwide.

It better be.

Ten years in the making, Sensor has cost more than $200 million to develop and start manufacturing, and will cost an additional $110 million to advertise it in its first year alone. Gillette, still recovering from years of turmoil when it was a repeated target of corporate raiders, is placing the biggest bet in its history on Sensor (see Exhibit 1).

If the new razor is a hit, it will cap the company's recent comeback and vindicate management's defense that its strategies would pay off for shareholders over the long run. If the razor flops, it undoubtedly will renew charges that Gillette executives entrenched themselves at the expense of stockholders.

"This is put up or shut up," says William Newbury, an analyst at College Retirement Equities Fund, a major Gillette shareholder that voted against management in a bitter proxy fight that narrowly failed to oust four incumbent directors last year.

"If we don't get sizable returns" on Sensor, concedes Gillette vice chairman Alfred M. Zeien, "we ought to be criticized for having wasted lots of money."

To substantially increase Gillette's profits, Sensor must perform a marketing miracle: halt a 15-year trend toward inexpensive disposable razors. At double the cost of shaving using disposables, Sensor will be a hard sell.

"Men are strange animals. They find something they like and stick to it," says Angela Aguiar, a buyer at Brooks Pharmacy, a New England chain. "It's difficult to get men to change their grooming habits. I've seen a lot of good products go by the wayside or grow slowly because men don't like to change."

Gillette executives would like nothing more than to prove their critics wrong and score a victory for mainstream, corporate America over Wall Street raiders. More than a battle over a company, the fight over Gillette in some ways epitomized the takeover wars of recent years. Takeover artists offered short-term profits. Management promised a bigger long-term payoff—if only shareholders were willing to wait for promising new products.

More than a few are rooting for Gillette, "What [raiders] are saying is that any time a stock price is below what we can get for it in frothy takeover market, we're entitled to liquidate the business" by selling it to the high bidder, says Louis Lowenstein, a Columbia Law School professor and critic of many takeovers. "That's not good industrial policy."

A bit stodgy, Gillette became a takeover target because of sluggish growth in the early and mid-1980s. Though it boasts some of the world's best-known brand names—among them Foamy shaving cream, Right Guard deodorant, Oral B toothbrushes, Papermate and Flair pens—earnings and sales stagnated because of lackluster mar-

EXHIBIT 1   Gillette after Its Showdown with the Raiders

It boosted productivity . . .

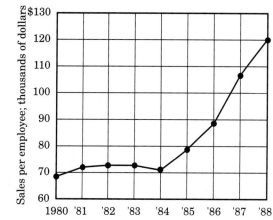

Raised ad spending . . .

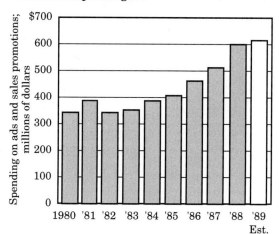

And increased profits . . .

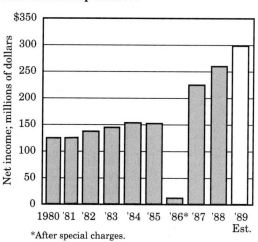

*After special charges.

Which helped its stock.

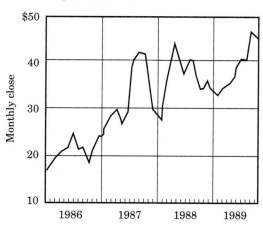

keting. Efforts to diversify into such disjointed businesses as computer accessories, eyewear, hearing aids and beauty centers didn't help.

Revlon Inc. made the first takeover bid in November 1986, but withdrew after being bought off with a $558 million payment for its stock. Gillette rebuffed two more overtures from Revlon a year later. In 1988, it fought off Coniston Partners, a New York investment firm, which had sought to oust four directors and sell the company.

Revlon was trying to buy the company on the cheap, Gillette insisted then—and now. In Gillette's defense, adds Colman Mockler Jr., its unassuming and shy chief executive, the rate of return on Gillette stock over the past decade has been 24 percent annually. "We're in the top 100 of the Fortune 500" over that period, he notes.

Gillette had made huge investments in new products and manufacturing efficiencies that curtailed earnings in the 1980s, but executives expect those investments to pay off in the 1990s. "I'm not criticizing [Revlon's Ronald] Perelman for perceiving Gillette as an undervalued asset," says Mr. Zeien. "We just said we're not going to let you steal this undervalued asset."

To the surprise of many on Wall Street, Gillette has fashioned a turnaround. Energized by its close shave with corporate raiders, it slashed employment 8 percent and dumped mediocre businesses (taking a $243 million pretax writeoff). It introduced a number of successful new products and increased ad spending. "Was Gillette a sleepy company beforehand? Did Perelman trigger change? Yeah," concedes Mr. Zeien. "But what it didn't do was change the fundamental way we do business."

The result: 1989 earnings are expected to reach $300 million, up from $181 million (before one-time charges) in 1986, and sales will approach $3.9 billion, up from $2.82 billion three years ago. Its writing-instruments business and Braun electric shaver and small appliance unit—which some analysts wanted Gillette to jettison a few years ago—are growing robustly. Only its toiletries and cosmetics business have remained laggards.

In fact, the company's stock, after dropping to the low $30s not long after Gillette won the proxy contest and the threat of a takeover diminished, has recovered. Now hovering in the mid $40s, it closed yesterday at $45.875 a share.

Many on Wall Street have climbed on the bandwagon. "I think that Gillette will ultimately vindicate itself, and there is some evidence that it already has," says Andrew Shore, an analyst at Shearson Lehman Hutton. And two of America's savviest investors have loaded up on Gillette stock. Warren Buffett bought $600 million of preferred stock, which is convertible into an 11 percent stake. And Fidelity Investment mutual fund guru Peter Lynch has added to Fidelity's holdings of late.

But critics remain. Revlon's last offer of $47 a share would have paid off handsomely for shareholders had they taken the money and reinvested it in the market, which has risen 25 percent this year. "We aren't too satisfied. They haven't done better than the market," says Jose Arau, principal investment officer at California Public Employees Retirement System, a Gillette holder that supported Coniston in its proxy fight. "It looks as if there's no value added here, so we can't be too happy."

So, to deliver on their promise to "maximize shareholder value,"

Gillette is gambling on Sensor, which will be announced Tuesday at a bash at New York's Pierre Hotel. Stores will start selling the razor after an ad blitz that kicks into high gear with commercials during the Super Bowl on Jan. 28.

For all its other businesses, Gillette means one thing to consumers world-wide: shaving. Gillette dominates the business in the United States, with a market share of about 64 percent. Razors and blades account for just one third of its sales—but two thirds of profits. "*Nothing* is as good as the razor business," says Derwin Phillips, a vice chairman. Gillette's operating profit margins from razors are 34 percent compared with 10.3 percent in all its other businesses combined.

Still, the shaving business hasn't been the same since disposable razors were introduced in the mid-1970s. Disposables, once used by relatively few, now are the razors of choice for more than half of all American shavers. But profits on them are thin, because they cost more to make yet sell for less than the cartridges used in permanent razors.

Sensor, Gillette believes, can reverse the trend by providing a better shave. But the big question isn't so much whether Sensor offers a better shave, but whether that matters to customers. The razor market isn't growing, so Sensor will have to win over shavers who use other razors, namely disposables, including its own.

New technology is the key to the Sensor. A man's face may look smooth to the naked eye. But magnified, it resembles the streets of New York City: there are potholes and bumps all over. "Current twin edge razors are like a car that doesn't have springs or shock absorbers," explains a research and development executive at Gillette. "They hit the whiskers at different points, so they leave different heights of whiskers. In some cases, the blades dig into skin" and cause irritation.

Sensor addresses this with a novel suspension system that allows the two blades to move separately. Each blade has tiny springs soldered to it. Thus, the blades move up, down and sideways with the contour of the face. Springs are attached to a guard below the twin blades. Because some shavers press too hard and some not hard enough, this feature, "like automatic transmission, will help to automatically adjust the force," the executive says.

The two blades are farther apart, allowing easier cleaning, and the razor has a mechanism making it easier to change cartridges. The head is slightly smaller than that of top-of-the-line Atra, so shavers will have to buy new razors to use Sensor blades.

To test the razor, Gillette has asked a number of employees to come in early every morning and shave at the factory here. Researchers measure their whiskers by mounting a microscopic camera on the razor that calibrates the shadow of the stub; they also collect the cut whiskers and measure them, using a microscope.

A prototype for what became the Sensor razor was first developed in 1979. Gillette had hoped to introduce the new system in 1984 or 1985, but it couldn't figure out how to mass produce the cartridges. (The long delay raised some eyebrows in the company. "It only took five years to fight World War II," grouses one marketing executive.)

The biggest obstacle was attaching the springs to the blades on a high-speed assembly line that makes 2½ cartridges a second. No commercial lasers could operate at the speed Gillette needed to weld the springs to the blades, so the company had to develop its own lasers. A test line in 1986 indicated its technology was feasible. Gillette spent the next two years—and $150 million—to build manufacturing equipment for mass production.

Though competitors such as Wilkinson, Bic, and Schick may get to license the technology in the future, they may be hampered because of the high cost and complexity of setting up manufacturing facilities. "To replicate [Sensor] would be a pretty tough undertaking," says one Gillette source.

Gillette figures that a portion of the profits will come as shavers who use top-of-the-line Atra and Trac II razors trade up to Sensor; they obviously are willing to pay a premium for a better shave. Sensor might win customers from rivals like Warner-Lambert Co.'s Schick division, Bic Corp. and Swedish Match's Wilkinson Sword unit. Since Gillette already has a huge market share, further gains won't be easy.

So the only way to increase profits substantially is to get users of disposables to switch. Can Sensor do it? A former Gillette shaving executive is skeptical. He asks: If products such as Atra already offer a closer shave, yet they haven't wooed a substantial number away from disposables, can Sensor, especially since its price will be 25 percent higher than Atra's?

Yes, insists John W. Symons, president of Gillette's North Atlantic shaving group, who headed Gillette's European business in the mid-1980s. Upset that disposables were making razors a commodity business in Europe, Mr. Symons mapped a counterattack with cartridge razors. At sales meetings, he would stand up with a disposable in one hand and a metal Atra razor in the other and demand, "Are you a plastic man or a steel man?" The strategy is working. In 1988, the unit market share of cartridges in Europe had risen to 36 percent from 33.8 percent in 1985.

Emboldened, Gillette stopped advertising disposables in the United States. Now, it promotes its cartridges as "the best a man can get." In the first six months of this year, cartridges captured 33 percent of the market, up from an all-time low of 31.7 percent last year. "That's the first time share has grown since disposables were launched in the mid-1970s," Mr. Symons chortles.

Case 5–6   *Highlights for Children, Inc.**

Elmer C. Meider, president of Highlights for Children, Inc., had just completed a lengthy meeting involving several of his managers. Each manager had been assigned the task of preparing recommendations that would allow Highlights for Children to more effectively utilize the three marketing channels currently being used. Meider felt that the company had not been taking full advantage of the capabilities of direct mail, telemarketing, and direct sales in terms of prospecting, lead distribution, current and new product sales, and overall profitability. Moreover, Meider contends that Highlights for Children needs to capitalize on the continuity of direct mail, the rapid follow-up possible via telemarketing, and the value of face-to-face customer contact available through direct sales.

Although Meider knew he had the authority to eliminate the direct sales force operation, he felt this would not be in the best interests of Highlights. Rumors were abundant about possible legal restrictions on telemarketing programs. In fact, several states were considering legislation that would greatly restrict when telephone calls could be made for sales purposes. One such law would limit telephone calls to specified times and no later than 7:00 P.M. Meider knew that such a limit would sharply curtail Highlights's successful telemarketing program. Moreover, the threat of increases in postal rates caused Meider concern about the future of Highlights's successful direct-mail program. These possible environmental changes provided support for Meider's position to keep the direct sales arm intact. Company experience revealed that the direct sales force was in a better position to learn about and resolve customer problems and concerns than either telemarketing or direct mail.

Managers from each of the three distribution methods had been asked to prepare recommendations concerning changes they would implement to improve the overall sales and profitability picture. Meider's task would be to review the various recommendations and prepare a final report to present to Garry C. Myers III, chief executive officer, who was present at the meeting. Also present at the meeting were Richard H. Bell, chairman of the board; Lynn Wearsch, national rep sales service manager; Chuck Rout, vice president—telemarketing; and Gayle Ruwe, mail marketing manager.

---

* Copyright © 1989 by Professor Neil M. Ford, University of Wisconsin-Madison. Adapted with permission of Highlights for Children, Inc., Columbus, Ohio.

Of the various recommendations, the one that provoked the most discussion was that Highlights for Children rely exclusively on tele-marketing and direct mail distribution and that the company elimi-nate the direct sales force. Richard Bell, responding to this suggestion, pointed out that it was the direct sales force that got the company started, and would keep the company going well into the future. He commented, "Highlights for Children might as well close its doors if the direct sales force is eliminated." One manager's response to Bell's defense of the direct sales force consisted of referring to the relative sales contributions from each source and how telemarketing and direct mail have grown faster. This manager noted the following:

> Telemarketing and direct sales are in a competitive position from a lead utilization standpoint. Profitability is greatly enhanced when leads are sent directly to telemarketing rather than to the direct sales force. Sure, repre-sentatives can sell a bigger package and a longer-term subscription than the other marketing arms, but the reps rely solely on company-generated leads and are not using referrals generated from customers, nor are they doing any local prospecting. The resources assigned to the direct sales force could be more profitably used by telemarketing and direct mail. Our opportunity costs, or losses, have been rising as a result of sending leads to the direct sales group. They cannot handle all of the leads, and by the time tele-marketing receives them they are stale and of little value.

Bell agreed in part with these observations but was quick to note that the size of the direct sales force had dropped from an all-time high of 750 to the current level of 265 independent sales reps, which in-cludes 65 area managers. "We need to be more effective recruiting new sales reps. Just doubling the direct sales force would produce signifi-cant benefits," noted Bell in his rejoinder. After this interchange, Garry Myers suggested that Elmer would take all proposals into con-sideration and attempt to arrive at a recommendation that would com-bine the best of everything.

THE COMPANY

General Information

Begun in 1946 as a children's publication, Highlights for Children, Inc., has become a multidivisional company, selling not only maga-zines but also textbooks, newsletters, criterion referenced tests, and other materials. The consumers include children, parents, and teach-ers.

The Mission Statement of Highlights for Children states:

> Highlights for Children, Inc.'s mission is to create, publish, produce, or distribute on a profitable basis quality products and services uniquely de-

signed for the educational development of children, their parents and teachers, and others with specific educational needs.

Each of the current divisions or subsidiaries operates within these guidelines.

Highlights emphasizes the fair and courteous treatment of its customers. Promotional offers are closely reviewed to ensure prospective customers are not being misled. Highlights is committed to maintaining a "pure" image in the marketplace in terms of marketing efforts as well as quality of its product.

Highlights for Children magazine is circulated to approximately 2 million subscribers. It is marketed through direct selling (via independent contractors), telephone marketing, and direct mail. Parents, teachers, doctors, and gift donors are targeted by the different marketing arms. In addition, Highlights sells various educational products that have been promoted through the introductory-offer school programs.

History

Dr. Garry C. Myers, Jr., and Caroline C. Myers founded Highlights for Children, Inc., in 1946 in Honesdale, Pennsylvania. Based on the belief that learning must begin early in order to fully develop a child's learning ability, the magazine was geared to challenge children's creative thinking and abilities. Today, the editorial offices are still in Honesdale, although the corporate headquarters are located in Columbus, Ohio, and the magazine is printed in Nashville, Tennessee.

At the time *Highlights for Children* was founded, magazines were sold almost exclusively by door-to-door salesmen. *Highlights for Children* followed suit. Today, Highlights continues to use direct selling in conjunction with telephone marketing and direct mail to market the magazine.

In 1955, Myers hit upon the idea of putting *Highlights for Children* in doctors' offices with lead cards. At about the same time, his wife came up with the introductory-offer program to be marketed to parents through the schools. This was the beginning of marketing *Highlights for Children* by mail. Both programs met with immediate and resounding success.

MAGAZINE CONTENT

Highlights for Children targets and services a diverse age group from 2 to 12. The material in the magazine ranges from easy to advanced. This conforms to the philosophy of challenging children: Rather than having material graded and directed to a particular age child, children are allowed to work at their own rate and are "encouraged" to achieve and understand more.

The tag line of *Highlights for Children* is "Fun with a Purpose." The *purpose* of the magazine is to educate and instruct, not merely entertain. The magazine is positioned as supplemental material to be used in the home, rather than in the classroom.

Highlights for Children likes to maintain the image of an educational magazine. No cut-outs or mark-ups are included in the magazine content, enhancing the idea of *lasting* quality. There is no paid advertising in *Highlights for Children,* which is in line with the educational image. Throughout the years, advertising has been considered at various times. Management continues to feel the magazine is more salable as an educational supplement without advertising. Highlights also believes that children are already subjected to more than enough advertising pressure through other sources, much of which is resented by parents and teachers. Recently, President Elmer Meider raised the advertising issue and suggested that advertising revenues might be a way to improve *Highlights's* profit performance.

THE MARKETING PROGRAM

Highlights for Children uses three different marketing arms to sell its products: direct selling, telephone marketing, and mail marketing. Each type is discussed in following sections. Exhibit 1 shows the current organization.

Direct Selling

The direct selling organization has two kinds of representatives: the school representatives and regular representatives. Almost all reps receive company-generated leads; however, school reps make most of their sales from self-generated "school drop" leads.

School Representatives.   Reps make their initial presentation to a school principal or superintendent. The object of the presentation is to gain permission to leave sample copies of *Highlights for Children* in grades K–4. If the school agrees to participate, a sample copy, along with a lead card, is sent home with each child. The child is instructed to return the card to the school if the parents are interested in ordering *Highlights*. Reps then pick up the lead cards from the schools. A school rep usually visits a particular school once every two to three years. Currently *Highlights for Children* has about 70 school reps.

EXHIBIT 1   Highlights for Children, Inc., Organization Chart

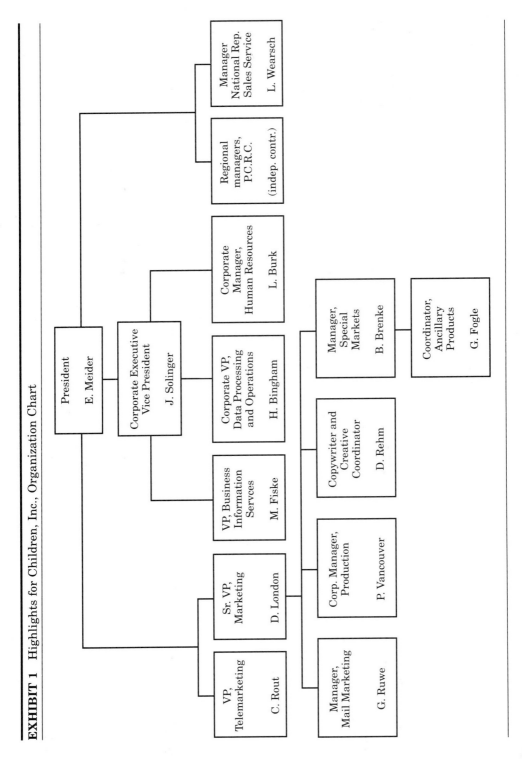

Regular Reps.   Regular reps contact the following company-generated leads:

1. *Parent inquiries (PI)* and *doctor inquiries (DI)*. These people have not had a subscription but have sent in a card indicating interest.
2. *Introductory-offer renewals (IO)*. These people have been sold the 6-month introductory offer through the school and are now up for renewal.
3. *Regular renewals (RR)*. These people have had a regular subscription (11 issues or more) and are up for renewal.
4. *Donor renewals (DR)*. These people have given a gift subscription (11 issues or more) and are up for renewal.

A rep has a set amount of time to work the leads (depending on the type). At the end of that time period, the lead automatically goes to either phone or mail for follow-up. Reps send back the leads marked "no contact" or "no sale" once they have been worked, so the other departments can follow up quickly.

Reps call on parents at home. The increasing number of women working and higher gasoline prices have made the rep's job more difficult over the years. When reps do find someone at home, their presentation hits mainly on what *Highlights for Children* is, how to use it, and its educational value. The rep can sell, on average, a 2.8-year term subscription.

There is a management structure in the regular rep program. Not all reps are under a manager; none reports directly to the home office. Managers receive an override on all area sales (personal and representative's sales).

The current rep structure is composed of about 265 active reps, of which about 65 are managers. The Columbus, Ohio, office has seven employees who are assigned to the direct-selling arm. Reps are independent contractors and as such are not paid a salary, but rather they earn a commission on their sales. Their commission is calculated by commission level times sales units. Units are determined by term sold: (five-year subscription = 1.4 units; three-year subscription = 1.0 unit; two-year subscription = .7 unit; and one-year subscription = .3 unit). *Highlights for Children* subscription rates are $49.95 for 33 issues (three years) and $79.95 for 55 issues (five years). For example, the commission for a three-year subscription is $24.97 (1.0 unit = .50; $49.95 × .50 = $24.97).

Telephone Marketing

Started over 10 years ago in response to the energy crisis and the possibility of the greatly reduced mobility of the representative selling arm, telephone marketing has grown and flourished from a staff of 3 to

190 telemarketing reps, all paid on a commission basis. Telemarketing commissions are about one half (23 percent) of direct-sales commissions. Commissions are not paid for sales that are canceled or never paid by the customers. These reps are located in Columbus along with 25 staff employees.

Telemarketing receives basically three types of leads: parent and doctor inquiries, introductory-offer renewals, and regular renewals. Telemarketing reps have a specified time period in which to contact and sell their leads before they go to mail marketing for follow-up. They attempt to contact leads, all types, 10 times before giving up. In one day's time, they can make up to four attempts. On average, telemarketing sells a 2.3-year term.

Mail Marketing

The Mail Marketing Department consists of three primary areas: creative, production/analysis, and list rental. Currently, 10 employees work in the mail marketing department. Major responsibilities, in addition to list rental, include acquiring *new customers* (through efforts such as the Christmas mailing and school teacher introductory-offer mailing), acquiring *new leads* (through the doctors' offices, doctor inquiries, and parent inquiries mailings), and converting leads (these leads may be new or renewals) to customers (typically after regular reps and/or phone reps have tried to convert). All activities are conducted through direct mail.

More specifically, all promotion packages (to acquire either a lead or a customer), space ads, package inserts, billing stuffers, preprinted computer forms, and so forth are created and produced through the efforts of this department. The actual mail production (merge/purge, lettershop, etc.) is also coordinated here. Finally, the analysis of the results is performed here as well.

Christmas Program.   The Christmas program is a multimedia effort to acquire one-year subscriptions targeting a donor. The mail program consists of over 5 million names, mailed from mid-September to mid-October.

Additionally, the Christmas program includes card inserts in the October, November, and December issues of *Highlights for Children* magazine, statement stuffers, approximately two million package inserts in outside packages (*Drawing Board, Current,* etc.) and space ads (*The Wall Street Journal, The New York Times, Christian Science Monitor,* etc.).

Introductory-Offer Program.   A mailing is made to teachers who hand out "take-home" slips on which the parents can subscribe. The subscription offer to the parents is for six months of *Highlights for Children,* an "introductory offer."

Parent Inquiry/Doctor Inquiry Program.   Several times a year, *Highlights for Children* purchases doctor lists for an outside mailing to produce doctor inquiries. General practitioners, pediatricians, dentists, any doctors who have children, and/or parents visiting their offices and waiting rooms are targeted. Doctors who subscribe are especially valuable because they provide a vehicle to reach parents, and the primary purpose of the doctor mailing is to eventually reach parents. Highlights for Children can send the magazine, complete with parent inquiry cards, into a doctor subscriber's office on a *monthly* basis, potentially reaching many parents.

MARKETING ARM EFFECTIVENESS

Background information revealed that mail marketing produced the most revenue for the last seven years. In 1983, telemarketing surpassed direct marketing in terms of revenue. Exhibit 2 shows sales by marketing arm since 1976. Order-per-lead ratios by marketing arm are as follows:

Telemarketing: over 30 percent.

Direct sales: over 20 percent.

Mail: over 5 percent.

Normally, order-per-lead ratios are higher for direct sales. In fact, for a given number of leads, say 50, the direct sales group will produce more orders than the telemarketing group. However, since the reps are asking for more leads than they can possibly handle, many end up

EXHIBIT 2   Highlights for Children, Inc.: Annual Gross Sales by Source, 1976–1985 ($000)

Year	Reps	Telephone	Mail
1976	11,400	860	10,700
1977	11,800	1,500	11,300
1978	12,100	2,300	12,100
1979	10,300	3,300	14,400
1980	10,400	6,400	16,300
1981	11,100	8,400	16,400
1982	12,400	9,000	21,400
1983	12,300	13,400	28,000
1984	10,800	20,400	36,000
1985	10,200	23,800	46,000

wasted and are not viable by the time they are received by telemarketing and direct mail.

The decline in the number of independent contractors has been of some concern for several years. Various programs have been initiated over the years to increase the number of reps. These programs have not met with much success as evidenced by the size of the direct sales force. Selling low-ticket items, however, limits how much a regular rep can earn. About one half of the regular reps worked part-time. Earnings range from as low as $1,000 a year for some reps to as high as six figures for those reps who are managers. Managers earn overrides on the sales of those reps that they have recruited into the sales organization, a common practice in direct selling programs. Exhibit 3 is typical of the literature used by Highlights to recruit new reps.

Meider and others are aware that this is a problem that others in direct selling have faced. Giants in the direct-selling industry such as Avon, Tupperware, Mary Kay, Amway, and so forth have all confronted this problem and have adopted various techniques to alleviate the negative impact that fewer reps have had on sales. A major con-

---

EXHIBIT 3   Sales Opportunity Fact Sheet

Highlights for Children is an educational magazine for children ages 2 through 12. There are 11 issues published each year, and the December issue includes an annual Resource Index, which turns that year's books into a home reference library for the whole family.

Highlights is available by enrollment only. It is not sold on any newsstand, contains no advertising, and is created primarily for family use. The vast majority of its subscribers are parents. *Highlights* contains a wide range of fiction, nonfiction, thinking and reasoning features, contributions from readers, and things to make and do. The high interest articles include humor, mystery, sports, folk tales, science, history, arts, animal stories, crafts, quizzes, recipes, action rhymes, poems, and riddles.

Dr. Garry Cleveland Myers and Caroline Clark Myers founded *Highlights for Children* in 1946 as the outcome of years of professional work in child psychology, family life, education, and publishing for children. *Highlights* has grown from a first issue circulation of 22,000 to over 1,500,000 in 1982 and is the world's most honored book for children.

Noted educator, psychologist, and author, Dr. Walter B. Barbe, is the editor-in-chief of *Highlights*. Dr. Barbe's books and professional publications have made him nationally renowned in education and in demand as an international speaker. The ongoing production of each issue is coordinated by a talented staff of educators, most of whom are parents. The editorial offices are located in Honesdale, Pennsylvania. The marketing arm for *Highlights for Children* is Parent and Child Resource Center, Inc., and the administrative offices are centered in Columbus, Ohio, where a dedicated representative sales staff plans and directs the business of selling and delivering *Highlights* all around the world.

EXHIBIT 3   *(concluded)*

Highlights for Children is sold nationally by authorized independent representatives directly to families, teachers, preschools, daycare centers, doctors' offices, and to any other person or place interested in the welfare and development of children. This is a direct, person-to-person sales opportunity.

As an independent contractor selling *Highlights'* products, you are free to work the hours you want and earn as much commission as possible. You are in business for yourself with exclusive leads and virtually no product competition. There is no investment required, and you are provided with the information and instruction you need to grow in skill, experience, and earnings. Your business will grow in proportion to the time, skill and resourcefulness you use in presenting the values of *Highlights* to families, individuals, or groups in your community. Your job is to visit with prospective customers, show them how *Highlights* will benefit their children, and write up the order. Statistics show that one out of three contacts will enroll.

You will find that selling *Highlights'* products is enjoyable, pleasant, and profitable. The only qualifications necessary are that you enjoy meeting people and have a sincere interest in children.

There is no limit to your earnings. Every home with children aged 2 through 12 is a potential customer. You retain a liberal commission on every enrollment at the time of the sale, plus additional commissions as your sales record grows. You receive bonuses for the quantity of sales you report, bonuses for the quality of the sale you make, and bonuses for recommending others as representatives. Your sales can also make you eligible to win incentive contests with case and/or merchandise prizes.

If you are interested in a sales career, complete the enclosed Confidential Information form and mail it today!

---

tributing factor has been the dramatic increase in the number of working mothers who are no longer home during the day.

The ability of people in direct selling to earn a reasonable level of income has been inhibited due to these trends. Many companies have adopted party plan selling programs in an attempt to increase the income earning opportunities of the reps. Other companies have expanded their product lines in order to provide their direct sales reps with more commission opportunities. Exhibit 4, a fact sheet published by the Direct Selling Association, provides a summary of the 1985 direct selling industry.

Meider, on the other hand, feels that despite these trends the direct sales reps are not working as hard as they should and are not following prescribed and proven methods of selling. Reps are supposed to ask customers who have ordered a subscription to *Highlights for Children* for the names of others who might be interested in subscribing. Since the reps knew that they could secure company-generated leads free, there was no financial incentive for them to ask for referrals. This referral process has been the mainstay method of direct selling not only for *Highlights for Children* but other direct selling companies as well. Reps are expected to engage in local prospecting, which involves locating residential areas occupied by parents of young children. These activities have been neglected, and reps today rely solely on company-generated leads.

Sales reps continually ask for more leads than they can process, resulting in lost opportunities. By the time the leads are sent back to Columbus, they are of limited value. Meider was particularly distressed to learn that several reps had established their own telemarketing operations to enhance their earnings opportunities. As a result of this practice, Highlights was paying the reps a commission that was twice the amount normally paid for telemarketing sales. A report prepared by Marilyn Fisk, vice president of business information services, added further to Meider's concern. Her report contained the following points:

EXHIBIT 4   Fact Sheet

Summary: 1985 Direct Selling Industry Survey

Total retail sales: $8,360,000

Percent of sales by major product group:

Personal care products	34.8%
Home/family care products	50.0%
Leisure/educational products	9.4%
Services/other	5.8%

Sales approach (method used to generate sales reported as a percent of sales dollars):

One-on-one contact	81.0%
Group sales/party plan	19.0%
In the home	77.0%
In a workplace	11.8%
At a public event*	2.5%
Over the phone	6.9%
Other	1.8%

Total salespeople: 2,967,887

Demographics of salespeople:

Independent	97.9%
Employed	2.1%
Full-time (30+ hours per week)	11.7%
Part-time	88.3%
Male	22.0%
Female	78.0%

* Such as a fair, exhibition, shopping mall, theme park, etc.

Source: Direct Selling Association, Washington, D.C.

- Telemarketing sales in general are for the magazine only; sales of other products are very limited.
- Telemarketing sales do not involve a down payment, hence there are more cancellations.
- Recruiting of additional direct-sales reps has declined, especially in those situations where the reps, with the assistance or blessing of their managers, have started their own telemarketing operations.

Meider's reaction to Fisk's report further solidified his decision that changes are needed. He could understand why the managers would favor telemarketing conducted by their direct reps. Each subscription netted a $4 override for the manager regardless of how it was secured, although suggestions had been made that the $4 override was not adequate. And, the direct reps received their usual commission. He had attempted at an earlier date to persuade the former national sales manager to do something about this practice only to be told that the direct reps were independent and would view this as interference. Besides, as the national sales manager indicated, "The reps view the annual Christmas mailing as a direct threat and want the program to be eliminated or at least share in the commissions on sales from their territories."

Sometime later, the national sales manager left Highlights for Children, due to a reorganization that eliminated the position. Meider hired two regional sales managers who work in the field and can provide closer supervision of the direct sales reps and their managers. Meider divided the United States into two regions: east and west. This move greatly reduced the span of control problems experienced by the former national sales manager.

Meider discussed these problems with Garry Myers III and asked for his reactions. Myers noted that it should not be surprising that reps rely totally on company-generated leads. As Myers stated, "Our reps want to make the most sales, and the best avenue is to call on people who have taken the effort to complete a card and mail it in to Highlights. Reps know that these leads are more likely to produce sales than what they are likely to obtain using the referral process." Myers likened the referral process to "cold-call selling" and company-generated leads as "warm-call selling." Regardless, Highlights for Children is losing profits as a result of these practices, and Myers hoped that Meider's report would be available soon.

Meider indicated that his initial report would contain a series of alternative recommendations that would be used to generate discussion. For example, Meider suggested that one alternative would be to eliminate company-generated leads. Another possibility, suggested by Meider, would place a limit on the number of company-generated leads that a rep could receive each month. The number received might be a function of previous referral sales or some other factor. Meider also suggested charging the managers and/or the reps for each company-generated lead. To offset these additional charges, one likely counter-suggestion would be to increase commissions paid to the reps. The Fisk report prompted another option: reducing the commission paid to reps for orders received without a down payment. This might curtail the use of telemarketing by the reps, a practice Meider wanted to stop. Finally, one manager suggested that the school reps be charged a small fee for all of the sample copies that are left at schools for K–4 distribution. The manager said, "If the regular reps are wasteful of the excessive leads that they receive, then the school reps may be just as guilty when they give away too many free samples."

Eliminating the independent reps is one alternative, as is increasing the number of reps. Meider did not agree with Bell that more reps was the best solution, although he did think that it was an alternative to consider. Expanding the product line to give the reps more items to sell and more commission opportunities was another alternative suggested to Meider. Currently, a three-year subscription at $49.95 produces a commission of $24.97. Meider knew that no one would suggest replacing the direct sales force with a company sales force. Such a move would increase overhead expenses by at least 15 percent to cover fringe benefits costs plus staff additions needed for purposes of governmental reporting. Eliminating the direct selling arm would be a better solution than creating a company sales force.

Myers thought that Meider's suggestions would indeed produce much discussion among his management team. At this juncture, he felt that Meider should narrow the alternatives down to a final set of recommendations.

Case 5–7 *Paper Mate**

The vice president of marketing for the Paper Mate Division of the Gillette Company, Derek Coward, was considering whether to recommend to top management the commercialization of a revolutionary new pen. He had just read the marketing plan presented by the product manager, David Melley, which proposed that the new pen—code name

* This case originally appeared in Victor P. Buell, *Marketing Management: A Strategic Planning Approach* (New York: McGraw-Hill, 1984), pp. 619–25. Reprinted by permission.

"Delta"—be introduced to the market. Delta represented a break-through in pen technology. It could be the first pen on the market containing truly erasable ink. Earlier pens, claiming erasability, had not sold successfully because the erasure resulted from abrading away the paper rather than removing the ink.

Paper Mate's technological breakthrough had been made several years earlier by Henry Peper of the Gillette R&D Department, who was credited as the author of the Paper Mate erasable ink patent. Mr. Peper described his invention as "a complicated process based on a simple idea." The idea was to combine ink with rubber cement. When erased, the ink adhered to the rubber cement rather than to the paper. Erasure could be made for several hours after writing, but after about 24 hours the ink became permanently absorbed in the paper. Although the combination of a special ink with rubber cement remained the basic technical concept, years of additional research and development had been necessary to bring the pen up to consumer use standards. To force the sticky fluid to flow around the ball point, for example, compressed nitrogen was sealed inside the ink container.

PAPER MATE HISTORY

In 1955 the Gillette Company acquired the Frawley Pen Company, maker of the Paper Mate brand of ball-point pens; this company formed the nucleus of what was to become the Paper Mate Division of Gillette.

The first commercially produced ball-point pen, developed by Milton Reynolds, had gone on sale at Gimbels' department store in New York City, October 29, 1945. Ten thousand pens were sold that day at $20 each. While the pens did not work too well, the potential advantages of the ball point versus the conventional fountain pen obviously had captured consumer interest. The Frawley Co. had introduced the Paper Mate brand of ball-point pen in 1949. This pen overcame the principal disadvantages of earlier ball-point pens and led to Gillette's interest in acquiring Frawley. Paper Mate's success over the years had come about because of both internally developed innovations and improvements on the innovations of others. With the addition of its Flair porous pen, the Paper Mate Division became the leader of the pen industry in terms of dollar sales. Paper Mate's divisional and division marketing organization charts are presented in Exhibits 1 and 2.

Paper Mate's parent, the Gillette Company, had net sales of $1.7 billion in 1978 and net profit after tax of $94.6 million. Percent of sales and profit contribution by major lines of business are shown in the next table.

EXHIBIT 1 Organization of the Paper Mate Division (July 1, 1979)

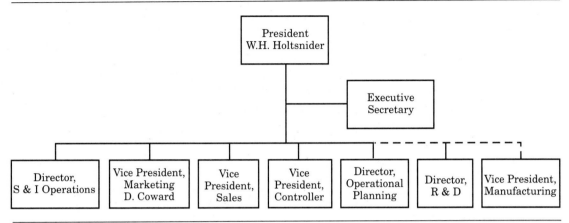

Business	Percent of Sales	Percent of Profit Contribution
Blades and razors	33%	72%
Toiletries and grooming aids	25	13
Braun products (electrical)	24	13
Writing instruments	8	6
Other	10	(4)
	100%	100%

The Paper Mate Division accounted for sales of $141 million and profit contribution of $12.7 million. Sales growth had been at a faster rate than the industry.

THE WRITING INSTRUMENT INDUSTRY[1]

Total industry unit sales grew modestly from 2.2 to 2.7 billion units (23 percent) between 1972 and 1978. Dollar sales grew considerably faster, however, from $319 million to $582 million (82 percent), as can be seen

---

[1] As defined by the Writing Instrument Manufacturers Association, the industry is composed of fountain, ball-point, and porous-tip pens; markers; mechanical pencils; and desk pen sets.

EXHIBIT 2   Marketing Organization, Paper Mate Division (effective February 15, 1979)

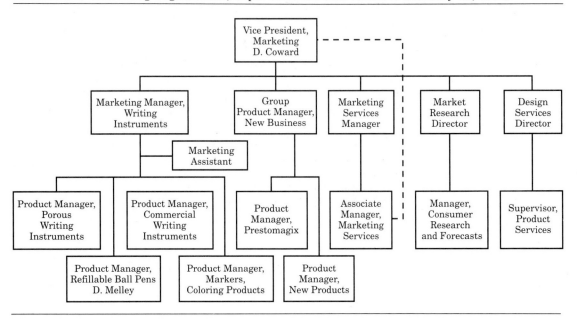

---

in Exhibit 3. Industry sales follow an uneven year-to-year pattern. Sales show a close correlation with gross national product. Inflation was partly responsible for the more rapid rise in dollar sales, but a more important reason was a shift in consumer demand toward higher-quality products. Exhibit 4 presents the percent change by product type in units and dollars between 1972 and 1978.

EXHIBIT 3   Estimated Writing Industry Instrument Sales, 1972–1978

Year	Units (millions)	Percent Change	Sales (millions)	Percent Change
1972	2,159		$319	
1973	2,341	8.4%	353	10.7%
1974	2,344		370	4.8
1975	2,120	(9.6)	365	(1.4)
1976	2,295	8.3	474	29.9
1977	2,438	6.2	538	13.6
1978	2,742	12.5	582	8.1

Source: Writing Instrument Manufacturers Association, Inc.

EXHIBIT 4 Percent Change by Type of Writing Instrument, 1972–1978

	Percent Change in Sales	
	Units	*Dollars*
Refillable ball point	(1.2%)	67.1%
Nonrefillable ball point	32.7	43.5
Total ball point pens	16.1	57.8
Total porous pens*	36.1	52.4
Markers	84.0	35.9
Mechanical pencils	17.3	21.9
Fountain pencils	(34.7)	60.1
Desk sets	(19.5)	47.9
Total industry	22.7%	82.3%†

* Not broken out by type in 1972.
† Includes products not available in 1972. When these are excluded, industry sales for the categories shown increased by 59 percent.

Source: Writing Instrument Manufacturers Association, Inc.

Exhibit 5 shows the breakdown of industry sales by type in 1978. The leading product is the ball-point pen followed by the porous-point pen. Ball-point and porous-point pens combined accounted for 88 percent of industry unit sales and 67 percent of dollar sales. Exhibit 6 shows an industry breakdown of writing instrument sales by channels and market segments.

Imports in 1974 were $23.6 million, but represented something less than 6 percent of the dollar value of domestic sales. Imports, however, were growing at a faster rate than the domestic industry between 1970 and 1974.[2]

Writing industry distribution channels are shown in Exhibit 7. Nearly half of industry shipments reach domestic consumers through a variety of retail outlets. Retailers purchase primarily from the four types of wholesalers shown; larger retailers may also buy direct from manufacturers. Over 30 percent of industry shipments are purchased by business organizations and institutions through channels such as commercial stationery dealers and specialty advertising houses. The latter imprint pens with company names and advertising messages. Approximately a fifth of total shipments go into export channels, and

[2] Source: *U.S. General Imports, Schedule A, Commodity by Country.* Bureau of the Census, U.S. Department of Commerce. Import data include categories of writing instruments not included in WIMA figures. For this reason imports probably were less than 6 percent if only the WIMA definition is used.

EXHIBIT 5   Percent of Industry Sales by Type of Writing
Instrument, 1978

Instrument	Percent of All Units Sold	Percent of Total Dollar Sales
Refillable ball point	29.3%	29.6%
Nonrefillable ball point	34.7	16.1
Total ball-point pens	64.0%	45.7%
Porous-point writing	19.3	19.3
Porous-point coloring	4.8	1.5
Total porous-point pens	24.1%	20.8%
Markers	8.8	7.0
Mechanical pencils	2.6	8.4
Fountain pens	0.3	4.5
Desk pen sets	0.1	1.8
Other	—	11.7
Total	99.9%	99.9%
Total ball-point and porous-point pens	88.1%	66.4%

Source: Writing Instrument Manufacturers Association, Inc.

the remaining 5 percent are sold to government and military installations.

Market Shares.   Exhibit 8 shows estimated market-share rankings of leading pen companies in 1978 based on dollar sales at retail prices. The information is reported separately for ball-point and porous-point pens. It should be noted that share data cover retail sales only.

EXHIBIT 6   Percent of Manufacturer Dollar Shipments, 1977 (by channel of distribution)*

Retail	45.6
Export	19.3
Specialty advertising	15.9
Commercial-industrial	14.1
Government	2.9
Military	2.1
Miscellaneous	0.1
	100.0

* "Channel of distribution" is the heading used by the WIMA. Marketing students will recognize that some categories are user markets rather than channels.

Source: Special survey in 1977 for the Writing Instrument Manufacturers Association, Inc.

EXHIBIT 7   Distribution Channels for Writing Instruments

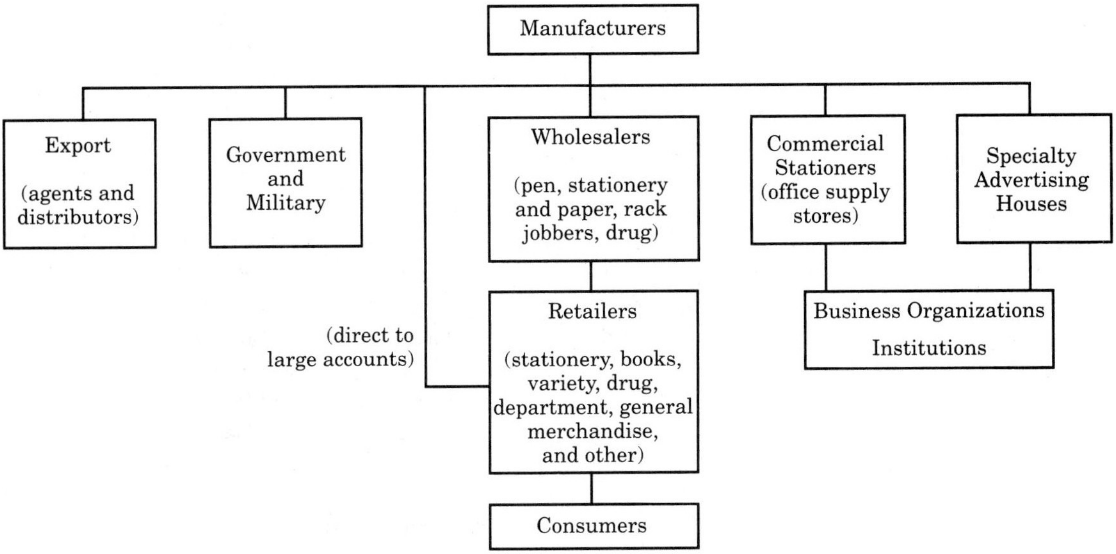

In 1978 five companies accounted for nearly 90 percent of the dollar value of ball-point pens sold at retail. Paper Mate and Bic were tied for first place. Paper Mate led in the medium- and higher-price refillable pen segments, while Bic led in the lower-price nonrefillable segments. Consequently, Bic was the industry leader in terms of units sold. Six companies accounted for approximately 75 percent of the dollar value of porous-point pens sold at retail. Paper Mate was the clear-cut leader in this pen segment, with Pentel in second place.

EXHIBIT 8   Market Share Rankings—Ball-Point and Porous-Point Pens (retail dollar value, 1978)

Ranking	Ball Point	Porous Point
1	Paper Mate and Bic (tied)	Paper Mate
2	Parker	Pentel
3	Cross	Sanford and Pilot (tied)
4	Sheaffer	Bic
5		Spree

Source: Market Research Department.

NEW-PRODUCT PLANNING AT PAPER MATE

During the several years that the erasable ink pen, Delta, had been in technical research and development, the Market Research Department of Paper Mate had conducted several consumer research studies to try to measure the market potential for an erasable ink pen. The advantage of being able to make corrections when writing with an ink pen had seemed sufficiently obvious to justify continued investment in R&D in the early years. The question remained, however, whether the idea was powerful enough to create a new and profitable market.

The first consumer use studies confirmed that there was significant consumer interest in erasability, but that the writing quality of the pens tested was not acceptable. After R&D had made improvements in writing quality, Paper Mate continued with market research. Three projects which marketing management felt provided significant information are described briefly: (1) a consumer use test; (2) the B/EST test, which provided information on trial and draw; and (3) the Yankelovich Laboratory Test, which showed whether people would buy the new pen under simulated market conditions.

Consumer Use Test. This test was conducted by Market Facts— New York, Inc., who placed products with families in two national consumer mail samples for extended in-home testing. The samples were balanced with U.S. Census data with respect to geographic region, population density, sex, age (between 12 and 54), household income, number in household, and occupation and education of male head of household.

The Delta pen with eraser was placed in 400 households. A branded ball-point pen (the *control* pen) was placed in a separate but matched sample of 400 households. The control pen was a standard ball-point pen with no eraser. Some of the comparative results are shown in Exhibit 9. Respondents were questioned twice–April and June–to see whether there was a difference in response after longer use. For convenience in presentation the results of the two responses have been averaged. While attitudes toward the test pen were generally favorable, potential problem areas were revealed as well.

B/EST Test. This test is designed to give indications of the strength of a new product concept—i.e., will it change people's perception of the marketplace enough to cause them to buy. (A first purchase is called *trial* in marketing idiom.) The test was conducted with panels of 200 consumers in three different shopping malls. The participants were screened to ensure that the panels were balanced with the general population in terms of sex and age and that they were users of ball-point pens. Each panel was shown a display board of eight pens, one of

EXHIBIT 9 Consumer Use Test—Delta versus Control Pen

(a) Ratings Results

	Percent of Users	
Rating	Delta	Control Pen
Very good	56%	55%
Good	39	37
Total	95%	92%
Fair	4	7
Poor		1
Don't know	1	
	100%	100%

(b) Preference Compared with Previous Pen Used Most Often

	Percent of Users	
Preference	Delta	Control Pen
Prefer test pen	78%	62%
Prefer previous pen	14	24
No preference	8	14
	100%	100%

(c) Positive and Negative Comments

Qualities Judged—Positive	Percent of Users Commenting Favorably		Qualities Judged—Negative	Percent of Users Commenting Negatively	
	Delta	Control Pen		Delta	Control Pen
Erasability	85%		Writing quality	50%	24%
Writing quality	34	76%	Physical characteristics	13	20
Physical characteristics	17	44	Erasability	6	
Writing immediacy and convenience	12	26	Writing immediacy and convenience	4	13

(d) Uses of Pens during Tests

	Percent of Users	
Used for	Delta	Control Pen
Making lists	90%	88%
Addressing envelopes, signing cards	69	72
Personal letters	67	68
Short notes or memos at work	62	61
Signing checks, legal documents	59	75
Working with a lot of numbers	58	48
Taking notes at classes, work or meetings	60	45
Writing lengthy reports	33	24
Homework	34	20

Source: Consumer use tests conducted by Market Facts–New York, Inc.

which was Delta. The balance consisted of a cross section of well-known brands of ball-point pens of varying prices. For purposes of the test, Delta was named "Ink Manager." It was presented differently to each panel as follows:

Panel A—$ .98 disposable.
Panel B—$1.29 disposable.
Panel C—$1.29 refillable.

Respondents first read a description of each product and then were shown the display board containing the eight pens. Respondents were then given 10 tokens each, with instructions to choose the three products they would be most likely to purchase. Each product chosen was assigned a minimum of one token. The remaining seven tokens were to be distributed among the same three products to indicate intensity of purchase interest. The results for "Ink Manager" were as follows:

	Panel A, $.98 Disposable	Panel B, $1.29 Disposable	Panel C, $1.29 Refillable
Percent of respondents who assigned any tokens to "Ink Manager"	43%	38%	44%
Percent tokens assigned to "Ink Manager"	15	14	15

"Ink Manager" was the third choice of all panels. In addition to the third-choice ranking and the information on pricing, other findings were reported. Twenty-nine percent of respondents said they were willing to try "Ink Manager." Before exposure to the erasability feature, consumers rated this quality as unimportant, but raised it to important after learning that such a feature was available. The product drew from ball-pen, porous-pen, and pencil users. Purchasers were more likely to be female than male and more likely to be 40 or older.

Yankelovich Laboratory Test. YLT is a market testing service for new products which attempts to simulate real-world market situations. It can be used by a company to determine whether to go to test market or as a partial substitute for test marketing where the company wishes to avoid market exposure of its new product to competition.

The YLT facility had interviewing rooms, a theater, an experimental store, and facilities for interviewing consumers by phone. Participants, drawn from various organizations such as PTAs and churches, visit the facility in groups. In all, 500 men and women aged 15 to 59 participated in the Delta test. Corrective factors were applied by YLT to compensate for demographic imbalances and biases introduced by the experimental technique. For purposes of this test Delta was named "Second Chance." It was presented in an attractive finished design as a refillable pen with an eraser on the top.

After obtaining demographic information on each participant—as well as the name, address, and phone number—the group saw a popular television show with its regular commercials, except that a commercial for the "Second Chance" erasable pen was also included. Following the show the participants were led into the convenience-type store and permitted to make purchases using their own money. However, all items were discounted proportionally to encourage buying. The store contained a pen section stocked with a representative sample of brands and included "Second Chance." After having the opportunity to shop, the group was broken into small focus groups for discussions about why the participants purchased what they did and why they rejected other brands. Consumers who bought "Second Chance" were contacted at home later by telephone at 30-day intervals to check for product satisfaction and willingness to repurchase at varying prices. The key results of the YLT were as follows:

1. 38 percent bought "Second Chance."
2. Of the people buying some type of writing instrument, 60 percent bought "Second Chance."
3. On the 30-day call back to purchasers of "Second Chance":
   a. 66 percent were completely satisfied.
   b. The main source of satisfaction was erasability, which had exceeded the expectations of most users.
   c. "Ink smearing/smudging" and "too light a writing line" were the primary performance negatives.
4. The willingness-to-repurchase rate was: after 30 days, 57 percent; after 60 days, 64 percent; and after 90 days, 64 percent.
5. Purchasers confirmed a willingness to pay between $1.50 and $2.00 for the product.[3]

THE PROBLEM

As Derek Coward reviewed the marketing plan for the erasable pen, he was mindful of the high proportion of promising new products that never attain commercial success. He was aware that Delta faced many

---

[3] For comparative purposes, the most popular ball-point refillable pens marketed under the Paper Mate brand name at that time ranged in price from $.98 to $1.49.

of the types of risks and trade-offs characteristic of new-product introductions generally. For example:

1. The new product had disadvantages as well as advantages.
2. The favorable results of the consumer sales tests had been obtained under simulated rather than real market conditions.
3. Consumers traditionally are skeptical before trial as to whether a new product will work as claimed.
4. Consumers' purchase habits are not easily broken.
5. Bankers' attitudes toward erasable ink might have an unfavorable effect on consumer purchases.
6. Erasability might prove to be a novelty that would wear off quickly.
7. Erasable pen sales could be expected to draw ("cannibalize") sales from existing Paper Mate products. If it drew from Paper Mate products, however, it should also draw from product sales of Paper Mate's competitors. The question was to what extent in each case.
8. The large commitment of promotional funds that would be required to support the new-product introduction could have a disastrous effect on divisional profits if consumer purchases fell much below the sales forecast.

Case 5–8 Comshare, Inc.*

A visitor to the attractively decorated corporate offices of Comshare, Inc., in Ann Arbor, Michigan, could not help but observe the air of excitement and anticipation. The firm had just announced its complementary marketing arrangement with IBM for the new decision support system (DSS) software product, System W. The firm was also finalizing a significant update to System W. Kevin Kalkhoven, group vice president, added to this enthusiasm when he stated, "With this latest release, System W will be easier to use than any of the competing products."

Comshare, Inc., was a computer service firm that was founded in 1966 to offer time-sharing services to industry, government, and other nonprofit organizations. These services made it possible for users to communicate with Comshare's computers in Ann Arbor via communi-

---

* This case was prepared as a basis for class discussion by Professors Donald W. Scotton, Allan D. Waren, and Bernard C. Reimann of Cleveland State University. Distributed by the Case Research Association. All rights reserved to the authors and the Case Research Association.

cation networks of telephone lines. The system was designed to provide instantaneous response, giving the user the impression of having his own computer. All of the usual data processing and accounting functions could be performed "long distance" on data stored at the computer center.

Since it started in business, Comshare had introduced many improvements to its time-sharing services. These included the addition of sophisticated databases, better methods for retrieving and displaying information, and the development of powerful and versatile modeling methods to help solve business and financial problems.

The latest and most significant of these developments was System W, an advanced Decision Support System (DSS) software product, which Comshare introduced late in 1982. This software made it possible for executives to enter or retrieve data from other mainframe or personal computers, build models to simulate their businesses, make forecasts, do statistical analyses, test assumptions or alternative scenarios, and even display their results in customized reports or graphs. While a substantial number of competitive products existed, Comshare executives considered System W to be a technological breakthrough in that it greatly facilitated modeling in multiple dimensions. Most of the competitive products were either limited to two-dimensional spreadsheets, or required extremely complex programming to achieve multidimensional modeling and analysis.

INDUSTRY TRENDS

Most computer hardware manufacturers, including IBM, focused their software efforts on systems software. Therefore, a potentially profitable and growing market segment became available for applications software. A rapidly growing number of "software houses" emerged to fill the need for high-quality applications software with an emphasis on ease of use and efficiency. Typical applications included material requirements planning, accounting and financial reporting, and database management.

Another factor that contributed to the rapid growth of this specialized software market was the inability of the data processing function, in most firms, to keep up with the burgeoning demand for its services. The resulting backlog of data processing projects led to an urgent need for highly sophisticated software which would be so easy to use that nonprogrammers, such as financial or marketing executives and their staffs, could develop their own custom-made applications.

At the same time, the increasing competitiveness and uncertainty of the business environment were creating a growing interest in strategic planning. This in turn led to a strong need for information systems to help top executives and strategic planners make decisions. One answer to this need was DSS (Decision Support System) applications software. This type of software made possible the bringing together of relevant information from both internal and external databases, and the use of complex models to simulate and analyze strategic alternatives before they were implemented.

There were fewer than 2,000 international computer software and service firms as reported in the 1982 Comshare Annual Report. Comshare, Inc., was one of the largest of these firms involved in the marketing of DSS software, which included data management, financial modeling, forecasting, analysis, reporting, and graphics. These DSS products were used by time-sharing customers via a worldwide computer network, as well as by customers who licensed the products for use on their mainframe computers and/or microcomputers.

The market for such DSS software and processing services, as reported in the 1983 Comshare Annual Report, was:

1981 sales	$549 million
1982 sales	729 million
1987 forecast	33.1 billion

The report also indicated that 1981 industry sales of all types of software, totaled $4.2 billion. Richard L. Crandall, president of Comshare, reported in an interview for this case that 17 percent, or $714 million, came from data management and financial software sales, the two main predecessors of DSS. He indicated also that "in 1975 barely one-half billion dollars of industry sales were in software." *Business Week,* in its February 27, 1984, issue, published a special report on "Software: The New Driving Force." This issue contained a forecast that software sales in the United States would "keep growing by a dizzying 32 percent a year, topping $30 billion in 1988."

DEVELOPMENT OF SYSTEM W

Corporate Goals and Planning

Comshare management developed their first long-range strategic plan in 1972. This plan contained the general goals for the firm, which were: (1) to be a profitable, high-technology, growth company and (2) to be the best firm in their chosen market segments. As a result of this planning process, the Comshare mission was redefined. Instead of considering its primary business to be the sales of general purpose time-sharing, management now viewed its main function as one of marketing business problem-solving assistance to its customers. Initial steps taken to implement this new focus included (1) making software tools available on their time-sharing network and (2) utilizing their support representatives to assist customers in solving business problems with these software tools.

Environmental Review

A major review of plans and strategies was undertaken in 1979. President Crandall, reflecting on this review, commented, "We were satisfied that the corporate goals spelled out in 1972 were still valid; however, the environment had changed and we needed to reassess it and its impact on our strategies."

The environmental review and assessment of company position revealed strengths, weaknesses, opportunities, and threats. Comshare was established in the international market and had a competitive sales force. There was sufficient talent in the organization to solve business problems. Market position was established in time-sharing. Comshare had the research and development capability to resolve the identified product gap in inquiry and analysis software. Finally the cash flow and cash position were sufficient to operate at a break-even point for several years.

Weaknesses included: (1) Comshare had no identifiable image in software, (2) the marketing organization lacked selling skills in software, (3) immediate market action could not be taken because of the recession and lack of a software product.

Several threats were present. The increasing presence of software firms and products for in-house computer use reduced the demand for time-sharing services. Software firms reduced prices to gain market shares. The advent of personal computers caused both computers and software to become available at lower costs.

Two major opportunities were identified as follows. (1) There existed increased demand for productivity software to augment the "first round" data management applications and financial modeling packages. More functional products were needed to solve a variety of problems. (2) A more functional and easier-to-use DSS was needed.

Product Focus and Development

Analysis of the environmental review caused Comshare to select Decision Support Software as its primary product that was to be delivered in as many ways as possible.

Comshare management also recognized the growing importance of distributed DSS, including both microcomputers, or PCs, and mainframes. However, PCs were not suited to be the only hardware in a total DSS. They did not have the capacity for storing and processing sufficient data for large-scale problems. The market segment to which Comshare was addressing System W included management decision makers who could use the system most efficiently, if it were easily accessible from their offices. A combination of personal and mainframe computers was needed for input and interface of data for management decision making. System W was developed to facilitate problem solving within these parameters.

IBM had not concentrated on DSS software. Rather, it exercised leadership in developing and producing mainframe and personal computers. Comshare elected to develop and market DSS software specifically designed for IBM computers. The product was to be a comprehensive, easy-to-use decision support system optimized to run on IBM systems.

Complementary Marketing Arrangement with IBM

A letter was received from IBM in September 1982 in which an invitation was extended to approximately 100 computer firms to attend an IBM-hosted conference. The purpose of the conference was to consider strategy for dealing with end-users of computers and related services. The emphasis was on applications software rather than data management and operating systems software. Mr. Crandall attended the conference and noted that most representatives of attending firms did not seem to take the new IBM direction seriously.

However, he felt that IBM was very serious in its desire to have outsiders provide applications software, while IBM concentrated on further developing its hardware—both mainframe and personal computers. This was a central part of IBM's new "Information Center" strategy, conceived to meet the pent-up demand among executives to use computers to satisfy their needs for relevant and timely information. This concept required the development of "user friendly" software that would allow nonprogrammer executive users to develop their own decision support systems. Since IBM did not have any strong offerings in this type of DSS software, Crandall envisioned a desire for IBM to work closely with a firm capable of developing and marketing superior DSS software.

Discussion continued between IBM and Comshare, and in early January 1984, a two-year complementary marketing arrangement was reached. As indicated in the January 9, 1984, issue of *Computerworld,* IBM would recommend System W for use in Information Centers using IBM 4300 computers. IBM and Comshare sales representatives would refer prospects to each other. In addition, provision was made for joint sales calls of IBM and Comshare personnel to prospective users of DSS.

The objective of IBM was to sell more hardware by making available the expertise and DSS software of Comshare to prospective customers on the theory that more hardware would be used if the customer problem was met properly. Finally, Comshare would continue its responsibility to users to install System W and conduct training programs.

COMPETITION

Kevin Kalkhoven estimated that the 1983 DSS industry leaders, their products, and sales (software exclusive of processing services) were:

Execucom	IFPS	$ 20 million
Management Decision Systems	Express	7–8 million
Comshare	System W	7–8 million
EPS, Inc.	FCS/EPS	6–7 million

Prior to the introduction of System W, Comshare had been a vendor of FCS/EPS on its time-sharing service. Comshare, however, still supported those time-sharing customers who were not willing to switch from FCS/EPS to System W.

There were more than 60 other competitors, at least 20 of whom had entered the business in the last two or three years. Two software products were identified as being particularly significant to Comshare. These were IFPS, a product originally developed for financial research functions, and Express, originally developed for marketing research. Both products had subsequently been enhanced and were being marketed as full function DSS systems. Comshare viewed IFPS as being particularly easy to use but lacking integrated functionality in areas such as data management, whereas Express was seen as a very hard to use product which was functionally well-integrated and quite powerful. Execucom had just announced a data management option for IFPS, which was intended to compensate for its weakness in this area.

In order to compete effectively in this market, Comshare felt it was essential to develop a product which was easier to use than IFPS and had more capabilities and was better integrated than Express. Thus System W was designed to take advantage of this opportunity for product positioning relative to the industry leaders.

Kevin Kalkhoven was confident that the most recent release of System W (including DATMAN) was much easier to use than any competing product. He pointed out that: "James Martin, an expert on applications software, has just completed his most recent comparative evaluation of financial planning software products. He ranked System W second only to Visicalc in user friendliness, ahead of IFPS and even Lotus 1-2-3." Visicalc was a limited spreadsheet program for personal computers and not considered as a competitor in the DSS software area.

Comshare management noticed that a number of other firms were waking up to the huge potential of the market. These firms were redoubling their efforts both in improving their products and in marketing them. Several firms had decided to "unbundle" their prices for total systems in order to be more competitive. Thus, a customer interested only in modeling, for example, could buy a starter system for as little as $10,000. If other capabilities, such as forecasting or graphics were desired, each of these additional modules could be purchased separately for $5,000–15,000 each. Another aspect of product pricing was the increasing willingness of some vendors to discount the prices of their software, especially for multiple purchases.

Another trend in competition concerned the way in which vendors handled the consulting portion of their DSS software business. Some, such as Management Decision Systems (Express Software) and Chase Interactive Data Corporation (Xsim Software), focused on selling a package of DSS software combined with their management consulting expertise. The consulting services were designed to help the users customize the products for their individual decision support requirements. As a result, the vendors' focus was less on the "user friendliness" of their products than on developing a staff of highly effective and personable consultants and technical specialists. These consultants and specialists were important adjuncts to the vendors' personal selling efforts to large corporations.

At the other end of the spectrum, as Mr. Crandall described it, "Firms like Integrated Planning (Stratagem) and GemNet (Fame) chose the strategy of developing and selling DSS products that allegedly required minimal consulting or technical support after the sale." They emphasized product development to make their software so "friendly" and flexible that nonprogrammers, such as financial or marketing executives, could use the software to create their own DSS with minimal outside assistance. Integrated Planning used the services of professional DSS consulting firms, such as Real Decisions Corporation, to assist customers in adapting Stratagem to their needs.

The degree of centralization of selling and technical support was another area in which strategies varied among competitors. Some of the newer and smaller vendors were highly centralized in these functions, due primarily to resource constraints. However, some of the larger firms that could afford to decentralize had concentrated their sales and technical support organizations in a central location. MDS, producers of Express Software, housed all of its consultants and technical support personnel at the headquarters in Waltham, Massachusetts. A toll-free 800 number "hot line" was available to users with problems. This hot line was staffed about 12 hours each working day by rotating shifts of experienced technical people. MDS believed that this allowed better use of their high-quality, specialized technical personnel. They felt that a decentralization strategy using local offices would spread these resources too thinly and result in a reduction of the quality of their customer services. However, a number of firms, such as Boeing Computer Services, Chase IDS, and Comshare chose the decentralized option of serving their users personally from a large number of geographically dispersed offices.

Another contrast in product-market strategies concerned the firms' focus on hardware compatibility. Some, such as Execucom, with its IFPS software, prided themselves on the fact that their software would run on almost every popular brand of hardware and type of operating system, i.e., DEC, HP, IBM, Prime, etc. Even some of the smaller vendors chose this strategy of making their software compatible with as many different types of hardware as possible. GemNet, for example, was in the process of developing FAME (its DSS software) simultaneously for three different operating systems.

Although the degree of competition had increased considerably by 1984, there were signs that rivalry could become more intense in the future. It was still relatively easy for a new firm to enter the DSS industry. Little start-up capital was needed. A few intelligent and hard working programmers could produce a new DSS software product within a year or two. A number of the most aggressive and successful new firms were founded by former employees of the older and more established firms. For example, Integrated Planning, the developer of Stratagem, was founded by several former employees of Automated Data Processing who had become dissatisfied with that company's supposed lack of effort to improve its products, TSAM and FML, to meet changing customer needs. Similarly, GemNet, developer of Fame software, was started by former members of Chase Interactive Data Corporation's technical staff. Software firms had become attractive acquisition targets for hardware manufacturers and others who were eager to share in the software boom. Acquisitions were of interest also to other software producers as a means to expand their product lines. For example, GemNet had recently received an acquisition offer from Citibank. The new ownership of GemNet would provide increased capitalization and staffing to permit the organization to realize its potential. In so doing it would be regarded as a competitive threat to other members of the industry.

There was also a trend for hardware manufacturers to become more interested in the highly profitable field of applications software. IBM and others seemed to be satisfied with cooperative ventures with software suppliers. However, firms such as Hewlett-Packard were making every effort to produce their own software.

One result of these competitive activities was a downward pressure on prices of applications software and some price discounting was observed in the DSS software industry as well. However, the potential benefits of the "right" software to users could outweigh the initial cost. The "wrong" product could cost several times as much as the acquisition cost in terms of extra implementation problems.

Another competitive threat arose through the actions of time-sharing firms such as Automated Data Processing and Data Resources International, a subsidiary of McGraw-Hill. These firms had developed software for use by their time-sharing customers. At the present time, they were exploring the possibility of selling and/or licensing these DSS products to other users who owned mainframe and personal computers. Data Resources International, for example, announced that it would release its DSS product, EPS, for sale in the fall of 1984.

MARKETING MIX STRATEGIES

Guiding Strategy

Richard L. Crandall said that "when we decided to develop a DSS software package, it was clear that we would be the new kid on the block as far as software sales were concerned. To be successful it was necessary to carve out a specific niche and to be easily distinguished from our competitors." The firm's strategic plan provided guidance in achieving these objectives.

The plan called for Comshare to develop the best possible DSS software product and furthermore to develop it specifically for IBM computer systems. In order to have the best DSS software it had to be more functional than the rest of the competition as well as being easier to use. In order to best fit with IBM systems, it was necessary to take advantage of as many of the IBM hardware and software features as possible.

Product

Analysis of the competitive considerations and threats mentioned above caused Comshare to:

1. Concentrate on developing decision support systems and software compatible with IBM computers.
2. Offer consulting and adaptation services for users of IBM machines and Comshare software.
3. Adopt the augmented product concept of locating facilities and per-

sonnel close to users. Thus face-to-face consulting could occur rather than obtaining impersonal information received from calling an 800 telephone number.

Pricing

It was observed that purchases of more than $100,000 usually required a series of approvals associated with major capital expenditures. Thus, the executive or group electing to purchase a DSS package must receive higher approval, which could be time consuming. This practice appeared to have imposed an average industry price ceiling of $75,000 for DSS packages.

Comshare conducted research with the use of videotaped focus groups to obtain customer and prospect reaction to System W. A number of considerations were examined such as price and acceptance of the product as to quality, concept, performance, and competition. Current environmental forces were examined and the following price strategies were selected for the introduction of System W in January 1983:

1. Competitive pricing would be utilized. For example, a scaled down version of System W would be sold for $50,000 to meet Execucom's price on its IFPS product.
2. Elements of target pricing would be employed so that profits would be realized within two years. This was consistent with the dynamics of product innovation and rapid changes in the competing firms.
3. System packages would be priced from $75,000 to less than $100,000.
4. The average price per package would be $80,000 as compared to the industry average of $75,000.
5. The policy of charging for consulting to adapt System W to specific user requirements would be continued.
6. Maintenance charges would be set at an annual rate of 15 percent of the purchase price. This would include program updates and related support services.

Promotion

System W was available in time-sharing applications before the end of 1982. However, the marketing plan called for the development of the "in-house" market. This segment comprised organizations owning and operating mainframe computers. In addition, some were using personal computers or were likely to own personal computers in the near future. The firm implemented its program of in-house sales and supporting advertising as of January 13, 1983.

Promotion of the product was carried out in several ways. First, news stories and product information were made available to the media through the public relations activities of the firm. System W reports appeared in *Computerworld, The Wall Street Journal,* and other computer and financial journals.

Colleges and universities were viewed as influencers. Comshare executives made themselves available for lectures and consultation about DSS and System W with universities and professional groups. Several universities were given System W packages for use by students. Another group of influencers was identified as business executives who might have use for System W in their positions and recommend it to others. This group was approached through conferences and "in-house tests."

Comshare's time-sharing customers provided another valuable avenue for product promotion. During the development of System W it was tested by 100 time-sharing customers. This test served to familiarize these potential users with the product. An additional purpose served by these customer trials was the testing of product modifications and adaptations to the specific user groups. Conferences were held with these time-sharing users to obtain their approvals of the product modifications, as well as their recommendations for use by others.

An advertising program was planned for the Spring of 1984 under the theme of "Safe Harbor." The relationship of Comshare and IBM under the marketing agreement provided the basis to inform potential users that purchasers would be in a safe harbor through the use of IBM in-house mainframes and personal computers with System W. Schedules were developed for advertising to appear in selected business journals. The advertising was to be selective and addressed to financial, marketing, and other senior executives. Not all senior executives would be contacted through the media. The conferences with senior executives mentioned above were viewed as one way to obtain coverage not presently affordable in the media coverage considered. It was recognized that the mass market of knowledgeable workers would be contacted presently through media advertising. Influencers were to be relied upon until sufficient revenues supported additional advertising.

Kevin Kalkhoven commented as follows about changing advertising requirements, "We used very limited advertising before System W since the time-sharing market does not require much advertising. However, the multitude of potential users for DSS software makes it necessary to communicate about System W through advertising."

Personal Selling

Comshare executives felt that improvements were needed in sales strategy and performance. Although some experience had been gained in the sale of software, it was believed that the sales organization did not really understand the best way to sell System W. Mr. Kalkhoven believed that the firm was very good in many other aspects of marketing such as promotion, publicity, and time-sharing sales, but that concerted effort was needed in the DSS software personal selling program.

Before System W was introduced, Comshare had initiated a five-year strategic plan for sales activity. That plan was applied to the major product lines, and System W was to be integrated fully. A one-year tactical plan was initiated under the five-year strategic plan for each product line. Every six months the yearly plan was updated to "roll over" the plan for the following 12 months. The directors of the product lines developed sales support action plans to include:

1. *Product and market development.* Plans for moving products through the markets were made and included things such as identification of users' and prospects' needs and adaptation to them; way of identifying needs and presenting solutions; sales and revenue plans; and management control of activities. Provisions were made for updating plans as the market and customer needs changed.
2. *Marketing materials.* Brochures, advertising reprints, and training manuals for salespeople and customers were developed.
3. *Consultants and technical support.* Consultants trained in adaptation of products to customer needs were made available to work with salespeople in meeting customer needs.
4. *Training.* Comshare developed an innovative computer-aided instruction system called the "Commander Learning Station." This combined the Apple IIe microcomputer and a videotape in such a way that potential users could learn System W in self-paced, interactive learning modules. Two versions were offered: a two-day "novice" program, and a half-day refresher program for infrequent, but experienced users.

Because time-sharing would continue to be the most significant portion of revenue for some time, salespeople would be involved in selling both time-sharing and System W. So salespeople were trained to work with and be supported by technical and local branch representatives in the sale and service of time-sharing.

Additional training was initiated to deal with Comshare time-sharing customers who were using FCS/EPS software originally recommended by Comshare salespeople. Comshare had offered support services for this software and felt obligated to continue to do this. However, they would not be able to support new releases of FCS/EPS.

Salespeople were trained to explain this situation and also to persuade customers to switch to System W. In addition, Comshare salespeople were informed of the possibility that clients might (1) seek a time-sharing service which supported new versions of FCS/EPS or (2) decide to purchase the FCS/EPS software outright for in-house use.

Distribution

Distribution of goods was of less importance in the time-sharing and software industry than others. Time-sharing operated through communication networks. Some hardware was required for adapting terminals to telephone lines. However, these were installed on a one-time basis and repetitive shipments of equipment were not required. Inventories were minimal and required little capital investment and management control.

This situation could change in the future. Richard L. Crandall said that it was possible that the vendors of decision support software might consider a new channel of distribution whereby software for microcomputers, personal computers, and mainframe computers would be sold through computer stores. Comshare was examining this possibility and considering the impact of such changes in distribution. For example, a marketing segmentation plan was considered in which Comshare salespeople would call on certain classes of customers and the remainder would be serviced by the computer stores. Another possibility was that other vendors could sell System W to market areas not covered by Comshare.

PRESENT AND FUTURE

Comshare's management viewed this firm as a planning-oriented organization that had evolved in a high-technology industry. Product innovation was the lifeblood of this company. However, strategic planning based on needs of the market place was equally important in directing the thrust of innovation and delivery products to significant markets.

System W was developed and offered under the aegis of strategic planning. Mr. Crandall identified Comshare as a marketing-oriented firm that translated corporate planning into strategic marketing action. Recognition of the changing environment caused the firm to meet changing needs in the market through delivery of System W. At the time of the marketing arrangement with IBM, Comshare was developing an enhancement to System W. It became available to users five months later as a fully integrated data management system named "DATMAN." This software made it possible for users to have access to total data management capability fully integrated with System W in terms of modeling, statistical analysis, reporting, etc.

Most competing products required users to utilize an additional data management software package (for example, ADABAS or INFO) which was difficult to interface with the DSS software. Therefore, Comshare's new product, DATMAN, was a major breakthrough. It provided a truly "user friendly" decision support system which would give the user full access to all data on its own or other computers (e.g., COMPUSTAT).

This rapidly changing market mandated the need to look constantly into the future. Mr. Crandall said, "System W and DATMAN are state-of-the-art today. I will leave you to conjecture on our next moves."

Case 5–9 Gap, Inc.*

The nation's merchants, many as glum as the Grinch this Christmas, are struggling to get through a retail recession by ballyhooing bargains, gift giveaways and even exotic vacations.

But not Gap Inc.

Its bright white Gap stores are oddly devoid of holiday hype. The company isn't displaying gimmicky merchandise to lure crowds. Its shelves are stocked with simple, all-cotton, no-frills clothing.

Nevertheless, the 21-year-old apparel chain is booming. It is benefiting from a sudden cachet with a wide spectrum of consumers—from teen-agers to celebrities. The current issue of *Gap Rap,* an in-house magazine, brags about the sighting of Jacqueline Onassis at a Manhattan Gap and reports recent purchases by Kathleen Turner, Arnold Schwarzenegger, and the Duchess of Kent.

The Gap has become hip as consumers, discarding their 1980s excesses, turn back to a "basics" frame of mind. Keds are popular, while Dove Bars and imported beers are passe. "It's a return to an earlier kind of Americana, when things weren't quite so complicated," say Mona Doyle, a consumer researcher.

The Gap brand of men's, women's and kids' clothes, the company contends, is now the third-largest-selling label in America—after Levi Strauss and Liz Claiborne sportswear. While competitors are strug-

---

* Source: Francine Schwadel, "Simple Success," *The Wall Street Journal,* December 12, 1990, pp. A1, 6. Reprinted by permission of *THE WALL STREET JOURNAL,* © 1990 Dow Jones & Company, Inc. All Rights Reserved Worldwide.

EXHIBIT 1   The Gap: Reaping the Rewards of Success

Earnings have jumped . . .

Annual net income, in millions

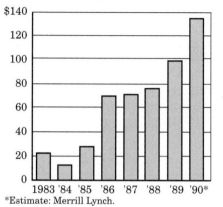

*Estimate: Merrill Lynch.

And stores proliferate . . .

Number of stores at year end

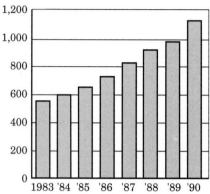

As it outpaces competitors . . .

Year-to-date same-store sales, in percent

	Percent change
Gap	**+15.0%**
Dillard Dept. Stores*	**+11.0**
Burlington Coat*	**+10.0**
Dayton Hudson*	**+6.8**
Limited	**+5.0**
Charming Shoppes	**+4.0**
TJX*	**+2.0**
May Dept. Stores*	**+1.4**
Nordstrom*	**+0.7**
Carter Hawley Hale	**-1.0**

*Estimate: Seidler Amdec Securities.
Source: Seidler Amdec Securities.

Benefiting investors.

Comparison of Gap stock vs. DJ Apparel Retailers index, Dec. 29, 1989=100

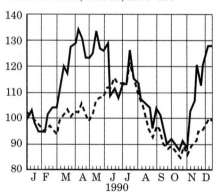

---

gling to match 1989 receipts, Gap's same-store sales have surged 15 percent this year. Its annual profit is expected to jump 35 percent (Exhibit 1). And Gap's results are even more impressive if its one struggling unit, Banana Republic, isn't included.

Gap is taking advantage of its good fortune—and the industry's bad times. Recession or not, Gap is plunging ahead with an ambitious, albeit risky, five-year expansion plan. It is bent on doubling sales—to nearly $4 billion by 1995—and its floor space. Next year alone, it plans to spend about $220 million, financed mostly from cash flow, and add as many as 165 new stores to its roster of 1,100 Gap, GapKids, and Banana Republic outlets.

"This is an opportunity to take market share," declares Donald Fisher, Gap's 62-year-old chairman and founder. He figures that Gap can woo discouraged customers away from weak, debt-laden chains that can't afford to keep stores looking sharp.

Gap isn't the only retailer prospering. Discounters Wal-Mart Stores Inc. and the Target unit of Dayton Hudson Corp. are faring well and see the economy's slide more as an opportunity than a threat. Target is even testing fashion ads aimed at department-store customers who might be trading down. One touts Target's $19.99 stirrup pants as "what to wear with a $175 Adrienne Vittadini sweater."

In a recession, Gap's basic clothes seem likely to retain their appeal. Its strategy of changing the colors of its stock every two months or so could keep Gap stores looking fresher than competitors'—while many of the competitors are trimming orders for new goods, leaving a jumble of old and new shades on their sales floors.

Furthermore, Gap's strategy could attract more bargain hunters: To move out slow-selling items quickly, the chain typically slashes prices by a third.

"The two things they offer—quality and value—are the things people put a premium on in tight times," says Thomas Flexner, a New York real-estate executive and Gap shopper.

Like other retailers, Gap expects slower sales growth through at least next year's first half. But it is predicting a still-healthy increase in roughly the 5 to 8 percent range at stores open at least a year.

A common item such as Gap's pocket T-shirt illustrates why. When consumers first began tightening their purse strings last summer, Gap already had positioned it as a stylish but inexpensive fashion statement. Singer Rickie Lee Jones and Twin Peaks heartthrob James Marshall wore it in Gap ads. The all-cotton shirt was available in a dozen colors, including trendy "chili" red as well as basic black and white. And Gap priced it at just $10.50—about 15 percent less than competitors were charging. Gap sold nearly a million.

In the fickle world of fashion, Gap could trip, of course. It has before. In 1987, it stumbled by sticking too long with such styles as shaker-knit sweaters and buffalo plaid shirts. In the fall of 1989, it introduced pastel-colored clothes that bombed. Its attempt to launch an upscale clothing chain called Hemisphere was a washout, triggering an after-tax charge of $6.5 million last year to close the nine shops.

But Gap's biggest swamp has been its 129-store Banana Republic chain.

In the mid-1980s, the chain expanded rapidly on the strength of its safari look, which was popular when Indiana Jones action films and "Out of Africa" were hot. But the safari craze fizzled in 1987, and the

Banana Republic chain struggled for two years with losses and declining same-store sales. Lately, the unit has staged a turn-around, posting three consecutive quarters of what Gap officials call "modest" profits. They add that they still see room for improvement—especially in Banana Republic's women's business.

"We're always trying things that don't work," acknowledges Millard "Mickey" Drexler, Gap's 46-year-old president. At the moment, he has doubts about a new $325 leather jacket that may be too expensive for Gap shoppers. He also worries that Gap managers may have overreacted to his call for simplicity and eliminated too many prints from the richly colored holiday assortment.

Gap didn't carry any clout when, in 1969, Mr. Fisher set out to sell a wide selection of Levi's. A real-estate executive then, Mr. Fisher hit on the idea of a jeans shop after failing to find Levi's in his common size at department stores. Initially, he also sold discounted records and tapes to draw shoppers into his first San Francisco store, but he quickly quit the music business because of losses to thieves.

His wife, Doris, coined the store's name after a cocktail party at which "the generation gap" was a hot topic. By the early 1980s, however, the Gap was having an identity crisis of its own. Levi's could be purchased almost everywhere; Sears sold them, and jeans shops were sprouting like weeds. Discounting was rampant—even at the Gap—and Mr. Fisher was worried.

So, in 1983, he recruited Mr. Drexler, who already had transformed the unprofitable Ann Taylor chain into a healthy, chic specialty store for working women. Previously, Mr. Drexler, the son of a New York garment-district worker, had worked at Bloomingdale's, Macy's and Abraham & Straus department stores.

Although the two executives initially considered starting a new chain, Mr. Drexler figured that he could do more for the Gap. He believed the company was squandering a good name by emphasizing low prices instead of fashion. He saw a market for casual clothes with "good style, good taste and good value."

Mr. Drexler made that point in his first day on the job by waving pictures ripped from magazines. One showed Fiat mogul Giovanni Agnelli in a Levi's chambray shirt; in another, designer Ralph Lauren posed in Levi's jeans and a jean jacket. "Good taste doesn't have to be more expensive," Mr. Drexler kept asserting.

Soon, Mr. Drexler discarded a dozen clothing labels, retaining only Levi's and the Gap brand he intended to build. He spruced up Gap stores. He also hired a team of seasoned Seventh Avenue designers—now numbering about 30—to study the world fashion scene and develop distinctive Gap collections.

Alan Millstein, publisher of the *Fashion Network Report* newsletter, contends that Gap designers "blaze no new trails" and "aren't the

Lewis and Clark of retailing." But, he adds, there's nothing wrong with that. He had just snapped up four long-sleeve Gap polo shirts that, at $30 each, cost about half of what department stores charge for a similar Ralph Lauren shirt.

Mr. Drexler also brought in Magdalene Gross, an Ann Taylor marketing expert, who changed Gap's image by advertising in places such as the *New York Times Magazine* and *Rolling Stone* instead of on television. She dreamed up the award-winning black-and-white "Individuals of Style" campaign showing actress Winona Ryder and other personalities in basic Gap T-shirts and jeans.

The results, at least initially, were disastrous. Net income slid 43 percent in 1984—a year the intense Mr. Drexler says he wouldn't want to relive. By 1985, however, profit was back on track: up 127 percent on a 25 percent sales rise. Mr. Drexler was rewarded handsomely. He received one million shares of restricted stock, some of which he cashed in earlier this year for $20.3 million. He still holds a 3 percent stake in Gap. Mr. Fisher's family owns 42 percent.

Except for 1987, when profit was flat, Mr. Drexler's record is impressive. Between 1984 and 1989, net income grew eightfold to $97.6 million on sales that tripled to $1.6 billion.

Still, the fast-talking Mr. Drexler isn't content. He spends most of his time at headquarters in product meetings or simply wandering around. His cavernous corner office is so barren it echoes when he talks. By contrast, the hallways and nearby offices are decorated with Lichtensteins, Calders, and other pieces from Mr. Fisher's modern-art collection.

Now, Mr. Drexler is pushing Gap's private-label jeans. They are priced a few dollars below Levi's but bring in bigger profits. And it is no coincidence that Gap's net income has ballooned as its sales of Levi's have shrunk; this year, Levi's will account for less than 5 percent of company sales, down from 23 percent in 1984.

At the stores, the emphasis is clearly on the house label. A large Gap store in San Francisco displays the line prominently on its first floor and relegates Levi's to a small area upstairs. A new store in Chicago doesn't carry Levi's at all. From time to time, Gap salespeople are paid extra for selling Gap jeans. A Levi Strauss marketing official says his company is "happy that they continue to carry Levi's products in whatever amounts."

Although Gap sometimes tests new styles—this spring, it will introduce a woman's sleeveless T-shirt that sold well at 35 stores in the South—Mr. Drexler operates largely on gut instinct. The four-year-old GapKids line was conceived at a meeting where he and other Gap executives shared frustrations about the difficulty of finding all-cotton clothes for their children. They tested the idea by displaying colorful sweatshirts in children's sizes in a Gap store in San Francisco. Despite inconclusive results, Mr. Drexler opened the first GapKids store anyway. "We loved what the clothes looked like," he says.

With 167 stores, GapKids is now the company's fastest-growing unit. A new babyGap line was added in February. Even though the tiny jean jackets go for $32 and pint-sized jeans and shaker-knit sweaters for $28 each, parents, many of them baby boomers, aren't balking at the prices. "Kids can wear them and wear them," says 34-year-old Linda Kirkendall of Warsaw, Ind., who stops at GapKids whenever she makes the two-hour drive to Chicago or Indianapolis.

On a recent afternoon, Mr. Drexler dropped in on a GapKids manager who was sitting on the floor and peering at sock designs with striped patterns. Mr. Drexler took a look.

"I think you'll do business on stripes," he announced, "but not on those stripes." He has trouble explaining why, saying finally that the colors are too dull. Gap clothes, he declares, should be "clean, all-American, simple good taste."

Case 5–10 *Thompson Respiration Products, Inc.**

Victor Higgins, executive vice president for Thompson Respiration Products, Inc. (TRP), sat thinking at his desk late one Friday in April 1982. "We're making progress," he said to himself. "Getting Metro to sign finally gets us into the Chicago market . . . and with a good dealer at that." Metro, of course, was Metropolitan Medical Products, a large Chicago retailer of medical equipment and supplies for home use. "Now, if we could just do the same in Minneapolis and Atlanta," he continued.

However, getting at least one dealer in each of these cities to sign a TRP Dealer Agreement seemed remote right now. One reason was the sizable groundwork required—Higgins simply lacked the time to review operations at the well-over 100 dealers currently operating in the two cities. Another was TRP's lack of dealer-oriented sales information that went beyond the technical specification sheet for each product and the company's price list. Still another reason concerned two conditions in the dealer agreement itself—prospective dealers sometimes balked

---

* This case was written by Professor James E. Nelson and DBA Candidate William R. Woolridge, the University of Colorado. Some data are disguised. © 1983 by the Business Research Division, College of Business and Administration and the Graduate School of Business Administration, University of Colorado. Used by permission.

at agreeing to sell no products manufactured by TRP's competitors and differed with TRP in interpretations of the "best efforts" clause. (The clause required the dealer to maintain adequate inventories of TRP products, contact four prospective new customers or physicians or respiration therapists per month, respond promptly to sales inquiries, and represent TRP at appropriate conventions where it exhibited.)

"Still," Higgins concluded, "we signed Metro in spite of these reasons, and 21 others across the country. That's about all anyone could expect—after all, we've only been trying to develop a dealer network for a year or so."

THE PORTABLE RESPIRATOR INDUSTRY

The portable respirator industry began in the early 1950s when polio-stricken patients who lacked control of muscles necessary for breathing began to leave treatment centers. They returned home with hospital-style iron lungs or fiber glass chest shells, both being large chambers that regularly introduced a vacuum about the patient's chest. The vacuum caused the chest to expand and, thus, the lungs to fill with air. However, both devices confined patients to a prone or semiprone position in a bed.

By the late 1950s TRP had developed a portable turbine blower powered by an electric motor and battery. When connected to a mouthpiece via plastic tubing, the blower would inflate a patient's lungs on demand. Patients could now leave their beds for several hours at a time and realize limited mobility in a wheelchair. By the early 1970s TRP had developed a line of more sophisticated turbine respirators in terms of monitoring and capability for adjustment to individual patient needs.

At about the same time, applications began to shift from polio patients to victims of other diseases or of spinal cord injuries, the latter group primarily a result of automobile accidents. Better emergency medical service, quicker evacuation to spinal-cord injury centers, and more proficient treatment meant that people who formerly would have died now lived and went on to lead meaningful lives. Because of patients' frequently younger ages, they strongly desired wheelchair mobility. Respiration therapists obliged by recommending a Thompson respirator for home use or, if unaware of Thompson, recommending a Puritan-Bennett or other machine.

Instead of a turbine, Puritan-Bennett machines used a bellows design to force air into the patient's lungs. The machines were widely used in hospitals but seemed poorly suited for home use. For one thing, Puritan-Bennett machines used a compressor pump or pressurized air to drive the bellows, much more cumbersome than Thompson's electric motor. Puritan-Bennett machines also cost approximately 50 percent more than a comparable Thompson unit and were relatively large and immobile. On the other hand, Puritan-Bennett machines were viewed by physicians and respiration therapists as industry standards.

By the middle 1970s TRP had developed a piston and cylinder design (similar in principle to the bellows) and placed it on the market. The product lacked the sophistication of the Puritan-Bennett machines but was reliable, portable, and much simpler to adjust and operate. It also maintained TRP's traditional cost advantage. Another firm, Life Products, began its operations in 1976 by producing a similar design. A third competitor, Lifecare Services, had begun operations somewhat earlier.

Puritan-Bennett

Puritan-Bennett was a large, growing, and financially sound manufacturer of respiration equipment for medical and aviation applications. Its headquarters were located in Kansas City, Missouri. However, the firm staffed over 40 sales, service, and warehouse operations in the United States, Canada, United Kingdom, and France. Sales for 1981 exceeded $100 million, while employment was just over 2,000 people. Sales for its Medical Equipment Group (respirators, related equipment, and accessories, service, and parts) likely exceeded $40 million for 1981; however, Higgins could obtain data only for the period 1977–

EXHIBIT 1 Puritan-Bennett Medical Equipment Group Sales ($ millions)

	1977	1978	1979	1980
Domestic sales:				
Model MA–1:				
Units	1,460	875	600	500
Amount	$ 8.5	$ 4.9	$ 3.5	$ 3.1
Model MA–2:				
Units	—	935	900	1,100
Amount	—	$ 6.0	$ 6.1	$ 7.8
Foreign sales:				
Units	250	300	500	565
Amount	$ 1.5	$ 1.8	$ 3.1	$ 3.6
IPPB equipment	$ 6.0	$ 6.5	$ 6.7	$ 7.0
Parts, service, accessories	$10.0	$11.7	$13.1	$13.5
Overhaul	$ 2.0	$ 3.0	$ 2.5	$ 2.5
Total	$28.0	$34.0	$35.0	$37.5

Source: *The Wall Street Transcript.*

80 (see Exhibit 1). Puritan-Bennett usually sold its respirators through a system of independent, durable medical equipment dealers. However, its sales offices did sell directly to identified "house accounts" and often competed with dealers by selling slower-moving products to all accounts. According to industry sources, Puritan-Bennett sales were slightly more than three fourths of all respirator sales to hospitals in 1981.

However, these same sources expected Puritan-Bennett's share to diminish during the 1980s because of the aggressive marketing efforts of three other manufacturers of hospital-style respirators: Bear Medical Systems, Inc., J. H. Emerson, and Siemens-Elema. The latter firm was expected to grow the most rapidly, despite its quite recent entry into the U.S. market (its headquarters were in Sweden) and a list price of over $16,000 for its basic model.

Life Products

Life Products directly competed with TRP for the portable respirator market. Life Products had begun operations in 1976 when David Smith, a TRP employee, left to start his own business. Smith had located his plant in Boulder, Colorado, less than a mile from TRP headquarters.

He began almost immediately to set up a dealer network and by early 1982 had secured over 40 independent dealers located in large metropolitan areas. Smith had made a strong effort to sign only large, well-managed, durable medical equipment dealers. Dealer representatives were required to complete Life Product's service training school held each month in Boulder. Life Products sold its products to dealers (in contrast to TRP, which both sold and rented products to consumers and to dealers). Dealers received a 20 to 25 percent discount off suggested retail price on most products.

As of April 1982, Life Products offered two respirator models (the LP3 and LP4) and a limited number of accessories (such as mouthpieces and plastic tubing) to its dealers. Suggested retail prices for the two respirator models were approximately $3,900 and $4,800. Suggested rental rates were approximately $400 and $500 per month. Life Products also allowed Lifecare Services to manufacture a respirator similar to the LP3 under license.

At the end of 1981 Smith was quite pleased with his firm's performance. During Life Products' brief history, it had passed TRP in sales and now ceased to see the firm as a serious threat, at least according to one company executive:

> We really aren't in competition with Thompson. They're after the stagnant market, and we're after a growing market. We see new applications and ultimately the hospital market as our niche. I doubt if Thompson will even

be around in a few years. As for Lifecare, their prices are much lower than ours, but you don't get the service. With them you get the basic product but nothing else. With us, you get a complete medical care service. That's the big difference.

Lifecare Services, Inc.

In contrast to the preceding firms, Lifecare Services, Inc., earned much less of its revenues from medical equipment manufacturing and much more from medical equipment distributing. The firm primarily resold products purchased from other manufacturers, operating out of its headquarters in Boulder as well as from its 16 field offices (Exhibit 2). All offices were stocked with backup parts and an inventory of respirators. All were staffed with trained service technicians under Lifecare's employ.

Lifecare did manufacture a few accessories not readily available from other manufacturers. These items complemented the purchased products and, in the company's words, served to "give the customer a complete respiratory service." Under a licensing agreement between Lifecare and Life Products, the firm manufactured a respirator similar to the LP3 and marketed it under the Lifecare name. The unit rented for approximately $175 per month. While Lifecare continued to service the few remaining Thompson units it still had in the field, it no longer carried the Thompson line.

Lifecare rented rather than sold its equipment. The firm maintained that this gave patients more flexibility in the event of recovery or death and lowered patients' monthly costs.

EXHIBIT 2   Lifecare Services, Inc., Field Offices

Augusta, Georgia	Houston, Texas
Baltimore, Maryland	Los Angeles, California
Boston, Massachusetts	New York, New York
Chicago, Illinois	Oakland, California
Cleveland, Ohio	Omaha, Nebraska
Denver, Colorado	Phoenix, Arizona
Detroit, Michigan	Seattle, Washington
Grand Rapids, Michigan*	St. Paul, Minnesota

* Suboffice.

Source: Trade literature.

THOMPSON RESPIRATION PRODUCTS, INC.

TRP currently employed 13 people, 9 in production and 4 in management. It conducted operations in a modern, attractive building (leased) in an industrial park. The building contained about 6,000 square feet of space, split 75/25 for production/management purposes. Production operations were essentially job shop in nature: Skilled technicians assembled each unit by hand on work-benches, making frequent quality control tests and subsequent adjustments. Production lots usually ranged from 10 to 75 units per model and probably averaged around 40. Normal production capacity was about 600 units per year.

Product Line

TRP currently sold seven respirator models plus a large number of accessories. All respirator models were portable but differed considerably in terms of style, design, performance specifications, and attendant features (see Exhibit 3). Four models were styled as metal boxes with an impressive array of knobs, dials, indicator lights, and switches. Three were styled as less imposing, overnighter suitcases with less prominently displayed controls and indicators. (Exhibit 4 reproduces part of the specification sheet for the M3000, as illustrative of the metal box design.)

Four of the models were designed as *pressure machines*, using a turbine pump that provided a constant, usually positive, pressure. Patients were provided intermittent access to this pressure as breaths per minute. However, one model, the MV Multivent, could provide either a constant positive or a constant negative pressure (i.e., a vacuum, necessary to operate chest shells, iron lungs, and body wraps). No other portable respirator on the market could produce a negative pressure. Three of the models were designed as *volume machines*, using a piston pump that produced intermittent, constant volumes of pressurized air as breaths per minute. Actual volumes were prescribed by each patient's physician based on lung capacity. Pressures depended on the breathing method used (mouthpiece, trach, chest shell, and others) and on the patient's activity level. Breaths per minute also depended on the patient's activity level.

Models came with several features. The newest was an assist feature (currently available on the Minilung M25 but soon to be offered also on the M3000) that allowed the patient alone to "command" additional breaths without having someone change the dialed breath rate. The sigh feature gave patients a sigh either automatically or on demand. Depending on the model, up to six alarms were available to indicate a

EXHIBIT 3 TRP Respirators

Model*	Style	Design	Volume (cc)	Pressure (cm H_2O)	Breaths per Minute	Weight (lbs.)	Size (ft.³)	Features
M3000	Metal box	Volume	300–3,000	+10 to +65	6 to 30	39	0.85	Sigh, four alarms, automatic switchover from AC to battery
MV Multivent	Metal box	Pressure (positive or negative)	n.a.	−70 to +80	8 to 24	41	1.05	Positive or negative pressure, four alarms, AC only
Minilung M15	Suitcase	Volume	200–1,500	+5 to +65	8 to 22	24	0.70	Three alarms, automatic switchover from AC to battery
Minilung M25 Assist (also available without the assist feature)	Suitcase	Volume	600–2,500	+5 to +65	5 to 20	24	0.70	Assist, sigh, three alarms, automatic switchover from AC to battery
Bantam GS	Suitcase	Pressure (positive)	n.a.	+15 to +45	6 to 24	19	0.75	Sigh, six alarms, automatic switchover from AC to battery
Compact CS	Metal box	Pressure (positive)	n.a.	+15 to +45	8 to 24	25	0.72	Sigh, six alarms, automatic switchover from AC to battery
Compact C	Metal box	Pressure	n.a.	+15 to +45	6 to 24	19	0.50	Sigh, four alarms, automatic switchover from AC to battery

n.a. = Not applicable.
* Five other models considered obsolete by TRP could be supplied if necessary.

Source: Company sales specification sheets.

EXHIBIT 4   The M3000 Minilung

M3000 MINILUNG

PORTABLE VOLUME VENTILATOR

The M3000 is a planned performance product designed to meet breathing needs. It is a significant step in the ongoing effort of a company which pioneered the advancement of portable respiratory equipment.

This portable volume ventilator sets high standards for flexibility of operation and versitility in use. The M3000 has gained its successful reputation as a result of satisfactory usage in hospitals, for transport, in rehabilitation efforts and in home care. This model grew out of expressed needs of users for characteristics which offered performance PLUS it is engineered to enable the user to have something more than just mechanical breathing.

Now breathing patterns can comfortably varied with the use of a SIGH, which can be obtained either automatically or manually.

Besides being sturdy and reliable, the M3000 can be adjusted readily.

Remote pressure sensing in the proximal airway provides for more accurate set up of the ventilator pressure alarms.

This model has the option of the patient-operated call switch.

AC-DC operation of the M3000 is accomplished with ease because automatic-swithch-over is provided on AC power failure, first to external battery, then to eternal battery.

THOMPSON takes pride in planning ahead

M3000 MINILUNG
Portable Volume Ventilator   See reverse for specifications

SPECIFICATIONS

300 to 3000 ml adjustable volume

10 to 65 cm water pressure

Automatic or Manual Sigh

Alarms
    Patient operated call alarm
    Low Pressure alarm and light
    High Pressure alarm and light
    Low Voltage light with delayed alarm
    Automatic switch-over provided on AC power failure,
        first to external battery, then to internal battery
    Alarm delay switch

Pilot lamps color-coded and labeled

Remote pressure connector

Self-contained battery for 2 hour operation—recharges automatically

Power sources
    120 volt, 60 hz; 12 volt external battery; and internal battery

Size 12 5/8 W   x   11 1/4 D   x   10 1/4 inches H

Weight 39 pounds (Shipping weight 48 pounds)

---

patient's call, unacceptable low pressure, unacceptable high pressure, low battery voltage/power failure, failure to cycle, and the need to replace motor brushes. All models but the MV Multivent also offered automatic switchover from alternating current to either an internal or an external battery (or both) in the event of a power failure. Batteries provided for 18 to 40 hours of operation, depending on usage.

Higgins felt that TRP's respirators were superior to those of Life Products. Most TRP models allowed pressure monitoring in the airway itself rather than in the machine, providing more accurate measurement. TRP's suitcase-style models often were strongly preferred by patients, especially the polio patients who had known no others. TRP's volume models offered easier volume adjustments, and all TRP models offered more alarms. On the other hand, he knew that TRP had recently experienced some product reliability problems of an irritating—not life threatening—nature. Further he knew that Life Products had beaten TRP to the market with the assist feature (the idea for which had come from a Puritan-Bennett machine).

TRP's line of accessories was more extensive than that of Life Products. TRP offered the following for separate sale: alarms, call switches, battery cables, chest shells, mouthpieces, plastic tubing, pneumobelts and bladders (equipment for still another breathing method that utilized intermittent pressure on a patient's diaphragm), and other items. Lifecare Services offered many similar items.

Distribution

Shortly after joining TRP, Higgins had decided to switch from selling and renting products directly to patients to selling and renting products to dealers. While it meant lower margins, less control, and more infrequent communication with patients, the change had several advantages. It allowed TRP to shift inventory from the factory to the dealer, generating cash more quickly. It provided for local representation in market areas, allowing patients greater feelings of security and TRP more aggressive sales efforts. It shifted burdensome paperwork (required by insurance companies and state and federal agencies to effect payment) from TRP to the dealer. It also reduced other TRP administrative activities in accounting, customer relations, and sales.

TRP derived about half of its 1981 revenue of $3 million directly from patients and about half from the dealer network. By April 1982 the firm had 22 dealers (see Exhibit 5), with 3 accounting for over 60 percent of TRP dealer revenues. Two of the three serviced TRP products, as did two of the smaller dealers; the rest preferred to let the factory take care of repairs. TRP conducted occasional training sessions for dealer repair personnel, but distances were great and turnover in the position high, making such sessions costly. Most dealers requested air shipment of respirators, in quantities of one or two units.

EXHIBIT 5   TRP Dealer Locations

Bakersfield, California	Salt Lake City, Utah
Baltimore, Maryland	San Diego, California
Birmingham, Alabama	San Francisco, California
Chicago, Illinois	Seattle, Washington
Cleveland, Ohio	Springfield, Ohio
Fort Wayne, Indiana	Tampa, Florida
Greenville, North Carolina	Tucson, Arizona
Indianapolis, Indiana	Washington, D.C.
Newark, New Jersey	
Oklahoma City, Oklahoma	Montreal, Canada
Pittsburgh, Pennsylvania	Toronto, Canada

Source: Company records.

EXHIBIT 6   Current TRP Respirator Price List

Model	Suggested Retail Rent/Month	Suggested Retail Price	Dealer Rent/Month	Dealer Price 1–2	Dealer Price 3 or More
M3000	$380	$6,000	$290	$4,500	$4,185
MV Multivent	270	4,300	210	3,225	3,000
Minilung M15	250	3,950	190	2,960	2,750
Minilung M25	250	3,950	190	2,960	2,750
Bantam GS	230	3,600	175	2,700	2,510
Compact CS	230	3,600	175	2,700	2,510
Compact C	200	3,150	155	2,360	2,195

Source: Company sales specification sheets.

Price

TRP maintained a comprehensive price list for its entire product line. (Exhibit 6 reproduces part of the current list.) Each respirator model carried both a suggested retail selling price and a suggested retail rental rate. (TRP also applied these rates when it dealt directly with patients.) The list also presented two net purchase prices for each model along with an alternative rental rate that TRP charged to dealers. About 40 percent of the 300 respirator units TRP shipped to dealers in 1981 went out on a rental basis. The comparable figure for the 165 units sent directly to consumers was 90 percent. Net purchase prices allowed an approximate 7 percent discount for orders of three or more units of each model. Higgins had initiated this policy early last year with the aim of encouraging dealers to order in larger quantities. To date, one dealer had taken advantage of this discount.

Current policy called for TRP to earn a gross margin of approximately 35 percent on the dealer price for 1–2 units. All prices included shipping charges by United Parcel Service (UPS); purchasers requesting more expensive transportation service paid the difference between actual costs incurred and the UPS charge. Terms were net 30 days with a 1.5 percent service charge added to past-due accounts. Prices were last changed in late 1981.

CONSUMERS

Two types of patients used respirators, depending on whether the need followed from disease or from injury. Diseases such as polio, sleep apnea, chronic obstructive pulmonary disease, and muscular dystrophy annually left about 1,900 victims unable to breathe without a respirator. Injury to the spinal cord above the fifth vertebra caused a similar result for about 300 people per year. Except for polio, incidences of the diseases and injury were growing at about 3 percent per year. Most patients kept one respirator at bedside and another mounted on a wheelchair. However, Higgins did know of one individual who kept eight Bantam B models (provided by a local polio foundation, now defunct) in his closet. Except for polio patients, life expectancies were about five years. Higgins estimated the total number of patients using home respirators in 1981 at 10,500:

Polio	3,000
Other diseases	6,500
Spinal cord injury	1,000

Almost all patients were under a physician's care as well as that of a more immediate nurse or attendant (frequently a relative). About 95 percent paid for their equipment through insurance benefits or foundation monies. About 90 percent rented their equipment. Almost all patients and their nurses or attendants had received instruction in equipment operation from respiration therapists employed by medical centers or by dealers of durable medical equipment.

The majority of patients were poor. Virtually none were gainfully employed, and all had seen their savings and other assets diminished to varying degrees by treatment costs. Some had experienced a divorce. Slightly more patients were male than female. About 75 percent lived in their homes, with the rest split between hospitals, nursing homes, and other institutions.

Apart from patients, Higgins thought that hospitals might be considered a logical new market for TRP to enter. Many of the larger and some of the smaller general hospitals might be convinced to purchase one portable respirator (like the M3000) for emergency and other use with injury patients. Such a machine would be much cheaper to purchase than a large Puritan-Bennett and would allow easier patient trips to testing areas, X-ray, surgery, and the like. Even easier to convince should be the 14 regional spinal-cord injury centers located across the country (Exhibit 7). Other medical centers that specialized in treatment of pulmonary diseases should also be prime targets. Somewhat less promising but more numerous would be public and private schools that trained physicians and respiration therapists. Higgins estimated the numbers of these institutions at:

General hospitals (100 beds or more)	3,800
General hospitals (fewer than 100 beds)	3,200
Spinal cord injury centers	14

EXHIBIT 7   Regional Spinal Cord Injury Centers

Birmingham, Alabama	Houston, Texas
Boston, Massachusetts	Miami, Florida
Chicago, Illinois	New York, New York
Columbia, Missouri	Philadelphia, Pennsylvania
Downey, California	Phoenix, Arizona
Englewood, Colorado	San Jose, California
Fishersville, Virginia	Seattle, Washington

Pulmonary disease treatment centers	100
Medical schools	180
Respiration therapy schools	250

DEALERS

Dealers supplying home care medical products (as distinct from dealers supplying hospitals and medical centers) showed a great deal of diversity. Some were little more than small areas in local drugstores that rented canes, walkers, and wheelchairs in addition to selling supplies such as surgical stockings and colostomy bags. Others carried nearly everything needed for home nursing care—renting everything from canes to hospital beds and selling supplies from bed pads to bottled oxygen. Still others specialized in products and supplies for only certain types of patients.

In this latter category, Higgins had identified dealers of oxygen and oxygen-related equipment as the best fit among existing dealers. These dealers serviced victims of emphysema, bronchitis, asthma, and other respiratory ailments—a growing market that Higgins estimated was about 10 times greater than that for respirators. A typical dealer had begun perhaps 10 years ago selling bottled oxygen (obtained from a welding supply wholesaler) and renting rather crude metering equipment to patients at home under the care of a registered nurse. The same dealer today now rented and serviced oxygen concentrators (a recently developed device that extracts oxygen from the air), liquid oxygen equipment and liquid oxygen, and much more sophisticated oxygen equipment and oxygen to patients cared for by themselves or by relatives.

Most dealers maintained a fleet of radio-dispatched trucks to deliver products to their customers. Better dealers promised 24-hour service and kept delivery personnel and a respiration therapist on call 24 hours a day. Dealers usually employed several respiration therapists who would set up equipment, instruct patients and attendants on equipment operation, and provide routine and emergency service. Dealers often expected the therapists to function as a sales force. The therapists would call on physicians and other respiration therapists at hospitals and medical centers, on discharge planners at hospitals, and on organizations such as muscular dystrophy associations, spinal cord injury associations, and visiting nurse associations.

Dealers usually bought their inventories of durable equipment and supplies directly from manufacturers. They usually received a 20 to 25 percent discount off suggested list prices to consumers and hospitals. Only in rare instances might dealers instead lease equipment from a manufacturer. Dealers aimed for a payback of one year or less, meaning that most products began to contribute to profit and overhead after 12 months of rental. Most products lasted physically for upwards of 10 years but technologically for only 5 to 6: Every dealer's warehouse contained idle but perfectly suitable equipment that had been superseded by models demanded by patients, their physicians, or their attendants.

Most dealers were independently owned and operated, with annual sales ranging between $5 million and $10 million. However, a number had recently been acquired by one of several parent organizations that were regional or national in scope. Such chains usually consisted of from 10 to 30 retail operations located in separated market areas. However, the largest, Abbey Medical, had begun operations in 1924 and now consisted of over 70 local dealers. Higgins estimated 1981 sales for the chain (which was itself acquired by American Hospital Supply Corporation in April 1981) at over $60 million. In general, chains maintained a low corporate visibility and provided their dealers with working capital, employee benefit programs, operating advice, and some centralized purchasing. Higgins thought that chain organizations might grow more rapidly over the next 10 years.

THE ISSUES

Higgins looked at his watch. It was 5:30 and really time to leave. "Still," he thought, "I should jot down what I see to be the immediate issues before I go—that way I won't be tempted to think about them over the weekend." He took a pen and wrote the following:

1. Should TRP continue to rent respirators to dealers?
2. Should TRP protect each dealer's territory (and how big should a territory be)?
3. Should TRP require dealers to stock no competing equipment?

4. How many dealers should TRP eventually have? Where?
5. What sales information should be assembled in order to attract high-quality dealers?
6. What should be done about the "best efforts" clause?

As he reread the list, Higgins considered that there probably were still other short-term–oriented questions he might have missed. Monday would be soon enough to consider them all.

Until then he was free to think about broader, more strategic issues. Some reflections on the nature of the target market, a statement of marketing objectives, and TRP's possible entry into the hospital market would occupy the weekend. Decisions on these topics would form a substantial part of TRP's strategic marketing plan, a document Higgins hoped to have for the beginning of the next fiscal year in July. "At least I can rule out one option," Higgins thought as he put on his coat. That was an idea to use independent sales representatives to sell TRP products on commission: a recently completed two-month search for such an organization had come up empty. "Like my stomach," he thought as he went out the door.

Case 5–11 *Northern Telecom, Inc.**

Hall Miller, vice president of marketing for the Central Office Switching Division of Northern Telecom, Inc., looked up from the magazine on his desk to a picture of a single, snow-covered log cabin with stately mountains rising in the background. The picture reminded him of his childhood in British Columbia.

His eyes moved from the picture to the window, where he could see traffic already starting to pile up on the portion of Interstate 40, which ran through Research Triangle Park, North Carolina between Durham, Chapel Hill, and Raleigh. It was mid-afternoon in March 1988 and the traffic would be bumper to bumper in another hour.

Hall smiled as he realized that the picture on the wall represented his perception of Northern's performance in the United States, while the impending traffic jam reminded him of the changing market conditions he felt the company would soon be facing.

* This case was prepared by Lew G. Brown, University of North Carolina at Greensboro, and Richard Sharpe. Appreciation is expressed to Northern Telecom for its support in developing this case.

Hall had been reviewing the results of a survey conducted by *Communications Week* in the fourth quarter of 1987. The purpose of the study was to identify purchase trends and priorities in the selection of central office telephone switching equipment. The survey respondents were primarily telephone company planners, who were directly involved with selecting and purchasing central office switches.

Hall was interested in the results of the *Communications Week* survey, since he wanted to use the information to prepare for the quarterly meeting of the regional marketing managers, which would be held in early April. These managers were assigned to each of the seven regions into which Northern Telecom had divided the United States for marketing purposes. It was these managers' responsibility to work with the sales force in each region to develop overall marketing strategies. They also worked on quotations and new business development in their regions.

Hall felt the time had come to get the group to step back and assess the overall market situation faced by the Central Office Switching Division and to identify potential changes in the division's marketing strategy.

HISTORY

Northern Telecom, Inc. (NTI), the U.S. subsidiary of Canadian-based Northern Telecom, Ltd (NTL), was originally part of the Bell System. Bell Canada, the parent company of NTL, was a subsidiary of AT&T until the late 1950s, when AT&T was ordered to divest its foreign subsidiaries. Prior to that divestiture and for some time afterward, Northern Telecom was known as Northern Electric, the Canadian counterpart of AT&T's U.S. manufacturing arm, Western Electric.

Despite the divestiture, Northern Telecom still had a captive customer in its parent, Bell Canada; and this relationship gave it roughly 80 percent of the Canadian market. However, Northern's management realized that if it were to survive it would have to design its own equipment. Previously, Northern had made copies of telephone equipment manufactured by Western Electric. To make its own equipment, Northern would have to be able to afford the massive research and development budgets required in the telecommunications equipment industry. The Canadian market alone would not support the required level of investment. Therefore, Northern broadened its market by establishing its presence in the United States in the 1960s and 1970s as a supplier of telephone switches.

A telephone switch is a device that routes individual calls from the person making the call to and through the telephone network. Once in the network, the call is routed from switch to switch until reaching the person being called. Initially, Northern Telecom had sold switches known as "private branch exchanges." These private branch exchanges were switches that were owned by the customer, such as a manufacturing company or a university, and were housed in the customer's facilities. Northern also sold the telephone sets that went with its systems.

Manufacturing and support facilities were established in West Palm Beach, Florida; Atlanta, Georgia; Richardson, Texas; Minnetonka, Minnesota; San Ramon, California; and Nashville, Tennessee, the U.S. headquarters of NTI. Northern's first facility in North Carolina opened in the early 1970s in Creedmoor, a small community north of Durham. It still amazed Hall to think that Northern had grown from 300 people at Creedmoor to 10,000 employees in the Raleigh area in less than a decade.

DEVELOPMENT OF THE DIGITAL SWITCH

Throughout the 1970s, Northern Telecom, in conjunction with Bell-Northern Research (BNR), Northern's R&D equivalent to Bell Labs, developed a process known as *digital* switching. Unlike *analog* signals—a continuous wave of electrical signals varying in amplitude and frequency in response to changes in sound—*digital* signals involve sampling the human voice at a rate of 8,000 times per second and breaking it into a stream of thousands of bits of electrical pulses in a binary code. As the pulses are routed through the network, they are multiplexed, which involves coding each pulse and sending them together in streams. Because each pulse is coded, it can be sent immediately and followed by other pulses from other conversations. This allows transmission of multiple conversations simultaneously on the same line. At each telephone switch, the pulses are either routed to another switch or are multiplexed (put back together) into voice signals and sent to the appropriate terminating party for the call.

Digital technology offered a number of advantages over analog switching, including faster and "cleaner" transmission, lower costs per line, and decreased floor space requirements for switching equipment (a digital switch required less than 50 percent the space of an analog switch).

In 1970, Northern developed the SP-1, a hybrid electromechanical switch whose functions were digitally controlled. In 1975, it introduced the first completely computerized telephone switch, the SL-1. The SL-1 was a significant technological advance over the analog and hybrid switches then in use and became a platform for a high-performance product line that allowed businesses to significantly reduce their telecommunications costs.

With its development of the digital switch, Northern entered the central office switch market. As opposed to private branch exchanges, central office switches are located in the telephone company's facilities. The customer's telephone sets are connected directly to the telephone company's switch, rather than to its own switch located in its facilities. Thus, Northern's customer became the telephone company, rather than individual businesses. Northern installed its first digital central office switch in 1979.

THE BREAKUP OF AT&T AND EQUAL ACCESS

Until the early 1980s, AT&T had a monopoly in the U.S. telephone market, providing local and long distance telephone service through the Bell System to more than 85 percent of the United States. Western Electric was the only supplier of telecommunications equipment to AT&T. The remaining 15 percent of the telephone service market was served by 1,200 "independent" telephone companies. Northern Telecom, along with other equipment vendors, sold its products to these independent telephone companies.

In 1982, through the provisions of the Modification of Final Judgment, which ordered the breakup of AT&T, AT&T divested the 22 local operating companies comprising the Bell System. Although the "new" AT&T retained the long distance portion of the business (called AT&T Communications), the newly formed Bell operating companies provided local telephone service and became distinct entities that were no longer tied to AT&T. As such, the Bell operating companies were now free to buy telecommunications equipment from other suppliers than Western Electric (renamed AT&T Technologies). For Northern Telecom and other vendors, divestiture was the end of a monopoly and the beginning of a highly competitive marketplace.

The Modification of Final Judgment also included the provision that the local telephone companies must provide exchange access to all long distance carriers (such as MCI and US Sprint) "equal in type, quality, and price to that provided to AT&T and its affiliates." To provide "equal access," many telephone exchanges (central office switches) had to be replaced with digital technology switches. Northern Telecom was well positioned at that time for success in the U.S. central office switching market, having a product lead in digital switching and being able to compete in an open market driven by equal access.

Thus began an era for Northern known to some observers in the industry as "one of the great marketing successes of recent times." Northern's sales went from U.S. $2.7 billion in 1983 to $4.2 billion in 1985, and it ranked second only to AT&T.

NORTHERN'S PRODUCTS

Hardware

Northern Telecom's digital central office switching components fell into four categories: systems, remotes, extensions, and lines. "Systems" equated to digital central office switches. Northern had three versions collectively known as the DMS Family (Digital Multiplex System)—the DMS-100, the DMS-100/200, and the DMS-200. The DMS-100 handled local lines only, the DMS-100/200 handled both local lines and toll trunks (trunks were lines between offices carrying long distance traffic), and the DMS-200 handled toll trunks only. Each DMS system had a maximum capacity of 100,000 lines.

Exhibits 1 and 2 show Northern Telecom's U.S. installed equipment base by customer type, by product category, and sales by year.

"Remotes" were digital switching units that extended central office features to remote areas. Northern's remotes ranged in size from 600 to 5,000 lines. Unlike central office systems, which were housed in buildings, remotes were often constructed in environmentally controlled cabinets and placed outside on concrete platforms in areas away from central offices. In addition to extending central office features and services, most remotes had some "stand-alone" capability (i.e., if the host central office switch went out of service for some reason, calls could still be made between customers being served by the same remote). Remotes also provided a cost savings in lines by performing a line-concentrating function, since all the subscribers who were served by a remote in a particular location were wired to the remote, rather than to the central office. Thus, all the customers on the remote were served by a single pair of wires extending from the remote to the central office. Remotes could be located up to 150 miles away from their hosts.

"Extensions" represented hardware additions and software upgrades to existing Northern switches.

"Lines" were reported in thousands; thus, as of year-end 1987, NTI had over 15.5 million lines in-service. A line represented the ability to serve one customer.

EXHIBIT 1 Northern Telecom, Inc., DMS-100 Family Installed Base by Customer Type, as of Year-end 1987

Customer	Systems	Remotes	Extensions	Lines (000)
Bell operating companies	658	248	1,106	9,841
Independent operating companies	434	1,303	1,120	5,686
Total U.S.	1,092	1,551	2,226	15,527

EXHIBIT 2   DMS-100 Family U.S. Sales by Year

Year	Systems	Remotes	Extensions	Lines (000)
1979	5			2
1980	13			75
1981	69	31	19	453
1982	51	86	41	492
1983	83	130	58	798
1984	116	210	152	1,379
1985	266	304	332	3,665
1986	235	359	604	3,962
1987	254	431	1,015	4,701
Total	1,092	1,551	2,226	15,527

Source: Northern Telecom Data.

Software

In addition to hardware, an important portion of Northern Telecom's product line was software. Northern Telecom's DMS switches were driven by both operating software (similar to DOS in a PC environment) and applications software performing specific functions (such as an accounting program to log and bill long distance calls).

Centrex (originally an AT&T brand name) had become a generic term describing any central office-based applications software package combining business-oriented voice, data networking, and control features bundled with intercom calling and offered to end users as a package. As a shared central office-based service, centrex was designed to replace applications served by equipment located at the customer's premises, such as key telephone systems and private branch exchanges. As opposed to investing in telephone switching equipment, the customer simply paid the telephone company a monthly fee per centrex line for access to a multitude of sophisticated business voice and high-speed data features. Call Forwarding and Call Waiting were examples of centrex basic voice features that had been offered to the residential market. Centrex (as an AT&T brand offering) was widespread throughout the 22 local Bell System telephone companies prior to divestiture. Centrex (as a generic product) was a major source of revenue for the telephone operating companies. The companies billed the customers each month for the features they had selected for use in their telephone systems.

AT&T STRATEGY

In the late 1970s, AT&T began what was known as a "migration" strategy, urging business customers to a private branch exchange (on-site) solution for their telecommunications needs, as opposed to a central office-based solution. Implementation of this strategy, which was designed to "bypass" the local telephone companies, intensified during and following divestiture. Telephone companies were directly affected by this strategy, for end users began purchasing their own private branch exchanges directly from AT&T and other vendors, rather than paying the telephone company's monthly per-line fees for central office-based business services. Telephone companies did not like this migration strategy, since it threatened their revenues.

Northern Telecom introduced its digital centrex applications software and was able to capitalize on the resentment telephone companies felt toward AT&T. Meridian Digital Centrex (MDC), Northern's centrex software offering, was introduced in 1982, and sales grew significantly from 1985 to 1987. Exhibit 3 shows NTI's MDC statistics by customer type.

Telephone companies purchased Northern's MDC software for their DMS switches for the purpose of reselling to end users the business services features the applications software provided. The telephone companies often renamed the service for the purpose of developing brand identity and loyalty (much as in the same way Sears bought appliances made by Whirlpool and sold them under the Kenmore label). BellSouth, for example, used John Naismith, the author of *Megatrends,* to advertise centrex as ESSX service. Exhibit 4 provides a

---

EXHIBIT 3 Meridian Digital Centrex Status—U.S.A., as of March 26, 1988 (1Q88)

	In-Service		*Shipped and In-Service*		*In-Service, Shipped, and Firm Orders*		
	Systems	*Lines*	*Systems*	*Lines*	*Systems*	*Lines*	*SRs**
Bell operating companies	594	1,610,166	696	1,956,973	757	2,087,921	44
Independent operating companies	265	292,633	280	387,810	288	401,299	6
Total U.S.	859	1,902,799	976	2,344,783	1,045	2,489,220	50

Numbers are cumulative across the page.
* "SRs"—Schedule Requests; jobs not yet firm orders.

Source: Northern Telecom data.

EXHIBIT 4   Meridian Digital Centrex Major End Users

Vertical Markets	Number of Major MDC End Users	Example
Universities	35	Indiana University
Government:		
—Municipal	30	—City of Las Vegas
—State	20	—Suncom (Florida)
—Federal	11	—Senate/White House
Major businesses	50	Ford Motor Company
Airports	15	Los Angeles Airport
Banks	27	Citicorp
Hospitals	16	Marquette Hospital
Telephone companies	11	NYNEX Headquarters

Source: Northern Telecom Data.

profile of some of the major MDC software end users by vertical markets served. Exhibit 5 provides a breakdown by line size of the Northern's DMS systems that had MDC software.

FINANCIAL PERFORMANCE

Exhibit 6 is a consolidated review of the financial performance of Northern Telecom Limited and its subsidiaries during the period 1979–87. As indicated, revenues for 1987 were $4.8 billion, up 11 percent from 1986. Net earnings for 1987 rose 15 percent to $329 million, up from $287 million in 1986.

EXHIBIT 5   Meridian Digital Centrex Line Size Distribution

Number of MDC Lines	Number of Installed Systems of This Size
1–1,999	658
2,000–9,999	241
10,000 +	71
MDC software, no lines	75
Total in-service, shipped and on order through 1Q88	1,045

Source: Northern Telecom data.

As noted in the bottom portion of Exhibit 6, Northern Telecom Limited had five principal business areas, Central Office Switching, Integrated Business Systems and Terminals, Transmission, Cable and Outside Plant, and Other. Central office switching, Hall's division, accounted for $2.6 billion, or 53 percent of total revenues in 1987.

The Integrated Business Systems and Terminals group sold on-premises customer equipment, such as private branch exchanges, local area networks, data terminals, electronic and key telephone systems, residential telephones, and special applications telephone systems. Many of the products sold by the Business Systems and Terminals group were offered under the Meridian product line name.

The Transmission group and Cable and Outside Plant group sold digital subscriber carrier systems, microwave radio transmission systems, fiber optic systems and cable, and network management systems.

Exhibit 7 presents a summary of Northern's income statements by geographic area for the 1985 to 1987 period. Although sales outside of the United States and Canada represented only a small percentage of total sales, Northern had scored a major breakthrough in 1985 by landing a five-year, $250 million contract with Nippon Telegraph and Telephone (NTT) and becoming the first foreign company to sell switches to NTT.

NTL had 48,778 employees as of year-end 1987, and 1987 earnings per share were $1.39.

THE CHANGING MARKETPLACE

Hall felt that Northern's success through the 1980s had been driven by five major factors:

1. A sustained product development lead in digital central office switching technology (AT&T did not introduce a digital central office switch until 1983).
2. Access to a huge market that had previously been restricted due to monopolistic constraints.
3. A willingness in that new market to be served by another vendor than AT&T (AT&T had moved from the position of supplier and parent organization to that of a competitor).
4. Equal access legislation requiring product replacement of old technology exchanges with new digital switches.
5. The ability to dilute the effect of AT&T's migration strategy on the Bell operating companies by providing them with revenue-generating features in MDC applications software for the DMS.

EXHIBIT 6 Consolidated 11-Year Review

Northern Telecom, Ltd., and Subsidiaries ($ millions)

	1987	1986	1985	1984	1983	1981	1979	1977
Earnings and related data:								
Revenues	$4,853.5	$4,383.6	$4,262.9	$3,374.0	$2,680.2	$2,146.1	$1,625.1	$1,149.7
Cost of revenues	2,895.8	2,730.5	2,078.9	2,074.1	1,713.3	1,542.5	1,117.0	821.4
Selling, general, and administrative expense	917.8	764.6	701.9	603.2	454.8	300.1	234.9	149.1
Research and development expense	587.5	474.5	430.0	333.1	263.2	151.8	117.6	64.2
Depreciation on plant and equipment	264.1	247.3	203.3	162.8	126.6	100.8	77.9	29.1
Provision for income taxes	141.5	127.9	132.8	120.3	79.3	29.8	30.3	45.5
Earnings before extraordinary items	347.2	313.2	299.2	255.8	183.2	92.1	97.4	76.3
Net earnings applicable to common shares	328.8	286.6	273.8	243.2	216.7	105.4	97.4	80.2
Earnings per revenue dollar (cents)	6.8	6.5	6.4	7.2	8.1	4.9	6.0	7.0
Earnings per common share (dollars):								
—before extraordinary items	1.39	1.23	1.18	1.06	0.83	0.45	0.53	0.48
—after extraordinary items	1.39	1.23	1.18	1.06	0.98	0.50	0.53	0.51
Dividends per share (dollars)	0.23	0.20	0.18	0.16	0.16	0.14	0.12	0.11
Financial position at December 31:								
Working capital	570.7	1,188.7	933.9	859.0	563.4	421.6	477.4	307.3
Plant and equipment (at cost)	2,345.6	1,975.2	1,737.5	1,458.0	1,152.2	829.8	602.4	356.9
Accumulated depreciation	1,084.2	877.3	672.4	591.5	506.4	355.0	237.8	184.3
Total assets	4,869.0	3,961.1	3,490.0	3,072.9	2,309.4	1,809.4	1,620.8	698.8
Long-term debt	224.8	101.1	107.6	100.2	102.3	207.5	165.0	48.0
Redeemable retractable preferred shares	153.9	281.0	277.5	293.6	—			
Redeemable preferred shares	73.3	73.3	73.3	—	—			
Common shareholders' equity	2,333.3	1,894.9	1,614.6	1,379.8	1,178.3	719.5	793.5	431.0
Return on common shareholders' equity	15.6%	16.3%	18.3%	19.0%	21.7%	15.7%	14.6%	19.4%
Capital expenditures	416.7	303.8	457.3	437.3	305.7	174.9	148.4	42.1
Employees at December 31	48,778	46,202	46,549	46,993	39,318	35,444	33,301	24,962

Quarterly Financial Data (unaudited) ($ millions, except per share figures)

	4th Qtr.		3rd Qtr.		2nd Qtr.		1st Qtr.	
	1987	1986	1987	1986	1987	1986	1987	1986
Revenues	$1,299.1	$1,314.4	$1,158.1	$1,032.2	$1,253.0	$1,067.4	$1,143.3	$969.6
Gross profit	584.9	536.1	479.1	404.5	489.9	389.4	403.8	323.1
Net earnings	140.0	132.2	69.5	66.0	77.6	64.9	60.1	50.1
Net earnings applicable to common shares	136.0	125.9	66.2	59.4	72.9	58.0	53.7	43.3
Earnings per common share	0.57	0.54	0.28	0.25	0.31	0.25	0.23	0.19
Weighted average number of common shares outstanding (thousands)	236,444	234,767	236,024	234,199	235,573	223,650	235,237	233,154

Revenues by Principal Product Lines ($ millions)

	1987	1986	1985	1984	1983
Central office switching	$2,577.2	$2,230.2	$2,141.3	$1,452.9	$ 981.9
Integrated business systems and terminals	1,302.0	1,284.7	1,256.6	1,162.9	985.8
Transmission	498.6	468.1	431.2	385.1	376.3
Cable and outside plant	408.2	348.4	373.4	314.9	275.5
Other telecommunications	67.5	51.5	60.4	58.9	60.7
Total	$4,853.5	$4,383.6	$4,262.9	$3,374.0	$2,680.2

EXHIBIT 7   Northern Telecom Ltd., Income by Geographic Area, 1985–87
($ millions)

	1987	*1986*	*1985*
Total revenues:			
United States	$3,103.0	$2,965.6	$2,967.3
Canada	2,140.3	1,771.1	1,792.8
Other	272.1	245.9	215.2
Less—inter-area transfers	(661.9)	(599.0)	(712.4)
Total all revenues	$4,853.5	$4,383.6	$4,262.9
Operating earnings:			
United States	$787.0	$674.2	$699.6
Canada	491.6	383.8	319.8
Other	(11.1)	18.8	12.0
Total all operating earnings	$1,267.5	$1,076.8	$1,031.4
Less—Research and development	($587.5)	($474.5)	($430.0)
Less—General corporate expenses	($227.6)	($188.3)	($179.3)
Net Operating Earnings	$452.4	$414.0	$422.1
Plus—Other income	36.3	27.1	9.9
Earnings before tax	$488.7	$441.1	$432.0
Identifiable assets:			
United States	$1,807.2	$1,749.6	$1,868.2
Canada	1,297.5	1,189.3	1,389.8
Other	181.1	210.1	264.2
Corporate assets*	332.4	460.3	204.6

* Corporate assets are principally cash and short-term investments and corporate plant and equipment.

Source: Northern Telecom, Ltd., 1987 annual report.

Despite Northern's success, however, Hall realized that the marketplace was changing and that Northern needed to reconsider its strategy to respond to these changes.

AT&T's 5ESS

Demand for digital switches had exceeded supply in the early 1980s, and AT&T had not entered the digital switching marketplace until 1983, with the 5ESS switch. As a result, Northern Telecom had a substantial competitive lead in both product/feature development and

EXHIBIT 8 Northern DMS and AT&T 5ESS System Shipments by Half Year

	Northern	AT&T
1H85	144	169
2H85	145	141
1H86	108	152
2H86	139	144
1H87	128	135
2H87	127	130

Source: Northern Telecom data; AT&T estimates.

in marketing its products to the telephone companies. AT&T had found itself in the unusual position of being an industry technology "follower," rather than the industry leader. Moreover, because of its monopoly position, AT&T had not been concerned previously with having to market its products.

Exhibit 8 compares Northern's DMS and AT&T's 5ESS shipments in half-year increments starting in 1985. Although only 13 of AT&T's 5ESS units were in-service by the end of 1983, with an additional 72 being placed in-service in 1984, pent-up demand in the telephone companies for additional products to help satisfy equal access requirements and the desire to have multiple suppliers helped sales of the 5ESS grow rapidly. Moreover, Northern experienced delivery problems in 1985, with one of its remote switch products and performance problems with a particular release of operating system software. Combined with the strong market demand for digital technology, these events helped to assure that AT&T's 5ESS would be a successful product. The U.S. telephone digital switching market became a two-supplier arena.

AT&T claimed to have 800 5ESS systems, 660 remotes, and 15 million lines in-service as of September 1987 (these figures included some switches located outside the United States and some within the AT&T system itself). Northern Telecom had 1,092 systems, 1,551 remotes, and 15.5 million lines in-service as of the end of 1987.

Pricing

Due to equal access, demand for digital switches exceeded supply from 1982–86. During this period, delivery was the primary determinant of which vendor would be chosen. Volume sales agreements negotiated with each regional or local telephone company for multiple changeouts of old technology switches were the norm, rather than the exception. Price was not a key selection criterion.

However, with supply exceeding the demand for digital switches from 1986 onward, the situation had become one of competitive bidding for each switch replacement, with bidding parties offering aggressive discounts. The objective was to win the initial system even at the sake of short-term profits, for winning the switch meant additional opportunities for revenue through software and hardware upgrades and extensions.

In 1987, the industry average price of a digital switch was estimated at $326 per line of capacity. However, discounts of up to 30 percent on this price were not uncommon. A switch with a 20,000 line capacity might be bid in the $4.5 million range. Switch prices ranged from $1 million to $10 million, with an average price of $2.5 million.

Hall had concerns that the discounts the vendors were offering often resulted in the winner leaving large sums of money on the table (e.g., coming in with a bid at $500,000 less than the next lowest competitor, when all that would have been necessary to win the switch was a $100,000 discount). Moreover, Hall did not want bids to be so low that the telephone companies would refuse to accept higher bids.

The End of Equal Access

In addition to increased competition and pricing pressures from AT&T, other factors were affecting the market. With the completion of the equal access process, telephone company construction budgets were declining 3–4 percent annually. Along with the decline in capital budgets was a corresponding increase in the expense budgets. As a result of this shift, telephone companies were expected to allocate more budget dollars toward upgrading equipment and less toward the purchase of new switches.

The Analog Switch Replacement Market

Following equal access, the next major determinant of growth in the U.S. telecommunications market was replacement of analog switches. These switches were analog stored program control (software driven) AT&T switches that were installed in the late 1960s and the 1970s. Exhibit 9 shows historical information and projections of the central office switch market by technology from 1988 through 1991. As indicated in Exhibit 9, analog switches accounted for 57 million lines of the total installed base in 1987, or 46 percent of the market, compared to a

EXHIBIT 9 Central Office Equipment Market by Technology, Total Market (thousands of lines)

| | 1986 | 1987 | Projected | | | |
			1988	1989	1990	1991
Installed base:						
Digital	27,048	36,560	45,230	54,072	62,693	72,057
Analog	56,143	57,022	57,426	57,854	56,750	54,800
Other	38,175	31,322	25,613	19,826	15,933	12,293
Total	121,366	124,904	128,269	131,752	135,376	139,150
Percent:						
Digital	22.3	29.3	35.3	41.0	46.3	51.8
Analog	46.3	45.6	44.8	43.9	41.9	39.4
Other	31.4	25.1	19.9	15.1	11.8	8.8
Demand:						
Digital	10,066	9,508	8,670	8,844	8,620	9,365
Analog	1,591	881	417	429	36	0
Total	11,657	10,389	9,087	9,273	8,656	9,365

Total Bell Operating Companies

	1986	1987	1988	1989	1990	1991
Installed base:						
Digital	14,509	21,341	27,389	33,553	39,997	46,966
Analog	53,899	54,729	55,114	55,451	54,317	52,379
Other	25,246	20,114	15,998	11,891	9,077	6,648
Total	93,654	96,184	98,501	100,895	103,391	105,993
Percent:						
Digital	15.5	22.2	27.8	33.3	38.7	44.3
Analog	57.6	56.9	56.0	55.0	52.5	49.4
Other	27.0	20.9	17.2	11.8	8.8	6.2
Demand:						
Digital	6,904	6,832	6,048	6,165	6,443	6,969
Analog	1,530	830	385	338	0	0
Total	8,434	7,662	6,432	6,502	6,443	6,969

Total Independent Operating Companies

	1986	1987	1988	1989	1990	1991
Installed base:						
Digital	12,539	15,219	17,841	20,519	22,696	25,091
Analog	2,244	2,293	2,312	2,403	2,433	2,421
Other	12,929	11,208	9,615	7,935	6,856	5,645
Total	27,712	28,720	29,768	30,857	31,895	33,157
Percent:						
Digital	45.2	53.0	59.9	66.5	71.0	75.7
Analog	8.1	7.9	7.8	7.8	7.6	7.3
Other	46.7	39.1	32.3	25.7	21.4	17.0
Demand:						
Digital	3,162	2,676	2,622	2,679	2,177	2,396
Analog	61	51	32	91	36	0
Total	3,223	2,727	2,654	2,770	2,213	2,396

Source: Northern Business Information, *Central Office Equipment Market: 1987 Edition.*

total of 36 million digital lines. The "Other" category represents older analog switches, which were electromechanical switches (no software).

Numerous factors were involved in analog replacement, which was estimated to be a $30 billion market over the next 30 years. Unlike other switches that had to be replaced, analog switches had been upgraded to support equal access requirements, since they were software driven. With depreciation service lives of 15–20 years, they would remain in the network until the early 1990s, assuming that the depreciation rates and regulatory positions did not change (switch replacement required approval from the appropriate state public utility commission). The latest versions of these switches offered a comprehensive set of centrex features, and they were large in terms of line size (30,000 to 55,000 lines). As such, a digital replacement switch would require both sufficient capacity and an equivalent set of centrex features.

These analog switches were usually housed in "wire centers," which were simply buildings that housed more than one type of central office switch and were typically located in high-growth metropolitan areas. Northern had a number of strategies to establish a presence in these wire centers, in the hope that this initial presence would provide a competitive advantage when an analog switch became available for digital replacement. Other vendors were marketing adjuncts for the analog switches, which were enhancements designed to prolong their life, while these same vendors worked to develop competitive digital switches. As such, these adjuncts were basically "stopgap" measures designed to meet a particular need and to buy additional time for R&D switch development.

ISDN

Beyond the replacement of analog switches, the next phase of telecommunications technology was called ISDN (Integrated Services Digital Network). ISDN would allow the transmission of voice, data, and video simultaneously over the same facilities. With existing technology, voice, high-speed data, and video had to be transmitted separately or over separate lines. While business telecommunications in 1988 were 90 percent voice and 10 percent data, this ration was predicted to move to 50 percent/50 percent. Cost, space, and time constraints would require that voice and data be integrated over one network.

ISDN would also allow standard interfaces between different pieces of equipment, such as computers; and it would free end users from concerns about whether new equipment from one vendor would interface with equipment made by another vendor, which an end user might already own.

Although universal standards for ISDN had yet to be resolved, useful applications were already apparent. Since ISDN phones were designed to display the calling number and the name assigned to the number on a small screen simultaneous with ringing, the party being called would be able to know where the call was coming from prior to answering. This call screening ability would provide opportunities to enhance 911 services (police, fire department, rescue squad, and the like) by immediately identifying the calling party's location and other useful information (such as a known medical condition or the location of the nearest fire hydrant) and by efficiently routing both the call and the information to all parties involved. A person served by ISDN could talk to her banker while looking at her account information on a computer terminal and send data instructions to move funds, simultaneously, on the same line.

ISDN was flexible, in that, from any ISDN telephone jack, one could connect a computer terminal, personal computer, file server, printer, facsimile or telex machine, or video camera. Equipment could be moved to any location without having to worry if a specific kind of cable were available. The various pieces of equipment could share a common ISDN loop for data and voice transmission, reducing or eliminating the need for modems and multiplexers. Data on an ISDN network could be transmitted at a rate of up to six times faster than standard analog networks but at a comparable cost.

Northern was positioning ISDN as its premier Meridian Digital Centrex software offering, since it offered both business voice features and high-speed data capabilities over a single line. Northern's strategy was to "migrate" end users from MDC to ISDN, stressing that existing MDC feature capabilities could serve customer needs today while ISDN standards and applications were being developed by industry regulatory organizations and other telecommunications equipment and computer vendors. In addition, MDC integrated with ISDN, with ISDN combining existing voice and data services while adding additional new features and sophisticated applications.

AT&T, on the other hand, had been advertising ISDN heavily to end users and was attempting to position it as a technologically superior *replacement* to centrex, rather than as a centrex enhancement. AT&T was pursuing this strategy since BRCS, its digital centrex offering, was perceived as being much less "feature-rich" than its analog centrex systems or Northern's Meridian Digital Centrex.

Northern Telecom placed the first successful ISDN phone call in the United States in November 1987, and it had a number of DMS sites inservice offering ISDN capabilities. In addition, both Northern Telecom and AT&T had numerous ISDN field trials and commercial applications scheduled with telephone companies and business end users throughout the country at specific sites during the 1988–90 time frame.

COMPETITION

In addition to the changing market and technological environments, Northern faced a number of strong competitors. Replacement of analog switches and ISDN were two potential markets attracting other equipment companies into the U.S. digital central office telecommunications market. Also, most of the telephone companies were interested in having a third equipment supplier, in addition to AT&T and Northern Telecom, to ensure that pricing and product development remained highly competitive.

Another potential opportunity/threat for Northern was that the seven Regional Holding Companies (RHCs) had petitioned Judge Green to lift the restrictions barring them from providing information services, going into the long distance business, and manufacturing terminals and central office switches through direct subsidiaries or joint ventures, or both.

Finally, although the level of competition was increasing, the number of competitors was actually decreasing. In 1979, there had been 30 major telecommunications equipment manufacturing companies in the developed world. Estimates were, however, that this number would decrease to 15 by 1989. Some experts estimated that a firm needed a 10 percent worldwide market share to survive. The worldwide telecommunications construction market was estimated to be $109 billion for 1988, up from $100 billion in 1987, with the United States accounting for 22 percent of this market.

Following is a discussion of some of Northern's competitors and the inroads each had made into the Bell operating companies.

Siemens

Siemens, a West German conglomerate, had sales of 8 billion DMs for its telecommunications segment in 1987 (sales for the entire company in 1987 were U.S. $20 billion). Seventy-three percent of Siemens' total sales for the year were from Germany and Europe, with 10 percent from North America.

The headquarters for Siemens's U.S. telecommunications division was in Boca Raton, Florida. An R&D facility was also located at Boca Raton, while manufacturing sites were located at Cherry Hill, New Jersey, and Hauppauge, New York. Siemens had 25,000 employees in the United States.

Siemens' digital central office offering was the EWSD. It was available in three versions: DE3, with a maximum capacity of 7,500 lines; DE4, with a maximum capacity of 30,000 lines; and DE5, with a maximum capacity of 100,000 lines.

Siemens had announced ambitious feature roll out plans for its offerings, promising both centrex and ISDN feature parity with both AT&T and Northern Telecom. However, whether it could effectively leapfrog the software development intervals incurred by the industry leaders remained to be seen.

Siemens had made inroads with five of the seven RHCs: Ameritech, BellSouth, Bell Atlantic, NYNEX, and Southwestern Bell. Siemens' progress had been based primarily on both competitive pricing and the desire of the Bell Operating Companies to increase competition in the central office switch market.

In spite of its recent success, industry consultants cited operational/maintenance problems with the EWSD regarding system reliability, architecture, and compliance to Bellcore standards (Bell Communications Research, or "Bellcore," was a standards organization jointly owned by the seven RHCs). However, heavy R&D efforts were underway to resolve these issues at Boca Raton, and Siemens was fully committed to adapting its products to U.S. market specifications.

Siemens had a $2.1 million contract with West Virginia University to develop computer-based training courses in the operation of EWSD central office equipment. In terms of joint ventures and acquisitions, the company purchased 80 percent of GTE's foreign transmissions operations in 1986.

Ericsson

Ericsson, a Swedish-based telecommunications company, had consolidated international sales of U.S. $5.5 billion in 1987. Europe and Sweden accounted for 84 percent of the geographic distribution of total sales for the year, with the United States and Canada contributing 7 percent. Like Siemens, Ericsson was attempting to crack the hold that Northern Telecom and AT&T shared on the U.S. central office switch market. Ericsson had targeted the Bell Operating Company market in BellSouth, NYNEX, Southwestern Bell, and US West.

Ericsson's digital central office offering was the AXE 10. Ericsson had already installed the AXE in 64 countries, had a worldwide installed base of over 11 million lines, and dominated markets in the developing world. Like Siemens, Ericsson had announced aggressive feature roll out plans (bypassing years of software development by AT&T Technologies and Bell-Northern Research), which it might not be able to deliver.

The AXE was manufactured in 16 countries and was being made available by Ericsson's Network Systems Division in Richardson, Texas. No plans were underway to construct manufacturing facilities for the AXE in the United States, although Ericsson was considered to have superior skills in setting up manufacturing plants in foreign countries and in training local workers for skilled jobs.

Ericsson had made a number of recent strategic moves intended to strengthen its position in the United States. The company had reorganized by regions to serve more effectively the RHC markets; moreover, it had reorganized marketing for the division into the functional areas of market development, marketing communications, systems engineering, and marketing systems. Plans had been announced for a Technical Training Center at the company's U.S. headquarters in Richardson, Texas. In addition, Ericsson had announced that it would be working with IBM to develop private networking capabilities.

NEC

NEC had $13 billion in sales in U.S. dollars for 1987, $4 billion of which was from its "communications" segment. Geographic sales distribution percentages were classified as "domestic" (Japan) at 67 percent and "overseas" at 33 percent.

NEC's digital central office offering was the NEAX61E. The switch was primarily an ISDN adjunct that interfaced analog systems and grew into a full central office. As such, it was basically an interim offering that was designed to extend the life of analog switches while buying time to improve the product in the hopes of having a competitive offering already when analog replacement began. NEC claimed that the NEAX61 was serving 4.8 million lines in over 250 sites in 40 countries.

NEC's U.S. headquarters was located in Irving, Texas, where production of the system was scheduled to begin by mid-1988. NEC had made inroads with four of the seven RHCs—Bell Atlantic, NYNEX, Pacific Telesis, and US West.

The company had recently announced plans for a Switching Technology Center in Irving, dedicated to developing software for central office switches and customer premises equipment. A second facility in San Jose, California, would develop software for intelligent transport networks, transmission systems, data communications, and network management systems. NEC claimed that it was moving its software development closer to its customers.

A major problem that NEC had to overcome was one of perception. NEC's first attempt to enter the U.S. market with the NEAX61 in the early 1980s met with little success. The product was highly touted, launched, and subsequently withdrawn due to numerous performance issues. Many industry experts felt that NEC was again entering the market prematurely with a product that was not powerful enough to meet U.S. requirements to support advanced business features or large capacities.

Stromberg-Carlson

Stromberg-Carlson was a division of Plessy, a British telecommunications corporation. Plessy had 1987 revenues of $2.45 billion from all product lines. Because Stromberg was a division, reliable data on its 1987 financial performance was not available. Stromberg-Carlson's product offering was the DCO (Digital Central Office). It was available in three versions: the DCO-CS, which was a toll version of the DCO (7,000 trunks, maximum); the DCO-SE (a 1,080 line switch designed to serve as a rural central office); and the DCO (32,000 lines, maximum). In addition, Stromberg-Carlson offered a full line of remotes, ranging in size from 90 lines to 10,000 lines.

Unlike Siemens, Ericsson, and NEC, Stromberg-Carlson had been a player in the U.S. telecommunications marketplace for a number of years. Stromberg was a primary supplier to the independent operating companies and was committed to maintaining strong ties with them. Stromberg's strategy was to target small to mid-size central offices (5,000–12,000 lines), focusing on rural applications. While Stromberg's lack of a large switch limited the market it could address, its niche strategy had served it well over the years, in that it could economically provide digital central capabilities in small line sizes.

However, Stromberg was now trying to crack the Bell operating company market as well. The company had made inroads with Bell-South and Pacific Telesis and had recently signed a volume supply agreement with South Central Bell for the 1989–90 time frame.

Stromberg-Carlson's U.S. headquarters and DCO manufacturing facility were located in Lake Mary, Florida (a suburb of Orlando). While Stromberg stated that it had a manufacturing capacity of 1 million lines per year at the Lake Mary facility, less than half of this capability was being used.

In response to its agreement with South Central Bell, Stromberg-Carlson had recently opened sales offices in Birmingham, Alabama. The company had a small installation force and was negotiating with AT&T to arrange to install some of its switches in South Central Bell.

Stromberg-Carlson shipped its 1,000th remote in December 1987 and placed its 2 millionth line in-service in January 1988. Two hundred switches, 400 remotes, and 400,000 lines were shipped by Stromberg-Carlson to the U.S. market in 1987.

Alcatel N.V.

Alcatel was established in France in 1985 as a subsidiary of Alcatel S.A. In December 1986, the firm's present name was adopted with the transfer of assets from its parent, Compagnie General d'Electricite (CGE). At the same time, CGE and International Telephone and Telegraph (ITT) combined their telecommunications activities, with ITT assuming 37 percent ownership of Alcatel. Alcatel offered digital switches, cable and fiber optic transmission networks, and radio and satellite transmission systems. 1986 sales were 10.6 million French francs.

The ITT deal allowed Alcatel to gain a position in West Germany, Italy, and Spain. While Alcatel had been insignificant in the world telecommunications market, the arrangement with ITT set the stage for it to become a major equipment manufacturer. Alcatel's strengths in transmission facilities offset ITT's weakness in this area. ITT contributed a dominant position in switching throughout the European market. Although the acquisition introduced Alcatel to the U.S. market, due to ITT's presence, it was not clear what effect this would have on the U.S. market. ITT had been working unsuccessfully for several years to develop a switch for the U.S. market.

CONCLUSION

Musing over the status of Northern's potential competitors, Hall Miller's gaze returned to the magazine on his desk. Overall, the *Communications Week* study had given Northern high marks relative to most of

EXHIBIT 10   Summary of Vendor Performance Rankings by Bell Operating Company Respondents

	AT&T	Ericsson	NEC	Northern Telecom	Siemens	Stromberg-Carlson
Initial cost	3.12	3.37	3.42	3.83	3.51	3.76
Life cycle cost	3.55	3.26	3.29	3.53	3.48	3.26
Strength of financial backing	4.66	3.48	3.74	4.24	4.05	3.05
Availability	3.90	3.36	3.29	4.17	3.40	3.56
Service/support	4.07	3.21	2.97	3.39	3.22	3.50
Reliability	4.06	3.31	3.08	3.52	3.47	3.24
Delivery	3.76	3.18	2.80	3.71	3.21	3.39
Experience in industry	4.88	3.97	3.34	4.29	3.78	3.91
High-technology company	4.63	3.77	3.69	4.28	4.08	3.23
Sound technical documentation	4.32	3.24	2.67	3.50	3.37	3.10
Breadth of product line	4.07	3.24	3.14	3.90	3.33	2.80
International experience	3.19	4.08	3.83	3.58	4.20	2.64
Long-term commitment to R&D	4.44	3.81	3.83	3.99	3.91	3.04

Scale of 1–5: 5 = excellent; 1 = poor. N = 497.

Source: *Communications Week.*

EXHIBIT 11   Summary of Vendor Performance Ranking by Independent Operating Company
Respondents

	AT&T	Ericsson	NEC	Northern Telecom	Siemens	Stromberg-Carlson
Initial cost	2.40	2.67	3.70	3.67	3.12	3.96
Life cycle cost	3.24	2.74	3.17	3.71	3.04	3.61
Strength of financial backing	4.65	3.31	3.69	4.34	3.65	3.50
Availability	3.56	2.61	3.22	4.06	2.93	4.03
Service/support	3.79	2.81	2.98	3.81	3.02	3.75
Reliability	4.23	2.80	3.41	4.08	3.25	3.63
Delivery	3.46	2.61	3.16	3.83	2.91	3.80
Experience in industry	4.74	3.27	3.55	4.58	3.62	4.19
High-technology company	4.72	3.35	3.93	4.45	3.84	3.72
Sound technical documentation	4.47	2.78	2.95	4.08	3.32	3.63
Breadth of product line	4.16	2.83	3.43	4.12	3.27	3.47
International experience	3.84	3.48	4.04	3.84	4.03	3.27
Long-term commitment to R&D	4.67	3.21	3.80	4.29	3.69	3.57

Scale of 1–5: 5 = excellent; 1 = poor. N = 1,047.

Source: *Communications Week.*

the competitors. However, there were shortcomings in particular areas
he wanted to address. (Exhibits 10 and 11 contain the results of the
study, segmented by Bell and independent operating company respondents.)

In terms of the changing market and increased competition, Hall felt
Northern had a competitive advantage, in that the company had the
largest installed base of digital switches of any vendor. This would
help generate revenue through hardware and software extensions and
new features prior to the replacement of analog switches. However,
Hall had seen AT&T's 5ESS shipments reach parity in a relatively
short time, and it seemed that competitors were popping up everywhere. In addition, 1988 MDC sales had been sluggish. Hall felt this
was largely due to customer confusion resulting from AT&T's hype of
ISDN.

Hall glanced out the window towards the Raleigh-Durham Airport.
It was 5:20 P.M., and the highway was packed with traffic. He decided
that he would develop a presentation for the regional marketing managers that outlined the division's position and presented a number of
possible changes in the marketing strategy that the division could
consider. This would generate discussion and help the group focus on
the options that needed more in-depth study before a decision could be
made.

Hall closed the magazine and placed it, along with several other pieces of information that had been gathered for him, in his briefcase. Despite the traffic and the work, he had to get home in time for his daughter's 6 P.M. soccer game. Perhaps he would be able to work on his analysis after supper.

Case 5–12   *J. W. Thornton Ltd.**

"Business is going great—I wish I knew why," laughed Peter Thornton, joint managing director of J. W. Thornton Ltd., a leading manufacturer and retailer of high-quality confectionery. Certainly there appeared reasons for his good humor; while the dismal economic situation in the United Kingdom was causing most retailers to show little volume growth and declining margins, four months into the financial year Thornton's sales from its 148 shops were 4 percent up on budget, and profits were even further ahead (Exhibit 1).

EXHIBIT 1   Some General U.K. Economic Indicators, 1970–1980

Year	Retail Sales	Sales of CTNs*	Company Profits†	Cost of Living Index
1970	100	100	100	100
1971	108	107	113	109
1972	133	121	126	117
1973	151	131	150	128
1974	175	155	160	148
1975	208	191	171	184
1976	238	223	219	213
1977	271	257	265	251
1978	310	285	300	274
1979	345	297	397	311
1980	389	351	468	360

* Retail sales of confectioners, tobacconists, and newspaper shops.
† Before providing for depreciation and stock appreciation.

Source: *U.K. Annual Abstract of Statistics.*

* Prepared by Peter Doyle, Bradford University, England. Copyright © 1981 by Professor P. Doyle. Reproduced with permission.

Nevertheless there were many decisions that needed to be taken on how to move the business forward. In particular it was not obvious how many new stores the company should aim to open, whether franchising offered an effective method of long-term growth, or whether the company should seek to manufacture confectionery for a broader range of retailers at home and overseas. Further, while the current situation looked satisfactory, in the recent past it had appeared much less rosy, and the directors felt that major mistakes had been made on pricing policy, advertising, and overhead cost control which had significantly curtailed profit performance. The board of directors, in discussing these issues, had identified the need for a corporate strategy to provide a longer-term perspective than that of the annual budget. Mr. Peter, as he was known in the company, had agreed and had offered to present a paper for the next meeting outlining his ideas about the strategic direction for the business.

COMPANY BACKGROUND

The company was founded in 1911 by J. W. Thornton, who began making hard-boiled sweets in a coke stove in the basement of his shop in Sheffield. He was soon joined by his two sons Norman and Stanley, who remain on the board to this day. In the years that followed, the company opened more shops and gradually expanded its product range. In 1925 the company's Special Toffee was developed which is still the shops' best-selling product. Another milestone was Stanley and Norman's decision to develop a really high-quality range of chocolates. During a continental holiday in 1953 the brothers visited the Basle School for Swiss Chocolatiers and recruited one of the top students. The result was the Thornton range of Continental Chocolates, which now sells 600 tons annually. By 1939 Thornton's had expanded to 35 shops in the Midlands and North of England. Further rapid growth followed the end of confectionery rationing in 1952, and advertising and seasonal promotions gradually increased consumer awareness of the Thornton name. By 1980 the company had over 1,000 employees, two factories, and 148 shops.

The company had always emphasized certain features. Most important was the commitment to product freshness and quality. Unwillingness to hazard the business's hard-won reputation in these areas accounted for management's long reluctance to sell confectionery outside their own shops despite many requests from interested retailers. This philosophy, together with the desire to develop a distinctive specialist confectionery image, also made them increasingly reluctant to buy products for their shops other than those produced from their factories. Bought-in goods (mainly greeting cards) now account for only five percent of shop turnover. A consequence was that the shops continued with a narrow range of products—three basic lines: chocolate, toffee, and hard-boiled sweets represented over 90 percent of sales.

The company has continued to emphasize traditional values. The shops have changed relatively little over the years, and there has been no major product introduction since the range of Continental Chocolates over 25 years earlier. Advertising made much of the products being "all made in the good old-fashioned way." Finally it remained very much a family business; all the shareholders and all eight members of the board including the president, the chairman, the two managing directors, and the company secretary were Thorntons. Hence the practice within the company of calling the directors Mr. Tony, Mr. Peter, etc., was not just quaint; it was necessary.

After the mid-1960s Mr. Norman's three sons Tony, Peter, and John, together with Mr. Stanley's son Michael, took an increasingly large part in running the business. In 1979 Peter and John became joint managing directors when Tony moved up from managing director to chairman. Previously both Peter and John had shared responsibility for the manufacturing side of the business. Under the new structure Peter's main sphere of responsibility covered marketing and retail, and John looked after manufacturing and product development. Stanley and Norman remained on the board as president and consultant, respectively.

Until the mid-1970s the company had seen almost uninterrupted progress (see Exhibit 2). Probably the peak year was in 1973, when the

EXHIBIT 2   J. W. Thornton Ltd., Selected Performance Data (£000)

Financial Year	Sales (excluding VAT)	Gross Profit	Pretax Net Profit	Total Assets*	Stock-holders' Funds	Number of Shops
1969–70	£ 2,262	£1,240	£237	£1,218	£ 809	107
1970–71	2,222	1,177	270	1,305	885	110
1971–72	2,783	1,517	336	1,503	1,043	122
1972–73	3,461	1,869	544	1,896	1,241	126
1973–74	4,270	2,263	581	2,373	1,488	130
1974–75	5,653	2,802	576	2,931	1,735	128
1975–76	7,091	3,824	709	3,425	2,002	130
1976–77	8,821	4,455	552	4,228	2,217	130
1977–78	10,887	5,532	704	4,749	2,661	132
1978–79	12,826	6,714	946	6,201	2,594	138
1979–80	15,551	8,360	668	7,515	3,113	148

* Assets valued on historic cost basis.

Source: Annual reports.

company earned a pretax margin of 16 percent and a return on net worth of 44 percent. Then, like many other retailers, business got more difficult as the slower growth of consumer expenditures and the rapid rise in inflation hit margins and cash flow.

RETAILING IN THE UNITED KINGDOM

The postwar years saw remarkable changes in the pattern of retailing in the United Kingdom. A number of forces created the stimuli for change. Car registrations grew from 2.5 million in 1950 to 13.5 million in 1973 when the majority of households had a car, which both increased their mobility and enabled them to carry more shopping in one trip. A second feature was the dispersal of population from major towns. While the drift to the suburbs was less dramatic than in the United States, it did result in a noticeable shift in retail buying power from the inner urban areas to the outer suburbs. A third factor was the rise in female employment, which increased the pressure for longer shop-opening hours and for facilities for shopping with the family. Finally, the overall level of spending rose sharply as a result of both a larger population and, more importantly, rising income levels. Real disposable income doubled between 1950 and 1980.

The most important responses to these stimuli were:

1. The growth of self-service across many sectors of retailing. Self-service offered savings both to the retailer and the shopper. In food, for example, supermarkets increased from only 500 in 1950 to over 30,000 in 1973.
2. A trend toward fewer, larger shops. The total number of food shops, for example, fell by one-half between 1960 and 1980, but the development of self-service in particular meant that on average the newer shops had much larger floor space.
3. Economies of scale in buying and marketing led to increased concentration in retailing. The major chains increased their share of trade at the expense of independent shops in all sectors of retailing.
4. A consequence of this greater retailing concentration was increasing bargaining power over manufacturers. Manufacturers' margins were squeezed as the larger retailers demanded their own private brands and larger discounts.
5. The extension of intertype retailing competition, or "scrambled merchandising." Retailers sought to strengthen their margins by broadening their merchandise assortments. Food retailers diversified into nonfoods, and nonfood businesses added on food lines.
6. The development of out-of-town retailing and the growth of new types of shops, such as supermarkets, shopping mall boutiques, dis-

count stores, and catalog showrooms. Many innovations took place during this period and grew rapidly at the expense of retailers which had reached the maturity state of the institutional life cycle.

7. Working wives, greater car ownership, and new types of mass merchandising encouraged the trend toward once-weekly one-stop shopping, increasingly at the large suburban superstore with ample parking.

After 1973, competition in retailing toughened noticeably, and retailers' profit margins halved between 1973 and 1980. The causes were the stagnation in consumer spending after 1973 and the rapid escalation in inflation. Larger retailers responded to the lack of market growth by price cutting to expand or maintain market shares, pressuring manufacturers even further for discounts and financial support, and boosting advertising budgets in an effort to strengthen the competitive position of their shops. During this period independent retailers had great difficulty in surviving, and several major retail groups ran into difficulties as they were squeezed by newer and more aggressive forms of retailing.

THE CONFECTIONERY MARKET

British confectionery consumption per capita, at almost 8½ ounces per week, is the highest in the world. The British eat twice as much candy as the Americans and French and four times as much as the Italians. Retail sales in 1980 exceeded £2,000 million [£2 billion] and amounted to over 700,000 tons.[1] The market is divided about equally in tonnage terms between chocolate and sugar confectionery, though chocolate's price makes that sector twice as valuable. Since 1960 there has been little difference in the volume or value growth [revenue] rates between the two sectors. A more detailed breakdown is given in Exhibit 3.

While overall market size has trebled in money terms between 1970 and 1980, there has been little volume growth: volume in 1980 was still marginally below the 1973 peak of 717,000 tons. This lack of growth is blamed on the recession, the sharp rise in cocoa and sugar prices, and the imposition of the value added tax (VAT) of 8 percent in 1974 (which rose to 15 percent in 1979). Unlike the United States, where consumption had been declining for many years, there was little evidence that diet or dental concerns were significantly affecting the market.

Confectionery manufacturing is fairly concentrated; seven companies account for 52 percent of sales strongly biased toward chocolate,

---

[1] £1 = 100p (pence). In 1980 £1 = $2.00 (U.S.) approximately.

EXHIBIT 3 U.K. Confectionery Tonnage by Product Group, 1974–1979*

	Tons (000)		
	1974	*1977*	*1979*
Chocolate:			
Milk chocolate bars with fruit, nuts, etc.	27	15	18
Plain chocolate bars	47	40	38
Count lines†	153	159	186
Chocolate assortments (including boxes)‡	65	51	51
Straight lines	51	47	47
Easter eggs novelties	18	20	21
Total	361	332	361
Sugar:			
Hard-boiled‡	95	87	75
Toffee, caramel, and fudge‡	66	75	68
Gums, jellies, pastilles	41	42	41
Liquorice	20	18	16
Chewing gum	15	16	14
Medicated	13	12	8
Other	78	71	72
Total	328	321	294

* U.K. sales by U.K. manufacturers only. Approximately an additional 50 tons of confectionery were imported in 1979.
† Count lines are items sold for individual consumption rather than by weight or quantity. Well-known examples are Kit Kat and Mars Bar, each with annual sales of over £40,000.
‡ Main sectors in which Thornton's competes.

while over 200 companies fight for the remaining 48 percent biased toward sugar. Cadbury's, Rowntree Mackintosh, and Mars are the three leading groups. Competition is fierce in advertising and brand development, especially in the filled chocolate bar/count line segment, which was the most buoyant and valuable sector of the whole confectionery market in recent years. Around £40 million was spent on advertising in 1980, making confectionery the most highly advertised of all product groups. There are many brands; the top 40 account for about 40 percent of the market. Other than Thornton's (which ranks about 16th), no major manufacturer is integrated forward into retailing.

Distribution of confectionery is extremely wide through a great variety of retailing outlets. The main channel, however, is still the mass of largely independent small confectioner/tobacconist/news agents (CTNs). Around 45,000 of these account for 38 percent of confectionery sales. But the number of CTNs has declined sharply in recent years, and their share of confectionery sales has dropped from 55 percent in 1960. Increasingly important are the large grocery supermarkets and superstores which have expanded their confectionery share from 20 to 32 percent since 1960. Other important outlets are cinemas, departments stores, and variety chains.

Women are the main purchasers of confectionery although children are the largest per capita consumers, especially in sugar. Women buy about 67 percent, men 20 percent, and children 13 percent. Fifty percent of purchases are made on Fridays and Saturdays. The average amount spent on each purchase occasion was about 33 pence in 1980. The gift market is very important, especially for Christmas, Easter, and Mother's Day. About 40 percent of spending is for gifts, mainly women for children and, secondly, men for women. A recent survey shows that among adult "heavy users" of confectionery, women consume more than men and that they are predominantly in the lower (C2D) income groups.[2]

THORNTON'S CHANNELS AND PRODUCTS

The company now had 148 shops controlled by a sales manager supervising 16 area managers. While in recent years shops had been opened in Scotland and the South of England, the majority of them were in the Midlands and North of England. Virtually all shops were in town centre shopping areas. Most of the shops were very small, the majority having under 300 square feet of selling space, although the company had tried to open somewhat larger units in recent years. The shops were not self-service, and queuing was a significant problem at peak periods. In 1980 the average turnover per shop was £110,000, though some of the better shops were doing two or three times this figure.

After 1974, under Mr. Tony's lead the company began to sell its confectionery through other shops. The real stimulus for this change in direction was the alarming rise in high street-shop rents, which if continued threatened to make many of Thornton's shops unprofitable. The most significant move was the decision to allow other shops (generally small CTNs) to sell Thornton's confectionery as part of their range on a franchise basis. In return for a small fee, franchisees could buy Thornton's at 25 percent off retail price. During its first five years franchising showed considerable growth (see Exhibit 4). Currently there were 45 shops with a Thornton franchise. The second important

---

[2] Survey researchers classify households and adults by social class. Broadly, A refers to upper middle-class households (3 percent of all households); B middle-class (13 percent); C1 lower-middle (22 percent); C2 skilled working-class (33 percent); D working-class (21 percent); E lowest levels of income (8 percent).

EXHIBIT 4   J. W. Thornton Ltd., Sales by Selected Channels of Distribution (£000, including VAT)

Financial Year	Thornton Shops	Franchise	Marks & Spencer	Other Chains	Export
1974–75	£ 6,049	£ 1	£ 3	£ 3	£ 3
1975–76	7,023	92	255	136	11
1976–77	8,351	392	661	167	24
1977–78	9,933	1,002	636	172	149
1978–79	11,845	1,303	462	205	184
1979–80	14,753	1,259	868	205	167

---

development was the request by Marks and Spencer, Britain's most successful variety store group, to sell Thornton's chocolate under its own private label. Currently this exceeded £800,000 in sales. Besides franchising and Marks and Spencer, small amounts were sold to a few other U.K. chains, and some £167,000 worth was exported to distributors in 14 countries overseas.

Thornton's was represented in product groups accounting for only about one third of the chocolate market (mainly assortments, straight lines, Easter eggs, etc.) and about two thirds of the sugar market (boiled, toffee, jellies, etc.). In particular they were not represented in "count lines" and filled chocolate bars, which made up the most profitable segment of the chocolate market. Besides confectionery the shops sold small amounts of bought-in greeting cards (£500,000 in 1979–80) and ice cream (£200,000). Percentage gross margins averaged 60 percent for sugar confectionery, 57 for chocolate, 50 for cards, and 30 for ice cream.

THE THORNTON'S CONSUMER

When Mr. Peter took over responsibility for the marketing operation in 1979, his lack of experience was balanced by an enthusiasm to get the business moving ahead again. He was critical that many important decisions had been neglected in the past due to differences of opinion and priorities on the board. In an early memorandum he said that product standards had dropped; production convenience was taking precedence over marketing needs; shortages at peak times were resulting in lost business; and shop display, hygiene, and stock control standards were all declining due to insufficient investment in shopfitting and management.

Peter inherited Tucker Advertising, a Manchester advertising agency appointed by Mr. Tony some months earlier. The agency convinced Peter of the need to undertake some research into Thornton's consumers and the confectionery market before a marketing strategy could be developed. Until then the company had undertaken little market research. But from Tucker's research and that conducted by the two agencies succeeding it, a fairly complete picture had been developed. The main research findings were:

1. In socioeconomic terms the Thornton's shopper profile was close to the average profile of confectionery buyers: AB 15 percent, C1 26 percent, C2 38 percent, D 18 percent, E 3 percent.

2. In areas where Thornton's had shops, 71 percent of confectionery eaters shop at Thornton's at least occasionally. The average expenditure per shopper was 70–99 pence in October 1978 and somewhat higher for the AB socioeconomic group.

3. Thornton's shoppers had very positive attitudes to the shops. A sample of 544 Thornton shoppers found 42 percent mentioning product quality as the most attractive feature; 21 percent, good service; and 11 percent, window displays. Only 20 percent of respondents could think of anything unattractive about the shops. Of the negative responses, "too small" and "queuing" were most frequently mentioned.

4. Price did not appear a problem. Respondents thought generally that Thornton's products were a little more expensive, but they believed the products to be of higher quality and good value for the money. This was especially true of chocolate, but boiled sweets were seen as neither more expensive nor of better quality than elsewhere. Chocolate and toffee were seen as of very good value by over 90 percent of Thornton shoppers.

5. Most Thornton customers bought more confectionery from other outlets than from Thornton's. As the agency noted, this is not surprising. "However good the product and reputation, however conveniently located the outlets, Thornton's accounts for a tiny proportion of confectionery distribution. When heavily advertised, well-established products are available at the checkout of a supermarket that Thornton's customers have to visit to buy groceries, it is not surprising that they purchase competitive brands. Customers typically buy a wide range of confectionery from a variety of outlets." Thornton's 148 shops competed with 127,000 other outlets selling confectionery.

6. Non-Thornton customers appeared to be much younger, to be often heavy confectionery eaters, especially of count lines (i.e., market leaders like Mars Bars, Kit-Kat, Yorkie), and to be more downmarket. Thornton's products appeared to appeal to older customers, especially women.

7. Gift purchasing was very important in confectionery, especially for boxes of chocolates. The majority of boxed chocolates were bought for family or friends. Self-consumption was more frequently the purchase motive for loose chocolates, toffee, and boiled sweets. Toffees and boiled sweets were the most favored purchases for children.

The advertising agencies came up with various proposals based on their research findings. Tucker Advertising recommended targeting on C1–C2–D housewives aged over 25 and focusing on increasing awareness of Thornton's traditional product quality. Penelope Keith, a well-known television comedy actress, was used in humorous TV and radio commercials to communicate the product benefits. Beaumont, Robock and King (BRK), a leading London agency which won the account early in 1979, defined the primary target as the "heavy confectionery purchaser" who was female, aged 16–34, in the C2–D–E groups with two to three children, and whose life-style might be summarized as "laugh and grow fat." Their creative approach was again humorous and traditional, based around singing confectionery workers at Thornton's factory. The creative proposition was aimed at expressing Thornton's shop as a "treasure trove" of high-quality confectionery and "a family firm making your family favourites." The Cundiff Partnership, a small London agency which gained the account in mid-1980, decided to target on "medium" confectionery buyers who were younger and more up-market (A–B–C1–C2) than the typical Thornton's consumer. Creatively they concentrated on telling straightforward product quality stories about the brands and linking with main gift-giving occasions, such as Christmas and Easter.

THORNTON'S MARKETING ORGANIZATION

In 1978 Mr. Tony asked Dr. John Riley, a professor of business administration at a local university, to take an overall look at the company's operation. Riley's report showed that profitability had significantly declined since 1970. He argued that this was due mainly to external factors: little market growth; the changing pattern of retailing, and high rates of inflation eroding margins. But he also suggested the problem had been worsened by (a) management cutting back on marketing investments, (b) falling shop volume, and (c) a switch in the product mix toward less-profitable items. On the positive side, he noted the remarkable growth of franchising, the success of Continental Chocolates, good cost control, and the margin protection the shops offered ("unlike other manufacturers Thornton's is not easily squeezed by the buying power of the major retail groups").

Mr. Peter accepted most of the points in the Riley report and began to attack these problems quickly. One difficulty he faced immediately was the lack of retail experience of his two senior managers: Joe Royston, the marketing manager, and Len Andrews, the sales manager. After much exasperation with his inability to get information and implementation from his marketing and salespeople, he hired a retail manager, Colin Shaw, in June 1980. The new man was not a retailer, but Peter felt that he was young and bright and that his experience in brand management would be very valuable. Andrews resigned around the same time, and Peter was hoping to find an experienced successor quickly.

Dr. Riley also drew attention to the need to improve the management information and planning procedures. Peter agreed that most of the information the directors received was still production oriented. A vast amount of information was available on manufacturing costs and standards but it was not easy to determine sales and profit performance trends of the products, channels of distribution, and shops. Evaluating price and promotional changes on different parts of the business was virtually impossible. One of the problems, he felt, was forcing the accounting department to give a greater priority to providing better information.

Thornton's had never undertaken formal longer-term planning. In recent years, however, the accountant had developed a useful annual

---

EXHIBIT 5

J. W. THORNTON LTD.
Income Statement and Budget
1980–1981
(£000)

	Actual 1978–79	*Actual 1979–80*	*Budget 1980–81*
Sales (excluding VAT)	£12,826	£15,551	£18,250
Direct costs	6,112	7,191	8,760
Gross profit	6,714	8,360	9,490
Wages and salaries	2,947	3,942	4,335
Pension scheme	94	116	125
Distribution	266	321	404
Repairs	354	405	460
Rent and rates	625	821	1,000
Postage, telephone, travel	166	240	267
Power	225	294	343
Legal and finance charges	242	307	284
Advertising	153	503	253
Display	48	52	53
Miscellaneous	90	147	149
Depreciation	508	553	650
Total trading overheads	5,718	7,701	8,323
Trading profit	996	659	1,167
Nontrading net income (expense)	(50)	9	(26)
Pretax profit	£ 946	£ 668	£ 1,141

budget, although it often did not appear until a few months into the financial year (beginning June 1). Another problem was that sales appeared as a residual rather than an output from a marketing forecast. Generally, overhead costs for the forthcoming year were taken as "given"; target net and gross profits were then agreed by the board; and turnover was subsequently defined as that level needed to balance these assumptions. It was perhaps not surprising that the sales volume figures generally proved optimistic. In the 1979–80 financial year this budgeting procedure had, however, produced more serious consequences (see Exhibit 5). Overhead costs in the budget had been allowed to escalate by a heavy commitment to advertising and a decision to introduce a new layer of management to strengthen the manufacturing team; but the level of sales needed to cover these costs proved to be much too high, and net profit suffered severely. The directors were determined not to let this mistake be repeated, and in the future they were sure that budgeted cost increases would be checked by realistic or even pessimistic budget sales forecasts.

BUSINESS AND MARKETING STRATEGY ISSUES

In thinking about the longer term, Peter felt that there were a number of areas where fundamental strategic decisions needed to be made. Getting these choices right would determine whether the business would have a successful future or not.

Shop Operations

This was perhaps the area where the most crucial decisions were needed. There were a number of obvious questions. Should Thornton's continue to see the shops as providing the vast majority of sales and profits? How many shops should they have? Where should the shops be located? What image should the shops aim to present to the public? Peter initially concluded that Thornton's own shop should be the dominant form of growth rather than outside sales. He argued, "In this age of the superstore and self-service with impersonal indifference, there is a demand for a specialist with a unique proposition. We are in a position to fill this role with our unique business. We have a fine manufacturing plant, involved people, strong street sites, and quality products to build on." He argued for opening as many shops as the company could afford, probably 10–20 a year.

Another area of concern was the shop image. Several observers believed that the stores were not right and that their appearance was confusing, lacking in impact, and old-fashioned. Over the years, the board had experimented with various piecemeal modifications to layout and window display, but there had been no real fundamental changes for many years. Worse, many of the older shops were now much in need of refitting and modernization. Peter, influenced by the successful remodeling ventures of a number of leading British retailers, became convinced that Thornton's shops needed a comprehensive repositioning guided by experts. After interviewing all the top retail designers, he commissioned Fitch and Company, the largest and most experienced of these organizations, to develop a complete shop redesign and corporate identity program for the group. Fitch's past clients included many of Britain's largest and most successful retail organizations. In October 1979 Fitch produced their models which proposed to completely redesign the shops, merchandising methods, packaging and company image. A program for implementing these changes at a cost of about £25,000 per shop was also defined in detail.

During the following six months, experience and changed circumstances led to some rethinking. One problem was that sales and profit were less buoyant than expected. Another was that rising costs of rents and staff and the failure of the advertising campaign to boost shop volume made the race to open new ones look very risky. In particular, the shops opened in new types of off-center locations—at the Tesco, Carrefour, and Fine Fare shopping mall complexes, for example—proved highly disappointing. Finally, there was the view on the board that while the Fitch proposals contained some good ideas, the complete shop redesign they proposed was really not the type of atmosphere that would appeal to Thornton's traditional customers.

Franchise Operations

Both Tony and Peter were less than enthusiastic about the Thornton franchise operation, and in 1978 they had agreed to halt further growth despite many requests for franchises. All the franchisees were independent CTN shops which sold Thornton's lines as part of their general ranges of tobacco, newspapers, other confectionery, and miscellaneous merchandise. Thus the shops retained their old names and trading formats, only agreeing to give a portion of their selling space (averaging 20–40 percent) over to the Thornton range. In general Peter believed that the profit potential was insufficient to attract people to devote their entire shop to the Thornton range. The limited commitment which resulted left Thornton's unhappy with the franchise business. The board felt these outlets generally failed to display the products properly and kept stock too long, threatening Thornton's quality image as well as its exclusivity. Finally, franchised confectionery offered a lower gross margin than through Thornton's own shops.

But both felt that now this attitude should be reconsidered. Average shop volume was slipping marginally nearly every year. Further Dr. Riley had pointed out that while the gross margin was higher in their own shops, when average shop operating costs were allowed for, the margin on franchise sales appeared to be at least as good. A report the directors had received the previous week from Mr. Michael and the company accountant supported this analysis. Their analysis estimated the gross and net trading margins as follows.[3]

	Gross Margin *(percent)*	*Trading Profit* *(percent)*
Thornton's shops	55%	6%
Franchise sales	45	14
Marks and Spencer	37	7
Other home sales	35	3
Export sales	33	−6

Two other points also counted. First, Thornton's franchise operation had developed too fast and without proper understanding of the problems involved. The directors felt they now had the experience to develop a much better control system which would overcome many of the past weaknesses. Second, with only 45 franchises there was undoubtedly vast sales growth potential from expanding the number of franchised outlets.

Marks and Spencer

With 255 stores in the United Kingdom and a turnover approaching £2 billion, Marks and Spencer is generally regarded as one of Britain's best-managed retailers. Since 1975 its business had become very important to Thornton's, M&S merchandising policy was based on developing very close, durable relationships with a small number of high-quality British manufacturers in each product field. Manufacturers had to follow M&S's exacting quality standards in supplying M&S with exclusive products sold under the "St. Michael" brand name. Thornton's was approached when M&S diversified into food and confectionery in the mid-1970s. In 1979–80 M&S purchased around £870,000 of Thornton's boxed chocolates and was also beginning to take Special Toffee and fudge on a trial basis.

Tony and Peter had always been hesitant about the M&S business. One reason was that the markup M&S required, exceeding 25 percent, meant it was a lower gross margin business for Thornton's. Profitabil-

---

[3] Some of the financial data in this case are disguised.

ity of the whole business was affected too, they believed, because M&S was reluctant to accept price increases not justified by corresponding manufacturer's cost increases. This was making it difficult to increase margins, and since Thornton's was not willing to be undercut in prices by M&S, the whole of Thornton's margin was held back. There were also strategic issues: M&S offered such large potential that Thornton's might risk becoming too dependent upon them in the future. In addition the directors asked: What is the differential advantage of a Thornton shop if the customer can buy its confectionery at Marks? M&S also interfered with Thornton's flexibility in other directions. They were unwilling to allow it to sell the products M&S bought to competitive retailers, severely limiting diversification options, though it was possible this objection could be overcome by introducing minor product differences which could differentiate the M&S range. Finally, M&S made life difficult for the factory: they could cancel or significantly increase orders with little notice. For example, in 1978–79, M&S purchases dropped substantially when for tax reasons they ceased to supply their Canadian stores with Thornton's confectionery. Finally, M&S orders were generally at peak times when capacity was already fully stretched. Nevertheless, in 1980–81, M&S orders were expected to top £1 million.

Export and Other Commercial Sales

The board believed there were many other exciting growth opportunities. In 1979–80 they exported some £167,000 of products to 14 countries, mainly through overseas distributors. While the volume was small, with sufficient management attention they felt it was possible to achieve major expansion, perhaps through overseas franchising. Thornton's toffee and chocolate had gained much favorable comment, many inquiries from interested buyers, and a number of prizes for quality at international confectionery exhibitions over the years. The board felt in many overseas markets Thornton's confectionery could offer a unique combination of very high quality at prices which were affordable by the average consumer.

At home, too, a large number of enquiries continually came into Thornton's from large department stores, supermarket groups, and other retailers interested in the lines. In recent years small customer accounts had been built up with a few retail groups, the largest being the Waitrose supermarket group, which in the last year had bought £70,000 of fudge and chocolates for sale under the Waitrose label. The Marks and Spencer constraint and the board's doubts about whether this was the right direction had restricted growth in this direction.

Finally, in the last year, mainly under the enthusiastic direction of Joe Royston, Thornton's had begun selling by mail order, with sales reaching around £4,000 over the period.

Product Line

On reflection Peter admitted that what Thornton's sold was largely based on tradition ("what we have always sold") and what the factory people thought they could produce rather than on much consideration of market opportunities. But even without a changed strategy, the market was shifting the nature of Thornton's business. In recent years it had become much more a chocolate and gift retailer. Volume sales of chocolate through the shops had increased by 40 percent since 1970, while sugar confectionery had dropped by over 10 percent. The highest growth was in boxed chocolates, which had almost doubled over the decade: the weakest area was the traditional boiled sweet, which had almost halved (Exhibits 6 and 7). Chocolate products now represented 43 percent of retail volume and over 61 percent of revenues.

EXHIBIT 6   Thornton's Shops: Confectionery Tonnage by Product Group, 1974–1980*

	Tons			
	1974	*1977*	*1979*	*1980*
Chocolate:				
Continental and other boxed chocolates	523	566	704	773
Continental—loose	241	250	282	279
Other chocolate—loose	567	458	489	491
Easter eggs, novelties	79	74	94	127
Misshapes	124	159	99	78
Total	1,534	1,507	1,668	1,748
Average price per ton	£1,850	£2,603	£3,884	£4,660
Sugar:				
Hard-boiled	620	529	421	409
Toffee	1,619	1,481	1,551	1,396
Fudge	185	190	219	179
Jellies	92	75	67	80
Total	2,516	2,275	2,258	2,064
Average price per ton	£1,031	£1,473	£1,862	£2,141

* Thornton shops only. Sales through other outlets amounted to 927 tons in 1980 (Exhibit 7).

EXHIBIT 7   J. W. Thornton's Sales by Product and Channel, 1980 (tons)

	Shops	Franchise	M&S	Other	Export
Chocolates:					
Boxed	773	145	183	25	28
Other	975	115	50	15	16
Hard-boiled	409	80	0	16	13
Toffee and miscellaneous	1,655	127	70	24	20

This change had not helped profits. Hard-boiled sweets in particular had high profit margins and a relatively low cost of sales. Further, the new growth areas that had compensated (i.e., chocolate boxes) had required additional investment which adversely affected return on assets and net profit. But there was probably little that could be done, since Thornton's hard-boiled, unlike its chocolate, had few distinctive features and the factory could not compete in unit cost with the large modern facilities of the major competitors.

Tony and Peter spent considerable time thinking about what products the shops should carry and "what business we are in." But defining the customer "need" or "want" Thornton's served in operational terms was not easy. The shops had sold at various times cigarettes, lemonade, and more recently greeting cards and ice cream. But the current view was that such extensions were inconsistent with the image of a unique specialist that Thornton's wished to create. However, they did not rule out certain complementary lines (e.g., cakes) in the future. Another possibility was broadening the confectionery lines carried by adding bought-in ranges to complement their own products. This had not been done in the past, Peter said, partly because there was a tendency in the company for the shops to be seen as an outlet for the factory.

John Thornton had a committee which met on a regular basis to consider new product development in the factory. Thornton's past advertising agencies had been eager to push the company into producing a count line or filled chocolate bar like Yorkie or Cadbury's Fruit and Nut to compete in those sectors representing up to 50 percent of the chocolate market and where Thornton's was unrepresented. But Thornton's felt this was unrealistic, since these often massively advertised products relied on virtually universal distribution and impulse purchasing for their sales. However, Thornton's was thinking about new lines. Additions and replacement items to the basic ranges of boiled sweets, toffee, and chocolates were being made continually. Up to 12 different centers or flavors might be introduced in a year. Four years ago "Traditional Assortment" had been introduced on a trial basis. This was a new range of super-quality, hand-finished chocolates selling at almost twice the price per pound of the Continental range. This was now in some 40 shops and generated a turnover last year of around £100,000. Other items on trial included additions to the children's confectionery lines and a small range of confectionery for diabetics.

Pricing Strategy

Like other retailers, Thornton's margins had been hit by the acceleration of inflation after 1973 and government price controls. But now they believed margins were under much better control. Peter said pricing strategy was based on the recognition that Thornton's products were high priced (e.g., a half-pound box of Continental was around 20 percent more expensive than a box of best-selling Cadbury's Dairy Milk) but that the consumer recognized their superior quality, and this allowed them to be perceived as good value for money. On the other hand, he believed that where their products were not unique they must be priced competitively. Recent experience, he believed, had proved his view. The Continental line had been unaffected by fairly steep price increases, whereas boiled sweets had shown impressive volume gains after a price cut—although he admitted that fudge had not shown a similar increase after the same policy had been applied.

Advertising and Promotion

During his first 12 months as managing director, Peter had spent an enormous amount of time with the advertising agency attempting to formulate a decisive marketing and advertising campaign. Between 1975 and 1978 Thornton's had tried to hold up net profit margins by restricting the growth of advertising and promotional expenditures. On taking over, Peter had felt this lack of investment had been a material cause of Thornton's recent sluggish performance. In 1979 Peter appointed BRK, a large London advertising agency, to handle this account. The advertising budget was trebled to over £500,000, and BRK developed a campaign employing television and a wide range of media to boost Thornton's image as a traditional and special type of confectionery shop. But the results were disappointing, and net profit was severely affected. In 1980 Peter began a serious reconsideration of advertising's role in the business.

He felt that a business of Thornton's size could not compete in advertising terms with Cadbury's or Rowntree's, which spent over £1 million supporting an individual brand. He also felt that broad "image" advertising for Thornton's was not the way. Instead he believed that advertising should be tailored to support Thornton's brands with the strongest identity—Special Toffee and Continental Chocolates—and to help build new ones.

A new agency, the Cundiff Partnership, was appointed in mid-1980 with a much reduced budget. Local radio was chosen as the prime medium on cost-efficiency grounds, with local press as a "top up." Advertising was targeted around the main gift seasons—Christmas, St. Valentine's Day, Mother's Day, and Easter. In addition a Special Toffee promotion was scheduled for October 1980 to restimulate volume.

With his new retail manager Colin Shaw, Peter was also seeking to strengthen Thornton's public relations. Thornton's retained the services of a local PR consultant at a reasonable fee and was also considering retaining Harry Shepherd's new PR consultancy in London. Mr. Shepherd had worked for 30 years as head of PR at Marks and Spencer and had recently resigned to start his own business. Peter felt that they were now on the right track as far as advertising and PR were concerned.

Marketing and Organization

The directors were fairly happy with the current situation. Important decisions were being taken, and there were some favorable features in the environment. For example, while in the late 70s Thornton's had been squeezed by rising commodity prices, cocoa was now trading at record lows. This year the price had dropped by £400 a ton, and since Thornton's was buying 1,000 tons annually, this was having a significant effect on profitability.

Besides changes in marketing strategy, Tony and Peter knew that changes in marketing organization were also needed. Currently, Colin Shaw was retail manager looking after advertising and promotion; Joe Royston was now responsible for exports, Marks and Spencer, and franchise and other home sales; and a new sales manager responsible for the shops was to be appointed. The last was felt to be particularly important, since there was much to do in the area of sales control and supervision. Training was poor, and the manuals detailing expected behavior from retail staff were now out of date and not used. Peter knew from experience that strategy would never be implemented properly without the right people and organization.

Case 5–13   Lee Co.*

For more than 50 years, the five-pocket blue jeans made by Lee Co. of Merriam, Kan., were the uniform of cowboys and farmhands.

Lee did a good, steady business, and that was enough to satisfy the dry-goods merchant Henry David Lee, who owned the company. But the once-stable jeans business has become extremely volatile, and the Lee brand has fallen on hard times. Today it is trying for a comeback.

In the 1960s of Bob Dylan and Vietnam, and even more so in the late '70s of designer jeans, Lee was riding high. The cotton denims, suddenly fashionable among women as well as men, crashed the gates of every American institution from high school to Studio 54.

Lee couldn't make pants fast enough. The company, which was acquired by VF Corp. in 1969, added new automated sewing plants and, in the '80s, laundries for stonewashing dungarees. The way Lee saw it, jeans were a permanent fixture, and the Lee name was spun gold.

But its vision proved myopic. In the early 1980s, the shrinking population of young people (age 12 to 24), the spreading body shapes of the older generation and the new popularity of sweat pants, warmup suits and khakis ended the boom. In 1989, only 387 million pairs of jeans were sold in the United States, down from 502 million in the peak year of 1981. After 1987, Lee experienced a two-year decline in U.S. jeans sales totaling 23 percent. VF had let inertia, not demand, steer the business.

Today, VF finally is aggressively trying to solve its Lee jeans problems, but the brand still is reeling (see Exhibit 1).

Boom and bust left Lee with too many factories and too much unsold stock. In the past two years it has closed 10 plants while working down its inventory. To attract more retail business, Lee this year has also cut wholesale prices 5 to 9 percent.

The brand now must recapture luster lost to neglect, while such parvenus as Gitano, Guess and private-label imports sold by Gap Inc. and other big retailers were cutting into the market. Lee is counting on the success of a new collection of casual pants, which are to be introduced in the fall—four long years after Lee's privately held rival, Levi Strauss Associates Inc., introduced its enormously successful Dockers brand. Lee also has to catch up in the thriving jeans markets overseas, where Levi, the inventor of blue jeans and ever the leader, has a beachhead.

---

* Source: Teri Agins, "Bottom Line," *The Wall Street Journal,* March 7, 1991, pp. A1, 4. Reprinted by permission of *THE WALL STREET JOURNAL,* © 1991 Dow Jones & Company, Inc. All Rights Reserved Worldwide.

EXHIBIT 1   VF Corp.: A Blue Jeans Market

Earnings have been hurt . . .

Annual net income, in millions

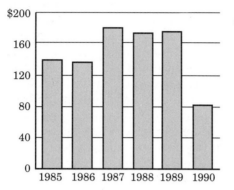

While business struggles . . .

Lines of business as a percent of 1990 revenue

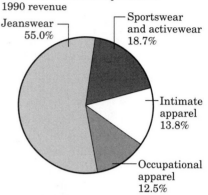

Jeanswear 55.0%

Sportswear and activewear 18.7%

Intimate apparel 13.8%

Occupational apparel 12.5%

In a fierce market . . .

1990 U.S. market share of leading jeans brands, in percent

Levi Strauss	22.0%
Lee*	**10.0**
Rustler*	**9.5**
Wrangler*	**5.5**
Gitano	3.7
Chic	2.5
Other	46.9

*Owned by VF Corp.
Source: Prudential Securities Inc. estimates.

And the stock lags.

Comparison of VF Corp. stock and DJ Textile and Apparel index, Dec. 29, 1989=100

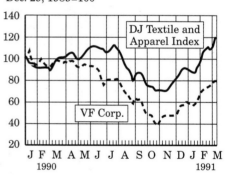

DJ Textile and Apparel Index

VF Corp.

J F M A M J J A S O N D J F M
1990   1991

Fourth quarter net income at Levi Strauss jumped 51.2 percent, to $75.3 million, boosted by international sales and strong demand for Dockers, which had 1990 sales of about $500 million.

While Lee continues to be a major force in the $6.3 billion U.S. jeans industry, second only to Levi, the brand's market share has slipped to about 10 percent. Fred Rowan, chief executive since 1989, figures it will take Lee two more years to accomplish "an architectural redesign" of its operations. "You can't get rid of your sins in six months," he says. All top executives in marketing, operations, and manufacturing have been replaced since 1989.

Meanwhile, Lee's parent, VF, is leaning on its other operations to keep shareholders happy. VF owns Wrangler, Rustler, and Girbaud jeanswear, all of which are in better shape than Lee; Vanity Fair lingerie; Jantzen sportswear; Red Kap uniforms; Bassett-Walker fleecewear (sweatshirts and such); and Health-Tex children's clothes.

On Feb. 12 VF announced a fourth-quarter net loss of $9.9 million, the result of, among other things, an $11.5 million restructuring charge from the Lee division and a $21 million provision for excess inventories at Lee. VF's jeanswear brands contributed some $1.4 billion of the $2.6 billion in sales. (Analysts estimate that Lee's sales account for about $600 million.)

Over the past two years, Lee's problems have cost VF some $100 million in profit, estimates Deborah Bronston, an analyst who follows the apparel stocks at Prudential Securities Inc.

In December, Standard and Poor's lowered VF's long-term debt ratings, cautioning that the extent of its progress on its turnaround "is still uncertain," S&P also cited softness in both retailing and the jeans market.

Just about everybody involved—stores, competitors, insiders—blames Lee's problems partly on VF and partly on the management of Lee. Critics say that VF ordered Lee to bolster corporate earnings by squeezing as much as it could from its basic jeans business while doing no long-term planning. Others say the Lee division itself was heavy with managers who had a "commodity mentality," meaning they would fill the retail pipeline with basic jeans and let retailers worry about how to sell them. "We had a management problem at Lee," says Lawrence Pugh, VF's chairman.

VF was just a lingerie company with annual sales of $69 million when it bought Lee in 1969, a year in which Lee had $87.5 million in sales. Lee could boast that it had outfitted World War I doughboys, dressed the actors on "Gunsmoke" and "The Beverly Hillbillies" and supplied the rodeo circuit. Then in 1972 Lee realized something that seemingly hadn't dawned on other big jeans makers: Women wanted jeans made for women, jeans that fit. Lee developed the Ms. Lee brand, and Lee today remains America's best-selling women's jeans. Its total jeans sales, men's and women's, doubled from 1972 to 1978 and grew another 70 percent between 1981 and 1985, even as the jeans industry overall was declining.

When jeans were the rage, Lee apparently gave little thought to anything other than boosting production. Lee jeans were in such demand that they sometimes were rationed to retail stores. But the company had a reputation for not servicing its retail accounts, of refusing, for example, to participate in cooperative ad campaigns with some stores.

"The managers at Lee were very conservative, they didn't encourage creativity, they wanted a safe output," says Kathy Ferguson, a former Lee vice president who left for Levi Strauss after 13 years.

As other jeans makers branched out into different styles, Lee clung to its basic Lee Rider, which Lee felt transcended faddishness. In 1978, Colonel Days, a chain of 34 Midwestern jeans stores with headquarters in St. Louis, did 80 percent of its business in four different styles and three different brands—all in dark indigo, the traditional color of blue jeans. "As long as you could procure product, it was a 'no-brainer' when it came to selling," says Gary Krosch, the chain's president.

Today the chain carries eight brands and 40 styles (including baggy jeans that everybody calls "anti-fit") in a range of colors from black and white to every conceivable shade of blue down to the ultrapale "ice washed" denim.

As jeans sales flattened in the early 1980s, Lee made the tactical blunder of broadening its distribution to mass-market chains such as Bradlees and Target. Discounters at the time were intent on replacing most of their private-label jeans with brand-name goods.

In a way, Lee's decision made sense. Mass merchants and discounters now sell more than a third of all jeans—more than specialty stores and department stores combined. Selling through discounters would, it was assumed, guarantee Lee an outlet. But the decision had unwanted effects.

"They figured they could grow their way out of the slump through production instead of trying to find ways to market fashion," says a former Lee sales executive.

Selling to discounters threw Lee into the hurly-burly competition with low-cost jeans importers like Gitano, which had a strong brand name and did a lot of advertising. Lee jeans were priced as much as 35 percent higher than other brands sold in discount stores, so, to move the merchandise, stores would mark down the jeans, at the expense of the stores' profit margins.

In a survey of discount-store shoppers by Leo J. Shapiro Associates, the top-selling brands in 1990 were Gitano, Sasson, Jordache, Hanes, and Chic. Lee, which had been the most popular brand in the same survey in 1989, fell to No. 21, as stores cut back on their orders of Lee jeans because the profit margins were slimmer.

When Lee started selling to discount chains, some department stores decided Lee was *declasse* and dropped their pants in favor of higher priced and more popular brands, including Girbaud jeans, now also a VF brand. (Lee continues to do much of its business with J. C. Penney, Sears and Montgomery Ward.) Meanwhile, Levi's jeans, priced higher and sold both by department stores and chains like the Gap, maintained their status.

"When the demand is down, everybody gets pickier, and a product with an OK image and an OK price will get squeezed out," says Robert Gregory, who was president of Lee in 1982 and 1983, then president of the parent, VF, from 1983 to 1990.

VF hit on another way as well to attempt to build market share, with its 1986 acquisition of Blue Bell Holdings Inc., the maker of Wrangler, Rustler, and Girbaud brand jeans. In buying Blue Bell, VF increased its domestic jeans market share to about 27 percent, compared with Levi Strauss's 22 percent, according to MRCA Services Inc., apparel marketing consultants.

The acquisitions should have been good for Lee. Wrangler was a popular brand with adult men; Rustler was popular with budget retailers—Kmart and Wal-Mart, which Lee doesn't deign to sell to; Girbaud is aimed at people with deeper pockets. Wall Street analysts believed VF would benefit from the merger by combining operations, but it didn't do that. Instead, VF continued to operate Wrangler and Lee separately. "They were killing all of this with the duplicate staffs," recalls Josie Esquivel, an apparel-industry analyst at Shearson Lehman Brothers Inc.

While Lee was preoccupied with trying to reinvigorate jeans sales, it failed to notice an emerging trend. More older consumers—the so-called "broad-butt market"—preferred other types of trousers.

Christine Rogers, a 38-year-old computer programmer from Fort Lee, N.J., says that she didn't buy jeans last year. She prefers now to wear sweatpants and leggings. "Jeans just aren't a big deal for me anymore," she says.

VF actually had a head start in casual clothes when, in 1984, it acquired Troutman Industries Inc., the maker of Skeets casual pants. But making the pants cost too much to sell them at a profit, VF concluded, so it closed Troutman in 1986. VF's chairman, Mr. Pugh, now thinks the move may have been a mistake. "In retrospect, [the product] was right," he says. "Perhaps we didn't give it enough time."

In 1986, Levi Strauss introduced its Dockers casual pants—tailored styles with a more generous cut in the legs and hips. Retailers ordered so much of the stuff that Dockers at first couldn't deliver the goods. Store buyers urged Lee's sales force to come out with competing products.

"You could have driven a Mack Truck through the opportunity we missed by not following Dockers," says a former Lee sales vice president, who says one Lee executive wore Dockers to work every day for a week to rub in the point.

"The last pair of jeans I bought was four years ago," says Mark Plummer, 30 years old, a part-time graduate student who works at Stephens Inc. a securities firm in Little Rock, Ark.

About "once every two weeks," he wears his old jeans, he says. "But when I want to be casual and I'm going out to eat, I'd rather wear Dockers or Haggar," cotton slacks that "are kind of loose and baggy and more comfortable."

This year, both Lee and Wrangler will introduce casual-pants collections. Wrangler's Timber Creek line will be out in the spring, and Lee says it will introduce its line, yet to be named, in the fall. But Dockers is already an entrenched, $500-million business.

As jeans sales fell, Lee started tinkering with its image, which had become as dowdy as its age-old ad slogan: "Lee, the brand that fits." For years Lee had eschewed close-up photos of rear ends in its ads. Finally it realized what Madison Avenue long knew: Sex sells. And, with advice from the ad agency Fallon McElligott, it changed its advertising to appeal to younger customers.

Inspired by the gritty, urban appeal of Levi's 501 button-fly jeans, Lee ran black and white ads on TV and in magazines showing kids in convertibles and at the laundromat wearing Lee Jeans. The ad agency won prizes, but customers didn't seem to get the message. VF chairman Mr. Pugh shudders at the very thought of that campaign: "Wrong, wrong, a big mistake," he says.

Lee's assault on youth exposed a number of its weaknesses. The brand added a number of fancier jeans to its repertoire—jeans with cargo pockets, jeans with embroidered detail. But Lee's factories—despite all their unused capacity—would have had to be retooled to make them. So Lee started using overseas contractors that were late and erratic in their deliveries. In the back-to-school selling season of 1989, just half of Lee's jeans shipments got to stores on time. As a result, orders were canceled. Hundreds of thousands of jeans were returned.

Today, VF is concentrating on integrating its businesses. With sweatpants outselling jeans at many stores, both Lee and Wrangler (a big supplier of desert fatigues to the Pentagon) are selling fleecewear manufactured by VF's Bassett-Walker division. Lee and Wrangler are retooling their factories to be more flexible. Wrangler now can produce some styles for VF's Girbaud brand that had been made by contractors.

Still, Lee has a long way to go. It is easy enough for VF to set goals for improving manufacturing operations, but it is harder to predict when, if ever, in a shrinking market consumers will again think that Lee jeans are hot.

Case 5–14   Color Tile, Inc.*

When you last tuned in, Fort Worth's Color Tile was concluding the final episode in a series of takeover bids.

Since becoming a subsidiary of Knoll International Holdings Inc. in a buyout engineered in October 1986 by Knoll and Color Tile executives, Color Tile has faded from view. Knoll's stock is not traded publicly and, even operationally, Color Tile has been quiet, adding no stores to the chain of 830 it has in the United States and Canada.

But that is about to change.

President Eddie Lesok, 39, says the company will open 50 stores in the next year, most of them in the Northeast, where its penetration is weak. Fifty more will open in 1989. And the company plans to keep up that pace into the 1990s.

And old stores will be made new. Soon 100 of the remaining stores will be redesigned and updated with new merchandising devices. Eventually, all will.

The aim: Improve market share in the home improvement field.

That may be a tall order, because, broadly defined, the home improvement field includes everything from Payless Cashways to your local spa dealer.

But narrowly defined, Color Tile already is faring well in market share. *Modern Floor Covering*, a trade publication, ranked Color Tile as the nation's largest retailer of floor coverings for 1987, surpassing Sears, the nation's largest retailer (see Exhibit 1).

This, even though Sears had more U.S. outlets, 759 to 665. This, even though Sears sells "soft surfaces" and Color Tile sells only "hard surfaces," in Lesok's terms.

The soft surface market is about 2.5 times as big as the hard surface market. Soft surface means carpeting; hard surface means ceramic tiles, vinyl and wood flooring.

No wonder Knoll International was interested in Color Tile. The company had become the No. 1 retailer of floor coverings competing with one hand tied behind its back, leaving the bulk of the market—carpeting—to others.

"Color Tile has enormous potential in a market where it was already dominant and could become more dominant through improved product

---

* Source: Tom Steinert-Threlkeld, "It's Been a Quiet Few Months for the Company, but Big Changes Are Afoot at Color Tile," *Fort Worth Star Telegram*, April 19, 1988, pp. 3, 5.

EXHIBIT 1   Top 10 Floor Covering Companies (includes tile, vinyl and carpet sales, 1987)

Store	Retail Volume ($ millions)*	Number of Locations
Color Tile Fort Worth, Texas	$335	665
Sears Chicago, Illinois	310	759
New York Carpet World Southfield, Michigan	306	99
Abbey Carpet Sacramento, California	166	269
Sherwin Williams Cleveland, Ohio	120	1,500
CarpetLand USA Munster, Indiana	115	57
Carpeteria Hollywood, California	95	67
Standard Brands Paint Torrance, California	75	136
ABC Carpets New York City	60	1
Carpet Fair Baltimore, Maryland	53	27

* Estimated.

Source: *Modern Floor Covering*, January 1988

offerings and customer support," Knoll Chairman Marshall Cogan says.

Customer support at Color Tile means doing such things as providing necessary tools for the job to customers rent-free and giving free advice on laying flooring—things competitors won't do.

"We're a fashion business," Color Tile Executive Vice President Larry Nagle says. "Part of our fashion is service. It's our luxury."

But more critically, it's also an opportunity to sell. An attentive salesperson gets the customer's ear. If that ear is attentive, other parts of the body may follow the instructions that are heard.

"You encourage them to do more and buy more," Cogan says succinctly.

Which has led, even in this seemingly dormant period for Color Tile, to substantial growth in the quiet world of unreported financial figures.

For the 12 months ended December 31 1987, Color Tile recorded $488 million in sales and an operating profit of $60 million (see Exhibit 2).

Those sales are about $100 million above sales reported in the last full year Color Tile was a public company, the 12-month period that ended June 30, 1986. Operating profits also were up nearly a third. Sales in that final fiscal year were $387 million, and operating profit was $45.8 million.

With growth like that without any new stores, "there's clearly great growth opportunity out there," Lesok says.

The push will be into the Northeast, where Lesok says the company's market share is light, and urban areas, where Knoll Managing Director Judith Woodfin says some home improvement retailers fear to tread.

"There is a do-it-yourself market that resides in cities," she asserts.

Achieving name recognition in those markets probably won't be difficult. In a nationwide survey conducted in November by New York's Grey Advertising Inc., Color Tile registered almost universal recognition among respondents who either had undertaken a do-it-yourself project in the last year or were planning one in the next year. Fully 97 percent of those respondents, 27 percent of all those surveyed, knew the Color Tile name and recognized it as selling hard floor coverings.

Even though that may translate into relatively low recognition among the public, it's the do-it-yourselfers that count.

"The important thing is that Color Tile is a store that is basically synonymous with do-it-yourself tile and wall-covering among the people who are doing that," says Tim Teran, Grey's vice president and associate director of marketing and research.

Both the new and retrofitted stores also will take on a new merchandising look aimed at boosting individual store sales. Walls, not just tables, will be used to display tiles. Product sample areas will be ex-

---

EXHIBIT 2   Color Tile Sales and Profit ($ millions)

Fiscal Year	Sales	Operating Profit*
6/30/83	$241.1	$32.4
6/30/84	282.8	35.7
6/30/85	347.2	45.9
6/30/86	387.1	45.8
12/31/87	488.0	60.0

* Profit before taxes, depreciation, interest.

Source: Color Tile, Inc.

panded. Merchandise will be stocked in a back room so the front of the store can focus on sales.

All that, Lesok hopes, will in turn create "more efficient visual merchandising," which in turn "will attract a more upscale customer." Not that Color Tile's average customer is a slouch now, with a typical household income of $45,000.

At the same time, the company will try to drive down costs. Knoll's policy is to make its subsidiaries the low-cost producers in their fields. One of the ways that can be achieved is through volume purchasing. Other Knoll subsidiaries, such as General Felt Industries, also buy adhesives to attach flooring to floors, so they are buying adhesives jointly to drive down the purchase price.

And like its electronic brethren at Tandy Corp., Color Tile manufactures products when needed. Three U.S. and three Canadian plants manufacture 38 percent of what the company sells. Color Tile buys the rest both domestically and abroad, again using volume to drive down costs. In Italy, which is the fashion leader in ceramic tile, Woodfin says, Color Tile buys 25 percent of all the tile produced.

Talk of expanding Color Tile's offerings to carpet frequently is heard, particularly now that the company is part of Knoll, which has other subsidiaries involved in carpet cushion.

So far, Color Tile management continues to reject a move to soft surfaces. The worries: Competing properly in carpet would require a huge devotion of resources, as well as development of talents the company doesn't have. It also could hurt sales of the company's bulwark products.

Still, Barry Witt, senior vice president and chief financial officer, says the company may begin testing carpet sales in some stores in a few years.

In the meantime, it will expand its offerings of hard surfaces. The aim, of course, is to be the hard-surface superstore, even at 4,200 square feet per store.

For instance, Tony Greco, the company's group vice president for marketing, this year is trying a new, high-priced line of tiles, Armstrong's Century Solarian line. At $2.39 a tile, "that's a high price point" for Color Tile, he says, but "it's taken off like a rocket."

The reason, he thinks, is that customers increasingly are upgrading their homes, seeking more prestigious surfaces. Indeed, 10 years ago one of the company's hottest sellers was tiles of—you guessed it—carpet. Now ceramic tiles account for 35 percent of sales.

Still, the offerings have to be broad enough and the service strong enough to keep the customer from going to Home Depot.

"When you've seen what we have," Lesok says, "you've seen what is available in the marketplace."

PART 6

Planning, Organizing, Implementing, and Controlling Marketing Strategy

STRATEGIC PLANNING

Preparation of the strategic marketing plan is one of the most demanding management responsibilities of the chief marketing executive. It requires folding together many different information-gathering and analysis activities into a comprehensive and integrated plan of action. Following a step-by-step approach in building the strategic plan will ensure that all components of the plan are covered and that their important interrelationships are recognized. The starting point is understanding the corporate strategic plan since the marketing plan is one of a bundle of functional strategies that must be combined to achieve corporate and business unit objectives.

Four important characteristics of the strategic marketing plan should be apparent. First, a logical process can and should be followed in developing the plan. Second, when the planning process raises relevant questions, management must supply the answers; decision makers develop strategic plans. Third, strategic marketing planning is a continuing activity that is adjusted and revised to take advantage of opportunities and avoid threats. Finally, marketing planning forms the leading edge of planning for the entire business unit. Marketing plans must be closely coordinated with research and development, operations, financial, and other business functions. Corporate and business unit objectives and strategies provide important marketing planning guidelines.

The major steps in the strategic marketing planning process are shown in Exhibit 1. Step 1, the marketing situation analysis, consists of product-market definition, customer analysis, key competitor analysis, environmental analysis, and marketing strategy assessment. Building on the findings of the situation analysis, Step 2 determines the market-target strategy. In Step 3, objectives for each market-target are formulated. Step 4 determines the marketing program positioning strategy for each market target. Coordinated strategies are developed for product, distribution, price, and promotion. Step 5 considers the organizational design and the allocation of responsibility for the activities included in the plan. In Step 6, the plan is assembled and the supporting financial budget is proposed. The plan is put into action in Step 7. Finally, in Step 8, the plan is evaluated and adjusted. Much of the actual work of managing involves strategic and tactical implementation, evaluation, and control of marketing operations. Successful performance of these activities relies heavily upon managers' understanding of the planning process. Strategic planning is a continuing cycle of making plans, launching them, tracking performance, identifying performance gaps, and then initiating problem-solving actions.

EXHIBIT 1   Steps in Preparing and Implementing the Strategic
Marketing Plan

In accomplishing strategic evaluation, management must select performance criteria and measures and then set up a tracking program to obtain the information needed to guide evaluation activities. When first establishing a strategic evaluation program (and periodically thereafter), a strategic marketing audit provides a useful basis for developing the program.

Strategic evaluation, the last stage in the marketing strategy process, is more aptly designated as the starting point (except perhaps in new-venture situations). Strategic marketing planning requires information from various ongoing monitoring and performance evaluation activities. Discussion of strategic evaluation has been delayed until this final part in order to have first examined the strategic areas that require evaluation and identified the kinds of information needed by the marketing strategist for assessing marketing performance.

FACILITATING IMPLEMENTATION

Plans, without proper implementation and control, are typically ineffective: A complete implementation plan should specify precisely:

- What activities are to be implemented.
- Who will be responsible for implementation.
- The time and location of implementation.
- How implementation will be accomplished.
- The performance measures and criteria to be used in evaluation.
- The nature and scope of the performance tracking program.
- How performance gaps will be identified.
- What actions will be taken under what circumstances.

Managers are important facilitators in the implementation process, and some are more effective than others. To be effective implementors, managers need:

- The ability to understand how others feel, as well as having good bargaining skills.
- The strength to be tough and fair in putting people and resources where they will be most effective.
- Effectiveness in focusing on the critical aspects of performance in managing marketing activities.
- The ability to create a necessary informal organization or network to match each problem that arises.[1]

---

[1] Thomas V. Bonoma, "Making Your Marketing Strategy Work," *Harvard Business Review,* March–April 1984, p. 75.

The implementation of marketing strategy may partially depend on external organizations such as marketing research firms, marketing consultants, advertising and public relations firms, channel members, and other organizations participating in the marketing effort. These outside organizations present a major management challenge when they actively participate in marketing activities. Their efforts should be programmed into the marketing plan and their roles and responsibilities clearly established and communicated. There is a potential danger in not informing outside groups of planned actions, deadlines, and other implementation requirements. For example, the advertising agency account executive and other agency staff members should be familiar with all aspects of the promotion strategy as well as the major dimensions of the marketing strategy. Restricting information from participating firms can adversely affect their contributions to strategy planning and implementation.

STRATEGIC EVALUATION AND CONTROL

The relationship between strategic planning and control is shown in Exhibit 2. Strategic planning is an ongoing process of making plans, implementing them, tracking performance, identifying performance gaps, and initiating actions to close the gap between desired and actual results. Management must establish performance criteria and measures so that information can be obtained for use in tracking performance. The purpose of evaluation may be to (1) find new opportunities or avoid threats, (2) keep performance in line with management's expectations, and/or (3) solve specific problems that exist.

Let us assume that we are concerned with establishing a strategic evaluation program for a business unit in which there has been no

EXHIBIT 2   Strategic Planning and Control Process

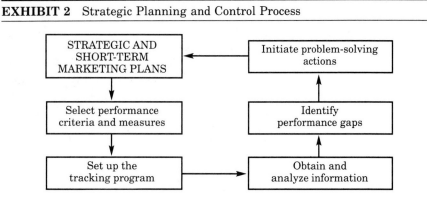

previous formal strategic marketing planning and evaluation program. Since evaluation essentially is comparing results with expectations, it is necessary to lay some groundwork before setting up a tracking program. The starting point is a *strategic marketing audit*. The audit is a comprehensive review and assessment of marketing operations. It includes a careful examination of:

1. Corporate mission and objectives.
2. Business composition and strategy.
3. Buyer analysis.
4. Competitor analysis.
5. Market-target strategy and objectives.
6. Marketing program positioning strategy.
7. Marketing program activities.
8. Marketing planning.
9. Implementation and management.

Examples of specific questions that should be addressed in examining each of these areas are shown in the appendix to Chapter 4.

There are other reasons for conducting a strategic marketing audit than its use in guiding the installation of a formal strategic marketing planning and evaluation program:

1. Organizational changes may bring about a complete review of marketing operations.
2. Major shifts in business involvement such as entry into new product and market areas, acquisitions, and other alterations in the composition of the business may require strategic audits.

While there is no norm as to how often a strategic audit should be conducted, the nature of the audit and costs involved suggest that the time span between audits should be at least three years and perhaps more, depending upon the company situation.

Cases for Part 6

The 15 cases in Part 6 continue the emphasis on program positioning strategy developed in Part 5. Cases in this part also focus on developing strategic plans and moving from the planning stage to action.

CASES

Case 6–1, Leykam Murztaler, describes the firm's strategy for marketing coated woodfree paper in Europe. In addition, it provides background information on the paper industry, major competitors, markets for coated woodfree paper, channels of distribution, and the buying process.

The California Valley Wine Company case (6–2) deals with a choice of introducing one of two potential new products. Both of the options present serious problems. The case analyst's challenge is to evaluate the merits of the options and make a recommendation.

Procter & Gamble Co. (Case 6–3) is competing in a maturing market for many of the company's staple products such as diapers and detergents. P&G chairman Edwin L. Artzt wants to turn the company into more of a fast-moving global marketer, particularly in high-growth areas such as cosmetics and health care. The case describes many of the actions P&G has taken during the early stages of transformation.

Robinson Chemical Company (Case 6–4) manufactures specialty chemicals—high performance engineering resins. The director of the firm's research labs is concerned about three products that have recently become available to the market. A marketing plan for one or more of the new resins is needed.

With domestic growth slowing, American Airlines (Case 6–5) is under pressure to broaden its international business to maintain its recent double-digit gains in revenues and passengers. The case describes

American's recent efforts to expand its presence in the international marketplace. The case analyst's challenge is to evaluate American's alternative international options and propose appropriate actions.

MeraBank (Case 6–6) operates in a turbulent environment and tough market. Competition is becoming more intensive and financial services customers are becoming more discriminating. The case provides an opportunity to study MeraBank's name change, market dynamics and strategic challenges, and particularly its services marketing and operations challenges.

Case 6–7, Motorola, Inc., describes problems the company has experienced competing in the microprocessor market. But, Motorola isn't giving up. It has taken aggressive action to become a major player in the fast-growing microprocessor market. What other actions should management consider? What should Motorola do now?

Case 6–8, Donaldson Company, Inc. (DCI), describes the world's largest manufacturer of heavy-duty filtration equipment. While enjoying considerable past success, the company has experienced major losses recently. A major focus of the case is the problem of coordinating worldwide selling and customer service efforts within the Original Equipment Group of DCI.

In becoming one of the world's largest providers of biological and chemical research services and a major supplier of laboratory animals and biotechnological products, Hazelton Laboratories Corporation (Case 6–9) faced the inevitable need to reorganize. However, following a major restructuring in 1990, the company still experienced organization-related problems. The case focuses on these problems and possible solutions.

Robert N. Maxwell Memorial Community Hospital (Case 6–10) is an established and well-known major hospital serving a large metropolitan area. The hospital's present marketing efforts are fractionalized and scattered among a number of people. Top management feels that the present marketing organization will be inadequate in the future.

Case 6–11, Aurora Lotion, describes a situation in which a Swiss subsidiary of a British company is plagued by parallel importing. The general manager of the Swiss subsidiary is concerned about the impact of this situation on salesforce morale and profitability.

Nike, Inc. (Case 6–12) is a fast-growing company. The organization that has evolved is informal; management decisions were based on collaboration, and communication among decision makers is direct and frequent. Growth, however, has put substantial strain on the informal organization structure. Phil Knight, company chairman, is considering the introduction of a more formal organization structure as well as a realignment of some business activities.

The Parke-Davis Professional Health Group (Case 6–13) examines the pharmaceutical market in Canada and the Parke-Davis salesforce strategy. Marvin Skripitsky, marketing director of the Professional Health Group, is considering several alternatives to deal with a perceived staffing problem.

Stop N Go (Case 6–14) is a chain of retail convenience stores. The total number of convenience stores in the United States leveled off in the late 1980s at 83,000. Industry profits fell 75 percent from 1988 to 1989. Stop N Go is overhauling merchandise and remodeling stores to remain competitive. The case provides interesting insight into one organization's efforts to reposition in a declining industry.

The final case in Part 6, Compaq Computer Corp. (6–15), examines the company's plans to enter the work station segment of the computer business. Management expects its new computers to lead annual sales from about $3.6 billion in 1990 to $15 billion by the year 2000. An appendix to the case provides a personal computer industry analysis.

Case 6–1   Leykam Mürztaler*

In February 1989, Dr. Gertrude Eder, Marketing Manager for Leykam Mürztaler AG, was reviewing a problem that had occupied her thoughts a great deal during the past few months. Although Leykam Mürztaler, like the paper industry in general, had been doing well in recent years, it was her opinion that it was time to think about ways to strengthen the company's ability to prosper as industry growth inevitably began slowing down. In particular, she was considering what recommendations to offer the Executive Board regarding the firm's branding strategy.

LEYKAM MÜRZTALER AG

The past few years had been good for the Leykam Mürztaler Group. Paralleling the industry's increased sales, the firm's total sales had risen from ASch4,842 million[1] in 1983 to ASch7,100 million in 1988, an increase of 47 percent. For Leykam Mürztaler AG, the principal

---

* This case was written by Professor H. Michael Hayes, University of Colorado at Denver. Copyright 1989 by IMEDE, Lausanne, Switzerland. The International Institute for Management Development (IMD), resulting from the merger between IMEDE, Lausanne, and IMI, Geneva, acquires and retains all rights. Reproduced by permission.

[1] ASch12.48 = $1.00 in December 1988.

operating component of the Group, 1988 revenues had reached ASch 6,300 million, an increase over 1986 of 41 percent, enhanced by the successful start-up of a new production line and by above average growth in demand for high-grade coated woodfree printing papers, the firm's main sales segment.

Leykam Mürztaler AG, together with its predecessor companies, had been a producer of paper for over 400 years. Headquartered in Gratkorn, Austria, the firm produced coated woodfree printing paper and newsprint, with integrated pulp production. Principal mills and offices were located at Gratkorn and Bruck, Austria. Export sales offices for coated woodfree paper were headquartered in Vienna.

In 1988, woodfree papers represented approximately 80 percent of sales, newsprint 13 percent and pulp 7 percent. Twenty-two percent of revenues came from Austria, 56 percent from Western Europe and 22% from exports to the rest of the world (including Eastern Europe). The highest share of exports was for coated woodfree papers at approximately 90 percent.

Production volumes in 1987 and 1988 are shown in Exhibit 1. The large increase in production of printing and writing paper in 1988 (to

---

EXHIBIT 1   Highlights of the Development of the Leykam-Mürztaler Group

	1987	*1988*	*Percent*
Production (in tons):			
Printing and writing papers	272,900	340,900	+24.9
Newsprint (Bruck)	98,200	99,200	+ 1.0
Paper total	371,100	440,100	+18.6
Chemical pulp	209,500	204,500	− 2.4
Mechanical pulp	30,900	32,100	+ 3.9
Deink pulp	58,900	62,700	+ 6.4
Total sales (gross, in ASch mn):			
Leykam-Mürztaler AG	5,234	6,300	+20.4
Export share	4,056	5,100	+25.7
Exports in %	78	81	—
Leykam-Mürztaler Group	5,906	7,100	+20.2
Capital expenditure and prepayments for fixed assets (in ASch mn)	1,418	1,500	+ 5.8
Cash flow (in ASch mn)	1,020	1,500	+47.1

Source: Annual Report.

340,900 tonnes) reflected successful selling of the output of the new coated woodfree paper machine at Gratkorn, with a capacity of 138,000 tonnes per year. The decline in pulp production reflected a change in product mix. External sales of pulp were declining as the company's pulp production was further integrated into the company's own paper production.

With the addition of the new production line, the company had become the European market leader in coated woodfree papers, with a market share of 8–10 percent. In December 1987 the Supervisory Board approved a project to establish a new production line at Bruck to produce mechanical coated printing papers (LWC) for magazines, catalogues and printed advertising materials. Planned capacity was 135,000 tonnes, to be put into operation at the end of 1989.

Despite the increased level of investment, financial results were very good. In 1987, the last year for which complete financial details were available, profit was down slightly from the previous year (see Exhibit 2), reflecting the greatly increased depreciation charges associated with the new paper machine and the decision to use the reducing-balance method of depreciation for it and some other equipment. Cash

EXHIBIT 2 Financial Results

	1983	*1984**	*1985*÷	*1986*	*1987*
Total sales (gross, in AS m)	4,842	5,367	5,420	5,187	5,906
Export sales (AS m)	2,973	3,413	3,537	3,331	4,062
Export share of Leykam-Mürztaler AG (%)	69	72	74	74	78
Capital investment (AS m)	313	253	444	2,461	1,518
Total depreciation (AS m)	374	344	337	476	1,064
thereof: reducing-balance depreciation (AS m)	—	—	—	125	674
Cash flow (AS m)	373	1,025	959	871	1,020
Profit for the year (AS m)	1	422	81	101	67
Personnel expenditure (AS m)	1,096	993	1,046	1,076	1,231
Number of employees (excluding apprentices) as of 31 December	2,918	2,424	2,364	2,578	2,825
Dividend and bonus (AS m)	—	54	81	101	67
(%)	—	4+4	4+8	4+8	8

* Excluding Niklasdorf Mill.
÷ Excluding Frohnierten Mill from 1 April 1985.

Source: Annual Report.

flow, however, was close to an all-time record, results were "clearly better than originally forecast," and operating profits were near the top of the European woodfree paper producers, on a percent-of-sales basis. Preliminary indications were that financial results for 1988 would be still better.

The company marketed its coated products under its MAGNO series brand (e.g., MAGNOMATT, MAGNOPRINT, MAGNOMATT K) principally through wholly owned merchants in Austria and other merchants throughout Western Europe. In addition, it sold to other kinds of merchants in Austria as well as to some printers and publishers directly. Paper merchants were contacted by sales representatives in Vienna and Gratkorn, sales subsidiaries in Germany, Italy, and France, and sales agents in other European countries. Some of its products were sold on a private-brand basis to certain large merchants.

Although Leykam Mürztaler served paper markets on a worldwide basis, this case focuses on coated woodfree papers for printing applications in Western Europe.

THE PULP AND PAPER INDUSTRY IN WESTERN EUROPE[2]

Despite its maturity, the pulp and paper industry was undergoing a major change. Characterized by high breakeven volumes, small fluctuations in demand could significantly impact profits, and there was some evidence that capacity was outgrowing demand. Despite the sophistication of paper-making technology, product differentiation was increasingly difficult to achieve. Some paper makers were integrating backwards to control the cost or assure the supply of pulp. Others were integrating forward, buying paper merchants in order to have better control of marketing. Still others were integrating horizontally to have a more complete product line.

Other changes were affecting the industry as well. Customers were being merged, acquired, or reorganized, thus changing established purchasing patterns. Changes in advertising were impacting traditional usage patterns. Paper merchants were merging to gain economies of scale. Some were emphasizing private brands to reduce their dependence on paper makers. Markets were fragmenting as new, small businesses were forming at a record rate. Consumption patterns were changing. In Europe, consumption ranged from 233kg per capita in Sweden to 60 in Portugal, but growth rates ranged from a high of 29.4 percent in Greece to a low of 2.4 percent in Denmark. There was some

---

[2] Western Europe included the 12 countries in the European Community plus Finland, Norway, Sweden, Austria, and Switzerland.

uncertainty about the implications of Europe's move toward a true common market in 1992, although trade barriers were not a significant factor in the industry.

Printing and Writing Paper

In the pulp and paper industry, the major and high-growth segment was printing and writing papers. Both coated and uncoated papers were produced from mechanically or chemically processed pulp to form four broad categories: coated woodfree, mechanical coated,[3] uncoated woodfree and mechanical uncoated. To be defined as coated, a paper had to have a surface coating of at least 5 grams per square meter (gsm).

Coated woodfree papers represented the highest quality category, in terms of printability, gloss, feel, ability to reproduce color and many other characteristics. Grades of coated woodfree papers were not precisely specified, but the industry had established further categories such as cast coated, art paper, standard, and low coated. (See Exhibit 3 for categories and prices.) The standard grade represented the bulk of sales. Within this category, however, there were many gradations—the amount of whiteness, brightness, stiffness and other characteristics. Leykam Mürztaler competed principally at the high end of the standard grade, but was planning to enter the art paper segment also.

EXHIBIT 3   Prices per Tonne (in $) of Woodfree Printing and Writing Papers in Western Europe (2nd quarter 1987 delivered)

Grade	West Germany	UK	France	Netherlands
Cast coated, sheets	2734	2324	2588	2480
Art paper, sheets	1897	1660	1837	1736
Standard, sheets	1283	1212	1235	1166
Standard, reels	1199	1145	1169	1091
Low coated, sheets	1172	1130	1136	1066

Note: Cast coated paper was estimated to represent 5% of the coated woodfree market, art paper 7–8%, standard coated 70%, and low coated less than 20%. Within the standard coated category, actual transaction prices could vary as much as 25% as a function of quality and as much as 10% due to competitive or other factors.

Source: EKONO *Strategic Study,* September 1988.

---

[3] Designated LWC or MWC, depending on the weight, although the dividing line was not precise.

Coated woodfree was the smallest printing and writing paper segment (17.8 percent of total consumption), but it was also the most dynamic, with an average growth rate of 8.4 percent from 1980 to 1987. Expectations were that 1988 consumption would exceed three million tonnes.

Markets for Printing and Writing Paper

Principal markets for printing and writing paper were magazines (33%), direct mail (17%), brochures and general print advertising (15%), copy paper (11%), other office paper (9%), and books (5%). For coated woodfree papers, it was estimated that advertising, direct and indirect, accounted for 85–90 percent of consumption.[4]

On a country-by-country basis, there was significant variation in the mix of advertising expenditures, however. In the UK, for instance, the bulk of advertising expenditures went to newspapers and TV, whereas in Germany advertising expenditures were split somewhat evenly among newspapers, magazines, catalogs, and direct mail.[5] Major uses for coated woodfree papers were direct mail, brochures, annual reports, etc. The dynamic growth of coated woodfree papers in recent years was largely fueled by the rapid increases in "nonclassical" advertising. Changes in this mix could significantly affect country consumption patterns for coated woodfree papers.

Despite cost pressures and shifts in individual markets and end uses, coated woodfree papers were benefiting from demand for more and better four-color printing as advertisers sought ways to improve the impact of their messages.

THE PRINTING INDUSTRY

The vast majority of orders for coated woodfree paper were placed by printers, either on the merchant or directly on the mill. In some instances, however, for very large orders, the order would be placed by either the printer or the publisher, depending on which seemed to have the strongest negotiating position with the supplier.

Selection of paper grade and manufacturer was a complex process that varied significantly according to end use, size of order, and sophistication of both the printer and the specifier or user. Almost without

---

[4] ECC International, Limited, 1987.
[5] Papis Limited.

exception, the printer had the final say in the selection of paper make and could significantly influence the grade of paper as well. The specifier (ad agency) or user (advertiser, publisher, mail order house, etc.) influenced paper selection, particularly with respect to grade, and could also influence selection of make, subject to final agreement by the printer.

For the printer, key paper characteristics were printability and runability. Surface characteristics, whiteness, and brightness were also important. Price was always important, especially when deciding between two suppliers with similar offerings or where paper costs represented a significant portion of the total cost of the printed product. Complaint handling, emergency assistance, speed, and reliability of delivery were key service components. Sales representative knowledge was also important. Within limits, relative importance of decision criteria varied from one country to another. In Italy and the UK, for instance, price and quality tended to be equally important, whereas quality and service factors tended to predominate importance rankings in Switzerland. There was some favoritism given producers for patriotic reasons, but seldom at the expense of quality or price.

The user or specifier considered many of the same characteristics as the printer. Printability and delivery were usually at the top of the list, but the major concern was the paper's suitability for the particular advertising message, within the constraints of the overall advertising budget.

Despite the apparent similarity of products offered by different mills, there was substantial variation in runability, which could only be determined by actual trial. According to one printer:

> The final test is how well the paper prints on our presses. This is a matter of "fit" between paper, ink, and press characteristics. We find there are variations between papers that meet the same specifications, which can only be determined by actual trial. This is not cheap as a trial involves printing 3,000 sheets. Because the paper characteristics cannot be completely specified, we like the idea of a mill brand. One time, we tested two merchant brands that we thought were different. Then we found out that the paper came from the same mill, so we really wasted our time on the second test.
>
> The merchant's sales representative is important, but we don't need him to call all that frequently. We like to talk to him about trends or problems we're having, but when we need something quickly, we call the merchant.
>
> Once we have selected a paper, it is critically important that its quality be consistent. Most suppliers are pretty good. Except for obvious flaws, however, we find they tend to want to blame problems on the ink or the press.

Over the past several years, the number of printers remained relatively constant, at about 15–20,000, with decreases from mergers and acquisitions offset by a growth in instant-print outlets. In the last 10 years, the number of commercial print customers doubled to over 500,000, half of whom used instant print outlets.

As the number of small businesses and the use of desktop publishing continued to grow, it was suggested that within 10 years traditional printers would perhaps only handle longer-run, full color work. Monochrome and spot color work would be produced in customers' offices, with the paper buying decision being made by people with little knowledge about paper or printing.[6] In-plant printing, however, was not expected to have a significant impact on the coated woodfree market.

PAPER MERCHANTS

Printers and publishers were reached in two principal ways: direct sales from the mill and sales from the mill through merchants, either independent or mill-owned. Direct sales were more common for high-volume products sold in reels, such as newsprint and LWC magazine paper. The pattern of distribution was influenced by characteristics of the transaction (see Exhibit 4) and the pattern varied significantly from one country to another (see Exhibit 5). For coated woodfree papers it was estimated that 70–80 percent of sales went through merchants.

As with all wholesalers, stocking to provide quick delivery in small quantities was a principal merchant function. Fragmentation of the fastest-growing market segments (business and small printers) had decreased the average order size and increased demand for a wide

---

EXHIBIT 4   Transaction Characteristics: A Comparison of the Roles of Manufacturers and Merchants

Characteristic	Manufacturer	Merchant
Order size (kg)	>1,500	200–500
Items carried	Small	2,500–5,000
Fixed costs	High	Low
Stock level (kg)	>2,000/item	500–1,750
Delivery	Often slow	24 hours
Service	None	Possible
Cash flow	Low	Low

Source: *The European Printing and Writing Paper Industry—1987.*

---

[6] By BIS Marketing Research Limited.

EXHIBIT 5   Market Shares per Distribution Channel (%)

Form of Distribution	*Country*			
	UK	France	Germany	Italy
Paper mills	48	50	59	80
Mill-owned merchants	} 52	50	—	} 20
Independent merchants		—	41	

Source: *The European Printing and Writing Paper Industry—1987.*

choice of paper grades, making it more difficult for mills to directly access these customers.

In warehousing, larger merchants had introduced expensive computer-controlled logistical systems, which reduced delivery times and the cost of preparing orders for delivery. Predictions were made that electronic interchange of information between merchants and their suppliers and larger customers would be the norm within the next few years. Merchants in the UK were spearheading an initiative to achieve industry standards for bar codes throughout Europe.

Changes in end-user profiles and new customer needs had forced merchants to expand the scope of their activities and customer support functions. As a result, the merchants' role broadened to include a number of additional services, including technical advice on paper choice and broader printing problems.

Private branding, supported by advertising, had long been used by some merchants to differentiate their products and service. Some large merchants had also invested in testing apparatus, similar to that found in mills, to check conformance to specifications and to support their desire to become principals, with full responsibility for product performance.

Merchant margins varied with location, type of sale, and nature of the transaction. For sales from stock, margins ranged from a low of 12 percent in Italy and 15 percent in Germany to 25 percent in France and Switzerland. Margins reduced to about 5 percent or less when a merchant acted as the intermediary solely for invoicing purposes.[7] (A typical income statement for a paper merchant is shown in Exhibit 6.)

Patterns of merchant ownership also varied from one country to another (see Exhibit 7). In the UK, for example, Wiggins Teape, a paper producer established in 1780, became a merchant in 1960 when existing merchants resisted introducing carbonless copy paper in the market. The company opened a network of offices to stimulate demand

---

[7] The European Printing and Writing Paper Industry—1987, IMEDE Case No. GM 375.

EXHIBIT 6 Typical Income Statement: Paper Merchant (%)

Sales	100
Cost of goods sold	75
Contribution	25
Other costs	23
Net profit	2
Depreciation	.5
Cash flow	2.5

Source: *The European Printing and Writing Paper Industry—1987.*

and provide technical support for the product. Between 1969 and 1984, the company acquired control of several major merchants operating in the UK, France, Belgium, Italy, and Finland. In 1984, sales of $480 million made Wiggins Teape the largest merchant in Europe.

On the other hand, Paper Union, one of the two largest merchants in Germany (turnover of $142 million and market share of 12 percent in 1984), was an independent merchant. It was formed in the early 1960s, from three smaller merchants, in an attempt to reach the critical size of 100,000 tonnes per year. Due to low margins in Germany, Paper Union had emphasized reducing operating costs and consistently fast delivery. Plans were being made, however, to introduce further services and advertising in an attempt to add value and increase customer awareness.

EXHIBIT 7 Paper Merchants: Ownership and Concentration per Country

Country	Merchants Totaling 80% of Country's Sales	Ownership
Sweden	2	Mill-owned
Denmark	3	Mostly mill-owned
Netherlands	5	Mill-owned
Belgium	5	Mill-owned
Switzerland	5	Mostly mill-owned
Austria	2 (70%)	Mill-owned
France	6	Mill-owned
West Germany	7	All independent
UK	Few big, many small ones	Partly mill-owned Mostly independent

Source: *Paper Merchandising, the Viewpoint of Independent Merchant.*

The move toward company-owned merchants was not without controversy. According to one independent merchant:

We believe that independent merchants are very much in the best interest of paper mills. We're aware, of course, that many mills are integrating forward, buying merchants in order to maintain access to distribution. It is our view, however, that this will cause a number of problems. No one mill can supply all the products that a merchant must offer. Hence, even mill-owned merchants must maintain relations with a number of other mills, who will always want to supply their full range of products to the merchant, including those which compete with the parent mill. This will create serious tensions and frequently will put the merchant in the position of having to choose between corporate loyalty and offering the best package to the customer. The parent can, of course, impose restrictions on the merchant with respect to selling competing products, but the sales force would have serious problems with this.

Our strong preference is for exclusive representation of a mill. This is particularly important where there are strong influencers, such as advertisers, to whom it is important for us to address considerable promotional effort. Also when we are an exclusive merchant, we provide the mill with extensive information on our sales, which allows the mill to do market analysis that both we and the mill find very valuable. We certainly would not provide this kind of information if the mill had intensive distribution. In a country like Switzerland, we can give the mill complete geographic and account coverage, so it's not clear to us why the mill needs more than one merchant. In our view, intensive distribution creates a situation where there is much more emphasis on price. While this first affects the merchant, it inevitably affects the mill as well.

If we do sell for a mill that has intensive distribution, we prefer to sell it under our brand, although we identify the mill, in small print. This is somewhat an historical artifact, going back to the days when mills did not attempt to brand their products, but if we're going to compete for business with another merchant, selling for the same mill, we feel having our name on the product helps us differentiate ourselves from the competitor.

At the same time, we should point out that we don't sell competing brands. There are about five quality grades within standard coated wood-free, and we handle two to three brands.

One industry expert predicted significant changes in distribution patterns.[8]

Looking to the future, it is predicted that there will be an increase in the number of paper grade classifications, moving from 4 just a few years ago to 20 or more. There will be an increasing number of different types of middlemen and distributors, and merchants will move into grades traditionally regarded as mill direct products (e.g., newsprint and mechanical grades) to bring these grades to the smaller customers.

---

[8] From a paper presented by BIS Marketing Research Limited.

Just as we have seen a technological revolution hit the traditional printing industry, we must now see a marketing revolution hit the traditional paper industry. Selection of the correct channel of distribution and the development of an active working relationship with that channel will be vital.

COMPETITION IN COATED WOODFREE PAPERS

In varying degrees, Leykam Mürztaler encountered at least 10 major European firms in the markets it served in Europe. Some, like KNP and Zanders, competed principally in coated woodfree papers. Others, like Stora and Feldmühle, produced a wide range of products, from coated woodfree papers to tissue to newsprint.

There was considerable variation in competitive emphasis among producers. Zanders, for instance, generally regarded as the highest quality producer, mostly produced cast coated and premium art paper,

EXHIBIT 8   Major Mill Reputation

Company	Comments on Reputation
Zanders (Germany)	Mercedes Benz in coated woodfrees. Excellent service. Strong promotion. Marketing activities have also been directed to advertising agencies, who can influence on choice of brand.
Leykam Mürztaler	Reliable supplier. Good service.
Arjomari (France)	Strong positions in France due to its own merchants.
Condat (France)	Good and stable quality.
Feldmühle (Germany)	Stable quality. Rapid deliveries and good stocking arrangements.
KNP (Netherlands)	Flexible supplier, also accepts small orders. Good service.
PWA Hallein (Germany)	Competes with price.
Scheufelen (Germany)	Good and stable quality. Reliable deliveries.
Stora Kopparberg (Sweden)	Reliable deliveries. Quality and service OK.

Source: *EKONO Strategic Study,* September 1988.

competed only at the top end of the standard coated range and was relatively unusual in its extensive use of advertising. Hannover Papier was particularly strong in service, offering fast delivery. PWA Hallein, which had tended to emphasize price over quality, had recently improved its quality but was keeping prices low in an apparent effort to gain market share. Arjomari, the biggest French producer, owned the largest merchant chain in France and had recently purchased merchants in the UK and Southern Europe. It had recently entered the premium art paper segment, generally regarded as difficult to produce for. Burgo, a large Italian conglomerate, concentrated principally on the Italian market. (See Exhibit 8 for a report on the image of selected suppliers.)

Rapid growth in the coated woodfree market had stimulated capacity additions by existing producers and was also stimulating conversion of facilities from uncoated to coated. Nordland of Germany, for instance, switched 100,000 tonnes of capacity from uncoated to coated by adding a coater in October 1988. Excellent in service, there was, however, some question about its ability to produce high quality.

Branding was a relatively new aspect of the industry. All the major producers had established brand names for major products or grades. To date, however, only Zanders had actively promoted its brand to the trade or to advertisers.

MARKETING AT LEYKAM MÜRZTALER AG

Marketing activities at Leykam Mürztaler were divided between the sales director, Wolfgang Pfarl, and the marketing manager, Gertrude Eder. Pfarl, a member of the executive board, was responsible for pricing as well as all personal selling activities, both direct and through merchants. Eder was responsible for public relations, advertising and sales promotion, and marketing research. As a staff member, she reported to Dr. Siegfried Meysel, the Managing Director.

Coated Woodfree Products and Markets

In coated woodfree papers, Leykam Mürztaler offered a comprehensive product line of standard coated papers under the MAGNO brand, for both sheet and web offset printing. These were produced in a wide variety of basis weights, ranging from 80–300 grams per square meter depending on the particular application. The firm targeted the high quality end of the standard coated category by offering higher coat weights, better gloss and print gloss, and better printability.

Using Austria as its home market, Leykam Mürztaler focused its principal efforts on countries in Europe. The majority of sales revenues came, in roughly similar amounts, from Austria, Italy, France, and the UK, with somewhat higher sales in Germany. Belgium, Holland, Switzerland, and Spain were important but smaller markets.

The firm also sold in a number of other countries, including the United States. Penetration of the US market by the European paper industry had been assisted by the favorable exchange rates during the early 1980s. The firm's policy, however, was to maintain its position in different countries despite currency fluctuations. As Gertrude Eder explained:

> We believe our customers expect us to participate in their markets on a long-term basis and to be competitive with local conditions. This may cost us some profits in the short term, as when we maintained our position in the UK despite the weak pound, but now that the pound is strong again, this investment is paying off. If we had reduced our presence when the exchange rate was unfavorable, it would have been very difficult to regain our position.

Channels of Distribution

Over the years, Leykam Mürztaler had sold most of its output through merchants. To some degree the method of distribution was influenced by the country served as the firm tended to follow the predominant trade practice in each country. In Switzerland, Germany, and the UK, all its business was done through merchants. In France, Italy, and Austria, there was a mixed pattern of distribution, but with a strong merchant orientation.

Merchants were carefully selected, and the firm did business only with stocking merchants who competed on service rather than price. In some countries (e.g., Holland) it used exclusive distribution, but this was not the normal pattern. Gertrude Eder explained:

> As a large producer, we have a volume problem. In the larger countries, one merchant simply can't sell enough product for us, plus we believe it is risky to commit completely to one merchant.

Similarly, Wolfgang Pfarl commented:

> In Germany, for instance, we could go to one merchant only, but to get the volume of business we need would require going into direct business with some nonstocking merchants, and that is something that neither we nor our stocking merchants want to happen.

To date, the trend toward mill ownership of merchants had not adversely affected the firm's ability to get good merchant representation. There was some concern, however, that with changing patterns of mill ownership, some merchants might be closed off to firms like Leykam Mürztaler in the future.

Service was also seen as a key to merchant relations. In this connection, the firm felt its computerized order system and new finishing facilities at the Gratkorn mill, highly automated, permitting flexibility in sheeting and packaging, and able to handle the total output of the new paper machine, provided great service capability and gave it a competitive advantage. As the mill superintendent put it:

> From a production standpoint, the ideal scenario is one in which we can run one grade of paper all year and ship it to customers in large reels. Reality is that meeting customer needs is critical, and I believe we have "state-of-the-art competence" in our ability to meet a tremendous variety of customer requirements efficiently.

Pricing

Pricing practices in the paper industry had a strong commodity orientation and, for coated woodfree papers, industry prices tended to serve as the basis for arriving at transaction prices. (See Exhibit 3 for information on industry prices and paper grades.) For sales to merchants, Leykam Mürztaler negotiated price lists, using the industry prices as a starting point, with final prices taking paper quality and other relevant factors into account. Price lists then remained in effect until there was a change in industry price levels. Routine orders were priced from the established price list. Large requirements, however, usually involved special negotiation.

According to one Leykam Mürztaler sales manager:

> We have some interesting discussions with our merchants about price. The customer knows we make a high quality product, so his principal interest is in getting it at the lowest possible price. In Europe there is no uniform classification of coated papers, as there is in the U.S.A. and Japan, so a standard approach is to try to get me to reclassify my product to a lower grade, and so a lower price. To some extent, though, my customer's preoccupation with price simply reflects price pressures he is experiencing from his customers. Still, it is frustrating because we believe we offer a lot more than just price and a good product. But I think we do a good job for the firm in getting the highest price possible.

Branding

In recent years, Leykam Mürztaler had followed the industry practice of branding its principal products. It did, however, supply products to certain merchants for private branding, a practice that was established when mill branding was not the norm. In 1988, some 30% of sales carried a merchant brand, largely reflecting the volume from Germany and the UK, where private branding was customary. Recently, however, the firm had started to identify most of its products by using a typical Leykam Mürztaler packaging, even for private labels.

Brands had been promoted primarily by the sales force, in direct contact with customers, using brochures and samples and by packaging. More recently, a series of superb visual messages was commissioned, using the theme "Dimensions in Paper" to suggest ways that high quality paper combined with printing could produce more effective communication. The script accompanying the visual messages was designed to appeal to both the advertisers, with emphasis on communication, and printers with emphasis on paper finish, touch, color, absorption, contrast and other key paper characteristics. On a limited basis, these messages had appeared in selected magazines and in brochures for customers.

There was general agreement within the firm that more emphasis needed to be placed on branding as a way to achieve product differentiation and convey the desired high quality image. There was less agreement on how much to spend promoting the brands or how to deal with merchants who were now buying Leykam Mürztaler products for sale under the merchants' labels. According to Gertrude Eder:

> Over the past few years we designed the corporate logo and corporate graphics and established blue, black, and white as the colors for all corporate communication. We have worked hard to establish a consistent presentation of our corporate identity. Feedback from customers and the sales department indicates that this has helped improve our visibility and image. Nevertheless, we are currently spending considerably less than 1 percent of sales on advertising. Zanders, on the other hand, a firm of about our size, has been spending a lot of money on advertising for years and as a result has better visibility than we do, particularly with advertising agencies, as well as an enviable reputation for quality and service.
>
> I don't know what the right number is for us, but we will need to spend substantially more if we are to establish the kind of brand awareness and image we desire. I think that to have any significant impact would take a minimum of ASch3–4 million for classical advertising (i.e., advertising in trade publications, in various languages) and ASch8–10 million for promotions, including brochures, leaflets, and trade fairs. In Western Europe we have to advertise in at least four to five languages, and sometimes more. In addition, the nature of the ads varies. In private brand countries, our ads emphasize the company name and focus on the Dimensions in Paper theme as well as the company's experience and modern production facilities. In other countries we emphasize the MAGNO brand.
>
> We are convinced that printers want to know what mill brand they are buying. Also, we believe that there is some subjectivity in selecting paper,

particularly by the advertiser, and we want to convince the advertiser that his message will come across better on Leykam Mürztaler paper.

The decision on supplying Leykam Mürztaler products for private branding was even more complex. As Wolfgang Pfarl commented:

I understand the position of the merchants who want to offer a private brand. The fact remains, however, that it is the mill that determines product characteristics and is responsible for meeting specifications. It is really a question of who is adding the value. In my view the merchant ought to emphasize those things which he controls, such as local stocks, good sales representation and service. Putting a merchant label on paper produced by Leykam Mürztaler misrepresents the value-added picture. Don't get me wrong. Our firm strongly believes in merchants. In fact, we avoid direct business wherever there are strong stocking merchants. It's just that we think mills and merchants have distinct roles to play, and they should not be confused.

Currently, we will still produce for a merchant's label, but we have started to insist that it also is identified as Leykam Mürztaler. The merchants aren't very happy about this, but we think it's the right thing to do.

Nevertheless, the situation with respect to existing merchants was difficult. As one of the senior sales managers said:

We have been supplying some of our merchants with paper to be sold under a private label for a long time, and they have invested substantial sums of money in establishing their own brands. I completely support the company's position on this, but I don't know how we can get the practice to change. If we insist on supplying products only under our own brand, there are a lot of competitors who would, I think, be happy to step in and take over our position with some merchants. If we can't convince a merchant to switch over to our brand, we could lose a lot of business, in one or two instances as much as 6,000 tonnes. On the other hand, if we aren't uniform on this, we will not be able to really exploit the potential of developing our own brands.

In addition to questions about branding policy, it was not clear how to capitalize on increased brand preference, if indeed it were achieved. As Wolfgang Pfarl said:

We might want to think in terms of higher prices or increased share, or some combination. Exactly what we would do could vary from market to market.

Personal Selling

Contact with merchants and with large, directly served accounts in Europe was mainly made by the company's own sales force headquartered in Vienna, by sales representatives in subsidiary companies in

Germany, Italy, and France, and by sales agents in other markets (e.g., the UK). Direct sales representatives numbered 20. Including clerical staff, Leykam had some 60 individuals in its sales department, most of whom had direct contact with customers.

The major activity of the sales force was making direct calls on large customers and on merchants. In addition, sales representatives made occasional calls on a merchant's customers, generally accompanied by the merchant's sales representative. Objectives usually included negotiating long-term contracts, "selling" the existing product line, new product introduction, and a review of customer requirements for products and service.

It was the firm's belief that its sales force was a major asset and that sales representatives could significantly influence relations with merchants. A major objective for all Leykam Mürztaler representatives was to do everything possible to develop close relations with assigned merchants. According to Wolfgang Pfarl:

> The average age of our sales force is between 35 and 40, and most of the individuals have spent their entire career in sales with Leykam Mürztaler. They are really committed to serve the customer, with on-time deliveries or any other aspects of our relationship, and the customer really respects their high level of service. In addition, they are good negotiators and represent Leykam effectively during contract negotiations. They do not need to be technical experts, but they make sure that our technical people provide technical information as required. Also, they monitor shipping performance, make presentations to merchants and may make joint customer calls with merchant sales representatives.

Mathias Radon, one of the Vienna based sales managers, made the following comments:

> In total we call on about 100 merchants in Europe. I work with our sales office in Italy, France, and Belgium and handle five merchants personally in the UK, in cooperation with our representative there. I call on the merchants two to three times a year and have extensive phone contact with our sales offices and representatives from Vienna.
>
> In general, the customer wants to talk about quantity, price, and service. We have conversations about private labelling. The new merchants would like us to give them private labels, but I think they know they can't get it. On the other hand, the ones to whom we are currently providing private labels don't want to give it up. The problem varies from country to country. In France, for instance, it's not such a big problem.
>
> One of my objectives is to encourage more stock business versus indent (merchant orders for direct mill shipment to the customer). This means we have to give them better service and provide back-up stocks.
>
> Some merchants handle mill brands that compete directly with Leykam Mürztaler, but most tend to do this under a private label.

From time to time we work to develop a new merchant, but generally we work on building long-lasting relationships with existing merchants. We encourage trips by merchant personnel to the mill. I will make short presentations to merchant sales representatives when I call on the merchant, but generally they are pretty knowledgeable about paper. We've tried contests and other incentives with merchants and are still thinking about it, but I'm not sure if that's what we should do.

From a quality standpoint, I try to stress whiteness, opacity, printability/ runability, and consistency. Lots of customers ask for lab figures, but I don't think you can rely just on lab reports. We have trial print runs every week by an independent printer to check our consistency. I think most printers feel the same way.

We tend to have lots of small problems rather than any one large problem—branding, for instance, pricing, friction when we appoint a new merchant, and country variations with regard to ways of doing business. I think branding will be important in all countries, but how we capitalize on it may have to vary.

After Sales Service

Problems in printing could arise due to a number of circumstances. There might be variations or flaws in the paper or in the ink. Presses could develop mechanical problems. Even changes in temperature and humidity could negatively affect printing quality. Because of the complexity of the printing process, the cause of a problem was not always clear, and reaching an equitable settlement could be difficult.

When problems did arise, the printer turned to the merchant or mill for technical advice and frequently wanted financial compensation for lost production. According to Wolfgang Pfarl:

When the printer encounters a production problem, it is important for us to be able to give him technical advice and work with him to solve the problem. Sometimes the sales representative can do this. More often, we have to involve one of our technical people from the mill. All too often, however, the printer is just looking for someone to compensate him financially, and we have to be very tough or we're likely to find ourselves paying for a lot of other people's mistakes.

Future Issues

Looking to the future, the firm was focusing its attention on managing "through the business cycle." As Wolfgang Pfarl put it:

Our real challenge is to strengthen our market position in Western Europe. Most of our coated woodfree paper goes into advertising. We have seen extraordinary growth in this market in the last few years, but we have to expect there will be a significant downturn in one or two years and that advertisers will then look intensely at their costs. In many cases this means the printer will suggest a lower cost grade as a substitute for coated wood-free. Our task is to differentiate MAGNO from the generic category and position it as "a paper for all seasons," so to speak. In other words, we want our customers to think of MAGNO as the "right" paper for high quality advertising, separately from coated woodfree.

In general, this means strengthening our corporate identity, being partners of the strongest merchants, and encouraging our merchants to support the MAGNO brand.

In a similar vein, Gertrude Eder commented:

This is a business where the impact of the business cycle is made worse by the tendency of merchants to overstock in good times and destock in bad times. Our objective, I think, should be to position Leykam as the last mill the merchant or printer would think of cancelling in a downturn.

Case 6–2 *California Valley Wine Company**

INTRODUCTION

On a March night in 1988, Maxwell Jones, new products/special project manager for California Valley Wine Company, leaned back in his chair in the office headquarters in Fresno, California. He glanced at the clock. It was already 10:30 P.M. on Wednesday. Max had been in the office since morning, but he was not sure that he was any closer to resolving the dilemma. Max had to make a recommendation which would shape the future of California Valley Wine Company (CVWC).

In recent years the company experienced diminishing sales and declining profitability (Exhibit 1). Several new product ideas were under consideration by CVWC management. Max received instructions to make a recommendation on what the new product was to be. For several months Max worked on the new product project and struggled with the decision. He gathered a large amount of information from trade sources, field salespeople, and executives at CVWC. By the end of the week, Max's recommendation was due to the New Product Evaluation Committee.

---

* This case was prepared by John E. Bargetto, MBA student, and Patrick E. Murphy, professor of marketing, University of Notre Dame. Copyright © 1990 by Patrick E. Murphy. Used with permission.

EXHIBIT 1   Sales and Profit for CVWC, 1980–1987 ($ millions)

Year	*1980*	*1981*	*1982*	*1983*	*1984*	*1985*	*1986*	*1987*
Sales	18.2	19.6	21.9	22.0	21.1	21.2	20.9	19.5
Earnings before taxes	2.1	1.8	1.9	1.6	.9	1.0	(.5)	.05

BACKGROUND OF CALIFORNIA VALLEY WINE COMPANY

CVWC was established in early 1934, shortly after the repeal of Prohibition. The founders, two cousins, George and Frank Lombardi, grew table grapes in Fresno, California, and saw the sudden demand in wine as a good opportunity to enter the wine business. The Lombardis purchased an old winery that had been vacated during Prohibition, and they began fermenting in the fall of 1934. In the early years they sold their wines mainly in barrels to restaurants, hotels, and liquor stores. In 1950 they constructed a major, modern winery on the outskirts of Fresno and planted additional vineyards.

In 1988 CVWC owned 1,600 acres of grapes, mostly Chenin Blanc, Thompson Seedless, and Ruby Cabernet. They marketed the wines in 1.5 and 3.0 liter bottles which retailed for $3.59 and $6.79, respectively. The three wines sold were Chenin Blanc (a white wine made from Chenin Blanc grapes), a Mountain Burgundy (a red wine made from Ruby Cabernet grapes), and a Mountain Rose (a rose wine made from a blend of red wine and Thompson Seedless).

CONTEMPORARY WINE INDUSTRY CONDITIONS

In recent years the wine business in California (where 90 percent of U.S. wine is produced) experienced particular difficulties. The so-called wine boom of the 1970s, when consumption levels of wine rose steadily, was over; per capita wine consumption recently declined (see Exhibit 2). The highest-ever consumption level occurred in 1985 and 1986, at 2.43 gallons per capita. However, in 1987 for the first time in 25 years, per capita consumption of wine decreased. Max knew well the reasons for the decline: growing health consciousness in society, greater awareness of physical problems associated with alcohol consumption, stiffer DUI laws and a rising drinking age, and the popularity of soft drinks with the younger generation. After 15 years of solid growth, total wine consumption (including coolers) in 1987 slipped to 581 million gallons.

EXHIBIT 2 Apparent Wine Consumption in the United States, 1934–1987

Year	Population* 1,000 Persons	Population* Percent Change	Wine Consumption† 1,000 Gallons	Wine Consumption† Percent Change	Per Capita Wine Consumption Gallons	Per Capita Wine Consumption Percent Change
1934	126,374	—	32,674	—	0.26	—
1935	127,250	0.7%	45,701	39.9%	0.36	38.5%
1936	128,053	0.6	60,303	32.0	0.47	30.6
1937	128,825	0.6	66,723	10.6	0.52	10.6
1938	129,825	0.8	67,050	0.5	0.52	0.0
1939	130,880	0.8	76,647	14.3	0.59	13.5
1940	131,954	0.8	89,664	17.0	0.68	15.3
1941	133,121	0.9	101,445	13.1	0.76	11.8
1942	133,920	0.6	133,038	11.4	0.84	10.5
1943	134,245	0.2	97,501	−13.7	0.73	−13.1
1944	132,885	−1.0	98,955	1.5	0.74	1.4
1945	132,481	−0.3	93,975	− 5.0	0.71	−4.1
1946	140,054	5.7	140,316‡	49.3	1.00‡	40.8
1947	143,446	2.4	96,660‡	−31.1	0.67‡	−33.0
1948	146,093	1.8	122,290	26.5	0.84	25.4
1949	148,665	1.8	132,567	8.4	0.89	6.0
1950	151,235	1.7	140,380	5.9	0.93	4.5
1951	153,310	1.4	126,514	−9.9	0.83	−10.8
1952	155,687	1.6	137,620	8.8	0.88	6.0
1953	158,242	1.6	140,796	2.3	0.89	1.1
1954	161,164	1.8	142,156	1.0	0.88	−1.1
1955	164,308	2.0	145,186	2.1	0.88	0.0
1956	167,306	1.8	150,039	3.3	0.90	2.3
1957	170,371	1.8	151,881	1.2	0.89	−1.1
1958	173,320	1.7	154,633	1.8	0.89	0.0
1959	176,289	1.7	156,224	1.0	0.89	0.0
1960	179,979	2.1	163,352	4.6	0.91	2.2
1961	182,992	1.7	171,632	5.1	0.94	3.3
1962	185,771	1.5	168,082	−2.1	0.90	−4.3
1963	188,483	1.5	175,918	4.7	0.93	3.3
1964	191,141	1.4	185,625	5.5	0.97	4.3
1965	193,526	1.2	189,677	2.2	0.98	1.0
1966	195,576	1.1	191,176	0.8	0.98	0.0
1967	197,457	1.0	203,403	6.4	1.03	5.1
1968	199,399	1.0	213,658	5.0	1.07	3.9
1969	201,385	1.0	235,628	10.3	1.17	9.3
1970	203,984	1.3	267,351	13.5	1.31	12.0
1971	206,827	1.4	305,221	14.2	1.48	13.0
1972	209,284	1.2	336,985	10.4	1.61	8.8
1973	211,357	1.0	347,481	3.1	1.64	1.9
1974	213,342	0.9	349,465	0.6	1.64	0.0
1975	215,465	1.0	368,029	5.3	1.71	4.3

EXHIBIT 2   *(concluded)*

Year	Population* 1,000 Persons	Percent Change	Wine Consumption† 1,000 Gallons	Percent Change	Per Capita Wine Consumption Gallons	Percent Change
1976	217,563	1.0	376,389	2.3	1.73	1.2
1977	219,760	1.0	400,972	6.5	1.82	5.2
1978	222,095	1.1	434,696	8.4	1.96	7.7
1979	224,567	1.1	444,375	2.2	1.98	1.0
1980	227,255	1.2	479,628	7.9	2.11	6.6
1981	229,637	1.0	505,684	5.4	2.20	4.3
1921	231,996	1.0	514,045	1.7	2.22	0.9
1983	234,284	1.0	528,076	2.7	2.25	1.4
1984	236,477	0.9	554,510	5.0	2.34	4.0
1985	238,736	1.0	580,292	4.6	2.43	3.8
1986	241,096	1.0	587,064	1.2	2.43	0.0
1987§	243,400	1.0	580,933	−1.0	2.39	−1.6

* All ages resident population in the United States on July 1.
† All wine, including wine coolers, entering distribution channels in the United States.
‡ Figures reflect excessive inventory accumulation by consumers and the trade in 1946, and subsequent inventory depletion in 1947; therefore, data for these years do not accurately reflect consumption patterns.
§ Preliminary.

Sources: Prepared by Economic Research Department, Wine Institute, on behalf of the California Wine Commission. Based on data obtained from reports of Bureau of Alcohol, Tobacco, and Firearms, U.S. Treasury Department, and Bureau of the Census, U.S. Department of Commerce.

During the 1970s, with its steady growth and romantic appeal, the wine industry drew many interested investors. The number of California wineries grew from 240 in 1970 to over 600 by 1980. While most of these were smaller wineries with whom CVWC did not compete directly, some aggressive competitors did enter the market. For example, in 1977 Coca-Cola purchased Taylor California Cellers and employed the same sophisticated marketing techniques—segmentation and slick advertising campaigns—used to sell Coke. (Coke sold Taylor to Seagrams in 1983, but Coke left behind the impact of much greater advertising expenditures by the entire wine industry.) With all of these new entrants, inventories swelled in most wineries and the industry suffered from excess supply.

To make matters worse, during the first half of the 1980s the dollar was overpriced in international markets. The wine market became flooded with inexpensive foreign wines, mainly from Italy, France, and Germany. In 1984, imports held 25.7 percent of the total wine market in the United States. Italian wines (such as the well-known brands of Riunite and Soave Bolla) dominated in the United States with 51 percent of the imported wine market.

During the 1980s consumption of hard booze such as whiskey and vodka dropped significantly. At the same time, low-alcohol wines (7–9 percent) as well as nonalcoholic wines entered the market. These changes reflected a growing concern about the need for greater moderation regarding the consumption of alcoholic beverages. Increased desire for good health and concern about the high caloric content of alcoholic beverages also discouraged alcoholic beverage consumption in the United States during the 1980s. In fact, a Gallup Poll taken in 1987 showed that 63 percent of Americans "occasionally drink alcohol" while a 1989 poll indicated that the percentage fell to 56 percent.

Social activist groups had recently directed consumers' attention toward the need for more moderate alcohol consumption. The growing attention about the dangers of alcohol use while driving gave rise to organizations such as MADD (Mothers Against Drunk Driving) and SADD (Students Against Driving Drunk). One organization, Stop Marketing Alcohol on Radio and Television (SMART), embarked on a major lobbying effort to restrict advertising of beer and wine because of health problems associated with alcoholic beverages and the companies appeal to younger and underage drinkers.

From his vantage point within the industry, Max was clearly aware that all these factors pointed to the changing attitude that Americans had toward the use of all alcoholic beverages. CVWC's sales had been affected by all of these developments. The sales of its red, white, and rose table wines bottled under the brand name California Valley continued to lose market share (Exhibit 3). It was time that CVWC did something and it was Max's responsibility to evaluate new product

EXHIBIT 3   CVWC Market Share of Jug Wines (1980–1987)

	Market Share
1980	14.0%
1981	15.0
1982	15.1
1983	14.9
1984	14.1
1985	14.6
1986	13.2
1987	10.4

possibilities. He had been with CVWC since 1962 when he joined as a sales representative. Over the years he was promoted to sales manager and eventually became the western states regional director of sales.

TWO POSSIBLE PRODUCTS

After considering several possible products, including sparkling wines, fruit wines, and blush wines, Max narrowed the field to two: a wine cooler or an inexpensive dessert wine. A wine cooler is a blend of carbonated water, fruit juice, and wine with an alcohol level of 4–6 percent. While wine coolers had been consumed for years, sometimes in the form of sangria, the surge in popularity had been a recent phenomenon (Exhibit 4). Coolers were first introduced as a commercial beverage in the early 1980s by California Cooler and there were numerous brands on the market. One concern expressed by the president at CVWC was the relatively high caloric content (225 per 12-ounce bottle) of the wine cooler. By 1987, the wine cooler segment of the wine industry had swelled to a $1.7 billion business representing 20 percent of the wine market.

The majority of the cooler market was divided between five market leaders. In 1987, Seagram's Wine Cooler and Gallo's Bartles and Jaymes together commanded nearly 48 percent of the market (Exhibit

EXHIBIT 4   Total Cases of Wine Coolers Sold, 1981–1987 (millions)

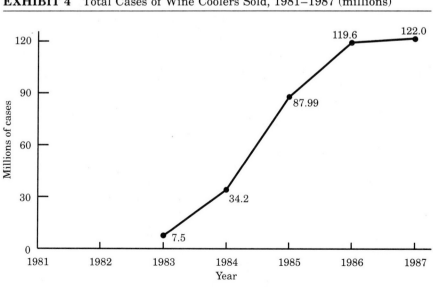

EXHIBIT 5   Wine Cooler Market Share (1987)

Cooler	Share
Seagrams	24.0%
Bartles & Jaymes	23.4
California Cooler	13.1
Sun Country	9.2
White Mountain	7.1
All others	23.2
Total	100.0%

---

5). Miller Brewing Company made a major product introduction of Matilda Bay malt-based cooler in 1987. Max was uncertain whether wine coolers were merely a fad or if they would become a permanent beverage option for consumers.

Although the rapid growth of the cooler market had ended, it represented a tremendous potential for sales. However, if CVWC were to enter this market, it would meet tough competition. A large advertising budget would be required to take market share from those brands already established, such as Bartles & Jaymes and Seagrams. For instance, Gallo allotted $80 million in 1985 to introduce its new cooler product.

CVWC could easily produce wine coolers from excess bulk wine. Other ingredients needed to make coolers are easily obtained. The same wine wholesalers through which CVWC sold its table wine can be utilized to distribute the cooler product. For example, the company used wholesalers and also sold directly to large retailers such as the Liquor Barn (a chain of California discount liquor stores) and out-of-state distributors in other places.

The Dessert Wine Option

Wines containing more than 14 percent alcohol are known as fortified or dessert wines because brandy has been added during the fermentation process to yield a beverage with higher alcohol content than table wines. Dessert wines can be contrasted with table wines that usually have an alcohol content of 10–14 percent. The most important advantage of the fortified wine option is profitability; the 22 percent net margins on these wines were larger than the 13 percent net margin on wine coolers. The varieties of grapes that CVWC grew were ideal for fortified wines, both for making the wine and the brandy required. Max had estimated that for $20,000 CVWC could set up an in-house brandy distillery which could supply all the brandy required to make fortified wines.

Although the same distributors would be used to get this product onto the market, Max was aware that some of the biggest liquor stores in California refused to carry low-end dessert wine products. In the words of a manager at one Liquor Barn, "We don't carry those products because we do not want the clientele in our store."

Dessert wines included a whole range of products from high-end Portugese ports ($15/bottle) to low-end muscatels ($1.99 bottle). During the 1940s and 1950s, these sweet ports and sherries represented a sizable portion of the wine consumed and they continued to grow until about 1970. The tastes of typical wine consumers for these sweet wines moved to a preference for drier table wines, and the market for fortified wines began to erode. In recent years, the majority of the fortified wines consumed were inexpensive brown bag purchases by street drunks. Although the image of these wines has changed, dessert wines have a noble past.

EXHIBIT 6   Wine Consumption in the United States, 1968–1986

Year	U.S.-Produced Other Special Natural Wine over 14 Percent Alcohol Consumed in the United States	All U.S.-Produced Wine Consumed in the United States (1,000 gallons)	Percent of Type
1968	12,591	191,447	6.6%
1969	12,221	210,936	5.8
1970	11,665	237,328	4.9
1971	11,631	269,065	4.3
1972	11,823	289,942	4.1
1973	10,944	292,041	3.7
1974	9,653	298,071	3.2
1975	10,918	318,071	3.4
1976	11,994	317,470	3.8
1977	12,396	331,766	3.7
1978	11,104	340,620	3.3
1979	10,084	352,206	2.9
1980	10,008	377,120	2.7
1981	10,288	390,971	2.6
1982	10,293	391,956	2.6
1983	11,055	397,070	2.8
1984	10,807	412,099	2.6
1985	11,724	441,034	2.7
1986	13,698	477,891	2.9

History of Fortified Wines.   Fortifying wine with the addition of brandy is a practice that dates back to the Roman period. The fortification process solved a practical problem of wine spoilage in ancient times. Wine spoilage especially posed a problem for those traveling who did not have the luxury of a cool cellar to protect the wine from damaging heat. Winemakers of that early era discovered that if wine was fortified by adding a concentrated spirit (like brandy) it would age longer. This practice was copied by the British living in Madeira, Portugal, who found that this fortification process allowed the wine to hold up better for the long sea journey home.

During the decades following the repeal of Prohibition in 1933, fortified wines such as sherries and ports represented a major portion of the wine consumed in the United States. These wines were typically enjoyed as an aperitif or as a dessert. However, as tastes changed and the variety of wines available broadened, wine drinkers began to consume more table wines. In 1970 dessert wines represented 27.7 percent of the wine market, but by 1986 they accounted for only 7.5 percent of the total wine market. Inexpensive fortified wine products are classified as special natural wines. As measured in volume, consumption of this product has been quite steady during the years 1968–1986 (Exhibit 6). Table wines saw a big increase in consumption during the 1970s and represented the vast majority of the nearly 600 million gallons consumed in the United States.

THE DILEMMA

Max was well aware, however, of the problems involved with entering the fortified wine market. Fortified wines presently available in the market were typically associated with the type of wines consumed by the destitute alcoholics who roamed the streets. Max was struck by an article he read some time ago in *The Wall Street Journal*. He reached for a copy of the article he had placed in a file folder and reread it closely. (The text of the article is shown in Exhibit 7.)

He was particularly sensitive about alcoholism because his father had suffered from the disease. He knew that many street drunks depended on these inexpensive fortified wines because it was the cheapest source of alcohol available. However, Max was not really sure what percentage of fortified wines were purchased by public drunks.

Max had wondered for some time about the ramifications of offering a fortified product to the market and whether or not it would add to the serious problem of alcoholism in this country. After reading *The Wall Street Journal* article, Max contacted the Wine Institute in San Francisco. The Wine Institute is an industry-funded organization whose purpose is to represent the California wineries and promote their

EXHIBIT 7

Misery Market: Winos & Thunderbird Are a Subject
Gallo Doesn't Like to Discuss

New York—In the dim light of a cold February morning, a grizzled wino shuffles into the Bowery Discount liquor store muttering, "Thunderchicken, it's good lickin.'" Fumbling for some change, he says: "Gimme one bird." Raymond Caba, the store clerk, understands the argot and hands over a $1.40 pint of Thunderbird, the top seller in what he calls "the bum section."

The ritual is repeated a thousand times a day in dead-end neighborhoods across the country. Cheap wines with down-and-dirty names—and an extra measure of alcohol— are the beverage of choice among down-and-out drunks. But winos are a major embarrassment to the big companies that manufacture these wines. With rare exceptions, they aren't eager to acknowledge their own products.

Thunderbird and Night Train Express are produced by the nation's largest wine company, E. & J. Gallo Winery, though you'll not learn that from reading the label on the bottle. MD 20/20 is made by Mogen David Wine Corp., a subsidiary of Wine Group Ltd., which refuses to talk about its product. Richards Wild Irish Rose Wine, the very best seller in the category, is produced by Canandaigua Wine Co. Canandaigua is volubly proud of the wine but quick to point out that it enjoys wide popularity with people who aren't alcoholics.

The Biggest Bang

People concerned about the plight of street alcoholics are critical of the purveyors of dollar-a-pint street wines made with cheap ingredients and fortified with alcohol to deliver the biggest bang for the buck. At 18% to 21% alcohol, these wines have about twice the kick of ordinary table wine, without any of the pretension.

The consumption of alcohol in the U.S. *is* declining in virtually every category, but the best selling of the low-end brands keep growing, in large part because customers can't stop drinking. Says Paul Gillette, the publisher of the Wine Investor in Los Angeles: "Makers of skid-row wines are the dope pushers of the wine industry."

Vintners generally try hard to filter their wines through the imagery of luxury and moderation, stressing vintage, touting quality. So they are understandably reluctant to be associated in any way with what some call a $500 million misery market.

Suppliers deny that the most popular street wines sell as well as they do because they appeal to dirt-poor, hardcore drinkers. Companies contend that their clientele is not like that at all, and besides, any alcoholic beverage can be abused. (The wine people say they face stiff competition from high-alcohol malt liquor and 200-milliliter bottles of cheap vodka.) The future for the high-proof business, vintners say, isn't particularly rosy in any case. The wine category they call "dessert" or "fortified"—sweet wines with at least 14% alcohol—has lost favor with drinkers.

Markedly Profitable

Wino wines are inexpensive to produce. They come in no-frills, screw-top packaging and require little or no advertising. Although they generally aren't the major part of vintners' product lineups, they are especially profitable. All told, net profit margins are 10% higher than those of ordinary table wines, Canandaigua estimates. Gallo says

EXHIBIT 7   *(continued)*

that isn't true for its products, but it won't say what is true.

The wines are also a rock-solid business. Of all the wine brands in America, the trade newsletter *Impact* says, Wild Irish Rose holds the No. 6 spot, Thunderbird is 10th and MD 20/20 is 16th. In contrast to the lackluster growth of most other wine brands, unit sales of the leading cheap labels, Wild Irish Rose and Thunderbird are expected to be up 9.9% and 8.6% respectively this year, *Jobson's Wine Marketing Handbook* estimates.

So unsavory is this market that companies go to great lengths to distance themselves from their customers. If suppliers are willing to talk about the segment—and few are— they still don't acknowledge the wino's loyal patronage. Gallo and Canandaigua leave their good corporate names off the labels, thus obscuring the link between product and producer.

The 'No-Name Market'

"This is the market with no name," says Clifford Adelson, a former executive director of sales at Manischewitz Wine Co., which once made low-end wines and was recently acquired by Canandaigua. "It's lots and lots of money, but it doesn't add prestige."

Cheap wines typically aren't even sold in many liquor stores. For instance, Frank Gaudio, who owns the big Buy-Rite Twin Towers Wine & Spirits store in New York's World Trade Center, doesn't stock any of these brands, though many homeless alcoholics spend their days just outside his door. "We don't want that clientele in our store," he says. "We could sell [fortified wines] and probably make money, but we don't." The wines, however, are staples of the bulletproof liquor stores of low-income neighborhoods. While you can't say the whole market for items like Thunderbird and Night Train consists of derelicts, down-and-outers do seem to be its lifeblood. Fifty current and reformed

drinkers interviewed for this article claim to have lived on a gallon a day or more of the stuff.

"The industry is manufacturing this for a selected population: the poor, the homeless, the skid-row individual," says Neil Goldman, the chief of the alcoholism unit at St. Vincent's Hospital in Manhattan's Greenwich Village.

*   *   *

Dawn finds a small bottle gang near the Bowery, chasing away the morning shakes with a bottle of Thunderbird they pass from hand to hand. Mel Downing tugs up the pant leg of his filthy jeans to reveal an oozing infection on his knee. He is drinking, he says, to numb the pain of this "wine sore" and other ones on his back before he goes to the hospital later in the morning. "We're used to this stuff," the 39-year-old Mr. Downing quickly adds. "We like the effect. We like the price."

A cheap drunk is the main appeal of the wines that winos call "grape" or "jug," but most often just "cheap." Winos say that these wines, even when consumed in quantity, don't make them pass out as readily as hard liquor would.

Walter Single, a recovering alcoholic, recalls that on a daily diet of nine pints of Wild Irish Rose, he still was able "to function well enough to panhandle the money he needed to drink all day and still have enough left for a wake-up in the morning."

Some drinkers say the high sugar content of the wines reduces their appetite for food, so they don't have to eat much. Others say they still can drink wine even after their livers are too far gone to handle spirits. Still others appreciate the portability of pint bottles.

"I feel more secure with a pint," explains Teddy Druzinski, a former carpenter. "It's next to me. It's in my pocket." Canandaigua

EXHIBIT 7   *(continued)*

estimates that low-end brands account for 43 million gallons of the dessert category's 55 million gallons and that 50% is purchased in pints.

Many people in the wine industry eschew producing skid-row wines. "I don't think Christian Brothers should be in a category where people are down on their luck—where some may be alcoholics," says Richard Maher, the president of Christian Brothers Winery in St. Helena, Calif. Mr. Maher, who once was with Gallo, says fortified wines lack "any socially redeeming values."

"The consumers are we alcoholics," agrees Patrick Gonzales, a 45-year-old wino who is undergoing a week of detoxification at a men's shelter on New York's Lower East side: "You don't see no one sitting at home sipping Mad Dog [MD 20/20] in a wine glass over ice."

Market Profile

Major producers see their customers otherwise. Robert Huntington, the vice president of strategic planning at Canandaigua, says the Canandaigua, N.Y., company sells 60% to 75% of its "pure grape" Wild Irish Rose in primarily black, inner-city markets. He describes customers as "not super-sophisticated," lower middle-class and low-income blue-collar workers, mostly men.

Daniel Solomon, a Gallo spokesman, maintains that Thunderbird "has lost its former popularity in the black and skidrow areas" and is quaffed mainly by "retired and older folks who don't like the taste of hard products."

According to accounts that Gallo disputes, the company revolutionized the skid-row market in the 1950s after discovering that liquor stores in Oakland, Calif., were catering to the tastes of certain customers by attaching packages of lemon Kool-Aid to bottles of white wine. Customers did their own mixing at home. The story goes that Gallo, borrowing the idea, created citrus-flavored Thunderbird. Other flavored high-proof wines then surged into the marketplace. Among them: Twister, Bali Hai, Hombre, Silver Satin and Gypsy Rose. Gallo says that the Kool-Aid story is "a nice myth" but that Thunderbird was "developed by our wine makers in our laboratories."

Vintners advertised heavily and sought to induce skid row's opinion leaders—nicknamed "bell cows"—to switch brands by plying them with free samples. According to Arthur Palombo, the chairman of Cannon Wines Ltd. and one of Gallo's marketing men in the 1950s and '60s, "These were clandestine promotions." He doesn't say which companies engaged in the practice.

Today, such practices and most brands have long since died out. Companies now resort to standard point-of-sale promotions and, in the case of Canandaigua, some radio and television advertising. There still is an occasional bit of hoopla. In New Jersey, Gallo recently named a Thunderbird Princess, and Canandaigua currently is holding a Miss Wild Irish Rose contest. But to hear distributors tell it, word of mouth remains the main marketing tool.

The market is hard to reach through conventional media. Winos will drink anything if need be, but when they have the money to buy what they want, they tend to hew to the familiar. (Sales resistance may help explain why the handful of low-end products that companies have tried to launch in the past 20 years mostly have bombed.) Besides, "it would be difficult to come up with an advertising campaign that says this will go down smoother, get you drunker and help you panhandle better," says Robert Williams, a reformed alcoholic and counselor at the Manhattan Bowery Corp.'s Project Renewal, a half-way house for Bowery alcoholics.

EXHIBIT 7   *(concluded)*

Companies see no reason to spend a lot of money promoting brands they don't want to be identified with. "Gallo and ourselves have been trying to convey the image of a company that makes fine products," says Hal Riney, the president of Hal Riney & Associates, which created the TV characters Frank Bartles and Ed Jaymes for Gallo's wine cooler. "It would be counterproductive to advertise products like this."

Richards Wild Irish Rose purports to be made by Richards Wine Co. The label on a bottle of Gallo's Night Train reads "vinted & bottled by Night Train Limited, Modesto, Ca." Gallo's spokesman, Mr. Solomon, says "The Gallo name is reserved for traditional [table] wines."

Industry people chime in that it isn't at all uncommon for companies to do business under a variety of monikers. But they also agree with Cannon's Mr. Palombo: "Major wine producers don't want to be associated with a segment of the industry that is determined to be low-end and alcoholic."

Winos have their own names for what they buy, Gallo's appellations notwithstanding. When they go to buy Night Train, they might say, "Gimme a ticket." They call Thunderbird "pluck," "T-Bird" or "chicken." In street lingo, Richards Wild Irish Rose is known as "Red Lady," while MD 20/20 is "Mad Dog."

If skid-row wines are cheap to market, they are even cheaper to make. They are generally concocted by adding flavors, sugar and high-proof grape-based neutral spirits to a base wine. The wine part is produced from the cheapest grapes available. Needless to say, the stuff never sees the inside of an oak barrel.

"They dip a grape in it so they can say it's made of wine," says Dickie Gronan, a 67-year-old who describes himself as a bum. "But it's laced with something to make you thirstier." Sugar probably. In any event, customers keep on swigging. Some are so hooked that they immediately turn to an underground distribution system on Sundays and at other times when liquor stores are closed. "Bootleggers," often other alcoholics, buy cheap brands at retail and resell them at twice the price. The street shorthand for such round-the-clock consumption is "24-7."

At nightfall, Mr. Downing, the member of the bottle gang with the leg infection, is panhandling off the Bowery "to make me another jug," as he puts it. As his shredded parka attests, he got into a fight earlier in the day with his buddy, Mr. Druzinski, who then disappeared. Mr. Downing also got too drunk to make it, as planned, to the hospital for treatment of his "wine sores."

A short while later, Mr. Druzinski emerges from the shadows. He has a bloodied face because he "took another header," which is to say he fell on his head. Nevertheless, in the freezing darkness, he joins his partner at begging once again.

"I'm feeling sick to my stomach, dizzy and mokus," Mr. Downing says. "But I still want another pint." He scans the deserted street and adds: "Another bottle is the biggest worry on our minds."

wines. The reply regarding this question of the so-called misery market came in a written letter.

> We reject the notion, however, that availability of "over 14 percent wine" encourages and/or causes abuse of the product. We know from a wide range of literature that alcohol abuse is a complex medical and social problem evolving from a vast array of generic biochemical predispositions, cultural norms, behaviors, expectations, and beliefs. We believe the most effective way to address alcoholism is through intervention, education, treatment, and prevention programs.

In doing some more research about the social implications of fortified beverages, Max had found an article in the *British Journal of Addiction*.[1] The article was titled, "A Ban of Fortified Wine in Northwestern Ontario and Its Impact on the Consumption Level and Drinking Pattern." The article described an experiment in which fortified wines were removed from store shelves in 10 communities in Ontario. The brands removed were those in the lower-price category, and considered to be the more popular beverage of public inebriates, many of whom were Native Indians. The researchers sought to compare the drinking patterns of people living in these 10 delisted communities with those in 18 communities where these fortified wines continued to be available. The researchers found that the ban of these fortified wines only led to an increased consumption of table wines, vodka, and Liquor Board wines and in some cases created additional social problems. Max felt that the presence of fortified wines in the American market did not cause alcoholism, but felt bothered by the idea that a large proportion of the customers for a CVWC fortified product might be these public drunks.

MARKETING STRATEGY

Whether Max recommended CVWC to enter the fortified wine market or the wine cooler market, he would be responsible for developing the appropriate marketing strategy. Max had a fairly clear vision in his mind of what the two potential products could be. In the case of the fortified wine, it would be made from the Thompson Seedless and French Colombard grapes and would contain about 15 percent sugar while having 18 percent alcohol. He thought perhaps the product could have an added orange or cherry flavor.

Given the potential image problems that a market for a fortified product could create for CVWC, Max felt that if they were to enter this

---

[1] "A Ban of Fortified Wine in Northwestern Ontario and its Impact on the Consumption Level and Drinking Patterns," *British Journal of Addiction,* 76 (1981), pp. 281–88.

market it would be best for CVWC to utilize an alternative brand name and a DBA (doing business as). The DBA is the name of the producer which, by law, has to be listed on the label. To protect the image of California Valley Wine Company, the bottom of the label could read "Produced and Bottled by CVWC Cellars," thereby disguising the producer of the wine. In addition to the DBA, as the *TWSJ* article mentioned, many wineries in California used second labels in order to protect the image of their main brand. For example, Gallo bottles its wines under a whole myriad of brand names: Carlo Rossi, Andre, and Polo Brindisi. Exhibit 8 lists the brand names, producers, and market shares of the leading fortified wine products. Although Max had not given much consideration to possible brand names for the fortified wine, Warm Nights had been tossed around by some of the salespeople.

Max felt that perhaps an upscale product with a distinctive label could be developed, one that commanded a higher price in the market and which in turn would yield a greater margin. It could be bottled in 750 milliliter bottles and positioned distinctively away from the low-end competition of MD 20/20 and Thunderbird. Certainly part of the reasons these wines were favorites of the public drunks was the inexpensive price. A 375-milliliter bottle of Night Train retailed for $1.09. The 750-milliliter bottles of Thunderbird and Wild Irish Rose could be purchased for as little as $1.99 and $2.32, respectively.

He wondered if the flat-shaped, pint-size bottle of Night Train had been intentionally designed to fit into a coat pocket. He thought that CVWC—in order to avoid the misery market—could market a product packaged with a fancy label in a corked bottle, and sell it for a higher

---

EXHIBIT 8   U.S. Fortified Wine Industry (fortified wines are sweet wines with at least 14 percent alcohol)

Wine	*Producer*	*Market Share (percent)*
Wild Irish Rose	Canandaigua	22%
Thunderbird	Gallo	18
All other Gallo dessert wines		16
MD 20/20	Wine Group Ltd.	7
Cisco	Canandaigua	4
Night Train Express	Gallo	3
All others: imported dessert wines, other domestic brands		30

Source: Industry estimates.

price, for example, $5.50. It could be positioned more as a sophisticated dessert wine. But then Max questioned whether or not customers would be willing to pay for this.

Max believed that the fortified wine was a liquor store item. Perhaps it would be feasible to selectively market this product, focusing on suburban stores. In this way the inner-city liquor stores, often frequented by public drunks, could be avoided. Max knew that once the product is out on the store shelves, the producer cannot influence who buys the product or how it is used. One idea that came to mind was that CVWC could print on the bottom of the labels "ENJOY IN MODERA-TION" like some other alcoholic beverage producers had done.[2] Perhaps this would help discourage abuse of the product. Max had bounced the idea off one of the salespeople, who replied, "Hey, Max, that's not our responsibility."

Promotion of fortified wines posed a particularly difficult problem. Max wondered how CVWC could promote the product and which product attributes could be highlighted. Max pulled out his *Code of Advertising Standards* that wine industry members were to voluntarily abide by. The following is a paragraph from the first section:

> Subscribers shall not depict or describe in their advertising: The consumption of wine or wine coolers for the effects their alcohol content may produce or make direct or indirect reference to alcohol content or extra strength, except as otherwise required by law or regulation.

There were certainly problems with promotion of this product, but one thing was certain. If CVWC was not able to promote the product it would be difficult to take market share away from the competition.

Of course, if Max were to recommend entering the wine cooler business, the problems associated with fortified wines would be avoided. If CVWC was to be successful in the wine cooler business, it would require some innovation. Max had thought that CVWC could develop a cooler with new flavors, for example, pomegranate or wild berry. They could be packaged in six packs potentially leading to greater sales over the typical four pack. He believed women could be targeted for this new product which could be sold as low calorie. Max considered whether CVWC might get some nationally known TV star to endorse the new product.

He turned on the PC near his desk and stared at the projections for both the fortified wine and wine cooler options. Exhibit 10 contains the actual numbers generated by the spreadsheet program. Both alternatives seemed to be viable and would help the bottom line of CVWC. He thought the numbers might even be a bit conservative.

---

[2] "Alco Beverage Company and Moderation Advertising," HBS case 9–387–070.

EXHIBIT 10 Projected CVWC Sales (1989–1991)

	Wine Cooler		
	1989	*1990*	*1991*
Sales (millions)*	5.00	6.00	7.00
Expenses			
Cost of goods sold	3.00	3.60	4.20
Selling and administrative	0.20	0.20	0.20
Salaries	0.15	0.17	0.19
Advertising	0.90	0.90	0.90
Interest	0.20	0.25	0.25
Total expenses	4.45	5.12	5.74
Earnings before taxes	0.55	0.88	1.26
	Fortified Wine		
Sales (millions)†	2.50	3.50	5.50
Expenses			
Cost of goods sold	1.00	1.40	2.20
Selling and administrative	0.20	0.20	0.20
Salaries	0.10	0.11	0.12
Advertising	0.20	0.20	0.20
Interest	0.15	0.15	0.15
Total expenses	1.65	2.06	2.87
Earning before taxes	0.85	1.44	2.63

* Based on \$11.42/case selling price.
† Based on \$14.75/case selling price.

Max was even more confounded by all of these considerations. But then again it was his responsibility to give the recommendation to the committee. Not only was he expected to present his recommendation regarding the new product to the New Product Evaluation Committee but he was also asked to discuss his strategy with the Social Responsibility Committee. This committee had been established in 1976 to oversee the activities of the various departments at CVWC because of its involvement in the alcoholic beverage industry.

When looking for some misplaced statistics on his cluttered desk, Max found a memo he had received from the vice president of marketing earlier in the day. The memo was marked "urgent" in red ink. It instructed Max to have his recommendation available by noon tomorrow. The memo concluded with a "Are there any other new product options you haven't explored? Max, see me in the morning." Max took a long breath and reached for the articles on the wine industry that covered his desk. Thumbing through them he hoped that a clear strategy would come to mind, one that he could sleep with.

Case 6–3   Procter & Gamble Co.*

Just after New Year's day, investment bankers for Revlon Inc. Chairman Ronald O. Perelman began quietly looking for someone to buy the glitzy cosmetics company. Within days, Procter & Gamble Co. came calling. Just a month later, P&G's relatively new chairman, Edwin Artzt, was meeting personally with Mr. Perelman, and P&G now appears the front-runner in an international competition for Revlon.

This hardly seems like the stodgy soap maker of Cincinnati. But P&G's aggressive interest in Revlon is just the latest move by Mr. Artzt to put his own stamp on the formal, slow-moving company.

In fact, Mr. Artzt has been on the warpath since he was named to P&G's top spot. He has told managers of faltering brands, like Citrus Hill orange juice, to get results or he'll sell the business. He has cut spending for once-sacred projects, like the fat substitute olestra, to focus on best-sellers like superconcentrated Tide detergent and Pert Plus shampoo. And he is clearing out managers who don't perform.

"I certainly don't want to have a short trigger with people and not give them a chance," he says. "But sure I've cleared out deadwood. Probably some of it was still breathing when it was cleared out."

P&G wasn't doing all that badly before Mr. Artzt took the helm. In fact, when the low-key John G. Smale stepped down in late 1989 after an 18 percent profit surge that fiscal year, Mr. Artzt was thought by many to be only a caretaker replacement.

But Mr. Artzt is confronting a maturing market for many of the company's staple products, such as diapers and detergents, while at the same time P&G's competitors have become more aggressive.

In response, Mr. Artzt wants to turn P&G into more of a fast-moving global marketer, particularly in high-growth areas such as cosmetics and health-care products.

The global race explains in part Mr. Artzt's urgency in seeking at least parts of Revlon, whose products include Max Factor lipstick and Halston perfume, and which is known for its international marketing and distribution operation.

Some competitors in the broad personal-care market, such as the Dutch Unilever Group and Kao Corp. of Japan, have been expanding into international markets at a much faster rate than P&G. Unilever,

---

* Source: Alecia Swasy, "Stodgy No More," *The Wall Street Journal,* March 5, 1991, pp. A1, 4. (Laurie P. Cohen contributed to this article.) Reprinted by permission of *THE WALL STREET JOURNAL,* © 1991 Dow Jones & Company, Inc. All Rights Reserved Worldwide.

for example, spent $3 billion to acquire 55 businesses in 1989 alone. The Dutch company, which had 1990 sales of $39.6 billion, operates in more than 75 countries, while P&G is in 46. P&G has been on the move, though; a decade ago, it had operations in just 22 countries.

Other companies—Unilever, Kao, and France's L'Oreal S.A.—also have expressed interest in all or parts of Revlon. But thus far, P&G has shown the most interest, sending teams to study Revlon businesses in Germany, Brazil, Spain, and Japan.

P&G got into the cosmetics business two years ago with the purchase of Noxell and its Cover Girl and Clarion brands, and, according to Mr. Artzt, it likes what it has seen. "I don't know of any place that's not a good beauty-care market," he says.

"Maybe not the Middle East," he adds. "I haven't peeked under those veils."

The eldest son of musicians, the 60-year-old Mr. Artzt won a basketball scholarship to the University of Oregon, where he studied journalism. After working as a sportswriter and a theater critic in Hollywood, he answered a newspaper ad for a P&G sales job.

At the company's Cincinnati headquarters, he soon earned the nickname "Prince of Darkness" because he spent so many nights at work. "We swore he slept upside down in his office hanging by his toes," says Lee Wotherspoon, who worked as a brand manager with Mr. Artzt.

He recalls how Mr. Artzt would descend the corporate elevators at 10 P.M, only to return to his office for more files. "He has an insatiable appetite for work," says Mr. Wotherspoon, now a career consultant in Newton, N.H.

It was work thousands of miles from Cincinnati that eventually won Mr. Artzt the CEO post. He is credited with reviving P&G's struggling overseas operations, from which the company will soon be deriving more than half of its sales. In Japan, for example, he turned a money-losing operation into a big profit center by tailoring diapers and detergents to local tastes.

Still, his appointment as chief executive surprised many associates, who'd expected the company's president, John E. Pepper, to be chosen. Mr. Artzt took over a company whose revenue of $24 billion last year was double that of a decade earlier. Net income for the fiscal year ended June 30 rose 33 percent, to $1.6 billion.

But that hasn't stopped Mr. Artzt from shaking things up. One of his first targets: the food and beverage division, where Fisher Nut, Citrus Hill, and Crisco shortening have stalled. For instance, sales of shortening have tumbled steeply since the mid-1980s, as consumers have reduced their fat intake, while Citrus Hill remains a lagging third behind Minute Maid and Tropicana orange juice.

"When he gets numbers he doesn't like, he'll be stalking the floors to find the people who produced them," says one manager, who notes that

Mr. Artzt is a frequent visitor these days to the food and beverage division. "If you see Ed coming down the hall, look out."

In a business review last year, Mr. Artzt didn't mince words about his disdain for a faltering nut business acquired by his predecessor. "Can I get my money back?" he asked.

Mr. Artzt describes his management style as "helpful and supportive." On a Harvard recruiting trip, he singled out a P&G intern, recalling in detail her summer projects. Nevertheless, he sometimes yells and curses when he is angry.

That hands-on approach unnerves some subordinates, but what challenges them the most is his demand for speed. As international chief, Mr. Artzt pushed for quick expansion of P&G's Always sanitary napkins. Within 31 months, the product was in 31 countries. Now it's the No. 1 or No. 2 brand in major markets, giving P&G about 12 percent of the $8 billion global market.

Today, product launches that once took years may take only months. Being quick is essential now that smaller competitors like Kimberly-Clark Corp. are moving faster. P&G's launch of ultra-thin diapers in the mid-1980s was supposed to give it a three- to five-year lead time, but Kimberly-Clark caught up within months.

"Historically, Procter was very patient and would take a long time to make a business work," says Gary Stibel of New England Consulting Group. It spent two decades researching olestra before seeking government approval. "Artzt is collapsing the P&G time frame," he says.

Lately, P&G has felt recession pressures as U.S. consumers limit purchases of its premium-priced products. While some overseas markets are growing faster than expected, in the United States "many consumer-product markets are off a percentage point or two," Mr. Artzt acknowledges. He has been closely reviewing the spending plans of every business segment and trimming some budgets. "We have to sharpen our priorities" for capital spending, he says.

A clear priority is building what he calls "world brands." He points to Pert Plus, a combination shampoo-conditioner that's now the world's best-selling brand. Launched first in the United States, Pert Plus is being rolled out quickly around the globe, although often under different labels. It's sold as Vidal Sassoon in Britain, for example, and Rejoy in Japan. "We'll definitely have more of our brands become world brands," Mr. Artzt says (see Exhibit 1).

That's part of the reason P&G is trying to expand in the beauty-care business, where there is strong demand in Japan and Europe and big potential elsewhere. P&G also needs cosmetics to freshen its product mix, since some of its items, like Duncan Hines cake mixes and Crisco shortening, are stale. "Nobody makes two-layer cakes or deep fries chicken anymore," says a former P&G staffer.

For P&G, which typically perfects products in the lab for years be-

---

EXHIBIT 1 Procter & Gamble: Looking After Consumers

After some tough years . . .

Annual net income, in billions

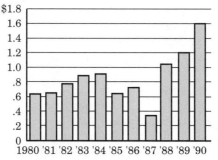

P&G businesses . . .

Lines of business as a percent of fiscal 1990 revenue

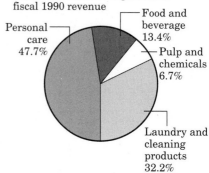

Personal care 47.7%

Food and beverage 13.4%

Pulp and chemicals 6.7%

Laundry and cleaning products 32.2%

Are market stalwarts . . .

Selected P&G brand names, as a percent of their respective markets

Pampers and Luvs diapers	50%
Crest	34
Oil of Olay*	24
Cover Girl	23
Secret	14
Pert Plus	13
Head & Shoulders	12
Clarion cosmetics	5

*As a percent of the mass market face creams and lotions
Source: Wertheim Schroder.

And investors gain.

Comparison of Procter & Gamble's stock and the DJIA, quarterly prices; DEC. 1979=100

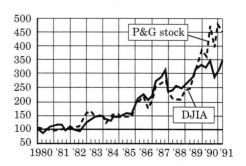

P&G stock

DJIA

---

fore doing painstaking market research, cosmetics is still foreign territory. This is a business where packaging often counts more than product quality, and advertising slogans promise "pure, raw sensuality," not "pure white" laundry.

But cosmetics companies increasingly are emphasizing skin protection and other health concerns, not just appearance. "That starts to come right down our alley," says Mr. Artzt.

P&G plans to use its enormous research and development base to launch new products for the Noxell cosmetic business. The company has long been famous for gaining market leadership by introducing products that offer an innovation, such as Tide with bleach.

At Noxell, it's also been cutting distribution costs while expanding markets for Cover Girl, Navy perfume, and other brands. And it has streamlined its traditionally cumbersome marketing methods. "If they want to change five or six makeup colors, we're not putting them through the same kind of procedures that we go through to change Tide or Pampers," Mr. Artzt says.

Upscale Revlon would give P&G, which already controls a good deal of supermarket and drug-store shelf space, the kind of greater mass essential to building profit margins and more global markets.

After meeting Mr. Perelman in Cincinnati, Mr. Artzt assigned teams of dozens of marketing, financial, operating, and legal staffers to review Revlon's businesses, mostly those overseas. The thorough nature of these examinations has surprised Revlon's top management, including Mr. Perelman, who recently noted to investment bankers that Revlon itself has bought companies on much less information than what P&G now possesses about his company.

It isn't clear whether P&G is interested in buying all of Revlon or simply certain pieces. The whole company might cost more than $3 billion.

Depending on what P&G goes after, there could be antitrust problems. P&G's Cover Girl has about 23 percent of the mass-market cosmetics business in all outlets, while Revlon's Max Factor and Almay and Revlon line account for 21 percent.

The Justice Department has already thwarted one of Mr. Artzt's earlier attempts to market Phone-Poulenc Rorer's Maalox because P&G already sells Pepto Bismol, a stomach remedy. Both P&G and Revlon lawyers have concluded that in the event of a merger, they would try to convince the government that the cosmetics market is more fragmented than what the mass market numbers show. They don't include, for example, the sales of door-to-door operations such as Avon Products Inc.

Last Thursday, Revlon officials feared their talks with P&G and others might be jeopardized when news of them surfaced. But Mr. Artzt telephoned Mr. Perelman to tell him that P&G still intended to go full speed ahead with the talks, people familiar with the conversation say.

Case 6–4   *Robinson Chemical Company**

THE FUTURE OF HPERS

Over the past seven years, John MacDougall, director of the research labs, supported research and development of high-performance engineering resins (HPERs) at the Chemical Division of the Robinson Company. Mr. MacDougall is concerned about the future of three products which have recently become available to the market. These products complement a specialty resin HPI–50, which in the past five years has found several applications. As head of the Plastics Business Group, Mr. MacDougall must now determine the best marketing approach for these resins for 1985 through 1987. Production estimates are needed due to the two-year lag between the time a capital request is granted and actual production begins. Bill Zerwiske, who is developing the market for these resins, also estimates a minimum of two years to get from the initial sampling of an engineering plastic to a commercial sale.

The HPER market has been targeted as a way for the Chemical Division to support the corporate financial objective of a 19 percent growth in earnings. But questions exist as to the performance of these resins against competitive products. Due to their recent development, little long-term performance data for these products is available. However, Mr. MacDougall feels confident in the products' acceptance if the correct markets can be identified. A survey of the competitors in this industry was obtained to help focus Robinson's future strategy (Appendix A).

COMPANY BACKGROUND

In 1981 the Robinson Company was one of the top five industrial process and control equipment companies in the United States, with revenues of $1.2 billion from its industrial equipment segment. Corporate dollar sales and earnings have grown at 13.6 percent and 18.7 percent, respectively, compounded annually from 1977 to 1981. The chemical segment contributed 19 percent of 1981 sales ($324 million) to the parent company. This segment develops, manufactures, and sells iso-

---

* This case was prepared by Peter J. LaPlaca, School of Business Administration, University of Connecticut at Storrs.

cyanates, polyurethane foams and elastomers, other specialty chemical intermediates, and metering and dispensing equipment used in the urethane foam industry. The chemical segment has evolved from a producer of a single product line based on one patented technology in the early 1950s into a vertically integrated specialty chemicals producer with a broad range of alternate technologies.

ISOCYANATE TECHNOLOGY

Isocyanates are derived from a complex reaction of petrochemical-based raw materials. Polyurethanes are formed by reacting the isocyanate with another liquid called a polyol in weight ratios from approximately 40:60 to 60:40. A diverse set of polyurethanes and modified urethanes is possible by using different isocyanates (Robinson produces 10 types), polyols (on the order of 100 industrywide), catalysts, and additives such as foaming agents. Urethanes can be either thermoset, where the product can neither be melted nor reused, or thermoplastic, where the product has a melt point and can be reprocessed by injection molding or extrusion, optionally with fillers or fibers.

Robinson markets isocyanates separately (drum or bulk quantity), systems which include both components, as well as pellets of the thermoplastic urethane (TPU—a key to the acronyms used in this case is given in Appendix B), polyoplast, in 50-pound bags. Applications include rigid foam insulation, seat cushions, shoe soles, fascia in car interiors, and even the artificial heart. The urethane industry is becoming mature in regard to its mainstay markets of automotive and housing, with growth rates of 3 to 4 percent annually and high price competition.

Other isocyanate-based polymers include the high-performance engineering resins (HPERs) polyamide, polyimide, polyesteramide (all based on a 60 percent to 70 percent isocyanate), and the latest entry, Superpoly, a high-performance TPU. A description of these products, their uses, properties, and target markets is given in Appendix C.

ISSUES: THE CHEMICAL DIVISION

Since 1980, sales and earnings of the Chemical Division have followed the severe downturn in the economy. Urethane sales to the automobile and building construction industries fell over 25 percent from 1981 to 1982, with a net divisional loss of over $30 million in 1982. Although 1983 sales are expected to improve, recovery is closely tied to the economy. The present situation of soft prices for isocyanates will be

EXHIBIT 1   Organizational Chart, 1983

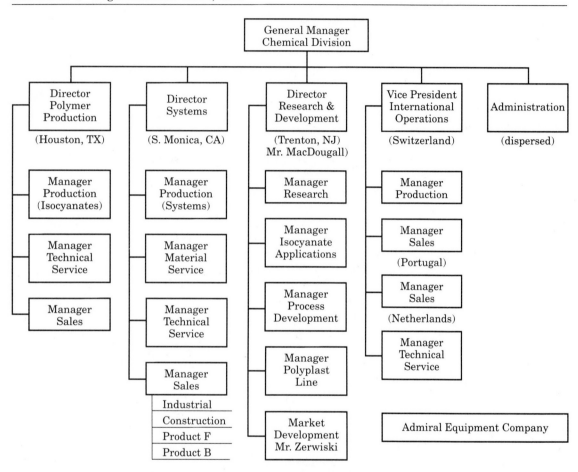

further aggravated by new production capacity from Robinson's joint venture in Portugal, which came onstream at the end of 1982.

Another issue involves the structure of the Chemical Division (Exhibit 1). The geographic dispersion of customer functions involved in supplying urethanes creates problems in interdepartment communications, in overlapping functions, and in providing a single face to buyers. The subsidiary which manufactures urethane processing equipment (Admiral Equipment Co.) operates independently of the Chemical Division. Admiral's functions could potentially be integrated with the Chemical Division's toward a common goal—that is, to meet fully the customers' needs in order to sell isocyanates.

While it is a publicly traded corporation, the Robinson Company is closely held and strongly identifies with its history in the industrial equipment industry. The following table indicates research and development and capital expenditures as a percentage of divisional sales, and total allocation. Corporate policy implies less support for long-term growth in the Chemical Division, vis-à-vis the Industrial Equipment Division.

| | Sales | Expenditure* | |
Division	Revenue	R&D	Capital
Industrial Equipment	65%	79% (10.7)*	76% (7.4)
Chemical	19	7 (3.1)	12 (4.2)
Agricultural	16	14 (7.5)	12 (4.8)
	100%	100%	100%

* Parentheses show percent of division sales.

Common marketing policies have been upheld for all divisions. Since equipment and controls are sold on quality, little market development has been needed. In selling industrial equipment and controls, high value added and little direct competition ensured high profit margins. During the 1970s these characteristics adequately described the Chemical Division. However, the competitive environment is rapidly changing for specialty chemicals. Intense competition puts pressure on prices; and growth in sales demands knowledge of market opportunities for new products.

PREVIOUS MARKETING STRATEGIES

With the objective of increasing isocyanate sales, Robinson's Chemical Division has developed various new applications for isocyanates. These new technologies provide a faster, more efficient process, greater flexibility in product design, or better performance-to-cost ratios than the existing technology. These are given in Exhibit 2, with their related industrial applications. Much of this technology is protected by patents but may be shared with prospective customers under written agreements.

The small size of Robinson's Chemical Division relative to other chemical companies does not hinder its efforts to support complete customer functions. Robinson provides research and development, production, technical service, and distribution. Although these functions are not physically consolidated, the technical resources are available.

Efforts are being made to improve the flow of communication between these groups. An ad hoc task force, consisting of members of the research, technical service, and sales segments was summoned to con-

EXHIBIT 2 Applications Served by Alternate Technologies

Applications

Applications	Laminated panel cores	Pour-in-place insulation	Structural foam	Flexible foam	Elastomers	Binder resin	Reinforcing fibers/fillers	Isocyanurates	Thermoplastics
Automotive Bumpers/fascia					●				
Seating				●					
Body panels							●	●	
Building construction: Wall insulation	●	●							
Particle boards						●			
Carpet underlay					●				
Adhesives/sealants					●				
Bedding/furniture			●	●					
Sporting goods					●				●
Electrical/electronic: Wire coatings					●				
Business machine housings			●				●	●	
Connectors					●				
Refrigeration	●						●		

Alternate technologies

centrate on product development problems, opportunities, etc. This task force was replaced by the Plastics Business Group, which involves market development, sales, and technical service representatives.

Due to Robinson's policy of promoting from within, most salespeople have experience in research or technical service. Specific knowledge regarding isocyanate technology allows the salespeople to field specific processing problems rather than returning to the research or technical service group for a solution.

Two approaches have been used to increase isocyanate sales. In an industry such as automotive or housing, the standard operating procedures and materials used have been established; high capital investments ensure the continuation of these operations. Therefore, to be sold on urethane bumpers or foam insulation, the industry must also be sold on the technology. Robinson has some background in the "nuts and bolts" side of the technology through its subsidiary, Admiral Equipment Co. Also, technical service provides the customer interaction necessary to increase the success rate. Quality control problems resulting from rushing the product through development have been identified, and appropriate corrective actions were taken. Technical service is crucial to solving these problems and protecting the company's image.

Most important for expanding the isocyanate markets is to achieve a final product which is superior to the present one, based on efficiencies gained in the process or final properties. Competitors in the urethane markets will emphasize one or two property improvements or a feature such as an internal release agent to sell a system. By integrating its function, the research group can request and test certain experimental isocyanates from the production facility. Salespeople can rely on technical service or research to try an idea which a customer suggests. This integration of functions has proven to be a useful strategic tool for developing isocyanate sales.

To reduce its dependence on the cyclical industries (automotive and building), Robinson supports product development in smaller, growth-oriented niches. These segments typically have low sales volume of 10–15 million pounds/year but provide high profit margins; additionally their specific needs require significant product innovation, which has contributed to Robinson's recognition as an innovator. Robinson has successfully targeted the sporting goods industry, among others, with its polyplasts line. Polyplasts are highly differentiated into systems that may have low-temperature flexibility (for ski boots), high abrasion resistance (for roller skate wheels), solvent resistance (for tubing), or high resilience (as membrane for the artificial heart).

PRODUCT INFORMATION

Two extremes of thermoplastic resins with different pricing and servicing strategies can be identified in order to differentiate the market: commodity resins and high-performance resins; however, there exists a continuum of products on this scale to sufficiently blur such a discrete categorization. Commodities are becoming highly specialized through developments in fiber reinforcement, additives, copolymer blends, etc., to match unique property requirements. Likewise, as the demand for high-performance engineering resins increases and proprietary knowledge becomes known to the industry, more competitors are drawn into the market. Keen competition and increasing volumes of high-performance engineering resins (HPERs) being sold create a market similar to that for the commodity resins. A definition proposed to simplify this situation is that high-performance engineering resins are not necessarily processed with fibers, fillers, or additives or otherwise blended to attain their outstanding properties.

COMMODITY PLASTICS

The commodity plastics, such as polyethylene, crystalline nylons, polypropylene, and polystyrene are available in grades ranging from general-purpose (GP) and impact grades to highly specialized resins for flexibility in processing techniques or to offer a specific property. For instance, polyethylene materials vary in physical properties from hard to soft, rigid to flexible, and tough to weak; it can be optically clear or opaque. Applications are equally diverse.

In this mature industry, commodity producers have striven to improve process technology, as this is the one point where they can exercise cost control. A company, such as Du Pont, which is integrated backward into energy and raw materials has a further advantage in cost control.

EXHIBIT 3   U.S. Commodity Resins

Resin	Consumption* (millions)	Growth Rate* (1982–1985)	Price† (per pound)	Sample Application
Polycarbonate	256 pounds	7.0%	$1.62	Business machine housings; bumpers; structural foam
Polyethylene				
High-density	4893	6.9	.45–.48	Bags; gas tanks; 55-gallon drums
Low-density	7725	4.9		
LD (except LLDPE)	6094	−6.2	.28–.37	Films; coatings
Linear low-density	1631	27.7	.35–.39	Chemical tanks; high-strength film
Polypropylene	3783	7.9	.40	Food packaging; automotive parts
Polystyrene				
(except expandable)	2990	5.5	.45	Computer housing
Expandable	442	5.7	.45	Insulation
Polyvinyl chloride	5380	4.2	.52–.58	Vinyl siding; pipe; records

* *Predicast Forecasts* (SIC 282), January 1983.
† *Chemical Marketing Reporter,* March 28, 1983, p. 53.

The similarity of each commodity resin across competitors means there are multiple sources. Price competition is keen. Price discounting in fractions of one cent per pound are common in truckload sales (40,000 pounds per truckload). Consumption of these resins is several billion tons annually, and growth rates are generally in the 4 to 7 percent range. An advance in technology, however, can offer substantial growth opportunity, as seen in linear low-density polyethylene (Exhibit 3). The technology for using these resins is well known, as they have existed for 20 years or more. Selling these resins requires a minimal technical background or backup. In fact, with the current price/earnings squeeze in the chemical industry, fewer salespeople are selling to wider geographical areas to improve their overall productivity.

ENGINEERING RESINS

Engineering resins are characterized by superior performance in hostile environments. HPERs retain their strength at elevated temperatures and may offer higher impact strength at low temperatures, be especially resistant to chemical attack, or have low frictional properties. Their applications often replace metals. Electrical resistivity and flame retardance also open new electrical/electronic applications. An optically clear HPER will find additional, unique applications. Due to these qualities, HPERs maintain high prices and profit margins relative to the commodity resins. Selected engineering resins, their properties, and uses are shown in Exhibit 4.

Growth of engineering resins in the United States is projected at 9.5 percent annually through 1986, with 1.3 billion pounds to be consumed in 1986, as seen in Exhibit 5. Providing technical support is essential to sales of these resins as they are generally new to the customers. HPERs often demand extra care in processing (such as drying) in order to maximize properties. A strong technical service group, with access to the customer's research and development, is essential for the "hand-holding" aspect of sales and to provide feedback to research for further product development.

The company that can provide three or four different resins, each differentiated within its line, stands a better chance of meeting customer needs by virtue of the breadth of specifications covered. Also, a discounting method is used in selling specialty resins where a buyer can combine purchases of several resins (weightwise) to sum to a truck load and thereby receive a discount in price.

EXHIBIT 4 Characteristics of Selected Unreinforced Engineering Resins

Properties[1] Resin/ASTM	Flammability (UL rating)[2]	Notched Izod Impact Strength (ft-lb/in)	Head Deflection Temperature (°F)	Load Bearing to 250°F	Moisture Absorption (D 570–A)	Optical Clarity
Acetal[4]	HB	1.4	277	Yes	0.25	No
6 nylon[4]	V–2	1.0	147	—[7]	1.6	No
Polycarbonate[4]	No	14.*	270	Yes	0.15*	Yes
Modified polyphenylene oxide[4]	V–0	7.0*	190	Yes	0.07*	No
Polyethylene terephthalate[4]	No	1.7	145	No	—	Yes
Polybutylene terephthalate[4]	V–0	0.5	135	No	0.09*	No
Acrylonitrile-utadiene-styrene	No	6.7*	180	No	0.3	No
612 nylon[5]	V–2	1.0	135	No	0.25	No
63T nylon	V–2	1.3	256	Yes	0.41	Yes
12 nylon	No	1.5	255	Yes	3.1[8]	Yes
Polyarylate[6]	V–0	4.2*	345*	Yes	0.27	Yes
Polyamide-imide[6]	V–0	2.5	525*	Yes*	0.28[8]	No
Polyetherimide[6]	V–0	1.0	392*	Yes	0.25	No
Thermoplastic polyurethane	No	22.*	194	No	0.17	No

* Superior performance.

[1] *Plastics Technology 1982/83*, mid-June 1982.

[2] UL ratings:

94 HB   *a.* Not having a burning rate exceeding 1.5 inches/minute over a 3.0-inch span for specimens having a thickness of 0.120–0.500 inch.

        b. Not have a burning rate exceeding 3.0 inches/minute over a 3.0-inch span for specimens having a thickness less than 0.120 inch.

        c. Cease to burn before the flame reaches the 4.0-inch reference mark.

V–0   *a.* Not have any specimen that burns for more than 10 seconds after either test flame application.

        b. Total combustion time is not to exceed 50 seconds for all 10 applications of the test.

        c. Not to have any specimen that burns to holding clamp.

        d. Not have any specimen that drips and ignites cotton 12 inches below.

        e. Not have any specimen with a glow time of more than 30 seconds after removal or second test flame.

Chemical Resistance	List Price[3] (per pound)	Sample Applications	Trade Name	Supplier
No	$ 1.55	Door handles; gears; appliances	Deirin 500	Du Pont
Yes	1.73	Tubing; moldings; hot-melt applications	Capron 8202	Allied
No	1.64	High-clarity film; medicine; light fixtures; packaging	Lexan 121	GE
No	1.31–1.92	Business machine housings; electrical; appliances	Noryl 190	GE
No	0.62	Clear bottles; food/beverage packages	Kodar PETG	Eastman
No	1.36–1.70	Interior panels; moldings	Celanex 2012	Celanese
No	0.64	Telephones; plumbing; appliances	Lustran 648	Monsanto
Yes	2.98	Wire jacketing; cable fasteners	Zytel 158L	Du Pont
Yes	3.60	Chemical site glass; electrical connectors	Trogamid T	Kay-Fries
—[9]	3.61	Filter housings; electrical connectors	Grilamid TR55	Emser
No	4.00	Lighting fixtures; snap conn.; appliances	Ardel D-100	Union Carbide
No	17.00	Engine parts: piston, intake valve, push rod	Torlon 4203	Amoco
Yes	4.25	Under-the-hood automobile circuit boards	Ultem 1000	GE
Yes	1.93	Bumpers; agricultural equipment; gears; wheels	Isoplast	Upjohn

V–2   *a.* Not have any specimen that burns for more than 30 seconds after either test flame application.
    b. Total combustion time is not to exceed 250 seconds for all 10 applications of the test.
    c. Not have any specimen that burns to holding clamp.
    d. Be permitted to have some specimens that drip flaming particles which ignite cotton 12 inches below.
    e. Not have any specimen with a glow time of more than 60 seconds after removal of second test flame.

[3] Bulk list prices: *Plastics Technology,* January 1983.
[4] Represents low end of HPERs.
[5] Generally sold with fillers, additives, etc.
[6] Represents high end of HPERs.
[7] Intermittent load-bearing capabilities to 250 F.
[8] Long-term moisture absorption.
[9] Resistant to hydrocarbons, aromatic and aliphatic solvents. Not resistant to strong acids or bases.

Source: *Modern Plastics Encyclopedia,* 1983.

EXHIBIT 5   U.S. HPER Consumption and Growth

Product	Pounds Consumed (millions)		Percent Growth Rate (1981–1986)
	1981	*1986*	
Nylons	280	402	7.5%
PC	245	422	11.5*
MPPO	130	210	10.0
Acetal	97	130	6.0
PBT/PET	60	121	15.0
Polysulphone/PPS	18	25	7.0
	830	1,310	9.5%†

* *Plastics World,* November 1982: 7–8 percent growth through 1980s; *Predicasts Forecasts,* January 1983: 9.1 percent annual growth for polycarbonates.
† Average.

Source: *Chemtech* (12), American Chemical Society, 1982, pp. 552–55.

INDUSTRY TRENDS

The engineering resin market has been characterized as risky due to a combination of high capital intensity and extended time period (e.g., 10–15 years) to achieve a positive cash flow. However, the HPER industry is seeing more competition, as it is a very desirable investment over the long term. A marketing communication prepared by Du Pont indicates a significant cost and energy advantage of engineering plastics over metals, as shown in Exhibit 6. A projection of HPERs' and metals' prices of the same report shows engineering plastics maintaining a very substantial volumetric cost advantage over metals for the next decade and probably into the next century (see Exhibit 7).

As patents terminate, the industry gains access to proprietary knowledge, and the time element in developing new technology is reduced. With technological advances, commodity resins are developing into higher-performance resins. Product improvements have been attained through mineral fillers, glass-fiber reinforcement, flame-retarding additives, etc., and through alloys of two or more resins. These products achieve good price/performance balance with a minimal risk. Examples of this type of product differentiation are GE's Lexan and NORYL product lines. (Appendix D details these product lines.)

EXHIBIT 6   Energy Requirements of Plastics and Metals

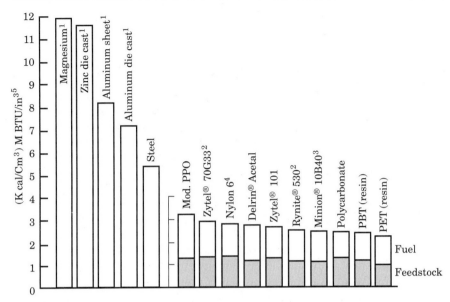

[1] Includes secondary metals usage of 34.5 percent for all sheet, 46 percent for die cast A1, 5 percent for Mg, 5 percent for zinc.
[2] Glass-reinforced.
[3] Mineral-reinforced.
[4] Includes energy credit for ammonium sulphate.
[5] Does not include energy to extract oil, gas, and coal from below ground.

Source: *Engineering Plastics News,* Du Pont Company, Marketing Communications Department.

As trends suggest, price competition in the industry is growing. GE's strength in having NORYL protected by patents does not preclude price attacks, since many resins compete directly for the same application. Also, many applications for resins are concentrated in the automotive market, putting the resin producers at a bargaining disadvantage.

A strong trend in the industry is toward international research, production, and sales functions. Robinson's international operations are increasing due to present cost advantages overseas. Petroleum raw materials can be purchased in the international market for isocyanate production in Portugal and Japan. Distribution costs to the Japanese and European markets are minimized by these overseas operations. However, investments overseas are subject to risks or price controls, fluctuations in currency exchange rates, and differing rates of economic growth.

EXHIBIT 7   Engineering Plastics and Metals Prices (historical and
projected)

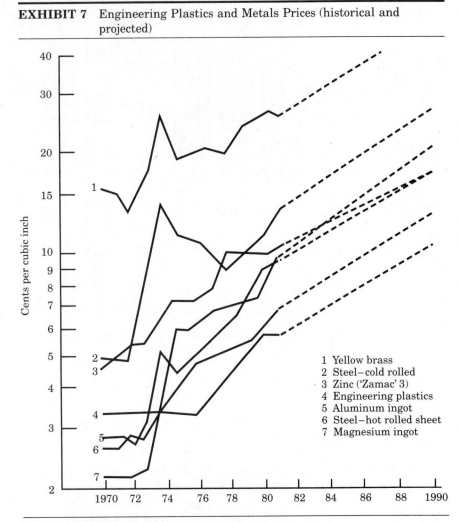

1 Yellow brass
2 Steel–cold rolled
3 Zinc ('Zamac' 3)
4 Engineering plastics
5 Aluminum ingot
6 Steel–hot rolled sheet
7 Magnesium ingot

Source: *Engineering Plastics News,* Du Pont Company, Marketing Communications Department.

FUTURE DECISIONS

MacDougall is faced with the problem of identifying an appropriate
marketing strategy for the Chemical Division in general and HPERs
in particular. This strategy will include identification of target markets, research and development priorities, and pricing, distribution,
and promotional strategies. MacDougall felt that the goals identified
by corporate would be possible but, given the resource constraints in
both R&D and capital expenditures, only if there were very tight controls imposed on a well-developed strategy.

Appendix A Competitors in the HPER Industry

Exhibit 8 is a summary of the following competitors' strengths and weaknesses and other descriptive information.

E. I. du Pont de Nemours & Co.

As the leader of U.S. chemical producers for 1982, Du Pont is positioned with several strategic advantages. In 1982 the company diversified into energy and chemical feedstocks with the purchase of Conoco Company. This ensures a stable and relatively cheap supply of raw materials for its plastics business. The company is now less vulnerable to cycles, resulting in a more stable stock. Also, Du Pont takes some of the cash generated by the mature fibers business and invests it in businesses that have more potential for growth, such as plastics.

Du Pont's strategy is founded on a strong technological base, with nearly $2 billion invested in R&D over the past three years. Research and development is aimed at cutting production costs and developing technically sophisticated products. Polymers such as Delrin (acetal resin), Sytel ST (the "world's toughest nylon"), and Kevlar (aramid reinforcing fiber) are examples. These products are used to replace metal parts and in electrical/electronic applications. Many of these compounds are patentable innovations which give substantial improvements over present products.

In the high-volume commodities, such as fibers, Du Pont competes on low cost, quality, and reliability. Capitalizing on the increased supply of raw materials, Du Pont recently announced its entry into high-density polyethylene.

Strategy in selling the high-performance polymers is based on developing niches with high value-in-use. Thus the highly differentiated product line. With 250 products in the high-performance polymer line, each application may consume only 10–15 million pounds/year but retain high profit margins due to this strategy. Sales depend heavily on technical service to educate the end user on processing techniques.

Du Pont promises to remain strong in the HPER industry, with plant additions noted for Hytrel (polyester elastomer) in Luxembourg and expanded production and marketing of Hytrel through a joint venture in Japan with Toray Industries. Production of Kevlar will triple to 45 million pounds/year with a $200 million investment in three U.S. plants, initiated this year. Kevlar is highly specialized, with prices ranging from $6 to $20 per pound.

One weakness noted is that Du Pont salespeople are responsible for the whole line of polymer products. Therefore they cannot be as responsive to individual property or processing needs. The sales force concentrates selling efforts on the high-volume commodities rather than the lower-volume, high-performance resins.

General Electric Co.

General Electric is a highly diversified manufacturer of consumer products, industrial equipment, aircraft engines, medical equipment, etc., with a strong commitment to innovation. The GE Credit Corporation has financed new prod-

EXHIBIT 8

Company	Strengths	Weaknesses
Du Pont	Integrated into petrochemicals and energy supplies Differentiated product line Pricing power Large commitment to HPERs	Undifferentiated sales force to market both commodities and specialty HPERs
General Electric	Full range of HPERs Backward integrated (phenols) Personal corporate interest High growth, investment plans	Diversified investment interests
Monsanto	Vertical integration backward (petrochemicals and energy supplies) Vertical integration forward (fabricated products) High R&D commitments	Largely a commodity supplier Sales dependent on economic cycles Undifferentiated sales force
Union Carbide	Proprietary processes/products Excellent properties of HPERs	Largest buyer of ethylene Weak balance sheet Needs strategic approach to market HPERs
Celanese	Vertical integration within company divisions International production	Dependent on externally supplied feedstocks Nonproprietary products/process
Upjohn	Vertical integration backward into chemical feedstocks Worldwide production and sales functions	Little product differentiation within HPER line Needs strategic approach to market specialty HPERs
Emser	Broad specialty chemicals base Worldwide production and sales functions	Dependent on externally supplied feedstocks Small size of operations
Huels	Vertical integration backward (petrochemicals and energy supplies) Worldwide sales force	Must purchase (more) feedstocks from external supplies Customer functions based in West Germany
Kay-Fries	Producer of chemical intermediates Worldwide production facilities	Limited customer funds in United States Depends on external supply for feedstocks Undifferentiated sales force
Dow	Active in oil and gas recovery and production Vertical integration into chemical feedstocks	Largely a commodity producer No price leverage; dependent on economic cycles Inexperience in product/market development of HPERs Alternate investment opportunities

ucts since 1943, although mostly from outside companies. With the sale of a natural resources interest in 1983, GE has $5 billion to invest in advanced technology such as factory automation, medical equipment, and man-made materials. The R&D budget of 3.0 percent of sales for 1982 supports this strategy.

GE wants to strengthen its one-third share of the worldwide $2.9 billion-per-year market for engineering resins. The company has a 20-year, $1.5 billion plan to expand, especially into foreign markets. GE is building a $105 million plant for NORYL in the Netherlands, for 1984 production. A $50 million joint venture in Japan will produce PPO resins. The company is building a $20 million technical center to expand the development and technical support capabilities of its plastics business. Recently GE expanded phenol production to assure a high-quality supply for several of its plastics. These plans have the personal support of the chairman and CEO, J. F. Welch, Jr., who rose through the engineering plastics operation to general manager of worldwide operations.

Today GE's line of engineering TPs includes polycarbonate, PPO-based resins, thermoplastic polyester, and the new polyetherimide, Ultem. Priced at $4.25 to $6.50 per pound, Ultem fills an intermediate position in the plastics spectrum in terms of price, properties, and processing.

Monsanto Company

As the largest U.S. chemical company in earnings for 1982, Monsanto's strength lies in its vertical integration. This includes oil and gas exploration and production, petrochemicals, plastic materials, and fabricated products. The commitment of $200 million to research and development (3.2 percent of sales) supports its technological efforts in the traditional areas, new materials, life science, and alternate energy sources. The strategy follows the pursuit of high-value businesses and maximum protection of foreign investments. This is seen in the divestiture of European fibers operations, including nylons (1978), polyesters (1980), and acrylic fibers (1983). Also, a polystyrene business was sold.

Monsanto agreed to join in a venture to produce nylon raw materials with an Italian company. An exchange of proprietary technology with Yoshino opens the Japanese market without a large investment.

Although Monsanto has flexibility in pricing, its position as a leading supplier of ABS and nylon is vulnerable to economic cycles. These products are dependent on the automobile and housing markets. Monsanto is tracking new opportunities in areas outside the acquired business.

Union Carbide Corporation

Union Carbide, number three in U.S. chemical producers' earnings for 1982, has recently completed a portfolio restructuring in an effort to insulate the corporation from cyclic fluctuations. Emphasis is on technological processing advantages of commodity monomers and polymers and some specialty chemicals. UCC is integrated from the basic products into value-added consumer products (e.g., Glad Wrap). It is not integrated into raw materials and is one of industry's largest purchasers of ethylene. Therefore UCC runs the risk of being denied adequate feedstocks during shortages. UCC's priority is to strengthen its balance sheet by trimming capital outlays (R&D expense is about 2.0 percent of sales) and through higher prices for its products.

UCC's entries in HPERs include polysulfone and polyarylsulfone, two specialty resins. The polysulfone capacity of 15 million pounds/year indicates a niche strategy. However, UCC must change its sales strategy to address the special applications suited for the polysulfones.

Celanese Corporation

Celanese is a diversified producer of fibers, petrochemicals, plastics, and specialty polymers, ranking eighth among U.S. chemical producers in 1982. Celanese Research Company performs basic research and development and advanced manufacturing technology. Celanese Mexicana is a multiproduct petrochemical producer. This plant and a proposed venture in Saudi Arabia would rely on local resources and turn out value-added products. Celanese Corporate is a major producer of bulk monomers and fibers. This company attempts to lead the market in reliability, manufacturing technology, or marketing.

Its high degree of vertical integration is apparent in the 19 percent of sales accounted for by other Celanese units. This company produces raw materials for Celcon (acetal copolymer) and nylon 6/6. Celanese also markets Celanex (PBT) and a PET resin, Petpac, for which it is dependent on external supplies for feedstocks. None of Celanese' products or processes are proprietary. Without a reliable supply of feedstocks, it is subject to shortages. Since the devaluation in Mexico, capital spending has been cut back in Celanese Mexicana.

Upjohn Co.

The Upjohn Co. is a diversified producer of pharmaceuticals, agricultural chemicals, and specialty chemicals. The Chemical Division produces the feedstocks and markets these feedstocks and complete systems for polyurethane foams, elastomers, and thermoplastics. As a small chemical company, relative to its competitors, Upjohn's strategy is to target unique opportunities for its specialty products. Manufacturing operations and sales are gaining a worldwide base. However, overseas sales were hurt last year by the strong U.S. dollar.

Over the last two years Upjohn added a high-performance polyamide and TPU to its polyurethane lines. The automotive and construction industries have been targeted in the past for the polyurethanes. In these mature markets, Upjohn competes on price rather than customer service. In order to be competitive with the new HPERs Upjohn, like UCC, must seek new markets for these resins and develop strong technical support.

Dynamit Nobel AG. (Kay-Fries, Inc.)

Dynamit Nobel AG. is a diversified West German company with interests in plastics, chemicals, and explosives. Worldwide sales for 1981 rank DN AG. fifth among U.S. chemical producers. As a recognized trendsetter, the Plastics

Division supplies materials for building construction, semifinished products, and high-precision injection molded parts. Manufacturing facilities are worldwide, as are sales subsidiaries. The U.S. subsidiary Kay-Fries is responsible for selling specialty chemicals, intermediate products, and HPERs. Dynamit Nobel's HPERs include high-performance PVC, nylon 12 (Trogamid), and engineering fluoropolymers. Kay-Fries supplies limited R&D and technical service in the United States. The broad product line implies less expertise in targeting markets for HPERs.

Emser Industries Incorporated

The companies of Swiss-based Ems-Chemie Holding AG (EMS) produce and market engineering plastics, synthetic fibers, and agrochemicals; generate electric power (mainly for their own plants); and license, design, and build plants. EMS—Grilon Holding, Inc., in the United States has a production facility (EMS—American Grilon) and a sales company (Emser Industries).

For a relatively young and small company, EMS has high industry recognition in HPERs. EMS's engineering plastics include nylon 6, nylon 12 (Grilamid TR 55) copolyamids, epoxies, and polyester resins. Corporate strategy concentrates on specialty products that are "tailor-made" and therefore difficult to substitute. EMS stresses solid know-how, highly developed application technology, as well as innovative consulting and assistance in the processing of products.

Chemische Werke AG. (Huels)

Huels is a U.S. subsidiary of the West German chemical company, Chemische Werke AG. Chemische has business in raw materials, energy, trading, and petrochemicals. It is 89 percent owned by Vepa, which in turn has proprietary interests in Deminex, an energy exploration concern. Taking advantage of the energy and petrochemical feedstocks available, Chemische Werke manufactures PVC, nylon 6, 6/6, 6/12, and (since 1982) nylon 12. Huels was formed in 1979 specifically for worldwide sales of the HPERs. The 11-member group at Huels offers samples of the nylon 12 and technical assistance. U.S. companies might hesitate to invest in Huels' products due to the research being overseas and the uncertain price-to-performance of this new product.

Dow Chemical Company

Ranking first in revenues and second in earnings for 1982, Dow Chemical Company leads basic chemicals and commodity resins production. Dow has recently gone on a "fitness" program, cutting capital expenditures, shedding assets to retire debt, and selling unprofitable overseas ventures. To increase profitability, Dow acquired a prescription drug manufacturer and has an interest in specialty chemicals and polymers. Dow announced it will be supplying polycarbonates by 1984. Combining its strength in commodities, monomer supplies, and established distribution channels, Dow could become a price leader in the low-to-middle range of the HPER market.

Appendix B Key to Acronyms

ABS	Acrylonitrile-butadiene-styrene
GP	General purpose
HPER	High-performance engineering resin
MPPO	Modified polyphenyleneoxide
PA	Polyamide
PAI	Polyamide-imide
PBT	Polybutylene terephthalate
PC	Polycarbonate
PEI	Polyetherimide
PET	Polyethylene terephthalate
PI	Polyimide
TPU	Thermoplastic urethane

Appendix C High-Performance Engineering Resins

Four isocyanate-based polymers form Robinson's bid in the HPER market. Characteristics are given below:

1. Superpoly, a chemical-resistant, low-moisture absorption engineering resin has exceptional impact resistance. Superpoly competes most directly with other high-impact engineering resins such as PC, impact-modified nylon, and PPO-based resins. Potential end uses range from automotive parts (bumper components, lamp housings) to sports equipment such as skis and tennis rackets. Good weather resistance suggests agricultural applications. This resin is priced at $2.00/pound.
2. HPA–70 is an amorphous nylon which has toughness, strength, solvent and moisture resistance, and a favorable impact strength compared to other nylons. The first application for HPA–70 is a filter bowl housing for motor fuels, although its chemical and alcohol resistance should open up more opportunities in replacing metals and in the electronics segment. HPA–70 is priced at $3.25/pound for truckload sales.
3. Elastamid, a polyesteramid, has good abrasion resistance and solvent resistance at elevated temperatures. It is used with reinforcing steel cable as a motorcycle belt drive. It is priced about the same as Superpoly.
4. A 10-year-old product, HPI–50 has high strength and chemical resistance at extreme temperatures. This HPER serves highly specialized, small-volume applications due to its price of more than $20/pound. HPI–50 is sold in pellet form, like the first three HPERs, or in a 20 percent solution. Recently a customer has developed a fiber-spinning process for the HPI–50 solution.

Appendix D   Product Differentiation in Engineering Resins

Two highly differentiated product lines GE offers are the PC, Lexan, and an MPPO, NORYL. Lexan is sold in 10 GP grades for optimum processing flexibility, two flame-retarded grades, one high-modulus grade for toughness and impact strength, two blow-molding grades, three glass-reinforced grades, and one high-heat grade. Another example is GE's modified phenylene oxide (NORYL) which includes 16 varieties and unlimited colors for total value versatility. Various grades of NORYL allow processing by injection molding, extrusion, and foam or thermoformed molding.

Case 6–5   American Airlines*

It's getting to be an old joke, but the head of American Airlines' international services, Hans Mirka, doesn't so much as chuckle. When his managers introduce themselves to travel officials in Europe, he says, the response often is, "Which American airline? You mean Pan Am?"

Pan Am and other global carriers may take some solace in this confusion over a generic-sounding name, but not much. That's because they know what the travel agents don't yet. American, the undisputed king of deregulated U.S. skies, is going global. And that is no laughing matter for the competition.

"They're an aggressive and expansionist airline," says British Airways spokesman David Burnside. "We admire them."

With domestic growth slowing, American is under pressure to broaden its international business to maintain its recent double-digit gains in passengers and revenue. Other former stay-at-home U.S. carriers—Delta, America West and USAir, among them—are seeking a stronger presence abroad for the same reason. But only American has its sights set on three continents at once.

The deep-pocketed carrier picked up Eastern Airlines' routes to South America for $310 million earlier this year. It has moved most aggressively into Europe, anticipating a surge in traffic when trade barriers come down in 1992. Several months ago, American agreed to buy Trans World Airlines' Chicago-London business for $195 million;

---

* Source: Bridget O'Brian, "Global Push," *The Wall Street Journal,* June 8, 1990, pp. A1, 7. Reprinted by permission of *THE WALL STREET JOURNAL,* © 1990 Dow Jones & Company, Inc. All Rights Reserved Worldwide.

American hopes to secure federal approval to fly the route sometime this summer. American is also seeking other European routes.

To supplement its single flight to Tokyo, American is competing against nine other U.S. carriers for six important new passenger routes to Japan, a market expanding five times as fast as the domestic one. The public counsel for the U.S. Department of Transportation is expected to issue a preliminary recommendation on the matter today.

American is in a strong position to maintain an international network. With 200,000 passengers a day, it has "the biggest, most mature domestic market in the world," Mr. Burnside of British Airways notes. That gives American considerable "feeder traffic" to funnel onto overseas flights.

American's drive to become an international powerhouse traces back to 1982, but the pace is accelerating. The airline is adding so many destinations so fast that some believe it could overtake the likes of Pan Am and TWA, international carriers for half a century, within several years. In Europe, however, Pan Am now serves 41 European cities, TWA 24, and American 11.

Why not simply buy Pan Am or TWA? "We've always said we don't want to buy another airline," says Robert L. Crandall, chairman of American and its parent, AMR Corp. "We don't want to acquire another airline's airplanes. We don't want another airline's people. We are only buying the right to fly." American wants to avoid the labor hassles of integrating union workers. And it disdains buying used planes, preferring to maintain a uniform fleet of airliners built to its specifications to keep down training and maintenance costs.

But American admits that its foreign offensive has been bumpy and fraught with missteps. Take its headlong rush last year into Stuttgart, Hamburg, and Geneva, with flights from the United States that passed through Brussels. Expensive landing fees and thin traffic on the last leg made the one-stop routes too costly and they had to be abandoned. American's route planners adopted a new rule as a result: nonstops or nothing.

Meanwhile, some of its hard-won international routes are being flown infrequently or not at all because American doesn't own enough long-haul aircraft. It has only two Boeing 747s, for instance. Even $20 billion in planes ordered in the past five years will provide limited relief when they roll in, because the order doesn't include enough widebodies. "To put the plainest face on it," says Mr. Crandall, "we guessed wrong."

This hasn't stopped American from aggressively seeking international passengers. Its newspaper and magazine ads seem ubiquitous on both sides of the Atlantic. In European ads, they always picture an American Airlines jet so readers know the ad refers to a specific airline.

American's high profile seems to rile Delta. Although Delta declined to comment for this article, it took a potshot in a recent employee publication. "While Delta has moved with less publicity," the statement read in part, "we believe our expansion has been more orderly and sure-footed." Delta has fewer routes to Europe, but more to Asia.

American has pulled out all the stops in its efforts to woo European travel agents and corporate travel managers, who hold greater sway over customers' travel decisions than their U.S. counterparts. American has been offering the agents free first-class trips, hoping its luxurious service will win them over "company by company, individual by individual," says Michael Gunn, American's head of marketing.

The carrier spares no expense on its first-class service. Passengers nestle into supple, sheepskin and leather seats that cost $24,000 a pair. The smell of bread and chocolate-chip cookies being baked inflight wafts through the cabin. Lobster fajitas are served on china with a vase of fresh flowers alongside. And should a traveler tire of the movie he has slipped into his personal video cassette player, he can recline his seat nearly horizontal to doze under oversized blankets.

American intends its service to rival that of heavyweights such as Swissair, Lufthansa, and Cathay Pacific. "We don't want to hear that Swissair does better than we do," declares Donald Carty, American's executive vice president of planning. "And we certainly don't want to hear that British Airways does better than we do."

But the carrier's marketing efforts will be wasted if it doesn't rectify its seat shortage, and soon. Acquisitions of foreign routes have outstripped aircraft deliveries, forcing American to accelerate its "musical planes" game. It bailed out of service to Lyon and Frankfurt this spring and postponed flights to Helsinki, Warsaw, and Barcelona—set to start this month —to free up enough jets to fly Chicago-London twice a day and the longest South American routes.

Such maneuvers may not bode well for the carrier's hopes for added route awards from the Transportation Department. The agency prefers to award routes to carriers that promise to make the most seats available, and it has appeared partial to fleets with lots of 747s. American doesn't much like 747s, preferring the more cost-efficient 200-seat Boeing 767. In any case, it would have to wait at least three years for new 747s because of Boeing's large backlog.

Big planes are especially important if American is to increase service to Japan and hopes to snare one of the new Soviet routes recently authorized. So, admittedly halfheartedly, "we're out rustling around looking for 747s," says American's operations chief, Robert Baker.

The plane American plans to use most in its international expansion, along with the 767, is the MD-11, a new, extremely economical plane from McDonnell Douglas. American has ordered 15 of the jets, whose flying range matches that of the 747, but which seat only about

250. The first MD-11s, originally due at American in the fall of 1990, are now expected in early 1991, but American executives fear the manufacturer could fall further behind.

American's jet shortfall could worsen considerably over the next couple of years if other carriers put desirable routes on the block that it feels compelled to snap up. Continuing financial difficulties at Pan Am and TWA make that a strong possibility.

Critics charge that American uses the excuse of too few planes to extricate itself from embarrassing, money-losing routes. In fact, American is open about its practice of abandoning a route that isn't profitable reasonably soon. "We either succeed, and succeed fairly fast," says Wesley Kaldahl, an American consultant who once ran the international operations, "or we say the hell with it. There are better things to do with our airplanes."

In 1983, American pulled out of Rio de Janeiro after nine months of losses. It ended its New York-Lyon run last week after the route failed to turn a profit.

Experimental routes such as Rio or Lyon do pay off in other ways, though. By flying untried routes, American has gained valuable international operating experience and bolstered its image as an international carrier in the minds of passengers, travel agents, and government officials. "They positioned themselves to take advantage of route opportunities that came up later," says William H. Pacelli, a manager at Avmark Inc., a consulting firm.

In going global, American has been barred from using some of its most successful domestic sales tools. Because of tight regulations in some European countries, it has had to forgo using its AAdvantage frequent-flier program. Nor can American engage in the kind of quick fare changes abroad that are common at home; fare changes overseas are subject to government reviews that can take weeks.

And, even though American is spending big money to bolster its international staff and improve ground service in the United States, it can't affect ground service much in certain European countries that rotate airport workers among carriers.

American has seized on some new sales tactics, however. It recently allied itself with the French rail service after discovering that passengers to Paris often took trains to their next destination. Combined ticketing for plane and train will be a boon for American when it takes affect later this year.

While waiting to be discovered by Europeans—and by Americans bound for Europe—American certainly isn't about to fly at less than capacity. If it isn't packing in the passengers, it'll pack in the cargo. "If you put 3,000 pounds of cargo on a passenger flight, that's like having 92 more passengers," said William Boesch, who heads American's cargo division. Last year, American's European passenger "load factor" hovered at a respectable 65.5%, while its cargo load factor regularly broke an enviable 80%.

Cargo doesn't have the cachet that passenger service does. But American seems to accept that becoming an international powerhouse may take time. "We haven't been, and are not going to be, an overnight sensation," sighs Mr. Mirka.

[Note: Additional information concerning American's international strategy options is provided in the Appendix to this case.]

Appendix   American's International Options

American Airlines flies one daily trip between Dallas/Fort Worth Airport and Tokyo and plans to begin service next spring to Australia and New Zealand. Otherwise, plans to expand its service across the Pacific to about a half-dozen destinations in Asia continue to progress slowly while the Fort Worth-based carrier awaits delivery of the first of up to 50 long-range McDonnell Douglas MD-11s late next year. Meanwhile, American executives are studying their options for expanding the airline's international operations in Europe and in Central and South America. Exhibit A-1 describes their options and the major advantages and disadvantages associated with each.

EXHIBIT A–1

Possible Action	Advantages	Disadvantages
Add three or four new routes between the U.S. and Europe each year through 1992, bypassing traditional gateway cities like New York and London.	Double or even triple service to Europe by 1995 while maintaining a tight control on costs; increase the number of U.S. gateways to Europe, thus reducing the need to fly to Europe via New York, usually on a competing carrier.	American still might trail some carriers, such as British Airways, in its share of the trans-Atlantic passenger market; might still be locked out of some of the traditional markets and key airports such as London's Heathrow.
Buy the Eastern Airlines Latin American division	Quick access to more than two dozen potentially profitable international routes from Miami to Central and South America; reduce competition at hubs in both Miami and San Juan, Puerto Rico; position American as a global carrier with service to five of the six inhabited continents.	Precludes buying all or part of either Pan Am's or TWA's more substantial international operations because of antitrust concerns; Central and South American markets are often volatile and sometimes politically unstable.

EXHIBIT A–1   (*concluded*)

Possible Action	Advantages	Disadvantages
Establish a European hub in partnership with a European airline	Gain access to more European destinations and passengers, possibly with favorable treatment from a European government because of the relationship with a carrier based there; gain rights to begin or increase service from nontraditional U.S. gateways such as Raleigh-Durham, N.C., and San Jose, Calif., where American has hubs.	Having to share some of the passengers and revenue with another airline; possibly having to make a significant equity investment in the European partner airline long before seeing any profits from the deal; lose some control over the quality of service experienced by American passengers when they travel on the European airline.
Buy all or part of financially beleaguered Pan American World Airways	Move overnight from a distant third to first place in U.S. carriers' trans-Atlantic market share; gain traditional New York-London, New York-Paris, New York-Frankfurt route rights, plus additional rights to serve other European cities and some Eastern bloc cities, including Moscow; gain Pan Am's service between West Berlin and cities throughout West Germany, possibly with the ability to expand to cities in rapidly changing eastern Europe; inherit tax advantages of Pan Am's $1.1 billion in operating loss carryforwards.	Inherit Pan Am's labor problems, its old inefficient fleet of planes, its negative net worth (currently $458 million) and $2.4 billion in liabilities; face threat of losing the German service rights as a result of rapid political changes; add debt to balance sheet and increase cost of borrowing money.
Buy all or parts of Trans World Airlines	Move overnight from a distant third to first place in U.S. carriers' trans-Atlantic market share; gain some traditional U.S.-Europe route rights; gain extensive route rights in southern Europe and in the eastern Mediterranean region; inherit TWA's $18.6 million in investment tax credits; gain access to the 20 Airbus A320s TWA has ordered for delivery in 1993.	Price believed to be about $500 million; must sell off most or all of TWA's domestic facilities and assets to avoid antitrust problems; inherit TWA's often rancorous labor problems, its old, inefficient fleet of planes, its route system in the politically volatile southern Europe and eastern Mediterranean regions, its negative net worth (currently $126 million) and its $4.4 billion in liabilities; add debt to balance sheet and increase cost of borrowing money.

Source: Dan Reed, "American Airlines, Domestic Pacesetter of the '80s, Is Still Spreading Its Wings," *Fort Worth Star Telegram,* Dec. 10, 1989, pp. 4–1, 2 and 3.

Case 6–6   *MeraBank**

MeraBank is one of the oldest and largest financial institutions in the Southwest. Formerly First Federal Savings and Loan, MeraBank changed its name, creating a new corporate identity to support and enhance its strong commitment to customer service and to facilitate new strategic thrusts. Now, MeraBank must consider the impact of its name and identity change, its expansion and repositioning strategies, and its basic services marketing challenges.

BACKGROUND

On January 1, 1986, First Federal Savings and Loan of Arizona gave banking a great new name, MeraBank. The rich history of First Federal was a foundation and catalyst for the emergence of MeraBank.

Brief History of MeraBank

Arizona was a frontier state in 1925 when State Building and Loan opened its doors for business. State Building and Loan was a forward-thinking company, an enthusiastic group of business people determined to grow with the needs of the nation's newest state. In 1938, the company became First Federal Savings and Loan and continued to grow, becoming the state's oldest and largest thrift.

First Federal was an appropriate name for this innovative company that achieved a long list of "firsts." For example, First Federal was the first Arizona savings and loan to open a branch office. This was achieved in 1948 when a branch office was opened in Yuma. First Federal was the first savings and loan in Arizona to exceed a billion dollars in assets. It was the first savings and loan to acquire other savings and loans with the acquisitions in 1981 of American Savings in Tuscon, Mohave Savings in northern and northwestern parts of Arizona, and the acquisition in 1982 of Mutual Savings in El Paso, Texas. After becoming a public company in 1983, First Federal was the

---

* This case was prepared by Michael P. Mokwa of Arizona State University, John A. Grant of Southern Illinois University—Carbondale, and Richard E. White of the University of North Texas, in cooperation with MeraBank and the First Interstate Center for Services Marketing at Arizona State University. The help of Robba Benjamin, Margaret B. McGuckin, and Barry Iselin of MeraBank is gratefully acknowledged.

first Arizona savings and loan to be listed on the New York and Pacific Stock Exchanges.

In 1984 and 1985, First Federal's growth accelerated, primarily due to the injection of capital from the stock conversion. The company progressed with its mission clearly defined—to be a leading real estate-based financial institution in the Southwest. To achieve its mission, activity centered on diversification with a real estate focus. Three companies were acquired—Realty World, a realty franchising business; First Service Title, a title and escrow service; and F.I.A. Associates, an investment consulting and advisory company. Consumer loan operations were expanded throughout eight western states. In 1985, the company changed its charter from a savings and loan association to a federal savings bank. First Federal officially became MeraBank on January 1, 1986.

In December 1986, MeraBank was acquired by Pinnacle West, formerly AZP, Inc. Pinnacle West is Arizona's largest corporation. Pinnacle West is a diversified group of subsidiaries that includes: Arizona Public Service Company, a public utility; Suncor Development Company, a real estate development company; El Dorado Investment Company, which invests through limited partnerships in private companies with significant growth potential; and Malapai Resources Company, which locates and develops fuel and uranium reserves. MeraBank with its $6.3 billion in assets and banking presence could be expected to improve short-term earnings and growth potential for the diversified Pinnacle West.

MeraBank's Business Lines

Throughout all of its changes, MeraBank has positioned itself as a family-oriented financial institution, capitalizing on its real estate expertise. For over 15 years, MeraBank has set the pace in residential mortgage lending in Arizona, with a market share nearly double that of its closest competitor. The company also has been a significant originator and syndicator of commercial real estate development and construction loans on a national basis. As illustrated in Exhibit 1, MeraBank's operations span eight western states. It is the 25th largest thrift in the United States, the largest thrift in Arizona, and the second largest financial institution in Arizona.

MeraBank has five major business lines: (1) retail banking; (2) consumer lending; (3) real estate lending and mortgage banking; (4) corporate banking; and (5) real estate development.

MeraBank has a well-established retail banking presence. The company offers the convenience of 78 branches, including 9 in Texas. Aside from MeraBank's commitment to the Texas region, expansion is being

EXHIBIT 1   MeraBank's Areas of Operation

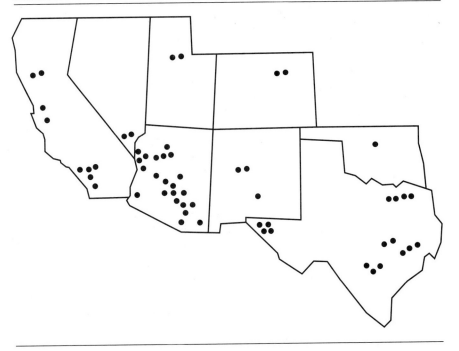

planned for other geographic areas in the Southwest. MeraBank's core products relate to checking and savings, but utilization of electronics and the potential for cross-selling are providing new opportunities in retail banking. Currently, MeraBank is a part of the largest ATM (automatic teller machine) system in the state of Arizona.

Phoenix is the largest and strongest area of operation for Mera-Bank's retail banking. MeraBank's market penetration is nearly 18 percent in Phoenix, which is significantly greater than in the smaller metropolitan areas of Tuscon and El Paso. The Phoenix area accounts for over 45 percent of the bank's business, while Tuscon is about 10.4 percent and El Paso is 8.8 percent. Other parts of Arizona account for 12.8 percent of the business, other areas of Texas are 4.1 percent, and other states are 18.2 percent. By reaching 15 percent of the Arizona market, MeraBank has a 7.1 percent share of the total deposit market. Exhibit 2 illustrates MeraBank's position in the total deposit market in comparison with other Arizona financial institutions. The exhibit shows each major competitor's share of the total deposit market. Valley National Bank (VNB) is the leader, followed by First Interstate Bank (FIB), The Arizona Bank (TAB), Western Savings (WS), Mera-Bank (MB), United Bank (UB), Pima Savings (PS), Great American

EXHIBIT 2 Consumer Banking—Total Deposit Market Share by
Competitors, Third Quarter 1987

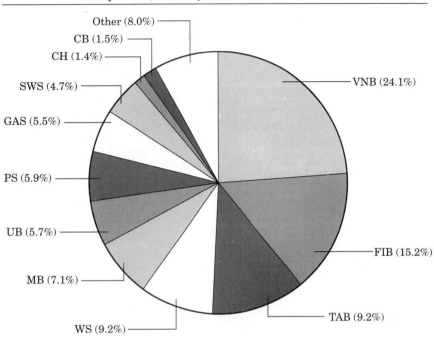

Savings (GAS), Southwestern Savings (SWS), Chase Bank (CH), and
CitiBank (CB).

In consumer lending, MeraBank offers customers a variety of secured and unsecured loans, including home equity lines of credit, car
loans, RV loans, and boat loans. Credit cards and lines of credit are
also important dimensions of the consumer lending package. Mera-
Bank views consumer lending as an expansion area and has opened
new consumer lending offices, called MeraFinancial Services Corporation, in key expansion areas of Colorado, California, and Texas. The
bank's goal in this area is to create as large a consumer loan portfolio
as possible, commensurate with sound underwriting. The consumer
lending group has instituted a detailed program of monthly loan reviews that will keep management well informed on the status of the
portfolio and how it is meeting underwriting standards.

A strong core of MeraBank's expertise lies in real estate financing.
The mortgage lending operations originate and service more loans in
Arizona than any other finance company. Exhibit 3 illustrates Mera-
Bank's dominance in the residential mortgage market by looking at
the largest of Arizona's counties. Additionally, Meracor Mortgage Cor-

poration offices operate in Arizona, California, Colorado, Nevada, New Mexico, Texas, and Utah. They handle residential, commercial, and construction loans. A further presence of MeraBank in the real estate lending market is the marketing of its realty brokerage office franchises. Meracor Realty Corporation holds the license for a large segment of the West and Southwest, having franchised more than 135 Realty World offices. Realty World brokers can offer MeraBank mortgages and services to clients, enabling the bank to reach new customers without adding its own branch office. Through ReaLoan, a computerized mortgage application system, a home buyer and broker can use a computer terminal to analyze the dozens of mortgages available through MeraBank.

In 1985, MeraBank expanded into title insurance. This service was designed to provide customers with title insurance and escrow services from national title insurance companies. Further expansion of the mortgage banking business is sought as MeraBank continues to pursue a program of nationwide lending to strengthen its position as a major force nationally in commercial and construction lending. F.I.A. Associates, the bank's real estate advisory and management company, manages over $1.5 billion in real estate properties and is viewed as a

EXHIBIT 3   Consumer Banking—New Residential Mortgages, Maricopa County, Third Quarter 1987

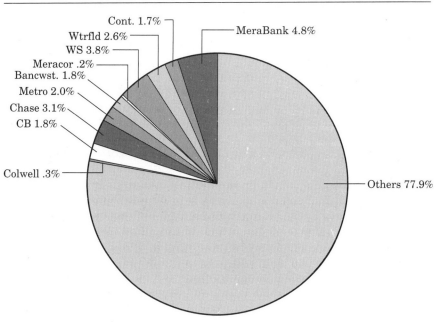

Cont. 1.7%
Wtrfld 2.6%
WS 3.8%
Meracor .2%
Bancwst. 1.8%
Metro 2.0%
Chase 3.1%
CB 1.8%
Colwell .3%
MeraBank 4.8%
Others 77.9%

way of diversifying in the real estate business through institutional investors.

Corporate banking provides both deposit and lending services to companies throughout the Southwest. MeraBank offers corporate clients a variety of deposit, checking, and lending services as well as financing, secured by accounts receivable and inventory. The bank finances equipment acquisition and plant expansions as well. Cash management accounts and high-yield bonds are products that were designed to meet the needs of the corporate banking customers. Corporate banking is a new area for savings institutions, and the bank is branching into this new and challenging business prudently.

MeraBank is also a significant competitor in real estate joint ventures, which include the marketing and property management of joint venture projects. This fifth business line, real estate development, is achieved through Meracor Development Corporation, the bank's joint venture and development company. Meracor activities focus on the management of profitable, high-quality projects in Arizona, and to a lesser extent in Texas, California, Colorado, and New Mexico. Management has made a strategic decision to reduce dependence on this area and to limit the size of joint venture development in the future to assure that MeraBank retains a conservative level of leverage.

The Competitive Market Environment

Competition in financial markets is expanding and intensifying as many new institutions are entering and as traditional market and service boundaries are eroding. The basic financial market in Arizona, MeraBank's largest area of operations, can be segmented fundamentally into (1) banks and (2) savings and loans. Information about MeraBank's major competitors in each of the segments can be found in Exhibit 4. In 1985, savings and loans totaled about 24 percent share of the Arizona deposit market, while banks maintained the largest overall market share with 70 percent of the deposits.

With product deregulation, savings and loan institutions have been given freedom to expand much more into consumer banking services. This has allowed saving and loan institutions to compete directly with the banks, which has resulted in a blurring of the distinction between banks and savings and loan institutions. Through mergers and acquisitions, which have taken place as a result of geographical deregulation, larger national and international bank holding companies have moved into the Arizona competitive environment and made their presence known. Of the six largest banks in Arizona, four changed hands in

EXHIBIT 4   Major Competitors: Arizona Financial Market—1986 (dollars in billions)

Competitor	Arizona Branches	Assets	Loans	Deposits
Banks:				
Valley National	272	$10.7	$7.3	$9.2
First Interstate	183	6.5	4.3	5.7
Arizona Bank	119	4.5	3.2	3.8
United Bank	47	2.7	1.8	2.2
MeraBank	68	6.3	5.1	4.0
Savings and loans:				
Western Savings	82	5.5	3.0	3.8
Great American	NA*			
Southwest Savings	50	2.1	1.7	1.5
Pima Savings	28	2.6	1.8	1.3

* Arizona operations combined with parent company.

1986. The two largest banks that have not changed hands during this period are Valley National Bank and First Interstate Bank.

Despite increased competition and activity, total deposits in the Arizona market have begun to decline. Arizona's deposit base increased by $11.2 billion from 1983 to 1986, reaching a peak of $33.4 billion. However, in 1987, total deposits declined from 1986. The leading financial institutions saw a stable or declining market share trend. First Interstate's market share dropped from 19 percent to 15.4 percent, while Valley National and MeraBank's market share declined 2.5 and 1.4 points, respectively. All major competitors experienced a positive annual growth rate between 1983 and 1986. But, in 1987, all but two competitors had a drop in the average deposit per branch from the first quarter of 1987 through the third quarter of 1987.

The decline in bank deposits appears to stem from consumers' desire for higher return investments. As the stock market enjoyed a record bull market period in the first three quarters of 1987, conservative banking products had a continuing decline. Certificates of deposits (CDs), which offer a guaranteed rate of return for a specified period of deposit time, declined while money market accounts (MMA), which offer a varying rate of interest with no time commitment on the deposit, exhibited a dramatic increase in sales. Passbook savings (PB) and interest-bearing checking accounts (NOW) steadily declined in 1987.

The Major Competitors

In the Arizona market, the most formidable competitor has been Valley National Bank, with nearly $10 billion in assets. Valley National remains as the only bank that is headquartered in Phoenix. Valley has 277 branches in Arizona. Valley National's 24.1 percent share of the total deposit market is maintained with 25 percent of the branches. Valley National's strategy seems centered on intense penetration and physical presence, supported by regional expansion.

Valley National is also the leader in the Arizona market for electronic banking and is planning further expansion. At present, the Valley National debit card is the one most widely accepted in the Arizona market and can be used to make purchases at grocery stores, service stations, convenience stores, and even department stores. This electronic funds transfer card has become known as a POS (point of sale). It allows a debit of the customer's bank account as payment for a purchase. The POS is expected to be expanded into more retail outlets by Valley National.

In the lending end of the business, Valley National has instituted a Loan by Phone program. The bank promises answers to loans in 30 minutes. These are some of the services that Valley focuses on in its advertising to create its image as "The Leader in Your Banking Needs."

First Interstate Bank has been very close in asset size to MeraBank but has over twice as many branch locations in Arizona. First Interstate has 15.2 percent of the deposit market share and 16.4 percent of the branches. The bank is also involved in POS capability, with its debit card being accepted at all but grocery store locations. First Interstate is an affiliate of First Interstate Bancorp, which is the eighth largest retail banking organization in the nation. First Interstate is a relatively new name for a long-standing competitor. Its advertising theme is "Serving Arizona for 110 years." First Interstate customers are the highest users of the automatic teller machines (ATMs) in Arizona, and First Interstate plans to continue to expand its ATMs, POS, and branches to stay on the leading edge in convenience banking.

The Arizona Bank is another competitor close to MeraBank in asset size, with just under $5 billion. The Arizona Bank, with 126 branches in Arizona, was acquired in October of 1986 by Security Pacific Corporation, the sixth largest bank holding company in the United States. The bank's image is tied closely with the state it serves. To convey an Arizona image, a native American Indian is used in the bank's logo, with the slogan "The Bank Arizona Turns To" and "Count on Us." The bank's plans include expansion of more branches in the Phoenix metropolitan area and some outlying communities.

The United Bank of Arizona has been a smaller competitor, with only 47 branch operations. It has maintained over $2 billion in assets. United Bank has a 5.7 percent share of the total deposits, with only a 3.9 percent share of the branches. United Bank was acquired by Union Bancorp in January of 1987. Union Bancorp is a holding bank in Los Angeles, a subsidiary of Standard Chartered PLC, an International Banking Network. United Bank has had the fastest percentage growth in assets, deposits, and loans of all major Arizona banks in the last five years. The bank's focus has been on responsiveness to the needs of middle-market growing businesses. This is reflected in the advertising theme, "Arizona's Business Bank for over 25 Years." Citicorp has been very interested in United Bank and would like to acquire it to enhance its own presence in Arizona.

In the savings and loan segment, the largest competitor has been Western Savings, with approximately $5.8 billion in assets. Headquartered in Phoenix, Western Savings has begun expansion into Tuscon and Flagstaff. In its major markets, Western Savings has located branch offices in popular grocery stores. To develop the image as "The Foresight People," Western Savings plans to continue to expand products and services. The company experienced about a 2 percent drop in CDs but has seen an increasing volume of retail deposits. Western Savings is the only thrift currently involved in POS. It has only been able to have its POS card accepted by about 200 Mobil service stations.

Great American, though substantially smaller, has been aggressively expanding in the Phoenix area, following a similar location strategy to that of Western Savings. Headquartered in San Diego, the company plans continued expansion in the Phoenix area, targeting high-income growth markets. Great American has experienced the largest increases in the MMAs and has seen a strong increase in the volume of retail deposits in the last year. The company presents itself in the image of a bank, trying to stress Great American, "Your Advantage Bank."

Southwest Savings is a smaller institution, with 53 branch operations. It has been an independent and closely held organization. Southwest has committed itself to serving the growing senior citizen population in Arizona. Southwest Savings has experienced the industry trend in product performance, with about a 2 percent drop in CDs, while MMAs were up sharply. However, overall total deposits have been down.

Pima Savings has operated out of Tuscon, where it has a 40 percent share of the total savings and loan deposits in Pima County. Pima Savings has a 5.9 percent market share of the total deposits in Arizona, with only 3.7 percent of the total branches. Pima Savings has seen continued growth in total deposits and in CDs. The company is viewed in the industry as the investment rate leader. Pima is rapidly expanding branches in the Phoenix area, frequently using Safeway grocery stores as outlets. Pima is owned by Pima Financial Corporation, which is a subsidiary of Heron Financial Corporation, a U.S. holding company for one of Europe's largest privately owned companies.

Other major competitors in the Arizona financial market began to arrive with the reinstatement of interstate banking in 1986. Among the newest financial institutions are: Citibank, which took over Great Western Bank & Trust of Arizona and is a subsidiary of Citicorp, the largest bank holding company in the United States; and Chase Bank of Arizona, a division of Chase, the second largest holding company in the country. Chase took over the former Continental Bank. These acquisitions should have an impact on the Arizona financial market in the near future. Interstate banking has provided the opportunity for the acquisitions of Arizona's financial institutions by out-of-state companies and could continue to be a factor in the competitive environment. Also considered as competitors in some segments of MeraBank's lines of business are insurance companies, finance companies, investment companies, money market funds, credit unions, and pension funds. Overall, many organizations are entering financial service markets.

THE NAME AND IDENTITY CHANGE

In 1985, the total population of Arizona was 3.2 million. The state had experienced a five-year increase in its total population, an increase of nearly 25 percent. Growth had been projected to continue. MeraBank's other dominant market, Texas, also had been growing. In 1985, it had a much larger population than Arizona, over 15 million people. At that time, First Federal operated 12 offices located throughout Texas in El Paso, Dallas, Austin, Houston, and Fort Worth.

Even though First Federal was well positioned in its highly competitive markets, banking deregulation and legislative changes were opening doors to interstate banking and to charter changes for thrift institutions. New products and services would soon be available, and a significant challenge confronted First Federal. Although First Federal offered a full range of products and services, most consumers perceived banks to be better—more full-service and service oriented—than savings and loans.

First Federal perceived a new change as a necessity, but the corporate priorities in 1985 were complex. The company hoped to demonstrate superior financial performance, while making customer service its most effective marketing tool. Moreover, the company hoped to protect its current market share from the threat of new competition, while increasing retail banking coverage in Texas and expanding beyond Arizona and Texas.

The board of directors has been considering a name change since the company went public in 1983. The name First Federal was a very common name in financial institutions. There were over 89 First Federals in Texas alone. If expansion was to be considered, the company needed a name it could grow with. Aside from expanding under one name and distinguishing itself to stockholders, the board wanted to include the word "bank" in its name and position itself as a bank in the market.

A market research company from New York was retained to help determine what the new name and bank image should be. However, the board felt the process would be easy, simply changing some signs and forms. The board decided that the First Federal logo could be maintained by simply changing the name to FedBank. The board dismissed the market research team, and, by 1984, it was ready to make the change. In August, a new senior vice president was given the task of implementing the name change. The initial step was to check out regulations regarding the use of the word "bank" in the name of a chartered savings and loan association. However, it was discovered in the legal search that the proposed use of Fed in the new name would violate federal law. There is a regulation banning private organizations from using a name that sounds like a federal agency. In this case, the proposed FedBank name was very similar to the federal bank known as the "Fed."

The task of changing the name would have to start over. The first market research company had left with some ill feelings. So in 1985, a new consulting firm, S & O Consultants, from San Francisco, was contracted for the project. S & O specialized in corporate identity. It had recently done the name change for First Interstate Bank in Arizona and was familiar with the financial institution market in the area.

The Project Objective

Objectives were established at the beginning of the project. The primary objective was to select a name that conveyed a positive image and new identity. The name needed to be legally available in all 50 states. It needed to fit all the business lines—everything from the title company to retail banking to real estate joint ventures. A distinctive identity was to be developed as well. The First Federal logo was very similar to other existing corporate identities and offered little value to the company as an identity. The new name needed to create excitement and set the tone for continued innovation and leadership. It needed to increase the employees' morale and help generate new business. However, the company did not have unlimited resources. So a very important objective was to accomplish everything within a strict, tight budget, and a short time frame.

The Process

Distinct phases were identified in the change process. First, the name itself had to be generated and selected. Second, the logo and identity surrounding the name had to be developed. Third, the identity needed to be communicated in a clear and concise way, and finally, evaluation must be undertaken.

Selecting the name was the first step. Criteria for the new name were established. These included implying stature and strength, being distinctive, memorable, and easy to pronounce. All the criteria were ranked and weighted in terms of perceived importance. The criteria of conveying a service-oriented bank and of implying stature and strength were ranked as the two most important criteria for the new name.

After a positioning statement was developed for the name itself, the process of generating the name began. Over 800 names were evaluated and critiqued. The top 20 names were further evaluated, using a mathematical scoring system, and all the top 20 names were legally searched in all 50 states. The evaluation of the final five that were considered is shown in Exhibit 5 (pages 774–75).

An early favorite was Merit Savings Bank. However, this name was being used elsewhere, particularly in California. And it was associated with a brand of cigarettes. However, the name had some interesting roots. After an arduous series of executive interviews, brainstorming sessions, and stormy meetings, a consensus was reached. The name MeraBank was selected.

In phase two, the logo and identity were developed. The company desired a design that would uniquely identify it and reach across all its business lines. The logo had to be instantly recognizable, even before the name was seen. The company wanted something that would emphasize a commitment to comprehensive financial services. The logo would have to be modern, make a strong retail statement, and incorporate a taste of Southwestern imagery, but not limit the bank to Arizona.

Choices were narrowed, and focus-group testing began. Focus-group reaction favored a multicolored logo. Group participants described the identity as "progressive," "modern," and "large." Obviously, this met the company's objectives. The colors were described as being "attractive" and "Southwestern." The vibrant yellow-gold and orange-red of the sunrise with the royal purple of the mountains were well-understood Southwestern images.

Several modifications were made to the logo, based on focus-group work. For example, the company has had a substantial senior citizen customer base. The seniors expressed some very strong dissatisfaction with the proposed typeface. They perceived the logo as very contemporary, but the typeface was perceived as very different and too modern. What resulted was a new and much more conservative typeface with the same multicolored contemporary logo. Perceptions were much more favorable.

Effective communication of the name and imagery were vital to establishing the identity and accomplishing performance-oriented objectives. A strategic decision was made to communicate the change from the inside out. To accomplish this, a large task force was assembled internally to cover literally every aspect of the identity change. The name-change task force began working in July of 1985. It included a project manager, seven project leaders, and 30 employees. The task force was responsible for the signage, forms, merchant notification, employee notification and promotion, media notification and promotion, and customer notification and promotion.

To direct and guide the task force, several objectives and strategic thrusts were outlined. The first objective was to gain employee awareness and enthusiasm for the name change. Employee support was essential to communicate the name from the inside out. A second objective of the task force was to develop a graphic plan and standards manual that clearly spelled out the proper representation and usage of the new logo. A high priority was given to the delicate task of communicating the change to primary stakeholders, including board members and the stockholders. A major undertaking involved identification and revision of all forms. The effort uncovered the opportunity to reduce by 30 percent the number of forms used.

The task force also needed to develop an advertising campaign and related promotions for customer notification. A TV spot would provide only 30 seconds to communicate the new identity; a billboard would provide less time A very complex message had to be refined to its strongest, simplest components. Also, the task force needed to develop branch employee training and information sessions, including the revision of the branch operations manual. Finally, the task force had to be prepared to handle any of the legal questions that could arise concerning the name change. Thus, one of the task force members was a staff attorney.

The plans to generate employee awareness and enthusiasm were initiated within tight time and resource constraints. The task force knew that employee support was essential to market acceptance. The name, but not the logo, was first announced to all employees at the

EXHIBIT 5 Summary of Name Choice Legal Search

Final Five Names	Estimated Probability of Successful Federal Registration	Prior Federal Registration	Prior State Registrations (if yes, how many states)	Prior Incidence of Litigation	Incidence of Common-Law Usage
Firstmark Savings Bank	5%	Yes, to FIRSTMARKCORP, for "consumer, commercial, and industrial financing"	Yes, 15 states	Yes, successfully precluded a savings and loan from use	Irrelevant
Interprise Savings Bank	50%, based upon similarity in sound to "ENTERPRISE"	No, but ENTERPRISE BANK is registered as ENTERPRISE LOANS	No, yes for ENTERPRISE in 2 states (incl. Calif. & Texas)	No	(1) ENTERPRISE S & L in Long Beach, Calif. (2) ENTERPRISE BANCORP in San Francisco, Calif.
Landmark Savings Bank	5%	Yes, to (1) SIGNAL LANDMARK for "residential and commercial construction" (2) LANDMARK PRIME LINE for "services"	Yes, 11 registrations in financial services category 10 registrations in real estate-related category	Yes	Numerous examples are: LANDMARK NATIONAL BANK (Denver) LANDMARK NATIONAL BANK (Dallas) LANDMARK THRIFT & LOAN (San Diego) LANDMARK REAL ESTATE (San Diego)

Merit Savings Bank	50%	No, but design mark registration of MERRITT COMMERCIAL S & L (Maryland), MERITLINE (product of CALIF. FIRST BANK OF SAN FRANCISCO)	No	Numerous examples are: (1) MERIT S & L (Los Angeles: 5 branches $280 million asset) (2) MERIT FINANCIAL in Denver, Dallas, and Houston
Pace Savings Bank	50%	No, but 3 similar word marks are registered: 1) PACE PLAN (product of COMMONWEALTH BANK in Penn.) 2) PACECARD (product of NATIONAL BANK OF COMMERCE W. VA.) 3) PACESETTER (product of NATIONAL BANK OF TULSA in Okla.)	Yes, as a word mark in Illinois and as initials (P.A.C.E.) in New Jersey	Not a common name for financial services and real estate but used by: 1) PACE MORTGAGE in Denver 2) PACE CO. REAL ESTATE in San Diego 3) PACE FINANCIAL MANAGEMENT in Dallas

company's big 60th birthday celebration in September 1985. Further internal communication was initiated through a new publication called *The MeraBanker.* The employee campaign even included a "mystery shopper" who went into the field asking employees questions about the name change.

A customer-awareness program began in November with a teaser advertising campaign. By December, more than 1,200 stationery forms and collateral pieces had been redesigned and printed. On January 1, 1986, the new signs and the major campaign theme, "First Federal Gives Banking a Great New Name," were unveiled. Throughout the customer awareness program, the *MeraBanker* term was consistently used for name and identity-related internal communication.

Extensive work was done with the press. Hundreds of press releases were sent out. Early releases included a question-and-answer piece that did not include the full identity. Later in the program, the logo, the name, and the advertising campaign were released to the press.

MeraBank wanted its identity to be comprehensive and wanted to maintain the integrity and power of the identity. So for the first time in the company's history, a graphic standards manual was developed to state how and for what purposes the logo could be used. This was necessary to determine proper use for advertising, promotions, and brochures, as well as use on checks, credit cards, debit cards, ATM cards, all banking forms, and annual reports. MeraBank even changed its hot-air balloon.

Results of the Name Change

The impact of the name change was very positive. Employees were enthusiastic about the change, and the name change scored extremely well on the mystery shopper quizzes. Over 96 percent of all employees answered questions about the new name correctly. The extensive amount of employee involvement in the name change stimulated a renewed sense of pride in the company. Moreover, the name change was the catalyst generating a new orientation: employees and management perceived themselves as a bank.

Market studies were undertaken to determine consumer response. Consumers were positive about the new name. Over two thirds recalled the new name, their primary source being television advertising. Fifty-five percent of consumers could identify the new name as MeraBank, and very few people perceived the name change as negative. Overall post-name change advertising was perceived a more meaningful than previous advertising. In fact, advertising recall doubled and achieved a significant breakthrough in terms of consumer scoring.

The new advertising was very successful in promoting the new MeraBank image. When surveys were conducted after the name change, people began to list MeraBank in the bank category and not with the savings and loan institutions. The ad campaign also helped to promote the trial of MeraBank. Of those surveyed who were likely to try MeraBank, most were impressed with the name change advertising and rated it as being very meaningful to them. Those who were willing to try MeraBank described the company as "progressive" and having a "high level of customer service."

A year after the name change, MeraBank's assets were up 20 percent, and its advertising recall was up almost 100 percent. MeraBank's retail banking and mortgage lending market share had dropped slightly. This was planned through new pricing strategies, which were undertaken to reduce the overall cost of funds. MeraBank, now positioned as a bank, lowered interest rates, getting these more in line with bank competitors versus savings and loan competitors.

THE NEW MERABANK

MeraBank began thinking of itself as a bank after the name change. Customers, employees, and the financial market began to refer to MeraBank as a bank, not as a thrift. However, changing the charter and creating new advertising campaigns were just the beginning. A complete repositioning in the market would be necessary to educate, attract, and serve "bank" customers. Changes in products, advertising, service, and facilities would be needed to complete the identity metamorphosis.

Several strategic changes occurred in conjunction with the name change. Advertising positioned MeraBank directly against the banks. Management dropped interest rates on savings deposits to bring them in line with bank rates. In the six months following the name change, the six-month CD rate dropped 1.1 percent. Through December 1987, the overall interest expense had been reduced by over $20 million as a result of this strategy. Interest rates and fees on credit cards were increased to be aligned with the pricing policies of banks. Customer service did not appear to suffer as a result of these changes. The number of total retail households served by MeraBank increased by 9 percent the first six months after the name change. By December 1987, the number of households served was up 22 percent.

The Marketing Group

Overall, changes were initiated to build a new corporate culture, emphasizing service and measuring performance against both banks and thrifts. Strategy implementation became the major responsibility of the marketing group. As a result of the successful name change, the senior vice president of marketing was promoted to executive vice president and chief administrative officer in charge of marketing, human resources, and long-range planning. She recruited a new senior vice president for the marketing group.

Headed by a senior vice president, the department is organized into four major divisions. The first division, Market Planning, Research, and Development, works on analyzing and segmenting the market and on keeping an accurate account of MeraBank's position in the financial market. Marketing Services develops and manages products, promotions, advertising, and print production for the company. Corporate Communications is responsible for public relations activities audio/visual productions, and employee communications. The fourth division, Directing Marketing, oversees direct-mail campaigns, telemarketing, customer service, and training. Though the reporting structure is set clearly, the functions interface frequently, and informal relationships appear to be very cooperative.

Consumer Market Segments

The primary demographic factors related to financial product usage appear to be age and income. Financial consumers for the banking industry often are segmented, using these two criteria. Segments with the strongest potential for heavy financial product usage are: mid-age middle-income; mid-age affluent; preretired middle income; preretired affluent; and retired high income groups. These segments represent 57 percent of the Phoenix Metropolitan population and 47 percent of the Tucson area.

Using segmentation profiles as a base, MeraBank has begun to target its distribution system as well as its products and communication efforts toward specific market segments, in particular more affluent population segments. A profile of MeraBank's customer segments appears in Exhibit 6. A major indicator of MeraBank's commitment to reach new segments and serve new needs can be seen in its direct marketing budget, which increased 200 percent from 1985 to 1986. As a result of the repositioning effort and the move to targeting, the total households that were served increased 15 percent, to well over a quarter of a million households.

EXHIBIT 6   Market Segmentation Profiles

Communication efforts to sell specific products/packages can be directed specifically to segments by learning more about financial styles of these groups.

Mid-Age, Middle Income—These households will be hard to target as an entire segment, because they are widely distributed across all financial styles and thus vary greatly in their attitudes toward financial matters. Households in this segment are family oriented. Much of their financial behavior is focused on protecting their families and planning for their children's future.

Mid-Age, Affluent—A large portion of this segment are Achievers and have the most-in-command financial style. They are likely to be receptive to marketing approaches that appeal to their self-image as successful, knowledgeable, and decisive people.

Households in this segment are value sensitive. They are receptive to distinctive product features and are able to make price/feature trade-offs. While households in this segment are price sensitive, they are willing to pay for services that they don't have time for, especially the dual-earner households. They have positive attitudes toward using electronics and are likely to own computers and other electronic/high-technology products.

Preretired, Middle Income—Half of the households in this segment are Belongers. Their financial style is predominantly more safe and simple. Many of these households will be receptive to marketing approaches that stress traditional, conservative values and emphasize the safety of the institution. In their efforts to minimize taxes and accumulate funds for retirement, these households will require conservative, lower-risk products.

Many of these households are shifting their focus away from their children to their own future retirement. Though the family is still important, these households' goals are changing as they enter a new life stage. They place a high value on the reputation of the financial institutions they use and on having trust in them.

Preretired, Affluent—The financial styles of the preretired affluent households are predominantly most in command and most comfortable. They are oriented toward the present and are concerned about retaining their present lifestyles during their retirement. They are sophisticated in their approach to financial matters. These households like having access to people that they perceive as competent, but they are receptive to using the telephone for financial dealings.

Retired, Higher Income—Households in this segment are the more safe and simple and prefer to keep their financial affairs uncomplicated and are generally unexperimental. Other households, called *most comfortable,* are sophisticated in their approach to their financial affairs. They view themselves as prosperous and financially secure. They highly value security and involvement in financial affairs. These retired households are likely to be receptive to social seminar-type events, because they have the time to attend and the interest in learning.

Service and Product Development

MeraBank launched two new retail banking services since the name change: the Passport Certificate Account and the Working Capital Account. These new accounts have brought in new deposits at a time when total deposits have been declining. Many existing product lines, such as CDs, have seen a decline in sales. MeraBank has suffered a loss of about 2 percent of its CD deposits. Passbook savings accounts have also been on a decline. However, MeraBank has increased its share of interest-bearing checking accounts—a conventional "bank" product, despite increases in the minimum balance of the NOW account from $100 to $500. Similarly, an increase in credit card fees has had only a minimal effect on the number of credit card accounts and card usage.

The Passport Certificate is targeted to the 55+ age group. The advertising campaign has used primarily newspapers. The core product is very traditional, a certificate of deposit. But the CD is augmented with free checking as well as free and discounted travel services, such as car rentals, insurance; even a 24-hour travel center is included. The account is made more tangible by giving each customer a wallet-sized passport card with the account number and the package benefits included.

The Working Capital Account is targeted to the affluent, middle-aged market segment. It is patterned after a money market account. It is a liquid investment with a very high yield tied to the one-year Treasury bill. The account requires a high minimum balance of $10,000 but permits unlimited access to the money. The investor can gain a high-yield CD rate but maintain checking privileges and access to the money. Once again, newspaper was the primary advertising medium for the product. The Working Capital Account provides its subscribers with monthly statements of the investment and the checking accounts. The account is the only product of its type in the Arizona market. In the first nine months after introduction, it generated a half billion dollars.

MeraBank has a strong commitment to customer service and convenience that goes beyond the traditional branch structure. The direct marketing division supervises the operations of Meratel, which is a customer service hotline and "telephone bank." Customers can open an account, obtain information, or transact business by calling 1-800-MERATEL. This convenience to customers has been well received. Call volume increased 300 percent during the year following the name change, from 75,000 calls in 1986 to 266,000 calls in 1987. To further improve the level of service performance, MeraBank has initiated direct marketing campaigns to retail customers, contacting them by mail and telephone. The intention is to expand this operation and begin a regular program of calling retail customers to enhance convenience.

MeraBank's management believes that its success is dependent on the capabilities and performance of employees. The company is recruiting and developing employees who are more sales oriented. Employees are expected to produce superior levels of performance, be customer oriented, have high standards of integrity, and work in unison with a team spirit. To ensure these service standards, a comprehensive training program has been instituted for the sales staff, with an incentive compensation system for frontline personnel. The commission program has resulted in doubling the cross-sales ratio at the front line. The training process has also been revised to reflect more product training and to amend a thrift vocabulary by incorporating banking terms. Periodically, the company will sponsor a contest to encourage high-quality service and improve morale. Internal newsletters provide employees with communication and inspiration to maintain quality service.

Community service also is an important orientation at MeraBank. In 1987, MeraBank contributed over $1.2 million to charity, and many of its employees work in behalf of civic and charitable endeavors. Contributions are divided among worthy cultural, civic, educational, health, and social welfare programs. In one project, MeraBank teamed with Realty World brokers to create a "Dream House." This project benefits victims of cerebral palsy. Strong community spirit is perceived to be a direct expression of MeraBank's service philosophy and culture.

Advertising and Promotion

Advertising and promotional strategy play a key role in positioning MeraBank. Following the name change, advertising objectives emphasized creating awareness and educating the public to the new identity. These objectives have evolved to emphasize increasing both deposits and branch traffic. The initial name-change campaign required an increase in promotional expenditures. However, the current advertising budget is only slightly more than it was for First Federal Savings. The primary media used are television and newspaper, while radio is used to a lesser extent. TV advertising is targeted at the 35+ age customer, while newspaper ads are aimed at an older 55+ customer. Direct-mail and billboard campaigns are used less often, but have been effective for some products.

MeraBank television advertising has incorporated the new identity of the institution, while maintaining the First Federal campaign theme of "We'll Be There." This theme has been used since 1985, and there are no plans to change the theme for general TV ads. However, MeraBank has tried to develop more sophisticated messages and imagery in the ads. Also, it runs special promotional campaigns, using television as the primary media. For example, MeraBank has become involved in an advertising campaign promoting CDs and a contest linked with ABC television stations and the 1988 Winter Olympics.

This campaign capitalized on patriotic interest in the Olympics and offered a free trip to the games in Canada as the grand prize. The winner of the contest was announced at the halftime of the 1988 Super Bowl. Additional prizes were large interest rates on CDs with Mera-Bank. TV, newspaper, and direct mail were utilized in this campaign. The campaign also included a contest for employees. Employee Olympics were held to spur interest in the promotion and to encourage outstanding service. Employees were able to nominate peers for sportsmanship, team spirit, and customer service.

Merchandising and Facility Management

Extending the emphasis placed on promotion, MeraBank has given more attention to branch merchandising. The entire point of sale "look" has been revised to reflect the new corporate identity. Signage, brochures, and point of purchase material incorporate the company logo and identity color scheme. Though thought has been given to a standardized interior appearance, there is not a uniform branch configuration. However, the newer and remodeled facilities reflect an interior design that is more open and modular in construction. Partitions are utilized to provide a flexible lobby setup. Both interior decor and career apparel that would embody MeraBank's corporate identity through style and color schemes have been under serious consideration. The basic design and exterior of branch locations also are under review.

MeraBank has essentially three prototypes for branch facilities: (1) a large regional center; (2) an intermediate size complex; or (3) a small shopping center style. However, a pilot project is being undertaken with the Circle K convenience stores. A MeraBank branch and Circle K convenience store are sharing the same building. Though no direct internal connection was made between the bank and store, the two facilities share a parking lot and the same foundation. This approach is viewed as a way of saving on construction costs for new branches as well as providing added security to the customers who use the ATM machine outside of the branch, because the convenience store is always open. It is not, however, regarded as an expansion strategy into retail grocery outlets—a strategy that has been popular with competitors.

MeraBank is planning a new corporate headquarters. The new office building is being designed based on a careful study of the company's history and image. The building is to personify the new positioning thrust and corporate culture of MeraBank.

Emerging Technology

MeraBank belongs to an automatic teller machine network that provides its customers with the most extensive coverage of any financial institution in Arizona. Expansion of the ATMs and a nationwide hookup are being planned. This could lead toward a future where most banking transactions could be done electronically at home using a computer terminal. Home banking appears to be a long-term technological goal of the banking industry.

The current trend in convenience bank merchandising is electronic fund transfers. Electronic fund transfers are used by many banks in the Phoenix area in the form of a debit card, POS. Though it looks like a credit card, it is used to facilitate payment at retail locations. Using the POS, a transaction is automatically debited to an account. While POS has been limited to market tests in most states, penetration in Arizona has been substantial.

A recent survey found the overall rate of POS acceptance to be 26 percent among financial service customers. The response varied by age groups. Younger age brackets had higher usage ratings. While the ratings may not seem impressive, they are when compared with the early ratings of ATM acceptance. Investment in POS technology is very high. However, market penetration might generate transaction volumes that reduce transaction costs considerably. Though many of the larger financial institutions have been involved in POS, MeraBank is taking a conservative stance toward electronic technology and is waiting to see how others fair before they follow.

Profitability Perspectives

Examining the profit picture at MeraBank, it is easiest to consider loans as the assets of the bank and deposits as the liabilities. A key to profitability is the diversity of the bank's assets and liabilities. MeraBank attempts to spread its investment risks and not invest too heavily in any one particular business line. Currently, the retail banking, consumer lending, real estate lending, and mortgage banking lines of business contribute most significantly. Corporate banking contributes to a lesser extent. On a limited basis, the real estate development line is profitable.

MeraBank is very competitive on consumer loans, such as auto loans, student loans, RV, and boat loans. Home and mortgage loans are a particular strength. The home equity loan is the fastest growing loan in the Arizona market. Commercial loans are a smaller segment of MeraBank's loan operations. Given that commercial interest rates vary on a case-by-case basis, it is difficult to generalize profitability in this line of business.

One area of consumer loans that could be developed into a more profitable position is credit cards. Profit in this area relates to volume and use of the card. Since the name change, MeraBank has offered the first year of the card with no fee but has added a $15 annual fee for each year after the first. The interest rate paid by the customer is 17.9 percent, which is comparable to other Arizona banks. Anyone may apply for a MeraBank credit card. The program is not tied to a deposit in the bank. Changes in the credit card program have brought Mera-Bank in line with the pricing policies of the major banks. However, credit card customers decreased when the changes were initiated. This is not thought to be a long-term setback.

On the liability side of the balance sheet, MeraBank offers several products that vary widely in their profit contribution. Certificates of deposit are the most profitable deposits. A bank can guarantee a certain return on the deposit, then pool them together and invest them at a higher rate. Passbook savings accounts would rank second in profitability potential. Low interest rate returns are the sacrifice for demand deposit accounts. Other less-profitable deposit products would be IRAs, followed by money market accounts. The least-profitable deposit account is the interest-bearing checking account, which serves as a loss leader to attract customers and to "cross-sell" other more profitable accounts. Automatic teller cards and point of sale cards also are only marginally profitable and serve mainly as loss leaders.

Financial planning, sales of securities, estate planning, administering trust, and private bankers are services provided by many major banks. These services are very competitive in the Arizona market and require experienced personnel with established performance. However, MeraBank has not expanded into these areas. Though these services have been studied, MeraBank views them as marginally profitable and does not consider them as a hedge against the risk of any loan segment going soft.

Expansion

The objectives of reaching new consumers and offering convenience to all consumers drive the expansion of branch locations. Since the name change, new branches have been added in the existing service areas of

Arizona and Texas, and further penetration of these states is being actively pursued.

Other expansion efforts seem to be evolving within the current eight-state Southwest region that already is served by divisions of MeraBank. The Southwest imagery that is projected in the corporate identity should fit well into such states as Colorado and California. Moreover, MeraBank management believes that the identity and the imagery of its logo would be acceptable to all parts of the country in any future expansion.

FUTURE CHALLENGES

MeraBank is no longer a small building and loan. It has grown in sophistication. MeraBank aspires to continue its tradition of innovation and leadership. The financial services market will become more complex and turbulent. Diversification and expansion present significant opportunities, but also tough questions. MeraBank envisions establishing and sustaining a competitive advantage in terms of its consumer service and service marketing strategies across its business lines and diverse geographic markets. With many different facilities, employees, and markets, setting appropriate objectives while creating the best strategies and programs to service its markets will be challenging.

MeraBank envisions using its identity as a means to powerfully exhibit who it is as a company and to provide evidence of its marketing presence. MeraBank believes that its identity can differentiate it from competitors and provide a distinct position in the market to generate sales and performance. The firm recognizes the problems of being a service provider with many intangibles to manage and market. Its identity must be considered all the way throughout service design, development, and delivery.

Increasingly, MeraBank has begun to consider fundamental service marketing challenges, such as making its services more tangible for its publics; controlling its service quality; developing its service culture; enhancing the productivity of its service encounters and environments; and protecting its new identity. MeraBank's new management orientation and renewed employee enthusiasm have generated a new strategic thrust and uncovered new challenges.

Case 6–7   Motorola, Inc.*

Motorola Inc. enjoys a stellar reputation for high-tech engineering. It fosters that image by trumpeting its Malcolm Baldrige National Quality Award from the U.S. government and Nikkei Prize for manufacturing from Japan.

But in the booming $2-billion-a-year market for computer microprocessors, the "brain" chips that run the machines, Motorola is winning booby prizes.

For a decade, it has trailed archrival Intel Corp. Last year it lost more market share by delaying improvements on its aging line of microprocessors. Today only one personal computer in 10 has a Motorola brain chip, and there's only a 28 percent chance, down from 79 percent in 1985, that an engineer's new workstation uses a Motorola microprocessor.

That isn't all. Motorola also is paying heavily for fumbling work on a new, speedier chip.

Thus, both Motorola's old and its new chip lines are being hit by major computer customers' defections, to Intel and to two upstarts, Sun Microsystems Inc. and Mips Computer Systems Inc.

How could Motorola, one of America's most admired companies and a master maker of other types of chips and of cellular phones, slide into such a predicament?

One reason is paradoxical: Motorola's obsession with technological excellence delayed new products at critical times. The other reason is an all-too-familiar case of infighting between champions of a new technology and defenders of a successful older one. Backers of Motorola's older microprocessors, the 68000 line, won crucial internal battles in the 1980s, and they siphoned off resources needed to develop a new, high-speed-chip technology, the so-called reduced-instruction-set computing. This RISC technology is faster because it combines more sophisticated circuit structures with more simplified internal software.

"We ran into a classic bureaucratic self-preservation reaction," recalls Roger Ross, who designed the RISC chip and later left Motorola in anger. Today's leader of the now-burgeoning RISC market, Sun, once considered abandoning its own chip in favor of Mr. Ross's. The Ross chip, called the 88000, didn't reach the market until 1989, more than a year behind rival RISC chips.

---

* Source: Stephen Kreider Yoder, "Computer Glitch," *The Wall Street Journal,* March 4, 1991, pp. A1, 4. Reprinted by permission of *THE WALL STREET JOURNAL,* © 1991 Dow Jones & Company, Inc. All Rights Reserved Worldwide.

"If I had to do it over again, I would have started earlier" on RISC, concedes Murray Goldman, who heads Motorola's microprocessor and memory group.

Motorola's mistakes hit at a bad time, a once-in-a-decade juncture when computer makers are choosing new chips to power future computers. Motorola "kind of lost the recipe in the last couple of years," says Willem Roelandts, vice president of Hewlett-Packard Co.'s networked-systems group. In fact, H-P, a big Motorola customer, delayed a new computer more than six months because Motorola was late with its new version of the 68000 series.

Motorola's mistakes aren't fatal. It still earns profits on microprocessors and dominates a larger market for processors that control products other than computers, ranging from car engines to washing machines. Its microprocessor sales are estimated at $500 million a year; its entire line of chips accounted for 30 percent of its $10.9 billion revenue last year (see Exhibit 1).

Moreover, Mr. Goldman is optimistic that the delayed new entry in its 68000 line, the 68040, will reclaim markets; Motorola finally started shipping the chip in volume last November.

And he contends that the snubbed 88000 RISC chip is the only one that can take markets from Intel. Motorola is betting that Apple Computer Inc., which now uses 68000-family chips, will plug the new RISC chip into its future Macintosh machines, spurring other computer makers to use it and making it a de facto standard.

But most computer experts give Motorola a slim chance of gaining ground on Intel, Sun, or Mips in computers.

Its problems started around 1980, when International Business Machines Corp. needed a chip to power its personal computer. Intel launched a marketing blitz, Operation Crush, to flog a microprocessor that it now concedes was inferior to Motorola's. IBM chose Intel's chip, which became the PC standard and now accounts for 80 percent of that market, compared with 9.7 percent for Motorola's, according to Dataquest Inc. That dominance spurred Intel's growth and compensated for its own slow entry into RISC technology; the first to market RISC chips were Mips and Sun, which calls its version the Sparc chip.

In 1985, Motorola did get a 79 percent share of the market for the microprocessors used in workstations, but workstation sales are less than a tenth the size of the PC market. Three years ago, moreover, Motorola's strength in workstations also began fading. Beginning in 1987, Motorola had promised significant gains in speed from the next-generation 68040 chip, but by 1989 the chip hadn't appeared.

That miscue illustrates one of Motorola's problems, computer makers say. Motorola customarily demands that its engineers create the best-designed, fastest and highest-quality product possible. But in the rapid-fire world of computer chips, that strategy often made Mo-

---

EXHIBIT 1   Motorola by the Numbers

Earnings benefited . . .

Annual net income, in $millions

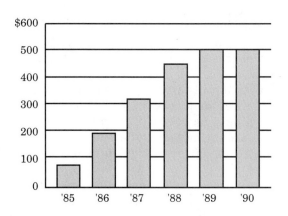

From diversification . . .

Lines of business as a percent of 1990 revenue
of $10.88 billion*

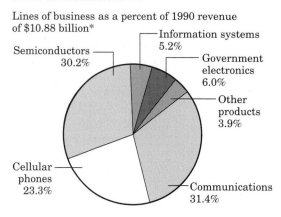

*Includes $476 million in adjustments and eliminations.

But it lost a key market . . .

World-wide personal computer sales by brand
of microprocessor, as a percent of units

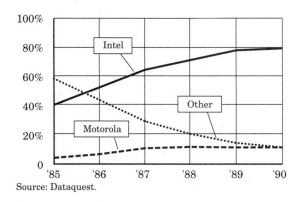

Source: Dataquest.

While investors wait.

Comparison of Motorola's stock price,
DJ Semi-conductor index and DJ Communications
index, monthly data, Dec. 1987=100

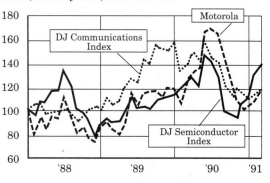

---

torola late to market. Mr. Goldman denies that this is a problem. "I'm
late [with the 68040] because we reached out so far," he says, but "we
have to leapfrog everybody."

Few observers agree. "It's a major problem, a situation where their
ongoing tendency to be late with the best hurts them," says James
Barlage, a Smith Barney analyst.

In March 1989, Motorola tried to steal Intel's fire by announcing the
68040 several weeks before Intel showed its rival 80486. Computer
experts praised Motorola's superior design, but, long after Intel had

shipped its chip to customers, Motorola was still revising its own. Unlike Intel, Motorola waited until it had got most of the bugs out of its chip.

For months, Motorola's exasperated customers waited for chips for new computers. Unisys Corp. salesmen began diverting customers to Intel-based machines. H-P, which predicted a year ago that 68040-based workstations would dominate its sales, began saying it expects many customers to switch to machines using H-P's own RISC chips. That hurt Motorola, which had already lost chip customers such as Tandem Computers Inc., Silicon Graphics Inc., and Sony Corp. to Mips.

"Not having the part two years ago set [Motorola] back irreparably in terms of keeping the Sparc and Mips guys from getting major chunks of the workstation business," says Michael Slater, editor of *Microprocessor Report,* a newsletter.

Motorola might have been better off if it had heeded Mr. Ross, whom it had hired from NCR Corp. in 1983 to explore RISC technology. Motorola could have kept the Sony account, for instance, if it had had a viable RISC chip, says Athol Foden, marketing manager for Sony's U.S. computer unit. Like other manufacturers, Sony learned in 1988 that the 88000 was only on the drawing board while Mips and Sun had working chips. But Motorola didn't push the 88000 hard, says James Christie, marketing vice president for Icon International Inc., which builds 88000 computers. "It was the ugly stepchild."

By 1986, Mr. Ross had designed a chip offering many times the power of Motorola's 68000 line. Mr. Ross says several executives at the company's headquarters in Schaumburg, Ill., were enthusiastic.

But in Austin, he says, officials froze the RISC team's staffing at five engineers even though it needed about 20 more. He says he finagled extra staff by waylaying engineers rotating through a new-recruits program; he got 17 of them and says they were "very critical" to the project. Executives also skimped on his capital expenditures, he says, forcing him to borrow computers from friends at Sun.

Mr. Ross's nemesis was Thomas Gunter, the father of Motorola's 68000 chip. Mr. Ross says Mr. Gunter lobbied against the RISC chip within Motorola and vied with him for customers. Mr. Ross says that he often went to a computer maker with data on the 88000's performance and that, afterward, "Tom would come in and make the same claims for the 68000."

Mr. Gunter, who refers to his relationship with Mr. Ross as "that soap opera," won't say much about it. Mr. Goldman calls Mr. Ross "unprofessional" and concedes the infighting was damaging: "We did have some jealousy back and forth."

The discord wasn't surprising, says James Norling, who heads all of Motorola's chip businesses. "Roger [Ross] was constantly beating the hell out of us" for more resources, he says, while the 68000 people, like any established group, were "not going to volunteer for their successors to take over their world."

Northern Telecom Inc.'s BN Research unit grew worried when Motorola management appeared apathetic toward Mr. Ross's chip, which Northern planned to use in a phone switch. As the Ross-Gunter feud boiled up, "I acted as a lobby on Roger's behalf," says John Perry, a Northern Telecom systems manager, who says he "made it very clear that if they wanted to be leaders in high-end microprocessors they had to develop RISC."

Motorola's bias toward the 68000 led to a loss that still haunts it. In 1985, Sun needed a new chip for its next-generation workstations. Because the 68000 chips Sun used didn't promise enough power, Sun engineers began to design the Sparc chip. But Sun saw merit in buying from a big, stable chip maker, says Bernard Lacroute, then Sun's executive vice president and now a partner in a venture-capital firm.

Sun discussed RISC options with Motorola between 1985 and 1987, Mr. Lacroute says, and at one time was willing to use the 88000 instead of its own Sparc. All Sun wanted from Mr. Goldman was a firm commitment to support the 88000, Mr. Lacroute says. Instead, he adds, Motorola kept pushing Sun to stay with the 68000.

"They weren't putting enough resources soon enough" into the 88000, he says.

In 1987, Sun introduced its Sparc chip. The chip overtook the 68000-family last year as the leader of workstation microprocessors, with 36 percent of the market, up from 1 percent in 1987. Sun, currently also the biggest maker of workstations, now buys only 2 percent of its microprocessors from Motorola—down from 80 percent in 1988.

Another ironic twist: Mr. Ross, the father of Motorola's 88000, is now president of Ross Technology Inc., which makes Sparc chips.

As RISC technology rapidly gained favor, Motorola finally stepped up its work on the new chip, and its 88000 looked promising at its 1988 debut. Some 50 companies agreed to use it; many of them joined a Motorola-backed alliance that was to assure that software for one 88000 computer could be used on another. At the chip's coming-out party, Mr. Goldman said it would bring "vast" new business.

The party didn't last. Companies that planned to use the 88000 say Motorola didn't spend enough to get software makers to modify programs for it. Oracle Corp., for instance, finally modified its popular data-base program last year to run on the 88000, but only after the alliance paid for it. Motorola was also slow to provide software "tools" that computer and software makers need to develop products around new chips.

Motorola's schizophrenia lingered on. Its executives touted the 88000's superiority, but marketers of the older 68000 line made equally ambitious claims. Motorola frustrated customers by not making clear which chip it would push, says Harry L. "Nick" Tredennick, who helped design the first 68000 and now runs a chip-design business. "I hadn't worked at Motorola for 10 years, and yet I was getting calls from their large customers asking if I knew what Motorola was going to do," he writes in Microprocessor Report. "I didn't, and I still don't."

Few manufacturers chose the 88000, and many of those that did have defected. In 1989, Status Computer Inc. switched to Intel's RISC chip. Last year, NCR dropped plans for an 88000 machine, Everex Systems Inc. scratched its 88000 computer after few sales, and Tektronix Inc. said it was ditching its workstation business, which included plans for 88000 machines. "The picture certainly is bleak," says Thomas Lacey, marketing vice president at Opus Systems, which uses the 88000 in computer boards.

A further blow came last month. Officials close to Compaq Computer Corp. said the company formed an industry alliance that would probably use the Mips chip for a new computer line. That dashed Motorola's hopes that Compaq would use the 88000 and jump-start its sales.

Motorola isn't giving up. It has slashed its 88000 prices, built a $500 million factory to make the chip and is pumping money into its 88000 alliance, which even rivals praise as well-organized. Mr. Goldman says Motorola will get a lift this year from the 88110, a faster, smaller version of the 88000. "I want to attack [Intel's market] with their own customers," he says. "The 88110 is the weapon of choice; 1991 is the time for the attack."

Case 6–8   *Donaldson Company, Inc.**

By 1985, Tom Baden, vice president of the Donaldson Company, Inc. (DCI) was convinced that the rules of competition in the industrial air and fluid filtration industry had changed. Two years earlier DCI had experienced its first loss in 50 years. While the situation improved in 1984, Baden realizes that a decision about his group's organizational structure is essential.

* This case was prepared by Shannon Shipp, M.J. Neeley School of Business, Texas Christian University. The U.S. Department of Education funded the preparation of this case under Grant #G00877027. Copyright © 1985 by the Case Development Center, University of Minnesota, School of Management, 271 19th Avenue South, Minneapolis, MN 55455.

Baden is vice president of DCI's Original Equipment Group (OEG), whose revenues in 1984 represented over 40 percent of DCI's 1984 annual sales of $250 million. Stated simply, Baden's task is to return OEG to financial performance levels of the 1975–79 period and establish a base for long-term growth in the markets served by OEG. Baden is also responsible for reinforcing DCI's corporate image as a high-quality, high-service provider of state-of-the-art products.

THE COMPANY

History

In 1915 Frank Donaldson, Sr., the original chairman of the company, invented the first effective air cleaner for internal combustion engines. Air is a necessary ingredient for the combustion process to occur. Before his invention, engines were extremely susceptible to "dusting out," or becoming inoperative due to excessive accumulation of dust entering the engine from unfiltered air.

In subsequent years, DCI led the industry in introducing new products, such as oil-washed filters, mufflers, multistaged air cleaners, and high-tech hydraulic filters. DCI became the world's largest manufacturer of heavy-duty air cleaners and mufflers and established a worldwide reputation for technology. Facilities grew from 200 square feet of manufacturing space in 1915 to more than 3 million square feet of manufacturing and office area worldwide in 1980.

Mission

By 1984 the company had broadly defined its mission: to design, manufacture, and sell proprietary products that "separate something unwanted from something wanted." The company's product line included air cleaners, air filters, mufflers, hydraulic filters, microfiltration equipment for computers, air pollution equipment, and liquid clarifiers. These products were developed, sold, and serviced by the organizational structure appearing in Exhibit 1. According to this exhibit, DCI has a functional organizational structure, with the nine worldwide support groups responsible for product development, manufacturing, administration, finance, and the four business groups responsible for selling and servicing products to their respective markets. The 1980 to 1984 sales of the four major business groups are listed in Exhibit 2. The fifth group listed, Microfiltration and Defense Products (MFD), was a part of the Business Development Group until 1984, when it was spun off to form a new business group.

EXHIBIT 1 DCI Organization Chart (1983)

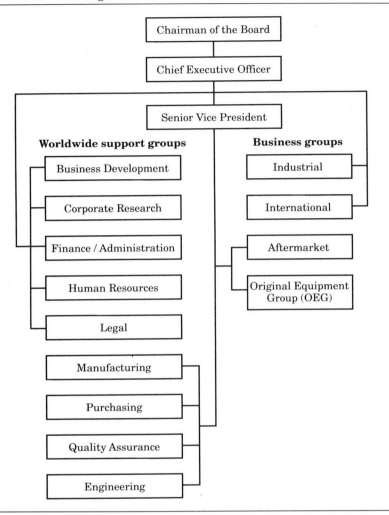

Source: Internal company documents.

EXHIBIT 2 DCI's Four Major Business Groups (annual sales, $ millions)

	1984	1983	1982	1981	1980
Original equipment group	$102.2	$ 63.9	$101.3	$104.6	$101.6
Aftermarket	22.6	17.6	20.5	20.1	17.0
Industrial	32.2	32.0	41.3	37.0	25.0
International	71.2	68.7	81.4	87.0	69.4
MFD	26.0	21.4	17.4	15.1	11.4
Total	$254.2	$203.6	$261.9	$263.8	$234.4

Source: DCI 1984 Annual Report.

1983–1984 Situation

In 1983 a peculiar set of external and internal causes combined to downgrade DCI's performance. Among external causes, sales of medium/heavy-duty trucks, buses, tractors and combines, construction equipment, and aftermarket replacement elements simultaneously hit five-year or all-time lows. These markets constituted the majority of sales for both the Original Equipment Group (OEG) and International. Although soft demand had been experienced in one or two of these markets before in a single year, never had all businesses declined so precipitously in the same year. Also, the strength of the dollar in 1982–84 was making DCI's customers less competitive in foreign markets. This in turn affected DCI's sales of replacement parts.

In 1984 DCI's operating results began to return to pre-1983 levels (see Exhibit 3). One reason was a success in the wet filtration area, particularly in high-stress environments. The primary reason was that

EXHIBIT 3   DCI Operating Results ($000)

	1984	*1983*	*1982*
Net sales	$254,052	$203,608	$262,018
Cost of sales	157,257	131,548	169,816
Gross earnings	96,795	72,060	92,202
Earnings (loss) before income taxes	20,238	(1,738)	12,805
Income taxes	10,546	1,800	5,572
Tax rate	52.1%	—	43.2%
Net earnings	9,692	(3,358)	7,233
Depreciation	7,694	8,320	8,518
Interest	2,670	2,076	2,345
Financial Position			
Current assets	$ 97,425	$81,668	$ 82,109
Current liabilities	45,022	32,796	35,574
Current ratio	2.2	2.5	2.3
Working capital	52,403	48,872	46,535
Long-term debt	19,549	21,791	18,752
Shareholder's equity	90,232	84,880	91,637
Capitalization ratio	22.1	22.1	21.2
Return on average shareholder's equity	11.1	(4.0)	7.9
Return on average invested capital	9.0	(3.3)	6.4
Property, plant, and equipment (gross)	$118,663	$118,182	$114,465
Property, plant, and equipment (net)	55,045	59,694	63,739
Total assets	$160,613	$148,083	$151,160

Source: DCI 1984 Annual Report.

sales by customers in DCI's worldwide markets, particularly heavy-duty trucks, began to return to pre-1983 levels. Because of the external causes described previously, however, DCI management thought it unlikely that sales by its customers would return to pre-1980 levels. To counter the effects of the decline in worldwide demand for DCI's products, Tom Baden concluded that OEG must address several critical internal problems.

Some of the internal problems included an inability to coordinate customer service to multinational customers, inability to provide accurate cost figures for given production quantities, and—especially for its small customers—"being difficult to buy from."

DCI found it difficult to coordinate customer service efforts for those customers with multiple purchasing or production facilities in different countries. Although DCI had offices in all of the countries where high sales potential existed (e.g., in West Germany, Brazil, and Mexico), lack of coordination among the offices caused spotty customer service. For example, customers were known to "shop" for the best prices among DCI offices. The different DCI offices were therefore competing against each other for the same business.

DCI was also unable to provide accurate cost figures for small production quantities. This hampered salespeople's efforts to quote prices that would cover DCI's costs, and yield profits. For example, setup costs in switching from producing one product to another were not factored into the costs of production runs, and hence omitted from the prices charged. Furthermore, account executives were measured primarily on sales rather than profits, thereby encouraging them to devote less attention to the costs of actually filling an order.

Although relationships with its largest customers were strong—based on its ability to work with those customers in solving problems—small customers complained to salespeople of slow response for engineering drawings and price quotes. They also complained of slow responses to questions about billing or order status. Very small customers (under $25,000 in annual sales) were not vocal with complaints about DCI because they were seldom contacted by DCI representatives.

ORIGINAL EQUIPMENT GROUP (OEG)

OEG Products and Markets

OEG constitutes the bulk of DCI's traditional businesses, such as heavy-duty trucks, and construction, mining, industrial, and agricultural equipment. It sells air and hydraulic filters, acoustical products (mufflers), and replacement elements to manufacturers and end users of heavy-duty mobile equipment in North America. OEG has not typically sold oil filters, as they are a commodity item and require much higher production runs than OEG traditionally makes. OEG is reviewing its position on producing oil filters because its customers often seek a single source for all their filter needs. About half of the annual worldwide sales of these products are in North America.

Current Organizational Structure for OEG

OEG is currently organized around the market segments it serves (see Exhibit 4). The construction, agriculture, industrial, and truck-bus market segments have their own market director and support staff that are responsible for all planning and administration as well as for maintaining good relations with the largest customers in the market. Each market group has outside salespeople who call directly on customers, as well as inside salespeople responsible for routing orders and customer service. A manager of marketing support is responsible for order-entry personnel and clerks. There are also two special project managers in OEG. The first special project manager coordinated the efforts of the worldwide action teams responsible for gathering information on competitors and customers. The second developed a marketing program to try to understand the needs of small original equipment manufacturers (OEMs) and the feasibility of using telemarketing to reach them.

EXHIBIT 4   OEG's Market-Based Organizational Structure

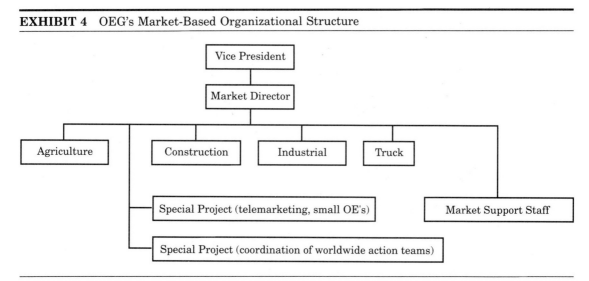

Source: Internal company documents.

OEG's Position Within DCI

OEG has primary worldwide responsibility to serve mobile heavy-equipment OEMs. The International Group supports OEG's efforts, while the Aftermarket Group competes with OEG for the same end-users. The International Group sells OEG's products in markets outside North America. Communication between OEG and International is crucial in providing high levels of customer service for multinational customers with plants in several countries. The Aftermarket Group competes with OEG by selling mobile heavy-equipment replacement elements under the Donaldson name through fleet specialists, heavy-duty distributors, and other outlets. These replacement parts compete with similar products sold by manufacturers' dealers supplied by OEG.

Within each market segment, customers are served by size. Large accounts (more than $250,000 in annual sales) are served by market directors or salespeople assigned to that account. Mid-sized customers (between $25,000 and $250,000 in annual sales) are called upon by a salesperson responsible for that territory. Small OEMs are served, if at all, by inside salespeople or order-entry personnel in the marketing support services group.

Organization by market segment offers a number of advantages to OEG, such as (1) easy tracking of changes in demand or customer usage characteristics and (2) an organizational structure similar to that in Engineering that facilitates good communications. Organization by market segment also has some problems, such as (1) some customers straddling several markets, making it difficult to assign the costs and profits from serving that customer to a specific market, and (2) an occasional inability to coordinate the engineering support for those customers who straddled market segments because an engineer from each of two market segments might be assigned to solve the same technical problem.

ACTION TEAM REPORTS AND ANALYSES

To regain OEG's previous market position, in early 1984 Tom Baden initiated a year-long strategic analysis to study all aspects of OEG operations. Reports were prepared by action teams from DCI offices around the world. These reports were the basis of a series of meetings that included all OEG executives and were used to obtain ideas for actions to improve OEG's organizational structure and marketing policies.

Baden must reach a decision on whether the existing marketing organization structure is best able to achieve OEG's goals or whether a new structure would be better. To make that decision, four elements of the year-long strategic analysis are considered: (1) competition, (2) customers, (3) marketing-mix strategies, and (4) telemarketing and global account management as alternatives to personal selling in reaching some customers.

Major Competitors

DCI is the traditional heavy-duty mobile-equipment market leader for heavy-duty filters. Major competitors include Fleetguard, Fram, Nelson, and Mann and Hummel. Other firms, such as Wix, Baldwin, Purolator, and AC/Delco, compete in certain market segments. In general, all of the competitors are on sound financial footing. Fleetguard and Fram have very healthy parent organizations (Cummins Engine and Allied/Bendix Corporation, respectively). Mann and Hummel and Nelson are healthy from good internal financial management. Research and development costs are generally lower for these organizations than for DCI because they tend to follow DCI's technological breakthroughs. Each competitor is strong in a particular market or through a particular channel, and most offer a full line of air and oil filters, which enables both customers and distributors to meet their filter needs through a single source.

OEG's Customers

OEG has over 600 customers, divided into three groups: large, mid-sized, and small.

Large Accounts. OEG's large customers (more than $250,000 in annual sales), consisting of 46 original equipment manufacturer (OEM) accounts and their dealers, constitute more than 90 percent of OEG sales and more than 40 percent of DCI sales. Thirty of these customers are headquartered in the United States, eight in Europe, and eight in Japan. A partial list of these customers appears in Exhibit 5. These customers are all large, and most have sales offices and production facilities in more than one country.

The competitive environment for large OEMs is undergoing rapid change. Some large OEMs, such as Caterpillar and Ford, are experiencing reduced sales due to increasing competition from non–U.S. manufacturers. The large OEMs are coping with the reduction in sales by calling on suppliers to reduce prices. For example, Caterpillar announced a three-year program beginning in 1983 and terminating in 1985 that required its suppliers to maintain stable prices even though inflation was predicted to increase 22 percent for that period. The

---

EXHIBIT 5 Some Large Current or Potential Customers for OEG

North America	*Europe*	*Japan*
Ford	Daimler-Benz	Hitachi
Caterpillar	IVECO	Isuzu
Champion	Leyland	Komatsu
Clark Equipment	Lister	Kubota
Cummins	Lombardini	Mitsubishi
Detroit Diesel	MAN	Nissan

Source: Internal company documents.

emphasis by large customers on cost containment is a major change from the 1970s (which emphasized product performance) and could squeeze OEG's margins and hurt DCI's performance.

According to meetings among salespeople and account executives, OEG's largest customers have common needs for filtration equipment. At a minimum, large customers desire state-of-the-art products at the lowest possible prices for products meeting specifications. Recent demand by large customers include:

1. Just-in-time deliveries.[1]
2. Long-term fixed source contracts.
3. Drop-ship arrangements to customers' dealers and/or manufacturing facilities for OE parts.
4. Worldwide availability of product.
5. The OE brand name on the product.
6. Electronic system tie-ins for improved order placement/followup and customer service and support.

These demands accompanied OEM efforts to consolidate their purchases to achieve stronger positions vis-à-vis their suppliers.

Large customers also perceive sales opportunities for replacement elements sales through their dealer networks. In North America, the large OEMs have 21,000 outlets, or original equipment dealers (OEDs), through which OEG could sell replacement elements. OEDs represent a new market opportunity for DCI. Traditionally, OEG has sold replacement elements to OEMs imprinted with the OEM's brand. Once the OEM takes title to the products, OEG expects the OEM to provide the necessary training and support to its distributors through which the products will be sold. Recently, OEDs are more actively

---

[1] Just-in-time deliveries occur when the supplier and customer have devised a schedule to ensure the next shipment of parts or supplies is delivered when the customer is about to use the last unit from the previous shipment.

looking for product lines to improve cash flow and profitability. Part of the impetus for the search for additional products is slow equipment sales. Service parts provide a logical line extension and source of steady cash flow for OEDs. To capitalize on the market in service parts, however, OEDs need extensive manufacturer support in terms of sales training, product knowledge, product literature, and merchandising, and complete lines of filters to service all makes of equipment, not just lines they represent.

Mid-Size and Small Accounts. Mid-size ($25,000 to $250,000 in annual sales) and small (less than $25,000 in annual sales) OEMs are offered only standard products from the OEG catalog. Custom engineering is rarely provided to these customers, unless they are willing to bear its full cost.

These smaller OEMs have different needs than large OEMs. In general, they desire state-of-the-art products but are willing to wait for a large OEM to install a new product first. They also desire consistent contact with OEG salespeople to keep abreast of changing filter prices (while realizing that they do not have the volumes to command the lowest available prices) and good product quality. Some OEMs often request the DCI name on the filters used in their equipment as a marketing tool, capitalizing on DCI's reputation for high quality among end users.

Marketing-Mix Strategies

Product and Price. DCI is known throughout the industry for its conservative management style, using strategic moves based on careful planning. OEG is no exception. OEG prefers serving selected, high-margin markets where customers are beginning to demand higher performance levels than those available from the products currently available. Pursuing these markets allows OEG to exploit its strengths of quality design and engineering, as well as allowing OEG to charge a premium price for its products. Price cutting is not a major component of OEG's market strategies.

Distribution. Distribution of OEG's products occurs through two primary channels. The first is directly to OEMs, which purchase products for installation on new equipment. In some markets, such as heavy-duty trucks and construction equipment, more than 70 percent of all new units shipped are factory-equipped with DCI products. OEMs depend on DCI as a reliable supplier of state-of-the-art products whose engineers design products for special applications or environmental conditions.

The second major channel is for replacement elements. These elements are often packaged and sold under the customer's name and logo and distributed through its dealer network. For example, OEG provides replacement elements for Caterpillar, International Harvester, J.I. Case, Freightliner, and Volvo, imprinted with their names and logos.

Promotion.   OEG products are promoted several ways, including advertising, direct mail, trade shows, and promotional literature. A distribution of OEG's promotional expenditures for 1984 appears in Exhibit 6. DCI encourages direct communication between OEG engineers and technicians and their customer counterparts. While this is not reflected in the promotional budget, it is an important element in OEG's communications with its customers. Other off-budget promotional expenses include sending OEG engineers to attend professional meetings and guiding customers on tours of the research and testing unit that contains some of the most modern filtration research facilities in the world.

Selling Methods.   OEG has traditionally relied on face-to-face selling to provide information to and solicit orders from customers. Two major problems exist with heavy reliance on personal selling. First, it is not cost efficient for OEG to use personal selling to reach mid-size and small customers unless a standard product already exists to fit the customer's application. As a result, service to these customers is provided primarily by local distributors or through DCI's Aftermarket

---

EXHIBIT 6   Promotional Budget (1984)

Item	Percent of Budget
Advertising	55%
Trade shows	16
Sales literature	13
Coop advertising	4
Photography	2
Public relations	2
Other sales materials	1
Advertising specialties	1
Audiovisual materials	1
Other	5
	100%

Source: Internal company documents.

Group. The lack of direct customer contact with these accounts has resulted in OEG having a low level of knowledge regarding their needs. Second, for large customers with multiple purchasing and usage sites, it is difficult to coordinate the activities of salespeople assigned to customers geographically. This problem becomes acute when the customer has purchasing or usage sites overseas, served through the International Division. This means that salespeople's activities have to be coordinated across geographic regions as well as across divisions within DCI.

Alternatives to Personal Selling

Two selling methods, telemarketing and global account management, are being considered as substitutes or supplements to the current selling method.

Telemarketing. Telemarketing involves organized, planned telephone communication between a firm and its customers. Telemarketing ranges from salespeople simply calling prospective customers to set up appointments, to complex systems with different employees responsible for different parts of selling, such as prospecting or customer service.

One special project manager explored the feasibility of telemarketing to small OEMs. The study's objective was to profile small OEMs that had purchased OEG products. These firms were questioned about their use of OEG products, needs for additional OEG support, and overall satisfaction with OEG products and services. Four hundred and sixty-one small OEMs were contacted during the month-long study, none with more than $25,000 in purchases from OEG the preceding year. Some study results appear in Exhibit 7.

Global Account Management. Global account management (GAM) is a method of assigning salespeople to accounts. Sellers use GAM when customers are large, with multiple purchase or usage points. Under a GAM system an account executive is responsible for all the communication between the customer and the seller, including (but not limited to) needs analysis, application engineering, field support, customer service, and order processing. Depending on the account size, the executive might have several subordinates provide necessary services. GAM's major advantage is communication coordination. Since all seller and buyer contact is monitored by the account manager, miscommunication is unlikely.

Implementing GAM would involve assigning teams to OEG's largest customers to improve support. Account teams would be composed of salespeople and applications engineers, with the number of people on

EXHIBIT 7   Telemarketing Study Results

	Number	*Percent of Responses*
Literature requests	211	46%
Satisfied customers	102	22
Not qualified as customers	58	13
Follow-up phone calls	17	4
Orders	9	2
Quotes	8	2
Terminations	5	1
Unavailable (not listed) duplicates	51	11
	461	100%

Source: Internal company documents.

the account proportional to its annual orders. Each team head, or Account Manager, would coordinate communications between all customer buying locations and OEG. Account managers would have worldwide profit and loss responsibility for their assigned customers. Sales representatives in district offices in other countries would report their customer activities to the lead account executive. Account executives are responsible for the subsidiaries of global customers in their geographic area. Account executives and sales representatives typically have multiple reporting relationships. A sample organizational chart appears in Exhibit 8. The boxes do not all represent people assigned full time to that account. For example, the account manager in

EXHIBIT 8   Global Account Management (sample organization chart)

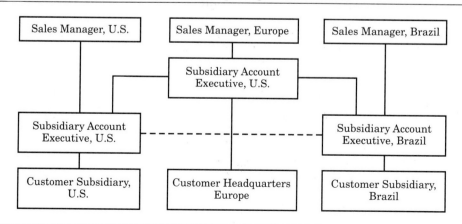

Source: Internal company documents.

Europe for Daimler-Benz would report to the sales manager in Europe. The Daimler-Benz account manager for Europe might also be a subsidiary account executive for Caterpillar in Europe, reporting to an account manager in the United States.

TOM BADEN'S DECISION

After attending the worldwide action team and OEG operations presentations, Tom Baden split OEG executives into two groups. Each group prepared a presentation explaining its vision for OEG's future corporate structure and marketing strategy.

Existing OEG Corporate Structure

One group maintained that the current organization structure (see Exhibit 4) would adequately meet the challenges posed by current external and internal problems. They believe that the 1983 problems were due to temporary forces and that the existing structure should not be changed.

Proposed New OEG Corporate Structure

Based on the results of the action team reports, the second group made several suggestions to improve OEG's performance. Two suggestions, global account management for large OEM's and telemarketing for small customers, were key features of the organizational structure proposed by the second group.

To incorporate these selling methods into OEG operations, the second group proposed the organization structure appearing in Exhibit 9 to replace the structure shown in Exhibit 4. The major difference is the replacement of the market groups (truck, agriculture, industrial, and construction) with the large-customer and mid-size and small-customer groups. The product/technical group is added to improve communication between engineering and marketing. Although this is a change from the current organizational structure, it is not a basis on which to accept or reject the new structure, since it could be appended to the current structure with little effort.

The suggested organizational structure would offer a number of advantages. Service to multinational customers would be coordinated under a single account manager. Current problems with lack of coordination among DCI offices could be minimized. Small OEMs would receive more attention. Although little deviation from standard products

EXHIBIT 9 Proposed Structure—Original Equipment Group

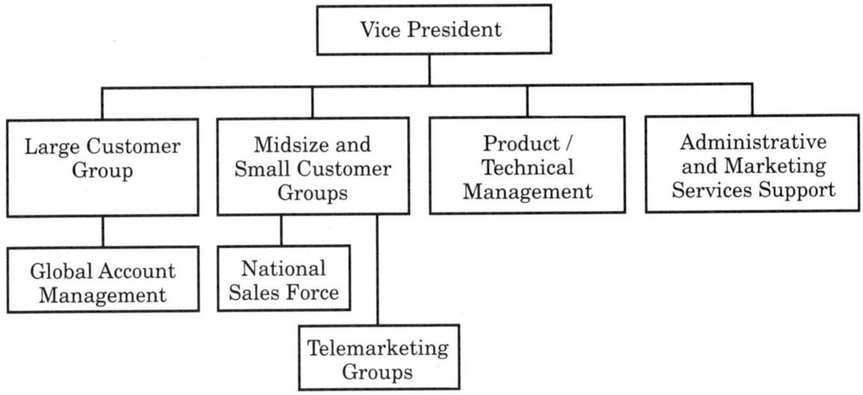

Source: Internal company documents.

would be permitted these customers, they would be contacted more frequently under telemarketing. Service to mid-size accounts would not change.

The proposed plan has several disadvantages as well. With fewer managers at the market director level, the number of workers each must supervise would increase. For the director of large accounts, that would involve 10 to 13 account managers for 30 to 40 accounts (some managers would be responsible for more than one account). Second, the reporting relationships (see Exhibit 8) grow rather complex under a GAM structure. This can obscure good and poor performance, making it more difficult to reward outstanding performance or detect poor performance. It could also make the salesperson's job more ambiguous as orders come from several bosses. Third, new-product development would be centered around applications for specific customers. With all salespeople focusing on specific customers, no one would be charged with maintaining a perspective on the market as a whole. Without a broad perspective on changing market conditions, it would be possible to miss a trend in customer usage characteristics, which could cause OEG to fail to become a technology leader in the new market. Narrow focus on a single customer's needs might also cause the salesperson or applications engineer to miss similar work performed for another account, thus duplicating effort.

THE DECISION

Baden must choose one of the two organizational structures to present to corporate management. Baden is aware that any organizational change inevitably causes staff upheaval, and he wants to ensure that the OEG structure chosen will remain in place for a long time. In deciding, he also must remember that the current organizational structure has been successful for many years and that any changes must be supported by sound reasoning. To help decide, he prepares the following questions to organize his presentation on the appropriate organizational structure to top DCI management.

1. How will customers react to both plans?
2. Which plan comes closest to solving the problems OEG faced in 1983?
3. Analyze the major strengths and weaknesses of each alternative. What conclusions can be drawn from the analysis?
4. Other than the alternatives presented, what organizational structures exist to accomplish the same goals? What dangers exist in suggesting an alternative organizational structure?

Case 6–9   *Hazleton Laboratories**

INTRODUCTION

The recent growth of Hazleton Laboratories Corporation (HLC), a globally disbursed and complex firm, was so phenomenal that, in 1990, the company underwent a second major organizational restructuring in two years. However, because the explosive growth in sales from $87 million in 1986 to $170 million in 1990 was forecasted to continue, Hazleton's CEO Donald Nielson, wondered about the need for still further organizational restructuring to meet the needs of the company's expanded international marketplace.

OVERVIEW

Hazleton Laboratories Corporation was founded in 1968. Headquartered in Herndon, Virginia, a suburb of Washington, D.C., the company's mission was to provide the highest quality in scientific services and products to organizations engaged in life sciences research. This

---

* This case was prepared by Professor John A. Pearce II of George Mason University and Sherry S. Chaples. Development of this case was sponsored by a Funds for Excellence grant from the State Council of Higher Education for Virginia.

area of research focused on products, processes, and diseases affecting man and the environment. The company grew to become one of the world's largest providers of biological and chemical research services and a major supplier of laboratory animals. A description of Hazleton's major facilities as of 1990 is provided in Exhibit 1.

EXHIBIT 1   Hazleton Facilities

The following discussion elaborates the services and products of each of Hazleton's North American, European, and Japanese locations.

Washington, D.C.

The suburbs of Washington, D.C., were the sites of three units of Hazleton Laboratories America (HLA). The majority of the laboratory facilities and the operational and scientific management were located in Vienna, Virginia, with additional animal laboratory facilities in Rockville, Maryland, and additional laboratory facilities in Kensington, Maryland. The Washington facilities had approximately 700 personnel and 340,000 square feet of laboratory and administrative space.

All Hazleton laboratories had their dossiers accepted by the Japanese ministry of agriculture, forestry, and fisheries and after inspection of its toxicology program by the Japanese ministry of health and welfare, the Washington laboratories were awarded an "A" rating. The immunotoxicology capabilities of the staff, coupled with the experience and facilities dedicated to primate toxicology, provided support to investigate the toxicology needs of biotechnology. The Washington laboratories served as the North American center for inhalation toxicology studies conducted by Hazleton. In addition, the laboratories participated in the National Toxicology Program for over 15 years and support basic research of investigators at the National Cancer Institute.

Due to HLA–Washington's location, it had ready access to the regulatory agencies. Coupled with its interaction with Hazleton's regulatory affairs personnel, this allowed them to provide total toxicology services to their clients. In addition to the offices in Washington, the Regulatory Affairs Division had offices in Harrogate, England; Paris, France; and Tokyo, Japan.

Vienna, Virginia

The Virginia facility was the original Hazleton toxicology laboratory. This laboratory, accredited by the Toxicology Laboratory Accreditation Board, was one of the first contract laboratories to automate the collection of study data. Its Immunochemistry Division provided biotechnological and chemistry services especially in the areas of development and testing.

Rockville, Maryland

Hazleton acquired this facility from Litton Bionetics, Inc., in September 1985. The laboratory's 100-person staff provided safety evaluation and

---

EXHIBIT 1   *(continued)*

---

toxicology studies to governmental and commercial clients since the early 1960s. The labs were housed in an 88,000-square-foot, state-of-the-art building specifically designed as a dual-corridor barrier facility operation. They had also participated for many years in the National Toxicology Program. The labs also supported basic research by investigators at the National Cancer Institute.

The Rockville Laboratories became an extension of the Vienna campus, adding needed capacity for both commercial and governmental clients. This division also provided specialized support in the field of inhalation toxicology.

Kensington, Maryland

This facility, which was acquired in 1985 from Litton Bionetics, became the Molecular Toxicology Division of Hazleton. Recognized as a world leader in molecular toxicology, the division had a staff of 80, occupying about 24,000 square feet of laboratory space. Laboratory operations consisted of both testing and research programs. In addition, the labs conducted studies that monitored human populations for genetic effects and others that analyzed possible effects on the immune system. Sponsors of their ongoing research programs included government agencies, private foundations, and associations, as well as selected research programs funded by the company. The capability in biotechnology services was also established at this location, and this capability fast became a major growth area for the corporation.

Madison, Wisconsin

The Hazleton Laboratory in Madison, Wisconsin, was located on a 26-acre site and provided services to its clients in the areas of chemistry, toxicology, and clinical sciences. Over 700 scientists and associated personnel worked in the 250,000 square feet of laboratory and office space to support the testing needs of the food, pharmaceutical, and chemical industries. This facility served industry in various chemical, toxicology, and biomedical disciplines since the company was founded.

The Chemistry Division at this location provided analytical testing services that included the determination of nutrient content of foods and feeds, identification of hazardous compounds in the environment, studies of metabolism and of the environmental fate of compounds, and of the migration of packaging components into foodstuffs.

The Madison Toxicology Division provided a full range of preclinical toxicology services that included all phases of classical toxicity testing. These tests were run in all the standard laboratory species, as well as in chickens, ducks, quail, and domestic livestock.

The resources included more than 75,000 square feet of animal and support facilities. Animal surgery capabilities within this group enabled the staff to conduct studies that required specialized surgical procedures. Additional facilities were available that allowed them to conduct domestic

---

EXHIBIT 1 (*continued*)

---

livestock programs in a variety of species, with specialization in dairy cattle studies.

Hazleton's clinical sciences provided clinical evaluation services in the areas of drug and personal care product development, OTC and consumer product evaluation, dental research, and biological and analytical chemistry testing services. Hazleton operated clinical facilities in the United States and in United Kingdom.

West Palm Beach, Florida

The Clinical Research Unit in West Palm Beach, Florida, was composed of 24 individual subject rooms, sample collection rooms, and a laboratory with state-of-the-art equipment to process samples for analysis.

Hazleton's West Palm Beach facility provided OTC product testing services for evaluating the safety and efficacy of cosmetic and proprietary products and the advertising claim substantiation of a product.

The Florida clinic also conducted dental studies and studies of the dermatological and health care products, such as sunscreen lotions, shampoos, cosmetics, and antiperspirants.

Denver, Pennsylvania

Hazleton Research Products (HRP) operated in five locations in the United States. Its headquarters and small animal breeding facilities were located in Denver, Pennsylvania. Its other facilities were located in Cumberland, Virginia; Reston, Virginia; Alice, Texas; and Kalamazoo, Michigan.

HRP was engaged in the breeding, importation, and sale of animals used exclusively for research. The animals were used to study the products of pharmaceutical and biotechnology and often were the final step in testing before compounds were introduced into human beings. This lab was also equipped to provide a variety of special services for client's research needs, including blood typing, ophthalmic testing, clinical chemistry, hematology, pathologic support services, and provides anti-sera production.

Harrogate, England

Headquarters of Hazleton Europe were at Harrogate in Yorkshire, England. The Harrogate laboratories employed over 400 scientists and support staff, who provided a full array of toxicology and chemistry services in a 180,000-square-foot facility. Their pharmaceutical and agrichemical company clients employed this facility to meet the requirement for registration of candidate materials anywhere in the world.

The metabolism staff worked with a fully computerized laboratory data capture and management system. Staff at the Madison, Wisconsin, laboratories was involved since the system had applicability at both sites.

In toxicology, the Harrogate laboratory was the European center for all inhalation toxicology studies conducted by Hazleton. This laboratory specialized in nose-only exposure for the international toxicology market.

EXHIBIT 1   *(continued)*

Chemistry and metabolism capabilities in Harrogate mirrored those of the Madison, Wisconsin, laboratories and regular cross-transfer of technology assists both units. Multinational clients took advantage of similar support on both sides of the Atlantic.

Leeds, England

The Hazleton Medical Research Unit was located at Springfield House, Leeds, adjacent to both the university medical school and general infirmary. This 48-bed facility opened in May 1986 and conducted studies in healthy volunteers, including safety and tolerance, drug metabolism studies, drug interactions, and postmarketing product support.

Support services were also offered in conjunction with the studies they conducted and on a "stand alone" basis to clients who are conducting their own clinical trials. Shipment of biotechnological products and other samples from single and multicenters was organized by Hazleton from any location in the world. Analysis of samples, coupled with data transmission where required, provided facility extension to Hazleton's clients.

Lyon, France

Hazleton France offered capabilities in toxicology and chemistry to domestic and international clients from the outskirts of France's second largest city, Lyon. Hazleton France had an internationally trained staff of 120 scientific, technical, and administrative personnel, who operated more than 88,000 square feet of laboratory and support facilities. This facility grew due to its strategic location and its international focus of the industry. Hazleton France was also the Hazleton center for acute toxicology.

Munster, West Germany

Hazleton Deutschland was located in Munster, West Germany, home of one of Germany's largest universities. Acquired in 1980, this laboratory was recognized worldwide as a leader in the field of primate reproduction studies. Clients from Europe, North America, and Japan used Hazleton Deutschland for those types of specialized research efforts.

The laboratory staff of 65 scientists and technicians operated in 40,000 square feet of modern laboratory space. The animal areas consisted of 26 primate rooms and 32 small animal rooms, which accommodated over 1,000 primates and up to 15,000 rodents.

Hazleton Deutschland served as the central laboratory for the performance of all primate reproduction studies in Hazleton. Technical links were maintained between this laboratory and other Hazleton facilities. This ensured that their clients benefited from shared technology development and scientific input.

Tokyo, Japan

Japan was a major market for Hazleton services and products, because of Japan's large pharmaceutical and chemical industries that served those markets worldwide. Requirements for Hazleton services by Japanese clients

EXHIBIT 1   *(concluded)*

reached then-record levels in 1985 and caused Hazleton to open this liaison office in Tokyo. Staffed by Hazleton employees, Nippon Hazleton coordinated with Japanese clients the services of all Hazleton laboratory facilities. This provided Hazleton's Japanese clients direct access to their services and also facilitates communications in English or Japanese.

Other services provided by Nippon Hazleton included:

- On-site assistance in protocol development and regulatory affairs.
- Assistance to off-shore clients serving the Japanese market.
- Expeditious coordination of communication between Hazleton Laboratories and Japanese clients.
- Professional representation of Hazleton Laboratories in other Far East nations.

Paris, France

The Paris office reported to the Lyon, France, office. It operated similarly to Tokyo, in that it was also a liaison office that provided access to Hazleton's services worldwide.

Hazleton's clients included research institutes; manufacturers of pharmaceuticals, chemicals, food, cosmetics, and biotechnology; other industrial companies; scientific research labs; and government agencies. The company employed 2,600 scientists, technicians, and administrative personnel who conducted operations in the United States, England, France, Japan, and West Germany. Although Hazleton was not a household name, thousands of popular consumer products were developed or tested by the company, particularly in the areas of cosmetic and drugs (prescription and over the counter). Moreover, many processed foods were tested or had their contents labeled by Hazleton.

In addition to research, product development, and testing, Hazleton also provided regulatory affairs consulting services. All industries served by Hazleton must meet regulatory and testing requirements before their products were distributed to the public. The Environmental Protection Agency (EPA), Food and Drug Administration (FDA), European Economic Community (EEC), and Organization for Economic Cooperation and Development (OECD) were just some of the agencies that require compliance with their regulations prior to releasing products. Because of the high impact nature of their work, more than 100 scientific papers were written, published, and presented worldwide by Hazleton's researchers each year.

DESCRIPTION OF HLC'S ACTIVITIES

Hazleton Laboratories Corporation was divided into five major types of activities that provided the various services and products needed to meet the needs of its clients. These activities were: toxicology, chemistry, human clinicals, animal products, and regulatory affairs.

Toxicology

Toxicology was concerned with the effects of daily exposure to potentially poisonous materials on humans in the home, workplace, and environment. In the toxicology laboratories, a battery of specialized tests was administered to various species of laboratory animals.

Professionals from a variety of disciplines were utilized to conduct the experiments and analyze the results. These tests lasted a few hours or continued throughout the animal's entire lifetime and revealed such findings as developmental and reproductive malformations, tumors, lethality, irritations, or other undesirable effects. Hazleton Laboratories established industry standards for excellence in toxicology studies. It was the first independent contract laboratory whose procedures were accredited by the Toxicology Laboratory Accreditation Board.

The areas of focus within this division included: acute, subchronic, chronic, oncogenicity, reproduction, inhalation, contract pathology, genetics, in vitro teratology, and immunotoxicology.

Chemistry

Chemistry determined the composition and chemical properties of various substances. This set of activities offered a wide range of in-house and contract services, such as formulations, metabolism, nutritional, pesticides, pharmaceutical, pharmacokinetics, and trace analysis. Hazleton's chemists verified the purity of test substances and determined their stability and concentration in the food and water of test animals, analyzed animal tissue or cultures after they were tested in other departments, provided government and industry with an understanding of the chemical behavior and residual environmental effects of particular products, and provided testing or analysis of how organisms were protected from disease.

Human Clinicals

Human clinicals conducted clinical investigations that analyzed the blood and urine of people that participated in studies conducted at Hazleton's facilities. Physicians, nurses, technicians, and medical assistants worked with pharmaceutical companies and regulatory agencies to determine the safety and effectiveness of new drugs and nutritional programs. A diverse population of human volunteers was carefully monitored to assess such effects as product efficacy, photosensitivity, and phytotoxic reactions.

This set of activities offered a wide range of services, including design and implementation of test protocols, data reduction and statistical analysis, and substantiation of advertising claims.

Animal Products

Animal products bred purpose-bred mongrels and beagles, rabbits, guinea pigs, and primates for laboratory use. The division also imported primates from various parts of the world. These animals are primarily used by the pharmaceutical, chemical, and agricultural industries for testing new drugs or chemicals before approval for marketing. In addition to offering animals for research, Hazleton was equipped to provide a variety of special services, which include antisera production, blood typing, ophthalamic testing, clinical chemistry, hematology, and pathology support services. Hazleton's laboratory units were the largest client for Hazleton's animal products.

Regulatory Affairs and Quality Assurance

Because of all the industries served by Hazleton were required to meet some of regulatory requirement before they could market their products, Hazleton's regulatory affairs and quality assurance operations complemented the company's emphasis on providing its clients with a product development package. This package enabled Hazleton's clients to be served from product inception, through market release, to maintaining its marketability. Hazleton personnel provided knowledge of national and international regulations, as well as skills in such areas as strategy design, petition preparation, and liasion assistance and counsel with regulatory agencies. Hazleton took great pride in maintaining constant contact with such agencies around the world as EPA, FDA, EEC, OECD; in designing test standards; and in helping to develop guidelines for regulatory approval.

THE MULTIDISCIPLINED NATURE OF HAZLETON

Most of Hazleton's laboratories were multidisciplined—that is, when testing was completed in one area of activity, the services of another area were often required to complete the analysis. Toxicology, one such discipline, usually referred to animal testing, and ultimately, to human testing. Animals were administered a compound to determine whether it caused a toxic reaction. If the compound did not cause adverse reactions, or if the toxic level was at a very high dose level, the compound could then be tested on humans. Toxicology was, therefore, safety testing, not efficacy testing. Hazleton conducted toxicology in five locations, two in the United States and three in Europe. Each toxicology housed several thousand rats and mice and several hundred dogs, primates, and rabbits.

The compounds were administered in a variety of ways: injection, inhalation, capsules, oral interbation, oral gavaging, or mixing the dose directly in the feed or water. Testing usually began with short-term studies that demonstrated at which dose level a significant reaction began. Dose levels were then decreased until no effect appeared. At this dose level the animals were monitored for long-term effects. The animal was then sacrificed and a total necropsy was performed. Such tissues as the heart, lungs, liver, kidneys, and pituitary glands were removed and examined.

For manufacturers of pesticides, Hazleton conducted residue studies. The pesticide was sprayed on crops, which were then harvested, taken to the laboratory, ground up, and tested for pesticide level. The testing was crucial because, if the pesticide level reached a critical level, the crops could not be sold.

Finally, in the chemistry labs, Hazleton obtained samples of blood or urine from animals or human beings and conducted analytical profiles. Metabolism chemistry involved measuring the air and performing tests on excreta and urine to determine what happened to the compound once it got into the system of the animal or human. Environmental chemistry involved obtaining samples of effluent in waste soil and liquids and performing content analyses. Nutritional chemistry involved testing for and establishing safe levels of chemicals in food products for the majority of the largest companies in the United States. Different foods were analyzed and labeled according to the FDA regulations.

The chemistry laboratories resembled traditional chemical laboratories, while both the animal and human clinics resembled hospitals. In the human clinic there were even cardiac care centers where a patient's heartbeat could be monitored by doctors and nurses on a 24-hour basis.

HISTORY OF THE COMPANY

Under the direction of Donald Nielsen, the company president since 1968, Hazleton acquired numerous companies, facilities, and product lines within the life sciences industries. In fact, in its 22-year history, the company had successfully completed 20 corporate mergers. Most notable was its acquisition of Raltech Laboratories in 1982, which expanded Hazleton's United States operations by 50 percent.

In April 1987, HLC was acquired by Corning, Inc., in an exchange of stock. Top executives at Hazleton cited the following reason for the merger: Hazleton's growth plans for the future required additional capital and greater expertise in international business operations; and these growth factors could be supplied by Corning. The merger would also provide Hazleton shareholders with an investment in a larger and more diversified enterprise, as well as expanding the laboratory science business of both companies. Additionally, this merger demonstrated Corning's commitment to a growth strategy in a technology-based industry, devoid of Japanese competition, in which they could quickly become a world leader—laboratory services.

Following the finalization of the merger, Hazleton became a subsidiary of Corning, with Hazleton's common stockholders receiving approximately one-half share of Corning for each share of Hazleton common stock. Although Hazleton was to benefit from Corning's technology and financial resources, Hazleton continued to operate as an independent subsidiary. Corning's confidence in Hazleton's management, philosophy, and policies were evidenced by Hazleton's continued self-management, with Donald Nielsen as CEO and all his top managers, who averaged 15 years of experience, remaining in key positions.

STRATEGY, STRUCTURE, AND THE FUTURE OF HAZLETON

In a presentation to the top management team in September 1989, Nielsen stated that to ensure the growth of the company an organization restructuring was required that was compatible with the firm's principles (as provided in Exhibit 2) and its successful strategy. He stated:

> The strategy dictates that we think globally, we act locally and globally; we cultivate fewer, but larger clients; we provide more services to each client; we have a closer relationship with each client; we develop new and creative information systems to track the progress of multiple studies, in multiple line disciplines which may be performed at multiple sites; and that we concentrate on clients not markets.
>
> To accomplish the above requires some changes in the way we operate. Over the next few years we need to bring all of Hazleton together so we act and think as one unit and our clients worldwide can be comfortable that any Hazleton unit will meet their requirements. The client needs to become

---

EXHIBIT 2   Hazleton Labs' Business Principles

In January 1989, Donald Nielsen established and distributed the following business principles, which were still in effect at the end of this case:

Business

- To provide superior scientific services and products that add value to organizations engaged in life sciences research.

Mission

- To help clients bring to market safe and effective new products and to maintain the marketability of existing products.
- To serve clients by providing services and products that may be needed to meet their own internal research or regulatory requirements, or both.
- To provide superior scientific services and products as quickly and economically as possible, commensurate with high quality and regulatory compliance.

Strategy

- To develop and sell worldwide those scientific services and products needed by the industries we serve to move their new products from the basic research stage through to the regulatory approval stage. Hazleton will also provide those scientific services necessary to keep existing products from falling out of compliance.

Goals

- To provide superior services and products to those clients we have the privilege of serving.
- To provide all employees with the opportunity to grow and develop to their full potential in a safe and attractive working environment.
- To provide our shareholders with an above-average rate of return on their investment.
- To be a good neighbor.

---

more assured that dealing with Hazleton will positively assist in accomplishing their worldwide development requirements.

We intend to gain a competitive advantage by stressing quality in everything we do, and by developing a true compound development capability through mega-sites.

ORGANIZATIONAL STRUCTURE

Growth during the first 20 years of the life of the company centered on an acquisition strategy, whereas from 1985 to 1990 the strategy shifted to concentrated growth and a global focus. The major challenge that the company faced was the design and activation of an appropriate organizational structure to accompany its recently adopted corporate strategy.

Pre-1989 Structure

Exhibit 3 presents the Hazleton organizational structure prior to 1989. At that time, the company was an organization of fairly independent entities that operated under the direction of a centralized management team, which felt the need for little communication or coordination among locations. Each location had an established client base and operated almost exclusively to satisfy its individual performance objectives.

Over a period of a few years in the mid-1980s, the marketplace forced the company to accept a global organization toward marketing, production, and customer service or risk its market position. A key impetus for change was Hazleton's need for coordinated efforts on large-scale contracts that it had been awarded. These multimillion-dollar contracts demanded the inputs from several labs. Thus, while globalization had been a long-range goal of the company, competitive market conditions forced an unanticipated rapid acceleration of Hazleton's growth plans. Realizing the need for organizational changes to reflect its dynamically evolving strategy, a new structure was created in 1989.

EXHIBIT 3   Pre-1989 Organizational Chart

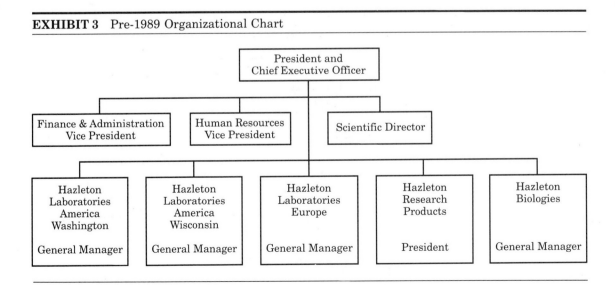

1989 Structure

Exhibit 4 illustrates the structure as it was redesigned in 1989. This modified matrix format was the company's first attempt to incorporate a global focus into its operations.

The operating units or labs were still independent. However, functional SBUs were created in an attempt to coordinate the functional areas of the company. Each location's general manager was responsible for costs, profits, lab utilization, and contract acquisition.

Under this arrangement, the company experienced problems with its organizational structure, most notably in three areas. First, coordination between facilities was lacking. When one location did not have the facilities to accommodate all phases of a contract, the general manager needed to contact other labs individually to negotiate an allocation of the work. Also, if a lab was contacted by a client for specific work and the lab did not have the needed capability or capacity, the search for an appropriate location would be necessary. This process of matching resources with client needs was complicated further if the job was highly varied, thus requiring the use of multiple Hazleton facilities.

EXHIBIT 4   1989 Organizational Chart

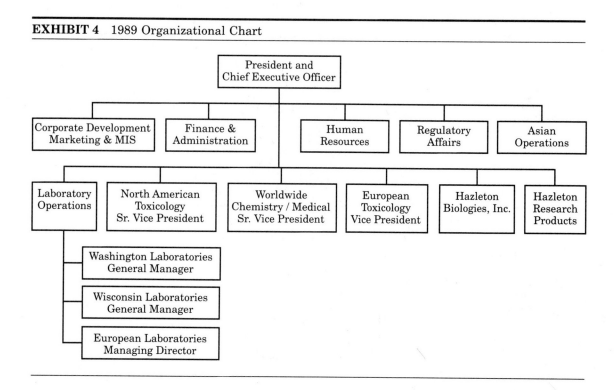

Second, the functional SBUs did not work well, especially in the area of toxicology. There was no coordination between the two vice presidents handling this functional area. As a result, there was little consistency on a companywide basis. The company did learn, however, that a global functional area, as operated in chemistry, worked much better. For example, through the amalgamation of chemistry, HLC was able to condense the time frame for bringing a compound to market, thereby substantially reducing costs.

Third, the managerial role conflict was substantial under the modified matrix structure. The general managers were too busy managing their lab operations to fully carry out their functional duties. With local issues taking precedence, the net result was that GMs were attempting to keep their labs full at the expense of attention to company's global goals.

1990 Structure

In an announcement in November 1989, Nielsen presented a reorganization of the company for 1990, in a further effort to integrate communication elements into the structure and to split the functional responsibilities from lab responsibilities. Exhibit 5 shows the relationships between the company's revised organizational chart and the functions carried out at each location.

The new structure established a vice president for marketing and business development, who was responsible for global marketing strategy, literature, and coordinating major programs. Reporting to him was the Regulatory Affairs Department, which addressed changing global conditions. Two directors of development (pharmachemicals and food, and chemicals and agrichemicals) were responsible for monitoring and responding to industry needs. R&D spending, new compounds in development, and new client requirements were just some of the areas they oversaw.

Also directly reporting to the vice president of marketing and business development were the key client executives. These executives were assigned to large clients and were responsible for the clients' programs within Hazleton. In addition, they had dotted line reporting responsibility to the labs where the programs were being conducted. These client executives were not physically located at headquarters.

The other newly established global functional division was the Science, Technology, and Quality Division. The vice president who headed the division was responsible for ensuring that the best available technology was being employed everywhere in the corporation. Such technology enabled the company to maximize productivity and standardize reporting. Like the vice president of marketing and busi-

EXHIBIT 5 1990 Organizational Chart

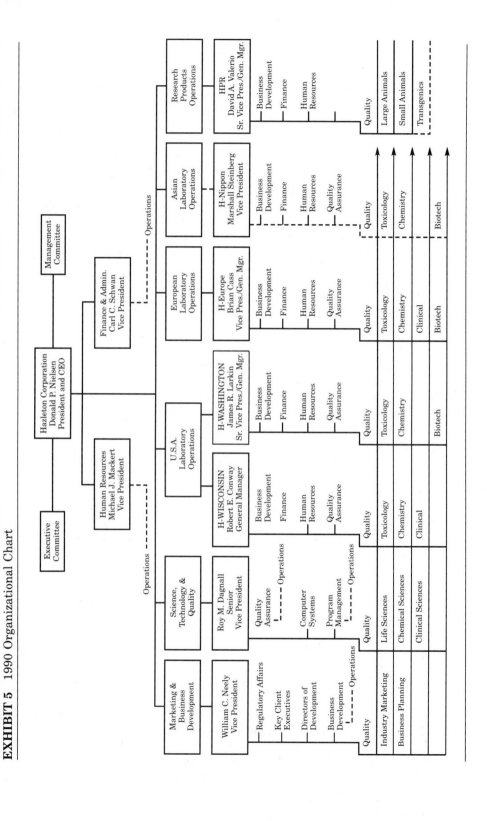

ness development, the VP of science, technology, and quality had global and across-boundaries authority and responsibility, yet lacked line manager authority.

The general managers of the laboratories also faced changes in their responsibilities—they were no longer fully independent managers. Those general managers who had succeeded in large part due to an entrepreneurial style were faced with culture shock when their power to negotiate client projects placements was removed. On the other hand, they recognized the need for greater interdependency among the company's labs. They knew that Nielsen's intent was not trying to decrease entrepreneurial spirit but to add the global dimension.

Under the general managers, each lab was operated as a profit center. Eventually, the labs were expected to be treated as factories or production centers—and measured on the efficiency of their production facilities. However, half of the GM's bonus was based on the achievement of the corporate goals. This was done to convince the GMs that they needed to be concerned with more than the profitability of their own operations.

In addition to overseeing operations, the GMs assisted in the selling function, which was done more inside the lab than outside. The business development person went out and called on a client, but the customer did not generally do business until he or she visited the lab. The general manager was a critical sales agent in such initial visits.

The organizational chart reflected other, more subtle, changes as well. For example, as of 1990, there were business development representatives at each location. They reported directly to the lab general manager, with dotted line responsibility to the vice president of marketing and business development. Since approximately 85 percent of business was still locally obtained, capturing business for their own lab was the primary responsibility of the business development representatives. However, the company established a bonus program, which provided incentives for the business development people to find or to develop clients that utilized labs beyond their home labs.

The final responsibility for placement of work was to be handled differently. If clients had a preference for a particular lab, the company attempted to accommodate their requests. If they could not place the work where the clients wanted, Hazleton would try to convince the clients to do it at another location so the work could be started immediately. The clients had the option to wait until their first preference lab (or even specific scientist) had open time periods. In general however, placement problems stemming from individual client preferences seldom arose, since major program clients typically required and expected multisite lab capability.

The major difficulties with work placement occurred when a specific lab did not have the functional capability to carry out a particular

---

EXHIBIT 6   Incentive Compensation Plan

	Percent of Bonus Tied to	
Year	*Corporate Goals*	*Local Goals*
For general managers:		
1987	0	100
1988	25	75
1989	50	50
1990	50	50
For business development executives and scientists:		
1988	0	100
1989	25	75
1990	25	75

---

stage of a study or when the lab was being fully utilized. Then the business development executive, who was responsible for deciding work placement, contacted other labs by telephone to determine companywide utilization levels. The company was working on a computer network system to facilitate this process. Essentially, then, the marketing and business development executives decided where such overflow work was placed.

Nielson experienced some resistance from his management team to these changes in authority and responsibility. Interpersonal conflicts among the new functional vice presidents and the general managers were a particular problem. There were also heightened sensitivities over coordination and communication needs since information flowed from the study director to the program manager to the key client executives to the client, or the reverse. Nielson tried to resolve the disputes by stressing the need for more centralization and focus on the company's global market goals.

Although not shown in the chart, reorganization was also used to reinforce the importance of a global company focus, and the Incentive Compensation Plan changed over the years, as reflected in Exhibit 6.

ORGANIZATIONAL ISSUES

Hazleton's organizational structure was becoming more centralized. However, the company remained complex as a result of the number of services and products it provided, in combination with its span of worldwide locations. Hazleton was considering what the next step should be to restructure the company so it could accomplish its global mission and goals.

A new organizational structure, if there was one, would need to address a number of specific issues:

a. Was more centralization necessary? Specifically, how should the company coordinate information and the receipt of contracts from its multiple entry points (i.e., business development, client executives, and multiple scientists all working with the same client)?

b. With the movement toward a more global focus in serving the world market, was the 1990 structure best? Or should the company be set up by markets served (e.g., drug companies, agricultural chemical companies)?

c. Should each facility become specialized in one functional or subfunctional area?

d. Some key client executives and industry specialists were also business development executives. Thus, reporting lines were sometimes confusing. How could this problem be eliminated?

e. Since the primary selling function was removed from the general manager's responsibilities, GMs could claim that the business development managers or key client executives were not doing the job of keeping the labs fully utilized. Would the GMs be justified in this claim?

f. Should the marketing and business development personnel continue to be the people to assign work? Or should the power revert back to the originating lab?

g. Should marketing and sales become a centralized function (with a single entry point to the company) or should they continue to be conducted at the individual lab level?

h. Who should be the point of contact for status reporting and answering customers' questions? As of 1990, clients were contacting company officials at multiple levels (the lab that obtained the contract, the lab doing the work in question, and the GM). Also, when one location could not handle a particular job and the job was placed at another lab, which lab should be ultimately responsible for this client and who should the client contact for contract updates?

i. Who should be responsible for the companywide utilization rates of all labs?

j. Who should be responsible (key client executive, program manager, and so on) when one lab of a multiple location study failed in its task?

k. To what extent would any proposed change extinguish the entrepreneurial spirit of the location or the firm as a whole?

l. Would it be better to continue an incremental structure change policy or to incorporate all changes into the structure at one time?

In essence, the challenge for the corporation is to answer the question: What are the best organizational structure and coordinating mechanisms for Hazleton Laboratories Corporation?

Case 6–10   *Robert N. Maxwell Memorial Community Hospital**

BACKGROUND AND HISTORY

The Robert N. Maxwell Memorial Community Hospital is a large 400-plus bed hospital serving a city of 842,000 in a county of 1,808,000 people. The hospital is one of eight major ones operating in the county and is ranked second in size in terms of number of beds and number of admissions per year. In addition, several small hospitals also operate in the county, but these are not considered to be major competitors.

The hospital has operated in the community for a number of years and is well known by area physicians and the community. Over 800 physicians are on the hospital's staff, and they provide the hospital with physician expertise in such areas as urology, pediatrics, OB–GYN, orthopedics, general practice, internal medicine, general surgery, neurosurgery, ophthalmology, ENT (ear-nose-throat), plastic surgery, proctology, thoracic medicine, and dental. Many of these 800 physicians are on the staffs of other area hospitals at the same time, but they do admit patients to Maxwell Hospital. It is common practice for many physicians to use more than one hospital, and thus a single physician could be on staff with a number of hospitals at the same time.

Originally the hospital had been called County General Hospital, but it was renamed Robert N. Maxwell Memorial Community Hospital during World War II. Robert N. Maxwell had been the 24-year-old son of a member of the hospital's board of directors, Joshua Maxwell. The younger Maxwell had been an Army Air Corps P-40 fighter pilot who had been killed early in the war in the Philippine Islands. The hospital had been renamed in his memory and was now commonly referred to simply as Maxwell Hospital. Few people in the community actually

---

* Reprinted from R. W. Haas and T. R. Wotruba, *Marketing Management: Concepts, Practice and Cases,* copyright © Business Publications, Inc., 1983, by permission of the publisher.

knew who Robert N. Maxwell had been or the derivation of the hospital's name.

Howard Hartley is the associate director of the hospital and functions in the capacity of its chief operating officer. A graduate of a Midwestern university with an MBA degree, Hartley is a very able and respected administrator. He is responsible for a host of departmental and functional activities, one of which is marketing. He is chairman of the hospital's loosely defined marketing committee and is therefore considered the top marketing officer in the organization. Hartley, however, does not consider himself a marketing authority and in fact is somewhat concerned about this. He has held this position for a number of years, dating back to when the hospital was relatively small. In those days, competition was not as strong as it had become in 1980, and the hospital itself was not as complex. Marketing had not been considered a really important activity. By 1980, the picture had changed—competition was fierce, and the organization was large and sometimes unwieldy. In addition, Hartley was concerned about his own ability to manage the marketing aspects of the company, since he was responsible for so many other activities at the same time. He did not feel he could give marketing the attention it needed.

THE PRESENT HOSPITAL ORGANIZATION

Exhibit 1 depicts the present general organization of the hospital. Five individuals make up the organization's top management team.

Paul Cashman holds the position of executive director and is for all purposes the equivalent of the organization's president. Well educated, articulate, and gracious, Cashman is an ideal top officer. He relates well with physician groups, with various hospital association people, with the area's political leaders, and with the community in general. In addition, he is a good buffer between the hospital and its board of directors. He does not, however, take an active interest in the day-to-day operations of the organization but leaves that to his subordinates. He relies heavily on Hartley to keep him informed in this area.

As has been stated, Howard Hartley is the hospital's associate director and acts as the chief operating officer. Cashman looks to Hartley to actually run the hospital. As the organization chart shows, Hartley is involved in many areas, heading up seven departments and chairing five functional committees as well.

Andre Dixon is an assistant director and is considered the hospital's top personnel officer. A college graduate with a degree in personnel management, Dixon has little interest or expertise in marketing. As the chart shows, his primary area of responsibility is in training and personnel development, although he is also involved in the administra-

EXHIBIT 1   Organization Chart

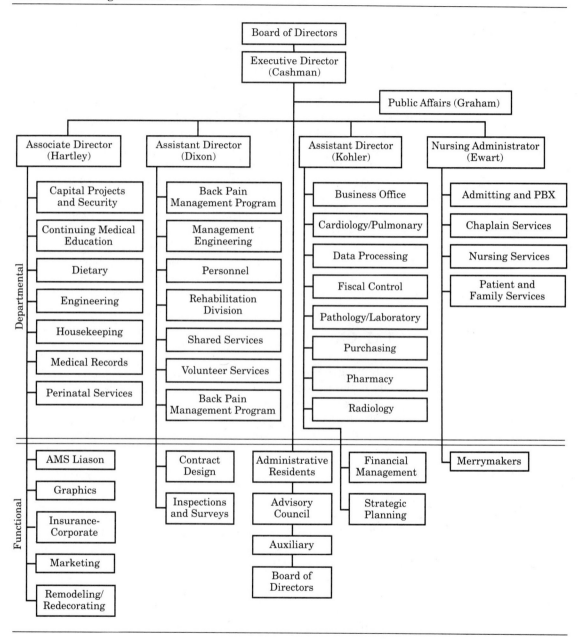

tion of the hospital's rehabilitation division and its back-pain management program. Both of these are medical programs headed by physicians. Dixon works closely with these physicians in the administration of these programs.

Terry Kohler is also an assistant director and is the organization's top financial officer. A recent MBA degree holder from an Ivy League university, Kohler is a financial, statistical, and data processing whiz. As the chart shows, his areas of responsibility are in fiscal control, purchasing, and data processing. He, like Dixon, is also involved in the administration of medical programs and departments, such as pathology and radiology. A very bright and able young administrator, Kohler is also responsible for the hospital's strategic planning program. In view of all his responsibilities, Kohler has little time for marketing activities although he does serve on the hospital's marketing committee.

The fifth top administrator is Nonny Ewart, the nursing administrator. Ms. Ewart has considerable nursing experience and is considered a very able nursing administrator. Well respected by her nurses, Ewart brings stability and professionalism to this important area of hospital administration. Her degree is in nursing, and she acknowledges openly that she has little awareness of what is involved in hospital marketing.

The primary marketing vehicle in the organization is the hospital's marketing committee. This committee is comprised of Dixon, Kohler, Ewart, and Hartley as chairman. Norman Graham, an outside consultant retained by the hospital, also serves on this committee. Graham heads the public affairs department which reports directly to Cashman as the chart indicates. This department is primarily responsible for publicity and public relations. Often, Paul Cashman attends committee meetings which typically take place on the first and third Thursdays of every month at 8:00 A.M. In addition, representatives from various departments, such as patient and family services, and public affairs, are often invited to attend. The committee meets to discuss marketing ideas and programs, and Hartley assigns various marketing activities to members when such activities are decided upon. This committee, while stretched thin, has fostered a genuine interest in strengthening the hospital's marketing orientation, which Hartley believes is a positive factor.

THE PROBLEM

A number of things are bothering Hartley regarding the hospital's marketing position.

First, the hospital's market share in terms of beds and admissions appears to be dropping. Hartley has analyzed these data between 1970

EXHIBIT 2 Robert N. Maxwell Hospital's Share of Beds and Admissions among Major Hospitals in the County Area, 1970 and 1980

Hospital	Beds				Admissions*			
	1970		*1980*		*1970*		*1980*	
	Number	*Percent*	*Number*	*Percent*	*Number*	*Percent*	*Number*	*Percent*
Maxwell	352	16.0%	401	15.7%	16,679	18.8%	14,793	15.6%
Canyon†	175	8.0	195	7.6	1,569	1.8	6,882	7.3
Claybourne	99	4.5	150	5.8	6,057	6.8	4,082	4.3
Greymont	234	10.6	234	9.1	13,175	14.8	12,039	12.7
Mercyhurst	498	22.6	511	20.0	21,599	24.3	21,140	22.3
Peninsula‡	150	6.8	150	5.9	4,277	4.8	4,391	4.6
Bayside	240	10.9	363	14.2	10,745	12.1	12,994	13.7
Doctors & Nurses	219	10.0	250	9.8	5,738	6.4	4,387	4.6
North County	232	10.6	306	11.9	9,096	10.2	14,202	14.9
Total	2,199	100.0%	2,560	100.0%	88,935*	100.0%	94,910*	100.0%

* Admission figures do not represent maximum number of patients possible, but rather the number of patients actually admitted in those years.
† Opened in mid-1972.
‡ Opened in 1974.

EXHIBIT 3   Age Distributions of Staff Physicians

Age Groups	Percent of General Practice Physicians		Percent of Internal Medicine Physicians	
	1970	1980	1970	1980
50 and under	69.6%	43.8%	81.3%	66.9%
51 and over	30.4	56.2	18.7	33.1
Total	100.0%	100.0%	100.0%	100.0%

and 1980, and the decline is illustrated in Exhibit 2. Hartley is concerned that if these trends continue, Maxwell Hospital could be in trouble in the future.

Second, a study conducted on the staff physicians indicates that the hospital may not be attracting enough young physicians. Reviewing age distributions for general practice and internal medicine physicians between 1970 and 1980, Exhibit 3 shows the data observed. Since both types of physicians are important in generating referrals, Hartley feels that the trends are not favorable.

Third, this same physician study indicates that a definite heavy-user pattern exists with physicians on staff. This is shown in Exhibit 4

EXHIBIT 4   Heavy-User Concept of Maxwell Hospital Physicians in 1980

Area	Total Number of Physicians	Number and Percent of Heavy Users		Patients Admitted by Heavy Users	
		Number	Percent	Number	Percent
Urology	37	6	16.2%	204	61.3%
Pediatrics	75	10	13.3	1,541	57.3
OB–GYN	94	16	17.0	2,942	57.1
Orthopedics	68	10	14.7	857	63.8
General practice	148	10	6.8	486	59.6
Internal	142	11	7.7	1,274	60.1
General surgery	93	10	10.8	751	62.9
Neurosurgery	18	6	33.3	256	92.6
Ophthalmology	59	6	10.2	156	88.1
ENT	26	5	19.2	249	83.3
Plastic surgery	16	5	31.2	55	84.4
Proctology	3	2	66.7	64	100.0
Thoracic	26	5	19.2	188	86.4
Dental	30	2	3.3	30	68.6
Total	835	104	12.4%	9,053	61.2%

which reveals that 12.4 percent of the staff physicians (104 of 835) admitted 61.2 percent of the patients (9,053 of 14,793 in 1980). Hartley believes this statistic is important, but he is unsure of its marketing implications.

Fourth, Hartley is concerned because there is no marketing specialist or professional on the marketing committee or in the entire hospital. He has read many health-care journal articles whose authors impress the need for hospitals to market more effectively in the changing health-care environment. These same authors also stress the need for

---

EXHIBIT 5

---

*DIRECTOR OF
HOSPITAL MARKETING*

A unique, growth opportunity now exists with our young, rapidly expanding National Health Care Management Company, for a highly motivated individual having a solid record of achieving significant quantifiable results.

The Director's responsibility is to achieve increased utilization and increased revenue for the Emergency Department's ancillary services, and in-patient units of general acute hospitals. The successful candidate would have authority to achieve, with his staff, census improvement results through physician contacts, community relations activity, public service health education programs, open-houses, interagency affiliations, and any other suitable techniques with which she or he might be familiar or might innovate. The qualified candidate might come from any of a variety of career backgrounds, but must be thoroughly familiar with hospital procedures and interrelationships. Such a candidate might be a Hospital Administrator, a Registered Nurse Consultant, a Nursing In-Service Director, a Clinic Manager, an Operations Executive of a Hospital Management Company, or an individual who has successfully marketed and developed management contracts for Hospital Ancillary Services.

If you are an ambitious executive seeking an environment where your growth and reward are contingent only upon your own performance, starting with an excellent salary and liberal fringe benefits, this is the unlimited opportunity you have been seeking.

Send your résumé and salary requirement to:

*BOX D-005NA,   TIMES
An Equal Opportunity Employer M/F*

hospitals to employ health-care marketing professionals to manage their marketing operations. He is also intrigued by the want ad which he had read in a major metropolitan newspaper (see Exhibit 5). Hartley cannot help but wonder if Maxwell Hospital has arrived at that point where marketing should be handled as a primary as opposed to a secondary activity.

MARKETING OBJECTIVES

A major responsibility of Hartley and the marketing committee had been to develop marketing objectives for the hospital. This was required as part of Kohler's strategic planning program. The committee put in many long hours on this and defined three target markets:

1. *The Physician Market.* Since most hospital patients are admitted by physicians, focusing marketing efforts on physicians in the area seemed most appropriate.
2. *The Patient Market.* Since patients can and do influence physicians in their selection of hospitals, the committee felt some form of patient marketing was needed.
3. *The Community Market.* Since the hospital must operate as a part of its community, marketing effort to promote Maxwell Hospital as a good citizen was logical.

The marketing committee then established objectives in each of these three target markets.

Overall Objective

To increase overall utilization of Robert N. Maxwell Memorial Community Hospital as a major community hospital in the county.

Physician Market Objectives

- To attract and retain a growing number of heavy-user physicians to the hospital.
- To continue to develop areas of specialization which will in turn attract physicians to the hospital because of the quality of services offered. This is currently being done with cardiovascular services, perinatal services, and rehabilitation services. (These were termed Commitment Level I services.)

- To create an awareness, liking, and preference for Maxwell Hospital among younger physicians and those recently arrived in the county.
- To increase the number of primary physicians (e.g., general practice and internal medicine) and thereby increasing the hospital's referral potential for other physicians.
- To increase the identification by present physicians with Maxwell Hospital and thus foster a closer relationship between the hospital and physicians using the hospital.
- To increase awareness by physicians in the state and surrounding area of the hospital's services, particularly in its areas of specialization.
- To increase awareness of the quality of services provided by Maxwell Hospital to strengthen the preference for Maxwell Hospital among all types of physicians in the county.

Patient Market Objectives

- To continue to provide the highest quality of patient care possible to foster favorable word-of-mouth promotion by patients to potential patients and to physicians in the marketplace.
- To develop the image of Maxwell Hospital as a quality provider of first-rate acute health care to potential patients in the marketplace.
- To attract health maintenance patients as well as acute health-care patients.
- To develop a file of patients of record so that more of the market has an existing relationship with Maxwell Hospital.
- To establish Maxwell Hospital as a complete source of information on health-care services and their availability in the county area.

Community Market Objectives

- To increase the level of public awareness in the county, and to broaden the image of Maxwell Hospital as not only a highly specialized hospital but also a total community hospital.
- To provide assistance and services to health-related institutions and to other community organizations.
- To increase the level of public awareness in the state and surrounding region of Maxwell Hospital's Commitment Level I Services.
- To establish the image of Maxwell Hospital as a good corporate citizen that is concerned and involved with community issues and problems.

The committee does not see the three markets as equals but recommends that marketing efforts be devoted toward the three in these proportions: 70 percent to the physician market, 20 percent to the patient market, and 10 percent to the community market.

Hartley believes the committee has done a good job and that the objectives are valid. He doubts, however, that these objectives could be attained with the hospital's existing marketing organization. In particular, he does not believe the hospital possesses the necessary marketing expertise or resources to develop strategies and programs to reach these objectives. He wonders how the hospital might best be organized to attain these objectives and reverse the trends he feels are alarming. Advise Mr. Hartley.

Case 6–11 *Aurora Lotion**

John Fairchild frowned as he hung up the telephone. He had just finished another conversation with Urs Brunner, the general manager of Produits Pour Femmes, SA (PPF), on a subject that had become increasingly troublesome over the last three years: how to respond to the problem of parallel importing of Aurora Lotion into Switzerland. Fairchild was the general manager of the Overseas Division of Smythe-Dabney International, Ltd., a British company which marketed Aurora and other women's cosmetics. A large portion of his job was devoted to offering information and recommendations to the managers of the subsidiary companies which made up the division.

The management of PPF, the Swiss subsidiary, had reported a growing rash of price cutting on Aurora Lotion, one of its most important products, by a group of independent distributors who were buying Aurora in England and bringing it to Switzerland themselves. This practice, which had been dubbed "parallel importing" or "black importing" in the trade, had put PPF's gross margins under pressure and squeezed the company's return on sales. The situation had reached the point

---

* This case was prepared by Thomas Kosnik, research associate, under the direction of Professor Christopher Gale. Copyright © 1978 by l'Institut pour l'Étude des Méthodes de Direction de l'Entreprise (IMEDE), Lausanne, Switzerland. Reproduced by permission.

that Urs Brunner had asked John Fairchild to intervene and recommend a strategy to counter the threat, including a substantial reduction of PPF's selling price for Aurora if necessary.

SMYTHE-DABNEY INTERNATIONAL, LTD.

The parent company for PPF was Smythe-Dabney International, Ltd. (SDI), with headquarters outside London. In 1977 SDI's sales were £25.8 million and its trading profits were £2.6 million. In the last 10 years earnings per share had increased at the compound rate of 20 percent a year. Sir Anthony Carburton, the chairman of SDI, felt that the impressive record was the result of several factors, including the quality of the company's product, the energies and talents of a close-knit management team, and the ability to stay a step ahead of competitors in the marketplace.

From the earliest days with the introduction of Aurora Lotion, SDI had marketed only products of high quality and had stressed that theme in advertising and promotion campaigns. As a result the various SDI cosmetics, under the Aurora name and in several other well-known brand families, enjoyed widespread brand recognition and consumer loyalty.

A keen sensitivity to the needs of both the channels of distribution and consumers caused the company's directors to search continually for ways to make their products and services more competitive. They had defined the market they served as the women's beauty care market and had acquired a wide line of products that complemented each other and ensured efficient utilization of the sales force and marketing staff. They quickly learned that the ability to supply the trade was critical and earned a reputation for having the company's products in stock in a timely fashion, providing a valuable service for their distributors. They used extensive television advertising to stimulate demand, and point-of-purchase displays in retail outlets to make it easier for consumers to select the products they needed.

The objectives of the company for the next three years were to increase sales and earnings per share 20 percent a year and to maintain a pretax income/sales ratio of 10 percent. The basic guidelines the corporate management had drafted to reach those objectives were to:

1. Increase unit volume of sales in all product lines.
2. Maintain historic direct (gross) margins.
3. Keep corporate overhead expenses low by maintaining a lean home office staff.

4. Give management of subsidiary companies decision-making authority on all tactical matters, with consultation with corporate management on strategic issues.

THE OVERSEAS DIVISION

SDI was composed of the UK Division and the Overseas Division. In 1977 the Overseas Division sold £10.8 million worth of women's beauty products in continental Europe, North America, and the Far East. In Europe, SDI had company-owned subsidiaries in France, Germany, and Switzerland and marketed its products in other countries through independent wholesale distributors.

Both Fairchild and Carburton shared the view that the most promising markets for future growth were in Europe and North America. In 1977 much of the 20 percent growth in sales and profits projected for the company as a whole was expected to come from the Overseas Division.

PRODUITS POUR FEMMES, SA

PPF was responsible for the marketing of Aurora and other SDI products in Switzerland. Its reporting relationship in the Overseas Division is shown in Exhibit 1. The organization was small, with 14 people in all comprising a sales force, marketing department, accounting department, and warehouse crew.

EXHIBIT 1   Smythe-Dabney International Ltd.—Overseas Division Organization Chart

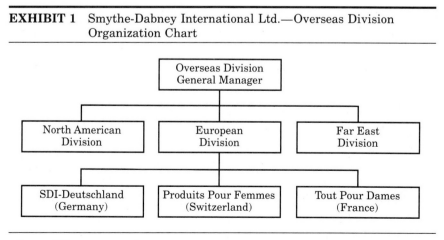

Source: SDI company records.

EXHIBIT 2

PRODUITS POUR FEMMES, SA DIVISION
Income Statement
1976 and 1977
(SFr. 000)

	1976	*1977*
Sales	3,525	4,300
Less: Cost of goods sold	1,160	1,720
Direct margin	2,365	2,580
Less:		
Advertising	405	403
Distribution	204	330
Promotion*	175	230
Other expenses†	55	70
Brand contribution	1,490	1,520
Less:		
Sales force expenses	410	430
General and administration	670	610
Trading profit (before tax)	410	480

* Does not include trade discounts on Aurora Lotion.
† Other expenses included marketing research, product research, public relations, depreciation, and inventory losses through obsolescence, damage etc.

Source: SDI company records (disguised).

Sales of the company in 1977 were SFr. 4.3 million, up 22 percent from the year before. Exhibit 2 shows PPF's income statement for 1976 and 1977.

Urs Brunner had recently taken over as general manager. He and his marketing manager were the key decision makers in day-to-day activities; John Fairchild and Dustin Cushman, the general manager for Europe, involved themselves with PPF only on matters of strategic importance.

THE PRODUCT

Aurora Lotion was a high-quality, all-purpose lotion for women. It was applied by being spread lightly over the skin of the face, arms, legs, and other parts of the body and then rubbing gently until the lotion was completely absorbed into the skin. The company stressed in its advertising that Aurora relieved dryness due to sun, wind, water, or detergents and made skin feel soft, clean, and gentle to the touch. It also stated that the effects of the lotion were longer lasting than those of many similar products. A single application of Aurora before bed-time each evening kept the skin "soft and beautiful," while it was necessary to apply other lotions as often as three or four times a day to get the same protection. The secret of Aurora's long-lasting effective-ness was a unique formula which allowed the lotion to penetrate the skin more completely than competing brands.

Aurora Lotion was the brand leader in a growing line of beauty products which included hand lotion, moisturizers, and bath prepara-tions. Exhibit 3 contains the Aurora product line's brand contribution statement to PPF. The company also marketed the full line of SDI products under other brands, including facial cosmetics, eye cosmetics, hair preparations, nail polish, and deodorants. In 1977 Aurora Lotion sales accounted for 20 percent of the total sales of PPF.

Over the years, Aurora Lotion had become increasingly familiar to women in many European countries. In fact, parallel importers capi-talized on this brand recognition and easily sold Aurora Lotion in Switzerland that had been shipped directly from Britain, even though the directions for use of the lotion were in English. Fairchild and Brunner estimated that 120,000 bottles of Aurora were parallel-im-ported into Switzerland in 1977, compared with PPF sales of 200,000 bottles in the same period.

EXHIBIT 3

AURORA PRODUCT GROUP PPF
Brand Contribution Statement
1976 and 1977
(SFr. 000)

	1976	1977
Sales	850	1,140
Less: Cost of goods sold	290	526
Direct margin	560	614
Less:		
Advertising	94	106
Distribution expenses	50	55
Promotion*	74	150
Other expenses†	15	12
Brand contribution	327	291

* Does not include trade discounts on Aurora Lotion.
† Other expenses included marketing research, product research, public relations, depre-ciation, and inventory losses.

Source: SDI company records (disguised).

COMPETITIVE PRODUCTS

All-purpose lotions for women were available in great variety and a wide range of price and quality. However, they tended to cluster in three main groups.

1. High-priced products.   These lotions were most often produced by companies making fashionable women's perfumes. They had the same scents as popular women's fragrances, so the consumer could use the lotion along with her favorite cologne or perfume. These lotions were sold for SFr. 20 to SFr. 50 in retail outlets, for bottles of 100 to 200 centiliters (cl). Some packages were annotated in grams rather than centiliters.

2. Medium-price lotions.   Many of these lotions were imported to Switzerland from France and England. They were attractively packaged and often made claims to characteristics that differentiated them from other lotions. Some were made by perfume houses to match less-expensive fragrances. They sold for between SFr. 7.50 and SFr. 15, and the most common bottle size was 200 cl.

EXHIBIT 4   Sample of All-Purpose Lotions Available in Switzerland

Product	Size of Selling Unit	Retail Selling Price per Selling Unit
High-price:		
Caron	120 cl	SFr. 28.00
Chanel	80 g	24.50
Je Reviens	100 cl	22.50
Amnioderm	200 cl	30.00
Medium-price:		
Aurora Lotion	200 cl	SFr. 15.00
Bea Kasser	150 cl	14.50
Janine D	200 cl	13.50
4711	200 cl	9.50
Ma Garde	125 cl	7.50
Oil of Olay	200 cl	7.50
Fenjal	250 cl	7.50
Winston's	300 cl	8.40
Low-price:		
Rose Milk	240 cl	SFr. 5.90
Nivea	250 cl	4.95
Kaloderma	300 cl	4.50
Jana Lait de Toilette (Migros)	430 cl	3.50

Source: Field research at retail outlets, Lausanne, Switzerland.

3. Low-price lotions. These products were the simple, functional answer to the everyday problems of dry, rough skin due to water, weather, and housework. Prices ranged from SFr. 3 to SFr. 6 for a plastic container of 240 cl to 450 cl.

Exhibit 4 provides examples of all-purpose lotions in the three price ranges. Aurora Lotion, with a suggested retail price of SFr. 15 for 200 cl, was positioned near the top of the middle range of lotions.

Consumers cited several problems that sometimes arose when using an all-purpose lotion. These related to the fragrance of the lotion and its ability to penetrate the skin. Some products had a heavy, sweet, or powerful scent that could potentially clash with or mask the fragrance of perfume. Some lotions left the skin feeling slippery, greasy, or wet after application, while others were not absorbed into the skin and washed off immediately upon contact with water. In the former case the lotion might stain clothing or furniture. In the latter case it was necessary to apply the lotion several times a day, after bathing, doing dishes, or returning from out of doors. The popularity of Aurora Lotion was due in large part to the fact that it had a light, clean scent that did not clash with perfumes and also that it penetrated deeply without leaving the skin slick or greasy.

THE BEAUTY CARE MARKET IN SWITZERLAND

Switzerland was a small, topographically rugged country in the center of Western Europe. The Swiss enjoyed a relatively high standard of living; the per capita GNP in 1975 was SFr. 22,500, the highest in Europe. The population was 6.4 million people, and the diversity of the Swiss was reflected in the fact that there were four official languages, as follows:

First Language	Percent of Population
German	65%
French	18
Italian	12
Romansh	1
Other	4
Total	100%

Source: Market research report, Swiss Federal Railway.

There were 3.28 million women in Switzerland who were distributed among the following age groups:

Age Group	Number of Women (000)
0–14	700
15–19	240
20–29	510
30–39	450
40–49	400
50–59	340
Over 60	640
Total	3,280

Source: *Consumer Europe 1977.*

Retail sales of all beauty products in Switzerland were SFr. 535.3 million in 1975. The per capita expenditure for the Swiss adult woman was nearly SFr. 210. The women's cosmetic market comprised several segments, which in 1975 accounted for the following percentages of the total retail sales:

Product Category	Percent of Beauty Product Sales
Face cosmetics	12%
Eye cosmetics	4
Hair preparations	22
Skin preparations	18
Fragrances	18
Deodorants	8
Bath preparations	4
Other	14
Total	100%

Source: *Consumer Europe 1977.*

Total sales of beauty products increased 12.6 percent from 1974 to 1975 in Switzerland. There were also changes in the structure of the market. Sales of fragrances and skin preparations, which included all-

EXHIBIT 5   Swiss Market for Skin Preparations, 1975

	Retail Sales (SFr. million)	*Unit Sales (packs)*	*Usership (million women)*	*Percent of Usership*
Hand cream/lotion	SFr. 22.8	7.8	1.85	72
Body cream/lotion	12.2	2.5	0.98	38
Moisturizers	7.5	1.2	0.73	29
All-purpose lotions	34.0	6.4	1.74	67
Others	18.8	+	+	+
	SFr. 95.3			

Source: *Consumer Europe 1977.*

purpose lotions, rose sharply, while there was a decline in the volume of face and eye cosmetics and bath preparations.

According to some experts, the potential for the skin preparations market varied significantly among European countries. Sales levels depended not only upon the predominant skin types in a country but also upon the affluence of the women. Partly because of the standard of living in Switzerland and the fact that a relatively large proportion of the women were fair skinned, the expenditure per adult woman on skin preparations was higher than in every other Western European country but Germany. In 1973 the "average" Swiss woman spent about SFr. 37 on skin lotions of various types. Exhibit 5 gives a breakdown of sales and usership of various categories of skin preparations, including all-purpose lotions.

CHANNELS AND PRICING

Smythe-Dabney products reached the buying public through a variety of channels of distribution, each with its own pricing arrangement. Aurora Lotion was manufactured in England and then sold in the United Kingdom to independent wholesalers or large retail chains. In countries with an SDI subsidiary, such as Switzerland, Aurora was sold to the affiliated company, which then resold it to wholesalers and retail stores. SDI billed all customers in pounds sterling. Company-owned subsidiaries were charged a transfer price, which was the standard manufacturing cost of the product, including:

- Raw materials.
- Direct labor.
- Factory overhead.
- Handling and warehousing.

The senior management of SDI adopted this transfer pricing arrangement in order to give the managers of each subsidiary maximum discretion over margins and profits. The reasons for this strategy were:

1. The majority of marketing costs were, in fact, incurred in the country where the product was sold.
2. Advertising, price promotions, and sales force management decisions were under the control of the subsidiary's management.
3. The practice reinforced the SDI concept of division autonomy on day-to-day decisions and fostered good relationships between subsidiary managers and corporate officers.

EXHIBIT 6   Percentage of Retail Sales of Women's Beauty Care Products Sold through Various Outlets in Switzerland

Outlet	Description	Percent of Total Sales
Department and cosmetics stores	Cosmetic departments of large department stores and small shops and "parfumeries" specializing in cosmetics.	20%
Drugstores and pharmacies	Drugstores sold cleaning compounds, preparations, and parapharmaceuticals; pharmacies sold prescription drugs and other products.	40
Multiple stores/hypermarkets	Large chains selling food items as well as many nonfood products, from clothing to hardware to beauty products, often at discount prices (e.g., Migros and Carrefour).	25
Direct sales	Door-to-door salespersons.	3
Supermarkets/food outlets	Small and medium-size retail stores selling mainly food, with some nonfood lines.	9
Other		3
Total		100%

Source: *Consumer Europe 1977.*

SDI's price to independent customers in Britain was standard manufacturing cost plus a percentage of the cost for contribution to overhead and profit. All customers paid freight charges from factory to their warehouses.

SDI gave independent distributors in the United Kingdom a 3.75 percent discount for cash purchases and up to 6 percent volume rebate for purchases of large amounts of any product. In addition, each month, the company ran price promotions for groups of products in order to encourage British distributors to increase the volume of products they carried.

In England, wholesalers' markups on cosmetics were usually between 15 percent and 25 percent; retail margins were 35 percent to 45 percent of the selling price to the consumer. On the other hand, wholesale margins for beauty products in Switzerland were between 40 percent and 55 percent of the selling price to retail outlets, and retail margins were 42 percent to 50 percent. In Switzerland, Aurora Lotion and other PPF products were sold at the retail level in a wide variety of outlets. Exhibit 6 shows the percentage of total sales of beauty care products that were sold through various outlets in 1975. While the data were incomplete, there was evidence of a rapid increase in the portion of total sales that were accounted for by hypermarkets in the last few years.

PARALLEL IMPORTS

Perhaps the biggest single problem that confronted the management of PPF was the parallel importing of Aurora Lotion. The difference in the wholesale price in Britain and Switzerland made it profitable for a distributor to send a buyer to England, purchase the product at the British wholesale price, and ship it to Switzerland for eventual resale to retail outlets. The process had become increasingly common in the last several years, and the management of PPF counted several large distributors who parallel imported Aurora Lotion among their main competitors in the marketplace. Although parallel importing was irritating to the sales force and management of PPF, it was not illegal and it was impossible to monitor.

There were three main reasons that the wholesale price of Aurora Lotion was lower in England than in Switzerland. First, retail prices were higher on the Continent than in Britain, reflecting a higher cost of living. Second, SDI conducted aggressive promotions in the United Kingdom each month, and the resulting average level of wholesale prices was lower than in Europe, where such promotions occurred less frequently. Finally, from 1972 through 1978 there had been a substantial decline in the value of the British pound against other currencies, including the Swiss franc. As a result of this trend, Swiss distributors had not had to increase the price of Aurora Lotion to the retail trade in five years, although SDI had hiked prices in Britain by as much as 25 percent a year in the same period. Since SDI billed its customers in pounds sterling, the fall of the pound against the Swiss franc had offset the British price increase.

Exhibit 7 contains a hypothetical example of the landed cost per bottle of parallel-imported Aurora Lotion.

A large British wholesaler purchased Aurora Lotion at £10.55 per case of 12 bottles. Normally the distributor was expected to take a 3.75 percent cash discount and to be eligible for a volume rebate of 6 percent of his net purchases. When reselling these goods in large volume, he was content to receive a 15 percent markup.

A wholesale distributor or large retailer doing business in Switzerland sent a representative across the English Channel to buy from the British supplier. He paid £0.93 for each bottle and incurred additional freight charges at 4 percent to 8 percent of the cost of goods, depending upon the volume shipped to Switzerland. Assuming at the time of the transaction an exchange rate of 3.75 Swiss francs per pound, his cost for a 200 cl bottle of Aurora Lotion landed in Switzerland was SFr. 3.70. The price list for PPF recommended the following price structure for the 200 cl bottle of Aurora (including freight):

PPF suggested list price to distributors	SFr. 5.00
Distributor's suggested list price to retail outlets	8.70
Retailer's suggested list price to consumers	15.00

EXHIBIT 7   Hypothetical Example of Parallel Importer's Cost per Bottle of Aurora Lotion*

SDI price/case	£10.55
SDI price/bottle	0.88
Less: 3.75 percent cash discount	0.04
Net purchase	0.84
Less: 6 percent volume rebate	0.05
British distributor's cost	0.79
Add: 15 percent markup	0.14
Wholesale price	0.93
Add: transport cost at 6 percent	0.06
Landed cost/bottle	£ 0.99
Landed cost/bottle†	SFr.3.70

* Figures have been rounded.
† Assumes 3.75 SFr./pound.

Source: Discussions with SDI directors.

EXHIBIT 8   Trends in Average Selling Price and Landed Cost of Aurora Lotion (200 cl) by Produits Pour Femmes, SA, 1975–1978

	1975	1976	1977	1978*
Average selling price per bottle (SFr.)†	5.00	4.70	4.30	4.00
Average landed cost per bottle (pounds)	0.35	0.40	0.45	0.50
Average exchange rate (SFr./£)‡	5.40	4.05	3.95	3.75

* 1978 is average for the first quarter of the year.
† "Average price" is list price less discounts given in trade promotions.
‡ Average rate during fourth quarter 1975–77; during first quarter 1978.

Source: SDI company records (disguised).

According to Urs Brunner, the retail price of Aurora Lotion had not declined in the last few years despite the parallel imports. Since the consumer was paying the same price, the channels were apparently enjoying higher margins.

It was difficult to assess the impact of parallel importing on PPF or SDI as a whole. On the one hand the average price of Aurora Lotion sold by PPF to the trade had declined over 20 percent in the past three years. Although PPF's list price for the product had not been reduced, the company had run a series of trade promotions which gave discounts to distributors, aimed at countering the competition from parallel imports. Exhibit 8 provides details in the trend of PPF's selling price for Aurora.

Sales of Aurora Lotion had increased in units and in Swiss francs, and Fairchild was not sure whether the increases were in spite of the parallel imports or because of them. Probable effects of the activity had been higher market penetration of the product and increased brand recognition, both of which were beneficial to PPF. Besides, from SDI's point of view, the sales of Aurora parallel imported from England benefited the parent company by the contribution from the SDI sales to the British wholesalers.

Even if the practice had mixed results Fairchild knew that he could not shrug off the situation. It was clear from his conversation with Brunner that it had resulted in low morale in the Swiss subsidiary's sales force. Salespersons were rewarded for units sold and wanted to cut the price of Aurora to make them more competitive with the parallel importers.

ALTERNATIVES

John Fairchild reviewed the possible responses he had considered to the problem at hand. One alternative was to lower PPF's recommended selling price for Aurora Lotion to distributors. He was concerned about the possible financial consequences of such a price cut, both for PPF and for SDI. Moreover he wondered what steps he should take to ensure that trading profits would not be sacrificed. He believed that related options included cutting the subsidiary's advertising budget, trimming the sales force, and raising the prices of other products.

On the other hand, he wondered whether PPF could simply adhere to the policy that had been followed in the past. Such a strategy would continue to consist of three elements:

1. Avoid direct competition in published list prices.
2. Use trade promotions such as price-off discounts or "buy two, get one free" to respond to competitive pricing.
3. Stress the advantages provided by PPF to the trade, such as continuity of supply, advertising to stimulate demand, and a full line of related products.

Although the problem of what to do about the price of Aurora Lotion demanded action in the short run, it also had implications for the future of the subsidiary over the long term. Fairchild wondered whether the independent Swiss wholesalers would begin to parallel import more SDI products across the channel. Aurora Lotion, which accounted for 20 percent of PPF sales, might only be the first of a growing number of products on which the subsidiary would face increasing price competition.

Perhaps the existence of parallel importers was a signal that PPF was not an efficient channel of distribution. SDI might be better off to conduct its business directly with the independent distributors in Switzerland. This issue took on added significance because of SDI's plans to expand abroad in the future. The corporate directors would be faced with the decision of whether to set up a company subsidiary or to sell SDI products through existing independent wholesalers each time they entered a market in a new country or region.

A meeting with Sir Anthony Carburton and the other SDI directors was scheduled soon. Fairchild decided that this would be the best time to present his views on the situation at PPF and make his recommendations to the group.

Case 6–12   Nike, Inc.*

During the fall of 1982, the Nike Company was recognized generally as one of the phenomenal success stories of the recent decade. From its small base in 1972, by 1981 the firm had blossomed into a $450 million giant and expected sales to reach $650 million in 1982. It had passed Adidas in the United States and held an estimated 30 percent of the American market. Most Nike executives were confident that a $1 billion sales year was imminent. Although the company owed much of its success to a vibrant management team, it was also very much the brainchild of a remarkable entrepreneur, Phil Knight, who still served as president, CEO, and major stockholder.

The Company's incredible growth rate was not without its problems. As Phil Knight reflected:

> There has been a severe overload on marketing compounded by our need to organize for new opportunities as our old products and markets mature. We are geared to handle existing lines where we have 30 percent or 40 percent of the market. But how about new areas which must be developed, like leisure products, international, the children's line, clothing, and cleated shoes? I question whether our existing approaches can successfully pioneer these many opportunity areas, particularly given the increase in competition and changes in consumer habits.

THE INDUSTRY

Nike competed in two industries: sports and athletic shoes; and also sportswear. Each of these categories was estimated to exceed $10 billion in 1982 sales. Starting from its running heritage, Nike had branched out rapidly into an assortment of other sports (tennis, soccer, basketball, etc.) as well as leisure ("look-like") markets. Running, still the company's wellhead, was essentially an American phenomenon, though it had been copied in varying degrees elsewhere. By 1980, however, the running boom showed signs of leveling off. In the words of Phil Knight: "We see only a couple more years of strong growth in running shoes in the United States, though we are sure fitness is here to stay."

* This case was written by Robert T. Davis, Professor of Marketing. The revision is by Professor Davis. Financial support was provided in part by the Marketing Management Program of the Graduate School of Business, Stanford University. Copyright © 1982 by the Board of Trustees of the Leland Stanford Junior University. All rights reserved.

Because of the industry's evolution, there was a wide range of competitors and strategies. In running, for example, there were Adidas (the largest firm in total, worldwide sales), Puma, Converse Rubber, Pony International, Asics (Tiger brand), New Balance, and Brooks (acquired by Wolverine in 1982), to mention the most obvious. Reliable data about these competitors was sketchy because many were either privately owed or divisions of larger companies. Moreover, market share estimates were based primarily on one commercial service that regularly surveyed 200 specialty retailers for competitive comparisons. Omitted from their sample were discounters, mass merchandisers, and most large department stores.

The market segments were diverse. In addition to the serious runners, the interested student might distinguish the faddist, the casual exerciser, the trend follower, the price buyer, the leisure-time devotee, the amateur sportsman, the high-fashion, status-conscious user, and any other number of variants. In recent months some observers felt that color coordination (between shoes and clothing) was a coming consumer preference. Indeed, one competitor (New Balance) had succeeded in drawing favorable comments about its grey, light brown, burgundy, and navy colors early in 1982. This same firm had recently increased its margins to the trade (to 55 percent compared to Nike's 48–50 percent), upped its innovation rate, and put heavy emphasis on the specialty retailers. These actions appeared to have increased that firm's penetration of the innovator segment.

The clothing business was even more fragmented, consisting of thousands of designers, cutters, finishers, stylists, knitters, weavers, and so forth. Raw materials ranged from cotton and wool to a great variety of synthetics and blends. In the relevant world of Nike, the key actors were such competitors as Levi Strauss, Head, Adidas, and hundreds of prestige designers (e.g., Pierre Cardin, Bill Blass). There were, in addition, many retailer brands such as Brooks Brothers, Saks and I. Magnin.

During the '60s and '70s, Levi Strauss grew spectacularly on the basis of its "Western-cowboy" look and, thanks partly to the well-publicized acceptance by James Dean and Marlon Brando, jeans became the uniform for every self-respecting teenager or young adult. By 1980, however, there was some speculation that "the look" was about to shift to a new life-style—the fit, the jock, the athlete-winner. If this shift materialized, the implications were great for the trade.

It was also reasonably obvious that traditional manufacturer labels in fashion merchandise were under siege by the aforementioned designer labels. Large numbers of department stores and mass merchandisers were trying to gain distinction handling such "prestige" labels and the use of the "boutique look" within their stores. It almost seemed that there were two fundamental strategies at work—the price-oriented mass-market appeal and the high-income, status appeal. The distinction between these two was somewhat clouded by the adoption of prestige labels by the more aggressive mass merchandisers. Even Sears Roebuck had relaxed its policy of carrying only house labels.

Adidas, Head, and Nike represented firms that had expanded into clothing from "hardware lines" (that is, shoes), whereas Levi Strauss experimented, not too successfully, with shoes. All of these firms, of course, vied for the same basic distribution system. At the retail level, the outlets could be classified as mass merchandisers (Sears), discounters (Marshalls and Mervyn's), department and specialty stores (R. H. Macy and I. Magnin), and a wide variety of small independents (sporting goods, shoe stores, running stores). These outlets could be reached through company salesmen, manufacturers' representatives, distributors, or even direct mail. Adidas, for example, covered the United States with four independent distributors; Levi Strauss used company salesmen; Nike employed manufacturers' representatives; and Sears Roebuck sold direct through mail order and/or retail stores.

Nike's niche in the industry was substantial. The firm appealed to the market on the basis of quality, technical innovation, and high performance, all of which attracted the serious runner. This acceptance by the experts was the lever to open up the mass markets. The product diffused into the channels starting with the high performance specialists and spreading into the mass outlets on the basis of this "expert" endorsement. Nike had also been aggressive in product-line extensions (such as leisure shoes and clothing). Whether or not to introduce a second label was a topic being discussed by senior management.

NIKE ORGANIZATION

One of the distinguishing characteristics of the company was its informal organization. From its beginning, Nike had been run as a small operation by a close-knit group of top managers. Most of them were sports enthusiasts and athletes and thus understood and appreciated the Nike line. A surprisingly large percentage also had legal or accounting backgrounds. But, as Phil Knight explained, "We mostly want people who are company experts, not functional experts." Problem solving, not specific technical knowledge, was the valued skill.

The organization chart shown in Exhibit 1 is therefore deceptive. It portrays the formal pieces of the organization, but not the way it works. Because apparel was a relatively new product line, it was still associated with footwear marketing (the same sales reps, for example, were involved), though sourcing and product development were separately handled.

EXHIBIT 1   Organization Chart

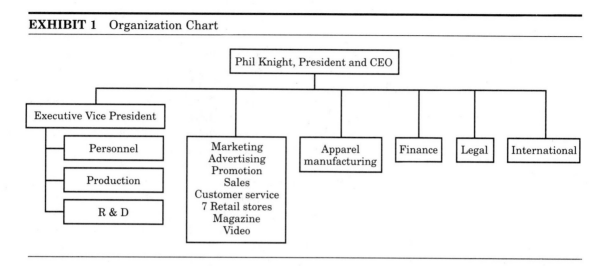

Management assignments across functions were normal. One senior manager had moved from legal to R&D, to lobbying, to marketing, and there were other equally dramatic assignment changes. Territorial imperatives were held to a minimum, and such words as budgeting, planning, and control were dirty ones—even though the company did have working systems. The emphasis was upon informality, willingness to change, experimentation, and mutual decision making. The Friday Club was the chief management tool of the company. This group of 11 top managers[1] was called together regularly, as Phil Knight laughingly described, "to shout at each other." The meetings were open and informal and everyone contributed with enthusiasm his ideas and solutions. Phil Knight played the catalyst role in eliciting ideas and in meshing the various personalities. There were no functional restrictions. The informality of these sessions was evident on one occasion when a visitor commented that Nike management "was a shambles." The next day at a follow-up meeting, each executive wore a T-shirt that said, "It's a shambles."

Even though the Friday Club was a key decision-making group, it wasn't as omnipotent as it might appear. In the first place, it was in practice a floating group with varying degrees of autonomy. There were five so-called old-timers who were really "the chairman's office" and who were considered the ultimate decision-making unit. The Friday Club itself could expand or shrink in size depending on the issue.

---

[1] These included in 1982: Chairman, Executive Vice President, Vice Presidents of Apparel, Finance, Production, Chief Counsel, Manager MIS, Vice President International, Director of Marketing, Treasurer, and Manager Far East Operation.

There had been some meetings, to illustrate, at which over 30 managers participated. Perhaps more important was the fact that reporting to these senior executives was a "conventional" organizational hierarchy. Marketing, to select one example, included research and advertising components while manufacturing had plant and quality assurance managers. The unique aspects of the Nike organization were the degree of mobility, the generalist perspective of the senior group, and the participative decision-making style.

HISTORY

Knight's enthusiasm for sports started early, and by his senior year in high school he was already an accomplished runner who had caught the eye of Bill Bowerman, the track and field coach at the University of Oregon. Knight attended that school and then received his MBA from Stanford in 1962. For one of his term papers, the budding entrepreneur developed an idea for a new business. He knew that running shoes were dominated by two German firms, Adidas and Puma, and he wondered why the Japanese couldn't do in shoes what they had already done in TV and cameras. After graduation from Stanford, Knight joined a CPA firm in Portland, Oregon, but as a sideline decided to import and sell Japanese running shoes. He traveled to Japan and contracted with Onitsuka to supply him with their Tiger line, as their exclusive agent for the 13 western states. He also persuaded his former track coach to join in the venture. Between them they invested $1,000 in inventory for shoes that cost $3.50 a pair but which they sold for $9.95. By 1966 the fledgling company had branched out to the East Coast, and by 1971 sales had reached just over $1,000,000. At this point Knight broadened his product line to include soccer, basketball, and tennis shoes.

In 1972 Onitsuka sought more control of its marketing and Knight decided to strike out on his own. Furthermore, even though his growth had been rapid—virtually doubling every year—it was still a small company and Knight was hard-pressed to obtain adequate financing. For each purchase, he had to put up a letter of credit that would tie up his credit for approximately 90 days. As luck would have it, he read a *Fortune* magazine article suggesting that Japanese trading companies could, among other things, extend credit on flexible terms, though at a slight premium. A few inquiries unearthed Nissho-Iwai, the sixth-largest trading company in Japan, and Knight and Nissho-Iwai soon agreed to a deal. Through Nissho-Iwai, Knight also acquired some manufacturing contacts who agreed to produce shoes to Nike's specifications.

The Nissho-Iwai deal gave Nike an important financial and business ally that made subsequent rapid growth possible. By putting up the necessary letters of credit every month, Nisshoi-Iwai freed Nike to concentrate on operating matters. In fact, the trading company went well beyond the strict limits of the agreement and gave Nike much needed flexibility. Nissho-Iwai served, furthermore, as the financial and administrative intermediary between Nike and the contract manufacturers. During these same early days, Phil established a strong accounts receivable group, which managed to keep receivables in line despite the explosive growth in sales.

The development of these contract manufacturers was an early preoccupation of top management. A traditional problem in the leisure shoe industry had been the lack of dependable supply and delivery, particularly for the retailers. Knight saw this as an opportunity. He first tied up a considerable percentage of the available shoe capacity in Japan and later in Taiwan and Korea. These vendors were delighted to supply such a fast-growing and profitable customer. By 1982 the company's production was centered in 28 plants, and over 80 percent of this production was in Taiwan and Korea. There were three plants in the United States. Knight also introduced a futures program for retailers, whereby the company guaranteed the price and delivery terms for any retailer who ordered six months in advance. Exhibit 2 shows how the system worked.

Since 65 percent of the orders followed this sequence, the futures program in effect served as a planning device by giving Nike reasonably accurate sales forecasts and shipment schedules. By 1982 monthly shipments were averaging 4.5 million pair. The other 35 percent of the

---

EXHIBIT 2   Illustrative Data

Date	Event	Elapsed Time
March 30	Retailer places order with Nike (order is noncancelable by the retailer and guaranteed by Nike)	0
April 15	Nike places order with NIAC (Nissho-Iwai American Corp.)	15 days
April 25	NIAC orders from the plant	25 days
July 30	Plant completes manufacturing and ships order	120 days
September 1	Shoes come to warehouse in Seattle, Boston, or Memphis	150 days
September 15	Shoes shipped to retailer	165 days

EXHIBIT 3   Cost Buildup

Cost to manufacturer (for a Korean plant)	$1.00
Price from Nissho-Iwai Corp. (Japan)	1.04
Price from Nissho-Iwai, U.S. (this is Nike cost)	1.08 + interest (near prime)
Price to the retail store	1.60
Price to the consumer	2.80–3.00

---

orders were placed by the dealers on a "when needed" basis. Delivery, in this second case, was not guaranteed.

Production costs were low and flexible, but quality was high because all output was made to Nike specifications and the firm maintained its own quality control staff at each plant. In fact, the first expatriate employee was assigned to Taiwan in 1976. Exhibit 3 summarizes the cost building from a hypothetical $1 manufacturing base.

As one of the early employees of the firm said: "Product control is our forte." Indeed, the plants had considerable product flexibility and could easily handle volume swings of 25 to 35 percent. The three U.S. plants were useful as a backup to the overseas contractors.

INNOVATION

Another early focus of Nike management was product innovation. Bowerman, for example, was a particularly creative individual who contributed the famous "waffle sole" (though at the expense of his wife's waffle iron). In fact, when Nike originally split from the Onitsuka group, the founders took with them two important product innovations that they had developed on their own time. Management's interest in innovation was so high that in 1974, while still small, the firm bought a factory in Exeter, New Hampshire, and dedicated it to R&D. This group subsequently developed a number of major innovations, including the airsole, the nylon top, and the full-cushioned mid-sole.

Innovation, in practice, was a constant give and take between marketing, production, and Exeter. For example, as marketing identified new product needs, it asked Exeter to conduct extensive research and testing in design and biomechanics.

Phil Knight, was an important innovator in an even broader sense—not only in product but also in several aspects of the operations. He was described by one colleague as "farsighted and alert to new opportunities." To be specific, Knight foresaw the desirability of expanding production out of Japan, the opportunity in a guaranteed retailer delivery system, the potential of manufacturing in China, and the advantages of working with a trading company instead of a bank. Moreover, he anticipated a number of market changes and moved his company into other sports shoes (basketball, court, cleated, etc.), a children's line, nonathletic leisure and work shoes, and clothing. The firm's early concentration on running represented superb timing (either by luck or brilliant deduction) and positioned Nike in the consumer's mind as "a running company."

MARKETING

The marketing program was developed over several years. To start, the company hired sales representatives who, of necessity, were new, enthusiastic, hardworking shoe amateurs. They were supervised by East Coast and West Coast field managers. The number of representatives was gradually increased and their territories decreased, until in 1982 there were 28 representative organizations employing 180 salespeople. Some carried other lines; some did not. But all had thrived under Nike and depended upon the firm for their well-being. Sales were so large that representative commissions averaged 2½ percent instead of the more traditional 6 percent.

The representatives sold to 8,000 retailers who operated 13,000 outlets. Almost 2,500 of these outlets were classified as mass merchandisers, 2,500 specialty (i.e., running) stores, 1,500 sporting goods, and the rest shoe stores and miscellaneous. The premier mass merchandiser for Nike was J. C. Penney, which was added in 1977 before Nike was particularly well known. (Adidas elected to go through J. C. Penney in 1981.) Quite obviously, the distribution system was effective and covered a wide range of clientele—from low-end to high-end specialty. Furthermore, the Nike line, priced between $19.95 and $70, was broad enough to accommodate each segment. Those relatively few dealers who sold primarily the top of the line to the serious, innovative runners were handled through a "Torch program" and received special attention. For all dealers, Nike offered a number of special inducements: a generous 46 percent margin, guaranteed prices and delivery, and a coordinated program of promotions, advertising, training, and sponsorships. As between footwear and apparel, the retail stores employed by Nike split out as follows: shoes only 25 percent; apparel only 25 percent; both 50 percent.

Nike also owned and operated seven retail stores. Their volume of $4 million was minor, but they were regarded as valuable training centers. There were no expansion plans.

The distribution story was different overseas where Nike was just beginning to expand. In Europe the jogging boom had not yet taken off, though Nike expected that it would. Adidas and Puma dominated the European distribution system and concentrated on the huge soccer market. These German competitors would not be easy to replace, particularly since their loss of market in the United States. As one industry executive stated: "Adidas and Puma will let the other American companies do whatever they want in Europe because they're not much of a threat. But after what Nike did to them in the U.S., they simply will not let themselves be embarrassed in their own backyards." It would not be easy for Nike to gain dealers whose livelihood depended on Adidas and Puma.

Japan was an easier target. Not only did the Japanese perceive American products as high quality, but also Nike had had years of contact with that market. England was another attractive market. Nike acquired its distributorships and also opened a manufacturing plant there to permit inexpensive access to the European markets.

Nike's promotion and advertising strategy was another ingredient of its success. The company to start, employed a pull, not a push, approach built around its distinctive "swoosh" trademark. Exhibit 4 shows how its recent $18 million budget was spent.

The critical part of Nike's selling approach was the endorsement by these athletic "heroes." From the firm's first endorsers—Steve Prefontaine and Geoff Petrie—the list grew to include 40 percent of the players in the National Basketball Association, a large percentage of the top runners, and such individual stars as John McEnroe, Sebastian Coe and Dan Fouts. As one of the Nike managers said: "These athletes are our promotional team."

The effectiveness of Nike's strategies was reflected in their financial statements. (See Exhibits 5 and 6.)

EXHIBIT 4   Budget Allocation (percent)

25%	Product advertising in such vertical publications as *Running* and *The Runner*—stressing general concepts like cushioning and shoe weight. Point-of-sale devices such as a retailer poster program, the use of technical tags and brochures, and dealer clinics.
25%	Dealer co-op advertising where Nike would match the dealers' advertising outlays up to a specified limit.
50%	Promotions that included free goods and/or cash payment to about 2,500 athletes as well as the sponsorship of selected athletic events (including a women's pro-tennis circuit).

EXHIBIT 5   Nike, Inc. Profit and Loss Summaries, 1981–1979

	1981	*1980*	*1979*
Revenues	457,742	269,775	149,830
Cost of sales	328,133	196,683	103,466
Selling and administrative	60,953	39,810	22,815
Interest	17,859	9,144	4,569
Other	92	107	(443)
Income before taxes	50,705	24,031	19,423
Taxes	24,750	11,526	9,700
Net income	25,955	12,505	9,723
Earnings per share	1.52	.77	.58
Breakdown of sales:			
Domestic footwear	398,852	245,100	143,400
Domestic apparel	33,108	8,100	2,200
Foreign sales	25,782	16,575	4,230
Total	457,742	269,775	149,830

CURRENT CONCERNS

Obviously, Nike had been a tremendous success. Nonetheless, size created its own problems and caused Phil Knight to review more specifically some of the important marketing issues. The channels, as a case in point, represented one such area of concern. To quote from a company document:

> Given the present management's obsession with increased "numbers," it is not surprising that we are witnessing an increased emphasis on self-service in branded footwear retail sales. You need only look as far as the local G. I. Joe's, J. C. Penney, Meir & Frank, or Athletic Shoe Factory Outlet to see why the technical portion of our line is so badly misunderstood. In self-service retail outlets, you are hard pressed to find any sales help, let alone well-informed assistance from users of athletic footwear. Perhaps it is a function of our stagnant economy, but every retailer is talking about how to reduce his "selling costs" by employing mass merchant mentality, i.e., read *Proportionally Fewer Customer Service-Oriented Retail Outlets* to intelligently sell our technical line.
>
> With a significantly smaller and diminishing percentage of our products being sold in specialty or Torch accounts, it is no wonder that our reputation is being redefined in the consumer's mind with descriptive phrases such as, "Low-End, Non-Technical, Pricepoint and Promotional." The bulk of our sales volume is now attributable to dealers who are providing less and less

EXHIBIT 6

NIKE, INC.
Balance Sheet
For Years Ended May 31, 1981, and 1980

	May 31, 1981	May 31, 1980
Assets		
Cash	1,792	1,827
Accounts receivable	87,236	63,861
Inventories	120,229	55,941
Deferred taxes	1,300	135
Prepaid expenses	2,487	2,151
Current assets	213,044	123,915
Property, plant, equipment	23,845	14,193
Accumulated depreciation	(7,673)	(4,027)
Other assets	1,073	534
Total assets	230,289	134,615
Liabilities		
Current portion of debt	6,620	3,867
Notes payable	61,190	36,500
Accounts payable	42,492	36,932
Accrued liabilities	15,401	10,299
Income taxes payable	12,654	6,693
Current liabilities	138,357	94,291
Long-term debt	8,611	11,268
Common stock	28,600*	71
Retained earnings	54,721	28,985
Total liabilities	230,289	134,615

* In 1981, Nike went public with the sale of 1,360,000 shares of common stock, with Knight retaining 51% of the outstanding shares.

point-of-purchase information about how our shoes perform to customers as retailers strive for more volume and fine tune their selling efficiency. The result of this shift in selling technique and brand identity puts increased pressure on Nike to pre-sell our products while making the shoes easily visible and recognizable as high-quality, innovative products.

In the midst of the recent frenzied growth of mass consumption of branded athletic footwear, there has developed a reaction among both the more technically aware and prestige-seeking, affluent consumers to distinguish themselves from the pack. With increased discretionary buying power, these consumers are demanding high-tech products and are willing to "pay a little more to get just what I wanted." This *is* the segment of the market we have ignored and, as a result, have been losing to New Balance, Tiger, and

Saucony. If Nike is going to continue to have mass volume sales and retain a strong share of the high-end sales, it is obvious we need to segment the product line and distinguish the product in this market so that it appeals to the high-tech, affluent consumers.

The High-Tech segment of the branded market is becoming substantially more crowded with new products and new brands. This is particularly true of running flats. Avia, for example, is gearing its entire entrance into the technical branded segments of the athletic footwear market with advertising and packaging that connotes high technology and new design innovations. Advanced technologies (materials, construction techniques) are creating a more confusing product environment for consumers to make buying decisions in. The expanded array of products and advertised product features, each (Puma, New Balance, Tiger) claiming to perform breakthroughs in sports research, is making our brand prey to slick (well-segmented) marketing strategies.

Of particular note was the recent incursion by some mass merchandisers into the high end of the shoe market. Mervyn's, to be specific, in early 1982 sold 300 pairs of Nike's newest technical product at very low prices. Nike received the income, to be sure, but was unable to capitalize in the consumer's mind on the technical advantage of the new product. To the consumer, it was only a price deal.

Another matter of worry had to do with individual responsibilities as opposed to companywide responsibilities. Size had increased the breadth and depth of the various lines. For example, there were over 200 shoe types alone. But, as no one was responsible for any one line, this led to a lack of focus and attention to details in several lines. Moreover, as implied earlier, there were few formal lines of communication and very little hierarchy between managers and locations. And finally, in Phil's opinion, the company was relying on too few key people who were close friends and saw the company as fun more than as a business.

It was within this special environment that Phil was considering his possible moves. It was not easy to trade off more control and formality against the current organizational culture. And yet he was very much aware that the market's and his own company's evolution required a new look at how to organize for growth.

Although he had thought about the implications and was well aware that there were other choices, Knight thought he might ask the Friday Club to consider the implications of eight alternatives.

1. *Do nothing.* Knight was sensitive to the real possibility that any kind of significant move might "spoil" the existing ambiance. After all, the organization had worked and had evolved a number of valuable attributes—informality, dynamism, and flexibility. Moreover, there was a minimum of territorial imperative within Nike: managers were not expected to build walls around their piece of the operation. On the contrary, open teamwork was expected. Over time, it was not surprising that the culture of the firm was well understood. The nuances of day by day interaction were as well developed as small talk between husband and wife.

Knight also considered it valuable that the footwear and apparel operations had been closely associated. Even though production for each was individually supervised, the marketing and sales were interdependent. The sales reps, to be specific, carried both lines.

It should be recognized, finally, that the organization with its functional orientation (namely marketing and manufacturing) focused upon these broad skills rather than separate products and markets. Presumably the functions would receive greater focus and hence deliver a higher level of generic expertise.

2. *Divisionalize (and decentralize) by product category.* But size and rapid growth still bothered Knight: Could the old informality continue? One alternative format is shown in Exhibit 7. Each division would be a profit center and control a number of key activities. If this option were accepted, there remained a number of knotty questions:

- Which activities would you assign to the divisions and which to corporate?

EXHIBIT 7

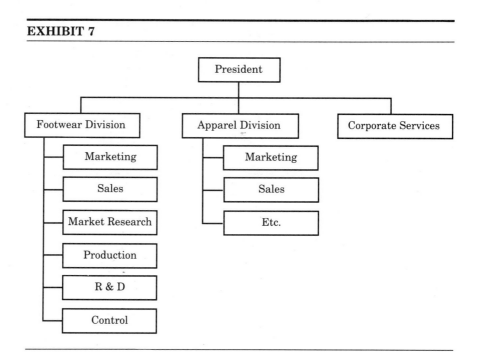

- Would you totally separate footwear and apparel and, if so, how would you handle the salesforce?
- Would the corporate services respond to divisional requests or initiate the requests?

3. *Organize by channel.* Since there were two levels of buyers, customers (or the retailers), and consumers, why not two levels of organization? The advertising and promotional efforts would be directed at consumer segments while the in-store selling and other channel efforts would be directed at retail segments. Thus, one might consider the format shown in Exhibit 8. Such an orientation would recognize the power of the trade and the need to comprehend the needs and strategies of each major retail type.

There would be, of course, some tough problems such as duplicate product managers since the channels are not mutually exclusive in their choice of products. This organizational variation would marry footwear and apparel, which would facilitate the use of a single salesforce. Unfortunately the distribution of retail outlets between shoes and apparel might cause complications.

Maybe the biggest problem would be that of finding executives sufficiently skilled in retail operations to make everything work.

4. *Organize by markets or segments.* This variation would be a further recognition that consumer segmentation is primary. Perhaps there should be geographic "operations" such as Nike east, west, south, and north. This orientation already existed to the extent that there was an international and domestic operation.

There were, needless to say, other segmentation alternatives such as demography, income, or application (runners versus spectators).

5. *Fragment the marketing function.* This approach would permit the various marketing activities (research, sales, advertising, etc.) to specialize and develop as "service centers" for the operations. The

---

EXHIBIT 8

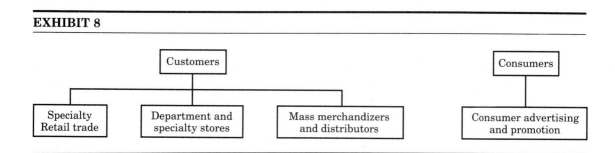

EXHIBIT 9

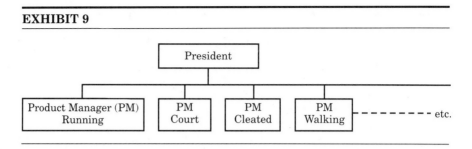

other extreme would be to pool all of these pieces into a centrally directed marketing department.

6. *Product management system.* This orientation might include the management shown in Exhibit 9. Each PM would be similar to a division manager but would probably have fewer responsibilities and be responsible primarily for the marketing mix.

In traditional product management systems, the manager has no direct authority over the separate business activities, rather the PM serves as a strategist, coordinator, and persuader who gets the job done through the efforts of others. One of the problems associated with this form of organization is to identify and develop young managers able to assume considerable responsibility without much authority.

7. *Split the marketing group into "established businesses" and "new opportunities."* Knight recognized that this organizational variation was a bit unorthodox, but he was intrigued with its recognition of two fundamental skills: old and new businesses. Whether such a split should include all the activities of the business or just selected ones, such as sales, R&D, and advertising, was an open question.

8. *Establish "task forces" to handle critical problem areas as they arise.* The comforting aspect of this alternative was that it was reasonably similar to the present policy of "throwing" people at problems. The concept of a series of task forces, however, was a bit more formal but had the potential danger of developing a "keep-your-hands-off" attitude among the teams.

Task forces, nevertheless, did reinforce the company's flexible approach to management and would permit the firm to concentrate on critical issues. The question might be raised, however, that task forces might be difficult to coordinate: the results might be a series of discrete, although separately effective, decisions.

Case 6–13   *Parke-Davis Professional Health Group**

In May 1984 Mr. Marvin Skripitsky, the marketing director of the Parke-Davis Professional Health Group, was in the process of preparing the 1985 Strategic Plan recommendations for his group. A formal presentation of his recommendations was to be made to Mr. Robert Serenbetz, the president of Warner-Lambert Canada, at the end of May. As Mr. Skripitsky reviewed the Group's situation, he was convinced that the most pressing problem facing the Group was the lack of detailing capacity in the sales force. The Professional Health Group was planning to introduce a number of new products over the next three years and there appeared to be insufficient sales force time available to adequately present new and existing products (i.e., to "detail" the products) to the medical community. He viewed this inability to properly promote the Group's pharmaceutical products as the major barrier to meeting the Group's growth objectives. Mr. Skripitsky knew that he, in consultation with Mr. Malcolm Seath, the general manager of the Health Care Division, and Mr. Gerry Gibson, the Group's director of sales, would have to make specific recommendations for dealing with the detailing capacity problem at the presentation to Mr. Serenbetz.

COMPANY

Parke-Davis was the pharmaceutical affiliate of Warner-Lambert, a major U.S.-based multinational. With worldwide sales of over $3.1 billion (U.S.) Warner-Lambert manufactured a wide range of pharmaceutical, personal care, and other products, including such well-known brands as Listerine, Chiclets and Schick. Parke-Davis had been founded in Detroit, Michigan, in 1866, and the company began operations in Canada in 1887, making it the second pharmaceutical company to operate in Canada. Over the years Parke-Davis had pioneered many significant health-care products including the first antidiptheric serum in 1893, Dilantin for the control of epilepsy in 1938, Benadryl the first antihistamine in North America in 1946, and in 1949 Chloro-

---

* This case was prepared by Professor Adrian B. Ryans. Copyright © 1985, The School of Business Administration, The University of Western Ontario. Used by permission.

mycetin the first wide-spectrum antibiotic to be discovered. Parke-Davis was acquired by Warner-Lambert in 1970. In 1979 Parke-Davis and Warner-Chilcott, the original pharmaceutical division of Warner-Lambert, were merged into one division to become the pharmaceutical component of Warner-Lambert Canada Inc. In 1983 Parke-Davis was merged with Warner Lambert's Personal Products business unit to form a new Health Care Division. In 1984 the Health Care Division was projected to have sales of $87 million with Parke-Davis accounting for $62 million of these sales.

Health Care Division

The mission of the Health Care Division was to be a Canadian leader in developing and providing pharmaceutical and personal care products for health and well-being while achieving steady growth in sales and profits. In the five-year strategic planning period beginning in 1985, the division was targeting for annual sales growth 4 percent above the level of inflation to achieve sales of approximately $133 million by 1989. Management of the Health Care Division believed that this objective was attainable, since the division enjoyed a number of major strengths, including a planned stream of major new products during the planning period, a broadly based product line that was not dependent on one or two major products or product categories, and a strong clinical trial and registration capability to expedite the approval of new pharmaceuticals and new claims for existing products. In addition, Parke-Davis had a strong image in the minds of consumers, pharmacists, doctors, and government. Most image studies placed Parke-Davis within the top five firms on almost every image criterion. This strong corporate image was useful in gaining access to doctors and the drug trade, and was helpful in developing and maintaining a consumer franchise for smaller nonprescription brands that could not support direct consumer advertising. While the broadly based product line was a strength in many respects, it also represented a weakness in that it made it difficult for the sales force to find the time to adequately detail all the products to the doctors. In addition, many physicians no longer viewed Parke-Davis as an innovator, since the product line was relatively old. A successful introduction of the planned new products was expected to correct this.

In Canada, the Health Care Division comprised two major groups: the Consumer Health Group and the Professional Health Group. Because both Warner-Chilcott and Parke-Davis had several big proprietary and OTC pharmaceuticals in 1979, the merger resulted in the

Consumer Health Group becoming the largest supplier of self-medication products in Canada, including such well-known brands as Benylin, Agarol, Sinutab and Gelusil.[1] These products were sold under the Parke-Davis name. The Consumer Health Group also marketed a wide range of personal care products (including Listerine, Bromo, Softsoap, Showermate, Schick, Topol, and Lensrins) that were distributed through drug stores and other convenient retail outlets. In addition to its extensive line of prescription ethical pharmaceuticals the Professional Health Group was responsible for promoting *selected* Consumer Health Group brands, such as Benylin, a major brand of cough syrup, to physicians. The general manager of the Health Care Division was Mr. Malcolm Seath.

Professional Health Group

The 1984 sales of the Professional Health Group were forecasted to be $33 million and the Group had an objective of increasing sales to over $50 million by 1989. Direct cost of goods sold and freight typically amounted to about 25 percent of selling price. During this period the Professional Health Group hoped to increase its market share in ethical (prescription) pharmaceuticals from 1.8 percent to 2.2 percent. The Professional Health Group was headed by the marketing director, Mr. Marvin Skripitsky. Reporting to the marketing director were two group product managers and the director of sales, Mr. Gerry Gibson. A simplified organization chart for the Group is shown in Exhibit 1. By 1984 the sales force consisted of 56 medical representatives, 4 medical information associates, 8 district managers and 3 regional managers.

The Professional Health Group was responsible for the 24 products or product groups shown in Exhibit 2. The Professional Health Group planned to add 15 products to this product line over the next three years, with these products having potential sales of over $25 million by 1989.

---

[1] Pharmaceutical products were usually divided into ethical and proprietary categories, depending on how they were marketed by the manufacturer. Ethical products were marketed directly to the medical profession, whereas proprietary products were promoted directly to the consumer. Ethical products were commonly divided into two further categories: prescription pharmaceuticals and over-the-counter (OTC) pharmaceuticals. As the name implies, prescription pharmaceuticals were available only on a prescription written by a physician. OTC pharmaceuticals could be purchased by the consumer without a prescription.

EXHIBIT 1 Partial Organization Chart of the Health Care Division

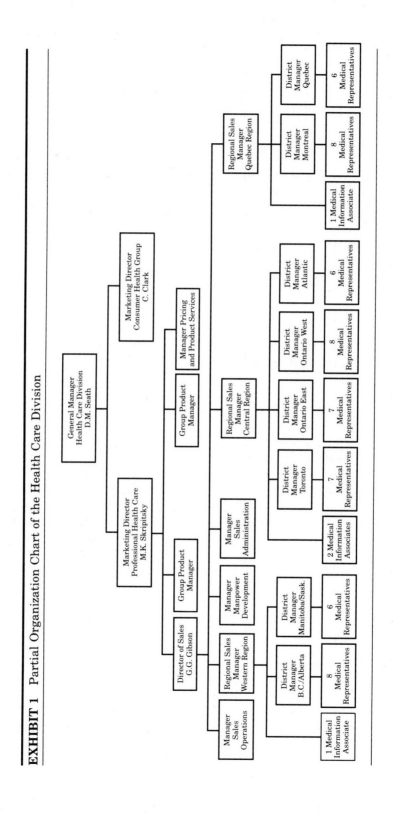

EXHIBIT 2   Parke-Davis Products

Anticonvulsants	Nardil
Prescription hemorrhoidals	Nicrostat
(Anusol)	Oral contraceptives
Amsa	Peritrate
Benadryl	Ponstan
Choledyl	Tucks
Chloro/Vira–A	Tedral
Colymycin	Thrombostat
Elase	Pyridium
Eryc	Mandelamine
Hose	Beben
Lopid	Vanquin
Mylanta	

INDUSTRY ENVIRONMENT

Management of the Health Care Division saw both threats and opportunities in the external environment. Health care costs were expected to continue to increase faster than the economy as a whole due to technological developments and an aging population. Although management felt that pharmaceuticals were the most cost-effective part of the health care system, they believed that pharmaceuticals would continue to attract the attention of politicians and others responsible for controlling health care costs. Some provinces had adopted "formularies" in an attempt to control pharmaceutical costs. In these cases the provincial government would only pay for pharmaceuticals listed in the formulary for people who were receiving government assistance in paying for pharmaceuticals. In addition, management believed that the increasing complexity of the health care system would force politicians to give more power to bureaucrats who would be perceived as "unbiased." In this environment access to key politicians and bureaucrats would be key.

Insurance companies, which paid at least some drug bills for 70 percent of Canadians, were expected to become increasingly important. Historically they had been passive participants in the health care system, paying whatever pharmacists charged for whatever pharmaceuticals were prescribed by doctors. Some were now attempting to restrict the choice of pharmaceuticals for which they would provide full reimbursement and in some cases they were attempting to force mandatory substitution of generic drugs.

On the more positive side there was a growing feeling in the industry that the federal government might change Canada's compulsory licensing laws to encourage more innovation in pharmaceuticals in Canada and to encourage more pharmaceutical firms to conduct more of their research in Canada. The compulsory licensing law in Canada required the patent-holding manufacturer to license patented products to other manufacturers.

Parke-Davis executives continued to believe that the keys to growth in the pharmaceutical industry in Canada would be the development of innovative new products and strong marketing of these products.

MARKET FOR PHARMACEUTICAL PRODUCTS IN CANADA

The total market for ethical and proprietary pharmaceutical products in Canada was more than $2.5 billion, with 17 percent of these sales being made to hospitals. The medical community in Canada comprised about 43,000 doctors and over 1,000 hospitals. There were also almost 5,000 retail pharmacies in Canada.

Competition

The overall pharmaceutical industry in Canada was highly competitive, with the largest company, American Home Products, having less than 8 percent market share of the combined ethical and proprietary pharmaceutical market sold through hospitals and drug stores. An additional 14 companies had market shares greater than 2 percent. The various divisions of Warner-Lambert had a combined market share of over 3 percent. Most of these companies were broad-line pharmaceutical companies. Competition in the industry seemed to be increasing, with the recent entry of major nonpharmaceutical companies through the acquisition of small pharmaceutical companies. Both Procter & Gamble and Dow Chemical had entered the market, using this mechanism, in the early 1980s.

By the end of 1983 there were a total of 55 pharmaceutical companies with sales forces operating in Canada. The number of medical representatives employed by these companies are shown in Exhibit 3. Some of the major competitors operated under more than one name and corporate structure. American Home Products operated under the Wyeth, Ayerst, and Whitehall names. Johnson & Johnson sold its products under the Ortho, Johnson & Johnson, McNeil, and Janssen names. Several companies, including both American Home Products and Johnson & Johnson, had more than one sales force. Merck Frosst, the company with the largest number of medical representatives in Canada had three different sales forces operating under different

EXHIBIT 3 Number of Medical Representatives Employed by Competitors in Canada

Size of Sales Force*	Number of Companies
0–10	3
11–20	4
21–30	9
31–40	4
41–50	15
51–60	13
61–70	6
71 or greater	1
Total number of sales forces	55

* Excludes managers and OTC representatives.

names, with almost 140 representatives at the end of 1983. When a company had more than one sales force, they usually operated under the names of different divisions (often the names of predecessor companies). Thus Johnson & Johnson had two sales forces operating under the McNeil and Ortho names individually. Earlier in 1984, one relatively small pharmaceutical company, Boehringer-Ingelheim, had added a second sales force. These two sales forces were using the same name, and the calling cards of the salespersons simply indicated that they were specialists in particular therapeutic classes. It was too early to measure the acceptance of this approach by the medical community. The large number of sales forces meant that the competition for a doctor's time was intense—Mr. Gibson estimated that some doctors could have as many as 40 to 50 medical representatives trying to see them in a given two-month period.

All the major brand name manufacturers of pharmaceuticals faced competition from generic manufacturers.

The Selling of Ethical Pharmaceuticals in Canada

Medical representatives (over 25,000 of them in North America alone) played a key role in the selling of ethical pharmaceuticals. Often called "detail men" (although they were increasingly women) for the details they provide doctors and pharmacists about pharmaceuticals, they played a key role in trying to convince doctors to prescribe their company's pharmaceuticals to the doctor's patients. Many market research studies concluded that doctors relied very heavily on medical representatives for information on prescribing pharmaceuticals. Some authorities suggested that the success of a new pharmaceutical could depend almost as much on the effectiveness of the medical representatives promoting the new product as on the product itself. The medical profession was faced with the difficult problem of keeping up with the flood of new pharmaceuticals that were continually becoming available. While the pharmaceuticals in major therapeutic product classes—such as those designed to treat heart disease—shared many similarities, the differences could be critical to the patients using the pharmaceutical. Detail men played a crucial role in providing the kind of information that would help a doctor decide whether a particular pharmaceutical was appropriate for a particular patient's condition. Many doctors, particularly harried general practitioners with a diverse practice, found it difficult to keep up with all the literature on the products that they might use in their practice, and they appreciated the information a detail man could provide. A well-trained detail man could provide the doctor with information on the chemical composition of the pharmaceutical, its possible side effects, and how it would interact with other medicines a patient might be taking. From the pharmaceutical company's point of view detail men provided a valuable feedback channel sometimes alerting the company to side effects that might not have been noticed before. Detail men also frequently organized symposia for groups of doctors, often bringing in outside medical authorities to help bring doctors up-to-date on current medical practice and pharmaceuticals. Major pharmaceutical companies regularly had their representatives set up displays in major hospitals in their territories. These displays of products and literature were staffed by the representative and many doctors dropped by after their morning rounds in the hospital or at the end of the working day.

One of the toughest jobs many detail men faced was getting past the receptionist or the nurse in a doctor's office, particularly when the office was crowded and the doctor was behind schedule. Increasingly, doctors were establishing rules that they would only see one medical representative a day. Parke-Davis representatives tried to make appointments with the doctor ahead of time, when this was possible. Even when the medical representative got into the doctor's office the doctor might keep the representative waiting and might be interrupted by a nurse or a telephone call during their conversation. The representative typically only had 5 to 10 minutes to make his presentation. During the presentation he might place primary emphasis on one or two products with brief reminders about one or two others. The pharmaceuticals presented to a particular doctor depended on the nature of the doctor's specialty and practice. Doctors frequently asked questions about products or might have questions about the appropriateness of particular products in a given situation.

Parke-Davis sales representatives were expected to make 5 to 6 calls per day on doctors, about two calls per day on retail pharmacies and perhaps one call every two days on a hospital. As did many other major pharmaceutical companies, Parke-Davis divided each year into six two-month sales cycles. A major planning issue was the decision as to which one or two products should get primary emphasis in each of these sales cycles for each medical specialty. Each medical representative attempted to call on all the doctors, retail pharmacies, and hospitals targeted by Parke-Davis at least once during each sales cycle. By 1984 Parke-Davis was targeting its sales force at some 18,000 doctors out of the 43,000 in Canada, and at over 80 percent of the retail pharmacies. The approximate Parke-Davis coverage of physicians and retail pharmacies by province is shown in Exhibit 4.

THE PROFESSIONAL HEALTH GROUP SALES FORCE

Organization

The field sales force of 60 persons was divided into two groups: the 56 medical representatives and 4 medical information associates (MIAs). The medical representatives were organized into eight geographical districts, each headed by a district manager, and had responsibility for detailing the full Professional Health Group product line to the medical community in their geographical territories.

In 1983 top management of the Professional Health Group had become very concerned about the ability of the medical representatives to detail their large existing product line, and at the same time introduce the large number of sophisticated new products that were planned in the future. The introduction of a sophisticated new pharmaceutical often required that the medical representative focus on key specialists and other potential opinion leaders. Since the medical representatives had largely been trying to maintain sales of existing products rather than introduce new ones over the preceding three or four years, they often were not actively working these key specialists. To overcome this problem, management decided to add a small number of more sophisticated representatives with stronger medical and pharmacological training, and very strong communication skills. These representatives would specialize in launching new products and would do the initial follow-up with doctors after the launch of the product. Given their strong educational background and the fact that at any point in time they would be focusing on a very small number of new products, it would be possible to provide them with more in-depth knowledge about each new product than could be given to the medical representatives.

EXHIBIT 4 Coverage of Physicians and Retail Pharmacies by Parke-Davis Sales Force (by province)

	British Columbia	Alberta	Saskatchewan	Manitoba	Ontario	Quebec	Atlantic Provinces	Total Canada
Physicians:								
Total physicians*	5,180	3,310	1,410	1,870	15,900	12,470	3,340	43,480
Covered by Parke-Davis	1,750	1,400	700	700	6,300	4,550	1,750	17,500
Percent covered	33.8%	42.3%	49.7%	37.4%	39.6%	36.5%	52.4%	40.2%
Retail pharmacies:								
Total retail pharmacies	593	559	229	285	1,648	1,079	502	4,965
Covered by Parke-Davis	400	320	160	160	1,440	1,040	400	4,000
Percent covered	67.5%	57.5%	53.5%	56.1%	87.4%	96.4%	79.7%	80.6%

* This includes all physicians registered in a province. Not all physicians registered in a province were active in a medical practice. For example, some were retired or employed in teaching, research, or administrative positions.

The company began to add the MIAs in 1983. They were also given geographical territories, but these territories were obviously much larger than those of the medical representatives, since four of them had to cover the whole of Canada. The four MIAs reported directly to the regional managers. Two were assigned to the Central Region and one each to the Quebec and Western Regions.

Recruiting and Selection

In selecting new representatives the Professional Health Group sought individuals with a strong background in one of the health sciences. Most recent recruits had Bachelor's degrees in Science, Nursing, or Pharmacy. Some were recruited directly out of university, but many had worked in the health care industry before joining Parke-Davis. One recent recruit was a registered nurse with several years of nursing experience in a hospital. Another was a pharmacist in his early 30s, who had become bored with the routine of dispensing pharmaceuticals and the long hours associated with operating a retail pharmacy.

Training

After joining Parke-Davis each medical representative attended two two-week training programs in Toronto. This training included material on Parke-Davis, and intensive training on biology and pharmacology, product information on the Parke-Davis product line, and some basic selling skills training. Between the sessions the representative was in his or her territory under the close supervision of the district manager. Training was a continuing process in any pharmaceutical company, with each representative receiving training in new products as they were introduced. When a major new product was introduced, it was common to provide the representatives with programmed learning materials, followed by an intensive two-day training meeting in Toronto. Many salespersons were also continually trying to update their skills by reading textbooks and a variety of other medical and pharmacological information made available to them by their companies. About every two years all medical representatives come to Toronto for an intensive "refresher" sales training course.

Compensation

Parke-Davis compensated its representatives using a base salary plus bonus compensation plan. In 1984 base salaries for representatives varied from $21,000 for a new sales trainee with no experience to

$36,000 for a senior sales representative. In addition, each representative was eligible for a regional bonus of up to 15 percent of base salary and an individual merit bonus of up to 10 percent of base salary. Thus a high-performing medical representative could earn as much as $45,000 plus fringe benefits and the use of a company automobile.

The regional bonus was based on the region's success in meeting sales objectives. For the purpose of calculating the regional bonus, the product line was divided into A, B, and C brands. "A" brands were those that in the opinion of management were the most profitable and had the greatest potential for future growth. "B" brands included high-volume brands with less potential for growth, but whose sales should be maintained. "C" brands included all other brands, which were not typically actively promoted. Management established objectives for each of the three groups of brands for each of the three regions and performance against these objectives was measured. Approximately 55 percent of the bonus was applied to the achievement of the A objective, 30 percent to the achievement of the B objective, and 15 percent to the achievement of the C objective. If a region met exactly 100 percent of its objectives for each group of brands each member of the regional team would receive a bonus of 10.5 percent of base salary. If 102 percent or more of the objective for each group was met, the full 15 percent bonus was awarded. Management did not believe it was feasible to do this monitoring at lower than a region level due to the difficulty of establishing exactly which representative or even district was responsible for a given sale. It was not uncommon for a prescription to be written by a doctor in one city, for the prescription to be filled at a retail pharmacy in another city, and for that pharmacy to have its drugs shipped from a warehouse in a different province.

The individual bonus was based on the district manager's judgment of the individual's contribution relative to others in the region. In order to make this judgment the district manager reviewed territory sales data, call activity and other activities, such as the number of symposia organized by the representative and the number of physicians who attended these symposia. The individual bonus decisions had to be reviewed and approved by the responsible regional manager and Mr. Gibson. District managers were in a good position to make this subjective judgment since they spent at least one day every month in the field with each of the representatives they supervised.

Performance Appraisal

Each representative was formally reviewed once a year by his or her manager. In this performance appraisal the district manager carefully reviewed the representative's achievements since the last review and any areas of concern. Particular attention was paid to the employee's skills in managing the work and in dealing with other people. The manager also focused on the individual's promotability and training and development needs. Each performance appraisal was reviewed by the regional manager and Mr. Gibson.

Motivation

A sales meeting was held once during each of the six sales cycles during the year. These meetings played an important role in the training and motivation of the sales force. Frequently these meetings would be held at the district level, but occasionally regional or national meetings would be held, particularly when a major new program or product was about to be launched.

THE DETAILING CAPACITY PROBLEM

In the strategic planning process for the Parke-Davis Professional Health Group in May 1984, Mr. Seath, Mr. Skripitsky, and Mr. Gibson viewed the Professional Health Group's lack of detailing capacity as its most pressing problem. The Group had launched Eryc, a major new antibiotic, in December 1983 with a first-year sales objective of $600,000. While the MIA sales force had played a major role in the prelaunch and launch activities for the product and was actively involved in the follow-up, the medical representatives would have to support it aggressively in their detailing calls for the next 18 months or so, if it was to achieve its market potential. In May 1984, Lopid, a major new cardiovascular pharmaceutical, was introduced with a first-year sales objective of almost $500,000. Again, the MIAs were playing a major role in the introduction. With three more new products slated for introduction in 1985, seven more in 1986, and at least five more in 1987, the detailing capacity problem was critical.

The magnitude of the problem was evident to Mr. Skripitsky and Mr. Gibson as they looked at the tentative 1985 Medical Promotion Schedule for the year beginning January 1, 1985, shown in Exhibit 5. Eryc and Lopid, the two new products, would require much of the available primary detailing time. In the case of general practitioners (GPs), 6 of the 12 available spots were taken up by the two new products, with an additional 2 of the 12 spots taken up by Choledyl SA, another relatively new product introduced early in 1983. Increasingly the inclusion of new products meant that important "bread and butter" products, many with good growth potential, would have to be dropped from active sales force promotion.

One brand that would fall in this category was Anusol HC, a pharmaceutically elegant prescription hemorrhoidal preparation, that was

EXHIBIT 5 Planned 1985 Medical Promotion Schedule (six two-month sales promotion cycles)

		1	2	3	4	5	6
General practitioners (GPs)	Primary	Lopid Benylin	Eryc Choledyl SA	Lopid Benadryl	Choledyl SA Lopid	Lopid Ponstan	Eryc Mylanta
	Reminder	Eryc Mylanta	Mylanta Anusol/Tucks	Ponstan Mylanta	Eryc Ponstan	Eryc Mylanta	Anusol/T Benylin
Surgeons	Primary	Mylanta Thrombostat	Anusol/Tucks	Mylanta Thrombostat	Mylanta	Thrombostat	Anusol/T
	Reminder	Hose	Hose	Anusol/Tucks Hose	Hose	Mylanta Hose	Mylanta Hose
Pediatricians	Primary	Benylin Choledyl Liquid	Benylin Choledyl Liquid	Benadryl Colymycin	Benadryl Vanquin	Choledyl Liquid Benylin	Benylin Choledyl Liquid
Obstetrics/ Gynecology (OB/GYNs)	Primary	Ponstan	Ponstan Mylanta	Ponstan	Ponstan	Mylanta Thrombostat	OC's Ponstan
	Reminder	Mylanta Tucks OC's	Tucks	Tucks OC's	OC's Tucks	Mylanta Tucks	Mylanta Hose
Internal medicine	Primary	Lopid	Lopid Nitrostat IV Eryc	Lopid Eryc	Lopid Nitrostat IV Eryc	Lopid Nitrostat IV	Lopid Eryc
	Reminder	Mylanta Eryc	Mylanta	Mylanta Benadryl	Mylanta	Mylanta Eryc	Mylanta Benylin
Hospital staff		Thrombostat Chloromycetin Mylanta	Nitrostat IV Benadryl Elase	Thrombostat Benadryl Mylanta	Nitrostat IV Elase	Thrombostat Chloromycetin Mylanta	Nitro IV Elase
Miscellaneous samples		Ponstan Hose	Hose Benylin	Hose Colymycin Eryc Anusol/Tucks	Benadryl Hose	Benadryl Hose Benylin	Ponstan Hose

---

EXHIBIT 6   Advertising and Promotion Budget for Prescription Anusol in
1984 and 1985 (planned)

	1984 (estimated) ($000)	*1985 (planned) ($000)*	*Percentage Change, 1984–85*
Promotion:			
"Loss of revenue"*	$221	$242	10%
Medical promotion	8	10	25
Mailing of samples	15	15	0
Samples (cost of goods)	224	307	37
Total	$468	$574	23%
Advertising:			
Print	$ 78	$150	92%
Print production	0	12	—
Agency fees	24	26	8
Audits and surveys	6	7	17
Total	$108	$195	81%
Total advertising and promotion budget	$574	$769	34%
As percent of sales	18%	22%	

* "Loss of revenue" was the estimated cost of price discounts and free-goods (buy 11 and get 1 free) that would be offered to the retail drug trade.

---

targeted at general practitioners, family physicians, and surgeons. With projected 1984 sales of $3.1 million, a market share of almost 50 percent in a market with a real growth rate of over 5 percent, and a manufacturing contribution margin of over 60 percent it was a major contributor to Parke-Davis's sales and profits. In 1984 total advertising and promotional spending on the product was expected to be over $500,000, with about 40 percent of this for samples. A breakdown of the actual advertising and promotion budget for 1984 and the planned budget for 1985 are shown in Exhibit 6. A projected 34 percent increase in the budget to support a 10 percent increase in sales was a partial response to the decreased availability of detailing time for the brand.

Alternatives under Consideration

As the management team of the Professional Health Group grappled with the problem of insufficient personal medical detailing time, it was apparent that there were several options open to them. The major options were:

1. Expand utilization of the MIAs to provide prelaunch, launch, and the entire postlaunch responsibility for new products for key specialists. This option would ensure that the new products would be very effectively detailed to the key potential prescribing specialists for a particular new product. The major disadvantage of this option was that the MIAs would be of little assistance in detailing the new products to general practitioners.

2. Increase the size of the regular sales force. This would allow the geographical territories to be smaller, permitting Parke-Davis to reach more doctors. However, management felt it was unlikely to increase the detailing time a salesperson could spend with key doctors for the Parke-Davis product line, since doctors would be unlikely to be willing to talk to the medical representative more than once during each two-month sales cycle. Thus the representative's capacity to detail more products to any one physician would not be enhanced.

3. Develop a second medical sales force for the Professional Health Group. The existing product line could be split between the two sales forces, perhaps with one sales force specializing in the cardiovascular and pulmonary products and the other sales force specializing in the anti-infective and anti-inflammatory products. If the few miscellaneous products in the Parke-Davis product line were also assigned to the second sales force, the two sales forces would have similar dollar volumes. Of the 15 new products planned for the 1985–87 period, 6 would be in the first group of products and 9 in the second group of products. With this option many physicians, drug stores, and hospitals would be detailed by two Parke-Davis medical representatives, thus doubling the number of products that could be detailed in any two-month sales cycle. However, management was unsure how the medical profession would react to this strategy—would doctors agree to see two different Parke-Davis sales representatives during a given two-month sales cycle, or would they only see one in each sales cycle? Management were also unsure how competition might react to this strategy. While some other competitors did have more than one sales force, with the exception of the recent move by Boehringer-Ingelheim these different sales forces operated under different names—often the names of predecessor companies.

4. Make no changes in the sales force, but make adjustments elsewhere to reflect the detailing capacity problem. Some managers felt it would be possible to revamp the detailing schedule to maximize the number of products on promotion. Substantial increases in the advertising and promotion support to brands might also reduce the need for detailing time on some of the products. To handle the large number of anticipated new-product introductions, these introductions could be delayed to provide a minimum four to six months' interval between the introduction of new brands. The detailing load could also be reduced by licensing the new products with low sales potential to other pharmaceutical manufacturers.

The Second-Sales-Force Option

By far the most radical of the four options under consideration was the addition of the second sales force. It was viewed to be quite risky, and if the decision to proceed with it was made, there were several major implementation issues that would need to be addressed.

In "fleshing out" the two-sales-forces option for discussion purposes, Mr. Skripitsky and Mr. Gibson thought that they would require 49 representatives for each sales force organized as shown in Exhibit 7. Where feasible, district managers would be responsible for medical representatives from only one of the sales forces, although in the more geographically dispersed areas such as Manitoba/Saskatchewan, rural Quebec, and the Atlantic Provinces, the district managers would have medical representatives from both sales forces reporting to them. Mr. Skripitsky and Mr. Gibson envisioned the continuance of the MIA sales force with five representatives assigned to it. The MIAs would support both sales forces as needed. The 1985 incremental cost of adding salespersons, managers, and support staff and facilities was estimated to average about $57,000 per person in the field; that is, $2.4 million for the 42 incremental persons that would be required to staff the two sales forces. Sales-force costs were expected to rise about 7 percent per year during the rest of the 1980s.

If a second sales force was added, the number of detailing slots available would be increased from 24 (four slots in each of the six sales cycles) to 48. In a preliminary look at the potential impact of this doubling of slots management thought that the 1985 Medical Promotion Schedule for general practitioners might be modified as shown in Exhibit 8. This would allow several more products to be detailed, some of them at high frequencies. In consultation with the product managers for the various products involved, Mr. Skripitsky and Mr. Gibson estimated that under the two-sales-forces option sales might be $1.3 million higher in 1985 than they would be with the continuance of current policies. Incremental sales of $4.6 million, $5.6 million, $7.9 million, and $9.5 million were expected in 1986, 1987, 1988, and 1989, respectively. The sources of these incremental sales are shown in Exhibit 9.

If the decision was made to add a second sales force there were several major implementation issues that needed to be addressed. A major concern was the naming of the two sales forces. Two major options had been proposed. Some managers thought that both sales forces

EXHIBIT 7 Proposed Sales Organization with Two Sales Forces

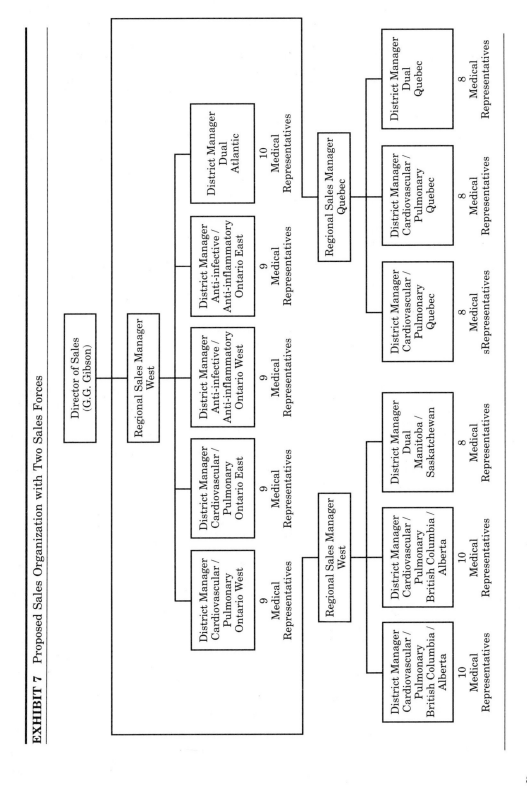

EXHIBIT 8   Change in 1985 Product Exposure to General Practitioners (GPs) with Second Sales Force

| | Frequency on Detail Schedule | | |
Product	Current Plan	Plan with Second Sales Force	Change
Lopid	4	5	1
Benylin	2	4	2
Eryc	5	4	(1)
Mylanta	5	6	1
Choledyl	2	4	2
Anusol/Tucks	2	5	3
Benadryl	1	2	1
Ponstan	3	3	—
Hose	—	3	3
Oral contraceptives	—	6	6
Colymycin Otic	—	1	1
Procan	—	5	5
	24	48	24

should operate clearly under the Parke-Davis name, with one sales force being called the Cardiovascular/Pulmonary Sales Group and the other the Anti-Infective/Anti-Inflammatory Sales Group. Others thought that the Parke-Davis name should be used but that the salespersons be represented as coming from two separate divisions. Suggestions for the division names included Research Laboratories Division of Parke-Davis, the Scientific Laboratories Division of Parke-Davis,

EXHIBIT 9   Estimated Impact of Second Sales Force on Sales ($000)

	1985	1986	1987	1988	1989
Incremental sales from existing ethical products	$ 615	$1,215	$1,680	$2,440	$3,040
Incremental sales from Consumer Health Group products*	300	350	400	450	500
Incremental sales from new products	400	3,000	3,500	5,000	6,000
Total incremental sales	$1,315	$4,565	$5,580	$7,890	$9,540

* Consumer Health Group products sold under the Parke-Davis brand (e.g., Benylin and Gelusil).

and the Warner Laboratories Division of Parke-Davis. The chosen name would appear on the representative's calling card. Another issue was whether all medical representatives should be trained on the full Parke-Davis product line, or just on the part of the product line sold by their sales force. As more new products were introduced, training on the full product line would probably require that the sales training program be lengthened. Perhaps the major implementation issue was how to introduce the idea of two Parke-Davis sales forces to the doctor and his or her receptionist/nurse. A negative reaction on their part could jeopardize the whole two-sales-forces plan. A continuing problem would be the need for the two sales representatives serving a particular geographical area to coordinate their activities so that they didn't end up calling on the same doctors at about the same time.

Mr. Gibson also wondered how the sales force would react if a second sales force were to be introduced. He could imagine some salespersons being concerned that an additional salesperson in their territory would make it more difficult for them to see their doctors and to gain as frequent access to hospitals. Many would be concerned about how any changes would affect their compensation and would want assurance that they wouldn't be expected to generate the same absolute dollar increases in sales on a reduced business base.

Possible Test

If the decision was made to add a second sales force, Mr. Skripitsky and Mr. Gibson wondered if they should first test the concept in one part of Canada, prior to introducing it nationally. If they proposed a test, they would have to recommend how it should be conducted, where it should be conducted, and how long it should last. The choice of a test area would not be an easy one. Every province or region of the country had significant drawbacks. British Columbia was geographically large and the Vancouver area had a very high ratio of physicians to people. Alberta had the advantages of being a relatively isolated market with little government intervention and having the Parke-Davis Western Region office in Edmonton. The latter would facilitate monitoring of any test. On the negative side it was a market in which Parke-Davis did extremely well and might not be representative from that point of view. The Alberta economy was also depressed in 1984. Both Saskatchewan and Manitoba were isolated markets, but both provincial governments had very restrictive formularies making them unrepresentative of the rest of Canada. Ontario's major disadvantage was its size. With over 36 percent of Canada's population, it seemed too large for a test market. If only part of the province was used, monitoring the results of the test would be extremely difficult and expensive, given the potential spillover effects of marketing activity in one part of the province into other areas. Quebec was also large and was a market where Parke-Davis was having some problems in early 1984. In addition, while the company had the capability to train French-speaking representatives, the burden of training people for the test would fall heavily on the shoulders of one individual. The Atlantic Provinces were viewed as being somewhat unique in Canada from a pharmaceutical marketing prospective, and Mr. Skripitsky and Mr. Gibson did not feel that any results obtained there would necessarily be projectable to the rest of the country.

THE SITUATION IN MAY 1984

As Mr. Skripitsky sat down in late May to decide what sales-force recommendations should be included in the five-year plan he knew that he would have to deal with a number of key issues that Mr. Seath was likely to bring up. Mr. Skripitsky felt that Mr. Seath would have major concerns about the two-sales-forces option. One of his concerns would be the large, continuing, fixed costs that would be associated with a second sales force. Warner-Lambert considered itself a very "people-oriented" company, and there would be no question of dismissing members of the second sales force if it did not work out. The investment of resources in a new salesperson was also considerable. Mr. Skripitsky felt the company's investment in a new salesperson could add up to $50,000 in the first two years the representative was with the company. Mr. Seath would want to be convinced that any additions to the sales-force head count would be fully warranted and that the additions were meeting a permanent need, not a temporary one. While Mr. Skripitsky expected that the 15 new products would be introduced, there was always the possibility that some of the introductions might have to be delayed or canceled if unforeseen problems occurred, such as a failure to get regulatory approval for a product. Mr. Seath would also want Mr. Skripitsky's assurance that the older products would in fact respond to more detailing time.

Mr. Skripitsky also knew that a key element of Mr. Seath's strategy for the Health Care Division was the continuing establishment of the Parke-Davis name as a highly respected brand name in the medical community. Mr. Seath would need to be convinced that the addition of a second sales force would not lead to any dilution of the Parke-Davis name.

Before presenting his recommendations Mr. Skripitsky knew he'd have to develop a detailed set of recommendations for whichever option he chose. If he decided on the two-sales-forces option, he would have to have specific recommendations on its size, timing, the naming of the sales forces, whether or not to test market the concept, and a host of implementation issues. He realized he had a lot of work to do within the next week to prepare his recommendations.

Case 6–14   Stop N Go*

As he takes a visitor on a whirlwind tour of the convenience-store business, V.H. "Pete" Van Horn passes a boarded-up Circle K store, a vivid symbol of the industry's past follies. With their archaic marketing techniques and crazy-quilt expansion, he says, his anger rising, "Circle K and 7-Eleven have created the impression that the industry is doomed."

The chief executive of National Convenience Stores Inc. is quickly pacified, however, by the sight of one of his own Stop N Go stores, which he brassily calls "the convenience store of the future." He marches through the store's wide aisles, extolling its virtues: bright lights and decorative wooden shelves stuffed with trendy products such as fresh pasta, expensive wine, Bart Simpson T-shirts and deli items. The store is a far cry from the industry's traditional shoe-box stands where beer, cigarettes and soda pop make up more than half of sales. "We're reinventing the business," Mr. Van Horn boasts.

The business could use some reinventing. Convenience stores once were little cash machines for their owners, where harried consumers were willing to pay more to pick up a few essentials without the hassle of wading through a supermarket. But that was before the spread of gas station mini-marts and before supermarkets fought back with express lanes and 24-hour operation. It was also before the industry's biggest chains, Circle K Corp. and Southland Corp.'s 7-Eleven, unwisely loaded up on debt and ended up in bankruptcy proceedings.

Now the two industry leaders have shed hundreds of stores. The total number of convenience stores in the United States, after growing explosively for years, leveled off in the late-1980s at 83,000. And industry profits plummeted 75 percent in 1989 from the year before, spurring much doomsday forecasting. "The convenience-store concept of offering less for more is outdated," says John Roscoe, a longtime industry consultant who predicts that "only small chains with stores in great locations will survive."

---

* Source: Kevin Hellider, "Off the Shelf," *The Wall Street Journal*, February 16, 1991, pp. A1, 10. Reprinted by permission of *THE WALL STREET JOURNAL*, © 1991 Dow Jones & Company, Inc. All Rights Reserved Worldwide.

Mr. Van Horn will have none of that. The problem, he insists, is that convenience store executives have been lousy marketers. "In an age of health-consciousness, customers walking into convenience stores are still greeted by racks of cigarettes, snuff, beer and beef jerky," he says. Another problem, he adds, is that operators continue to plop down cookie-cutter stores. "In ethnic neighborhoods, we've never had products or signage indicating we recognize that most of our customers are, say, Hispanic," he says.

So Mr. Van Horn is overhauling merchandise and remodeling his 1,071-store chain—the seventh largest—and designing store prototypes for three kinds of neighborhoods: mainstream, upscale, and Hispanic. He is tracking product performance store by store with a sophisticated point-of-sale scanning system, pretty advanced stuff for what has been a doggedly low-tech business. And in joint ventures with companies including Pizza Hut, NCS is about to install fast-food eateries in Stop N Go stores.

The industry is watching closely to see if Stop N Go can lure enough minorities and working women to replace the industry's shrinking traditional customer base: blue-collar men, especially blue-collar white men. At the handful of stores that have received complete overhauls, Mr. Van Horn says, sales are up about 20 percent and sales from women up nearly 100 percent. After operating losses in three of the last four years—attributable partly to huge investments required to redefine and redesign the chain—NCS expects to post a large enough operating profit this year to break even after paying a $3.2 million preferred-stock dividend. It had sales last fiscal year of $1.06 billion.

But the effort is expensive, risky and hasn't always gone smoothly. Some of Mr. Van Horn's previous ideas, such as selling television sets and bicycles at a few stores, have flopped. His ethnic-targeted stores have been criticized for stereotyping. The immediate results of some of the changes have been disappointing.

Varying the product mix from store to store could dilute the chain's buying power. And higher-class inventory costs a lot more to carry if sales languish. Fresh sandwiches and produce will introduce significant new spoilage costs. "A can of Coke isn't as difficult to manage as a piece of fruit, and it has a longer shelf life and national advertising behind it," says Coney Elliot, an industry consultant.

Moreover, many still doubt that the stores can overcome their blue-collar image. "I spent a whole day looking at stores with Pete," says Mr. Roscoe, the consultant. "When a guy walked out of Stop N Go in a suit and tie, Pete yelled, 'That's our new market!' Hell, it was the only guy in a suit and tie we saw all day."

The reaction of professional women like Kim Kindred illustrates the problem. As the 24-year-old Houston restaurant-company manager waits in line at an Apple Tree grocery here with pasta and wine, she's told she could get the same things at the Stop N Go next door—without the wait. "Convenience stores are glorified gas stations," she responds. "I don't buy my dinner at gas stations."

There are other problems, too. Oil companies still have thousands of stations they can convert into stores, and, like Stop N Go, they are beginning to experiment with larger units that offer more nontraditional merchandise such as deli food. "In four or five years, oil companies will be the giants of the convenience-store industry," predicts David Glass, chief executive of WalMart Stores Inc., which recently bought the nation's largest convenience-store supplier, McLane Co.

Officials of Ito-Yokado Co., the Japanese franchiser of 7-Eleven stores that is seeking to assume control of Southland, has indicated that it, too, will introduce new products and install point-of-sale systems to discern customer habits. "Changing life styles and the aging of the baby-boom generation mean that our product mix has to change, and it will," says Southland spokeswoman Cecilia Norwood, adding that 7-Eleven will begin downplaying cigarettes and emphasizing healthier items.

And some say that whole strategy is wrong anyway. Circle K officials, in fact, say it was their attempt to add new products and services that—along with heavy debt taken on in an unsuccessful expansion—helped land the company in bankruptcy proceedings. "By getting into movie rentals, lottery tickets, ATM machines, fast food and a bunch of other sexy new products, the company took its eye off the ball," says Karen Simon, the new senior vice president of marketing. Circle K's reorganization plan calls for the company to return its focus to what it calls the "power categories"—beer, cigarettes, and soda pop. As for Mr. Van Horn's strategy, Ms. Simon laughs and says, "All I can say is, 'Good luck, Pete.'"

Mr. Van Horn, who is 52 years old, says luck has nothing to do with it. Reared by a rich oil man who refused to share his wealth with the kids, believing they should earn their own success, Mr. Van Horn worked his way through school delivering newspapers and pumping gas, then abandoned a planned career in oil to join NCS in 1966 as a store manager. He rose through district manager, Southwest division manager and vice president of stores before becoming CEO in 1975. Since then, he says, he has invested "virtually all" of his net worth in NCS stock, of which he now owns a 2 percent stake (worth about $2 million). "My life and career are invested in this," he says. "Not to mention my ego."

Until 1985, his ego was doing just fine. Profits rose every quarter, and the company's stock, adjusted for splits and stock dividends, rose 2,138 percent from 1975 to 1984. But the '80s oil bust devastated Houston, the company's largest market, at the same time that oil companies started using that market to launch an aggressive expansion of their mini-mart program. As a result, long before hard times hit the rest of the industry, profits disappeared at NCS and its stock plummeted from nearly $20 a share in 1984 to $4.75 yesterday.

At the same time, Karl Eller, then chief of Circle K, was considering a takeover attempt, Mr. Van Horn says, but backed off after Cincinnati financier Carl Lindner—the largest shareholder of both NCS and Circle K—declined to back him without Mr. Van Horn's approval. Mr. Van Horn took advantage of Circle K's seemingly insatiable appetite for growth, selling the Phoenix-based company 186 stores in nine cities as part of his effort to concentrate on fewer markets. "I sold Karl Eller a bunch of crap," he says. (Mr. Eller and Mr. Lindner didn't return calls seeking comment for this article.)

At the same time, Mr. Van Horn bought all of Southland's 7-Eleven stores in Houston and San Antonio, giving Stop N Go a dominant market share in those cities.

When the dust settled, NCS was operating nearly the same number of stores in eight markets that it operated in 21 five years before. Mr. Van Horn then quadrupled his advertising budget to $12 million a year to saturate those markets. Still, the trimmed-down Stop N Go didn't take off.

In 1988, some retail repositioning specialists took Mr. Van Horn on a cross-country tour of successful businesses such as Nordstrom's, the Walt Disney Store chain, and Simon David, a Dallas gourmet grocery. Intoxicated by their fancy offerings, he came back to Houston determined to lure the affluent away from supermarket express lanes. "The average person in a supermarket express lane has 10 items, and seven of them are available in the typical convenience store," he says. "It's the other three that's always killed us."

From lists showing household income by zip code, he and other company officials identified 200 Stop N Go stores serving affluent neighborhoods in Houston. Using the point-of-sale scanners, the company was able to identify 200 slow-selling items to clear out, including Guns & Ammo magazine, Sugar Pops cereal, and Hamburger Helper. Next, they drew up a fancier list: rich cheeses, gourmet pastries, *The New Yorker* magazine.

The expected flood of yuppies failed to materialize. For one thing, company marketing managers, feeling pressure from Mr. Van Horn to increase sales, were spending ad dollars promoting cigarettes, soda pop, and beer, items they knew they could move.

After four months, even after that problem was corrected, sales in many stores had declined.

Recalling his tour of one of the Walt Disney stores, with its video screens, bright colors and creative shelves, Mr. Van Horn decided the problem was visual. "Our idea of presentation was stacking up 20 cases of Coca-Cola and putting a sign on top," He says. Back at the drawing board, company officials sketched in potted plants, wooden shelves, fancy display tables and a reading area beside magazine racks, as well as improved signs and lighting outside. They also devised an employee dress code of white shirts, bow ties and green aprons.

The first unit boasting those changes opened here last April, and sales immediately shot up 20 percent over the same month a year earlier, a trend that has continued. Leaving the store recently with some fruit and a bagel, Julie Jeffers, a college student majoring in dietetics, says, "It's nice not to have to go into a big grocery store for these items."

Meantime, company officials last summer studied the Hispanic market. Internal data showed that ice cream and beverage sales were 30 percent higher in Hispanic-area Stop N Go stores than elsewhere—crucial information in determining how to stock an expressly-for-Hispanics store. A design firm hired by Mr. Van Horn gave the store its logo: a Mayan welcome sign painted outside. The first Hispanic store opened here in late September. Since then, sales are up more than 20 percent, led by Mexican-made products such as Gamesa Iced Wheelies (a cookie) and some U.S. brands that have long been sold in Mexico.

The company's ethnic strategy could also backfire because it calls for loading up the stores with fatty foods and salty snacks. Even store manager Roy Enriquez, a big admirer of his Hispanic prototype store, says that its merchandise is based on "a bit of a misconception that Hispanics aren't as health-conscious as other people."

Mr. Van Horn says the Hispanic store mix is based on statistics rather than stereotypes, and he says that in certain categories Hispanics are in fact more health-conscious consumers. For instance, they buy fewer cigarettes, he says, so cigarettes aren't emphasized in the Hispanic prototype.

Mr. Van Horn junked the idea of a black-oriented store after concluding from his point-of-sale data that blacks' buying habits didn't differ significantly from those of blue-collar whites. To serve both groups, he is planning to unveil a mainstream prototype in March that he says will feature products from both the Hispanic and "upscale" prototypes. While continuing to emphasize traditional products such as beer and cigarettes, the mainstream store will carry fresher and more fashionable items. Already, all Houston Stop N Go stores offer sandwiches made fresh daily.

Despite the fatter margins produced by the made-over stores, Mr. Van Horn says he won't be rolling out new ones quickly. Conversions cost tens of thousands of dollars per store, a considerable burden for a company that already has long-term debt of nearly $190 million. The company estimates that fewer than 150 stores will have been repositioned by midyear.

Repositioning customer attitudes could take even longer. Mr. Van Horn goes quickly from elation to deflation one day as he watches two men in ties and sport coats deliberate over Stop N Go's new fresh-daily

$3.50 sandwiches, then opt instead for an old standby: 99-cent hot dogs. "The industry has been offering stale products so long," he says, "the customer isn't trained to buy anything else."

Case 6–15   *Compaq Computer Corp.**

Computer customers like Richard Gonzalez really bug Compaq Computer Corp.

The personal-computer maker couldn't do much when Great West Life Assurance Co., acting on Mr. Gonzalez's recommendation, replaced Compaq's personal computers with work stations from Sun Micro-systems Inc. "When we saw Sun's workstations, we knew they were more powerful than anything Compaq had," says Mr. Gonzalez, an administration executive at the Denver insurer.

Not for long, if Compaq has its way. The Houston-based company, which successfully challenged International Business Machines Corp. to win a small but profitable niche among corporate PC customers, now wants to be all things to all business computer users. Last week, Compaq took an important step in that direction: It spent $135 million for a 13 percent stake in Silicon Graphics Inc. and another $50 million for access to the workstation maker's sophisticated graphics technology.

Another piece of the strategy fell into place yesterday in New York, when Compaq, along with 20 other companies, created the Advanced Computing Environment. The new 21-company alliance, led by Compaq, software giant Microsoft Corp. and minicomputer maker Digital Equipment Corp., hopes to establish a standard for computers based on Reduced Instruction Set Computing (RISC) technology from Mips Computer Systems Inc. By roping in other suppliers and computer makers, the companies hope to persuade software makers to create programs for the ACE machines, which ACE members will need to challenge established RISC players such as Sun Microsystems Inc. and IBM.

Although the group didn't show an ACE computer or even offer a complete list of technical specifications, the ACE announcement was important for the whole computer industry. Previously, the only standards for advanced systems were set on an *ad hoc* basis as established

---

* Source: Jim Bartimo, "Pushing Ahead," *The Wall Street Journal*, April 10, 1991, pp. A1, 4. Reprinted by permission of *THE WALL STREET JOURNAL*, © 1991 Dow Jones & Company, Inc. All Rights Reserved Worldwide.

players gained market share. Even if the group isn't completely successful, it has set a standard with which established companies must contend and software makers must figure into their plans.

Compaq views its new ACE computers, which it will build in cooperation with Silicon Graphics and expects to market sometime in 1992, as the basis of its future product strategy. Compaq believes that ACE will let it build computers that will act like a PC but still do anything that advanced computers from Sun, IBM, DEC, or Hewlett-Packard Inc. can do—and do it better. Instead of cabinet-sized machines, the Compaq office of the future would be run by PC-sized systems, in various size combinations, that have a mainframe's capabilities but also can run much of the software currently available for PCs. And as in the PC market, Compaq hopes to benefit by being able to assemble its new machines from off-the-shelf parts instead of proprietary technology.

This strategy, a Compaq insider predicts, will increase annual sales to about $15 billion by the year 2000 from the current $3.6 billion— and at least half those sales will come out of the hides of advanced-computer rivals.

"We're not predicting the end of IBM and DEC," says Joseph "Rod" Canion, Compaq's chief executive. "But they'll have a difficult time competing and catching up."

If that sounds arrogant for a company known mainly for making clones of IBM PCs, well, that's Compaq. Advanced computers may be a tough, technologically sophisticated market filled with deep-pocket rivals and demanding customers, but Compaq believes that it has little choice if it wants to maintain its healthy growth rate. "If you don't lead the market, you're at the whim of the leaders," says Michael Swavely, Mr. Canion's chief strategist, who recently took a six-month leave for personal reasons.

With sales slowing and competition intensifying in the PC market, Compaq fears that its premium-price strategy is vulnerable to discounters such as Dell Computer Corp. Dell recently slashed prices and derided Compaq as the "Top of the Markups" in aggressive comparison ads. In notebook computers, some 40 new competitors, including some with machines underpricing Compaq's by as much as $2,000, have entered the market this year and are threatening a stronghold that brought in 17 percent of Compaq's 1990 U.S. revenue, according to David R. Korus, an analyst at Kidder, Peabody & Co. In Europe, which provided more than half of Compaq's 1990 revenue, Compaq expects more discounting and flat sales this year. The company's U.S. revenue growth skidded to just 6 percent last year from 24 percent a year earlier (see Exhibit 1).

And some analysts wonder whether Compaq's clone-maker philosophy will transfer smoothly into the advanced-computer arena. Can the company, which relies heavily on other manufacturers to supply the

---

EXHIBIT 1   Compaq Computer: Facing the Future

To keep growth strong . . .

Annual revenue, in billions

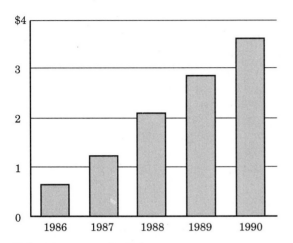

Compaq's business . . .

Compaq's 1990 revenue by business segment

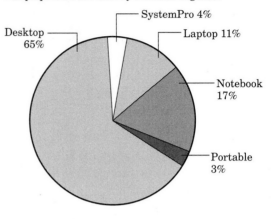

Will fight entrenched rivals . . .

1990 minicomputer market share

IBM	**19.85%**
Digital Equipment	**14.95**
Groupe Bull	**5.91**
Unisys	**5.60**
Hewlett-Packard	**5.56**
Fujitsu	**5.12**
NEC	**4.45**
AT & T Data Systems Group	**3.45**
NCR	**3.34**
Tandem Computers	**3.27**
Other vendors	**28.49**

Source: Dataquest.

And try to bolster the stock.

Comparison of Compaq's stock and the DJ Computer index, Dec. 31, 1990=100

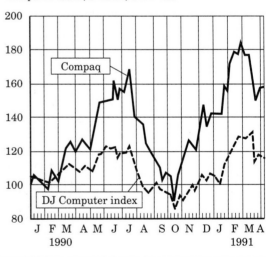

---

guts of its machines and on independent dealers to sell and service them, compete with makers of mainframes, work stations, and mini-computers, companies that develop much of their own proprietary hardware and operating systems and maintain sizable in-house sales and support staffs?

Nobody is dismissing Compaq's chances; this is a company that has usually been able to back up its cockiness with deeds. Formed by a group of former Texas Instruments Inc. executives in 1982, Compaq set itself apart from dozens of now-forgotten PC "clone makers" by convincing buyers and dealers that it offered a high-quality, competitively priced alternative to IBM's new PC. And in 1986, Compaq cemented its reputation by building an IBM-compatible computer based on Intel Corp.'s new 80386 chip before IBM did.

Even when IBM fought back with its Micro Channel computer architecture and its OS/2 operating system, which were supposed to establish a new PC standard that the clone makers couldn't follow, Compaq wiggled out of the trap. The company formed PC hardware and software makers into the "Gang of Nine" to establish its own standard in 1988. In reality, the standard war proved little; both systems could run much of the existing software. However, IBM never captured as much market share as many expected, and Compaq gained stature through its defiance of the industry giant.

By then, Compaq was already hunting for new products for its big customers. What it came up with was SystemPro, a so-called file server that, like a minicomputer, acts as the storage and communications hub for a PC network. Though lacking the power of a minicomputer, SystemPro was aimed at customers traditionally served by the more powerful machines.

But although compaq has declared its first venture outside the pure PC world a success—it gave the company $200 million in first-year revenue and new cachet among business users—SystemPro has had some bumpy moments. Introduced in 1989, SystemPro sold about 6,500 units last year, less than Compaq had anticipated, according to people close to the company.

Some analysts cite SystemPro's problems as proof that Compaq's collegial approach to product development might be ill-suited to the advanced-computer market. Suppliers took months to deliver the software needed to make SystemPro function as the hub of a PC network. Even now, Novell Inc. hasn't been able to finish customizing its popular networking software to take advantage of one of SystemPro's main selling points, its multiple microprocessors. As a result, companies wanting the Novell software usually buy a lower-priced, single-chip version of the system.

The SystemPro also showed Compaq that its 2,000 computer dealers were no match for the technical wizards that sell and support DEC and IBM machines. Ronan McGrath, a vice president of information systems for Canadian National Railways, which owns more than 3,000 Compaq PCs, has complained that his dealer couldn't answer technical questions about the SystemPro models. That kind of technical expertise is supplied routinely by big computer companies' engineers, but most dealers can't afford the $80,000 or more in salary such experts command.

"It's like running a Ferrari in Romania," Mr. McGrath says. "The performance is great, but you can't get it serviced."

In reaction, Compaq said in February that it would anoint 10 percent of its dealers as specialists in the complex new machines and train them. It also promised to convert another 10 percent of the dealer network later. The remaining 1,600 U.S. dealers could sell customers a Compaq service contract.

How effective Compaq's "superdealers" will be against competitors' staff experts remains to be seen. Avery More, president of CompuCom Inc., one of the dealers chosen, decided to replace his own IBM minicomputers with a couple of SystemPros to show customers that the Compaq product could do the job. But Mr. More had trouble persuading one of his own board members to approve the switch. "You can't run a whole company with that, are you crazy?" Mr. More recalls the director's saying. A letter from a Compaq executive promising a seamless transfer eventually convinced the director.

The expertise of Compaq's dealers will become even more important when the company introduces its ACE machines and seeks a share of huge new markets. Last year, some $30 billion of mainframes, $28 billion of minicomputers and $7.3 billion of work stations were sold, according to one estimate. Compaq has prospered with just 3½ percent of the $36.7 billion world-wide PC market, although some experts question whether the company can maintain its healthy profit margins in cutthroat markets such as work stations.

The new alliance has stirred a lot of skepticism. Sun's president, Scott McNealy, has denigrated Compaq's technological prowess. "Compaq doesn't do computers," Mr. McNealy sniffs. "They do handles and sheet metal."

That theme crops up repeatedly. Although Compaq has proved adept at combining existing technologies to build quality machines, it has yet to prove itself an innovator in computer science. And most computer standards have emerged from innovators, not from groups devising common-denominator standards that suit every company. "The cowards of our industry don't want to be first," says Aaron Goldberg, a vice president for International Data Corp., a market-research firm, "so they band together for 'coop-etition.'"

Companies such as Sun, IBM, and DEC have broad-based technical staffs that program operating software and design processor chips. Apple Computer Inc.'s control over its operating system ensured that no clone makers copied the Apple Macintosh; that gave Apple an edge in competing with IBM and others.

In the past, relying on other companies for key components has given Compaq headaches. A shortage of Intel chips and flat-panel screens this year delayed early shipments of Compaq's notebook computers. Compaq was even wait-listed for some super-small hard disks from Conner Peripherals Inc., even though Compaq owns a 21 percent stake in the company.

Mr. Goldberg says he doesn't see much hope that Compaq can become a major, full-line computer maker. "How many $4 billion computer companies don't have a field presence?" he asks.

[Note: Additional information about the personal computer industry is provided in the Appendix to this case.]

Appendix   *Personal Computer Industry Analysis**

A sea change is roiling the personal-computer industry and especially the market leaders, International Business Machines and Compaq Computer.

Compaq yesterday disclosed that it expects second-quarter sales to drop a surprising 15 percent, causing an 80 percent drop in estimated earnings to 25 cents a share and contributing to an inventory glut. The news drove its stock down 27 percent as analysts slashed year-end projections. Last month, IBM said its personal-computer sales sagged 17 percent in the quarter.

But meanwhile, sales are booming at clone makers such as AST Research and Dell Computer. Also faring well is Sun Microsystems, whose powerful desktop computers are increasingly being used as PCs. Apple Computer reported an 85 percent jump in unit sales of its Macintosh PCs, aided by price cuts and its edge in software.

Ironically—for a high-tech industry in which companies' main fear usually is competitors' innovations—the two biggest PC makers are being hurt because innovation is scarce. PCs have become so standardized around Intel's powerful microprocessors and Microsoft's operating software that Compaq and IBM have done little to differentiate their desktop machines from others, and so they can't justify higher prices and profit margins. In fact, user surveys find some clones rated higher than Compaq and IBM machines in performance and quality.

"Almost everything we buy is a no-name clone," says Glenn Thomas, information-services manager at Hudson Foods Inc., of Rogers, Ark. Mr. Thomas once bought almost exclusively from IBM and Compaq but now buys clones from Gateway 2000, of North Sioux City, S.D., and Taiwan's DTK Computer. Clones use essentially the same inner workings as more expensive brethren do, he adds, and some "have PCs that outperform IBM."

The trend is being greatly accelerated by the recession, which has caused large corporate buyers to either cut back on computer purchases or seek

* Source: Stephen Kreider Yoder and G. Pascal Zachary, "Shifting Fortunes," *The Wall Street Journal*, May 16, 1991, pp. A1, 6. Reprinted by permission of *THE WALL STREET JOURNAL*, © 1991 Dow Jones & Company, Inc. All Rights Reserved Worldwide.

cheaper machines. In a recent survey, Robertson Stephens & Co., a securities firm, found that these buyers planned to roll back purchases 21 percent this year.

Compaq and IBM are especially vulnerable to the cutbacks because they depend the most heavily on the big companies. Clone makers and Apple, on the other hand, derive a greater percentage of sales from individuals and small businesses.

AMR Corp.'s American Airlines says it plans to buy fewer PCs this year than last year. Ford Motor Co., which has 70,000 desktop PCs, says it will purchase fewer than half as many PCs this year as in previous years. Phillips Petroleum Co. plans to buy 1,100 PCs this year, 377 fewer than last year, because "we have less places where we need them now," says John R. Smith, the Bartlesville, Okla., company's procurement manager.

Like Mr. Thomas, increasing numbers of companies are bypassing Compaq and IBM when they do buy. Chrysler Corp. has added clone makers to its approved-vendors list and last year leased 3,000 PCs made by South Korea's Lucky Goldstar Group. Says Irene Hession, a PC buyer for Polaroid Corp.: "We have definitely gone toward clones."

IBM and Compaq belatedly struck back at the clones last month by cutting prices on popular machines as much as 34 percent. The move is too late, says Denins Cox, marketing director at Packard Bell Electronics, a clone-maker and the nation's fifth-largest PC seller last year. "They've been forced to narrow the gap."

Despite the turmoil, the PC industry's world-wide sales are expected to increase 11 percent this year, after a 9 percent gain last year, says Infocorp. However, Stella Kelly, an analyst at the Santa Clara, Calif., market-research firm, says that growth "hinges on several factors," most notably continued high demand for notebook PCs powered by Intel's 386sx chip, desktop models powered by Intel's 386sx chip, desktop models powered by Intel's 486 chip and Apple's lower-priced Macintosh models.

Apple has also slashed prices on its lowest-cost Macintoshes, sparking a surge in sales that promises to double its share of the PC market, to nearly 20 percent. Computer buyers say Compaq and IBM will eventually benefit from their price cuts as well. "We do expect that Compaq has essentially closed the gap with the quality clones and that their demand will come back," says Ed Anderson, president of Computer-Land Corp.'s USA retail chain.

Moreover, the worrisome inventory glut at Compaq and other companies may be magnified by a recent spate of mergers between big retail chains, which now are reducing combined inventories. "To do that, you stop buying for a little while," Mr. Anderson says. "We don't expect to turn it back on for 60 days. It isn't an inventory buildup in the sense of demand being stopped."

Joseph "Rod" Canion, Compaq's chief executive, says he isn't sure how much inventory is clogging the dealer channel, but he says "the glut will certainly hurt us for the rest of the second quarter and well into the third quarter." Compaq's earnings comparisons also will suffer because of the strong European business that boosted profits in the past.

Some industry analysts expect similar problems at Apple and IBM very soon. "The dealer channel is all mucked up, and it's going to get more mucked up," says JoeAnn Stahel of Storeboard/Computer Intelligence, which tracks

PC sales through retailers. "Compaq is not alone in having excess product in some categories."

But even when sales recover, Compaq and IBM can kiss their once-juicy profit margins goodbye. Compaq, for instance, has traditionally reported after-tax margins three to four times higher than those of Sun Microsystems. One omen: Apple's slashing of its prices last fall led to an 11 percent decline in profit margins in the first three months of this year.

And it will be increasingly difficult to generate steamy growth in dollar sales after unusually sharp price cuts, even if those cuts attract new computer users. Apple's dollar sales, for instance, grew only 19 percent in the last quarter despite the 85 percent jump in unit sales. PC sales in the five years between 1990 and 1994 will grow just 44 percent, down from the industry's heady 100 percent growth in the five years preceding 1989, says International Data Corp., market-research firm in Framingham, Mass.

All that's a big switch from the 1980s bonanza days for IBM and Compaq. Conservative corporate PC buyers, still nervous about the new technology represented by the PCs they were purchasing to replace typewriters, bought largely from IBM. Meanwhile, Compaq racked up huge growth by offering machines with a technological edge over IBM's. Compaq beat out IBM and others by months with the first PC that used Intel's new 80386 chip in 1986.

As long as Big Blue and Compaq were the first with innovations and held a quality edge over the clones, which tended to trail in the use of new technology, the two leaders could charge 30, 40 and 50 percent more for their PCs. But that was when desktop PCs were the site of the computer industry's most striking innovations. In those early days, a slew of innovations conspired to make the desktop computer one of the hottest items around, a powerful new tool. The laser printer, floppy drive, mouse pointing device and other features were introduced between 1980 and 1985.

But the desktop PC is no longer awash in innovation. Since 1985, its basic features have been essentially unchanged. There have been some innovations in software; for instance, both Apple and Microsoft have improved their system software, which controls the basic operations. But PC makers have mainly relied on weary standards, and their few initiatives have centered on arcane features such as internal channels invisible to customers.

Innovations are occurring, but in portable computers and workstations, the industry's fastest-growing segments. In recent years, new types of display screens, hard-disk drives, semiconductor memory and communications devices have appeared first on notebook and hand-held computers. Compaq is having trouble keeping its 386 portable in stock, while its other models pile up in inventory. Apple and IBM are suffering from the relative unpopularity of their less-sleek portables.

Even as portables are stealing away desktop PC sales because of miniaturization, workstations are cutting into PC sales because they offer brute power and solid, if somewhat unimaginative, networking. Sun continues to post big gains partly because of its inroads into PC rivals (see Exhibit A–1).

The same is true for Hewlett-Packard and IBM, which also have strong workstation products. "We're at a turning point," says George Dodd, head of computer science at General Motors' research labs. "Because of the drastically reduced prices of these machines," he says, GM engineers will soon be doing

---

EXHIBIT A–1 Workstations' Growth

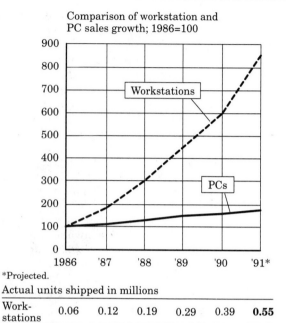

Comparison of workstation and
PC sales growth; 1986=100

*Projected.

Actual units shipped in millions

Work- stations	0.06	0.12	0.19	0.29	0.39	**0.55**
PCs	15.06	16.79	19.17	22.21	23.99	**26.99**

Source: Dataquest.

---

tasks they once only dreamed of, such as crash-testing cars on desktop computers instead of smashing into concrete walls, or designing car parts completely by computer.

Even when change comes to the desktop PC, clone makers are quick to seize it. Nothing illustrated this better than when Intel, the chief purveyor of the "brain" chips in PCs, introduced a cheaper version of its advanced chip, the 486. The next day, a dozen clone makers announced machines based on the chip and so cheap that IBM, Compaq and others had to slash prices on older machines.

PC makers are realizing that standards such as Intel chips cut both ways and that, to prosper, they need to incorporate some unique, tangible features in their PCs. Stewart Alsop, editor of *PC Letter*, says companies are focusing more on competing by design innovation than by putting together coalitions around different technical standards. "They have begun to realize that what customers want is new value, even more than standards," he says.

The race to innovate is most apparent in miniaturization and graphics. Hewlett-Packard, an also-ran in PCs, wowed the industry last month with a new $700 palm-sized PC that can send and receive data via satellite. Many computer makers disparaged hand-held PCs as toys and left them to Japanese consumer-electronics concerns. Now they may follow Hewlett-Packard with similar devices.

IBM is planning a new emphasis as well. For instance, it has a "skunk works" in Florida building a radically new computer designed to accept handwriting from an electronic pen. Like Apple a laggard in notebook PCs, IBM hopes its future pen-based machine—due out as early as next year—will revive its innovative image. Xerox is taking the power of new microprocessors to a different dimension: Rather than create more powerful desktop machines, researchers at its Palo Alto Research Center are designing computers the size of legal pads and Post-it notes.

Even relatively successful Apple is eyeing fresh markets, particularly joint ventures with Sony of Japan to develop a new portable computer and a repackaged Macintosh for the home-electronics market to compete with Nintendo. "It's a question of bringing to market products people don't know us for," says John Sculley, Apple's chief executive officer.

Mr. Sculley bluntly concedes that Apple has so far missed the explosive wave in portable and, even smaller, notebook computers, but he vows that won't happen again. "We are putting more attention on breakout areas," he says.

For these companies, and other traditional PC powerhouses such as Tandy Corp., another key is mastering a diverse set of networking and multimedia technologies, which figures to be the foundation for the desktop computer of the mid-1990s. Just this week, Digital Equipment, another also-ran in PCs, introduced a very fast PC based on Intel's 486 chip with networking capabilities and workstation quality graphics built in.

Future machines from some makers are expected to manage and transmit "files" of sound and images as easily as text is handled today. While "some hoary technical issues must be overcome, the big question is how do vendors stuff these capabilities into their machines without making them too expensive," Mr. Alsop says.

The extra wallop of computer power will bring sweeping changes for the average PC user, too. With power to spare, computer and software designers say, PCs of the 1990s will talk to users in human voices, show movie-quality video images, play 15-piece orchestra music in stereo.

The greater appeal of such machines may slow the trend toward portables, which have been in such demand that some experts predict the end of the desktop. Outfitted with new capabilities, the desktop PC will reassert its dominance in personal computing, says William Gates, Microsoft's chief executive. Mr. Gates doubts that a new class of notebook PCs, armed with built-in radio communicators, will satisfy customers. "What is so urgent that you can't wait to get back to your desktop machine?" he asks.

Index of Cases